SMITH & HOGAN
CRIMINAL LAW

Cases and Materials

Ninth Edition

David Ormerod

Professor of Criminal Law, University of Leeds
Barrister of the Middle Temple, 18 Red Lion Court

OXFORD
UNIVERSITY PRESS

OXFORD

UNIVERSITY PRESS

Great Clarendon Street, Oxford OX2 6DP

Oxford University Press is a department of the University of Oxford.
It furthers the University's objective of excellence in research, scholarship,
and education by publishing worldwide in

Oxford New York

Auckland Cape Town Dar es Salaam Hong Kong Karachi
Kuala Lumpur Madrid Melbourne Mexico City Nairobi
New Delhi Shanghai Taipei Toronto

With offices in

Argentina Austria Brazil Chile Czech Republic France Greece
Guatemala Hungary Italy Japan Poland Portugal Singapore
South Korea Switzerland Thailand Turkey Ukraine Vietnam

Oxford is a registered trade mark of Oxford University Press
in the UK and in certain other countries

Published in the United States
by Oxford University Press Inc., New York

British Library Cataloguing in Publication Data

Data available

Library of Congress Cataloging in Publication Data

Data available

Typeset by Newgen Imaging Systems (P) Ltd., Chennai, India
Printed in Great Britain
on acid-free paper by
Ashford Colour Press Ltd., Gosport, Hampshire

ISBN 978–0–40–697729–8

3 5 7 9 10 8 6 4

Contents

Preface

This book, which serves as a companion to *Smith and Hogan Criminal Law*, has been popular with generations of students. Its selection of significant cases which provide a clear account of the law, coupled with its thought-provoking questions, are a testament to the great teaching abilities of Sir John Smith and Brian Hogan. I was privileged to have worked with J.C. Smith at the University of Nottingham and subsequently to have followed in Brian Hogan's footsteps at the University of Leeds. I was honoured when, in the course of completing the last edition J.C. invited me to collaborate with him in writing subsequent editions. Sadly there was no opportunity to do so before he passed away, and responsibility for this ninth edition fell to me alone.

Although law school class sizes make it increasingly difficult to adopt the casebook method of teaching, some institutions maintain the tradition. My own experiences of teaching criminal law by the casebook method at Nottingham and Leeds Universities have been rewarding and enjoyable. The book is not, of course, restricted to use only in formal casebook teaching. It provides a comprehensive but accessible collection of materials which will complement a criminal law course delivered by lectures and seminars. The increased availability of legal materials from free and commercial databases on the internet has rendered even the most obscure case accessible to nearly all law students. However, the availability of such a range of materials does not diminish the need for a collection such as this. Students are increasingly likely to be overwhelmed by the volume of cases to which they have immediate access, and it is therefore as important as ever for them to have a collection structured so as to guide their learning.

I have followed the structure and style of previous editions, with the emphasis being on case extracts of a sufficient length to allow students to develop important skills in reading legal judgments. I have, however, made some changes, and more will no doubt follow in future editions. In particular, in this edition, there is greater reference to the European Convention on Human Rights and a few more extracts from academic writings. I have also included references for further reading at the end of each chapter. Recent years have seen a steady increase in the volume of appellate decisions on criminal law and, in particular, the House of Lords now deliver more judgments on substantive criminal law. Inevitably this has led to a substantial number of new cases to be included in this edition. On recklessness, there is the landmark decision of the House of Lords in *G*, and on intention the Court of Appeal's explanation of *Woollin* in *Matthews* and *Alleyne*. The House of Lords' decision on the ECHR compatibility of reverse burden provisions in *Attorney-General's Reference (No 4 of 2002)* is also included. On causation, the drug dealing cases continue to provoke controversy with *Kennedy No 2* being the Court of Appeal's latest offering. Similarly, the courts' struggle with the limits of the defence of provocation persists, and the Privy Council's opinion in *A-G for Jersey v Holley* was delivered just in time to be included in Chapter 18. The decision in the House of Lords in *Hasan* on duress, and that of the Court of Appeal in *Quayle* on necessity were also late additions to this edition. Other cases of significance include *Misra* on manslaughter, *Bryce* on participation, *Sofroniou* on obtaining services by deception and *Dica* and *Konzani* on HIV transmission and offences against the person. Aside from the case law, legislative changes led to a completely new chapter on sexual offences. I have incorporated many of the valuable extracts from the Law Commission's reports and consultation papers and other significant proposals for reform including those on fraud, murder and partial defences to murder. In my experience, seminar discussions on the present law are often enlivened and enhanced by consideration of the future shape the law might take.

I am grateful to David Gruner, Ruth Armstrong and Ben Fitzpatrick who read those chapters in which I have made substantial change. Their comments were of great assistance but of course I remain responsible for any errors. This is the first edition of this book to be published by Oxford University Press, and I would like to thank Natalie Williams and Gabriella La Cava for their invaluable assistance. Finally, on a more personal note, thanks are due to Olivia for her forbearance when, weeks after the textbook had been completed, this book continued to devour my time. Updates of significant changes in the law will be included in the Online Resource Centre at www.oxfordtextbooks.co.uk/orc/smithhogan_casebook9e/.

David Ormerod
July 2005

Acknowledgements

Grateful acknowledgement is made to all the authors and publishers of copyright material which appears in this book, and in particular to the following for permission to reprint material from the sources indicated:

Crown copyright material is reproduced under Class Licence Number C01P0000148 with the permission of the Controller of HMSO and the Queen's Printer.

Peter Carter QC for extract from unreported case. *Sinclair* (1998) Court of Appeal Criminal Division.

The Incorporated Council of Law Reporting for extracts from *Appeal Court Reports*, *Weekly Law Reports*, and *Family Division* (Law Reports).

Juta and Company Ltd for extract from *The South African Law Reports*.

Oxford University Press for extracts from Patrick Devlin: 'Statutory Offences' in *Samples of Law Making* (OUP, 1962) and Andrew Ashworth: 'Belief and Intent in Criminal Liability' in J. Eekelaar and J. Bell (eds) *Oxford Essays in Jurisprudence* (OUP, 1987); also extract from G. Mead: 'Contracting into Crime: A Theory of Criminal Omissions (1991) 11 *Oxford Journal of Legal Studies* 147.

Reed Elsevier (UK) Ltd trading as Lexis Nexis Butterworths for extracts from *All England Law Reports* [All ER] and extract from M. A. Millner: *Negligence in Modern Law* (Butterworths, 1967).

Professor G. R. Sullivan for extract from letter to *The Times*, 29 March 2002.

Sweet & Maxwell Ltd for extracts from J. C. Smith: 'Responsibility in Criminal Law' in *Barbara Wootten: Essays in her Honour* edited by P. Bean and D. Whynes (Tavistock, Taylor & Francis Books, 1986); Glanville Williams: *Criminal Law: The General Part* (Stevens, 2nd edn, 1961); Lord Cooke of Thorndon: from *One Golden Thread* (Hamlyn Lectures, Stevens, 1996), J. C. Smith: from *Justification and Excuse in the Criminal Law* (Hamlyn Lectures, Stevens, 1989); and Barbara Wootten: *Crime and Criminal Law: Reflections of a Magistrate and a Social Scientist* (Hamlyn Lectures, Stevens, 1963); extracts from *Criminal Law Review*: The Hon Mrs Justice Arden: 'Criminal Law at the Crossroads: The Impact of Human Rights from the Law Commission's Perspective and the Need for a Code' (1999) Crim LR 439; Andrew Ashworth (in reply): 'The Human Rights Act and the Substantive Criminal Law: A Non-Minimalist View' (2000) Crim LR 564; Lord Bingham: 'Must we wait forever?' (1998) Crim LR 694; Lord Justice Buxton: 'The Human Rights Act and the Substantive Criminal Law' (2000) Crim LR 331; J. Gobert: 'A Corporate Criminality: New Crimes for the Times' (1994) Crim LR 722; Edward Griew: 'Dishonesty. The Objection to *Feely* and *Ghosh*' (1985) Crim LR 341; J. Horder: 'How Culpability Can and Cannot be Denied in Under-age Sex Crimes' (2001) Crim LR 15; and 'A Critique of the Correspondence Principle in Criminal Law' (1995) Crim LR 759; F. Leverick: 'Is English Self-Defence Law Incompatible with Article 2 of the ECHR?' (2002) Crim LR 347; R. D. Mackay: 'The Abnormality of Mind Factor in Diminished Responsibility' (1999) Crim LR 117;

R. D. Mackay and C. Gearty: 'On being insane in Jersey—the case of *Attorney General v Jason Prior*' (2001) Crim LR 560; Sir Brian MacKenna: 'Blackmail' (1966) Crim LR 467; B. Mitchell: 'In Defence of a Principle of Correspondence' (1999) Crim LR; A. Norrie: 'After *Woollin*' (1999) Crim LR 532; A. T. H. Smith: 'The Idea of Criminal Deception' (1982) Crim LR 721; Sir John Smith: response to F. Leverick (above) (2002) Crim LR 952; J. C. Smith, commentary on *DPP v Stonehouse* (1977) Crim LR 544; and 'The Element of Chance in Criminal Liability' (1971) Crim LR 63; J. R. Spencer: 'The Theft Act' (1979) Crim LR 24; and 'The Sexual Offences Act 2003 (2) Child and Family Offences' (2004) Crim LR 347; P. Sutherland and C. Gearty: 'Insanity and the ECHR' (1992) Crim LR 418; C. Wells: 'The Decline and Rise of English Murder: Corporate Crime and Individual Responsibility' (1988) Crim LR 788; and Glanville Williams: 'Necessity' (1978) Crim LR 128; extracts from cases reported in *Criminal Law Review*; extracts from *Law Quarterly Review*; Andrew Ashworth: 'The Scope of Criminal Liability for Omissions' (1989) 105 LQR 424; R. Goff: 'The Mental Element in the Crime of Murder' (1988) 104 LQR 30; S. Gough 'Intoxication and Criminal Liability: The Law Commission's Proposed Reforms' (1996) LQR 335; J. Horder: 'Strict Liability, Statutory Construction, and the Spirit of Liberty' (2002) LQR 458; and Glanville Williams: 'Criminal Omissions: The Conventional View' (1991) 107 LQR 86; also extracts from *Road Traffic Reports* [RTR] and from *Criminal Appeal Reports* [Cr App R].

Thomson Legal & Regulatory Ltd for extract from *Commonwealth Law Reports* (1969), vol 121 published by the © Lawbook Co, part of Thomson Legal & Regulatory Ltd, www.thomson.com.au.

Vathek Publishing for extract from B. Fitzpatrick: 'Strict Liability and Article 6(2) of the European Convention on Human Rights: Non School-Attendance Offence' (2004) 68 *Journal of Criminal Law* 11.

Every effort has been made to trace and contact copyright holders prior to going to press but this has not been possible in every case. Although we are continuing to seek the necessary permissions up to publication, if notified, the publisher will undertake to rectify any errors or omissions at the earliest opportunity.

Table of Statutes

References in **bold** type indicate where the section of an Act is set out in part or in full.

Table of Cases

References in **bold** indicate where a case is set out.

Abbreviations

The following are the abbreviations used for the principal textbooks and legal journals cited in this book. References are to the latest editions, as shown below, unless it is specifically stated otherwise. The particulars of other works referred to in the text are set out in the relevant footnotes.

Andenaes, GPCL	*The General Part of the Criminal Law of Norway* (1965) by J. Andenaes.
Archbold	*Criminal Pleading, Evidence and Practice* by J. F. Archbold (2005) by P. J. Richardson and others.
Ashworth, POCL	*Principles of Criminal Law* (4th edn, 2003) by A. Ashworth.
Blackstone	*Blackstone's Criminal Practice* (2005) by P. Murphy and others.
Blackstone, *Commentaries*, i	*Commentaries on the Laws of England* by Sir William Blackstone, vol i (4 vols) (17th edn, 1830) by E. Christian.
Burchell and Hunt, SACLP	*South African Criminal Law and Procedure*, vol I, *General Principles* (1983) by F. M. Burchell, J. R. L. Milton and J. M. Burchell.
Butler	Report of the Committee on Mentally Abnormal Offenders (1975) Cmnd 6244.
CLJ	Cambridge Law Journal.
Cal Law Rev	California Law Review.
Can Bar Rev	Canadian Bar Review.
Co I Inst	*Institutes of the Laws of England* by Sir Edward Coke, vol I (4 vols) (1797).
Col LR	Columbia Law Review.
Crime, Proof and Punishment	*Crime, Proof and Punishment: Essays in Honour of Sir Rupert Cross* edited by C. F. H. Tapper (1981).
Criminal Law Essays	*Criminal Law: Essays in Honour of J. C.* Smith edited by P. F. Smith (1987).
Crim LR	Criminal Law Review.
CLP	Current Legal Problems.
CLRC/OAP/R	Criminal Law Revision Committee, Fourteenth Report, *Offences Against the Person* (1980) Cmnd 7844.
CLRC/OAP/WP	Criminal Law Revision Committee, Working Paper on Offences Against the Person (1976).
CLRC/SO/WP	Criminal Law Revision Committee, Working Paper on Sexual Offences (1980).
Draft Code	*A Criminal Code for England and Wales*, Law Com No 177 (1989).

East, I PC	*A Treatise of the Pleas of the Crown* by E. H. East, vol I (2 vols) (1803).
Edwards, *Mens Rea*	*Mens Rea in Statutory Offences* (1955) by J. Ll. J. Edwards.
Foster	*A Report on Crown Cases and Discourses on the Crown Law* by Sir Michael Foster (3rd edn, 1792) by M. Dodson.
Gordon	*Criminal Law of Scotland* (2nd edn, 1978) by G. H. Gordon.
Griew, *Theft*	*The Theft Acts 1968 and 1978* (7th edn, 1995) by E. J. Griew.
Hale, I PC	*The History of the Pleas of the Crown* by Sir Matthew Hale, vol i (2 vols) (1736).
Hall, *General Principles*	*General Principles of Criminal Law* (2nd edn, 1960) by J. Hall.
Halsbury	*The Laws of England* by the Earl of Halsbury and Other Lawyers (4th edn, 1973–) by Lord Hailsham of St Marylebone.
Harv LR	Harvard Law Review.
Hawkins, I PC	*A Treatise of the Pleas of the Crown* by W. Hawkins, vol I (2 vols) (8th edn, 1795) by J. Curwood.
Holdsworth, I HEL	*A History of English Law* by Sir William Holdsworth, vol i (14 vols) (1923–64).
Howard, SR	*Strict Responsibility* (1963) by Colin Howard.
J Crim L	Journal of Criminal Law (English).
J Cr L & Cr	Journal of Criminal Law and Criminology (USA).
JSPTL	Journal of the Society of Public Teachers of Law.
Kenny, *Outlines*	*Outlines of Criminal Law* by C. S. Kenny (19th edn, 1965) by J. W. C. Turner.
LQR	Law Quarterly Review.
LS	Legal Studies, the Journal of the Society of Legal Scholars.
MACL	*The Modern Approach to Criminal Law* edited by L. Radzinowicz and J. W. C. Turner (1948).
Med Sci & L	Medicine, Science and the Law.
MLR	Modern Law Review.
NZ Essays	*Essays on Criminal Law in New Zealand* edited by R. S. Clark (1971).
OJLS	Oxford Journal of Legal Studies.
Perkins, *Criminal Law*	*Criminal Law* (2nd edn, 1969) by R. Perkins.
Perkins and Boyce, *Criminal Law*	*Criminal Law* (3rd edn, 1982) by R. Perkins and R. Boyce.
Pollock and Maitland, I HEL	*The History of English Law before the Time of Edward I* by Sir Frederick Pollock and F. W. Maitland, vol I (2 vols) (2nd edn).

RCCP	Report of the Royal Commission on Capital Punishment (1953) Cmd 8932.
Reshaping the Criminal Law	*Reshaping the Criminal Law: Essays in Honour of Glanville Williams* edited by P. R. Glazebrook (1978).
Russell	*Crime* by Sir W. O. Russell (12th edn, 1964) by J. W. C. Turner (2 vols).
Simester and Sullivan	*Criminal Law Theory and Doctrine* (2nd edn, 2003).
Smith, *Justification and Excuse*	*Justification and Excuse in the Criminal Law* by J. C. Smith (The Hamlyn Lectures, 1989).
Smith, *Property Offences*	*Property Offences* (1994) by A. T. H. Smith.
Smith, *Theft*	*The Law of Theft* (8th edn, 1997) by J. C. Smith.
SALJ	South African Law Journal.
Stephen, *Digest*	*A Digest of the Criminal Law* by Sir James Fitzjames Stephen (9th edn, 1950) by L. F. Struge.
Stephen, HCL	*A History of the Criminal Law of England* by Sir James Fitzjames Stephen, (19th edn, 1950) by L. F. Sturge.
U Pa Law Rev	University of Pennsylvania Law Review.
Williams, CLGP	*Criminal Law: The General Part* (2nd edn, 1961) by G. L. Williams.
Williams, TBCL	*Textbook of Criminal Law* (2nd edn, 1983) by G. L. Williams.
Wilson, *Central Issues*	*Central Issues in Criminal Theory* (2002) by W. Wilson.
YLJ	Yale Law Journal.

1

Introduction

1. SOURCES OF CRIMINAL LAW

Unlike most jurisdictions, England and Wales has no criminal code. From very early times Parliament has created criminal offences. These have always taken effect in the context of the common law of crime, that is, the law made by the judges in the decided cases. The doctrine of precedent requires judges to follow the decisions of higher courts. Those courts—the Administrative Court, the Court of Appeal Criminal Division, and the House of Lords—consider themselves bound, with some exceptions, by their own decisions. These decisions therefore make the law—unless they are overturned by Parliament or by a higher court, or the court itself in one of the exceptional cases in which it is free to do so.

The general principles of criminal liability are nearly all to be found in common law, not in an Act of Parliament. The great majority of crimes are now defined by statute but some very important crimes are not, particularly murder and manslaughter. Whether the law concerning a crime is to be found in the common law or in a statute is frequently a matter of historical accident.

Decided cases may, however, be no less important in relation to statutory than to common law offences. When we seek to find the law the statute must always be the starting point but statutes have to be construed by the courts. Once the statute has been construed by a higher court it is that construction which counts. If it differs from the meaning which would naturally be put upon statute by the ordinary reader, it is the construction which prevails. The reader of s 3(1) of the Theft Act 1968 must learn that the words in that section, 'the rights of an owner', mean 'a right of an owner', because the House of Lords has so decided (below, p **759**). The Law Commission has pointed out (Consultation Paper No 122, 1992, para 7.11) that the most important offences under the Offences Against the Person Act 1861 'have become in effect common law crimes, the context of which is determined by the case law and not by statute.' The words of the Act, when not positively misleading, are virtually irrelevant. That is an extreme case but, even in a modern statute like the Theft Act 1968, the words of a section may be misleading to a reader who is unaware of the case law. Hence the emphasis put upon cases in this book.

2. CODIFICATION OF CRIMINAL LAW

Much effort has gone into proposals to codify our criminal law—so far, in vain. Criminal Law Commissioners worked from 1833 to 1849 (and two major Bills based on their work were introduced in 1853) but made no progress, largely because of the opposition by the judges to codification of the common law. Then a judge who was also a great criminal lawyer, Sir James Fitzjames Stephen, prepared a draft code which, he said, represented the labour of many of the best years of his life and which was introduced into Parliament in 1878 and again in 1879. Again the effort failed, probably because of opposition by the judges, especially Lord Cockburn CJ.

Modified versions of Stephen's Code became the law in Canada, New Zealand and many other jurisdictions but nothing significant happened in England until 1967 when the Home Secretary of the time, Mr Roy Jenkins, made a speech in favour of codification. Almost immediately, the Law Commission, in its second programme (1968), stated its objective of a comprehensive examination of the criminal law with a view to its codification. It established a working party which produced a series of valuable papers on the general principles of criminal law. In 1980 the Commission appointed a Criminal Code Team to consider and make proposals in relation to a code. The team reported in 1985 with a draft Criminal Code Bill covering general principles of liability and offences against the person (Law Com No 143). The generally favourable reception given to the report encouraged the Commission to proceed with the preparation of a more complete code covering, in Part I, general principles and, in Part II, the range of specific offences which would be expected in a code. A report and draft Criminal Code Bill (Law Com No 177) was published in 1989. The draft Bill is intended for the most part to be a restatement of the existing law but it also incorporates law reform proposals made by official bodies such as the Criminal Law Revision Committee and the Law Commission itself.

There now appears to be substantial support for codification. See, in particular, Lord Bingham CJ, 'Must We Wait for Ever?' [1998] Crim LR 694.

The arguments in favour of codification are what they have always been. First, it would bring clarity and accessibility to the law. As the Attorney-General put it in the House of Commons 119 years ago:

'Surely, it is a desirable thing that anybody who may want to know the law on a particular subject should be able to turn to a chapter of the Code, and there find the law he is in search of explained in a few intelligible and well-constructed sentences; nor would he have to enter upon a long examination of Russell on Crimes, or Archbold, and other text-books, because he would have a succinct and clear statement before him. (Hansard, HC, April 3, 1879, vol. 245 (3rd series), col. 316)' Secondly, a code would bring coherence to this branch of the law. Sir John Smith has expressed his general disbelief in codes—a disbelief which I for my part share—but he continued: 'The criminal law is entirely different. It is incoherent and inconsistent. State almost any general principle and you find one or more leading cases which contradict it. It is littered with distinctions which have no basis in reason but are mere historical accidents. I am in favour of codification of the criminal law because I see no other way of reducing a chaotic system to order, of eliminating irrational distinctions and of making the law reasonably comprehensible, accessible and certain. These are all practical objects. Irrational distinctions mean injustice. A is treated differently from B when there is no rational ground for treating him differently; and this is not justice. (Codification of the Criminal Law, Child & Co. Lecture, 1986)' Sir John has entertained generations of students, practitioners and judges by highlighting the anomalies in our present law. As the present Chairman of the Law Commission has herself said, the cure now can only be achieved by codification; it cannot be provided by the courts alone. Thirdly, a code would bring greater certainty to the law, and in this of all fields the law should be so far as possible certain. The arguments for incremental development of the law, persuasive elsewhere, have no application here. It is not just that a defendant should be held punishable for an act which would not have been thought criminal when he did it; and if he is held not liable for conduct which would at that time have been thought criminal, the almost inevitable consequence is that others have been unjustly punished. Incorporation of the European Convention reinforces the need for certainty if the principle of legality is to be observed. Even the most breathless admirer of the common law must regard it as a reproach that after 700 years of judicial decision-making our highest tribunal should have been called upon time and again in recent years to consider the mental ingredients of murder, the oldest and most serious of crimes.... One hopes that parliamentary time may yet be found to achieve something that has eluded our predecessors but would, I think, come to be recognised as an important milestone in our legal and public life.

A government paper, 'Criminal Justice: The Way Ahead', included plans for 'a consolidated, modernised core criminal code' and work is proceeding at the Law Commission. But it would be unrealistic to suppose that codification is imminent or that the whole Code could be enacted in a single Act. It would necessarily have to be done by a series of Acts which would then be consolidated. The Law Commission's Report (Law Com No 218), 'Legislating the Criminal Code' (1993), proposes to begin with non-fatal offences against the person and contains a draft Bill covering these offences and, most importantly, some provisions governing general principles of liability which would be applicable to all offences. In February 1998 the Home Office published a Consultation Paper, 'Violence: Reforming the Offences Against the Person Act 1861' with a revised draft Bill, discussed [1998] Crim LR 317. This seemed to give real hope of a significant start on the enactment of the Code but no more was heard of the outcome of the consultation process and progress seems to have stalled, pending the Law Commission's reconsideration of the draft Code. Subsequently, other aspects of the Commission's Codification proposals have been taken forward into legislation (for example, the provisions relating to Non Accidental Deaths and Serious Injury to Children (2003), now found in the Domestic Violence, Crime and Victims Act 2004; and the fraud reform proposals from Report No 276, *Fraud* (2002), currently in the Fraud Bill 2005).

Provisions of the draft Code are, however, useful in understanding and scrutinizing the present law and will be found at appropriate points in the following pages.

On codification generally, see G. de Búrca and S. Gardner, 'Codification of the Criminal Law' (1990) 10 OJLS 559.

3. THE HUMAN RIGHTS ACT 1998

In addition to the primary and secondary legislation of the UK Parliament, and the decisions of the English and Welsh courts, it is increasingly important to consider other legal sources which will impact on the way that English Criminal Law is defined and applied. Although the ECHR impact is most significant in the context of evidence and procedure, the ECHR also has a direct impact on the operation of the substantive criminal law in many ways. In terms of definition of crimes, the greatest impact might have been expected to be through Article 7, which proscribes retrospective criminalization, including a prohibition on criminal laws which are too vague and uncertain.

Article 7 provides:

(1) No one shall be held guilty of any criminal offence on account of any act or omission which did not constitute a criminal offence under national or international law at the time when it was

committed. Nor shall a heavier penalty be imposed than the one that was applicable at the time the criminal offence was committed.

(2) This Article shall not prejudice the trial and punishment of any person for any act or omission which, at the time it was committed, was criminal according to the general principles of law recognised by civilised nations.

The European Court held in *Kokkinakis v Greece* (1994) 17 EHRR 397, and has reiterated many times since, that

Article 7 is not confined to prohibiting the retrospective application of the criminal law to an accused's disadvantage: it also embodies, more generally, the principle that only the law can define a crime and prescribe a penalty (*nullum crimen, nulla poena sine lege*) and the principle that the criminal law must not be extensively construed to an accused's detriment, for instance by analogy....it follows that an offence must be clearly defined in the law. *SW v UK* [1995] 21 EHRR 363, para 35.

The Court looks to whether the individual can know from the wording of the relevant provision and, if need be, with the assistance of the courts' interpretation of it, what acts and omissions will make him criminally liable.

This is not a prohibition on the development of the common law. As the Court noted in *SW*:

However clearly drafted a legal provision may be, in any system of law, including criminal law, there is an inevitable element of judicial interpretation. There will always be a need for elucidation of doubtful points and for adaptation to changing circumstances. Indeed, in the United Kingdom, as in the other Convention States, the progressive development of the criminal law through judicial law-making is a well entrenched and necessary part of legal tradition. Article 7 of the Convention cannot be read as outlawing the gradual clarification of the rules of criminal liability through judicial interpretation from case to case, provided that the resultant development is consistent with the essence of the offence and could reasonably be foreseen.

To date the English courts have taken a very narrow view of the protection afforded by Article 7 and have failed to accept that common law crimes such as manslaughter by gross negligence (*Misra* (below, Ch 18 p 651) and public nuisance (*Goldstein* [2003] EWCA Crim 3450), are incompatible with Article 7 on the grounds of their vagueness.

As the Human Rights Act was being implemented, leading commentators debated the likely impact this aspect of the ECHR might have in producing greater certainty in the substantive criminal law.

Lord Justice Buxton, 'The Human Rights Act and the Substantive Criminal Law'
[2000] Crim LR 331

...

There are two, somewhat different, types of reason why certainty is desirable in the criminal law. The first directly engages human rights interests: the citizen is entitled to know what he can do and what he cannot, and in particular is entitled to be protected from the arbitrariness of state action that must attend punishment for breaches of a law that is erratic in its operation. The second is that uncertainty in, or difficulty of access to, the criminal law makes criminal trials not only unpredictable in their outcome but also unduly lengthy and expensive. The ECHR is not concerned with the latter problem....

The ECHR is however at least in principle concerned with the other aspect of this problem, the rights of the citizen and his protection from excess of power on the part of the state; but here again the ECHR has disappointingly little to offer in practice. That is because it is very difficult to discern in the ECHR jurisprudence any general principle that the criminal law must be accessible and certain above a very modest level; and where certainty of criminal law has come into issue in ECHR questions, the standards required by the Convention jurisprudence have been distinctly undemanding. I deal with those two criticisms in reverse order from that just set out.

Articles 7–11 of the ECHR provide various freedoms (e.g. freedom of expression, Article 10), which the national state may however restrict in accordance with certain conditions: conditions that in each case must be 'prescribed by', or 'in accordance with', 'law'. Thus, in relation to what is characterised in ECHR terms as an interference with, for instance, private life, under Article 8, no justification can be pleaded by the national state if the justificatory reasons are not prescribed by any law at all (Halford v. United Kingdom (1997) 24 E.H.R.R. 523). And when a national state tries to rely on a provision of national law for this purpose it has to remember that:

> 'a norm cannot be regarded as a "law" unless it is formulated with sufficient precision to enable the citizen to regulate his conduct: he must be able—if need be with appropriate advice—to foresee, to a degree that is reasonable in the circumstances, the consequences which a given action may entail' (Silver v. United Kingdom (1983) 5 E.H.R.R. 347 [87]–[88]).

However, this apparently promising appeal to the virtues of certainty has severe limitations. It does not require the law to be in statutory form; and not only the common law of contempt of court (Sunday Times v. United Kingdom (1979) 2 E.H.R.R. 245) but even the notoriously elusive common law concept of breach of the peace (Steel v. United Kingdom [1998] Crim.L.R. 893) have been held by the Strasbourg Court to pass the Silver test. True it is that the other possible basis on which a binding order can be made, that the respondent's conduct was contra bonos mores, has been found to be insufficiently precise to count as 'law' (Hashman v. United Kingdom, The Times, December 1, 1999 and [2000] Crim.L.R. 185, sub nom. Hashman and Harrap v. United Kingdom); but it would have been extraordinary if any other conclusion had been reached, in view of the conclusion of the English Law Commission that to impose restrictions on the basis of that concept is contrary to elementary English notions of fair process (Law Com. 222 (1994), at para. 4.34).

This very cautious approach has been carried through in the interpretation of Article 7 of the ECHR, which purports to establish a more general principle of certainty in the criminal law by providing that:

No-one shall be held guilty of any criminal offence on account of any act or omission which did not constitute a criminal offence under national or international law at the time when it was committed.

Although Article 7 ostensibly requires scrutiny of all aspects of the certainty of penal laws (See Kokkinakis v. Greece (1994) 17 E.H.R.R. 397), its main application has been in relation to retrospective or allegedly retrospective criminal laws: to which topic we now turn.

Retrospectivity

No English criminal lawyer needs to be told that criminal penalties should not be imposed in respect of conduct that was not criminal at the time at which it was committed. However, the ECHR's explication of this principle is, again, somewhat limited.

The issue was explored in SW v. United Kingdom ((1996) 21 E.H.R.R. 363), a complaint resulting from the conviction of a husband for raping his wife that was only upheld by the abolition of the marital rape exemption by the House of Lords in R (Rape: Marital Exemption) (above). The Strasbourg Court concluded, in line with the foreseeability rationale that it adopts in respect of other issues of certainty of law, that:

> 'Article 7…cannot be read as outlawing the gradual clarification of the rules of criminal liability through judicial interpretation from case to case, provided that the resultant development is consistent with the essence of the offence and could be reasonably foreseen' (para. 36).

This is, however, foresight of a somewhat special sort. The accretion of exceptions to the martial rape exemption might on one view be described as an 'evolution [that] had reached a stage where judicial recognition of the absence of immunity had become a reasonably foreseeable development of the law; (para. 43)' but might equally have been thought to indicate that the basic exemption, on which the complainant in SW v. United Kingdom relied, remained intact and could only be altered by legislation. That was certainly the view of the Law Commission, which published a working paper on rape within marriage shortly before the matter came to a head in the courts (Law Commission Working Paper No. 116, especially at para. 2.08), and of a number of first instance judges who, however reluctantly, had seen themselves as bound by the rule (See in particular the full and careful judgment of Rougier J., commenting on some decisions in a contrary sense, in R. v. J. [1991] 1 All E.R. 759). While hesitating to appeal here to Lord Simonds' famous comparison of foresight and hindsight (In The Wagon Mound [1961] A.C. 388 at 424), if one posits an (admittedly unlikely) visit to his solicitor by Mr R to ask for advice about trying to have intercourse with his wife, it is far from clear that he would have been told with any confidence that (whatever else might be said about his conduct) he was facing a criminal conviction and a sentence of three years imprisonment.

It would therefore seem that a 'criminal offence' under Article 7 can be an offence merely in gremio, provided that its appearance can be said to be foreseeable on the basis of a not very demanding standard of foresight. That adds nothing to the protection of the individual that is provided by English domestic principle, and indeed falls short of what English principle has always been thought to require.

The requirement of certainty of law and the HRA

Even in those very limited cases where the jurisprudence of the ECHR does affect the substance of criminal or near criminal provisions, the only available example being binding over in respect of conduct considered to be contra bonos mores, it is difficult to speak with confidence about the effect of that finding in English domestic law. That is because, as cannot be too often or too strongly stressed, the ECHR is not by the HRA 'incorporated' into English law in the same way as the law of the European Union directly became also English law, and just like any other part of domestic law, by the operation of sections 2 and 3 of the European Communities Act 1972. Rather, Convention rights, with the same content as they are given by ECHR jurisprudence, are enforced in English law by the special methods envisaged by the HRA. It is therefore necessary first to investigate the terms of the right, and then to see how that right fits into the special HRA machinery.

The right identified in Hashman v. United Kingdom was a right not to be prevented, by the application of the domestic law on binding over, from exercising another Convention right, the right to freedom of expression under Article 10. As we have seen, under the ECHR the object of that right of non-interference is the state. The courts are in ECHR terms an organ of the state; and are also, under section 6 of the HRA, public authorities that must act compatibly with Convention rights. It might be thought to follow that, should the facts of Hashman repeat themselves, the English court should simply refuse to enforce or apply the law of binding over. That course is not, however, open to the English court where an offending provision is statutory rather than part of the common law. In that case, even if the court thinks, and declares, that the provision is incompatible with the ECHR, by section 4(6) of the HRA the provision continues to bind…There are of course good English constitutional and ECHR human rights reasons why the product of a democratically-elected legislature should be better protected from attack by the courts than are the rules of the common law. It however seems very unlikely that it could be right for a domestic court to refuse to apply a rule of the common law on the grounds that it was incompatible with the ECHR when that course is not open to it in respect of a statutory rule.

English courts and Convention rights

The foregoing issue does not however arise until the English court concludes that a national rule or practice is indeed incompatible with the ECHR. There is currently some disagreement about how the English court should approach that question in cases, which will be the majority, where the claim of incompatibility is made without specific foundation in the case law of the Strasbourg Court. It seems, however, inevitable that the English court, faced with that problem, must apply the Strasbourg jurisprudence garnered from other cases: that is, to try to determine how the Strasbourg Court would decide the case were it to come before it. That intellectual process is complicated by the reluctance of the Strasbourg Court to differ from the national court in matters of judgment exercised in criminal cases...; and more generally by the frequent recourse of the Strasbourg Court to the doctrine of the margin of appreciation, which is not a doctrine directly available to, or logically to be applied by, the national court. Nevertheless, that the Strasbourg Court sees the terms of the ECHR, including Article 6, as allowing for the application by it of the doctrine of the margin of appreciation necessarily demonstrates that it is difficult to draw from the bare wording of those provisions anything more than very general and flexible principles (this point is strikingly made by Judge de Mayer in his dissenting judgment in Z v. Finland [1997] E.H.R.L.R. 439 at 442–443). The national judge, when asked to apply an Article of the ECHR to a situation not specifically addressed by existing Convention law, must therefore recognise that generality and flexibility is the nature of Convention jurisprudence, fashioned by the Strasbourg Court out of the ECHR itself (Lord Hope of Craighead in R. v. DPP, ex p. Kebilene [1999] 3 W.L.R. 972 at 993H:).

Simply to ignore the view taken by the Strasbourg Court of the ambit and nature of the ECHR, and to try to apply the wording of the ECHR effectively as if it were an English statute...., would lead in logic, as the Law Commission has indeed recently suggested, to a distinctly stronger line being taken in the national courts on the protection of Convention rights than would necessarily be evident in Strasbourg (L.C.C.P. No 155, para. 5.48). Not only does it seem extraordinary in itself that London should know better than Strasbourg what the Strasbourg jurisprudence requires..., but also the suggestion hardly sits well with the English court's obligation, imposed by section 2(1) of the HRA, to take the Strasbourg jurisprudence into account.... In practice, however, English judges may be expected to pay close attention to the spirit of that jurisprudence; with what may be expected to be the result that they will hesitate long before concluding that a provision of the English common law would necessarily be found to be incompatible with the ECHR.

...

In reply, Andrew Ashworth, 'The Human Rights Act and the Substantive Criminal Law: A Non-Minimalist View'
[2000] Crim LR 564

I will not review that literature, but will advance just a few arguments contrary to Sir Richard's position on Convention rights and substantive criminal law. For many practitioners and teachers the normative question of what the approach ought to be is no less important than the predictive question of what approach the courts are likely to take in October 2000. Thus far, there is little indication of this. As Lord Chief Justice, Lord Bingham made it clear that he did not expect judges to take divergent views on the application of the Human Rights Act; but already there are differences apparent in the cases...

Some Common Ground

In laying the foundations for his argument, Sir Richard Buxton makes a number of important points that bear repetition. To refer to the Human Rights Act as 'incorporating' the Convention is loose: the powers and duties in the Act are much more specific, and apply only to those Convention rights listed in Schedule 1. In the sphere of criminal justice the greatest impact will be upon criminal procedure and evidence, with sentencing and the substantive criminal law much less affected. Indeed, on some issues English law already grants rights more extensive than those required by the Convention (e.g. many of the provisions of the Police and Criminal Evidence Act 1984), and this is to be expected. The purpose of the Convention is to declare only minimum rights.

Some of those who advocate(d) 'incorporation' of the Convention into English law tend to pay insufficient attention to its deficiencies. As an international document on human rights it can be criticised as somewhat narrow and old-fashioned. Turning to the Strasbourg jurisprudence, this is patchy and in some respects disappointing. In terms of fairness and even self-consistency there are judgments of the European Court of Human Rights which do not achieve a high standard. Sir Richard Buxton mentions two of these. The judgment in Steel v. U.K. (above) begins by considering whether the offence of conduct likely to cause a breach of the peace attains the standard of certainty required by the 'quality of law' test that applies wherever the State seeks to rely upon the lawfulness of arrest or detention. The Court held that English law on this point, which Sir Richard describes as 'notoriously elusive', does satisfy the certainty requirements. The judgment in SW v. U.K. (above) propounds the test of 'reasonable foreseeability', if necessary with legal advice, for determining whether a judicial extension of the law amounts to retrospective criminalisation contrary to Article 7. But, as Sir Richard observes, there must be doubts about the consistency of the judgment when the Court went on to hold that the marital rape conviction satisfied this test.

Applying the Human Rights Act

The above remarks suggest that the Convention and its case-law do not always shine as beacons of enlightenment. However, there are many other decisions which are not open to such strictures. Moreover, the Human Rights Act requires English courts and other public authorities to take a certain approach. By section 6 they must act compatibly with Convention rights. By section 3 they must interpret statutes 'so far as is possible' in a way that is compatible with Convention rights. And by section 2 the courts must 'take account of' the Strasbourg jurisprudence on the Convention.

These provisions will usher in a new judicial approach. Sir Richard states that it is hardly surprising that the European Court has held that binding a person over not to act contra bonos mores fails the certainty requirement in the 'quality of law' test (Hashman and Harrup v. U.K. [2000] Crim. L.R. 185), since the Law Commission had already concluded that the 'concept is contrary to elementary English notions of fair process.' (But the fact is that the English courts have allowed the notion to be used for many years, without calling it into question. Now, under the Human Rights Act, a court would be failing in its section 6 duty if it were to rely on contra bonos mores to bind a person over. It should apply section 2 and section 6 and decline any application of this nature. The Human Rights Act gives courts a much clearer direction than did the common law on matters of this kind. Sir Richard argues that it is unlikely that the Act allows a court to refuse to apply a rule of common law, on grounds of incompatibility with a Convention right, when it has no such power in respect of a statutory rule. But there is nothing in the Act to support his interpretation. The Act requires a higher court to make a 'declaration of incompatibility' when the power of interpretation in section 3 cannot be used to remove the incompatibility, so as to preserve the sovereignty of Parliament. No such concern for sovereignty is needed where it is a matter of altering a common law rule. On this view a court may (and, in view of section 6 of the Act, should) decline to bind a person over not to act contra bonos mores. Equally, a court should attempt to amend the scope of the common law defence of parental chastisement if a case is heard before the government introduces amending legislation, because by section 6 the court is bound to act so as to ensure compatibility with Article 3 of the Convention, and the current defence violates Article 3 (A. v. U.K. (1999) 28 E.H.R.R. 603 [1998] Crim. L.R. 892). Further, it is not clear that an English court's function should be to predict how a particular point would be decided in Strasbourg: a court should take account of any Strasbourg decisions, but there seems no reason why it should not develop those decisions and fill in gaps where they exist, taking a principled rather than a predictive approach.

I would therefore submit that the Human Rights Act empowers, nay commands, the courts to amend common law rules so as to ensure compatibility with the Convention (A. Lester and D. Pannick (eds), Human Rights Law and Practice (1999), para. 2.6.3, n.3.). Now Sir Richard argues that there are some cases in which such an amendment would infringe the Article 7 rights of the defendant, by (effectively) enlarging the scope of an offence retrospectively. That is an important argument in principle, but it will rarely be applicable. It would not apply to either of the examples above, binding over or parental chastisement: even though compatibility with Convention rights requires a contraction in the scope of the latter defence, it is 'reasonably foreseeable' with legal advice that an English court will now follow Strasbourg. Moreover, as mentioned earlier, the Strasbourg court has taken a rather conservative view of Article 7, and it will rarely bite if the seeds of a change in the law have been sown in previous decisions. Sir Richard is right to say that English courts that rely on the Human Rights Act to amend common law rules must remain aware of Article 7, but it is doubtful whether it is as strong a restraint as he implies.

Many of the other Articles of the Convention will also affect the scope of definition of existing and future crimes. As with other areas of law, the criminal court is obliged to 'take account' of the ECHR jurisprudence in construing English law. This is problematic since much of the Strasbourg jurisprudence is vague and general in nature and not in the familiar form of common law case precedents.

The Convention rights

Many of the ECHR rights as specified in the Human Rights Act 1998, Sch 1 will be of importance in determining the appropriate scope and application of offences. These are set out here for ease of reference.

Article 2

2. (1) Everyone's right to life shall be protected by law. No one shall be deprived of his life intentionally save in the execution of a sentence of a court following his conviction of a crime for which this penalty is provided by law.

(2) Deprivation of life shall not be regarded as inflicted in contravention of this Article when it results from the use of force which is no more than absolutely necessary:
(a) in defence of any person from unlawful violence;
(b) in order to effect a lawful arrest or to prevent the escape of a person lawfully detained;
(c) in action lawfully taken for the purpose of quelling a riot or insurrection.

Article 2 will impact on the scope of the protection offered by the law of homicide and the qualifications on the scope of self-defence. This is considered in Chapter 12 below.

Article 3

3. No one shall be subjected to torture or to inhuman or degrading treatment or punishment.

Article 3 will regulate, for example, the parental administration of corporal punishment.

Article 5

5. (1) Everyone has the right to liberty and security of the person. No one shall be deprived of his liberty save in the following cases and in accordance with a procedure prescribed by law:
(a) the lawful detention of a person after conviction by a competent court;

(b) the lawful arrest or detention of a person for non-compliance with the lawful order of a court or in order to secure the fulfilment of any obligation prescribed by law;

(c) the lawful arrest or detention of a person effected for the purpose of bringing him before the competent legal authority on reasonable suspicion of having committed an offence or when it is reasonably considered necessary to prevent his committing an offence or fleeing after having done so;

(d) the detention of a minor by lawful order for the purpose of educational supervision or his lawful detention for the purpose of bringing him before the competent legal authority;

(e) the lawful detention of persons for the prevention of the spreading of infectious diseases, of persons of unsound mind, alcoholics or drug addicts or vagrants;

(f) the lawful arrest or detention of a person to prevent his effecting an unauthorised entry into the country or of a person against whom action is being taken with a view to deportation or extradition.

(2) Everyone who is arrested shall be informed promptly, in a language which he understands, of the reasons for his arrest and of any charge against him.

(3) Everyone arrested or detained in accordance with the provisions of paragraph (1)(c) of this Article shall be brought promptly before a judge or other officer authorised by law to exercise judicial power and shall be entitled to trial within a reasonable time or to release pending trial. Release may be conditioned by guarantees to appear for trial.

(4) Everyone who is deprived of his liberty by arrest or detention shall be entitled to take proceedings by which the lawfulness of his detention shall be decided speedily by a court and his release ordered if the detention is not lawful.

(5) Everyone who has been the victim of arrest or detention in contravention of the provisions of this Article shall have an enforceable right to compensation.

Article 5 will affect, for example, the manner in which defendants found unfit to plead or not guilty by reason of insanity will be treated. This is considered in Chapter 11 below.

Article 6

6. (1) In the determination of his civil rights and obligations or of any criminal charge against him, everyone is entitled to a fair and public hearing within a reasonable time by an independent and impartial tribunal established by law. Judgment shall be pronounced publicly but the press and public may be excluded from all or part of the trial in the interest of morals, public order or national security in a democratic society, where the interests of juveniles or the protection of the private lives of the parties so require, or to the extent strictly necessary in the opinion of the court in special circumstances where publicity would prejudice the interests of justice.

(2) Everyone charged with a criminal offence shall be presumed innocent until proved guilty according to law.

(3) Everyone charged with a criminal offence has the following minimum rights:

(a) to be informed promptly, in a language which he understands and in detail, of the nature and cause of the accusation against him;

(b) to have adequate time and facilities for the preparation of his defence;

(c) to defend himself in person or through legal assistance of his own choosing or, if he has not sufficient means to pay for legal assistance, to be given it free when the interests of justice so require;

(d) to examine or have examined witnesses against him and to obtain the attendance and examination of witnesses on his behalf under the same conditions as witnesses against him;

(e) to have the free assistance of an interpreter if he cannot understand or speak the language used in court.

Article 6 could on one interpretation affect the legitimacy of an offence of strict liability offences, as discussed in Chapter 8. Its impact will be very obvious in relation to the burden of proof discussed below, p 176.

The concept of a 'criminal charge' is an autonomous Convention concept, and the national courts can readily avoid any categorical determination for the purposes of English law: *Engel v Netherlands* [1976] 1 EHRR 647. The European Court has determined that if domestic law classifies the proceeding as criminal, this will be decisive, but where domestic law classifies the proceeding as non-criminal, the ECtHR will consider the true nature of the proceedings, taking into account the severity of the penalty which may be imposed looking especially at whether imprisonment is a possible penalty; whether the rule applies only to a specific group or to the public generally; whether there is a 'punitive or deterrent element' to the process; whether the imposition of any penalty is dependent upon a finding of culpability; and whether other Member States classify such conduct as criminal.

Article 8

8. (1) Everyone has the right to respect for his private and family life, his home and his correspondence.

(2) There shall be no interference by a public authority with the exercise of this right except such as is in accordance with the law and is necessary in a democratic society in the interests of national security, public safety or the economic well-being of the country, for the prevention of disorder or crime, for the protection of health or morals, or for the protection of the rights and freedoms of others.

Article 8 will be relevant in protecting the rights of consenting adults to engage in sexual behaviour as discussed below in Chapter 20.

Article 9

9. (1) Everyone has the right to freedom of thought, conscience and religion; this right includes freedom to change his religion or belief and freedom, either alone or in community with others and in public or private, to manifest his religion or belief, in worship, teaching, practice and observance.

(2) Freedom to manifest one's religion or beliefs shall be subject only to such limitations as are prescribed by law and are necessary in a democratic society in the interests of public safety, for the protection of public order, health or morals, or for the protection of the rights and freedoms of others.

Article 9 could impact on the law of blasphemy or the right of a religion to conduct a service in public, or on the right to perform ritual male circumcision.

Article 10

10. (1) Everyone has the right to freedom of expression. This right shall include freedom to hold opinions and to receive and impart information and ideas without interference by public authority and regardless of frontiers. This Article shall not prevent States from requiring the licensing of broadcasting, television or cinema enterprises.

(2) The exercise of these freedoms, since it carries with it duties and responsibilities, may be subject to such formalities, conditions, restrictions or penalties as are prescribed by law and are necessary in a democratic society, in the interests of national security, territorial integrity or public safety, for the prevention of disorder or crime, for the protection of health or morals, for the protection of the reputation or rights of others, for preventing the disclosure of information received in confidence, or for maintaining the authority and impartiality of the judiciary.

Article 10 could be relevant when defendants are charged with offences in which they are expressing themselves in the form of protest—criminal damage or public order being the most obvious.

Article 11

11. (1) Everyone has the right to freedom of peaceful assembly and to freedom of association with others, including the right to form and to join trade unions for the protection of his interests.

(2) No restrictions shall be placed on the exercise of these rights other than such as are prescribed by law and are necessary in a democratic society in the interests of national security or public safety, for the prevention of disorder or crime, for the protection of health or morals or for the protection of the rights and freedoms of others. This Article shall not prevent the imposition of lawful restrictions on the exercise of these rights by members of the armed forces, of the police or of the administration of the State.

Article 11 could affect the way the public order restrictions on a meeting are enforced.

Article 14

14. The enjoyment of the rights and freedoms set forth in this Convention shall be secured without discrimination on any ground such as sex, race, colour, language, religion, political or other opinion, national or social origin, association with a national minority, property, birth or other status.

Article 14 could impact on the way that the criminal law discriminates against spouses or non-married couples.

In the case of Articles 2 and 3 the rights are absolute. With Articles 8–10, the rights are qualified. Thus, although there may be a prima facie breach of the right, it is open to the Crown to show that the restriction on the exercise of that right is (i) prescribed by law (or in accordance with law), and (ii) is necessary in a democratic society for one or more specified objectives (such as the protection of public order, health or morals, or the rights of others), and (iii) that it is a proportionate interference with the right in order to promote those specified objectives. For example, where D is prosecuted for possession of cannabis and claims his conduct was in accordance with his religion (Article 9), it will be for the Crown to establish that the law relating to misuse of drugs is sufficiently clearly prescribed by law, and that the offence is necessary and proportionate to protect public order or prevent crime, etc.

It was thought that the enactment of the Human Rights Act 1998 might serve as a catalyst for the implementation of the Criminal Code.

The Hon. Mrs Justice Arden DBE 'Criminal Law at the Crossroads: The Impact of Human Rights from The Law Commission's Perspective and The Need for a Code'
[1999] Crim LR 439

Our criminal law is a mixed system of statutory provisions and common law. The judges can within limits keep the common law up to date. Statute law, however, has to be kept up to date by Parliament.

For many years there has been legislative inertia. The situation is that there is an accumulated back-log of work for Parliament leaving large areas of criminal statutes needing reform.... The enactment of the Human Rights Act 1998 creates a new and pressing need for reform.

In 2005, there is still no sight of the Code being enacted.

FURTHER READING

P. ALLDRIDGE, 'Making Criminal Law Known', S. Shute and A. Simester (eds) *Criminal Law Theory* (2002)

On codification in other jurisdictions

P. R. FERGUSON, 'Codifying Criminal Law: The Scots and English Draft Codes Compared' [2004] Crim LR 105

J. P. MCCUTCHEON and K. QUINN, 'Codifying Criminal Law in Ireland' (1998) Statute Law Review 131

2

The elements of a crime

1. ACTUS REUS AND MENS REA

Anyone who thinks about it will readily appreciate that crime ordinarily involves a mental element. Suppose I take your bicycle from the rack in which you have left it, ride it home and put it in my garage. Have I stolen it? The question cannot be answered without considering my state of mind at the time of the taking. Perhaps I mistook your bicycle for my own similar model which I had left in the same shed. Or perhaps I mistakenly supposed that you had said I could borrow the bicycle; or, though I knew it was your bicycle and that I was taking it without your consent, I only intended to borrow it for a day or two. In none of these cases have I stolen it. But, if I knew it was your bicycle and that I did not have your consent and I dishonestly intended to keep it permanently for myself, I am guilty of theft. The act is the same in every case. The difference is in the state of mind with which the act is done. If D, driving his car, runs V down and kills him this will be murder if D did so intending to kill V; manslaughter if, though he wished no harm to anyone, he was driving with such gross negligence as a jury thinks to deserve condemnation as that offence; and accidental death if the collision occurred in spite of the fact that he was concentrating on what he was doing and exercising the care that a prudent and reasonably skilful driver should.

Virtually all crimes require proof of a mental element of some sort. It has to be proved with the same degree of strictness as the other elements of the crime as the case of *Woolmington*, p 172, below, demonstrates. Lawyers have long found it convenient to distinguish the mental element for the purposes of exposition of the law and have called it 'mens rea'. This phrase derives from a maxim quoted by Coke in his *Institutes* (ch 1, fo 10) 'Actus non facit reum nisi mens sit rea', an act does not make a man guilty of a crime unless his mind also be guilty. The expression, 'actus reus', is much more recent, having apparently been coined by Kenny in the first edition of his *Outlines of Criminal Law* in 1902 (see Jerome Hall, *General Principles of Criminal Law*, p 222, footnote 24) but it is now used throughout the common law world to designate the elements of an offence other than the mental element. These expressions are only analytical tools. The only thing that exists in law is the crime. The term 'mens rea' has long been used by the courts to denote whatever mental element is in issue. Recently 'actus reus' has also been utilized by courts with predictably uncertain results. See *Antoine* below, p 368. Courts and writers use the expressions in different senses and it cannot be asserted that one usage is correct and others wrong. Glanville Williams (*Criminal Law: The General Part* (2nd edn, 1961), p 18) writes:

…actus reus means the whole definition of the crime with the exception of the mental element—and it even includes a mental element in so far as that is contained in the definition of an act. This meaning of actus reus follows inevitably from the proposition that all the constituents of a crime are either actus reus or mens rea….

Actus reus includes, in the terminology here suggested, not merely the whole objective situation that has to be proved by the prosecution, but also the absence of any ground of justification or excuse, whether such justification or excuse be stated in any statute creating the crime or implied by the courts in accordance with general principles (though not including matters of excuse depending on absence of mens rea). [See also, Williams, TBCL, ch 2.]

This is a particularly useful description of the concepts but it involves two points of controversy.

(1) The actus reus generally requires proof that the defendant did an act. It is argued that since an act is essentially a voluntary movement and not a spasm or convulsion, 'voluntariness', though a mental element, is part of the actus reus. Moreover, the word that describes the act may imply some further mental element. There are for example many offences where the actus reus consists in possession of proscribed articles. It has long been recognized that 'possess' imports a mental as well as a physical element. (See *Warner*, p 243, below.) Some writers and judges have described these mental elements as part of the mens rea. However, the only thing that really matters is whether they are elements in the crime. If they are, it is immaterial whether they are assigned to the actus reus or to the mens rea.

(2) The second question is whether actus reus should include the absence of justification or excuse. The actus reus of murder may be described as the killing of a human being; but if the killer, in the days of capital punishment, was the public executioner carrying out his duty to hang a convicted traitor it might seem strange to describe this as an actus reus. Similarly if the killer was acting in lawful self-defence. Where the actor knows of the circumstances of justification it might seem equally strange to describe his state of mind as mens rea. Neither the public executioner nor the person acting in self-defence had a 'guilty mind'. Courts sometimes treat the mental element in the broader sense. In *Gladstone Williams* (1987) 78 Cr App R 276 at 280, below, p 453, Lord Lane CJ said: 'The mental element necessary to constitute guilt [of assault] is the intent to apply unlawful force to the victim. We do not believe that the mental element can be substantiated by simply showing an intent to apply force and no more.'

If the defendant believed (though under a mistake) in circumstances which would justify the degree of force he used, in the opinion of Lord Lane, he lacked the mens rea for an assault.

There is however something to be said for having terms to describe the particular elements of a crime without thereby invoking all the possible defences. If the Latin expressions are regarded merely as technical terms which do not in themselves necessarily import guilt, the difficulty of so using them disappears. Professor Lanham has said ([1976] Crim LR 276): 'As a matter of analysis we can think of a crime as being made up of three ingredients, actus reus, mens rea and (a negative element) absence of a valid defence.'

According to that view a person may cause an actus reus with mens rea but not be guilty of the crime in question because of the existence of a defence. Gladstone Williams was such a person.

In favour of this approach is the fact that defences also may require mental as well as external elements. For example, the defence of provocation on a murder charge requires evidence not only of provocative facts but also an actual loss of self-control on the part of the defendant (p 585, below). If the object is clarity of exposition, there may, therefore, be something to be said for treating elements of offences and elements of defences separately.

The theory underlying the draft Code is the same as Professor Lanham's analysis. It treats the definition of the offence and the definition of any defences separately. For example, it provides that a person is guilty of murder if 'he causes the death of another ... intending to cause death.' If the Code stopped there, the public executioner (capital punishment being then the penalty for treason) would have been guilty of murder—all the elements of the offence are present. Of course that would be absurd and the Code does not stop there. Clause 45, which is in Part I of the Code under the cross-heading, 'Defences', provides that:

45. Acts justified or excused by law
A person does not commit an offence by doing an act which is justified or excused by—

  (a) any enactment; or

  (b) any 'enforceable Community right' as defined in section 2(1) of the European Communities Act 1972; or

  (c) any rule of the common law continuing to apply by virtue of section 4(4)

The act of the executioner in hanging a person condemned to death for treason would then have been justified by various Treason Acts. Similarly, a person who intentionally killed another would be guilty of no offence if his act was justified or excused by cl 44 of the Code as self-defence. A soldier who killed an enemy in battle would be justified by the common law.

The separation of the definition of offences from that of defences in the Code is for convenience in stating the law. There are numerous possible defences to every crime but the definition of a particular crime never states them. They are assumed to apply unless excluded. Sometimes the definition includes the word 'unlawfully' and this is sometimes said to incorporate the available defences—it means 'without justification or excuse'. But many statutory definitions do not use that word and it makes no difference; the defences are still available. So it makes sense to distinguish between the elements of offences and the elements of defences.

The distinction has practical importance. Suppose that an offence has three elements, A, B and C, that is, three facts which the prosecution must prove in order to obtain a conviction; and that a particular defence has three elements, X, Y and Z. If the prosecution fail to prove any of the elements of the offence, A, or B, or C, the case must be dismissed. But if A, B and C are proved, the defendant (call him Dan) will be convicted unless there is evidence of a defence. So, unless the prosecution have obligingly produced evidence of X, Y and Z (sometimes they do), it will be for Dan to try to do so. As we shall see (below, Ch 6), Dan usually does not have to *prove* these facts—it is enough if his evidence induces the court or jury to think that there is a reasonable possibility that X, Y *and* Z are present. But if his evidence fails to raise the possibility in respect even of only one of them, or if the prosecution prove that one of them does not exist, the defence fails.

In *More* (1986) 86 Cr App R 234, (1988) Crim LR 176, HL, M was charged with various offences of dishonesty and set up the defence of duress. The court said that the defence had three ingredients: (i) that the alleged threats were made; (ii) that M was impelled by them to commit the offences; and (iii) that a sober person of reasonable firmness would have been so impelled. Hodgson J (at 246) said:

Once there is evidence from which the jury could come to the conclusion that the defendant had acted under duress, then it is for the prosecution to satisfy them so that they are sure that the defence is not made out... The prosecution's first task is to satisfy each juror (ignoring the question of majority verdicts) that every ingredient of the offence has been made out. Failure as to one ingredient in the case of one juryman makes a conviction impossible. But, in the case of duress, once one juryman is sure that one of the three ingredients of the defence is not made out, then the defence cannot succeed and the best the defendant can hope for is a disagreement.

It is common to speak of 'a defence' where the defendant merely denies the existence of one or more elements of the offence—A, B and C in the above example. In a murder trial he denies that he caused the death or that he intended to do so. The question then is simply whether the prosecution have proved the existence of that element as well as all the other elements of the offence. 'Defence' is here used in a sense different from that of the preceding discussion: only the elements of the offence are in issue.

A comparison of the two following cases demonstrates the importance of distinguishing between the elements of an offence and the elements of a defence.

2. CONSTITUENTS OF AN ACTUS REUS

R v Deller
(1952) 36 Cr App R 184, Court of Criminal Appeal

(Hilbery, McNair and Streatfeild JJ)

The appellant was charged with obtaining from C a car No DYW 29 'by falsely pretending that he was the owner of a Standard motor car No FXF 372, that the said car was free from all encumbrances, that there was no money owing upon the said car, and that he was free to deal with the said car'. The appellant had previously signed documents which purported to effect a sale by him of FXF 372 to Great Western Motors and a hiring back to him by the Central Wagon and Finance Co. If the transaction was in reality a loan to the appellant on the security of the car, it was a bill of sale and void because not registered under the Bills of Sale Act 1878. The appellant was convicted and appealed on the ground that the documents were a bill of sale and that he spoke the truth when he said that the car was free from encumbrances.

[**Hilbery J** (delivering the judgment of the court) having stated the facts continued:]

It has been argued that, because a document was in existence purporting to represent as between the parties an agreement of hire and purchase, the false pretence was established when the appellant said that it was his car and not encumbered, because he must have believed that and known that there was in existence this agreement. It is to be observed that the false pretence which was alleged was not that he falsely pretended that there was not in existence any hire-purchase agreement in respect of the car; and that in fact he made no such representation was clearly established in the cross-examination of Mr Clarke when before the magistrates, as appears from the depositions.

In those circumstances, if the direction given to the jury was a clear direction that, in the event of their finding that this was in truth a loan transaction on the security of the car and not a genuine sale with a hiring back, the right verdict would be Not Guilty, the verdict of Guilty by the jury would be tantamount to a finding by them that the transaction was not one merely of loan but was in fact a genuine transaction of sale and hiring back to the man who had, prior to that sale, been the owner of the car. Unfortunately, whereas the issue that the jury had to try was correctly put in the summing-up, there was matter later on in the summing-up which, in our opinion, prevents us from taking that view of the verdict and vitiates the summing-up, having regard to the exact terms of the false pretences alleged in the indictment … [The judge examined the direction to the jury and continued:] Of course, once the jury came to the conclusion that in fact the transaction was one of loan and not of sale of the car, but loan on the attempted security of the car, the documents as a matter of law were void documents and that the learned Deputy Chairman must have known. But in one and the same breath he was asking the jury to say, if they thought it was a loan, to look upon the documents as being the security for the loan and saying to the jury that, whatever they thought about the strict ownership of the car, when they came to the representation that it was unencumbered, here were these documents which were a charge upon the car. In truth, if they came to the conclusion that the transaction was a loan, as a matter at law the documents were void; they were no more than pieces of paper. The charge to the jury ought to have been: if they came to the conclusion that the documents represented only a transaction of loan on the security of the car, then the documents were all void and of no effect, and the falsity of every one of the alleged representations was not proved because, it may be quite accidentally and, strange as it may sound, dishonestly, the appellant had told the truth. In the circumstances, it seems to us to be quite clear that the jury may well have thought that, although these were documents to cloak a loan transaction and to give a loan transaction the colour of a sale and a hiring back, yet none the less they were a charge on the car, and to say it was unencumbered became a false pretence. Having regard, therefore, to the indictment and the direction in the summing-up, we are of opinion that this conviction must be quashed.

Conviction quashed

Questions

1. An element of the offence of obtaining by false pretences (as now of obtaining by deception under s 15 of the Theft Act 1968) was the making of a false statement. Was this element proved in *Deller*? If not, could Deller properly be convicted of the offence even though the other elements, including the mens rea, a dishonest intention to obtain by false pretences, were proved?

If he could not be convicted of the offence, the question arises whether he could be convicted of an attempt to commit it; and this is considered below, p 519.

2. *Should* Deller have been guilty of an offence? Would it be desirable to have a law stating: 'A person who does any act with intent thereby to commit an offence is guilty of an offence and liable to be punished as if he had committed the offence he intended to commit'?

R v Dadson

(1850) 4 Cox CC 358, Court for Crown Cases Reserved

(Pollock CB, Wightman J, Williams J, Talfourd J and Martin B)

The prisoner was tried and convicted before Erle J, at the last Maidstone Assizes, but the learned judge entertaining some doubt as to the propriety of the conviction, reserved the following case:

George Dadson was indicted for shooting at William Waters, with intent to do him grievous bodily harm. It appeared that he, being a constable, was employed to guard a copse, from which wood had been stolen, and for this purpose carried a loaded gun. From this copse he saw the prosecutor come out, carrying wood, which he was stealing, and called to him to stop. The prosecutor ran away, and the prisoner, having no other means of bringing him to justice, fired, and wounded him in the leg. These were the facts on which the prisoner acted. It was alleged in addition that Waters was actually committing a felony, he having been before convicted repeatedly of stealing wood, but these convictions were unknown to the prisoner, nor was there any reason for supposing that he knew the difference between the rules of law relating to felony and those relating to less offences. I told the jury that shooting with intent to wound amounted to the felony charged, unless from other facts there was a justification; and that neither the belief of the prisoner that it was his duty to fire if he could not otherwise apprehend the prosecutor, nor the alleged felony, it being unknown to him, constituted such justification. Upon this the prisoner was convicted of felony, and let out on his recognisances to come up for judgment, if required. I have to request the opinion of the judges whether this conviction was right.

Cur adv vult

Pollock CB, delivered the judgment of the court. [After stating the facts as above]—We are all of opinion that the conviction is right. The prosecutor not having committed a felony known to the prisoner at the time when he fired, the latter was not justified in firing at the prosecutor; and having no justifiable cause, he was guilty of shooting at the prosecutor with intent to do him grievous bodily harm, and the conviction is right.

Conviction affirmed

In order to understand *Dadson* it is necessary to know something about the law then in force. The court assumes that it was then lawful to use deadly force if that was necessary to arrest a person whom the arrester knew to be a felon. Larceny was a felony but growing wood (which Waters was alleged to have stolen) was not larcenable at common law because it was part of the land. However, under the Larceny Act 1827, s 39, stealing growing wood was a misdemeanour or, if the thief had two previous convictions for that offence, a felony.

Dadson was charged under the Offences Against the Person Act 1828, s 12, by which it was felony to:

'... unlawfully and maliciously shoot at any person ... with intent ... to maim, disfigure or disable such person or to do some other grievous bodily harm to such person.'

Dadson has been the subject of much debate. Glanville Williams argues (CLGP, p 24) that it is wrong: that there was no actus reus—Waters was in fact a felon and therefore it was lawful to use deadly force to arrest him. Dadson had mens rea—he intentionally shot at Waters, unaware of any grounds justifying or excusing such conduct—but that was immaterial if there was no actus reus.

That is Williams' argument; but consider whether all the elements of the offence under s 12 of the 1828 Act *were* proved. If they were not, then Dadson, like Deller, should have been acquitted; but if they were proved, the next question is whether Dadson had made out a defence. We then have to ask, what are the elements of the defence? If there is only one element—the arrestee was a fleeing felon who could not be stopped except by shooting—then, again, Dadson should have been acquitted because the arrestee was a felon. But the court holds that there is a second element—that the defendant knew him to be a felon. Why should not the court so decide? What are the arguments for and against?

Williams argues that, if *Dadson* is rightly decided, it follows that a British soldier who kills an enemy in action, believing himself to be killing his own drill sergeant is guilty of murder—which is preposterous. Does this absurd result follow? Murder (below, p 554) is the unlawful killing of a person under the Queen's Peace with malice aforethought. The enemy soldier in battle is not 'under the Queen's Peace'. Have all the external elements of the offence been proved? Or is this a case like *Deller* and materially different from *Dadson*?

The court in *Dadson* remarks that there was no reason for supposing that the defendant knew the difference between the rules relating to felony and those relating to lesser offences. Was this relevant? Suppose that, before he fired, Dadson had recognized Waters as the man he had twice successfully prosecuted for stealing wood from the copse but that he knew nothing about the law of felonies and misdemeanours—he knew the facts justifying his conduct but not the law. Should he have had a defence?

Dadson is considered further, below, p 468, in relation to the modern law of arrest. See also R. L. Christopher 'Unknowing Justification and the Logical Necessity of the Dadson Principle in Self-Defence' (1995) 15 OJLS 229.

3. AN ACT; AND AUTOMATISM

Reduced to its lowest terms, an act is merely a muscular movement—for example, the crooking of a finger. But this is a very narrow view. Reference to an act generally includes some of the circumstances surrounding the movement, and its consequences. For instance, if, when D crooked his finger, it was gripping the trigger of a loaded gun pointing at V's heart, to say that 'D crooked his finger' would be a most incomplete and misleading way of describing what D did. We would naturally say, 'D *shot* V', taking into account the relevant circumstances and consequences. If we say, 'D *murdered V*' we take into account still more circumstances—not only the state of mind with which D pulled the trigger, but also the absence of circumstances of justification or excuse—for example, D was not a soldier in battle shooting at an enemy, V, nor was he acting in self-defence against an aggressor who was attempting to kill him. 'Murder', unlike 'kill', connotes a particular offence and therefore an actus reus (including the absence of excuse).

Ryan v R
(1969) 121 CLR 205, High Court of Australia

(Barwick CJ, Taylor, Menzies, Windeyer and Owen JJ)

Ryan entered a service station, pointed a sawn-off rifle at the attendant and demanded money. The rifle was loaded and cocked with the safety catch off. The attendant placed money on the counter. Still pointing the rifle with one hand, Ryan attempted to tie the attendant up. When the attendant moved suddenly Ryan pressed the trigger and shot him dead. By the law of New South Wales killing, an act done in the course of committing a felony (in this case, robbery) was murder—but the act had to be a voluntary act. At his trial for murder Ryan's defence was that he pressed the trigger involuntarily. He was convicted and his appeal to the High Court of Australia was dismissed.

[**Barwick CJ**, having held that a jury could not dismiss Ryan's account as incredible:]

There were therefore, in my opinion, at least four possible and distinctly different views of the discharge of the gun which, upon all the material before them, could be taken by the jury. First, the applicant's explanation could be disbelieved, and it could be concluded that he had fired the gun intentionally—that is to say, both as a voluntary act and with the intention to do the deceased harm. Second, that he fired the gun voluntarily, not intending to do any harm to the deceased but merely to frighten him as a means of self-protection. Third, that being startled, he voluntarily but in a panic, pressed the trigger but with no specific intent either to do the deceased any harm or to frighten him.

Fourth, that being startled so as to move slightly off his balance, the trigger was pressed in a reflex or convulsive, unwilled movement of his hand or of its muscles. I shall later refer to these conclusions of fact as the possible views identifying each by number ...

An occasion such as the fourth view of the evidence in the instant case (ante) would, in my opinion, be an instance of a deed not the result of a culpable exercise of the will to act. But such an occasion is in sharp contrast to the third view of those facts from which it needs carefully to be distinguished. If voluntariness is not conceded and the material to be submitted to the jury wheresoever derived provides a substantial basis for doubting whether the deed in question was a voluntary or willed act of the accused, the jury's attention must be specifically drawn to the necessity of deciding beyond all reasonable doubt that the deed charged as a crime was the voluntary or willed act of the accused. If it was not then for that reason, there being no defence of insanity, the accused must be acquitted. No doubt care will be taken by the presiding judge that the available material warrants the raising of this specific issue. In doing so, he will of course have in mind that the question for him is whether upon that material a jury would be entitled to entertain a reasonable doubt as to the voluntary quality of the act attributed to the accused. Also, the presiding judge where the circumstances of the case are like those of the instant case will explain the difference between the third and fourth views (ante) so that the jury are given to understand the precise question to which they have relevantly to address themselves. Although a claim of involuntariness is no doubt easily raised, and may involve nice distinctions, the accused, if the material adduced warrants that course, is entitled to have the issue properly put to the jury.

Windeyer J. ... The conduct which caused the death was of course a complex of acts all done by the applicant—loading the rifle, cocking it, presenting it, pressing the trigger. But it was the final act, pressing the trigger of the loaded and levelled rifle, which made the conduct lethal. When this was said to be a reflex action, the word 'reflex' was not used strictly in the sense it ordinarily has in neurology as denoting a specific muscular reaction to a particular stimulus of a physical character. The phrase was, as I understood the argument, used to denote rather the probable but unpredictable reaction of a man when startled. He starts. In doing so he may drop something which he is holding, or grasp it more firmly. Doctor Johnson in his Dictionary—and his definition has been in substance repeated by others—said that 'to start' means 'to feel a sudden and involuntary twitch or motion of the animal frame on the apprehension of danger'. The *Oxford Dictionary* speaks of a start as a 'sudden involuntary movement of the body occasioned by surprise, terror, joy or grief ...'. But assume that the applicant's act was involuntary, in the sense in which the lexicographers use the word, would that, as a matter of law, absolve him from criminal responsibility for its consequences? I do not think so. I do not think that, for present purposes, such an act bears any true analogy to one done under duress, which, although done by an exercise of the will, is said to be involuntary because it was compelled. Neither does it, I think, bear any true analogy to an act done in convulsions or an epileptic seizure, which is said to be involuntary because by no exercise of the will could the actor refrain from doing it. Neither does it, I think, bear any true analogy to an act done by a sleep-walker or a person for some other reason rendered unconscious whose action is said to be involuntary because he knew not what he was doing.

Such phrases as 'reflex action' and 'automatic reaction' can, if used imprecisely and unscientifically, be, like 'blackout', mere excuses. They seem to me to have no real application to the case of a fully conscious man who has put himself in a situation in which he has his finger on the trigger of a loaded rifle levelled at another man. If he then presses the trigger in immediate response to a sudden threat or apprehension of danger, as is said to have occurred in this case, his doing so is, it seems to me, a consequence probable and foreseeable of a conscious apprehension of danger, and in that sense a voluntary act. The latent time is no doubt barely appreciable, and what was done might not have been done had the actor had time to think. But is an act to be called involuntary merely because the mind worked quickly and impulsively?

Apart from the anxieties and tensions necessarily experienced by anyone taking part in an armed robbery, Ryan was not, so far as appears, suffering from an abnormality of any kind. More commonly—at least in the reported cases—the defendant who relies upon automatism claims that he had a 'blackout' and that this was due to a condition of mind or body—a tumour on the brain, arteriosclerosis (hardening of the arteries) cutting off the supply of blood to the brain, epilepsy, hyperglycaemia (high blood sugar) caused by diabetes, hypoglycaemia (low blood sugar) caused by the administration of too much insulin to control diabetes, or sleepwalking; or he may say that he was suffering from concussion following a blow on the head or that he was affected by the administration by his dentist of an anaesthetic. If the defendant was indeed in a state of automatism at the time of the alleged act as a result of any of these conditions he cannot be guilty of the crime charged; but there is a question whether he should be simply acquitted or found not guilty by reason of insanity. If the alleged condition amounts to 'a disease of the mind' within the M'Naghten Rules of 1843 (a question of law) then the proper verdict is not guilty by reason of insanity. The importance of this is that the defendant is then liable to various types of restraint which the court may impose on him (below, Ch 11).

Whether the defence succeeds at all may depend on how it is classified in law. If the alleged condition is a disease of the mind the onus is on the defendant to prove, on the balance of probabilities, that he was suffering from that condition and that it caused the automatism; but if it does not amount to a disease of the mind all that the defendant has to do is to adduce evidence of those facts which might reasonably be true and then it is for the prosecution to prove beyond reasonable doubt that the relevant facts, or one of them, did not exist.

Bratty v Attorney-General for Northern Ireland
[1963] AC 386, [1961] 3 All ER 523, House of Lords

(Viscount Kilmuir LC, Lord Tucker, Lord Denning, Lord Morris of Borth-y-Gest and Lord Hodson)

The accused killed a girl whom he was driving in his car by taking off her stocking and strangling her with it. He gave evidence that a 'blackness' came over him and that 'I didn't know what I was doing. I didn't realise anything.' There was evidence that he might have been suffering from psychomotor epilepsy which could cause ignorance of the nature and quality of acts done. At the trial the defences of automatism and insanity were raised. The trial judge rejected the defence of insanity. The Court of Criminal Appeal in Northern Ireland dismissed an appeal against conviction for murder. The appellant appealed to the House of Lords.

[**Viscount Kilmuir LC** made a speech dismissing the appeal.]

[**Lord Tucker** agreed.]

Lord Denning. My Lords, in *Woolmington v Director of Public Prosecutions* Viscount Sankey LC said:

> 'When dealing with a murder case the Crown must prove (a) death as the result of a voluntary act of the accused and (b) malice of the accused.'

The requirement that it should be a voluntary act is essential, not only in a murder case, but also in every criminal case. No act is punishable if it is done involuntarily: and an involuntary act in this context—some people nowadays prefer to speak of it as 'automatism'—means an act which is done by the muscles without any control by the mind such as a spasm, a reflex or a convulsion; or an act done by a person who is not conscious of what he is doing such as an act done whilst suffering from concussion or whilst sleep-walking. [But see *Burgess*, p 30, below.] The point was well put by Stephen J in 1889:

'…can anyone doubt that a man who, though he might be perfectly sane, committed what would otherwise be a crime in a state of somnambulism, would be entitled to be acquitted? And why is this? Simply because he would not know what he was doing';

see *Tolson*. The term 'involuntary act' is, however, capable of wider connotations: and to prevent confusion it is to be observed that in the criminal law an act is not to be regarded as an involuntary act simply because the doer does not remember it. When a man is charged with dangerous driving, it is no defence for him to say 'I don't know what happened. I cannot remember a thing': see *Hill v Baxter* [[1958] 1 QB 277, [1958] 1 All ER 193]. Loss of memory afterwards is never a defence in itself, so long as he was conscious at the time; see *Russell v HM Advocate* [1946 JC 37]; *Podola* [see p 365, below]. Nor is an act to be regarded as an involuntary act simply because the doer could not control his impulse to do it. When a man is charged with murder, and it appears that he knew what he was doing, but that he could not resist it, then his assertion 'I couldn't help myself' is no defence in itself: see *A-G for South Australia v Brown* [[1960] AC 432, [1960] 1 All ER 734]: though it may go towards a defence of diminished responsibility, in places where that defence is available, see *Byrne* [see p 578, below]: but it does not render his act involuntary so as to entitle him to an unqualified acquittal. Nor is an act to be regarded as an involuntary act simply because it is unintentional or its consequences are unforeseen. When a man is charged with dangerous driving, it is no defence for him to say, however truly, 'I did not mean to drive dangerously'. There is said to be an absolute prohibition against that offence, whether he had a guilty mind or not (see *Hill v Baxter* per Lord Goddard CJ), but even though it is absolutely prohibited, nevertheless he has a defence if he can show that it was an involuntary act in the sense that he was unconscious at the time and did not know what he was doing (see *HM Advocate v Ritchie* [1926 JC 45], *Minor* [(1955) 15 WWRNS 433] and *Cooper v McKenna, ex p Cooper* [[1960] Qd R 406]).

Another thing to be observed is that it is not every involuntary act which leads to a complete acquittal. Take first an involuntary act which proceeds from a state of drunkenness. If the drunken man is so drunk that he does not know what he is doing, he has a defence to any charge, such as murder or wounding with intent, in which a specific intent is essential, but he is still liable to be convicted of manslaughter or unlawful wounding for which no specific intent is necessary; see *Beard's* case [see p 190, below]. Again, if the involuntary act proceeds from a disease of the mind, it gives rise to a defence of insanity, but not to a defence of automatism. Suppose a crime is committed by a man in a state of automatism or clouded consciousness due to a recurrent disease of the mind. Such an act is no doubt involuntary, but it does not give rise to an unqualified acquittal, for that would mean that he would be let at large to do it again. The only proper verdict is one which ensures that the person who suffers from the disease is kept secure in a hospital so as not to be a danger to himself or others. That is, a verdict of guilty but insane.

Once you exclude all the cases I have mentioned, it is apparent that the category of involuntary acts is very limited. So limited indeed that until recently there was hardly any reference in the English books to this so-called defence of automatism. There was a passing reference to it in 1951 in *Harrison-Owen* [[1951] 2 All ER 726] where a burglar, who broke into houses, said he did not know what he was doing. I should have thought that, in order to rebut this defence, he could have been cross-examined about his previous burglaries: but the Court of Criminal Appeal ruled otherwise. I venture to doubt that decision. The next is the singular case of *Charlson* [[1955] 1 All ER 859]. Stanley Charlson, a devoted husband and father, hit his ten-year-old son on the head with a hammer and threw him into the river and so injured him. There was not the slightest cause for the attack.

He was charged with causing grievous bodily harm with intent, and with unlawful wounding. The evidence pointed to the possibility that Charlson was suffering from a cerebral tumour in which case he would be liable to a motiveless outburst of impulsive behaviour over which he would have no control at all. Now comes the important point—no plea of insanity was raised, but only the defence of automatism. Barry J directed the jury in these words [[1955] 1 All ER 859 at 864]:

> 'If he did not know what he was doing, if his actions were purely automatic and his mind had no control over the movement of his limbs, if he was in the same position as a person in an epileptic fit and no responsibility rests on him at all, then the proper verdict is "not guilty" ...'

On that direction the jury found him not guilty. In striking contrast to *Charlson* is *Kemp*. A devoted husband of excellent character made an entirely motiveless and irrational attack on his wife. He struck her violently with a hammer. He was charged with causing her grievous bodily harm. It was found that he suffered from hardening of the arteries which might lead to a congestion of blood in the brain. As a result of such congestion, he suffered a temporary lack of consciousness, so that he was not conscious that he picked up the hammer or that he was striking his wife with it. It was therefore an involuntary act. Note again the important point—no plea of insanity was raised but only the defence of automatism. Nevertheless, Devlin J put insanity to the jury. He held that hardening of the arteries was a 'disease of the mind' within the M'Naghten rules and he directed the jury they ought so to find. They accordingly found Kemp guilty but insane.

My Lords, I think that Devlin J was quite right in *Kemp* in putting the question of insanity to the jury, even though it had not been raised by the defence. When it is asserted that the accused did an involuntary act in a state of automatism, the defence necessarily puts in issue the state of mind of the accused man: and thereupon it is open to the prosecution to show what his true state of mind was. The old notion that only the defence can raise a defence of insanity is now gone ... [see Ch 11, below].

On the other point discussed by Devlin J namely, what is a 'disease of the mind' within the M'Naghten rules, I would agree with him that this is a question for the judge. The major mental diseases, which the doctors call psychoses, such as schizophrenia, are clearly diseases of the mind. But in *Charlson*, Barry J seems to have assumed that other diseases such as epilepsy or cerebral tumour are not diseases of the mind, even when they are such as to manifest themselves in violence. I do not agree with this. It seems to me that any mental disorder which has manifested itself in violence and is prone to recur is a disease of the mind. At any rate it is the sort of disease for which a person should be detained in hospital rather than be given an unqualified acquittal.

It is to be noticed that in *Charlson* and *Kemp* the defence raised only automatism, not insanity. In the present case the defence raised both automatism and insanity. And herein lies the difficulty because of the burden of proof. If the accused says he did not know what he was doing, then, so far as the defence of automatism is concerned, the Crown must prove that the act was an involuntary act; see *Woolmington's* case. But so far as the defence of insanity is concerned, the defence must prove that the act was an involuntary act due to disease of the mind; see *M'Naghten's Case*. This apparent incongruity was noticed by Sir Owen Dixon, Chief Justice of the High Court of Australia, in an address which is to be found in 31 Australian Law Journal 255 and it needs to be resolved. The defence here say: Even though we have not proved that the act was involuntary, yet the Crown have not proved that it was a voluntary act: and that point at least should have been put to the jury.

My Lords, I think that the difficulty is to be resolved by remembering that, whilst the *ultimate* burden rests on the Crown of proving every element essential in the crime, nevertheless in order to prove that the act was a voluntary act, the Crown is entitled to rely on the presumption that every man has sufficient mental capacity to be responsible for his crimes: and that if the defence wish to displace that *presumption* they must give some evidence from which the contrary may reasonably be inferred. Thus a drunken man is presumed to have the capacity to form the specific intent necessary to constitute the crime, unless evidence is given from which it can reasonably be inferred that he was incapable of forming it; see the valuable judgment of the Court of Justiciary in *Kennedy v HM Advocate* [1944 JC 171 at 177] which was delivered by the Lord Justice-General (Lord Normand). So also it seems to me that a man's act is presumed to be a voluntary act unless there is evidence from which it can reasonably be inferred that it was involuntary. To use the words of Devlin J the defence of automatism 'ought not to be considered at all until the defence has produced at least prima facie evidence', see *Hill v Baxter* [[1958] 1 QB 277 at 285, [1958] 1 All ER 193 at 196]; and the words of North J in New Zealand 'unless a proper foundation is laid', see *Cottle* [[1958] NZLR 999 at 1025]. The necessity of laying this proper foundation is on the defence: and if it is not so laid, the defence of automatism need not be left to the jury, any more than the defence of drunkenness (*Kennedy v HM Advocate* [1944 JC 171]) provocation (*Gauthier* [(1943) 29 Cr App Rep 113]) or self-defence (*Lobell* [[1957] 1 QB 547, [1957] 1 All ER 734]) need be.

What, then, is a proper foundation? The presumption of mental capacity of which I have spoken is a provisional presumption only. It does not put the legal burden on the defence in the same way as the presumption of sanity does. It leaves the legal burden on the prosecution, but nevertheless, until it is displaced, it enables the prosecution to discharge the ultimate burden of proving that the act was voluntary. Not because the presumption is evidence itself, but because it takes the place of evidence. In order to displace the presumption of mental capacity, the defence must give sufficient evidence from which it may reasonably be inferred that the act was involuntary. The evidence of the man himself will rarely be sufficient unless it is supported by medical evidence which points to the cause of the mental incapacity. It is not sufficient for a man to say 'I had a black-out': for 'black-out' as Stable J said in *Cooper v McKenna, ex p Cooper* [[1960] Qd R 406 at 419] 'is one of the first refuges of a guilty conscience, and a popular excuse'. The words of Devlin J in *Hill v Baxter* [[1958] 1 QB 277 at 285, [1958] 1 All ER 193 at 197] should be remembered:

> 'I do not doubt that there are genuine cases of automatism and the like, but I do not see how the layman can safely attempt without the help of some medical or scientific evidence to distinguish the genuine from the fraudulent.'

When the only cause that is assigned for an involuntary act is drunkenness, then it is only necessary to leave drunkenness to the jury, with the consequential directions, and not to leave automatism at all. When the only cause that is assigned for it is a disease of the mind, then it is only necessary to leave insanity to the jury, and not automatism. When the cause assigned is concussion or sleepwalking, there should be some evidence from which it can reasonably be inferred before it should be left to the jury. If it is said to be due to concussion, there should be evidence of a severe blow shortly beforehand. If it is said to be sleepwalking, there should be some credible support for it. His mere assertion that he was asleep will not suffice. Once a proper foundation is thus laid for automatism, the matter becomes at large and must be left to the jury. As the case proceeds, the evidence may weigh first to one side and then to the other: and so the burden may appear to shift to and fro. But at the end of the day the legal burden comes into play and requires that the jury should be satisfied beyond reasonable doubt that the act was a voluntary one.... There was [in the present case] no evidence of automatism apart from insanity. There was therefore no need for the judge to put it to the jury.... I would therefore dismiss the appeal.

[**Lord Morris of Borth-y-Gest** made a speech dismissing the appeal with which **Lord Hodson** agreed.]

Appeal dismissed

The law distinguishes between 'insane' and 'non-insane' automatism—a distinction which turns on whether the cause is an 'internal' or an 'external' factor. If it is an internal factor, the plea is, in law, one of not guilty by reason of insanity. If it is an external factor, it is a simple plea of not guilty. The judge must decide which it is. Very important consequences follow from his decision. If the defence is one of insanity —

(i)   the burden of proof (on the balance of probabilities) shifts from the prosecution to the defence;

(ii) it must be supported by the written or oral evidence of two or more registered medical practitioners at least one of whom is 'duly approved': Criminal Procedure (Insanity and Unfitness to Plead) Act, 1991, s 1 (below, p 367); and

(iii) if the defence succeeds, the defendant will be found not guilty by reason of insanity but will not necessarily walk free. He may be made the subject of a hospital order or other measure authorized by the Criminal Procedure (Insanity) Act 1964 s 5(2), as amended, see below p 381).

Where the automatism is alleged to arise from an external factor the defendant bears only an evidential burden—he does not have to prove anything, but must introduce such evidence as might leave a reasonable jury in reasonable doubt whether he was in the state alleged. If the jury think he may have been in that state, they must acquit him.

Question

Dan and Ed are jointly charged with murder. Each says that he was unaware of what he was doing at the material time, Dan because he was suffering from psychomotor epilepsy, Ed because he was suffering from concussion. Each defence is supported by medical evidence. How should the judge direct the jury on the burden of proof? If the jury, having considered the evidence, return to inform the judge that they consider that both defences are, as likely as not, true, and ask for further directions, what should the judge tell them? Is the result satisfactory?

R v Quick and Paddison
[1973] 3 All ER 347, Court of Appeal, Criminal Division

(Lawton LJ, Mocatta and Milmo JJ)

The appellants were nurses employed at a mental hospital. They were convicted of assault occasioning actual bodily harm to a paraplegic spastic patient at the hospital. Quick called medical evidence to show that he was diabetic and that at the time of the alleged assault he was suffering from hypoglycaemia and was unaware of what he was doing. He submitted that the evidence established a defence of automatism. Bridge J ruled that the defence raised was one of insanity, whereupon Quick changed his plea to guilty. Paddison was convicted by the jury on the basis that he had abetted Quick. Quick appealed on the ground that the judge's ruling was wrong and that a diabetic in a temporary and reversible condition of hypoglycaemia was not, while in that condition, suffering from any defect of reason from disease of the mind.

[**Lawton LJ**, delivering the judgment of the court, reviewed the evidence and the decisions in *Bratty, Kemp, Hill v Baxter* [1958] 1 All ER 193, [1958] 1 QB 277 and *Kay v Butterworth* (1945) 173 LT 191, and continued:]

In this quagmire of law seldom entered nowadays save by those in desperate need of some kind of defence, *Bratty v A-G for Northern Ireland* provides the only firm ground. Is there any discernible path? We think there is—judges should follow in a common sense way their sense of fairness. This seems to have been the approach of the New Zealand Court of Appeal in *Cottle* [[1958] NZLR 999] and of Sholl J in *Carter* [[1959] VR 105]. In our judgment no help can be obtained by speculating (because that is what we would have to do) as to what the judges who answered the House of Lords' questions in 1843 [see p 374, below] meant by disease of the mind, still less what Sir Matthew Hale meant in the second half of the 17th century [(1682) Vol I, Ch IV]. A quick backward look at the state of medicine in 1843 will suffice to show how unreal it would be to apply the concepts of that age to the present time. Dr Simpson had not yet started his experiments with chloroform, the future Lord Lister was only 16 and laudanum was used and prescribed like aspirins are today. Our task has been to decide what the law means now by the words 'disease of the mind'. In our judgment the fundamental concept is of a malfunctioning of the mind caused by disease. A malfunctioning of the mind of transitory effect caused by the application to the body of some external factor such as violence, drugs, including anaesthetics, alcohol and hypnotic influences cannot fairly be said to be due to disease. Such malfunctioning, unlike that caused by a defect of reason from disease of the mind, will not always relieve an accused from criminal responsibility. A self-induced incapacity will not excuse (see *Lipman* [see p 200, below]) nor will one which could have been reasonably foreseen as a result of either doing, or omitting to do something, as for example, taking alcohol against medical advice after using certain prescribed drugs, or failing to have regular meals whilst taking insulin. From time to time difficult borderline cases are likely to arise. When they do, the test suggested by the New Zealand Court of Appeal in *Cottle* is likely to give the correct result, viz can this mental condition be fairly regarded as amounting to or producing a defect of reason from disease of the mind?

In this case Quick's alleged mental condition, if it ever existed, was not caused by his diabetes but by his use of the insulin prescribed by his doctor. Such malfunctioning of his mind as there was, was caused by an external factor and not by a bodily disorder in the nature of a disease which disturbed the working of his mind. It follows in our judgment that Quick was entitled to have his defence of automatism left to the jury and that Bridge J's ruling as to the effect of the medical evidence called by him was wrong. Had the defence of automatism been left to the jury, a number of questions of fact would have had to be answered. If he was in a confused mental condition, was it due to a hypoglycaemic episode or to too much alcohol? If the former, to what extent had he brought about his condition by not following his doctor's instructions about taking regular meals? Did he know that he was getting into a hypoglycaemic episode? If Yes, why did he not use the antidote of eating a lump of sugar as he had been advised to do? On the evidence which was before the jury Quick might have had difficulty in answering these questions in a manner which would have relieved him of responsibility for his acts. We cannot say, however, with the requisite degree of confidence, that the jury would have convicted him. It follows that his conviction must be quashed on the ground that the verdict was unsatisfactory.

Appeals allowed

Questions

1. What would have been the result if the court had found that it was the diabetes and not the insulin which caused the automatism? See *Hennessy*, below.

2. Is it accurate to say that 'a self-induced incapacity will not excuse'? Did not a self-induced incapacity excuse to some extent even in *Lipman* below, p 200? He was not convicted of murder.

3. Was the incapacity not 'self-induced' in the present case? Quick administered the insulin to himself. What difference would it have made if his condition had been brought about by failure to follow the doctor's instructions about regular meals? Which is more likely to recur—forgetting to administer insulin or forgetting to eat having done so?

R v Hennessy

(1989) 89 Cr App R 10, Court of Appeal, Criminal Division

(Lord Lane CJ, Rose and Pill JJ)

H, a diabetic, was charged with taking a conveyance and driving while disqualified. His defence was that at the relevant time he had failed to take his proper dose of insulin due to stress, anxiety and depression and consequently was suffering from hyperglycaemia (excessive blood sugar) and was in a state of automatism. The trial judge ruled that the condition, if it existed, was caused by diabetes, a disease, so that the defence was one of insanity under the M'Naghten Rules. H then pleaded guilty. He appealed arguing that the judge's ruling was wrong and that his depression and marital troubles were a sufficiently potent external factor to override the effect of the diabetic shortage of insulin.

Lord Lane CJ quoted from the judgment of Devlin J in *Hill v Baxter* [1958] 1QB 277 at 285:

> 'I have drawn attention to the fact that the accused did not set up a defence of insanity. For the purposes of the criminal law there are two categories of mental irresponsibility, one where the disorder is due to disease and the other where it is not. The distinction is not an arbitrary one. If disease is not the cause, if there is some temporary loss of consciousness arising accidentally, it is reasonable to hope that it will not be repeated and that it is safe to let an acquitted man go entirely free. But if disease is present the same thing may happen again, and therefore, since 1800, the law has provided that persons acquitted on this ground should be subject to restraint.'

That is the submission made by Mr Owen as a basis for saying the judge's decision was wrong and that this was a matter which should have been decided by the jury.

In our judgment, stress, anxiety and depression can no doubt be the result of the operation of external factors, but they are not, it seems to us, in themselves separately or together external factors of the kind capable in law of causing or contributing to a state of automatism. They constitute a state of mind which is prone to recur. They lack the feature of novelty or accident, which is the basis of the distinction drawn by Lord Diplock in *R v Sullivan* (infra). It is contrary to the observations of Devlin J, to which we have just referred in the case of *Hill v Baxter* (supra). It does not, in our judgment, come within the scope of the exception 'some external physical factor such as a blow on the head or the administration of an anaesthetic.' ...

Appeal dismissed

Question

A and B are diabetics. Both commit similar 'offences' while in a similar state of automatism. A is suffering from hypoglycaemia because he has taken too much insulin. B is suffering from hyperglycaemia because he has failed to take his proper dose. Has either of them a defence? Is there any valid ground for distinguishing between them?

R v Sullivan

[1983] 2 All ER 673, House of Lords

(Lords Diplock, Scarman, Lowry, Bridge and Brandon)

Lord Diplock. My Lords, the appellant, a man of blameless reputation, has the misfortune to have been a lifelong sufferer from epilepsy. There was a period when he was subject to major seizures known as grand mal; but as a result of treatment which he was receiving as an out-patient of the Maudsley Hospital from 1976 onwards these seizures had, by the use of drugs, been reduced by 1979 to seizures of less severity known as petit mal, or psychomotor epilepsy, though they continued to occur at a frequency of one or two per week.

One such seizure occurred on 8 May 1981, when the appellant, then aged 51, was visiting a neighbour, Mrs Killick, an old lady aged 86 for whom he was accustomed to perform regular acts of kindness. He was chatting there to a fellow visitor and friend of his, a Mr Payne aged 80, when the epileptic fit came on. It appears likely from the expert medical evidence about the way in which epileptics behave at the various stages of a petit mal seizure that Mr Payne got up from the chair to help the appellant. The only evidence of an eye-witness was that of Mrs Killick, who did not see what had happened before she saw Mr Payne lying on the floor and the appellant kicking him about the head and body, in consequence of which Mr Payne suffered injuries severe enough to require hospital treatment.

As a result of this occurrence the appellant was indicted on two counts: the first was of causing grievous bodily harm with intent, contrary to s 18 of the Offences Against the Person Act 1861; the second was of causing grievous bodily harm, contrary to s 20 of the Act. At his trial, which took place at the Central Criminal Court before his Honour Judge Lymbery QC and a jury, the appellant pleaded not guilty to both counts. Mrs Killick's evidence that he had kicked Mr Payne violently about the head and body was undisputed and the appellant himself gave evidence of his history of epilepsy and his absence of all recollection of what had occurred at Mrs Killick's flat between the time that he was chatting peacefully to Mr Payne there and his returning to the flat from somewhere else to find that Mr Payne was injured and that an ambulance had been sent for. The prosecution accepted his evidence as true. There was no cross-examination....

[His Lordship stated that the judge had ruled that, he would direct the jury that, if they accepted this evidence, they would be bound to return a verdict of not guilty by reason of insanity, whereupon the appellant changed his plea to guilty of assault occasioning actual bodily harm and was sentenced to three years' probation. He reviewed the M'Naghten Rules and *Bratty*, p 22, above and continued:]

In the instant case, as in *Bratty*'s case, the only evidential foundation that was laid for any finding by the jury that the appellant was acting unconsciously and involuntarily when he was kicking Mr Payne was that when he did so he was in the post-ictal stage of a seizure of psychomotor epilepsy. The evidential foundation in the case of Bratty, that he was suffering from psychomotor epilepsy at the time he did the act with which he was charged, was very weak and was rejected by the jury; the evidence in the appellant's case, that he was so suffering when he was kicking Mr Payne, was very strong and would almost inevitably be accepted by a properly directed jury. It would be the duty of the judge to direct the jury that if they did accept the evidence the law required them to bring in a special verdict and none other. The governing statutory provision is to be found in s 2 of the Trial of Lunatics Act 1883. This says 'the jury *shall* return a special verdict'.

My Lords, I can deal briefly with the various grounds on which it has been submitted that the instant case can be distinguished from what constituted the ratio decidendi in *Bratty*'s case, and that it falls outside the ambit of the M'Naghten Rules.

First, it is submitted the medical evidence in the instant case shows that psychomotor epilepsy is not a disease of the mind, whereas in *Bratty*'s case it was accepted by all the doctors that it was. The only evidential basis for this submission is that Dr Fenwick said that in medical terms to constitute a 'disease of the mind' or 'mental illness', which he appeared to regard as interchangeable descriptions, a disorder of brain functions (which undoubtedly occurs during a seizure in psychomotor epilepsy) must be prolonged for a period of time usually more than a day, while Dr Taylor would have it that the disorder must continue for a minimum of a month to qualify for the description 'a disease of the mind'.

The nomenclature adopted by the medical profession may change from time to time; Bratty was tried in 1961. But the meaning of the expression 'disease of the mind' as the cause of 'a defect of reason' remains unchanged for the purposes of the application of the M'Naghten Rules. I agree with what was said by Devlin J in *R v Kemp* [1956] 3 All ER 249 at 253, [1957] 1QB 399 at 407 that 'mind' in the M'Naghten Rules is used in the ordinary sense of the mental faculties of reason, memory and understanding. If the effect of a disease is to impair these faculties so severely as to have either of the consequences referred to in the latter part of the rules, it matters not whether the aetiology of the impairment is organic, as in epilepsy, or functional, or whether the impairment itself is permanent or is transient and intermittent, provided that it subsisted at the time of commission of the act. The purpose of the legislation relating to the defence of insanity, ever since its origin in 1880, has been to protect society against recurrence of the dangerous conduct. The duration of a temporary suspension of the mental faculties of reason, memory and understanding, particularly if, as in the appellant's case, it is recurrent, cannot on any rational ground be relevant to the application by the courts of the M'Naghten Rules, though it may be relevant to the course adopted by the Secretary of State, to whom the responsibility for how the defendant is to be dealt with passes after the return of the special verdict of not guilty by reason of insanity.

To avoid misunderstanding I ought perhaps to add that in expressing my agreement with what was said by Devlin J in *R v Kemp*, where the disease that caused the temporary and intermittent impairment of the mental faculties was arteriosclerosis, I do not regard that judge as excluding the possibility of non-insane automatism, for which the proper verdict would be a verdict of not guilty, in cases where temporary impairment not being self-induced by consuming drink or drugs, results from some external physical factor such as a blow on the head causing concussion or the administration of an anaesthetic for therapeutic purposes. I mention this because in *R v Quick* [1973] 3 All ER 347, [1973] QB 910 Lawton LJ appears to have been inconsistent with the speeches in this House in *Bratty's* case, where *R v Kemp* was alluded to without disapproval by Viscount Kilmuir LC and received the express approval of Lord Denning. The instant case, however, does not in my view afford an appropriate occasion for exploring possible causes of non-insane automatism.

The only other submission in support of the appellant's appeal which I think it necessary to mention is that, because the expert evidence was to the effect that the appellant's acts in kicking Mr Payne were unconscious and thus 'involuntary' in the legal sense of that term, his state of mind was not one dealt with by the M'Naghten Rules at all, since it was not covered by the phrase 'as not to know the nature and quality of the act he was doing'. Quite apart from being contrary to all three speeches in this House in *Bratty's* case, the submission appears to me, with all respect to counsel, to be quite unarguable. Dr Fenwick himself accepted it as an accurate description of the appellant's mental state in the post-ictal stage of a seizure. The audience to whom the phrase in the M'Naghten Rules was addressed consisted of peers of the realm in the 1840s when a certain orotundity of diction had not yet fallen out of fashion. Addressed to an audience of jurors in the 1980s it might more aptly be expressed as: he did not know what he was doing.

My Lords, it is natural to feel reluctant to attach the label of insanity to a sufferer from psychomotor epilepsy of the kind to which the appellant was subject, even though the expression in the context of a special verdict of not guilty by reason of insanity is a technical one which includes a purely temporary and intermittent suspension of the mental faculties of reason, memory and understanding resulting from the occurrence of an epileptic fit. But the label is contained in the current statute, it has appeared in this statute's predecessors ever since 1800. It does not lie within the power of the courts to alter it. Only Parliament can do that. It has done so twice; it could do so once again.

Sympathise though I do with the appellant, I see no other course open to your Lordships than to dismiss this appeal.

[The other Law Lords agreed.]

Appeal dismissed

R v Burgess
[1991] 2 All ER 769, Court of Appeal, Criminal Division

(Lord Lane CJ, Roch and Morland JJ)

Burgess and his friend and neighbour, Miss Curtis, spent an evening at her flat watching video tapes. She fell asleep. While she was asleep he hit her over the head with a bottle and the video recorder and then grasped her round the throat. When she cried out he appeared to come to his senses and showed great anxiety over what he had done. He was charged with wounding with intent. His defence was that he lacked the mens rea because he was sleepwalking which, he argued, was non-insane automatism. The judge ruled that, assuming that he was not conscious at the time of the act, the medical evidence was evidence of insanity. He was found not guilty by reason of insanity and ordered to be detained in a secure hospital. He appealed on the ground that the judge's ruling was wrong.

[**Lord Lane CJ**, delivering the judgment of the court:]

The appellant plainly suffered from a defect of reason from some sort of failure (for lack of a better term) of the mind causing him to act as he did without conscious motivation. His mind was to some extent controlling his actions, which were purposive rather than the result simply of muscular spasm, but without his being consciously aware of what he was doing. Can it be said that that 'failure' was a *disease* of the mind rather than a defect or failure of the mind not due to disease? That is the distinction, by no means always easy to draw, upon which this case depends, as others have depended in the past.

One can perhaps narrow the field of inquiry still further by eliminating what are sometimes called the 'external factors' such as concussion caused by a blow on the head. There were no such factors here. Whatever the cause may have been, it was an 'internal' cause. The possible disappointment or frustration caused by unrequited love is not to be equated with something such as concussion. On this aspect of the case, we respectfully adopt what was said by Martin JA giving the judgment of the court in the Ontario Court of Appeal in *R v Rabey* (1977) 17 OR (2d) 1 at 17, 22, which was approved by a majority in the Supreme Court of Canada (see [1980] SCR 513 at 519) (where the facts bore a similarity to those in the instant case although the diagnosis was different):

> 'Any malfunctioning of the mind, or mental disorder having its source primarily in some subjective condition or weakness internal to the accused (whether fully understood or not), may be a "disease of the mind" if it prevents the accused from knowing what he is doing, but transient disturbances of consciousness due to certain specific external factors do not fall within the concept of disease of the mind...In my view, the ordinary stresses and disappointments of life which are the common lot of mankind do not constitute an external cause constituting an explanation for a malfunctioning of the mind which takes it out of the category of a "disease of the mind". To hold otherwise would deprive the concept of an external factor of any real meaning.'

[His Lordship quoted from the speech of Lord Diplock in *Sullivan*, above, p 28, and that of Lord Denning in *Bratty*, above, p 22, concluding with Lord Denning's opinion that 'any mental disorder which has manifested itself in violence and is prone to recur is a disease of the mind. At any rate it is the sort of disease for which a person should be detained in hospital rather than be given a qualified acquittal.' Lord Lane continued:]

It seems to us that if there is a danger of recurrence that may be an added reason for categorising the condition as a disease of the mind. On the other hand, the absence of the danger of recurrence is not a reason for saying that it cannot be a disease of the mind. Subject to that possible qualification, we respectfully adopt Lord Denning's suggested definition.

There have been several occasions when during the course of judgments in the Court of Appeal and the House of Lords observations have been made, obiter, about the criminal responsibility of sleepwalkers, where sleepwalking has been used as a self-evident illustration of non-insane automatism.

[His Lordship referred to Lord Denning's remarks and his reference to Stephen J in *Bratty*, above, p 23, and continued:]

We have also been referred to a Canadian decision, *R v Parks* (1990) 56 CCC (3d) 449. In that case the defendant was charged with murder. The undisputed facts were that he had, whilst according to him he was asleep, at night driven his motor car some 23 km to the house of his wife's parents where he had stabbed and beaten both his mother-in-law and his father-in-law. His mother-in-law died as a result and his father-in-law sustained serious injuries. A number of defence witnesses, including experts in sleep disorders, gave evidence to the effect that sleepwalking is not regarded as a disease of the mind, mental illness or mental disorder, and the trial judge directed the jury that if the accused was in a state of somnambulism at the time of the killing, then he was entitled to be acquitted on the basis of non-insane automatism. The defendant was acquitted of the murder of his mother-in-law and subsequently acquitted of the attempted murder of his father-in-law.

The Crown Court appealed from the accused's acquittal and it was held by the Ontario Court of Appeal that the appeal should be dismissed. The court concluded that sleep is a normal condition and 'the impairment of the respondent's faculties of reason, memory and understanding was caused not by any disorder or abnormal condition but by a natural, normal condition—sleep (at 465–66).' [The Crown's further appeal to the Supreme Court of Canada was dismissed, distinguishing *Burgess* (1992) 95 DLR (4th) 27].

We accept of course that sleep is a normal condition, but the evidence in the instant case indicates that sleepwalking, and particularly violence in sleep, is not normal.... [*Parks*] apart, in none of the other cases where sleepwalking has been mentioned, so far as we can discover, has the court had the advantage of the sort of expert medical evidence which was available to the judge here.

One turns then to examine the evidence upon which the judge had to base his decision and for this purpose the two medical experts called by the defence are the obvious principal sources. Dr d'Orban in examination-in-chief said:

> 'On the evidence available to me, and subject to the results of the tests when they became available, I came to the same conclusion as Dr Nicholas and Dr Eames, whose reports I had read, and that was that [the appellant's] actions had occurred during the course of a sleep disorder.'

He was asked, 'Assuming this is a sleep associated automatism, is it an internal or external factor?' He answered: 'In this particular case, I think that one would have to see it as an internal factor.'
Then in cross-examination:

> '*Q*. Would you go so far as to say that it was liable to recur? *A*. It is possible for it to recur, yes.
> *Judge Lewis*. Is this a case of automatism associated with a pathological condition or not? A. I think the answer would have to be Yes, because it is an abnormality of the brain function, so it would be regarded as a pathological condition.'

Dr Eames in cross-examination agreed with Dr d'Orban as to the internal rather than the external factor. He accepted that there is a liability to recurrence of sleepwalking. He could not go so far as to say that there is no liability of recurrence of serious violence but he agreed with the other medical witnesses that there is no recorded case of violence of this sort recurring.

The prosecution, as already indicated, called Dr Fenwick, whose opinion was that this was not a sleepwalking episode at all. If it was a case where the appellant was unconscious of what he was doing, the most likely explanation was that he was in what is described as a hysterical dissociative state. That is a state in which, for psychological reasons, such as being overwhelmed by his emotions, the person's brain works in a different way. He carries out acts of which he has no knowledge and for which he has no memory. It is quite different from sleepwalking.

He then went on to describe features of sleepwalking. This is what he said:

> 'Firstly, violent acts in sleepwalking are very common. In just an exposure of one day to a sleepwalking clinic, you will hear of how people are kicked in bed, hit in bed, partially strangled—it is usually just arms round the neck, in bed, which is very common. Serious violence fortunately is rare. Serious violence does recur, or certainly the propensity for it to recur is there, although there are very few cases in the literature—in fact I know of none—in which somebody has come to court twice for a sleepwalking offence. This does not mean that sleepwalking violence does not recur; what it does mean

is that those who are associated with the sleeper take the necessary precautions. Finally, should a person be detained in hospital? The answer to that is: Yes, because sleepwalking is treatable. Violent night terrors are treatable. There is a lot which can be done for the sleepwalker, so sending them to hospital after a violent act to have their sleepwalking sorted out, makes good sense.'

Dr Fenwick was also of the view that in certain circumstances hysterical dissociative states are also subject to treatment.

It seems to us that on this evidence the judge was right to conclude that this was an abnormality or disorder, albeit transitory, due to an internal factor, whether functional or organic, which had manifested itself in violence. It was a disorder or abnormality which might recur, though the possibility of it recurring in the form of serious violence was unlikely. Therefore, since this was a legal problem to be decided on legal principles, it seems to us that on those principles the answer was as the judge found it to be. It does however go further than that. Dr d'Orban as already described, stated it as his view that the condition would be regarded as pathological. Pathology is the science of diseases. It seems therefore that in this respect at least there is some similarity between the law and medicine.

The judge was alive to the apparent incongruity of labelling this sort of disability as insanity. He drew attention, as we would also wish to do, to the passage of the speech of Lord Diplock in *R v Sullivan* [1983] 2 All ER 673 at 678, [1984] AC 156 at 173 [cited, above, p 30 (penultimate paragraph)].

This appeal must accordingly be dismissed.

Appeal dismissed

In *A-G's Reference (No 2 of 1992)* (1993) 99 Cr App R 429, [1994] Crim LR 692, D, a professional lorry driver, was charged with causing death by reckless driving. He had driven for six hours out of 12 (but breached no regulation) when he drove at 40 mph about half a mile along the hard shoulder of a motorway and ran into the back of a stationary van which had broken down, pushing it into the recovery vehicle. On the evidence of an expert witness, Professor Brown, that D was 'driving without awareness' the judge left automatism to the jury who acquitted. The Attorney-General referred the case to the Court of Appeal who ruled that automatism ought not to have been left to the jury.

Lord Taylor CJ said: Mr Pert QC [for D]…conceded that despite Professor Brown's phrase 'driving without awareness,' the Professor's description of the condition shows that it amounts only to reduced or imperfect awareness. There remains the ability to steer the vehicle straight. There is also usually a capacity to react to stimuli appearing in the road ahead. In the present case the respondent admitted he had actually seen the flashing lights a quarter of a mile from the scene.

Mr Pert confined his argument to the question whether Professor Brown's evidence properly raised the issue of automatism, which is the sole point of the reference. However, he wished to reserve the question whether the Professor's evidence might have been relevant to refute recklessness (see *Toner* (1991) 93 Cr App R 382).

[Lord Taylor referred to the cases (above) distinguishing between 'internal' and 'external' causes and continued:]

Here, Mr Pert argues that the precipitating cause of the condition described by Professor Brown was the external factor of motorway conditions. However that may be, the proper approach is that prescribed by Lord Lane CJ in *Burgess* at pages 43 and 96C as follows:

'Where the defence of automatism is raised by a defendant, two questions fall to be decided by the judge before the defence can be left to the jury. The first is whether a proper evidential foundation for the defence of automatism has been laid. The second is whether the evidence shows the case to be one of insane automatism, that is to say a case which falls within the *M'Naghten* Rules, or one of non-insane automatism.'

The first of those questions is the one raised by this reference. In our judgment the 'proper evidential foundation' was not laid in this case by Professor Brown's evidence of 'driving without awareness.' As the authorities cited above show the defence of automatism requires that there was a total destruction of voluntary control on the defendant's part. Impaired, reduced or partial control is not enough. Professor Brown accepted that someone 'driving without awareness' within his description, retains some control. He would be able to steer the vehicle and usually to react and return to full awareness when confronted by significant stimuli.

Accordingly, in our judgment, the learned recorder ought not to have left the issue of automatism to the jury in this case and the answer to the point of law as formulated is: no.

Question

As the driver's condition did not amount to automatism, the question whether it was caused by an external or an internal condition did not arise. But, if 'the ordinary stresses and disappointments of life which are the common lot of mankind do not constitute an external cause' (*Rabey* above, p 31, per Martin JA) does not the same apply to the conditions which all motorists encounter on motorways? Should a person who is so exceptionally susceptible to these conditions that he is in fact reduced to a state of automatism and causes injury or damage remain free from any restraint to do it again?

4. COINCIDENCE OF ACTUS REUS AND MENS REA

In order to constitute a crime the actus reus and the mens rea must coincide (a) in point of law and (b) in point of time.

(1) COINCIDENCE IN LAW

All the elements of the crime charged must be proved. It is not therefore sufficient to prove that the defendant caused the actus reus of crime X with the mens rea of crime Y. Cf *Pembliton*, below, p 35. It must be remembered, however, that sometimes the same mens rea is sufficient for two or more crimes; an intention to cause grievous bodily harm is a sufficient mens rea both for the offence of causing such harm with intent contrary to s 18 of the Offences Against the Person Act 1861 and for murder. An intention to cause some less than grievous bodily harm is sufficient for the offence of maliciously causing grievous bodily harm contrary to s 20 of the Offences Against the Person Act 1861 and for manslaughter.

Transferred malice

If D, with the mens rea of a particular crime, causes the actus reus of the same crime, he is guilty of that crime even though the victim, or object, of the offence is different from that which D intended or foresaw or ought to have foreseen. This common law doctrine is restated by the Draft Code, cl 24, and appears in the following terms in the draft Criminal Law Bill, cl 32:

32. Transferred fault and defences
　(1) In determining whether a person is guilty of an offence, his intention to cause, or his awareness of a risk that he will cause, a result in relation to a person or thing capable of being the victim

or subject-matter of the offence shall be treated as an intention to cause or, as the case may be, an awareness of a risk that he will cause, that result in relation to any other person or thing affected by his conduct.

(2) Any defence on which a person might have relied on a charge of an offence in relation to a person or thing within his contemplation is open to him on a charge of the same offence in relation to a person or thing not within his contemplation.

A provision to similar effect (but applicable only to the non-fatal offences in the draft Bill) is included in the draft Bill annexed to the Home Office Consultation Paper, 'Violence, Reforming the Offences Against the Person Act 1861' February 1998).

Attorney-General's Reference (No 3 of 1994)
[1997] 3 All ER 936, House of Lords

(Lords Goff, Mustill, Slynn, Hope and Clyde)

D stabbed his girl friend, F, whom he knew to be pregnant. E recovered; but there was evidence that the child, V, was born prematurely as a result of the wound and, as a result of the premature birth, died after 121 days. D was charged with the murder of V. The judge directed an acquittal on the ground that no conviction of murder or manslaughter was possible in law. (A foetus is not a person in law and cannot be the victim of murder or manslaughter.) On the reference, the Court of Appeal held that there was evidence that D murdered V, his intent to cause grievous bodily harm (the mens rea of murder) to E being 'transferred' to V. They also held that the foetus before birth was to be regarded as an integral part of the mother, like her arm or leg; so an intention to kill or cause grievous bodily harm to the foetus was an intention to cause grievous bodily harm to a person in being, the mother.

Lord Mustill held that the foetus is not a part of the mother: The mother and the foetus are two distinct organisms, living symbiotically, not a single organism with two aspects. So an intention to kill or injure the foetus is not an intention to cause gbh to a person—it is not the mens rea of murder. He accepted that the doctrine of transferred malice was sound law and continued.

The sources in more recent centuries are few. Of the two most frequently cited the earlier is *R v Pembliton* (1874) LR 2 CCR 119, [1874–80] All ER Rep 1163. In the course of a fight the defendant threw a stone at others which missed and broke a window. He was indicted for that he 'unlawfully and maliciously did commit damage, injury and spoil upon a window...' The jury found that he did not intend to break the window. On a case stated to the Court for Crown Cases Reserved it was argued for the prosecution that 'directly it is proved that he threw a stone...without just cause, the offence is established'. The ancient origins of this argument need no elaboration, and indeed the report of the argument as it developed showed that it was based on a conception of general malice. The interventions in argument are instructive. After the prosecutor had relied on the fact that the prisoner was actuated by malice, Blackburn J responded (at 120): 'But only of a particular kind, and not against the person injured.' Later, in reply to a reliance on a passage from Hale, the same judge said (at 121):

> 'Lord Coke, 3 Inst., p 56, puts the case of a man stealing deer in a park, shooting at the deer, and by the glance of the arrow killing a boy that is hidden in a bush, and calls this murder; but can any one say that ruling would be adopted now?'

This most learned of judges continued:

> 'I should have told the jury that if the prisoner knew there were windows behind, and that the probable consequence of his act would be to break one of them, that would be evidence for them of malice.'

The conviction was quashed. It is sufficient to quote briefly from the judgment of Blackburn J (at 122):

> 'We have not now to consider what would be malice aforethought to bring a given case within the common law definition of murder; here the statute says that the act must be unlawful and malicious…The jury might perhaps have found on this evidence that the act was malicious, because they might have found that the prisoner knew that the natural consequence of his act would be to break the glass, and although that was not his wish, yet he was reckless whether he did it or not; but the jury have not so found…'

This decision was distinguished in *R v Latimer* (1886) 17 QBD 359, [1886–90] All ER Rep 386. Two men quarrelled in a public house. One of them struck at the other with his belt. The glancing blow bounced off and struck the prosecutrix, wounding her severely. The assailant was prosecuted and convicted for having unlawfully and maliciously wounded her, contrary to s 20 of the Offences against the Person Act 1861. Counsel for the defendant relied on *R v Pembliton*. In his judgment, Lord Coleridge CJ said ((1886) 17 QBD 359 at 361, [1886–90] All ER Rep 386 at 387):

> 'It is common knowledge that a man who has an unlawful and malicious intent against another, and, in attempting to carry it out, injures a third person, is guilty of what the law deems malice against the person injured, because the offender is doing an unlawful act, and has that which the judges call general malice, and that is enough.'

A similar theme is found in the brief judgments of the other members of the court, who were able to distinguish *R v Pembliton* which, as Bowen LJ put the matter: '…was founded—not upon malice in general—but upon a particular form of malice, viz., malicious injury to property.' Bowen LJ put the case thus ((1886) 17 QBD 359 at 362, [1886–90] All ER Rep 386 at 388):

> 'It is quite clear that the act was done by the prisoner with malice in his mind. I use the word "malice" in the common law sense of the term, viz., a person is deemed malicious when he does an act which he knows will injure either the person or property of another.'

My Lords, I find it hard to base a modern law of murder on these two cases. The Court in *R v Latimer* was, I believe, entirely justified in finding a distinction between their statutory backgrounds and one can well accept that the answers given, one for acquittal, the other for conviction, would be the same today. But the harking back to a concept of general malice, which amounts to no more than this, that a wrongful act displays a malevolence which can be attached to any adverse consequence, has long been out of date. And to speak of a particular malice which is 'transferred' simply disguises the problem by idiomatic language. The defendant's malice is directed at one objective, and when after the event the court treats it as directed at another object it is not recognising a 'transfer' but creating a new malice which never existed before. As Dr Glanville Williams pointed out in *Criminal Law: The General Part* (2nd edn, 1961) p 184, the doctrine is 'rather an arbitrary exception to general principles'. Like many of its kind this is useful enough to yield rough justice, in particular cases, and it can sensibly be retained notwithstanding its lack of any sound intellectual basis. But it is another matter to build a new rule upon it.

I pause to distinguish the case of indiscriminate malice from those already discussed, although even now it is sometimes confused with them. The terrorist who hides a bomb in an aircraft provides an example. This is not a case of 'general malice' where under the old law any wrongful act sufficed to prove the evil disposition which was taken to supply the necessary intent for homicide. Nor is it transferred malice, for there is no need of a transfer. The intention is already aimed directly at the class of potential victims of which the actual victim forms part. The intent and the actus reus completed by the explosion are joined from the start, even though the identity of the ultimate victim is not yet fixed. So also with the shots fired indiscriminately into a crowd. No ancient fictions are needed to make these cases of murder.

Lord Mustill said that the question of manslaughter had caused him great anxiety, but he was persuaded by the opinion of Lord Hope.

Lord Hope, having made a detailed examination of the law of involuntary manslaughter (below, p 622) concluded:

I think, then, that the position can be summarised in this way. The intention which must be discovered is an intention to do an act which is unlawful and dangerous. In this case the act which had to be shown to be an unlawful and dangerous act was the stabbing of the child's mother. There can be no doubt that all sober and reasonable people would regard that act, within the appropriate meaning of this term, as dangerous. It is plain that it was unlawful as it was done with the intention of causing her injury. As the defendant intended to commit that act, all the ingredients necessary for mens rea in regard to the crime of manslaughter were established, irrespective of who was the ultimate victim of it. The fact that the child whom the mother was carrying at the time was born alive and then died as a result of the stabbing is all that was needed for the offence of manslaughter when the actus reus for that crime was completed by the child's death. The question, once all the other elements are satisfied, is simply one of causation. The defendant must accept all the consequences of his act, so long as the jury are satisfied that he did what he did intentionally, that what he did was unlawful and that, applying the correct test, it was also dangerous. The death of the child was unintentional, but the nature and quality of the act which caused it was such that it was criminal and therefore punishable. In my opinion that is sufficient for the offence of manslaughter. There is no need to look to the doctrine of transferred malice for a solution to the problem raised by this case so far as manslaughter is concerned.

Lords Goff, Slynn and Clyde agreed with the speeches of Lords Mustill and Hope.

Questions

1. Lord Mustill criticized the doctrine of transferred malice as having 'no sound intellectual basis' and involving a fiction. Do you agree that this is true of the doctrine as stated in the Draft Code?

2. Does the rule that an intention to cause gbh is a sufficient mens rea for murder involve a fiction? No one pretends that it is an intention to kill.

3. Does the prosecution's argument involve a 'double' transfer of intent?

4. Would Lord Mustill have decided differently if D had intended to *kill* the mother, thus eliminating one of his 'fictions'? Or if D had intended (as was the fact) to cause gbh to the mother and, the child having suffered gbh as a result of the premature birth but survived, D had been charged with causing gbh to it with intent?

5. It is held that D could be guilty of manslaughter because, by the unlawful and dangerous act done to the mother, he caused the death of the child. How, if at all, does this differ from transferred malice? But it was not merely 'an unlawful and dangerous act'. It was an act done with the mens rea of murder; and it admittedly caused death. So why is it not murder?

Note

The Court of Appeal rejected arguments advanced by Glanville Williams (i) that 'an unexpected difference of mode will be regarded as severing the chain of causation if it is sufficiently far removed from the intended mode, and (ii) that the doctrine 'should be limited to cases where the consequence was brought about by negligence in relation to the actual victim.' These arguments were not advanced in the House of Lords.

As cl 32(2), above, shows, if D shoots at V and, unforeseeably, kills, and is charged with killing, X, he can rely on any defence, such as provocation or self-defence which he could have relied on had he killed, and been charged with killing, V. Cf *Gross* (1913) 23 Cox CC 455.

For the place of transferred fault in criminal damage to property, see below, p 946.

J. Horder, 'A Critique of the Correspondence Principle in Criminal Law'
[1995] Crim LR 759 (references omitted)

. . .

The correspondence principle (hereinafter, the 'C' principle) concerns the relationship between actus reus and mens rea. Its definition and justification are well expressed by Ashworth and Campbell ('Recklessness in Assault—And in General?' (1991) 107 L.Q.R. 187 at p.192.):

'[I]f the offence is defined in terms of certain consequences and certain circumstances, the mental element ought to correspond with that by referring to those consequences or circumstances. If a mental element as to a lesser consequence were acceptable, this would amount to constructive criminal liability.'

An example may serve as an illustration. An assault is committed when D's conduct causes V to apprehend immediate physical contact only if D realised that his conduct might cause V's apprehension. Assault is thus a crime that appears to satisfy the C principle, because one is not to be held liable unless one's mens rea (what one realised might happen) refers to the prohibited consequence in question (what V apprehended). The C principle remains very much an ideal, if anything, rather than an accurate descriptive generalisation about crimes. Even amongst crimes requiring mens rea, not all exemplify the principle to anything like the full extent. The real problem is to decide when the C principle makes sense, even as an ideal.

In this regard, Ashworth argues that the C principle is a concrete illustration of a more abstract general principle at work within the criminal law, the principle of individual autonomy. The autonomy principle dictates that people are not to be held criminally liable unless, inter alia, they can be shown to have chosen to do, or had control over the doing of, the harm or wrong in question. At first sight, the autonomy principle's emphasis on choice and control appears to provide an attractive theoretical grounding for a subjectivist understanding of the C principle. On the subjectivist view, the C principle limits criminal liability to harms or wrongs that are intended or consciously risked; and harms or wrongs intended or consciously risked would seem to be paradigm examples of things over whose occurrence one has choice or control. On closer analysis, though, it becomes clear that the C principle cannot so easily be derived theoretically from the autonomy principle. Suppose D throws a brick from a window and, in so doing, intends to, or realises that he may, hit V. In these circumstances, if V is struck by the brick, the C principle dictates that D may be held criminally liable for the striking, because D's mens rea related to that possible outcome as an element in the actus reus. Yet, at this very point, the C principle appears to part company with the autonomy principle, as stated. When D let go of the brick, he ceased to have control over events. Since the brick would have missed V if it had been blown off course, or if V had suddenly moved, the actual fact that V was struck was as much a matter of chance as of choice or control. No doubt, D is still rightly regarded as causing the striking; but no one is in control of everything they cause to occur. So, seemingly contrary to the C principle, the autonomy principle dictates that D should be held criminally liable for no more than endangering V by throwing the brick, since that action was all that D chose to do or controlled.

One might still argue that the two principles do not really conflict. Everything depends on whether the two principles are, on the one hand, what one might call 'permissive' principles or, on the other hand, 'restrictive' principles of liability. The autonomy principle appears to be broadly 'permissive' in character: if D chose to do wrong (or, say, controlled the wrongdoing of another), the imposition of criminal liability is permitted just in virtue of the choice or control. On the other hand, the C principle seems 'restrictive' in character: it restricts liability, howsoever permitted or justified by other principles, to conduct or consequences that D intended or foresaw. Seen as a restrictive principle of liability, the C principle seems to amount to no more than a hypothetical imperative: if D is to be held responsible for consequences beyond his control, he must at least have adverted to the possibility of those consequences coming about. This being so, ironically, the C principle will only make sense as an ideal in legal systems which do not respect the autonomy principle; because only then will issues arise of liability for consequences of one's conduct beyond one's control. But in spite of these difficulties, there is clearly a deeper theoretical link between the so-called autonomy principle and the C principle. Observance of the autonomy principle prevents any element of 'moral luck'—responsibility for consequences of one's conduct beyond one's control—from finding a place within the conditions of criminal liability. Observance of the C principle is meant to ensure that if a (morally unlucky) D is to be held criminally liable for the consequences of her conduct beyond her control, such liability should not be regarded as fair unless D intended to bring about, or adverted to the possibility of bringing about, those consequences. For, unless this mens rea condition is satisfied, D will not have been representatively labelled when held criminally responsible for those consequences.

. . .

The principle of representative labelling requires that there be a close match between the label or name attached to a crime, such as 'murder' or 'manslaughter', and the nature and gravity of what the defendant has done, whether or not there was an element of chance in bringing about the outcome in question. The C principle insists that one cannot be representatively labelled as a 'murder' or as a 'manslaughterer' unless one's mens rea (intention or foresight) related to the forbidden consequence itself, the unlawful killing. As is well known, in English law both murder and manslaughter fall short of this requirement. As Ashworth puts it, speaking of murder:

'a person may be convicted of murder if he . . . intended to cause grievous bodily harm. However, the latter species of fault breaches the principle of correspondence: the fault element does not correspond with the conduct element (which is, causing death), and so a person is liable to conviction for a higher crime than contemplated.'

Unfortunately, it is not clear that there is such a smooth connection between the C principle and the principle of representative labelling. Suppose D decides to speed unlawfully, realising that by so doing he makes it more likely that he will kill any pedestrian who steps out in front of him. A child runs out into the road, and is killed by the speed of the impact with D's car. Given that D foresaw killing as a possible consequence of his unlawful conduct, there could be no compromise of the C principle in convicting D of murder. Yet the principle of representative labelling would be compromised by a conviction for murder, because D did not intend to inflict any harm at all: intention to kill or seriously to injure is partly constitutive of the wrong of murder. These principle of representative labelling may thus insist on intention as the form of mens rea, even where the C principle is satisfied by foresight alone. A C principle theorist might reply that all this point demonstrates is that the two principles interact in the construction of criminal wrongs; but this response is unsatisfactory. A broader theory of how mens rea (and in particular, intention) can be partly constitutive of the wrongdoing in some crimes, when combined with the principle of representative labelling, threatens to make the C principle redundant in any analysis of such crimes.

...

Intention rarely operates as a mere 'fault element' in the criminal law. Its main role is in changing the normative significance of conduct. If, in appropriating your property, I intend permanently to deprive you of it, that intention does not simply make me more 'at fault' in what I do. It may turn my conduct from something neutral (like putting goods in a shopping basket) into a substantive criminal offence. Intention plays the same role in all 'precursor' offences where it is the mental element, and in criminal attempts. Without the intention to commit the crime, there is not only no fault; there is simply no wrong. Unless one also insists on an intention to (try to) produce the prohibited outcome in a criminal attempt, more than merely preparatory steps taken towards the outcome merge with a different wrong: endangerment. In all these cases, of course, the C principle appears to be satisfied, since subjective mens rea will relate to the actus reus; but the appearance is misleading because the principle is doing no work. In such cases (crimes of 'specific intent'), once one has understood the role of intention in defining the limits of the criminal wrong, there is nothing left for the C principle to do. A similar point can be made about more controversial cases, where the representative labelling principle is satisfied, but the C principle is not.

Suppose D forcibly removes V's kidney during a coerced and gratuitous operation, giving no thought to whether V will survive. V dies of shock. We have seen that Ashworth draws on the C principle to argue that this kind of case is inappropriate for a murder conviction, because although D intends to inflict grievous bodily harm, he was not subjectively aware that V might die. But as the example of the speeding driver shows, even where D does realise that someone may be unlawfully killed as a result of his conduct, this is not enough in itself to constitute sufficient mens rea for murder, for the purposes of representative labelling. So, in murder cases, it turns out that the claims of the C principle are dependent for their plausibility on making the assumption that the defendant had at least an intention to inflict grievous bodily harm, in any event. Consistency with the principle of representative labelling demands no less, precisely because the present law seeks to distinguish murder from involuntary manslaughter (as representative labels) by regarding the wrong of murder as constituted by killing with no less than such an intention. The C principle only comes into play once one is already dealing with a fully constituted wrong; but in crimes of specific intent, once one has defined the wrong one may (by definition) already have accounted for the mental element. Arguably, this is true of murder. 'Murder' is a strongly evaluative label that is meant to be reserved for the worst kinds of killing. Yet, in clearly demarcating its province—for representative labelling purposes—from that of manslaughter, there need be no special theoretical link (just as there is no historical link made, in this regard, between murder and intended killing. Even if, other things being equal, an intentional killing is somehow worse than an unintentional killing brought about through (say) the intended and wrongful removal of a kidney, further argument is needed before we must accept that someone guilty of the latter act is not representatively labelled as a murderer.

...

The C principle is thus a principle whose relevance, if any, is confined largely to crimes of basic intent, where mens rea plays an attributional role focused on the degree of one's fault in committing an admitted wrong. So, in cases where it is admitted that D was at fault in grievously harming V, contrary to section 20 of the Offences Against the Person Act 1861, the C principle dictates that D should not be criminally liable unless D foresaw at least the possibility of nothing less than grievous harm stemming from his or her conduct. On this view the law, which holds that it is enough to fulfil the requirements of 'malice' to show that D foresaw the possibility of no more than some physical harm, is too harsh...

B. Mitchell, 'In Defence of a Principle of Correspondence'
[1999] Crim LR 195 (references omitted)

...

Of paramount importance to the debate is the definition of relevant concepts and principles, and Dr Horder appears to have adopted rather narrower interpretations of subjectivism and the C principle than many subjectivists would advocate. The C principle commonly appeals to those who support a subjectivist approach to criminal liability, but Dr Horder seems to confine this to cases where the proscribed result or circumstance is intended or knowingly risked—the latter being construed as subjective recklessness. However, it is suggested that this is unduly restrictive and that a more justifiable concept of subjectivism is one which incorporates what superficially looks like a form of objectivism but which on closer examination is seen to be rather different. The proposed species of subjectivism is one which includes cases where D inadvertently risks the proscribed result or circumstance but had the capacity to have recognised it and thus ought to have done so, the latter constituting what might be termed 'latent' recklessness. It would be incorrect to describe this as an objective test since the question is not simply whether D's awareness and actions matched up to those of the hypothetical reasonable person; instead, the focus is on what could justifiably have been expected of the individual charged.

Such an approach is by no means especially novel or controversial. Rehearsing the arguments favouring criminal liability for negligence, Ashworth remarks that 'a person who negligently causes harm could have done otherwise' and provided 'the individuals have the capacity to behave otherwise, it is fair to impose liability in those situations where there are sufficient signals to alert the reasonable citizen to the need to take care'. This 'focus on capacity should not be dismissed as "objective", for that would be an undiscriminating use of the term'. On this basis, 'objectivism' becomes narrower than some lawyers have traditionally assumed, and would be confined to cases in which D is measured against the hypothetical reasonable man whilst ignoring the danger that D may have been incapable of conforming to the reasonable man's standards . . .

In accordance with this wider view of subjectivism, the C principle requires that D either knowingly caused or risked the proscribed harm or failed to exercise his capacity to recognise it when he could and ought to have done so. In these latter cases, D may have given no thought to the risk of the proscribed harm or he may have mistakenly thought (or assumed) there was no risk. In either instance D may, for example, have been under the influence of drugs or medication, or he may simply have failed to make the best use of his ability. The point is that he could have recognised there was an unjustifiable risk, he ought to have exercised that capacity, and ought not to have taken the risk.

Indeed, it is further suggested that Dr Horder's omission to address the role of capacity in the assessment of liability is a significant deficiency in his critique. The essential issue here is to determine the circumstances in which a person should be held liable under the criminal law for the consequences of his action. Professor Hart, one of the most influential jurists in recent years, advocated the liberal view that a person should only be held legally responsible for his actions if he had the capacity and fair opportunity to conform to the law's expectations and can thus be said to have chosen not to do so. To hold D criminally responsible for results or states of affairs consequent upon actions which he could not or could not reasonably have avoided offends our sense of individual justice and cannot be rationalised on utilitarian grounds. The issue of capacity arises however not only at this most basic level of D's ability to regulate his conduct (at the actus reus level), but also in relation to D's state of mind (his mens rea). Given the significance of mens rea in criminal law in ensuring adequate fault to justify liability, a person ought not to be held liable for those harms which he could not reasonably have been expected to foresee. Although this appears to represent acceptance of objectivism—in that D has failed to do what could reasonably have been expected of him—the fact that the particular D could reasonably have acted so as to conform to the law shows that his liability is ultimately subjectivist.

...

The first point of criticism raised by Dr Horder is that the C principle is not entirely consistent with the IA principle [individual autonomy]...Again, however, it appears that terminology is being used rather loosely. As Ashworth explains, we should recognise that people generally have sufficient capacity and free choice so that they should only be held criminally liable for what they chose to do or could control. When D throws the brick he is aware (albeit latently) that, for example, V might suddenly move or he might be wearing body armour beneath his clothing. If cross-examined at the critical moment when he lets go of the brick D would surely acknowledge that for some such reason V might not actually be struck by it or suffer no real injury. But he still chose to throw the brick in the expectation that V would or might well be struck; he exercised a good deal of control over the brick by deliberately throwing it towards V. Although he could not be absolutely certain that it would strike V or that it would cause the injury which he imagined, he clearly chose to take the risk. What matters is that the actual outcome of throwing the brick is the sort of thing which D envisaged—it came within the range of outcomes which D had expected.

...

Dr Horder seeks to show that there is no 'smooth connection between the C principle and the principle of representative labelling' [RL] and offers the example of the motorist who deliberately drives at speed, aware that he is thereby more likely to kill any pedestrian who steps out in front of him. A child runs out into the road and is killed by the motorist driving at speed. Dr Horder states that the RL principle would require an intent—presumably, to kill—for murder, whereas the C principle would happily treat the motorist as a murderer. The latter is at best misleading. The C principle readily holds the motorist criminally liable for causing the child's death and regards him as criminally liable for such death, but it does not necessarily categorise him as a murderer. Rather the C principle accepts that the precise offence category is a separate issue and would happily accommodate the motorist as a manslayer, provided the motorist knew or had the capacity to have been aware of the risk of killing. The C principle is wholly consistent with the RL principle's desire to reflect variations in personal culpability following the intention/recklessness distinction.

...

Dr Horder argues that in criminal law intention has a special significance in that it not only provides the fault element in crimes of specific intent but also constitutes the wrongness in D's conduct, and that this ultimately renders the C principle redundant. However, as Gardner (who had previously put the same argument about the role of intention) illustrated [John Gardner, 'Criminal Law and the Uses of Theory: A Reply to Laing' (1994) 14(2) O.J.L.S. 217 at 221, 222], numerous crimes do not demonstrate the same significance of intention. Moreover, there is another, fundamental objection to Dr Horder's claim which is that even in the main example he uses, namely theft, it is highly misleading to import such relative significance to the intent to permanently deprive. Many allegations of theft turn on the issue of dishonesty—for example, cases in which a shop assistant 'borrows' money from the till, saying that he intended to replace an equivalent sum a short while later. All the other elements of the crime are present and guilt depends solely on whether the court thinks the defendant acted (dis)honestly. Indeed, there is a similar lack of any special significance of intention in crimes, such as those involving deception, where intention is merely one of two or more elements of mens rea.

...

See also J. Horder 'Questioning the Correspondence Principle—A Reply' [1999] Crim LR 206.

Question

Whose view is (i) most attractive; (ii) most closely reflects the current state of the law?

R v Taafe

[1984] 1 All ER 747, House of Lords

(Lords Fraser, Scarman, Roskill, Bridge and Brightman)

Lord Scarman. My Lords, the certified question in this appeal by the Crown from the decision of the Court of Appeal quashing the respondent's conviction in the Crown Court at Gravesend neatly summarises the assumed facts on which the recorder ruled that, even if they were proved to the satisfaction of a jury, the respondent would not be entitled to be acquitted. The question is in these terms:

> 'When a defendant is charged with an offence, contrary to section 170(2) of the Customs and Excise Management Act 1979 [below, p 44], of being knowingly concerned in the fraudulent evasion of the prohibition on the importation of a controlled drug—Does the defendant commit the offence where he: (a) imports prohibited drugs into the United Kingdom; (b) intends fraudulently to evade a prohibition on importation; but (c) mistakenly believes the goods to be money and not drugs; and (d) mistakenly believes that money is the subject of a prohibition against importation.'

In effect, the recorder answered the question in the affirmative and the Court of Appeal in the negative.

There was no trial, for the respondent changed his plea to guilty after the recorder's ruling. On his appeal against conviction, the judgment of the Court of Appeal was delivered by Lord Lane CJ. The judgment recites the history of the case and the assumptions on which a decision had to be taken (see [1983] 2 All ER 625, [1983] 1 WLR 627). It is unnecessary to burden the House with a repetition of what is there so clearly set forth.

Lord Lane CJ construed the subsection under which the respondent was charged as creating an offence not of absolute liability but as one of which an essential ingredient is a guilty mind. To be 'knowingly concerned' meant, in his judgment, knowledge not only of the existence of a smuggling operation but also that the substance being smuggled into the country was one the importation of which was prohibited by statute. The respondent thought he was concerned in a smuggling operation but believed that the substance was currency. The importation of currency is not subject to any prohibition. Lord Lane CJ concluded ([1983] 2 All ER 625 at 628, [1983] 1WLR 627 at 631):

> 'He [the respondent] is to be judged against the facts that he believed them to be. Had this indeed been currency and not cannabis, no offence would have been committed.'

Lord Lane CJ went on to ask this question:

> 'Does it make any difference that the [respondent] thought wrongly that by clandestinely importing currency he was committing an offence?'

The Crown submitted that it did. The court rejected the submission: the respondent's mistake of law could not convert the importation of currency into a criminal offence; and importing currency is what it had to be assumed that the respondent believed he was doing.

My Lords, I find the reasoning of Lord Lane CJ compelling. I agree with his construction of s 170(2) of the 1979 Act; and the principle that a man must be judged on the facts as he believes them to be is an accepted principle of the criminal law when the state of a man's mind and his knowledge are ingredients of the offence with which he is charged.

The other Law Lords agreed.

Notes

1. The defendant had committed the actus reus of the offence because he had in fact imported drugs, the importation of which was forbidden by the 1979 Act. He also had *an intention to break the law forbidding importation* because he believed (wrongly) he was importing currency and he also believed (wrongly) that the importation of currency was prohibited. But since the act he intended to do was not actually prohibited by law—it was not an actus reus—his intention, however morally reprehensible, was not a mens rea. It is the same in this respect as the case of a man who has sexual intercourse with a 17-year-old girl, believing that the law prohibits sexual intercourse with girls under the age of 18. He has an intention to break the law prohibiting sexual intercourse with girls but he does not intend an actus reus.

2. Section 170(2) of the Customs and Excise Management Act 1979 provides:

…if any person is, in relation to any goods, in any way knowingly concerned in any fraudulent evasion or attempt at evasion:

    (a) of any duty chargeable on the goods;

    (b) of any prohibition or restriction for the time being in force with respect to the goods under or by virtue of any enactment; or

    (c) of any provision of the Customs and Excise Acts 1979 applicable to the goods,
       he shall be guilty of an offence under this section and may be arrested.

If the defendant is mistaken as to the nature of the goods, whether he is guilty will depend on the nature of the mistake. If, on the facts he believed to exist, he would be committing the actus reus of the offence charged and he was in fact committing the actus reus of the same offence, actus reus and mens rea would coincide and he would be guilty. The mistake is immaterial. For example, he believes he is smuggling a crate of Irish whiskey. In fact the crate contains Scotch whisky. He believes he is importing a dutiable item and he is importing a dutiable item. He knows, because his belief and the facts coincide in this respect, that he is evading the duty chargeable on the goods in the crate. If the crate contained only an item which was not dutiable, there would be no actus reus of the full offence; but D might be guilty of an attempt. See Ch 15, below.

Where D believes he is smuggling dutiable goods and the goods are not merely dutiable but prohibited, the answer may be different. In principle, it should depend on whether the mens rea and the actus reus coincide. If sub-s (2) created a single offence it should be immaterial that D thought he was committing an offence under para (a) whereas in fact he was committing an offence under para (b) because they are then the same offence—it is the same in principle as the case where D shoots to kill a person whom he believes to be a man, W, but who is in fact a woman, V. He is guilty of murder. With the mens rea of murder, he caused the actus reus of murder. The mistake is immaterial.

Whether sub-s (2) creates one offence or separate offences under paras (a), (b) and (c) respectively is a question of the interpretation of the section, to which there is no certain answer. What is certain is that an evasion or attempted evasion (contrary to para (b)) of a prohibition under s 3 of the Misuse of Drugs Act 1971 is a separate offence from the general offence of importing prohibited goods. This is because such an offence carries a higher penalty than is generally available under sub-s (2) and, under the principle in *Courtie* [1984] 1 All ER 740, [1984] AC 463, it must be a separate offence. The principle is that where an offence carries a higher penalty when a particular element is present, the offence with that element is a separate offence from the offence without it. It follows that there are several such separate offences under para (b) because the maximum penalty varies according to the class of drug—for Class A drugs, life, for Class B drugs, 14 years and for Class C drugs, five years. The maximum for prohibited goods generally is two years. Thus para (b) creates no less than four offences—unless the courts decide that this is so inconvenient a result that it could not have been intended by Parliament: *DPP v Butterworth* [1994] 3 All ER 289, [1995] 1 AC 381.

The effect of the application of the general principle would be that, if D is concerned in the importation of a drug which he believes to be pemoline (a Class C drug) but which is in fact pethidine (a Class A drug), he would be not guilty of any complete offence under para (b), because there is no coincidence of the actus reus and mens rea of any offence. However, in *Shivpuri* [1986] 2 All ER 334, [1987] AC 1, below, p 547, the House of Lords, looking at the case law and the legislative history, concluded that Parliament intended that the only mens rea necessary for an offence under para (b) should be knowledge that the goods were subject to a prohibition on importation. If there are four offences, the mens rea is the same for each. In the case put above, D would be guilty of the 'life' offence, although the offence he believed he was committing was punishable with only five years. He would, at the same time, be guilty of an attempt to commit the five-year offence, because that is the offence he intends to commit. These results would be reversed if he was in fact importing pemoline, believing it to be pethidine—that is, he would be guilty of the five-year offence and of an attempt to commit the 'life' offence. In *Bett* [1999] 1 Cr App R 361, [1999] Crim LR 218 the court took a similar view of the offences of permitting premises to be used for supplying a controlled drug, contrary to s 8(b) of the Misuse of Drugs Act 1971. The penalties differ according to the class of drug, A, B, or C, involved. There are three offences; but it is necessary to prove only that D knew the premises were being used for supplying *a* controlled drug—any controlled drug, whatever it might turn out to be. The mens rea is the same for each offence, whether it be a two-year, a three-year, or a five-year offence. This may be the necessary implication of the statute, but is it just?

See *Ellis, Street and Smith* (1986) 84 Cr App R 235, [1987] Crim LR 44 and commentary; *Siracusa* (1989) 90 Cr App R 340, [1989] Crim LR 712. 'Evasion' and 'attempt at evasion' are not two separate offences but two different ways of committing a single offence: *Latif* [1996] 1 All ER 353 at 365–366, HL, per Lord Steyn, below, p 57.

In *Taafe* the defendant believed that he was concerned in the importation of something which did not fall within any of the three paragraphs of sub-s (2). Consequently, he did not have the mens rea for an offence under the section. He believed that he was committing an offence, but his mistake was one of criminal law. Nor could he have been convicted of an attempt. See p 543, below.

(2) COINCIDENCE IN POINT OF TIME

R v Jakeman

(1983) 76 Cr App R 223, Court of Appeal, Criminal Division

(Eveleigh LJ, Wood and McCullough JJ)

Jakeman (J) booked a flight from Accra to Rome and thence to London. When she checked in at Accra she booked two suitcases through to London. They contained cannabis, the importation of which into the UK is prohibited by s 3(1) of the Misuse of Drugs Act 1971. The flight to Rome was cancelled. The passengers were flown to Paris. J left her luggage there, and flew to Rome and then to London. Customs officials in Paris assumed the luggage had been misrouted and sent the suitcases to London where the cannabis was discovered. J was convicted under the Customs and Excise Management Act 1979, s 170(2): '... if any person is, in relation to any goods, in any way knowingly concerned in any fraudulent evasion ... (b) of any prohibition ... for the time being in force with respect to the goods ... he shall be guilty of an offence.' J's defence was that on leaving Accra she decided to have nothing more to do with the enterprise and so did not collect the suitcases in Paris and tore up the baggage tags. The judge ruled that this was no answer. She appealed.

Wood J. . . . We will deal first with the application for leave to appeal against conviction. Mr Mansfield first submits that the learned judge was wrong in the ruling which he gave. He submits that for the offence under section 170(2) of the 1979 Act, the participation of the applicant and her mens rea must continue throughout the offence—in this case at least until the wheels of the aircraft touched down at Heathrow Airport.

In developing his submission on the first ground of appeal, Mr Mansfield relied upon the applicant's assertion that she had changed her mind immediately on leaving Accra and on the facts that she did not collect her suitcases in Paris, that she tore up the baggage tags on arrival at Heathrow and that she did not seek to claim her suitcases. He submitted that whether one referred to 'withdrawal' or 'abandonment or lack of mens rea' as the necessary ingredient of the defence, assistance was to be obtained from such cases as *Croft* (1944) 29 Cr App R 169, [1944] 1 KB 295 and *Becerra and Cooper* (1975) 62 Cr App R 212. These cases are concerned with accomplices and secondary parties to crime, not to the principal offender, and in the view of this court are not of assistance to test the submission which is made. It is our view that the correct approach is to analyse the offence itself, but before turning to consider the wording of the section as a whole, it is valuable to look at decided cases and to see what assistance can be derived from them.

The following propositions are supported by decisions of this court. First, that the importation takes place when the aircraft bringing the goods lands at an airport in this country. See *Smith (Donald)* (1973) 57 Cr App R 737, 748, [1973] QB 924, 935G. Secondly, acts done abroad in order to further the fraudulent evasion of a restriction on importation into this country are punishable under this section, see *Wall (Geoffrey)* (1974) 59 Cr App R 58, 61, [1974] 1 WLR 930, 934C.

For guilt to be established the importation must, of course, result as a consequence, if only in part, of the activity of the accused. If, for example, in the present case the applicant had taken her two suitcases off the carousel at Charles de Gaulle airport in Paris, removed all the luggage tags, placed the suitcases in a left luggage compartment and thrown the key of that compartment into the Seine, and then subsequently, in a general emergency, all left luggage compartments had been opened, a well-known English travel label had been found on her suitcase and those suitcases had been sent to the Travel Agents' agency, care of Customs and Excise at Heathrow, then that undoubted importation would not be the relevant one for the purposes of a charge against the applicant. . . .

Although the importation takes place at one precise moment—when the aircraft lands—a person who is concerned in the importation may play his part before or after that moment. Commonly, the person responsible for despatching the prohibited drugs to England acts fraudulently and so does the person who removes them from the airport at which they have arrived. Each is guilty. *Wall* (supra) is an example of the former and *Green* (1976) 62 Cr App R 74, [1976] QB 985 of the latter.

There is no doubt that, putting aside the question of duress, as we have done, the applicant had a guilty mind when at Accra she booked her luggage to London. By that act, she brought about the importation through the instrumentation of innocent agents. In this way, she caused the airline to label it to London, and the labels were responsible for the authorities in Paris sending it on to London.

What is suggested is that she should not be convicted unless her guilty state of mind subsisted at the time of importation. We see no reason to construe the act in this way. If a guilty mind at the time of importation is an essential, the man recruited to collect the package which has already arrived and which he knows contains prohibited drugs commits no offence. What matters is the state of mind at the time the relevant acts are done, ie at the time the defendant is concerned in bringing about the importation. This accords with the general principles of common law. To stab a victim in a rage with the necessary intent for murder or manslaughter leads to criminal responsibility for the resulting death regardless of any repentance between the act of stabbing and the time of death, which may be hours or days later. This is so even if, within seconds of the stabbing, the criminal comes to his senses and does everything possible to assist his victim. Only the victim's survival will save him from conviction for murder or manslaughter.

The applicant alleged that she repented as soon as she boarded the aircraft; that she deliberately failed to claim her luggage in Paris, that she tore up the baggage tags attached to her ticket and so on, but none of this could have saved her from being held criminally responsible for the importation which she had brought about by deliberate actions committed with guilty intent. Thus, the learned judge was right in the ruling he made....

Appeal dismissed

Questions

1. Do you agree that the defendant would not have been guilty if she had removed the luggage in Paris as envisaged by the judge? D leaves a poisoned apple for his wife, V, intending to kill her. He then repents and conceals the apple. V finds it, eats it and dies. Is D guilty of murder?

2. Was D already guilty of an attempt to commit the offence when, in Accra, she booked the suitcases through to London? Cf Criminal Attempts Act 1981, Ch 15, below.

3. Is an intention to do a merely preparatory act a sufficient mens rea if, unexpectedly, the preparatory act causes the actus reus of the offence? D prepares a poisoned apple with the intention of giving it to his wife, V, tomorrow. V finds the poisoned apple today, eats it and dies. Or, D is cleaning his gun with the intention of shooting V tomorrow. The gun goes off accidentally and kills V. Is D guilty of murder?

Thabo Meli v R
[1954] 1 All ER 373, Privy Council

(Lord Goddard CJ, Lord Reid and Mr L. M. D. da Silva)

The appellants, in accordance with a prearranged plan, took a man to a hut, gave him beer so that he was partially intoxicated and then struck him over the head. Believing him to be dead, they took his body and rolled it over a low cliff, dressing the scene to look like an accident. In fact the man was not dead, but died of exposure when unconscious at the foot of the cliff.

Lord Reid.... The point of law which was raised in this case can be simply stated. It is said that two acts were done: first, the attack in the hut; and, secondly, the placing of the body outside afterwards—and that they were separate acts. It is said that, while the first act was accompanied by mens rea, it was not the cause of death; but that the second act, while it was the cause of death, was not accompanied by mens rea; and on that ground, it is said that the accused are not guilty of murder, though they may have been guilty of culpable homicide. It is said that the mens rea necessary to establish murder is an intention to kill, and that there could be no intention to kill when the accused thought that the man was already dead, so their original intention to kill had ceased before they did the act which caused the man's death. It appears to their Lordships impossible to divide up what was really one series of acts in this way. There is no doubt that the accused set out to do all these acts in order to achieve their plan, and as parts of their plan; and it is much too refined a ground of judgment to say that, because they were under a misapprehension at one stage and thought that their guilty purpose had been achieved before, in fact, it was achieved, therefore they are to escape the penalties of the law. Their Lordships do not think that this is a matter which is susceptible of elaboration. There appears to be no case, either in South Africa or England, or for that matter elsewhere, which resembles the present. Their Lordships can find no difference relevant to the present case between the law of South Africa and the law of England; and they are of the opinion that by both laws there can be no separation such as that for which the accused contend. Their crime is not reduced from murder to a lesser crime merely because the accused were under some misapprehension for a time during the completion of their criminal plot.

Their Lordships must, therefore, humbly advise Her Majesty that this appeal should be dismissed.

Appeal dismissed

R v Le Brun
[1991] 4 All ER 673, Court of Appeal, Criminal Division

(Lord Lane CJ, Auld and Judge JJ)

While the appellant and his wife were walking home at about 2 am they got into a heated argument. He hit her on the jaw, knocking her down unconscious. He then attempted to lift or drag her away from the scene but she slipped from his grasp and hit her head causing a fracture to the skull from which she died. He was charged with murder and convicted of manslaughter.

[**Lord Lane CJ**, delivering the judgment of the court:]

The main thrust of [the argument of Mr Wilson-Smith for the appellant] is to be found in ground 3 of the notice of appeal, which I will now read:

> 'The learned judge erred in law in directing the jury that they could convict the appellant of murder or manslaughter (depending on the intention with which he had previously assaulted the victim) if they were sure that, having committed the assault with no serious injury resulting, the appellant had accidentally dropped the victim causing her death whilst either: (a) attempting to move her to her home against her wishes, including any wishes she may have expressed prior to the previous assault, and/or (b) attempting to dispose of her body or otherwise cover up the previous assault.'

Problems of causation and remoteness of damage are never easy of solution. We have had helpful arguments from both counsel on this point, the point in the present case being, to put it in summary before coming to deal with it in more detail, that the intention of the appellant to harm his wife one way or another may have been separated by a period of time from the act which in fact caused the death, namely the fact of her falling to the ground and fracturing her skull. That second incident may have taken place without any guilty mind on the part of the appellant.

The learned editors of Smith and Hogan *Criminal Law* (6th edn, 1988 [see 11th edn, p 56]) p 320 say:

> 'an intervening act by the original actor will not break the chain of causation so as to excuse him, where the intervening act is part of the same transaction; but it is otherwise if the act which causes the *actus reus* is part of a completely different transaction. For example, D, having wounded P, visits him in hospital and accidentally infects him with smallpox of which he dies.'

The problem in the instant case can be expressed in a number of different ways, of which causation is one. Causation on the facts as the jury in this case must have found them—I say at the best from the point of view of the appellant—is in one sense clear. Death was caused by the victim's head hitting the ground as she was being dragged away by the appellant. The only remoteness was that between the initial unlawful blow and the later moment when the skull was fractured causing death.

The question can be perhaps framed in this way. There was here an initial unlawful blow to the chin delivered by the appellant. That, again on what must have been the jury's finding, was not delivered with the intention of doing really serious harm to the wife. The guilty intent accompanying that blow was sufficient to have rendered the appellant guilty of manslaughter, but not murder, had it caused death. But it did not cause death. What caused death was the later impact when the wife's head hit the pavement. At the moment of impact the appellant's intention was to remove her, probably unconscious, body to avoid detection. To that extent the impact may have been pro tanto accidental. May the earlier guilty intent be joined with the later non-guilty blow which caused death to produce in the conglomerate a proper verdict of manslaughter?

It has usually been in the context of murder that the problem has arisen in the previous decisions....

[His Lordship referred to *Thabo Meli*, above, p 47, and to *Moore and Dorn* [1975] Crim LR 229 and continued:]

However, it will be observed that the present case is different from the facts of those two cases in that death here was not the result of a preconceived plan which went wrong, as was the case in those two decisions which we have cited. Here the death, again assuming the jury's finding to be such as it must have been, was the result of an initial unlawful blow, not intended to cause serious harm, in its turn causing the appellant to take steps possibly to evade the consequences of his unlawful act. During the taking of those steps he commits the actus reus but without the mens rea necessary for murder or manslaughter. Therefore the mens rea is contained in the initial unlawful assault, but the actus reus is the eventual dropping of the head on the ground.

Normally the actus reus and the mens rea coincide in point of time. What is the situation when they do not? Is it permissible, as the Crown contends here, to combine them to produce a conviction for manslaughter?

The answer is perhaps to be found in the next case to which we were referred, and that was *R v Church* [1965] 2 All ER 72, [1966] 1 QB 59. In that case the defendant was charged with the murder of a woman whose body was found in a river. The cause of death was drowning. The defendant had it seemed attacked the woman and rendered her semi-conscious. He thought she was dead and in his panic he threw her into the river. He was acquitted of murder but convicted of manslaughter....

[His Lordship quoted from the judgment of the court given by Edmund Davies J adopting as sound Glanville Williams' view (CLGP 174) that 'If a killing by the first act would have been manslaughter, a later destruction of the supposed corpse should also be manslaughter;' and holding that, if the jury regarded the conduct of the appellant as 'a series of acts which culminated in her death... it mattered not whether he believed her to be alive or dead when he threw her in the river.' His Lordship continued:]

It seems to us that where the unlawful application of force and the eventual act causing death are parts of the same sequence of events, the same transaction, the fact that there is an appreciable interval of time between the two does not serve to exonerate the defendant from liability. That is certainly so where the appellent's subsequent actions which caused death, after the initial unlawful blow, are designed to conceal his commission of the original unlawful assault.

It would be possible to express the problem as one of causation. The original unlawful blow to the chin was a causa sine qua non of the later actus reus. It was the opening event in a series which was to culminate in death: the first link in the chain of causation, to use another metaphor. It cannot be said that the actions of the appellant in dragging the victim away with the intention of evading liability broke the chain which linked the initial blow with the death.

In short, in circumstances such as the present, which is the only concern of this court, the act which causes death and the necessary mental state to constitute manslaughter need not coincide in point of time....

[Having quoted extensively from the summing-up, His Lordship continued:]

The complaint made by Mr Wilson-Smith is primarily directed at the portion of that passage which we have read, namely the passage which runs: 'if he was doing that because he was determined to make her come home even though she had refused to do so...'

The argument advanced on behalf of the appellant is this. There has to be shown by the Crown in order to succeed a continuing transaction, or an unbroken chain of causation between the act which proved the mens rea and the final incident which resulted in death before it can be said that there is a sufficient connection between the mens rea and the actus reus. The mere fact that this man attempts to get his wife home when she is unconscious, it is argued, coupled with her earlier unwillingness to go home, is not enough to show a continuing transaction of an unbroken chain as has to be shown.

In every case, and this is no exception, the summing up has to be read against the background of fact which lies behind the whole of the case. Part of the background is, as we have already indicated when trying to set out the facts of the case, that the dispute between the two was certainly in part, and probably very largely, about whether she was going to go home or not....

[His Lordship referred again to the summing-up and continued:]

The judge was drawing a sharp distinction between actions by the appellant which were designed to help his wife and actions which were not so designed: on the one hand that would be a way in which the prosecution could establish the connection if he was not trying to assist his wife; on the other hand if he was trying to assist his wife, the chain of causation would have been broken and the nexus between the two halves of the prosecution case would not exist....

[His Lordship said that the direction given to the jury in relation to manslaughter was satisfactory.]

Appeal dismissed

Questions

1. There was no doubt that Le Brun caused the death of his wife (V). There was a problem of causation only if the prosecution relied upon the blow to the jaw as the cause of death. If it was, this was a straightforward case of manslaughter. V did not die of any injury directly inflicted by that blow but it rendered her unconscious. She would not have died as she did if she had not been unconscious. Was the blow then a cause of death? It is sufficient to establish liability for homicide that the act alleged is one of two or more causes of death. Was it? Cf *Masilela*, below.

2. If the blow was a cause of death, did it matter whether Le Brun was trying to take his wife home against her will or was doing his best to help her? What if a passer-by had tried to carry her to get help and dropped her as Le Brun did? Does intervention by a third party 'break that chain of causation' where the accused's own act would not do so?

3. If dropping her was the sole cause of death, the 'series of acts' or transaction principle comes into play. Would the series of acts have come to an end if Le Brun had been attempting to get her to hospital? Or if he had thought that, whatever she had said before the blow, in the changed circumstances, she would have wished to go home?

Note

Where the first act is a cause of death. In *S v Masilela* 1968 (2) SA 558 (AD) the appellants (DD) struck and throttled V in his house with intent to kill him. DD threw him, unconscious, on to his bed. Having ransacked the house they set it on fire. V died of carbon monoxide poisoning. They may have believed V to be dead when they started the fire. On the assumption that this was so, their convictions for murder were, nevertheless, upheld. The majority held that the strangulation injuries (which were inflicted with intent to kill) were a material and direct contributory cause of death. But for the injuries V would have had no difficulty in escaping from the fire. Hart and Honoré, *Causation*, p 334, refer to a German case OGHBZSt 2 (1949), 285 where D turned on the gas in the matrimonial bedroom, intending to kill his sleeping wife, V, and went away. Three hours later he returned and, believing V to be dead, turned on the gas a second time to simulate an accident. The Supreme Court of the British Zone decided that D was guilty of murder as his act on the first occasion contributed to V's death by weakening her condition. What if a third party had turned on the gas on the second occasion?

Attorney-General's Reference (No 4 of 1980)
[1981] 2 All ER 617, Court of Appeal, Criminal Division

(Ackner LJ, Tudor Evans and Drake JJ)

In the course of an argument on the landing of a maisonette the accused pushed the deceased causing her to fall backwards over a handrail and head first onto the floor below. Almost immediately afterwards the accused tied a rope round the deceased's neck and dragged her upstairs by it. He then placed her in the bath and cut her neck with a knife to let out her blood, with the purpose of cutting up her body and disposing of it, which he then did. The body was never found. The accused was charged with manslaughter. There was evidence that the deceased died either as a result of being pushed down the stairs or by being strangled by the rope or by having her throat cut, but the Crown conceded that it was impossible to prove which of those acts had caused the death. In response to a submission by the defence at the close of the Crown's case that there was no case to go to the jury, the judge decided to withdraw the case from the jury and directed an acquittal on the ground that the Crown had failed to prove the cause of the death. The Attorney-General referred to the court for its opinion the question whether, if an accused person killed another by one or other of two or more different acts, each of which was sufficient to establish manslaughter, it was necessary to prove which act caused the death in order to found a conviction.

Ackner LJ. ... On the above facts this reference raises a single and simple question, viz, if an accused kills another by one or other of two or more different acts each of which, if it caused the death, is a sufficient act to establish manslaughter, is it necessary in order to found a conviction to prove which act caused the death? The answer to that question is No, it is not necessary to found a conviction to prove which act caused the death. No authority is required to justify this answer, which is clear beyond argument, as was indeed immediately conceded by counsel on behalf of the accused.

What went wrong in this case was that counsel made jury points to the judge and not submissions of law. He was in effect contending that the jury should not convict of manslaughter if the death had resulted from the 'fall', because the push which had projected the deceased over the handrail was a reflex and not a voluntary action, as a result of her digging her nails into him. If, however, the deceased was still alive when he cut her throat, since he then genuinely believed her to be dead, having discovered neither pulse nor sign of breath, but frothy blood coming from her mouth, he could not be guilty of manslaughter because he had not behaved with gross criminal negligence. What counsel and the judge unfortunately overlooked was that there was material available to the jury which would have entitled them to have convicted the accused of manslaughter, whichever of the two sets of acts caused her death. It being common ground that the deceased was killed by an act done to her by the accused and it being conceded that the jury could not be satisfied which was the act which caused the death, they should have been directed in due course in the summing up, to ask themselves the following questions: (i) 'Are we satisfied beyond reasonable doubt that the deceased's "fall" downstairs was the result of an intentional act by the accused which was unlawful and dangerous?' If the answer was No, then they would acquit. If the answer was Yes, then they would need to ask themselves a second question, namely: (ii) 'Are we satisfied beyond reasonable doubt that the act of cutting the girl's throat was an act of gross criminal negligence?' If the answer to that question was No, then they would acquit, but if the answer was Yes, then the verdict would be guilty of manslaughter. The jury would thus have been satisfied that, whichever act had killed the deceased, each was a sufficient act to establish the offence of manslaughter.

The facts of this case did not call for 'a series of acts direction' following the principle in *Thabo Meli v R* [p 47, above]....

Note

The defendant was certainly guilty of manslaughter if he acted with the fault required on both occasions; but should he not also have been guilty if he acted with that fault on the first occasion only? If he in fact thereafter killed while disposing of what he believed to be a corpse was not this part of the 'same transaction' (*Thabo Meli*) or 'a series of acts which culminated in death' (*Church*)? But, if the jury were not satisfied with the fault required on the first occasion, acquittal must follow.

FURTHER READING

A. Ashworth, 'Defining Offences Without Harm' in A. T. H. Smith (ed) *Criminal Law: Essays in Honour of J.C. Smith* (1987)

P. H. Robinson, 'Should the Criminal Law Abandon the Actus Reus-Mens Rea Distinction?' in

S. Shute, J. Gardner and J. Horder (eds) *Action and Value in Criminal Law* (1993)

A. T. H. Smith, 'On Actus Reus and Mens Rea' in P. Glazebrook (ed) *Reshaping the Criminal Law: Essays in Honour of Glanville Williams* (1978)

3
Causation

Introduction

Where the definition of a crime includes a result, it must be proved that D caused that result. An act done with intent to cause the result may be an attempt to commit the crime but it will not be the full offence unless it actually causes it. It makes no difference that the *event* desired by D happens if it does not happen as a result of his act. So in *White* [1910] 2 KB 124, below, p 54, where D administered poison to V with intent to kill her and she died not of poison but of a heart attack, he was guilty of attempted murder but not of murder. It would have been different if the poison had precipitated the heart attack. The death of V was the event which D desired to bring about but it was not the result of his act.

The discussion of causation usually occurs in the context of homicide, but it is an important feature in all result crimes. It is especially so in cases of strict liability where, in the absence of mens rea elements, disputes over causation become the most critical issue in determining liability. (See for example, on environmental offences: N. Padfield, 'Clean Water and Muddy Causation' [1995] Crim LR 683.) Causation is also an important aspect of many property crimes. Where D tells lies to V in order to persuade him to give him money and V is not deceived but sends the money, D is not guilty of obtaining by deception: *Mills* (1857) 7 Cox CC 263, but is guilty of an attempt to obtain: *Hensler* (1870) 11 Cox CC 570. In these cases V would not have sent the money if D had not asked for it, so in that sense D's act was a cause of the obtaining; but the law requires that the property be obtained *by deception*, that is, that the *deception* be the cause of the obtaining, and it was not.

Arguably, the criminal law places too much emphasis on the result occurring (which is sometimes a matter of luck) and not enough on the blameworthiness of D's conduct in seeking to bring about that result. See A. Ashworth, 'Belief Intent and Criminal Liability' in J. Eekelaar and J. Bell (eds) *Oxford Essays in Jurisprudence* (1989).

General approach to issues of causation

1. Is D's conduct a 'but for' cause ('but for' D's act would the result have occurred)?

2. Is D's conduct potentially a relevant legal cause:
   (a) D's conduct need not be the sole cause;
   (b) D's conduct must be a culpable cause;
   (c) D's conduct need not be a direct cause;
   (d) D's conduct must be more than merely *de minimis*.

3. Is there any intervening act between D's conduct and the prohibited result which breaks the chain of causation? Consider the type of intervention:
   (a) naturally occurring events;
   (b) third party interventions;

(c) the exceptional case of the medical profession;

(d) victim's conduct.

The courts have commonly asserted that causation is simply a question of fact to be answered by the application of common sense. That is difficult to reconcile with the existence of a book, *Causation in the Law*, of over 500 pages with a 24-page table of cases by two eminent professors, Hart and Honoré. The difficulty was recognized by the House of Lords in the *Empress* case, below, p 59. Whether that case helps to overcome the difficulty is a matter for debate.

1. BUT FOR CAUSATION

Consider *White* [1910] 2 KB 124. But for D's act of poisoning, would V have died anyway? There is a danger with taking but for causation too far. If D invites V to dinner and V is run over by X and killed on the way to D's house, V would not have died but for the invitation; but as a matter of common sense, no one would say 'D killed V', and D has not caused his death in law. The 'but for' test serves to filter out irrelevant factors, but cannot be regarded as any more than a starting point in the causation inquiry.

2. LEGAL CAUSES

(1) MULTIPLE CAUSES

A result may have more than one cause. It is sufficient for criminal liability that D's act was one of two or more causes. If the result would not have occurred as and when it did *but for* D's act that is usually enough to fix him with responsibility for it. If V is already dying of meningitis when D strikes him and the blow accelerates V's death, D is guilty of homicide. If a fatal collision occurs because two motorists are driving dangerously, both are guilty of causing death by dangerous driving. Usually it is simply a question of fact whether the act caused the result, but the matter is more complex when an act by some other person or some event intervenes between D's act and the result.

(2) A CULPABLE CAUSE?

A person while acting with the fault required for an offence may cause the forbidden result, yet there may be no connection between the fault and the result. Should he be held responsible for the result?

In *Clarke* (1990) 91 Cr App R 69 it was argued that a person who drives a car when so affected by drink that there was an obvious and serious risk that his driving would cause injury to the person or substantial damage to property was thereby guilty of reckless (as then defined in *Caldwell* and *Lawrence*, below, pp 146 and 148) driving. Russell LJ responded to this argument as follows:

Suppose a person gets into a car when indisputably unfit through drink to drive it; he drives at a snail's pace and is involved in a collision that is wholly the other driver's fault; the other driver is killed. On Mr Elias's [appellant's counsel's] definition the driver drives recklessly because he is driving while unfit through drink to do so. If another road user happens to be killed, he is guilty of causing death by reckless driving. That, in our view, cannot be correct.

Obviously it is not correct; but is that because the driver is not driving recklessly or because his reckless driving did not cause the death? Consider *Crossman*, [1986] RTR 49, where it was held that a lorry driver was guilty of reckless driving, however slowly and carefully he drove, if he was ignoring an obvious and serious risk that the load on his lorry was liable to fall off and cause injury. The load fell on to and killed a pedestrian and Crossman was held to be guilty of causing death by reckless driving. Assuming that Crossman was rightly held to be reckless (which he might not now be under the subjective test of recklessness see below, p 156) this was right because there was a connection between the recklessness and the death. But suppose that a child had run in front of the lorry so that, notwithstanding his slow and careful driving, he could not avoid running over and killing him. Plainly he should not be held guilty of causing death by reckless driving. He was committing the offence of reckless driving when he ran over and killed the child, but the death was not due to his recklessness.

Reckless driving has now been abolished but Crossman's conduct would amount to dangerous driving (below, p 168 and see *Woodward* [1995] 2 Cr App R 388, [1995] Crim LR 487 and commentary) and, where death was caused by the insecure load, to causing death by dangerous driving. Should the reasoning of Russell LJ, above, be applied to convict him of causing death in the hypothetical case of the child? Consider the next case.

R v Dalloway
(1847) 2 Cox CC 273, Stafford Crown Court

(Erle J)

The prisoner was indicted for the manslaughter of one Henry Clarke, by reason of his negligence as driver of a cart.

It appeared that the prisoner was standing up in a spring-cart, and having the conduct of it along a public thoroughfare. The cart was drawn by one horse. The reins were not in the hands of the prisoner, but loose on the horse's back. While the cart was so proceeding down the slope of a hill, the horse trotting at the time, the deceased child, who was about three years of age, ran across the road before the horse, at the distance of a few yards, and one of the wheels of the cart knocking it down and passing over it, caused its death. It did not appear that the prisoner saw the child in the road before the accident.

Spooner, for the prosecution, submitted that the prisoner, in consequence of his negligence in not using reins, was responsible for the death of the child, but Erle J, in summing up to the jury, directed them that a party neglecting ordinary caution, and, by reason of that neglect, causing the death of another, is guilty of manslaughter; that if the prisoner had reins, and by using the reins could have saved the child, he was guilty of manslaughter; but that if they thought he could not have saved the child by pulling the reins, or otherwise by their assistance, they must acquit him.

The jury acquitted the prisoner.

(3) DIRECT CAUSES

The connection between D and the result need not be direct. In *R v Mitchell* (1983) 76 Cr App R 293, CA, D entered a post office in which there was a lengthy queue. D tried to push in, an elderly man intervened and complained to D. D hit this man who fell back onto an 89-year-old lady who suffered a broken leg and died as a result of complications from that injury. D's conviction for manslaughter was upheld: 'We can see no reason of policy for holding that an act calculated to harm A cannot be manslaughter if, in fact it kills B. The criminality of the doer of the act is precisely the same . . . .' per Staughton J at p 296.

(4) DE MINIMIS CAUSES

Some factual causes are so minute that they can be ignored in law. In *R v Kimsey* [1996] Crim LR 35 D was convicted of causing death by dangerous driving. He had been racing another car driven by the deceased. D argued that the reason V crashed was because of her loss of control of the car, not because of D's collision with her car. The prosecution argued that D's conduct, by racing and/or colliding and/or driving too closely had caused V's loss of control and led to her death. The Court of Appeal confirmed that the test is whether the 'contribution of the dangerous driving to the death was more than minute.'

This can give rise to difficult questions of degree in cases of the killing of terminally ill individuals. The question of how much acceleration of impending death needs to be established to show that D has caused V's death raises complex and controversial issues of euthanasia. There have been a number of high profile cases in which doctors have been prosecuted for murder where they have 'eased the passing' of a terminally ill patient, often reducing life expectancy by only hours. A recent example was that of Dr Cox (1992) 12 BMLR 38 ('Hard cases make bad law (Mercy killing and Dr Cox)' (1992) 142 NLJ 1293), and a more significant one was that of Bodkin Adams, reported at [1957] Crim LR 365.

3. NOVUS ACTUS INTERVENIENS

This is a notoriously difficult area of law and the courts have struggled to produce clear principles. The diversity of factual circumstances in which interventions arise, encourages the courts to distinguish cases too readily. In addition, decisions are very heavily influenced by policy considerations, particularly since most are homicide cases in which D has performed a culpable act with mens rea. The following categories of intervening event can be considered.

(1) NATURAL EVENTS

According to a leading American writer, R. M. Perkins, if D knocks down V and leaves him unconscious on the floor of a building which collapses in a sudden earthquake and kills him, D is not guilty of homicide even if it is certain that V would not have been in the building if D had not knocked him down. But if D had struck V on the sea shore and left him unconscious in the path of the incoming tide, D would be responsible for V's death by drowning. (Examples given by Perkins (1946) 36 J Cr L & Cr at 393.) The sea shore example was followed in *Hallett* [1969] SASR 141, on similar facts; and the court said it would have been different if the unconscious victim had been left above the highwater mark but drowned by a wholly exceptional tidal wave resulting from an undersea earthquake.

Suppose a hospital is struck by lightning and set on fire so that everyone in it perishes. Are all the patients who were there because they had been assaulted now the victims of homicide?

(2) INTERVENING ACTS OF OTHERS

The law struggles to distinguish precisely between voluntary and involuntary actors intervening after the defendant's conduct and before the prohibited result. It is generally accepted that where X, the intervening party has acted in an involuntary manner, if his act is foreseeable, it will not break the chain of causation and D will remain liable. On the other hand a free deliberate informed act by X would break the chain of causation, whether foreseeable or not.

R v Latif; R v Shahzad
[1996] 1 All ER 353

(Lords Keith, Jauncey, Mustill, Steyn and Hoffmann)

Shahzad in Pakistan had heroin worth £3.2 m. He wanted to export it to England. Unknown to him, his principal courier, Honi, was a paid informer. With customs officials, Honi received the heroin from Shahzad and the officers arranged to export it to England. With the co-operation of the officers, Honi came to England and persuaded Shahzad to come to England. Shahzad and his accomplice, Latif met Honi at an appointed place and received from him what they believed to be the heroin (in fact, Horlicks!).

The defendants were convicted of being knowingly concerned in the fraudulent evasion or attempt at evasion of the prohibition of the importation of heroin, contrary to s 170(2)(b) of the Customs and Excise Management Act 1979 (set out above, p 44). Their appeal was dismissed by the Court of Appeal [1995] 1 Cr App R 270 who held that the words 'fraudulent evasion' extend to 'any conduct which is directed and intended to lead to the importation of goods covertly in breach of a prohibition on import'.

Lord Steyn (with whose speech Lords Keith, Jauncey, Mustill and Hoffmann agreed) said that the prosecution did not try to support this reasoning in the House of Lords and, after reference to a commentary in [1994] Crim LR 751–752, continued:

Counsel for the prosecution attempted to support the conviction on a different basis. He submitted that there was in truth a criminal evasion because Shahzad delivered the heroin intending that it should be imported into the United Kingdom: it was imported into the United Kingdom; and Shahzad sought to take delivery in England of the heroin. Counsel emphasized the continuing nature of the offence. He said it did not matter that the customs officers acted for their own purpose. The problem, as Sir John Smith pointed out in the note in the *Criminal Law Review*, is one of causation. The general principle is that the free, deliberate and informed intervention of a second person, who intends to exploit the situation created by the first, but is not acting in concert with him, is held to relieve the first actor of criminal responsibility: see *Hart and Honoré, Causation in the Law*, 2nd ed (1985), 325 et seq.; *Blackstone's Criminal Practice* (1995), 13–15. For example, if a thief had stolen the heroin after Shahzad delivered it to Honi, and imported it into the United Kingdom, the chain of causation would plainly have been broken. The general principle must also be applicable to the role of the customs officers in this case. They acted in full knowledge of the content of the packages. They did not act in concert with Shahzad. They acted deliberately for their own purposes whatever those might have been. In my view consistency and legal principle do not permit us to create an exception to the general principle of causation to take care of the particular problem thrown up by this case. In my view the prosecution's argument elides the real problem of causation and provides no way of solving it.

That is, however, not the end of the matter. There is another principle solution to be considered, namely the alternative argument of the prosecution in the Court of Appeal, *viz* that Shahzad was guilty of an attempted evasion under section 170(2). Initially, counsel for the prosecution did not on the hearing before your Lordships rely on this alternative argument. After your Lordships raised the question counsel for the prosecution did advance this alternative argument. On this question your Lordships heard oral submissions and subsequently received further written submissions.

Shahzad delivered the heroin to Honi in Pakistan for the purpose of exportation to the United Kingdom and subsequently Shahzad tried to collect the heroin from Honi for distribution in the United Kingdom. In these circumstances the guilt of Shahzad of an offence under that part of section 170(2) which creates the offence of an attempt at the evasion of a prohibition is plain. Counsel for Shahzad suggested that the jury might have viewed Shahzad's conduct as mere preparatory steps falling short of an attempted evasion. In my view that would have been a wholly unrealistic suggestion. In common sense and law that was only one possible answer: Shahzad committed attempts at evasion in Pakistan and in England. Indeed I am confident that counsel would not have devalued his speech to the jury with a suggestion that on the prosecution case there was no attempt at evasion. For my part I have no doubt that this case must be approached on the basis that the guilt of Shahzad of an attempt at evasion under section 170(2) cannot seriously be disputed.

Counsel for Shahzad also argued that if the movement of the heroin from Pakistan to England was not a fraudulent evasion it was impossible for Shahzad to be guilty of an offence of attempt at evasion. It will be recalled that I accepted that the customs officer, who brought the heroin to England, committed an offence under section 50(3) of the Customs and Excise Management Act 1979 and further that I assumed that the customs officer also committed an offence under section 170(2) of the same Act. In these circumstances the argument apparently falls away. In any event, Shahzad committed the attempt at evasion in Pakistan and nothing that the customs officer subsequently did could deprive Shahzad's conduct of its criminal character. And Shahzad's attempt at evasion by distribution of heroin in England was an offence. It was sufficient to prove that Shahzad intended to commit the full offence and was guilty of acts which were more than merely preparatory to the commission of the full offence.

Counsel for Shahzad further submitted that in the circumstances of this case an English court would not have had jurisdiction to try an offence of an attempt at evasion under section 170(2) in England. The attempted evasion in Pakistan, as well as the attempted evasion in England, were respectively directed at importation into the United Kingdom and associated with an importation into the United Kingdom. In these circumstances counsel's submission in regard to the attempt at evasion, which Shahzad committed in Pakistan, is destroyed by the decision of the House of Lords in *DPP v Stonehouse* [1977] 2 All ER 909, [1978] AC 55. The English courts have jurisdiction over such criminal attempts even though the overt acts take place abroad. The rationale is that the effect of the criminal attempt is directed at this country.

Appeals dismissed

Notes and questions

1. The case serves as a strong authority recognizing unequivocally the orthodox position that X's act will break the chain of causation started by D where X's act is a free deliberate and informed act.

2. After reading *Latif,* would you consider that D could be liable for V's death where D supplies heroin to V, a sane adult, who then injects himself? Is V's act a free informed and deliberate one? See *Kennedy No 2* below.

Empress Car Co v National Rivers Authority
[1998] 1 All ER 481, House Lords

(Lords Browne-Wilkinson, Lloyd, Nolan, Hoffmann and Clyde)

The question was whether the company had caused the pollution of a river, contrary to s 85(1) of the Water Resources Act 1991, by installing a tank of diesel oil in a position where, if the tap was turned on, the oil would flow into the river, and omitting to provide a proper lock or other protection against misuse. The tap was turned on by a person unknown and the entire contents flowed into the river. The House upheld the conviction of the company. Lord Hoffmann, having remarked on the many cases in which justices who have attempted to apply their common sense to the issue of causation have been reversed by the Divisional Court, went on to offer some guidance.

The first point to emphasise is that commonsense answers to questions of causation will differ according to the purpose for which the question is asked. Questions of causation often arise for the purpose of attributing responsibility to someone, for example, so as to blame him for something which has happened or to make him guilty of an offence or liable in damages. In such cases, the answer will depend upon the rule by which responsibility is being attributed. Take, for example, the case of the man who forgets to take the radio out of his car and during the night someone breaks the quarterlight, enters the car and steals it. What caused the damage? If the thief is on trial, so that the question is whether he is criminally responsible, then obviously the answer is that he caused the damage. It is no answer for him to say that it was caused by the owner carelessly leaving the radio inside. On the other hand, the owner's wife, irritated at the third such occurrence in a year, might well say that it was his fault. In the context of an inquiry into the owner's blameworthiness under a non-legal, commonsense duty to take reasonable care of one's own possessions, one would say that his carelessness caused the loss of the radio.

Not only may there be different answers to questions about causation when attributing responsibility to different people under different rules (in the above example, criminal responsibility of the thief, commonsense responsibility of the owner) but there may be different answers when attributing responsibility to different people under the same rule. In *National Rivers Authority v Yorkshire Water Services Ltd* [1995] 1 All ER 225, [1995] 1 AC 444 the defendant was a sewerage undertaker. It received sewage, treated it in filter beds and discharged the treated liquid into the river. One night someone unlawfully discharged a solvent called iso-octanol into the sewer. It passed through the sewage works and entered the river. The question was whether the defendant had caused the consequent pollution. Lord Mackay of Clashfern LC, with whom the other members of the House agreed, said ([1995] 1 All ER 225 at 231, [1995] 1 AC 444 at 452):

> '...I am of opinion that Yorkshire Water Services having set up a system for gathering effluent into their sewers and thence into their sewage works there to be treated, with an arrangement deliberately intended to carry the results of that treatment into contro58lled waters, the special circumstances surrounding the entry of iso-octanol into their sewers and works do not preclude the conclusion that Yorkshire Water Services caused the resulting poisonous, noxious and polluting matter to enter the controlled waters, notwithstanding that the constitution of the effluent so entering was affected by the presence of iso-octanol.'

So in the context of attributing responsibility to Yorkshire Water Services under s 85(1) (then s 107(1)(a) of the Water Act 1989), it had caused the pollution. On the other hand, if the person who put the iso-octanol into the sewer had been prosecuted under the same subsection, it would undoubtedly have been held that he caused the pollution....

I turn next to the question of third parties and natural forces. In answering questions of causation for the purposes of holding someone responsible, both the law and common sense normally attach great significance to deliberate human acts and extraordinary natural events. A factory owner carelessly leaves a drum containing highly inflammable vapour in a place where it could easily be accidentally ignited. If a workman, thinking it is only an empty drum, throws in a cigarette butt and causes an explosion, one would have no difficulty in saying that the negligence of the owner caused the explosion. On the other hand, if the workman, knowing exactly what the drum contains, lights a match and ignites it, one would have equally little difficulty in saying that he had caused the explosion and that the carelessness of the owner had merely provided him with an occasion for what he did. One would probably say the same if the drum was struck by lightning. In both cases one would say that although the vapour-filled drum was a necessary condition for the explosion to happen, it was not caused by the owner's negligence. One might add by way of further explanation that the presence of an arsonist workman or lightning happening to strike at that time and place was a coincidence....

I would also wish to avoid the language of foreseeability in relation to the inquiry into causation. In deciding whether some particular factor has played so important a part that any activity by the defendant should be seen as entirely superseded as a causative element, it is not a consideration of the foreseeability, or reasonable foreseeability, of the extraneous factor which seems to me to be appropriate, but rather its unnatural, extraordinary or unusual character. Matters of fault or negligence are not of immediate relevance in the present context and the concepts particularly related to those matters should best be avoided.

Notes and questions

1. What has become of the general principle stated in *Latif*, above (where Lord Hoffmann concurred with Lord Steyn)? *Latif* was not cited in *Empress*. Was it simply overlooked? Are the cases, on this issue, distinguishable?

2. The House decided only that the justices were *entitled to find*, on the evidence, that Empress caused the pollution. But the facts were not in dispute. Could the justices have properly decided that Empress did *not* cause the pollution? Should not *the law* say either that this was the offence, or that it was not?

3. If the factory owner does not cause the explosion where the workman deliberately drops his match into the oil drum, why did Empress cause the pollution when the unknown person turned on the tap? Can you see any difference? In both cases the intervention was 'free, deliberate and informed.' See *Pagett*, below, at p 61. Could it be that the outcome in *Empress* resulted from the current concern to prevent pollution? See *Alphacell v Woodward*, below, p 241.

4. Lord Hoffmann referred to *Stansbie v Troman* [1948] 1 All ER 599 where a decorator working alone in a house was held liable in the tort of negligence when he left the front door unlocked while he went out to buy wallpaper and a thief entered the house and stole items he found there. Cases of this kind are rarely relevant in the criminal law because the absence of mens rea means that the question of causation simply does not arise. No one would suggest that the decorator was guilty of theft (or that Lord Hoffmann's careless husband was guilty either of criminal damage to [his wife's] car or theft of her radio).

But *Empress* concerned a case of strict liability where the court held that the only question was whether D 'caused' the pollution; and there is no suggestion that the word 'cause' imports any requirement of mens rea. In the rare cases where negligence is sufficient fault in the criminal law, the tort cases may be in point. Consider the next question.

5. If a swimmer had swallowed the oil-polluted water and died, or a passerby had been killed by the exploding drum, could the owner have been guilty of manslaughter by gross negligence?

6. Lord Hoffmann says that he wishes to avoid the language of foreseeability and the question is whether the event was 'unnatural, extraordinary or unusual'. How, if at all, does this differ from the question whether it was foreseeable?

7. Consider again the case of D who supplies V with a syringe of heroin and V self-injects. Applying *Empress*, would V's act break the chain of causation? Always? What factors would determine whether D remained liable? See *Kennedy No 2* below.

R v Pagett

(1983) 76 Cr App R 279, Court of Appeal, Criminal Division

(Robert Goff LJ, Cantley and Farquharson JJ)

Pagett (P), armed with a shotgun, took a girl, Gail Kinchen (K), who was six months pregnant by him, from the home of her mother and stepfather by force, wounding the stepfather, and violently assaulting her mother. P took K to a block of flats, pursued by the police. The police called on P to come out. Eventually he did so, holding K in front of him as a shield. He approached two police officers and fired the shotgun. The officers fired back instinctively not taking any particular aim. K was struck by three bullets and died. P was convicted of, inter alia, manslaughter. He appealed on the ground that the judge had misdirected the jury that, on these facts, he had caused K's death.

[**Robert Goff LJ** delivered the judgment of the court:]

We turn to the first ground of appeal, which is that the learned judge erred in directing the jury that it was for him to decide *as a matter of law* whether by his unlawful and deliberate acts the appellant caused or was a cause of Gail Kinchen's death. It is right to observe that this direction of the learned judge followed upon a discussion with counsel, in the absence of the jury; though the appellant, having dismissed his own counsel, was for this purpose without legal representation. In the course of this discussion, counsel for the prosecution referred the learned judge to a passage in Professor Smith and Professor Hogan's *Criminal Law* (4th edn (1978), p 272), which reads as follows:

> 'Causation is a question of both fact and law. D's act cannot be held to be the cause of an event if the event would have occurred without it. The act, that is, must be a *sine qua non* of the event and whether it is so is a question of fact. But there are many acts which are *sine qua non* of a homicide and yet are not either in law, or in ordinary parlance, the cause of it. If I invite P to dinner and he is run over and killed on the way, my invitation may be a *sine qua non* of his death, but no one would say I killed him and I have not caused his death in law. Whether a particular act which is a *sine qua non* of an alleged *actus reus* is also a cause of it is a question of law. Where the facts are admitted the judge may direct the jury that a particular act did, or did not, cause a particular result.'
>
> There follows a reference to *Jordan* [p 71, below].

For the appellant, Lord Gifford criticised the statement of the learned authors that 'Whether a particular act which is a *sine qua non* of an alleged *actus reus* is also a cause of it is a question of law.'

He submitted that that question had to be answered by the jury as a question of fact. In our view, with all respect, both the passage in Smith and Hogan's *Criminal Law*, and Lord Gifford's criticism of it, are oversimplifications of a complex matter....

Now the whole subject of causation in the law has been the subject of a well-known and most distinguished treatise by Professors Hart and Honoré, *Causation in the Law*. Passages from this book were cited to the learned judge, and were plainly relied upon by him; we, too, wish to express our indebtedness to it. It would be quite wrong for us to consider in this judgment the wider issues discussed in that work. But, for present purposes, the passage which is of most immediate relevance is to be found in Chapter XII, in which the learned authors consider the circumstances in which the intervention of a third person, not acting in concert with the accused, may have the effect of relieving the accused of criminal responsibility. The criterion which they suggest should be applied in such circumstances is whether the intervention is voluntary, ie whether it is 'free, deliberate and informed.' We resist the temptation of expressing the judicial opinion whether we find ourselves in complete agreement with that definition; though we certainly consider it to be broadly correct and supported by authority. Among the examples which the authors give of non-voluntary conduct, which is not effective to relieve the accused of responsibility, are two which are germane to the present case, viz a reasonable act performed for the purpose of self-preservation, and an act done in performance of a legal duty.

There can, we consider, be no doubt that a reasonable act performed for the purpose of self-preservation, being of course itself an act caused by the accused's own act, does not operate as a *novus actus interveniens*. If authority is needed for this almost self-evident proposition, it is to be found in such cases as *Pitts* (1842) Car & M 284, and *Curley* (1909) 2 Cr App R 96. In both these cases, the act performed for the purpose of self-preservation consisted of an act by the victim in attempting to escape from the violence of the accused, which in fact resulted in the victim's death. In each case it was held as a matter of law that, if the victim acted in a reasonable attempt to escape the violence of the accused, the death of the victim was caused by the act of the accused. Now one form of self-preservation is self-defence; for present purposes, we can see no distinction in principle between an attempt to escape the consequences of the accused's act, and a response which takes the form of self-defence. Furthermore, in our judgment, if a reasonable act of self-defence against the act of the accused causes the death of a third party, we can see no reason in principle why the act of self-defence, being an involuntary act caused by the act of the accused, should relieve the accused from criminal responsibility for the death of the third party. Of course, it does not necessarily follow that the accused will be guilty of the murder, or even of the manslaughter, of the third party; though in the majority of cases he is likely to be guilty at least of manslaughter. Whether he is guilty of murder or manslaughter will depend upon the question whether all the ingredients of the relevant offence have been proved; in particular, on a charge of murder, it will be necessary that the accused had the necessary intent....

No English authority was cited to us, nor we think to the learned judge, in support of the proposition that an act done in the execution of a legal duty, again of course being an act itself caused by the act of the accused, does not operate as a novus actus interveniens....Even so, we agree with the learned judge that the proposition is sound in law, because as a matter of principle such an act cannot be regarded as a voluntary act independent of the wrongful act of the accused. A parallel may be drawn with the so-called 'rescue' cases in the law of negligence, where a wrongdoer may be held liable in negligence to a third party who suffers injury in going to the rescue of a person who has been put in danger by the defendant's negligent act. Where, for example, a police officer in the execution of his duty acts to prevent a crime, or to apprehend a person suspected of a crime, the case is surely *a fortiori*. Of course, it is inherent in the requirement that the police officer, or other person, must be acting in the execution of his duty that his act should be reasonable in all the circumstances: see section 3 of the Criminal Law Act 1967. Furthermore, once again we are only considering the issue of causation. If intervention by a third party in the execution of a legal duty, caused by the act of the accused, results in the death of the victim, the question whether the accused is guilty of the murder or manslaughter of the victim must depend on whether the necessary ingredients of the relevant offence have been proved against the accused, including in particular, in the case of murder, whether the accused had the necessary intent.

The principles which we have stated are principles of law. This is plain from, for example, the case of *Pitts* (1842) Car & M 284, to which we have already referred. It follows that where, in any particular case, there is an issue concerned with what we have for convenience called *novus actus interveniens*, it will be appropriate for the judge to direct the jury in accordance with these principles. It does not however follow that it is accurate to state broadly that causation is a question of law. On the contrary, generally speaking causation is a question of fact for the jury. Thus in, for example, *Towers* (1874) 12 Cox CC 530, the accused struck a woman; she screamed loudly, and a child whom she was then nursing turned black in the face, and from that day until it died suffered from convulsions. The question whether the death of the child was caused by the act of the accused was left by the judge to the jury to decide as a question of fact. But that does not mean that there are no principles of law relating to causation, so that no directions on law are ever to be given to a jury on the question of causation. On the contrary, we have already pointed out one familiar direction which is given on causation, which is that the accused's act need not be the sole, or even the main, cause of the victim's death for his act to be held to have caused the death.

Appeal dismissed

Questions

1. In what way were the police officers' acts capable of being described as 'involuntary'? What is the purpose of firearms training if officers are going to fire their weapons involuntarily?

2. In *R v DPP, ex p P Jones* [2000] Crim LR 858, DC, there was evidence that M, the managing director of E Ltd, had failed to set up a safe system of work for the operation of a grab bucket crane and that a death resulting from the operation of the crane would not have occurred if such a system had been established and observed. The immediate cause of death was an inadvertent movement of the joystick of the crane by the operator, H. The court ordered the DPP to reconsider his decision not to prosecute M or E Ltd for manslaughter by gross negligence. The court clearly thought there was no evidence of a break in the chain of causation. Even if H's act was negligent, it was hardly 'free, deliberate and informed'. What if it had been grossly negligent (so that H would have been guilty of manslaughter)?

Kennedy (No 2)
[2005] EWCA Crim 685, Court of Appeal, Criminal Division

(Woolf CJ, Davis and Field JJ)

K, supplied heroin to MB ('the deceased'). K prepared a 'hit' of heroin for MB and gave him the syringe ready for injection. MB injected himself and returned the syringe to K. K left the room. The heroin resulted in MB's breathing being affected. Although an ambulance was summoned, the injection resulted in the death of MB. On his conviction, K appealed and the Court of Appeal upheld his conviction ([1999] Crim LR 65) on the basis that (a) K was a secondary party to MB's act of self-injection (this is wrong and has now been accepted to be so by the Court of Appeal—see below, Ch 9, p 275); (b) that MB's act of self-injection was not a break in the chain of causation. Subsequent decisions of the Court of Appeal cast doubt on these conclusions and the case was referred back to the Court of Appeal by the Criminal Cases Review Commission.

The Lord Chief Justice:
[His lordship referred to the first appeal and the case of *Dalby* [1982] WLR 425]

21. Turning to the decisions which have taken place since that judgment [the first appeal] was given, they are most conveniently treated in chronological order. The first case to which it is necessary to refer is that of *Dias* [2002] 2 Cr. App. R. 5. The facts in *Dias* were very similar to the facts of this appeal. The most distinctive factual feature of *Dias* was that both the deceased and the defendant injected themselves with syringes prepared by Dias.

23. …Lord Justice Keene, in giving the judgment of this court, considered that it was not possible to rely on the unlawful supply of the heroin because 'the chain of causation was probably broken by (the) intervening act of the deceased injecting himself' (paragraph 8). Keene LJ found difficulty in seeing any distinction between the circumstances which were considered in Dalby, and the circumstances which were considered on the first appeal in this case (paragraph 21).

24. This court decided that, for the purposes of the offence of manslaughter, the unlawful act was 'essentially the injection of the heroin rather than the possession of it'. Keene LJ also stated that the defendant could only have been guilty of manslaughter as a secondary party and not as a principal. If that was the position, then 'who [was] the principal of manslaughter?' As there was no offence of self-manslaughter, the court considered it was difficult to see how the defendant could be guilty of that offence as a secondary party merely because he encouraged or assisted the deceased to inject himself with the drug. [That aspect of the case is dealt with in Ch 18 below.] The appeal was, therefore, allowed.

25. The decision in *Dalby* was followed by the decision in *Richards* [2002] EWCA Crim 12…

The next case was *Rogers* [2003] 1 WLR 1374. The important point in *Rogers* was that the defendant applied a tourniquet to the deceased's arm while the deceased injected himself with heroin. Rose VP agreed with Keene LJ in *Dias* and accepted that Waller LJ (Junior)'s reasoning in the first appeal was incorrect 'insofar as the reasoning was based on self-injection being an unlawful act'. Rose VP, like Keene LJ in *Dias*, approved of the criticism of Waller LJ's judgment on the first appeal contained in the commentary on that decision of Sir John Smith in *The Criminal Law Review* [1999] Crim LR 65. [This aspect of the case is dealt with in Ch 9 below on participation.]…

28. Pausing, before turning to the final case in the series, it is important to point out where the authorities that we have already cited take us;

    i) That a person who kills himself is not committing a crime.

    ii) Contrary to part of the judgment of Waller LJ (Junior) on the first appeal, even though a person may encourage another to take his own life, he is not an accessory to manslaughter on this ground alone as there is no principal of whom he is the accessory.

    iii) If, however, the role played by the defendant, in concert with the deceased, amounts to administering or causing the drug to be administered, then that person will have committed an offence under s.23 of the 1861 Act and he will be guilty of an unlawful act. The fact that the deceased may die does not affect that situation. Furthermore, if the defendant participates in an offence involving the administration of the drug, there could be no question of difficulties in relation to causation.

    iv) On the first appeal, Waller LJ (Junior) was right when he regarded 'the critical question to which the jury must direct its mind, where (as in the instance case) there is an act causative of death performed by, in this case the deceased himself, is whether the appellant can be said to be *jointly responsible* for the carrying out of that act.' (Emphasis added)

v) The critical comments in relation to the judgment on the first appeal are directed to other parts of Waller LJ's judgment, when he indicates that it would be sufficient if the appellant was an accessory. Waller LJ, for example, stated 'if the appellant *assisted in and wilfully encouraged* that unlawful conduct [i.e. the self-injection] he would himself be acting unlawfully.' (Emphasis added) If the encouragement is isolated from the assisting, then there would be a basis for the criticism....

31. The last case in the series is the case of *Finlay* [2003] EWCA Crim 3868.

32. [In *Finlay*] the trial judge, anticipating the judgment of this court in *Rogers*, gave a ruling stating:

'So it seems to me that subject to one further point, to which I will turn almost immediately, cooking up heroin, loading it into a syringe, and then giving the syringe to someone who is clearly going to inject themselves almost immediately, is capable of coming within the terms of section 23. Whether or not it does so in any given case is a question of fact which falls for the jury and not the court to decide.

The last remaining point in relation to section 23 is this. In order to establish limb two of their case, the prosecution would have to prove that the defendant caused the heroin to be administered to, or be taken by, the deceased. In my view it is not necessary for the Crown to prove that the defendant's actions were the sole cause of the deceased injecting heroin. Here, by cooking up, loading the syringe, and handing it to the deceased, the defendant produced a situation in which the deceased could inject and in which an injection by her into herself was entirely foreseeable. It was not a situation in which injection could be regarded as something extraordinary. That being the case, it seems to me that on the authority of *Environment Agency v Empress Car Company Limited* (above), that it would be open to the jury to conclude that the defendant's action caused heroin to be administered to, or to be taken by, the deceased.

At the end of the day this is a question of fact for the jury to decide.'

33. Of this part of the ruling on the appeal, Buxton LJ said:

'That clearly sets out the law as it was understood by this court in the case of *R v Rogers*. The test is one of causation. In this case, could it be said that the act of the deceased in taking up the syringe and using it on herself, which are to be assumed to be the facts, prevented Mr Finlay's previous acts being causative of the injection. The judge rightly referred to *Environment Agency v Empress Car Company* [1999] 2 AC 22. In that case Lord Hoffmann said that the prosecution need not prove that the defendant did something which was the immediate cause of death. When the prosecution had identified an act done by the defendant, the court had to decide, particularly when a necessary condition of the event complained of was the act of a third party, whether that act should be regarded as a matter of ordinary occurrence which would not negative the effect of the defendant's act; or something extraordinary, on the other hand which would leave open a finding that the defendant did not cause the criminal act or event. That, said Lord Hoffmann, with the agreement of the rest of the House of Lords, was a question of fact and degree to which, in the case before him, the justices had to apply their common sense, as in a jury trial the jury has to apply its common sense. That was exactly the way in which the judge directed himself in his observations on the application that count 2 should be removed from the jury....

Whether or not the defendant caused heroin to be administered to or taken by the deceased is a question of fact and degree which you have to decide, and you should decide it by applying your common sense and knowledge of the world to the facts that you find to be proved by the evidence. The prosecution do not have to show that what the defendant did or said was a sole cause of the injection of heroin into the deceased. Where the defendant has produced the situation in which there is the possibility for heroin to be administered to or taken by [the victim], but the actual injection of heroin involves an act on part of another—in this case [the victim] herself—then if the injection of heroin is to be regarded in your view as a normal fact of life, in the situation proved by the evidence, then the act of the other person will not prevent the defendant's deeds or words being a cause, or one of the causes, of that injection. On the other hand, if in the situation proved by the evidence, injection is to be regarded as an extraordinary event, then it would be open to you to conclude that the defendant did not cause heroin to be administered to or taken by the deceased....

Mr Gibson-Lee really advances two reasons why the judge should not have taken that view, and why he should have considered that count 2 should not have gone to the jury. The first is that on the assumption that it was the deceased who injected herself, that act of itself breaks the chain of causation between whatever it was that the accused did and the actual event of injection. That is a view that is also taken in a critical commentary on the decision in *Rogers* in the *Criminal Law Review* [see [2003] Crim LR 555]. We have to say that that approach is not correct. It seeks to make the existence of what used to be called a *novus actus interveniens*, and can now more simply be regarded as an act of another person, as something that as a matter of *law* [emphasis added] breaks the chain of causation. It was that view or assumption that was rejected by the House of Lords in the *Empress Car* case. Intervening acts are only a factor to be taken into account by the jury in looking at all the circumstances, as the judge told them to do.

Secondly, Mr Gibson-Lee says that in any event the facts of this case were such that it simply was not open to the jury to conclude that Mr Finlay had caused the injection. He had done no more than form part of the background, or provide the opportunity of which the deceased availed herself:—in other words, that the case was so extreme or so clear that it was not appropriate for the jury to look at it as a case of causation at all. The judge did not take that view, nor do we. The unhappy circumstances of this case, and in particular the unhappy circumstances of this lady's life and condition, in our view indicate that it was certainly open to a jury to conclude in *Empress Car* terms that in those circumstances, and we emphasise that, it was what Lord Hoffmann described as an "ordinary" occurrence for the purpose of the law of causation that she should have taken advantage of whatever it was that Mr Finlay did towards her or with her. It is not necessary for that conclusion to decide, as Mr Gibson-Lee suggested it was that she was incapable of knowing what she was doing or had ceased entirely to be a rational being. All that is necessary, in our judgment, is that the circumstances should be such that it could properly be said to fall within the ambit of possible and ordinary events that she will take the opportunity given her. We quite accept that, on facts different from these, there might be more difficulty in coming to that conclusion.'

34. It was because of his view that the test to be applied was 'one of causation' that Buxton LJ, like the judge, referred to Lord Hoffmann's speech in *Environment Agency v Empress Car Company Limited*. By focusing on the issue of causation, and by proceeding on the footing that the issue under s.23 was whether the defendant had caused to be administered the drug, Buxton LJ was departing somewhat from the approach of Rose VP in *Rogers*. If Finlay's actions were part and parcel of the administering of the drug or the causing the drug to be administered for the purposes of s.23 of the 1861 Act, then there really could be no problem as to causation as Rose VP indicated in *Rogers*. Of course, if the jury had taken the view that the activities of Finlay formed no more than 'part of the background' to the drug taking or simply 'provide[d] the opportunity of which the deceased availed herself', then the position would be different. Questions of causation would be determined otherwise.

35. The reliance by Buxton LJ on what Lord Hoffmann said in the *Empress* case as to causation is criticised by the Commission and the appellant and in academic articles (see for example, Criminal Law Review 2004 pp 463–7). This raises the question, as the Commission and Mr Bentley point out on behalf of the appellant, whether the *Empress* approach is intended to be of general application, or confined to situations similar to that which was being considered in the *Empress* case.

[His lordship referred to the *Empress* case]…

We cite these statements of Lord Hoffmann to emphasise that he was very much concerned with the context in which the issue arose for decision. This is of importance because, later in his speech, [his lordship] made clear foreseeability was not the proper test [see the extract above, p **60**].

40. In *Finlay*, Buxton LJ was suggesting that the approach the House of Lords appropriately applied in the *Empress* case to a statute dealing with pollution could be applied equally here to the issues of causation where the statutory context is very different. It is, however, to be noted that the question of causation can arise on a charge of manslaughter when s.23 of the 1861 Act is not relied upon, and in two different circumstances when s.23 is relied upon. It can arise on the general question of whether the defendant's unlawful action caused the deceased's death. It can also arise on the question of whether the defendant caused to be administered 'any poison or other destructive or noxious thing contrary to s.23'. These are distinct situations.

41. In his summing-up in *Finlay*, the trial judge referred to the need for the prosecution, in relation to the s.23 offence, to prove that the defendant caused the heroin to be administered to, or to be taken by, the deceased. In that context he referred to the *Empress* case. As we understand the position, it was to this context that Buxton LJ was addressing himself when he referred with approval to the approach of the judge to establishing causation in accordance with Lord Hoffmann's speech in the *Empress* case. In that context, this appears to us to be, with respect, an unnecessary sophistication. All the jury had to decide as to causation was whether Finlay's actions were as a matter of fact causative of the deceased taking the action to administer the drug. If it was, his conduct contravened s.23 and was unlawful. Otherwise it was not.

42. It has to be remembered that when considering whether the defendant's act has caused death, what amounts to causation in a case of this nature is not dependent upon a particular statutory context. Accordingly if a defendant is acting in concert with the deceased, what the deceased does in concert with the defendant will not break the chain of causation, even though the general principles as to causation have to be applied. This was recognised by Lord Steyn when he qualified the general position when saying in *R v Latif & Others* [1996] 2 Cr. App. R. 92 at p 104:

'The free, deliberate and informed intervention of a second person, who intends to exploit the situation created by the first, *but is not acting in concert with him* is held to relieve the first actor of criminal responsibility.' (Emphasis added)

43. If Kennedy either caused the deceased to administer the drug or was acting jointly with the deceased in administering the drug, Kennedy would be acting in concert with the deceased and there would be no breach in the chain of causation.

44. The exception made for the person 'acting in concert' is of considerable importance. The fact that a person who takes his own life does not commit an unlawful act by so doing, does not mean that a person who helps him to commit that act, if that helping act is contrary to s.23, does not commit an unlawful act. On the contrary, the helper does commit an unlawful act and could be charged under s.23 and convicted. He could also be convicted of manslaughter if the person he was helping dies in consequence. The requirement of an unlawful act is fulfilled. There should, in the appropriate case, be no difficulty in establishing foreseeability of risk. Nor should there be difficulty in establishing causation because the participants were acting in concert.

45. The Commission, in their Statement of Reasons, suggest that if the defendant cannot be an accessory, then nor can he be a joint principal. However, this approach ignores the significance of the independent unlawful act under s.23. If the defendant is guilty of an unlawful act under s.23 of the 1861 Act, this in turn can result in his being guilty of the different offence of

manslaughter. So if the defendant is properly proved to have committed an offence under one or other of the limbs of s.23, then, subject to the other requirements of establishing manslaughter, he will be guilty of manslaughter. Insofar as the Commission and Mr Bentley submitted otherwise, we reject their contentions, which are, in any event, inconsistent with previous decisions of this Court which are binding upon us. Keene LJ in *Dias* also recognised that an approach based on s.23 may result in the offence of manslaughter being established 'so long as the chain of causation was not broken'.

46. The Commission argue that taking the reasoning in *Finlay* to its logical conclusion, the outcome would be that a person who assists another to commit suicide by providing a loaded syringe of heroin to another, in order that that person can take his own life, would now become a principal to murder. It is suggested by the Commission that such 'assisted suicide' type situations are analogous to the *Finlay/Kennedy* type situation, save that in the former instance there is a joint intention to kill.

47. In the *Finlay/Kennedy* type situation, the Commission argue that the 'helper' would have the necessary mens rea (intent to cause death or really serious bodily harm, foresight of such consequences providing evidence of the necessary intent; quite different from motive or desire) and, by virtue of the reasoning in *Finlay*, they would also be committing the *actus reus* of murder (performing an act that was a substantial cause of death) even though the "helper" may not himself have administered the fatal dose or injection.

[His lordship considered the argument relating to the Suicide Act 1961 considered below, Ch 18)]...

Conclusions

51. In view of the conclusions that we have come to as a result of our examination of the authorities, it appears to us that it was open to the jury to convict the appellant of manslaughter. To convict, the jury had to be satisfied that, when the heroin was handed to the deceased 'for immediate injection', he and the deceased were both engaged in the one activity of administering the heroin. These were not necessarily to be regarded as two separate activities; and the question that remains is whether the jury were satisfied that this was the situation. If the jury were satisfied of this then the appellant was responsible for taking the action in concert with the deceased to enable the deceased to inject himself with the syringe of heroin which had been made ready for his immediate use.

52. In our view, the jury would have been entitled to find (and indeed it is an appropriate finding) that in these circumstances the appellant and the deceased were jointly engaged in administering the heroin. This was the conclusion of this Court on the first appeal, as we understand Waller LJ's judgment, and we do not feel it necessary to take a different view, though we do accept that the issue could have been left by the trial judge to the jury in more clear terms than it was.

53. The point in this case is that the appellant and the deceased were carrying out a 'combined operation' for which they were jointly responsible. Their actions were similar to what happens frequently when carrying out lawful injections: one nurse may carry out certain preparatory actions (including preparing the syringe) and hand it to a colleague who inserts the needle and administers the injection, after which the other nurse may apply a plaster. In such a situation, both nurses can be regarded as administering the drug. They are working as a team. Both their actions are necessary. They are interlinked but separate parts in the overall process of administering the drug. In these circumstances, as Waller LJ stated on the first appeal, they 'can be said to be jointly responsible for carrying out that act'.

54. Whether the necessary linkage existed between the actions of the appellant and the deceased was very much a matter for the jury to determine. The question then arises as to whether the trial judge in the summing up expressed the issue in sufficiently clear terms for the jury? As to this, we share similar reservations to those expressed by Waller LJ in his judgment on the first appeal. There was no need for the jury to find the encouragement that Waller LJ thought was necessary. However, the jury did have to find that the appellant and the deceased were acting in concert in administering the heroin.

Appeal dismissed

Questions

1. The Lord Chief Justice provides an example of a nursing team working together to prepare and administer an injection. But surely this works against his lordship's conclusion: the nursing 'team' is injecting 'another'—the patient. Is that not a legally significant difference?

2. D hands P bullets for his gun. P shoots V. Has D caused V's death?

3. To which crimes does this novel 'joint responsibility' doctrine apply?

4. Where does liability, according to *Kennedy*, begin? Does it begin when D opens an injection pack, or when he cooks up the heroin, or when the syringe is loaded? See D. C. Ormerod and R. Fortson [2005] Crim LR 819.

(3) INTERVENING MEDICAL TREATMENT

It has been noted that many of the difficult issues on causation arise in cases of homicide. In those cases a common problem is that following the defendant's infliction of injury on V, V is treated by medical professionals in a less than perfect manner. In what circumstances will the medical intervention break the chain of causation? Bear in mind that the judgments in these cases are laden with policy—the courts do not want to be 'letting off' D who has culpably caused some injury with mens rea when V dies, particularly when the medical profession are compelled to treat V, and often to do so in under-resourced circumstances.

R v Cheshire
[1991] 3 All ER 670, Court of Appeal, Criminal Division

(Beldam LJ, Boreham and Auld JJ)

During an argument in a fish and chip shop about midnight on 9/10 December 1987 D produced a handgun and shot V in the thigh and stomach. During his treatment in hospital V developed respiratory problems and a tracheotomy tube was placed in his windpipe. He died in hospital on 15 February 1988. At the post-mortem it was found that V's windpipe had become obstructed due to narrowing near the site of the tracheotomy scar.

D was charged with murder. The pathologist who conducted the post-mortem gave evidence that the immediate cause of death was cardio-respiratory arrest 'due to a condition which was produced as a result of treatment to provide an artificial airway in the treatment of gunshot wounds of the abdomen and leg.'

And he said, 'In other words, I give as the cause of death cardio-respiratory arrest due to gunshot wounds of the abdomen and leg.'

For the appellant it was conceded that the sequence of events which had led to the deceased's death was that described by the pathologist but a consultant surgeon, Mr Eadie, gave it as his opinion that by 8 February 1988 the wounds of the thigh and the abdomen no longer threatened the life of the deceased and his chances of survival were good. In his view, 'The cause of his death was the failure to recognise the reason for his sudden onset and continued breathlessness after the 8th February [and the] severe respiratory obstruction, including the presence of stridor [on 14 February] ...'

Mr Eadie said that V would not have died if his condition had been diagnosed and properly treated. The doctors had been negligent and this was the cause of death; but they had not, in his opinion, been grossly negligent or reckless.

Judge Lowry QC directed the jury that 'the bullets caused the death, even if the treatment was incompetent, negligent. For you to find that the chain was broken, the medical treatment or lack of medical treatment must be reckless ... Reckless conduct is where somebody could not care less. He acts or fails to act careless of the consequences, careless of the comfort or safety of another person ...' D was convicted of murder.

[**Beldam LJ**, having quoted from the judgment of Robert Goff LJ in *Pagett*, above, p 61, and his expression of indebtedness to Hart and Honoré, continued:]

We too are indebted to section IV of Chapter 12 of that work (2nd edn, 1985). Under the heading 'Doctor's or victim's negligence' the authors deal with cases in which an assault or wounding is followed by improper medical treatment or by refusal of treatment by the victim or failure on his part to take proper care of the wound or injury. The authors trace from *Hale's Pleas of the Crown* and *Stephen's Digest of the Criminal Law* the emergence of a standard set by Stephen of common knowledge or skill which they suggest appears to require proof of something more than ordinary negligence in order that one who inflicts a wound may be relieved of liability for homicide. And they refer to most American authorities as requiring at least gross negligence to negative causal connection. English decisions, however, have not echoed these words. In conclusion the authors state (at 362):

> 'Our survey of the place of doctor's and victim's negligence in the law of homicide, where differences of policy between civil and criminal law might be expected to make themselves felt, yields a meagre harvest. (i) On Stephen's view, which has some modern support, there is no difference between civil and criminal law as regards the effect of medical negligence: in each case gross negligence ("want of common knowledge or skill") is required to negative responsibility for death.'

Whatever may be the differences of policy between the approach of the civil and the criminal law to the question of causation, there are we think reasons for a critical approach when importing the language of the one to the other.

Since the apportionment of responsibility for damage has become commonplace in the civil law, judges have sought to distinguish the blameworthiness of conduct from its causative effect. Epithets suggestive of degrees of blameworthiness may be of little help in deciding how potent the conduct was in causing the result. A momentary lapse of concentration may lead to more serious consequences than a more glaring neglect of duty. In the criminal law the jury considering the factual question, did the accused's act cause the deceased's death, will we think derive little assistance from figures of speech more appropriate for conveying degrees of fault or blame in questions of apportionment. Unless authority suggests otherwise, we think such figures of speech are to be avoided in giving guidance to a jury on the question of causation. Whilst medical treatment unsuccessfully given to prevent the death of a victim with the care and skill of a competent medical practitioner will not amount to an intervening cause, it does not follow that treatment which falls below that standard of care and skill will amount to such a cause. As Professors Hart and Honoré comment, treatment which falls short of the standard expected of the competent medical practitioner is unfortunately only too frequent in human experience for it to be considered abnormal in the sense of extraordinary. Acts or omissions of a doctor treating the victim for injuries he has received at the hands of an accused may conceivably be so extraordinary as to be capable of being regarded as acts independent of the conduct of the accused but it is most unlikely that they will be.

We have not been referred to any English authority in which the terms of the direction which should be given to a jury in such a case have been considered. We were referred to *R v Jordan* (1956) 40 Cr App R 152 in which the appellant, who had been convicted of murder, sought leave to call further evidence about the cause of the victim's death. The application was granted and evidence was received by the court that the stab wound from which the victim died eight days later was not the cause of the victim's death. The deceased had died from the effects of sensitivity to Terramycin which had been given to him after his intolerance to it was established and in abnormal quantity. The court considered that the introduction into the system of the victim of a substance shown to be poisonous to him and in quantities which were so great as to result in pulmonary oedema leading to pneumonia were factors which ought to have been before the jury and which in all probability would have affected their decision.

R v Jordan was described in the later case of *R v Smith* [1959] 2 All ER 193, [1959] 2 QB 35 as a very particular case dependent upon its exact facts. The appellant in *R v Smith* had been convicted at court-martial of the murder of another soldier by stabbing him. The victim had been dropped twice while being taken to the medical reception station and was subsequently given treatment which was said to be incorrect and harmful. Lord Parker CJ, giving the judgment of the Court-Martial Appeal Court, rejected a contention that his death did not result from the stab wound. He said ([1959] 2 All ER 193 at 198, [1959] 2QB 35 at 42–43):

> 'It seems to the court that, if at the time of death the original wound is still an operating cause and a substantial cause, then the death can properly be said to be the result of the wound, albeit that some other cause of death is also operating. Only if it can be said that the original wounding is merely the setting in which another cause operates can it be said that the death does not result from the wound. Putting it in another way, only if the second cause is so overwhelming as to make the original wound merely part of the history can it be said that the death does not flow from the wound.'

Both these cases were considered by this Court in *R v Malcherek; R v Steel* [1981] 2 All ER 422, [1981] 1 WLR 690 in which it had been argued that the act of a doctor in disconnecting a life support machine had intervened to cause the death of the victim to the exclusion of injuries inflicted by the appellants. In rejecting this submission Lord Lane CJ, after considering *R v Jordan* and *R v Smith*, said ([1981] 2 All ER 422 at 428, [1981] 1 WLR 690 at 696):

> 'In the view of this court, if a choice has to be made between the decision in *R v Jordan* and that in *R v Smith*, which we do not believe it does (*R v Jordan* being a very exceptional case), then the decision in *R v Smith* is to be preferred.'

Later in the same judgment Lord Lane CJ said ([1981] 2 All ER 422 at 428–429, [1981] 1 WLR 690 at 696–697):

> 'There may be occasions, although they will be rare, when the original injury has ceased to operate as a cause at all, but in the ordinary case if the treatment is given bona fide by competent and careful medical practitioners, then evidence will not be admissible to show that the treatment would not have been administered in the same way by other medical practitioners. In other words, the fact that the victim has died, despite or because of medical treatment for the initial injury given by careful and skilled medical practitioners, will not exonerate the original assailant from responsibility for the death.'

In those two cases it was not suggested that the actions of the doctors in disconnecting the life support machines were other than competent and careful. The court did not have to consider the effect of medical treatment which fell short of the standard of care to be expected of competent medical practitioners.

A case in which the facts bear a close similarity to the case with which we are concerned is *R v Evans and Gardiner (No 2)* [1976] VR 523. In that case the deceased was stabbed in the stomach by the two applicants in April 1974. After operation the victim resumed an apparently healthy life but nearly a year later, after suffering abdominal pain and vomiting and undergoing further medical treatment, he died. The cause of death was a stricture of the small bowel, a not uncommon sequel to the operation carried out to deal with the stab wound inflicted by the applicants. It was contended that the doctors treating the victim for the later symptoms ought to have diagnosed the presence of the stricture, that they had been negligent not to do so and that timely operative treatment would have saved the victim's life.

The Supreme Court of Victoria held that the test to be applied in determining whether a felonious act has caused a death which follows, in spite of an intervening act, is whether the felonious act is still an operating and substantial cause of the death.

The summing up to the jury had been based on the passage already quoted from Lord Parker CJ's judgment in *R v Smith* and the Supreme Court indorsed a direction in those terms. It commented upon the limitations of *R v Jordan* and made observations on the difference between the failure to diagnose the consequence of the original injury and cases in which medical treatment has been given which has a positive adverse effect on the victim. It concluded (at 528):

> 'But in the long run the difference between a positive act of commission and an omission to do some particular act is for these purposes ultimately a question of degree. As an event intervening between an act alleged to be felonious and to have resulted in death, and the actual death, a positive act of commission or an act of omission will serve to break the chain of causation only if it can be shown that the act or omission accelerated the death, so that it can be said to have caused the death and thus to have prevented the felonious act which would have caused death from actually doing so.'

Later in the judgment the court said (at 534):

> 'In these circumstances we agree with the view of the learned trial Judge expressed in his report to this Court that there was a case to go to the jury. The failure of the medical practitioners to diagnose correctly the victim's condition, however inept or unskilful, was not the cause of death. It was the blockage of the bowel which caused death and the real question for the jury was whether that blockage was due to the stabbing. There was plenty of medical evidence to support such a finding, if the jury chose to accept it.'

It seems to us that these two passages demonstrate the difficulties in formulating and explaining a general concept of causation but what we think does emerge from this and the other cases is that when the victim of a criminal attack is treated for wounds or injuries by doctors or other medical staff attempting to repair the harm done, it will only be in the most extraordinary and unusual case that such treatment can be said to be so independent of the acts of the accused that it could be regarded in law as the cause of the victim's death to the exclusion of the accused's acts.

Where the law requires proof of the relationship between an act and its consequences as an element of responsibility, a simple and sufficient explanation of the basis of such relationship has proved notoriously elusive.

In a case in which the jury have to consider whether negligence in the treatment of injuries inflicted by the accused was the cause of death we think it is sufficient for the judge to tell the jury that they must be satisfied that the Crown have proved that the acts of the accused caused the death of the deceased, adding that the accused's acts need not be the sole cause or even the main cause of death, it being sufficient that his acts contributed significantly to that result. Even though negligence in the treatment of the victim was the immediate cause of his death, the jury should not regard it as excluding the responsibility of the accused unless the negligent treatment was so independent of his acts, and in itself so potent in causing death, that they regard the contribution made by his acts as insignificant.

It is not the function of the jury to evaluate competing causes or to choose which is dominant provided that they are satisfied that the accused's acts can fairly be said to have made a significant contribution to the victim's death. We think the word 'significant' conveys the necessary substance of a contribution made to the death which is more than negligible.

In the present case the passage in the summing up complained of has to be set in the context of the remainder of the direction given by the judge on the issue of causation. He directed the jury that they had to decide whether the two bullets fired into the deceased on 10 December caused his death on 15 February following. Or, he said, put in another way, did the injuries caused cease to operate as a cause of death because something else intervened? He told them that the prosecution did not have to prove that the bullets were the only cause of death but that they had to prove that they were one operative and substantial cause of death. He was thus following the words used in *R v Smith*.

The judge then gave examples for the jury to consider before reverting to a paraphrase of the alternative formulation used by Lord Parker CJ in *R v Smith*. Finally, he reminded the jury of the evidence which they had heard on this issue. We would remark that on several occasions during this evidence the jury had passed notes to the judge asking for clarification of expressions used by the medical witnesses, which showed that they were following closely the factual issues they had to consider. If the passage to which exception has been taken had not been included, no possible criticism could have been levelled at the summing up. Although for reasons we have stated we think that the judge erred when he invited the jury to consider the degree of fault in the medical treatment rather than its consequences, we consider that no miscarriage of justice has actually occurred. Even if more experienced doctors than those who attended the deceased would have recognised the rare complication in time to have prevented the deceased's death, that complication was a direct consequence of the appellant's acts, which remained a significant cause of his death. We cannot conceive that, on the evidence given, any jury would have found otherwise.

Accordingly, we dismiss the appeal.

Appeal dismissed

Notes and questions

1. It is important not to lose sight of the issue in a criminal trial of this nature. D is charged with the offence of murder or manslaughter. The question is whether the medical intervention has broken the chain of causation so that D is absolved of liability for the death (he may be liable for the injury or an attempt). It is not a question of whether the medical professional is 'guilty'.

2. The intervening medical treatment may involve an omission. In *R v McKechnie* (1992) Cr App R 51 DD beat up an elderly man, V, who suffered very serious head injuries and remained unconscious for weeks. Doctors discovered that V had a duodenal ulcer but decided that it would be too dangerous to operate because he was still unconscious from his beating. V died as a result of the ulcer bursting. DD were convicted and appealed inter alia on the direction as to causation. The Court of Appeal upheld the conviction: 'The Recorder's statement of the question of the intervening events—the doctor's decision not to operate on the duodenal ulcer because [V's] head injuries made such an operation dangerous—properly directed the jury, not to the correctness of the medical decision, but to its reasonableness', per Auld J at 58.

3. In what way does a test based on 'potency' or 'independence' differ from asking whether the act of the medical professional was 'foreseeable' and 'reasonable'? To what extent is the negligence or recklessness of the medical professional important in determining whether a break in the chain of causation has occurred?

4. What if, having been shot by D, V's wounds were healing well when he contracted MRSA in the hospital and died? Cf *Gowans* [2003] EWCA Crim 3935 where V contracted fatal septicaemia in hospital.

(4) THE VICTIM'S CONDUCT AS A BREAK IN THE CHAIN OF CAUSATION

This is, again, an area in which the courts have struggled to define any clear principles. A number of difficult issues arise:

- To what extent does it matter that V 'acts' and exacerbates his position rather than 'omits to save himself'?
- If D 'takes his victim as he finds him' does this extend beyond taking V's physical infirmities to include also V's psychological abnormalities?
- To what extent does D take only V's pre-existing conditions as found?

R v Blaue
[1975] 3 All ER 446, Court of Appeal, Criminal Division

(Lawton LJ, Thompson and Shaw JJ)

The appellant was convicted of manslaughter on the ground of diminished responsibility. He had inflicted four serious stab wounds on the deceased, one of which pierced a lung. The deceased, a Jehovah's Witness, refused to have a blood transfusion because it was contrary to her religious beliefs, and acknowledged this refusal in writing, despite the surgeon's advice that without the transfusion she would die. The Crown conceded at the trial that had she had the blood transfusion she would not have died. Blaue appealed on the ground (inter alia) that Mocatta J, following *Holland* (1841) 2 Mood & R 351, in effect directed the jury to find causation proved.

[**Lawton LJ** delivered the judgment of the court:]

...In *Holland* [(1841) 2 Mood & R 351] the defendant, in the course of a violent assault, had injured one of his victim's fingers. A surgeon had advised amputation because of danger to life through complications developing. The advice was rejected. A fortnight later the victim died of lockjaw: '...the real question is', said Maule J [2 Mood & R 351 at 352], 'whether in the end the wound inflicted by the prisoner was the cause of death?' That distinguished judge left the jury to decide that question as did the judge in this case. They had to decide it as juries always do, by pooling their experience of life and using their common sense. They would not have been handicapped by a lack of training in dialectics or moral theology.

Maule J's direction to the jury reflected the common law's answer to the problem. He who inflicted an injury which resulted in death could not excuse himself by pleading that his victim could have avoided death by taking greater care of himself: see Hale [*Pleas of the Crown* (1800), pp 427, 428]. The common law in Sir Matthew Hale's time probably was in line with contemporary concepts of ethics. A man who did a wrongful act was deemed *morally* responsible for the natural and probable consequences of that act. Counsel for the appellant asked us to remember that since Sir Matthew Hale's day the rigour of the law relating to homicide has been eased in favour of the accused. It has been—but this has come about through the development of the concept of intent, not by reason of a different view of causation. Well known practitioner's textbooks, such as *Halsbury's Laws* [3rd edn, vol 10, p 706] and *Russell on Crime* [12th edn (1964), vol 1, p 30], continue to reflect the common law approach. Textbooks intended for students or as studies in jurisprudence have queried the common law rule. See Hart and Honoré, *Causation in the Law* [1959, pp 320, 321], and Smith and Hogan [*Criminal Law* (3rd edn, 1973) p 214].

The physical cause of death in this case was the bleeding into the pleural cavity arising from the penetration of the lung. This had not been brought about by any decision made by the deceased girl but by the stab wound.

Counsel for the appellant tried to overcome this line of reasoning by submitting that the jury should have been directed that if they thought the girl's decision not to have a blood transfusion was an unreasonable one, then the chain of causation would have been broken. At once the question arises—reasonable by whose standards? Those of Jehovah's Witnesses? Humanists? Roman Catholics? Protestants of Anglo-Saxon descent? The man on the Clapham omnibus? But he might well be an admirer of Eleazar who suffered death rather than eat the flesh of swine [see 2 Maccabees, ch 6, vv 18–31] or of Sir Thomas More who, unlike nearly all his contemporaries, was unwilling to accept Henry VIII as Head of the Church in England. Those brought up in the Hebraic and Christian traditions would probably be reluctant to accept that these martyrs caused their own deaths.

As was pointed out to counsel for the appellant in the course of argument, two cases, each raising the same issue of reasonableness because of religious beliefs, could produce different verdicts depending on where the cases were tried. A jury drawn from Preston, sometimes said to be the most Catholic town in England, might have different views about martyrdom to one drawn from the inner suburbs of London. Counsel for the appellant accepted that this might be so; it was, he said, inherent in trial by jury. It is not inherent in the common law as expounded by Sir Matthew Hale and Maule J. It has long been the policy of the law that those who use violence on other people must take their victims as they find them. This in our judgment means the whole man, not just the physical man. It does not lie in the mouth of the assailant to say that his victim's religious beliefs which inhibited him from accepting certain kinds of treatment were unreasonable. The question for decision is what caused her death. The answer is the stab wound. The fact that the victim refused to stop this end coming about did not break the causal connection between the act and death…

Appeal dismissed

Questions

1. Was not the wound a substantial and operating cause (*Smith*, above, p 71) of death? If so, did it matter whether the victim's rejection of the blood transfusion was also a cause of death? Could it be said that the rejection of the blood transfusion was 'the immediate and sufficient cause' of death (Code, cl 17(2) below p 77)? Was not the victim dying of the wound when the transfusion was offered to save her?

2. Suppose that the victim had been a child who had been abducted by her parents so as to avoid the transfusion and had died. Would the defendant still have been guilty of manslaughter? Would the parents also have been guilty? See *Re S* [1993] 1 FLR 376.

3. In *Pigney v Pointer's Transport Services Ltd* [1957] 2 All ER 807 V's suicide, resulting from depression (not amounting to insanity under the M'Naghten Rules, below, p 374), resulting from injuries inflicted by D, was held to be caused by D for the purposes of the law of tort. Was D guilty of homicide? Was V's suicide the free, deliberate and informed act of a responsible person such as to break the chain of causation? Is this a case where D must take V as he finds him? Would he—and should he—avoid liability under Code, cl 17(2), below, p 77?

4. Compare the approach taken in the cases where V seeks to escape from D and in doing so suffers a fatal injury. In *R v Pitts* (1842) Car & M 284 it was held that 'If a person, being attacked, should from an apprehension of immediate violence, an apprehension which must be well grounded and justified by the circumstances, throw himself for escape into a river, and be drowned, the person attacking him is guilty of murder' (at p 284). In *R v Williams* (1992) 95 Cr App R 1 V, a hitch-hiker, leapt from a moving car and died from his injuries. The other occupants of the car were convicted of V's manslaughter, and robbery of V. On the question as to whether V had broken the chain of causation between the unlawful act of robbery and his death, the Court of Appeal held:

The jury should consider…whether the deceased's reaction in jumping from the moving car was within the range of responses which might be expected from a victim placed in the situation which he was. The jury should bear in mind any particular characteristic of the victim and the fact that in the agony of the moment he may act without thought and deliberation. per Stuart-Smith L J at p 8.

5. In *R v Dear* [1996] Crim LR 595 D stabbed V with a stanley knife after allegations that V had sexually abused D's 12-year-old daughter. V died. D claimed that V had broken the chain of causation by either re-opening the wounds (suicide) or if the wounds had reopened naturally, by failing to stop the bleeding. The Court of Appeal held there was no need to enquire whether V had behaved negligently or grossly negligently:

…the cause of the deceased's death was bleeding from the artery which the defendant had severed. Whether or not the resumption or continuation of that bleeding was deliberately caused by the deceased, the jury were entitled to find that the [defendant's] conduct made a operative and significant contribution to the death.

Is the correct test to apply that from *Williams* (was V's act 'daft') or that from *Blaue*?

4. CRITICISMS AND REFORM

Any law that exists on the question of causation in the criminal law is common law. Clause 17 of the Draft Criminal Code is an attempt to restate the common law principles. Whether it does so successfully is disputed but its principal critic, Glanville Williams, remarks ([1989] CLJ at 405–406) that 'it concentrates the mind wonderfully' and it at least provides a basis for discussion. Clause 17 provides:

17. Causation
(1) Subject to subsections (2) and (3), a person causes a result which is an element of an offence when—
   (a) he does an act which makes a more than negligible contribution to its occurrence; or
   (b) he omits to do an act which might prevent its occurrence and which he is under a duty to do according to the law relating to the offence.

(2) A person does not cause a result where, after he does such an act or makes such an omission, an act or event occurs—

    (a) which is the immediate and sufficient cause of the result;

    (b) which he did not foresee; and

    (c) which could not in the circumstances reasonably have been foreseen.

(3) A person who procures, assists or encourages another to cause a result that is an element of an offence does not himself cause that result so as to be guilty of the offence as a principal except when—

    (a) section 26(1)(c) [procuring an act by an innocent agent] applies; or

    (b) the offence itself consists in the procuring, assisting or encouraging another to cause the result.

The exemption that would be created by this subsection is criticized by Glanville Williams ('*Finis* for *Novus Actus*' (1989) CLJ 391) as being both too wide and too narrow.

Is clause 17(2) too wide?

Williams argues (at p 400) that the sub-section is too wide in that it provides that an event, as well as an act, may break the chain of causation:

At common law there is an important difference in respect of criminal causation between a human act and an event: the intervening act of a responsible person has an effect on imputable causation that an 'act of God' has not.

Williams cites no authority for the alleged common law of 'act of God'. Is he right? Cf the examples provided by Perkins above, p 56, of D knocking down V and leaving him unconscious on the floor of a building which collapses in a sudden earthquake and kills V and leaving V on the sea shore unconscious in the path of the incoming tide.

Williams argues that, 'Under the present law when *novus actus* excludes the responsibility of the first actor it offers the prosecution the later actor as a substitutional defendant.' Of course it is not possible to prosecute the homicidal earthquake or thunderbolt but why should that affect the actor's responsibility for the death? Does the law—or should it—insist that someone must be responsible for every killing?

Professor Williams goes on (p 401):

When there is a new intervening act but no substitutional defendant—when the later actor is not responsible for what he does, as when the first actor instigates a child under ten, or a person who does not realise the incriminating circumstances, to commit the criminal act—*novus actus* normally does not operate to break causation. The first actor remains liable as perpetrator for the result, the reason being that the second actor does not exercise a free and informed volition. This is the position under the present law; but it would be changed by the Draft Code. Under clause 17(2), even if the intervening actor is non-culpable his act will insulate the first actor from responsibility for the result if the first actor could not reasonably have foreseen the intervention; and it makes no difference that there is no substitutional defendant. This is not codifying the existing law but radically changing it, and moreover changing it without explicit acknowledgement or explanation.

If D *instigates* a nine-year-old child to commit a crime, of course D commits the crime himself through an innocent agent. Clause 17(2) does not apply. See below, p 274. But if the intervention of the nine-year-old is unforeseen and not reasonably foreseeable, why should D be held responsible for it? If, while the victim of the assault envisaged above is lying unconscious, a nine-year-old comes along and cuts his throat, is D liable—and should he be liable—for homicide? Is the case distinguishable, so far as D's responsibility is concerned, from the case of the earthquake? Should it make any difference to the liability of D that the cut-throat is aged nine or nineteen?

Williams' theory receives some support from Hart and Honoré, p 336:

Acts of persons under a disability. In criminal as in civil law the intervening act of a child, insane person, or one who is incapacitated through drink or illness, does not in general negative causal connection.

The authorities cited, however, are not inconsistent with cl 17(2). The first is *Michael* (1840) 9 C & P 356. D's child, V, was in the care of a nurse, X. D, intending to murder the child, gave X a large quantity of laudanum, telling her it was a medicine to be administered to V. X did not think the child needed any medicine and left it untouched on the mantelpiece of her room. In X's absence, one of her children, Y, took the laudanum and administered a large dose to V who died. All the judges held that the jury were rightly directed that this administration by 'an unconscious agent' was murder by D. Hart and Honoré criticize this reasoning on the ground that the child, Y,

...was not in any sense an agent, conscious or unconscious, of the mother [sc D] who intended [X] alone to give the poison to [V]; but the decision may be justified on the ground that, in our terminology, the act of the child of five did not negative causal connection between the accused's act and the death.

Williams thinks that Michael was rightly convicted but that she would get off under cl 17(2) on the ground that Y's act was not foreseeable (though in TBCL 394 he wrote: 'It seems very likely that the boy of five who had administered it to the baby had been told or had otherwise come to believe that it was the baby's medicine...').

Would cl 17(2) exempt Michael? It depends on how we construe 'act or event'. If the act or event was the administration of laudanum to V and V's consequent death, this was not merely foreseen but intended by D, so that cl 17(2) would not preclude the court from holding that D caused that result. Cf Williams, TBCL 394: 'Michael intended to poison her baby with laudanum administered by the hand of another, and this very thing happened.' It is only if we construe 'act or event' to mean administration *by Y* that cl 17(2) would apply. The case is certainly very different from that of the nine-year-old cut-throat, above.

Williams (TBCL 394) considers a variation of *Michael*. Suppose that, contrary to the finding of the jury, she did not intend killing by a single dose but a slow killing by the cumulative effect of a series of small doses. Y in fact administered half the bottle. The trial judge, Alderson B, appears to have taken the view that, in those circumstances, D would not be guilty. Williams thinks otherwise. Who is right? Was the massive dose an 'act or event' foreseen by D or reasonably foreseeable? (Note that administration of the first of a projected series of doses is attempted murder according to *White*, above, p 54.)

When Michael gave the laudanum to X, she was guilty of attempted murder. This was the last act that she intended and needed to do in order to bring about the death of V. No reasonable jury could fail to find that she had done a more than merely preparatory act with intent to commit murder. If an act done with intent to kill does kill, murder is committed even if the killing is caused in an unforeseen and unforeseeable way. D shoots at V's head, but the bullet misses, ricochets and kills V by striking him in the back. However improbable this sequence of events, no one will doubt that D has killed V and is guilty of murder. If the 'act or event' of cl 17(2) is 'shooting V', it was foreseen and has happened. But what if (to take an even more bizarre case) the bullet misses V but cuts through a rope, causing a ton weight to fall and kill him? It would be absurd to say that D has not killed V. Would cl 17(2) compel this absurd result? Or can 'act or event' be construed to avoid the absurdity?

The second case cited by Hart and Honoré is *Lowe* (1850) 3 Car & Kir 123. D, an engineer at a colliery was responsible for a steam engine used for raising miners to the surface. He left the engine in charge of an ignorant boy who told D he was not competent to manage the engine. In consequence of his mismanagement a miner was killed. D was convicted of manslaughter by negligence. Here, plainly, the act of the boy was foreseeable and its foreseeability was indeed the basis of D's liability. Clause 17(2) would not help him.

Hart and Honoré's third case is *Johnson v Alabama* 142 Ala 70 (1905). Officers were attempting to arrest D's insane parent, E. D freed E's hands thereby enabling him to attack and kill an officer. It was held that D had caused V's death. If the attack was foreseeable this is plainly right and cl 17(2) would not apply. But if it was not foreseeable, why should D be held to have caused it any more than in the example of the nine-year-old cut-throat, above? Is the controller of a mental hospital guilty of homicide if a patient whom he has released for the weekend unforeseeably goes berserk and kills?

Is clause 17(2) too narrow?

Williams' argument here is that the effect of cl 17 is that:

  (i) a general who orders his troops into a battle where some of them will inevitably be killed has caused their deaths; and

  (ii) a tobacco company might be held liable for manslaughter in causing the deaths of the smokers;

and that this is too wide—that is, that sub-s (2) does not exclude all the cases it should.

The general

The first thing to notice is that the general, even if he is taken to intend that the deaths be caused (below, p **120**), will not be criminally liable. The act which he does is justified by the common law and the Draft Code provides:

  45. A person does not commit an offence by doing an act which is justified or excused by—...
       (c) any rule of the common law continuing to apply by virtue of section 4(4).

Clause 4(4) preserves rules of the common law unless they are replaced by or are inconsistent with the provisions of the Code.

Sometimes it is lawful to send men to their deaths; and this is such a case. The questions, whether the general causes the death of his men, and whether he intends their death, are therefore unlikely ever to arise in a criminal court. Nevertheless, Williams' criticism deserves an answer. Suppose the general's place is taken by an impostor who sends a regiment on a hazardous and wholly unjustified raid, either because he wants to assist the enemy or because he believes he is a latter-day Napoleon, a military genius who will win the war. The regiment is wiped out by enemy fire. Are we really going to say that he has not caused their deaths? A voluntary intervening act usually breaks the chain of causation; but the enemy soldiers are like innocent agents: they are doing their duty and commit no offence. And, so far as causation goes, is there any difference between the impostor and the general? In both cases it is the enemy fire which directly causes death and in both cases it is the order to attack which sends them to their death.

The tobacco case

Is it really impossible here to say that the tobacco company has caused the death or injury of the smokers? The matter may be put to the test before long in the civil courts; but it should be remembered that proof of causation is only the first step towards establishing civil or criminal liability. Here too questions of justification or excuse will arise for risks may lawfully be taken with the lives of others where there is sufficient social justification and smoking, however much some of us may dislike it, might be argued to have a social purpose though a diminishing one.

Williams also relies on *Beatty v Gillbanks* (1882) 9 QBD 308. It was held that the Salvation Army was acting lawfully in holding its meeting in Weston-super-Mare, although its officers knew from experience that this would cause a hostile organization, the Skeleton Army, to attack them. Williams argues that, under the Code, the Salvationists would be liable for 'the disorder' on the ground of causation. But is this so? Can a person be convicted of assaulting himself? In fact, the Skeletons were the principal offenders. The Salvationists could only be liable as accessories. Would it not be absurd to contend that they were aiding, abetting, counselling or procuring an attack on themselves? The Code, cl 40(6), restating the common law, would specifically authorize the Salvationists to use force to resist the attack:

…subsection (1) [authorising the use of force] may apply although the occasion for the use of force arises only because he does anything that he may lawfully do [in this case, hold the meeting], knowing that such an occasion may arise.

How could the Salvationists be guilty of an assault which they were entitled to resist? What if the Skeletons had broken a shop window in the course of the attack? They would be guilty of criminal damage. Could the Salvationists be convicted of procuring that offence? See below, p **282**.

FURTHER READING

A. ASHWORTH, 'Defining Offences Without Harm' in P. F. Smith (ed) *Criminal Law: Essays in Honour of J. C. Smith* (1987)

R. HEATON, 'Dealing in Death' [2003] Crim LR 497

A. NORRIE, 'A Critique of Criminal Causation' (1991) 54 MLR 685

A. NORRIE, *Crime Reason and History* (2nd edn, 2001), ch 7

S. SHUTE, 'Causation: Foreseeability v Natural Consequences' (1992) 55 MLR 584

J. STANNARD, 'Criminal Causation and the Careless Doctor' (1992) 55 MLR 577

4
Omissions

Criminal liability for pure omissions is exceptional at common law. The generally accepted definitions of most offences include a verb like 'kill', 'assault', 'damage' or 'take' which (at first sight, at least) requires an action of some kind. There are few common law crimes of omission. In *Dytham* [1979] 3 All ER 641, a police officer, D, was on duty at 1 am when he saw a man, V, being ejected from a night-club and being kicked and beaten by a number of bouncers. D took no steps to intervene. V died. D was charged with misconduct whilst acting as an officer of justice in that he deliberately failed to carry out his duties as a police constable by wilfully omitting to take any steps to preserve the peace or to protect V or to arrest or otherwise bring to justice the assailants. The conviction was upheld. (On misconduct in public office see now *A-G's Reference (No 3 of 2003)* [2004] EWCA Crim 868.)

However, many statutes make it a specific offence to omit to do something, for example, a motorist who fails to give his name and address after an accident or a company which fails to make a prescribed return under the relevant Companies Acts may be guilty of an offence. These offences, although they provide that D is liable for a criminal offence by omission are uncontroversial. Most of them are of a regulatory nature. They seem to respect the principles of fair labelling and fair warning since the conviction is explicitly for the failure to act. Liability for omissions (though exceptional) is not limited to crimes expressly defined by statute as omission offences. The more controversial question is whether, and if so how, the criminal law should impose liability for omissions in relation to general offences such as murder, manslaughter and assault.

1. THE DEBATE OVER GENERAL CRIMINAL LIABILITY FOR OMISSIONS

Andrew Ashworth, 'The Scope of Criminal Liability for Omissions'
(1989) 105 LQR 424

Although the paradigm of criminal liability is a prohibition on the culpable doing of a certain act, all systems of criminal law seem to include offences of omission. Some will have been drafted expressly so as to penalise an omission, e.g. 'failing to...,' usually in the context of an undertaking or activity such as running a business or driving a motor vehicle. There may be other offences worded in a way which leaves open the possibility that they may be committed by omission as well as by acts. References to omissions should not, of course, be taken to imply that we may be said to omit to do everything that we do not do each day. The term 'omission' is properly applied only to failure to do things which there is some kind of duty to do, or at least things which it is reasonable to expect a person to do (on the basis of some relationship or role).

What the scope of such duties should be is therefore a major question for the legislature when considering criminal law reform and for the courts when developing the common law or interpreting statutes. Two contrasting positions may be identified, the 'conventional view' and the 'social responsibility view.' They are not polar opposites, and in a practical sense the difference between them is a matter of the extent of the duties recognised. But the two views do proceed from different theoretical foundations, and these are important when considering reasons for and against particular instances of criminal liability for omissions. What it is proposed to call the 'conventional view'—though one cannot be sure how settled or how prevalent it is—maintains that the criminal law should be reluctant to impose liability for omissions except in clear and serious cases. It is accepted that there are many activities in modern society which must, to some extent, be regulated by criminal offences, of which some will properly be offences of omission; it is also accepted that citizens have duties to support the collective good by paying taxes, etc., and that such duties may be reinforced by offences of omission; but the distinctive argument is that our duties towards other individuals should be confined to duties towards those for whom we have voluntarily undertaken some responsibility. Whereas we owe negative duties (e.g. not to kill or injure) to all people, it is right that we should owe positive duties (e.g. to render assistance, to support) only to a circumscribed group of people with whom there exists a special relationship. When supporters of the conventional view are pressed to justify this limitation, they might tend to argue that there is moral distinction between acts and omissions, maintaining that failure to perform an act with foreseen bad consequences is morally less bad than performing an act with the identical foreseen bad consequences.

...

Adherents to the 'social responsibility view' would draw attention to the co-operative elements in social life, and would argue that it may be fair to place citizens under obligations to render assistance to other individuals in certain situations. This does not commit them to the view that the criminal law should enforce general duties to help all persons at all times. But it leads them to doubt whether the existence of some relationship or voluntary undertaking should be regarded as a precondition of criminal omissions liability. And it may also lead them to attack the argument that there is a general moral distinction between failing to perform an act with foreseen bad consequences and performing an act with identical bad consequences. All types of offence vary in their seriousness, of course, and even if it were true that on the whole omissions are less culpable than acts, it would not follow that omissions are less suitable for criminal prohibition than acts. On the 'social responsibility view,' then, there is no reason to accept the limitation imposed on omissions liability by the 'conventional view.'

...

The conventional view embodies a minimalist stance on criminal liability for omissions. It accepts that criminal law is the sharpest end of a legal structure which aims to ensure both that respect for social values is enforced and that essential social needs are provided for. It therefore accepts criminal liability for such omissions as non-payment of taxes. But it regards it as exceptional, and as requiring special justification, for the criminal law to impose duties to assist other individuals. Apart from special relationships (such as parent-child) and other voluntarily undertaken duties, there should be no criminally enforceable duties to assist others or to perform socially useful acts.

The main buttress is an argument from individual autonomy and liberty. Each person is regarded as an autonomous being, responsible for his or her own conduct. One aim of the law is to maximise individual liberty, so as to allow each individual to pursue a conception of the good life with as few constraints as possible. Constraints there must be, of course, in modern society: but freedom of action should be curtailed only so far as is necessary to restrain individuals from causing injury or loss to others. Setting these outer limits to freedom of action is, however, much more acceptable than requiring certain actions of a citizen, especially at times and in circumstances which may be inconvenient and may conflict with one's pursuit of one's personal goals. To impose a duty to do X at a certain time prevents the citizen from doing anything else at that time, whereas the conventional prohibitions of the criminal law leave the citizen free to do whatever else is wanted apart from the prohibited conduct. Moreover, the criminal law should recognise an individual's choices rather than allowing liability to be governed by chance, and the obligation to assist someone in peril may be thrust upon a chance passer-by, who may well prefer not to become involved at all. If I am driving to a concert 50 miles away which is to feature a soloist who is being heard for the last time in this country, should I be obliged to stop and render assistance to the victims of a road accident in which I was not involved, at the risk of missing part or the whole of the concert? It is no argument to say that such a journey is always open to the possibility of chance happenings, such as engine failure in the car, a road blocked by a fallen tree, and so on, because in the case of the accident victims I am physically free to drive on to my destination whereas the other happenings amount to physical prevention, and render me incapable of reaching my destination on time. Thus it is no argument to say that all arrangements are vulnerable to chance, since the law can strive to minimise its effect and to keep individual choice as wide as possible. There is a choice whether to stop and offer assistance or to continue on my way to the concert, but an offence requiring a citizen to stop and render assistance would effectively foreclose that choice, coercing me to sacrifice the pursuit of my own interests in favour of alleviating the misfortunes of others to whom I have not voluntarily assumed any duty. By its 'chance' nature, the incidence of such a duty reduces the predictability of one's obligations and impinges on the liberty to pursue one's conception of the good life. On the conventional view, then, I deserve moral praise if I stop to assist the accident victims and thereby lose the opportunity to attend the (whole) concert, but it does not follow that I deserve blame if I do not stop. Praise may be appropriate for an act of 'saintliness' going beyond duty, whereas the duties themselves require only the basic conditions of peaceful co-existence. Stopping to help is part of the morality of aspiration, not the morality of duty.

In thus equating individual autonomy with negative liberty (i.e. liberty not to do certain acts), the conventional view rejects broad duties to others as paternalistic, and as failing to respect each individual's right to self-determination. Any obligation to help others in peril begs the question of who is to decide what 'peril' is. Individuals may choose to engage in amateur boxing or in motor cycle racing, knowing of the high risk of injury but deciding that it is worth the risk in order to enjoy the excitement of the sport. Are these boxers or motor cyclists 'in peril'? Few would extend a citizen's obligation to intervene (where it exists) to these cases, probably because the individual's decision to engage in the sport may be assumed to be an informed and settled decision. Self-determination, a value closely entwined with individual autonomy, would be impaired by the intervention of others. But what about the person who decides to commit suicide and jumps from a bridge into the River Thames? Should the passing citizen be obliged to alert the emergency services or, if the conditions are favourable, to mount a rescue attempt? The passing citizen is unlikely to know about the potential suicide's state of mind. It is known that some attempts at suicide proceed from an unbalanced state of mind, and some are merely attempts to draw attention to the person's problems rather than to relinquish life. On the conventional view these possibilities for paternalistic intervention should not be made the basis of any legal duty. If a citizen sees what appears to be an attempted suicide, the citizen's freedom from non-voluntary obligations together with the potential suicide's right to self-determination are sufficient to conclude the case against a duty to intervene.

A third argument looks to the social consequences of the opposite, 'social responsibility' view. Its effect in requiring each citizen to offer assistance to others in peril might on the one hand reduce the autonomy and privacy of others in pursuing their own objectives and enjoyment, however dangerous it may appear to others, and might on the other hand make citizens into busybodies who believe that they must be constantly advising others to avoid risk and danger. In other words, it might be too intrusive and too onerous—both tendencies which go against the maximisation of liberty which is the keynote of the conventional view.

Fourthly, there is the argument that the 'social responsibility' view is unpractical because it would require each of us to avert or alleviate large numbers of situations which we know about. One strand of this argument calls attention to the problem of setting limits to the individuals duties on the social responsibility view: must I sell my car and my house, live at subsistence level and devote all my surplus earnings and time to preventing so many people from 'sleeping rough' in London, or to provide towards the relief of starvation in Africa? In what way do perils of these kinds differ materially from the accident victims or the person who jumps into the River Thames? A second strand of the argument is that the 'social responsibility' view may lead to the inculpation of large numbers of people, e.g. all the members of a crowd who witness someone being beaten up by others. It is excesses of this nature, in the depth and breadth of the obligations imposed, which are seen as sufficient to condemn the 'social responsibility' view as an unworkable moral or legal standard.

A fifth argument draws strength from the principle of legality: it maintains that citizens are so unaccustomed to thinking in terms of legal duties to act (as distinct from the well-known prohibitions) that it is unfair to impose such burdens except in circumstances which are well-defined and well-publicised. Protagonists might add that few provisions on general liability for omissions attain these standards, and that the obligation to take reasonable steps to assist a person in peril is much too uncertain to meet these standards. The social consequence is likely to be that ignorance of the law is a frequent occurrence, which cannot be good either for society or for the individuals concerned. Wide conceptions of social responsibility must therefore be rejected as a basis for criminal legislation: the conventional view, with its few well-known and voluntarily assumed duties to others, is the preferable approach.

THE INDIVIDUALISM OF THE CONVENTIONAL VIEW DOUBTED

The arguments for the conventional view may appear strong and practical, but they depend on a narrow, individualistic conception of human life which should be rejected as a basis for morality and (although this raises further issues) as a basis for criminal liability. Let us look again at the arguments, in turn.

The first argument, based on individual autonomy and freedom, is altogether too pure. To the extent that the conventional view relies on 'social fact' for some of its justifications, it is worth pointing out that rarely is individual autonomy promoted as a supreme value throughout a moral or legal system. For example, paternalistic considerations are taken to outweigh it when imposing a duty to wear a seat belt in the front seat of a car: this restricts individual liberty and self-determination, and it may be justified by reference to the known dangers of travelling without a seat-belt, combined with the relatively large benefit (in the social costs of health care) reaped from such a comparatively minor infringement of freedom of action. Systems of criminal law typically include a wide range of offences which impose duties to act, in relation to taxation, motoring and business activities....

The second and third arguments for the conventional view establish, however, that limits must be set to the obligations to others if the ideal of individual autonomy is not to be submerged beneath a welter of duties imposed on each person. The resolution of these conflicts of theory and practice is no easy matter, but the 'social responsibility' view would at least start from the assumption that duties to others are not necessarily alien to individual autonomy, and would have to reconcile this with the desirability of individuals safeguarding their own interests too. This dilemma, which also underlies the fourth argument for the conventional view, demonstrates the need for principled debate about the extent of social co-operation necessary to realise individual autonomy. Those who advocate 'social responsibility' bear the heavy burden of formulating defensible and workable criteria for the imposition of duties to act. Indeed, as the fifth argument showed, attention is also necessary to the promulgation of such rules. In so far as it is true that people do not consider that they have legal duties to assist others, any legislation to introduce such duties must be phrased as precisely as possible, and must be supported by a programme of education and information. These represent considerable challenges for the 'social responsibility' view on criminal liability for omissions.

...

On the 'social responsibility' view there are arguments for imposing certain obligations on individuals as citizens. These arguments are not founded on a simple benefit/burden calculation, that whoever takes the benefits of living in a certain society must in fairness expect to have to submit to its burdens. Such an approach leaves many unanswered questions about the quantum of burden which must be borne in order to have access to certain benefits. The reasoning is rather that the imposition of certain minimal duties shows a concern for the rights of other members of the community and there-fore for the community itself, and so tends to promote the maximisation of liberty. However, the idea of maximum liberty relates to each individual as a member of the community rather than to each individual in isolation. Thus an apparent diminution of the freedom of one citizen (by requiring that citizen to take reasonable steps to prevent a harm or to call the emergency services) may be justifiable by reference to the augmentation of the freedom of another citizen (who is under attack or otherwise in danger), and such justification is in the context of striving towards a community in which the liberty of each and all can be maximised.

Once the case for imposing some citizenship duties is made out, there remain difficult questions about the proper extent and scope of these duties. Duties towards the collective good such as the duty to pay taxes may be established fairly easily, but duties towards other individuals who are strangers require further justification. It is thought that the arguments above establish the case for a duty to take steps to save other citizens in peril. It is true that this duty must be hedged about with qualifications, so as to ensure that the obligations are neither too dangerous nor too onerous for the citizen upon whom they fall....

Glanville Williams, 'Criminal Omissions—The Conventional View'
(1991) 107 LQR 86

...Ashworth says that there is no moral difference between (i) a positive act and (ii) an omission when a duty is established. But even if this is so, he has already conceded a difference between the two when he says that an omission is culpable only when there is duty to act. The duty requirement sometimes involves considerations that are irrelevant to crimes of commission. Of course, every crime is a breach of legal duty not to commit the crime, but this is part of the meaning of the word 'crime.' The point is that no requirement of a particular duty not to act (over and above the specification of the crime) applies to wrongs of commission.

...

First,...omissions liability should be exceptional, and needs to be adequately justified in each instance. Secondly, when it is imposed this should be done by clear statutory language. Verbs primarily denoting (and forbidding) active conduct should not be construed to include omissions except when the statute contains a genuine implication to this effect—not the perfunctory and fictitious implication that judges use when they are on the lawpath instead of the purely judge-path. Thirdly, maximum penalties applied to active wrongdoing should not automatically be transferred to corresponding omissions; penalties for omissions should be rethought in each case.

The case for the conventional view
The arguments for this philosophy may be briefly stated. (I would have thought them too obvious to need statement.) First, society's most urgent task is the repression of active wrongdoing. Bringing the

ignorant or lethargic up to scratch is very much a secondary endeavour, for which the criminal process is not necessarily the best suited.

Secondly, our attitudes to wrongful action and wrongful inaction differ. There may be instances where our blood boils at the same temperature on account of both, but these are very exceptional. The only likely instance that comes to my mind is that of parents who are charged with killing their baby (i) by smothering it or (ii) by starving it to death. In this instance we are likely to feel more angry and sad about the slow starvation (an omission) than about the comparatively merciful infliction of death with a pillow. But on other occasions we almost always perceive a moral distinction between (for example) killing a person and failing to save his life (the former being the worse); and similarly between other acts and corresponding omissions.

This moral distinction, which we express in our language, reflects differences in our psychological approach to our own acts and omissions. We have much stronger inhibitions against active wrong-doing than against wrongfully omitting. This again is coupled with the fact that it is in every way easier not to do something (personal needs apart) than to do it. Also, a requirement to do something presupposes the ability to do it (the physical ability, and often the financial and educational ability as well), whereas almost everyone has the ability to refrain from ordinary physical acts.

Thirdly, serious crimes of commission can usually be formulated merely by stating the forbidden conduct, but laws creating crimes of omission are rarely directed against the whole world. They are intended to operate only against particular classes of person (and sometimes only for the protection of particular classes), in which case these persons must be singled out in the statement of the crime. To take an example: the courts can, in theory, punish everyone (with exceptions) who knowingly kills, but they cannot punish everyone who fails to save life, without some minimum specification of whose lives are to be saved. I cannot be made criminally responsible when I knowingly fail to save (and do not even try to save) the lives of unfortunate inhabitants of the Ganges delta who are drowned in floods; yet I could do something to help them by selling my house and giving the money to a suitable charity. Ashworth meets the point by saying that the requirement of duty 'establishes moral responsibility and delineates in time and space the number of people who may be said to have omitted'.... Very well, but this looks like translating law into morals rather than morals into law. Anyway, Ashworth does not propose that everything that may be regarded as a moral duty should automatically become a legal duty. So when we propose to punish omissions we are left with the problem of defining the scope of legal duty.

Fourthly, when crimes are expressed with the use of verbs implying action, it is a breach of the principle of legality to convict people of them when they have not acted; and it is unfair 'labelling' (Ashworth's expression) to convict non-doers of acts under the name of doers.

Fifthly, and perhaps most important of all, the law enforcement agencies (including the courts) have their work cut out to deal with people who offend by active conduct. The prisons, it is scarcely necessary to recall, are packed with them. To extend the campaign by attempting to punish all (or large groups of) those who contribute to the evil result by failing to co-operate in the great endeavour of producing a happier world would exceed the bounds of possibility.

Ashworth says of the conventional view that the supporting arguments 'depend on a narrow, individualistic conception of human life which should be rejected as a basis for morality and (although this raises further issues) as a basis for criminal liability'...I leave it to the reader to judge whether the arguments as I have formulated them deserve this stricture.

In justifying the conventional view I have made no reference to the philosophy of individualism or to the autonomy principle, both of which Ashworth (erroneously I think) regards as the foundation of the conventional view. How far the State should provide financial succour and social services for those in need has nothing to do with the question whether individuals should be criminally punishable for not providing others with these advantages. To bring these considerations based on general social policy into the discussion simply muddies the waters. The same remark applies to Ashworth's support for legislation requiring the wearing of seat-belts, support which is now platitudinous, as well as being irrelevant to his attack on 'the conventional view.' The argument against treating omissions in the same way as positive acts does not go to the extent of saying that omissions running contrary to the public interest should never be punishable. Those who oppose seat belt legislation (among whom I am not to be counted) do so on the ground that it unjustifiably restricts bodily liberty, not on the ground that it wrongly punishes omissions. The legislation forbids one to drive in a car without belting up, and the forbidden conduct is a hybrid act/omission, which is legally classified as an act, not an omission.

Question

Which view do you find most convincing?

2. THE PRESENT LAW

The court's approach to the imposition of liability for omissions requires consideration of four issues:

  (i) Does the law recognize that the particular offence may be committed by omission? Some offences may, some may not.

 (ii) If the offence is capable of being committed by omission, who was under a duty to act? The result has occurred, so no one prevented it from occurring but, clearly, not everyone in the jurisdiction of the court is liable for failing to do so. What are the criteria for selecting the culprit?

(iii) Where the definition of the crime requires proof that D caused a certain result, can he be said to have caused that result by doing nothing?

These three questions cannot be completely separated and sometimes two or all three of them arise in the same materials which follow. Each of them may also give rise to yet another question:

 (iv) Is D's conduct properly categorized as an omission, or as an act?

(1) OFFENCES CAPABLE OF BEING COMMITTED BY OMISSION

Statutory interpretation

Professor Glanville Williams is opposed in principle to the interpretation of result crimes so as to be capable of commission by omission. See (1987) 7 LS 92 at 97, 'What should the Code do about Omissions?'

I would like to see the Code say that enactments creating offences in words primarily referring to acts are not to be interpreted to include mere omissions unless the enactment expressly so provides. There can surely be no argument that 'harass' and 'obstruct' primarily refer to positive acts. If Parliament wishes to penalize omissions it must direct its mind to the subject and make its meaning clear.

But Professor Williams concedes that 'some words can legitimately be held to "specify" both acts and omissions, even though they refer expressly to neither,' instancing the word 'neglect' (p 97). Is this not true of the word, 'obstruct'? If I am standing in a narrow passage blocking your way, and I refuse to move, does not my omission 'obstruct' you? And is not 'obstruction' a result crime, rather than a conduct crime?

In *Shama* [1990] 2 All ER 602, [1990] 1 WLR 661 a conviction for falsifying a document required for an accounting purpose contrary to the Theft Act 1968, s 17(1)(a), was upheld although D had entirely omitted to fill in a form which it was his contractual duty (as an employee of British Telecom) to complete. Where a person makes an account or record or document he may, as s 17(2) makes clear, falsify it by omitting material particulars. There is no difficulty about that: he has made a false document and is liable for that act. But in *Shama* D made no document. The case was one of pure omission. Can the words, 'falsifies any document' fairly be read to include that case?

In *Firth* (1989) 91 Cr App R 217, [1990] Crim LR 326 a doctor was held to have deceived a hospital contrary to the Theft Act 1978, s 2(1) (below, p **858**), by failing to inform the hospital that certain patients were private patients, knowing that they had been admitted as NHS patients and that he would not be billed for services for which he should have been charged. Can he fairly be said to have 'deceived' the hospital by his inactivity?

In *Ahmad* (1986) 84 Cr App R 64, [1986] Crim LR 739 it was held that the words 'does acts' in the Protection from Eviction Act 1977 were not satisfied by proof of an omission. D commits an offence if he 'does acts' likely to interfere with the peace or comfort of a residential occupier with intent to cause him to give up occupation of the premises. D having done such acts without any such intent, omitted with the specified intention to rectify the situation he had created.

However, even the use of the word 'act' does not always exclude liability for omissions. Thus in *Speck* [1977] 2 All ER 859 it was held that a man 'commits an act of gross indecency with...a child', contrary to the Indecency with Children Act 1960 by totally passive submission to an act done by the child.

Homicide

At common law it is established that there can be liability for murder and manslaughter (gross negligence) by an omission: *Gibbons and Procter* below, (murder); *Stone and Dobinson* below (manslaughter). The offences which the Law Commission proposes to replace involuntary manslaughter may not be committed by omission, 'unless the omission is in breach of a duty at common law': Law Com No 237 (1996), below p **663**.

Particular problems in offences against the person

Some take the view that the offences against the person are crimes of action—wounding, assaulting, battering—and should not be capable of commission by omission (see for example, Wilson, *Central Theories*, p **101**).

The CLRC in its Fourteenth Report on offences against the person identified those of its proposed offences against the person which were to be capable of being committed by omission—murder, manslaughter, causing serious injury with intent, unlawful detention, kidnapping, abduction and aggravated abduction. Other offences against the person, for example, assault, would not be capable of being committed by omission. The Code Team included in their Bill (Law Com No 143) a clause to give effect to this recommendation: an offence was to be capable of being committed by omission only if the enactment creating it so specified and the Code specified the chosen offences against the person. These provisions have no place in the current draft Code. The Law Commission was persuaded by an article by Professor Glanville Williams ((1987) 7 LS 92) that it would make important changes in the law on which there had been no consultation (and which indeed had not been foreseen) and which, therefore, could not be justified. Williams pointed out that in a number of cases statutory offences had been held to be capable of being committed by omission, although there was no express provision that they might be so committed. The Code Team's proposals would have reversed those cases; and no consideration had been given as to whether they ought to be reversed. The draft Code does not specify which offences may be committed by omission. It leaves that question, as under the present law, to the courts. But cl 17(1) makes it clear that, under the Code, results 'may be caused' by omission and defines offences against the person in terms of 'causing' death (rather than 'killing') or other relevant harm. Some other offences (notably offences of damage to property) are also defined in terms of 'causing' so as to leave it fully open to the courts to decide that the offence should be capable of commission by omission if they think it appropriate.

In Law Com No 218, which deals with only non-fatal offences against the person, the Law Commission specifies which of those offences should be capable of commission by omission. It broadly follows the approach of the CLRC and specifies intentionally causing serious injury, torture, unlawful detention, kidnapping, abduction and aggravated abduction. As in the draft Code, the draft Non-Fatal Offences Against the Person Bill makes no attempt to specify who is under a duty to act. Clause 19(1) provides:

An offence to which this section applies may be committed by a person who, with the result specified for the offence, omits to do an act that he is under a duty to do at common law.

Clause 19(1) does not apply to cl 3 (recklessly causing serious injury, which would replace OAPA 1861, s 20), cl 4 (intentionally or recklessly causing injury which would replace OAPA 1861, s 47) or cl 6 (assault) so, if the draft Bill were enacted, it would be settled that these offences could not be committed by omission. The draft Bill annexed to the Home Office Consultation Paper of February 1998 is to the same effect.

Consider the following case which was much discussed in the CLRC.

D, a cleaner, puts polish on the floor and then, in breach of his duty, omits to display the notice with which he has been provided warning users of the building of the dangerous state of the floor. V slips on the polish and falls.

Was it a mere omission?

This example was put to the CLRC as a case of omission and was so treated by them. But one member of the committee, Glanville Williams, has had second thoughts ((1987) 7 LS at 92) about this: 'in such circumstances of act/omission the total conduct could and should be regarded as an act, so the cleaner could be guilty of the offence of causing injury recklessly . . .' If D put the polish on the floor with intent that V should fall on it, there is no difficulty in saying that D has caused the fall by an act; but what if he spread the polish with no thought of anyone falling and then either decided, or forgot, to place the notice? Does not the fault then lie purely in omitting? But even if Williams is right, the problem may be salvaged because he recognizes that, if it was the duty, not of the cleaner but of the janitor, to place the notice on polishing days, it could not be said that the janitor had caused the injury by an act, for he did no act whatever. Williams would convict the cleaner in the original case but acquit the janitor in the alternative version. He would be prepared to tolerate this fine distinction because, as he rightly says, all legal rules are capable of producing fine distinctions. This is all right if the distinction is sound in principle; but is the distinction between act/omission and omission sound? Cf *Miller*, below, p **93**.

The effect of a mere omission

Let us consider further the case which is acknowledged to be an omission: the janitor (J) does not display the notice, V falls and (a) suffers no injury, (b) suffers slight injury, (c) suffers serious injury or (d) is killed. If J is charged with assault or causing injury (less than serious, injury), the prosecution under the Code (and perhaps under the existing law) will fail because there is no actus reus; but if he is charged with murder, manslaughter, or intentionally causing serious injury, the prosecution will not fail for this reason. J will, prima facie, be guilty of any of these offences for which he has the appropriate mens rea. Can these distinctions be justified?

Does the difference in effect depend on the presence or absence of a duty?

Whatever the outcome, J is under a duty in the civil law to display the notice—not to do so is a breach of contract. Is he always under a duty in the criminal law? Suppose, when J omits to display the notice, he foresees that V may fall and sustain serious injury but 'couldn't care less'. V does fall, sustains serious injury and, a week later, dies of the injury. J is not guilty of causing serious injury but is guilty of manslaughter. At the time of the omission, either he was under a duty or he was not. Can his innocence of recklessly causing injury be said to depend on the absence of a duty to display the notice?

Is there a causation problem in these cases?

Of course the spreading of the polish was a cause but J did not spread the polish and the question is whether the omission to display the notice was also a cause. Would the injury not have occurred *but for* that failure? If V was blind and would not have seen the notice anyway, the omission to display it was not a cause. Is causation proved only if we are *certain* that V would have seen the notice and then taken sufficient care not to fall? Cf *Morby*, below p **104**. Could we ever be certain of that?

(2) WHO IS UNDER A DUTY TO ACT?

Though an offence is capable of being committed by omission, it does not follow that everyone is under a duty to act. The courts have recognized a number of categories in which a duty to act arises, each of which is discussed below ((a)–(f)). For discussion see L. Alexander, 'Criminal Liability for Omissions' in S. Shute and A. Simester, *Criminal Law Theory: Doctrines of the General Part* (2002).

Contract

In *Pittwood* (1902) 19 TLR 37 D, a gatekeeper on a railway line had a contractual duty to his employer to keep the gate closed. D opened the gate and forgot to close it. V, assuming that the way was safe as the gate was open was then killed by a passing train. D's counsel argued that D only owed a duty to his employers under his contract, but the court held that a man might incur liability arising from such a contract.

Questions

1. What types of contract will give rise to such a duty? Is it only contracts involving a protective or 'health and safety' based purpose?

2. Does a lecturer owe a duty to the students in his lecture—to protect against injury from defective premises? From attack by homicidal lecture gatecrashers?

3. Aside from the difficulty of which contracts are sufficient to establish a duty, there is the question of the content and scope of the duty. If D is a lifeguard employed by Leeds Council, does his duty to save a drowning stranger in the council's pool apply when D has formally clocked off work for the day? Does D's liability under contract depend on V's knowledge that D is under contract with X (for example, the council or the railway company)?

Voluntary undertakings

In *Instan* [1893] 1 QB 450 D lived with and maintained V, her aunt aged 73. For the final few days before her death V was completely incapacitated. D bought food with her aunt's money, but failed to give her any. Nor did D summon medical help. Death ensued from exhaustion and gangrene. D was convicted of manslaughter. The court affirmed her conviction. Coleridge LCJ concluded that a there was a duty—a 'legal common law duty is nothing else than the enforcing by law of that which is a moral obligation without legal enforcement.'

See further, G. Mead, 'Contracting into Crime: A Theory of Criminal Omissions' (1991) 11 OJLS 147, at 168 arguing that a person who has voluntarily undertaken responsibility ought to be under a duty because:

First he is more likely to be aware that a person may be in a position of peril and in need of assistance. He will know of the vulnerability of the victim in a way that others may not. Second, he may be more capable of carrying out the required task than will a third party. We might assume that, in most cases where D undertakes to do a particular thing, he feels he has the ability to do it, whereas a third party, who has not given such an undertaking will not necessarily possess the required skills to do what is needed in order to avert danger to V. The third point is that if other people are aware of the undertaking they might feel it unproductive for them to get involved as well. They might reasonable think that they would be simply getting in the way and hinder the completion of the task in question.

Questions

1. Was D's duty, in *Instan*, a result of her voluntary undertaking? Her relationship? Her cohabitation? Her being paid by her aunt?

2. Is the existence of a moral duty a sufficient basis for the imposition of criminal liability?

3. If D assumes some responsibility for V, it seems less objectionable for the law to impose liability for his subsequent omissions. But what of the objections based on principles of fair

labelling and fair warning? Is the scope of the duty and its content sufficiently clearly prescribed to satisfy these principled concerns?

Special relationships

The most obvious type of relationship in which it has been held that a duty to act arises is that between parent and child. This is supported by the statutory obligations such as the Children and Young Persons Act 1933, s 1. The failure of parents to feed and care for their children has given rise to liability for manslaughter and even in one case for murder: *Gibbons and Procter* (below, p **105**). It remains unclear which other categories of relationship will give rise to such a duty.

In *Stone and Dobinson* [1977] 2 All ER 341, [1977] QB 354, CA, S and D, S's mistress, allowed S's sister, Fanny, to lodge with them. The sister became infirm while lodging with them and died of toxaemia from infected bed sores and prolonged immobilization. S and D had made only half-hearted and wholly ineffectual attempts to secure medical attention for the sister. Upholding the convictions of S and D for manslaughter, the court said:

There is no dispute, broadly speaking, as to the matters on which the jury must be satisfied before they can convict of manslaughter in circumstances such as the present. They are: (1) that the defendant undertook the care of a person who by reason of age or infirmity was unable to care for himself; (2) that the defendant was grossly negligent in regard to his duty of care; (3) that by reason of such negligence the person died. It is submitted on behalf of the appellants that judge's direction to the jury with regard to the first two items was incorrect.

At the close of the Crown's case submissions were made to the judge that there was no, or no sufficient, evidence that the appellants, or either of them, had chosen to undertake the care of Fanny.

That contention was advanced by counsel for the appellant before this court as his first ground of appeal. He amplified the ground somewhat by submitting that the evidence which the judge had suggested to the jury might support the assumption of a duty by the appellants did not, when examined, succeed in doing so. He suggested that the situation here was unlike any reported case. Fanny came to this house as a lodger. Largely, if not entirely due to her own eccentricity and failure to look after herself or feed herself properly, she became increasingly infirm and immobile and eventually unable to look after herself. Is it to be said, asks counsel for the appellants rhetorically, that by the mere fact of becoming infirm and helpless in these circumstances, she casts a duty on her brother and Mrs Dobinson to take steps to have her looked after or taken to hospital? The suggestion is that, heartless though it may seem, this is one of those situations where the appellants were entitled to do nothing; where no duty was cast on them to help, any more than it is cast on a man to rescue a stranger from drowning, however easy such a rescue might be.

This court rejects that proposition. Whether Fanny was a lodger or not she was a blood relation of the appellant Stone; she was occupying a room in his house; Mrs Dobinson had undertaken the duty of trying to wash her, of taking such food to her as she required. There was ample evidence that each appellant was aware of the poor condition she was in by mid-July. It was not disputed that no effort was made to summon an ambulance or the social services or the police despite the entreaties of [neighbours]. A social worker used to visit [Stone]. No word was spoken to him. All these were matters which the jury were entitled to take into account when considering whether the necessary assumption of a duty to care for Fanny had been proved.

This was *not* a situation analagous to the drowning stranger. They *did* make efforts to care. They tried to get a doctor; they tried to discover the previous doctor. Mrs Dobinson helped with the washing and the provision of food. All these matters were put before the jury in terms which we find it impossible to fault. The jury were entitled to find that the duty had been assumed. They were entitled to conclude that once Fanny became helplessly infirm, as she had by 19 July, the appellants were, in the circumstances, obliged either to summon help or else to care for Fanny themselves...

Questions

1. Is the duty imposed because of the cohabitation? The relationship? The decision by D and S to assist Fanny? All of these? Given the limited capacity of the defendants, were their ineffectual efforts not enough to satisfy any duty that arose?

2. Such a duty can arise as a matter of marriage (*Hood* [2004] 1 Cr App R (S) 431), so the duty surely cannot be based on blood relationships. Is its true basis one of interdependence? Should a strong 14-year-old owe a duty to his ailing mother? Should a duty extend between siblings? Does a student D owe a duty to his anorexic flatmate, V to call for medical treatment for her? To feed her?

3. What is the extent of a duty imposed by relationships? Is it a duty to do what is reasonable? What D believes to be reasonable? That which is necessary to avert the danger from V?

4. Note the offence under s 5 of the Domestic Violence, Crime and Victims Act 2004 relating to carers' responsibilities for death or serious injury to a child.

Many of the cases involving relationships also involve a voluntary undertaking by the party, and it is unclear to what extent the courts would impose a duty on the basis of a relationship per se.

Creation of a dangerous situation or 'supervening fault'

Clause 23 of the draft Code is concerned with a particular type of liability for omission which is not, in terms, limited to particular crimes. It is restated in cl 31 of the Draft Criminal Law Bill (Law Com No 218) as follows:

31. Supervening fault
Where it is an offence to be at fault in causing a result and a person lacks the fault required when he does an act that may cause or does cause, the result, he nevertheless commits the offence if—

    (a) being aware that he has done the act and that the result may occur or, as the case may be, has occurred and may continue, and

    (b) with the fault required,

he fails to take reasonable steps to prevent the result occurring or continuing and it does occur or continue.

This clause was intended to restate and generalize the principle applied by the House of Lords in the following case.

R v Miller
[1983] 1 All ER 978, House of Lords

(Lords Diplock, Keith, Bridge, Brandon and Brightman)

The defendant lay on a mattress in a house in which he was a squatter and lit a cigarette. He fell asleep and woke to find the mattress on fire. He went into the next room and fell sleep.

The house caught fire and £800 worth of damage was done. He was charged with arson, contrary to s 1(1) and (3) of the Criminal Damage Act 1971, in that he 'damaged by fire a house … intending to do damage to such property or recklessly as to whether such property would be damaged'. He was convicted and his appeal to the Court of Appeal was dismissed. He appealed to the House of Lords. Note that at the time of this decision the mens rea for the offence was governed by the test of recklessness in *Caldwell* (below, p **146**).

Lord Diplock. The first question is a pure question of causation; it is one of fact to be decided by the jury in a trial on indictment. It should be answered No if, in relation to the fire during the period starting immediately before its ignition and ending with its extinction, the role of the accused was at no time more than that of a passive bystander. In such a case the subsequent questions to which I shall be turning would not arise. The conduct of the parabolical priest and Levite on the road to Jericho may have been indeed deplorable, but English law has not so far developed to the stage of treating it as criminal; and if it ever were to do so there would be difficulties in defining what should be the limits of the offence.

If, on the other hand the question, which I now confine to: 'Did a physical act of the accused start the fire which spread and damaged property belonging to another?', is answered 'Yes', as it was by the Jury in the instant case, then for the purpose of the further questions the answers to which are determinative of his guilt of the offence of arson, the conduct of the accused, throughout the period from immediately before the moment of ignition to the completion of the damage to the property by the fire, is relevant; so is his state of mind throughout that period.

Since arson is a result-crime the period may be considerable, and during it the conduct of the accused that is causative of the result may consist not only of his doing physical acts which cause the fire to start or spread but also of his failing to take measures that lie within his power to counteract the danger that he has himself created. And if his conduct, active or passive, varies in the course of the period, so may his state of mind at the time of each piece of conduct. If, at the time of any particular piece of conduct by the accused that is causative of the result, the state of mind that actuates his conduct falls within the description of one or other of the states of mind that are made a necessary ingredient of the offence of arson by s 1(1) of the Criminal Damage Act 1971 (ie intending to damage property belonging to another or being reckless whether such property would be damaged), I know of no principle of English criminal law that would prevent his being guilty of the offence created by that subsection. Likewise I see no rational ground for excluding from conduct capable of giving rise to criminal liability conduct which consists of failing to take measures that lie within one's power to counteract a danger that one has oneself created, if at the time of such conduct one's state of mind is such as constitutes a necessary ingredient of the offence. I venture to think that the habit of lawyers to talk of 'actus reus', suggestive as it is of action rather than inaction, is responsible for any erroneous notion that failure to act cannot give rise to criminal liability in English law.

No one has been bold enough to suggest that if, in the instant case, the accused had been aware at the time that he dropped the cigarette that it would probably set fire to his mattress and yet had taken no steps to extinguish it he would not have been guilty of the offence of arson, since he would have damaged property of another being reckless whether any such property would be damaged.

I cannot see any good reason why, so far as liability under criminal law is concerned, it should matter at what point of time before the resultant damage is complete a person becomes aware that he has done a physical act which, whether or not he appreciated that it would at the time when he did it, does in fact create a risk that property of another will be damaged, provided that, at the moment of awareness, it lies within his power to take steps, either himself or by calling for the assistance of the fire brigade if this be necessary, to prevent or minimise the damage to the property at risk …

My Lords, in the instant case the prosecution did not rely on the state of mind of the accused as being reckless during that part of his conduct that consisted of his lighting and smoking a cigarette while lying on his mattress and falling asleep without extinguishing it. So the jury were not invited to make any finding as to this. What the prosecution did rely on as being reckless was his state of mind during that part of his conduct after he awoke to find that he had set his mattress on fire and that it was smouldering, but did not then take any steps either to try to extinguish it himself or to send for the fire brigade, but simply went into the other room to resume his slumbers, leaving the fire from the already smouldering mattress to spread and to damage that part of the house in which the mattress was.

The recorder, in his lucid summing up to the jury (they took 22 minutes only to reach their verdict), told them that the accused, having by his own act started a fire in the mattress which, when he became aware of its existence, presented an obvious risk of damaging the house, became under a duty to take some action to put it out. The Court of Appeal upheld the conviction, but its ratio decidendi appears to be somewhat different from that of the recorder. As I understand the judgment, in effect it treats the whole course of conduct of the accused, from the moment at which he fell asleep and dropped the cigarette onto the mattress until the time the damage to the house by fire was complete, as a continuous act of the accused, and holds that it is sufficient to constitute the statutory offence of arson if at any stage in that course of conduct the state of mind of the accused, when he fails to try to prevent or minimize the damage which will result from his initial act, although it lies within his power to do so, is that of being reckless whether property belonging to another would be damaged....

My Lords, these alternative ways of analysing the legal theory that justifies a decision which has received nothing but commendation for its accord with common sense and justice have, since the publication of the judgment of the Court of Appeal in the instant case, provoked academic controversy. Each theory has distinguished support. Professor J C Smith espouses the 'duty theory' (see [1982] Crim LR 526 at 528); Professor Glanville Williams who, after the decision of the Divisional Court in *Fagan v Metropolitan Police Comr* [below, p **96**] appears to have been attracted by the duty theory, now prefers that of the continuous act (see [1982] Crim LR 773). When applied to cases where a person has unknowingly done an act which sets in train events that, when he becomes aware of them, present an obvious risk that property belonging to another will be damaged, both theories lead to an identical result; and, since what your Lordships are concerned with is to give guidance to trial judges in their task of summing up to juries, I would for this purpose adopt the duty theory as being the easier to explain to a jury; though I would commend the use of the word 'responsibility', rather than 'duty' which is more appropriate to civil than to criminal law since it suggests an obligation owed to another person, ie the person to whom the endangered property belongs, whereas a criminal statute defines combinations of conduct and state of mind which render a person liable to punishment by the state itself.

[**Lords Keith**, **Bridge**, **Brandon** and **Brightman** agreed.]

Appeal dismissed

Questions

1. Was the defendant held liable for damaging the house by falling asleep while smoking? Or for damaging the house by failing to take reasonable steps to put out the burning bed?

2. What if the defendant had found that his nine-year-old child had set the bed on fire and had left it to burn? Or the fire had originated in an electrical fault in the wiring of the house when he switched on his electric blanket?

3. What if the defendant's fellow squatter had (a) sustained grievous bodily harm or (b) died in the fire?

Fagan v Metropolitan Police Commissioner
[1968] 3 All ER 442, Queen's Bench Division

(Lord Parker CJ, Bridge and James JJ)

The defendant was directed by a constable to park his car close to the kerb. He drove his car on to the constable's foot. The constable said, 'Get off, you are on my foot.' The defendant replied, 'Fuck you, you can wait', and turned off the ignition. He was convicted by the magistrates of assaulting the constable in the execution of his duty and his appeal was dismissed by Quarter Sessions who were in doubt whether the driving on to the foot was intentional or accidental but were satisfied that he 'knowingly, unnecessarily and provocatively' allowed the car to remain on the foot.

James J [with whom **Lord Parker CJ** concurred]...In our judgment, the question arising, which has been argued on general principles, falls to be decided on the facts of the particular case. An assault is any act which intentionally—or possibly recklessly—causes another person to apprehend immediate and unlawful personal violence. Although 'assault' is an independent crime and is to be treated as such, for practical purposes today 'assault' is generally synonymous with the term 'battery', and is a term used to mean the actual intended use of unlawful force to another person without his consent. On the facts of the present case, the 'assault' alleged involved a 'battery'. Where an assault involved a battery, it matters not, in our judgment, whether the battery is inflicted directly by the body of the offender or through the medium of some weapon or instrument controlled by the action of the offender. An assault may be committed by the laying of a hand on another, and the action does not cease to be an assault if it is a stick held in the hand and not the hand itself which is laid on the person of the victim. So, for our part, we see no difference in principle between the action of stepping on to a person's toe and maintaining that position and the action of driving a car on to a person's foot and sitting in the car while its position on the foot is maintained.

To constitute this offence, some intentional act must have been performed; a *mere* omission to act cannot amount to an assault. Without going into the question whether words alone can constitute an assault, it is clear that the words spoken by the appellant could not alone amount to an assault; they can only shed a light on the appellant's action. For our part, we think that the crucial question is whether, in this case, the act of the appellant can be said to be complete and spent at the moment of time when the car wheel came to rest on the foot, or whether his act is to be regarded as a continuing act operating until the wheel was removed. In our judgment, a distinction is to be drawn between acts which are complete—though results may continue to flow—and those acts which are continuing. Once the act is complete, it cannot thereafter be said to be a threat to inflict unlawful force on the victim. If the act, as distinct from the results thereof, is a continuing act, there is a continuing threat to inflict unlawful force. If the assault involves a battery and that battery continues, there is a continuing act of assault. For an assault to be committed, both the elements of actus reus and mens rea must be present at the same time. The 'actus reus' is the action causing the effect on the victim's mind: see the observations of Parke B, in *R v St George* [(1840) 9 C & P 483 at 490, 493]. The 'mens rea' is the intention to cause that effect. It is not necessary that mens rea should be present at the inception of the actus reus; it can be superimposed on an existing act. On the other hand, the subsequent inception of mens rea cannot convert an act which has been completed without mens rea into an assault.

In our judgment, the justices at Willesden and quarter sessions were right in law. On the facts found, the action of the appellant may have been initially unintentional, but the time came when, knowing that the wheel was on the officer's foot, the appellant (i) remained seated in the car so that his body through the medium of the car was in contact with the officer, (ii) switched off the ignition of the car, (iii) maintained the wheel of the car on the foot, and (iv) used words indicating the intention of keeping the wheel in that position. For our part, we cannot regard such conduct as mere omission or inactivity. There was an act constituting a battery which at its inception was not criminal because there was no element of intention, but which became criminal from the moment the intention was formed to produce the apprehension which was flowing from the continuing act. The fallacy of the appellant's argument is that it seeks to equate the facts of this case with such a case as where a motorist has accidentally run over a person and, that action having been completed, fails to assist the victim with the intent that the victim should suffer.

We would dismiss this appeal.

Bridge J. I fully agree with my lords as to the relevant principles to be applied. No mere omission to act can amount to an assault. Both the elements of actus reus and mens rea must be present at the same time, but the one may be superimposed on the other. It is in the application of these principles to the highly unusual facts of this case that I have, with regret, reached a different conclusion from the majority of the court. I have no sympathy at all for the appellant, who behaved disgracefully; but I have been unable to find any way of regarding the facts which satisfied me that they amounted to the crime of assault. This has not been for want of trying; but at every attempt I have encountered the inescapable question: after the wheel of the appellant's car had accidentally come to rest on the constable's foot, what was it that the appellant *did* which constituted the act of assault? However the question is approached, the answer which I feel obliged to give is: precisely nothing. The car rested on the foot by its own weight and remained stationary by its own inertia. The appellant's fault was that he omitted to manipulate the controls to set it in motion again.

Neither the fact that the appellant remained in the driver's seat nor that he switched off the ignition seem to me to be of any relevance. The constable's plight would have been no better, but might well have been worse, if the appellant had alighted from the car leaving the ignition switched on. Similarly, I can get no help from the suggested analogies. If one man accidentally treads on another's toe or touches him with a stick, but deliberately maintains pressure with foot or stick after the victim protests, there is clearly an assault; but there is no true parallel between such cases and the present case. It is not, to my mind, a legitimate use of language to speak of the appellant 'holding' or 'maintaining' the car wheel on the constable's foot. The expression which corresponds to the reality is that used by the justices in the Case Stated. They say, quite rightly, that he 'allowed' the wheel to remain.

With a reluctantly dissenting voice, I would allow this appeal and quash the appellant's conviction.

Appeal dismissed. Leave to appeal to the House of Lords refused

Notes and questions

1. Was there a 'continuing act' in *Miller* or in *Fagan*? Under the Draft Code (p **93**, above) does it matter? Should it matter?

2. D, a motorist, without fault on his part skids on an oil-covered surface and injures V. D stops and sees that V is unconscious and bleeding. He could easily drive V to a nearby hospital. He drives off leaving V by the roadside. V bleeds to death. His life could have been saved had he been driven to the hospital. Is D liable to conviction for (a) manslaughter or (b) causing death by dangerous driving according to: (i) *R v Miller* or (ii) the Draft Code, cl 23 (cl 31 of the Draft Criminal Law Bill, above, p **93**)? Should it be different if D injured V by (i) careless driving or (ii) dangerous driving? (For dangerous driving, see below, p **168**.)

3. James LJ's definition of assault (above p **96**) appears to be taken almost verbatim from the first edition of Smith & Hogan, *Criminal Law* (1965), p 262. We wrote '(possibly) recklessly' because the law was then uncertain. It is now clear that recklessness is enough. See *Venna*, below, p **673**, *Savage and Parmenter*, p **160** and *Ireland*, p **670**.

4. In *Santana–Bermudez* [2003] EWHC 2908 (Admin) S-B, a drug user, had assured a police officer about to search him that he was carrying no 'sharps'. The officer stabbed her finger on a syringe needle in his pocket during the search. Applying *Miller*, Maurice Kay J said:

…where someone (by act or word or a combination of the two) creates a danger and thereby exposes another to a reasonably foreseeable risk of injury which materialises, there is an evidential basis for the *actus reus* of an assault occasioning actual bodily harm. It remains necessary for the prosecution to prove an intention to assault or appropriate recklessness.

5. Does the *Miller* principle apply in a case in which D has created the dangerous situation as a result of a justifiable act, rather than one of inadvertence? (See *State ex rel Kuntz v Montana thirteenth District Court* 995 P 2d 951 (Mont) (2000).)

Dangerous pursuits

In *Khan and Khan* [1998] Crim LR 830 the appellants abandoned a 15-year-old girl when she was distressed by taking an excessive quantity of drugs which they had supplied to her and she died. Quashing their conviction for manslaughter 'by omission,' that is, by a grossly negligent omission, the court said:

To extend the duty to summon medical assistance to a drug dealer who supplies heroin to a person who subsequently dies on the facts of this case would undoubtedly enlarge the class of person to whom, on previous authority, such a duty may be owed. It may be correct to hold that such a duty does arise. However before that situation can occur, the judge must first make a ruling as to whether the facts as proved are capable of giving rise to such a duty and, if he answers that question in the affirmative, then to give an appropriate direction which would enable them to answer the question whether on the facts as found by them there was such a duty.

The judge had made no such ruling or given any such direction. But in *Gurphal Singh* [1999] Crim LR 582 in a summing up which the Court of Appeal described as 'a model of its kind' the judge directed the jury that, as a matter of law, the defendant owed a duty to V, an occupant of the lodging house in which he worked as a 'maintenance man', in respect of the safety of the gas fire. V died from carbon monoxide poisoning from the defective fire. The conviction for manslaughter was upheld. The jury must have found that a reasonably prudent person would have known that there was a serious and obvious risk of death and that D's negligence was a substantial cause. See further below, p **649**.

Sinclair
[1998], unreported 21 Aug, Court of Appeal Criminal Division
(We are grateful to Mr Peter Carter QC for providing further details)

Sinclair (S), a methadone user and his close friend Coleman, who had limited experience of taking methadone, went to J's flat to buy drugs. Earlier S and Coleman had been drinking and taking other drugs supplied by Smith. S and Coleman each injected themselves there with the methadone they had bought. Ten minutes later Coleman became unconscious.

He never regained consciousness and died the next morning. Following his collapse, Smith and J went out to purchase more drugs. J expressed concern about Coleman's condition and injected him with a saline solution in the hope of restoring consciousness. Other ineffective attempts to bring Coleman round, including slapping him and pouring cold water over him failed.

At the conclusion of the prosecution's case, submissions were made on behalf of both appellants that there was no case to go to the jury. This was on the basis first that the Crown had failed to prove that either of the defendants owed a duty of care to the deceased and secondly that there was no sufficient evidence that the omissions of either appellant were such as to be a substantial cause of death. It was conceded that the court was bound by the decisions of the Court of Appeal, in relation to duty by *R Stone & Dobinson* [1977] 1 QB 354, and in relation to causation by *R v Cato*, [1976] 1 WLR 110. A considerable number of authorities were referred to. The judge ruled that it was for the jury to decide whether the defendants had voluntarily assumed the care of the deceased so as to assume a legal duty of care to him and that there was sufficient evidence on causation to be left to the jury.

The judge's ruling and summing up in relation both to duty of care and causation were at the heart of the appeals of both appellants.

On behalf of Sinclair, Mr Peter Carter QC submitted that there is no authority in which a duty of care has been held to exist in circumstances such as the present. The distinction between acts and omissions is an important one in the law of manslaughter. A doctor has a duty to act and to act appropriately in a non-negligent fashion but the criticism of Sinclair was based solely on omission. It is important for people to know where they stand in relation to the Criminal Law and, to this end, concepts of liability should be clear....

Mr Carter submitted that the effect of the judge's direction about which he complained,... was to cast... on the jury the sole responsibility of determining whether a legal duty of care existed. The judge should have directed the jury that, if they found proved such facts as he identified, they should find there was a legal duty of care. In the present case there were no facts justifying such a finding and therefore the case should have been withdrawn from the jury at the close of the prosecution. Acts done benevolently rather than maliciously should not found liability in manslaughter. On seeing that Coleman was unconscious Sinclair could have turned on his heels and gone home without incurring criminal liability. If, out of humanity, he stayed with his friend and tried to do what he could, that did not give rise to a legal duty of care. The court should set the hurdle for establishing a legal duty at a higher level.

Mr Cassel [Counsel for J] further submitted that there is no authority in England which imposes a duty of care on a medically unqualified stranger following a relationship of only a few hours duration. Authorities in other jurisdictions point to a contrary conclusion. He referred to *The People v Beardsley* 118 North Western Reporter 1128 (1907) a decision of the Supreme Court of Michigan where the presence of a woman friend in the defendant's house when both took liquor and the woman took drugs was held not to create a legal duty such as exists in the case of husband and wife. Mcalvay CJ, giving what appears to have been the judgment of the court, at page 1131 said:

> 'Had this been a case where two men underlike circumstances had voluntarily gone on debauchery together and one had attempted suicide, no one would claim that this doctrine of legal duty could be invoked to hold the other criminally responsible for omitting to make effort to rescue his companion.'

Mr Cassell also referred to a decision of the New South Wales Supreme Court in *Tak Tak* 1988 NSWLR 226 which emphasised, as a pre-condition for a legal duty of care to arise, the need for the disabled person to be secluded by the defendant to prevent others from affording aid. In the present case, he submitted, Johnson did not undertake to provide necessities for the deceased nor did he confine him. He distinguished *Stone & Dobinson* because, in that case, the deceased had lived with the appellant for 3 years and, as is apparent from page 357B of the report, the prosecution case was put on the basis that, during that period, the appellants had assumed responsibility for the deceased, prior to the final days of neglect.

Accordingly, submitted Mr Cassell, the judge was wrong to reject the submission of no case to answer on Johnson's behalf. He failed to make a ruling as to whether the facts proved were capable of giving rise to a legal duty [see per Swinton Thomas LJ in *R v Khan & Khan*, above p **98**]. Alternatively, if he was right to leave the matter to the jury, he should have explained to them what facts would need to be proved for them to find that Johnson had a legal as well as a moral duty of care. They should have been directed that only if they felt sure that Johnson had, by words or actions undertaken to provide V with the necessities of life and knew that he alone was responsible for Coleman well being could he have been under a legal duty.

Mr Cassell further submitted that the judge failed to put Johnson's defence in particular that he had only met Coleman once before and was not responsible for selling drugs to him and that no duty of care resulted from their relationship.

On behalf of the Crown, Mr Corkery QC drew attention to the Law Commission Report No 237, in particular paras 3.14 and 3.15, where the difficulties of codifying the law in relation to the extent of a duty to act are emphasised. He submitted that the law has to remain uncertain and that there can be a deliberate assumption of care on the spur of the moment. If, as Mr Cassell had submitted, seclusion of the disabled person is a requirement for a duty to exist this would defeat the public interest in preserving life. He relied on *Stone & Dobinson* as showing that seclusion is not an element of English Law, because in that case there were 3 others, apart from the defendants, with access to the house.

In the present case, he submitted, Sinclair owed a duty of care because he had been a friend of the deceased for 13 or 14 years, they had lived together for 18 months to 2 years , they were described as 'like brothers' and Sinclair himself had said 'I wouldn't walk away and leave him: he is my friend'. Pegler [a visitor] had advised that an ambulance be called and, between 7 and 9pm, according to McKie, Sinclair had been to his house because of his concern about Coleman. All these factors pointed to the voluntary assumption by Sinclair of a duty of care. As to Johnson, his flat was a recognised place for acquiring and injecting methadone. Needles and syringes were provided. He knew that Coleman had taken methadone. He had prepared and administered saline injections to him and had put him to bed knowing that serious efforts had been made, by face slapping and throwing water, to revive him.

…

[The court disposed of the appeal on the basis of arguments relating to causation] But, in deference to the arguments which have been addressed to us in relation to the existence of a legal duty of care, we propose to say something on this aspect of the matter without embarking on an exhaustive review of the authorities.…

So far as Johnson is concerned, there is no English authority in which a duty of care has been held to arise, over a period of hours, on the part of a medically unqualified stranger. *Beardsley and Tak Tak* are both persuasive authorities pointing away from the existence of any such duty, although we do not accept, in the light of *Stone and Dobinson*, that the concept of seclusion is in, English Law, a necessary pre-requisite to the existence of a legal duty of care. But Johnson did not know the deceased. His only connection with him was that he had come to his house and there taken methadone and remained until he died. Others were coming and going in the meantime. The fact that Johnson had prepared and administered to the deceased saline solutions does not, as it seems to us, demonstrate on his part a voluntary assumption of a legal duty of care rather than a desultory attempt to be of assistance. In our judgment, the facts in relation to Johnson were not capable of giving rise to a legal duty of care and the judge should have withdrawn his case from the jury for this further reason.

Sinclair was in a different position. The evidence was that he was a close friend of the deceased for many years and the two had lived together almost as brothers. It was Sinclair who paid for and supplied the deceased with the first dose of methadone and helped him to obtain the second dose. He knew that the deceased was not an addict. He remained with the deceased throughout the period of his unconsciousness and, for a substantial period, was the only person with him. In the light of this evidence, there was in our judgment material on which the jury properly directed, could have found that Sinclair owed the deceased a legal duty of care. The judge was therefore correct to leave Sinclair's case to the jury on this aspect. We do accept however, that there is force in Mr Carter's submission that, in the law of manslaughter, it is important to distinguish between acts of commission and omission and that, even if it is appropriate, in criminal as well as in civil law, for the circumstances in which a duty of care exists to expand incrementally, it is undesirable there should be such elasticity in that expansion that potential defendants are unaware until after the event whether their conduct is capable of being regarded as criminal....

Appeals against conviction for manslaughter allowed; third appellant's appeal against sentence allowed

Question

Should the existence of a duty be a question of law or of fact? What criteria could a jury apply? Would not juries reach inconsistent results if the issue was for them?

A general duty of rescue?

Proposals have often been made for the imposition of a general duty, particularly to save others from death or serious injury. A famous early example was the proposal by Edward Livingston for his Draft Code (never enacted) for Louisiana. It was to the effect that a person shall be guilty of homicide who omits to save life which he could save 'without personal danger or pecuniary loss'. This seems at first sight to be an attractive solution to the 'child in the shallow pool' case. The Commissioners who in 1838 reported on the Indian Penal Code thought the proposal open to serious objection (Macaulay, *Works*, vol 7, 494.) If this were the only test of a duty it would certainly be quite inadequate; the common law duty quite properly requires the person owing it to incur 'pecuniary loss'.

A parent may be unable to procure food for an infant without money. Yet the parent, if he has the means, is bound to furnish the infant with food, and if, by omitting to do so, he voluntarily causes its death, he may with propriety be treated as a murderer. [*Ibid* 494–495]

As a test for an *additional* duty its defects are less obvious; but it would, apparently, have been unacceptable to the Commissioners.

They put the case of a surgeon, the only person in India who could perform a certain operation. If the operation is not performed on a particular patient he will certainly die. The surgeon could perform the operation without personal danger or pecuniary loss—in fact he will be well paid. But, for personal reasons it is extremely inconvenient for him to do so—he wishes to return to Europe or has other plans incompatible with the performance of the operation. The Commissioners thought it self-evident that he should not be guilty of murder. The example is an unusual one, highly unlikely to arise in practice, but not easy to distinguish in principle from the 'shallow pool' case. The difference, if there is one, seems to lie in the immediacy of the impending death in the shallow pool case. If Macaulay's surgeon were to witness an accident and, knowing that he was the only doctor present and that only immediate medical assistance could save an injured man's life, were to pass on because it was inconvenient to stop, it would seem less extravagant to convict him of an offence.

Macaulay excused what he thought might appear to be the excessive leniency of the Commissioners' proposals on the following grounds:

It is, indeed, most highly desirable that men should not merely abstain from doing harm to their neighbours, but should render active services to their neighbours. In general, however, the penal law must content itself with keeping men from doing positive harm, and must leave to public opinion, and to the teachers of morality and religion, the office of furnishing men with motives for doing positive good. It is evident that to attempt to punish men by law for not rendering to others all the service which it is their duty to render to others would be preposterous. We must grant impunity to the vast majority of those omissions which a benevolent morality would pronounce reprehensible, and must content ourselves with punishing such omissions only when they are distinguished from the rest by some circumstances which marks them out as peculiarly fit objects of penal legislation.

Not everyone accepts this point of view. Professor Millner (*Negligence in the Modern Law*, p 33), writing in the context of the civil law of negligence, says:

There is, however, nothing absolute about this immunity from liability, and no reason why changing attitudes should not bring some of the more callous types of indifference within the reach of the law, at least in cases where inaction amounts to calculated indifference to the fate of others, as in the case where an injured pedestrian is left to lie in the path of oncoming traffic by those who know of his plight and could remedy it; or where a person is allowed, without warning, to cross thin ice or a crumbling bridge by one who is aware that the other, in his innocence is courting disaster; or where a person who, being in a position to take *some* action, yet allows a helpless and solitary invalid to starve to death. It is hard to imagine that anyone would be affronted if the law in such cases were to raise a duty of care in favour of the victim of this kind of callous indifference to the fate of one's fellows.

For a powerful supporting argument for such liability see Ashworth (above p **82**). There is a wealth of literature on this topic, see especially J. Feinberg, *Harm to Others* (OUP, 1984), ch 4. See also M. Menlove, 'The Philosophical Foundations of a Duty to Rescue' and A. McCall Smith, 'The Duty to Rescue and the Common Law' in M. Menlove and A. McCall Smith (eds) *The Duty to Rescue: The Jurisprudence of Aid* (1993).

There is also the option of creating a specific statutory offence of the form found in many jurisdictions which criminalize the failure to take reasonable steps to rescue. Such statutes do not impose liability for the prohibited harm that V suffers (death or injury, etc), but the appropriately labelled offence of failure to rescue with an appropriate punishment. See for detailed examination of the French system, A. Ashworth and E. Steiner, 'Criminal Omissions and Public Duties: The French Experience' (1990) 10 LS 153.

(3) OMISSIONS AND CAUSATION

Assuming that the offence in question is one which can be interpreted so as to be committed by omission and that there is a relevant category of duty, the question remains, how can D cause any harm by omission? Stephen, in his *Digest of the Criminal Law* (4th edn, 1887), art 212, stated the general rule for offences against the person as follows: 'It is not a crime to cause death or bodily injury, even intentionally, by any omission ...'

It will be noted that Stephen does not seem to have doubted that death or bodily injury may be caused by omission. He assumes that these results may be so caused, but denies that it is an offence. He gave the following famous illustration: 'A sees B drowning and is able to save him by holding out his hand. A abstains from doing so in order that B may be drowned, and B is drowned. A has committed no offence.'

Stephen went on to state exceptional cases where A would be guilty of murder—where A is B's parent for example. If A and a stranger, C, were walking past together it is impossible to say, as a matter of fact, that A has, and that C has not, caused the death of the child. Either could have saved him equally easily and each deliberately refrained from doing so. The difference is that, in law, A has a duty to act but C does not.

It has been argued (Brian Hogan, 'Omissions and the Duty Myth' in *Criminal Law Essays in Honour of J. C. Smith*, p 85) that it is not true that results can be 'caused' by omission and that it ought to follow that no one should be liable for a 'result crime' because of a mere omission. 'If grandma's skirts are ignited by her careless proximity to the gas oven, the delinquent grandson cannot be said to have killed her by his failure to dowse her. No sensible doctor would enter as the cause of her death, say, failure to telephone the fire brigade.' Professor Hogan continues:

If any proposition is self-evident (and, arguably, none is) it is that a person cannot be held to have caused an event which he did not cause. Hence my delinquent child cannot sensibly be said to have caused the death of his grandmother simply by a failure to take steps (which may or may not have been successful anyway) to prevent that death. To say to the child, 'You have killed your grandmother' would simply be untrue.

This is not to say that I am against liability for omissions. There would be nothing in principle objectionable in Parliament enacting a law which made it an offence for a member of a household to fail to take steps reasonably available to him to prevent or minimize harm to other members of the household. There are of course numerous instances where Parliament (and a handful where the common law) has penalised omissions but what is noteworthy is that the defendant is penalised for the omission but not visited with liability for the consequences of that omission....

So in no sense am I against liability for omission. I would ask only two conditions of a law punishing omissions. One is that it be clearly articulated and the other is that it seeks to punish the defendant for his dereliction and does not artificially treat him as a cause of the event he has not brought about by his conduct....

Thus far I have discussed cases where by no stretch of the imagination can it be said that the defendant has caused a result by his inaction. The question then arises whether a result may ever be caused by inaction. My answer is: No. On the other hand a result may be caused by the defendant's *conduct* and the totality of the defendant's conduct causing a result may properly include what he has not done as well as done. In such cases I doubt whether it is very, or at all, helpful to analyze each phase of the defendant's conduct as one of omission or commission. The question is simply: did the defendant's *conduct* cause the result?

Take a simple example. X, driving his car, sees Y beginning to cross the road ahead. X realizes that unless he takes some action, such as removing his foot from the accelerator to the brake or turning to left or right, he will run down Y. In fact he takes no action whatsoever and runs down Y. Charged with an offence in relation to the harm done to Y, X would surely be laughed out of court if he said: I did not do anything to cause harm to Y. We would not have the slightest difficulty in saying that X ran down Y and was the cause of the harm to Y. *R v Miller* [above, p **93**] holds, and with respect rightly, that one who inadvertently (or otherwise faultlessly, presumably) starts a chain of events causing harm may be properly held liable if, having become aware that he was the cause, he fails to take steps reasonably available to him to prevent or minimize the damage that will ensue. A fortiori the driver X. There is nothing inadvertent about his causing of harm to Y. X chooses to stay with a course of conduct which he knows will cause harm to Y.

Compare the views of A. Leavens, 'A Causation Approach to Criminal Omissions' (1888) 76 Cal LR 547.

Such a view of causation is flawed because its inquiry is too limited. It depends on a definition of the status quo as the existing physical state of affairs at the precise time of the omission...Our everyday notions of causation, however, are not so limited because we understand that the status quo encompasses more than the physical state of affairs at a given time. Indeed, in everyday usage the status quo is taken to include expected patterns of conduct, including actions designed to avert certain unwanted results. When, for example, a driver parks a car on a steep hill, it is normal to set the parking brake and put the car in gear. If the driver forgets to do so and the car subsequently rolls down the hill, smashing into another car, we would say that the failure to park properly was a departure from the status quo. This failure, not the visibly steep hill or the predicate act of pulling the car to the curb, was the cause of the collision. Once we realize that a particular undesirable state of affairs can be avoided by taking certain precautions, we usually incorporate these precautions into what we see as the normal or at rest state of affairs. A failure to engage in the preventative conduct in these cases can thus be seen as an intervention that disturbs the status quo. When such a failure to act is a necessary condition (a 'but for' cause) of a particular harm, then that failure fairly can be said to cause that harm. In the above example, the driver's failure to park the car in a proper manner caused the accident as surely as if he had actually driven his car into the other....

Notes

The authors of the draft Code accepted that results may be caused by omission. Clause 17(1) (above, p **76**) provides that a person causes a result which is an element of an offence when: '(b) he omits to do an act which might prevent its occurrence and which he is under a duty to do according to the law relating to the offence.'

It has been cogently argued that this would extend liability beyond the present law, and beyond what is desirable, by including results which the act D omitted to do *might* have prevented and that it should be restricted to results which that act *would* have prevented. See Glanville Williams (1987) 7 LS 92 at 106–107.

In *Morby* (1882) 15 Cox CC 35 D was convicted of manslaughter of his son, a child under the age of 14. D knew that the child was suffering from small pox. D did not summon a doctor because he was one of the 'Peculiar People' who did not believe in medical aid but trusted in prayer and anointment. The child died of small pox. In the Court for Crown Cases Reserved (Lord Coleridge CJ, Grove, Stephen, Mathew and Cave JJ) D's counsel admitted that he could not contend that D was not guilty of breach of a statutory duty but argued that death was not caused by breach of that duty. Lord Coleridge CJ said:

We are all clearly of opinion that the conviction cannot be supported. The jury may have thought that, as there had been a neglect of his duty by the parent, it was right to mark their sense of it by their verdict. Nothing could be more cautious than the answers given by the medical witness to the questions put to him. It was not enough to sustain the charge of manslaughter to show that the parent had neglected to use all reasonable means of saving the life of his child; it was necessary to show that what the parent neglected to do had the effect of shortening the child's life. The utmost that the doctor would say, giving his evidence under a strong responsibility, in answer to the question, 'In your judgment, if medical advice and assistance had been called in at any stage of this disease, might the death have been averted altogether?' was, 'I cannot say that death would probably have been averted. I think it probable that life might have been prolonged. I can only say probably might, because I did not see the case during life; had I done so I might have been able to answer the question.' That evidence is far too vague to allow this conviction to stand when all that the skilled witness could say was that probably the life of the boy might have been prolonged if medical assistance had been called in.

Questions

1. Was the court in *Morby* right? If so, is this an answer to cases like Hogan's example of the incinerated granny? The steps omitted 'may not have been successful anyway'—proof that they would have been successful would rarely, if ever, be possible. But what if the child, observing that granny's skirt was beginning to scorch had deliberately refrained from telling her, in the expectation—or even the hope—that it would burst into flames? *But for* the child's omission to warn, Granny's life *would* have been saved. Is it then unreasonable to say that the child caused her death?

2. V has a heart attack and reaches for the pills which would save his life. (i) D, a stranger, pushes the bottle out of his reach. (ii) The bottle is just out of V's reach. D could easily give it to him but does nothing. In both cases D wants V to die and V in fact dies. In (i) D is guilty of murder. In (ii) he apparently commits no offence. Are the cases morally distinguishable? Is one more deserving of punishment than the other? Should the law distinguish between them? Can D be said to have *caused* death in (i) but not in (ii)?

R v Gibbins and Proctor

(1918) 13 Cr App R 134, Court of Criminal Appeal

(Darling, McCardie and Salter JJ)

Walter Gibbins and Edith Proctor were living together with Gibbins' daughter, Nelly, aged seven, and other children. The children were healthy except for Nelly, who was kept upstairs apart from the others and was starved to death. There was evidence that Proctor hated Nelly and cursed and hit her, from which the jury could infer that she had a very strong interest in Nelly's death. Gibbins was in regular employment, earning good wages, all of which he gave to Proctor. According to Gibbins's counsel, it was his duty to provide the money; it was Proctor's to provide the food. When Nelly died, Proctor told Gibbins to bury her out of sight which he did, in the brickyard where he worked. Gibbins and Proctor were tried together and convicted of murder of Nelly. They appealed, inter alia, on the ground of misdirection.

[**Darling J**, delivering the judgment of the court:]

.... the misdirection here complained of is on a crucial matter, where [the judge] told the jury what they must find in order to convict either prisoner of murder. He said, 'The charge against the prisoners is, in the first place, that they killed this child Nelly, or caused her death, by malice aforethought. That means they intended she should die and acted so as to produce that result.' If that is a misdirection it is one in favour of the prisoners.... 'If you think that one or other of those prisoners wilfully and intentionally withheld food from that child so as to cause her to weaken and to cause her grievous bodily injury, as the result of which she died, it is not necessary for you to find that she intended or he intended to kill the child then and there. It is enough if you find that he or she intended to set up such

a set of facts by withholding food or anything as would in the ordinary course of nature lead gradually but surely to her death.' In our opinion that direction amply fulfils the conditions which a judge
should observe in directing the jury in such a case as this....

'If the omission to provide necessary food or raiment was accompanied with an intention to cause
the death of the child, or to cause some serious bodily injury to it, then it would be malicious in the
sense imputed by this indictment, and in a case of this kind it is difficult, if not impossible, to understand how a person who contemplated doing serious bodily injury to the child by the deprivation of
food, could have meditated anything else than causing its death.' The word used is 'contemplated', but
what has to be proved is an intention to do grievous bodily injury. In our opinion the judge left the question correctly to the jury, and there is no ground for interfering with the convictions for those reasons.

It has been said that there ought not to have been a finding of guilty of murder against Gibbins. The
court agrees that the evidence was less against Gibbins than Proctor, Gibbins gave her money, and as
far as we can see it was sufficient to provide for the wants of themselves and all the children. But he
lived in the house and the child was his own, a little girl of seven, and he grossly neglected the child.
He must have known what her condition was if he saw her, for she was little more than a skeleton. He
is in this dilemma; if he did not see her the jury might well infer that he did not care if she died; if he
did he must have known what was going on. The question is whether there was evidence that he so
conducted himself as to shew that he desired that grievous bodily injury should be done to the child.
He cannot pretend that he shewed any solicitude for her. He knew that Proctor hated her, knew that
she was ill and that no doctor had been called in, and the jury may have come to the conclusion that
he was so infatuated with Proctor, and so afraid of offending her, that he preferred that the child
should starve to death rather than that he should be exposed to any injury or unpleasantness from
Proctor. It is unnecessary to say more than that there was evidence that Gibbins did desire that
grievous bodily harm should be done to the child; he did not interfere in what was being done, and he
comes within the definition which I have read, and is therefore guilty of murder.

The case of Proctor is plainer. She had charge of the child. She was under no obligation to do so or to
live with Gibbins, but she did so, and receiving money, as it is admitted she did, for the purpose of supplying food, her duty was to see that the child was properly fed and looked after, and to see that she had
medical attention if necessary. We agree with what Lord Coleridge CJ said in *Instan* [1893] 1 QB 450:
'There is no case directly in point, but it would be a slur upon, and a discredit to the administration of,
justice in this country if there were any doubt as to the legal principle, or as to the present case being
within it. The prisoner was under a moral obligation to the deceased from which arose a legal duty
towards her; that legal duty the prisoner has wilfully and deliberately left unperformed, with the consequence that there has been an acceleration of the death of the deceased owing to the non-performance
of that legal duty.' Here Proctor took upon herself the moral obligation of looking after the children;
she was *de facto*, though not *de jure*, the wife of Gibbins and had excluded the child's own mother. She
neglected the child undoubtedly, and the evidence shews that as a result the child died....

Appeals dismissed

Questions

1. Was Gibbins held liable for an omission upon an omission?—that is, because he failed to
interfere to prevent Proctor's failure to feed Nelly?

2. Proctor was not related, in blood or in law, to Nelly. Why was she under a duty to feed
Nelly?

3. Can it be seriously argued (cf above, p 103) in such a case as this that death is not *caused*
by an omission? Or might the case be put on the ground that preventing Nelly from having

access to the food which was sufficient to keep the other children in good health was not a mere omission but a continuing act or series of acts?

5. Does it follow from the decision that, if Nelly had not died but had sustained grievous bodily harm, the appellants would have been guilty of causing gbh with intent contrary to s 18 of OAPA 1861?

In *A (children) (conjoined twins: surgical separation* [2001] Fam 147, [2000] 4 All ER 961, below, p **440**, Mary's heart and lungs were too deficient to keep her alive. She lived only because Jodie was able to circulate sufficient oxygenated blood for both of them. The evidence was that, if they were not separated, both would die. Separation would kill Mary but give Jodie a good chance of a normal life. The parents, Roman Catholics, refused their consent to the operation on religious grounds. **Ward LJ**:

I know there is a huge chasm in turpitude between these stricken parents and the wretched parents in *R v Gibbins* (1918) 13 Cr App R 134 who starved their child to death. Nevertheless I am bound to wonder whether there is strictly any difference in the application of the principle. They know they can save her. They appreciate she will die if not separated from her twin. Is there any defence to a charge of cruelty under s 1 of the Children and Young Persons Act 1933 in the light of the clarification of the law given by *R v Sheppard* [1980] 3 All ER 889, [1981] AC 394 which in turn throws doubt on the correctness of *Oakey v Jackson* [1914] 1 KB 216? Would it not be manslaughter if Jodie died through that neglect? I ask these insensitive questions not to heap blame on the parents. No prosecutor would dream of prosecuting. The sole purpose of the inquiry is to establish whether either or both parents and doctors have come under a legal duty to Jodie, as I conclude they each have, to procure and to carry out the operation which will save her life. If so then performance of their duty to Jodie is irreconcilable with the performance of their duty to Mary. Certainly it seems to me that if this court were to give permission for the operation to take place, then a legal duty would be imposed on the doctors to treat their patient in her best interests, ie to operate upon her. Failure to do so is a breach of their duty. To omit to act when under a duty to do so may be a culpable omission. Death to Jodie is virtually certain to follow (barring some unforeseen intervention). Why is that not killing Jodie?

Question

If the parents had prevented the operation by abducting the twins and both had died would this have been murder or manslaughter of both twins, or only of Jodie, or of neither?

(4) ACT OR OMISSION?

It will be obvious from the above, that the distinction between acts and omissions is often tenuous and certainly too fine to bear the strain of distinguishing between circumstances in which there is no criminal liability and where there is liability in full measure. Some of the most striking examples of the difficulty in distinguishing acts and omissions arise in the medical context.

Dr Arthur's case

John Pearson was born at 7.55 am on 28 June 1980. It was immediately recognized that he was suffering from Down's syndrome. When his mother was informed, she rejected the baby. Dr Arthur, a highly respected consultant paediatrician, saw the parents at noon.

There was a discussion as to whether the mother should keep the child. Following that discussion, Arthur wrote in his case notes: 'Parents do not wish the baby to survive. Nursing care only.' This meant that the child would be given water but no food. He entered on the treatment chart a prescription for a drug, dihydrocodeine (DF118) to be given 'as required' at four-hourly intervals by the nurse in charge. Dr Arthur was alleged to have said to a police officer '(DF118) is a sedative which stops the child seeking sustenance.' In a later written statement he said that the purpose of the drug was to reduce suffering. The baby died at 5.10 am on 1 July 1980, $57\frac{1}{4}$ hours after birth. The cause of death was stated to be broncho-pneumonia as a result of Down's syndrome.

Following an allegation that the baby had been drugged and starved to death there was a police investigation and Arthur was charged with murder before Farquharson J and a jury at Leicester Crown Court. The prosecution alleged that death was caused by DF118 poisoning but, following defence evidence that the child might have died from inherent defects from which it was suffering before birth, the murder charge was dropped and replaced by one of attempted murder. In the course of a lengthy summing up:

[**Farquharson J** directed the jury:]

... the prosecution must prove not only an act which you as a jury decide is an attempt to cause the death of John Pearson, but an act accompanied by an intent that the child should die at the time the act was carried out.

[The defence say that] Arthur was not committing an act, a positive act, at all; he was simply prescribing a treatment which involved the creation of a set of circumstances whereby the child would peacefully die, and that there is all the difference in the world between the one and the other ...

The prescription of that drug, dihydrocodeine, is a matter that is of consequence in this case. The importance that you attach to it is—and I must repeat—something for you to say as to whether the prosecution have, (a) proved that there was an attempt here or (b) that there was an act properly so-called on the part of Dr Arthur, as distinct from simply allowing the child to die ...

Not only is it a possibility but it is a real possibility, say the defence, that in the ensuing days as [the mother] becomes more in control of herself and recovers from the trauma of giving birth to the child she could change her mind. This is a very vital part of the case because one of the main contentions of the defence here is that what was being done by Dr Arthur in prescribing this treatment had no sort of finality; it was in the nature ... of a holding operation. If the mother had changed her mind then different treatment and management would have been given to the child ...

However serious the case may be; however much the disadvantage of a mongol or, indeed, any other handicapped child, no doctor has the right to kill it ...

But what has been perhaps the most agonizing part of this case is that it has become very clear, you may think, that it is a very difficult area to decide precisely where a doctor is doing an act, a positive act, or allowing a course of events or a set of circumstances to ensue ...

If a child is born with a serious handicap—the instance we have been given is duodenal atresia where a mongol has an ill-formed intestine whereby the child will die of the ailment if he is not operated on—a surgeon may say: as this child is a mongol, handicapped in the way I have already been discussing with you, I do not propose to operate; I shall allow (and you have heard this expression several times) nature to take its course.

No one could say that the surgeon was committing an act of murder by declining to take a course which would save the child.

Equally, if a child not otherwise going to die, who is severely handicapped, is given a drug in such an excessive amount by the doctor that the drug itself will cause his death and the doctor does that intentionally it would be open to the jury to say: yes, he was killing, he was murdering the child ...

[Dr Arthur did not give evidence. He was acquitted by the jury.]

Questions

1. Is the duty owed to a newly-born severely handicapped child different from, and of a lower order than, that owed to a normal child? Consider the cases where parents and a surgeon agree that an operation to rectify duodenal atresia which would save the child's life shall not be performed (a) on a severely handicapped child, (b) on a normal healthy child.

2. Is withholding food properly equated with not performing a surgical operation?

3. Is any of the following a 'positive act'? (i) withholding food; (ii) instructing others to withhold food; (iii) administering a drug; (iv) instructing others to administer a drug. Consider the following evidence of expert witnesses, of which the judge reminded the jury.

Professor Campbell: 'There is an important difference between allowing a child to die and taking action to kill it. Withholding food is, I think, a negative, not a positive act.'

Dr Dunn: 'I regard it as a negative act, withholding food...Many respected members of the profession regard the not giving of food as allowing nature to take its course....I know of no paediatrician who withholds treatment in the sense which we are talking [that is, withholding food] who regards what he has done as killing the child.'

4. What is the relevance of the fact that eminent paediatricians do not regard the withholding of food as a 'positive act'? Who determines the scope of the criminal law?

5. If Dr Arthur had prescribed a course of treatment which would result in the child's death, what was the relevance of the fact that it was revocable, 'a holding operation', and that, if the mother had changed her mind in time, he expected that the child could have been fed and its life saved? Should a doctor leave it to the mother to decide, in effect, whether such a child should live or die?

For discussion of *Arthur*'s case, see M. Gunn and J. C. Smith [1985] Crim LR 705 and I. Kennedy, *Treat Me Right*, ch 8.

Airedale National Health Service Trust v Bland
[1993] 1 All ER 821, House of Lords

(Lords Keith of Kinkel, Goff of Chieveley, Lowry, Browne-Wilkinson and Mustill)

In 1989 Anthony Bland, then aged 17, was injured in the Hillsborough Stadium disaster suffering irreversible brain damage and thereafter was in a persistent vegative state (PVS)—no cognitive function, no sight, hearing, capacity to feel pain, move his limbs or communicate in any way. Being unable to swallow, he was fed by naso-gastric tube. Repeated infections were treated by antibiotics. The consensus of medical opinion was that there was no hope of his improvement or recovery.

On the application (with the support of Bland's parents) of the Airedale NHS Trust, in whose hospital Bland was a patient, Sir Stephen Brown P granted a declaration that the Trust might lawfully (1) discontinue all life-sustaining treatment including ventilation, nutrition and hydration by artificial means and (2) discontinue medical treatment except for the purpose of enabling Bland to die peacefully with the greatest dignity and least distress. The Court of Appeal (Bingham MR, Butler-Sloss and Hoffmann LJJ) dismissed an appeal by the Official Solicitor who appealed to the House of Lords. He submitted that the withdrawal of artificial feeding would constitute murder. The House, though accepting that their decision in this civil action would not be legally binding on a criminal court, unanimously dismissed the appeal.

[**Lord Keith** made a speech dismissing the appeal.]

Lord Goff. Why is it that the doctor who gives his patient a lethal injection which kills him commits an unlawful act and indeed is guilty of murder, whereas a doctor who, by discontinuing life support, allows his patient to die may not act unlawfully and will not do so if he commits no breach of duty to his patient? Professor Glanville Williams has suggested (see *Textbook of Criminal Law* (2nd edn, 1983) p 282) that the reason is that what the doctor does when he switches off a life support machine 'is in substance not an act but an omission to struggle' and that the 'omission is not a breach of duty by the doctor, because he is not obliged to continue in a hopeless case'.

I agree that the doctor's conduct in discontinuing life support can properly be categorised as an omission. It is true that it may be difficult to describe what the doctor actually does as an omission, for example where he takes some positive step to bring the life support to an end. But discontinuation of life support is, for present purposes, no different from not initiating life support in the first place. In each case, the doctor is simply allowing his patient to die in the sense that he is desisting from taking a step which might, in certain circumstances, prevent his patient from dying as a result of his pre-existing condition: and as a matter of general principle an omission such as this will not be unlawful unless it constitutes a breach of duty to the patient. I also agree that the doctor's conduct is to be differentiated from that of, for example, an interloper who maliciously switches off a life support machine because, although the interloper may perform exactly the same act as the doctor who discontinues life support, his doing so constitutes interference with the life-prolonging treatment then being administered by the doctor. Accordingly, whereas the doctor, in discontinuing life support, is simply allowing his patient to die of his pre-existing condition, the interloper is actively intervening to stop the doctor from prolonging the patient's life, and such conduct cannot possibly be categorized as an omission.... If the justification for treating a patient who lacks the capacity to consent lies in the fact that the treatment is provided in his best interests, it must follow that the treatment may, and indeed ultimately should, be discontinued where it is no longer in his best interests to provide it. The question which lies at the heart of the present case is, as I see it, whether on that principle the doctors responsible for the treatment and care of Anthony Bland can justifiably discontinue the process of artificial feeding upon which the prolongation of his life depends.

It is crucial for the understanding of this question that the question itself should be correctly formulated. The question is not whether the doctor should take a course which will kill his patient, or even take a course which has the effect of accelerating his death. The question is whether the doctor should or should not continue to provide his patient with medical treatment or care which, if continued, will prolong his patient's life. The question is sometimes put in striking or emotional terms, which can be misleading. For example, in the case of a life support system, it is sometimes asked: should a doctor be entitled to switch it off, or to pull the plug? And then it is asked: can it be in the best interests of the patient that a doctor should be able to switch the life support system off, when this will inevitably result in the patient's death? Such an approach has rightly been criticized as misleading, for example by Professor Ian Kennedy (in his paper in *Treat Me Right, Essays in Medical Law and Ethics* (1988)), and by Thomas J in *Auckland Area Health Board v A-G* [1993] 1 NZLR 235 at 247. This is because the question is not whether it is in the best interests of the patient that he should die. The question is whether it is in the best interests of the patient that his life should be prolonged by the continuance of this form of medical treatment or care.

The correct formulation of the question is of particular importance in a case such as the present, where the patient is totally unconscious and where there is no hope whatsoever of any amelioration of his condition. In circumstances such as these, it may be difficult to say that it is in his best interests that the treatment should be ended. But, if the question is asked, as in my opinion it should be, whether it is in his best interests that treatment which has the effect of artificially prolonging his life should be continued, that question can sensibly be answered to the effect that it is not in his best interests to do so.

[**Lords Lowry** and **Browne-Wilkinson** made speeches dismissing the appeal.]

Lord Mustill. After much expression of negative opinions I turn to an argument which in my judgment is logically defensible and consistent with the existing law. In essence it turns the previous argument on its head by directing the inquiry to the interests of the patient, not in the termination of life but in the continuation of his treatment. It runs as follows. (i) The cessation of nourishment and hydration is an omission not an act. (ii) Accordingly, the cessation will not be a criminal act unless the doctors are under a present duty to continue the regime. (iii) At the time when Anthony Bland came into the care of the doctors decisions had to be made about his care which he was unable to make for himself. In accordance with *F v West Berkshire Health Authority* [1989] 2 All ER 545, [1990] 2 AC 1 these decisions were to be made in his best interests. Since the possibility that he might recover still existed his best interests required that he should be supported in the hope that this would happen. These best interests justified the application of the necessary regime without his consent. (iv) All hope of recovery has now been abandoned. Thus, although the termination of his life is not in the best interests of Anthony Bland, his best interests in being kept alive have also disappeared, taking with them the justification for the non-consensual regime and the correlative duty to keep it in being. (v) Since there is no longer a duty to provide nourishment and hydration a failure to do so cannot be a criminal offence.

My Lords, I must recognise at once that this chain of reasoning makes an unpromising start by transferring the morally and intellectually dubious distinction between acts and omissions into a context where the ethical foundations of the law are already open to question. The opportunity for anomaly and excessively fine distinctions, often depending more on the way in which the problem happens to be stated than on any real distinguishing features, has been exposed by many commentators, including in England the authors above-mentioned, together with Smith and Hogan *Criminal Law* (6th edn, 1988) p 51, Beynon 'Doctors as murderers' [1982] Crim LR 17 and Gunn and Smith '*Arthur's* case and the right to life of a Down's syndrome child' [1985] Crim LR 705. All this being granted, we are still forced to take the law as we find it and try to make it work. Moreover, although in cases near the borderline the categorisation of conduct will be exceedingly hard, I believe that nearer the periphery there will be many instances which fall quite clearly into one category rather than the other. In my opinion the present is such a case, and in company with Compton J in *Barber v Superior Court of Los Angeles County* 147 Cal App 3d 1006 at 1017 (1983) amongst others I consider that the proposed conduct will fall into the category of omissions.

I therefore consider the argument to be soundly based. Now that the time has come when Anthony Bland has no further interest in being kept alive, the necessity to do so, created by his inability to make a choice, has gone; and the justification for the invasive care and treatment together with the duty to provide it have also gone. Absent a duty, the omission to perform what had previously been a duty will no longer be a breach of the criminal law.

Notes and questions

1. Is there really a difference between the questions: (i) 'is it in the best interests of the patient that he should die?' and (ii) 'is it in the best interests of the patient that his life should be prolonged by this treatment?'

2. 'How can it be lawful to allow a patient to die slowly, though painlessly, over a period of weeks from lack of food but unlawful to produce his immediate death by a lethal injection, thereby saving his family from yet another ordeal to add to the tragedy that has already struck them?'—per Lord Browne-Wilkinson—who thought this was 'undoubtedly the law'. Have you an answer? See M J Gunn (1995) 7 Child and Family Law Quarterly.

3. In *Re A (children)*, the case of the conjoined twins, above, p **107**, below, p **440**, Johnson J, the trial judge, held that the reasoning in *Bland* could be applied to that case. He thought that the course proposed by the doctors was not 'a positive act but merely the withdrawal of Mary's blood supply.' It was as if Jodie stood in the same relation to Mary as the various machines did in relation to Bland. But none of the judges in the Court of Appeal agreed— though Robert Walker LJ did say at one point that, following separation, Mary 'would die because tragically her own body, on its own, is not and never has been viable.' Ward LJ went so far as to say that the distinction between act and omission was irrelevant: 'It is important to stress that it makes no difference whether the killing is by act or by omission. That is a distinction without a difference.' He referred to the speeches of Lords Lowry, Browne-Wilkinson and Mustill in Bland's case. But was not the distinction between act and omission the foundation of the decision in Bland's case, unhappy though their lordships were with it? See Lord Browne-Wilkinson's remarks with which Lord Mustill agreed, in Question 2, above. If Mary were not being kept alive by Jodie, it seems clear that it would not have been unlawful to omit to take steps which might briefly have prolonged her life. Yet Johnson J's conclusion was not justified. Bland's case was materially different. This was not a case of discontinuing treatment. Mary was not receiving treatment. The operation would be a positive act. It would involve the use of the scalpel and 'a number of invasions of Mary's body ... before the positive step was taken of clamping the aorta and bringing about Mary's death.'

4. In *R (on the application of Pretty) v DPP* [2002] 1 All ER 1, HL, P was suffering from motor neurone disease, a progressive degenerative disease from which she had no hope of recovery. The disease had deprived her of the capacity to commit suicide but her intellect and capacity to make decisions were in no way impaired. Her husband was willing to assist her to kill herself, provided that the DPP would undertake not to prosecute him under s 2(1) of the Suicide Act 1961, below, p **618**. The DPP would not do so. P applied for judicial review of his decision, seeking a declaration that it infringed her human rights under the European Convention. It was held that it did not. P's appeal to the ECtHR was unsuccessful. But, where a Miss B was kept alive only by life-support machines, Butler-Sloss P held in *Re B* [2002] that, since B had full capacity to make decisions, she had a right to require the support to be withdrawn, so that she would die. Professor R. Sullivan, in a letter to *The Times* (29 March 2002) criticizes the distinction drawn between the two cases.

Yet the distinction drawn is doubtful. The removal of life support will require acts to be carried out by medical personnel. Were life support to be removed without the consent of a sentient patient, we would clearly be confronted with a case of an act ending life. Yet the presence of consent does not change the involvement of doctors and nurses from acts into omissions.

What, of course, changes is the moral quality of the intervention when consent is present. In Miss B's case patient autonomy is respected: in Mrs Pretty's case it is denied. This differential treatment can only be justified, if it is justifiable at all, in terms of relevant moral differences between the two cases. It cannot be justified by spurious manipulation of the distinction between acts and omissions.

Is the distinction between P's case and B's any different from that acted on by the House of Lords in Bland's case? Is there a moral distinction between the two cases? Is there a moral difference between letting nature take its course—where that will result in death—and killing by a positive act?

In *R (on the application of Burke) v General Medical Council* [2004] EWHC 1879 (Admin) B was suffering from a progressively degenerative disorder that would require his treatment by way of artificial nutrition and hydration (ANH) as his condition worsened. He sought clarification from the courts as to when treatment could lawfully be withdrawn and applied for judicial review of the guidance issued by the defendant (GMC) on withholding and withdrawing of life prolonging treatments. The court held that the guidance was defective. It failed sufficiently to acknowledge that it was the duty of a doctor who was unwilling or unable to carry out the wishes of a patient to go on providing the treatment until he found another doctor who would do so; and failed sufficiently to acknowledge the heavy presumption in favour of life-prolonging treatment and to recognize that the touchstone of best interests was intolerability; and to spell out the legal requirement to obtain prior judicial sanction for the withdrawal of ANH. The court stated the summary of its 78-page judgment:

Summary of conclusions

(a) Once a patient has been received or admitted into a National Health Service hospital a duty to care arises—a duty to provide and go on providing treatment —, whether the patient is competent or incompetent, conscious or unconscious.

(b) Once the duty to care has arisen, the doctor and the hospital are under a continuing obligation that cannot lawfully be shed unless arrangements are made for the responsibility to be taken over by someone else.

(c) The duty to care is, in principle, a duty to provide that treatment which is in the best interests of the patient.

(d) The evaluation of a patient's best interests involves a welfare appraisal in the widest sense, taking into account, where appropriate, a wide range of ethical, social, moral, emotional and welfare considerations.

(e) Doctors can properly claim expertise on medical matters; but they can claim no special expertise on the many non-medical matters which go to form the basis of any decision as to what is in a patient's best interests. Medical opinion, however eminent, can never be determinative of what is in a patient's best interests.

(f) In the final analysis it is for the patient, if competent, to determine what is in his own best interests. If the patient is incompetent and has left no binding and effective advance directive then in the final analysis it is for the court to decide what is in his best interests.

(g) Personal autonomy—the right of self-determination—and dignity are fundamental rights, recognised by the common law and protected by Articles 3 and 8 of the Convention.

(h) The personal autonomy which is protected by Article 8 embraces such matters as how one chooses to pass the closing days and moments of one's life and how one manages one's death.

(i) The dignity interests protected by the Convention include, under Article 8, the preservation of mental stability and, under Article 3, the right to die with dignity and the right to be protected from treatment, or from a lack of treatment, which will result in one dying in avoidably distressing circumstances.

(j) An enhanced degree of protection is called for under Articles 3 and 8 in the case of the vulnerable.

(k) Treatment is capable of being 'degrading' within the meaning of Article 3, whether or not there is awareness on the part of the victim. However unconscious or unaware of ill-treatment a particular patient may be, treatment which has the effect on those who witness it of degrading the individual may come within Article 3. It is enough if judged by the standard of right-thinking bystanders it would be viewed as humiliating or debasing the victim, showing a lack of respect for, or diminishing, his or her human dignity.

(l) A failure to provide life-prolonging treatment in circumstances exposing the patient to 'inhuman or degrading treatment' will in principle involve a breach of Article 3. Where the National Health Service has assumed responsibility for treating a terminally ill patient's condition and he has become reliant on the medical care he is receiving, there will prima facie be a breach of Article 3 if that care is removed in circumstances where this will subject him to acute mental and physical suffering and lead to him dying in avoidably distressing circumstances. Moreover, even if the patient's suffering does not reach the severity required to breach Article 3 a withdrawal of treatment in such circumstances may nonetheless breach Article 8 if there are sufficiently adverse effects on his physical and moral integrity or mental stability.

(m) If the patient is competent (or, although incompetent, has made an advance directive which is both valid and relevant to the treatment in question) his decision as to where his best interests lie, and as to what life-prolonging treatment he should or should not have, is in principle determinative. Important as the sanctity of life is, it has to take second place to personal autonomy.

(n) The personal autonomy protected by Article 8 means that in principle it is for the competent patient, and not his doctor, to decide what treatment should or should not be given in order to achieve what the patient believes conduces to his dignity and in order to avoid what the patient would find distressing. A competent patient's Article 8 rights—his rights to physical and psychological integrity, to autonomy and dignity—must prevail over any rights or obligations located in Articles 2 and 3. Any positive obligations of the State under Article 2 or Article 3 necessarily cease at the point at which they would otherwise come into conflict with or intrude into the competent patient's rights of autonomy and self-determination under Article 8. Article 3 does not entitle anyone to force life-prolonging treatment on a competent patient who refuses to accept it. Nor does Article 2.

(o) If the patient is incompetent, the test is best interests. There is a very strong presumption in favour of taking all steps which will prolong life, and save in exceptional circumstances, or where the patient is dying, the best interests of the patient will normally require such steps to be taken. In case of doubt that doubt falls to be resolved in favour of the preservation of life. But the obligation is not absolute. Important as the sanctity of life is, it may have to take second place to human dignity. In the context of life-prolonging treatment the touchstone of best interests is intolerability. So if life-prolonging treatment is providing some benefit it should be provided unless the patient's life, if thus prolonged, would from the patient's point of view be intolerable.

(p) Reference to Article 2 does not add anything in this type of case. Article 2 does not entitle anyone to force life-prolonging treatment on a competent patient who refuses to accept it. Article 2 does not entitle anyone to continue with life-prolonging treatment where to do so would expose the patient to "inhuman or degrading treatment" breaching Article 3. On the other hand, a withdrawal of life-prolonging treatment which satisfies the exacting requirements of the common law, including a proper application of the intolerability test, and in a manner which is in all other respects compatible with the patient's rights under Article 3 and Article 8, will not give rise to any breach of Article 2.

      ...

(r) ….A competent patient, properly advised by a doctor, may elect to choose a form of treatment which is not the one that the doctor would recommend. But this does not release the doctor from his continuing duty to care for his patient, unless perhaps, that is, he finds himself conscientiously unable to do so. In any event, if a doctor is for any reason unable to carry out the wishes of his patient, his duty is to find another doctor who will do so.

…

214 … (e) …I find it hard to envisage any circumstances (other, perhaps, than those envisaged by Professor Higginson [an expert witness in the case]) in which a withdrawal of ANH in such circumstances—that is from a sentient patient, whether competent or incompetent—could be compatible with the Convention.

(f) But the position will be different once the claimant has entered into the final stage and has finally lapsed into a coma. Assuming that the patient is otherwise being treated with dignity, and in a manner which is in all other respects compatible with his rights under Article 3 and Article 8, there will not be any breach either of Article 3 or of Article 8 or of Article 2 if ANH is withdrawn in circumstances where it is serving absolutely no purpose other than the very short prolongation of the life of a dying patient who has slipped into his final coma and lacks all awareness of what is happening. For it can then properly be said that the continuation of ANH would be bereft of any benefit at all to the patient and that it would indeed be futile.

(g) Where it is proposed to withhold or withdraw ANH the prior authorisation of the court is required as a matter of law (and thus ANH cannot be withheld or withdrawn without prior judicial authorisation): (i) where there is any doubt or disagreement as to the capacity (competence) of the patient; or (ii) where there is a lack of unanimity amongst the medical professionals as to either (1) the patient's condition or prognosis or (2) the patient's best interests or (3) the likely outcome of ANH being either withheld or withdrawn or (4) otherwise as to whether or not ANH should be withheld or withdrawn; or (iii) where there is evidence that the patient when competent would have wanted ANH to continue in the relevant circumstances; or (iv) where there is evidence that the patient (even if a child or incompetent) resists or disputes the proposed withdrawal of ANH; or (v) where persons having a reasonable claim to have their views or evidence taken into account (such as parents or close relatives, partners, close friends, long-term carers) assert that withdrawal of ANH is contrary to the patient's wishes or not in the patient's best interests.

Note that this decision was overturned in *R (Burke) v GMC* [2005] EWCA Civ 1003. The Court of Appeal held the GMC's guidance to be lawful.

FURTHER READING

L. ALEXANDER, 'Criminal Liability for Omissions: An Inventory of Issues' in S. Shute and A. Simester (eds) *Criminal Law Theory: Doctrines of the General Part* (2000)

P. GLAZEBROOK 'Criminal Omissions: The Duty Requirements in Offences Against the Person' (1960) 76 LQR 386

B. HOGAN, 'Omissions and the Duty Myth' in P. F. Smith (ed), *Criminal Law: Essays in Honour of J. C. Smith* (1987)

G. HUGHES, 'Criminal Omissions'(1958) 67 Yale LJ 590

I. KENNEDY, 'Switching Off Life Support Machines: The Legal Implications' [1977] Crim LR 443

J. KEOWN, 'Beyond Bland: A critique of the BMA Guidance on Withholding and Withdrawing Medical Treatment' (2000) 20 LS 66

J. C. SMITH, 'Liability for Omissions in Criminal Law' (1984) 4 LS 88

5
Fault

There are some offences, generally minor offences, called 'offences of strict liability', where a person may be convicted although he was not at fault in any way. Generally, however, the law requires proof of fault of some kind. Offences of strict liability are considered in Chapter 8, below. In the present chapter we consider the different types of fault which the criminal law requires.

Criminal Code Bill, cl 6, provides—

fault element; means an element of an offence consisting—

   (a) of a state of mind with which a person acts; or

   (b) of a failure to comply with a standard of conduct; or

   (c) partly of such a state of mind and partly of such a failure…

We saw at the outset that crime generally involves a mental element, mens rea. Where the defendant has caused some result which is forbidden by the criminal law the fault is usually the state of mind with which that result was caused. There are degrees of fault. The most blameworthy mental element is an *intention* to bring about the forbidden result. Also blameworthy, but less so, is *recklessness* whether that result be caused. So, intentional killing is murder and reckless killing is manslaughter. 'Intentionally' and 'recklessly' are ordinary words of the English language but experience shows that they are capable of different meanings. The ordinary people who sit on juries, as well as philosophers, may well differ as to whether a particular state of mind constitutes intention, or recklessness, or neither of these. Many of the most important and difficult cases in recent years have been concerned with the meaning of these terms.

Sometimes the fault which must be proved is guilty knowledge of some sort. For example, when a person is found in possession of stolen goods, say a car, he commits a crime only if he knew or believed that the car was stolen. If he bought it in perfect good faith, it is his misfortune, not his fault. He may be guilty of the tort of conversion because the car still belongs to its original owner. The tort requires no fault. He may have to return the car or account to the owner for its value and may have lost the price he paid. But the innocent buyer of stolen goods commits no crime. If, however, he knew or believed the car was stolen when he bought it, he is guilty of the crime of handling stolen goods.

Fault is not limited to states of mind. A person who did not foresee a harmful result of his conduct obviously did not intend it but it may be that he *ought* to have foreseen the risk of causing it and avoiding doing so, as a reasonably prudent person would. For some crimes, this is sufficient fault. The prosecution have to prove only that the defendant behaved as no reasonably prudent person would and, in the case of a result crime, thereby caused the proscribed result. This is negligence. There may be degrees of negligence. Any deviation from the standard of care to be expected of a reasonable person is sufficient for civil liability in the tort of negligence; but if the criminal law imposes liability for negligence, it sometimes requires 'gross' negligence—a very serious deviation from the required standard.

1. MENS REA IS LEGAL NOT MORAL FAULT

While there is a moral basis for the notions of fault and degrees of fault in the criminal law, legal 'fault' does not necessarily import moral blameworthiness as the following case shows.

R v Kingston
[1994] 3 All ER 353, House of Lords

(Lords Keith, Goff, Browne-Wilkinson, Mustill and Slynn)

With a view to blackmailing the appellant (K) who had paedophiliac homosexual inclinations, F arranged for Penn (P) to obtain damaging information against K. P lured a 15-year-old boy to his flat and surreptitiously drugged him. While the boy was asleep P invited K to abuse him sexually. K did so and was photographed and taped. K's defence to a charge of indecent assault (see now the offence of sexual assault and the child sex offences discussed in Chapter 20) was that P had laced his drink, that he saw the boy lying on the bed but remembered nothing more. The judge directed the jury that they should acquit if they thought he may have been so affected by drugs that he did not intend to commit the inde-cent assault; but that, if they were sure that he did intend to commit an indecent assault, he was guilty because a drugged intent was still an intent. He was convicted but the Court of Appeal quashed his conviction on the ground that, if he had formed an intention to assault which he would not have formed but for the surreptitious administration of drugs which had caused him to lose self-control, the involuntary intoxication negatived mens rea. The Crown appealed to the House of Lords.

[**Lord Mustill**, having said that the decision of the Court of Appeal was founded on what that court believed to be a general principle that a person should be acquitted as lacking mens rea if his intent 'arose out of circumstances for which he bears no blame', continued:]

My Lords, with every respect I must suggest that no such principle exists or, until the present case, had ever in modern times been thought to exist. Each offence consists of a prohibited act or omission coupled with whatever state of mind is called for by the statute or rule of the common law which cre-ates the offence. In those offences which are not absolute the state of mind which the prosecution must prove to have underlain the act or omission—the 'mental element'—will in the majority of cases be such as to attract disapproval. The mental element will then be the mark of what may properly be called a 'guilty mind'. The professional burglar is guilty in a moral as well as a legal sense; he intends to break into the house to steal, and most would confidently assert that this is wrong. But this will not always be so. In respect of some offences the mind of the defendant, and still less his moral judgment, may not be engaged at all. In others, although a mental activity must be the motive power for the pro-hibited act or omission the activity may be of such a kind or degree that society at large would not criticise the defendant's conduct severely or even criticise it at all. Such cases are not uncommon. Yet to assume that contemporary moral judgments affect the criminality of the act, as distinct from the punishment appropriate to the crime once proved, is to be misled by the expression 'mens rea', the ambiguity of which has been the subject of complaint for more than a century. Certainly, the 'mens' of the defendant must usually be involved in the offence; but the epithet 'rea' refers to the criminality of the act in which the mind is engaged, not to its moral character. If support from the commentators for this proposition is necessary it may be found in Smith and Hogan *Criminal Law* (7th edn, 1992), pp 79–80, Glanville Williams *Textbook of Criminal Law* (2nd edn, 1983), p 221 and also p 75 and *Russell on Crime* (12th edn, 1964), vol 1, pp 80, 86.

My Lords, it is hard to discuss the respondent's contrary argument at length, for no decided case has been cited to support it; nor indeed was any cited against it, and this is not surprising, since there can have been few occasions in modern times when the dissociation between the mental and the moral aspects of a crime has been doubted. By coincidence, however, this very question has recently been considered by the Judicial Committee of the Privy Council. In *Yip Chiu-cheung v R* [1994] 2 All ER 924, [1995] 1 AC 111 the appellant was charged with conspiracy to traffic in a dangerous drug, contrary to the common law and s 4 of the Dangerous Drugs Ordinance of Hong Kong. So far as material the facts were as follows. The case for the prosecution was that the appellant had a series of meetings in Thailand with a man named Needham, who unknown to the appellant was an undercover drug enforcement officer of the United States of America. In the course of these meetings it was arranged that Needham would act as courier to carry a consignment of drugs by air from Hong Kong to Australia, the plan being that Needham would travel to Hong Kong, collect the drugs and fly on to Australia. Needham said that throughout his dealings with the appellant he kept the authorities in Hong Kong and Australia informed of the plans and they agreed that he would not be prevented from carrying the drugs out of Hong Kong and into Australia. Although Needham fully intended to carry it out this scheme foundered for practical reasons and he never in fact went to Hong Kong. On an appeal against conviction one of the arguments for the appellant was that he could not be guilty of conspiring with Needham since Needham himself had committed no offence. In an opinion delivered by Lord Griffiths after the conclusion of the arguments in the present appeal, the Board dismissed this contention in the following terms (at 927–928):

> 'On the principal ground of appeal it was submitted that the trial judge and the Court of Appeal were wrong to hold that Needham, the undercover agent, could be a conspirator because he lacked the necessary mens rea or guilty mind required for the offence of conspiracy. It was urged upon their Lordships that no moral guilt attached to the undercover agent who was at all times acting courageously and with the best of motives in attempting to infiltrate and bring to justice a gang of criminal drug dealers. In these circumstances it was argued that it would be wrong to treat the agent as having any criminal intent, and reliance was placed upon a passage in the speech of Lord Bridge of Harwich in *R v Anderson* [1985] 2 All ER 961 at 965 [below, p **498**]; but in that case Lord Bridge was dealing with a different situation from that which exists in the present case. There may be many cases in which undercover police officers or other law enforcement agents pretend to join a conspiracy in order to gain information about the plans of the criminals, with no intention of taking any part in the planned crime but rather with the intention of providing information that will frustrate it. It was to this situation that Lord Bridge was referring in *Anderson*. The crime of conspiracy requires two or more persons to commit an unlawful act with the intention of carrying it out. It is the intention to carry out the crime that constitutes the necessary mens rea for the offence. As Lord Bridge pointed out, an undercover agent who has no intention of committing the crime lacks the necessary mens rea to be a conspirator. The facts of the present case are quite different. Nobody can doubt that Needham was acting courageously and with the best of motives; he was trying to break a drug ring. But equally there can be no doubt that the method he chose and in which the police in Hong Kong acquiesced involved the commission of the criminal offence of trafficking in drugs by exporting heroin from Hong Kong without a licence. Needham intended to commit that offence by carrying the heroin through the customs and on to the aeroplane bound for Australia.'

I would therefore reject that part of the respondent's argument which treats the absence of moral fault on the part of the appellant as sufficient in itself to negative the necessary mental element of the offence.

Before proceeding to the next stage two remarks must be made. The first is that in the passage above-quoted the Court of Appeal echoed part of a dictum in *Pearson's Case* (1835) 2 Lew CC 144, 168 ER 1108: 'If a party be made drunk by stratagem, or the fraud of another, he is not responsible.' If it is an essential part of the reasoning of the court that the intervention of a third party is involved I must join with Sir John Smith in pointing out that a loss of self-control through the acts of a third party does not in general constitute a defence, as witness the example given by Sir John [[1993] Crim LR 784] of a man who severely injures the victim when enraged by lies told by a third party against the victim. In such a case there is substantial mitigation but no defence recognised by law. Secondly I have felt some concern about whether, in the discussion so far, the principle relied upon has been correctly stated. That counsel was arguing for the proposition that mens rea is to be equated with moral fault is clear, for he gave as an example of the absence of mens rea a mother who took goods from a supermarket without payment in order to feed a starving child: an example which in fact demonstrates as clearly as any could the difference between mitigation and defence. I have however wondered whether the Court of Appeal meant something different and more narrow, namely that there is no mens rea if the intent is set in motion by a condition which the defendant did not bring about by his own deliberate act. This proposition was not separately argued and I hesitate to say anything about it, except that if it were right as a matter of general law an irresistible impulse brought about by an inherent medical condition would, aside from all questions of insanity and diminished responsibility, be a defence at common law; which it is not.

Appeal allowed

Other aspects of this case are considered below, p **188**.

Notes and questions

1. The Court of Appeal said that 'A man is not responsible for a condition produced by "strategem or the fraud of another".' The man is not responsible *for the condition*; but does it follow that he is not responsible for acts done in that condition? Iago's strategem and fraud caused Othello's jealousy, which caused him to kill Desdemona; but would not Othello be properly convicted of murder?

2. Writing after the decision of the Court of Appeal but before that of the House of Lords in *Kingston*, G. R. Sullivan argued that *Kingston* exemplifies 'a welcome readiness to acquit rather than merely mitigate despite the presence of conventional mens rea and the absence of compelled behaviour. The essence of non-culpability would appear to be that D is in a state of unblameworthy disequilibrium and in that condition engages in untypical behaviour which is essentially the product of the exceptional circumstances prevailing at the time of the offence': [1994] Crim LR 272 at 274. Does this opinion provide the basis for a workable defence to crime?

3. In *Dodman* [1998] 2 Cr App R 338, C-MAC, D was convicted of conduct contrary to good order and air-force discipline, contrary to s 59 of the Air Force Act 1955. His offence consisted in taking full-time civilian employment while still serving in the RAF and signing himself into an RAF station mess as being on duty there, which was not true. The Court-Martial was directed, in accordance with the Manual of Air Force Law, that they must be satisfied that D knew his conduct was 'blameworthy', in that he knew or ought to have known that his conduct was wrongful. It was held that the Manual was seriously misleading. Mens rea does not involve blameworthiness. Here it consisted in D's intention to

do those acts (basic mens rea) which were objectively contrary to good order and air-force discipline, whether or not he knew that.

4. It is only by examining the definition of the particular crime that we can learn what kind of fault, if any, is required. The next question is what do the fault terms ('intention', etc) mean.

2. INTENTION

The word 'intention' and the phrase 'with intent to' are commonly found in the definition of offences. There has been much controversy as to the proper meaning of intention. Some, including Sir John Salmond and Dr J. W. C. Turner, thought that a result is intended only when it is desired.

At the other extreme, it has sometimes been maintained that a result is intended where it is not desired but is foreseen by a person as a *probable* result of his act. This opinion appeared to have had the approval of a majority of the House of Lords in *Hyam v DPP* [1975] AC 55, p **562**, below. The House did not, however, decide anything about the nature of intention. They did decide that a person has the mens rea of murder if, when he does the act which kills, he knows that it is highly probable that he will cause death or grievous bodily harm. Ackner J directed the jury to that effect and his direction was held by the majority of the House to be correct. Ackner J described that state of mind as 'the necessary intent'. The House, though agreeing that this was the mens rea of murder, did not decide that it was 'intent'. Lord Hailsham, one of the majority, emphatically said that it was not. See below, p **563**, Viscount Dilhorne and Lord Cross, though disposed to think it did amount to intention, decided only that it was a sufficient mens rea for murder. The minority differed only as to what it is that must be foreseen. They agreed that it was sufficient that the relevant result (in their opinion, death, not merely grievous bodily harm) should be foreseen as probable. Lord Diplock (one of the minority), however, took a view of the ratio decidendi different from that stated above because he said in *Whitehouse; Lemon* [1979] AC 617 at 638:

When Stephen (*History of the Criminal Law of England*) was writing in 1883, he did not then regard it as settled law that, where intention to produce a particular result was a necessary element of an offence, no distinction was to be drawn in law between the state of mind of one who did an act because he desired it to produce that particular result and the state of mind of one who, when he did the act, was aware that it was likely to produce that result but was prepared to take the risk that it might do so, in order to achieve some other purpose which provided his motive for doing what he did. It is by now well-settled law that both states of mind constitute 'intention' in the sense in which that expression is used in the definition of a crime whether at common law or in a statute. Any doubts on this matter were finally laid to rest by the decision of this House in *R v Hyam* [*Hyam v DPP*] [1975] AC 55.

In the next case, *Moloney*, the House began with the assumption that the mens rea of murder is an intention to kill or to cause grievous bodily harm. Consequently, the question in issue *was* the meaning of intention.

R v Moloney
[1985] 1 All ER 1025, House of Lords

(Lord Hailsham LC, Lords Fraser, Edmund-Davies, Keith and Bridge)

The appellant (M) and his stepfather (S) drank heavily at the ruby wedding anniversary of the appellant's maternal grandparents. The rest of the family retired at 1 am but M and S remained and were heard laughing and talking in an apparently friendly way until nearly 4 am when a shot rang out. M telephoned the police, saying, 'I've just murdered my father.' He stated that they had had a disagreement as to who was quicker at loading and firing a shotgun. At S's request he got two shotguns and cartridges. M was first to load. S said 'I didn't think you'd got the guts, but if you have pull the trigger.' M stated 'I didn't aim the gun. I just pulled the trigger and he was dead.'

Stephen Brown J directed the jury that the prosecution had to prove that M intended to kill S or to cause him some really serious injury. He gave the following direction on intent:

When the law requires that something must be proved to have been done with a particular intent, it means this: a man intends the consequence of his voluntary act (a) when he desires it to happen, whether or not he foresees that it probably will happen and (b) when he foresees that it will probably happen, whether he desires it or not.

M was convicted of murder and his appeal was dismissed by the Court of Appeal. He appealed to the House of Lords.

Lord Hailsham LC and Lords Fraser, Edmund-Davies and Keith said that they agreed with the speech of Lord Bridge.

Lord Bridge, having held that the direction given by Stephen Brown J was unsatisfactory and potentially misleading, continued:

The golden rule should be that, when directing a jury on the mental element necessary in a crime of specific intent, the judge should avoid any elaboration or paraphrase of what is meant by intent, and leave it to the jury's good sense to decide whether the accused acted with the necessary intent, unless the judge is convinced that, on the facts and having regard to the way the case has been presented to the jury in evidence and argument, some further explanation or elaboration is strictly necessary to avoid misunderstanding. In trials for murder or wounding with intent, I find it very difficult to visualise a case where any such explanation or elaboration could be required, if the offence consisted of a direct attack on the victim with a weapon, except possibly the case where the accused shot at A and killed B, which any first year law student could explain to a jury in the simplest of terms. Even where the death results indirectly from the act of the accused, I believe the cases that will call for a direction by reference to foresight of consequences will be of extremely rare occurrence. I am in full agreement with the view expressed by Viscount Dilhorne that, in [*Hyam v DPP*] [1975] AC 55, 82 itself, if the issue of intent had been left without elaboration, no reasonable jury could have failed to convict. I find it difficult to understand why the prosecution did not seek to support the conviction, as an alternative to their main submission, on the ground that there had been no actual miscarriage of justice.

I do not, of course, by what I have said in the foregoing paragraph, mean to question the necessity, which frequently arises, to explain to a jury that intention is something quite distinct from motive or desire. But this can normally be quite simply explained by reference to the case before the court or, if necessary, by some homely example. A man who, at London airport, boards a plane which he knows to be bound for Manchester, clearly intends to travel to Manchester, even though Manchester is the last place he wants to be and his motive for boarding the plane is simply to escape pursuit. The possibility that the plane may have engine trouble and be diverted to Luton does not affect the matter. By boarding the Manchester plane, the man conclusively demonstrates his intention to go there, because it is a moral certainty that that is where he will arrive....

[Rejecting the suggestion in *DPP v Smith* that the Act, to amount to murder, must be 'aimed at' someone, Lord Bridge continued:]

But what of the terrorist who plants a time bomb in a public building and gives timely warning to enable the public to be evacuated? Assume that he knows that, following evacuation, it is virtually certain that a bomb disposal squad will attempt to defuse the bomb. In the event the bomb explodes and kills a bomb disposal expert. In our present troubled times, this is an all too tragically realistic illustration. Can it, however, be said that in this case the bomb was 'aimed' at the bomb disposal expert?...

Starting from the proposition established by *R v Vickers* [1957] 2 All ER 741, [1957] 2 QB 664, as modified by *DPP v Smith* [1961] AC 290 that the mental element in murder requires proof of an intention to kill or cause really serious injury, the first fundamental question to be answered is whether there is any rule of substantive law that foresight by the accused of one of those eventualities as a probable consequence of his voluntary act, where the probability can be defined as exceeding a certain degree, is equivalent or alternative to the necessary intention. I would answer this question in the negative....

I am firmly of opinion that foresight of consequences, as an element bearing on the issue of intention in murder, or indeed any other crime of specific intent, belongs, not to the substantive law, but to the law of evidence. Here again I am happy to find myself aligned with my noble and learned friend, Lord Hailsham of St Marylebone LC, in [*Hyam v DPP*] [1974] 2 All ER 41, [1975] AC 55, where he said, at p 65: 'Knowledge or foresight is at the best material which entitles or compels a jury to draw the necessary inference as to intention.' A rule of evidence which judges for more than a century found of the utmost utility in directing juries was expressed in the maxim: 'A man is presumed to intend the natural and probable consequences of his acts.' In *DPP v Smith* [1961] AC 290 your Lordships' House, by treating this rule of evidence as creating an irrebuttable presumption and thus elevating it, in effect, to the status of a rule of substantive law, predictably provoked the intervention of Parliament by section 8 of the Criminal Justice Act 1967 [below, p **179**] to put the issue of intention back where it belonged, viz, in the hands of the jury, 'drawing such inferences from the evidence as appear proper in the circumstances.' I do not by any means take the conjunction of the verbs 'intended or foresaw' and 'intend or foresee' in that section as an indication that Parliament treated them as synonymous; on the contrary, two verbs were needed to connote two different states of mind.

I think we should now no longer speak of presumptions in this context but rather of inferences. In the old presumption that a man intends the natural and probable consequences of his acts the important word is 'natural'. This word conveys the idea that in the ordinary course of events a certain act will lead to a certain consequence unless something unexpected supervenes to prevent it. One might almost say that, if a consequence is natural, it is really otiose to speak of it as also being probable.

Section 8 of the Criminal Justice Act 1967 leaves us at liberty to go back to the decisions before that of this House in *DPP v Smith* [1961] AC 290 and it is here, I believe, that we can find a sure, clear, intelligible and simple guide to the kind of direction that should be given to a jury in the exceptional case where it is necessary to give guidance as to how, on the evidence, they should approach the issue of intent.

I know of no clearer exposition of the law than that in the judgment of the Court of Criminal Appeal (Lord Goddard CJ, Atkinson and Cassels JJ) delivered by Lord Goddard CJ in *R v Steane* [1947] KB 997 where he said, at p 1004:

> 'No doubt, if the prosecution prove an act the natural consequence of which would be a certain result and no evidence or explanation is given, then a jury may, on a proper direction, find that the prisoner is guilty of doing the act with the intent alleged, but if on the totality of the evidence there is room for more than one view as to the intent of the prisoner, the jury should be directed that it is for the prosecution to prove the intent to the jury's satisfaction, and if, on a review of the whole evidence, they either think that the intent did not exist or they are left in doubt as to the intent, the prisoner is entitled to be acquitted.'

In the rare cases in which it is necessary to direct a jury by reference to foresight of consequences, I do not believe it is necessary for the judge to do more than invite the jury to consider two questions.

First, was death or really serious injury in a murder case (or whatever relevant consequence must be proved to have been intended in any other case) a natural consequence of the defendant's voluntary act? Secondly, did the defendant foresee that consequence as being a natural consequence of his act? The jury should then be told that if they answer yes to both questions it is a proper inference for them to draw that he intended that consequence.

Appeal allowed

Note

Moloney is expressed to apply to 'specific intents' generally—that is (probably), any requirement of intention as distinct from recklessness or lesser forms of fault—and was soon applied to the 'intent to cause the residential occupier of any premises ... to give up the occupation of the premises' required by s 1(3)(a) of the Protection from Eviction Act 1977: *AMK (Property Management) Ltd* [1985] Crim LR 600, CA.

The terrorist and the bomb

Lord Bridge's example (above, p 122) assumes that the terrorist is guilty of murder. The terrorist intends the bomb squad to attempt to defuse the bomb because he knows that it is a virtually certain result of his act that they will do so. But can it be said that he knows that death or serious injury is virtually certain, highly probable, or even probable? Do officers in charge of bomb squads send their men and themselves to virtually certain death? (If a bomb goes off while being defused, the chances of escaping without serious injury are negligible but it may be successfully defused.) Cf the Fourteenth Report of the Criminal Law Revision Committee where it is proposed that an extension of the law of murder is necessary if the terrorist envisaged is to be guilty of that crime. See A. Pedain, 'Intention and the Terrorist Example' [2003] Crim LR 579 (below).

A possible justification

A result which is desired is intended, even though the actor knows that the chances of achieving it are remote. Because he wants to kill V, he takes great care in aiming a gun at him and pulling the trigger; but V is half a mile away and he knows his chances of hitting him are remote. Surely, he intends to kill V. A result which is known to be an inevitable concomitant of the desired result must also be intended. A much used illustration (see draft Code, illustration 18(ii)) is that of D who plants a bomb in a plane, timed to explode in mid-Atlantic and destroy the cargo in order to enable him to obtain the insurance money. D wishes the crew no ill—he would be delighted if they should, by some miracle, escape—but he knows that, if his plan succeeds, their deaths are, for all practical purposes, inevitable. It is generally agreed that D intends to kill the crew. Suppose, however, that D knows that this particular type of bomb has a 50 per cent failure rate. There is an even chance that the bomb will not go off. He still intends to destroy the cargo because that is what he wants to do. Does it not follow that he also intends to kill the crew? This is neither a certain result nor a desired result but it is suggested that it is enough that it is the inevitable concomitant of a desired result. Lord Bridge's terrorist of course wants the bomb to go off. If he wants it to go off at a time when he knows the bomb squad will be attempting to defuse it, the case is indistinguishable from that of the bomb in the plane; but if he is merely indifferent whether the squad will be working on the bomb at the time, it is difficult to see that he intends to kill or injure them.

R v Hancock and Shankland
[1986] 1 All ER 641, House of Lords

(Lords Scarman, Keith of Kinkel, Roskill, Brightman and Griffiths)

Hancock (H) and Shankland (S) were miners on strike. They objected to a miner (X) going to work. X was going to work in a taxi driven by the deceased, Wilkie (W). H and S pushed a concrete block weighing 46 lbs and a concrete post weighing 65 lbs from a bridge over the road along which X was being driven by W with a police escort. The block struck the taxi's windscreen and killed W. H and S were prepared to plead guilty to manslaughter but the Crown decided to pursue the charge of murder. The defence was that H and S intended to block the road but not to kill or do serious bodily harm to anyone. Mann J directed the jury in accordance with the *Moloney* 'guidelines', p **123**, above.

H and S were convicted of murder. The Court of Appeal quashed their conviction. The Crown appealed to the House of Lords.

[**Lord Scarman** having reviewed *Moloney*:]

It is only when Lord Bridge of Harwich turned to the task of formulating guidelines that difficulty arises. It is said by the Court of Appeal that the guidelines by omitting any express reference to probability are ambiguous and may well lead a jury to a wrong conclusion. The omission was deliberate. Lord Bridge omitted the adjective 'probable' from the time-honoured formula 'foresight of the natural and probable consequences of his acts' because he thought that 'If a consequence is natural, it is really otiose to speak of it as also being probable' [1985] AC 905, 929B. But is it?

Lord Bridge of Harwich did not deny the importance of probability. He put it thus, p 925H:

> 'But looking on their facts at the decided cases where a crime of specific intent was under consideration, including *Hyam v DPP* [1974] 2 All ER 41, [1975] AC 55 itself, they suggest to me that the probability of the consequence taken to have been foreseen must be little short of overwhelming before it will suffice to establish the necessary intent.'

In his discussion of the relationship between foresight and intention, Lord Bridge of Harwich reviewed the case law since the passing of the Homicide Act 1957 and concluded at p 928F that

> 'foresight of consequences, as an element bearing on the issue of intention in murder, or indeed any other crime of specific intent, belongs, not to the substantive law, but to the law of evidence.'

He referred to the rule of evidence that a man is presumed to intend the natural and probable consequences of his acts, and went on to observe that the House of Lords in *Smith's* case [1960] 3 All ER 161, [1961] AC 290 had treated the presumption as irrebuttable, but that Parliament intervened by section 8 of the Criminal Justice Act 1967 to return the law to the path from which it had been diverted, leaving the presumption as no more than an inference open to the jury to draw if in all the circumstances it appears to them proper to draw it.

Yet he omitted any reference in his guidelines to probability. He did so because he included probability in the meaning which he attributed to 'natural'. My Lords, I very much doubt whether a jury without further explanation would think that 'probable' added nothing to 'natural'. I agree with the Court of Appeal that the probability of a consequence is a factor of sufficient importance to be drawn specifically to the attention of the jury and to be explained. In a murder case where it is necessary to direct a jury on the issue of intent by reference to foresight of consequences the probability of death or serious injury resulting from the act done may be critically important. Its importance will depend on the degree of probability: if the likelihood that death or serious injury will result is high, the probability of that result may, as Lord Bridge of Harwich noted and the Lord Chief Justice emphasised, be seen as overwhelming evidence of the existence of the intent to kill or injure. Failure to explain the relevance of probability may, therefore, mislead a jury into thinking that it is of little or no importance and into concentrating exclusively on the causal link between the act and its consequence. In framing his guidelines Lord Bridge of Harwich emphasised [1985] AC 905, 929G, that he did not believe it necessary to do more than to invite the jury to consider his two questions. Neither question makes any reference (beyond the use of the word 'natural') to probability. I am not surprised that when in this case the judge faithfully followed this guidance the jury found themselves perplexed and unsure. In my judgment, therefore, the *Moloney* guidelines as they stand are unsafe and misleading. They require a reference to probability. They also require an explanation that the greater the probability of a consequence the more likely it is that the consequence was foreseen and that if that consequence was foreseen the greater the probability is that that consequence was also intended. But juries also require to be reminded that the decision is theirs to be reached upon a consideration of all the evidence.

Accordingly, I accept the view of the Court of Appeal that the *Moloney* guidelines are defective. I am, however, not persuaded that guidelines of general application, albeit within a limited class of case, are wise or desirable. The Lord Chief Justice formulated in this case guidelines for the assistance of juries but for the reason which follows, I would not advise their use by trial judges when summing up to a jury....

[**Lords Keith**, **Roskill**, **Brightman** and **Griffiths** agreed.]

Appeal dismissed

R v Nedrick

[1986] 3 All ER 1, Court of Appeal, Criminal Division

(Lord Lane CJ, Leggatt and Kennedy JJ)

Nedrick, having threatened to 'burn out' a woman against whom he bore a grudge, poured paraffin through the letter box of her house and set it alight. The woman's child died in the fire. Nedrick was charged with murder. The direction given to the jury before the publication of the speeches in *Moloney*, was based on the passage in *Archbold* which was disapproved in that case and was to the effect that the defendant was guilty of murder if he knew that it was highly probable that his act would result in serious bodily injury to somebody in the house. The Court of Appeal quashed the conviction and substituted a verdict of manslaughter.

Lord Lane CJ. We have endeavoured to crystallise the effect of their Lordships' speeches in *R v Moloney* and *R v Hancock* in a way which we hope may be helpful to judges who have to handle this type of case.

It may be advisable first of all to explain to the jury that a man may intend to achieve a certain result whilst at the same time not desiring it to come about....[Lord Lane discussed Lord Bridge's illustration of the man boarding a plane at London Airport, above, p **121**, and Lord Scarman's criticism of the *Moloney* guidelines in *Hancock*].

Where the charge is murder and in the rare cases where the simple direction is not enough, the jury should be directed that they are not entitled to infer the necessary intention unless they feel sure that death or serious bodily harm was a virtual certainty (barring some unforeseen intervention) as a result of the defendant's actions and that the defendant appreciated that such was the case.

Where a man realises that it is for all practical purposes inevitable that his actions will result in death or serious harm, the inference may be irresistible that he intended that result, however little he may have desired or wished it to happen. The decision is one for the jury to be reached on a consideration of all the evidence.

Appeal allowed

R v Woollin
[1998] 4 All ER 103, House of Lords

(Lords Browne-Wilkinson, Nolan, Steyn, Hoffmann and Hope of Craighead)

The facts are stated by Lord Steyn, with whose speech Lord Noland and Lord Hope agreed. Lord Browne-Wilkinson and Lord Hoffmann agreed that the appeal should be allowed.

Lord Steyn. The appellant lost his temper and threw his three-month-old son on to a hard surface. His son sustained a fractured skull and died. The appellant was charged with murder. The Crown did not contend that the appellant desired to kill his son or to cause him serious injury. The issue was whether the appellant nevertheless had the intention to cause serious harm. The appellant denied that he had any such intention. Subject to one qualification, the Recorder of Leeds (Judge Savill QC) summed up in accordance with the guidance given by Lord Lane CJ in *R v Nedrick* [1986] 3 All ER 1 at 4…

But towards the end of his summing up the judge directed the jury that if they were satisfied that the appellant—

> 'must have realised and appreciated when he threw that child that there was a substantial risk that he would cause serious injury to it, then it would be open to you to find that he intended to cause injury to the child and you should convict him of murder.'

The jury found that the appellant had the necessary intention; they rejected a defence of provocation; and they convicted the appellant of murder. On appeal to the Court of Appeal (Criminal Division) the appellant's principal ground of appeal was that by directing the jury in terms of substantial risk the judge unacceptably enlarged the mental element of murder. The Court of Appeal ([1997] 1 Cr App R 97) rejected this ground of appeal and dismissed the appeal. Giving the judgment of the Court of Appeal Roch LJ (at 107) observed about *R v Nedrick* that—

> 'although the use of the phrase "a virtual certainty" may be desirable and may be necessary, it is only necessary where the evidence of intent is limited to the admitted actions of the accused and the consequences of those actions. It is not obligatory to use that phrase or one that means the same thing in cases such as the present where there is other evidence for the jury to consider.'

[Lord Steyn reviewed the cases leading up to the decision in *Nedrick*.]

The direct attack on *Nedrick*
It is now possible to consider the Crown's direct challenge to the correctness of *R v Nedrick*. First, the Crown argued that *R v Nedrick* prevents the jury from considering all the evidence in the case relevant to intention. The argument is that this is contrary to the provisions of s 8 of the 1967 Act. This provision reads:

> 'A court or jury, in determining whether a person has committed an offence,—(a) shall not be bound in law to infer that he intended or foresaw a result of his actions by reasons only of its being a natural and probable consequence of those actions; but (b) shall decide whether he did intend or foresee that result by reference to all the evidence, drawing such inferences from the evidence as appear proper in the circumstances.'

Paragraph (a) is an instruction to the judge and is not relevant to the issues on this appeal. The Crown's argument relied on para (b), which is concerned with the function of the jury. It is no more than a legislative instruction that in considering their findings on intention or foresight the jury must take into account all relevant evidence: see Professor Edward Griew 'States of mind, presumptions and inferences' in *Criminal Law: Essays in Honour of J C Smith* (1987) pp 68, 76–77. *R v Nedrick* is undoubtedly concerned with the mental element which is sufficient for murder. So, for that matter, in their different ways were *Smith, Hyam, Moloney* and *Hancock*. But, as Lord Lane CJ emphasised in the last sentence of *R v Nedrick* [1986] 3 All ER 1 at 4: 'The decision is one for the jury to be reached on a consideration of all the evidence.' *R v Nedrick* does not prevent a jury from considering all the evidence: it merely stated what state of mind (in the absence of a purpose to kill or to cause serious harm) is sufficient for murder. I would therefore reject the Crown's first argument.

In the second place the Crown submitted that *R v Nedrick* is in conflict with the decision of the House in *R v Hancock*. Counsel argued that in order to bring some coherence to the process of determining intention Lord Lane CJ specified a minimum level of foresight, namely virtual certainty. But that is not in conflict with the decision in *R v Hancock*, which, apart from disapproving Lord Bridge's 'natural consequence' model direction, approved *R v Moloney* in all other respects. And in *R v Moloney* [1985] 1 All ER 1025 at 1036 Lord Bridge said that if a person foresees the probability of a consequence as little short of overwhelming this 'will suffice to *establish* the necessary intent' (my emphasis). Nor did the House in *R v Hancock* rule out the framing of model directions by the Court of Appeal for the assistance of trial judges. I would therefore reject the argument that the guidance given in *R v Nedrick* was in conflict with the decision of the House in *R v Hancock*.

The Crown did not argue that as a matter of policy foresight of a virtual certainty is too narrow a test in murder. Subject to minor qualifications, the decision in *R v Nedrick* was widely welcomed by distinguished academic writers: see Professor J C Smith QC's commentary on *R v Nedrick* [1986] Crim LR 742 at 743–744, Glanville Williams 'The mens rea for murder: leave it alone' (1989) 105 LQR 387, J R Spencer 'Murder in the dark: a glimmer of light?' [1986] CLJ 366–367 and Ashworth *Principles of Criminal Law* (2nd edn, 1995) p 172. It is also of interest that it is very similar to the threshold of being aware that it *will* occur 'in the ordinary course of events' in the Law Commission's draft Criminal Code (see *Criminal Law: Legislating the Criminal Code: Offences against the Person and General Principles* (Law Com No 218 (1993) (Cm 2370), App A (Draft Criminal Law Bill with Explanatory Notes) pp 90–91): cf also Professor J C Smith QC 'A note on "intention"' [1990] Crim LR 85 at 86. Moreover, over a period of 12 years since *R v Nedrick* the test of foresight of virtual certainty has apparently caused no practical difficulties. It is simple and clear. It is true that it may exclude a conviction of murder in the often cited terrorist example where a member of the bomb disposal team is killed. In such a case it may realistically be said that the terrorist did not foresee the killing of a member of the bomb disposal team as a virtual certainty. That may be a consequence of not framing the principle in terms of risk-taking. Such cases ought to cause no substantial difficulty since immediately below murder there is available a verdict of manslaughter which may attract in the discretion of the court a life sentence. In any event, as Lord Lane eloquently argued in a debate in the House of Lords, to frame a principle for particular difficulties regarding terrorism 'would produce corresponding injustices which would be very hard to eradicate' (see 512 HL Official Report (5th series) col 480). I am satisfied that the *Nedrick* test, which was squarely based on the decision of the House in *R v Moloney*, is pitched at the right level of foresight.

The argument that *Nedrick* has limited application

The Court of Appeal ([1997] 1 Cr App R 97 at 107) held that the phrase 'a virtual certainty' should be confined to cases where the evidence of intent is limited to admitted actions of the accused and the consequences of those actions. It is not obligatory where there is other evidence to consider. The Crown's alternative submission on the appeal was to the same effect. This distinction would introduce yet another complication into a branch of the criminal law where simplicity is of supreme importance. The distinction is dependent on the vagaries of the evidence in particular cases. Moreover, a jury may reject the other evidence to which the Court of Appeal refers. And in preparing his summing up a judge could not ignore this possibility. If the Court of Appeal's view is right, it might compel a judge to pose different tests depending on what evidence the jury accepts. For my part, and with the greatest respect, I have to say that this distinction would be likely to produce great practical difficulties. But, most importantly, the distinction is not based on any principled view regarding the mental element in murder. Contrary to the view of the Court of Appeal, I would also hold that s 8(b) of the 1967 Act does not compel such a result.

In my view the ruling of the court of Appeal was wrong. It may be appropriate to give a direction in accordance with *R v Nedrick* in any case in which the defendant may not have desired the result of his act. But I accept that the trial judge is best placed to decide what direction is required by the circumstances of the case.

[Lord Steyn said that the conviction of murder was unsafe and must be quashed.]

The status of *Nedrick*

In my view Lord Lane CJ's judgment in *R v Nedrick* provided valuable assistance to trial judges. The model direction is by now a tried and tested formula. Trial judges ought to continue to use it. On matters of detail I have three observations, which can best be understood if I set out again the relevant part of Lord Lane CJ's judgment. It was:

> '(A) When determining whether the defendant had the necessary intent, it may therefore be helpful for a jury to ask themselves two questions. (1) How probable was the consequence which resulted from the defendant's voluntary act? (2) Did he foresee that consequence? If he did not appreciate that death or serious harm was likely to result from his act, he cannot have intended to bring it about. If he did, but thought that the risk to which he was exposing the person killed was only slight, then it may be easy for the jury to conclude that he did not intend to bring about that result. On the other hand, if the jury are satisfied that at the material time the defendant recognised that death or serious harm would be virtually certain (barring some unforeseen intervention) to result from his voluntary act, then that is a fact from which they may find it easy to infer that he intended to kill or do serious bodily harm, even though he may not have had any desire to achieve that result ... (B) Where the charge is murder and in the rare cases where the simple direction is not enough, the jury should be directed that they are not entitled to infer the necessary intention unless they feel sure that death or serious bodily harm was a virtual certainty (barring some unforeseen intervention) as a result of the defendant's actions and that the defendant appreciated that such was the case. (C) Where a man realises that it is for all practical purposes inevitable that his actions will result in death or serious harm, the inference may be irresistible that he intended that result, however little he may have desired or wished it to happen. The decision is one for the jury to be reached on a consideration of all the evidence.' (See [1986] 3 All ER 1 at 3–4.)

First, I am persuaded by the speech of my noble and learned friend Lord Hope of Craighead that it is unlikely, if ever, to be helpful to direct the jury in terms of the two questions set out in (A). I agree that these questions may detract from the clarity of the critical direction in (B). Secondly, in their writings previously cited Glanville Williams, Professor Smith and Andrew Ashworth observed that the use of the words 'to infer' in (B) may detract from the clarity of the model direction. I agree. I would substitute the words 'to find'. Thirdly, the first sentence of (C) does not form part of the model direction. But it would always be right for the just to say, as Lord Lane CJ put it, that the decision is for the jury upon a consideration of all the evidence in the case.

Notes and questions

1. *Inferring intention from foresight.* The notion that intention can be inferred from foresight goes back at least to Lord Hailsham's speech in *Hyam*. In *Moloney* (above p **122**) Lord Bridge seemed to think that the notion derived support from s 8 of the Criminal

Justice Act 1967. What the section says is that the court or jury must decide whether D 'did intend or foresee that result, drawing such inferences from the evidence as appear proper in the circumstances.'

'The evidence', it seems, is the nature of the act done by D and the relevant circumstances in which it was done—all objective facts. Depending on the nature of those facts, a court or jury might conclude that:

(1) D wanted to cause that result—it was his aim, object or purpose; or—

(2) though he did not want to cause that result—
   (a) he foresaw that he would do so—it was certain or virtually certain to happen; or
   (b) he foresaw that he might—it was (i) highly probable, or (ii) probable, or at least (iii) possible.

None of these alternatives involves inferring one state of mind from another—a notion which some regard as impossible. The question in practice is whether intention is limited to (1) and (2) (a) or extends to (2)(b)(i) or (ii).

2. The House rejects 'infer' in favour of 'find'. Is there any difference?

3. At one point in his speech ([1998] 4 All ER 110 (not in the above extract)) Lord Steyn said 'The effect of the critical direction [in *Nedrick*] is that a result foreseen as virtually certain *is* an intended result' (author's italics). Peter Mirfield argues, [1999] Crim LR 246, that 'we can, as a matter of ordinary language and logic be sure that if I am *entitled* to find A only when B and C are present, I am also entitled not to find it where both are present. Therefore whatever else A (intention) is, it is not B (virtual certainty), nor a combination of the two.' Is Lord Steyn's statement, above, inconsistent with his decision?

4. When a jury finds that D foresaw that the relevant result was virtually certain, by what criteria are they to decide whether to exercise their 'entitlement' to find that it amounted to intention? How should the judge direct them, if they ask?

5. See also the article, 'After *Woollin*' [1999] Crim LR 532 by A. Norrie and below, p **564**.

Matthews and Alleyne
[2003] 2 Cr App R 30 [2003] Crim LR 553, Court of Appeal, Criminal Division

(Rix LJ, Crane J and Maddison HHJ)

M and A were convicted of the robbery, kidnapping and murder of Jonathan. J was attacked on leaving a club in the early hours of the morning, and ultimately thrown off a bridge 25' high into a river 64' wide. J could not swim and drowned. A co-accused gave evidence that J had said he could not swim. One ground of appeal was that the judge had directed the jury that foresight of virtual certainty of consequences *was* intention.

Rix LJ:
[His lordship reviewed the facts and positions taken by the various co defendants]
22 The judge went on to say:

'The prosecution say that the defendants did actually intend to kill, but at least in the case of a non swimmer who was thrown off the middle of a bridge into a river as wide as this was drowning was a virtual certainty, and the defendants appreciated that, and in the absence of any desire, or attempt, to save him, and if they also realised that the others were not going to save him too they must have had the intentions of killing him.'

23 This direction was regarded as incorporating what has become known as the *Nedrick* or *Woollin* direction, after the cases of *R. v Nedrick* (1986) 83 Cr.App.R. 267, [1986] 1 WLR 1025 and *R. v Woollin* [1999] 1 Cr.App.R. 8, [1999] 1 AC 82. The classic form of that direction, repeated in the JSB model direction, is as follows:

'Where the charge is murder and in the rare cases where the simple direction is not enough, the jury should be directed that they are not entitled to find the necessary intention, unless they feel sure that death [or serious bodily harm] was a virtual certainty (barring some unforeseen intervention) as a result of the defendants actions and that the defendant appreciated that such was the case.'

24 We have emphasised the word find in that direction, because the original direction of Lord Lane CJ in *Nedrick* contained the word infer. The only change made by the House of Lords in *Woollin* was to substitute find for infer (see Lord Steyn at pp.20 and 96H and Lord Hope of Craighead at pp. 21 and 97D).

25 The essential ground of appeal argued on behalf of both Alleyne and Matthews is that the judges direction on intent was a misdirection, and that in consequence their convictions for murder are unsafe....

29 .... Two criticisms are here made on behalf of both Alleyne and Matthews. The first is that the alternatives presented to the jury in the judges ... directions ... might, by implication, lead the jury to think that they could convict of murder ... even if they had already rejected ... a specific intention [to kill] actually in the mind/s of the defendants. The second is that ... the judges amended form of a *Woollin* direction is put as a substantive rule of law (will only succeed in proving this intent by making you sure that etc) rather than as a rule of evidence.

30 We will consider this second criticism first, as it is the more general one. Indeed Mr Coker was inclined to concede that there had been a misdirection if, contrary to his primary submission, the speech of Lord Steyn in *Woollin* is to be interpreted as laying down a mere rule of evidence. He submits, however, that acting deliberately with an appreciation of a virtual certainty of death is an intention to kill, and not merely evidence from which intent to kill can be inferred. In this connection he relies on the following matters.

31 In his speech in *Woollin* Lord Steyn reviewed the earlier cases which had considered what state of mind must be found to exist for a conviction of murder where the defendant denied an intent to kill or commit grievous bodily harm, put forward a different intent or purpose for his actions, and yet did so in circumstances which made it difficult to understand how death or grievous bodily harm was not foreseen or appreciated as highly probable or indeed (barring unforeseen interventions) almost inevitable. In *Director of Public Prosecutions v. Smith* (1960) 44 Cr.App.R. 261, [1961] AC 290 the defendant in the course of attempting to avoid arrest had killed a policeman by driving off with the policeman clinging to the car. The House of Lords ruled both that it was sufficient that death or grievous bodily harm was foreseen as likely, and that a defendant foresaw what a reasonable person in his position would have foreseen. The first rule put the threshold for the mental element of murder at a low level, and the second rule introduced an objective test of foresight. Parliament reversed the second rule by s.8 of the Criminal Justice Act 1967, which provides that [his lordship referred to s 8 (above), and *Hyam, Moloney, Hancock, Nedrick* and *Woollin* (above).]

39 Mr Coker for the Crown on this appeal submits that in *Woollin* the House of Lords has finally moved away from a rule of evidence to a rule of substantive law. In this connection he drew attention

to a sentence in Lord Steyn's speech at pp.17 and 93F where he says, immediately after setting out Lord Lane's observations in *Nedrick*, that the effect of the critical direction is that a result foreseen as virtually certain is an intended result.

40 He also relies on what Professor Sir John Smith has to say in his note on *R. v Woollin* [1998] Crim LR 890 and in Smith and Hogan, *Criminal Law*, 10th edition, at 70ff. Thus in the former, Professor Smith said this:

> 'A jury might still fairly ask We are all quite sure that D knew that it was virtually certain that his act would cause death. You tell us we are entitled to find that he intended it. Are we bound to find that? Some of us want to and some do not. How should we decide? The implication appears to be that, even now, they are not so bound. But why not? At one point Lord Steyn says of *Nedrick* "The effect of the critical direction is that a result foreseen as virtually certain is an intended result". If that is right, the only question for the jury is, Did the defendant foresee the result as virtually certain? If he did, he intended it. That, it is submitted is what the law should be; and it now seems that we have at last moved substantially in that direction. The *Nedrick* formula, however, even as modified (entitled to find), involves some ambiguity with the hint of the existence of some ineffable, undefinable, notion of intent, locked in the breasts of the jurors.'

41 Moreover, in the latter treatise (at 72) Professor Smith cites Lord Lane speaking in the debate on the report of the House of Lords Select Committee on Murder (HL Paper, 78-I, 1989) as follows:

> 'in *Nedrick* the court was obliged to phrase matters as it did because of earlier decisions in your Lordships House by which it was bound. We had to tread very gingerly indeed in order not to tread on your Lordships toes. As a result, *Nedrick* was not as clear as it should have been. However, I agree with the conclusions of the committee that intention should be defined in the terms set out in para.195 of the report on p.50. That seems to me to express clearly what in *Nedrick* we failed properly to explain.'

42 The definition referred to, as Smith and Hogan goes on to explain, is that stated in cl.18(b) of the Draft Code (itself referred to by Lord Steyn in *Woollin*) as follows:

> 'A person acts intentionally with respect to a result when he acts either in order to bring it about or being aware that it will occur in the ordinary course of events.'

43 In our judgment, however, the law has not yet reached a definition of intent in murder in terms of appreciation of a virtual certainty. Lord Lane was speaking not of what was decided in *Nedrick* (or in the other cases which preceded it) nor of what was thereafter to be decided in *Woollin*, but of what the law in his opinion should be, as represented by the cl.18(b) definition. Similarly, although the law has progressively moved closer to what Professor Smith has been advocating (see his commentaries in the Criminal Law Review on the various cases discussed above), we do not regard *Woollin* as yet reaching or laying down a substantive rule of law. On the contrary, it is clear from the discussion in *Woollin* as a whole that *Nedrick* was derived from the existing law, at that time ending in *Moloney and Hancock*, and that the critical direction in *Nedrick* was approved, subject to the change of one word.

44 In these circumstances we think that the judge did go further than the law as it stands at present permitted him to go in redrafting the *Nedrick/Woollin* direction into a form where, as Mr Coker accepts (although we have some doubt about this), the jury were directed to find the necessary intent proved provided they were satisfied in the case of any defendant that there was appreciation of the virtual certainty of death. This is to be contrasted with the form of the approved direction which is in terms of not entitled to find the necessary intention, unless.

45 Having said that, however, we think that, once what is required is an appreciation of virtual certainty of death, and not some lesser foresight of merely probable consequences, there is very little to choose between a rule of evidence and one of substantive law. It is probably this thought that led

Lord Steyn to say that a result foreseen as virtually certain is an intended result. Lord Bridge had reflected the same thought when he had said, in *R. v Moloney* (1985) 81 Cr.App.R. 93, 101, [1985] AC 905, 920C, that if the defendant there had had present to his mind, when he pulled the trigger, that his gun was pointing at his stepfathers head at a distance of six feet and its inevitable consequence, then the inference was inescapable, using words in their ordinary, everyday meaning, that he intended to kill his stepfather. Lord Lane had also spoken in *Nedrick* of an irresistible inference.

46 We also think that on the particular facts of this case, reflected in the judges directions, the question of the appellants intentions to save Jonathan from drowning highlight the irresistible nature of the inference or finding of intent to kill, once the jury were sure both that the defendants appreciated the virtual certainty of death (barring some attempt to save him) and that at the time of throwing Jonathan from the bridge they then had no intentions of saving him. If the jury were sure that the appellants appreciated the virtual certainty of Jonathan's death when they threw him from the bridge and also that they then had no intention of saving him from such death, it is impossible to see how the jury could not have found that the appellants intended Jonathan to die.

47 We turn then to the first criticism made of the judges direction on intent to kill, namely that the jury might be led to think that they could convict a defendant ... even if they had not been sure under alternative (i) of this specific intention actually in the mind/s of the defendants. It would perhaps have been better to frame alternative (i) specifically in terms of the Crown's primary case that the defendants purpose or desire had been to kill, to silence, Jonathan. The contrast highlighted by the alternatives would then have been between an intent to kill proved by a finding that the appellants had purposed or desired Jonathan's death and an intent to kill proved by a finding that the appellants appreciated the virtual certainty of his death, whether they purposed or desired it or not. However, we think that the jury could not possibly have misunderstood the alternative cases put before them. The first represented the Crown's primary case, the second its fall-back position, itself a response to the defendants case, at any rate express in the defences of Dawkins and Canepe [the codefendants], that this was merely a terrible prank which had gone disastrously wrong, that they simply had not appreciated the virtual certainty of death.

48 Thus, throughout the direction under consideration, and throughout his summing-up the judge constantly repeated the refrain of the offence of murders need for an intent, here the intent to kill. The judge told the jury that the offence of murder is committed when a person kills another with intent to kill. He emphasised that the prosecution had said from first to last that the defendants intended to kill. He directed them that they had to be sure that at the time Jonathan was thrown from the bridge each defendant then intended to kill him (or was party to a joint enterprise with others, knowing or realising that it was then their intention to kill him). He then directed the jury that the prosecution would only succeed in proving this intent in one of the two alternative ways discussed. He went on to quote prosecution counsel:

> 'Mr Coker said: However, wicked, however cruel, or nauseating, their conduct may have been they are only guilty of murder if they intended to kill Jonathan. I agree with that and, indeed that is the law.'

Appeal dismissed

Notes and questions

1. Care should be taken with the use of the alternative forms of intention—direct and oblique. In *MD* [2004] EWCA Crim 1391 the Court of Appeal described oblique intention as:

designed to help the prosecution fill a gap in the rare circumstances in which a defendant does an act which caused death without the purpose of killing or causing serious injury, but in circumstances where death or serious bodily harm had been a virtual certainty (barring some unforeseen intervention) as a result of the defendant's action and the defendant had appreciated that such was the case. *Woollin* is not designed to make the prosecution's task more difficult, many murderers whose purpose was to kill or cause serious injury would escape conviction if the jury was only given a *Woollin* direction the man who kills another with a gun would be able to escape liability for murder if he could show [this seems to be an error and the court can be presumed to mean the prosecution show] that he was such a bad shot that death or serious bodily harm was not a virtual certainty or that the defendant had thought that death or serious bodily harm was not a virtual certainty.

2. When the oblique intention direction is delivered, what should a judge say to a jury who ask—'what are we seeking to "find" which may turn this state of mind of foresight of virtual certainty into one of intention?' Is the answer that the should look for some undefinable moral aspect to the state of mind?

(1) REFORM OF THE LAW CONCERNING INTENTION

Since *Nedrick* the law concerning intention has been considered in three reports. The Law Commission Report on Codification (April 1989) proposed a definition which would apply, unless the context otherwise requires, to all code offences which require proof of intention. A Select Committee of the House of Lords on Murder and Life Imprisonment (The Nathan Committee, HL Paper 78–1, 24 July 1989) recommended that, for the purposes of the law of murder (the only offence within the Committee's terms of reference), intention should be defined in the lines proposed in the Codification Report.

The Law Commission's Report 'Legislating the Criminal Code: Offences Against the Person and General Principles' (Law Com No 218, 1993) makes proposals in relation only to non-fatal offences against the person. See below (footnotes omitted).

The Commission's proposed definition of intention (set out below) is substantially reproduced in the Home Office consultation paper of February 1998. *Woollin* shows that the definition is, in one respect, too narrow. It was not Woollin's purpose to kill or cause serious injury, so he did not come within cl 1(a)(i); and, clearly, he had no other purpose— except to vent his anger, which is not a purpose to cause a result. So he would not come with para (ii) either. Paragraph (ii) might be amended to read:

…*he knows that* it will occur in the ordinary course of events, or that it would do so if he were to succeed in his purpose of causing some other result.

The italicized words would leave open to the jury the possibility of finding that Woollin intended the result.

'Intention'
Introduction
7.1 Clause 1(a) of the Criminal Law Bill provides for the purposes of the offences in Part I of the Bill that:

'a person acts…"intentionally" with respect to a result when—

(i) it is his purpose to cause it; or

(ii) although it is not his purpose to cause that result, he knows that it would occur in the ordinary course of events if he were to succeed in his purpose of causing some other result.'

7.2 To define 'intention' by statute involves a different policy from that adopted, in the context of the law of homicide, by the House of Lords. However, in that context the absence of definition, whether by statute or in the practice of the courts, has been productive of serious difficulty, in particular in relation to a result of conduct that, although not desired by the actor, is known by him to be the certain, or overwhelmingly likely, outcome of his actions. As the authorities stand the jury, in a case where it appears that the defendant did not desire the relevant result of his actions, are only told that they may nevertheless *infer* [now 'find'] his intention to cause that result if he recognised that result to be a 'virtually certain' consequence of his actions. This form of direction falls short of asserting that such recognition of virtual certainty is in law a case of intention; and thus does not clarify the nature of the state of mind that the jury may 'infer'.

7.3 In LCCP we drew attention to the criticism of that position that had been made not only in the Code Report but also by the Nathan Committee. We therefore proposed that for the purposes of the Criminal Law Bill there should be a statutory definition of intention, and suggested a formula in terms almost identical to those set out above. There was on consultation little disagreement either with the general proposition that 'intention' should be defined for the purposes of the non-fatal offences against the person dealt with in the Bill, or with the terms of the definition that we proposed. We therefore now recommend the adoption of a statutory definition in the terms of clause 1(a) of the Criminal Law Bill.

The basic definition: intention as 'purpose'

7.4 In all but the most unusual case, courts and juries will only be concerned with the basic rule in clause 1(a) (i) of the Criminal Law Bill: that a person acts intentionally with respect to a result when it is his purpose to cause that result.

7.5 The concept of purpose is ideally suited to express the idea of intention in the criminal law, because that law is concerned with results that the defendant causes by his own actions. Those results are intentional, or intentionally caused, on his part when he has sought to bring them about, by making it the purpose of his acts that they should occur. It is for that reason that distinguished judges have naturally spoken of the concept of intention in the criminal law in terms of 'purpose'. We are confident that courts and juries will find the statutory confirmation of this central nature of intention, when that word is used in the definition of offences, both easy and helpful to use.

A special and limited case

7.6 Therefore, in almost all cases when they are dealing with a case of intention, courts will not need to look further than paragraph (i) of clause 1(a). Paragraph (ii) is however aimed at one particular type of case that, it is generally agreed, needs to be treated as a case of 'intention' in law, but which is not covered by paragraph (i) because the actor does not act in order to cause, or with the purpose of causing, the result in question. Because this case is less straightforward than that just discussed it takes up more space in this part of our report than, we have to say, would be justified if the only consideration were the frequency with which the case is likely to trouble courts in practice.

7.7 The point was formulated by Lord Hailsham of St Marylebone in *Hyam*. A person must be treated as intending 'the means as well as the end and the inseparable consequences of the end as well as the means'. If he acts in order to achieve a particular purpose, knowing that that cannot be done without causing another result, he must be held to intend to cause that other result. The other result may be a *pre-condition*: as where D, in order to injure P, throws a brick through a window behind which he knows P to be standing; or it may be a *necessary* concomitant of the first result: as where (to use a much-quoted example) D blows up an aeroplane in flight in order to recover on the insurance covering the cargo, knowing that the crew will inevitably be killed. D intends to break the window and he intends the crew to be killed.

7.8 There is, of course, no absolute certainty in human affairs. D's purpose *might* be achieved without causing the further result; P *might* fling up the window while the brick is in flight; the crew *might* make a miraculous escape by parachute. These, however, are only remote possibilities, as D (if he contemplates them at all) must know. The further result will occur, and D knows that it will occur, 'in the ordinary course of events'. This expression was used in clause 18 of the Draft Code to express the near-inevitability, as appreciated by the actor, of the further result.

7.9 It is desirable to stress, because the point has been misunderstood in some quarters, that this way of defining 'intention' does not have the effect of treating some cases of recklessness as cases of intention by extending liability for an offence requiring intention to every case where the actor foresees the further result as highly likely to occur. On the contrary, the definition extends the meaning of 'intention' only very slightly beyond the primary meaning adopted in clause 1(a)(i) of 'purpose'. The point of the phrase 'in the ordinary course of events' is to ensure that 'intention' covers the case of a person who knows that the achievement of his purpose will *necessarily* cause the further result in question in the absence of some wholly improbable supervening event. The phrase had earlier been used by the CLRC in explaining their use of the word 'intention' in the context of offences against the person. The Nathan Committee recommended adoption of the Draft Code definition for the purpose of the law of murder. The Lord Chief Justice expressed approval of it in the House of Lords debate on that committee's report.

7.10 Reference to 'the ordinary course of events' can, therefore, now be made with some confidence in this part of the definition of 'intention'. That is the approach of clause 1(a)(ii) of the Criminal Law Bill. However, the Bill's definition, while being fundamentally that of the Draft Code, seeks to improve on and tighten the Draft Code in three respects.

7.11 First, in order to re-emphasise that this part of the definition is not dealing with a case of recklessness, it specifically requires the actor to *know*, and not merely to be aware (of a risk), that the further result would occur in the ordinary course of events if he succeeded in his purpose of causing the result at which he was actually aiming.

7.12 Second, the formulation has to cater for the case in which the actor is not sure that his main purpose will be achieved—he cannot be *sure*, for example, that the bomb that he places on the plane will, as he intends, go off in flight. In such a case he does not know that the secondary result (the death of the crew) will occur. Yet he ought to be guilty of murder if the crew do die because he knows that they *will* die *if* the bomb goes off as he intends. So the definition of 'intention' should treat a person as intending a result that he knows to be, in the ordinary course of events, a necessary concomitant of achieving his main purpose *if* that purpose is achieved.

7.13 Third, it is prudent to provide specifically that a result that it is the actor's purpose to *avoid* cannot be intended. The definition adopted in the Draft Code was criticised on this ground in the House of Lords debate on the Nathan Report by Lord Goff of Chieveley. He argued that, since the Draft Code definition spoke in unlimited terms of results that the actor was aware would occur in the ordinary course of events, it would convict of an offence of serious injury, for instance, a man who threw a child from a burning building, knowing that the child would thereby almost inevitably be injured, even though the inevitable consequence of inaction would be the child's death from burning. It might be a matter for some argument whether this case was in fact covered by the definition in the Draft Code, and a judicial commentator on LCCP 122 argued strongly that since such a case would not in practice be prosecuted the Criminal Law Bill should not seek to address it. Nevertheless it is undesirable that there should be any even arguable doubt on that point. The objection is avoided in clause 1(a)(ii) of the Criminal Law Bill, which restricts secondary results that are caused intentionally under its provisions to such results that only occur if the actor succeeds in his primary purpose. In the example just cited, the father (on the assumption that his case legitimately attracts sympathy) has as his purpose to *prevent* injury to the child. He acts to achieve that purpose, however difficult or unlikely that may be the circumstances. If, applying clause 1(a) (ii), he were to succeed in his purpose, injury to the child would, of necessity and by definition, not occur. Clause 1(a)(ii) therefore excludes any suggestion that in a (hypothetical) case of the type mentioned above injuries that in fact occur, though sought to be avoided, were inflicted intentionally.

7.14 The extended definition of 'intention' employed in clause 1(a)(ii) of the Criminal Law Bill thus takes account of the above three points. It makes plain that the definition is not confined to cases where the actor is certain that he will succeed in his principal objective. However, it treats as intended any result that the actor recognises at the time that he acts as inevitable if his purpose is to be achieved; and he is treated thereafter as having intended that result whether or not the purpose at which he aimed is in fact achieved.

R v Steane

[1947] 1 All ER 813, Court of Criminal Appeal

(Lord Goddard CJ, Atkinson and Cassels JJ)

The facts appear in the judgment of the court.

[**Lord Goddard CJ** read the judgment of the court.]

The appellant was convicted at the Central Criminal Court before Henn Collins J on an indictment which charged him under the Defence (General) Regulations, reg 2A, with doing acts likely to assist the enemy with intent to assist the enemy…

The count on which he was convicted charged him with entering the service of the German Broadcasting System on a date in January 1940, and it was common ground and admitted by the appellant that he did so enter that service and on several occasions broadcast certain matters through that system.…[His Lordship described the evidence of threats of internment in a concentration camp and of physical violence which had been made against the appellant and his family.] The appellant also asserted again and again and said that he had done so in the written report of 5 July, which, as we have already said, was not produced, that he never had the slightest idea or intention of assisting the enemy and what he did was done to save his wife and children, and that what he did could not have assisted the enemy except in a very technical sense. Unlike the evidence which has been adduced in many other similar cases, there was no record of the actual broadcasts made by the appellant. This again was, no doubt, inevitable, but unfortunate, as the actual tone of the broadcast might have thrown some light on the motives and intentions of the appellant, but, in the opinion of the court, there was undoubtedly evidence from which a jury could infer that the acts done by the appellant were acts likely to assist the enemy.

The far more difficult question that arises, however, is in connection with the direction to the jury with regard to whether these acts were done with the intention of assisting the enemy. The case as opened, and, indeed, as put by the learned judge, appears to this court to be this: A man is taken to intend the natural consequences of his acts. If, therefore he does an act which is likely to assist the enemy, it must be assumed that he did it with the intention of assisting the enemy. Now, the first thing which the court would observe is that where the essence of an offence or a necessary constituent of an offence is a particular intent, that intent must be proved by the Crown just as much as any other fact necessary to constitute the offence. The wording of the regulation itself shows that it is not enough merely to charge a prisoner with doing an act likely to assist the enemy. He must do it with the particular intent specified in the regulation. While, no doubt, the motive of a man's act and his intention in doing the act are in law different things, it is none the less true that in many offences a specific intention is a necessary ingredient and the jury have to be satisfied that a particular act was done with that specific intent, although the natural consequences of the act might, if nothing else was proved, be said to show the intent for which it was done. To take a simple illustration, a man is charged with wounding with intent to do grievous bodily harm. It is proved that he did severely wound the prosecutor. Nevertheless, unless the Crown can prove that the intent was to do the prosecutor grievous bodily harm, he cannot be convicted of that felony. It is always open to the jury to negative by their verdict the intent and to convict only of the misdemeanour of unlawful wounding. Or again, a prisoner may be charged with shooting with intent to murder. Here, again, the prosecution may fail to satisfy the jury of the intent, although the natural consequence of firing, perhaps at close range, would be to kill. The jury can find in such a case an intent to do grievous bodily harm, or they might find that, if the person shot at was a police constable, the prisoner was not guilty on the count charging intent to murder but was guilty of intent to avoid arrest. The important thing to notice in this respect is that where an intent is charged in the indictment, the burden of proving that intent remains throughout on the prosecution. No doubt, if the prosecution prove an act the natural consequences of which would be a certain result and no evidence or explanation is given, then a jury may, on a proper direction, find that the prisoner is guilty of doing the act with the intent alleged, but if, on the totality of the evidence, there is room for more than one view as to the intent of the prisoner, the jury should be directed that it is for the prosecution to prove the intent to the jury's satisfaction, and if, on a review of the whole evidence, they either think that the intent did not exist or they are left in doubt as to the intent, the prisoner is entitled to be acquitted....

In this case the court cannot but feel that some confusion arose with regard to the question of intent by so much being said in the case with regard to the subject of duress. Duress is a matter of defence where a prisoner is forced by fear of violence or imprisonment to do an act which in itself is criminal. If the act is a criminal act, the prisoner may be able to show that he was forced into doing it by violence, actual or threatened, and to save himself from the consequences of that violence. There is very little learning to be found in any of the books or cases on the subject of duress and it is by no means certain how far the doctrine extends, though we have the authority both of Hale and of Fitzjames Stephen, that, while it does not apply to treason, murder and some other felonies, it does apply to misdemeanours, and offences against these regulations are misdemeanours. But here again, before any question of duress arises, a jury must be satisfied that the prisoner had the intention which is laid in the indictment. Duress is a matter of defence and the onus of proving it is on the accused.* As we have already said, where an intent is charged on the indictment, it is for the prosecution to prove it, so the onus is the other way.

Another matter which is of considerable importance in this case, but does not seem to have been brought directly to the attention of the jury, is that very different considerations may apply where the accused at the time he did the acts is in subjection to an enemy power and where he is not. British soldiers who were set to work on the Burma road or, if invasion had unhappily taken place, British subjects who might have been set to work by the enemy digging trenches would, undoubtedly, have been doing acts likely to assist the enemy. It would be unnecessary surely in their cases to consider any of the niceties of the law relating to duress, because no jury would find that merely by doing this work they were intending to assist the enemy. In our opinion, it is impossible to say that where acts were done by a person in subjection to the power of another, especially if that other be a brutal enemy, an inference that he intended the natural consequences of his acts must be drawn merely from the fact that he did them. The guilty intent cannot be presumed and must be proved. The proper direction to the jury in this case would have been that it was for the prosecution to prove the criminal intent, and that, while the jury would be entitled to presume that intent if they thought that the act was done as the result of the free, uncontrolled action of the accused, they would not be entitled to presume it if the circumstances showed that the act was done in subjection to the power of the enemy or was as equally consistent with an innocent intent as with a criminal intent, eg a desire to save his wife and children from a concentration camp. They should only convict if satisfied by the evidence that the act complained of was, in fact, done to assist the enemy and if there was doubt about the matter, the prisoner was entitled to be acquitted....

Appeal allowed

* This dictum goes too far. The accused who wishes to set up duress may bear an evidential burden; but once he has introduced evidence of duress, the burden of disproving it lies on the Crown: *Gill* [1963] 2 All ER 688, [1963] 1 WLR 841.

Glanville Williams, *The Mental Element in Crime*, p 21, commenting on *Steane*

The chief English authority against the view that intention may be held to include foresight of certainty is *Steane* [p **136**, above]. Although this is frequently cited as an important authority in discussions of intention, its importance derives chiefly from its rejection of the proposition that a person is to be deemed to intend the natural consequence of his acts. The actual decision in *Steane* seems highly disputable; it could have been reached more readily and more acceptably by recognising duress as a defence. Undoubtedly the element of duress caused the Court of Criminal Appeal to be sympathetic towards the defendant; and in cases where such sympathy is absent, foresight of certainty (or knowledge of existing circumstances) is regularly taken to be equivalent to intention. Thus in *Arrowsmith v Jenkins* [1963] 2 QB 561, [1963] 2 All ER 210, the defendant's knowledge that a meeting she was addressing was obstructing the highway made her guilty of 'wilfully' obstructing the highway, even though she had no particular desire to create an obstruction as such.

Lord Denning's treatment of *Steane* in his Lionel Cohen lecture [*Responsibility before the Law* (Jerusalem, Israel, 1961)] seems hard to reconcile with his principal thesis, which is that the word 'intent' in law includes recklessness unless there is some statutory indication of a narrower meaning. I should have thought that this view would have led him to disapprove the decision in *Steane*, but Lord Denning agrees with it; and the reason he gives is that the statutory offence of doing an act likely to assist the enemy with intent to assist the enemy obviously required desire or purpose. 'This man Steane had no desire or purpose to assist the enemy. The Gestapo had said to him: "If you don't obey, your wife and children will be put in a concentration camp." So he obeyed their commands. It would be very hard to convict him of an "intent to assist the enemy" if it was the last thing he desired to do.'

I cannot myself see that the statutory language rebutted Lord Denning's wide meaning of 'intention' if there is such a wide meaning. As a matter of policy, the draftsman would surely have wished to catch the man who did an act knowing that it was likely to assist the enemy, but not caring whether it did so or not; and he has not used any language to negative this meaning except the overriding phrase 'with intent to assist the enemy', which Lord Denning does not regard as sufficient to negative recklessness. However, let me assume, with Lord Denning, that the formula is restricted to acts done with intent (in the sense of desire or purpose) to assist the enemy. Steane's predominant intent was to save his family, and in order to do that he broadcast for the enemy. On any intelligible use of language, he intentionally (purposely) broadcast. He did not broadcast by mistake or accident or in a state of automatism. If it is thought too strong to say that he desired to broadcast, at least he knew he was broadcasting, which is enough to establish wilfulness or intent. No doubt he did so reluctantly, as the lesser of two evils; but many people go to work in the morning for precisely the same reason.

But, it may be said, it is not enough to assert that Steane intentionally broadcast; what has to be established is that he intended to assist the enemy. On this, there may even be an initial doubt whether he assisted the enemy. The enemy presumably hoped and thought that the broadcasts would assist them, but it would be hard to determine whether or not the broadcasts did so. The answer to this doubt is that the notion of assisting the enemy as used in the statute is obviously not limited to acts that can be shown to have assisted the enemy to win a military victory or otherwise to have promoted their cause. It would be no defence to a traitor to show that a campaign in which he assisted the enemy turned out to be disastrous to the enemy and caused them to lose the war. 'Assisting the enemy' means assisting the enemy in the war effort, whether the outcome is successful or not, Steane's intentional participation in the enemy broadcasts was an intentional assistance to the enemy, whether or not the broadcasts in fact helped them. It could perhaps be said that Steane desired to help the enemy in this way in order to save his family; but even if this formula is objected to, he certainly knew that he was assisting the enemy's war project, and therefore intentionally assisted the enemy. The case can either be regarded as one of voluntary action in known circumstances, or as taking part in the causation of a result (the transmission of radio waves) which is foreseen as certain; on either view it is one of intention.

The concept of intention cannot distinguish between the man who assists the enemy in order to save his family and the man who assists the enemy in order to earn a packet of cigarettes. It is only the law of duress that can make a distinction. That is why Steane should have been acquitted by reason of the defence of duress, and not because he lacked intent to assist the enemy.

Notes

1. *Steane* is by no means the only case in which 'intent' is construed to mean, in effect, purpose. In *Burke* [1988] Crim LR 839, CA it was held that a person commits an offence under s 1(3) of the Protection from Eviction Act 1977 when he does an act with intent to cause a residential occupier to give up the occupation of premises although the act (storage of furniture in a bathroom), when done without any such intention, is an act which he is perfectly entitled to do. The act must be one which is 'calculated'—meaning 'likely'—to interfere with the peace or comfort of the residential occupier, but that is the sole requirement of the actus reus. The essence of the offence is the intent with which the act is done. The commentary at [1988] Crim LR 841 reads:

Under the principle stated in *Moloney*, as subsequently interpreted, a person may be held to intend a result though it is not his purpose to cause it, if he is aware that it is a virtually certain result of his act. That is evidence from which a jury may 'infer' that he intended the result. It was presumably this principle which the present appellant's counsel had in mind when he argued that it would be easy for the prosecution to prove the necessary intent. Suppose, he argued, that H, on being told that the landlord wanted to use the bathroom to store the surplus furniture but did not want him to leave, had said, 'But if you do not remove the furniture I will have to leave' and the landlord had said, 'Well, I will be very sorry if you do but I do not propose to remove the furniture.' Counsel submitted that this would be evidence from which a jury could, and would, infer that the landlord had formed the intention that H should leave. The court did not accept this as an accurate analysis but, with respect, it is a perfectly accurate analysis if we apply the law about intention stated in the murder cases of *Moloney*, *Hancock* and *Nedrick*—except that whether the jury would have 'inferred' an intention is a matter of speculation. The court stated:

'A landlord whose intention is to do an act which may interfere with the peace and comfort of a residential occupier but which he is entitled to do as a matter of contract, and which he does for some reason quite distinct from an intention to get the occupier to leave, is clearly not guilty of the offence under this section.'

So the departure of the occupier must be the defendant's 'reason' for doing the acts likely to interfere with peace or comfort; it must be his purpose, motive or object to get rid of the occupier. No doubt the basis of counsel's argument was that the law would be much too severe, and unsound in principle, if a landlord committed an offence merely by doing an act which he could lawfully do but which he knew would cause the tenant to leave. The argument was directed to inducing the court to hold that the act must be an unlawful one; but the court found a different way of putting the law on an acceptable basis. An offence consisting in doing any act, lawful or not, is tolerable if there is a requirement that it be done with the purpose of causing some evil; but it is likely to be found intolerable if the only requirement is that the defendant should know that it will cause that result.

Such a meaning of 'with intent to...' is not new. In practice this is, and always has been, its meaning in the law of burglary. In that context, there is no room for the wider meaning found in the murder cases. Entry 'with intent to' commit a felony or one of the offences specified in the Theft Act 1968, s 9(2), has always meant, in substance, 'with the purpose of' committing one of those offences.

2. In *Ahlers* [1915] 1 KB 616 a German consul, who assisted German nationals to return home after the declaration of war in 1914, was held to intend to do his duty as consul and not to intend to aid the King's enemies. In *Thorne v Motor Trade Association* [1937] AC 797, [1937] 3 All ER 157, HL Lord Atkin thought that to put a trader's name on a 'stop list' so that his business would certainly be ruined might be 'an act done in lawful furtherance of business interests, and ... without any express intent to injure the person whose name is published'. In *Sinnasamy Selvanayagam v R* [1951] AC 83 the Privy Council thought that if D remained in occupation of his home in defiance of a lawful order to quit, knowing that the owner of the property would be annoyed, his 'dominant intention' was simply to retain his home and he was not guilty of an offence under the Ceylon Penal Code of remaining in occupation with intent to annoy the owner. (This was obiter since the court declined to find that the defendant contemplated that he would induce in the mind of the 'owner' (a government superintendent) 'an emotion so inappropriate to a government officer and so unprofitable, as annoyance'.)

Are the expressions 'express intent' and 'dominant intention' simply a way of describing purpose?

3. RECKLESSNESS

R v G and another

[2003] UKHL 50, [2003] 4 All ER 765, [2004] Crim LR 369, House of Lords

(Lords Bingham of Cornhill, Browne-Wilkinson, Steyn, Hutton, and Rodger of Earlsferry)

G and R, aged 11 and 12 went camping without their parents' permission. During the night they set fire to newspapers in the yard at the back of a shop and threw the lit newspapers under a wheelie bin. They left without putting out the fire. The fire spread to the wheelie bin and to the shop causing £1m worth of damage. The boys' case was that they expected the newspapers to burn themselves out on the concrete floor. Neither appreciated the risk of the fire spreading as it did. They were charged with arson contrary to s 1(1) and (3) of the 1971 Act. The judge directed the jury in accordance with *Caldwell*, [1982] AC 341, expressing reservations about that being a harsh test. The Court of Appeal upheld the convictions stating that *Caldwell* had been rightly applied and certified the issue of recklessness as one of general public importance.

Lord Bingham of Cornhill: [1] My Lords, the point of law of general public importance certified by the Court of Appeal to be involved in its decision in the present case is expressed in this way:

> 'Can a defendant properly be convicted under s 1 of the Criminal Damage Act 1971 on the basis that he was reckless as to whether property was destroyed or damaged when he gave no thought to the risk but, by reason of his age and/or personal characteristics, the risk would not have been obvious to him, even if he had thought about it?'

The appeal turns on the meaning of 'reckless' in that section. This is a question on which the House ruled in *R v Caldwell* [1981] 1 All ER 961, [1982] AC 341, a ruling affirmed by the House in later decisions. The House is again asked to reconsider that ruling.

[His Lordship referred to the facts and the trial judge's direction on the law.]

THE HISTORICAL BACKGROUND

[8] Section 51 of the Malicious Damage Act 1861 provided, so far as relevant:

> 'Whosoever shall unlawfully and maliciously commit any damage, injury, or spoil to or upon any real or personal property whatsoever ... the damage, injury, or spoil being to an amount exceeding 5l., shall be guilty of a misdemeanour ...'

The defendant in *R v Pembliton* (1874) LR 2 CCR 119, [1874–80] All ER Rep 1163 was charged under this section. He had been fighting in the street and had picked up a large stone and thrown it at the people he had been fighting with. The stone missed its human target but broke a window causing damage of a value exceeding £5. The jury convicted the defendant, although finding that he had not intended to break the window, and the recorder referred the case to the Court of Crown Cases Reserved (Lord Coleridge CJ, Blackburn J, Pigott B, Lush J and Cleasby B) which quashed the conviction. The words 'unlawfully and maliciously' were very widely used in the Malicious Damage Act 1861 and the issue on appeal was whether the defendant had acted 'maliciously'. Lord Coleridge CJ said ((1874) LR 2 CCR 119 at 122, [1874–80] All ER Rep 1163 at 1164):

> '[I]t seems to me that what is intended by the statute is a wilful doing of an intentional act. Without saying that if the case had been left to them in a different way the conviction could not have been supported, if, on these facts, the jury had come to a conclusion that the prisoner was reckless of the consequence of his act, and might reasonably have expected that it would result in breaking the window, it is sufficient to say that the jury have expressly found the contrary.'

Blackburn J was of the same opinion ((1874) LR 2 CCR 119 at 122, [1874–80] All ER Rep 1163 at 1165):

> 'The jury might perhaps have found on this evidence that the act was malicious, because they might have found that the prisoner knew that the natural consequence of his act would be to break the glass, and although that was not his wish, yet that he was reckless whether he did it or not; but the jury have not so found, and I think it is impossible to say in this case that the prisoner has maliciously done an act which he did not intend to do.'

Thus the court interpreted 'maliciously' as requiring proof of intention, but were inclined to accept that intention could be shown by proof of reckless disregard of a perceived risk. This was also the approach followed in *R v Welch* (1875) 1 QBD 23, where the defendant faced charges of unlawfully and maliciously killing, maiming and wounding a mare contrary to s 40(1) of the Malicious Damage Act 1861. The trial judge was held to have been right to direct the jury to convict if they found that the defendant in fact intended to kill, maim or wound the mare or, in the alternative, that he knew that what he was doing would or might kill, maim or wound the mare and nevertheless did what he did recklessly and not caring whether the mare was injured or not.

[9] The first eight sections of the Malicious Damage Act 1861 all related to arson and all used the expression 'unlawfully and maliciously'. In the first edition of his *Outlines of Criminal Law* published in 1902, Professor Kenny addressed the meaning of 'maliciously' with particular reference to arson. He wrote (pp 163–165, footnotes omitted):

'(a) "Maliciously." Burning a house by any mere negligence, however gross it be, is, as we have seen, no crime; (an omission in our law which may well be considered as deserving the attention of the legislature). Even the fact that this gross negligence occurred in the course of the commission of an unlawful act, or even of a felonious one, will not suffice to render the consequent burning-down indictable as an arson. For in any statutory definition of a crime, "malice" must, as we have already seen, be taken-not in its vague common law sense as a "wickedness" in general, but-as requiring an actual intention to do the particular kind of harm that in fact was done. Consequently, if a criminal, when engaged in committing some burglary or other felony, negligently sets fire to a house, he usually will not be guilty of arson…But it must not be supposed that everyone who has maliciously set fire to some article which it is not arson to burn, will necessarily become guilty of arson if the fire should happen to spread to an arsonable building. For when a man mischievously tries to burn some chattel inside a house, and thereby, quite accidentally and unintentionally, sets fire to the house, this does not constitute an arson. And even if his setting fire to this chattel inside the building was intrinsically likely to result in setting fire to the building itself, he still will not necessarily be guilty of arson. For it is essential to arson that the incendiary either should have intended the building to take fire, or, at least, should have recognised the probability of its taking fire and have been reckless as to whether or not it did so. Of course the mere fact that this probability was an obviously manifest one will be strong evidence to warrant the jury in finding, if they think fit, that the prisoner did, in fact, thus recognise the danger and regard it with indifference.'

One of the cases cited by Professor Kenny was *R v Harris* (1882) 15 Cox CC 75, where the charge was of setting fire to a dwelling house. The judge (at 77) directed the jury:

'Again, if you think that the prisoner set fire to the frame of the picture with a knowledge that in all probability the house itself would thereby be set on fire, and that he was reckless and utterly indifferent whether the house caught fire or not, that is abundant evidence from which you may, if you think fit, draw the inference that he intended the probable consequences of his act, and if you draw that inference, then, inasmuch as the house was in fact set on fire through the medium of the picture frame, the prisoner's crime would be that of arson.'

This was consistent with the ratio of *R v Child* (1871) LR 1 CCR 307 (also cited by Professor Kenny) where it was held that the defendant had not intended to set fire to a house and had thought that what he was doing would not do so. Another case cited by Professor Kenny was *R v Faulkner* (1877) 13 Cox CC 550, decided in the Irish Court of Crown Cases Reserved. The defendant had set fire to a ship while stealing rum from its hold. He had been boring a hole by candlelight and some rum had spilled out and been ignited. It was conceded that he had not intended to burn the vessel, and his conviction was quashed. Barry J said (at 555):

'[*R v Pembliton* (1874) LR 2 CCR 119, [1874–80] All ER Rep 1163] must be taken as deciding that to constitute an offence under the Malicious Injuries to Property Act, sect. 1, the act done must be in fact intentional and wilful, although the intention and will may (perhaps) be held to exist in, or be proved by, the fact that the accused knew that the injury would be the probable result of his unlawful act, and yet did the act reckless of such consequences.'

[10] *R v Pembliton* was again relied on in *R v Cunningham* [1957] 2 All ER 412, [1957] 2 QB 396. The defendant in that case had wrenched a gas meter from the wall and stolen it. Gas had escaped. He was charged under s 23 of the Offences Against the Person Act 1861 with unlawfully and maliciously causing a noxious thing, namely coal gas, to be taken by the victim. He pleaded not guilty but was convicted. Giving the reserved judgment of the Court of Criminal Appeal, Byrne J said ([1957] 2 All ER 412 at 414, [1957] 2 QB 396 at 399–400):

> 'We have considered those cases [among others, *R v Pembliton* and *R v Faulkner*], and we have also considered, in the light of those cases, the following principle which was propounded by the late Professor C. S. Kenny in the first edition of his *Outlines of Criminal Law* published in 1902, and repeated in the sixteenth edition, edited by Mr. J. W. Cecil Turner, and published in 1952 (ibid., at p. 186): " ... in any statutory definition of a crime, 'malice' must be taken not in the old vague sense of 'wickedness' in general, but as requiring either (i) an actual intention to do the particular kind of harm that in fact was done, or (ii) recklessness as to whether such harm should occur or not (i.e. the accused has foreseen that the particular kind of harm might be done, and yet has gone on to take the risk of it). It is neither limited to, nor does it indeed require any ill-will towards, the person injured." The same principle is repeated by Mr. Turner in his tenth edition of *Russell on Crime* [vol 2, p 1592].'

That was accepted as an accurate statement of the law. In the course of his able address, Mr Perry [for the Crown] pointed out, correctly, that the words quoted had not appeared in the first (1902) edition written by Professor Kenny. It does not, however, appear that the later summary misrepresents what the professor had written, quoted at [9], above.

[11] *R v Mowatt* [1967] 3 All ER 47, [1968] 1 QB 421 arose from the robbery by the defendant of a victim W. When W retaliated, the defendant struck him in the face. He was charged with wounding with intent to do grievous bodily harm contrary to s 18 of the Offences Against the Person Act 1861, on which an alternative verdict of unlawful wounding contrary to s 20 of that Act was open to the jury. The trial judge gave no direction to the jury on the meaning of 'maliciously' and the jury convicted under s 20. The defendant's appeal against conviction on the ground of this non-direction failed. In a judgment of the Court of Appeal (Diplock LJ, Brabin and Waller JJ) reference was made to *R v Cunningham* and the court ([1967] 3 All ER 47 at 49, [1968] 1 QB 421 at 425) cast no doubt on the proposition that ' "maliciously" in a statutory crime postulates foresight of consequence', but the court regarded Professor Kenny's more general statement as inapposite to the specific alternative statutory offences described in ss 18 and 20. The court held ([1967] 3 All ER 47 at 50, [1968] 1 QB 421 at 426) that 'maliciously' imports an awareness that an act may have the consequence of causing some physical harm to some other person, even if the harm foreseen was relatively minor. The court ruled:

> 'But where the evidence for the prosecution, if accepted, shows that the physical act of the accused which caused the injury to another person was a direct assault which any ordinary person would be bound to realise was likely to cause some physical harm to the other person (as, for instance, an assault with a weapon or the boot or violence with the hands) and the defence put forward on behalf of the accused is not that the assault was accidental or that he did not realise that it might cause some physical harm to the victim, but is some other defence such as that he did not do the alleged act or that he did it in self-defence, it is unnecessary to deal specifically in the summing-up with what is meant by the word "maliciously" in the section ... In the absence of any evidence that the accused did not realise that it was a possible consequence of his act that some physical harm might be caused to the victim, the prosecution satisfy the relevant onus by proving the commission by the accused of an act which any ordinary person would realise was likely to have that consequence.'

THE 1971 ACT

[12] In its second programme of law reform the Law Commission, then under the chairmanship of Scarman J, envisaged the codification of the criminal law. As part of that project it examined a

number of specific offences, among them the law of malicious damage, on which it published its Working Paper No 23 in April 1969. This described the Malicious Damage Act 1861, despite five later amending statutes, as 'unsatisfactory' (p 1 (para 2)). In a brief statistical introduction the Law Commission drew attention (pp 4–5 (para 9)) to the prevalence of malicious damage offences among the youngest criminal age group (the 10–14-year-olds) as well as among other juveniles, and to the fact that more than half of those convicted of the most serious offence (arson) were under 21. In a section on 'The Mental Element' the Law Commission referred to a working party which was formulating draft propositions on the mental element in crime and observed (p 19 (para 31)):

> 'For the present purpose, we assume that the traditional elements of intention, knowledge and reck-lessness (in the sense of foresight and disregard of consequences or awareness and disregard of the likelihood of the existence of circumstances) will continue to be required for serious crime.'

The Law Commission identified (p 20 (para 33)) 'intent to do the forbidden act or recklessness in relation to its foreseen consequences' as the 'essential mental element in the existing malicious dam-age offences' and quoted with apparent approval the passage from *R v Cunningham* which is set out at [10], above. The Law Commission considered that the word 'maliciously' should be avoided (p 21 (para 34)) and favoured its replacement by 'wilful or reckless' (p 35 (para 64)). It proposed (p 37 (para 68)) that the new group of offences should require—

> 'traditional mens rea, in the sense of intention or recklessness in relation to prescribed consequences, and, where appropriate, knowledge or recklessness in relation to prescribed circumstances.'

The working paper does not suggest that the law as then understood was thought to be lead-ing to unjustified acquittals. In a published comment on the working paper ('Malicious Damage: The Law Commission's Working Paper' [1969] Crim LR 283), Professor Brian Hogan wrote (at 288)...

> 'What is implicit in "maliciously" in the present law will appear explicitly as intention or recklessness in the new code. No doubt the meanings ascribed to intention and recklessness in the codification of the general principles will be applied mutatis mutandis to offences of damage to property.'

[13] In its Report on Offences of Damage to Property (Law Com no 29) published in July 1970, the Law Commission broadly followed, in respects relevant to this appeal, the lines of the working paper. On the mental element of criminal damage offences the Law Commission said (p 17):

> '44. In the area of serious crime (in contrast to offences commonly described as "regulatory offences" in which the test of culpability may be negligence, or even a test founded on strict liability) the elements of intention, knowledge or recklessness have always been required as a basis of liability. The tendency is to extend this basis to a wider range of offences and to limit the area of offences where a lesser mental element is required. We consider, therefore, that the same elements as are required at present should be retained, but that they should be expressed with greater simplicity and clarity. In particular, we prefer to avoid the use of such a word as "maliciously", if only because it gives the impression that the mental element differs from that which is imposed in other offences requiring traditional mens rea. It is evident from such cases as *R. v. Cunningham* ([1957] 2 All ER 412, [1957] 2 QB 396) and *R. v. Mowatt* ([1967] 3 All ER 47, [1968] 1 QB 421) that the word can give rise to difficulties of interpretation. Furthermore, the word "maliciously" conveys the impression that some ill-will is required against the person whose property is damaged.'

It does not appear from the report that the Law Commission's consultation had elicited any complaint that the existing law was unduly favourable to defendants. Annexed to the report was a draft Bill: in this cl 1(1) and (2) were exactly as enacted in the 1971 Act, but what became s 1(3) was omitted. On 16 June 1970, a month before this report was published, the Law Commission had published its

Codification of the Criminal Law: General Principles: The Mental Element in Crime (Working Paper No 31). In that working paper a definition of recklessness was proposed (p 48):

'A person is reckless if, (a) knowing that there is a risk that an event may result from his conduct or that a circumstance may exist, he takes that risk, and (b) it is unreasonable for him to take it having regard to the degree and nature of the risk which he knows to be present.'

In the 1971 Act as passed all except six sections of the Malicious Damage Act 1861, a lengthy Act, were repealed, very much as the Law Commission had proposed.

[14] Enactment of the 1971 Act did not at once affect the courts' approach to the causing of unintentional damage. In *R v Briggs* [1977] 1 All ER 475, [1977] 1 WLR 605 the defendant had been charged under s 1(1) of the 1971 Act as a result of damage caused to a car and the appeal turned on the trial judge's direction on the meaning of 'reckless'. The appeal succeeded since the judge had not adequately explained that the test to be applied was that of the defendant's state of mind. The Court of Appeal (James LJ, Kenneth Jones and Peter Pain JJ) ruled ([1977] 1 All ER 475 at 477–478, [1977] 1 WLR 605 at 608):

'A man is reckless in the sense required when he carries out a deliberate act knowing that there is some risk of damage resulting from that act but nevertheless continues in the performance of that act.'

This definition was adopted but modified in *R v Parker* [1977] 2 All ER 37, [1977] 1 WLR 600 where the defendant in a fit of temper had broken a telephone by smashing the handset violently down on to the telephone unit and had been convicted under s 1(1) of the 1971 Act. The court (Scarman and Geoffrey Lane LJJ and Kenneth Jones J) ([1977] 2 All ER 37 at 39–40, [1977] 1 WLR 600 at 603–604) readily followed *R v Briggs* but held that the defendant had been fully aware of all the circumstances and that if—

'he did not know, as he said he did not, that there was some risk of damage, he was, in effect, deliberately closing his mind to the obvious-the obvious being that damage in these circumstances was inevitable.'

The court accordingly modified the *R v Briggs* definition in this way:

'A man is reckless in the sense required when he carries out a deliberate act knowing or closing his mind to the obvious fact that there is some risk of damage resulting from that act but nevertheless continuing in the performance of that act.'

This modification made no inroad into the concept of recklessness as then understood since, as pointed out by Professor Glanville Williams *Textbook of Criminal Law* (1st edn, 1978) p 79, cited by Lord Edmund-Davies in his dissenting opinion in *R v Caldwell* [1981] 1 All ER 961 at 970, [1982] AC 341 at 358:

'A person cannot, in any intelligible meaning of the words, close his mind to a risk unless he first realises that there is a risk; and if he realises that there is a risk, that is the end of the matter.'

[15] The meaning of 'reckless' in s 1(1) of the 1971 Act was again considered by the Court of Appeal (Geoffrey Lane LJ, Ackner and Watkins JJ) in *R v Stephenson* [1979] 2 All ER 1198, [1979] QB 695. The defendant had tried to go to sleep in a hollow he had made in the side of a haystack. Feeling cold, he had lit a fire in the hollow which had set fire to the stack and damaged property worth £3,500. He had been charged and convicted under s 1(1) and (3) of the 1971 Act. The defendant however had a long history of schizophrenia and expert evidence at trial suggested that he may not have had the same ability to foresee or appreciate risks as the mentally normal person. Giving the reserved judgment of the court, Geoffrey Lane LJ ([1979] 2 All ER 1198 at 1201–1203, [1979] QB 695 at 700–703) reviewed the definition of recklessness in the Law Commission's Working Paper No 31 (see [13], above), the acceptance of that definition by the leading academic authorities and the

House of Lords' adoption of a subjective meaning of recklessness in tort in *British Railways Board v Herrington* [1972] 1 All ER 749, [1972] AC 877. The court thought it fair to assume that those who were responsible for drafting the 1971 Act were intending to preserve its legal meaning as described in Kenny and expressly approved in *R v Cunningham*. The court then continued:

> 'What then must the prosecution prove in order to bring home the charge of arson in circumstances such as the present? They must prove that (1) the defendant deliberately committed some act which caused the damage to property alleged or part of such damage; (2) the defendant had no lawful excuse for causing the damage (these two requirements will in the ordinary case not be in issue); (3) the defendant either (a) intended to cause the damage to the property, or (b) was reckless whether the property was damaged or not. A man is reckless when he carries out the deliberate act appreciating that there is a risk that damage to property may result from his act. It is however not the taking of every risk which could properly be classed as reckless. The risk must be one which it is in all the circumstances unreasonable for him to take. Proof of the requisite knowledge in the mind of the defendant will in most cases present little difficulty. The fact that the risk of some damage would have been obvious to anyone in his right mind in the position of the defendant is not conclusive proof of the defendant's knowledge, but it may well be, and in many cases doubtless will be, a matter which will drive the jury to the conclusion that the defendant himself must have appreciated the risk.'

The appeal was accordingly allowed. But the court recognised that what it called the subjective definition of recklessness produced difficulties. One of these was where a person by self-induced intoxication deprived himself of the ability to foresee the risks involved in his actions. The court suggested that a distinction was to be drawn between crimes requiring proof of specific intent and those, such as offences under s 1(1) of the 1971 Act, involving no specific intent ([1979] 2 All ER 1198 at 1204, [1979] QB 695 at 704):

> 'Accordingly it is no defence under the 1971 Act for a person to say that he was deprived by self-induced intoxication of the ability to foresee or appreciate an obvious risk.'

[16] In *Archbold's Pleading, Evidence and Practice in Criminal Cases* (40th edn, 1979) p 958 (para 1443c), on which jury directions were no doubt routinely based at the time, the better view was said to be—

> 'that whereas "intent" requires a desire for consequences or foresight of probable consequences, "reckless" only requires foresight of possible consequences coupled with an unreasonable willingness to risk them.'

R v CALDWELL

[17] *R v Caldwell* [1981] 1 All ER 961, [1982] AC 341 was a case of self-induced intoxication. The defendant, having a grievance against the owner of the hotel where he worked, got very drunk and set fire to the hotel where guests were living at the time. He was indicted upon two counts of arson. The first and more serious count was laid under s 1(2) of the 1971 Act, the second count under s 1(1). He pleaded guilty to the second count but contested the first on the ground that he had been so drunk at the time that the thought there might be people in the hotel had never crossed his mind. His conviction on count 1 was set aside by the Court of Appeal which certified the following question ([1981] 1 All ER 961 at 964, [1982] AC 341 at 344):

> 'Whether evidence of self-induced intoxication can be relevant to the following questions-(a) Whether the defendant intended to endanger the life of another; and (b) Whether the defendant was reckless as to whether the life of another would be endangered, within the meaning of Section 1(2)(b) of the Criminal Damage Act 1971.'

In submitting that the two questions should be answered (a) Yes and (b) No, counsel for the Crown did not challenge the correctness of *R v Briggs* or *R v Stephenson*.

[18] In a leading opinion with which Lord Keith of Kinkel and Lord Roskill agreed, but from which Lord Wilberforce and Lord Edmund-Davies dissented, Lord Diplock discounted ([1981] 1 All ER 961 at 964–965, [1982] AC 341 at 351) Professor Kenny's statement of the law approved in *R v Cunningham* (see [10], above) as directed to the meaning of 'maliciously' in the Malicious Damage Act 1861 and having no bearing on the meaning of 'reckless' in the 1971 Act. It was, he held, no less blameworthy for a man whose mind was affected by rage or excitement or drink to fail to give his mind to the risk of damaging property than for a man whose mind was so affected to appreciate that there was a risk of damage to property but not to appreciate the seriousness of the risk or to trust that good luck would prevent the risk occurring. He observed ([1981] 1 All ER 961 at 965, [1982] AC 341 at 352):

'My Lords, I can see no reason why Parliament when it decided to revise the law as to offences of damage to property should go out of its way to perpetuate fine and impracticable distinctions such as these, between one mental state and another. One would think that the sooner they were got rid of the better.'

Reference was made to *R v Briggs*, *R v Parker* and *R v Stephenson*, but Lord Diplock saw no warrant for assuming that the 1971 Act, whose declared purpose was to revise the law of damage to property, intended 'reckless' to be interpreted as 'maliciously' had been ([1981] 1 All ER 961 at 966, [1982] AC 341 at 353). He preferred the ordinary meaning of 'reckless' which—

'surely includes not only deciding to ignore a risk of harmful consequences resulting from one's acts that one has recognised as existing, but also failing to give any thought to whether or not there is any such risk in circumstances where, if any thought were given to the matter, it would be obvious that there was. If one is attaching labels, the latter state of mind is neither more nor less "subjective" than the first. But the label solves nothing. It is a statement of the obvious; mens rea is, by definition, a state of mind of the accused himself at the time he did the physical act that constitutes the actus reus of the offence; it cannot be the mental state of some non-existent hypothetical person.'

To decide whether a person had been reckless whether harmful consequences of a particular kind would result from his act it was necessary to consider the mind of 'the ordinary prudent individual' ([1981] 1 All ER 961 at 966, [1982] AC 341 at 354). In a passage which has since been taken to encapsulate the law on this point, and which has founded many jury directions (including that in the present case) Lord Diplock then said ([1981] 1 All ER 961 at 967, [1982] AC 341 at 354):

'In my opinion, a person charged with an offence under s 1(1) of the 1971 Act is "reckless as to whether or not any property would be destroyed or damaged" if (1) he does an act which in fact creates an obvious risk that property will be destroyed or damaged and (2) when he does the act he either has not given any thought to the possibility of there being any such risk or has recognised that there was some risk involved and has none the less gone on to do it. That would be a proper direction to the jury; cases in the Court of Appeal which held otherwise should be regarded as overruled.'

On the facts Lord Diplock concluded ([1981] 1 All ER 961 at 967, [1982] AC 341 at 355) that the defendant's unawareness, owing to his self-induced intoxication, of the risk of endangering the lives of hotel residents was no defence if that risk would have been obvious to him had he been sober. He held ([1981] 1 All ER 961 at 967, [1982] AC 341 at 356) that evidence of self-induced intoxication was relevant to a charge under s 1(2) based on intention but not to one based on recklessness.

[19] In his dissenting opinion Lord Edmund-Davies expressed ([1981] 1 All ER 961 at 969, [1982] AC 341 at 357) 'respectful, but profound, disagreement' with Lord Diplock's dismissal of Professor Kenny's statement which was—

'accurate not only in respect of the law as it stood in 1902 but also as it has been applied in countless cases ever since, both in the United Kingdom and in other countries where the common law prevails ...'

Lord Edmund-Davies drew attention to the Law Commission's preparation of the 1971 Act and its definition of recklessness in Working Paper No 31 and continued:

> 'It was surely with this contemporaneous definition and the much respected decision of *R v Cunningham* in mind that the draftsman proceeded to his task of drafting the 1971 Act.'

He observed ([1981] 1 All ER 961 at 970, [1982] AC 341 at 358):

> 'In the absence of exculpatory factors, the defendant's state of mind is therefore all-important where recklessness is an element in the offence charged, and s 8 of the Criminal Justice Act 1967 has laid down that: "A court or jury, in determining whether a person has committed an offence,-(a) shall not be bound in law to infer that he intended or foresaw a result of his actions by reason only of its being a natural and probable consequence of those actions; but (b) shall decide whether he did intend or foresee that result by reference to all the evidence, drawing such inferences from the evidence as appear proper in the circumstances." (Emphasis added.)'

Lord Edmund-Davies differed from the majority on the relevance of evidence of self-induced intoxication: in his opinion ([1981] 1 All ER 961 at 972, [1982] AC 341 at 361) such evidence was relevant to a charge under s 1(2) whether the charge was based on intention or recklessness.

R v LAWRENCE

[20] Judgment was given by the House in *R v Lawrence* [1981] 1 All ER 974, [1982] AC 510 on the same day as *R v Caldwell*, although only two members (Lord Diplock and Lord Roskill) were party to both decisions. The defendant had ridden a motor cycle along an urban street after nightfall and had collided with and killed a pedestrian. He had been charged and convicted under s 1 of the Road Traffic Act 1972 which made it an offence to cause the death of another person by driving a motor vehicle on a road recklessly. His appeal had succeeded on the ground of an inadequate direction to the jury. The issue on appeal to the House concerned the mental element in a charge of reckless driving.

[21] Lord Hailsham of St Marylebone LC ([1981] 1 All ER 974 at 975, 978, [1982] AC 510 at 516, 520, 521), agreeing with Lord Diplock and with the majority in *R v Caldwell*, understood recklessness to evince 'a state of mind stopping short of deliberate intention, and going beyond mere inadvertence…' Lord Diplock ([1981] 1 All ER 974 at 982, [1982] AC 510 at 526) rehearsed the history of motoring offences based on recklessness beginning with s 1 of the Motor Car Act 1903 and applied essentially the same test as laid down in *R v Caldwell*, by reference to the 'ordinary prudent individual'. He formulated an appropriate jury direction to the same effect, mutatis mutandis, as that in *R v Caldwell*. But he added ([1981] 1 All ER 974 at 982, [1982] AC 510 at 527):

> 'It is for the jury to decide whether the risk created by the manner in which the vehicle was being driven was both obvious and serious and, in deciding this, they may apply the standard of the ordinary prudent motorist as represented by themselves. If satisfied that an obvious and serious risk was created by the manner of the defendant's driving, the jury are entitled to infer that he was in one or other of the states of mind required to constitute the offence and will probably do so; but regard must be given to any explanation he gives as to his state of mind which may displace the inference.'

Lord Fraser of Tullybelton, Lord Roskill and Lord Bridge of Harwich agreed with Lord Hailsham of St Marylebone LC and Lord Diplock.

LATER CASES

[22] The decisions in *R v Caldwell* and *R v Lawrence* were applied by the House (Lord Diplock, Lord Keith of Kinkel, Lord Bridge of Harwich, Lord Brandon of Oakbrook and Lord Brightman) in *R v Miller* [1983] 1 All ER 978, [1983] 2 AC 161 [above, p **93**], although subject to a qualification germane to the facts of that case but not to the facts of the present case ([1983] 1 All ER 978 at 983, [1983] 2 AC 161 at 179).

[23] In *Elliott v C (a minor)* [1983] 2 All ER 1005, [1983] 1 WLR 939 the defendant was a 14-year-old girl of low intelligence who had entered a shed in the early morning, poured white spirit on the floor and set it alight. The resulting fire had flared up and she had left the shed, which had been destroyed. She was charged under s 1(1) of the 1971 Act and at her trial before justices the prosecution made plain that the charge was based not on intention but on recklessness. The justices sought to apply the test laid down in *R v Caldwell* [1981] 1 All ER 961, [1982] AC 341 but inferred that in his reference to 'an obvious risk' Lord Diplock had meant a risk which was obvious to the particular defendant. The justices acquitted the defendant because they found that the defendant had given no thought at the time to the possibility of there being a risk that the shed and contents would be destroyed, and this risk would not have been obvious to her or appreciated by her if she had thought about the matter ([1983] 2 All ER 1005 at 1007–1008, [1983] 1 WLR 939 at 945). The prosecutor's appeal was allowed. Glidewell J, giving the first judgment, accepted the submission that—

> 'if the risk is one which would have been obvious to a reasonably prudent person, once it has also been proved that the particular defendant gave no thought to the possibility of there being such a risk, it is not a defence that because of limited intelligence or exhaustion she would not have appreciated the risk even if she had thought about it.'

Robert Goff LJ felt constrained by the decisions of the House in *R v Caldwell, R v Lawrence* and *R v Miller* to agree, but he expressed his unhappiness in doing so and plainly did not consider the outcome to be just. A petition for leave to appeal against this decision was dismissed by an appeal committee.

[24] The defendant in *R v Stephen Malcolm R* (1984) 79 Cr App R 334 had thrown petrol bombs at the outside wall of the bedroom of a girl who he believed had informed on him in relation to a series of burglaries. He had admitted throwing the bombs but claimed he had done so to frighten the girl and without realising that if a bomb had gone through the window it might have killed her. He was charged with arson under s 1(2) of the 1971 Act, on the basis of recklessness. At trial, it was submitted on the defendant's behalf that when considering recklessness the jury could only convict him if he did an act which created a risk to life obvious to someone of his age and with such of his characteristics as would affect his appreciation of the risk (at 337). On the trial judge ruling against that submission the defendant changed his plea and the issue in the Court of Appeal (Ackner LJ, Bristow and Popplewell JJ) was whether the ruling had been correct. The court held that it had: if the House had wished to modify the *Caldwell* principle to take account of, for instance, the age of the defendant, the opportunity had existed in *Elliott's* case and it had not been taken. Although concerned at the principle it was required to apply, the court had little doubt that on the facts of the case the answer would have been the same even if the jury had been able to draw a comparison with what a boy of the defendant's age would have appreciated.

[25] On his appeal to the House (Lord Keith of Kinkel, Lord Roskill, Lord Ackner, Lord Goff of Chieveley and Lord Browne-Wilkinson) in *R v Reid* [1992] 3 All ER 673, [1992] 1 WLR 793 the defendant, convicted of causing death by reckless driving contrary to s 1 of the Road Traffic Act 1972, later re-enacted in s 1 of the Road Traffic Act 1988, asked the House to reconsider its decision in *R v Lawrence* on which the trial judge's jury direction had been based. The House unanimously affirmed its earlier decision as correct in principle for essentially the reasons which Lord Diplock had given. Lord Keith, however, accepted ([1992] 3 All ER 673 at 675, [1992] 1 WLR 793 at 796) that Lord Diplock's suggested jury direction might call for modification or addition—

> 'where the driver acted under some understandable and excusable mistake or where his capacity to appreciate risks was adversely affected by some condition not involving fault on his part. There may also be cases where the driver acted as he did in a sudden dilemma created by the actions of others.'

Lord Ackner ([1992] 3 All ER 673 at 684, [1992] 1 WLR 793 at 806) drew attention to Lord Diplock's acceptance that 'regard must be given to any explanation [the defendant] gives as to his state of mind which may displace the inference' (see [21], above) and commented:

> 'I read this as no more than a cautionary instruction to the jury that, while it would be open to them at first sight to find that the accused was driving recklessly from the mere manner of his driving, if it shows a clear disregard for the lives or safety of others without any explanation for this conduct, yet before reaching any firm conclusions they must have regard to any explanation which accounts for his conduct. In short, they must have regard to all the available evidence.'

Lord Ackner, Lord Goff and my noble and learned friend Lord Browne-Wilkinson ([1992] 3 All ER 673 at 683, 685, 694, [1992] 1 WLR 793 at 805, 807, 816–817, respectively) all, with varying degrees of emphasis, made plain that their observations were directed to recklessness in the context of driving and not to recklessness in the context of s 1 of the 1971 Act or any other context.

[26] In *R v Coles* [1995] 1 Cr App R 157 a 15-year-old defendant convicted under s 1(2) of the 1971 Act on the basis of recklessness again challenged, unsuccessfully, the rule laid down by Lord Diplock in *R v Caldwell*. Since recklessness was to be judged by the standard of the reasonable, prudent man, it followed that expert evidence of the defendant's capacity to foresee the risks which would arise from his setting fire to hay in a barn had been rightly rejected.

[27] In the present case the Court of Appeal (Dyson LJ, Silber J and Judge Beaumont QC) reviewed the authorities ([2002] EWCA Crim 1992 at [18], [2003] 3 All ER 206 at [18]) but was in no doubt that the *Caldwell* test had been rightly applied. It acknowledged (at [23]) that the *Caldwell* test had been criticised and had not been applied in a number of Commonwealth jurisdictions and saw great force in these criticisms but held that it was not open to the Court of Appeal to depart from it.

Conclusions

[28] The task confronting the House in this appeal is, first of all, one of statutory construction: what did Parliament mean when it used the word 'reckless' in s 1(1) and (2) of the 1971 Act? In so expressing the question I mean to make it as plain as I can that I am not addressing the meaning of 'reckless' in any other statutory or common law context. In particular, but perhaps needlessly since 'recklessly' has now been banished from the lexicon of driving offences, I would wish to throw no doubt on the decisions of the House in *R v Lawrence* and *R v Reid*.

[29] Since a statute is always speaking, the context or application of a statutory expression may change over time, but the meaning of the expression itself cannot change. So the starting point is to ascertain what Parliament meant by 'reckless' in 1971. As noted at [13], above, s 1 as enacted followed, subject to an immaterial addition, the draft proposed by the Law Commission. It cannot be supposed that by 'reckless' Parliament meant anything different from the Law Commission. The Law Commission's meaning was made plain both in its report (Law Com no 29) and in Working Paper No 23 which preceded it. These materials (not, it would seem, placed before the House in *R v Caldwell*) reveal a very plain intention to replace the old-fashioned and misleading expression 'maliciously' by the more familiar expression 'reckless' but to give the latter expression the meaning which *R v Cunningham* [1957] 2 All ER 412, [1957] 2 QB 396 and Professor Kenny had given to the former. In treating this authority as irrelevant to the construction of 'reckless' the majority fell into understandable but clearly demonstrable error. No relevant change in the mens rea necessary for proof of the offence was intended, and in holding otherwise the majority misconstrued s 1 of the Act.

[30] That conclusion is by no means determinative of this appeal. For the decision in *R v Caldwell* was made more than 20 years ago. Its essential reasoning was unanimously approved by the House in *R v Lawrence*. Invitations to reconsider that reasoning have been rejected. The principles laid down have been applied on many occasions, by Crown Court judges and, even more frequently, by justices.

In the submission of the Crown, the ruling of the House works well and causes no injustice in practice. If Parliament had wished to give effect to the intention of the Law Commission it has had many opportunities, which it has not taken, to do so. Despite its power under *Practice Statement (Judicial Precedent)* [1966] 3 All ER 77, [1966] 1 WLR 1234 to depart from its earlier decisions, the House should be very slow to do so, not least in a context such as this.

[31] These are formidable arguments, deployed by Mr Perry with his habitual skill and erudition. But I am persuaded by Mr Newman QC for the appellants that they should be rejected. I reach this conclusion for four reasons, taken together.

[32] First, it is a salutary principle that conviction of serious crime should depend on proof not simply that the defendant caused (by act or omission) an injurious result to another but that his state of mind when so acting was culpable. This, after all, is the meaning of the familiar rule actus non facit reum nisi mens sit rea. The most obviously culpable state of mind is no doubt an intention to cause the injurious result, but knowing disregard of an appreciated and unacceptable risk of causing an injurious result or a deliberate closing of the mind to such risk would be readily accepted as culpable also. It is clearly blameworthy to take an obvious and significant risk of causing injury to another. But it is not clearly blameworthy to do something involving a risk of injury to another if (for reasons other than self-induced intoxication (see *DPP v Majewski* [1976] 2 All ER 142, [1977] AC 443)) one genuinely does not perceive the risk. Such a person may fairly be accused of stupidity or lack of imagination, but neither of those failings should expose him to conviction of serious crime or the risk of punishment.

[33] Secondly, the present case shows, more clearly than any other reported case since *R v Caldwell* [1981] 1 All ER 961, [1982] AC 341, that the model direction formulated by Lord Diplock (see [18], above) is capable of leading to obvious unfairness. As the excerpts quoted at [6]–[7], above, reveal, the trial judge regretted the direction he (quite rightly) felt compelled to give, and it is evident that this direction offended the jury's sense of fairness. The sense of fairness of 12 representative citizens sitting as a jury (or of a smaller group of lay justices sitting as a bench of magistrates) is the bedrock on which the administration of criminal justice in this country is built. A law which runs counter to that sense must cause concern. Here, the appellants could have been charged under s 1(1) of the 1971 Act with recklessly damaging one or both of the wheelie-bins, and they would have had little defence. As it was, the jury might have inferred that boys of the appellants' age would have appreciated the risk to the building of what they did, but it seems clear that such was not their conclusion (nor, it would appear, the judge's either). On that basis the jury thought it unfair to convict them. I share their sense of unease. It is neither moral nor just to convict a defendant (least of all a child) on the strength of what someone else would have apprehended if the defendant himself had no such apprehension. Nor, the defendant having been convicted, is the problem cured by imposition of a nominal penalty.

[34] Thirdly, I do not think the criticism of *R v Caldwell* expressed by academics, judges and practitioners should be ignored. A decision is not, of course, to be overruled or departed from simply because it meets with disfavour in the learned journals. But a decision which attracts reasoned and outspoken criticism by the leading scholars of the day, respected as authorities in the field, must command attention. One need only cite (among many other examples) the observations of Professor John Smith [1981] Crim LR 392 at 393–396 and Professor Glanville Williams 'Recklessness Redefined' (1981) 40 CLJ 252. This criticism carries greater weight when voiced also by judges as authoritative as Lord Edmund-Davies and Lord Wilberforce in *R v Caldwell* itself, Robert Goff LJ in *Elliott v C (a minor)* [1983] 2 All ER 1005, [1983] 1 WLR 939 and Ackner LJ in *R v Stephen Malcolm R* (1984) 79 Cr App R 334. The reservations expressed by the trial judge in the present case are widely shared. The shop floor response to *R v Caldwell* may be gauged from the editors' commentary, to be found in *Archbold's Pleading, Evidence and Practice in Criminal Cases* (41st edn, 1982) pp 1009–1010 (para 17–25). The editors suggested that remedial legislation was urgently required.

[35] Fourthly, the majority's interpretation of 'reckless' in s 1 of the 1971 Act was, as already shown, a misinterpretation. If it were a misinterpretation that offended no principle and gave rise to no injustice there would be strong grounds for adhering to the misinterpretation and leaving Parliament to correct it if it chose. But this misinterpretation is offensive to principle and is apt to cause injustice. That being so, the need to correct the misinterpretation is compelling.

[36] It is perhaps unfortunate that the question at issue in this appeal fell to be answered in a case of self-induced intoxication. For one instinctively recoils from the notion that a defendant can escape the criminal consequences of his injurious conduct by drinking himself into a state where he is blind to the risk he is causing to others. In *R v Caldwell* it seems to have been assumed (see [18], above) that the risk would have been obvious to the defendant had he been sober. Further, the context did not require the House to give close consideration to the liability of those (such as the very young and the mentally handicapped) who were not normal, reasonable adults. The overruling by the majority of *R v Stephenson* [1979] 2 All ER 1198, [1979] QB 695 does however make it questionable whether such consideration would have led to a different result.

[37] In the course of argument before the House it was suggested that the rule in *R v Caldwell* might be modified, in cases involving children, by requiring comparison not with normal, reasonable adults but with normal, reasonable children of the same age. This is a suggestion with some attractions but it is open to four compelling objections. First, even this modification would offend the principle that conviction should depend on proving the state of mind of the individual defendant to be culpable. Second, if the rule were modified in relation to children on grounds of their immaturity it would be anomalous if it were not also modified in relation to the mentally handicapped on grounds of their limited understanding. Third, any modification along these lines would open the door to difficult and contentious argument concerning the qualities and characteristics to be taken into account for purposes of the comparison. Fourth, to adopt this modification would be to substitute one misinterpretation of s 1 for another. There is no warrant in the Act or in the travaux preparatoires which preceded it for such an interpretation.

[38] A further refinement, advanced by Professor Glanville Williams (1981) 40 CLJ 252 at 270–271, adopted by the justices in *Elliott*'s case and commented upon by Robert Goff LJ in that case is that a defendant should only be regarded as having acted recklessly by virtue of his failure to give any thought to an obvious risk that property would be destroyed or damaged, where such risk would have been obvious to him if he had given any thought to the matter. This refinement also has attractions, although it does not meet the objection of principle and does not represent a correct interpretation of the section. It is, in my opinion, open to the further objection of over-complicating the task of the jury (or bench of justices). It is one thing to decide whether a defendant can be believed when he says that the thought of a given risk never crossed his mind. It is another, and much more speculative, task to decide whether the risk would have been obvious to him if the thought had crossed his mind. The simpler the jury's task, the more likely is its verdict to be reliable. Robert Goff LJ's reason for rejecting this refinement ([1983] 2 All ER 1005 at 1011–1012, [1983] 1 WLR 939 at 950) was somewhat similar.

[39] I cannot accept that restoration of the law as understood before *R v Caldwell* would lead to the acquittal of those whom public policy would require to be convicted. There is nothing to suggest that this was seen as a problem before *R v Caldwell*, or (as noted at [12]–[13], above) before the 1971 Act. There is no reason to doubt the common sense which tribunals of fact bring to their task. In a contested case based on intention, the defendant rarely admits intending the injurious result in question, but the tribunal of fact will readily infer such an intention, in a proper case, from all the circumstances and probabilities and evidence of what the defendant did and said at the time. Similarly with recklessness: it is not to be supposed that the tribunal of fact will accept a defendant's assertion that he never thought of a certain risk when all the circumstances and probabilities and evidence of what he did and said at the time show that he did or must have done.

[40] In his printed case, Mr Newman advanced the contention that the law as declared in *R v Caldwell* was incompatible with art 6 of the European Convention for the Protection of Human Rights and Fundamental Freedoms 1950 (as set out in Sch 1 to the Human Rights Act 1998). While making no concession, he forbore to address legal argument on the point. I need say no more about it.

[41] For the reasons I have given I would allow this appeal and quash the appellants' convictions. I would answer the certified question obliquely, basing myself on cl 18(c) of the Criminal Code Bill annexed by the Law Commission to its report *A Criminal Code for England and Wales* (1989) (Law Com no 177) vol 1, Report and Draft Criminal Code Bill):

'[A] person acts…"recklessly" [within the meaning of s 1 of the 1971 Act] with respect to-(i) a circumstance when he is aware of a risk that it exists or will exist; (ii) a result when he is aware of a risk that it will occur; and it is, in the circumstances known to him, unreasonable to take the risk…'

Lord Steyn

…

[45] In my view the very high threshold for departing from a previous decision of the House has been satisfied in this particular case. In summary I would reduce my reasons to three propositions. First, in *R v Caldwell* the majority should have accepted without equivocation that before the passing of the 1971 Act foresight of consequences was an essential element in recklessness in the context of damage to property under s 51 of the Malicious Damage Act 1861. Secondly, the matrix of the immediately preceding Law Commission recommendations shows convincingly that the purpose of s 1 of the 1971 Act was to replace the out of date language of 'maliciously' causing damage by more modern language while not changing the substance of the mental element in any way. Foresight of consequences was to remain an ingredient of recklessness in regard to damage to property. Thirdly, experience has shown that by bringing within the reach of s 1(1) cases of inadvertent recklessness the decision in *R v Caldwell* became a source of serious potential injustice which cannot possibly be justified on policy grounds.

…

[52] In the case before the House the two boys were 11 and 12 respectively. Their escapade of camping overnight without their parents' permission was something that many children have undertaken. But by throwing lit newspapers under a plastic wheelie-bin they caused £1m of damage to a shop. It is, however, an agreed fact on this appeal that the boys thought there was no risk of the fire spreading in the way it eventually did. What happened at trial is highly significant. The jury were perplexed by the *Caldwell* directions which compelled them to treat the boys as adults and to convict them. The judge plainly thought this approach was contrary to common sense but loyally applied the law as laid down in *R v Caldwell*. The view of the jurors and the judge would be widely shared by reasonable people who pause to consider the matter. The only answer of the Crown is that where unjust convictions occur the judge can impose a lenient sentence. This will not do in a modern criminal justice system. Parliament certainly did not authorise such a cynical strategy.

[53] Ignoring the special position of children in the criminal justice system is not acceptable in a modern civil society. In 1990 the United Kingdom ratified the United Nations *Convention on the Rights of the Child* (New York, 20 November 1989; TS 44 (1992); Cm 1976) (the UN convention) which entered into force on 15 January 1992. Article 40(1) provides:

'States Parties recognize the right of every child alleged as, accused of, or recognized as having infringed the penal law to be treated in a manner consistent with the promotion of the child's sense of dignity and worth, which reinforces the child's respect for the human rights and fundamental freedoms of others and which takes into account the child's age and the desirability of promoting the child's rein-tegration and the child's assuming a constructive role in society.' (My emphasis.)

This provision imposes both procedural and substantive obligations on state parties to protect the special position of children in the criminal justice system. For example, it would plainly be contrary to art 40(1) for a state to set the age of criminal responsibility of children at, say, five years. Similarly, it is contrary to art 40(1) to ignore in a crime punishable by life imprisonment, or detention during Her Majesty's pleasure, the age of a child in judging whether the mental element has been satisfied. It is true that the UN convention became binding on the United Kingdom after *R v Caldwell* was decided. But the House cannot ignore the norm created by the UN convention. This factor on its own justified a reappraisal of *R v Caldwell*.

[54] If it is wrong to ignore the special characteristics of children in the context of recklessness under s 1 of the 1971 Act, an adult who suffers from a lack of mental capacity or a relevant personality disorder may be entitled to the same standard of justice. Recognising the special characteristics of children and mentally disabled people goes some way towards reducing the scope of s 1 of the 1971 Act for producing unjust results which are inherent in the objective mould into which the *Caldwell* analysis forced recklessness. It does not, however, restore the correct interpretation of s 1 of the 1971 Act. The accepted meaning of recklessness involved foresight of consequences. This subjective state of mind is to be inferred 'by reference to all the evidence, drawing such inferences from the evidence as appear proper in the circumstances' (per Lord Edmund-Davies [1981] 1 All ER 961 at 970, [1982] AC 341 at 358, citing s 8 of the Criminal Justice Act 1967). That is what Parliament intended by implementing the Law Commission proposals.

[55] This interpretation of s 1 of the 1971 Act would fit in with the general tendency in modern times of our criminal law. The shift is towards adopting a subjective approach. It is generally necessary to look at the matter in the light of how it would have appeared to the defendant. Like Lord Edmund-Davies I regard s 8 of the 1967 Act, as of central importance. There is, however, also a congruence of analysis appearing from decisions of the House. In *Director of Public Prosecutions v Morgan* [1975] 2 All ER 347, [1976] AC 182 [below, p **181**] the House ruled that a defence of mistake must be honestly rather than reasonably held. In *Beckford v R* [1987] 3 All ER 425 at 432, [1988] AC 130 at 145 per Lord Griffiths [below, p **451**], the House held that self-defence permits a defendant to use such force as is reasonable in the circumstances as he honestly believed them to be. *B (a minor) v Director of Public Prosecutions* [2000] 1 All ER 833, [2000] 2 AC 428 concerned the offence contrary to s 1(1) of the Children Act 1961 [see below, p **216**]. The House held that the accused's honest belief that a girl was over 14 need not be based on reasonable grounds. Lord Nicholls of Birkenhead observed ([2000] 1 All ER 833 at 837, [2000] 2 AC 428 at 462):

> 'Considered as a matter of principle, the honest belief approach must be preferable. By definition the mental element in a crime is concerned with a subjective state of mind, such as intent or belief.'

To same effect is *R v K* [2001] UKHL 41, [2001] 3 All ER 897, [2002] 1 AC 462 [below, p **221**] where it was held that while a girl under the age of 16 cannot in law consent to an indecent assault, it is a defence if the defendant honestly believed she was over 16. It is true that the general picture is not entirely harmonious. Duress requires reasonable belief (see Lord Lane CJ in *R v Graham* [1982] 1 All ER 801 at 806, [1982] 1 WLR 294 at 300, approved by the House of Lords in *R v Howe* [1987] 1 All ER 771, [1987] AC 417; *R v Martin* [1989] 1 All ER 652). Duress is a notoriously difficult corner of the law. However, in *R v Graham* [1982] 1 All ER 801 at 806, [1982] 1 WLR 294 at 300 [below, p **407**] Lord Lane CJ stated that in judging the accused's response the test is:

> '...have the prosecution made the jury sure that a sober person of reasonable firmness, sharing the characteristics of the defendant, would not have responded to whatever he reasonably believed [the threatener] said or did by taking part in the [offence].' (My emphasis.)

The age and sex of the defendant (but possibly no other characteristics) are relevant to the cogency of the threat (see *R v Bowen* [1996] 4 All ER 837, [1997] 1 WLR 372). In regard to provocation a wider view of the impact on defendant has prevailed (see *R v Smith* [2000] 4 All ER 289, [2001] 1 AC 146 (by a three to two majority) [below, p **600**]).

[56] These developments show that what Lord Diplock described in *R v Caldwell* [1981] 1 All ER 961 at 966, [1982] AC 341 at 353 as an 'esoteric meaning' of recklessness was also consistent with the general trend of the criminal law.

CONCLUSION ON CALDWELL

[57] The surest test of a new legal rule is not whether it satisfies a team of logicians but how it performs in the real world. With the benefit of hindsight the verdict must be that the rule laid down by the majority in *R v Caldwell* failed this test. It was severely criticised by academic lawyers of distinction. It did not command respect among practitioners and judges. Jurors found it difficult to understand: it also sometimes offended their sense of justice. Experience suggests that In *R v Culdwell* the law took a wrong turn.

[58] That brings me to the question whether the subjective interpretation of recklessness might allow wrongdoers who ought to be convicted of serious crime to escape conviction. Experience before *R v Caldwell* did not warrant such a conclusion. In any event, as Lord Edmund-Davies explained ([1981] 1 All ER 961 at 970, [1982] AC 341 at 358), if a defendant closes his mind to a risk he must realise that there is a risk and, on the evidence, that will usually be decisive. One can trust the realism of trial judges, who direct juries, to guide juries to sensible verdicts and juries can in turn be relied on to apply robust common sense to the evaluation of ridiculous defences. Moreover, the endorsement by Parliament of the Law Commission proposals could not seriously have been regarded as a charter for the acquittal of wrongdoers.

[59] In my view the case for departing from *R v Caldwell* has been shown to be irresistible.

[60] I agree with the reasons given by Lord Bingham of Cornhill. I have nothing to add to his observations on self-induced intoxication.

Appeal allowed

Notes and questions

1. The law is returned to what it was intended to be. Recklessness in criminal damage is to be construed in a subjective sense—by looking to the state of mind of the individual defendant.

2. Although the decision in *Caldwell* has now been overruled and is to be regarded as wrong as regards its conclusions on recklessness, it deserves some further consideration. For criticism of *Caldwell* see commentary, [1981] Crim LR 393; E. Griew [1981] Crim LR 743; G. Syrota [1982] Crim LR 97; Glanville Williams, 'Recklessness Redefined' [1981] CLJ 252. See also J. McEwan and St John Robilliard, 'Recklessness: the House of Lords and the Criminal Law' (1981) LS 267 and the response of G. Williams (1992) LS 189.

3. The majority in *Caldwell* had ruled:

a person charged with an offence under s 1(1) of the 1971 Act is 'reckless as to whether or not any property would be destroyed or damaged' if (1) he does an act which in fact creates an obvious risk that property will be destroyed or damaged and (2) when he does the act he either has not given any thought to the possibility of there being any such risk or has recognised that there was some risk involved and has none the less gone on to do it.

Was recklessness under the *Caldwell* definition a 'state of mind'? Was it really mens rea? (Cf *Kingston* above.) Glanville Williams wrote that to describe giving no thought as a state of mind was 'an abuse of language' [1981] CLJ 252.

4. Was *Caldwell* recklessness a form of negligence? It was pointed out by critics of the *Caldwell/Lawrence* test of recklessness that the only thing that prevented it from being a straightforward gross negligence test was that a person who did give thought to the possibility of there being a risk and concluded, grossly negligently, that there was no risk, was not guilty of recklessness under either of Lord Diplock's alternatives. This escape hole became known as 'the lacuna'. Some writers disputed whether it existed at all; but its existence was essential if any credence was to be given to Lord Diplock's insistence that he was describing two states of mind. A good illustration of the so-called lacuna is to be found in the facts of *Crossman* (1986) 82 Cr App R 333, [1986] Crim LR 406 though the point of law was not taken. D, a lorry driver, rejected the advice of the loaders of a piece of heavy machinery on his lorry that it was unsafe unless chained and sheeted. D said it was 'as safe as houses'. When he drove away, the load fell off and killed a pedestrian. D's defence, that reckless driving must have something to do with the handling or control of the vehicle, was rejected. He then pleaded guilty to causing death by reckless driving. The same point was taken on appeal and the appeal was dismissed. But could D be said to have failed to give thought to the possibility of there being any risk when that possibility had been drawn to his attention, considered and rejected by him? And could he be said to have recognized that there was some risk involved if he really believed that the load was 'as safe as houses'? Should not the case have gone to the jury with a direction that, if D believed, or may have believed, that the load was as safe as houses, recklessness was not proved? He may have been grossly negligent in forming his opinion. If so, he would now be guilty of causing death by dangerous driving, below, p **168** and his liability for manslaughter would depend on whether his negligence created a risk to life, bad enough, in the opinion of the jury, to deserve condemnation as that offence. In *R v Reid* [1992] 3 All ER 673, House of Lords the House acknowledged the lacuna. Lord Browne-Wilkinson agreeing with Lords Ackner and Goff. 'There may be cases where, despite the defendant being aware of the risk and deciding to take it, he does so because of a reasonable misunderstanding, sudden disability or emergency which renders it inappropriate to characterise his conduct as being reckless.' See L. Leigh, 'Recklessness after Reid' (1993) 56 MLR 208.

5. The House of Lords in *G* made clear that the principle espoused in *Caldwell* was unacceptable for serious crimes (see in particular Lord Bingham at [32]). In this respect the House of Lords is endorsing its recent commitment to subjectivism (oddly enough it has done so at a time when Parliament keeps creating serious offences based on objective fault elements as in sexual offences and, for example, offences of money laundering under the Proceeds of Crime Act 2002).

6. One of the interesting aspects of *Caldwell* was that it caused commentators to consider important questions about what the approach to recklessness *ought* to be. *Should* a person be held to be reckless only if:
   (a) he is aware of the risk; or
   (b) he is aware of the risk or he would have been aware of it if *he* had given thought to the matter (compare *Briggs* and *Stephenson* referred to in Lord Bingham's judgment); or
   (c) he is aware of the risk or a person of his age and with his relevant characteristics who gave thought to the matter would have been aware of it (see the rejected argument in *Stephen Malcolm R*); or
   (d) he is aware of the risk or a reasonably prudent man who gave thought to the matter would have been aware of it?

(e) Should what matters be D's attitude to the risk of harm rather than his foresight of it? Which test—*Caldwell* or *G* – better reflects that? See further, D. Birch [1988] Crim LR 4.

In *Caldwell* (p **144**, above), Lord Diplock had suggested that there is no difference in culpability between a defendant who has given no thought to the possibility that there might be a risk and one who knows there is a risk and decides to take it. Do you agree? Consider the case of the South Wales bus driver who in 1982 attempted to drive his 13ft 9in double-decker under a railway bridge 10ft 6in high, killing six people and injuring several others. (See *The Times*, 7 October 1982, 2 November 1982 and 13 January 1983.) It appears that he had driven the route regularly for 10 years but had never taken a double-decker on the route before. When he hit the bridge he thought, 'My God, a double-decker.' He knew he was driving a double-decker because, only two stops before the crash, he had told passengers boarding the bus that there was plenty of room upstairs. But, as he approached the bridge, he had apparently forgotten that he was driving a double-decker. It was stated at the inquest that the Director of Public Prosecutions did not consider there was evidence for a charge of manslaughter or causing death by dangerous (meaning, presumably 'reckless', dangerous driving having been, at that time, abolished) driving. The driver subsequently pleaded guilty to driving without due care and attention.

7. Although *G* was a unanimous decision, Lord Rodger was clearly not as committed to the subjectivist approach to recklessness as his brethren:

Lord Rodger of Earlsferry:

[65] It is no secret that, for a long time, many of the leading academic writers on English criminal law have been 'subjectivists'. By that I mean, at the risk of gross over-simplification, that they have believed that the criminal law should punish people only for those consequences of their acts which they foresaw at the relevant time. Those who subscribe to that philosophy will tend to approve the concept of recklessness in *R v Cunningham* [1957] 2 All ER 412, [1957] 2 QB 396. The late Professor Glanville Williams and the late Professor John Smith, who were members of the influential Criminal Law Revision Committee, were two of the most distinguished proponents of such views.

    ...

[68] it is equally clear that other views are not only possible but have actually been adopted by English judges at different times over the centuries. Their judgments reveal many strands of thinking (see J Horder 'Two Histories and Four Hidden Principles of Mens Rea' (1997) 113 LQR 95). There is therefore no reason to treat the concept of recklessness expounded in *R v Cunningham* either as being the quintessence of the historic English criminal law on the point or as necessarily providing the best solution in all circumstances. Indeed in *R v Stephenson* [1979] 2 All ER 1198, [1979] QB 695, a case on s 1(1) of the 1971 Act, Geoffrey Lane LJ recognised that the subjective approach was problematical in certain situations. Having made it quite clear that in his view the test of recklessness under the 1971 Act remained subjective and that the knowledge or appreciation of risk of some damage must have entered the defendant's mind, he commented ([1979] 2 All ER 1198 at 1204, [1979] QB 695 at 704):

> 'There is no doubt that the subjective definition of "recklessness" does produce difficulties. One of them which is particularly likely to occur in practice is the case of the person who by self-induced intoxication by drink or drugs deprives himself of the ability to foresee the risks involved in his actions. Assuming that by reason of his intoxication he is not proved to have foreseen the relevant risk, can he be said

to have been "reckless"? Plainly not, unless cases of self-induced intoxication are an exception to the general rule. In our judgment the decision of the House of Lords in *Director of Public Prosecutions v Majewski* ([1976] 2 All ER 142, [1977] AC 443) makes it clear that they are such an exception.'

In *R v Caldwell* just the kind of problem envisaged by Geoffrey Lane LJ arose: the defendant said that he was so drunk that it did not occur to him that there might be people in the hotel whose lives might be endangered if he set fire to it. Part of what Lord Diplock did to confront the kind of difficulty identified by Geoffrey Lane LJ was to adopt a wider definition of recklessness that covered culpable inadvertence. In so doing, as the House now holds, he misconstrued the terms of the 1971 Act.

[69] It does not follow, however, that Lord Diplock's broader concept of recklessness was undesirable in terms of legal policy. On the contrary, there is much to be said for the view that, if the law is to operate with the concept of recklessness, then it may properly treat as reckless the man who acts without even troubling to give his mind to a risk that would have been obvious to him if he had thought about it. This approach may be better suited to some offences than to others. For example, in the context of reckless driving the House endorsed and re-endorsed a more stringent version (see *R v Lawrence* [1981] 1 All ER 974, [1982] AC 510; *R v Reid* [1992] 3 All ER 673, [1992] 1 WLR 793). I refer in particular to the discussion of the policy issues by Lord Goff of Chieveley in *R v Reid* [1992] 3 All ER 673 at 686–689, [1992] 1 WLR 793 at 808–812. Moreover, the opposing view, that only advertent risk-taking should ever be included within the concept of recklessness in criminal law, seems to be based, at least in part, on the kind of thinking that the late Professor Hart demolished in his classic essay, 'Negligence, Mens Rea and Criminal Responsibility' (1961), reprinted in HLA Hart Punishment and Responsibility (1968) pp 136–157.

[70] Because the decision in *R v Caldwell* involved this legitimate choice between two legal policies, I was initially doubtful whether it would be appropriate for the House to overrule it. An alternative way to allow the appeal by reanalysing Lord Diplock's speech and overruling *Elliott v C (a minor)* [1983] 2 All ER 1005, [1983] 1 WLR 939 might well have been found. But, for the reasons that I have already indicated, I have come to share your Lordships' view that we should indeed overrule *R v Caldwell* and set the law back on the track that Parliament originally intended it to follow. If Parliament now thinks it preferable for the 1971 Act to cover culpably inadvertent as well as advertent wrongdoers, it can so enact. The Law Commission recognised that, if codifying the law, Parliament might wish to adopt that approach (see A Criminal Code for England and Wales (1989) (Law Com no 177) vol 2, Commentary on Draft Criminal Code Bill, p 366 (para 8.21), pp 446–447 (para 17.6)).

Do you agree that 'there is much to be said for the view that, if the law is to operate with the concept of recklessness, then it may properly treat as reckless the man who acts without even troubling to give *his* mind to a risk that would have been obvious to him if he had thought about it?'

8. Was the House of Lords right to reject a modified position of the *Caldwell* approach to deal only with cases involving children? Why should the law tolerate a child's incapacities any more than those of an adult with a relevant disability?

9. Can juries be trusted to decide whether the defendant did see the risk of the harm or not? Consider D, an absent minded professor who when arriving late for a lecture opens the car door and knocks a cyclist off causing injury and damage to the bike. Is he reckless? How easy will it be for him to deny recklessness by saying merely that he did not stop to look in the wing mirror? (Remember that the burden of proof remains on the prosecution.)

10. The definition of recklessness approved by Lord Bingham is that [A] person acts... 'recklessly' [within the meaning of s 1 of the 1971 Act] with respect to—(i) a circumstance

when he is aware of a risk that it exists or will exist; (ii) a result when he is aware of a risk that it will occur; and it is, in the circumstances known to him, unreasonable to take the risk…' Foresight of 'a' risk of the criminal damage is sufficient, provided it was not justifiable for D to take that risk in the circumstances. Should the law be stricter still and require foresight of a 'substantial' or 'real' risk?

11.   Might it be said that Lord Diplock was reckless in producing his model direction in failing to refer to the Law Commission work on the definition intended for the 1971 Act?!

12.   Although explicitly a decision on the criminal damage offences, G is it seems being accepted as providing the correct test for recklessness in any offence for which that state of mind suffices as the fault element. In *Attorney-General's Reference (No 3 of 2003)* [2004] EWCA Crim 868, [2004] 2 Cr App R 23 the defendant police officers had arrested V who had been injured in a fight and had become abusive and aggressive towards hospital staff when receiving treatment. Following medical confirmation that V was fit to be detained, he was placed partially face down wearing handcuffs in the custody suite but developed breathing difficulties and died. The officers were charged with gross negligence manslaughter and misconduct in a public office. They were acquitted on the judge's direction because (i) there was a lack of causation on the gross negligence counts, and (ii) there was insufficient evidence of recklessness for a conviction for misconduct. On the reference by the Attorney-General, the court considered the subjective approach to recklessness pronounced in G. The Crown sought to restrict the impact of G in two ways. First, it was argued that the House of Lords expressly limited its conclusions on recklessness to criminal damage. It was argued that in conduct crimes such as misconduct in public office, the issue of recklessness ought to be focused on the misconduct itself, not in the likelihood of any result being caused. The Crown argued that the prosecution ought to succeed on proof that there has been misconduct by the defendant and he was '*indifferent*' as to whether the acts or omissions constituting the misconduct may have any consequences. The court rejected any such limitation on the subjective approach in G. Secondly, the Crown argued that in crimes in which liability arises because of a duty situation an objective test of recklessness ought to apply so that those who do not advert to the risk of harm to particular individuals ought to be found reckless. The Court of Appeal rejected the argument. The court considered the House of Lords' interpretation of 'wilful neglect' in the case of duty as in *Sheppard* [1981] AC 394 (dealing with child neglect), and emphasized that in its view *Sheppard* imposed a subjective test in which the characteristics of the individual defendant were to be taken into consideration. The Court of Appeal's conclusion was that *Sheppard* 'did not impose a lower duty on the prosecution than G' [para 27]. For the purposes of wilful neglect or misconduct it was necessary for the offender to have subjective awareness of the duty to act or a subjective recklessness as to the existence of the duty.

4. MALICE

In much nineteenth century criminal legislation it was common to require that offences be committed 'unlawfully and maliciously'. As we have seen, the word 'unlawfully' meant 'without justification or lawful excuse' and in most instances it probably had no effect because a defendant could have relied on any justification or excuse recognized by the law

even if the word had not been used. The word 'maliciously' however imported a requirement of mens rea. It was not given its natural meaning of 'spitefully' or 'with ill-will'. Professor C. S. Kenny in his *Outlines of Criminal Law* (1902) derived from *Pembliton* (1874)
and *Latimer* (above, in the speech of Lord Bingham p **141**), the general proposition that:

...in any statutory definition of a crime, 'malice' must...be taken—not in its vague common law
sense as 'wickedness' in general, but—as requiring an actual intention to do the particular kind of
harm that in fact was done (or at least a recklessness as to doing it). (15th edn, p 189)

In *Cunningham* [1957] 2 All ER 412 D, in order to steal money from a gas meter, ripped the
meter away from the supply pipes and released a cloud of noxious coal gas into the house
next door. D was charged with *maliciously* administering a noxious substance (the gas) to
the neighbour so as thereby to endanger her life, contrary to s 23 of the Offences Against the
Person Act 1861. The Court of Criminal Appeal stated that 'in any statutory definition of a
crime "malice" must be taken not in the old vague sense of "wickedness" in general, but as
requiring either (1) an actual intention to do the particular *kind* of harm that in fact was
done, or (2) recklessness as to whether such harm should occur or not (i.e. the accused has
foreseen that the particular kind of harm might be done, and yet has gone on to take the
risk of it)' (*Outlines of Criminal Law*, 1902).

As the word 'maliciously' was used throughout the Offences Against the Person Act 1861
and the Malicious Damage Act 1861, these central parts of the criminal law were governed
by a consistent principle. A person was liable for causing the relevant harm only if either—
(a) he intended to cause harm of that kind or (b) he took a deliberate risk of doing so.

R v Savage; R v Parmenter
[1991] 4 All ER 698, House of Lords

(Lords Keith, Brandon, Ackner, Jauncey and Lowry)

Savage. There was bad feeling between Savage (S) and another young woman, Beal (B). S,
with a nearly full pint glass of beer in her hand, pushed her way through to a table in a pub
where B was sitting with friends. S said 'Nice to meet you darling' and threw the contents of
the glass over B. Contrary to S's evidence, she must have let go of the glass because it broke
and a piece of it cut B's wrist. S was charged with unlawfully and maliciously wounding B,
contrary to s 20 of the Offences Against the Person Act 1861 (OAPA). The jury were
directed that deliberately throwing the contents of the glass over B was an assault and that,
if S unintentionally let go of the glass causing the wound, she was guilty. The Court of
Appeal, following *Mowatt* [1968] 1QB 421, 426, quashed her conviction of the s 20 offence
because the jury ought to have been directed that S was guilty of that offence only if she
foresaw that some physical harm might result from her act; but the court substituted a
conviction for assault occasioning actual bodily harm (abh) contrary to OAPA, s 47. It was
common ground that S committed an assault by the act of throwing the beer and the only
remaining question was whether that act 'occasioned', or caused, abh.

Spratt [1991] 2 All ER 210, [1990] 1 WLR 1073. In this case another division of the Court
of Appeal delivered judgment on the same day as the court in *Savage* and reached different
conclusions. Neither court was aware of the other's judgment. Spratt fired an air pistol
from his flat into the square below. Two pellets struck a girl playing there. He said that he
was aiming at the sign on a rubbish chute, that he did not know anyone was there and
would not have fired if he had known. He pleaded guilty to assault occasioning actual

bodily harm (OAPA, s 47) on the advice of counsel who told the judge that the plea was based on recklessness in failing to give thought to the possibility of a risk of abh. On an appeal against sentence, doubt was raised about the correctness of the plea and the case was adjourned to enable an appeal to be made against conviction. The court allowed the appeal, holding that D was not guilty of the offence under s 47 unless he foresaw that he might occasion abh.

Parmenter. P was convicted on four counts of unlawfully and maliciously inflicting gbh (OAPA, s 20) on his son between the child's birth on 8 February 1988 and 11 May 1988. His defence was that he did not appreciate the frailty of a very young child and did not realize that the way he handled the child was likely to cause injury. The judge, using the words of Diplock LJ in *Mowatt*, directed the jury that it was 'enough that he should have foreseen that some physical harm to the person, albeit of a minor character, might result.' The Court of Appeal quashed the conviction. It was *not* enough that P *should have* foreseen. He was guilty only if he actually foresaw that some physical harm might be done. The court, preferring *Spratt* to *Savage*, declined to substitute a conviction of assault occasioning abh, contrary to s 47, because it was not implicit in the verdict of the jury that P foresaw that he might occasion abh.

The courts in *Savage* and *Parmenter* gave leave to appeal to the House of Lords.

Lord Ackner, with whom all of their Lordships agreed, formulated four questions arising in these appeals. (At this point we are not concerned with the first question.)

Lord Ackner: II *Can a verdict of assault occasioning actual bodily harm be returned upon proof of an assault together with proof of the fact that actual bodily harm was occasioned by the assault, or must the prosecution also prove that the defendant intended to cause some actual bodily harm or was reckless as to whether such harm would be caused?*

Your Lordships are concerned with the mental element of a particular kind of assault, an assault 'occasioning actual bodily harm'. It is common ground that the mental element of assault is an intention to cause the victim to apprehend immediate and unlawful violence or recklessness whether such apprehension be caused (see *R v Venna* [1975] 3 All ER 788, [1976] QB 421). It is of course common ground that Mrs Savage committed an assault upon Miss Beal when she threw the contents of her glass of beer over her. It is also common ground that however the glass came to be broken and Miss Beal's wrist thereby cut, it was, on the finding of the jury, Mrs Savage's handling of the glass which caused Miss Beal 'actual bodily harm'. Was the offence thus established or is there a further mental state that has to be established in relation to the bodily harm element of the offence? Clearly the section, by its terms, expressly imposes no such requirement. Does it do so by necessary implication? It uses neither the word 'intentionally' nor the word 'maliciously'. The words 'occasioning actual bodily harm' are descriptive of the word 'assault', by reference to a particular kind of consequence.

In neither *R v Savage* nor *R v Spratt* nor in *R v Parmenter* was the court's attention invited to the decision of the Court of Appeal in *R v Roberts* (1971) 56 Cr App R 95, [1972] Crim LR 27. This is perhaps explicable on the basis that this case is not referred to in the index to *Archbold's Criminal Pleading, Evidence and Practice* (43rd edn, 1988). The relevant text states (para 20–117): 'The mens rea required [for actual bodily harm] is that required for common assault', without any authority being provided for this proposition.

It is in fact *R v Roberts* which provides authority for this proposition. Roberts was tried on an indictment which alleged that he indecently assaulted a young woman. He was acquitted on that charge, but convicted of assault occasioning actual bodily harm to her. The girl's complaint was that while travelling in the defendant's car he sought to make advances towards her and then tried to take her coat off. This was the last straw and, although the car was travelling at some speed, she jumped out and sustained injuries. The defendant denied he had touched the girl. He had had an argument with her and in the course of that argument she suddenly opened the door and jumped out. In his direction to the jury the chairman of quarter sessions stated: 'If you are satisfied that he tried to pull off her coat and as a result she jumped out of the moving car then your verdict is guilty.'

It was contended on behalf of the appellant that this direction was wrong since the chairman had failed to tell the jury that they must be satisfied that the appellant foresaw that she might jump out of the car as a result of his touching her before they could convict. The court rejected that submission. The test was, said the court (at 102):

> 'Was it [the action of the victim which resulted in actual bodily harm] the natural result of what the alleged assailant said and did, in the sense that it was something that could reasonably have been foreseen as the consequence of what he was saying or doing? As it was put in one of the old cases, it had got to be shown to be his act, and if of course the victim does something so "daft", in the words of the appellant in this case, or so unexpected, not that this particular assailant did not actually foresee it but that no reasonable man could be expected to foresee it, then it is only in a very remote and unreal sense a consequence of his assault, it is really occasioned by a voluntary act on the part of the victim which could not reasonably be foreseen and which breaks the chain of causation between the assault and the harm or injury.'

[His Lordship quoted from the summing up to the jury.]

Thus, once the assault was established, the only remaining question was whether the victim's conduct was the natural consequence of that assault. The words 'occasioning' raised solely a question of causation, an objective question which does not involve inquiring into the accused's state of mind.

In *R v Spratt* [1991] 2 All ER 210 at 219, [1990] 1 WLR 1073 at 1082 McCowan LJ said:

> 'However, the history of the interpretation of the 1861 Act shows that, whether or not the word "maliciously" appears in the section in question, the courts have consistently held that the mens rea of every type of offence against the person covers both actual intent and recklessness, in the sense of taking the risk of harm ensuing with foresight that it might happen.'

McCowan LJ then quoted a number of authorities for that proposition. [His Lordship examined the cases.] Thus, none of the cases cited was concerned with the mental element required in s 47 cases. Nevertheless, the Court of Appeal in *R v Parmenter* at 415 preferred the decision in *R v Spratt* to that of *R v Savage* because the former was 'founded on a line of authority leading directly to the conclusion there expressed'.

My Lords, in my respectful view, the Court of Appeal in *R v Parmenter* was wrong in preferring the decision in *R v Spratt*. The decision in *R v Roberts* (1971) 56 Cr App R 95, [1972] Crim LR 27 was correct. The verdict of assault occasioning actual bodily harm may be returned upon proof of an assault together with proof of the fact that actual bodily harm was occasioned by the assault. The prosecution are not obliged to prove that the defendant intended to cause some actual bodily harm or was reckless as to whether such harm would be caused.

III *In order to establish an offence under s 20 of the 1861 Act, must the prosecution prove that the defendant actually foresaw that his act would cause harm, or is it sufficient to prove that he ought to have foreseen?*

Although your Lordships' attention has been invited to a plethora of decided cases, the issue is a narrow one. Is the decision of the Court of Criminal Appeal in *R v Cunningham* [1957] 2 All ER 412, [1957] 2 QB 396 still good law, subject only to a gloss placed upon it by the Court of Appeal, Criminal Division in *R v Mowatt* [1967] 3 All ER 47, [1968] 1 QB 421, or does the later decision of your Lordships' House in *R v Caldwell* [1981] 1 All ER 961, [1982] AC 341 provide the answer to this question?

These three decisions require detailed consideration.

R v Cunningham

As previously stated this case concerned a charge brought under s 23 of the 1861 Act, which makes it an offence 'unlawfully and maliciously' to administer etc to any person any poison or other noxious thing so as to endanger life or inflict grievous bodily harm. Cunningham, in stealing a gas meter and its contents from the cellar of a house, fractured a gas pipe, causing coal gas to escape. This percolated through the cellar wall to the adjoining house and entered a bedroom, with the result that Mrs Wade, who was asleep, inhaled a considerable quantity of the gas, with the result that her life was endangered. Cunningham's conviction was quashed because of the misdirection of the trial judge as to the meaning of 'maliciously' in s 23 of the Act.

Byrne J, in a reserved judgment given on behalf of the court, accepted as accurate the following statement of the law propounded by Professor CS Kenny in the first edition of his *Outlines of Criminal Law* published in 1902 and set out in the 16th edition (1952) p 86:

> '...in any statutory definition of a crime, "malice" must be taken not in the old vague sense of wickedness in general, but as requiring either (1) an actual intention to do the particular *kind* of harm that in fact was done, or (2) recklessness as to whether such harm should occur or not (ie the accused has foreseen that the particular kind of harm might be done, and yet has gone on to take the risk of it). It is neither limited to, nor does it indeed require any ill-will towards the person injured.'

The court held that the jury should have been left to decide whether, even if the appellant did not intend the injury to Mrs Wade, *he* foresaw that the removal of the gas meter might cause injury to someone but nevertheless removed it.

R v Caldwell

Mr Sedley QC has not invited your Lordships to reconsider the majority decision of your Lordships' House. He chose a much less ambitious task. He submits that *R v Cunningham* cannot be bad law, since it is inconceivable that your Lordships' House, in its majority judgment, would have steered such a careful path around it. Your Lordships, having power to overrule it, would, so he submits, have felt obliged to do so in order to avoid creating a false double standard of 'recklessness'. He further submits that it is a significant that Lord Diplock, whose speech represented the views of the majority of your Lordships, nowhere suggests that his own judgment in *R v Mowatt* [1967] 3 All ER 47, [1968] 1 QB 421, which clarified or modified *R v Cunningham*, was of doubtful validity.

In the light of these submissions it is necessary to deal in some detail with *R v Caldwell*...

[His Lordship quoted extensively from Lord Diplock's speech in *Caldwell*.]

Before returning to the submission made by Mr Sedley, to which I have referred above, I think it is now convenient to go back in time to the decisions of the Court of Appeal in *R v Mowatt* [1967] 3 All ER 47, [1968] 1 QB 421, to which reference has already been made. The facts of that case were simple. On 30 September 1966 in the early hours of the morning the defendant and a companion stopped a third man in the street and asked him whether there was a pub anywhere nearby. The defendant's companion then snatched a £5 note from the third man's breast-pocket and ran off. The third man chased him without success and returned to the defendant, grasping him by the lapels and demanding to know where his companion had gone. The defendant then struck the third man, knocking him down. Two police officers saw the defendant sit astride the third man and strike him repeated blows in the face, pull him to his feet and strike him again, knocking him down and rendering him almost unconscious. The defendant admitted inflicting the first blow but claimed it was self-defence. He was tried on an indictment which included a count for wounding with intent to do grievous bodily harm contrary to s 18 of the Offences against the Person Act 1861. In summing up on this count the trial judge told the jury they were entitled to return a verdict of unlawful wounding under s 20 of the Act. However in his summing up, while explaining the meaning of the word 'unlawfully' so far as it was relevant to the defence of self-defence, he gave no direction as to the meaning of 'maliciously'.

The importance of this case is that the Court of Appeal considered *R v Cunningham* and, although modifying or explaining an important feature of that decision, in no way queried its validity. The judgment of the Court of Appeal, to which I have already made references, was, as previously stated, given by Diplock LJ, as he then was. It is of course one of Mr Sedley's points that, although *R v Mowatt* was not referred to in *R v Caldwell*, it was most unlikely that its existence was overlooked, particularly by Lord Diplock. Diplock LJ observed that 'unlawfully and maliciously' was a fashionable phrase of parliamentary draftsmen in 1861 (see [1967] 3 All ER 47 at 49, [1968] 1 QB 421 at 425). It ran as a theme, with minor variations, through the Malicious Damage Act 1861, and the Offences against the Person Act 1861. He then referred to the 'very special' facts in *R v Cunningham* and observed:

> 'No doubt on these facts the jury should have been instructed that they must be satisfied before convicting the accused *that he was aware* that physical harm to some human being was a possible consequence of his unlawful act in wrenching off the gas meter. In the words of the court " 'maliciously' in a statutory crime postulates foresight of consequence" (see [1957] 2 All ER 412 at 414, [1957] 2 QB 396 at 399), and on this proposition we do not wish to cast any doubt.' (My emphasis.)

Subsequently, he added ([1967] 3 All ER 47 at 50, [1968] 1 QB 421 at 426):

> 'In the offence under s 20, and in the alternative verdict which may be given on a charge under s 18— for neither of which is any specific intent required—the word "maliciously" does import on the part of the person who unlawfully inflicts the wound or other grievous bodily harm an *awareness* that his act may have the consequence of causing some physical harm to some other person. That is what is meant by "the particular kind of harm" in the citation from *Professor Kenny's Outlines of Criminal Law* (18th edn, 1962, para 158a, p 202). It is quite unnecessary that the *accused* should have foreseen that his unlawful act might cause physical harm of the gravity described in the section, ie, a wound or serious physical injury. It is enough that *he* should have foreseen that some physical harm to some person, albeit of a minor character, might result.' (My emphasis.)

Mr Sedley submitted that in *R v Caldwell* your Lordships' House could have followed either of two possible paths to its conclusion as to the meaning of 'recklessly' in the 1971 Act. These were: (a) to hold that *R v Cunningham* (and *R v Mowatt*) were wrongly decided and to introduce a single test, wherever recklessness was an issue; or (b) to accept that *R v Cunningham* (subject to the *R v Mowatt* 'gloss' to which no reference was made) correctly states the law in relation to the Offences against the Person Act 1861, because the word 'maliciously' in that statute was a term of legal art which imported into the concept of recklessness a special restricted meaning, thus distinguishing it from 'reckless' or 'recklessly' in modern 'revising' statutes then before the House, where those words bore their then popular or dictionary meaning.

I agree with Mr Sedley that manifestly it was the latter course which the House followed. Therefore in order to establish an offence under s 20 the prosecution must prove either that the defendant intended or that he actually foresaw that his act would cause harm.

IV *In order to establish an offence under s 20 is it sufficient to prove that the defendant intended or foresaw the risk of some physical harm or must he intend or foresee either wounding or grievous bodily harm?*

It is convenient to set out once again the relevant part of the judgment of Diplock LJ in *R v Mowatt* [1967] 3 All ER 47 at 50, [1968] 1 QB 421 at 426. Having considered Professor Kenny's statement, which I have quoted above, he then said:

> 'In the offence under s 20...for...which [no] specific intent is required—the word "maliciously" does import...an awareness that his act may have the consequence of causing some physical harm to some

other person. That is what is meant by the "particular kind of harm" in the citation from *Professor Kenny's Outlines of Criminal Law* (18th edn, 1962, para 158a, p 202). It is quite unnecessary that the accused should have foreseen that his unlawful act might cause physical harm of the gravity described in the section, ie a wound or serious physical injury. *It is enough that he should have foreseen that some physical harm to some person, albeit of a minor character, might result.*' (My emphasis.)

Mr Sedley submits that this statement of the law is wrong. He contends that, properly construed, the section requires foresight of a wounding or grievous bodily harm. He drew your Lordships' attention to criticisms of *R v Mowatt* made by Professor Glanville Williams and by Professor J C Smith in their textbooks and in articles or commentaries. They argue that a person should not be criminally liable for consequences of his conduct unless he foresaw a consequence falling into the same legal category as that set out in the indictment.

Such a general principle runs contrary to the decision in *R v Roberts* (1971) 56 Cr App R 95, [1972] Crim LR 27, which I have already stated to be, in my opinion, correct. The contention is apparently based on the proposition that, as the actus reus of a s 20 offence is the wounding or the infliction of grievous bodily harm, the mens rea must consist of foreseeing such wounding or grievous bodily harm. But there is no such hard and fast principle. To take but two examples, the actus reus of murder is the killing of the victim, but foresight of grievous bodily harm is sufficient and, indeed, such bodily harm need not be such as to be dangerous to life. Again, in the case of manslaughter death is frequently the unforeseen consequence of the violence used.

The argument that, as ss 20 and 47 have both the same penalty, this somehow supports the proposition that the foreseen consequences must coincide with the harm actually done, overlooks the oft-repeated statement that this is the irrational result of this piecemeal legislation. The act 'is a rag-bag of offences brought together from a wide variety of sources with no attempt, as the draftsman frankly acknowledged, to introduce consistency as to substance or as to form' (see Professor J C Smith in his commentary on *R v Parmenter* ([1991] Crim LR 41)).

If s 20 was to be limited to cases where the accused does not desire but does foresee wounding or grievous bodily harm, it would have a very limited scope. The mens rea in s 20 crime is comprised in the word 'maliciously'. As was pointed out by Lord Lane CJ, giving the judgment of the Court of Appeal in *R v Sullivan* [1981] Crim LR 46, the 'particular kind of harm' in the citation from Professor Kenny was directed to 'harm to the person' as opposed to 'harm to property'. Thus it was not concerned with the degree of the harm foreseen. It is accordingly in my judgment wrong to look upon the decision in *R v Mowatt* [1967] 3 All ER 47, [1968] 1 QB 421 as being in any way inconsistent with the decision in *R v Cunningham* [1957] 2 All ER 412, [1957] 2 QB 396.

My Lords, I am satisfied that the decision in *R v Mowatt* was correct and that it is quite unnecessary that the accused should either have intended or have foreseen that his unlawful act might cause physical harm of the gravity described in s 20, ie a wound or serious physical injury. It is enough that he should have foreseen that some physical harm to some person, albeit of a minor character, might result.

In the result I would dismiss the appeal in *Savage's* case but allow the appeal in *Parmenter's* case, but only to the extent of substituting, in accordance with the provisions of s 3(2) of the Criminal Appeal Act 1968, verdicts of guilty of assault occasioning actual bodily harm contrary to s 47 of the 1861 Act for the four s 20 offences of which he was convicted.

Appeal in *R v Savage* dismissed; appeal in *R v Parmenter* allowed in part and conviction of assault occasioning actual bodily harm substituted.

Note

Note that in the penultimate paragraph of his speech Lord Ackner used the phrase, 'should have foreseen', which, when used in directing a jury, led to the quashing of convictions in several cases, including *Parmenter*. Although all their Lordships concurred in Lord Ackner's speech, the use of this phrase must be regarded as a slip and not as casting doubt on the proposition clearly stated by Lord Ackner that 'the prosecution must prove either that the defendant intended or that he *actually foresaw* that his act would cause harm' [authors' italics].

Savage confirms not only the decisions in *Cunningham* and *Mowatt* but also a series of cases decided after *Caldwell* and *Lawrence*. It left no doubt that the subjective form of mens rea—that D must himself foresee a risk of the prohibited harm and go on unjustifiably to take it—is applicable to the offences against the person.

5. KNOWLEDGE

The cases discussed above raise a more general problem about knowledge in the criminal law. Does a person 'know' a fact which is not present to his mind at the relevant moment, though he is quite capable of recalling it—as the bus driver recalled that he was driving a double-decker at the moment of impact? Professor Glanville Williams at one time thought he does. The following passage in the first edition of his *Textbook* (p 79) does not appear in the second edition but it is not clear whether he has changed his mind. He is discussing *Parker* (discussed in Lord Bingham's speech in *G* see p 145, above). D, in a telephone kiosk, being frustrated by his inability to get through, twice slammed the telephone down on to its cradle. On the second occasion he smashed it. Charged with criminal damage, he said that he did not realize at the time he acted that he was likely to break the telephone. The Court of Appeal held he was rightly convicted because 'a man is reckless when he carried out the deliberate act knowing or closing his mind to the obvious fact that there is some risk of damage resulting from that act, but nevertheless continued the performance of that act.'

The facts were so eloquent of recklessness that the appeal might well have been dismissed on the ground that no miscarriage of justice had actually occurred, even if the direction was regarded as misleading. Parker must have slammed the receiver down extremely hard to break the plastic, and it is impossible to believe that he did not know the risk of damaging it. It is a misunderstanding of the legal requirement to suppose that this knowledge of risk must be a matter of conscious awareness at the moment of the act. We grow up in a world in which we come to know, from the earliest age, that things are broken by rough treatment. Some things are more resistant than others: one could, in a temper, kick a farm tractor or the wheel of a lorry without doing damage. But is there anyone who does not know that a telephone receiver can be damaged by being violently slammed down? The fact that it is slammed down because of a feeling of frustration is nothing to the purpose.

If this is right, what was all the fuss over *DPP v Smith* (p 561, below) about? Smith, rightly suspected by a police officer of having stolen goods in his car, drove off at speed with the officer hanging on to the car and pursued an erratic course until he was thrown off in the path of an oncoming vehicle and killed. The whole incident lasted about 10 seconds: [1961] AC at 298 and 302. The Court of Criminal Appeal, whose judgment seems now to be rehabilitated (below, p 561), thought the relevant question was as to the state of mind of the defendant during those 10 seconds of panic. But if when Smith was sitting quietly at home, relaxed in his armchair, someone had said to him, 'Jim, if you were to drive off in your car at top speed in a busy street with a copper clinging to the bonnet, do you think it is likely that he would suffer serious injury?' would not his reply have been an unprintable affirmative? The Court of Appeal in that case, however, thought that the relevant question was what Smith thought in a moment of panic and the 10 seconds which the whole episode occupied. Was not this right?

(1) 'WILFUL BLINDNESS'

A requirement of knowledge has frequently been held to be satisfied by proof of what is sometimes called 'wilful blindness'. It has indeed been stated in the House of Lords that—

... it is always open to the tribunal of fact, when knowledge on the part of a defendant is required to be proved, to base a finding of knowledge on evidence that the defendant had deliberately shut his eyes to the obvious or refrained from inquiry because he suspected the truth but did not want to have his suspicions confirmed.

(*Westminster City Council v Croyalgrange Ltd* [1986] 2 All ER 353 at 359)
In so far as this states a universal rule it goes too far. In handling stolen goods (below, p 935) a person is not taken to 'know' that the goods are stolen merely because he suspects that they may be stolen and asks no questions because he prefers not to know.

Wilful blindness as described in *Croyalgrange* is indistinguishable from advertent recklessness as to circumstances. The draft Code, cl 18(a), defines it rather more narrowly:

... a person acts—
'knowingly' with respect to a circumstance not only when he is aware that it exists or will exist, but also when he avoids taking steps that might confirm his belief that it exists or will exist.

As the law stands, the question whether 'knowingly' includes wilful blindness is one of construction and may vary according to the context in which the word is used. Consider, for example, ss 2 and 3 of the Criminal Damage Act 1971. Since it is sufficient in these sections that D knows that the threatened conduct '*is likely* to endanger' life, does it not follow that it is sufficient that he is aware that life-endangering circumstances are likely to exist, but not sufficient that he is aware that they may possibly exist?

6. NEGLIGENCE

Before *Caldwell* a clear line was drawn by jurists between recklessness and negligence. Recklessness was advertent risk-taking. Negligence was inadvertent risk-taking. In both cases the risk was an unreasonable risk that a prudent person would not take but the reckless person was aware of the risk, the negligent person ought to have been aware of it but was not. Thus for Jerome Hall (GPCL 114–115):

Recklessness is like [intentionality] in that the actor is conscious of a forbidden harm, he realizes that his conduct increases the risk of its occurrence, and he has decided to create that risk;

whereas—

... negligence implies inadvertence, ie that the defendant was completely unaware of the dangerousness of his behaviour although actually it was unreasonably increasing the risk of the occurrence of an injury.

Similarly for Dr J. W. C. Turner (writing as editor of *Russell on Crime* (12th edn) pp 41–42) a reckless person is one who:

acts with full knowledge that he is taking the chance that this secondary result will follow... His precise mental attitude will be one of two kinds (a) he would prefer that the harmful result should not occur, or (b) he is indifferent as to whether it does or does not occur. Whichever it may be the common law makes no distinction in his liability.

Whereas (p 43):

Negligence... in this connection connotes *inadvertence*...

Glanville Williams (CLGP, 100) wrote:

Responsibility for some crimes may be incurred by the mere neglect to exercise due caution, where the mind is not actively but negatively or passively at fault. This is inadvertent negligence. Since advertent negligence has a special name (recklessness) it is convenient to use 'negligence' generally to mean inadvertent negligence.

Under *Caldwell* this distinction between advertent and inadvertent risk-taking was no longer synonymous with the distinction between recklessness and negligence in English criminal law. Most inadvertent risk-taking probably arises from a failure to give thought to the existence of a risk and so amounted to *Caldwell* recklessness. The only distinction between *Caldwell* recklessness and negligence lay in the existence of the so-called 'lacuna' discussed above, p 156.

(1) NEGLIGENCE IN ROAD TRAFFIC OFFENCES

The offences of reckless driving and causing death by reckless driving were abolished by the Road Traffic Act 1991, following the recommendation of the Road Traffic Law Review Report, HMSO, 1988 (the 'North Report'), discussed by J. R. Spencer [1988] Crim LR 707. The 1991 Act, following the recommendations of North, substitutes new ss 1 and 2 in the Road Traffic Act 1988, which create offences of causing death by dangerous driving and dangerous driving respectively. Section 2 of the 1991 Act substitutes a new s 3 in the 1988 Act and, not following the advice of North, extends the offence of careless and inconsiderate driving to include, as well as motor vehicles, mechanically propelled vehicles which are not motor vehicles and to public places which are not roads. All these are offences of negligence.

1. Causing death by dangerous driving
A person who causes the death of another person by driving a mechanically propelled vehicle dangerously on a road or other public place is guilty of an offence.

2. Dangerous driving
A person who drives a mechanically propelled vehicle dangerously on a road or other public place is guilty of an offence.

2A. Meaning of dangerous driving
  (1) For the purposes of sections 1 and 2 above a person is to be regarded as driving dangerously if (and, subject to subsection (2) below, only if)—
     (a) the way he drives falls far below what would be expected of a competent and careful driver, and

(b) it would be obvious to a competent and careful driver that driving in that way would be dangerous.

(2) A person is also to be regarded as driving dangerously for the purposes of sections 1 and 2 above if it would be obvious to a competent and careful driver that driving the vehicle in its current state would be dangerous.

(3) In subsections (1) and (2) above 'dangerous' refers to danger either of injury to any person or of serious damage to property; and in determining for the purposes of those subsections what would be expected of, or obvious to, a competent and careful driver in a particular case, regard shall be had not only to the circumstances of which he could be expected to be aware but also to any circumstances shown to have been within the knowledge of the accused.

(4) In determining for the purposes of subsection (2) above the state of a vehicle, regard may be had to anything attached to or carried on or in it and to the manner in which it is attached or carried.

3. Carelessness and inconsiderate driving. If a person drives a mechanically propelled vehicle on a road or other public place without due care and attention, or without reasonable consideration for other persons using the road or place, he is guilty of an offence.

Causing death by dangerous driving is punishable by 14 years' imprisonment, dangerous driving by two and careless driving is triable only summarily and punishable by a fine at level 4.

Lord Diplock, in a passage in *Lawrence* referred to with approval by Lord Ackner in *Reid* [1992] 3 All ER 673 at 680, said of s 3's predecessor that it—

creates an absolute offence in the sense in which that term is commonly used to denote an offence for which the only mens rea needed is simply that the prohibited physical act (actus reus) done by the accused was directed by a mind that was conscious of what his body was doing, it being unnecessary to show that his mind was also conscious of the possible consequences of his doing it. So s3 takes care of this kind of inattention or misjudgment to which the ordinarily careful motorist is occasionally subject without its necessarily involving any moral turpitude, although it causes inconvenience and annoyance to other users of the road.

The dangerous driving offences under ss 1 and 2 are also offences which require proof of no state of mind beyond the fact (if it be disputed) that the defendant was voluntarily driving the vehicle. Are they not then just as 'absolute' as careless driving? But all the offences require fault in the sense of failure to attain a prescribed standard of conduct. For careless driving, the defendant must be shown to have fallen below the standard, for dangerous driving, 'far' below it. Are not the offences more accurately described as offences of negligence than as 'absolute' or even 'of strict liability'? Cf *Gosney*, below, p **170**.

Why do we need an offence of mere carelessness or lack of consideration in the handling of vehicles when we do not have one in relation to other dangerous articles such as chainsaws? The North Report offered an answer:

the careless use of chainsaws does not contribute to over 5,000 deaths every year. It is because the danger associated with the widespread use of motor vehicles is so great that society has decided to attempt to restrain the use of vehicles so as to reduce this danger. And there are parallels between road traffic law and other bodies of regulatory law covering areas of activity such as health and safety at work, and building standards. Some of these areas of law contain offences which could be the result of mere carelessness such as, for example, polluting a river or leaving a machine unguarded. The common element between such offences is the degree of danger that may be caused to innocent parties.

North also replied to the argument that a careless driving offence is unnecessary because the self-interest of drivers in avoiding an accident is enough. The Report said that, if the offence were abolished:

at least part of it would have to be replaced or there would be some serious instances of bad driving which would go unpunished. In our view it is likely that the issues here are confused by the amount of attention which is focussed on the common shorthand term for this offence—careless driving. But what is required to establish the section 3 offence is more than this. The course of driving must be found to be lacking in *due* care or *reasonable* consideration. Cases where no accident is caused, involving momentary inattention for example, by a driver with an unblemished driving career should not, in our opinion, lead to an appearance in court. But a series of bad overtaking decisions might, if such driving came to police attention, warrant prosecution, even if no accident resulted.

What is the difference between 'lacking in due care' and carelessness? Is not 'momentary inattention' lack of due 'care'?

In *Reid*, Lord Goff gave the following example:

Take the simple case of a man driving his car on the motorway in a group of other cars, all travelling at say 60 mph, and he fails for a moment or so to keep his eye on the car in front—perhaps his attention is caught by a pretty girl in the car alongside—with the result that he does not notice that the car in front has had to brake suddenly and he drives straight into it causing it damage. This is a classic case of careless driving; I do not think that on these simple facts anybody would say that he was driving recklessly. This is not a case of a man driving dangerously (in the sense described by Lord Diplock) and nevertheless failing to address his mind to the possibility of risk; it is a case of a man who failed to drive with due care and attention, and no more.

If no accident occurs the man is certainly unlikely to be prosecuted for dangerous driving. But is he any less guilty of the offence?

Consider *Gosney* [1971] 3 All ER 220, [1971] 2 QB 674. At about midnight Mrs G was driving her car at about 30 mph in the fast lane of a dual carriageway, when she met a police car. There was nothing wrong with G's driving except that she was going in the wrong direction. She was charged with the former offence of dangerous driving, contrary to the Road Traffic Act 1960. She sought to prove by her testimony and by the production of maps and plans that it was not her fault that she was driving on the wrong carriageway; that she had turned right at a junction with which she was unfamiliar and that there was no indication by road sign or otherwise that a right turn into that carriageway was prohibited. The trial judge, following a decision by the Court of Appeal that dangerous driving was an absolute offence, refused to admit this evidence. It was irrelevant because driving in the wrong direction in the fast lane of a dual carriageway was dangerous driving and it was immaterial whether she was to blame for doing so. The Court of Appeal, disapproving its earlier decision, held that dangerous driving was not an absolute offence. It required fault—that is, a falling below the standard of care or skill of a competent and experienced driver. The excluded evidence was relevant to this question so G's conviction was quashed.

How would we now decide whether G was guilty of careless, or of the new dangerous, driving? The excluded evidence would be admissible on either charge. We have to envisage a competent and careful driver (call him Pat) arriving at the junction at night and in the same conditions of weather, etc, as G. Unless we are satisfied that Pat would not have made the same mistake as G, she must be acquitted of both offences. But if we are satisfied that

Pat would not have made that mistake, how do we distinguish between careless and dangerous? Is it that, for careless, we must be sure that the true state of affairs would have been obvious to Pat; for dangerous, that it would have been *blindingly* obvious? If not, what is the test?

FURTHER READING

J. BRADY, 'Recklessness, Negligence, Indifference and Awareness' (1980) 43 MLR 381

R. A. DUFF, 'The Obscure Intentions of the House of Lords' [1986] Crim LR 771

E. GRIEW, 'Consistency, Communication and Codification—Reflections on Two Mens Rea Words' in P. R. Glazebrook (ed) *Reshaping the Criminal Law* (1978), 57

H. L. A. HART, 'Negligence Mens Rea and Criminal Responsibility' in *Punishment and Responsibility* (1968)

J. HORDER, 'Intention in the Criminal Law—A Rejoinder' (1995) MLR 678

N. LACEY, 'A Clear Concept of Intention' (1993) 56 MLR 621

N. LACEY, 'In(de)terminable Intentions' (1995) 58 MLR 692

LORD GOFF, 'The Mental Element in the Crime of Murder' (1988) 104 LQR 30

A. W. NORRIE, 'Oblique Intention and Legal Politics' [1989] Crim LR 793

A. PEDAIN 'Intention and the Terrorist Example' [2003] Crim LR 579

S. SHUTE, 'Knowledge and Belief in the Criminal Law' in S. Shute and A. Simester (eds) *Criminal Law Theory: Doctrines of the General Part* (2002), 171

A. P. SIMESTER, 'Can Negligence be Culpable' in J. Horder, *Oxford Essays in Jurisprudence* (2000)

J. C. SMITH, 'A Note on Intention' [1990] Crim LR 85

J. C. SMITH, 'Intention in Criminal Law' (1974) 27 CLP 93

G. R. SULLIVAN, 'Knowledge, Belief and Culpability' ibid, 207;

V. TADROS, 'Recklessness and the Duty to Take Care' in S. Shute and A. Simester (eds) *Criminal Law Theory* (2002)

M. WASIK and M. P. THOMPSON, 'Turning a Blind Eye as Constituting Mens Rea' (1981) 32 NILQ 328

G. WILLIAMS, 'Oblique Intention' [1987] CLJ 417

G. WILLIAMS, 'The mens rea for murder—Leave it alone' (1989) 105 LQR 387

6
Proof

1. THE PRESUMPTION OF INNOCENCE

Woolmington v Director of Public Prosecutions
[1935] All ER Rep 1, House of Lords

(Lord Sankey LC, Lord Hewart CJ, Lords Atkin, Tomlin and Wright)

After a few months of marriage, the appellant's wife left him and went to live with her mother. The appellant was anxious for her to return but she did not. One morning he called at her mother's house and shot her dead. His story was that he decided to take an old gun which was in the barn at his employer's farm, show it to his wife and tell her that he was going to commit suicide if she did not come back. He sawed off the two barrels and loaded the gun with the two cartridges which were in the barn. He attached a piece of wire flex to the gun so that he could suspend it from his shoulder underneath his coat. When he asked his wife if she would come back, she replied that she was going to work as a domestic servant. He then threatened to shoot himself and went on to show her the gun. As he brought it across his waist, it somehow went off. It was, he said, a pure accident.

[**Swift J**, having quoted the passage from *Foster's Crown Law* cited below, directed the jury as follows:]

Once it is shown to a jury that somebody has died through the act of another, that is presumed to be murder, unless the person who has been guilty of the act which causes the death can satisfy a jury that what happened was something less, something which might be alleviated, something which might be reduced to a charge of manslaughter, or was something which was accidental, or was something which could be justified.

At the end of his summing up he added:

The Crown has got to satisfy you that this woman, Violet Woolmington, died at the prisoner's [sic] hands. They must satisfy you of that beyond any reasonable doubt. If they satisfy you of that, then he has to show that there are circumstances to be found in the evidence which has been given from the witness-box in this case which alleviate the crime so that it is only manslaughter, or which excuse the homicide altogether by showing that it was a pure accident.

The accused was convicted and his appeal was dismissed by the Court of Criminal Appeal. He appealed to the House of Lords.

[**Lord Sankey LC** (with whom all their Lordships concurred), having stated the facts continued:]

It is true, as stated by the Court of Criminal Appeal, that there is apparent authority for the law as laid down by the learned judge. But your Lordships' House has had the advantage of a prolonged and exhaustive inquiry dealing with the matter in debate from the earliest times, an advantage which was not shared by either of the courts below. Indeed your Lordships were referred to legal propositions dating as far back as the reign of King Canute (994–1035). I do not think it is necessary for the purpose of this opinion to go as far back as that. Rather would I invite your Lordships to begin by considering the proposition of law which is contained in *Foster's Crown Law*, written in 1762, and which appears to be the foundation for the law as laid down by the learned judge in this case. It must be remembered that Sir Michael Foster, although a distinguished judge, is for this purpose to be regarded as a textbook writer, for he did not lay down the doctrine in any case before him, but in an article which is described as 'The Introduction to the Discourse of Homicide'. In the folio edition, published at Oxford at the Clarendon Press in 1762, at p 255, he states:

> 'In every charge of murder, the fact of killing being first proved, all the circumstances of accident, necessity, or infirmity, are to be satisfactorily proved by the prisoner, unless they arise out of the evidence produced against him; for the law presumeth the fact to have been founded in malice until the contrary appeareth. And very right it is, that the law should so presume. The defendant in this instance standeth upon just the same foot that every other defendant doth: the matters tending to justify, excuse, or alleviate must appear in evidence before he can avail himself of them.'

Now the first part of this passage appears in nearly every textbook or abridgment which has been since written....

The question arises: Is that statement correct law? Is it correct to say, and does Sir Michael Foster mean to lay down, that there may arise in the course of a criminal trial a situation at which it is incumbent upon the accused to prove his innocence? To begin with, if that is what Sir Michael Foster meant, there is no previous authority for his proposition, and I am confirmed in this opinion by the fact that in all the textbooks no earlier authority is cited for it....

If at any period of a trial it was permissible for the judge to rule that the prosecution had established its case and that the onus was shifted on the prisoner to prove that he was not guilty, and that, unless he discharged that onus, the prosecution was entitled to succeed, it would be enabling the judge in such a case to say that the jury must in law find the prisoner guilty and so make the judge decide the case and not the jury, which is not the common law. It would be an entirely different case from those exceptional instances of special verdicts where a judge asks the jury to find certain facts and directs them that on such facts the prosecution is entitled to succeed. Indeed, a consideration of such special verdicts shows that it is not till the end of the evidence that a verdict can properly be found and that at the end of the evidence it is not for the prisoner to establish his innocence, but for the prosecution to establish his guilt. Just as there is evidence on behalf of the prosecution so there may be evidence on behalf of the prisoner which may cause a doubt as to his guilt. In either case, he is entitled to the benefit of the doubt. But while the prosecution must prove the guilt of the prisoner, there is no such burden laid on the prisoner to prove his innocence, and it is sufficient for him to raise a doubt as to his guilt; he is not bound to satisfy the jury of his innocence.

This is the real result of the perplexing case of *Abramovitch* (1912) 7 Cr App Rep 145 which lays down the same proposition, although, perhaps, in somewhat involved language. Juries are always told that, if conviction there is to be, the prosecution must prove the case beyond reasonable doubt. This statement cannot mean that in order to be acquitted the prisoner must 'satisfy' the jury. This is the law as laid down in the Court of Criminal Appeal in *Davies* [1913] 1 KB 573 the head-note of which correctly states that where intent is an ingredient of a crime there is no onus on the defendant to prove that the act alleged was accidental. Throughout the web of the English criminal law one golden thread is always to be seen—that it is the duty of the prosecution to prove the prisoner's guilt subject to what I have already said as to the defence of insanity and subject also to any statutory exception. If, at the end of and on the whole of the case, there is a reasonable doubt, created by the evidence given by either the prosecution or the prisoner, as to whether the prisoner killed the deceased with a malicious intention, the prosecution has not made out the case and the prisoner is entitled to an acquittal. No matter what the charge or where the trial, the principle that the prosecution must prove the guilt of the prisoner is part of the common law of England and no attempt to whittle it down can be entertained. When dealing with a murder case the Crown must prove (*a*) death as the result of a voluntary act of the accused and (*b*) malice of the accused. It may prove malice either expressly or by implication. For malice may be implied where death occurs as the result of a voluntary act of the accused which is (i) intentional and (ii) unprovoked. When evidence of death and malice has been given (this is a question for the jury) the accused is entitled to show by evidence or by examination of the circumstances adduced by the Crown that the act on his part which caused death was either unintentional or provoked. If the jury are either satisfied with his explanation or, upon a review of all the evidence, are left in reasonable doubt whether, even if his explanation be not accepted, the act was unintentional or provoked, the prisoner is entitled to be acquitted. [His Lordship accordingly held that the jury had been misdirected and the appeal must be allowed.]

Although the House of Lords in *Woolmington* declared that they were stating what had always been the law, it is likely that they were in fact changing it and that, in the nineteenth century, the onus of proving common law defences was on the accused. See Lord Devlin giving the opinion of the Privy Council in *Jayasena v R* [1970] 1 All ER 219, 212. It was many years before the effect of *Woolmington* was fully recognized by the courts. Woolmington was simply denying an allegation made by the Crown—namely that he intentionally shot his wife—and supporting that denial by his own account of what actually happened. But the same principle applies where the defendant admits the elements of the offence and asserts new facts amounting to a justification or excuse for what would otherwise be the crime charged—for example, he relies on self-defence, duress or provocation. In these cases the defendant may have to satisfy an evidential burden—that is, unless the elements of the defence appear in the evidence tendered by the prosecution, he must introduce some evidence of them or the defence will not be left to the jury at all. The evidential burden is not a burden of *proof*—the defendant does not have to satisfy the jury of the existence of the elements of the defence. Once evidence of those elements has been given, the jury must acquit, unless they are satisfied that one or more of them does not exist. The onus of proof is on the prosecution to disprove at least one element of the defence.

Exceptions to Woolmington

Woolmington admitted of only two exceptions—insanity (the only exception at common law) and 'any statutory exception'. In *H v United Kingdom* Appn No 15023/89, 4 April 1990 (unreported) the European Commission found no infringement of Article 6(2) in requiring a defendant to establish a defence of insanity.

There are many statutory exceptions—cases where the enactment declares that the onus of proving a particular defence is to be on the defendant. In these cases, as in the case of the insanity defence, the standard of proof required is not proof beyond reasonable doubt but proof on the balance of probabilities. If the jury think it just a little more likely than not that the elements of the defence exist—51 per cent to 49 per cent—the defence is made out. But if, as must sometimes happen, the jury find that they simply cannot decide whether the defendant's story is true or not, the law is that they must convict.

One particularly important statutory exception is provided by s 101 of the Magistrates' Courts Act 1980:

101. Where the defendant to an information or complaint relies for his defence on any exception, exemption, proviso, excuse or qualification, whether or not it accompanies the description of the offence or matter of complaint in the enactment creating the offence or on which the complaint is founded, the burden of proving the exception, exemption, proviso, excuse or qualification shall be on him; and this notwithstanding that the information or complaint contains an allegation negativing the exception, exemption, proviso, excuse or qualification.

The effect of the section is limited to 'enactments' but the great majority of offences are to be found in enactments. It is also limited to summary trial in magistrates' courts; but it applies to all offences which are tried summarily—and the great majority of indictable offences may be tried summarily—they are 'triable either way'. In *Hunt* [1987] 1 All ER 1, [1987] AC 352 the House of Lords accepted that it would be absurd that the allocation of the burden of proof in an offence triable either way should differ according to whether the offence happened to be tried summarily or on indictment. But that absurdity arises unless the common law rules governing the burden of proof of statutory defences, which still apply in the Crown Court, are the same as those stated in s 101. The effect is the same as if s 101 applied in all courts. In practice, s 101 seems to be often overlooked. See, for example, Criminal Damage Act 1971, s 5, as applied in *Jaggard v Dickinson*, below, p 209. (On *Hunt*, see D. J. Birch, 'Hunting the Snark' [1987] Crim LR 221.)

Notes

1. For discussion of *Woolmington*, see J. C. Smith, 'The Presumption of Innocence' 38 NILQ 223 and Lord Cooke of Thorndon, 'One Golden Thread' in *Turning Points of the Common Law* (the Hamlyn Lectures, 1996), 28.

2. The application of the burden of proof in criminal trials is a matter of the law of evidence and procedure and lies beyond the scope of this work. Reference should be made to relevant textbooks on the law of evidence.

2. THE PRESUMPTION OF INNOCENCE AND ARTICLE 6(2) OF THE ECHR

Article 6 of the Convention provides:

1. In the determination of his civil rights and obligations or of any criminal charge against him, everyone is entitled to a fair and public hearing within a reasonable time by an independent and impartial tribunal established by law…

2. Everyone charged with a criminal offence shall be presumed innocent until proved guilty according to law.

The House of Lords has been called on to consider, on four occasions, the compatibility with Article 6(2) of statutory provisions which appear to place a burden of proof on the accused in a criminal trial.

Attorney-General's Reference (No 4 of 2002); Sheldrake (Respondent) v Director of Public Prosecutions (Appellant)
[2004] UKHL 43

(Lord Bingham of Cornhill, Lords Steyn, Phillips of Worth Matravers, Rodger of Earlsferry, Carswell)

Lord Bingham of Cornhill

My Lords,

1. Sections 5(2) of the Road Traffic Act 1988 and 11(2) of the Terrorism Act 2000, conventionally interpreted, impose a legal or persuasive burden on a defendant in criminal proceedings to prove the matters respectively specified in those subsections if he is to be exonerated from liability on the grounds there provided. That means that he must, to be exonerated, establish those matters on the balance of probabilities. If he fails to discharge that burden he will be convicted. In this appeal by the Director of Public Prosecutions and this reference by the Attorney General these reverse burdens ("reverse" because the burden is placed on the defendant and not, as ordinarily in criminal proceedings, on the prosecutor) are challenged as incompatible with the presumption of innocence guaranteed by article 6(2) of the European Convention for the Protection of Human Rights and Fundamental Freedoms (1953) (Cmd 8969). Thus the first question for consideration in each case is whether the provision in question does, unjustifiably, infringe the presumption of innocence. If it does the further question arises whether the provision can and should be read down in accordance with the courts' interpretative obligation under section 3 of the Human Rights Act 1998 so as to impose an evidential and not a legal burden on the defendant. An evidential burden is not a burden of proof. It is a burden of raising, on the evidence in the case, an issue as to the matter in question fit for consideration by the tribunal of fact. If an issue is properly raised, it is for the prosecutor to prove, beyond reasonable doubt, that that ground of exoneration does not avail the defendant.

[...his lordship referred to the pre-Convention law, the cases on the presumption of mens rea (below Ch 8) and Article 6]

9. The right to a fair trial has long been recognised in England and Wales, although the conditions necessary to achieve fairness have evolved, in some ways quite radically, over the years, and continue to evolve. The presumption of innocence has also been recognised since at latest the early 19th century, although (as shown by the preceding account of our domestic law) the presumption has not been uniformly treated by Parliament as absolute and unqualified. There can be no doubt that the underlying rationale of the presumption in domestic law and in the Convention is an essentially simple one: that it is repugnant to ordinary notions of fairness for a prosecutor to accuse a defendant of crime and for the defendant to be then required to disprove the accusation on pain of conviction and punishment if he fails to do so. The closer a legislative provision approaches to that situation, the more objectionable it is likely to be. To ascertain the scope of the presumption under the Convention, domestic courts must have regard to the Strasbourg case law. It has there been repeatedly recognised that the presumption of innocence is one of the elements of the fair criminal trial required by article 6(1): see, for example, *Bernard v France* (1998) 30 EHRR 808, para 37.

[his lordship referred to *X v United Kingdom* (1972) 42 CD 135]

11. The leading Strasbourg authority on the presumption of innocence is *Salabiaku v France* (1988) 13 EHRR 379. The applicant, a Zaïrese national living in Paris, went to the airport to collect, as he said, a parcel of foodstuffs sent from Africa. He could not find this, but was shown a locked trunk, which he was advised to leave alone. He however took possession of it, went through the green customs channel and was detained. The trunk was opened and found to contain drugs. He was charged with the criminal offence of illegally importing narcotics and with the customs offence, also

criminal, of smuggling prohibited goods. At trial the applicant was convicted of both offences: on the first he was sentenced to a term of imprisonment and was prohibited from residing in France; on the second he was fined. On his appeal, his conviction of the first offence was set aside: the facts were not sufficiently proved, and he was given the benefit of the doubt. His conviction of the second offence was upheld since

> '…any person *in possession* (*détention*) of goods which he or she has brought into France without declaring them to customs is presumed to be legally liable unless he or she can prove a specific event of *force majeure* exculpating him; such *force majeure* may arise only as a result of an event beyond human control which could be neither foreseen nor averted….' (p 382)

This was an application of article 392(1) of the French Customs Code, as elaborated by judicial decisions, and was held by the Court of Cassation, on further appeal, to be proper. It appeared that the severity of an apparently irrebuttable presumption had been to some extent moderated by court decisions upholding the trial court's unfettered power of assessing evidence and giving a broad meaning to *force majeure*. The trial court could also take account of extenuating circumstances when imposing penalties. In the result the Strasbourg court rejected the applicant's complaint that article 392(1) infringed the presumption of innocence, relying on the features just noted and the courts' freedom to give an accused the benefit of the doubt even where the offence was one of strict liability. It was noted that the French courts had been careful to avoid resorting automatically to the presumption laid down in article 392(1), and had exercised their power of assessment on the basis of the evidence adduced by the parties before them. Thus the French courts had not applied article 392(1) in a way which conflicted with the presumption of innocence.

12. The Court's decision in *Salabiaku* is important less perhaps for what it decided than for the indications it gives of the correct approach in principle. First of all, it is recognised that member states may, generally speaking, attach criminal consequences to defined facts:

> '27. As the Government and the Commission have pointed out, in principle the Contracting States remain free to apply the criminal law to an act where it is not carried out in the normal exercise of one of the rights protected under the Convention and, accordingly, to define the constituent elements of the resulting offence. In particular, and again in principle, the Contracting States may, under certain conditions, penalise a simple or objective fact as such, irrespective of whether it results from criminal intent or from negligence. Examples of such offences may be found in the laws of the Contracting States.'

It also sanctions, but in a qualified way, the application of factual and legal presumptions:

> '28.… Presumptions of fact or of law operate in every legal system. Clearly, the Convention does not prohibit such presumptions in principle. It does, however, require the Contracting States to remain within certain limits in this respect as regards criminal law. If, as the Commission would appear to consider, paragraph 2 of article 6 merely laid down a guarantee to be respected by the courts in the conduct of legal proceedings, its requirements would in practice overlap with the duty of impartiality imposed in paragraph 1. Above all, the national legislature would be free to strip the trial court of any genuine power of assessment and deprive the presumption of innocence of its substance, if the words "according to law" were construed exclusively with reference of domestic law. Such a situation could not be reconciled with the object and purpose of article 6, which, by protecting the right to a fair trial and in particular the right to be presumed innocent, is intended to enshrine the fundamental principle of the rule of law.
>
> Article 6(2) does not therefore regard presumptions of fact or of law provided for in the criminal law with indifference. It requires States to confine them within reasonable limits which take into account the importance of what is at stake and maintain the rights of the defence. The Court proposes to consider whether such limits were exceeded to the detriment of Mr Salabiaku.'

Thus the question in any case must be whether, on the facts, the reasonable limits to which a presumption must be subject have been exceeded.

[his lordship reviewed several European Court authorities]

21. From this body of authority certain principles may be derived. The overriding concern is that a trial should be fair, and the presumption of innocence is a fundamental right directed to that end. The Convention does not outlaw presumptions of fact or law but requires that these should be kept within reasonable limits and should not be arbitrary. It is open to states to define the constituent elements of a criminal offence, excluding the requirement of mens rea. But the substance and effect of any presumption adverse to a defendant must be examined, and must be reasonable. Relevant to any judgment on reasonableness or proportionality will be the opportunity given to the defendant to rebut the presumption, maintenance of the rights of the defence, flexibility in application of the presumption, retention by the court of a power to assess the evidence, the importance of what is at stake and the difficulty which a prosecutor may face in the absence of a presumption. Security concerns do not absolve member states from their duty to observe basic standards of fairness. The justifiability of any infringement of the presumption of innocence cannot be resolved by any rule of thumb, but on examination of all the facts and circumstances of the particular provision as applied in the particular case.

29. [His lordship reviewed the leading English authorities *R v Director of Public Prosecutions, ex p Kebilene* [2000] 2 AC 326 and *R v Lambert* [2001] UKHL 37, [2002] 2 AC 545; *R v Johnstone* [2003] UKHL 28, [2003] 1 WLR 1736]

29. ....An enlarged Court of Appeal (Lord Woolf CJ, Judge LJ, Gage, Elias and Stanley Burnton JJ) in *Attorney General's Reference No 1 of 2004* [2004] EWCA Crim 1025 [heard] four appeals heard at the same time. In its judgment the court considered much of the authority to which I have referred...and detected (para 38) a 'significant difference in emphasis' between the approach of Lord Steyn in *R v Lambert* [2002] 2 AC 545 and that of Lord Nicholls in *R v Johnstone* [2003] 1 WLR 1736. Making plain its preference for the latter, the court prefaced its guidance to the courts of England and Wales by ruling that (para 52A):

'Courts should strongly discourage the citation of authority to them other than the decision of the House of Lords in *Johnstone* and this guidance. *Johnstone* is at present the latest word on the subject.'

Relying on this judgment, Mr Perry, for the Director of Public Prosecutions and the Attorney General, submitted in his printed case and (more tentatively) in argument that there was clearly a difference of emphasis between the approach of Lord Steyn in *R v Lambert* and that of Lord Nicholls in *R v Johnstone*, and that the latter was to be preferred. Mr Turner QC, for Mr Sheldrake, made a submission to the opposite effect, that the reasoning of the House in *R v Johnstone* should not be followed.

30. Both *R v Lambert* and *R v Johnstone* are recent decisions of the House, binding on all lower courts for what they decide. Nothing said in *R v Johnstone* suggests an intention to depart from or modify the earlier decision, which should not be treated as superseded or implicitly overruled. Differences of emphasis (and Lord Steyn was not a lone voice in *R v Lambert*) are explicable by the difference in the subject matter of the two cases. Section 5 of the Misuse of Drugs Act 1971 [*Lambert*] and section 92 of the Trade Marks Act 1994 [*Johnstone*] were directed to serious social and economic problems. But the justifiability and fairness of the respective exoneration provisions had to be judged in the particular context of each case. I have already identified the potential consequence to a section 5 defendant who failed, perhaps narrowly, to make good his section 28 defence. He might be, but fail to prove that he was, entirely ignorant of what he was carrying. By contrast, the offences under section 92 are committed only if the act in question is done by a person 'with a view to gain for himself or another, or with intent to cause loss to another.' Thus these are offences

committed (if committed) by dealers, traders, market operators, who could reasonably be expected (as Lord Nicholls pointed out) to exercise some care about the provenance of goods in which they deal. The penalty imposed for breaches of section 92 may be severe (see, for example, *R v Gleeson* [2001] EWCA Crim 2023, [2002] 1 Cr App R (S) 485, but that is because the potential profits of fraudulent trading are often great.

31. The task of the court is never to decide whether a reverse burden should be imposed on a defendant, but always to assess whether a burden enacted by Parliament unjustifiably infringes the presumption of innocence. It may nonetheless be questioned whether (as the Court of Appeal ruled in para 52D) 'the assumption should be that Parliament would not have made an exception without good reason'. Such an approach may lead the court to give too much weight to the enactment under review and too little to the presumption of innocence and the obligation imposed on it by section 3.

[His lordship went on to apply the reasoning to the cases before the House.]

Notes and questions

1. The House unanimously reversed the decision of the Divisional Court in *Sheldrake v DPP*. In prosecutions under the Road Traffic Act 1988, s 5(2) for being in charge of a motor vehicle after consuming so much alcohol that the proportion of it in blood, breath or urine exceeded the specified limit, a defendant bears a full legal burden of proving that there was no likelihood of his driving the vehicle while in that condition.

2. The House, by a bare majority, reversed the Court of Appeal's ruling in *A-G's Reference (No 4 of 2002)*. In prosecutions for the offence under s 11 of the Terrorism Act 2000 of 'belonging or professing to belong to a proscribed organisation', the defence under s 11(2) imposed only an evidential burden for D to prove—(a) that the organization was not proscribed on the last (or only) occasion on which he became a member or began to profess to be a member, and (b) that he had not taken part in the activities of the organization at any time while it was proscribed. That provision was to be 'read down' in accordance with the Human Rights Act 1998, s 3 so as to impose only an evidential burden.

3. Does the case really provide any useful guidance to trial judges faced with an offence containing a provision which states that 'it shall be for the defendant to prove . . .'? Compare the views of A. Ashworth [2005] Crim LR 218, and I. Dennis, 'Reverse Onuses and the Presumption of Innocence [2005] Crim LR (Dec).

3. PROOF OR DISPROOF OF STATES OF MIND

(1) THE CRIMINAL JUSTICE ACT 1967, S 8

8. A court or jury, in determining whether a person has committed an offence—
    (a) shall not be bound in law to infer that he intended or foresaw a result of his actions by reason only of its being a natural and probable consequence of those actions; but
    (b) shall decide whether he did intend or foresee that result by reference to all the evidence, drawing such inferences from the evidence as appear proper in the circumstances.

In 1960 the House of Lords in *DPP v Smith* laid down a largely objective test of liability in murder. The test was 'not what the defendant contemplated, but what the ordinary reasonable man or woman would in all the circumstances of the case have contemplated as the natural and probable result'. This decision was heavily criticized and referred to the Law Commission. The Commission's Report ('Imputed Criminal Intent: *DPP v Smith*') contained two draft clauses. The second, defining the mens rea of murder, was never enacted. But the first became s 8 of the Criminal Justice Act 1967. It was intended to put on a statutory basis a rule that, 'where intent or foresight is required in the criminal law, such intent or foresight must be subjectively proved . . .'. It will be noted that the provision was not intended to require proof of intent or foresight in crimes where it was not previously required. It was not intended to alter the definition of the mens rea of any crime. That was why the first clause re-defined the mens rea of murder—but that clause was not enacted. Nevertheless, in *Hyam v DPP* [1974] 2 All ER 41, [1975] AC 55 the House of Lords held that s 8 had changed the mens rea of murder: the test now *was* what the defendant contemplated; what the ordinary reasonable person would have contemplated was only evidence of what the defendant contemplated. Murder was the only crime where the mens rea was held to have been changed by s 8. It did not affect the law of manslaughter: *Lipman* (1969) (below, p **200**).

In 1987 in *Frankland and Moore v R*, below, p **561**, the Privy Council (comprised of five judicial members of the House of Lords) held that, in so far as it laid down an objective test of liability, *Smith* did not represent the common law of England. The Privy Council cannot formally overrule a decision of the House of Lords but, for all practical purposes, it can now be taken that *Smith* was wrongly decided. This removes an anomaly from legal theory: s 8 did not, after all, modify the law of murder any more than it modified the definition of any other crime.

Section 8 and mistake of fact

Section 8 is concerned only with *results* of actions. If a distinction is taken between foresight of results and knowledge of circumstances, it appears to have no application to the latter. However, as O. W. Holmes J pointed out, knowledge of circumstances and foresight of consequences are inextricably related. Foresight of consequences 'is a picture of a future state of things called up by knowledge of the present state of things, the future being viewed as standing to the present in the relation of effect to cause' (*The Common Law* (John Harvard Library edn, 1963), p 46). Because of the circumstance that the gun is loaded, the man at whom it is pointed will be killed when the trigger is pulled. It is impossible to apply s 8 to the results of acts without also applying it to circumstances of this kind. Not all legally relevant circumstances, however, are related to the physical consequences of the act in this way. Some circumstances have no bearing on the *occurrence* of the consequences but are relevant to the *legal effect* of those consequences. The fact that the man at whom the gun is pointed is not 'under the Queen's peace' (he is an enemy soldier in battle) is legally relevant, because it is not murder to kill him. The *consequence* relevant to the law of murder—death of a human being—may occur whether this circumstance exists or not; but if the circumstance does not exist, the consequence is not a crime. Of course, it may perfectly properly be said that 'killing a human being under the Queen's peace' is a different *consequence* from 'killing a human being who is not under the Queen's peace'. If 'results' were interpreted to include *all* legally relevant circumstances then s 8 would have had a far-reaching effect in relation to the defence of mistake; but it has not been so interpreted.

This limitation on the effect of s 8 was important while the courts maintained the opinion that a mistake of fact was no answer to a charge of crime unless it was a reasonable mistake. It is now, however, established by the decision of the House of Lords in *DPP v Morgan*, below that a mistake *which precludes mens rea negatives liability*, even though the mistake is an unreasonable one. The prosecution must establish mens rea and they cannot do so if the defendant was making a mistake, whether reasonably or not, which prevented him from having mens rea. *Morgan* also decided that, at common law, on a charge of rape the prosecution must prove that the defendant knew that the woman was not consenting or was indifferent as to whether she consented or not. The decision on the law of rape has now been superseded by the Sexual Offences Act 2003 but *Morgan* remains of great importance on the question of general principle. The decision does for mistake of fact precisely what s 8 does for a failure to foresee results. Like s 8, it does not affect the substantive law of any crime (except rape before the 1976 Act). We must look to the substantive law of the particular offence to find whether knowledge of the existence, or the possibility of the existence, of a particular fact is required and if it is so required, then the defendant is not guilty of that offence if he did not have that knowledge, even though his mistake was entirely unreasonable. When a court holds that a mistake is not a defence because it is an unreasonable mistake, it must be on the ground that the definition of the particular offence does not require knowledge of the existence, or the possibility of the existence of the fact in question. If the bigamy cases, such as *Tolson*, below, stated the law correctly, it is because the law of bigamy does not require knowledge of the existence, or the possibility of the existence, of the first marriage. It is sufficient that the defendant *ought* to know that his wife is alive, or that the marriage has not been dissolved or annulled, as the case may be; bigamy is an offence of negligence, so far as this element of the crime is concerned.

(2) DISPROVING ALLEGED MISTAKE

Director of Public Prosecutions v Morgan
[1975] 2 All ER 347, House of Lords

(Lords Cross of Chelsea, Hailsham of St Marylebone, Simon of Glaisdale, Edmund-Davies and Fraser of Tullybelton)

The appellant Morgan was a senior NCO in the Royal Air Force, the other appellants younger and junior members of that service. On the night of the offences Morgan invited the other three to return to his house and suggested to them that they should all have intercourse with his wife, the prosecutrix. The young men, who were complete strangers to Mrs Morgan, were at first incredulous but were persuaded that Morgan's invitation was intended seriously when he told them stories of his wife's sexual aberrations and provided them with condoms to wear. They also said in effect that Morgan told them to expect some show of resistance on his wife's part but that they need not take this seriously since it was a mere pretence whereby she stimulated her own sexual excitement. This part of the conversation was denied by Morgan.

Mrs Morgan's account of what happened, in substance, was that she was awakened from sleep in a single bed in a room which she shared with one of her children. Her husband and the other men in part dragged and in part carried her out on to a landing and thence into another room which contained a double bed. She struggled and screamed and shouted to her son to call the police, but one of the men put a hand over her mouth. Once on the double bed the appellants had intercourse with her in turn, her husband being the last to do so. During intercourse with the other three she was continuously being held, and this, coupled with her fear of further violence, restricted the scope of her struggles, but she repeatedly called out to her husband to tell the men to stop.

The three men gave evidence of her manifesting her sexual co-operation and enjoyment in a way which could only indicate that she was consenting. Any element of resistance on her part was, according to this account, no more than play-acting.

The appellant Morgan's statement to the police was equivocal, but in evidence he asserted that his wife agreed in advance to have intercourse with the three friends he had brought home and, in the event, indicated her pleasure in doing so. According to Morgan, the only protest voiced by his wife related to the fact that one of the men who had intercourse with her was not wearing a condom.

The three younger men were convicted of rape and aiding and abetting rape and Morgan was convicted of aiding and abetting rape. The judge directed the jury that the men were guilty of rape even if they in fact believed that Mrs Morgan consented if such belief was not based on reasonable grounds. See the passage quoted by Lord Hailsham, below. They were convicted and their appeal to the Court of Appeal was dismissed.

Lord Cross of Chelsea.... If the words defining an offence provide either expressly or impliedly that a man is not to be guilty of it if he believes something to be true, then he cannot be found guilty if the jury think that he may have believed it to be true, however inadequate were his reasons for doing so. But, if the definition of the offence is on the face of it 'absolute' and the defendant is seeking to escape his prima facie liability by a defence of mistaken belief, I can see no hardship to him in requiring the mistake—if it is to afford him a defence—to be based on reasonable grounds. As Lord Diplock said in *Sweet v Parsley*, there is nothing unreasonable in the law requiring a citizen to take reasonable care to ascertain the facts relevant to his avoiding doing a prohibited act. To have intercourse with a woman who is not your wife is, even today, not generally considered to be a course of conduct which the law ought positively to encourage and it can be argued with force that it is only fair to the woman and not in the least unfair to the man that he should be under a duty to take reasonable care to ascertain that she is consenting to the intercourse and be at the risk of a prosecution if he fails to take such care. So if the Sexual Offences Act 1956 had made it an offence to have intercourse with a woman who was not consenting to it, so that the defendant could only escape liability by the application of the 'Tolson' principle, I would not have thought the law unjust.

But, as I have said, s 1 of the 1956 Act does not say that a man who has sexual intercourse with a woman who does not consent to it commits an offence; it says that a man who rapes a woman commits an offence. Rape is not a word in the use of which lawyers have a monopoly and the question to be answered in this case, as I see it, is whether according to the ordinary use of the English language a man can be said to have committed rape if he believed that the woman was consenting to the intercourse and would not have attempted to have it but for his belief, whatever his grounds for so believing. I do not think that he can. Rape, to my mind, imports at least indifference as to the woman's consent. I think, moreover, that in this connection the ordinary man would distinguish between rape and bigamy. To the question whether a man who goes through a ceremony of marriage with a woman believing his wife to be dead, though she is not, commits bigamy, I think that he would reply 'Yes,—but I suppose that the law contains an escape clause for bigamists who are not really to blame.' On the other hand, to the question whether a man, who has intercourse with a woman believing on inadequate grounds that she is consenting to it, though she is not, commits rape, I think that he would reply 'No...'. For these reasons, I think that the summing up contained a misdirection.

The question which then arises as to the application of the proviso [to s 2(1) of the Criminal Appeal Act 1968] is far easier of solution... The jury obviously considered that the appellants' evidence as to the part played by Mrs Morgan was a pack of lies. So I would apply the proviso and dismiss the appeal.

Lord Hailsham of St Marylebone.... The learned judge [at the trial] said:....

'Further, the Prosecution have to prove that each defendant intended to have sexual intercourse with this woman without her consent. Not merely that he intended to have intercourse with her but that he intended to have intercourse without her consent. Therefore if the defendant believed or may have believed that Mrs Morgan consented to him having sexual intercourse with her, then there would be no such intent in his mind and he would be not guilty of the offence of rape, but such a belief must be honestly held by the defendant in the first place. He must really believe that. And, secondly, his belief must be a reasonable belief; such a belief as a reasonable man would entertain if he applied his mind and thought about the matter. It is not enough for a defendant to rely upon a belief, even though he honestly held it, if it was completely fanciful; contrary to every indication which could be given which would carry some weight with a reasonable man. And, of course the belief must be not a belief that the woman would consent at some time in the future, but a belief that at the time when intercourse was taking place or when it began that she was then consenting to it.'

My first comment upon this direction is that the propositions described 'in the first place' and 'secondly' in the above direction as to the mental ingredient in rape are wholly irreconcilable. In practice this was accepted by both counsel for the appellants and for the respondent, counsel for the appellants embracing that described as 'in the first place' and counsel for the respondent embracing the 'secondly', and each rejecting the other as not being a correct statement of the law. In this, in my view, they had no alternative.

If it be true, as the learned judge says 'in the first place', that the prosecution have to prove that 'each defendant intended to have sexual intercourse without her consent, not merely that he intended to have intercourse with her but that he intended to have intercourse without her consent', the defendant must be entitled to an acquittal if the prosecution fail to prove just that. The necessary mental ingredient will be lacking and the only possible verdict is 'not guilty'. If, on the other hand, as is asserted in the passage beginning 'secondly', it is necessary for any belief in the woman's consent to be 'a reasonable belief' before the defendant is entitled to an acquittal, it must either be because the mental ingredient in rape is not 'to have intercourse and to have it without her consent' but simply 'to have intercourse' subject to a special defence of 'honest and reasonable belief', or alternatively to have intercourse without a reasonable belief in her consent. Counsel for the Crown argued for each of these alternatives, but in my view each is open to insuperable objections of principle. No doubt it would be possible, by statute, to devise a law by which intercourse, voluntarily entered into, was an absolute offence, subject to a 'defence' of belief whether honest or honest and reasonable, of which the 'evidential' burden is primarily on the defence and the 'probative' burden on the prosecution. But in my opinion such is not the crime of rape as it has hitherto been understood. The prohibited act in rape is to have intercourse without the victim's consent. The minimum mens rea or guilty mind in most common law offences, including rape, is the intention to do the prohibited act, and that is correctly stated in the proposition stated 'in the first place' of the judge's direction. In murder the situation is different, because the murder is only complete when the victim dies, and an intention to do really serious bodily harm has been held to be enough if such be the case.

The only qualification I would make to the direction of the learned judge's 'in the first place' is the refinement for which, as I shall show, there is both Australian and English authority, that if the intention of the accused is to have intercourse *nolens volens*, that is recklessly and not caring whether the victim be a consenting party or not, that is equivalent on ordinary principles to an intent to do the prohibited act without the consent of the victim.

The alternative version of the learned judge's direction would read that the accused must do the prohibited act with the intention of doing it without an honest and reasonable belief in the victim's consent. This in effect is the version which took up most of the time in argument, and although I find the Court of Appeal's judgment difficult to understand, I think it the version which ultimately commended itself to that Court. At all events I think it the more plausible way in which to state the learned judge's 'secondly'. In principle, however, I find it unacceptable. I believe that 'mens rea' means 'guilty or criminal mind', and if it be the case, as seems to be accepted here that mental element in rape is not knowledge but intent, to insist that a belief must be reasonable to excuse is to insist that either the accused is to be found guilty of intending to do that which in truth he did not intend to do, or that his state of mind, though innocent of evil intent, can convict him if it be honest but not rational ...

I believe the law on this point to have been correctly stated by Lord Goddard in *Steane* [1947] KB 997 at 1004 (p **136**, above), when he said:

> 'if on the totality of the evidence there is room for more than one view as to the intent of the prisoner, the jury should be directed that it is for the prosecution to prove the intent to the jury's satisfaction, and if, on review of the whole evidence, they either think the intent did not exist or they are left in doubt as to the intent, the prisoner is entitled to be acquitted.'

That was indeed, a case which involved a count where a specific, or, as Professor Smith has called it, an ulterior, intent was, and is required to be, charged in the indictment. But, once it be accepted that an intent of whatever description is an ingredient essential to the guilt of the accused I cannot myself see that any other direction can be logically acceptable. Otherwise a jury would in effect be told to find an intent where none existed or where none was proved to have existed. I cannot myself reconcile it with my conscience to sanction as part of the English law what I regard as logical impossibility, and, if there were any authority which, if accepted would compel me to do so, I would feel constrained to declare that it was not to be followed. However for reasons which I will give I do not see any need in the instant case for such desperate remedies. [His Lordship referred to *Tolson* (p **217**, below), *Sweet v Parsley* (p **249**, below) and *Warner v Metropolitan Police Comr* (p **243**, below).]

... it is logically impermissible as the Crown sought to do in this case, to draw a necessary inference from decisions in relation to offences where mens rea means one thing, and cases where it means another, and in particular from decisions on the construction of statutes, whether these be related to bigamy, abduction or the possession of drugs, and decisions in relation to common law offences. It is equally impermissible to draw direct or necessary inferences from decisions where the mens rea is, or includes, a state of opinion, and cases where it is limited to intention (a distinction I referred to in *Hyam*, post), or between cases where there is a special 'defence', like self defence or provocation and cases where the issue relates to the primary intention which the prosecution has to prove.

Once one has accepted, what seems to me abundantly clear, that the prohibited act in rape is non-consensual sexual intercourse, and that the guilty state of mind is an intention to commit it, it seems to me to follow as a matter of inexorable logic that there is no room either for a 'defence' of honest belief or mistake, or of a defence of honest and reasonable belief and mistake. Either the prosecution proves that the accused had the requisite intent, or it does not. In the former case it succeeds, and in the latter it fails. Since honest belief clearly negatives intent, the reasonableness or otherwise of that belief can only be evidence for or against the view that the belief and therefore the intent was actually held, and it matters not whether, to quote Bridge J (see [1975] 2 All ER at 389), 'the definition of a crime includes no specific element beyond the prohibited act'. If the mental element be primarily an intention and not a state of belief it comes within his second proposition and not his third. Any other view, as for insertion of the word 'reasonable' can only have the effect of saying that a man intends something which he does not.

By contrast, the appellants invited us to overrule the bigamy cases from *Tolson* onwards and perhaps also *Prince* (the abduction case) as wrongly decided at least in so far as they purport to insist that a mistaken belief must be reasonable. The arguments for this view are assembled, and enthusiastically argued, by Professor Glanville Williams in his treatise on Criminal Law between pages 176 and 208, and by Messrs Smith and Hogan (see Smith and Hogan, at pp 148, 149 of their textbook (3rd edn)).

Although it is undoubtedly open to this House to reconsider *Tolson* supra and the bigamy cases, and perhaps *Prince* (supra) which may stand or fall with them, I must respectfully decline to do so in the present case. [See now *B (a minor) v DPP* and *K*, below, pp **216** and **221**]. Nor is it necessary that I should. I am not prepared to assume that the statutory offences of bigamy or abduction are necessarily on all fours with rape, and before I was prepared to undermine a whole line of cases which have been accepted as law for so long, I would need argument in the context of a case expressly relating to the relevant offences. I am content to rest my view of the instant case on the crime of rape by saying that it is my opinion that the prohibited act is and always has been intercourse without consent of the victim and the mental element is and always has been the intention to commit that act, or the equivalent intention of having intercourse willy-nilly not caring whether the victim consents or no. A failure to prove this involves an acquittal because the intent, an essential ingredient, is lacking. It matters not why it is lacking if only it is not there, and in particular it matters not that the intention is lacking only because of a belief not based on reasonable grounds. I should add that I myself am inclined to view *Tolson* as a narrow decision based on the construction of a statute, which prima facie seemed to make an absolute offence, with a proviso, related to the seven year period of absence, which created a statutory defence. The judges in *Tolson* decided that this was not reasonable, and, on general jurisprudential principles, imported into the statutory offence words which created a special 'defence' of honest and reasonable belief of which the 'evidential' but not the probative burden lay on the defence. I do not think it is necessary to decide this conclusively in the present case. But if this is the true view there is a complete distinction between *Tolson* and the other cases based in statute and the present.

I may also add that I am not impressed with the analogy based on the decision in *Wilson v Inyang* [1951] 2 KB 799 at 803 which has attracted the attention of some academic authors. That clearly depends on the construction of the words 'wilfully and falsely' where they are used in the relevant statute. Also, though I get some support from what I have been saying from the reasoning of the decision in *Smith* [1974] 1 All ER 632, [1974] 1 QB 354 (p **940**, below), I nevertheless regard that case as a decision on the Criminal Damage Act 1971, rather than a decision covering the whole law of criminal liability.

For the above reasons I would answer the question certified in the negative, but would apply the proviso to the Criminal Appeal Act on the ground that no miscarriage of justice has or conceivably could have occurred. In my view, therefore, these appeals should be dismissed.

[**Lord Fraser of Tullybelton** made a speech applying the proviso and dismissing the appeal.]

[**Lord Simon of Glaisdale** and **Lord Edmund-Davies** made dissenting speeches.]

Appeal dismissed

Notes and questions

1. The mens rea for rape has now been reformed in the Sexual Offences Act, s 1 with the effect of reversing *Morgan*. D's belief that V is consenting to the sexual acts must be a reasonable one for him to hold. The jury are to have regard to any steps he took to ascertain whether V was consenting. See the discussion below, Ch 20.

2. *Morgan* was concerned with the requirement of mens rea in relation to an element in the definition of an offence. The same principles do not necessarily apply when we are considering the mental element of a defence. A person charged with an offence against the person may claim that he was acting in self-defence because he believed he was being attacked. Is it sufficient that he honestly held that belief, or must the belief have been based on reasonable grounds? In *Albert v Lavin* [1981] 1 All ER 628, [1982] AC 546 the Divisional

Court reluctantly followed a long line of dicta asserting that D's belief must be based on reasonable grounds. They interpreted Lord Hailsham's speech in *Morgan* to accept that this was so; they noted that the two dissenting judges in *Morgan*, uncontradicted by the majority, asserted that this was 'clear law'; and that Glanville Williams had stated that *Morgan* was 'a formidable obstacle to an argument in favour of the subjective rule'. Nevertheless, in *Gladstone Williams* [1987] 3 All ER 411 the Court of Appeal, disapproving of *Albert v Lavin*, cited the CLRC's recommendation that legislation should provide 'that a person may use such force as is reasonable in the circumstances *as he believes them to be* [emphasis added] in the defence of himself or any other person'; and Lord Lane CJ added: 'In the view of this Court that represents the law as expressed in *DPP v Morgan* and in *Kimber* (1983) 77 Cr App Rep 225, [1983] Crim LR 630.' Note, however, that Lord Lane considered that he was concerned with the mens rea of assault, rather than with the mental element of a defence: above, p 15. Note also that the subjective principle has not been accepted for all defences— in duress, D's belief that he was being threatened is no answer if it was not based on reasonable grounds. See further *Beckford*, below, p 451, *Hasan* below, p 387.

FURTHER READING

A. ASHWORTH, 'Commentary' [2005] Crim LR 215

I. DENNIS, 'Reverse Onuses and the Presumption of Innocence' [2005] Crim LR (Dec)

S. TIERNEY and V. TADROS, 'The Presumption of Innocence and the Human Rights Act' [2004] MLR 402.

7

Intoxication

1. VOLUNTARY AND INVOLUNTARY INTOXICATION

Many offences are committed by persons who are intoxicated by alcohol or other drugs. Many of these offences would not have been committed if the offender had not been intoxicated. Alcohol weakens the restraints and inhibitions which normally govern a person's conduct. It also impairs perception and judgement so that a drunken person is liable to have accidents which would not happen if he were sober. It has never been a defence for a person simply to say, however truthfully, that he would not have committed the offence if he had not been drunk—that 'it was the drink that did it'. If that is all, his intoxicated condition is, at most, a matter to be taken into account in imposing sentence. The fact that he had been drinking may sometimes mitigate the gravity of the offence, sometimes—as in dangerous driving—it may aggravate it.

A different problem arises when the definition of the offence includes a mental element and the defendant claims that he lacked that mental element because he was drunk—he failed to foresee a result which he would have foreseen had he been sober or he made a mistake of fact which he would not have made when sober. If he is, or may be, telling the truth and the failure to foresee or the mistake negatives the mens rea of the offence, the prosecution has not proved its case. If the drunkenness is 'involuntary'—the defendant was unaware that his lemonade had been heavily laced with vodka—he will be acquitted. But where the intoxication is voluntary the law has never allowed this defence in all cases. A distinction is made between offences requiring 'specific intent' and other cases. Intoxication negativing specific intent is an answer to the charge, intoxication negativing any lesser form of mens rea—usually referred to as 'basic intent'—is not. The defendant will be convicted of the offence of basic intent even though the mental element, which must be proved in the case of all sober defendants, has not been proved against him. This is known, after the leading case, as 'the *Majewski* approach'.

Cases involving intoxication may usefully be approached by considering three questions:

(1) Is the intoxication voluntary or involuntary? If involuntary, and D lacks mens rea at the time of the actus reus, D is to be acquitted of any mens rea crime. But a drunken intent is still an intent, so the negation of mens rea must be complete.

(2) If the intoxication is voluntary, the next issue is whether the crime charged is one of specific 'intent' or 'basic' intent? The courts have failed to distinguish these with any principled precision, but as a working rule, crimes with mens rea of intent are specific intent and those of recklessness or negligence are basic intent. If the crime is one of specific intent and D was voluntarily intoxicated so that he lacked the mens rea for the crime, he should be acquitted of that crime.

(3) If the crime is one of basic intent, the next question is whether the drug involved is one of a dangerous nature (that is, one known to create states of unpredictability or aggression). If so, in assessing his guilt, the jury or magistrates should ignore his intoxication in considering whether he was reckless as to the harm caused/whether he was negligent as to the harm caused. If the drug is one of a non-dangerous form (for example, a soporific drug such as valium) D will be guilty of the crime charged if he was reckless as to becoming unpredictable or aggressive by taking that drug.

The operation of these questions which focus on the three key distinctions drawn in the law may be illustrated by a hypothetical case. In an actual case (below, p **205**) D stabbed his friend, V, believing, because he was drunk, that he was stabbing a theatrical dummy. Suppose that V had survived and D had been charged with wounding with intent to cause gbh, contrary to OAPA 1861, s 18. The intoxication was voluntary—it was not a case of D's drink being laced or of D taking prescribed medicines in accordance with the medical instructions. The crime under s 18 involves an 'intent to cause gbh' and is a specific intent crime and, as D obviously had no such intent, he must be acquitted. If D is charged with unlawful and malicious wounding, contrary to OAPA 1861, s 20, however, he will be convicted: that is a basic intent crime only. Section 20 requires proof that the accused was aware that his act might cause physical harm to a person but that requirement is not a specific intent. D, believing that he was stabbing a dummy, was not aware that his act might cause physical harm to any person: but, since his lack of awareness arose from intoxication, he is liable to conviction. In the actual case, V died. D was not guilty of murder because murder requires a specific intent: but he was guilty of manslaughter which does not.

Mistakes and failures to foresee arising from intoxication are not an answer to offences requiring negligence because they amount to a failure to comply with the standard of conduct which the law requires. The reasonable, prudent person is not voluntarily intoxicated. *A fortiori*, such mistakes and failures are not an answer to offences of strict liability, not requiring fault. This accords with general principles. It is in respect of offences which have a fault element of recklessness that a special rule prevails because recklessness is not 'specific intent'.

R v Kingston
[1994] 3 All ER 353, House of Lords

(Lords Keith, Goff, Browne-Wilkinson, Mustill and Slynn)

The facts are stated, above, p **117**. Having rejected the respondent's argument on general principle and having found no authority to support it, Lord Mustill thought it necessary to consider the law laid down in *Majewski*. He concluded that, as in other common law jurisdictions, evidence of voluntary intoxication is excluded, except in 'specific intent' cases, as a matter of policy. He continued:

There remains the question by what reasoning the House put this policy into effect. As I understand it two different rationalisations were adopted. First that the absence of the necessary consent is cured by treating the intentional drunkenness (or more accurately, since it is only in the minority of cases that the drinker sets out to make himself drunk, the intentional taking of drink without regard to its possible effects) as a substitute for the mental element ordinarily required by the offence. The intent is transferred from the taking of drink to the commission of the prohibited act. The second rationalisation is that the defendant cannot be heard to rely on the absence of the mental element when it is absent because of his own voluntary acts. Borrowing an expression from a far distant field it may be said that the defendant is estopped from relying on his self-induced incapacity.

Your Lordships are not required to decide how these two explanations stand up to attack, for they are not attacked here. The task is only to place them in the context of an intoxication which is not voluntary. Taking first the concept of transferred intent, if the intoxication was not the result of an act done with an informed will there is no intent which can be transferred to the prohibited act, so as to fill the gap in the offence. As regards the 'estoppel' there is no reason why the law should preclude the defendant from relying on a mental condition which he had not deliberately brought about. Thus, once the involuntary nature of the intoxication is added the two theories of *Majewski* fall away, and the position reverts to what it would have been if *Majewski* had not been decided, namely that the offence is not made out if the defendant was so intoxicated that he could not form an intent. Thus, where the intoxication is involuntary *Majewski* does not *subtract* the defence of absence of intent; but there is nothing in *Majewski* to suggest that where intent is proved involuntary intoxication *adds* a further defence.

Lord Mustill went on to consider authorities in other jurisdictions. In particular he discussed a number of Scottish decisions involving involuntary intoxication. These make it clear that, in Scotland, a defence is made out if it is 'based . . . on an inability to form mens rea due to some factor which was outwith the accused's control and which he was not bound to foresee'; or if he was 'suffering from a total alienation of reason rendering him incapable of controlling or appreciating what he was doing'. These and the other dicta quoted all require an inability to form the intent. Should the defence be limited to the case of inability, or should it extend to the case where a person capable of forming an intent fails to do so because he is involuntarily intoxicated?

Kenny gives a vivid illustration (also referred to by Lord Denning in *Gallagher*, below) of a nurse who got so drunk at a christening that she put the baby on the fire in mistake for a log of wood. She was clearly capable of forming an intent to make up the fire so she must have been *capable* of forming an intent to kill, however improbable it was that she would do so. Equally clearly she did not form that intention and so must be acquitted of murder: *Pordage* [1975] Crim LR 575. Being voluntarily intoxicated, she would have no defence to a charge of manslaughter or any offence of basic intent. If she had merely dropped the supposed log, causing the baby a slight injury, she would have had no defence to a charge of assault occasioning actual bodily harm. Suppose, however, that her intoxication was due, not to her too liberal indulgence in the champagne, but to her orange juice having been heavily laced, without her knowledge, with vodka. Even if she was *capable* of committing an assault, is there any ground for convicting her of that offence? Or of manslaughter, if the baby died as a result of being dropped, or put on the fire? Cf *Goring* [1999] Crim LR 670.

Questions

1. Should D's intoxication be regarded as involuntary where he knew he was drinking alcohol, but under-estimated the strength of the alcohol? *Allen* [1988] Crim LR 698.

2. What of D who becomes intoxicated through taking brandy administered to D after an accident? Involuntary intoxication?

2. 'SPECIFIC' AND 'BASIC' INTENT

Director of Public Prosecutions v Majewski
[1976] 2 All ER 142, House of Lords

(Lord Elwyn-Jones LC, Lords Diplock, Simon of Glaisdale, Kilbrandon, Salmon, Edmund-Davies and Russell of Killowen)

The appellant was convicted on three counts of assault occasioning actual bodily harm and on three counts of assault on a police constable in the execution of his duty. The evidence which was largely undisputed showed that the offences were committed in the Bull public house in Basildon and that during a fierce struggle Majewski shouted at the police: 'You pigs, I'll kill you all, you f . . . pigs, you bastards.' He had consumed large quantities of drugs and alcohol shortly before the offences. He was a drug-addict, and admitted that he had previously 'gone paranoid' but said that this was the first time he had 'completely blanked out'. He claimed not to have known what he was doing. The medical evidence suggested that such a state, called 'pathological intoxication', was possible but unlikely: it was quite possible for an intoxicated person to know what he was doing at the time and to suffer an 'amnesic patch' later. Judge Petre directed the jury to 'ignore the subject of drink and drugs as being in any way a defence' to the assaults. An appeal to the House of Lords was unanimously dismissed.

Lord Elwyn-Jones LC . . . If a man consciously and deliberately takes alcohol and drugs not on medical prescription, but in order to escape from reality, to go 'on a trip', to become hallucinated, whatever the description may be, and thereby disables himself from taking the care he might otherwise take and as a result by his subsequent actions causes injury to another—does our criminal law enable him to say that because he did not know what he was doing he lacked both intention and recklessness and accordingly is entitled to an acquittal?

Originally the common law would not and did not recognise self-induced intoxication as an excuse. Lawton LJ [[1975] 3 All ER 296 at 305, 306] spoke of the 'merciful relaxation' to that rule which was introduced by the judges during the 19th century, and he added:

'Although there was much reforming zeal and activity in the 19th century Parliament never once considered whether self-induced intoxication should be a defence generally to a criminal charge. It would have been a strange result if the merciful relaxation of a strict rule of law had ended, without any Parliamentary intervention, by whittling it away to such an extent that the more drunk a man became, provided he stopped short of making himself insane, the better chance he had of an acquittal . . . The common law rule still applied but there were exceptions to it which Lord Birkenhead LC [*DPP v Beard*] tried to define by reference to specific intent.'

There are, however, decisions of eminent judges in a number of Commonwealth cases in Australia and New Zealand (but generally not in Canada nor in the United States), as well as impressive academic comment in this country, to which we have been referred, supporting the view that it is illogical and inconsistent with legal principle to treat a person who of his own choice and volition has taken drugs and drink, even though he thereby creates a state in which he is not conscious of what he is doing, any differently from a person suffering from the various medical conditions like epilepsy or diabetic coma and who is regarded by the law as free from fault. However, our courts have for a very long time regarded in quite another light the state of self-induced intoxication. The authority which for the last half century has been relied on in this context has been the speech of Lord Birkenhead LC in *DPP v Beard* [[1920] AC 479 at 494, [1920] All ER Rep 21 at 25]:

'Under the law of England as it prevailed until early in the nineteenth century voluntary drunkenness was never an excuse for criminal misconduct; and indeed the classic authorities broadly assert that voluntary drunkenness must be considered rather an aggravation than a defence. This view was in terms based upon the principle that a man who by his own voluntary act debauches and destroys his will power shall be no better situated in regard to criminal acts than a sober man.'

Lord Birkenhead LC made an historical survey of the way the common law from the 16th century on dealt with the effect of self-induced intoxication on criminal responsibility. This indicates how, from 1819 on, the judges began to mitigate the severity of the attitude of the common law in such cases as murder and serious violent crime when the penalties of death or transportation applied or where there was likely to be sympathy for the accused, as in attempted suicide. Lord Birkenhead LC [[1920] AC 479 at 499, 500, [1920] All ER Rep 21 at 27, 28] concluded that (except in cases where insanity was pleaded) the decisions he cited:

'establish that where a specific intent is an essential element in the offence, evidence of a state of drunkenness rendering the accused incapable of forming such an intent should be taken into consideration in order to determine whether he had in fact formed the intent necessary to constitute the particular crime. If he was so drunk that he was incapable of forming the intent required he could not be convicted of a crime which was committed only if the intent was proved. . . . In a charge of murder based upon intention to kill or to do grievous bodily harm, if the jury are satisfied that the accused was, by reason of his drunken condition, incapable of forming the intent to kill or to do grievous bodily harm . . . he cannot be convicted of murder. But nevertheless unlawful homicide has been committed by the accused, and consequently he is guilty of unlawful homicide without malice aforethought, and that is manslaughter: per Stephen J in *Doherty's* case [(1887) 16 Cox CC 306 at 307]. [He concluded the passage:] the law is plain beyond all question that in cases falling short of insanity a condition of drunkenness at the time of committing an offence causing death can only, when it is available at all, have the effect of reducing the crime from murder to manslaughter.'

From this it seemed clear—and this is the interpretation which the judges have placed on the decision during the ensuing half-century—that it is only in the limited class of cases requiring proof of specific intent that drunkenness can exculpate. Otherwise in no case can it exempt completely from criminal liability. . . .

[His Lordship discussed *A-G for Northern Ireland v Gallagher* (p **204**, below) and *Bratty v A-G for Northern Ireland* (p **22**, above).]

The seal of approval is clearly set on the passage of the *Beard* decision. In no case has the general principle of English law as described by Lord Denning in *Gallagher's* case and exposed again in *Bratty's* case [[1963] AC 386, [1961] 3 All ER 523] been overruled in this House and the question now to be determined is whether it should be.

I do not for my part regard that general principle as either unethical or contrary to the principles of natural justice. If a man of his own volition takes a substance which causes him to cast off the restraints of reason and conscience, no wrong is done to him by holding him answerable criminally for any injury he may do while in that condition. His course of conduct in reducing himself by drugs and drink to that condition in my view supplies the evidence of mens rea, of guilty mind certainly sufficient for crimes of basic intent. It is a reckless course of conduct and recklessness is enough to constitute the necessary mens rea in assault cases: see *Venna* [[1975] 3 All ER 788 at 793] per James LJ. The drunkenness is itself an intrinsic, an integral part of the crime, the other part being the evidence of the unlawful use of force against the victim. Together they add up to criminal recklessness. On this I adopt the conclusion of Stroud [[1920] 36 LQR at 273] that:

'It would be contrary to all principle and authority to suppose that drunkenness (and what is true of drunkenness is equally true of intoxication by drugs) can be a defence for crime in general on the ground that "a person cannot be convicted of a crime unless the *mens* was *rea*". By allowing himself to get drunk and thereby putting himself in such a condition as to be no longer amenable to the law's commands, a man shows such regardlessness as amounts to mens rea for the purpose of all ordinary crimes.'

This approach is in line with the American Model Code [s 2.08(2)]:

'When recklessness establishes an element of the offence, if the actor, due to self-induced intoxication, is unaware of a risk of which he would have been aware had he been sober, such unawareness is immaterial.'

Acceptance generally of intoxication as a defence (as distinct from the exceptional cases where some additional mental element above that of ordinary mens rea has to be proved) would in my view undermine the criminal law and I do not think that it is enough to say, as did counsel for the appellant, that we can rely on the good sense of the jury or of magistrates to ensure that the guilty are convicted. It may well be that Parliament will at some future time consider, as I think it should, the recommendation in the Butler Committee Report on Mentally Abnormal Offenders [(1975) Cmnd 6244] that a new offence of 'dangerous intoxication' should be created. But in the meantime it would be irresponsible to abandon the common law rule, as 'mercifully relaxed', which the courts have followed for a century and a half ...

The final question that arises is whether s 8 of the Criminal Justice Act 1967 has had the result of abrogating or qualifying the common law rule. That section emanated from the consideration the Law Commission gave to the decision of the House in *DPP v Smith* [[1961] AC 290, [1960] 3 All ER 161]. Its purpose and effect was to alter the law of evidence about the presumption of intention to produce the reasonable and probable consequences of one's acts. It was not intended to change the common law rule. In referring to 'all the evidence' it meant all the *relevant* evidence. But if there is a substantive rule of law that in crimes of basic intent, the factor of intoxication is irrelevant (and such I hold to be the substantive law), evidence with regard to it is quite irrelevant. Section 8 does not abrogate the substantive rule and it cannot properly be said that the continued application of that rule contravenes the section. For these reasons, my conclusion is that the certified question should be answered Yes, that there was no misdirection in this case and that the appeal should be dismissed.

My noble and learned friends and I think it may be helpful if we give the following indication of the general lines on which in our view the jury should be directed as to the effect on the criminal responsibility of the accused of drink or drugs or both, whenever death or physical injury to another person results from something done by the accused for which there is no legal justification and the offence with which the accused is charged is manslaughter or assault at common law or the statutory offence of unlawful wounding under s 20, or of assault occasioning actual bodily harm under s 47 of the Offences against the Person Act 1861.

In the case of these offences it is no excuse in law that, because of drink or drugs which the accused himself had taken knowingly and willingly, he had deprived himself of the ability to exercise self-control, to realise the possible consequences of what he was doing or even to be conscious that he was doing it. As in the instant case, the jury may be properly instructed that they 'can ignore the subject of drink or drugs as being in any way a defence to' charges of this character.

[**Lord Diplock** said that he agreed with the speech of Lord Elwyn-Jones LC.]

Lord Simon ... still have the temerity to think that the concept of 'crime of basic intent' is a useful tool of analysis; and I explained what I meant by it in the passage in *Morgan* [[1975] 2 All ER 347 at 363, 364] generously cited by my noble and learned friend, Lord Elwyn-Jones LC. It stands significantly in contrast with 'crime of specific intent' as that term was used by *Stephen's Digest* and by Lord Birkenhead LC in *Beard* [[1920] AC 479, [1920] All ER Rep 21]. The best description of 'specific intent' in this sense that I know is contained in the judgment of Fauteux J in *George* [(1960) 128 CCC 289 at 301]:

'In considering the question of mens rea, a distinction is to be made between (i) intention as applied to acts considered in relation to their purposes and (ii) intention as applied to acts apart from their purposes. A general intent attending the commission of an act is, in some cases, the only intent required to constitute the crime while, in others, there must be, in addition to that general intent, a specific intent attending the purpose for the commission of the act.'

In short, where the crime is one of 'specific intent' the prosecution must in general prove that the purpose for the commission of the act extends to the intent expressed or implied in the definition of the crime...

As I have ventured to suggest, there is nothing unreasonable or illogical in the law holding that a mind rendered self-inducedly insensible (short of M'Naghten [M'Naghten's case (1843) 10 Cl & Fin 200, [1843–60] All ER Rep 229 [p **374**, below]] insanity), through drink or drugs, to the nature of a prohibited act or to its probable consequences is as wrongful a mind as one which consciously contemplates the prohibited act and foresees its probable consequences (or is reckless whether they ensue). The latter is all that is required by way of mens rea in a crime of basic intent. But a crime of specific intent requires something more than contemplation of the prohibited act and foresight of its probable consequences. The mens rea in a crime of specific intent requires proof of a purposive element. This purposive element either exists or not; it cannot be supplied by saying that the impairment of mental powers by self-induced intoxication is its equivalent, for it is not. So that the 19th century development of the law as to the effect of self-induced intoxication on criminal responsibility is juristically entirely acceptable; and it need be a matter of no surprise that Stephen stated it without demur or question.

[**Lord Kilbrandon** said that he agreed with the speech of Lord Elwyn-Jones.]

Lord Salmon ... an assault committed accidentally is not a criminal offence. A man may, eg, thoughtlessly throw out his hand to stop a taxi, or open the door of his car and accidentally hit a passer-by and perhaps unhappily cause him quite serious bodily harm. In such circumstances, the man who caused the injury would be liable civilly for damages but clearly he would have committed no crime. It is, I agree, possible to commit assault and other crimes of violence recklessly, not caring whether or not what you do causes injury. There are no doubt some contexts, eg, commercial contracts in which the words 'very carelessly' and 'recklessly' are synonymous, but I do not think that this is usually true in the context of the criminal law, except perhaps in the case of manslaughter. I do not, however, wish to take up your Lordships' time in discussing this topic further for it is hardly relevant to the question before this House.

There are many cases in which injuries are caused by pure accident. I have already given examples of such cases: to these could be added injuries inflicted during an epileptic fit, or whilst sleep-walking, and in many other ways. No one, I think, would suggest that any such case could give rise to criminal liability.

It is argued on behalf of the appellant that a man who makes a vicious assault may at the material time have been so intoxicated by drink or drugs that he no more knew what he was doing than did any of the persons in the examples I have given and that therefore he too cannot be found guilty of a criminal offence.

To my mind there is a very real distinction between such a case and the examples I have given. A man who by voluntarily taking drink and drugs gets himself into an aggressive state in which he does not know what he is doing and then makes a vicious assault can hardly say with any plausibility that what he did was a pure accident which should render him immune from any criminal liability. Yet this in effect is precisely what counsel for the appellant contends that the learned judge should have told the jury.

A number of distinguished academic writers support this contention on the ground of logic. As I understand it, the argument runs like this. Intention, whether special or basic (or whatever fancy name you choose to give it), is still intention. If voluntary intoxication by drink or drugs can, as it admittedly can, negative the special or specific intention necessary for the commission of crimes such as murder and theft, how can you justify in strict logic the view that it cannot negative a basic intention, eg, the intention to commit offences such as assault and unlawful wounding? The answer is that in strict logic this view cannot be justified. But this is the view that has been adopted by the common law of England, which is founded on common sense and experience rather than strict logic. There is no case in the 19th century when the courts were relaxing the harshness of the law in relation to the effect of drunkenness on criminal liability in which the courts ever went so far as to suggest that drunkenness, short of drunkenness producing insanity, could ever exculpate a man from any offence other than one which required some special or specific intent to be proved . . .

[**Lord Edmund-Davies** and **Lord Russell of Killowen** made speeches dismissing the appeal.]

Appeal dismissed

Questions

1. Is the decision confined to the case where 'a man consciously and deliberately takes alcohol and drugs . . . in order to escape from reality, to go "on a trip", to become hallucinated . . .'? Or does it apply to cases of ordinary social drinking?

2. If 'specific intent' requires proof of a 'purposive element'—as Lord Simon says—is (a) murder, (b) rape or (c) taking a conveyance without the consent of the owner (see *MacPherson* [1973] RTR 157) a crime of specific intent?

3. Was it justifiable to uphold the conviction on the ground that the appellant was reckless? Was there any finding that he was reckless in the sense in which that term is used in *Venna* (p **673**, below) at the time he took the drink?

4. If 'the drunkenness is itself an intrinsic, an integral part of the crime', can the prosecution make out their case by adducing evidence that the defendant was drunk?

5. In *Fotheringham* (1988) 88 Cr App R 206, [1988] Crim LR 846 D had sexual intercourse with his 14-year-old baby-sitter, V, who made no resistance but did not in fact consent. V was in the matrimonial bed, as D's wife had advised in view of their late return. D's defence was that because he had taken so much drink he believed that he was having intercourse with his wife. If so, he did not intend to commit rape because a man could not then be convicted of rape of his wife; and, presumably, he would have believed she was consenting (at that time it need not have been a reasonable belief). The judge directed that the drunken mistake could be no defence. D's appeal was dismissed. Watkins LJ said that 'in rape self-induced intoxication is no defence, whether the issue be intention, consent or, as here, mistake as to the identity of the victim.' D obviously intended to have sexual intercourse but, if his story was true, he did not intend to commit rape. Recklessness as to consent was a sufficient mens rea, so his drunken mistake was no answer to that allegation. But what about his belief that V was his wife? Suppose that, when it was still the law that a man could not rape his wife, a sober man (in the dark) had thought of a sleeping woman, 'Is this my wife? I am not sure—but I'll have intercourse anyway.' It was not his wife. Should he have been guilty of rape?—that is, was recklessness enough?

(1) DISTINGUISHING BETWEEN OFFENCES OF SPECIFIC AND BASIC INTENT

As a result of *Majewski* and *Caldwell* (below, p **199**) it now seems settled that any offence which may be committed by recklessness will be regarded as 'an offence of basic intent'. Unfortunately that is not so simple a rule as it seems.

(i) The statutory definition of some offences spells out alternative mental elements—intention or recklessness. The Criminal Damage Act 1971 is a conspicuous example. D may be charged in a single count with 'intentionally or recklessly' causing damage and in that case the offence charged is one of basic intent: the prosecution succeeds if they can prove only recklessness. But sometimes the prosecution may use two counts, one alleging intention and the second recklessness, in order to obtain the verdict of the jury on the issue to assist the judge in sentencing. In that event the first count charges an offence of specific intent, the second an offence of basic intent. The jury may take intoxication into account on the first count but not on the second.

(ii) An offence may require proof of two mental elements, one a basic, the other a specific, intent. Under s 18 of the OAPA 1861 there is an offence of unlawfully and maliciously wounding with intent to resist lawful apprehension. It is settled that the words 'unlawfully and maliciously' when used in s 20 of the OAPA import only a basic intent—that is, *Cunningham* recklessness. Presumably they have the same effect in s 18. So far as wounding goes, s 18 is an offence of basic intent; but the intent to resist lawful apprehension seems clearly to be a specific intent. D, who is drunk, intends to resist arrest but, because of his intoxication, does not foresee the risk of wounding, might be convicted notwithstanding his lack of *Cunningham* recklessness. But if, because of intoxication, he does not realize he is resisting lawful apprehension, he must be acquitted. The Law Commission (Law Com No 229, para 1.42) assert that their latest proposals would 'remove the distinction drawn in the present law between offences of specific and basic intent, replacing it by a distinction between states of mind.' If the above analysis is correct, that distinction already exists although the courts have not had occasion to invoke it. The Commission (para 5.39) cite the s 18 example from Smith and Hogan, *Criminal Law* (7th edn), pp 222–223, which is, of course, discussing the present law.

The difficulties noticed in the last paragraph are not insuperable when we are concerned only with the elements of the offence. They are more formidable if we are required to distinguish between offences of specific and basic intent for the purposes of the mental element in a defence (below, p **206**). If D's defence to the s 18 offence (above) is self-defence, how do we decide whether he is charged with an offence of specific or of basic intent?

S. Gough, 'Intoxication and Criminal Liability: The Law Commission's Proposed Reforms'
(1996) LQR 335, 342

...

THE SPECIFIC-BASIC DISTINCTION
The origins of the terminology of 'specific intent'

The distinction between offences of specific and basic intent has been a persistent headache for criminal lawyers, especially over the last two or three decades. The terminology of 'specific' intent is traceable to the midnineteenth century. Patterson J. spoke in *Cruse* (1838) [8 C. & P. 541] of intoxication's ability to defeat the 'positive intention' required by murder, while in *Monkhouse* (1849) [4 Cox C.C. 55.] Coleridge J. noted that drunkenness would not lead to an acquittal unless, inter alia, it deprived the defendant of 'the power of forming any specific intention.' Most importantly, Lord Birkenhead L.C. referred to specific intent in *D.P.P. v. Beard* (1920):

'Where a specific intent is an essential element in the offence, evidence of a state of drunkenness rendering the accused incapable of forming such an intent should be taken into consideration in order

to determine whether he had in fact formed the intent necessary to constitute the particular crime.'
[[1920] A.C. 479, at p. 499]

Yet these cases gave no indication that a 'specific intent' was different from an ordinary intent. Indeed, other intoxication cases of the period omit any reference to 'specific' intent and speak simply of intoxication's ability to negate intent. [*Meakin* (1836) 7 C. & P. 297] *Beard* is particularly confusing in that, having used the language of 'specific intent' in the first half of his opinion, Lord Birkenhead switches to the language of intent simpliciter in the second half. [[1920] A.C. 479 at pp. 504–505.] In short, the terms 'intent' and 'specific intent' seem to have been used interchangeably.

Why, then, did some judges use the term 'specific intent' instead of just 'intent'? In answering this question we must bear in mind the 19th and early 20th century approach to mens rea. Stephen, writing in the late 19th century, points to 'malice' as a sufficient mental element for most offences. The word carried its common meaning of moral depravity or 'wickedness', [*General View of the Criminal Law of England*. (1863), 82.] and there is no indication that any subjective mental state was required. This is confirmed by Harris who, writing around the same time, noted that

> 'Malice is found not only in cases: i) Where the mind is actively or positively in fault, as where there is a deliberate design to defraud, but also: ii) Where the mind is passively or negatively to blame, that is, where there is culpable or criminal inattention or negligence.' [Harris, *Principles of the Criminal Law*, (1st ed, 1877), 14.]

In any event, as Harris pointed out, many offences would have been satisfied even in the absence of malice:

> 'When the law expressly declares an act to be criminal, the question of intention or malice need not be considered; at least, except by the judge in estimating the amount of punishment.' [ibid]

Early 20th century criminal lawyers paint a similar picture. [Kenny. *Outlines of Criminal Law* (1st ed, 1902),]

Intoxicatedly inadvertent behaviour would have been perfectly consistent with liability for an offence with a mental element of malice or less. As Kenny noted around the turn of the century, '[D's] mens rea in allowing himself to become intoxicated is sufficient to supply the ordinary mental element of guilt to any criminal act which may ensue from it.' [p. 60] The key words here are 'ordinary mental element'. Some offences, as Kenny later points out, required mental elements that were out of the ordinary. In these cases intoxication might, depending on the nature of the mental element required, operate to negate liability for that offence:

> '[Intoxication] may disprove the presence of some additional mens rea that is essential to the definition of some particular crime. It may, for instance, disprove the presence of murderous malice, or of an intent to do grievous bodily harm, or of an intent to commit a felony.' [p. 61.]

Here, then, is an explanation for the occasional use of words like 'specific' or 'positive' in the early cases. The ordinary mental element required by offences at this time was 'malice', a form of negligence that intoxication would obviously not negate. There were, though, a few offences that specifically (or positively or explicitly) required specific (or particular or positive) mental states. Depending on their exact nature, these extra mental requirements might be incompatible with extreme intoxication. In other words, 'specificity' was not a characteristic of the intent required by an offence, although 'specifically requiring intent' might be a characteristic of offences themselves.

The specific-basic distinction in modern law
The casually used terminology of specific intent has been pressed into service in modern law to ensure that the kinds of offences that would have allowed liability for (objective) intoxicated wrongdoing in the past can continue to do so despite their more recent subjectivist overhaul. In simple terms, where the offence is one of 'specific intent', the defendant cannot be liable unless he acted with

the necessary mental state. It makes no difference that his lack of mens rea was the result of intoxication. On the other hand, where, apart from his mental state, the defendant satisfies the conditions of liability for an offence that is not one of 'specific intent' (that is, of a 'basic intent' offence), he will (effectively) be held liable irrespective of his lack of mens rea. However, this explanation leaves at least two questions unanswered. How can modern offences that ostensibly require a subjective mens rea be satisfied by inadvertent intoxicated wrongdoing? And why is it that only some (ostensibly) subjective offences can be treated in this way while other (actually) subjective offences cannot?

There have been several attempts to explain the mechanism by which intoxicated wrongdoing satisfies the requirements of subjective offences. The Law Commission [*Legislating the Criminal Code: Intoxication and Criminal Liability* (1995). Law Com. No. 229.] considered two approaches, one that treats intoxicated wrongdoing as a substitute for subjectively reckless wrongdoing and another that presumes that there is subjectively reckless wrongdoing where intoxicated wrongdoing is shown to be present. Neither approach is particularly attractive. Intoxicated wrongdoing is not a direct alternative to subjectively reckless wrongdoing, and that is a good reason for not presuming it to be. Rather, there are differences between the two types of wrongdoing that may need to be reflected in different sentences or—and this is the important point—in different offence headings.

Considerations of fair labelling, the set of principles governing the assimilation of particular types of wrongdoing under particular offence headings, have driven the specific-basic distinction into the law. Intoxicated wrongdoing is not equivalent to subjective wrongdoing, but where it is perceived to share the salient characteristics of the wrong or family of wrongs associated with a particular offence heading, including any characteristics given salience by being specified in the offence heading itself, there will be little objection to assimilating it under that heading. Any remaining differences between the two types of wrongdoing will be minor enough to be taken into account at the sentencing stage. There are, on the other hand, some offence headings that do not exhibit this degree of flexibility. Killing in drunken inadvertence, for example, while it is a very serious form of wrongdoing, could hardly be considered equivalent to the specific and serious wrongs normally associated with murder. Or, at least, to treat it as murder would so broaden the types of wrongdoing associated with that offence as to risk diluting the special opprobrium attaching to it. Similarly, where a heading gives salience to particular characteristics of the wrongs prohibited by explicitly specifying them—wounding with intent to do grievous bodily harm, for example—it would be paradoxical to use it to convict the unthinking drunken wounder whose wrongdoing exhibits no such characteristic.

This is not to say that the specific-basic distinction can be explained solely in terms of fair labelling. The common law judges have had to work with existing offence headings and there are certain types of intoxicated wrongdoing that do not fit particularly neatly under any of these. Where such wrongdoing is considered relatively venial, the temptation may be to sacrifice the conviction of deserving offenders in order to preserve the coherence of the law's labelling scheme. Perhaps thoughtless drunken trespass or appropriation ought to be criminal, but it would seem wrong to deal with such offenders under the ancient and emotive headings of burglary and theft, and in the absence of appropriate existing offence headings they go free. Where the intoxicated wrongdoing is considered more serious, by contrast, the temptation may be to sacrifice the principles of fair labelling in order to secure the conviction of deserving offenders. The classification of rape as a basic intent offence may be an example of this type of compromise. There are serious doubts whether the rapist who drunkenly believes his victim to be consenting should be dealt with under the same opprobrious heading as the advertent rapist who knowingly risks that they are not. Since there is no other appropriate offence heading, though, it is better to convict the intoxicated individual under the rape heading than to acquit completely.

Objections to the specific-basic distinction

I should mention three objections that might be raised against this approach to the specific-basic distinction.

(1) It may be objected that the process of tacitly extending offences to cover closely related but not explicitly prohibited wrongs is contrary to the rule of law (in that it involves retrospective criminalisation and judicial legislation) or that it is impractical (in that its role in securing the conviction of a handful of admittedly deserving individuals does not justify the complexity and difficulty that it introduces). Such objections are not particularly persuasive. Judicial extension of offences to cover closely related types of wrongdoing is not confined to the intoxication rules: it is a common technique used to give flexibility to offence headings, to circumvent the letter of the law and give effect to its spirit..... Consider also the non-contemporaneity cases like *Church*. [[1966] 1 Q.B. 59.] *Thabo Meli* [1954] 1 W.L.R. 228] (and, it may be added, *Gallagher* [[1963] A.C. 349]). The defendants had all committed wrongs similar to the central wrong prohibited by murder save only that their behaviour did not satisfy the contemporaneity requirements of that offence. That is, while they had intended to kill and had caused death, the acts causing death had not involved an intent to kill. The instinct of the courts in each case was to ignore the minor difference between the actual and the required wrongdoing and convict under the murder heading. To the extent that it would be undesirable to rewrite the law in these various respects and allow plainly culpable individuals to get off scot-free, perhaps it is not the specific-basic distinction that we should be rethinking but our assumptions about the practical and constitutional difficulties presented by the current intoxication rules.

(2) A second objection rejects the specific-basic distinction as unprincipled because it cannot be reduced to a neat general formula. Many people have attempted to find such a formula—some have tried to identify specific intent with ulterior intent, others with purpose, others with subjective recklessness. All of these enterprises make the mistake, identified above, of assuming 'specificity' to be a quality of the mental elements required by certain offences and, as a result, they all fail to capture the common law distinction. Some of them require counterintuitive amendments to the accepted categorisations of offences as specific or basic—under the 'purpose' of 'ulterior intent' approaches, for example. Murder would have to be reclassified as a basic intent offence because neither of those mental states is necessary for its commission. Others overconfidently classify as specific or basic offences like rape over which the common law has understandably dithered.

In fact, to search for a neat reduction of the specific-basic distinction is to misunderstand its nature. 'Specific intent offence' is an (inapt) label given to offences which, for the kinds of reasons already discussed, cannot appropriately be extended to cover inadvertent intoxicated wrongdoing. We do not expect a general formula to tell us whether a certain offence heading should cover a certain objectively reckless wrong, subjectively reckless wrong, intentional wrong, or wrong characterised by a special quality like dishonesty or indecency. It is similarly misguided to expect a general theory to tell us whether a particular offence heading should cover a given intoxicated wrong.

...

(3) Finally, many have wanted to deal with intoxicated wrongdoing under a special heading ('dangerous intoxication', for example) rather than, as at present, under ordinary offences. While there many be an argument to be made along these lines, it is difficult to imagine that it would be very persuasive. In particular, it seems implausible to claim, as advocates of a new offence must be claiming, that the reasons against grouping intoxicated vandals alongside advertent vandals under the existing criminal damage heading are more powerful than the reasons against grouping intoxicated vandals alongside intoxicated killers under some new offence. The underlying mistake is the assumption that wrongs should be grouped primarily according to their mental components and with

little reference to their other characteristics. Not only have offence labels always reflected the non-mental characteristics of the wrongs they prohibit, but in many cases such characteristics are the only basis for a labelling distinction—consider the separate classification of murder as opposed to section 18 wounding, or of common assault as opposed to section 47 actual bodily harm, or of attempted offences as opposed to completed offences. Why should we apologise for distinguishing between intoxicated killers and intoxicated vandals on the same grounds? All this being said, it is doubtful how many of the advocates of a new offence realise they are making this implausible argument. Most of them are, I suspect, motivated by a vague and unfocused objection to objective liability per se. The attempt to reconcile such extreme subjectivist views with an uneasy acceptance that it would not be right or, at least, not politically acceptable for intoxicated offenders to get off leads to the rather sloppy conclusion that there should be a special offence—a criminal law ghetto in which the slightly fishy intoxicated wrongs are kept separate from 'proper' (subjective) criminal wrongdoing.

The introduction of one bland offence heading to cover all criminal intoxicated wrongdoing may well be undesirable, but we should not rule out the possibility that a range of narrowly circumscribed new offences should be introduced to cover forms of intoxicated wrongdoing that are difficult to categorise at present. On the other hand, there are dozens of other considerations bearing on whether such reforms should be introduced. Should the law be made even more complex? How far would the new offences be open to abuse? How, for example, would deterrence and respect for the law be affected if enough real rapists were able to bluff themselves into a new 'forcible intercourse' category designed to catch inadvertent offenders? Even leaving these difficulties aside, though, it is hard to accept that very many intoxicated wrongs sit uncomfortably under their existing basic intent offence headings. Even if we were given carte blanche to rewrite the specific-basic distinction and to introduce new offences where necessary, I doubt that we would want to change very much. Certainly, it seems unlikely that we would want to bring intoxicated killers under any other category than manslaughter, or intoxicated vandals under any other category than criminal damage. or intoxicated wounders under any other categories than unlawful wounding or assault occasioning actual bodily harm.

Would a crime of being 'criminally intoxicated' be useful?

3. *CALDWELL* AND INTOXICATION

In *Caldwell* [1981] 1 All ER 961 at 968, p **146**, above, Lord Diplock said:

...classification into offences of specific and basic intent is irrelevant where being reckless whether a particular harmful consequence will result from one's act is a sufficient alternative mens rea.

This was right when, under *Caldwell*, there was an obvious risk and the defendant had not given any thought to the possibility of it. However intoxicated he was, he had the fault required for the crime and was liable. D might say that he did consider whether there was a risk and decided there was none. He was then not *Caldwell* reckless. But, if he would have appreciated the existence of the risk had he been sober, he will still be liable because of *Majewski*. Since *G*, overruling *Caldwell*, the application of intoxication to that form of recklessness need no longer be considered.

4. INTOXICATION CAUSING AUTOMATISM

R v Lipman

[1969] 3 All ER 410, Court of Appeal, Criminal Division

(Widgery and Fenton Atkinson LJJ and James J)

The facts appear in the judgment. Milmo J directed the jury:

He would be guilty of manslaughter if the jury were to find either—(1) that he must have realised before he got himself into the condition he did by taking the drugs, that acts such as those he subsequently performed and which resulted in the death, were dangerous; or (2) that the taking of the drugs which the defendant took that night was dangerous and that the [defendant] must have realised that by taking them he was incurring a risk of some harm, not necessarily serious harm, to some other person or persons; or (3) that in taking these drugs in the circumstances in which he took them, the [defendant] was grossly negligent and reckless and this involves the jury considering whether or not he thought that what he was doing was safe so far as other people were concerned. [See [1970] 1 QB 152.]

The jury found the defendant not guilty of murder but guilty of manslaughter by reason of grounds (1) and (3) above. The defendant appealed.

[**Widgery LJ** delivered the judgment of the court:]

Both the applicant and the victim were addicted to drugs and on the evening of 16 September 1967 both took a quantity of a drug known as LSD. Early on the morning of 18 September the applicant (who is a United States citizen) hurriedly booked out of his hotel and left the country. On the following day (19 September) Delbarre's landlord found her dead in her room. She had suffered two blows on the head causing haemorrhage of the brain, but she died of asphyxia as a result of some eight inches of sheet having been crammed into her mouth.

The applicant was returned to this country by extradition proceedings, and at the trial he gave evidence of having gone with Delbarre to her room and there experienced what he described as an LSD 'trip'. He explained how he had the illusion of descending to the centre of the earth and being attacked by snakes, with which he had fought. It was not seriously disputed that he had killed the victim in the course of this experience, but he said he had no knowledge of what he was doing and no intention to harm her. He was charged with murder, but the jury evidently accepted that he lacked the necessary intention to kill or to do grievous bodily harm, as to manslaughter, the jury was directed that it would suffice for the Crown to prove that:

> '…he must have realised, before he got himself into the condition he did by taking the drug, that acts such as those he subsequently performed and which resulted in the death were dangerous'.

In this court counsel for the applicant contends that this was a misdirection, and that the jury should have been directed further that it was necessary for the Crown to prove that the applicant had intended to do acts likely to result in harm, or foresaw that harm would result from what he was doing.

For the purposes of criminal responsibility we see no reason to distinguish between the effect of drugs voluntarily taken and drunkenness voluntarily induced. As to the latter there is a great deal of authority. [His Lordship quoted from the speeches of Lord Birkenhead in *Beard's* case and Lord Denning, in *Bratty's* case [see p 22, above] and *Gallagher's* case [see p 204]].

These authorities show quite clearly, in our opinion, that it was well established that no specific intent was necessary to support a conviction for manslaughter based on killing in the course of an unlawful act and that, accordingly, self-induced drunkenness was no defence to such a charge.

In a case of manslaughter by neglect, however, it has been recognised that some mental element must be established, and for this I turn to *Andrews v DPP* [see p **638**, below]. In that case Lord Atkin dealt in some detail with the mental element involved in manslaughter by neglect. [His Lordship cited a passage from Lord Atkin's speech, p **639**, below.]

It is to be observed that in that case there are two references to mens rea; and the next case in which a similar reference is made is *Church* [see p **624**, below]. This seems to be the first case in which a reference to mens rea occurs when the killing was the result of an allegedly unlawful act, and the crucial passage appears in the judgment of Edmund Davies J. Before I turn to that passage, I should say that in *Church* the appellant, who threw the unconscious body of the victim into a river where she drowned, pleaded that he thought she was already dead. The jury were directed that if they thought that that was the state of the prisoner's mind the proper verdict was manslaughter, and this direction was criticised by the Court of Criminal Appeal on the ground that on the facts of that case it was equivalent to saying the commission of any unlawful act from which death resulted would be manslaughter. [His Lordship cited a passage from the judgment of Edmund Davies J, p **624**, below.]

This passage forms the basis of the applicant's submission before us, namely, that by 1965 (the date of *Church*) it had become recognised that guilt of manslaughter derived from the accused's having intended or foreseen that some harm should befall the victim as a result of his action. It is accepted in this argument that at that time the so-called objective test was applied to the state of the accused's mind, so that the issue was concluded against him if ordinary sober and reasonable people would recognise that harm was likely to be caused. But it is nevertheless maintained that the theoretical basis of guilt was the accused's supposed intent or foresight.

The final step in the argument is that s 8 of the Criminal Justice Act 1967 has replaced the objective test by a subjective one, so that the jury are now required to consider the actual state of the accused's own mind at the relevant time. [His Lordship quoted s8, p **179**, above.]

If the applicant's argument be sound, it follows that we have come a long way since *DPP v Beard* [see p **191**, above] and that events have moved very fast. In our judgment, there is a flaw in the applicant's argument; and the flaw lies in the assumption that *Church* introduced a new element of intent or foreseeability into this type of manslaughter. All that the judgment in *Church* says in terms is that whereas, formerly, a killing by any unlawful act amounted to manslaughter, this consequence does not now inexorably follow unless the unlawful act is one in which ordinary sober and responsible people would recognise the existence of risk. The development recognised by *Church* relates to the type of act from which a charge of manslaughter may result, not in the intention (real or assumed) of the prisoner. It is perhaps unfortunate that a reference to mens rea, which had been found unhelpful by Lord Atkin, was repeated in *Church*, and to give it the effect now contended for would be contrary to *DPP v Beard* and the other authorities which we have cited. The decision in *Church* was referred to in this court later in *Lamb* [see p **624**, below] where the accused had pointed a revolver at the victim in the belief, as he said, that there was no round in the chamber, but the revolver had fired and the victim was killed. It was pointed out in this court that no unlawful act on the part of the prisoner had been proved in the absence of the necessary intent to constitute an assault. But this is intention of a different kind. Even if intent has to be proved to constitute the unlawful act, no specific further intent is required to turn that act into manslaughter. Manslaughter remains a most difficult offence to define because it arises in so many different ways and, as the mental element (if any) required to establish it varies so widely, any general reference to mens rea is apt to mislead.

We can dispose of the present application by reiterating that when the killing results from an unlawful act of the accused no specific intent has to be proved to convict of manslaughter, and self-induced intoxication is accordingly no defence. Since in the present case the acts complained of were obviously likely to cause harm to the victim (and did, in fact, kill her) no acquittal was possible and the verdict of manslaughter, at the least, was inevitable.

Appeal dismissed

Questions

1. Why is it relevant whether a person knows it is dangerous to cram eight inches of bedsheet into a woman's mouth if he has no idea that he is going to do, or is doing, such an act?

2. The cases distinguish between (i) manslaughter by an unlawful act, p 622, below and (ii) manslaughter by 'gross negligence' or 'recklessness' p 638, below. Which of these doctrines was invoked by (a) Milmo J, in his direction and (b) the Court of Appeal in upholding the conviction?

3. According to (i) Milmo J's summing up and (ii) the Court of Appeal, was the act for which Lipman was responsible (a) the taking of the drugs or (b) the acts done to Delbarre? If they differ, which is right?

4. The court concedes, 'even if intent has to be proved to constitute the unlawful act . . .' Was any intent proved with respect to the unlawful acts done to Delbarre?

5. In *DPP v Kellet* [1994] Crim LR 916 it was held that, even if a sober person does not 'allow' a dog to be unmuzzled in a public place, contrary to the Dangerous Dogs Act 1991, s 1(7), unless he knows and consents, a person who accidentally allows the dog out because he is drunk is guilty: it is an offence of 'basic intent'. But if D does not 'allow' there is no actus reus. Voluntary intoxication negatives the requirement of a basic intent but can it ever negative the requirement of an actus reus? Even in *Lipman*, D 'killed'. Did Kellett 'allow'?

5. RECKLESS INTOXICATION

R v Hardie
[1984] 3 All ER 848, Court of Appeal, Criminal Division

(Parker LJ, Stuart-Smith and McCowan JJ)

The defendant's relationship with the woman with whom he was living broke down and she left him. He became upset and took several tablets of valium, a sedative drug, belonging to the woman. Later he started a fire in the bedroom of the flat while the woman and her daughter were in the sitting room. Charged with an offence under s 1(2) of the Criminal Damage Act 1971, he argued that the effect of the drug was to prevent him having the mens rea. The judge directed the jury that this could be no defence because the drug was self-administered. He appealed on grounds of misdirection.

Parker LJ . . . in *R v Bailey* [1983] 2 All ER 503, [1983] 1 WLR 760 this court had to consider a case where a diabetic had failed to take sufficient food after taking a normal dose of insulin and struck the victim over the head with an iron bar. The judge directed the jury that the defence of automatism, ie that the mind did not go with the act, was not available because the incapacity was self-induced. It was held that this was wrong on two grounds: (a) because on the basis of *DPP v Majewski* it was clearly available to the offence embodying specific intent and (b) because although self-induced by the omission to take food it was also available to negative the other offence which was of basic intent only.

Having referred to *DPP v Majewski* and *R v Lipman* Griffiths LJ, giving the considered judgment of the court, said ([1983] 2 All ER 503 at 507, [1983] 1 WLR 760 at 764–765):

'It was submitted on behalf of the Crown that a similar rule should be applied as a matter of public policy to all cases of self-induced automatism. But it seems to us that there may be material distinctions between a man who consumes alcohol or takes dangerous drugs and one who fails to take sufficient food after insulin to avert hypo-glycaemia. It is common knowledge that those who take alcohol to excess or certain sorts of drugs may become aggressive or do dangerous or unpredictable things; they may be able to foresee the risks of causing harm to others, but nevertheless persist in their conduct. But the same cannot be said, without more, of a man who fails to take food after an insulin injection. If he does appreciate the risk that such a failure may lead to aggressive, unpredictable and uncontrollable conduct and he nevertheless deliberately runs the risk or otherwise disregards it, this will amount to recklessness. But we certainly do not think that it is common knowledge, even among diabetics, that such is a consequence of a failure to take food; and there is no evidence that it was known to this appellant. Doubtless he knew that if he failed to take his insulin or proper food after it he might lose consciousness, but as such he would only be a danger to himself unless he put himself in charge of some machine such as a motor car, which required his continued conscious control. In our judgment, self-induced automatism, other than that due to intoxication from alcohol or drugs, may provide a defence to crimes of basic intent. The question in each case will be whether the prosecution has proved the necessary element of recklessness. In cases of assault, if the accused knows that his actions or inaction are likely to make him aggressive, unpredictable or uncontrolled with the result that he may cause some injury to others and he persists in the action or takes no remedial action when he knows it is required, it will be open to the jury to find that he was reckless.'

In the present instance the defence was that the valium was taken for the purpose of calming the nerves only, that it was old stock and that the appellant was told it would do him no harm. There was no evidence that it was known to the appellant or even generally known that the taking of valium in the quantity taken would be liable to render a person aggressive or incapable of appreciating risks to others or have other side effects such that its self-administration would itself have an element of recklessness. It is true that valium is a drug and it is true that it was taken deliberately and not taken on medical prescription, but the drug is, in our view, wholly different in kind from drugs which are liable to cause unpredictability or aggressiveness. It may well be that the taking of a sedative or soporific drug will, in certain circumstances, be no answer, for example in a case of reckless driving, but if the effect of a drug is merely soporific or sedative the taking of it, even in some excessive quantity, cannot in the ordinary way raise a *conclusive* presumption against the admission of proof of intoxication for the purpose of disproving mens rea in ordinary crimes, such as would be the case with alcoholic intoxication or incapacity or automatism resulting from the self-administration of dangerous drugs.

In the present case the jury should not, in our judgment, have been directed to disregard any incapacity which resulted or might have resulted from the taking of valium. They should have been directed that if they came to the conclusion that, as a result of the valium, the appellant was, at the time, unable to appreciate the risks to property and persons from his actions they should then consider whether the taking of the valium was itself reckless. We are unable to say what would have been the appropriate direction with regard to the elements of recklessness in this case for we have not seen all the relevant evidence, nor are we able to suggest a model direction, for circumstances will vary infinitely and model directions can sometimes lead to more rather than less confusion. It is sufficient to say that the direction that the effects of valium were necessarily irrelevant was wrong.

Appeal allowed

Questions

1. Are drugs to be divided into two categories—alcohol and 'dangerous' drugs which attract the operation of *Majewski* and other drugs which do not?

2. Is it permissible for the court to apply a 'conclusive presumption' of recklessness in the light of s 8 of the Criminal Justice Act 1967, p **179**, above?

6. DRINKING 'WITH INTENT'

Attorney-General for Northern Ireland v Gallagher
[1961] 3 All ER 299, House of Lords

(Lords Reid, Goddard, Tucker, Denning and Morris of Borth-y-Gest)

The facts appear sufficiently in the speech of Lord Denning. The Court of Criminal Appeal in Northern Ireland quashed the conviction for murder because the Lord Chief Justice, in their view, had directed the jury to apply the M'Naghten test (p 374, below) not to the time when the accused killed his wife but to the morning of that day, before he opened the bottle of whisky.

[**Lord Tucker**, with whom Lords Goddard and Reid agreed, held that the jury had not been misdirected.]

Lord Denning. My Lords, every direction which a judge gives to a jury in point of law must be considered against the background of facts which have been proved or admitted in the case. In this case the respondent did not give evidence himself. And the facts proved against him were: He had a grievance against his wife. She had obtained a maintenance order against him and had been instrumental in getting him detained in a mental hospital. He had made up his mind to kill his wife. He bought a knife for the purpose and a bottle of whisky—either to give himself Dutch courage to do the deed or to drown his conscience after it. He did in fact carry out his intention. He killed his wife with the knife and drank much of the whisky before or after he killed her. There were only two defences raised on his behalf: (i) Insanity; (ii) Drunkenness. . . .

My Lords, this case differs from all others in the books in that the respondent, whilst sane and sober, before he took to the drink, had already made up his mind to kill his wife. This seems to me to be far worse—and far more deserving of condemnation—than the case of a man who, before getting drunk, has no intention to kill, but afterwards in his cups, whilst drunk, kills another by an act which he would not dream of doing when sober. Yet, by the law of England, in this latter case his drunkenness is no defence even though it has distorted his reason and his will-power. So why should it be a defence in the present case? And is it made any better by saying that the man is a psychopath? The answer to the question is, I think, that the case falls to be decided by the general principle of English law that, subject to very limited exceptions, drunkenness is no defence to a criminal charge nor is a defect of reason produced by drunkenness. This principle was stated by Sir Matthew Hale in his *Pleas of the Crown*, Vol 1, p 32, in words which I would repeat here:

> 'This vice [drunkenness] doth deprive men of the use of reason, and puts many men into a perfect, but temporary frenzy . . . by the laws of England such a person shall have no privilege by this voluntary contracted madness, but shall have the same judgment as if he were in his right senses.'

This general principle can be illustrated by looking at the various ways in which drunkenness may produce a defect of reason: (a) It may impair a man's powers of perception so that he may not be able to foresee or measure the consequences of his actions as he would if he were sober. Nevertheless, he is not allowed to set up his self-induced want of perception as a defence. Even if he did not himself appreciate that what he was doing was dangerous, nevertheless, if a reasonable man in his place, who was not befuddled with drink, would have appreciated it, he is guilty; see *Meade* [[1909] 1KB 895], as explained in *DPP v Beard* [see p **191**, above]. (b) It may impair a man's power to judge between right or wrong, so that he may do a thing when drunk which he would not dream of doing while sober. He does not realise he is doing wrong. Nevertheless, he is not allowed to set up his self-induced want of moral sense as a defence. In *Beard's* case Lord Birkenhead LC distinctly ruled that it was not a defence for a drunken man to say he did not know he was doing wrong. (c) It may impair a man's power of self-control so that he may more readily give way to provocation than if he were sober.

Nevertheless, he is not allowed to set up his self-induced want of control as a defence. The acts of provocation are to be assessed, not according to their effect on him personally, but according to the effect they would have on a reasonable man in his place. The law on this point was previously in doubt (see the cases considered in *Beard's* case), but it has since been resolved by *McCarthy* [[1954] 2 QB 105; [1954] 2 All ER 262], *Bedder v DPP* [see p **591**, below] and s3 of the Homicide Act 1957.

The general principle which I have enunciated is subject to two exceptions: (i) If a man is charged with an offence in which a specific intention is essential (as in murder, though not in manslaughter), then evidence of drunkenness, which renders him incapable of forming that intent, is an answer; see *Beard's* case. This degree of drunkenness is reached when the man is rendered so stupid by drink that he does not know what he is doing (see *Moore* [(1852) 3 Car & Kir 319]) as where, at a christening, a drunken nurse put the baby behind a large fire, taking it for a log of wood (18 Gentleman's Magazine, 1748, p 570); and where a drunken man thought his friend (lying in his bed) was a theatrical dummy placed there and stabbed him to death ((1951) Times, 13 January). In each of those cases it would not be murder. But it would be manslaughter. (ii) If a man by drinking brings on a distinct disease of the mind such as delirium tremens, so that he is temporarily insane within the M'Naghten rules, that is to say, he does not at the time know what he is doing or that it is wrong, then he has a defence on the ground of insanity; see *Davis* [(1881) 14 Cox CC 563], and *Beard's* case.

Does the present case come within the general principle or the exceptions to it? It certainly does not come within the first exception. The respondent was not incapable of forming an intent to kill. Quite the contrary. He knew full well what he was doing. He formed an intent to kill, he carried out his intention and he remembered afterwards what he had done. And the jury, properly directed on the point, have found as much, for they found him guilty of murder. Then does the case come within the second exception? It does not to my mind; for the simple reason that he was not suffering from a disease of the mind brought on by drink. He was suffering from a different disease altogether. As the Lord Chief Justice observed in his summing-up: 'If this man was suffering from a disease of the mind, it wasn't of a kind that is produced by drink.' So we have here a case of the first impression. That man is a psychopath. That is, he has a disease of the mind which is not produced by drink. But it is quiescent. And, whilst it is quiescent, he forms an intention to kill his wife. He knows it is wrong, but still he means to kill her. Then he gets himself so drunk that he has an explosive outburst and kills his wife. At that moment he knows what he is doing but he does not know it is wrong. So in that respect—in not knowing it is wrong—he has a defect of reason at the moment of killing. If that defect of reason is due to the drink, it is no defence in law. But, if it is due to the disease of the mind, it gives rise to a defence of insanity. No one can say, however, whether it is due to the drink or to the disease. It may well be due to both in combination. What guidance does the law give in this difficulty? That is, as I see it, the question of general public importance which is involved in this case.

My Lords, I think the law on this point should take a clear stand. If a man, whilst sane and sober, forms an intention to kill and makes preparation for it, knowing it is a wrong thing to do, and then gets himself drunk so as to give himself Dutch courage to do the killing, and whilst drunk carries out his intention, he cannot rely on this self-induced drunkenness as a defence to a charge of murder, nor even as reducing it to manslaughter. He cannot say that he got himself into such a stupid state that he was incapable of an intent to kill. So, also, when he is a psychopath, he cannot by drinking rely on his self-induced defect of reason as a defence of insanity. 'The wickedness of his mind before he got drunk is enough to condemn him, coupled with the act which he intended to do and did do. A psychopath who goes out intending to kill, knowing it is wrong, and does kill, cannot escape the consequences by making himself drunk before doing it. That is, I believe, the direction which the Lord Chief Justice gave to the jury and which the Court of Criminal Appeal found to be wrong. I think that it was right, and for this reason I would allow the appeal. I would agree, of course, that if, before the killing, he had discarded his intention to kill or reversed it—and then got drunk—it would be a different matter. But when he forms the intention to kill and without interruption proceeds to get drunk and carry out his intention, then his drunkenness is no defence, and none the less so because it is dressed up as a defence of insanity. There was no evidence in this case of any interruption, and there was no need for the Lord Chief Justice to mention it to the jury.

I need hardly say, of course, that I have here only considered the law of Northern Ireland. In England, a psychopath such as this man might now be in a position to raise a defence of diminished responsibility under s 2 of the Homicide Act 1957....

I would allow this appeal and restore the conviction of murder.

Appeal allowed

Notes and questions

1. *Archbold* (1992 edn) para 17–147, commenting on *Gallagher's* case:

If A with the intention of killing B enrages a gorilla with the result that the gorilla in fact kills B, A is clearly guilty of murder and, under the old law, as a principal in the first degree. What difference does it make if for the gorilla he substitutes himself?

2. What if Gallagher, getting up in the night to relieve himself, had blundered drunkenly into the grandfather clock on the landing and knocked it down the stairs, killing his wife who had just arrived home?

7. INTOXICATION AND DEFENCES

We have seen (above, p 15) that, just as a state of mind is a necessary element in the definition of an offence, so also it is a necessary element in some defences. Just as intoxication may cause a person to *lack* the mens rea of an offence so it may cause him to *have* the necessary mental element of a defence. It is necessary for a defendant who relies on self-defence to offer evidence that he believed he was being attacked in such a way as to justify or excuse the force which he used to defend himself. What if that belief was mistaken—he was not under attack at all—and the mistake was made because he was drunk at the time? The CLRC's answer to this was that it depended on the offence with which he was charged: if it was an offence of specific intent, then he could rely on the drunken belief; but, if it was not an offence of specific intent, he could not. D, being charged with murder, could rely on his drunken belief that he was using the minimum of force to defend himself from a deadly attack; but if the jury acquitted him of murder on that ground, they could convict him of manslaughter because his drunken belief would not avail him on the latter charge, manslaughter not being an offence requiring specific intent. Similar results would follow in relation to the offences under ss 18 and 20 of the OAPA 1861.

The Code Team incorporated this recommendation in cl 29(6) of their draft (Law Com No 143) and the Law Commission included it, though in different terms, in the Draft Code, cl 22(1)(b) and (2) set out below, p 212.

The law has however developed differently. Consider the next case.

R v O'Grady
[1987] 3 All ER 420, Court of Appeal, Criminal Division

(Lord Lane CJ, Boreham and McCowan JJ)

The defendant (O) and his friend, the deceased (M), had been drinking heavily and fell asleep in O's flat. O said that he awoke to find M hitting him, that M had a piece of glass in one hand and that he, O, picked up a piece of glass and hit M. M died of the injury caused. At the instance of counsel for the prosecution, Judge Underhill gave the following additional direction to the jury:

It might be a view that you might take, I know not, that this defendant thought he was under attack from the other man mistakenly and made a mistake in thinking that he was under attack because of the drink that was in him. If he made such a mistake in drink he would nevertheless be entitled to defend himself even though he mistakenly believed that he was under attack. He would be entitled in those circumstances to defend himself. But if in taking defensive measures, then he went beyond what is reasonable either because of his mind being affected by drink or for any other reason, then the defence of self-defence would not avail him because, as I told you earlier on, you are entitled to defend yourself if it is necessary so to do, but the defensive measures that you take must be reasonable ones and not go beyond what is reasonable.

O was convicted of manslaughter and appealed on the grounds, inter alia, that the judge was wrong to limit the reference to mistake as to the *existence* of an attack and should have included a reference to the possibility of a mistake as to the *severity* of it; and that the judge had 'in effect divorced the reasonableness of the appellant's reaction from the appellant's state of mind at the time.'

Lord Lane CJ [having said that the court had found no case directly in point which was binding]:

As McCullough J [the single judge, giving leave to appeal] pointed out helpfully in his observations for the benefit of the court:

'Given that a man who *mistakenly* believes he is under attack is entitled to use reasonable force to defend himself, it would seem to follow that, if he *is* under attack and mistakenly believes the attack to be more serious than it is, he is entitled to use reasonable force to defend himself against an attack of the severity he believed it to have. If one allows a mistaken belief induced by drink to bring this principle into operation, an act of gross negligence (viewed objectively) may become lawful even though it results in the death of the innocent victim. The drunken man would be guilty of neither murder nor manslaughter.'

How should the jury be invited to approach the problem? One starts with the decision of this court in *R v Williams* [1987] 3 All ER 411, namely that where the defendant might have been labouring under a mistake as to the facts he must be judged according to that mistaken view, whether the mistake was reasonable or not. It is then for the jury to decide whether the defendant's reaction to the threat (real or imaginary) was a reasonable one. The court was not in that case considering what the situation might be where the mistake was due to voluntary intoxication by alcohol or some other drug.

We have come to the conclusion that, where the jury are satisfied that the defendant was mistaken in his belief that any force or the force which he in fact used was necessary to defend himself and are further satisfied that the mistake was caused by voluntarily induced intoxication, the defence must fail. We do not consider that any distinction should be drawn on this aspect of the matter between offences involving what is called specific intent, such as murder, and offences of so called basic intent, such as manslaughter. Quite apart from the problem of directing a jury in a case such as the present where manslaughter is an alternative verdict to murder, the question of mistake can and ought to be considered separately from the question of intent. A sober man who mistakenly believes he is in danger of immediate death at the hands of an attacker is entitled to be acquitted of both murder and manslaughter if his reaction in killing his supposed assailant was a reasonable one. What his intent may have been seems to us to be irrelevant to the problem of self-defence or no. Secondly, we respectfully adopt the reasoning of McCullough J already set out.

This brings us to the question of public order. There are two competing interests. On the one hand the interest of the defendant who has only acted according to what he believed to be necessary to protect himself, and on the other hand that of the public in general and the victim in particular who, probably through no fault of his own, has been injured or perhaps killed because of the defendant's drunken mistake. Reason recoils from the conclusion that in such circumstances a defendant is entitled to leave the court without a stain on his character....

We have therefore come to the conclusion that a defendant is not entitled to rely, so far as self-defence is concerned, on a mistake of fact which has been induced by voluntary intoxication.

As already indicated, the judge's addendum to his summing up, which he made at the suggestion of prosecuting counsel, was unnecessary and erred in favour of the appellant.

The appeal against conviction is accordingly dismissed.

Appeal dismissed

Notes and questions

1. As O was appealing from a conviction of manslaughter, could the opinion of the court as to the correct direction on a charge of murder be any more than an obiter dictum?

2. The court was much influenced its assumption that, if the drunken mistake founded a defence to murder, it also founded a defence to manslaughter. Was this assumption correct? See below, p **468**. Was McCullough J right to say that, if the appellant's arguments were right, 'an act of gross negligence (viewed objectively) may become lawful even though it results in the death of an innocent victim'? Why is it not manslaughter simply because it is a case of causing death by gross negligence?

3. The CLRC (of which McCullough J was a member) gave the following illustration (OAP Report, para 278) of what they thought the law should be:

...a householder who mistakenly believes that a police officer, who has entered his house to look around on finding the front door open, is a burglar about to attack him and strikes him down in self-defence would probably be acquitted on the indictment. But if his mistaken belief was due to voluntary intoxication the effect of our proposals would be that he would be acquitted of murder but convicted of manslaughter.

Why should not McCullough J and the Court of Appeal, in the absence of any contrary authority, have held that proposition to be the law? (Cf the comparable situation in *Williams (Gladstone)*, below, p **453**.) Is not this course still open to the court?

4. Is there anything to be said in favour of Judge Underhill's opinion that a defendant might rely on a drunken mistake to show that he believed he was under attack but not to show how deadly he thought the attack to be?

5. The proposition in *O'Grady* that a drunken mistake could not found a defence of self-defence on a murder charge was subjected to heavy criticism.

The Law Commission, in declining to follow that proposition in the draft Code said (Law Com No 177, para 8.42):

... it would, we believe, be unthinkable to convict of murder a person who thought, for whatever reason, that he was acting to save his life and who would have been acting reasonably if he had been right.

The Court of Appeal, however, continued to think the unthinkable in *O'Connor* [1991] Crim LR 135. They were aware of the heavy criticism of *O'Grady* but declared that the case was binding on them. This too appears to be obiter, being unnecessary to the decision because O'Connor's conviction of murder was quashed on the ground that the judge omitted to direct the jury that voluntary intoxication could have prevented the appellant from forming the specific intent to kill or cause gbh.

6. The Law Commission (Consultation Paper No 122, para 21.9 and Law Com No 218, para 45.3) accepted that the dicta in *O'Connor* and *O'Grady* represented the present law and their draft Non Fatal Offences Bill, cl 33(1), would have codified the law as stated in those cases pending their law reform consideration of intoxication. They now confirm (Law Com No 229, para 7.11) that they still regard the result (which they would have codified!) as unthinkable and propose instead (para 7.12) that a person should be able to rely on his intoxicated belief only where the offence requires proof of intention, purpose, knowledge, belief, fraud or dishonesty. This means that he could not rely on it where the offence requires proof only of recklessness, negligence or imposes strict liability and is substantially the same as the CLRC proposal and cl 22 of the Draft Code; but the legislative technique proposed to achieve it is much more complex. As below, p **212**, the proposals in Law Com No 229 have not been adopted by the Home Office and it seems likely that the Commission will have to think again. All these proposals seem to be subject to the difficulty that an offence may require intention, etc, as to one element and be satisfied with recklessness as to another. Is there any way of solving that problem?

7. D is charged with murder. He hit V in the face with a beer glass, causing a cut from which V bled to death. D says (a) he was acting in self-defence and (b) he had no intent to cause death or gbh. V was not in fact attacking him but D says that, in his drunken condition, (a) he believed V was attacking him with a broken glass so as to threaten his life; (b) he forgot he had a glass in his own hand. Following *O'Grady* and *O'Connor*, so far as (a) is concerned, the jury must treat D as if he were not drunk (would he have known that he was not being attacked if he had not been drunk?), whereas for (b) they must take his drunkenness into account. His drunkenness is relevant to the question whether he knew he had a glass in his own hand (because that goes to specific intent) but not to the question whether he believed there was a glass in V's hand (because that goes to self-defence). Can this be justified?

Jaggard v Dickinson
[1980] 3 All ER 716, Queen's Bench Division

(Donaldson LJ and Mustill J)

The defendant lived in a house belonging to one Heyfron. Making her way home drunk, she went by mistake to the wrong house, found it locked and did damage by breaking in. She was charged with an offence under s 1(1) of the Criminal Damage Act 1971. She relied on s 5(2) of the Act, p **946**, below, saying that she believed that Heyfron would have consented to her doing the damage in the circumstances. The magistrates held that this drunken belief could not be a defence.

Mustill J . . . It is convenient to refer to the exculpatory provisions of s 5(2) as if they created a defence whilst recognising that the burden of disproving the facts referred to by the subsection remains on the prosecution. The magistrates held that the appellant was not entitled to rely on s 5(2) since the belief relied on was brought about by a state of self-induced intoxication.

In support of the conviction counsel for the respondent advanced an argument which may be summarised as follows. (i) Where an offence is one of 'basic intent', in contrast to one of 'specific intent', the fact that the accused was in a state of self-induced intoxication at the time when he did the acts constituting the actus reus does not prevent him from possessing the mens rea necessary to constitute the offence: see *DPP v Morgan* [p **181**, above], *DPP v Majewski* [p **190**, above], (ii) Section 1(1) of the 1971 Act creates an offence of basic intent: see *R v Stephenson* [1979] 2 All ER 1198, [1979] QB 695. (iii) Section 5(3) has no bearing on the present issue. It does not create a separate defence, but is no more than a partial definition of the expression 'without lawful excuse' in s 1(1). The absence of lawful excuse forms an element in the mens rea: see *R v Smith* [1974] 1 All ER 632 at 636, [1974] QB 354 at 360 [p **940**, below]. Accordingly, since drunkenness does not negative mens rea in crimes of basic intent, it cannot be relied on as part of a defence based on s 5(2).

Whilst this is an attractive submission, we consider it to be unsound, for the following reasons. In the first place, the argument transfers the distinction between offences of specific and of basic intent to a context in which it has no place. The distinction is material where the defendant relies on his own drunkenness as a ground for denying that he had the degree of intention or recklessness required in order to constitute the offence. Here, by contrast, the appellant does not rely on her drunkenness to displace an inference of intent or recklessness; indeed she does not rely on it at all. Her defence is founded on the state of belief called for by s 5(2). True, the fact of the appellant's intoxication was relevant to the defence under s 5(2) for it helped to explain what would otherwise have been inexplicable, and hence lent colour to her evidence about the state of her belief. This is not the same as using drunkenness to rebut an inference of intention or recklessness. Belief, like intention or recklessness, is a state of mind; but they are not the same states of mind.

It was, however, urged that we could not properly read s 5(2) in isolation from s 1(1), which forms the context of the words 'without lawful excuse' partially defined by s 5(2). Once the words are put in context, so it is maintained, it can be seen that the law must treat drunkenness in the same way in relation to lawful excuse (and hence belief) as it does to intention and recklessness, for they are all part of the mens rea of the offence. To fragment the mens rea, so as to treat one part of it as affected by drunkenness in one way and the remainder as affected in a different way, would make the law impossibly complicated to enforce.

If it had been necessary to decide whether, for all purposes, the mens rea of an offence under s 1(1) extends as far as an intent (or recklessness) as to the existence of a lawful excuse, I should have wished to consider the observations of James LJ, delivering the judgment of the Court of Appeal in *R v Smith* [1974] 1 All ER 632 at 636, [1974] QB 354 at 360. I do not however find it necessary to reach a conclusion on this matter and will only say that I am not at present convinced that, when these observations are read in the context of the judgment as a whole, they have the meaning which the respondent has sought to put on them. In my view, however, the answer to the argument lies in the fact that any distinctions which have to be drawn as to the relevance of drunkenness to the two subsections arises from the scheme of the 1971 Act itself. No doubt the mens rea is in general indivisible, with no distinction being possible as regards the effect of drunkenness. But Parliament has specifically isolated one subjective element, in the shape of honest belief, and has given it separate treatment and its own special gloss in s 5(3). This being so, there is nothing objectionable in giving it special treatment as regards drunkenness, in accordance with the natural meaning of its words.

Appeal allowed

Questions

1. Why did not s 101 of the Magistrates' Courts Act 1980, p 175, above, apply so as to put the onus of proving the defence on the defendant?

2. Would the defendant have been liable if she had believed (through intoxication or otherwise) that the house was her own? Cf *Smith*, p 940, below. Would it be sensible for the law to distinguish between the two cases?

3. Is there a distinction between using intoxication to rebut an inference of recklessness and to rebut evidence of belief? What if the belief is that there is no risk?

4. Did *Smith*, p 940, below, decide that the absence of lawful excuse forms an element in the mens rea?

5. In *Richardson and Irwin* [1999] 1 Cr App R 392, [1999] Crim LR 494 it was held, following *Aitken* (1992) 95 Cr App R 304, C-MAC, that a drunken belief that the victim of 'horse-play' was consenting to a dangerous act was a defence to a charge of unlawfully and maliciously inflicting gbh contrary to s 20 of the Offences Against the Person Act 1861. In *Aitken* the court considered the judge-advocate's direction under two heads, 'Unlawfully' and 'Maliciously'. They discussed intoxication only under 'maliciously', and effect of the alleged belief in consent only under 'unlawfully', as if belief went to the issue of actus reus rather than mens rea. But, where actual consent would be a defence (as appears to be the case here), the absence of a belief that the victim consents is an element in the mens rea. Section 20 being an offence of basic intent, D would not have been allowed to rely on his intoxication to show he did not foresee that he might cause any injury. Why should he be able to rely on it to show belief in consent? Is this another instance of the fragmentation of mens rea which Mustill J thought Parliament required him to tolerate in *Jaggard v Dickinson*, above, p 210? But Parliament has said nothing about the absence of consent in the s 20 offence. Was it necessary or desirable to differentiate between the two elements of mens rea?

The effect of cl 22(1)(b) of the Draft Code would have been to reverse *Jaggard v Dickinson* because 'it created an anomalous distinction (between a mistake as to the non-existence of an element of an offence and a mistake as to the existence of a circumstance affording a defence) which it be wrong to perpetuate in the Code.' The Law Commission's Non-Fatal Offences Bill would have abandoned cl 22 but would have reversed *Jaggard v Dickinson* by an amendment to the Criminal Damage Act. The Commission's proposals in Law Com No 229 (para 7.17) would achieve that result by applying the same rules to statutory defences as to defences generally.

8. REFORM OF THE LAW

The Draft Code, cl 22 is intended to represent the existing law. It does not restate a rule for specific intents because that is merely an application of the ordinary principle that any evidence which is relevant to the existence or non-existence of a fact is admissible: evidence of intoxication may be relevant to rebut an inference that D intended a natural consequence of his act. It is only the special rule regarding recklessness and lesser degrees of fault that needs to be stated.

22. Intoxication

(1) Where an offence requires a fault element of recklessness (however described), a person who was voluntarily intoxicated shall be treated—
   (a) as having been aware of any risk of which he would have been aware had he been sober;
   (b) as not having believed in the existence of an exempting circumstance (where the existence of such a belief is in issue) if he would not have so believed had he been sober.

(2) Where an offence requires a fault element of failure to comply with a standard of care, or requires no fault, a person who was voluntarily intoxicated shall be treated as not having believed in the existence of an exempting circumstance (where the existence of such a belief is in issue) if a reasonable sober person would not have so believed.

(3) Where the definition of a fault element or of a defence refers, or requires reference, to the state of mind or conduct to be expected of a reasonable person, such person shall be understood to be one who is not intoxicated.

(4) Subsection (1) does not apply—
   (a) to murder (to which section 55 [see p **662**, below] applies); or
   (b) to the case (to which section 36 [see p **382**, below] applies) where a person's unawareness or belief arises from a combination of mental disorder and voluntary intoxication.

(5) —
   (a) 'Intoxicant' means alcohol or any other thing which, when taken into the body, may impair awareness or control.
   (b) 'Voluntary intoxication' means the intoxication of a person by an intoxicant which he takes, otherwise than properly for a medicinal purpose, knowing that it is or may be an intoxicant.
   (c) For the purposes of this section, a person 'takes' an intoxicant if he permits it to be administered to him.

(6) An intoxicant, although taken for a medicinal purpose, is not properly so taken if—
   (a) —
      (i) it is not taken on medical advice; or
      (ii) it is taken on medical advice but the taker fails then or thereafter to comply with any condition forming part of the advice; and
   (b) the taker is aware that the taking, or the failure, as the case may be, may result in his doing an act capable of constituting an offence of the kind in question; and accordingly intoxication resulting from such taking or failure is voluntary intoxication.

(7) Intoxication shall be taken to have been voluntary unless evidence is given, in the sense stated in section 13(2), that it was involuntary.

The Law Commission, when preparing the Non-Fatal Offences Against the Person Bill, were not satisfied with the present law and undertook a full review. A consultation paper (LCCP 127) put forward six possible options for reform. The Commission's two preferred options would both have abolished the *Majewski* approach, so that intoxication would be taken into account like other relevant evidence in every case in determining whether the defendant had the required mental element. The second of these options would have combined the abolition of the *Majewski* approach with the creation of a new offence of (in effect) causing the actus reus of an offence while 'deliberately intoxicated'. These options, however, did not find favour with some influential consultees, particularly judges and practitioners. In the end, the Commission decided to recommend (Law Com No 229, *Legislating the Criminal Code: Intoxication and Criminal Liability*, 1995) codification of the present law with some minor amendments. They intended to incorporate their draft Criminal Law (Intoxication) Bill into their draft Non-Fatal Offences Against the Person Bill. Unfortunately, the drafting of the intoxication provisions is such as to have elicited the following conclusion from a learned commentator (Mr Ewan Paton [1995] Crim LR 382 at 392):

> Ironically, the most likely legislative outcome (if there is one) may be a return to the intoxication provisions of the Offences against the Person Report. These implement the preferred policy with considerably more economy and clarity than do some of the new report's tortured provisions.

Mr Paton's prophecy seems likely to be fulfilled. The Home Office Consultation Paper clearly prefers the earlier proposals. The provisions are substantially the same as those in the Draft Code, cl 22. The authors share Mr Paton's preference for the provisions in the Offences Against the Person Bill (this Bill, dealing only with non-fatal offences, goes back, with some variation in wording, to the Law Commission's earlier proposals. See J. C. Smith [1998] Crim LR 317 at 321) but these apply only to offences against the person, whereas those of the Intoxication Bill are general and would replace the common law on the subject. If the OAP Bill's provisions were preferred, the logical consequence would be a reversion in due course to the general provisions of the Draft Code, possibly modified in the light of the Law Commission's further consideration of the matter.

FURTHER READING

S. Gough, 'Surviving without *Majewski*' [2000] Crim LR 719

J. Horder, 'Pleading Involuntary Lack of Capacity' (1993) 52 CLJ 298

A. C. E. Lynch, 'The Scope of Intoxication' [1982] Crim LR 139

G. Orchard, 'Surviving without *Majewski*' [1993] Crim LR 426

R. Smith and L. Clements, 'Involuntary Intoxication, The threshold of inhibition and the instigation of crime' (1995) 46 NILQ 210

8

Strict liability

In the entire field of criminal law there is no more important doctrine than that of mens rea, embedded as are its roots in the principle that no man shall be punished for committing a crime unless a guilty mind can be imputed to him. Since the turn of the last century this principle has been assailed in no uncertain manner by the legislature. Long before then, however, Parliament had been prepared to use the sanctions of the criminal law as a means of securing a well-ordered structure of social and economic conduct. Two world wars, with their vast output of regulations creating new offences, have served to foster and enlarge this practice, in which it has become increasingly common to by-pass the above cardinal principle. In its place there has arisen a theory of strict liability in which the question of a guilty mind is wholly irrelevant. (J. Ll. Edwards, *Mens rea in Statutory Offences* (1950), p.xiii.)

1. MEANING OF STRICT LIABILITY

Most offences are now defined by statute. It is a question of statutory construction whether the offence requires a mental element and, if so, what that mental element is. Often the definition uses a word or a phrase—'knowingly', 'with intent to', 'recklessly', 'wilfully', 'dishonestly', and so on—which gives guidance to the court. Often the definition uses a verb or noun which imports a mental element of some kind—'permits' and 'possesses', are examples—so that there cannot be an actus reus without that mental element.

It does not follow that, where no word or phrase importing a mental element is used, the court will find that mens rea is not required. On the contrary the courts have frequently asserted that there is a presumption in favour of mens rea which must be rebutted by the prosecution; but the application of this presumption has been far from consistent. All earlier cases must now be reconsidered in the light of the two leading cases, *B (a minor) v DPP* and *K*, which follow. The presumption of mens rea is re-asserted with particular emphasis. It applies to all statutory offences, unless excluded expressly or by necessary implication. According to Lord Steyn, 'It can only be displaced by specific language, ie, an express provision or a necessary implication.' What distinguishes these from earlier pronouncements is not only the fact they are two unanimous decisions of the House of Lords but also the fact that they effectively overrule *Prince* (1875), regarded as the leading case on strict liability for 125 years, and many cases which applied it. Prince was convicted of taking a girl under 16 out of the possession of her parents although he believed on reasonable grounds that she was 18. The principles stated by the House are not limited to age-related elements of the actus reus; there is a presumption of mens rea in respect of every element of it. It is, however, too early to say with confidence what will be the effect on existing strict liability offences and it remains necessary to consider the old learning.

Distinction from absolute liability

It is commonly said that, in offences of strict liability, 'no mens rea' need be proved. Indeed, it was held in *Sandhu*, below, p **229**, that mens rea not only need not, but must not, be proved. As the cases in this chapter will show, this usually relates to mens rea with respect to one or more elements of the offence. It does not mean that no mental element whatever need be proved. Lord Edmund-Davies in *Whitehouse; Lemon* [1979] 1 All ER 898 at 920 cited the statement in *Smith and Hogan* (see 9th edn, p 98) that 'an offence is regarded— and properly regarded—as one of strict liability if no mens rea need be proved as to a single element in the actus reus.' The single element is, however, usually one of crucial importance so the effect is that a person with no moral culpability may be convicted.

Distinction from negligence

Strict liability means liability without fault, not even negligence, in respect of one or more elements of the offence. The offence of failing to take all reasonable steps to secure that a ship is operated in a safe manner (Merchant Shipping Act 1988, s 31, since repealed by s 314 of the Merchant Shipping Act 1995) was, by definition an offence of negligence, not, as the court in *Seaboard Offshore v Secretary of State for Transport* [1993] Crim LR 611 seemed to think, strict liability. See also *Peterssen v RSPCA* [1993] Crim LR 852.

2. WHEN WILL STRICT LIABILITY BE IMPOSED?

A modern example of a long line of cases imposing liability without fault is *Pharmaceutical Society of Great Britain v Storkwain Ltd* [1986] 2 All ER 635, [1986] 1 WLR 903, HL (discussed by B. S. Jackson in 'Storkwein: A Case Study in Strict Liability and Self Regulation' [1991] Crim LR 892). The Medicines Act 1968, s 58(2) provides that no person shall sell by retail specified medicinal products except in accordance with a prescription given by an appropriate medical practitioner. The defendant supplied specified drugs on prescriptions purporting to be signed by Dr Irani. The prescriptions were forged. There was no finding that the defendants acted dishonestly, improperly or even negligently. So far as appeared, the forgery was sufficient to deceive the sellers without any shortcoming on their part. Yet the House of Lords held that the Divisional Court had rightly directed the magistrate to convict. The court cited the following summary of principles stated by Lord Scarman, giving the advice of Privy Council in *Gammon (Hong Kong) Ltd v A-G of Hong Kong* [1984] 2 All ER 503:

(1) there is a presumption of law that mens rea is required before a person can be held guilty of a criminal offence; (2) the presumption is particularly strong where the offence is 'truly criminal' in character; (3) the presumption applies to statutory offences, and can be displaced only if this is clearly or by necessary implication the effect of the statute; (4) the only situation in which the presumption can be displaced is where the statute is concerned with an issue of social concern; public safety is such an issue; (5) even where a statute is concerned with such an issue, the presumption of mens rea stands unless it can be shown that the creation of strict liability will be effective to promote the objects of the statute by encouraging greater vigilance to prevent the commission of the prohibited act.

The Divisional Court said that the statute applied to an issue of social concern (what statute imposing criminal liability does not?) and public safety; and strict liability would be effective to promote its objects. The House discerned the intention of Parliament to create an offence of strict liability in the facts that (i) express requirements of mens rea are to be found in other sections of the Act but not in s 58(2)(a), and (ii) exercising a power under the Act, the Minister had provided for an exemption where the seller, having exercised all due diligence, believes on reasonable grounds that the product is not a 'prescription only' medicine. Storkwain of course knew that the medicine was 'prescription only', but believed on reasonable grounds that the prescription was valid. The Minister had not provided an exemption for that. For a criticism, see [1986] Crim LR at 814. How does the exercise of powers by a Minister after the Act has been passed reveal the intention of Parliament in passing it?

3. THE PRESUMPTION OF MENS REA

B (a minor) v Director of Public Prosecutions
[2000] 1 All ER 833, House of Lords

(Lord Irvine LC, Lords Mackay, Nicholls, Steyn and Hutton)

The Indecency with Children Act 1960, s 1(1) provided that 'Any person who commits an act of gross indecency with or towards a child under 14 [subsequently raised to 16, see now the Sexual Offences Act 2003, s 8, p 737] or who incites a child under that age to such an act with him or another' is guilty of an offence. The offence at the time of this case was punishable with two years' imprisonment on indictment. B, a boy of 15, was sitting next to a 14-year-old girl on a bus and asked her to give him what he described as a 'shiner', meaning not a black eye, but an act of oral sex. He was charged with inciting her, contrary to the 1960 Act. On a preliminary point of law, a Magistrates' Court ruled that s 1(1) imposed strict liability and that a mistaken belief, however reasonable, that the child was 14 or over, was no defence. B then pleaded guilty. On an appeal by way of case stated to the Divisional Court, Brooke LJ, Rougier and Tucker JJ delivered judgments, reluctantly dismissing the appeal. The Crown appealed to the House of Lords.

[Lords **Irvine**, for the reasons given by Lord Nicholls, and **Mackay**, for the reasons given by Lords Nicholls Steyn and Hutton, agreed that the appeal should be allowed.]

   Lord Nicholls of Birkenhead. My Lords, an indecent assault on a woman is a criminal offence. So is an indecent assault on a man. Neither a boy nor a girl under the age of 16 can, in law, give any consent which would prevent an act being an assault. These offences have existed for many years. Currently they are to be found in ss 14 and 15 of the Sexual Offences Act 1956. They have their origins in ss 52 and 62 of the Offences Against the Person Act 1861. [See now Ch 20, below.]
   In the early 1950s a lacuna in this legislation became apparent. A man was charged with indecent assault on a girl aged nine. At the man's invitation the girl had committed an indecent act on the man. The Court of Criminal Appeal held that an invitation to another person to touch the invitor could not amount to an assault on the invitee. As the man had done nothing to the girl which, if done against her will, would have amounted to an assault on her, the man's conduct did not constitute an indecent assault on the girl. That was *Fairclough v Whipp* [1951] 2 All ER 834. Two years later the same point arose and was similarly decided regarding a girl aged 11: see *DPP v Rogers* [1953] 2 All ER 644, [1953] 1 WLR 1017. Following a report of the Criminal Law Revision Committee in August 1959 (*First Report* (*Indecency with Children*) (Cmnd 835)), Parliament enacted the Indecency with Children Act 1960. Section 1(1) of this Act makes it a criminal offence to commit an act of gross

indecency with or towards a child under the age of 14, or to incite a child under that age to such an act. The question raised by the appeal concerns the mental element in this offence so far as the age ingredient is concerned.

The answer to this question depends upon the proper interpretation of the section. There are, broadly, three possibilities. The first possible answer is that it matters not whether the accused honestly believed that the person with whom he was dealing was over 14. So far as the age element is concerned, the offence created by s 1 of the 1960 Act is one of strict liability. The second possible answer is that a necessary element of this offence is the absence of a belief, held honestly and on reasonable grounds by the accused, that the person with whom he was dealing was over 14. The third possibility is that the existence or not of reasonable grounds for an honest belief is irrelevant. The necessary mental element is simply the absence of an honest belief by the accused that the other person was over 14.

The common law presumption

As habitually happens with statutory offences, when enacting this offence Parliament defined the prohibited conduct solely in terms of the proscribed physical acts. Section 1(1) says nothing about the mental element. In particular, the section says nothing about what shall be the position if the person who commits or incites the act of gross indecency honestly but mistakenly believed that the child was 14 or over.

In these circumstances the starting point for a court is the established common law presumption that a mental element, traditionally labelled mens rea, is an essential ingredient unless Parliament has indicated a contrary intention either expressly or by necessary implication. The common law presumes that, unless Parliament indicated otherwise, the appropriate mental element is an unexpressed ingredient of every statutory offence. On this I need do no more than refer to Lord Reid's magisterial statement in the leading case of *Sweet v Parsley* [1969] 1 All ER 347 at 349–350, [1970] AC 132 at 148–149:

> '... there has for centuries been a presumption that Parliament did not intend to make criminals of persons who were in no way blameworthy in what they did. That means that, whenever a section is silent as to mens rea, there is a presumption that, in order to give effect to the will of Parliament, we must read in words appropriate to require mens rea ... it is firmly established by a host of authorities that mens rea is an essential ingredient of every offence unless some reason can be found for holding that that is not necessary.'

Reasonable belief or honest belief

The existence of the presumption is beyond dispute, but in one respect the traditional formulation of the presumption calls for re-examination. This respect concerns the position of a defendant who acted under a mistaken view of the facts. In this regard, the presumption is expressed traditionally to the effect that an honest mistake by a defendant does not avail him unless the mistake was made on reasonable grounds. Thus, in *R v Tolson* (1889) 23 QBD 168 at 181, [1886–90] All ER Rep 26 at 34 Cave J observed:

> 'At common law an honest and reasonable belief in the existence of circumstances, which, if true, would make the act for which a prisoner is indicted an innocent act has always been held to be a good defence. This doctrine is embodied in the somewhat uncouth maxim "actus non facit reum, nisi mens sit rea." Honest and reasonable mistake stands in fact on the same footing as absence of the reasoning faculty, as in infancy, or perversion of that faculty, as in lunacy ... So far as I am aware it has never been suggested that these exceptions do not equally apply in the case of statutory offences unless they are excluded expressly or by necessary implication.'

The other judges in that case expressed themselves to a similar effect. In *Bank of New South Wales v Piper* [1897] AC 383 at 389–390 the Privy Council likewise espoused the 'reasonable belief' approach: '... the absence of mens rea really consists in an honest and reasonable belief entertained by the accused of facts which, if true, would make the act charged against him innocent.'

In *Sweet v Parsley* Lord Diplock referred to a general principle of construction of statutes creating criminal offences, in similar terms:

> '...a general principle of construction of any enactment, which creates a criminal offence [is] that, even where the words used to describe the prohibited conduct would not in any other context connote the necessity for any particular mental element, they are nevertheless to be read as subject to the implication that a necessary element in the offence is the absence of a belief held honestly and on reasonable grounds in the existence of facts which, if true, would make the act innocent.' (See [1969] 1 All ER 347 at 361, [1970] AC 132 at 163.)

The 'reasonable belief' school of thought held unchallenged sway for many years. But over the last quarter of a century there have been several important cases where a defence of honest but mistaken belief was raised. In deciding these cases the courts have placed new, or renewed, emphasis on the subjective nature of the mental element in criminal offences. The courts have rejected the reasonable belief approach and preferred the honest belief approach. When mens rea is ousted by a mistaken belief, it is as well ousted by an unreasonable belief as by a reasonable belief. In the pithy phrase of Lawton LJ in *R v Kimber* [1983] 3 All ER 316 at 319, [1983] 1 WLR 1118 at 1122 it is the defendant's belief, not the grounds on which it is based, which goes to negative the intent. This approach is well encapsulated in a passage in the judgment of Lord Lane CJ in *R v Williams* [1987] 3 All ER 411 at 415:

> 'The reasonableness or unreasonableness of the defendant's belief is material to the question of whether the belief was held by the defendant at all. If the belief was in fact held, its unreasonableness, so far as guilt or innocence is concerned, is neither here nor there. It is irrelevant. Were it otherwise, the defendant would be convicted because he was negligent in failing to recognise that the victim was not consenting ... and so on.'

Considered as a matter of principle, the honest belief approach must be preferable. By definition the mental element in a crime is concerned with a subjective state of mind, such as intent or belief. To the extent that an overriding objective limit ('on reasonable grounds') is introduced, the subjective element is displaced. To that extent a person who lacks the necessary intent or belief may nevertheless commit the offence. When that occurs the defendant's 'fault' lies exclusively in falling short of an objective standard. His crime lies in his negligence. A statute may so provide expressly or by necessary implication. But this can have no place in a common law principle, of general application, which is concerned with the need for a mental element as an essential ingredient of a criminal offence.

The traditional formulation of the common law presumption, exemplified in Lord Diplock's famous exposition in *Sweet v Parsley*, cited above, is out of step with this recent line of authority, in so far as it envisages that a mistaken belief must be based on reasonable grounds. This seems to be a relic from the days before a defendant in a criminal case could give evidence in his own defence. It is not surprising that in those times juries judged a defendant's state of mind by the conduct to be expected of a reasonable person....

[Lord Nicholls discussed *DPP v Morgan*, above, p **181**, *Kimber* [1983] 3 All ER 316, *Williams*, below, p **454**, and *Blackburn v Bowering*, below, p **675**]

The Crown advanced no suggestion to your Lordships that any of these recent cases was wrongly decided. This is not surprising, because the reasoning in these cases is compelling. Thus, the traditional formulation of the common law presumption must now be modified appropriately. Otherwise the formulation would not be an accurate reflection of the current state of the criminal law regarding mistakes of fact. Lord Diplock's dictum in *Sweet v Parsley* [1969] 1 All ER 347 at 361, [1970] AC 132 at 163 must in future be read as though the reference to reasonable grounds were omitted.

I add one further general observation. In principle, an age-related ingredient of a statutory offence stands on no different footing from any other ingredient. If a man genuinely believes that the girl with whom he is committing a grossly indecent act is over 14, he is not intending to commit such an act with a girl under 14. Whether such an intention is an essential ingredient of the offence depends upon a proper construction of s 1 of the 1960 Act. I turn next to that question.

The construction of s 1 of the Indecency with Children Act 1960

In s 1(1) of the 1960 Act Parliament has not expressly negatived the need for a mental element in respect of the age element of the offence. The question, therefore, is whether, although not expressly negatived, the need for a mental element is negatived by necessary implication. 'Necessary implication' connotes an implication which is compellingly clear. Such an implication may be found in the language used, the nature of the offence, the mischief sought to be prevented and any other circumstances which may assist in determining what intention is properly to be attributed to Parliament when creating the offence.

I venture to think that, leaving aside the statutory context of s 1, there is no great difficulty in this case. The section created an entirely new criminal offence, in simple unadorned language. The offence so created is a serious offence. The more serious the offence, the greater is the weight to be attached to the presumption, because the more severe is the punishment and the graver the stigma which accompany a conviction. Under s 1 conviction originally attracted a punishment of up to two years' imprisonment. This has since been increased to a maximum of ten years' imprisonment. The notification requirements under Pt I of the Sex Offenders Act 1997 now apply, no matter what the age of the offender: see Sch 1, para 1(1)(b). Further, in addition to being a serious offence, the offence is drawn broadly ('an act of gross indecency'). It can embrace conduct ranging from predatory approaches by a much older paedophile to consensual sexual experimentation between precocious teenagers of whom the offender may be the younger of the two. The conduct may be depraved by any acceptable standard, or it may be relatively innocuous behaviour in private between two young people. These factors reinforce, rather than negative, the application of the presumption in this case.

The purpose of the section is, of course, to protect children. An age ingredient was therefore an essential ingredient of the offence. This factor in itself does not assist greatly. Without more, this does not lead to the conclusion that liability was intended to be strict so far as the age element is concerned, so that the offence is committed irrespective of the alleged offender's belief about the age of the 'victim' and irrespective of how the offender came to hold this belief.

Nor can I attach much weight to a fear that it may be difficult sometimes for the prosecution to prove that the defendant knew the child was under 14 or was recklessly indifferent about the child's age. A well-known passage from a judgment of that great jurist, Sir Owen Dixon, in *Thomas v R* (1937) 59 CLR 279 at 309, bears repetition:

> 'The truth appears to be that a reluctance on the part of courts has repeatedly appeared to allow a prisoner to avail himself of a defence depending simply on his own state of knowledge and belief. The reluctance is due in great measure, if not entirely, to a mistrust of the tribunal of fact—the jury. Through a feeling that, if the law allows such a defence to be submitted to the jury, prisoners may too readily escape by deposing to conditions of mind and describing sources of information, matters upon which their evidence cannot be adequately tested and contradicted, judges have been misled into a failure steadily to adhere to principle. It is not difficult to understand such tendencies, but a lack of confidence in the ability of a tribunal correctly to estimate evidence of states of mind and the like can never be sufficient ground for excluding from inquiry the most fundamental element in a rational and humane criminal code.'

Similarly, it is far from clear that strict liability regarding the age ingredient of the offence would further the purpose of s 1 more effectively than would be the case if a mental element were read into this ingredient. There is no general agreement that strict liability is necessary to the enforcement of the law protecting children in sexual matters. For instance, the draft Criminal Code Bill prepared by the Law Commission in 1989 (*A Criminal Code of England and Wales* (Law Com No 177)) proposed a compromise solution. Clauses 114 and 115 of the Bill provided for committing or inciting acts of gross indecency with children aged under 13 or under 16. Belief that the child is over 16 would be a defence in each case: see vol 1, report and draft Criminal Code Bill, p 81.

Is there here a compellingly clear implication that Parliament should be taken to have intended that the ordinary common law requirement of a mental element should be excluded in respect of the age ingredient of this new offence? Thus far, having regard especially to the breadth of the offence and the gravity of the stigma and penal consequences which a conviction brings, I see no sufficient ground for so concluding.

Indeed, the Crown's argument before your Lordships did not place much reliance on any of the matters just mentioned. The thrust of the Crown's argument lay in a different direction: the statutory context. This is understandable, because the statutory background is undoubtedly the Crown's strongest point. The Crown submitted that the law in this field has been regarded as settled for well over 100 years, ever since the decision in *R v Prince* (1875) LR 2 CCR 154, [1874–80] All ER Rep 881. That well known case concerned the unlawful abduction of a girl under the age of 16. The defendant honestly believed she was over 16, and he had reasonable grounds for believing this. No fewer than 15 judges held that this provided no defence. Subsequently, in *R v Maughan* (1934) 24 Cr App Rep 130 the Court of Criminal Appeal (Lord Hewart CJ, Avory and Roche JJ) held that a reasonable and honest belief that a girl was over 16 could never be a defence to a charge of indecent assault. The court held that this point had been decided in *R v Forde* [1923] 2 KB 400, [1923] All ER Rep 477. The court also observed that in any event the answer was to be found in *R v Prince*. Building on this foundation Mr Scrivener QC submitted that the 1956 Act was not intended to change this established law, and that s 1 of the 1960 Act was to be read with the 1956 Act. The preamble to the 1960 Act stated that its purpose was to make 'further' provision for the punishment of indecent conduct towards young people. In this field, where Parliament intended belief as to age to be a defence, this was stated expressly: see, for instance, the 'young man's defence' in s 6(3) of the 1956 Act.

This is a formidable argument, but I cannot accept it. I leave on one side Mr O'Connor QC's sustained criticisms of the reasoning in *R v Prince* and *R v Maughan*. Where the Crown's argument breaks down is that the motley collection of offences, of diverse origins, gathered into the 1956 Act displays no satisfactorily clear or coherent pattern. If the interpretation of s 1 of the 1960 Act is to be gleaned from the contents of another statute, that other statute must give compelling guidance. The 1956 Act as a whole falls short of this standard. So do the two sections, ss 14 and 15, which were the genesis of s 1 of the 1960 Act.

Accordingly, I cannot find, either in the statutory context or otherwise, any indication of sufficient cogency to displace the application of the common law presumption. In my view the necessary mental element regarding the age ingredient in s 1 of the 1960 Act is the absence of a genuine belief by the accused that the victim was 14 years of age or above. The burden of proof of this rests upon the prosecution in the usual way. If Parliament considers that the position should be otherwise regarding this serious social problem, Parliament must itself confront the difficulties and express its will in clear terms. I would allow this appeal.

I add a final observation. As just mentioned, in reaching my conclusion I have left on one side the criticisms made of *R v Prince* and *R v Maughan*. Those cases concerned different offences and different statutory provisions. The correctness of the decisions in those cases does not call for decision on the present appeal. But, without expressing a view on the correctness of the actual decisions in those cases, I must observe that some of the reasoning in *R v Prince* is at variance with the common law presumption regarding mens rea as discussed above. To that extent, the reasoning must be regarded as unsound. For instance, Bramwell B ((1875) LR 2 CCR 154 at 174, [1874–80] All ER Rep 881 at

884) seems to have regarded the common law presumption as ousted because the act forbidden was 'wrong in itself'. Denman J ((1875) LR 2 CCR 154 at 178, [1874–80] All ER Rep 881 at 896) appears to have considered it was 'reasonably clear' that the 1861 Act was an Act of strict liability so far as the age element was concerned. On its face this is a lesser standard than necessary implication. And in the majority judgment, Blackburn J reached his conclusion by inference from the intention Parliament must have had when enacting two other, ineptly drawn, sections of the 1861 Act. But clumsy parliamentary drafting is an insecure basis for finding a necessary implication elsewhere, even in the same statute. *R v Prince*, and later decisions based on it, must now be read in the light of this decision of your Lordships' House on the nature and weight of the common law presumption.

Appeal allowed

In a commentary in [2000] Crim LR 404 it was suggested by J. C. Smith that B's case would have far-reaching consequences. The editors of *Archbold* (2001 edn, 17–12), however, 'submitted that this significantly overstates its significance because it is far from clear what it decides other than in relation to the particular offence with which their Lordships were concerned.' Then came the following case.

R v K

[2001] 3 All ER 897, House of Lords

(Lords Bingham, Nicholls, Steyn, Hobhouse and Millett)

The facts are stated in the speech of Lord Bingham.

Lord Bingham of Cornhill. [1] My Lords, the appellant K was indicted on a single count of indecent assault committed against a girl C who at the time was aged 14, contrary to s 14(1) of the Sexual Offences Act 1956 [see now the offence of sexual assault under s 3 of the Sexual Offences Act 2003, below, **p 729**]. His defence was to be that the sexual activity between him and C was consensual, that she had told him she was 16 and that he had had no reason to disbelieve her. He is a man of good character, aged 26 at the date of the offence charged against him. Before the trial a preliminary issue was raised on behalf of K: whether, to establish K's guilt under the section, the prosecution had to prove that at the time of the incident K did not honestly believe that C was 16 or over. Argument on this issue was heard by Judge Thorpe at the Crown Court at Chichester. He ruled, in favour of K, that the prosecution did have to prove an absence of genuine belief on the part of the accused that the victim was aged 16 or over. In so ruling the judge relied on the recent decision of the House of Lords in *B (a minor) v DPP*. The prosecution appealed against that ruling under s 35 of the Criminal Procedure and Investigations Act 1996. The Court of Appeal (Criminal Division) (Roch LJ, Rougier and Gray JJ) allowed the appeal and held that such absence of genuine belief did not have to be proved ([2001] Crim LR 134 and commentary) The court certified the following point of law of general public importance:

> '(a) Is a defendant entitled to be acquitted of the offence of indecent assault on a complainant under the age of 16 years, contrary to s 14(1) of the 1956 Act, if he may hold an honest belief that the complainant in question was aged 16 years or over? (b) If yes, must the belief be held on reasonable grounds?'

Leave to appeal was refused by the Court of Appeal but granted by the House.

[2] Section 14 of the 1956 Act is in these terms:

> '(1) It is an offence, subject to the exception mentioned in subsection (3) of this section, for a person to make an indecent assault on a woman.
> (2) A girl under the age of sixteen cannot in law give any consent which would prevent an act being an assault for the purposes of this section.

(3) Where a marriage is invalid under section two of the Marriage Act 1949, or section one of the Age of Marriage Act 1929 (the wife being a girl under the age of sixteen), the invalidity does not make the husband guilty of any offence under this section by reason of her incapacity to consent while under that age, if he believes her to be his wife and has reasonable cause for the belief.

(4) A woman who is a defective cannot in law give any consent which would prevent an act being an assault for the purposes of this section, but a person is only to be treated as guilty of an indecent assault on a defective by reason of that incapacity to consent, if that person knew or had reason to suspect her to be a defective.'

This section is matched by a parallel section, s 15, which makes it an offence for a person to make an indecent assault on a man. Subsections (2) and (3) of s 15 are to the same effect, in relation to men, as sub-ss (2) and (4) in relation to women.

[3] If the provisions of s 14 were part of a single, coherent legislative scheme and were read without reference to any overriding presumption of statutory interpretation, there would be great force in the simple submission which Mr Scrivener, resisting this appeal on behalf of the Crown, based upon them: sub-ss (3) and (4) define circumstances in which a defendant's belief, knowledge or suspicion exonerate a defendant from liability for what would otherwise be an indecent assault; if it had been intended to exonerate a defendant who believed a complainant to be 16 or over, this ground of exoneration would have been expressed in sub-s (2); the omission of such a provision makes plain that no such ground of exoneration was intended.

[4] It is, however, plain that s 14 was not part of a single, coherent legislative scheme. The 1956 Act was a consolidation Act. Its provisions derived from diverse sources. The rag-bag nature of the 1956 Act and its predecessor statutes has been the subject of repeated comment: see, for example, the observations of the draftsman of the Offences Against the Person Act 1861 Act quoted in *B (a minor) v DPP* [2000] 1 All ER 833 at 848, [2000] 2 AC 428 at 473; the criticisms of Lord Nicholls of Birkenhead in the same case (see [2000] 1 All ER 833 at 841, [2000] 2 AC 428 at 465); the description of the Act by Professor Lacey as 'a patchwork of pre-existing offences' in 'Beset by Boundaries: The Home Office Review of Sex Offences' [2001] Crim LR 3; the recognition of the Home Office in 'Setting the Boundaries: Reforming the law on sex offences; Vol 1, p 35, para 3.2.3 (July 2000) that the present legislation 'does not form a coherent code'.

[5] Section 14(1) derives from s 52 of the 1861 Act. At common law there was no offence of indecent assault. Section 52 of the 1861 Act criminalised 'any indecent Assault upon any Female'. The maximum penalty was two years; imprisonment. Since conduct is not generally an assault in law if done with the consent of the alleged victim, it seems clear that the consent of the victim, whatever her age, defeated a charge under this section as originally enacted.

[6] Plainly this provision gave inadequate protection to children, whose inherent immaturity was understandably regarded as impairing any consent they might give. There was legitimate public concern when a defendant accused of indecently assaulting a child of six years relied successfully on the consent of the child. There could have been no belief on the defendant's part that the child was over the age of consent, so that issue did not arise. In the Criminal Law Amendment Act 1880 it was provided that it should be no defence to a charge of indecent assault on a young person under the age of 13 to prove that he or she consented to the act of indecency. This provision was re-enacted in s 1 of the Criminal Law Amendment Act 1922 (with an increase of the age to 16). It is the source of s 14(2).

[7] Until 1929 England and Wales adhered to the old canon law rule that boys could be married at 14 and girls at 12. The Age of Marriage Act of that year provided that a marriage between persons either

of whom was under the age of 16 should be void. This enactment was subject to a proviso that in any proceedings against a person charged under s 5(1) of the Criminal Law Amendment Act 1885 or with indecent assault it should be a sufficient defence to prove that at the time when the offence was alleged to have been committed he had reason to believe that the alleged victim was his wife. This proviso was repealed by the Marriage Act 1949 (which re-enacted the age limit) but the repeal was itself repealed in 1953. Section 14(3) thus derives from sources quite different from the other provisions of the 1956 Act with which the House is concerned.

[8] Section 14(4) derives from s 56(3) of the Mental Deficiency Act 1913 which provided that no consent should be any defence in any proceedings for an indecent assault upon any defective, if the accused knew or had reason to suspect that the person in respect of whom the offence was committed was a defective....

[Lord Bingham discussed *Prince* and subsequent cases of strict liability, particularly the provision of the 'young man's defence' to a charge of sexual intercourse with a girl under 16 which originally appeared in the Criminal Law Amendment Act 1885 and was at that time in s 6 of the Sexual Offences Act 1956. This defence did not apply to indecent assault where the courts imposed unmitigated strict liability. The fact that the defence was available on the graver charge (sexual intercourse) and not on the lesser (indecent assault) was constantly criticized by the courts, being described as 'grotesque' and 'amazing.']

[**19**] In *B (a minor) v DPP* [2000] 1 All ER 833, [2000] 2 AC 428 the House considered s 1(1) of the 1960 Act in the light of the presumption that guilty knowledge is an essential ingredient of a statutory offence unless it is shown to be excluded by express words or necessary implication. It found no express words and no necessary implication having that effect. It was accordingly necessary for the prosecution to prove the absence of a genuine belief on the part of the defendant, whether reasonable or not, that the victim had been 14 or over. The House was invited in that case to treat the Acts of 1956 and 1960 as part of a single code (see [2000] 2 AC 428 at 457, 473), and that approach seems to me to be plainly correct. It is at once obvious that if an absence of genuine belief as to the age of an underage victim must be proved against a defendant under s 1 of the 1960 Act but not against a defendant under s 14 of the 1956 Act, another glaring anomaly would be introduced into this legislation. But that conclusion does not relieve the House of the need to carry out, in relation to s 14, the task that it carried out in relation to s 1.

[**20**] Neither in s 14 not elsewhere in the 1956 Act is there any express exclusion of the need to prove an absence of genuine belief on the part of a defendant as to the age of an underage victim. Had it been intended to exclude that element of mens rea it could very conveniently have been so provided in or following sub-s (2).

[**21**] For reasons already given, significance cannot be attached to the inclusion of grounds of exoneration in sub-ss (3) and (4) and the omission of such a ground from sub-s (2), although sub-ss (3) and (4) do reflect parliamentary recognition that a defendant should not be criminally liable if he misapprehends a factual matter on which his criminal liability depends. There is nothing in the language of this statute which justifies, as a matter of necessary implication, the conclusion that Parliament must have intended to exclude this ingredient of mens rea in s 14 any more than in s 1. If the effect of the presumption is read into s 14, with reference to the defendant's belief as to the age of the victim, no absurdity results. With the wisdom of hindsight it can be seen that Avory J was right to hold, in *R v Forde*, that the statutory defence in s 2 of the 1922 Act could not be read into s 1 of that Act, but he was wrong in failing to apply to s 1 of the 1922 Act the overriding presumption referred to in [17] above. He may, no doubt, have been misled by the now discredited authority of

R v Prince (1875) LR 2 CCR 154, [1874–80] All ER Rep 881, which although not apparently cited will have been very familiar to him.

[**22**] I consider that Judge Thorpe reached the right conclusion. The Court of Appeal gave more weight to the re-enactment of the relevant provisions in 1956 than was appropriate for a consolidation Act.

[**23**] I would accordingly give an affirmative answer to the first certified question. It is common ground that a negative answer should be given to the second question. In giving those answers I would make the following concluding points: (1) Nothing in this opinion has any bearing on a case in which the victim does not in fact consent. While s 14(2) provides that a girl under the age of 16 cannot in law give any consent which would prevent an act being an assault, she may in fact (although not in law) consent. If it is shown that she did not consent, and that the defendant did not genuinely believe that she consented, any belief by the defendant concerning her age is irrelevant, since her age is relevant only to her capacity to consent. (2) While a defendant's belief need not be reasonable provided it is honest and genuine, the reasonableness or unreasonableness of the belief is by no means irrelevant. The more unreasonable the belief, the less likely it is to be accepted as genuine (see *R v Gladstone Williams* [1987] 3 All ER 411 at 415.) (3) Although properly applied to s 1 of the 1960 Act and s 14 of the 1956 Act, the presumption cannot be applied to ss 5 and 6 of the 1956 Act. Those sections as a pair derive directly from corresponding sections in the 1871 Act, as demonstrated above. The statutory or young man's defence was introduced into what is now s 6. Its omission from what is now s 5 is plainly deliberate. A genuine belief that a child three years under the age of consent was over that age would in any event defy credulity. Section 6(3) of the 1956 Act plainly defines the state of knowledge which will exonerate a defendant accused under that section, and this express provision necessarily excludes the more general presumption. (4) Nothing in this opinion should be taken to minimise the potential seriousness of the offence of indecent assault. While some instances of the offence may be relatively minor, others may be scarcely less serious than rape itself. This is reflected in the maximum penalty, now increased to ten years' imprisonment, and the mandatory requirement that those convicted be subject to the notification requirements of the Sex Offenders Act 1997. These considerations make it more rather than less important that, in any forthcoming recasting of the law on sexual offences, the mens rea requirement should be defined with extreme care and precision. Parliament is sovereign and has the responsibility to decide where the boundaries of criminal activity should be drawn. . . . I would allow this appeal.

[**Lord Nicholls** agreed, **Lords Steyn** and **Hobhouse** made concurring speeches.]

Lord Millett. [**40**] My Lords, I have had the advantage of reading in draft the speech of my noble and learned friend Lord Bingham of Cornhill, with which I agree. For the reasons he gives I would allow the appeal and answer the certified questions as he proposes.

[**41**] I do so without reluctance but with some misgiving, for I have little doubt that we shall be failing to give effect to the intention of Parliament and will reduce s 14 of the Sexual Offence Act 1956 to incoherence. The section creates a single offence of indecent assault. It is intended for the protection of women. Subsection (2) and the first part of sub-s (4) extend the scope of the section. They are intended to protect women who are particularly vulnerable and who by reason of age or mental infirmity may be prevailed upon to give their consent to what would otherwise be an indecent assault. Subsection (3) and the proviso to sub-s (4) afford the defendant a limited defence based on the defendant's state of mind.

[**42**] The need for such a defence in the case of a woman with impaired mental faculties is obvious. Her mental state may well not be apparent, and it would be manifestly unjust to deny

a defence where the defendant believed that she was normal and had no reason to suspect that she was not. The absence of a similar proviso to sub-s (2), while suggesting that no similar defence is intended in the case of underage girls, does not lead inevitably to that conclusion. But sub-s (3) is a different matter. Introduced when the age of marriage was raised to 16, its policy is self-evident. There is no need to extend the scope of the section, designed to protect women from assault and young girls from exploitation, to a girl whom the defendant believes he has married. In such a case the defendant has not taken advantage of her age for his own sexual gratification. On the contrary, he is labouring under the belief that he has undertaken a lifelong responsibility towards her.

[43] Yet sub-s (3) requires the defendant's mistaken belief in the subsistence of a valid marriage to be reasonable as well as honest. To afford a defendant who has not married the girl a more generous defence than one who believes he has is grotesque. It cannot have been the intention of Parliament, either in 1929 when it introduced the sub-s (3) defence, or when it consolidated the law in 1956. Parliament must have known that it was a commonplace for men to be convicted of the offence despite their genuine belief that the girl was over 16, a matter which went to mitigation but not defence. Parliament not only viewed this state of affairs with equanimity, but on the earlier occasion at least legislated on a basis which made no sense unless this was the law.

[44] But the age of consent has long since ceased to reflect ordinary life, and in this respect Parliament has signally failed to discharge its responsibility for keeping the criminal law in touch with the needs of society. I am persuaded that the piecemeal introduction of the various elements of s 14, coupled with the persistent failure of Parliament to rationalise this branch of the law even to the extent of removing absurdities which the courts have identified, means that we ought not to strain after internal coherence even in a single offence. Injustice is too high a price to pay for consistency.

Appeal allowed

Notes and questions

1. The offences in issue in these cases have been replaced by those in the Sexual Offences Act 2003 (which itself contains numerous strict liability offences) see below Ch 20. The cases remain important authorities on the presumption of mens rea generally. It would be misleading however to think that since *B* and *K* the courts have consistently rejected strict liability. Far from it. There are numerous instances of provisions being interpreted as imposing strict liability see for example, *Mohammed* [2002] EWCA Crim 1856; 2 WLR 1050 (materially contributing to insolvency by gambling carrying two years' imprisonment) and *Matudi* [2004] EWCA Crim 697 (importing prohibited animal products). In those cases the court had found the presumption rebutted by necessary implication having regard to the usual criteria: the words of the statute, seriousness of the offence, stigma attaching, legislative purpose, statutory context, ease of proof, etc.

2. As long ago as 1953 Glanville Williams (CLGP (1st edn) 260, 2nd edn, 243) subjected *Prince* to the same kind of heavy criticism as, nearly 50 years later, influenced the House of Lords in these two cases to describe it as a 'relic from an age dead and gone', 'unsound' and 'discredited'—though not yet formally overruled. Williams went on to write that subsequent legislation was clearly based on the assumption that *Prince* was rightly decided and concluded that 'The general development makes it clear that *Prince* is now riveted upon English law in respect of the question of age until reversed by Parliament', adding that there was no need for it to be extended to questions other than age. Note that Williams formed this view before the consolidating Sexual Offences Act of 1956—and that enactment could only add weight to his opinion. Did not Lord Millett acknowledge the truth—that the House, having lost patience with Parliament, was ignoring its plain intention? Can this be justified? Is it a breach of the constitutional principle that Parliament is sovereign?

3. Lord Bingham observes that a man who has sexual intercourse with a girl aged 12 is unlikely to be able plausibly to assert that he believed her to be 16 but (i) it is not impossible, (ii) that does not affect the principle and (iii) the 'man'—who may be a boy—may easily have believed her to be 13 or 14. See the discussion below p **733** of the mens rea in relation to the corresponding offences under the Sexual Offences Act 2003.

4. In *Kumar* [2005] Crim LR 470, [2004] EWCA Crim 3207, K's conviction for buggery, contrary to s 12 of the Sexual Offences Act 1956, following consensual anal intercourse with the 14-year-old complainant was quashed by the Court of Appeal. It was held that the mental element had not been excluded expressly from s 12 by any compellingly clear or truly necessary implication, and that such a construction did not give rise to any internal inconsistency. Buggery stemmed from a common law offence and was unlike the age based offences in the 1956 Act.

5. In practical terms is the presumption of mens rea worth taking seriously when around half of the offences to be found in *Archbold* (the practitioners' manual used in the Crown Court) contain an element of strict liability? See A. Ashworth and M. Blake, 'The Presumption of Innocence in English Criminal Law' [1996] Crim LR 306.

6. The cases of *B* and *K* met with warm approval from some (Sir John Smith at [2000] Crim LR 403 and [2001] Crim LR **993**), and harsh criticism from others (for example, P. Glazebrook, 'How old do *you* think she was?' [2001] CLJ 26).

J. Horder, 'How Culpability Can, and Cannot, be Denied in Under-age Sex Crimes'
[2001] Crim LR 15 (references omitted)

. . . .

The decision of the House of Lords [in *B*], a decision that flies in the face of Legislation and case law across much of the rest of the common law world (e.g. *R. v. Hess*; *R. v. Nguyen* [1990] 2 S.C.R. 906), can be attributed more or less directly to the pervasive influence of a subjectivist understanding of the so-called 'correspondence principle' in criminal law theory. According to subjectivists, this theory requires that defendants should not in general be held criminally liable unless they intended to bring about, or realised that they might bring about, the forbidden consequences in the forbidden circumstances. Here is Smith and Hogan's statement of this article of faith:

> 'An ideal rule would seem to be [one] requiring intention or recklessness as to all the elements in the actus reus. Presumably, no element is included in the definition of an actus reus unless it contributes to the heinousness of the offence. If the accused is blamelessly inadvertent with respect to any one element in the offence . . . is it then proper to hold him responsible for it?' (J. C. Smith and B. Hogan, *Criminal Law* (9th ed), (1999, Butterworths), p. 72).

. . .

The so-called 'ideal rule' entails that where D believes that any element of the actus reus is absent, no matter how morally insignificant it may have been to the crime's definition, he or she is not criminally culpable. Applying the 'ideal rule' to section 1(1), the House of Lords concerned itself exclusively with whether D realised that V might be, as section 1(1) demands, aged under 14. That concern is with the wrong issue. Whether V is aged just under or over 14 years is, for the purposes of section 1(1), in itself a matter of moral insignificance, in spite of its legal import. There is no moral distinction to be drawn between a case in which a man invites a girl aged just under 14 to commit an act of gross indecency, and a case in which a man does the same to a girl aged just over 14. Even supposing it to be a true belief, a belief that V is aged 14 has—in and of itself (an important qualification, as we shall see)—no bearing on what D is morally permitted to do, in so far as inciting acts of gross indecency with young girls is concerned. It follows that a mistaken belief that V is aged 14 has no moral bearing on whether D is to be blamed for engaging in the actus reus, by (as in the instant case) inciting an act of gross indecency with a young girl. If one accepts this, and accepts (as the House of Lords appears to do) that a concern for mens rea is a concern about moral culpability, then one ought also to accept that under section 1(1) D's belief that V is aged 14 has, by itself, no legal bearing on his culpability. And the logic of the argument dictates that this will remain true, however reasonable D's belief about V's age may have been. Once these points have been accepted it becomes possible to focus on the main issue, overlooked by the House of Lords. This is the need to identify an element of the actus reus, bearing on D's liability, that does have practical moral significance. Once one has identified such an element it will follow, on now generally accepted legal principles, that a belief that it is absent is also a matter of practical moral significance, and hence a basis for denying culpability (mens rea) even when the actus reus was fulfilled.

. . . .

2. The Irrationality of the Subjectivist Approach to B's Belief

. . . . . . Suppose D, an adult paedophile, invites V, who is in fact 13, to commit an act of gross indecency with him. D believes V is over 14. D's belief is based, however, solely on an inference drawn from the character of previous sexual experiences he has had with V, as compared to his numerous sexual experiences with other children both younger and older than V. The law as it stands after *B. (A Minor) v. DPP* would acquit D in this example, even though it was nothing more than his experience as a paedophile that led him to believe that V was over 14. . . .

3. Law, Morality and the Significance of Age

. . . Take a case in which D has sexual intercourse with the 15-year-old V, reasonably believing that she is 16, and is charged with having had sexual intercourse with an under-age girl contrary to section 6 of the Sexual Offences Act 1956. As is well-known, the Statute provides for a denial of mens rea in only very limited circumstances. There is a case, however, for the general availability of a defence of lack of mens rea, where D honestly (and, I would add reasonably) believed that V was 16. That exact age, as the age of consent, is a guiding reason, giving those over that age permission to engage in consensual sexual intercourse. The stipulation of exactly 16 as the age of consent is in law what I earlier referred to as an example of determinatio. Moral reason suggests that the law should protect those whose mental, social and moral development is below that at which the full significance to the giving of consent to sexual activity is appreciated. And in practice (or as we assume), it is best to do this through a general prohibition on sexual advances towards those below a certain age, even though different individuals' mental, social and moral development may proceed at somewhat different rates. Moral and practical thinking of this kind does not, however, dictate any particular age (within the bounds of reason) at which the general prohibition cuts in: that is where the stipulative role of determinatio in law comes into play. Even so, unlike (say) the fixing of a speed limit at exactly 50 or 70, the legal settlement of the age of consent as 16 is neither arbitrary nor (now) without moral significance, whatever the position may have been when the law was changed to raise the age of consent from 13 to 16 in 1885. It is not just that birthdays are commonly regarded across cultures as having in themselves a moral and social significance that would make the setting of the age of consent at, say, 15 and a half far more arbitrary. It is that, as the Home Office Consultation Paper puts it, 'The present age of sixteen is well established, well understood and well supported'; it has, in other words 'gathered moral import with age, and . . . contribute[d] to structuring people's moral thinking' (see note 1). In this regard, I venture to suggest that what distinguishes the age of 16 from the age of 14, the age at issue in section 1 of the ICA 1960, is that the age of 14 has little or no moral resonance, and has not structured people's moral thinking in any significant way. This is the thought that lies behind my earlier suggestion that a mistaken belief that V is aged 14 is a mistake about a matter of moral indifference, unlike a mistaken belief that V is aged 16.

. . .

The criteria relevant to culpability ought only to be those which relate to guiding moral reasons for the actions in question; and D's belief that V is aged 14 is not such a guiding reason. It is not in itself a moral reason for doing as he does . . .

A subjectivist might reply in the following way. The subjectivist might say, in relation to section 1(1), that a belief about V's age can operate as a guiding reason, for D him or herself. D, a paedophile, might have a self-imposed restriction that he seeks to have sexual relations only with children over 14 because it would be 'going too far' to interfere with children under that age. If he then incites a child who is in fact aged under 14, but whom he believes to be 14, should this belief not operate as a denial of mens rea? The problem with this subjectivist reply, is that it only gains plausibility by making it open to defendants themselves to determine the standards by which their culpability is judged. On the contrary, putting aside cases where D's lack of capacity is in issue, culpability is rightly assessed by reference to general, not individual standards. . . .

Note

1. Consider the offences under ss 5–16 of the Sexual Offences Act 2003 below, p **733**.

4. THE RELEVANCE OF 'STATES OF MIND' IN STRICT LIABILITY

Devlin J, 'Statutory Offences'
4 JSPTL (NS) 206 at 212, Samples of Law Making (OUP, 1962)

. . . it is said that there must be mens rea but that it is supplied by the intent to do the forbidden act. This phrase, as Dr Glanville Williams has shown, does not stand up to analysis. Take, for example, the offence of selling adulterated milk. The forbidden act is selling *adulterated* milk: it is not selling milk. So the reasoning has to go something like this:

    (1) I intend to sell this can of milk;

    (2) This can of milk is adulterated;

    (3) Therefore I intend to sell adulterated milk.

So it is said, there is an intent to do the forbidden act.

One ought not to brush aside the conception simply because it is expressed in that inelegant way. The conception is a workable one. Mens rea consists of two elements. It consists first of all of the intent to do an act, and secondly of a knowledge of the circumstances that make that act a criminal offence. Take, for example, firing a gun within forty yards of the highway. There must be an intention to do it—there must be an intention to pull the trigger. If the trigger is pulled accidentally, then without going any further, there is no mens rea. But there must also be a knowledge of the circumstances that make the act forbidden—a knowledge that you are standing within forty yards of the highway. What this formula does is to call the act, as distinct from knowledge of its circumstances and effects, the forbidden act. In every case of crime you have to identify one act that makes the crime; the man's state of mind has to be determined at the time of that act. What was his knowledge of the circumstances and his intention at that time? It is difficult to find a convenient word for the act; let me call it the cardinal act, because the crime hinges on its commission. It is the deed that is at the heart of the crime. That is what those who have stated the law in this form intend it to mean. The effect of stating the law in this way is that if you do the cardinal act, eg the act of selling, you do it at your peril. The prosecution need not prove that you knew of any of the factors that make the selling criminal.

This is one way of stating what is meant by absolute liability in statutory offences. But it is a way which involves a state of mind. It means that you have got deliberately to do the cardinal act and then the intentional doing of that act supplies the mens rea. You cannot sell milk in your sleep, but there are some things that you can do in a semi-conscious state and it is those things which have begun to raise the problem of what is the proper way of stating the law. Is it that the doing of the act supplies the mens rea? Or is it simply that state of mind is quite immaterial and that there is no need for the prosecution to prove any intent at all? Stephen J stated it in the second way as long ago as 1889 in *Tolson* (1889) 23 QBD 168. More recently Goddard CJ has put it both ways; in the first way in 1951 in *Kat v Diment* [1951] 1 KB 34, [1950] 2 All ER 657 and in the second way in the following year in *Gardner v Akeroyd* [1952] 2 QB 743, [1952] All ER 306. This difference is not merely of theoretical interest to students of law; it may be of prime importance, though only in a minority of cases. Last year in *Hill v Baxter* [1958] 1QB 277, [1958] 1 All ER 193, the justices acquitted a man of dangerous driving and of failing to conform to traffic signals because they held he was in a state of automatism and did not know what he was doing. This brought up the point quite acutely though, as it turned out, it was not specifically dealt with. The facts raised the question of whether you were to say that the state of mind was immaterial or whether you were to say that there must be an intent at least to drive. Two of the judges in the Divisional Court arrived at their conclusion without dealing with the point specifically but, I think, by assuming that state of mind was immaterial; and the third judge, whom I must confess to be myself, evaded the issue. Thus these two schools of thought have never been formally arrayed in opposition one to another....

R v Sandhu
[1997] Crim LR 288

(Lord Bingham CJ, Sachs and Toulson JJ)

The appellant had bought a Grade II Listed Building which was in extremely poor condition. He applied for and was granted listed building consent. Between July 1993 and April 1995 the appellant caused works to be carried out to the building. He was charged with various offences of causing works to be executed for the alteration of a listed building without authorisation, contrary to s 9(1) of the Planning (Listed Buildings and Conservation Areas) Act 1990. These were offences of strict liability. At trial the prosecution sought to adduce evidence that the appellant had been clearly warned both by the local authority's representative and by his own surveyor as to what he could and could not do to the building, but that he had chosen to ignore those warnings. The appellant made a preliminary submission to the judge that that evidence should be excluded on the ground that it did nothing to answer the five matters required to be proved in s 7 of the Act, but simply went to impugn the motives of the appellant in a manner that had no place in proof of an offence of strict liability. The judge rejected the submission. He stated (i) that although the prosecution was not required to prove mens rea the evidence was relevant as to how the actus reus had been caused; (ii) that if the evidence was excluded a defendant would be in a better position in a strict liability offence than where the prosecution had to prove mens rea, where such evidence would undoubtedly be admissible and (iii) that without the surveyor's evidence, the jury would have a distorted view of the true picture and there was no reason why they should not be apprised of how the surveyor came to be involved with the appellant and what his advice to him had been. The prosecution therefore led the evidence and the appellant was convicted. He appealed on the ground that the evidence should not have been admitted.

Held, allowing the appeal, the evidence should not have been admitted as the judge's reasons were unsound. So far as the first reason was concerned, an offence of strict liability was one which involved no proof of mens rea, it was complete when the specified elements of the offence were established. To adduce evidence which went beyond proof of those elements was not an optional extra, it was to adduce inadmissible evidence and to adduce inadmissible evidence which was prejudicial to the interests of the accused was objectionable. With regard to the second point, it was certainly true that, inasmuch as an offence of strict liability involved no proof of mens rea, proof of motive, intention, knowledge and so on could not be relevantly adduced. Indeed a defendant was in a worse position since an innocent state of mind afforded him no defence. It was not therefore generally true to say that the defendant to a charge which was of strict liability was better placed than in the ordinary class of case. So far as the third point was concerned, it was open to the prosecution to adduce evidence of the surveyor as to what he had seen on each occasion as to the work that had been done and how it had come to be done. That, however, did not involve his giving evidence as to the advice which he had given the appellant, still less giving evidence to the effect that the appellant had flouted and overridden his advice. That was material which was irrelevant to what the Crown had had to prove to establish the charge. In cases of this kind it was important to have regard to the principles which had to be observed. Any evidence adduced by the prosecution, was relevant if and to the extent and it went to answer any one of these five question in s 7. Evidence which did not go to answer one of those questions was irrelevant and therefore inadmissible. There might be cases in which evidence, although irrelevant and inadmissible, was not prejudicial to a defendant and thus would not threaten the safety of a conviction, such was the case where evidence was neutral. But where evidence was irrelevant, inadmissible and damaging to a defendant, then it was in truth mere prejudice. Its admission would serve no purpose other than to incline a jury to think badly of that particular defendant.

Commentary. 'The main general rule governing the entire subject [of evidence] is that all evidence which is sufficiently relevant to an issue before the court is admissible and all that is irrelevant, or insufficiently relevant should be excluded': Cross and Tapper, *Evidence* (8th ed), p 51, fundamental though this rule is, it is all too often overlooked. The first of the two propositions it embodies was overlooked by the Court of Appeal in *Potamitis* [1994] Crim LR 434 and *Irish* [1994] Crim LR 922. See commentaries thereon. In the present case the trial judge, in the opinion of the Court of Appeal, failed to apply the second proposition.

At first sight, it is a little surprising to find a conviction being quashed because the prosecution have, or may have, proved that the defendant had a *mens rea* with respect to the *actus reus* with which he is charged, something more than the prosecution need prove. We now know they *must not* prove, or seek to prove, it. Obviously a person who, with full *mens rea*, commits the *actus reus* of an offence of strict liability is guilty of that offence. If *Prince* ((1875) LR 2 CCR 154) had known perfectly well that the girl he was taking out of the possession of her father was only 13 years old, he would have been no less guilty of the offence—but it now appears that, in such a case, the prosecution would be well advised to take care not to adduce any evidence suggesting that he knew. Sometimes evidence going to prove that the defendant committed the *actus reus* may incidentally (if believed) prove that he had *mens rea*. In that case, the evidence is admissible—it is part of the *res gestae* in one of the quite different senses in which that much-abused phrase is used. An argument that this was so in the present case was rejected. It is not inconceivable that evidence relevant to the issue whether the defendant *caused* the *actus reus* (which the prosecution must prove) would also show that he intentionally caused it with full knowledge of all the circumstances. If the defence was that the defendant had not caused the *actus reus* because a dishonest builder, without the defendant's knowledge, had replaced listed window frames, a letter from the defendant instructing the builder to ignore the listing would obviously be relevant and admissible, although it would prove guilty knowledge. Though the judge would instruct the jury that it was irrelevant in law whether he knew or not, it is hard to see how they could sensibly be instructed to ignore any part of this evidence—it is not divisible into parts.

Wider implications of the decision. The decision could have far-reaching effects. Presumably it applies to any evidence tending to show that the defendant is guilty of an offence greater than that charged. If D is charged with manslaughter by an unlawful and dangerous act, evidence that he acted with intent to kill or to do grievous bodily harm is irrelevant. If he is charged with common assault, evidence that the assault occasioned actual bodily harm or that the victim was a constable acting in the course of his duty is irrelevant and, presumably, prejudicial. All this suggests that it is prudent for the prosecution to charge the most serious offence which the evidence warrants and to avoid, as far as possible, the admission of any evidence suggesting that the defendant was guilty of an offence greater than that charged.... [J. C. Smith]

5. RECOGNITION OF OFFENCES OF STRICT LIABILITY

One problem, a serious one, is the identification of offences of strict liability, or, more precisely, the identification of the element or elements in the offence which will attract strict liability.

The factors commonly cited as influencing the decision whether the presumption of mens rea is rebutted in any case include:

(1) the use of verbs and adverbs importing a mental element—knowingly, wilfully, etc.

(2) the social context of the crime:
  (i) is it a 'real crime' or a quasi crime or regulatory offence?
  (ii) whether the crime is one of general or special prohibition—the latter making it more likely that the presumption will be rebutted;
  (iii) the ease with which those affected by the regulation might comply;
  (iv) the social danger involved.

(3) the severity of the punishment.

In the passage in *Gammon*, cited above, p **215**, Lord Scarman attempts to give some guidance by listing the five criteria, but this must now be read in the light of *B (a minor) v DPP* and *K*.

Lord Scarman says that the presumption which always favours mens rea is particularly strong where the offence is truly criminal. The presumption can only be displaced where the statute is concerned with an issue of social concern. Even here the presumption in favour of mens rea remains unless it can be shown that the creation of strict liability will be effective to promote the objects of the statute by creating greater vigilance. Can all this be reconciled with the assertion by Lord Steyn in *K* that the presumption 'can only be displaced by specific language, ie, an express provision or a necessary implication?' Up to an uncertain point it is possible to identify offences, or elements in offences, which were, and perhaps still are, likely to attract strict liability. Usually, though by no means invariably, the offence is one created in a statute which seeks to regulate the activities of a particular class of persons such as licensees, or the sellers of food and drugs, or employers in industry and commerce. Hence the expression 'regulatory offences', namely, offences which are meant to regulate the carrying on of particular activities. It might be convenient, it would certainly be simpler, if all such offences could be classified as offences of strict liability but it is not as straightforward as that. Parliament is (or the parliamentary draftsmen are) unhelpful in that the use of a mens rea word (such as 'knowingly' or 'permitting') in one provision and its absence in another provision (or sometimes in the same provision) appears to be haphazard and without any underlying rationale.

In *Harrow London Borough of v Shah and Shah* [1999] 3 All ER 302, [2000] Crim LR 692, DC, the Shahs, newsagents, were charged with selling a national lottery ticket to a boy under 16, contrary to the National Lottery Act 1993, s 13(1)(c) and the National Lottery Regulations 1994, reg 3. They had taken all reasonable steps to ensure that the regulations were complied with and they were not present in the shop when the lottery ticket was sold by their employee, who reasonably believed that the boy was at least 16 years old. The magistrates dismissed the information. The Divisional Court remitted the case with a direction to continue the hearing.

Section 13 provides:

(1) If any requirement or restriction imposed by regulations made under section 12 is contravened in relation to the promotion of a lottery that forms part of the National Lottery—
   (a) the promoter of the lottery shall be guilty of an offence, except if the contravention occurred without the consent or connivance of the promoter and the promoter exercised all due diligence to prevent such a contravention,
   (b) any director, manager, secretary or other similar officer of the promoter, or any person purporting to act in such a capacity, shall be guilty of an offence if he consented to or connived at the contravention or if the contravention was attributable to any neglect on his part, and
   (c) any other person who was a party to the contravention shall be guilty of an offence.

(2) A person guilty of an offence under this section shall be liable—
   (a) on summary conviction, to a fine not exceeding the statutory maximum;
   (b) on conviction on indictment, to imprisonment not exceeding two years, to a fine or to both.

Mitchell J. Section 13 has two important features. First, whereas in subsection (1) paragraphs (a) and (b) the liability of the promoter and the promoter's, directors, managers and the like is tempered by the provision of a statutory defence, in subsection (1)(c) the liability of 'any other person' who was a party to the contravention of the regulation is not expressed to be subject to a statutory defence. Second, although the maximum sentence for conviction on indictment is two years, a fine or both, those penalties apply to all persons who are guilty of any offence under the section including the promoter. The maximum of two years cannot therefore be said to be tailormade for a contravention of reg 3 by a shopkeeper. . . .

[Having cited various authorities, particularly Lord Reid in *Sweet v Parsley* [1969] 1 All ER 347 at 350, Mitchell J continued:]

Having regard to those observations, for my part I do not regard a contravention of reg 3 as being truly criminal in character. [**Kennedy LJ** agreed.]

Taking the second of Mitchell J's two 'features' first, s 13 creates three distinct offences. Offence (a) can be committed as a principal only by the promoter, offence (b) only by one of the specified officers and offence (c) can be committed by anyone. If it were a single offence, it might be argued that the high penalty of two years' imprisonment was provided for the deterrence of the officers and not intended for lesser mortals like shopkeepers; but, as they are obviously distinct offences, the maximum is no less 'tailormade' for (c) than for (a) and (b). It is true that liability in (a) is 'tempered by the provision of a statutory defence' but this is not true of (b). Whereas, in (a) there is at least an evidential, and possibly a legal, burden

(Magistrates' Courts Act 1980, s 101) on D to establish an exception (b) expressly requires a degree of fault (consent, connivance or neglect) which must be proved by the prosecution.

The common law presumption of mens rea is qualified for (a) and (b) but it is unqualified for (c). (a) and (b) exhibit a descending degree of strictness as the seniority of the officer descends. If that descent is carried on to (c)—the shopkeeper or his employee—full mens rea is required. There is nothing in (c) which is inconsistent with the application of the presumption.

Can the imposition of strict and vicarious liability be justified, particularly in the light of the later decisions in *B (a minor) v DPP* and *K*?

Strangely, the section nowhere provides that it is an offence to contravene the regulation. Should this have been taken to mean that it is an offence 'like abetting suicide' for persons who assist or encourage another to do an act which it is not an offence for him to do? Or must 'a party to the contravention' be taken to be, or to include, the contravenor?

Cundy v Le Cocq
[1884] 13 QBD 207, DC

(Stephen and Mathew JJ)

Case stated by one of the magistrates of the Metropolis, on a complaint by the respondent against the appellant under s 13 of the Licensing Act 1872, charging that the appellant, being the keeper of certain licensed premises had on the 14th of January, 1884, unlawfully sold intoxicating liquor to a drunken person.

Upon the hearing of the information it was proved that there had been a sale of intoxicating liquor and that the person served was drunk. It was proved in answer to the complaint that neither the appellant nor his servants had noticed that the person served was drunk; that he had, whilst on the licensed premises, been quiet in his demeanour and had done nothing to indicate insobriety; and that there were no apparent indications of intoxication.

It was contended for the appellant that there was nothing to shew any knowledge or means of knowledge on the part of the appellant or his servants that the person served was drunk; but the magistrate held that the offence was complete on proof that a sale had taken place, and that the person served was drunk, and deemed it unnecessary to determine whether there had been on the part of the appellant or his servants a knowledge or means of knowledge of the drunkenness of the drunken person. He accordingly convicted the appellant.

The question for the opinion of the court was whether the construction placed by the magistrate on the section was right, or whether in arriving at his decision it was necessary for him to consider whether or not the appellant or his servants knew or had the means of knowing, or whether they could with ordinary care have detected, that the person served was drunk.

The Licensing Act 1872 (35 & 36 Vict c 94), s13, enacts:

> 'If any licensed person permits drunkenness or any violent quarrelsome, or riotous conduct to take place on his premises, or sells any intoxicating liquor to any drunken person, he shall be liable to a penalty not exceeding for the first offence, 10/, and not exceeding for the second and any subsequent offence, 20/.
>
> Any conviction for any offence under this section shall be recorded on the licence of the person convicted, unless the convicting magistrate or justices shall otherwise direct.'

Stephen J. I am of opinion that this conviction should be affirmed. Our answer to the question put to us turns upon this: whether the words of the section under which the conviction took place, taken in connection with the general scheme of the Act, should be read as constituting an offence where the licensed person knows or has means of knowing that the person served with intoxicating liquor is drunk, or whether the offence is complete where no such knowledge is shewn. I am of opinion that the words of the section amount to an absolute prohibition of the sale of liquor to a drunken person, and that the existence of a bonâ fide mistake as to the condition of the person served is not an answer to the charge, but is a matter only for mitigation of the penalties that may be imposed. I am led to that conclusion both by the general scope of the Act, which is for the repression of drunkenness, and from a comparison of the various sections under the head 'offences against public order'. Some of these contain the word 'knowingly', as for instance s14, which deals with keeping a disorderly house, and s16, which deals with the penalty for harbouring a constable. Knowledge in these and other cases is an element in the offence; but the clause we are considering says nothing about the knowledge of the state of the person served. I believe the reason for making this prohibition absolute was that there must be a great temptation to a publican to sell liquor without regard to the sobriety of the customer, and it was thought right to put upon the publican the responsibility of determining whether his customer is sober. Against this view we have had quoted the maxim that in every criminal offence there must be a guilty mind; but I do not think that maxim has so wide an application as it is sometimes considered to have. In old times, and as applicable to the common law or to earlier statutes, the maxim may have been of general application; but a difference has arisen owing to the greater precision of modern statutes. It is impossible now, as illustrated by the cases of *R v Prince* ((1875) LR 2 CCR 154) and *R v Bishop* ((1880) 5 QBD 259), to apply the maxim generally to all statutes, and the substance of all the reported cases is that it is necessary to look at the object of each Act that is under consideration to see whether and how far knowledge is of the essence of the offence created. Here, as I have already pointed out, the object of this part of the Act is to prevent the sale of intoxicating liquor to drunken persons, and it is perfectly natural to carry that out by throwing on the publican the responsibility of determining whether the person supplied comes within that category.

I think, therefore, the conviction was right and must be affirmed.

[**Mathew J** concurred.]

Conviction affirmed

Notes and questions

1. Stephen J said that the presumption, or 'maxim', as he prefers it, of mens rea, was no longer of general application after *Prince* and its successors. But *Prince* is now discredited (*B (a minor) v DPP* and *K*) and the presumption is said by the House of Lords to apply to all statutory offences unless excluded expressly or by necessary implication from the words of the enactment. Can *Cundy* now be considered a reliable authority or is it, like *Prince*, discredited?

2. Notice that s 13 of the 1972 Act created two offences, one of permitting and one of selling. In *Somerset v Wade* [1891–4] All ER Rep 1228, DC, it was held that the offence of permitting requires knowledge of what is alleged to have been permitted. If 'selling' must be strictly prohibited because it is necessary for the repression of drunkenness and the preservation of public order, is the permission 'of drunkenness or any violent, quarrelsome or riotous conduct' any less in need of strict prohibition?

Sherras v De Rutzen
[1895] 1 QB 918, DC

(Day and Wright JJ)

The appellant was the licensee of a public-house, and was convicted before a Metropolitan Police Magistrate under s16, sub-s (2), of the Licensing Act, 1872, for having unlawfully supplied liquor to a police constable on duty without having the authority of a superior officer of such constable for so doing.

[By s 16 of the Licensing Act 1872:

'If any licensed person

(1) Knowingly harbours or knowingly suffers to remain on his premises any constable during any part of the time appointed for such constable being on duty ... or

(2) Supplies any liquor or refreshment whether by way of gift or sale to any constable on duty unless by authority of some superior officer of such constable, or

(3) Bribes or attempts to bribe any constable ...

he shall be liable to a penalty ...']

It appeared that the appellant's public-house was situated nearly opposite a police-station, and was much frequented by the police when off duty, and that on 16 July 1894, at about 4.40, the police constable in question, being then on duty, entered the appellant's house and was served with liquor by the appellant's daughter in his presence. Prior to entering the house the police constable had removed his armlet, and it was admitted that if a police constable is not wearing his armlet that is an indication that he is off duty. The armlet is removed at the police-station when a constable is dismissed, and a publican seeing the armlet off would naturally think the police constable off duty. The police constable was in the habit of using the appellant's house, and was well known as a customer to the appellant and his daughter. Neither the appellant nor his daughter made any inquiry of the police constable as to whether he was or was not on duty, but they took it for granted that he was off duty in consequence of his armlet being off, and served him with liquor under that belief. The appellant and his daughter were in the habit of serving a number of police constables in uniform with their armlets off each day, and the question whether they were or were not on duty was never asked when the armlet was seen to be off.

The appellant appealed to quarter sessions against the conviction, contending that in order to constitute an offence under s16, sub-s2 of the Licensing Act 1872, there must be shewn to be either knowledge that the police constable was on duty, or an intentional abstention from ascertaining whether he was on duty or not. The court of quarter sessions, however, upheld the conviction, considering that knowledge that the police constable, when served with liquor, was on duty, was not an essential ingredient of the offence; but stated this case for the opinion of the court.

Day J. I am clearly of opinion that this conviction ought to be quashed. This police constable comes into the appellant's house without his armlet, and with every appearance of being off duty. The house was in the immediate neighbourhood of the police-station, and the appellant believed, and he had very natural grounds for believing, that the constable was off duty. In that belief he accordingly served him with liquor. As a matter of fact, the constable was on duty; but does that fact make the innocent act of the appellant an offence? I do not think it does. He had no intention to do a wrongful act; he acted in the bonâ fide belief that the constable was off duty. It seems to me that the contention that he committed an offence is utterly erroneous. An argument has been based on the appearance of the word 'knowingly' in sub-s (1) of s 16, and its omission in sub-s (2). In my opinion the only effect of this is to shift the burden of proof. In cases under sub-s (1) it is for the prosecution to prove the knowledge, while in cases under subs (2) the defendant has to prove that he did not know. That is the only inference I draw from the insertion of the word 'knowingly' in the one subsection and its omission in the other.

It appears to me that it would be straining the law to say that this publican, acting as he did in the bonâ fide belief that the constable was off duty, and having reasonable grounds for that belief, was nevertheless guilty of an offence against the section, for which he was liable both to a penalty and to have his licence indorsed.

Wright J. I am of the same opinion. There are many cases on the subject, and it is not very easy to reconcile them. There is a presumption that mens rea, an evil intention, or a knowledge of the wrongfulness of the act, is an essential ingredient in every offence; but that presumption is liable to be displaced either by the words of the statute creating the offence or by the subject-matter with which it deals, and both must be considered: *Nichols v Hall* ((1873) LR 8 CP 322). One of the most remarkable exceptions was in the case of bigamy. It was held by the judges, on the statute 1 Jac 1, c 11, that a man was rightly convicted of bigamy who had married after an invalid Scotch divorce, which had been obtained in good faith, and the validity of which he had no reason to doubt: *Lolley's Case* ((1812) Russ & Ry 237). Another exception, apparently grounded on the language of a statute, is *Prince's Case* ((1875) LR 2 CCR 154), where it was held by fifteen judges against one that a man was guilty of abduction of a girl under sixteen, although he believed, in good faith and on reasonable grounds, that she was over that age. Apart from isolated and extreme cases of this kind, the principal classes of exceptions may perhaps be reduced to three. One is a class of acts which, in the language of Lush J in *Davies v Harvey* ((1874) LR 9 QB 433), are not criminal in any real sense, but are acts which in the public interest are prohibited under a penalty. Several such instances are to be found in the decisions on the Revenue Statutes, eg, *A-G v Lockwood* ((1842) 9 M & W 378), where the innocent possession of liquorice by a beer retailer was held an offence. So under the Adulteration Acts, *R v Woodrow* ((1846) 15 M & W 404) as to innocent possession of adulterated tobacco; *Fitzpatrick v Kelly* ((1873) LR 8 QB 337) and *Roberts v Egerton* ((1874) LR 9 QB 494) as to the sale of adulterated food. So under the Game Acts, as to the innocent possession of game by a carrier: *R v Marsh* ((1824) 2 B & C 717). So as to the liability of a guardian of the poor, whose partner, unknown to him, supplied goods for the poor: *Davies v Harvey* ((1874) LR 9 QB 433). To the same head may be referred *R v Bishop* ((1880) 5 QBD 259), where a person was held rightly convicted of receiving lunatics in an unlicensed house, although the jury found that he honestly and on reasonable grounds believed that they were not lunatics. Another class comprehends some, and perhaps all, public nuisances: *R v Stephens* ((1866) LR 1 QB 702) where the employer was held liable on indictment for a nuisance caused by workmen without his knowledge and contrary to his orders; and so in *R v Medley* ((1834) 6 C & P 292) and *Barnes v Akroyd* ((1872) LR 7 QB 474). Lastly, there may be cases in which, although the proceeding is criminal in form, it is really only a summary mode of enforcing a civil right: see per Williams and Willes JJ in *Morden v Porter* ((1860) 7 CBNS 641), as to unintentional trespass in pursuit of game; *Lee v Simpson* ((1847) 3 CB 871), as to unconscious dramatic piracy; and *Hargreaves v Diddams* ((1875) LR 10 QB 582), as to a bonâ fide belief in a legally impossible right to fish. But, except in such cases as these, there must in general be guilty knowledge on the part of the defendant, or of someone whom he has put in his place to act for him, generally, or in the particular matter, in order to constitute an offence. It is plain that if guilty knowledge is not necessary, no care on the part of the publican could save him from a conviction under s 16, sub-s (2), since it would be as easy for the constable to deny that he was on duty when asked, or to produce a forged permission from his superior officer, as to remove his armlet before entering the public house. I am, therefore, of opinion that this conviction ought to be quashed.

Conviction quashed

Notes and questions

1. Is it still true to say, as Wright J did, that the presumption of mens rea can be displaced either by the words of the statute creating the offence *or the subject matter with which it deals*?

2. Neither *Lolley's Case* nor *Prince* can, since *B (a minor) v DPP* and *K*, be regarded as good law.

3. Wright J's class of acts which are not 'criminal in any real sense' perhaps marks the beginning of an influential source of strict liability so, in subsequent cases, we find constant references to prohibited acts which are not 'truly criminal' or are 'quasi-criminal'. This theory was canonized through its approval by the greatly—and rightly—respected Lord Reid in *Sweet v Parsley* (below, p **249** at p **250**) and Lord Reid's opinion is cited with approval in *B (a minor) v DPP* and *K*. We have seen a striking instance of it application in *Harrow London Borough Council v Shah*, above, p **232**. What sort of 'truth' are the judges talking about when they say that an offence like that in issue in *Shah* is not 'truly' criminal? Parliament has declared it punishable on indictment with two years' imprisonment. The offence must be tried in the criminal courts in accordance with the rules of criminal procedure and evidence and the offender may be imprisoned as a convicted criminal for up to two years. Is not the inescapable truth that it *is* criminal? The judges may think it ought not to be a crime—but, in the case of statutory offences, it is not from them to decide. Cf Lord Mustill's opinion in *Kingston*, above, p **118** ('the epithet "rea" refers to the criminality of the act in which the mind is engaged, not to its moral character'). All the jurists who have attempted to define a crime have concluded that it is impossible to say whether an act is crime by looking at it in isolation from the law, for the obvious reason that an act which is not a crime today may well become one tomorrow, and vice versa. The only test can be whether the act is prohibited by statute or common law with criminal sanctions. Is not the truth that the Shahs—like many others—were convicted of a crime on a false premise?

4. If we delete the 'not criminal in any real sense' category in Wright J's judgment, what is left?

Mohammed

[2002] EWCA Crim 1856; [2003] WLR 1053

(Dyson LJ, Silber J and HHJ Goddard QC)

The facts appear in the judgment of Dyson LJ.

Dyson LJ

[1] On 12 April 2002 in the Crown Court at Middlesex Guildhall, the appellant was convicted of the offence of materially contributing to the extent of his insolvency by gambling contrary to section 362(1)(a) of the Insolvency Act 1986 ('the 1986 Act'). He sought leave to appeal against his conviction and the Registrar referred his application to the full court, because there are a number of cases pending in the crown court in which the same issue arises. The question raised on this appeal is whether the offence under section 362(1)(a) of the 1986 Act requires a mental element, or mens rea. The judge ruled that it does not, and that the offence is one of strict liability.

[13] In *Sweet v Parsley* [1970] AC 132, 149G, Lord Reid spoke again of 'quasi-criminal acts' in respect of which 'one can safely assume that, when Parliament is passing new legislation dealing with this class of offences, its silence as to mens rea means that the old practice [viz of recognising them as absolute offences] is to apply'. But, he said, where it comes to acts of 'a truly criminal character', different considerations apply. The first of these is that 'a stigma still attaches to any person convicted of a truly criminal offence, and the more serious or more disgraceful the offence the greater the stigma. So he [viz the reasonable legislator] would have to consider whether, in a case of this gravity, the public interest really requires that an innocent person should be prevented from proving his innocence in order that fewer guilty men may escape'.

[14] It is not clear to us whether an offence under section 362(1)(a) would have been classified by Lord Reid as 'quasi-criminal', or 'truly criminal'. A maximum penalty of two years imprisonment is by no means insignificant, although it is towards the lower end of the scale of maximum custodial

sentences. On the other hand, it is open to doubt whether, at any rate in 2002, such an offence would be regarded as 'truly criminal'. Classificatory difficulties of this kind may well be the reason why Lord Scarman's second proposition and, in particular, the passage in the speech of Lord Nicholls were expressed in the terms that we have seen.

[15] The question whether the presumption of law that mens rea is required applies, and, if so, whether it has been displaced can be approached in two ways. One approach is to ask whether the act is truly criminal, on the basis that, if it is not, then the presumption does not apply at all. The other approach is to recognise that any offence in respect of which a person may be punished in a criminal court is, prima facie, sufficiently 'criminal' for the presumption to apply. But the more serious the offence, the greater the weight to be attached to the presumption, and conversely, the less serious the offence, the less weight to be attached. It is now clear that it is this latter approach which, according to our domestic law, must be applied.

[16] The starting point, therefore, is to determine how serious an offence is created by section 362(1)(a), and accordingly how much weight, if any, should be attached to the presumption. Some weight must undoubtedly be given to the presumption, but in our judgment it can be readily displaced. As we have said, the maximum sentence indicates that Parliament considered this to be an offence of some significance, but not one of the utmost seriousness. This is not surprising. We do not believe that great stigma attaches to a conviction of this offence. [We note the government's proposal to repeal the provision altogether and deal with it as misconduct leading to a bankruptcy restriction order. This may indicate no more than a change of heart since 1986, and not be a reliable indication of the intention of Parliament when enacting the 1986 Act. But it does in our view lend some support for the proposition.] In our view, this is not, and never has been, a particularly serious offence. . . .

[18] First, the 1986 Act created a clear and coherent regime. The majority of the offences include an express requirement of a mental element. This is achieved either in the section which creates the offence (for example, section 356(2)); or by reference to section 352 (which contains a reverse onus of proof provision). Only a few, of which section 362(1)(a) is one, do not specify a mental element. In our judgment, this is a clear pointer to Parliament's intention in relation to section 362(1)(a). But it is not sufficient by itself. As Lord Reid said in *Sweet v Parsley* [below p **249**]

[19] Further support for the displacement of the presumption in relation to section 362(1)(a) emerges when a comparison is made of the maximum sentences provided for by the various offences created in Chapter VI of the 1986 Act. The offences where no mental element is specified, for the most part, attract considerably lower maximum sentences than those where a mental element is specified. Thus all the offences where a mental element is expressly required in the sections which create the offence, and (with two exceptions) all the offences to which section 352 applies, provide a maximum sentence of 7 years imprisonment. The maximum for all those offences where no mental element is specified is 2 years imprisonment.

[20] The next point relied on by Mr Eadie is the fact that gambling which harms a gambler's creditors is a matter of social concern. That is obviously right. It follows that this is a case where the fourth and fifth of Lord Scarman's propositions are engaged. So too they were in *Harrow London Borough Council v Shah* [1999] 2 Cr App Rep 457. In that case, the Divisional Court had to decide whether the offence of selling National Lottery tickets to a person under the age of 16 was an offence of strict liability. The court decided that it was. In giving the leading judgment, Mitchell J said (p 463E) that the legislation dealt with an issue of social concern, and (p 464A) that it was an excellent example of the sort of legislation contemplated by Lord Scarman's fifth proposition. He said: 'That strict liability

attaches to this offence will unquestionably encourage greater vigilance in preventing the commission of the prohibited act'....

[22] It is self-evident that section 362(1)(a) is aimed at an issue of social concern. We do not understand Mr Campbell-Tiech to contend otherwise. His point is that an offence of strict liability does not achieve the object of the statute any more effectively than an offence which requires a mental element. We do not agree. If the offence is absolute, then all that has to be proved is that in the two years before petition the bankrupt materially contributed to, or increased the extent of, his insolvency by gambling. This may have the result that, for some persons at least, the only way to avoid running the risk of committing the offence is to gamble only for low stakes. If that is so, then an offence of strict liability may have a more chilling effect on gambling that may materially contribute to insolvency than an offence which requires a mental element. We are satisfied that strict liability will encourage greater vigilance to prevent gambling which will or may materially contribute to insolvency....

[33] Accordingly, we dismiss the appeal.

Questions

1. Having asserted the importance of the presumption of mens rea in *B* and *K*, have the courts then undermined the significance of that presumption by failing to provide clear guidelines on when the presumption will be rebutted?

2. Does the case assist in determining whether it is possible properly to distinguish 'quasi-criminal offences' from crimes involving the 'disgrace of criminality' as Lord Reid suggests? On what principle should the line be drawn? On which side of the line would the following offences fall:

   (i)   driving with a blood-alcohol concentration in excess of the prescribed limit;
   (ii) driving while uninsured against third-party liability;
   (iii) the sale by a butcher of meat unfit for human consumption?

J. Horder, 'Strict Liability, Statutory Construction, and the Spirit of Liberty'
[2002] LQR 458

In interpreting the scope of criminal offences created by statute, English courts have always claimed to take very seriously a responsibility to protect personal liberty. Lord Goddard C.J. once explained how it is that the courts have sought to do this in a principled way:

> 'It is of the utmost importance for the protection of the liberty of the subject that a court should always bear in mind that, unless a statute, either clearly or by necessary implication, rules out mens rea as a constituent part of a crime, the court should not find a man guilty of an offence against the criminal law unless he has a guilty mind.' [*Brend v. Wood* (1946) 62 T.L.R. 462 at p. 463]

In a broad sense, it is simply more 'just' that criminal conviction should generally follow only when the mens was rea; but fault requirements focused on whether defendants knew (or could have known) that they might be engaged in acts or omissions amounting to an offence also minimise the encroachment on liberty involved in criminalisation. Such requirements can ensure that those who did all that could reasonably have been done to avoid falling foul of the criminal law will remain free from its clutches....

The courts' understanding of personal liberty emerges from what they regard as a key distinction between 'real' and 'regulatory' crime, between mala in se, crimes that are said to be 'truly criminal' in character, and mala prohibita, crimes said to be focussed on 'regulation of a particular activity involving potential danger'. On a number of important occasions, the House of Lords has implied mens rea requirements into a criminal statute because that statute was concerned with wrongdoing conviction for which carries great stigma with it (such as sex-related or drug-related criminal wrongdoing). Such wrongdoing is conceived of as being 'truly criminal'. On other occasions, the House of Lords has refused to imply mens rea requirements into a criminal statute, because that statute concerned conduct prohibited solely because it exemplified bad (risky; unsafe) practice in a context in which there are public or industry standards of good practice. Such conduct is made criminal only as an aid to regulation, and conviction is not thought to attract stigma. The difference in approach towards the two kinds of cases reflects an underlying assumption that liberty is at stake, and must hence be protected by an implication of mens rea, only in cases involving 'truly criminal' wrongdoing, wrongdoing conviction for which attracts stigma.

There is certainly an important kind of liberty, freedom from undeserved stigma, at stake in cases involving 'truly criminal' wrongdoing. Conviction for some statutory crimes (such as sex-related crimes) carries with it a tendency, to use the older language of libel law, to vilify someone, and bring him or her into hatred, contempt and ridicule. Someone exposed to such a risk clearly has his or her prospects for autonomous life significantly reduced. Quite apart from whatever adverse official consequences of conviction that there may be, one's plans, projects, relationships, and so forth, that can be successfully pursued only in common with others may be undermined by widespread distrust or disregard fomented amongst those others by knowledge of one's conviction. Accordingly, a determination to imply (in the absence of legislative provision to the contrary) mens rea requirements in statutory provisions creating such crimes ensures—assuming that the courts imply the right kind of mens rea requirements—that adverse consequences of this kind are not undeservedly imposed.

When it comes to the interpretation of criminal statutes and the possible imposition of strict liability, however, there may be a different but equally important kind of liberty at stake in many 'regulatory' criminal cases, whether or not conviction in such cases attracts stigma. The imposition of strict liability in a 'regulatory' context may seriously threaten the participation of individuals in activities of intrinsic worth to their pursuit of an autonomous life. To give some examples from the case law, for the butcher, baker, pharmacist, corner-shop owner, farmer, dogowner, antique gun collector or amateur radio broadcaster, there is what has been termed an 'action' reason, and not (or not just) an 'outcome' reason, to participate in their livelihood or hobby respectively. In other words, for such people it is engaging in the activity itself or, in some occupational cases, engaging in the role that one's activities give one (say, within the local community), rather than simply securing a given outcome (say, profit) of the activity, that contributes to their wellbeing and hence to their individual autonomy. As Raz puts it, 'freedom [autonomy] consists in the pursuit of valuable forms of life, and . . . its value derives from the value of that pursuit' (my emphasis). [J. Raz, *The Morality of Freedom* (1986) at p. 395] Moreover, for Raz, forms of life include 'socially defined and determined pursuits and activities', meaning recognised and socially organised hobbies as well as (say) occupations serving the community.

By using the deterrent weapon of strict liability to convict people of a criminal offence when, perhaps by unhappy mischance, they have fallen into bad practice in the pursuit of an intrinsically valuable activity, in Raz's sense, the courts are ignoring the importance of action-reasons to people's freedom, and posing undue threats to their prospects for an autonomous life. A more nuanced approach to criminal statutes and to strict liability is hence required, if the courts' claim to be champions of personal liberty is to be comprehensively vindicated. First, the courts should seek to distinguish between statutes dealing with activities with largely instrumental value—like transport—where strict liability may in principle be more easily justified, and statutes dealing with activities that may have intrinsic value for the participants. Secondly, where the latter are in issue, the courts must further consider whether the outcome-value of strict liability is so overwhelming that even considerations of personal autonomy must give way to it. This second stage may look much like the familiar contrast between 'the policy of objective liability' (supporting strict liability) and 'the principle of mens rea,' in statutory interpretation; but it should in fact give the courts considerably less scope to find strict liability justified than the familiar contrast does. This is because the courts would no longer treat the question whether to imply a culpability requirement as a simple matter of balancing conflicting outcome-reasons: i.e. the outcome reasons that favour such an implication (less chance of conviction, and greater scope to err for defendants), as against the outcome reasons that militate in favour of strict liability (greater deterrent effect; more chance of conviction). The courts would also be asking whether those falling foul of the statute's criminal provisions will, when they do so, be likely to have been engaged in activities whose intrinsic value lies in their being constitutive of an autonomous life. Taking this question seriously ought, at the very least, to lead to a new class of cases in which strict liability is, on the grounds of liberty, found to be an implication that is unwarranted despite the social concerns that justified criminalisation in the first place.

6. STRICT LIABILITY IN RELATION TO PARTICULAR CRIMES

(1) OFFENCES AFFECTING THE ENVIRONMENT

Alphacell Ltd v Woodward

[1972] 2 All ER 475, House of Lords

(Lord Wilberforce, Viscount Dilhorne, Lords Pearson, Cross of Chelsea and Salmon)

The facts are taken from the speech of Lord Cross.

The appellants in the course of their business caused large quantities of polluted effluent to flow into a settling tank on the bank of the River Irwell. The tank would have inevitably overflowed with the result that the effluent would have entered the river had not the appellants installed two pumps to keep the level of the water in the tanks low enough to prevent any overflow. At the base of the pumps there are or were metal 'roses' with holes of a diameter of 3/4 inch designed to allow water to reach the pump freely but to prevent any solid matter which might get into the tank from passing through the roses and coming into contact with the impeller.

On Tuesday 25 November 1969, the pumps failed to prevent the settling tank from overflowing, the reason for the failure being—as was subsequently discovered—that a quantity of brambles, leaves and other vegetable matter had found its way through the holes in the 'roses' and was wound round the impellers. The evidence, which the justices accepted, was to the effect that the 'roses' had been regularly inspected each weekend since they had been installed a year previously, that no vegetable matter had been in them when the pumps were inspected a few days before the overflow, and indeed that no vegetable matter had ever been found in the pumps before. How all these brambles and leaves had found their way through the roses in the course of the two or three days before 25 November was an unsolved mystery.

Lord Wilberforce. My Lords, the enactment under which the appellants have been convicted is the Rivers (Prevention of Pollution) Act 1951. The relevant words are 'if he causes or knowingly permits to enter a stream any poisonous, noxious or polluting matter'.

The subsection evidently contemplates two things—*causing*, which must involve some active operation or chain of operations involving as the result the pollution of the stream; *knowingly permitting*, which involves a failure to prevent the pollution, which failure, however, must be accompanied by knowledge. I see no reason either for reading back the word 'knowingly' into the first limb, or for reading the first limb as, by deliberate contrast, hitting something which is unaccompanied by knowledge. The first limb involves causing and this is what has to be interpreted.

In my opinion, 'causing' here must be given a common sense meaning and I deprecate the introduction of refinements, such as causa causans, effective cause or novus actus. There may be difficulties where acts of third persons or natural forces are concerned but I find the present case comparatively simple. The appellants abstract water, pass it through their works where it becomes polluted, conduct it to a settling tank communicating directly with the stream, into which the polluted water will inevitably overflow if the level rises over the overflow point. They plan, however, to recycle the water by pumping it back from the settling tank into their works; if the pump works properly this will happen and the level in the tank will remain below the overflow point. It did not happen on the relevant occasion due to some failure in the pumps.

In my opinion, this is a clear case of causing the polluted water to enter the stream. The whole complex operation which might lead to this result was an operation deliberately conducted by the appellants and I fail to see how a defect in one stage of it, even if we must assume that this happened without their negligence, can enable them to say they did not cause the pollution. In my opinion, complication of this case by infusion of the concept of mens rea, and its exceptions, is unnecessary and undesirable. The section is clear, its application plain. I agree with the majority of the Divisional Court ([1971] 2 All ER 910) who upheld the conviction, except that rather than say that the actions of the appellants were *a cause* of the pollution I think it more accurate to say that the appellants caused the polluting matter to enter the stream. . . .

The actual question submitted to this House under the Administration of Justice Act 1961 [sic. 1960 is meant], s 1 (2) is:

'Whether the offence of causing polluting matter to enter a stream contrary to section 2 of the Rivers (Prevention of Pollution) Act 1951 can be committed by a person who has no knowledge of the fact that polluting matter is entering the stream and has not been negligent in any relevant respect.'

The answer to this, I suggest, should be 'Yes', it being understood that the test is whether the person concerned caused or knowingly permitted the poisonous, noxious or polluting matter to enter the stream. As, in my opinion, the appellants did so cause, I would dismiss the appeal.

[**Viscount Dilhorne, Lord Pearson, Lord Cross of Chelsea** and **Lord Salmon** made speeches dismissing the appeal.]

See also *Hart v Anglian Water Services Ltd* [2003] EWCA Crim 224 (causing sewage effluent to be discharged).

Notes and questions

1. Viscount Dilhorne and Lord Salmon, thought the Act dealt with acts 'not criminal in any real sense'. Cf above, pp **236–237**, above.

2. A repetition or continuation of an offence under s 2(1) was punishable with six months' imprisonment. If D, who had a previous conviction, was charged with another offence under the Act, would it still be 'not criminal in any real sense'?

3. Should the criminal law require a person to do more than is reasonable to prevent a particular harm occurring?

4. Lord Pearson pointed out: 'There was no intervening act of a trespasser and no act of God. There was not even any unusual weather or freak of nature.' Lord Cross also appears to have thought the decision might have been different if there had been such evidence. Why?

5. R. W. L. Howells (35 MLR p 663) writes:

The appellants' contention was, in essence that having set up a system which would, in ordinary circumstances, prevent pollution, they were entitled to provide a 'second line' system for the disposal of their effluent into the river, in the event of an unforeseen failure of their 'first line' system. Disposal into the river would be, at the same time, the simplest and cheapest for them, as well as the very activity the Act was designed to prevent. An alternative, but obviously less convenient, 'second line' system would have been one that provided for the automatic stopping of their operation whenever their effluent recovery system failed. But it was obviously far more economic for the company, in the event of a pump failure, to continue their operations, and to take their chance with a plea that they had not 'caused' pollution within section 2(a) when their effluent had emptied itself into the river.

Looked at this way, is it not true to say that the appellants had *intentionally* caused the pollution? The provision of the channel into the river showed that, in a certain event, which they thought to be unlikely and hoped to prevent, they intended the effluent to flow into the river. A conditional intention is still intention. Was the case then, one of strict liability? But could this be said of the *Empress Car* case, above, p 59?

6. Is the case a good illustration of the argument that strict liability crimes are more efficient? In regulatory offences the claim is often made that 'negotiated compliance' by regulatory authority is more efficient. Does it deter this individual in the future? Does it deter others? See J. Rowan-Robinson, P. Q. Watchman and C. R. Barker, 'Crime and Regulation' [1988] Crim LR 211; and especially G. Richardson, 'Strict Liability for Regulatory Crime: The Empirical Research' [1987] Crim LR 295. Richardson reports that 'the majority of enforcement officers regard [strict liability] with favour and urge its retention. Although prosecution and its direct threat are seldom used, routine enforcement is conducted against a background of the criminal law and the implicit threat of its invocation. The fewer the uncertainties which attach to the law, therefore, the stronger the agencies' bargaining power' (p 303).

(2) DRUGS OFFENCES

Warner v Metropolitan Police Commissioner
[1968] 2 All ER 356, House of Lords

(Lords Reid, Morris of Borth-y-Gest, Guest, Pearce and Wilberforce)

The appellant, a floor-layer, sold scent as a side-line. He went to a café and inquired whether anything had been left for him. The proprietor told him there was something under the counter. The appellant found two boxes there and took them away. He was stopped by the police. One box contained scent, the other 20,000 tablets containing amphetamine sulphate, a prohibited drug under the Drugs (Prevention of Misuse) Act 1964. He was charged with being in possession of a prohibited drug, contrary to s 1 of the Act. The appellant said that he assumed that both boxes contained scent. The jury were directed that lack of knowledge of what the box contained went only to mitigation. The jury returned a verdict of guilty after three minutes. The chairman asked the jury whether they thought the appellant knew he had possession of drugs. The foreman answered that he did not know, he had not asked the jury. At the chairman's invitation, the jury retired again and shortly returned to say that they found that the appellant did know. The chairman made it clear that this was his own view and sentenced Warner to two years' imprisonment. The Court of Appeal dismissed his appeal against conviction and sentence. On appeal to the House of Lords, it was held that the jury had been misdirected but that no reasonable jury would have accepted the appellant's story and the conviction was upheld under the proviso to s 4(1) of the Criminal Appeal Act 1907.

Lord Reid... I understand that this is the first case in which this House has had to consider whether a statutory offence is an absolute offence in the sense that the belief, intention, or state of mind of the accused is immaterial and irrelevant. It appears from the authorities that the law on this matter is in some confusion, there being at least two schools of thought. So I think it necessary to begin by making some observations of a general character.

There is no doubt that for centuries mens rea has been an essential element in every common law crime or offence. Equally there is no doubt that Parliament, being sovereign, can create absolute offences if so minded; but we were referred to no instance where Parliament in giving statutory form to an old common law crime has or has been held to have excluded the necessity to prove mens rea. There is a number of statutes going back for over a century where Parliament in creating a new offence has transferred the onus of proof so that, once the facts necessary to constitute the crime have been proved, the accused will be held to be guilty unless he can prove that he had no mens rea. We were not referred, however, to any except quite recent cases in which it was held that it was no defence to a charge of a serious and truly criminal statutory offence to prove absence of mens rea.

On the other hand there is a long line of cases in which it has been held with regard to less serious offences that absence of mens rea was no defence. Typical examples are offences under public health, licensing and industrial legislation. If a person sets up as say a butcher, a publican, or manufacturer and exposes unsound meat for sale, or sells drink to a drunk man or certain parts of his factory are unsafe, it is no defence that he could not by the exercise of reasonable care have known or discovered that the meat was unsound, or that the man was drunk or that his premises were unsafe. He must take the risk and when it is found that the statutory prohibition or requirement has been infringed he must pay the penalty. This may well seem unjust, but it is a comparatively minor injustice and there is good reason for it as affording some protection to his customers or servants or to the public at large. Although this man might be able to show that he did his best, a more skilful or diligent man in his position might have done better, and when we are dealing with minor penalties which do not involve the disgrace of criminality it may be in the public interest to have a hard and fast rule. Strictly speaking there ought perhaps to be a defence that the defect was truly latent so that no one could have discovered it; but the law has not developed in that way, and one can see the difficulty if such a defence were allowed in a summary prosecution. These are only quasi-criminal offences and it does not really offend the ordinary man's sense of justice that moral guilt is not of the essence of the offence.

[His Lordship reviewed the authorities and continued:]

The only thing that makes me hesitate about this case is the severity of the penalty and the fact that this would be regarded as a truly criminal and disgraceful offence, so that a stigma would attach to a person convicted of it. Applicants for employment, permits or other advantages are often asked whether they have been convicted of any offence. Admission of a conviction of an ordinary offence of this class ought not to be too seriously regarded—and the conviction might be of the man's company and not of the man himself. A man who had, however, to admit a conviction with regard to dangerous drugs might be at a grave disadvantage, and this might not be removed by an explanation that he had only suffered a small penalty. He might even be dismissed by his employer. This makes me hesitate to impute to Parliament an intention to deprive persons accused of these offences of the defence that they had no mens rea. I would think it difficult to convince Parliament that there was any real need to convict a man who could prove that he had neither knowledge of what was being done nor any grounds for suspecting that there was anything wrong.

I dissent emphatically from the view that Parliament can be supposed to have been of the opinion that it could be left to the discretion of the police not to prosecute, or that if there was a prosecution justice would be served by only a nominal penalty being imposed . . . The object of this legislation is to penalise possession of certain drugs. So if mens rea has not been excluded what would be required would be the knowledge of the accused that he had prohibited drugs in his possession. It would be no defence, though it would be a mitigation, that he did not intend that they should be used improperly. And it is a commonplace that, if the accused had a suspicion but deliberately shut his eyes, the court or jury is well entitled to hold him guilty. Further, it would be pedantic to hold that it must be shown that the accused knew precisely which drug he had in his possession. Ignorance of the law is no defence and in fact virtually everyone knows that there are prohibited drugs. So it would be quite sufficient to prove facts from which it could properly be inferred that the accused knew that he had a prohibited drug in his possession. That would not lead to an unreasonable result. In a case like this Parliament, if consulted, might think it right to transfer the onus of proof so that an accused would have to prove that he neither knew nor had any reason to suspect that he had a prohibited drug in his possession; I am unable to find sufficient grounds for imputing to Parliament an intention to deprive the accused of all rights to show that he had no knowledge or reason to suspect that any prohibited drug was on his premises or in a container which was in his possession.

It was suggested in argument that it may always be a defence, even to an absolute offence, to prove absence of mens rea. There are some dicta to that effect, but I do not think that your lordships would introduce such a far reaching doctrine without statutory authority. When we are dealing with the original type of absolute offence—a person engaging in a business where he does certain things at the peril of a pecuniary penalty—it is clearly established that absence of mens rea is no defence. And a right to prove absence of mens rea would sometimes go too far. Mens rea or its absence is a subjective test, and any attempt to substitute an objective test for serious crime has been success-fully resisted. If, however, there is to be a halfway house between the common law doctrine and absolute liability, there could be an objective test: not whether the accused knew, but whether a rea-sonable man in his shoes would have known or have had reason to suspect that there was something wrong. I would not support an objective test where the ordinary member of the public is concerned, but it is not unreasonable to say that if a person engages in some particular business he must behave as, and have the capacity of, the ordinary reasonable man. . . .

In considering what is the proper construction of a provision in any Act of Parliament which is ambiguous one ought to reject that construction which leads to an unreasonable result. As a legal term 'possession' is ambiguous at least to this extent: there is no clear rule as to the nature of the mental element required. All are agreed that there must be some mental element in possession, but there is no agreement as to what precisely it must be. Indeed the view which prevailed in *R v Ashwell* [(1885) 16 QBD 190] and was approved in *Hudson* [[1943] KB 458, [1943] 1 All ER 642] went so far that a per-son who received a sovereign thinking it to be a shilling was held not to possess the sovereign until he discovered the mistake. There it was argued that 'possession' in this context should be given a popular and not a legal meaning; but even if that were a legitimate way to construe a well-known legal term, I think that it would lead to the same ambiguity. If the ordinary reasonable man were asked what he thought 'possession' meant in this context he would probably say that is a puzzle for the lawyers, and if he ventured his own opinion he might say it meant control; but if asked whether the innkeeper con-trols the contents of a box handed to him for safekeeping, I think that he would most probably say 'No'.

Lockyer v Gibb was relied on by the Court of Appeal as the case most nearly in point. There the accused had been in a café with some people when the police came in. A man, whom apparently she did not know, gave her a bottle containing tablets 'to look after for him'. She put them at the bottom of her shopping bag and when she went out she was stopped by the police. She was prosecuted under a regulation made under the Dangerous Drugs Act 1965 for being in possession of a scheduled drug. The magistrate held that there was a possibility that she did not know that the tablets contained any of the scheduled drugs. She may have been a very stupid woman, for I would think that any normal person being given a bottle of tablets in such circumstances would know perfectly well that the tablets must contain prohibited drugs which the man did not want the police to find in his possession. With regard to possession Lord Parker CJ, said:

> 'In my judgment, it is quite clear that a person cannot be said to be in possession of some article which he or she does not realise is, or may be, in her handbag, in her room, or in some other place over which she had control. That, I should have thought, is elementary, if something were slipped into one's basket and one had not the vaguest notion it was there at all, one could not possibly be said to be in possession of it.'

I entirely agree; but that destroys any contention that mere physical control or custody without any mental element is sufficient to constitute possession under that enactment. If something is slipped into my bag I have as much physical control over it as I have over anything else in my bag. I can carry it where I will and I can transfer the whole contents of my bag to some other person without ever realising that this particular thing is included. Then, however, Lord Parker went on to say:

> '... in my judgment, under this provision, while it is necessary to show that the appellant knew she had the articles which turned out to be a drug, it is not necessary that she should know that in fact it was a drug of a particular character.'

With that I cannot agree for reasons which I have already given. I do not think that this distinction will bear critical examination and I do not know what the result would be on this view if, in the present case, both the scent and the drugs had been in the same parcel. The appellant, if his story were accepted, would have rightly believed that the parcel contained scent, but would have been ignorant of the fact that drugs had been slipped in with the scent. Could it be right that if the appellant had taken possession of the parcel of scent and thereafter the drugs had been slipped in without his knowledge he would be innocent (which is Lord Parker's view), but that if the drugs had been slipped in without his knowledge before he took possession then he would be guilty? That seems to me to be quite unreasonable and it seems to me to be equally unreasonable that the fact that there were two parcels and not one should make all the difference between guilt and innocence.

If this case is to be decided on this narrower ground I accept the view of my noble and learned friends, Lord Pearce and Lord Wilberforce. It enables justice to be done in all cases which resemble this case. But it still leaves subject to injustice persons who in innocent circumstances take into their possession what they genuinely and reasonably believe to be an ordinary medicine, if in fact the substance turns out to be a prohibited drug. Nevertheless this ground is sufficient to show that the learned trial judge must be held to have misdirected the jury in the present case.

[**Lord Morris** held that the accused could be convicted of possession of a prohibited drug only if it were proved that he was knowingly in control of the substance or container in circumstances which enabled him to know or discover (or could have enabled him, had he so wished, to know or discover) what it was that he had, before assuming control of it or continuing to be in control of it.]

[**Lord Guest** held that possession of the parcel amounted to possession of the contents and no proof need be given of the knowledge of the nature of the contents.]

[**Lord Pearce**, having considered certain authorities and held that Lord Parker CJ in *Lockyer v Gibb* was right to hold that a person did not have possession of something which had been 'slipped into his bag' without his knowledge continued:].

One may, therefore, exclude from the 'possession' intended by the Act of 1964 the physical control of articles which have been 'planted' on him without his knowledge; but how much further is one to go? If one goes to the extreme length of requiring the prosecution to prove that 'possession' implies a full knowledge of the name and nature of the drug concerned, the efficacy of the Act is seriously impaired, since many drug pedlars may in truth be unaware of this. I think that the term 'possession' is satisfied by a knowledge only of the existence of the thing itself and not its qualities, and that ignorance or mistake as to its qualities is not an excuse. This would comply with the general understanding of the word 'possess'. Though I reasonably believe the tablets which I possess to be aspirin, yet if they turn out to be heroin I am in possession of heroin tablets. This would be so I think even if I believed them to be sweets. It would be otherwise if I believed them to be something of a wholly different nature. At this point a question of degree arises as to when a difference in qualities amounts to a difference in kind. That is a matter for a jury who would probably decide it sensibly in favour of the genuinely innocent but against the guilty.

The situation with regard to containers presents further problems. If a man is in possession of the contents of a package, prima facie his possession of the package leads to the strong inference that he is in possession of its contents; but can this be rebutted by evidence that he was mistaken as to its contents? As in the case of goods that have been 'planted' in his pocket without his knowledge, so I do not think that he is in possession of contents which are quite different in kind from what he believed. Thus the prima facie assumption is discharged if he proves (or raises a real doubt in the matter) either (a) that he was a servant or bailee who had no right to open it *and* no reason to suspect that its contents were illicit or were drugs or (b) that although he was the owner he had no knowledge of (including a genuine mistake as to) its actual contents or of their illicit nature and that he received them innocently and also that he had had no reasonable opportunity since receiving the package of acquainting himself with its actual contents. For a man takes over a package or suitcase at risk as to its contents being unlawful if he does not immediately examine it (if he is entitled to do so). As soon as may be he should examine it and if he finds the contents suspicious reject possession by either throwing them away or by taking immediate sensible steps for their disposal....

The direction to which the appellant was entitled would, in my opinion, be approximately as follows. The Drugs (Prevention of Misuse) Act 1964 forbids possession of these drugs. Whether he possessed them with an innocent or guilty mind or for a laudable or improper purpose is immaterial, since he is not allowed to possess them. If he possessed them, he is guilty. If a man has physical control or possession of a thing that is sufficient possession under the Act of 1964 provided that he knows that he has the thing; but a man does not (within the meaning of the Act of 1964) possess things of whose existence he is unaware. The prosecution have here proved that he possessed the parcel, but have they proved that he possessed its contents also? There is a very strong inference of fact in any normal case that a man who possesses a parcel also possesses its contents, an inference on which a jury would in a normal case be justified in finding possession. A man who accepts possession of a parcel normally accepts possession of the contents. That inference, however, can be disproved or shaken by evidence that, although a man was in possession of a parcel, he was completely mistaken as to its contents and would not have accepted possession had he known what kind of thing the contents were. A mistake as to the qualities of the contents, however, does not negative possession. Many people possess things of whose exact qualities they are unaware. If the accused knew that the contents were drugs or were tablets, he was in possession of them, though he was mistaken as to their qualities. Again if, though unaware of the contents, he did not open them at the first opportunity to ascertain (as he was entitled to do in this case) what they were, the proper inference is that he was accepting possession of them. (It would be otherwise if he had no right to open the parcel.) Again, if he suspected that there was anything wrong about the contents when he received the parcel, the proper inference is that he was accepting possession of the contents by not immediately verifying them. (This would, in my opinion, apply also to a bailee.)

In the present case you may think that the difference between scent and tablets is a sufficient difference in kind to entitle the accused to an acquittal if on the whole of the evidence it appears that he may have genuinely believed that the parcel contained scent, and that he may not have had any suspicions that there was anything illicit in the parcel, and that he had no opportunity of verifying its contents. For in that case it is not proved that he was in possession of the contents of the parcel.

The appellant has, therefore, been deprived of the chance of putting before the jury a defence which was in theory open to him on the facts of this case; but the evidence against him was so strong that no jury properly directed would have acquitted him. In my opinion, therefore, the proviso should be applied and I would dismiss the appeal.

[**Lord Wilberforce** held that there was one single question to be answered—'What kind of control with what mental element does the Act intend to prohibit?' On the question of making clear to the jury what is required in order to establish possession, he associated himself with the observations of Lord Pearce.]

Appeal dismissed

Notes and questions

1. The judges got into great difficulties over the concept of possession. Would any of these difficulties have arisen if the offence had been interpreted to require mens rea?

2. D is found carrying a sealed package which contains heroin. How would the judges have dealt with him if he believed:
  (i)   the box was empty;
  (ii) the box contained aspirin, or sweets, or jewellery, or stolen jewellery, or explosives, or something, but he had no idea what?

3. When *Warner* was tried, the offence was understood to be one of strict liability, requiring no mental element as to the nature of the thing (in fact, a drug) which was in the defendant's control. Was there any reason why the jury should have given any thought to the question whether he knew that the boxes contained drugs? Was the chairman right to ask the jury their opinion? Was the opinion of the jury (given after they had returned their verdict) of any value? Should evidence have been admitted as to the defendant's knowledge, or lack of it, at the trial? See *Sandhu*, above, p **229**.

4. Manifestly it is relevant in determining the sentence to be imposed on the defendant that the court should know whether the defendant acted knowingly or unwittingly. In *Dalas* [1966] Crim LR 692, CCA, D, charged with the unlawful possession of three and a half kilos of cannabis, claimed that he got it from a woman who owed him £150 and that he thought it was Indian culinary herbs which he planned to sell in order to recoup his debt. The jury found him guilty but, since the offence was one of strict liability, the jury's verdict did not show whether they believed his innocent explanation or not. The trial judge, however, said that he did not believe it and sentenced D to three years' imprisonment; a sentence which would have been indefensible if the judge had concluded that D believed he was in possession of curry powder.

Affirming the conviction in *Dalas* the CCA acknowledged that the trial judge, by virtue of the application of strict liability, might have to decide a difficult question of fact without the aid of the jury. It was decided in *Newton* (1982) 77 Cr App R 13, CA, that disputed facts affecting sentence may be determined by the trial judge after conviction, now referred to as a '*Newton* hearing'. So is it the case that all the imposition of strict liability does is to remove the determination of an important, often crucial, issue of fact from the jury to the judge? Or is there a case for convicting the defendant who is free of fault, and for punishing him, to ensure greater vigilance either in (i) the defendant; or (ii) in others?

7. STRICT LIABILITY, MENS REA AND THE BURDEN OF PROOF

Sweet v Parsley
[1969] 1 All ER 347, House of Lords

(Lords Reid, Morris of Borth-y-Gest, Pearce, Wilberforce and Diplock)

Miss Sweet, a schoolteacher, was the sub-tenant of a farm in Oxfordshire. Finding it impracticable to travel into Oxford, she let the rooms in the farmhouse to tenants at low rentals allowing them the common use of the kitchen. She retained one room for her own use and visited the farm occasionally to collect rent and see that all was well. The police found evidence that cannabis was smoked in the farmhouse. She was convicted by the magistrates of being concerned in the management of premises which were used for the purpose of smoking cannabis, contrary to s 5(b) of the Dangerous Drugs Act 1965. The magistrates found that 'she had no knowledge whatever that the house was being used for the purpose of smoking cannabis' and that 'once or twice when staying overnight at the farmhouse the appellant shouted if there was excessive noise late at night but otherwise she did not exercise any control over the tenants except that she collected rent from them'. Miss Sweet's appeal to the Divisional Court was dismissed. She appealed to the House of Lords.

Lord Reid . . . How has it come about that the Divisional Court has felt bound to reach such an obviously unjust result? It has, in effect, held that it was carrying out the will of Parliament because Parliament has chosen to make this an absolute offence. And, of course, if Parliament has so chosen, the courts must carry out its will, and they cannot be blamed for any unjust consequences. But has Parliament so chosen? I dealt with this matter at some length in *Warner v Metropolitan Police Comr* [p **244**, above]. On reconsideration I see no reason to alter anything which I there said. But I think that some amplification is necessary. Our first duty is to consider the words of the Act; if they show a clear intention to create an absolute offence, that is an end of the matter. But such cases are very rare. Sometimes the words of the section which creates a particular offence make it clear that mens rea is required in one form or another. Such cases are quite frequent. But in a very large number of cases there is no clear indication either way. In such cases there has for centuries been a presumption that Parliament did not intend to make criminals of persons who were in no way blameworthy in what they did. That means that, whenever a section is silent as to mens rea, there is a presumption that, in order to give effect to the will of Parliament, we must read in words appropriate to require mens rea.

Where it is contended that an absolute offence has been created, the words of Alderson B in *A-G v Lockwood* [(1842) 9 M & W 378 at 398] have often been quoted:

'The rule of law, I take it, upon the construction of all statutes, and therefore applicable to the construction of this, is, whether they be penal or remedial, to construe them according to the plain literal and grammatical meaning of the words in which they are expressed unless that construction leads to a plain and clear contradiction of the apparent purpose of the act or to some palpable and evident absurdity.'

That is perfectly right as a general rule and where there is no legal presumption. But what about the multitude of criminal enactments where the words of the Act simply make it an offence to do certain things but where everyone agrees that there cannot be a conviction without proof of mens rea in some form? This passage, if applied to the present problem, would mean that there is no need to prove mens rea unless it would be 'a plain and clear contradiction of the apparent purpose of the Act' to convict without proof of mens rea. But that would be putting the presumption the wrong way round; for it is firmly established by a host of authorities that mens rea is an essential ingredient of every offence unless some reason can be found for holding that that is not necessary. It is also firmly established that the fact that other sections of the Act expressly require mens rea, for example because they contain the word 'knowingly', is not in itself sufficient to justify a decision that a section which is silent as to mens rea creates an absolute offence. In the absence of a clear indication in the Act that an offence is intended to be an absolute offence, it is necessary to go outside the Act and examine all relevant circumstances in order to establish that this must have been the intention of Parliament. I say 'must have been', because it is a universal principle that if a penal provision is reasonably capable of two interpretations, that interpretation which is most favourable to the accused must be adopted.

What, then, are the circumstances which it is proper to take into account? In the well known case of *Sherras v De Rutzen* [above, p **234**] Wright J only mentioned the subject-matter with which the Act deals. But he was there dealing with something which was one of a class of acts which 'are not criminal in any real sense, but are acts which in the public interest are prohibited under a penalty'. It does not in the least follow that, when one is dealing with a truly criminal act, it is sufficient merely to have regard to the subject-matter of the enactment. One must put oneself in the position of a legislator. It has long been the practice to recognise absolute offences in this class of quasi-criminal acts, and one can safely assume that, when Parliament is passing new legislation dealing with this class of offences, its silence as to mens rea means that the old practice is to apply. But when one comes to acts of a truly criminal character, it appears to me that there are at least two other factors which any reasonable legislator would have in mind. In the first place, a stigma still attaches to any person convicted of a truly criminal offence, and the more serious or more disgraceful the offence the greater the stigma. So he would have to consider whether, in a case of this gravity, the public interest really requires that an innocent person should be prevented from proving his innocence in order that fewer guilty men may escape. And equally important is the fact that, fortunately, the press in this country are vigilant to expose injustice, and every manifestly unjust conviction made known to the public tends to injure the body politic by undermining public confidence in the justice of the law and of its administration. But I regret to observe that, in some recent cases where serious offences have been held to be absolute offences, the court has taken into account no more than the wording of the Act and the character and seriousness of the mischief which constitutes the offence.

The choice would be more difficult if there were no other way open than either *mens rea* in the full sense or an absolute offence; for there are many kinds of case where putting on the prosecutor the full burden of proving *mens rea* creates great difficulties and may lead to many unjust acquittals. But there are at least two other possibilities. Parliament has not infrequently transferred the onus as regards *mens rea* to the accused, so that, once the necessary facts are proved, he must convince the jury that, on balance of probabilities, he is innocent of any criminal intention. I find it a little surprising that more use has not been made of this method; but one of the bad effects of the decision of this House in *Woolmington v DPP* [p **172**, above] may have been to discourage its use. The other method would be in effect to substitute in appropriate classes of case gross negligence for mens rea in the full sense as the mental element necessary to constitute the crime. It would often be much easier to infer that Parliament must have meant that gross negligence should be the necessary mental element than to infer that Parliament intended to create an absolute offence. A variant of this would be to accept the view of Cave J in *Tolson* [p **217**, above]. This appears to have been done in Australia where authority appears to support what Dixon J said in *Proudman v Dayman* [(1941) 67 CLR 536]:

> 'As a general rule an honest and reasonable belief in a state of facts which, if they existed, would make the defendant's act innocent affords an excuse for doing what would otherwise be an offence.'

It may be that none of these methods is wholly satisfactory, but at least the public scandal of convicting on a serious charge persons who are in no way blameworthy would be avoided. If this section means what the Divisional Court have held that it means, then hundreds of thousands of people who sublet part of their premises or take in lodgers or are concerned in the management of residential premises or institutions are daily incurring a risk of being convicted of a serious offence in circumstances where they are in no way to blame. For the greatest vigilance cannot prevent tenants, lodgers or inmates or guests whom they bring in from smoking cannabis cigarettes in their own rooms. It was suggested in argument that the appellant brought this conviction on herself because it is found as a fact that, when the police searched the premises, there were people there of the 'beatnik fraternity'. But surely it would be going a very long way to say that persons managing premises of any kind ought to safeguard themselves by refusing accommodation to all who are of slovenly or exotic appearance, or who bring in guests of that kind. And, unfortunately, drug taking is by no means confined to those of unusual appearance. Speaking from a rather long experience of membership of both Houses, I assert with confidence that no Parliament within my recollection would have agreed to make an offence of this kind an absolute offence if the matter had been fully explained to it. So, if the court ought only to hold an offence to be an absolute offence where it appears that that must have been the intention of Parliament, offences of this kind are very far removed from those which it is proper to hold to be absolute offences.

I must now turn to the question what is the true meaning of s 5 of the Act of 1965. [His Lordship held that the 'purpose' referred to in s 5 of the 1965 Act was the purpose of the management and, as the appellant had no such purpose, the conviction must be quashed.]

[**Lords Morris** and **Pearce** held that it was necessary to prove that the accused had knowledge of the particular purpose to which the premises were being put in order to secure a conviction, and that the appeal should be allowed.]

[**Lord Wilberforce** held that the 'purpose' which must be proved under the section must be that of the manager; and that the appeal should be allowed.]

[**Lord Diplock**, held that criminal statutes are to be read subject to the implication that a necessary element in the offence is the absence of a belief held honestly and on reasonable grounds.]

See the comments of Lord Nicholls on Lord Diplock's speech.

Appeal allowed

Notes and questions

1. Is it a 'bad effect' (per Lord Reid, pp **249–250**, above) of *Woolmington* (p **172**, above) that it has discouraged the courts from putting an onus of proof on the accused? Consider the concluding passage of Lord Cooke of Thorndon's 1996 Hamlyn Lecture on *Woolmington*, 'One Golden Thread', at p 47.

Sir John Smith ended his 1987 MacDermott Lecture on *The Presumption of Innocence* (38 NILQ 223) with the indisputable proposition that in England the golden thread has always been broken at some points, adding 'It would be a great day for our law if the golden thread could be made to run truly throughout the tangled web'. I am, with full respect, not so sure. But it does seem odd that in the home of *Woolmington* absolute (or 'strict') liability is so extensively accepted by the courts, and with some equanimity. It is as if the great case has created a judicial mindset which recoils at a shifting of the onus, yet tolerates a harsher solution. The New Zealand via media cannot be claimed to solve all the problems and awaits further working out. Perhaps, though, it would at least be worth looking at in England.

Ultimately the issue is one of relative values. In the eyes of common lawyers and probably in the eyes of the Common People of the Hamlyn Trust, absolute liability for alleged criminal conduct goes against the grain. Nevertheless, for lesser offences, the English courts accept it from time to time, usually in the name of legislative intent—even although in truth the legislature may have been content to leave a practical solution to the courts. A practical solution must allow for the dictates of public expediency in the matter of regulatory offences. The creation of such offences may be the most efficient method of controlling conduct in an industry, but because of the limitations of the prosecution's knowledge the difficulty of proof may be excessively demanding. Then the public interest may well be sufficiently served by casting a burden of proof, or [sic] the balance of probabilities, on the defendant. Justice is not denied to the individual if, in the typical case where the defence of total absence of fault can be allowed, it is recognised that he enters a field of activity having a public impact, knowing that in cases of doubt it will be for him to prove that he runs a tight ship.

2. Did *Woolmington* decide anything about mistaken beliefs? Particularly, did it decide that an unreasonably mistaken belief is no defence?

3. Lord Reid in his speech in *Sweet v Parsley*, above, p **249**, said that there were many kinds of case where putting on the prosecution the full burden of proving mens rea created great difficulty for the prosecutor and might lead to unjustified acquittals. It would be interesting to know what 'kinds of case' Lord Reid had in mind. Any case, and *Woolmington* was surely one of them, may present the prosecutor with formidable problems in proving beyond reasonable doubt that the defendant acted deliberately rather than accidentally. Is it any more difficult to prove that the defendant knew that the contents of the parcel he possessed contained cannabis than to prove that the defendant discharged a gun deliberately? Lord Reid thought that in the unspecified kinds of case he had in mind, one alternative was to transfer the onus of proof as regards mens rea to the accused. Once the necessary facts are proved by the prosecution, it would be up to the accused to prove, on balance of probabilities, that he was innocent of any criminal intention. Lord Reid's alternative appears to have informed s 28 of the Misuse of Drugs Act 1971 which provides:

> (1) This section applies to offences under any of the following provisions of this Act, that is to say section 4(2) and (3) [producing and supplying controlled drugs], section 5(2) and (3) [possession of controlled drugs], section 6(2) [cultivation of cannabis] and section 9 [prohibition of certain activities relating to opium].
>
> (2) Subject to subsection (3) below, in any proceedings for an offence to which this section applies it shall be a defence for the accused to prove that he neither knew of nor suspected nor had reason to suspect the existence of some fact alleged by the prosecution which it is necessary for the prosecution to prove if he is to be convicted of the offence charged.
>
> (3) Where in any proceedings for an offence to which this section applies it is necessary, if the accused is to be convicted of the offence charged, for the prosecution to prove that some substance or product involved in the alleged offence was the controlled drug which the prosecution alleges it to have been, and it is proved that the substance or product in question was that controlled drug, the accused:
>
> (a) shall not be acquitted of the offence charged by reason only of proving that he neither knew nor suspected nor had reason to suspect that the substance or product in question was the particular controlled drug alleged; but

(b) shall be acquitted thereof:
   (i) if he proves that he neither believed nor suspected nor had reason to suspect that the substance or product in question was a controlled drug; or
   (ii) if he proves that he believed the substance or product in question to be a controlled drug, or a controlled drug of a description, such that, if it had in fact been that controlled drug or a controlled drug of that description, he would not at the material time have been committing any offence to which this section applies.

(4) Nothing in this section shall prejudice any defence which it is open to a person charged with an offence to which this section applies to raise apart from this section.

If D is charged with possession of a particular controlled drug it continues to be necessary for the prosecution to prove that he was in possession of the substance which was in fact the drug alleged. This requires the prosecution to prove whatever mental element is necessary to establish possession of the substance. Otherwise there is no actus reus. But, prima facie, that is all the prosecution have to prove. Section 28(3)(a) makes it clear that the prosecution does not have to prove that D knew that, or was reckless whether, the substance was *that* drug. If no further evidence is offered, D should be convicted. Clearly the presumption of mens rea as stated in *B (a minor) v DPP* is excluded expressly or, at least, by necessary implication: *Lambert* [2001] 3 All ER 577, HL [68], per Lord Hope, [128] per Lord Clyde and [182] per Lord Hutton. Section 28(3)(b) makes it clear that it is a defence for D to 'prove' that he believed on reasonable grounds that the substance in his possession was talcum powder, Horlicks—or anything other than a controlled drug.

The burden of proof

In *Woolmington*, above, p 172, the House of Lords recognized that there are statutory exceptions to the rule that the onus of proof of all issues is on the Crown. Statutes frequently provide that 'it shall be for the defendant to prove . . . .' Such a provision is commonly said to create a 'reverse onus'. In *Carr-Brant* [1943] 2 All ER 156, [1943] KB 607 the judge had directed the jury that such a provision in the Prevention of Corruption Act 1916, s 2, required D to prove his innocence beyond reasonable doubt. The court, quashing the conviction on another ground held that this was wrong.

In our judgment, in any case where, either by statute or at common law [that is, the defence of insanity], some matter is presumed against an accused person 'unless the contrary is proved,' the jury should be directed that it is for them to decide whether the contrary is proved; that the burden of proof required is less than that required at the hands of the prosecution in proving the case beyond a reasonable doubt; and that the burden may be discharged by evidence satisfying the jury of the probability of that which the accused is called upon to establish.

The court said that the burden on the accused was the same as that on the claimant in a civil case—that is, 'the preponderance of probability'. This was universally accepted as the correct principle and subsequent statutes were clearly enacted on that assumption. Then came the Human Rights Act 1998. In *Lambert*, above, the House of Lords, Lord Hutton dissenting, held, obiter, that s 28, so interpreted, violated the presumption of innocence guaranteed in Article 6(2) of the European Convention on Human Rights (see Ch 2 and Ch 5 above). Lord Steyn said,

. . . I am satisfied that the transfer of the legal burden in s 28 does not satisfy the criterion of proportionality. Viewed in its place in the current legal system, s 28 of the 1971 Act is a disproportionate reaction to perceived difficulties facing the prosecution in drugs cases. It would be sufficient to impose an evidential burden on the accused. It follows that s 28 is incompatible with convention rights.

The 'evidential burden' is a term coined by Glanville Williams in CLGP (1st edn, 1953, s 225, 2nd edn, 1961 s 287) to mean 'The burden of introducing sufficient . . . evidence to get before the jury . . .' In the case of a criminal defendant, that means such evidence as *might* raise a doubt in the minds of a reasonable jury. Once D has introduced such evidence he has satisfied the evidential burden. But it is plain that this is not a burden of *proof*. He has not proved anything, not even—yet—raised a doubt. The jury may still properly convict him of the offence.

In *Lambert*, however, it was held, obiter, Lord Hutton dissenting, that s 3(1) of the Human Rights Act—'So far as it is possible to do so, primary legislation and subordinate legislation must be read and given effect in a way which is compatible with Convention rights'— enabled and required the House to hold that 'proves' means satisfy the evidential burden. This decision was much influenced by an article, 'The Logic of Exceptions' [1988] CLJ 261 at 265 by Glanville Williams arguing that 'unless the contrary is proved' can be taken, in relation to a defence to mean 'unless sufficient evidence is given to the contrary'. In *R v DPP, ex p Kebilene* [1999] 4 All ER 801, 837, Lord Cooke said '. . . for evidence that it is a possible meaning one could hardly ask for more than the opinion of Professor Glanville Williams . . .' and this opinion was relied on in *Lambert*. But did the great jurist's very proper aversion to reverse onuses carry him too far on this occasion? If, in s 28(2), we substitute for 'prove', 'introduce sufficient evidence that', is not the result nonsense? It cannot be, and the judges certainly do not intend it to be, a 'defence' merely to introduce evidence that may raise a reasonable doubt. They intend it to be a defence only if the jury are in fact left in reasonable doubt. So we have to read 'prove' to mean 'raise a reasonable doubt whether'. Is that a possible meaning of 'prove'? Cf 'Commentary' at [2001] Crim LR 807 and Professor Sullivan [2002] Crim LR at 157: '[Lambert] completely undermines the legislative provision subjected to "interpretation"; an evidential burden is not, as some claim, a form of halfway house between a probative burden and its absence, but something that arises quite spontaneously in any trial where the prosecution has made a case which requires an answer.'

R v McNamara

[1988] 87 Cr App R 246, Court of Appeal, Criminal Division

(Lord Lane CJ, Drake and Henry JJ)

A cardboard box containing 20 kg of cannabis resin was found on the back of McNamara's motorcycle. His explanation was that he was delivering the box for a man he refused to name and thought it contained pornographic material or pirate videos. He was charged under s 5(3) of the Misuse of Drugs Act 1971 with having a controlled drug in his possession with intent to supply it to another. The judge directed the jury: 'You should convict . . . if you are satisfied so that you are sure that he had possession of the contents of the cardboard box, which admittedly was cannabis resin, and knew that the box contained something, unless on the balance of probabilities he has proved that he neither knew, suspected nor had reason to suspect the contents of the box was any controlled drug.'

[**Lord Lane CJ**, having cited s 28(2) of the Misuse of Drugs Act 1971 (above, p **252**):]

If one reads those words literally, they seem in effect to cast upon the defendant the burden of disproving all facts adduced by the prosecution in support of the charges. This, one imagines, cannot possibly have been the intention of the draftsman.

We have had our attention drawn by Mr Kamlish to the decision of this Court in the case of *Ashton-Rickhardt* [1978] 1 All ER 173, [1978] 1 WLR 37. The view of the Court in that case was certainly that subsection (2) of section 28 did not have that extraordinary effect. . . .

[His Lordship referred to the speeches in *Warner* (above, p **243**).]

The situation in the present case with which we are dealing is, to pick up Lord Wilberforce's words, a non-ideal form of possession, namely, holding by the defendant of a box and its contents, which perhaps it is convenient to refer to as box-possession, observing, as we do, that we appreciate the danger of begging the question altogether by the use of the word 'possession'. The defendant admittedly has control of a box which he knows contains a 'thing' which he has not seen. If he knows what the thing is, no problem arises. But what if the defendant knows that the box contains something, but is mistaken as to the nature of that thing? That is to say, in terms of the present case, what if he knew that the box contained something, but he thought it was pornographic or pirated video films, whereas in fact it was undoubtedly cannabis resin?

Prior to the passing of the 1971 Act, the House of Lords, in *Warner v Metropolitan Police Commissioner* tackled this question. Unhappily it is not altogether easy to extract from the speeches of their Lordships the *ratio decidendi*. But doing the best we can, and appreciating that we may not have done full justice to the speeches, the following propositions seem to us to emerge.

First of all a man does not have possession of something which has been put into his pocket or into his house without his knowledge: in other words something which is 'planted' on him, to use the current vulgarism. Secondly, a mere mistake as to the quality of a thing under the defendant's control is not enough to prevent him being in possession. For instance, if a man is in possession of heroin, believing it to be cannabis or believing it perhaps to be aspirin.

Thirdly, if the defendant believes that the thing is of a wholly different nature from that which in fact it is, then the result, to use the words of Lord Pearce, would be otherwise. Fourthly, in the case of a container or a box, the defendant's possession of the box leads to the strong inference that he is in possession of the contents or whatsoever it is inside the box. But if the contents are quite different in kind from what he believed, he is not in possession of it . . .

It seems to us that it was with a view to elucidating some of the problems which arise from the speeches in that case that the 1971 Act was passed. First of all the preamble to the Act reads as follows: 'An Act to make new provision with respect to dangerous or otherwise harmful drugs and related matters, and for purposes connected therewith.' No doubt Parliament was stimulated to make this enactment by reason, partially at any rate of what Lord Pearce said at p 307 of the report, which reads as follows: 'It would, I think, be an improvement of a difficult position if Parliament were to enact that when a person has ownership or physical possession of drugs he shall be guilty unless he proves on a balance of probabilities that he was unaware of their nature or had reasonable excuse for their possession.'

It seems to us, in order to make sense of the provisions of section 28, and also to make as clear as can be possible the decision in *Warner v MPC* (supra), the draftsman of the Act intended that the prosecution should have the initial burden of proving that the defendant had, and knew that he had, in these circumstances the box in his control and also that the box contained something. That, in our judgment, establishes the necessary possession. They must also of course prove that the box in fact contained the drug alleged, in this case cannabis resin. If any of those matters are unproved, there is no case to go to the jury.

The speeches in *Warner v MPC* (supra) then seem to have qualified that comparatively simple concept by saying that the defendant has the burden thereafter to show or suggest that he had no right or opportunity to open the box or reason to doubt the legitimacy of the contents and that he believed the contents were different in kind, and not merely quality, than what they actually were.

To implement those considerations as they stood, and explain them so the jury can understand them, would have been a daunting task for a judge. Accordingly, in our view, it is to those matters that the words of section 28, and particularly section 28(3)(b)(i) are directed [His Lordship read the subsection (above, p **252**)]. Once the prosecution have proved that the defendant had control of the box, knew that he had control and knew that the box contained something which was in fact the drug alleged, the burden, in our judgment is cast upon him to bring himself within those provisions. Thus in our judgment the direction of the judge in the present case was correct.

Appeal dismissed

Questions

1. In *Lambert* [2001] 3 All ER 577, HL, Lord Hutton said that in his opinion the law was correctly stated by Lord Lane in *McNamara* 'save that the illuminating analysis of s 28 by Lord Justice General, Lord Rodger, in *Salmon v HM Advocate* 1999 JC 67 demonstrates that where a defendant advances the defence that he did not know that the bag or other container which he was carrying contained a controlled drug, and believed it contained a different type of article such as a video film, this defence arises under s 28(2) and not under s 28(3).'

Is not sub-s (3) in fact a qualification of the more general defence under sub-s (2)? If D is charged with being in possession of heroin and he proves that he believed on reasonable grounds that what he possessed was cannabis, would he not have a defence under sub-s (2) if sub-s (3) were not there? That the substance was heroin is a fact which the prosecution has to prove and D can prove that he neither knew nor suspected nor had reason to suspect its existence; but sub-s (3)(a) denies him a defence.

2. The court referred to Lord Pearce's proposition (above, p **247**) that a person would not be in possession of a thing if he believed that it was of 'a wholly different nature' from that which it was in fact. Was that proposition applied? What would have been the result of its application? Is the effect of the decision that we now have a simpler and more effective concept of possession under the 1971 Act?

See commentary on *McNamara* [1988] Crim LR 440 at 441 and *Lewis* (1988) 87 Cr App R 270, [1988] Crim LR 517, CA and commentary.

3. How would *Warner's* case (p **243**, above) be decided under the Misuse of Drugs Act 1971?

4. Section 8 of the Misuse of Drugs Act provides: 'A person commits an offence if, being the occupier or concerned in the management of premises, he knowingly permits or suffers any of the following activities to take place on those premises, that is to say . . . (d) administering or using a controlled drug which is unlawfully in any person's possession at or immediately before the time when it is administered or used.'

How would *Sweet v Parsley* now be decided?

5. In *Irving* [1970] Crim LR 642, CA, the accused was found in possession of a bottle which contained stomach pills and an amphetamine tablet. He said that the tablet had been prescribed for his wife and she must have put it in the bottle by accident when she was refilling it with stomach pills for his use and that he had no idea it was there. It was held the jury had been wrongly directed that, if he was knowingly in possession of the bottle, he was in possession of the contents; it was akin to the case where a drug is slipped into a person's pocket without his knowledge. In *Marriott* [1971] 1 All ER 595, [1971] 1 WLR 187, CA, the accused was convicted of being in possession of cannabis when he had a penknife with 0.03

grains of cannabis resin, representing at most one-thirtieth of a single cannabis cigarette, adhering to a broken blade. A direction that the accused was guilty if he knew he was in possession of the penknife, even if he did not know that there was foreign matter adhering to the knife, was held to be wrong. It was necessary at least to prove that he knew that there was some foreign matter adhering to the knife. The court thought it may be that no further mens rea was necessary—so that the accused would be guilty if he believed on reasonable grounds that the matter was tobacco or toffee—though, 'Perhaps the law does not go as far as that'. If the facts of *Irving* and *Marriott* were to recur after the Act came into force:

(a) Would it be for Irving to 'prove' (cf *Lambert*) that he did not know that the tablet was in the bottle or for the Crown to prove that he did know it was there?

(b) Would it be for Marriott to 'prove' that he did not know there was anything on the knife or for the Crown to prove that he did? If he had said that he knew there was something on the knife but thought it was toffee, where would the onus of proof lie?

8. ARTICLE 6 AND STRICT LIABILITY OFFENCES

Barnfather v London Borough of Islington Education Authority
[2003] EWHC 418, Queen's Bench Divisional Court

(Maurice Kay and Elias JJ)

The facts appear in the judgment.

Mr Justice Maurice Kay:

1. On 6 February 2002 the Appellant was convicted at Highbury Corner Magistrates' Court of an offence under section 444(1) of the Education Act 1996. She was fined £75 and ordered to pay prosecution costs of £50. Section 444(1) provides:

   'If a child of compulsory school age who is a registered pupil at a school fails to attend regularly at the school, his parent is guilty of an offence.'

… Counsel for the Appellant raised a preliminary issue as to whether the offence as prescribed by section 444(1) is compliant with the European Convention on Human Rights and Fundamental Freedoms (ECHR). The case for the Appellant was and is that section 444(1) is not ECHR compliant because it is a strict liability offence which does not require proof of any knowledge or fault on the part of the parent. The Crown Court ruled that the offence is ECHR compliant. However, the appeal to the Crown Court remains unresolved because of the present appeal to the Administrative Court by Case Stated in relation to the preliminary issue. The questions posed by the Case Stated for the opinion of this court are:

   '1. Is section 444(1) of the Education Act 1996 as interpreted by the higher courts prior to the enactment of the Human Rights Act 1998 compatible with the provisions of the European Convention on Human Rights?

   2. If not, can the section be reinterpreted compatibly with the Convention pursuant to section 3 of the Human Rights Act 1998 and, if so, how?'

…

7. The authorities prior to the coming into force of the Human Rights Act 1998 consistently demonstrated the strict liability imposed by section 444(1) and its predecessors.

…

The human rights issue.

11. In a nutshell, Mr. Owen's submission is that section 444(1) is not compliant with Article 6.2 of the ECHR. Although initially he was minded to contend that this court should read words into section 444(1) pursuant to section 3 of the Human Rights Act so as to render it compliant, he no longer pursues that approach and now seeks a declaration of incompatibility pursuant to section 4 . . .

Article 6.2

12. Article 6 is headed 'Right to a fair trial'. It is appropriate that I refer to Article 6.1 and 6.2. They are in the following terms:

> '1. In the determination of his civil rights and obligations or of any criminal charge against him, everyone is entitled to a fair and public hearing within a reasonable time by an independent and impartial tribunal established by law . . .
> 2. Everyone charged with a criminal offence shall be presumed innocent until proved guilty according to law.'

At fist sight it is not obvious how Article 6.2 might impact on the issue of a strict liability offence. Its subject matter appears to be procedural and evidential rather than substantive. It is therefore necessary to refer to the Strasbourg Jurisprudence upon which Mr. Owen bases his submissions.

The leading case is *Salabiaku v. France* (1988) 13 EHRR 379 [see above p **176**] . . . .

14. If counsel in the present case agree on one thing it is that the reasoning in *Salabiaku* is not always easy to follow. Mr. Owen submits that the reasoning enables a court to subject a strict liability offence to scrutiny to see whether it is confined 'within reasonable limits' on a proportionality basis. He founds this submission on the passage in paragraph 27 which observed that Contracting States may penalise 'a simple or objective factor as such, irrespective of whether it results from criminal intent or negligence', but only '*under certain conditions*'. He then refers to passages in paragraph 28 including the reference to Contracting States being required 'to remain within certain limits in this respect as regards criminal law'. Finally, he points to the later passage concerning the requirement that States 'confine them *within reasonable limits* which take into account the importance of what is at stake and maintain the rights of the Defendants'.

15. The next piece in Mr. Owen's jigsaw is *Hansen v. Denmark*, an admissibility decision of the European Court of Human Rights sitting on 16 March 2000 (application number 28971/95). Its context is the requirement for rest periods in relation to lorry drivers who are monitored by tachographs. The Danish courts had convicted a driver and also Mr. Hansen, the managing director of the company. The relevant statutory provision was that

> 'liability of a fine can be imposed on an employer for violation of . . . sections 7 and 8 (i) and (iii) when the driving was carried out in his interest, although the violation cannot be imputed to his intent or negligence.'

Mr. Hansen sought to rely on Article 6.2. The Court expressly adopted the passages in paragraphs 27 and 28 of the judgment in *Salabiaku*, in particular the references to 'under certain conditions' and 'within reasonable limits'. However, it concluded that the Danish law was 'well within the reasonable limits which take into account what is at stake'. The complaint was therefore held to be inadmissible. Nevertheless, Mr. Owen relies upon the decision as an example of the Strasbourg Court scrutinising a strict liability offence by reference to Article 6.2 and the 'reasonable limits test' set out in *Salabiaku*.

The diligent researches of counsel have not unearthed any subsequent case or leading text in which *Hansen* has been considered. *Salabiaku* has been considered in a number of cases including by the

House of Lords in *Lambert* (above) in which Lord Clyde, when dealing with Article 6.2 in the context of the burden imposed upon a defendant by section 28 of the Misuse of Drugs Act 1971, quoted extensively from *Salabiaku*....

16. On behalf of the Secretary of State, Mr. Lewis (supported by Mr. Auburn on behalf of Islington) submits that strict liability offences do not attract the application of Article 6.2 in the manner for which Mr. Owen contends. He further submits that the specific ingredients of an offence, including whether it is an offence which requires *mens rea* to be established or whether a particular defence should be available, are matters of substantive criminal law which is exclusively a matter for the Contracting State. If it does not prescribe *mens rea* for a particular offence, Article 6.2 simply does not arise. The presumption of innocence relates to proof of the elements of the offence. It does not require that elements which are not part of the offence be added to it. Nor does it require that certain defences must be made available. All this is a matter for the national legislature, subject to the possibility of the engagement of other Articles in the ECHR which may arise in some cases ... but do not arise in the present case where only Article 6.2 is relied upon.

Discussion

17. It is important to keep in mind the essential nature of the offence prescribed by section 444(1). Whilst it is fairly described as an offence of strict liability, it is not one built upon any reversal of the burden of proof. To obtain a conviction, a local authority must prove to the criminal standard (1) that the child is a registered pupil at a relevant school; (2) that he is of compulsory school age; (3) that he has failed to attend regularly; and (4) in a case where such an issue is raised, that the reason for absence was not with leave or by reason of his sickness or any unavoidable cause. I have previously referred to the restricted way in which this fourth requirement has been interpreted in the courts. A reverse burden does arise in relation to section 444(4) (walking distance and transport) and section 444(6) (children of no fixed abode) but nothing in this case turns on that. It follows that the case for the Claimant is not based on the most obvious concern of Article 6.2 which is the presumption of innocence.

18. In *Salabiaku* the Strasbourg Court emphasised the words 'proved guilty according to law' in Article 6.2 and held that the 'law' in question is not to be construed exclusively with reference to domestic law. However, the question is whether Article 6.2 provides a criterion against which the *substance* of a domestic offence can be scrutinised or whether it is confined to procedural matters and the way in which such an offence may be proved. I have no doubt that the issue in *Salabiaku* was of the latter rather than of the former kind. It related to the method of proof of the customs offence and the deployment of a presumption, akin to a reverse burden, in that regard. When, in paragraph 28, the Court referred to Article 6.2 requiring States to 'confine within reasonable limits' it did so specifically in relation to 'presumptions of fact or of law'. Likewise the reference to remaining 'within certain limits' earlier in that paragraph. Moreover, the passage in paragraph 27—

> ' "in principle, the Contracting States, may, *under certain conditions*, penalise a simple or objective fact as such, irrespective of whether it results from criminal intent or negligence"—
> does not seem to me to be alluding to conditions deriving from Article 6.2 which may impact on the substantive elements of an offence. Nor, in my judgment, does the passage in the speech of Lord Clyde in *Lambert*, ... adumbrate any wider ambit of Article 6.2.'

Mr. Lewis submits that this limitation of Article 6.2 to procedural and evidential matters is supported by recent cases in the Court of Appeal, Criminal Division. In *Daniel* [2002] EWCA Crim 959 there was a consideration of section 354(1)(b) of the Insolvency Act 1986 and the offence of concealing a debt, in relation to which there is a defence of 'no intention' on the basis of a reverse burden (section 354)....

24. In my judgment, for the reasons I have given, neither *Salabiaku* nor anything else relied upon by Mr. Owen in his formidable submissions provides a basis for holding section 444(1) to be incompatible with Article 6.2. Accordingly I would answer the first of the questions posed by the Case Stated in the affirmative and the second does not arise.

....

Mr Justice Elias:

34. I agree with Maurice Kay J that this application fails on the grounds that Article 6.2 does not impose any restrictions on the power of Parliament to create strict liability offences. It follows that the courts are not entitled to use Article 6.2 to import a defence into a strict liability offence where Parliament has not done so, nor can they make any declaration of incompatibility because of the absence of any such defence. On this fundamental ground this application must fail. However, partly in deference to the careful and attractive arguments advanced by Mr Owen Q.C for the claimant, and also because I have the misfortune to take a different view from Maurice Kay J as to whether section 444(1) of the Education Act 1996 would infringe Article 6.2 if that provision did permit strict liability offences to be reviewed, I have prepared a short judgment of my own. I gratefully adopt Maurice Kay J's account of the background to this appeal, and his recitation of the relevant statutory provisions. I will not repeat them here....

....

Article 6.2 and strict liability offences.

45. ...I do not think that *Salabiaku* –admittedly not an easy case to understand— establishes the principle for which Mr. Owen contends, for the reasons Maurice Kay J gives. I gratefully adopt his analysis of both that and the *Hansen* decisions. I accept, however, that one of the consequences of the courts not having this power is that it will sometimes be fortuitous whether a particular statute can be reviewed under Article 6 or not. It may be a matter of chance how a criminal provision is framed, and yet the power of the courts to intervene will depend on whether it can find a legitimate peg on which to hang Convention principles. For example, in *Salabiaku* itself the European Court of Human Rights was able to require a defence of what it described as 'force majeure' to qualify an apparently irrebuttable presumption that possession of certain contraband goods was sufficient to establish guilt to a charge of smuggling, precisely because it was formulated as a presumption. However, as Mr Owen submits, if he is wrong in his submissions then it means that they could not have questioned an offence which simply made possession in the airport of certain contraband goods itself an offence. I also accept that the logic of rejecting Mr Owen's arguments is that a state's laws are subject to fuller review when they include a defence which places the burden on the defence than they are when no defence at all is conferred.

46. However, it seems to me that this inevitably follows simply from the principle that the purpose of Article 6 is to ensure that a trial is conducted fairly. I recognise, as Mr Owen points out, that the Convention jurisprudence has developed certain principles of procedural fairness, such as the right to silence and the privilege against self incrimination, which are not to be found in terms in Article 6 itself. However, they do not touch in any way the substance of the laws which a state has imposed. Strasbourg has no power to question the substance of the laws unless they contravene some specific

Convention Article. In my judgment the courts should be slow to extend the control over the content of the laws by a creative construction of Article 6....

49. It follows that in my view Mr Owen is contending for a principle which would infringe the integrity of the Convention jurisprudence. There is much to be said for such a principle, and something very akin to it has been developed by the common law, but I have doubts whether it could properly be brought within the scope of Article 6, even recognising that the Convention is a living instrument whose interpretation may change over time. In any event, it is not for this court to make such a singular leap from procedure to substance, and I resist the enticing overtures of Mr Owen to do so....

50. I turn briefly to consider the issue of justification.... The relevant question, however, is whether it is proportionate to that objective to impose criminal liability without fault, or, indeed, without even any knowledge that the child is not attending school. Does the plainly desirable social policy of securing school attendance justify the imposition of (admittedly small) criminal penalties, even on the parent who has done his or her honest best and taken reasonable steps to achieve that objective? In this context I make the obvious but nevertheless relevant observation that the parent is being made liable for the failure of a third party— the child- who has a mind of his or her own capable of frustrating the best of parental endeavours. Whilst it is not strictly accurate to describe this as a 'vicarious' liability, as Mr Owen contends, since the child is not in breach of any duty cast directly on him or her, nonetheless it must be recognised that liability is being imposed for failing to achieve a result which simply cannot in some cases be secured.

51. The alleged justification for imposing such liability as explained by Ms. Scales [of the Education Dept], is as follows:

> 'The offence is simple and relatively easy to prove.... This straightforward, easily provable offence, with limited penal consequences, is considered to be a useful tool within the local education authority armoury to assist them in making parents face up to and discharge their responsibilities and enforcing the parental duty to ensure that children receive full time education.'

52. I do not consider that this meets the burden of proving justification. No doubt it is convenient for the prosecution to have an easily provable offence. That is always the case, but it is hardly a justification for doing away with mens rea. The premise in this part of the argument is that the lack of mens rea must be justified, and the benefits to the prosecutor cannot conceivably constitute such justification otherwise that safeguard could always be overridden. In any event, in my opinion any problems of proof could in large part be dealt with by imposing a reverse burden on the parent to require him or her to demonstrate what steps had been taken and to satisfy the court that they were reasonable.

53. Nor in my view is it enough simply to assert that the existence of a strict liability offence is a useful tool for the authorities. It is far from self evident that it will be. Indeed, it may be thought positively to discourage parents who need encouragement from taking responsibility for their children for them to know that they may be taken to court even if they do all they can to secure the child's school attendance. I would have expected some indication, for example, of the circumstances in which it might be thought proper to prosecute a parent under section 444(1) rather than using section 444(1A), and why it is considered that this would help to achieve the objective of securing attendance. Does this assumption rely on anything more than impression, or perhaps anecdotal information?

54. Mr. Lewis for the Secretary of State strongly contended that it was relevant in assessing the justification for these provisions to analyse them in context. He referred to various features of the

legislation which he submitted demonstrates that prosecutions were carefully controlled. For example, the relevant guidance ensures that in practice parents will be informed that their child is not attending ... Only the local education authority may institute a prosecution (s.446). Moreover, before doing so it must consider the option of applying for an education supervision order with respect to the child (s.447). The effect of this order is to place the child's education under the supervision of the designated local education authority. Exceptionally, if the child is beyond parental control, the authority can seek a care order from the courts so as to take the child away from the home environment altogether.

55. I do not consider that these arguments advance Mr. Lewis' case. Indeed, they come very close to a submission that in fact there will be no prosecution unless there is fault on behalf of a defendant. It seems to me to be no answer to a charge that these provisions are not justified or are unfair to say that the education authority controls the prosecution and can ensure that there is only a prosecution in an appropriate case. Will it in general be an appropriate case only if the authority considers that there is fault? If so, then it means that the authority instead of a court will be deciding as a matter of executive discretion whether there is fault. No doubt that is highly convenient to the prosecution, but it is constitutionally unacceptable to permit the executive to make that decision. That is precisely what Article 6 is trying to avoid. Conversely, if an appropriate case can include cases where the parents are not at fault, notwithstanding the battery of safeguards identified by Mr Lewis, then it is necessary to ask what such exceptional prosecutions will achieve. The fact that the prosecution of blameless persons will be rare or that there are other routes for achieving the objectives of the statute seem to me to point strongly against the need for the legislation at all rather than in support of it. Furthermore, it is of no benefit to an innocent parent successfully prosecuted to be told that he or she is something of a rare specimen.

56. Moreover, it must be remembered that where a prosecution is now brought under section 444(1A), the court can convict as an alternative under section 444(1). Accordingly, even if the education authority had a general policy of seeking to prosecute only those whom it considered to be at fault in some way, liability under section 444(1) would no doubt frequently be established if the defendant successfully resisted the liability based on fault.

57. I recognise that the penalties are small, being only a fine, and that is a factor which can properly be considered when determining whether an offence of strict liability is justified. However, in my opinion there is nonetheless a real stigma attached to being found guilty of a criminal offence of this nature. It suggests either an indifference to one's children, or incompetence at parenting, which in the case of the blameless parent will be unwarranted. It is worthy of note that in *Crump* and the later case of *Bath and Somerset District Council v Warman* [1999] ELR 81 which followed it, the Divisional Courts in both cases recommended to the magistrates that they might think it proper to give an absolute discharge. That seems to me to be consistent with the view that justice is not served by prosecuting the innocent. If they ought not to be prosecuted, neither in my view ought there to be legislation permitting them to be. I bear in mind that the courts should pay due regard to the fact that Parliament has chosen to adopt legislation of this nature. However, the onus is on the Secretary of State to satisfy the court that the provision is justifiable. Had we been able to question section 444(1) under Article 6.2, I would have held that he has failed to discharge that burden. The strict liability offence is disproportionate to the objective to be achieved.

58. In the event, however, this appeal fails on the grounds that Article 6 does not entitle the courts to question the justification for strict liability offences.

B. Fitzpatrick, 'Strict Liability and Article 6(2) of the European Convention on Human Rights: School Non-Attendance Offence'
[2004] 68 J Crim L 11

... Two questions arguably remain. The first asks, as a matter of principle, whether the purported dichotomy between procedure and substance is quite so clear. Substantive questions of strict liability are, on one view, also procedural questions about (the lack of a requirement of) proof. Where the net result concerns the liability of a defendant, there is arguably not a great moral difference between the situation where that liability arises as a result of the manner in which the substantive elements of an offence are configured and the situation in which the defendant's liability is determined by a procedural rule which places a burden upon him or her. As the court in the present case acknowledges, the procedure/substance dichotomy can have two problematic consequences: first, the arbitrariness of the distinction can lead to the arbitrary availability of an avenue of review under Article 6; secondly, through sufficiently careful drafting, a legislature could avoid all possibility of Article 6 review, by framing all potentially reviewable matters squarely within the parameters of substance, rather than procedure.

The second question asks whether, as a matter of practice, it will always be possible to distinguish between a situation in which a statute is reviewable on a procedural basis from one in which it is non-reviewable as a matter of substance. Consider the offence in the Sexual Offences Act 2003 of rape of a child under 13 (s. 5). That offence will require proof of the fact of sexual intercourse and of the age of the child. If that were all there were to it, then the provision would appear to be non-reviewable using Article 6, on the basis that it raises only matters of substance. However, it is equally arguable that the offence of 'rape' necessarily implies a lack of consent, and that that lack of consent is presumed in cases where the victim is under 13. If the latter analysis is preferred, then the provision may be reviewable under Article 6, following *Salabiaku*. It might also be suggested that if it is susceptible to review as a matter of law, then it is only a matter of time before it is challenged, on the basis that it imposes strict liability for a very serious offence, and arguably does not 'take into account the importance of what is at stake [or] maintain the rights of the defence' (*Salabiaku*).

Cf P. Roberts, 'The Presumption of Innocence Brought Home? Kebilene Deconstructed' [2002] 118 LQR 41, 50: 'Article 6(2) has no bearing on the reduction or elimination of mens rea requirements, and is therefore perfectly compatible with offences of strict or even absolute liability.'

9. CRIMINAL LIABILITY WITHOUT AN ACT

The cases so far considered in this chapter all involved the commission of an act by the defendant. But Parliament can do anything and has occasionally enacted that a person may be liable because something happens to him in certain circumstances—that is, he 'is found' in a particular situation.

R v Larsonneur

(1933) 24 Cr App R 74, Court of Criminal Appeal

(Lord Hewart CJ, Avory and Humphreys JJ)

On 14 March 1933, the appellant, who was a French citizen, landed at Folkestone with a French passport, which was endorsed 'Leave to land granted at Folkestone this day on condition that the holder does not enter any employment, paid or unpaid, while in the

United Kingdom.' On 22 March 1933, the condition was varied by the following endorsement signed by an Under-Secretary of State: 'The condition attached to the grant of leave to land is hereby varied so as to require departure from the United Kingdom not later than the 22nd March 1933.'

The appellant went on that day to the Irish Free State. This did not count as a departure from the United Kingdom for the purposes of the order. An order for her deportation therefrom was made by the executive authorities of that country, and on 20 April she was brought to Holyhead in the custody of the Irish Free State police. There she was handed over to the Holyhead police and detained by them until the arrival of a police officer from London. On the following day she was taken to London in custody, and on 22 April she was charged before a police magistrate there.

At the trial, on a charge under Article 18(1)(b) of the Aliens Order 1920 (below) the jury returned a verdict of 'Guilty through circumstances beyond her own control', and the Chairman passed a sentence of three days' imprisonment and made an order recommending the appellant for deportation.

By the Aliens Order 1920, Article 1(3): 'Leave shall not be given to an alien to land in the United Kingdom unless he complies with the following conditions, that is to say . . . (g) he has not been prohibited from landing by the Secretary of State.'

By Article 1(4), as amended by SR & O No 326 of 1923, and No 715 of 1931: '. . . an alien who is found in the United Kingdom at any time after the expiration of the period limited by any such condition shall for the purposes of this Order be deemed to be an alien to whom leave to land has been refused . . .'

By Article 18(1)(b), as amended by SR & O No 326 of 1923: 'If any alien, having landed in the United Kingdom in contravention of art 1 of this Order, is at any time found within the United Kingdom, he shall be guilty of an offence against this Order.'

The judgment of the court was delivered by:

Lord Hewart CJ: In fact, the appellant went to the Irish Free State and afterwards, in circumstances which are perfectly immaterial, so far as this appeal is concerned, came back, to Holyhead. She was at Holyhead on 21 April 1933, a date after the day limited by the condition on her passport.

In these circumstances, it seems to be quite clear that art 1(4) of the Aliens Order 1920 (as amended by the Orders of 1923 and 1931), applies. . . . The appellant was, therefore, on 21 April 1933, in the position in which she would have been if she had been prohibited from landing by the Secretary of State and, that being so, there is no reason to interfere with the finding of the jury. She was found here and was, therefore, deemed to be in the class of persons whose landing had been prohibited by the Secretary of State, by reason of the fact that she had violated the condition on her passport. The appeal, therefore, is dismissed and the recommendation for deportation remains.

Appeal dismissed

Questions

1. Did the offence consist in 'being found' or in 'landing and being found'? If the latter, was the court justified in saying that the circumstances in which Larsonneur came back to Holyhead were 'perfectly immaterial'? 'Being found' may not require a voluntary act on the part of the accused, but is that also true of 'landing'?

2. *Larsonneur* no longer stands alone. In *Winzar v Chief Constable of Kent* (1983) The Times, 28 March, D was taken to hospital on a stretcher but was found to be drunk and told to leave.

When he was seen slumped on a seat in the corridor the police were called and they took him to a police car parked in the hospital forecourt on W Road and drove him to the police station. He was convicted of being found drunk in a highway, W Road, and his conviction was upheld by the Divisional Court. 'Found drunk' meant perceived to be drunk. It was enough that he was present in a highway and there perceived to be drunk. 'Perceive' means to become aware of. Did the police become aware of D's state in the highway? Or in the hospital or its forecourt?

3. *Larsonneur* has been generally condemned by the writers but it is defended by D. J. Lanham [1976] Crim LR 276. He considers why the accused should have been denied the 'most readily acceptable' of all defences, physical compulsion.

Clear though compulsion may be as a defence it is, unlike infancy, not an absolute defence. It may, at least with regard to certain types of crime, be defeated If the defendant has been at fault in bringing about the situation which has exposed him to compulsion. An authority for this proposition is the Australian case *O'Sullivan v Fisher* ([1954] SASR 33) D was in effect charged with being found drunk in a public place. He had been forced from private premises into a public place by police officers. Reed J accepted that the offence charged was strict in the sense that it was not necessary to prove that D intended to get drunk or to be in the public place. The learned judge ruled however that compulsion was capable of being a defence. His Honour considered three types of case:

    (a) where the defendant was forced into the public place by unlawful force;
    (b) where the defendant was arrested and taken into the public place;
    (c) where the defendant was ejected from the private place by lawful force.

In the first two cases the judge thought that compulsion would be a defence. In the third case compulsion would provide no excuse.

The first and third cases are clear. If a man gets drunk in his own house and is kidnapped by terrorists and taken into the street there can be no possible justification for denying him the defence of compulsion. If a man trespasses in his neighbour's house and drinks himself silly he cannot plead compulsion if his neighbour lawfully decants him into the street. Case (b) however may need qualification. If the defendant is drunk in his own house and is unexpectedly arrested there by the police and is taken into the street he should have the defence whether he is guilty of the crime for which the arrest is made or not. But if the defendant is on the run from the police and gets himself drunk on private premises when his arrest is imminent, he should not be able to rely on the defence.

Though Reed J did not express himself in these terms it is suggested that the principle which emerges from the case of *O'Sullivan v Fisher* is that in cases of strict liability a person can rely on the defence of compulsion unless he has culpably brought about the situation in which the compulsion was used. He will, for example, lose the defence if the compulsion was reasonably foreseeable.

[Having examined the evidence in the case, Professor Lanham concludes that Larsonneur brought upon herself the act of compulsion which led to her being charged.]

No one could claim that *Larsonneur* stood as a shining example of English jurisprudence. But it can hardly be regarded as the last word in judicial depravity. If Miss Larsonneur had been dragged kicking and screaming from France into the United Kingdom by kidnappers and the same judgment had been given by the Court of Criminal Appeal, the defence of unforeseeable compulsion would truly have been excluded and the case would be the worst blot on the pages of the modern criminal law. But she wasn't and it wasn't and it isn't.

See also Rakesh C. Doegar [1998] Crim LR 791, response at [1999] Crim LR 100, and correspondence at [1999] Crim LR 684.

10. STRICT LIABILITY: PROS AND CONS

Barbara Wootton, *Crime and the Criminal Law*
(1963)

Nothing has dealt so devastating a blow at the punitive conception of the criminal process as the proliferation of offences of strict liability; and the alarm has forthwith been raised. Thus Dr J Ll J Edwards has expressed the fear that there is a real danger that the 'widespread practice of imposing criminal liability independent of any moral fault' will result in the criminal law being regarded with contempt. 'The process of basing criminal liability upon a theory of absolute prohibition', he writes, 'may well have the opposite effect to that intended and lead to a weakening of respect for the law' [Edwards, J Ll J, *Mens Rea in Statutory Offences* (Macmillan, 1955) p 247]. Nor, in his view, is it an adequate answer to say that absolute liability can be tolerated because of the comparative unimportance of the offences to which it is applied and because, as a rule, only a monetary penalty is involved; for, in the first place, there are a number of important exceptions to this rule (drunken driving for example); and, secondly, as Dr Edwards himself points out, in certain cases the penalty imposed by the court may be the least part of the punishment. A merchant's conviction for a minor trading offence may have a disastrous effect upon his business.

Such dislike of strict liability is not by any means confined to academic lawyers. In the courts, too, various devices have been used to smuggle mens rea back into offences from which, on the face of it, it would appear to be excluded. To the lawyer's ingenious mind the invention of such devices naturally presents no difficulty. Criminal liability, for instance, can attach only to voluntary acts. If a driver is struck unconscious with an epileptic seizure, it can be argued that he is not responsible for any consequences because his driving thereafter is involuntary: indeed he has been said not to be driving at all. If on the other hand he falls asleep, this defence will not serve since sleep is a condition that comes on gradually, and a driver has an opportunity and a duty to stop before it overpowers him. Alternatively, recourse can be had to the circular argument that anyone who commits a forbidden act must have intended to commit it and must, therefore, have formed a guilty intention. As Lord Devlin puts it, the word 'knowingly' or 'wilfully' can be read into acts in which it is not present; although as his Lordship points out this subterfuge is open to the criticism that it fails to distinguish between the physical act itself and the circumstances in which this becomes a crime [Devlin, Lord, *Samples of Law Making* (OUP, 1962) pp 71–80, p **228**, above]. All that the accused may have intended was to perform an action (such as firing a gun or driving a car) which is not in itself criminal. Again, in yet other cases such as those in which it is forbidden to permit or to allow something to be done the concept of negligence can do duty as a watered down version of mens rea for how can anyone be blamed for permitting something about which he could not have known?

All these devices, it cannot be too strongly emphasised, are necessitated by the need to preserve the essentially punitive function of the criminal law. For it is not, as Dr Edwards fears, the criminal law which will be brought into contempt by the multiplication of offences of strict liability, so much as this particular conception of the law's function. If that function is conceived less in terms of punishment than as a mechanism of prevention these fears become irrelevant. Such a conception, however, apparently sticks in the throat of even the most progressive lawyers. Even Professor Hart, in his Hobhouse lecture on *Punishment and the Elimination of Responsibility* [Hart, HLA, *Punishment and the Elimination of Responsibility* (Athlone Press, 1962) pp 27, 28] seems to be incurably obsessed with the notion of punishment, which haunts his text as well as figuring in his title. Although rejecting many traditional theories, such as that punishment should be 'retributive' or 'denunciatory', he nevertheless seems wholly unable to envisage a system in which sentence is not automatically equated with 'punishment'. Thus he writes of 'values quite distinct from those of retributive punishment which the system of responsibility does maintain, and which remain of great importance even if our aims in *punishing* are the forward-looking aims of social protection'; and again 'even if we *punish* men not as wicked but as nuisances ...' while he makes many references to the principle that liability to punishment must depend on a voluntary act. Perhaps it requires the naïveté of an amateur to suggest that the forward-looking aims of social protection might, on occasion, have absolutely no connection with punishment.

If, however, the primary function of the courts is conceived as the prevention of forbidden acts, there is little cause to be disturbed by the multiplication of offences of strict liability. If the law says that certain things are not to be done, it is illogical to confine this prohibition to occasions on which they are done from malice aforethought; for at least the material consequences of an action, and the reasons for prohibiting it, are the same whether it is the result of sinister malicious plotting, of negligence or of sheer accident. A man is equally dead and his relatives equally bereaved whether he was stabbed or run over by a drunken motorist or by an incompetent one; and the inconvenience caused by the loss of your bicycle is unaffected by the question whether or no the youth who removed it had the intention of putting it back, if in fact he had not done so at the time of his arrest. It is true, of course, as Professor Hart has argued [op cit, pp 29, 30], that the material consequences of an action by no means exhaust its effects. 'If one person hits another, the person struck does not think of the other as *just* a cause of pain to him ... If the blow was light but deliberate, it has a significance for the person struck quite different from an accidental much heavier blow.' To ignore this difference, he argues, is to outrage 'distinctions which not only underlie morality, but pervade the whole of our social life'. That these distinctions are widely appreciated and keenly felt no one would deny. Often perhaps they derive their force from a purely punitive or retributive attitude; but alternatively they may be held to be relevant to an assessment of the social damage that results from a criminal act. Just as a heavy blow does more damage than a light one, so also perhaps does a blow which involves psychological injury do more damage than one in which the hurt is purely physical.

The conclusion to which this argument leads is, I think, not that the presence or absence of the guilty mind is unimportant, but that mens rea has, so to speak—and this is the crux of the matter— *got into the wrong place*. Traditionally, the requirement of the guilty mind is written into the actual definition of a crime. No guilty intention, no crime, is the rule. Obviously this makes sense if the law's concern is with wickedness: where there is no guilty intention, there can be no wickedness. But it is equally obvious, on the other hand, that an action does not become innocuous merely because whoever performed it meant no harm. If the object of the criminal law is to prevent the occurrence of socially damaging actions, it would be absurd to turn a blind eye to those which were due to carelessness, negligence or even accident. The question of motivation is *in the first instance* irrelevant.

But only in the first instance. At a later stage, that is to say, after what is now known as a conviction, the presence or absence of guilty intention is all-important for its effect on the appropriate measures to be taken to prevent a recurrence of the forbidden act. The prevention of accidental deaths presents different problems from those involved in the prevention of wilful murders. The results of the actions of the careless, the mistaken, the wicked and the merely unfortunate may be indistinguishable from one another, but each case calls for a different treatment. Tradition, however, is very strong, and the notion that these differences are relevant only after the fact has been established that the accused committed the forbidden act seems still to be deeply abhorrent to the legal mind. Thus Lord Devlin, discussing the possibility that judges might have taken the line that all 'unintentional' criminals might be dealt with simply by the imposition of a nominal penalty, regards this as the 'negation of law'. 'It would' [Devlin, Lord, *Samples of Law Making* (OUP, 1962) p 73], he says, 'confuse the function of mercy which the judge is dispensing when imposing the penalty with the function of justice. It would have been to deny to the citizen due process of law because it would have been to say to him, in effect: "Although we cannot think that Parliament intended you to be punished in this case because you have really done nothing wrong, come to us, ask for mercy, and we shall grant mercy".... In all criminal matters the citizen is entitled to the protection of the law … and the mitigation of penalty should not be adopted as the prime method of dealing with accidental offenders.'

Within its own implied terms of reference the logic is unexceptionable. If the purpose of the law is to dispense punishment tempered with mercy, then to use mercy as a consolation for unjust punishment is certainly to give a stone for bread. But these are not the implied terms of reference of strict liability. In the case of offences of strict liability the presumption is not that those who have committed forbidden actions must be punished, but that appropriate steps must be taken to prevent the occurrence of such actions.

J. C. Smith, 'Responsibility in Criminal Law', in Barbara Wootton, *Essays in Her Honour* (eds Bean and Whynes, 1986), 141, at p 149

Judging the intentions of others

The law relating to responsibility, Lady Wootton rightly says, 'presumes an ability to make judgments about other men's intentions and the degree of their iniquity, the validity of which cannot ever be objectively demonstrated' (Wootton 1981: 64). It is certainly true that the doctrine of *mens rea* does presume this ability. If the presumption is baseless the doctrine is a sham and should be abolished as soon as possible. It should not be accepted that it is baseless, however, because its validity cannot be 'objectively demonstrated', in the way that the rules of science may be demonstrated in a laboratory. We can often be as certain that a man had a particular state of mind as we can be certain of anything. Does any rational being doubt that armed men who enter a bank and demand money at gunpoint intend to steal, that they dishonestly intend to appropriate property belonging to the bank and permanently to deprive the bank of it? That a man who lies in wait for a girl in a dark lane, knocks her down, and has sexual intercourse with her, intends to have sexual intercourse with her without her consent? That a man who applies a loaded shotgun to another's knee and pulls the trigger intends to cause grievous bodily harm? In such cases we can be just as certain that the defendant had the intention as that he did the act. That, indeed, is what the law requires. The judge tells the jury that they must be convinced not only that the defendant did the act, but that he did it with *mens rea*. Evidence is always admissible to challenge the inference and, if it casts doubt on even the most overwhelming inference of *mens rea*, the defendant is entitled to be acquitted.

Moreover, Lady Wootton herself assumes that these matters would be taken into account at the sentencing stage. 'The prevention of accidental death presents different problems from those involved in the prevention of wilful murders' (1981: 48). But it is no easier to answer the question at the one stage than the other. While we retain our present procedures it will be the magistrates who will have to answer the question at whatever point it arises. In the Crown Court it becomes a question of whether the matters which really determine the fate of the defendant are to be decided by the judge or by the jury. It would not be appropriate here to attempt to assess the relative virtues of the judge and jury in matters of fact-finding; but there would certainly be grave disquiet in many quarters if the jury were relegated to the role of answering only the question, 'Did he do it?.

No doubt there is a greater difficulty in answering the second point: can we properly assess the degree of iniquity? We can, however, assess reasonably objectively the gravity of the harm caused; and, if the defendant chose to cause that harm, or to take a risk of causing it, this seems to afford a reasonable measure by which to assess 'iniquity'. This assumes that the defendant could and did choose.

[Having discussed *Tolson*, above, p **217**, and *Ball* (1966) 50 Cr App R 266.] This brings me to what I regard as the major difficulty in Lady Wootton's theory. It is essentially a practical one. The only question for the court of trial is to be 'Did he do it?' Whether he did it intentionally, recklessly, negligently, or by sheer accident is irrelevant. In any event the person who did it is to be passed on to the 'sentencer' who will consider what should be done to ensure that he does not do it again. Now if the court of trial has to disregard the question of fault, so too surely do the police and the prosecuting authority (or whatever takes its place). If we allow the police or prosecutor to decide to proceed or not on the basis of whether or not the defendant was at fault, we do indirectly what we will not permit to be done directly. We allow the crucial decision which is now made formally and openly on proper evidence in court to be made informally, privately, and on whatever evidence the prosecutor, in his wisdom, or lack of it, considers relevant. The logic of the system requires the prosecution of *all* cases because even if the forbidden result has resulted from 'sheer accident', the sentencer is under a duty to consider whether there is anything to be done to ensure that the 'offender' does not have such accidents again. Everyone who causes an injury to another person, everyone who damages another's property, could, and should, be brought to court. Every buyer or seller of goods who makes an innocent misrepresentation, every bona-fide purchaser of goods in fact stolen, the surgeon whose patient dies on the operating table, the Good Samaritan who innocently gives help to a person escaping after committing an arrestable offence—all these have brought about the harm which it is the object of the law to prevent; so they should be subject to process of law so as to ensure that they do not cause the harm again. The business of the courts would be enormously multiplied. And to what purpose? What is to be done with all those who (like Ball and Mrs Tolson) have behaved reasonably and have had the misfortune to cause the forbidden result by sheer accident—except to tell them to continue to behave reasonably?

It is reasonably safe to assume that what would in fact happen is that, however illogically, the fault test would be applied at the police or prosecution stage. This would be prompted, not only by the natural sense of justice of those operating the system, but also by their realization of the futility of invoking legal process against one who has behaved entirely reasonably.

A further practical difficulty is that the system would put enormous discretion into the hands of the sentencer. He would apparently have the same power in law over one who caused death accidentally as over a murderer. It is difficult to believe that such a large discretion would be tolerable. It would dilute, if not destroy, the criminal law as a moral force and that at a time when the decline of religious belief has, as Lady Wootton herself says, created a dangerous vacuum. The shift from punishment to prevention may be intended to remove the moral basis of the law; but if, as some believe, one of the major reasons why people do not commit crimes is the sense of guilt which attaches to them, should not the aim be to enhance the sense of guilt rather than otherwise? To remove the element of fault is to empty the law of moral content. If murder were, in law, no different from accidental death, should we be so inhibited from committing murder as most of us are?

11. NO STOPPING AT THE 'HALFWAY HOUSE'?

Many common law countries have developed a so-called 'halfway house' between strict liability and a full mens rea requirement. It takes various forms but, in general, the effect is that the prosecution has to prove the commission of the actus reus but then the onus shifts to the defendant to prove, on the balance of probabilities, that he did not have mens rea and was not negligent. Sometimes it does not go so far but imposes a merely evidential burden on the defendant. See, for example, *R v City of Sault Ste Marie* (1978) 85 DLR 3d 161, where the Canadian Supreme Court acknowledged a defence for the defendant to 'avoid liability by proving that he took all reasonable care. This involves consideration of what a reasonable man would have done in the circumstances. The defence would be available if the accused reasonably believed in a mistaken set of facts which, if true, would render the act or omission innocent, or if he took all reasonable steps to avoid the particular event' (p 181).

Lord Cooke, a distinguished New Zealand judge who sees merit in the halfway-house noted in his Hamlyn lectures (see p 251 above, and Devlin J, p 228, above. See also: G. Orchard, 'The Defence of Absence of Fault in Australasia and Canada' in P. Smith, (ed) *Essays in Honour of J. C. Smith* (1987)). that the doctrine had made no headway in England. Subsequently the theory was rejected in *B (a minor) v DPP* and not referred to in *K*. It seems that it has no future in England unless included in the statute in question.

Hostility to statutory reverse onuses, following the enactment of the Human Rights Act 1998 (cf *Lambert*, above, p 254) makes it even less likely that the courts will depart from the *Woolmington* principle unless statute requires, and the European Convention permits, them to do so. See the discussion in Ch 6 above, p 175.

12. DUE DILIGENCE DEFENCES

It is common for the drastic effect of a statute imposing strict liability to be mitigated by the provision of a statutory 'due diligence' defence. Such defences usually impose on the defendant a burden of proving both that he had no mens rea and that he took all reasonable precautions and exercised all due diligence to avoid the commission of an offence. Thus one who sells feeding stuffs containing deleterious ingredients is liable even if he proves that the commission of the offence was due to a mistake or an accident or some other cause beyond his control unless he also proves that he took all reasonable precautions, etc: Agriculture Act 1970, ss 73 and 82. See too Weights and Measures Act 1985, s 34; Trade Descriptions Act 1968, s 24. The effect of such provisions is that the prosecution need do no more than prove that the accused did the prohibited act and it is then for him to establish, if he can, that he did it innocently. Such provisions are a distinct advance on unmitigated strict liability; but they are still a deviation from the fundamental principle that the prosecution must prove the whole of their case. See for discussion, D. Parry, 'Judicial Approaches to Due Diligence' [1995] Crim LR 695.

13. REFORM

It seems clear that the presumption requires mens rea in respect of every element in the actus reus and it is assumed above that this means either intention or recklessness with respect to each element. If that is right, we may now have reached the position stated in the Draft Criminal Code Bill, cl 20:

(1) Every offence requires a fault element of recklessness with respect to each of its elements other than fault elements, unless otherwise provided.

(2) Subsection 1 does not apply to pre-Code offences....

The recklessness referred to is *Cunningham*, not *Caldwell*, recklessness.

The Law Commission considered a suggestion that the presumption in favour of mens rea should be displaceable only by an *express* provision requiring some fault other than recklessness, or stating that no fault is required. But, said the Commission, 'We do not think that this would be appropriate. We are mindful of the "constitutional platitude" pointed out by

Lord Ackner in *Hunt* [1987] AC 352 at 380, that the courts must give effect to what Parliament has provided not only "expressly" but also by "necessary implication". If the terms of a future enactment creating an offence plainly implied an intention to displace the presumption created by clause 20(1), the courts would no doubt feel obliged to give effect to that intention even if the present clause were to require express provision for the purpose.'

A word of caution is necessary because the terms 'mens rea' and 'strict liability' have no universally recognized meaning in law. For example Lord Bingham in *K* says (para [18]) that the description of the offence under s 14(1) of the Sexual Offences Act 1956 of indecent assault on a child under 16 as an offence of strict liability before the decision in *K* was a misnomer because 'There always had to be such deliberation in the conduct of the defendant as would be necessary to prove an assault.' But the 'assault' in an indecent assault on a consenting child under 16 is, as pointed out in the commentary on the decision of the Court of Appeal, [2001] Crim LR at 135–136, pure fiction. So this amounts to saying that, if an offence requires proof of a voluntary act, it is not one of strict liability. The only offences of strict liability would be situational offences, like 'being found' in certain circumstances. Is this a helpful concept of strict liability or (if the converse is mens rea) of mens rea? Compare the opinion of Lord Edmund-Davies, above, p 215. Which view is to be preferred?

FURTHER READING

P. Brett, 'Strict Responsibility: Possible solutions' (1974) 37 MLR 417

J. Horder, 'Strict Liability, Statutory Construction and the Spirit of Liberty' (2002) 118 LQR 458

L. H. Leigh, *Strict and Vicarious Liability* (1982)

9
Parties to offences

1. INTRODUCTION

The person who does the forbidden act is not necessarily the only one who is liable to be convicted of the crime thereby committed. Suppose that Dawn visits Peter, a 'contract killer', and tells him that she wants him to kill her husband, Victor. Dawn is now liable to conviction for inciting Peter to commit murder. Incitement to commit a crime is itself a crime, committed as soon as the act of incitement is done. It would make no difference if Peter said he would have nothing to do with the proposal; the offence of incitement consists in the act of incitement. If Peter agrees to commit the murder, the pair of them are guilty of conspiracy to murder. Conspiracy to commit a crime is another distinct offence, committed as soon as the agreement is made. It would make no difference to liability to conviction of conspiracy (though it would affect the sentence) that, immediately afterwards, they thought better of it and decided to abandon the plan.

If Peter goes ahead and kills Victor he is guilty of murder. So is Dawn. She may be miles away at the time but she is equally responsible in law with Peter for Peter's act. Suppose that Peter has taken into his confidence two friends, Carl, who lent him a gun with which to shoot Victor, and Eric who drove him to Peter's house and kept watch outside while Peter did the deed inside. Carl and Eric are also guilty of the murder of Victor. Dawn, Peter, Carl and Eric are all equally liable to be convicted of murder and liable to the same punishment—which, for murder, must be life imprisonment. Peter who actually did the deed is called the principal and the others are described as secondary parties or accessories. In the case of crimes other than murder, where the judge has a discretion in imposing sentence, the permissible maximum is the same for all; but sentences may vary according to the responsibility of each party. The principal is not necessarily the most blameworthy. An accessory may be the 'mastermind' and the dominant personality.

There may be more than one principal. If D1 and D2 attack V, intending to murder him, and the combined effect of their blows is to kill him, both are guilty of murder as principals. Consider whether Gibbins in *Gibbins v Proctor*, above, p **105**, was a joint principal or an accessory.

In this chapter we are concerned to examine the nature and extent of secondary participation in a crime. As the above example shows, secondary participation is closely inter-related with incitement and conspiracy; but as they are distinct crimes they are separately considered, along with the crime of attempt with which they are closely associated, in Chapters 13–15. There may be secondary participation in incitement, conspiracy and attempt as in other crimes.

(1) THE DERIVATIVE NATURE OF SECONDARY LIABILITY

The distinctive feature of secondary liability is that, subject to the principle in *Millward*, below, p **276**, it is derivative; the liability of Dawn, Carl and Eric derives from that of Peter. See D. Lanham, 'Primary and Derivative Criminal Liability: An Australian Perspective' [2000] Crim LR 707.

When Peter points the gun at Victor, Dawn, Carl and Eric have done everything necessary to become murderers, but whether they do so depends on whether Peter pulls the trigger. If he changes his mind at the last moment, of course, none of them would be guilty of murder, for no murder has been committed. The liability of the secondary party derives from the *guilt* of the principal, not from his *conviction*. If, after killing Victor, Peter kills himself, or goes abroad and is never heard of again, Dawn, Carl and Eric may still be convicted of the murder Peter committed. If, at their trial, it is proved that the absent Peter committed the murder and that they played the parts described, Peter's absence and the fact that he is unconvicted are immaterial. Where the alleged principal has been convicted, his conviction is, since s 74 of PACE 1984 came into force, admissible evidence on the trial of an alleged accessory to prove that he committed the offence. If, when the conviction is admitted in evidence, the defendant denies that the offence was committed, he must prove it on a balance of probabilities. Where the alleged principal has not been convicted, the prosecution must prove by other evidence and beyond reasonable doubt that he did commit the crime.

These are the rules of the common law. Over the centuries, a wide variety of verbs were used by the courts and by Parliament to describe the acts which amount to secondary participation but in modern times they have been generally, though not invariably, limited to four, 'aid, abet, counsel or procure'. The rules of secondary participation apply automatically to every offence unless expressly or impliedly excluded. When Parliament creates a new offence it does not usually provide that anyone who aids, abets, counsels or procures it will be guilty. There is no need to do so. The common law rule is now embodied in statute law.

Accessories and Abettors Act 1861

8. Abettors in misdemeanours
Whosoever shall aid, abet, counsel, or procure the commission of any indictable offence, whether the same be an offence at common law or by virtue of any Act passed or to be passed, shall be liable to be tried, indicted, and punished as a principal offender.

Magistrates' Courts Act 1980

44. Aiders and abettors
(1) A person who aids, abets, counsels or procures the commission by another person of a summary offence shall be guilty of the like offence and may be tried (whether or not he is charged as a principal) either by a court having jurisdiction to try that other person or by a court having by virtue of his own offence jurisdiction to try him.

(2) Any offence consisting in aiding, abetting, counselling or procuring the commission of an offence triable either way (other than an offence Listed in Schedule 1 to this Act) shall by virtue of this sub-section be triable either way.

2. PRINCIPALS, INNOCENT AGENTS AND ACCESSORIES

Notwithstanding the above provisions of the Accessories and Abettors Act and the Magistrates' Courts Act, it is sometimes necessary to distinguish between the principal and secondary parties:

(i) in the case of all offences of strict liability for, even in these cases, secondary parties must be proved to have mens rea;

(ii) in all cases where the offence is so defined that it can be committed as a principal in the first degree only by a member of a specified class (for example, the holder of a justices' licence);

(iii) where vicarious liability is in issue. In some offences vicarious liability may be imposed for the act of another who is a principal or does the act of a principal; but there is no vicarious liability for the act of a secondary party.

Where there are several participants in a crime we define the principal as the participant 'whose act is the most immediate cause of the actus reus'. It may be that the *person* whose act is the most immediate cause of the actus reus is not a participant in the crime at all. For example D and E prepare a letter bomb addressed to V and D posts it. The letter passes through several hands in the Post Office and is put through V's letterbox by F, an unsuspecting postman. V opens it and is injured or killed. F's act is the most immediate cause of the killing but F is not a participant in the crime. Obviously D is the principal. F and the other Post Office employees who handled the letter are described as 'innocent agents'.

See P. Alldridge, 'The Doctrine of Innocent Agency' (1990) 2 Criminal Law Forum 45; G. Williams, 'Innocent Agency and Causation' (1992) Criminal Law Forum 289.

The Draft Code, cl 26(1)(c) identifies three categories of innocent agents. It provides that a person is guilty as a principal if he procures, assists or encourages the relevant act:

by another who is not himself guilty of the offence because:
  (i) he is under ten years of age; or
  (ii) he does the act or acts without the fault required for the offence; or
  (iii) he has a defence.

Our postman falls into category (ii). A man who persuaded a nine-year-old child to smother a baby would be an example of category (i); and a man (D) who compelled another (X) by threats of death to wound a third person (Y) would be an example of (iii). If charged with wounding, X would have the defence of duress. If Y died of his wounds and D and X were charged with murder, X would now be the alleged principal and D the alleged accessory because duress is not a defence to murder.

(1) COMPLICITY AND CAUSATION

Suppose that Dawn hires Peter to beat up Victor and Peter does so. Section 18 of the Offences Against the Person Act 1861 provides that:

Whosoever shall unlawfully and maliciously... cause any grievous bodily harm to any person... with intent... to do some grievous bodily harm to any person...

shall be liable to imprisonment for life. Peter has committed this offence as a principal and Dawn who counselled and procured him to do so is liable as a secondary party. But why is not Dawn a principal? Has she not *caused* grievous bodily harm to Victor with intent—the very thing which the statute forbids? The beating up occurred only because she hired Peter to do it. In a very real sense Dawn did cause gbh to Victor; but in law she is not regarded as having caused the harm. The intervening voluntary act by Peter breaks the chain of causation. If this were not so, the legal distinction between principals and secondary parties would break down because in many, though not all, cases of secondary liability the secondary party, like Dawn in the example, *in fact* is a cause of the actus reus.

When the Code Team agreed on what is now cl 17(1) of the Draft Code:

... a person causes a result which is an element of an offence when:
   (a) he does an act which makes a more than negligible contribution to its occurrence...

and cl 54—

A person is guilty of murder if he causes the death of another:
   (a) intending to cause death...

they realized that, if they stopped there, Dawn who procured Peter to commit murder would herself be a principal murderer. So, in order to preserve the distinction between principal and accessory, they added a sub-s (3) to cl 17:

A person who procures, assists or encourages another to cause a result that is an element of an offence does not himself cause that result so as to be guilty of the offence as a principal except when:
   (a) section 26(1) applies...

Cf G. Williams, 'Finis for Novus Actus' [1989] CLJ 391. It is an unexpressed assumption on which the law of accessories depends. So when Dawn procures Peter to kill or cause gbh in the above examples, she has not committed the criminal offence herself but has procured Peter to do so and is liable not as a principal but as an accessory.

The Court of Appeal has, in a series of recent cases, seemingly undermined this principle. In *Finlay* [2003] EWCA Crim 3868 and *Kennedy No 2* [2005] EWCA Crim 685 the Court of Appeal held that where D hands V a syringe and V self-injects, the jury are entitled to find that they are jointly engaged in the offence of administering heroin. It is submitted that the decision ought to be read in its specific and very narrow context. D had handed to the deceased 'for immediate injection' and D was found by the jury to have been 'engaged' in the administration. It would be premature to apply the case beyond this narrow bound by suggesting for example that by supplying the gun to P (a sane adult acting of his own volition) for him to execute V, D becomes a murderer rather than an accessory to murder.

(2) CAUSATION THROUGH AN INNOCENT AGENT

Clause 17(3) makes an exception where s 26(1) applies. That sub-section applies to the cases of innocent agency, noted above, p 274. So if Dawn procures a nine-year-old, or the postman (who acts without the fault required for the offence), or an insane person (who has a defence) to do the act which kills or causes gbh, she causes the harm in law as well as in fact and is liable accordingly as the principal. Once the causation point is satisfied, she fits the definition of the offence. She has herself done what the law forbids. But it is not every offence which can be committed through an agent. Consider bigamy. A, knowing that

B's wife is alive, tells B that she is dead and persuades him to marry C. B has committed the actus reus of bigamy ('being married, marries') but is not guilty of that offence because he lacks mens rea. A has knowingly procured the commission of the actus reus but is it possible to say that he has himself committed it? He may be a bachelor but, whether he is or not, can it be said that he has 'married'? Is bigamy—except in the case of a proxy marriage—a crime which is capable of commission through an innocent agent? Consider the following case.

R v Millward

[1994] Crim LR 527, Court of Appeal

(McCowan LJ, Scott Baker and Blofeld JJ)

H and M were charged with causing death by reckless driving. H was the driver and M was charged as an aider, abettor, counsellor or procurer. The alleged recklessness was not in the manner of the driving but in taking the vehicle, a tractor with a defective towing mechanism, on the road. The trailer became detached and collided with an oncoming vehicle, causing death. The jury acquitted H and convicted M who appealed, arguing that the actus reus of the offence was never committed.

McCowan LJ. We have been referred to a number of authorities.... The first is the case of *Thornton v Mitchell* [1940] 1 All ER 339. In that case a bus driver was charged with driving without due care and attention and driving without reasonable consideration for other road users contrary to section 12 of the Road Traffic Act 1930. The conductor was charged with aiding and abetting the offences. The bus had to be reversed. It was the duty of the conductor to signal to the driver that the road was clear, because the driver could not see. The conductor erroneously signalled that it was clear. Unfortunately, two pedestrians were knocked down and the injuries to one of them proved fatal. The driver of the bus was acquitted of the two charges against him, but the conductor was convicted. It was held that the conductor could not be convicted of aiding and abetting the principal in what the principal was not doing. He could not be convicted as a principal because, on the particular wording of section 12, only the driver could be guilty of the principal offence.

It seems to us that the ratio of this case is that the driver did not commit the *actus reus* of the offence of careless driving. He had driven with due care and attention. He had relied on the conductor's signals.

The second case is *R v Millar* [1970] 2 QB 54 (below, p **344**).... That case does not take matters a great deal further so far as this appeal is concerned, because the driver of the vehicle was also convicted. It is the case of *R v Cogan and Leak* [1975] 2 All ER 109, [1976] QB 217 that, in the view of this court, provides the greatest assistance as regards this appeal. In that case, Cogan was charged with the rape of Leak's wife. Leak was charged with aiding and abetting, counselling and procuring Cogan to commit the rape. Both men were convicted. The material facts can be summarised as follows. Leak took Cogan back to his house and told his wife that Cogan wanted to have sexual intercourse with her and he was going to see that she did. Leak's wife was unwilling but frightened of Leak. She did have intercourse with Cogan and did not struggle, although she was sobbing throughout the whole incident. Leak's statement amounted to a confession that he had procured Cogan to have sexual intercourse with his wife. Cogan was convicted upon the basis that although he genuinely believed that Leak's wife was consenting, he had no reasonable grounds for that belief. On the state of the law as perceived at that time, Cogan was, on that basis, guilty of rape. But between the trial and the appeal the case of *R v Morgan* (above, p **181**) was decided by the House of Lords. In *Morgan* it was held that the all important matter was the defendant's genuine belief, and not whether there were reasonable grounds for it. Cogan's conviction was therefore quashed and Leak contended that his conviction could not stand following Cogan's acquittal.

Certain passages in that authority are of importance. Lawton LJ, giving the judgment of the court, said at 223 C:

> 'Her ravishment had come about because Leak had wanted it to happen and had taken action to see that it did by persuading Cogan to use his body as the instrument for the necessary physical act. In the language of the law the act of sexual intercourse without the wife's consent was the actus reus: it had been procured by Leak who had the appropriate mens rea, namely, his intention that Cogan should have sexual intercourse with her without her consent. In our judgment it is irrelevant that the man whom Leak had procured to do the physical act himself did not intend to have sexual intercourse with the wife without her consent. Leak was using him as a means to procure a criminal purpose.
>
> Before 1861 a case such as this, pleaded as it was in the indictment, might have presented a court with problems arising from the old distinction between principals and accessories in felony. Most of the old law was swept away by section 8 of the Accessories and Abettors Act 1861 and what remained by section 1 of the Criminal Law Act 1967. The modern law allowed Leak to be tried and punished as a principal offender. In our judgment he could have been indicted as a principal offender. It would have been no defence for him to submit that if Cogan was an "innocent" agent, he was necessarily in the old terminology of the law a principal in the first degree, which was a legal impossibility as a man cannot rape his own wife during cohabitation. [See now, below, p **728**.] The law no longer concerned itself with niceties of degrees in participation in crime; but even if it did Leak would still be guilty. The reason a man cannot by his own physical act rape his wife during cohabitation is because the law presumes consent from the marriage ceremony...'

The law on that has since changed.

> 'Had Leak been indicted as a principal offender, the case against him would have been clear beyond argument. Should he be allowed to go free because he was charged with "being aider and abettor to the same offence"? If we are right in our opinion that the wife had been raped (and no one outside a court of law would say that she had not been), then the particulars of offence accurately stated what Leak had done, namely, he had procured Cogan to commit the offence. This would suffice to uphold the conviction. We would prefer, however, to uphold it on a wider basis. In our judgment convictions should not be upset because of mere technicalities of pleading in an indictment. Leak knew what the case against him was and the facts in support of that case were proved. But for the fact that the jury thought that Cogan in his intoxicated condition might have mistaken the wife's sobs and distress for expressions of her consent, no question of any kind would have arisen about the form of pleading. By his written statement Leak virtually admitted what he had done. As Judge Chapman said in *R v Humphreys* [1965] 3 All ER 689, 692: "It would be anomalous if a person who admitted to a substantial part in the perpetration of a misdemeanour as aider and abettor could not be convicted on his own admission merely because the person alleged to have been aided and abetted was not or could not be convicted." In the circumstances of this case it would be more than anomalous: it would be an affront to justice and to the common sense of ordinary folk. It was for these reasons that we dismissed the appeal against conviction.'

In our judgment, what is of particular relevance in this case, as emerges from the case of *Cogan and Leak*, is whether the actus reus has been committed by the principal offender. In the present case Hodgson, the co-defendant, was acquitted because he lacked, in the view of the jury, the necessary element of mens rea.

Mr MacDonald [for the appellant] seeks to distinguish *Cogan and Leak* on two grounds. In the first place, he says that in this area of the law each case has to be decided and dealt with upon its own facts. Secondly, he says that *Cogan* was in reality a case of aiding and abetting rather than of procuring. He contends that this is an important distinction. He says too that in that case Leak was present and that he could not, in such circumstances, have been convicted in his absence. In our view, whilst there may in many cases be an overlap between aiding and abetting, on the one hand, and counselling or procuring on the other, we do not think that that is of any significance in this case. Essentially, it would seem to us, the case of *Cogan and Leak* was a case of procuring, as indeed is the present case. In this court's view, it is impossible to find any significant distinction between the case of *Cogan and Leak* and the present case.

Support is to be found in *Blackstone's Criminal Practice* 3rd edn 1993, p 69 where the author says, having made earlier reference to *Cogan and Leak*:

> 'There is some debate over the precise principle involved in these cases but everyone agrees that the result is just. To say that the liability is really that of a principal acting through an innocent agent can cause problems where the accused lacks some characteristic essential for liability as a principal, for example, if in *Cogan* it had been a woman, rather than Mrs Leak's husband, who had terrorised her into submitting to intercourse. The definition of rape in the Sexual Offences Act 1956, s 1, requires it to be committed by a man, whereas there is no problem in convicting a person as accessory to an offence which he or she cannot commit as a principal (see *Ram* (1893) 17 Cox CC 609, woman as accessory to rape). Thus it is probably preferable to adopt the principle that an accessory can be liable provided that there is the actus reus of the principal offence even if the principal offender is entitled to be acquitted because of some defence personal to himself.
>
> It may well be, however, that this principle is limited to cases where the accessory has procured the *actus reus* (ie, has caused it to be committed as in the case of *Bourne* and *Cogan*). This would also be consistent with the position stated above that procuring does not mean a common intention between the accessory and the principal, whereas other forms of aiding and abetting generally do. If the principal lacks the *mens rea* of the offence there can hardly be a common intention that it should be committed. But this is not required for procuring.'

In our view, that passage from Blackstone correctly sets out the law. It is necessary to refer briefly to one further authority. That is the case of *R v Calhaem* [below, p **292**] . . .

[McCowan LJ quoted from the judgment and continued:]

> Then this sentence appears:
>
> > 'Of course, the law is that the offence must have been committed before anyone can be convicted as an abettor or counsellor of it.'

We do not think that too much should be read into those words of Parker LJ in that case. In the first place, what the case was concerned with was causal connection. But it may well be that what he was in reality saying was that before anyone can be convicted as abettor or counsellor, the actus reus of the offence must be committed. In any event, the earlier decision in *Cogan and Leak* does not appear to have been referred to, or considered at all, by the court in *Calhaem*.

In this court's view, it is the authority of *Cogan and Leak* that is relevant to the decision that we have to make. In this court's view, the actus reus in the present case was the taking of the vehicle in the defective condition on to the road so as to cause the death of the little boy. It was procured by this appellant. The requisite mens rea was, in our judgment, present on the jury's finding. The appellant caused Hodgson to drive that vehicle in that condition just as Leak had caused Cogan to have sexual intercourse with his wife.

Appeal dismissed

The principle in *Millward* can apply only where there has been an actus reus. Causing death by reckless driving, which was the offence in issue in that case, has since been replaced by the offence of causing death by dangerous driving. The actus reus of the new offence is more precisely defined (above, p **169**) and it includes the situation where 'it would be obvious to a competent and careful driver that driving the vehicle in its current state would be dangerous.' In *Loukes* [1996] 1 Cr App R 444, [1996] Crim LR 341, the propellor shaft of a tipper truck broke while it was being driven on a motorway, causing the truck to crash into a car and kill its driver. The judge directed the jury to acquit the driver of causing death by dangerous driving: there was no evidence on which a jury could find that it would have been obvious to a competent and careful driver that driving the vehicle in its current state would be dangerous. The judge directed that the appellant, L, who was responsible for the maintenance of the vehicle could be guilty as a secondary party to the offence. His conviction was quashed: there was no actus reus, so he could not be held to have procured one. *Was* the mere taking of the defective vehicle on to the road in *Millward* the actus reus of reckless driving? See commentary on *Loukes* [1996] 1 Cr App R 444, [1996] Crim LR 341.

Millward had already been followed in *Wheelhouse* [1994] Crim LR 756 where P and W were charged with burglary by stealing a car from V's garage. P took the car and it was alleged that W procured him to do so. The jury acquitted P, probably because they thought that W may have persuaded P that the car belonged to him, and convicted W. W's appeal was dismissed. But was it necessary to invoke the controversial decision in *Millward*? It is ancient law that burglary may be committed by an innocent agent. Hale (1736) I PC 55, wrote:

If A, being a man of full age take a child of seven or eight years old well instructed by him in this villainous art, as some such there be, and the child goes in at the window, takes goods out and delivers them to A who carries them away, this is burglary in A, tho the child, that made the entry, be not guilty by reason of his infancy.

So if the wife in the presence of her husband by his threats or coercion breaks and enters the house of B in the night, this is burglary in the husband, tho the wife, that is the immediate actor, is excused by the coercion of the husband.

In *DPP v K & B* [1997] 1 Cr App R 36, [1997] Crim LR 121, DC, two girls, K aged 14 and B aged 11 (but responsible because *doli capax*, that is, they knew that what they were doing was seriously wrong, as the law then required), procured an unidentified boy, X, who was not younger than 10, but may have been under 14, and may have been *doli incapax*, to have sexual intercourse with a girl, W, aged 14, without her consent. It was held, following *Millward*, that K and B were guilty of rape, even if X, being *doli incapax*, was not. 'The actus reus was proved. The respondents procured the situation which included the actus reus.'

It is necessary to invoke the *Millward* principle only where the crime is one which is incapable of being committed by an innocent agent, like rape, bigamy or a driving offence. The problem has been much discussed since *Bourne* (1952) 36 Cr App R 125, CCA, where a man was held guilty of aiding and abetting his wife to commit buggery with a dog, although she could not have been convicted because she was acting under duress by him. Cross (68 LQR 354) argued that the decision was in accordance with principle because 'The wife committed the "actus reus" with the "mens rea" required by the definition of the crime in question and the husband participated in that "mens rea"'. The wife had mens rea because she knew exactly what she was doing. That would not explain *Cogan and Leak* where Cogan may have believed that Mrs Leak was consenting to the sexual intercourse, in which case he committed the actus reus without mens rea. Lawton LJ gave two reasons:

(i) That Leak might have been convicted as a principal; but everything that Leak did could have been done by a woman and it would be nonsense to say that a woman could be guilty of rape (which requires penile penetration) as a principal.

(ii) That Leak had procured the *crime of rape* (cf Glanville Williams, TBCL, 371–372)—
      'no one outside a court of law would say that Mrs Leak had not been [raped]'
      (above, p 276), but Lawton LJ was *in* a court of law.

It would take a bold person to tell Mrs Leak that she had not been raped; but, if Cogan thought
she was consenting, she had not been raped by him—any more than your bike has been stolen
if it has gone for ever from the place where you left it, taken in good faith by X, who owns an
exactly similar model and thought yours was his. You think your bicycle has been stolen, but
you are wrong. However, rightly or wrongly, the second reason given by the court in *Cogan and
Leak* was that Leak had procured not merely the actus reus, but the offence, of rape by Cogan.
Was either ratio decidendi of *Cogan and Leak*—(i) L was a principal, or (ii) L procured the
commission of *the offence*—applicable to *Millward*? The theory (advanced in every edition of
Smith and Hogan, that procuring the actus reus of an offence is the offence, is criticized by
Kadish (*Essays in Criminal Law*, 180) saying that it 'at least technically…amounts to creating
a new crime.' The Law Commission (*Assisting and Encouraging Crime*, Consultation Paper No
131, para 4.207), writing before *Millward*, are also sceptical:

'A prime danger of such a rule is that, in its anxiety to meet cases of the type just discussed
(including *Bourne* and *Cogan and Leak*) it will reach too far.'

Is the principle of *Millward* limited to procurers, as distinct from aiders, abettors and coun-
sellors—who assist or encourage but do not, by their own acts, *cause*, the commission of the
offence by another? X, a married man, believes on reasonable grounds that his wife, Y, is dead.
D knows she is alive. He persuades X to marry Z. E and F also know that Y is alive. E acts as best
man at the wedding and F gives the bride away. Are D, E and F guilty of bigamy? Or only D?

(3) SEMI-INNOCENT AGENTS

R v Burke and Clarkson
[1987] 1 All ER 771, House of Lords

(Lord Hailsham LC, Lords Bridge, Brandon, Griffiths and Mackay)

Burke shot a criminal on the doorstep of Botton's house. The prosecution alleged that he did
this at the request of Clarkson who was anxious to prevent Botton from giving evidence against
him. Clarkson's defence was that he had nothing to do with the shooting. Burke's defence was
that he had agreed to shoot Botton only out of fear of Clarkson; but that in the event the gun
went off accidentally and the killing was unintentional and therefore only manslaughter. Both
were convicted of murder. The judge directed that if Burke was guilty only of manslaughter
and not murder, then Clarkson could be found guilty at worst of manslaughter. On appeal,
Burke argued, inter alia, that this was a misdirection and that it may have induced the jury
to return a perverse verdict against him simply to ensure that they could convict of murder
Clarkson whom they believed to be the real villain. The appeal was dismissed by the Court
of Appeal. The second question certified for the House of Lords was 'can one who incites or
procures by duress another to kill or be a party to a killing be convicted of murder if that other
is acquitted by reason of duress?' (Other aspects of this case are considered below, p 416.)

[**Lords Hailsham, Bridge, Brandon** and **Griffiths** dismissed the appeal.]

Lord Mackay. I turn now to the second certified question. In the view that I take on the first question the second question does not properly arise. However, I am of opinion that the Court of Appeal
reached the correct conclusion on it as a matter of principle.

Giving the judgment of the Court of Appeal Lord Lane CJ said ([1986] 1 All ER 833 at 839–840, [1986] QB 626 at 641–652):

'The judge based himself on a decision of this court in *R v Richards (Isabelle)* [1973] 3 All ER1088, [1974] QB 776. The facts in that case were that Mrs Richards paid two men to inflict injuries on her husband which she intended should "put him in hospital for a month". The two men wounded the husband but not seriously. They were acquitted of wounding with intent but convicted of unlawful wounding. Mrs Richards herself was convicted of wounding with intent, the jury plainly, and not surprisingly, believing that she had the necessary intent, though the two men had not. She appealed against her conviction on the ground that she could not properly be convicted as accessory before the fact to a crime more serious than that committed by the principals in the first degree. The appeal was allowed and the conviction for unlawful wounding was substituted. The court followed a passage from *Hawkins's Pleas of the Crown* (2 Hawk PC (8th edn) p442): "I take it to be an uncontroverted rule that [the offence of the accessory can never rise higher than that of the principal]; it seeming incongruous and absurd that he who is punished only as a partaker of the guilt of another, should be adjudged guilty of a higher crime than the other." James LJ, delivering the judgment in *R v Richards* [1973] 3 All ER 1088 at 1092, [1974] QB 776 at 780, had this to say: "If there is only one offence committed, and that is the offence of unlawful wounding, then the person who has requested that offence to be committed, or advised that that offence be committed, cannot be guilty of a graver offence than that in fact which was committed." The decision in *R v Richards* has been the subject of some criticism (see for example Smith and Hogan *Criminal Law* (5th edn, 1983) p140). Counsel before us posed the situation where A hands a gun to D informing him that it is loaded with blank ammunition only and telling him to go and scare X by discharging it. The ammunition is in fact live (as A knows) and X is killed. D is convicted only of manslaughter, as he might be on those facts. It would seem absurd that A should thereby escape conviction for murder. We take the view that *R v Richards* was incorrectly decided, but it seems to us that it cannot properly be distinguished from the instant case.'

I consider that the reasoning of Lord Lane CJ is entirely correct and I would affirm his view that, where a person has been killed and that result is the result intended by another participant, the mere fact that the actual killer may be convicted only of the reduced charge of manslaughter for some reason special to himself does not, in my opinion, in any way result in a compulsory reduction for the other participant.

Notes and questions

1. The House had decided that duress could never be a defence to murder so the question certified could not arise. If duress were a defence to murder, the supposed killer would be guilty of no offence and it seems perfectly obvious that the duressor would be guilty of murder through an innocent agent.

2. Question 2 did not raise the question posed by *Richards* and by Burke's defence (above) but Lord Mackay, probably obiter, affirmed the Court of Appeal's opinion on that issue. Probably everyone will agree with the court's example of the loaded gun. But how can this be justified in theory in view of the derivative nature of secondary liability? Professor Kadish's solution (*Essays in Criminal Law*, 183) is that in such a case A can properly be said to have caused X's death because D's actions are not 'fully voluntary': because of D's ignorance of a material fact, he was not fully aware of what he was doing or its consequences. The general rule—that one who aids, abets, counsels or procures another to commit an actus reus is not regarded as causing it (above, pp 274–275)—is displaced. Glanville Williams (TBCL, 373) would describe E as a semi-innocent agent—'he is an innocent agent in respect of part of the responsibility of the secondary party.' Is not the effect of Kadish's theory that there are two offences of homicide, two principals and no

secondary party? A has caused death with intent to kill—murder; D has caused death with intent to frighten—manslaughter (at worst). It is not then the case, which Hawkins found incongruous and absurd, of the guilt of the accessory rising higher than that of the principal (cf the similar problem in joint enterprise cases, below, p 324).

3. Kadish however thinks *Richards* was rightly decided: 'she could not be blamed for an assault that did not take place... an actual assault took place (and Mrs Richards is liable for it) but an aggravated assault did not take place.... It did not take place because those committing the assault did not intend to commit grievous bodily harm.' Do you agree? Certainly, if A incites B to assault V whom A, but not B, believes to be a constable on duty and B does assault V (who is not a constable on duty) it is clear that A is not guilty of the aggravated assault: the aggravated assault did not take place—there was no actus reus for it. *Richards* is not so easy because the actus reus of the aggravated assault did take place—it was wounding, which is the same for both s 18 and s 20. Is it significant that the actions of the two men in *Richards* were 'fully voluntary'? They knew perfectly well what they were doing.

4. D sends a letter bomb through the post to V. E, the postman, notices wires sticking out of the envelope and is aware that letter-bombs have been sent recently by terrorists with fatal results. He thinks, 'This could be a letter-bomb—but I'm in a hurry—I'll risk it' and pushes the envelope through V's letterbox. It explodes and kills V. If E is guilty of manslaughter, can D be convicted of murder? Are the postman's actions 'fully voluntary'? Is he a 'semi-innocent' agent?

3. ACCESSORIES

(1) AIDING, ABETTING, COUNSELLING OR PROCURING

Attorney-General's Reference (No 1 of 1975)
[1975] 2 All ER 684, Court of Appeal, Criminal Division

(Lord Widgery CJ, Bristow and May JJ)

The facts appear in the question for the court.

[**Lord Widgery CJ** delivered the following judgment of the court:]

This case comes before the court on a reference from the Attorney General under s 36 of the Criminal Justice Act 1972, and by his reference he asks the following question:

> 'Whether an accused who surreptitiously laced a friend's drinks with double measures of spirits when he knew that his friend would shortly be driving his car home, and in consequence his friend drove with an excess quantity of alcohol in his body and was convicted of the offence under the Road Traffic Act 1972, s 6(1) is entitled to a ruling of no case to answer on being later charged as an aider and abettor, counsellor and procurer, on the ground that there was no shared intention between the two, that the accused did not by accompanying him or otherwise positively encourage the friend to drive, or on any other ground.'

The language in the section which determines whether a 'secondary party', as he is sometimes called, is guilty of a criminal offence committed by another embraces the four words 'aid, abet, counsel or procure'. The origin of those words is to be found in s 8 of the Accessories and Abettors Act 1861 which provides:

> 'Whosoever shall aid, abet, counsel, or procure the commission of any misdemeanor, whether the same be a misdemeanor at common law or by virtue of any Act passed or to be passed, shall be liable to be tried, indicted, and punished as a principal offender.'

Thus, in the past, when the distinction was still drawn between felony and misdemeanor, it was sufficient to make a person guilty of a misdemeanor if he aided, abetted, counselled or procured the offence of another. When the difference between felonies and misdemeanors was abolished in 1967, s1 of the Criminal Law Act 1967 in effect provided that the same test should apply to make a secondary party guilty either of treason or felony.

Of course it is the fact that in the great majority of instances where a secondary party is sought to be convicted of an offence there has been a contact between the principal offender and the secondary party. Aiding and abetting almost inevitably involves a situation in which the secondary party and the main offender are together at some stage discussing the plans which they may be making in respect of the alleged offence, and are in contact so that each knows what is passing through the mind of the other.

In the same way it seems to us that a person who counsels the commission of a crime by another, almost inevitably comes to a moment when he is in contact with that other, when he is discussing the offence with that other and when, to use the words of the statute, he counsels the other to commit the offence.

The fact that so often the relationship between the secondary party and the principal will be such that there is a meeting of minds between them caused the trial judge in the case from which this reference is derived to think that this was really an essential feature of proving or establishing the guilt of the secondary party and, as we understand his judgment, he took the view that in the absence of some sort of meeting of minds, some sort of mental link between the secondary party and the principal, there could be no aiding, abetting or counselling of the offence within the meaning of the section.

So far as aiding, abetting and counselling is concerned we would go a long way with that conclusion. It may very well be, as I said a moment ago, difficult to think of a case of aiding, abetting or counselling when the parties have not met and have not discussed in some respects the terms of the offence which they have in mind. But we do not see why a similar principle should apply to procuring. We approach s8 of the 1861 Act on the basis that the words should be given their ordinary meaning, if possible. We approach the section on the basis also that if four words are employed here, 'aid, abet, counsel or procure', the probability is that there is a difference between each of those four words and the other three, because, if there were no such difference, then Parliament would be wasting time in using four words where two or three would do. Thus, in deciding whether that which is assumed to be done under our reference was a criminal offence we approach the section on the footing that each word must be given its ordinary meaning.

To procure means to produce by endeavour. You procure a thing by setting out to see that it happens and taking the appropriate steps to produce that happening. We think that there are plenty of instances in which a person may be said to procure the commission of a crime by another even though there is no sort of conspiracy between the two, even though there is no attempt at agreement or discussion as to the form which the offence should take. In our judgment the offence described in this reference is such a case.

If one looks back at the facts of the reference: the accused surreptitiously laced his friend's drink. This is an important element and, although we are not going to decide today anything other than the problem posed to us, it may well be that in similar cases where the lacing of the drink or the introduction of the extra alcohol is known to the driver quite different considerations may apply. We say that because where the driver has no knowledge of what is happening, in most instances he would have no means of preventing the offence from being committed. If the driver is unaware of what has happened, he will not be taking precautions. He will get into his car seat, switch on the ignition and drive home and, consequently, the conception of another procuring the commission of the offence by the driver is very much stronger where the driver is innocent of all knowledge of what is happening, as in the present case where the lacing of the drink was surreptitious.

The second thing which is important in the facts set out in our reference is that following and in consequence of the introduction of the extra alcohol, the friend drove with an excess quantity of alcohol in his blood. Causation here is important. You cannot procure an offence unless there is a causal link between what you do and the commission of the offence, and here we are told that in consequence of the addition of this alcohol the driver, when he drove home, drove with an excess quantity of alcohol in his body.

Giving the words their ordinary meaning in English, and asking oneself whether in those circumstances the offence has been procured, we are in no doubt that the answer is that it has. It has been procured because, unknown to the driver and without his collaboration, he has been put in a position in which in fact he has committed an offence which he never would have committed otherwise. We think that there was a case to answer and that the trial judge should have directed the jury that an offence is committed if it is shown beyond reasonable doubt that the accused knew that his friend was going to drive, and also knew that the ordinary and natural result of the additional alcohol added to the friend's drink would be to bring him above the recognised limit of 80 milligrammes per 100 millilitres of blood.

It was suggested to us that, if we held that there may be a procuring on the facts of the present case, it would be but a short step to a similar finding for the generous host, with somewhat bibulous friends, when at the end of the day his friends leave him to go to their own homes in circumstances in which they are not fit to drive and in circumstances in which an offence under the Road Traffic Act 1972 is committed. The suggestion has been made that the host may in those circumstances be guilty with his guests on the basis that he has either aided, abetted, counselled or procured the offence.

The first point to notice in regard to the generous host is that that is not a case in which the alcohol is being put surreptitiously into the glass of the driver. That is a case in which the driver knows perfectly well how much he has to drink and where to a large extent it is perfectly right and proper to leave him to make his own decision.

Furthermore, we would say that if such a case arises, the basis on which the case will be put against the host is, we think, bound to be on the footing that he has supplied the tool with which the offence is committed. This of course is a reference back to such cases as those where oxy-acetylene equipment was bought by a man knowing it was to be used by another for a criminal offence [*Bainbridge*, p **292**, below]. There is ample and clear authority as to the extent to which supplying the tools for the commission of an offence may amount to aiding and abetting for present purposes.

Accordingly, so far as the generous host type of case is concerned we are not concerned at the possibility that difficulties will be created, as long as it is borne in mind that in those circumstances the matter must be approached in accordance with well-known authority governing the provision of the tools for the commission of an offence, and never forgetting that the introduction of the alcohol is not there surreptitious, and that consequently the case for saying that the offence was procured by the supplier of the alcohol is very much more difficult.

Our decision on the reference is that the question posed by the Attorney-General should be answered in the negative.

Determination accordingly

Bryce

[2004] EWCA Crim 1231, [2004] 2 Cr App R 592, [2004] Crim LR 936, Court of Criminal Appeal, Criminal Division

(Potter LJ, Hooper and Astill JJ)

D was convicted of murder as an aider and abettor. In the course of a drug dealers' dispute D assisted X, who was acting on the orders of another, Black, by transporting X and a gun to a caravan near V's home so that X could carry out the murder. 12 hours after D had left X at the scene, he shot V with the gun. D assisted in disposing of evidence after the killing. D's appeal was focused on the issue of causation—that what D did was too remote in time and place to the killing and that at that stage when D assisted, X had not yet formed the intention to commit any criminal offence.

Potter LJ:

[72] So far as causation is concerned..., in order to establish the liability of a secondary party, the precise extent to which it is necessary to prove a causative link between the act of assistance alleged against the secondary party and the substantive crime committed by the perpetrator is by no means clearly established in our criminal law. In the case of one charged with 'procuring' an offence, it is clear that a causal link must indeed be demonstrated. In *Attorney General's Reference (No. 1 of 1975)* [1975] QB 773, [1975] 2 All ER 684 the court stated at 780B

> 'You cannot procure an offence unless there is a causal link between what you do and the commission of the offence.'

Further, in no less an authority than Stephen's Digest (4th ed) Art 39, it is stated that, not only one who procures but one who 'counsels' or 'commands' is liable, and by implication only liable, when the crime committed by the perpetrator

> '...is committed in consequence of such counselling, procuring, or commandment.'

[73] It has been held that 'counselling' need not be the cause of the commission of the offence in the sense of showing that, without such counselling, the offence would not have been committed: see *A-G v Able* [1984] QB 795, [1984] 1 All ER 277 at 812. It has also been held that proffered advice or encouragement which has no effect on the mind of the perpetrator is not counselling: *R v Clarkson* [1971] 3 All ER 344, [1971] 1 WLR 1402. Nonetheless, for secondary party liability there must be some causal connection between the act of the secondary party relied on and the commission of the offence by the perpetrator. In *R (on the application of Morgan) v Assistant Recorder of Kingston-upon-Hull* Lord Parker CJ, in distinguishing the offence of incitement from the liability of an accomplice, observed:

> 'It is of the essence of the offence established by 'counselling, procuring or commanding' that, as a result of the counselling, procuring or commanding, something should have happened which constituted either the full offence or the attempt...' (emphasis added)

[74] On the other hand, it seems clear that the requirement for a causal connection is given a wide interpretation where a secondary party prior to the crime has counselled or assisted the perpetrator in actions taken by him which are directed towards the commission of the crime eventually committed. In *Attorney General's Reference (No.1 of 1975)*, when considering the word 'counsel' and giving it its ordinary meaning of 'advise, solicit or something of that sort', this court stated:

> 'There is no implication in the word itself that there should be any causal connection between counselling and the offence. [But] there must clearly be, first, contact between the parties, and, second, a connection between the counselling and the murder. So long as there is counselling...so long as the

principal offence is committed by the one counselled and so long as the one counselled is acting within the scope of his authority … we are of the view that the offence is made out.'

[75] It thus appears that in such circumstances liability will be established unless:

'Considered as a matter of causation there … [is] … an overwhelming supervening event which is of such a character that it will relegate into history matters which would otherwise be looked upon as causative factors'

per Lord Parker CJ in *R v Anderson and Morris* [1966] 2 QB 110, [1966] 2 All ER 644 at 120, when considering the question of the liability of an accomplice for acts of a perpetrator which have gone beyond the parties' common purpose. Absent some such 'overwhelming supervening event', if the secondary party is to avoid liability for assistance rendered to the perpetrator in respect of steps taken by the perpetrator towards the commission of the crime, only an act taken by him which amounts to countermanding of his earlier assistance and a withdrawal from the common purpose will suffice.

Questions

1. Can there be a case of aiding, abetting or counselling where the parties have not met and have not discussed the offence? Cf *Mohan v R* [1967] 2 All ER 58, [1967] 2 AC 187, PC.

2. The court in *A-G's Reference (No 1 of 1975)* holds that Parliament must have intended the four words, 'aid, abet, counsel and procure' to have different meanings but the court did not have the advantage of an exposition of the history of secondary participation and might have arrived at a different conclusion if it had. See J. C. Smith, 'Aid, Abet, Counsel or Procure' in *Reshaping the Criminal Law* (ed, Glazebrook, 1978) p 120. The Code Team and the Law Commission thought that the scope of secondary participation as defined in the case law is accurately described by three words, 'procure, assist, or encourage'. Professor Kadish, with whom Glanville Williams agrees, thinks that only two types of activity are involved—'intentionally influencing the decision of the primary party to commit the crime, and intentionally helping the primary actor to commit the crime': *Blame and Punishment*, 135, 151. Does this formula adequately cover a case like the *A-G's Reference*? See discussion at [1991] Crim LR 765 and 930.

Williams, TBCL, 339 writes: 'In so far as *Attorney-General's Reference* purports to decide that merely causing an offence can be said to be a procuring of it, it should be regarded as too incautious a generalisation.' He refers to *Beatty v Gillbanks*, above, p **80** as a case where a party, the Salvation Army, caused the commission of an offence but should not be liable for it. But Lord Widgery said, 'to procure means to produce by *endeavour*'. What is the significance of the words, 'by endeavour'? Even if the Salvation Army can be said to have caused the riot, can they be said to have caused it 'by endeavour'?

Note the paradox that, if the procurer must be proved to have caused the offence (for example, grievous bodily harm) in fact, he does not cause it in law (above, pp **79–80**), or he would be not merely a procurer but a principal offender.

Lord Widgery's generous host fills the bibulous guest's glass as rapidly as he empties it and may be aware that the guest, who has come alone in his car, will drive home with an excess of alcohol. Does the host cause this result? Does he cause it by *endeavour*?

Blakely and Sutton v Director of Public Prosecutions
[1991] RTR 405, Queen's Bench Division

(Bingham LJ and McCullough J)

Blakely (B) was associating with Taft (T), a married man who was in the process of divorcing his wife. T sometimes spent the night with B. On 26 October 1988 T met B in a pub and told her that at the end of the evening he intended to drive home to his wife. B was upset. She knew that, when T intended to drive home, it was his invariable practice to drink two pints of beer and, thereafter, tonic water. After T had drunk his two pints, at Sutton's (S's) suggestion, B and S added vodka to T's tonic water. B intended to tell T what she had done when the time came for him to leave. B and S believed that T would not be willing to drive with an excess of alcohol. At closing time T went to the lavatory and then drove off before B and S could tell him what they had done. T was charged with, and pleaded guilty to, driving with an excess of alcohol. B and S were convicted by the justices, and on appeal by the Crown Court, of jointly aiding, abetting, counselling, procuring or commanding T to commit the offence.

The judge directed the justices that the defendants would be guilty of procuring if the jury were satisfied so as to be sure that the defendants deliberately set out to cause Taft to consume an amount of alcohol in excess of the level permitted for drivers and did so; and that in doing so they either knew that he would drive or were reckless as to whether or not he would drive. The judge adopted the definition of 'recklessness' given by Lord Diplock in *Lawrence* (above, p 148).

B and S appealed by way of case stated.

[**McCullough J** said that, although the charge was framed so compendiously, the prosecution had alleged only that the defendants had 'procured' T to commit the offence; so the only issue was the mens rea of procuring which (it was not disputed) included an intention to do the act which, to a significant extent at least, caused the commission of the offence. He went on:]

The more pertinent question is what must be proved to have been the state of the accused's mind in relation to the offence which the principal offender went on to commit. Has it to be shown that he knew that it would (or would in the ordinary course of events) be committed, or that it might well be; is it enough that he gave no thought to the obvious risk that it might? And how willing must he have been that it should? Must he have intended it to follow, or is it enough that he was prepared to act realising that it might do so? The questions are linked; they have arisen in cases concerning all types of secondary parties and the emphasis placed on each has necessarily varied from case to case.

As to his belief in the likelihood of the offence resulting, the principal question for consideration, having regard to the fact that the defendants might have been convicted under limb (a) [of the *Lawrence* definition of recklessness], is whether an alleged procurer may be convicted if, at the time of his own act, he gave no thought to the possibility that the principal might go on to commit the offence that he did commit.

[Having stated the arguments of counsel, the judge went on:]

I turn first to *Carter v Richardson* [1974] RTR 314. The facts were that Carter was supervising Collin, a learner driver, whose blood-alcohol level exceeded the prescribed limit. Carter was a principal in the second degree. The argument in the magistrates' court seems to have turned on whether there had to be evidence that Carter knew the exact amount of alcohol in the driver's blood or whether it was enough that he knew that the driver had consumed such a quantity of alcohol that the level in his blood must have been above the prescribed limit. The justices preferred the latter view and Carter was convicted. This court, presided over by Lord Widgery CJ, held that they were right.

The word 'reckless' appears only once in the judgments. In *Carter v Richardson* [1974] RTR 314 Lord Widgery CJ said, at p 317H:

'Going on through the justices' case, we find that they give as their opinion that: "… it was impossible for the defendant to know exactly how many milligrammes of alcohol there were in a millilitre of Collin's blood and that it sufficed that an aider and abettor was aware that the principal had consumed an excessive amount of alcohol or was reckless as to whether he had done so"—I pause there to say that for my part I think that is a correct statement of the law.'

This passage, however, stands alone. Everywhere else in his judgment Lord Widgery CJ spoke in terms of Carter's 'knowledge' or 'awareness': see the following, at p 318A, D–F:

'The justices were right if they took the view that it was sufficient if the defendant was aware that the principal offender had consumed excessive alcohol… What is apparent from the case is that the justices saw fit to draw the inference that the defendant knew that Collin had had too much to drink, if I may put it in the colloquial sense… In my judgment they were perfectly entitled on the primary facts found to draw the further inference not only that the defendant knew that Collin had been drinking, but that the defendant knew that Collin had been drinking to such an extent that it was probable that his blood-alcohol content was over the limit. If that is established then the offence is established.'

MacKenna J, who agreed with the judgment of Lord Widgery CJ, said, at p 318H:

'… the justices were entitled to infer that he, when the car was stopped, either knew that Collin had too much alcohol in his blood or at least believed that it was probable that he had.'

May J said no more than that he agreed.

There was thus the single reference to 'recklessness'. It did not form part of the ratio of the case. There is, in any event, nothing to suppose that, when Lord Widgery CJ gave his approval to the passage which contained the word, he was thinking of anything other than advertent recklessness.

[Having considered various authorities, the judge went on:]

For these reasons I would state my conclusions on the question of the mens rea of an alleged accessory before the fact as follows. While it may nowadays be the law that advertent recklessness to the consequences of his deliberate act of assistance may suffice to convict some, if not all, those accused of being an accessory before the fact, it is clear that inadvertent recklessness does not. It must, at the least, be shown that the accused contemplated that his act would or might bring about or assist the commission of the principal offence: he must have been prepared nevertheless to do his own act, and he must have done that act intentionally. The requirements match those needed to convict principals in the second degree. And they fit well with the liability of the parties to a joint enterprise.

In relation to those accused only of 'procuring' and perhaps also those accused only of 'counselling and commanding', it may be, as the judgment of Lord Goddard CJ in *Ferguson v Weaving* [1951] 1 KB 814, 819 would permit and as the judgment of Lord Widgery CJ in *A-Gs Reference (No 1 of 1975)* [1975] RTR 473, 477H–J strongly suggests, that it is necessary to prove that the accused intended to bring about the principal offence. The present case does not, however, require this to be decided.

It follows that, in my judgment, the direction which the judge gave to the justices was wrong.

Finally, I must deal with an alternative submission advanced by Mr McCahill. It is that since (i) the defendants laced Taft's drink with the intention of putting his blood-alcohol level over the statutory limit, (ii) at that time they knew that Taft intended to drive, and (iii) it was in consequence of their action that, when he drove, his blood-alcohol level was over the limit, it follows that they procured his offence.

I cannot accept this. The facts that Mr McCahill Lists omit the defendants' belief that when they, as they intended, told Taft what they had done he would not be prepared to drive. Mr McCahill seeks to relegate this important fact to oblivion by labelling it a 'secret hope' and saying that it derived from their motive, which was that he should spend the night with Blakely rather than drive home. This, in my view, is unreaListic. I accept that their motive was that he should spend the night with Blakely, but their intention to prevent him from driving was just as real as their knowledge that he intended to drink so little that he would be able lawfully to drive. On the facts which they found the court may well have convicted the defendants on the basis that they gave no thought to the risk that, despite their intention to tell him that they had laced his drink, he might nevertheless drive. On my understanding of the law that would have been wrong.

So I would quash these convictions and answer the stated questions as follows: (1) the use of the word 'recklessness' is best avoided when considering the mens rea required of someone accused of procuring the commission of a substantive offence; (2) in so far as the correct approach to that mens rea accords with the concept of 'recklessness', no.

[**Bingham LJ** gave judgment allowing the appeal.]

Appeal allowed

Questions

The Draft Code, cl 27, which is intended to restate the present law, provides that—

a person is guilty of an offence as an accessory if:

(a) he intentionally procures or assists or encourages the act which constitutes or results in the commission of the offence by the principal; and

(b) he knows that, or (where recklessness suffices in the case of the principal) is reckless with respect to, any circumstance that is an element of the offence . . .

Carter (in *Carter v Richardson*, above, p **287**) would be guilty under this provision because he intentionally assisted or encouraged the act of driving, being reckless whether the driver had an excess of alcohol in his blood; but Blakely, while she intended the *circumstance* (the excess of alcohol), did not intentionally procure the *act of driving* because her object was to prevent T from driving. Is the Code right? Or should it be the law that she was guilty if she knew there was a risk that T might drive with excess alcohol?

(2) CAUSING ANOTHER TO COMMIT A CRIME BY CREATING A MOTIVE TO COMMIT IT

A related problem on which there is little authority is that of the person who intentionally causes another to commit a crime by providing him with a motive. Stephen (II HCL, 8) thought that if A told B of facts which gave B a motive to murder C and B did so, 'it would be an abuse of language to say that A had killed C, though no doubt he has been the remote cause of C's death.' He discusses Shakespeare's play, *Othello*. Iago wanted Othello to murder his wife, Desdemona, and caused him to do so by persuading him that Desdemona was committing adultery with his lieutenant, Cassio. Stephen remarks:

I am inclined to think that Iago could not have been convicted as an accessory before the fact to Desdemona's murder, but for one single remark—'do it not with poison, strangle her in her bed'.

Sanford Kadish (*Essays*, 135 at p 166) disagrees with this reasoning, pointing out that it is not necessary to prove that a secondary party to murder 'killed', only that his actions make him responsible for killing by another. Iago has certainly in fact caused Othello's act but, as

Othello is the principal, Iago is not regarded in law as having caused Desdemona's death. But this is true of secondary parties generally. Is there any reason why, if the above facts were proved, Iago should not be held liable as an accessory, even if he had never expressly encouraged Othello to kill? Did he not procure the killing by endeavour?

Of course Iago was telling Othello a pack of lies and Kadish thinks the problem is different if the alleged accessory was telling the truth. Lies are evidence, or corroboration, of the intent. Suppose Desdemona really had been up to no good with Cassio and Iago had told Othello no more than the truth, but with the same object of provoking him into killing her.

Kadish (p 166) writes:

Volunteering the truth to another is different. It is as consistent with an innocent state of mind as with a culpable one.... To make this the basis of accessory liability invited judicial examination of how far the disclosure was motivated by Othello's expected reaction rather than duty or friendship.

The intent point is debatable. Even where lies are told, there is a serious problem of proof. Deceiving a man into thinking that his wife is committing adultery falls well short of prima facie evidence of an intention that he should murder her. Iago might have told the same lies to get Othello to send Desdemona to a nunnery or divorce her, never contemplating that he would murder her, and, in that case, he certainly could not be liable for murder. There is a problem of proof in either case. Is the fact that the difficulty of proof is greater when the truth is told a sufficient foundation for a distinction in principle? Suppose that it is possible to prove the evil motive.

Kadish is also concerned about the propriety of convicting a person of an offence for telling the truth. 'Making telling of the truth an element of criminal liability casts a long shadow over proper social behaviour' (p 167).

Can a person commit a crime by doing no more than telling the truth? In a television play, 'Mother Love', shown on BBC2 in November 1989, members of a family have good reason to believe that a woman will commit suicide if she finds out that her son is seeing her divorced husband, his father. The son has in fact been seeing his father regularly for years but this has been carefully concealed from the mother. Suppose (to depart from the facts of the play) that someone, wanting her to die, tells her the truth and, as he hopes and expects, she duly commits suicide. Is he guilty of procuring her to commit suicide, an offence under the Suicide Act 1961 (below, p 618), by telling her the truth? Should the fact that the defendant has told the truth necessarily exempt him from criminal liability? Has he not produced the result by endeavour?

Suppose that Adam is just getting over a serious operation when his son, Abel, is killed. The surgeon says that on no account must Adam be told of Abel's death until he has fully recovered. Until then, the shock will kill him. Adam's other son, Cain, wishing to accelerate his inheritance of his father's property, brusquely tells Adam that Abel is dead, whereupon Adam collapses and dies. Should it be an answer to a charge of murder that Cain was only telling the truth? That of course is not a case of secondary liability but, if a person can be guilty as a principal by telling the truth, should not this, *a fortiori*, be possible in the case of an accessory? Is not the only problem (a serious problem, of course) one of proof?

(3) ENCOURAGEMENT

Where D did not 'procure' the commission of the offence and did not 'aid' the principal, the prosecution may rely on the fact that he encouraged ('abetted') its commission.

Must there be an intention to encourage? If X and Y agree to race in a dangerous manner on the highway and one of them runs down and kills a pedestrian, both are guilty of causing death by dangerous driving and possibly of manslaughter. It is immaterial that it is impossible to identify the actual killer: the one who did not kill was an accessory and may be indicted and convicted as a principal: *Swindall and Osborne* (1846) 2 Car & Kir 230, 175 ER 95. Williams (TBCL 360) suggests that this result depends on the agreement to race. He contrasts the following case:

D1, driving a car, passes D2. D2, angered by this, accelerates to pass D1; and so a kind of competition develops between the two drivers, and each drives at a negligent speed. A pedestrian is killed by one of the drivers, it is not known which. Only the driver who killed the pedestrian is guilty of manslaughter; and if his identity cannot be established, neither driver can be convicted of this crime. Here neither driver wished the other to drive at speed or intended to give him encouragement in the affair. Knowingly causing another person to act is not sufficient to constitute incitement to do it.

Perhaps it is not sufficient to constitute *incitement* but it does not necessarily follow that it is not sufficient to constitute aiding and abetting. If D1 and D2 are passing and re-passing each must know that his conduct is an encouragement to the other. Although he may not wish to encourage the other, does he not intend to do so in the sense of *Moloney/Hancock* intention?

Williams cites *Mastin* (1834) 6 C & P 396, 172 ER 1292. In that case two brothers, John and William Mastin, were riding fast on the highway. William, following John, rode against another rider and killed him. It was argued by Curwood for the prosecution, 'As both prisoners were racing, the act of one is the act of both.' Patteson J responded: 'I think that if two are riding fast, and one of them goes by without doing any injury to anyone, he is not answerable because the other, going equally fast, rides against someone and kills him'; and he directed the acquittal of John.

The facts seem to have been substantially the same in *Turner* [1991] Crim LR 57, where the parties were not riding horses but driving cars. The court accepted that there was no suggestion that there had been any prior arrangement to race. L lost control, collided with an oncoming car and killed his own passenger. He had pleaded guilty to causing death by reckless driving. The prosecution's case against T was that he aided and abetted L. T's appeal against conviction for causing death by reckless driving was dismissed. The jury had been properly directed that they had to be sure, first, that L and T were racing and, second, that the racing was a cause of the passenger's death.

L's conviction was held to have been properly admitted in evidence under PACE, s 74 (above, p 273). This (it is submitted) proved not only that L drove recklessly but also that L's reckless driving caused death. If so, the only remaining issue on the trial of T was whether T abetted L's reckless driving; but the court seems to have assumed that it was necessary to prove—and had been proved—that T's driving itself caused the death. Was this necessary? If it was, T was guilty as a principal. If the case against T was that he was a principal, should L's conviction have been admitted? Was it relevant that L had committed the offence?

If two drivers are racing (whether by prior agreement or not) does it necessarily follow that each is encouraging the other to drive recklessly (or, now, dangerously)? Or should the jury be directed that they must be sure that the principal was in fact encouraged, and the alleged abettor knew that he was encouraging him?

R v Calhaem

[1985] 2 All ER 266, Court of Appeal, Criminal Division

(Parker LJ, Tudor Evans J and Sir John Thompson)

The prosecution alleged that Calhaem (C) hired Zajac (Z) to murder Mrs Rendell (R), C's rival for the affections of her solicitor. Z, the principal witness for the prosecution, testified to the hiring and said that he went to R's house, armed but with no intention of killing her; that he intended only to act out a charade so that C and R would think an attempt had been made; but that, when R screamed, he went berserk and killed her. It was argued, inter alia, that the judge had misdirected the jury by not telling them that, as in the case of procuring, the counselling by C must have been a 'substantial cause' of the killing. C's appeal was dismissed.

[**Parker LJ**, having cited *A-G's Reference (No 1 of 1975)*, above, continued:]

We must therefore approach the question raised on the basis that we should give to the word 'counsel' its ordinary meaning, which is, as the judge said, 'advise', 'solicit', or something of that sort. There is no implication in the word itself that there should be any causal connection between the counselling and the offence. It is true that, unlike the offence of incitement at common law, the actual offence must have been committed, and committed by the person counselled. To this extent there must clearly be, first, contact between the parties, and, second, a connection between the counselling and the murder. Equally, the act done must, we think, be done within the scope of the authority or advice, and not, for example, accidentally when the mind of the final murderer did not go with his actions. For example, if the principal offender happened to be involved in a football riot in the course of which he laid about him with a weapon of some sort and killed someone who, unknown to him, was the person whom he had been counselled to kill, he would not, in our view, have been acting within the scope of his authority; he would have been acting entirely outside it, albeit what he had done was what he had been counselled to do.

Question

What is the difference between 'connection' and 'cause'?

(4) SECONDARY PARTICIPATION IN A 'TYPE' OF CRIME

R v Bainbridge

[1959] 3 All ER 200, Court of Criminal Appeal

(Lord Parker CJ, Byrne and Winn JJ)

[**Lord Parker CJ** delivered the following judgment of the court:]

The appellant in this case was convicted at the Central Criminal Court of being accessory before the fact to office-breaking and was sentenced to four years' imprisonment. He now appeals against his conviction only on a point of law.

The facts were these. On the night of 30 October 1958, the Stoke Newington branch of the Midland Bank was broken into by cutting the bars of a window, the doors of the strong room and of a safe inside the strong room. They were opened by means of oxygen cutting equipment and nearly £18,000 was stolen. The cutting equipment was all left behind, and it was later found that that cutting equipment so left behind by the thieves had been purchased by the appellant some six weeks earlier. The case against him was that he had bought this cutting equipment on behalf of one or more of the thieves with the full knowledge that it was going to be used, if not against the Stoke Newington branch of the Midland Bank, at any rate for the purposes of breaking and entering premises. The appellant's case, as given in his evidence, was this: 'True, I had bought this equipment from two different firms. I had gone there with a man called Shakeshaft to buy it for him. As a result of conversation which I had with him, I was suspicious that he wanted it for something illegal. I thought it was for breaking up stolen goods which Shakeshaft had received, and, as the result, in making those purchases I gave false names and addresses; but I had no knowledge that the equipment was going to be used for any such purpose as that for which it was used.'

The complaint here is that Judge Aarvold, who tried the case, gave the jury a wrong direction in regard to what it was necessary for them to be satisfied of in order to hold the appellant guilty of being an accessory before the fact. The passages in question are these:

'To prove that, the prosecution have to prove these matters; first of all, they have to prove that the felony itself was committed. Of that there is no doubt. That is not contested. Secondly, they have to prove that the [appellant] knew that a felony of that kind was intended and was going to be committed, and with that knowledge he did something to help the felons commit the crime. The knowledge that is required to be proved in the mind of [the appellant] is not the knowledge of the precise crime. In other words, it need not be proved that he knew that the Midland Bank, Stoke Newington branch, was going to be broken and entered, and money stolen from that particular bank, but he must know the type of crime that was in fact committed. In this case it is a breaking and entering of premises and the stealing of property from those premises. It must be proved that he knew that that sort of crime was intended and was going to be committed. It is not enough to show that he either suspected or knew that some crime was going to be committed, some crime which might have been a breaking and entering or might have been disposing of stolen property or anything of that kind. That is not enough. It must be proved that he knew that the type of crime which was in fact committed was intended.'

There are other passages to the same effect; in particular, when the jury returned for further directions before they came to their verdict, the learned judge said this:

'If in fact, before it has happened, [the appellant], knowing what is going to happen, with full knowledge that a felony of that kind is going to take place, deliberately and wilfully helps it on its way, he is an accessory ... If he was not present he would not be guilty as a principal, but then you would have to decide whether he helped in purchasing this equipment for Shakeshaft knowing full well the type of offence for which it was going to be used, and, with that knowledge, buying it and helping in that way.'

Counsel for the appellant, who argued this case very well, contended that that direction was wrong. As he put it, in order that a person should be convicted of being accessory before the fact, it must be shown that, at the time when he bought the equipment in a case such as this, he knew that a particular crime was going to be committed; and by 'a particular crime' counsel meant that the premises in this case which were going to be broken into were known to the appellant and contemplated by him, and not only the premises in question but the date when the crime was going to occur; in other words, that he must have known that on a particular date the Stoke Newington branch of the Midland Bank was intended to be broken into.

The court fully appreciates that it is not enough that it should be shown that a person knew that some illegal venture was intended. To take this case, it would not be enough if the appellant knew—he says that he only suspected—that the equipment was going to be used to dispose of stolen property. That would not be enough. Equally, this court is quite satisfied that it is unnecessary that knowledge of the intention to commit the particular crime which was in fact committed should be shown, and by 'particular crime' I am using the words in the same way as that in which counsel for the appellant used them, namely, on a particular date and particular premises.

It is not altogether easy to lay down a precise form of words which will cover every case that can be contemplated. But, having considered the cases and the law, this court is quite clear that the direction of Judge Aarvold in this case cannot be criticised. Indeed, it might well have been made with the passage in Foster's *Crown Cases* (3rd edn) (1792) at p 369, in mind, because the learned author says:

> 'If the principal totally and substantially varieth, if being solicited to commit a felony of one kind he *wilfully and knowingly* committeth a felony of another, *he* will stand single in that offence, and the person soliciting will not be involved in his guilt. For on *his* part it was no more than a fruitless ineffectual temptation.'

The converse of course is that, if the principal does not totally and substantially vary the advice or the help and does not wilfully and knowingly commit a different form of felony altogether, the man who has advised or helped, aided or abetted, will be guilty as an accessory before the fact.

Judge Aarvold in this case, in the passages to which I have referred, makes it clear that there must be not merely suspicion but knowledge that a crime of the type in question was intended, and that the equipment was bought with that in view. In his reference to the felony of the type intended it was, as he states, the felony of breaking and entering premises and the stealing of property from those premises. The court can see nothing wrong in that direction.

Appeal dismissed

Questions

1. Is this case authority for the proposition that the supplier of equipment for use in committing a particular type of crime is liable for *all* crimes of that type which are committed by the person supplied, using that equipment? Does the fact that the equipment was left behind suggest that it was for use on one occasion only?

2. A South African judge, Schreiner JA, suggests that the supplier of an implement to a burglar may be liable only for those offences which he knew, or perhaps ought to have known, were specifically in the contemplation of the burglar when he gave it to him: *Toni* 1941 (1) SA 109 at 116 (AD). Is this a workable test? What if no specific offences are contemplated by the burglar or no specific offences are known by the supplier to be contemplated by the burglar at the time of supply of the implement?

3. D knows that E makes his living by armed robberies. He supplies E with a revolver and ammunition. Is D liable for murder if E with the revolver deliberately shoots (i) a policeman who is impeding his escape after a robbery; (ii) his wife, with whom he has had a sudden quarrel?

4. D knows that E is a burglar. He supplies him with a jemmy. E, using the jemmy, breaks into D's mother's house and steals. D is furious. Is he liable for burglary? What if E had committed the burglary in D's house?

Note

See Law Commission Working Paper No 43, Proposition 10:

Where a principal is helped in the commission of more than one offence by a single act of help, the accessory who afforded that help shall not, after having been convicted of one or more of such offences, be convicted of another of such offences of equal or lesser gravity.

(A proposition not adopted in the Draft Code, pp **289**, above.)

Director of Public Prosecutions for Northern Ireland v Maxwell
[1978] 3 All ER 1140, House of Lords Note

(Viscount Dilhorne, Lords Hailsham of St Marylebone, Edmund-Davies, Fraser of Tullybelton and Scarman)

Court of Criminal Appeal in Northern Ireland
[1978] 3 All ER 1151 Note

(Lowry LCJ, Jones and McGonigal LJJ)

The appellant, a member of the Ulster Volunteer Force, proscribed in Northern Ireland, had guided terrorists to the Crosskeys Inn by leading them in his car. The trial judge found that the appellant knew there was to be 'an attack on the Crosskeys bar, not a casual or social visit or mere reconnaissance' and that 'the attack would be one of violence in which people would be endangered or premises seriously damaged.' However the appellant did not know precisely what offence was to be committed. Although the appellant was charged as a principal in the offence, of planting a pipe bomb in the Crosskeys Inn, contrary to s 3(1)(a) of the Explosive Substances Act 1883, the true nature of his role was that of an aider and abettor. He appealed against conviction on the ground that he must be shown to have known the type of crime intended to be committed and the kind of means of offence being carried to the scene.

Lowry LCJ [delivering the judgment of the Court of Criminal Appeal in Northern Ireland:] ... Suppose the intending principal offender (whom I shall call 'the principal') tells the intended accomplice (whom I shall call 'the accomplice') that he means to shoot A or else leave a bomb at A's house and the accomplice agrees to drive the principal to A's house and keep watch while there, it seems clear that the accomplice would be guilty of aiding and abetting whichever crime the principal committed, because he would know that one of two crimes was to be committed, he would have assisted the principal and he would have intended to assist him. Again, let us suppose that the principal tells the accomplice that the intention is to murder A at one house but, if he cannot be found or the house is guarded, the alternative plan is to go to B's house and leave a bomb there or thirdly to rob a particular bank (or indeed murder somebody, or bomb somebody's house or rob any bank, as to which see *Bainbridge* ([1960] 1 QB 129, [1959] 3 All ER 200)) and requests the accomplice to make a reconnaissance of a number of places and report on the best way of gaining access to the target. The accomplice agrees and makes all the reconnaissances and reports, and the principal then, without further communication, selects a target and commits the crime. It seems clear that, whichever crime the principal commits, all the ingredients of the accomplice's guilt are present. In each of these examples the accomplice knows exactly what is contemplated and the only thing he does not know is to which particular crime he will become an accessory when it is committed. His guilt springs from the fact that he contemplates the commission of one (or more) of a number of crimes by the principal and he intentionally lends his assistance in order that such a crime will be committed. In other words, he knows that the principal is committing or about to commit one of a number of specified illegal acts and with that knowledge he helps him to do so.

The situation has something in common with that of two persons who agree to rob a bank on the understanding, either express or implied from conduct (such as the carrying of a loaded gun by one person with the knowledge of the other), that violence *may* be resorted to. The accomplice knows, not that the principal will shoot the cashier, but that he may do so; and if the principal does shoot him, the accomplice will be guilty of murder. A different case is where the accomplice has only offence A in contemplation and the principal commits offence B. Here the accomplice, although morally culpable (and perhaps guilty of conspiring to commit offence A), is not guilty of aiding and abetting offence B.

The principle with which we are dealing does not seem to us to provide a warrant, on the basis of combating lawlessness generally, for convicting an alleged accomplice of *any* offence which, helped by his preliminary acts, a principal may commit. The relevant crime must be within the contemplation of the accomplice and only exceptionally would evidence be found to support the allegation that the accomplice had given the principal a completely blank cheque....

The facts found here show that the appellant, as a member of an organisation which habitually perpetrates sectarian acts of violence with firearms and explosives, must, as soon as he was briefed for his role, have contemplated the bombing of the Crosskeys Inn as not the only possibility but one of the most obvious possibilities among the jobs which the principals were likely to be undertaking and in the commission of which he was intentionally assisting. He was therefore in just the same situation, so far as guilty knowledge is concerned, as a man who had been given a list of jobs and told that one of them would be carried out. And so he is guilty of the offence alleged against him in count 1 ...

[The court certified the following point of law of general importance:

'If the crime committed by the principal, and actually assisted by the accused, was one of a number of offences, one of which the accused knew the principal would probably commit, is the guilty mind which must be proved against an accomplice thereby proved against the accused?'

The House of Lords dismissed the appeal. All of their Lordships approved the judgment of Lowry LCJ. Lord Edmund-Davies said that to do more than approve it would be a sleeveless errand; but he agreed with the view (below) of Viscount Dilhorne.]

Viscount Dilhorne....No objection could be taken to the form of these counts as by statute [Accessories and Abettors Act 1861, s 8; Criminal Law Act 1967, s 1(2)] aiders and abettors can be charged as principals, but the particulars to each count give no indication of the case the prosecution intended to present and which the appellant had to meet. In the particulars to the first count, he is charged with placing the bomb in the Crosskeys Inn; in the particulars to the second with having had it in his possession or under his control. The prosecution did not attempt to prove that he had placed the bomb or that he had been present when the bomb was put in the inn, nor was any attempt made to establish that at any time he had the bomb in his possession or under his control. It is desirable that the particulars of the offence should bear some relation to the realities and where, as here, it is clear that the appellant was alleged to have aided and abetted the placing of the bomb and its possession or control, it would in my opinion have been better if the particulars of offence had made that clear.

[**Lord Scarman** (having quoted from the judgment of Lowry LCJ):] Lowry LCJ continues:

'The relevant crime must be within the contemplation of the accomplice and only exceptionally would evidence be found to support the allegation that the accomplice had given the principal a completely blank cheque.'

The principle thus formulated has great merit. It directs attention to the state of mind of the accused: not what he ought to have in contemplation, but what he did have. It avoids definition and classification, while ensuring that a man will not be convicted of aiding and abetting any offence his principal may commit, but only one which is within his contemplation. He may have in contemplation only one offence, or several; and the several which he contemplates he may see as alternatives. An accessory who leaves it to his principal to choose is liable, provided always the choice is made from the range of offences from which the accessory contemplates the choice will be made. Although the court's formulation of the principle goes further than the earlier cases, it is a sound development of the law and in no way inconsistent with them. I accept it as good judge-made law in a field where there is no statute to offer guidance.

Appeal dismissed

In *Taylor, Harrison and Taylor* [1998] Crim LR 582 the court said that the 'proper practice, urged by the House of Lords [in *Maxwell*, above], but almost universally ignored, that where the allegation is one of secondary liability, and there is information available to the prosecution that indicates that, that allegation should be specifically set out in the particulars.'

(5) PRINCIPAL EXCEEDING AUTHORITY

S v Robinson
1968 (1) SA 666, Supreme Court of South Africa, Appellate Division

(Steyn CJ, Potgieter and Holmes JJA)

Because of dire financial distress and for the purpose of insurance gain to his widow and to avoid imprisonment for fraud, the deceased conspired with Robinson (the first appellant), his wife (the second appellant) and Esterhuizen (the third appellant) that he be shot. Robinson was to do the shooting and the deceased agreed to go on with the plan 'no matter what happens'. Robinson drove the deceased to the agreed place. At the last minute, the deceased withdrew his consent to die. Robinson then shot him. The three appellants were convicted of murder.

Steyn CJ. . . . The remark by the deceased 'No matter what happens, we must go through with it', is explained by the fact that, on at least one previous occasion, an attempt to execute the murder as planned and desired by the deceased had been frustrated, because the deceased's courage failed him and he declined to go through with it. Although the use of the word 'we' renders it less clear, this remark was in all probability intended to convey to the first appellant that he must not be deterred from the deed if the deceased should once again revoke his consent to be killed. What is perfectly clear from this evidence, is that the deceased did in fact, by saying that he could not go through with it at all, resile from the pact of murder by consent. When, in spite of that, the first appellant shot him, he was no longer a consenting or willing party. He had countermanded the arrangement, at least as between himself and the second and third appellants. He had been the author and originator of that arrangement and his willingness and desire to be killed, was an essential feature of it. There can be no doubt that, had it not been for his own wish and readiness to die, no such arrangement would have come into existence, and there can, I think, equally be no doubt that death without his consent was no part of it. He was, as all concerned must have been aware, in control of the situation he had created for himself and at liberty at any time to withdraw from it. It was precisely as a result of this that the earlier attempt had failed. Because he could not go through with it, the first appellant desisted. It is true that on the day of his death the second appellant, his wife, after he had suggested suicide by both of them, told him that, because such suicide would not achieve the purposes of his death, he 'must go through with it'. That amounted to no more than an implied exhortation not to flinch again from being killed. I cannot find in it a variation of the then existing arrangement, having the effect that he was to be killed whether or not he withdrew his consent at the crucial moment, and there is no ground for holding that it was so intended by the second appellant or so understood by the third appellant, or that anything to that effect was conveyed to the first appellant, who was not present on this occasion. The witness Kleynhans does not say that the third appellant displayed any dissatisfaction when the above-mentioned report was made to him, but that takes the matter no further. Assuming that his assent may be inferred from the absence of evidence of dissatisfaction, acquiescence, without protest ex post facto in what the first appellant had done, would not show that it was part of the common purpose. Had the deceased not told the first appellant that they must go through with it, no matter what happens, it may well be that the latter would again have refrained from the fatal deed. The common purpose was murder with the consent of the victim. In shooting the deceased after he had retracted his consent, the first appellant acted outside the common purpose. There is no evidence to show or from which it could be inferred with any certainty that the second and third appellants foresaw the possibility that the first appellant might kill the deceased even if he withdrew his consent, and that they were reckless whether or not he did so kill him. It follows that an intention on their part that the deceased was to be murdered also in such an event, has not been proved. The suggestion that the deceased was so drunk that his withdrawal of consent is to be ignored is without substance. From his remarks and reactions, as described by the first appellant, it is quite clear that he knew full well what the two of them were about. In the result, the second and third appellants have, in my opinion, not been shown to be guilty of murder.

But that is not the end of the matter. When the deceased told the appellants that they were to go through with it, no matter what happened, that did not have the effect of cancelling the arrangement of murder by consent. It merely added, as between the deceased and the first appellant, an instruction to proceed even if consent should be revoked. Had the deceased not retracted and had he been killed with his consent, it could hardly have been contended that this added instruction removed the killing from the ambit of the common purpose. Up to the point where the deceased recoiled from execution of the common purpose and said that he could not go through with it at all, the first appellant was applying himself to the achievement of that purpose. As the deceased, in relief, fell forward with his head on to the steering wheel, the first appellant pulled the trigger. The inference is justified that at that stage he had the revolver in his hand, ready to shoot. That he then had the firm intention to kill is obvious from the fact that a moment later he fired the fatal shot. In relation to the common purpose, there was, shortly before the shot was fired, a completed attempt to murder in the execution of that purpose. The fact that the first appellant proceeded beyond his attempt to a murder without consent, does not mean that at this stage he had not committed the crime of attempted murder with consent. In my view the second and third appellants cannot be absolved from complicity in this crime of attempted murder....

[**Potgieter JA** concurred in the judgment of Steyn CJ.]

Holmes JA.... What is needed here is a robust conspectus of the circumstances as a whole... looking squarely at the whole train of events, the conspiracy was fulfilled in death, and there is no room for exquisite niceties of logic about the exact limits of the mandate in the conspiratorial common purpose. The three members of the trial Court held that the appellants were all equally a party to this planned and urgently sought death. On the facts, I consider as a matter of justice that the trial Court was entitled to come to that conclusion, and there is no basis for disturbing it. To hold that, in the known desperate circumstances of the deceased, his final instruction (ie to go through with it 'whatever happens') took the matter outside the conspiracy of death, would in my view be at odds with the realities; and it would produce an air of artificiality...

Appeal dismissed

Questions

1. Is the opinion of the majority preferable to that of Holmes JA?

2. A employs B to follow his wife C and, if he finds she is committing adultery, to kill her. B finds that C is not committing adultery. He nevertheless kills her. What is the liability of A?

(6) ACCESSORY'S KNOWLEDGE OF FACTS

Johnson v Youden
[1950] 1 All ER 300, King's Bench Division

(Lord Goddard CJ, Humphreys and Lynskey JJ)

It was an offence under s 7(1) of the Building Materials and Housing Act 1945 for a builder to sell a house at a price in excess of that fixed by the local authority in the licence to build the house. The three respondents, partners in a firm of solicitors, were charged with aiding and abetting a builder in an offence under this section and acquitted. The prosecutor appealed by way of case stated.

Lord Goddard CJ.... In this case the builder had a licence which entitled him to sell the house for £1,025. He induced a railway porter to agree to buy the house for £1,275, ie £250 more than the controlled price, and he instructed a firm of solicitors, in which the three respondents are partners, to act as his solicitors for the sale. The builder was charged with an offence against s 7(1) of the Act of 1945 and was convicted, but the three respondents were acquitted on charges of aiding and abetting him.

In regard to the respondents, the justices found that, until 6 April 1949, none of them knew anything about the extra £250 which the builder was receiving, and that the first two respondents, Mr Henry Wallace Youden and Mr George Henry Youden, did not know about it at any time, as the builder deliberately concealed the fact and even refused to give the purchaser a receipt for that £250. The justices, therefore, were right, in our opinion, in dismissing the information against the first two respondents on the ground that they could not be guilty of aiding and abetting the commission of the offence as they did not know of the matter which constituted the offence. If they had known that the builder was receiving the extra £250 and had continued to ask the purchaser to complete, they would have committed an offence by continuing to assist the builder to offer the property for sale, contrary to the provisions of s 7(1) of the Act of 1945, and, as ignorance of the law is no defence, they would have been guilty of the offence even if they had not realised that they were committing an offence, but a person cannot be convicted of aiding and abetting the commission of an offence if he does not know of the essential matters which would constitute the offence.

In regard to their partner, Mr Brydone, the third respondent, the facts are different. Until 6 or 7 April 1949, he was as ignorant as were his partners that the builder had insisted on receiving £250 beyond what he was entitled to charge, but on 6 April he received a letter from the purchaser's solicitor saying:

'I duly received your letter of 26 March informing me that you are ready to settle at any time and that the amount payable on completion is £925.'

The sum was £925, because the controlled price was £1,025, and £100 had been paid as deposit. The letter continued:

'I think I ought to let you know the reason why I have not as yet proceeded to completion. It is that I have felt compelled to report to the town clerk what I consider to be a breach by your client of the provisions of s 7 of the Building Materials and Housing Act 1945.'

This letter naturally put the third respondent, who was dealing with the matter, on inquiry, and he thereupon read the relevant provisions of the Act of 1945 and also spoke to the builder who told him a story which, even if it were true, was on the face of it obviously a colourable evasion of the Act. The builder's story was that he had placed the extra £250 in a separate deposit account and that it was to be spent on payment for work as and when he (the builder) would be lawfully able to execute it in the future on the house on behalf of the purchaser.

It seems impossible to imagine that anyone could believe such a story. Who has ever heard of a purchaser, when buying a house from a builder, putting money into the builder's hands because he may want some work done thereafter? I think that the third respondent could not have read s 7(5) of the Act as carefully as he should have done, because I cannot believe that any solicitor, or even a layman, would not understand that the bargain which the builder described was just the kind of transaction which the Act prohibits. Section 7(5) provides:

> 'In determining for the purposes of this section the consideration for which a house has been sold or let, the court shall have regard to any transaction with which the sale or letting is associated...'

If the third respondent had read and appreciated those words he would have seen at once that the extra £250 which the builder was getting was in regard to a transaction with which the sale was associated, and was, therefore, an unlawful payment. Unfortunately, however, he did not realise it, but either misread the Act or did not read it carefully, and on the following day he called on the purchaser to complete. He was, therefore, clearly aiding and abetting the builder in the offence which the builder was committing. The result is that, so far as the first two respondents are concerned, the appeal fails and must be dismissed, but, so far as the third respondent is concerned, the case must go back to the justices with an intimation that an offence has been committed, and there must be a conviction.

Humphreys J. I agree.

Lynskey J. I also agree.

Appeal dismissed in respect of the first two respondents and allowed in respect of the third respondent. Case remitted to the justices with a direction to convict the third respondent. No order as to costs

Questions

1. Brydone's fault seems to have been that, on this occasion, he was not as good at, or perhaps as careful in, statutory interpretation, as he ought to have been. Is that a good ground for convicting him as an aider and abettor?

2. If Brydone had consulted his partners and they had all concluded that the proposed transaction would be lawful and should proceed, would they have been guilty of conspiracy? Cf Criminal Law Act 1977, s 1, p **488**, below.

Ferguson v Weaving
[1951] 1 All ER 412, King's Bench Division

(Lord Goddard CJ, Hilbery and Devlin JJ)

The respondent was the licensee of a hotel with several rooms in which intoxicating liquor was served. She was charged with aiding, abetting, counselling and procuring customers to consume liquor after hours, contrary to s 4(b) of the Licensing Act 1921, and acquitted. She had given signals to indicate the approach, and arrival, of closing time. (The law did not then allow 'drinking-up time'.) Waiters, in breach of the instructions given by the respondent, failed to collect glasses from the offending customers in the concert room. She was performing her duties in another part of the hotel; and the magistrate found that she had done everything she could to see that the requirements of the law were complied with. The prosecutor appealed.

[**Lord Goddard CJ**, reading the judgment of the court:]

We will assume for the purpose of this case that the respondent had delegated to the waiters the conduct and management of the concert room, and if the Act of 1921 had made it an offence for a licensee knowingly to permit liquor to be consumed after hours then the fact that she had delegated the management and control of the concert room to the waiters would have made their knowledge her knowledge. In this case there is no substantive offence in the licensee at all. The substantive offence is committed only by the customers. She can aid and abet the customers if she knows that the customers are committing the offence, but we are not prepared to hold that knowledge can be imputed to her so as to make her, not a principal offender, but an aider and abettor. So to hold would be to establish a new principle in criminal law and one for which there is no authority. If Parliament had desired to make a licensee guilty of an offence by allowing persons to consume liquor after hours it would have been perfectly easy so to provide in the section. A doctrine of criminal law that a licensee who has knowledge of the facts is liable as a principal in the second degree is no reason for holding that, if she herself had no knowledge of the facts but someone in her employ and to whom she may have entrusted the management of the room did know them, this makes her an aider and abettor. As no duty is imposed on her by the section to prevent the consumption of liquor after hours there was no duty in this respect that she could delegate to her employees. While it may be that the waiters could have been prosecuted for aiding and abetting the consumers, as to which we need express no opinion, we are clearly of opinion that the respondent could not be. To hold the contrary would, in our opinion, be an unwarranted extension of the doctrine of vicarious responsibility in criminal law. The appeal will be dismissed with costs.

Appeal dismissed

Note

In connection with Lord Goddard's remarks on delegation and vicarious responsibility, compare *Vane v Yiannopoullos*, p 338, below.

Questions

1. Why should the knowledge of the waiters be imputed to the licensee where the licensee is charged as a principal and not where he is charged as an abettor? If the licensee should be treated as if he knew that which he does not know for the one purpose, why not for the other?

2. If the Licensing Act had made it an offence for a licensee to permit liquor to be consumed after hours, would Weaving have been guilty of that offence?

(7) ACCESSORY'S INTENTION

National Coal Board v Gamble
[1958] 3 All ER 203, Queen's Bench Division

(Lord Goddard CJ, Slade and Devlin JJ)

The Board was convicted of having aided, abetted, counselled and procured the commission of the offence of using a motor lorry on a road with a load weighing more than that permitted, in contravention of the Motor Vehicles (Construction and Use) Regulations 1995, regs 68 and 104. The lorry was driven by one Mallender whose employers were convicted of the offence as principals. The Board appealed by way of case stated. The facts appear sufficiently in the judgment of Devlin J.

[**Lord Goddard** delivered judgment dismissing the appeal.]

Devlin J. A person who supplies the instrument for a crime or anything essential to its commission aids in the commission of it; and if he does so knowingly and with intent to aid, he abets it as well and is therefore guilty of aiding and abetting. I use the word 'supplies' to comprehend giving, lending, selling or any other transfer of the right of property. In a sense a man who gives up to a criminal a weapon which the latter has a right to demand from him aids in the commission of the crime as much as if he sold or lent the article, but this has never been held to be aiding in law (see *Lomas* (1913) 110 LT 239, and *Bullock* [1955] 1 All ER 15, [1955] 1 WLR 1). The reason, I think, is that in the former [sic., presumably 'latter' is intended] case there is in law a positive act and in the latter [sic., presumably 'former' is intended] only a negative one. In the transfer of property there must be either a physical delivery or a positive act of assent to a taking; but a man who hands over to another his own property on demand, although he may physically be performing a positive act, in law is only refraining from detinue [a tort now abolished]. Thus in law the former act is one of assistance voluntarily given and the latter is only a failure to prevent the commission of the crime by means of a forcible detention, which would not even be justified except in the case of felony. Another way of putting the point is to say that aiding and abetting is a crime that requires proof of mens rea, that is to say, of intention to aid as well as of knowledge of the circumstances, and that proof of the intent involves proof of a positive act of assistance voluntarily done. These considerations make it necessary to determine at what point the property in the coal passed from the Coal Board and what the Coal Board's state of knowledge was at that time. If the property had passed before the Coal Board knew of the proposed crime, there was nothing they could legally do to prevent the driver of the lorry from taking the overloaded lorry out on to the road. If it had not, then they sold the coal with knowledge that an offence was going to be committed.

The Coal Board called no evidence, so that a good deal was left to inference; but the conclusions of fact reached by the magistrates have not been seriously disputed. The Coal Board had an instalment contract with the Central Electricity Authority for a supply of coal to be delivered at the colliery into lorries sent by a carrier on behalf of the authority. The quantity of each instalment was not prescribed and the inference is that the Coal Board were to deliver and the carrier to receive as much as each lorry could carry (which means of course as much as it could legally and safely carry) until the contract quantity was exhausted. The method of delivery was for the lorry to be loaded by hopper and then to proceed to a weighbridge; there were off-loading facilities if the load was found to be overweight. At the weighbridge a ticket was issued in accordance with the Weights and Measures Act 1889, s21(1), which provides that where any quantity of coal exceeding two hundredweight is delivered by means of any vehicle to any purchaser, the seller of the coal shall deliver or send by post to the purchaser or his servant, before any part of the coal is unloaded, a ticket or note in the prescribed form. On this occasion the carrier's lorry was driven by one Mallender and its maximum legal load (after allowing for the tare weight) was 11 tons 12 hundredweights. It was loaded at the hopper, Mallender telling the operator when to stop. Mallender then took the lorry to the weighbridge. The weighbridge operator, one Haslam, weighed the lorry and its load and informed Mallender that his load was nearly four tons over-weight. Haslam asked Mallender whether he intended taking the load and Mallender said he would risk it; he then took the weight ticket from Haslam and left the colliery.

In these circumstances prima facie the property in the coal passed on delivery to the carrier in accordance with r5 of s18 of the Sale of Goods Act 1893. If the delivery was complete after loading and before weighing, the Coal Board had not until after delivery any knowledge that an offence had been committed; but where weighing is necessary for the purpose of the contract, as for example in order to ascertain the price of an instalment, the property does not pass until the weight has been agreed....

It was contended on behalf of the Coal Board that Haslam had no option after weighing but to issue the ticket for the amount then in the lorry. I think that this contention is unsound. In the circumstances of this case the loading must be taken as subject to adjustment; otherwise, if the contract were for a limited amount, the seller might make an over-delivery or an under-delivery which could not thereafter be rectified and the carrier might be contractually compelled to carry away a load in excess of that legally permitted. I think that the delivery of the coal was not completed until after the ascertained weight had been assented to and some act was done signifying assent and passing the property. The property passed when Haslam asked Mallender whether he intended to take the load and Mallender said he would risk it and when the mutual assent was, as it were, sealed by the delivery and acceptance of the weight ticket. Haslam could, therefore, after he knew of the overload have refused to transfer the property in the coal.

This is the conclusion to which the justices came. Counsel for the Coal Board submits that it does not justify a verdict of guilty of aiding and abetting. He submits, first, that even if knowledge of the illegal purpose had been acquired before delivery began, it would not be sufficient for the verdict; and secondly, that if he is wrong about that, the knowledge was acquired too late, and the Coal Board was not guilty of aiding and abetting simply because Haslam failed to stop the process of delivery after it had been initiated.

On his first point counsel submits that the furnishing of an article essential to the crime with knowledge of the use to which it is to be put does not of itself constitute aiding and abetting; there must be proved in addition a purpose or motive of the defendant to further the crime or encourage the criminal. Otherwise, he submits, there is no mens rea.

I have already said that in my judgment there must be proof of intent to aid. I would agree that proof that the article was knowingly supplied is not conclusive evidence of intent to aid. *Fretwell* ((1862) Le & Ca 161) is authority for that. *Steane* [p **136**, above] in which the defendant was charged with having acted during the war with intent to assist the enemy contrary to the defence regulations then in force, makes the same point. But prima facie—and *Steane* makes this clear also—a man is presumed to intend the natural and probable consequences of his acts and the consequence of supplying essential material is that assistance is given to the criminal. It is always open to the defendant, as in *Steane* to give evidence of his real intention; but in this case the defence called no evidence. The prima facie presumption is therefore enough to justify the verdict, unless it is the law that some other mental element besides intent is necessary to the offence.

This is what counsel for the Coal Board argues, and he describes the additional element as the purpose or motive of encouraging the crime. No doubt evidence of an interest in the crime or of an express purpose to assist it will greatly strengthen the case for the prosecution, but an indifference to the result of the crime does not of itself negative abetting. If one man deliberately sells to another a gun to be used for murdering a third, he may be indifferent whether the third man lives or dies and interested only in the cash profit to be made out of the sale, but he can still be an aider and abettor. To hold otherwise would be to negative the rule that mens rea is a matter of intent only and does not depend on desire or motive.

The authorities, I think, support this conclusion, though none has been cited to us in which the point has been specifically argued and decided. The Lord Chief Justice has quoted the statement of the law in *Ackroyds Air Travel Ltd v DPP* ([1950] 1 All ER 933), which is consistent with the results reached in the earlier cases of *Cook v Stockwell* ((1915) 84 LJKB 2187) and *Cafferata v Wilson; Reeve v Wilson* ([1936] 3 All ER 149) and with the later case of *Bullock* ([1955] 1 All ER 15, [1955] 1 WLR 1). The same principle has been applied in civil cases where the seller has sued on a contract for the supply of goods which he knew were to be used for an illegal purpose. In some of the authorities there is a suggestion that he could recover on the contract unless it appeared that in addition to knowledge of the purpose he had an interest in the venture and looked for payment to the proceeds of the crime. In *Pearce v Brooks* ((1866) LR 1 Exch 213) Pollock, CB (ibid, at p 217) stated the law as follows:

'...I have always considered it as settled law, that any person who contributes to the performance of an illegal act by supplying a thing with the knowledge that it is going to be used for that purpose, cannot recover the price of the thing so supplied. If, to create that incapacity, it was ever considered necessary that the price should be bargained or expected to be paid out of the fruits of the illegal act (which I do not stop to examine), that proposition has been overruled by the cases I have referred to [viz. *Cannan v Bryce* (1819) 3 B & Ald 179 and *M'Kinnell v Robinson* (1838) 3 M & W 434], and has now ceased to be law.'

The case chiefly relied on by counsel for the Coal Board was *Coney* ((1882) 8 QBD 534). In this case the defendants were charged with aiding and abetting an illegal prize fight at which they had been present. The judgments all refer to 'encouragement', but it would be wrong to conclude from that that proof of encouragement is necessary to every form of aiding and abetting. Presence on the scene of the crime without encouragement or assistance is no aid to the criminal; the supply of essential material is. Moreover, the decision makes it clear that encouragement can be inferred from mere presence. Cave J, who gave the leading judgment, said of the summing up (ibid, at p 543):

'It may mean either that mere presence unexplained is evidence of encouragement, and so of guilt, or that mere presence unexplained is conclusive proof of encouragement, and so of guilt. If the former is the correct meaning, I concur in the law so laid down, if the latter, I am unable to do so.'

This dictum seems to me to support the view which I have expressed. If voluntary presence is prima facie evidence of encouragement and therefore of aiding and abetting, it appears to me to be a fortiori that the intentional supply of an essential article must be prima facie evidence of aiding and abetting.

As to counsel for the Coal Board's alternative point, I have already expressed the view that the facts show an act of assent made by Haslam after knowledge of the proposed illegality and without which the property would not have passed. If some positive act to complete delivery is committed after knowledge of the illegality, the position in law must, I think, be just the same as if the knowledge had been obtained before the delivery had been begun. Of course, it is quite likely that Haslam was confused about the legal position and thought that he was not entitled to withhold the weight ticket. There is no mens rea if the defendant is shown to have a genuine belief in the existence of circumstances which, if true, would negative an intention to aid; see *Wilson v Inyang* ([1951] 2 KB 799, [1951] 2 All ER 237). This argument, however, which might have been the most cogent available to the defence, cannot now be relied on, because Haslam was not called to give evidence about what he thought or believed....

[**Slade J** dissented, holding that an aider and abettor must be shown to have assisted or encouraged and that 'assist' and 'encourage' necessarily import motive. There was no evidence that Haslam was inspired by a desire to encourage Mallender to commit the offence.]

Appeal dismissed

Notes and questions

1. The court accepted the Board's invitation to identify the Board with their servant and to treat the Board as answerable for the servant's offence. Slade J felt doubtful of the court's jurisdiction to do so on a criminal charge. But for this invitation, the Board could not have been convicted. It could not be held vicariously liable for aiding and abetting, as distinct from committing the offence in question (see *Ferguson v Weaving*, p 300, above) and Haslam was much too inferior a servant for his acts to be regarded as the acts of the Board. See below, p 337 and *John Henshall (Quarries) Ltd v Harvey* [1966] 1 All ER 725, [1965] 2 QB 233.

2. Professor Williams argues, relying principally on *Hodgson v Temple* (1813) 5 Taunt 181, that a seller can enforce a sale of goods made in the ordinary course of business although he knew of the buyer's illegal purpose, at least if the illegality is a minor one and does not

involve great immorality; and that this inevitably implies that he is not a party to a crime (CLGP, p 372). Other civil cases hold that the seller may not sue on the contract but Professor Williams thinks it is settled that *Hodgson v Temple* is the case which would be followed today. A different view however is taken by other writers. Professor Williams distinguishes sale from letting on the ground that the lessor is involved more continuously in the known illegality than the seller. *Pearce v Brooks* was a case of hire purchase though no distinction was drawn between letting and sale and Devlin J treats it as an authority on 'supply' which would cover both. Is the distinction between sale and hire a valid one?

3. Should we distinguish between major illegalities known to be contemplated by buyers which would both disable the seller from suing on the contract and make him liable for the buyer's crime—and minor illegalities which would not disable the seller from suing and would leave him free from criminal liability? On what principle should the distinction be based? See J. C. Smith [1972B] CLJ 197, 208–211. Devlin J distinguishes sharply between the sale or loan of an article on the one hand and the surrender of an article to its owner on the other. It follows that there is a distinction between one who enters into an agreement to sell or to let, knowing from the start of the illegal purpose of the buyer or hirer, and one who only discovers that illegal purpose after the transaction has passed the point at which the other party acquires proprietary rights. Is this a valid distinction?

4. D agrees: (a) to sell, (b) to let on hire, his car to E. D knows that E intends to drive the car himself and—(i) has no licence to drive; or (ii) has no insurance against third party risks; or (iii) is disqualified; or (iv) is subject to epileptic fits. Is D liable for offences that E commits by driving the car?

5. D agrees: (a) to sell, (b) to let, his house to E. D knows that E intends to use the house (i) as a brothel (cf Sexual Offences Act 1956, s 34); (ii) as a residence for his mistress (cf *Upfill v Wright* [1911] 1 KB 506, where it was held that the landlord could not recover the rent because he knew that the tenant had such an immoral purpose); (iii) as a centre for espionage. Is D liable for offences that E commits in the house?

6. In *Lomas*, the accused was held to be not guilty of aiding and abetting a burglary by returning to the burglar, one King, a jemmy which the accused had borrowed from him. How do you think Devlin J would have dealt with an action by King in tort to recover his jemmy from Lomas?

Bryce

[2004] EWCA Crim 1231, [2004] 2 Cr App R 592, [2004] Crim LR 936, Court of Criminal Appeal, Criminal Division

(Potter LJ, Hooper and Astill JJ)

D was convicted of murder as an aider and abettor. In the course of a drug dealers' dispute D assisted X, who was acting on the orders of another, Black, by transporting X and a gun to a caravan near V's home so that X could carry out the murder. 12 hours after D had left X at the scene, he shot V with the gun. D assisted in disposing of evidence after the killing. D's appeal was focused on the issue of causation—that what D did was too remote in time and place to the killing and that at that stage X had not yet formed the intention to commit any criminal offence.

Potter LJ [stated the facts and the grounds of appeal:]

[41] The required mens rea is the same for aiding, abetting counselling and procuring: see *R v Rook* [1993] 2 All ER 955 and [1993] Crim LR 698 and commentary thereto. As stated in *Smith & Hogan: Criminal Law* (10th ed)

'In the modern law, secondary participation almost invariably consists simply in assisting or encouraging the commission of the crime and it is generally irrelevant whether the secondary participant is present or absent or whether his assistance or encouragement was given before or at the time of the offence. The only possible exception may be the procurer who succeeds in causing the principal to commit the crime (as in the *A-G's Reference [No.1 of 1975]*) without doing anything which could be fairly described as encouragement or assistance.' (p.145)

[42] ... [I]t is necessary to show firstly that the act which constitutes the aiding, abetting etc was done intentionally in the sense of deliberately and not accidentally and secondly that the accused knew it to be an act capable of assisting or encouraging the crime. In this case, as in most cases, the first requirement will not be in issue. The act of taking X to the caravan with the gun was obviously done deliberately. However, on the defence which the appellant sought to advance through his counsel, the second requirement was implicitly in issue in that Mr Foy wished to submit to the jury that the appellant's actions were intended to impede rather than assist.

[43] ... [I]t is now well established that it is not necessary to prove that the secondary party at the time of the act of aiding, abetting etc intended the crime to be committed.

[44] As Devlin J said in *National Coal Board v Gamble* [1958] 3 All ER 203, [1959] 42 CAR 240 at 250:

'If one man deliberately sells to another a gun to be used for murdering a third, he may be indifferent whether the third man lives or dies and interested only in the cash profit to be made out of the sale, but he can still be an aider and abetter.'

[45] Thus, if it is proved that the defendant intended to do the acts of assistance or encouragement, it is no defence that he hoped that events might intervene to prevent the crime taking place. So, where the defendant drove the perpetrator to a place where he knew that the perpetrator intended to murder a policeman, his intentional driving of the car to that place amounted to an aiding and abetting of the offence despite his unwillingness that the killing should take place: see *Lynch v DPP for Northern Ireland* [1975] AC 653, [1975] 1 All ER 913, at 678, in which Lord Morris of Borth-y-Gest stated:

'If in the present case the jury were satisfied that the car was driven towards the garage in pursuance of a murderous plan and that the appellant knew that that was the plan and intentionally drove the car in execution of that plan, he could be held to have aided an abetted even though he regretted the plan or indeed was horrified by it. However great his reluctance, he would have intended to aid and abet.'

[46] It not being necessary to show that the secondary party intended the crime to be committed by the perpetrator, what must be his state of mind vis a vis the commission of the crime? As was stated by Lord Goddard CJ in *Johnson v Youden* [1950] 1 KB 544, [1950] 1 All ER 300 at 446:

'Before a person can be convicted of aiding and abetting the commission of an offence he must at least know the essential matters which constitute that offence.'

He went on to say:

'He need not actually know that an offence has been committed, because he may not know that the facts constitute an offence and ignorance of the law is not a defence. If a person knows all the facts and is assisting another person to do certain things, and it turns out that the doing of those things constitutes an offence, the person who is assisting is guilty of aiding an abetting that offence.'

This statement was approved by the House of Lords in *Maxwell v DPP for Northern Ireland* [1978] 3 All ER 1140, (1979) 68 Crim App R 128 HL.

[47] Sir Robert Lowry CJ in *Maxwell* (supra) at 140–141 stated:

'[The secondary party's] guilt springs from the fact that he contemplates the commission of one (or more) of a number of crimes by the principal and he intentionally lends his assistance in order that such a crime shall be committed. In other words, he knows that the principal is committing or about to commit one of a number of specified illegal acts and with that knowledge helps him to do so.'

[48] But does the secondary party actually have to know that the crime will be committed, as this passage suggests, or is something less sufficient? Lord Simon in Lynch 698G-699B cited Devlin J in *National Coalboard v Gamble* [1959] 1 QB 11, [1958] 3 All ER 203, 20 and continued:

'The act of supply must be voluntary (in the sense I tried to define earlier in this speech), and it must be *foreseen* that the instrument or other object or service supplied will *probably (or possibly and desiredly)* be used for the commission of a crime.' (Emphasis added)

[49] Those words were uttered in respect of a person participating at the time of the commission of the offence by the actual perpetrator. However, in the context of a person charged as an accessory who has rendered assistance prior to the commission of the crime by the perpetrator, the circumstances in respect of which knowledge is sufficient for liability may go wider than that of the specific crime actually committed. This is because, as pointed out in *Blackstone's Criminal Practice* (2004) at A6.5 (p.75), it is inappropriate and unworkable to require knowledge of the essential matters constituting the offence in a situation where the offence is yet to be committed in the future or by a person of whose precise intentions the accused cannot be certain in advance. It is thus sufficient for the accused to have knowledge of the type of crime in contemplation. Thus where a person supplies equipment to be used in the course of committing an offence of a particular type, he is guilty of aiding and abetting the commission of any such offence committed by the person to whom he supplies the equipment, providing that he knows the purpose to which the equipment is to be put or realises that there is a real possibility that it will be used for that purpose and the equipment is actually used for that purpose: see *R v Bullock* [1955] 1 All ER 15, 38 Crim App R 151 and *R v Bainbridge* [1960] 1 QB 129, [1959] 3 All ER 200.

.... [His lordship considered *Rook]*

[58] *Rook* is, in our view, authority for the proposition that it is not necessary to show that the secondary party intended the commission of the principal offence and that it is sufficient if the secondary party at the time of his actions relied on as lending assistance or encouragement contemplates the commission of the offence, that is knows that it will be committed or realises that it is a real possibility that it will be committed.

[59] The issue in the present case is whether, in addition to proving that the act of assistance relied on was deliberate and that the secondary party contemplated the commission of the offence, the prosecution must prove an intention to assist. It was the defendant's case through his counsel that his intention was not to assist, but to hinder, the plan which was apparently in existence between Black and X.

[60] We have already seen that Devlin J, in *National Coal Board v Gamble* referred to an intent to aid and that in *Maxwell*, Sir Robert Lowry CJ referred to intentionally lending his assistance in order that the crime shall be committed, in a passage cited with approval by Lloyd LJ in *Rook*. Although in *Rook* the endorsement of the passage from Smith and Hogan and of the written direction includes no reference to intent to assist, the Court had earlier approved the direction that the appellant must have done the various things 'intending to assist [the principals] to commit a murder.'

[61]   In *Criminal Law Theory and Doctrine*, Simester and Sullivan, 2000 the authors state that a secondary party must intend 'that his conduct will help or encourage P's actions' (page 198). 'It is the assistance, not the ultimate crime, that must be intended by' the secondary party.

[62]   *Blackstone's Criminal Practice 2004* (paragraph A 5.4, page 73) relying upon the passage from Devlin J in *National Coal Board v Gamble* which we have already cited, also states that there must be an intention to aid. The authors consider the case of Lynch:

> 'Thus in DPP for Northern Ireland v Lynch [1975] AC 653 the accused's alleged opposition to the principal offence did not preclude a finding that he intended to aid.'

[63]   The authors then consider the authorities such as *R. v Woollin* [1999] AC 82 which decide that a person may still intend to do something even though he does not desire it. The authors continue:

> '*Gillick v West Norfolk and Wisbech Area Health Authority* [1986] AC 112 is an example of a type of case where the uncertainties of the precise meaning of intention effectively confer a perhaps welcome discretion on whether to impose responsibility. That case concerned, inter alia, the question of whether a doctor giving contraceptive advice or treatment to a girl under the age of 16 could be liable as accessory to a subsequent offence of unlawful sexual intercourse committed by the girl's sexual partner. The House of Lords held that generally this would not be the case (the action was a civil one for a declaration) since the doctor would lack the necessary intention (even though he realised that his actions would facilitate such intercourse). One rationale for the decision would be that a jury would not infer intention in such circumstances if they thought that the doctor was acting in what he considered to be the girl's best interests.
>
> Similar reasoning could be applied to a troublesome group of cases involving the supply of articles for use in crime which the recipient already has some sort of civil right to receive. The general position seems to be that this is not aiding and abetting (see, for example, *Lomas* (1913) 9 Cr App R 220 concerning the return of a jemmy to its owner) because the alleged accessory does not intend to aid the offence but rather merely to comply with his supposed civil-law duties. Critics of this general position rightly point out that it can hardly apply to a person returning a revolver to its owner knowing that he is then going to use it to carry out a murder. But here a jury probably would infer intention to aid from the accused knowledge of the effects of his action, and the flexibility of the notion of intention enables an appropriate solution to be found to situations for which it is difficult to formulate precise rules in advance.
>
> It is particularly important to stress the need for an intention to aid where the accused may not personally appreciate the natural and probable consequences of his action as in *Clarkson* [1971] 1 WLR 1402 where there was 'at least the possibility that a drunken man with his self-discipline loosened by drink … might not intend that his presence should offer encouragement to rapers; … he might nor realise that he was giving encouragement' (at p. 1406). The reference to intoxication underlines the fact that complicity normally requires intention rather than recklessness (*Blakely v DPP* [1991] Crim LR 763) and that, for the purposes of the Majewski rule (*DPP v Majewski* [1977] AC 443: see A3.10), complicity can be regarded as requiring specific intent.'

[64]   Mr Farrell relies upon *Lynch, Powell and English* [below, p **316**] and *Rook* in support of his argument that no such intent is required. We have already examined *Rook* and conclude that it is not authority for Mr Farrell's proposition. In *Powell and English* the appeals related, per Lord Hutton at page 16, to:

> 'the liability of a participant in a joint criminal enterprise when another participant in that enterprise is guilty of a crime, the commission of which was not the purpose of the enterprise'

[65]   Lord Hutton cited, amongst other authorities, the High Court of Australia in *McAuliffe v R* 69 ALJR 621, at 624 for the proposition that 'each of the parties to an arrangement or understanding

is guilty of any crime falling within the scope of the common purpose which is committed in carrying out that purpose' and concluded at page 27:

> 'it is sufficient to found a conviction for murder for a secondary party to have realised that in the course of the joint enterprise the primary party might kill with intent to do so or with intent to cause grievous bodily harm.'

[66] However, because *Powell and English* is another 'joint enterprise' case concerned with the extent of the liability of a secondary party for acts going beyond the scope of a joint enterprise to which he was a party, it does not help the resolution of the instant case in which the question raised was whether there was any intent on the part of the secondary party to assist at all. Mr Farrell did not argue for the Crown that the fact that the Appellant took X to the caravan with a gun, albeit almost certainly an offence against the Firearms legislation, was sufficient in itself to bring the principles in *Powell and English* into play. The issue was whether the appellant intended to hinder rather than assist in violence against the victim; it was an issue whether there was any common purpose or intention to assist at all.

[67] We return to *Lynch*. In that case, the principal issue related to the defence of duress. The House by a majority held that the defence of duress was available to a secondary party, a conclusion subsequently overruled in *Howe* [1987] AC 417. The second certified question was:

> 'Where a person charged with murder as an aider and abettor is shown to have intentionally done an act which assists in the commission of the murder with knowledge that the probable result of his act, combined with the acts of those whom his act is assisting, will be the death or serious bodily injury of another, is his guilt thereby established *without the necessity of proving his willingness to participate in the crime*?' (emphasis added)

[68] The emphasised words show that the second question was concerned with whether the secondary party must intend the crime to be committed. We have already set out the view of Lord Morris on that issue (see paragraph 45 above).

[69] Lord Simon said at 698F that the majority in the Court of Appeal had held, rightly in his view, that the mens rea 'did not involve "a specific intent" '. Lord Simon continued at 698G–699B:

> 'As Devlin J said in *National Coalboard v Gamble* [1959] 1 QB 11, 20:
>
>> A person who supplies the instrument for a crime or anything essential to its commission aids in the commission of it; and if he does so knowingly and with intent to aid, he abets it as well and is therefore guilty of aiding and abetting.
>>
>> The actus reus is the supplying of an instrument for a crime or anything essential for its commission. On Devlin J's analysis the mens rea does not go beyond this. The act of supply must be voluntary (in the sense I tried to define earlier in this speech), and it must be foreseen that the instrument or other object or service supplied will probably (or possibly and desiredly) be used for the commission of a crime. The definition of the crime does not in itself suggest any ulterior intent; and whether anything further in the way of mens rea was required was precisely the point at issue in *Gamble's* case. Slade J thought the very concept of aiding and abetting imported the concept of motive. But Lord Goddard CJ and Devlin J disagreed with this. So do I. Slade J thought that abetting involved assistance or encouragement, and that both implied motive. So far as assistance is concerned, this is clearing not so. One may lend assistance without any motive, or even with the motive of bringing about a result directly contrary to that in fact assisted by one's effort.'

[70] Despite that passage, it seems to us, as to the authors *of Blackstone* (paragraph 63 above) that *Lynch* is not authority for the proposition that there does not have to be an intent to assist. We do not think that those words of Lord Simon were intended to go further than the words of Devlin J which he was approving. Lynch was concerned primarily with duress and secondly with whether it was necessary to show that the secondary party intended the commission of the crime committed by the perpetrator.

[71] We are of the view that, outside the *Powell and English* situation (violence beyond the level anticipated in the course of a joint criminal enterprise), where a defendant, D, is charged as the secondary party to an offence committed by P in reliance on acts which have assisted steps taken by P in the preliminary stages of a crime later committed by P in the absence of D, it is necessary for the Crown to prove intentional assistance by D in the sense of an intention to assist (and not to hinder or obstruct) P in acts which D knows are steps taken by P towards the commission of the offence. Without such intention the mens rea will be absent whether as a matter of direct intent on the part of D or by way of an intent sufficient for D to be liable on the basis of 'common purpose' or 'joint enterprise'. Thus, the prosecution must prove:

(a) an act done by D which in fact assisted the later commission of the offence,

(b) that D did the act deliberately realising that it was capable of assisting the offence,

(c) that D at the time of doing the act contemplated the commission of the offence by A ie he foresaw it as a 'real or substantial risk' or 'real possibility' and,

(d) that D when doing the act intended to assist A in what he was doing.

Callow v Tillstone
(1900) 83 LT 411, Queen's Bench Division

(Lawrence and Kennedy JJ)

A heifer belonging to a farmer, Lintott, became very ill in consequence of eating yew leaves. Lintott killed the heifer which would probably have died in a few minutes. Callow, a veterinary surgeon, accompanied by Lintott and Grey, a butcher, examined the carcase and certified that it was sound and healthy. The examination was negligently conducted. If Callow had exercised due care, he must have discovered that the meat was unsound. Grey offered the meat for sale and was convicted by the justices of exposing for sale meat which was unsound and unfit for human consumption. Subsequently Callow was convicted by the justices of aiding and abetting Grey's offence. The justices found that Callow had been guilty of negligence and that such negligence had caused the exposure of the unsound meat for sale. The justices stated a case, asking 'Was the negligence of which the justices found Callow had been guilty sufficient to support the conviction for aiding and abetting . . .?'

Lawrence J. In this case we have no doubt that the justices came to a wrong conclusion in finding that the appellant Callow was guilty of the offence charged against him. What they had found him guilty of was only negligence, and the question now arises upon that finding whether Callow, who was the veterinary surgeon called in in the case, can be found guilty of aiding and abetting the exposing for sale of this unsound meat, when all that the justices find against him is negligence. The justices found that Callow had been guilty of negligence and thereby abetted Grey, and upon that they convicted him. We think that is not sufficient, and the case of *Benford v Simms* [1898] 2 QB 641 is very strong to show that it is not sufficient. In that case, where there was a conviction, the defendant, a veterinary surgeon, had— according to the finding of the justices—knowingly counselled the owner of a horse to cause the act of cruelty in question and Channell J says at the end of his judgment, that the decision of the court in that case 'afforded no ground whatever for supposing that a veterinary surgeon who gives a wrong opinion and commits an error in judgment is liable to be convicted of cruelty if the effect of his opinion being followed is that the act of cruelty does in fact result'. I think, therefore, the appeal must be allowed.

Kennedy J: I am entirely of the same opinion. It seems to me that all that is found by the justices against the appellant is negligence, and to my mind a person cannot be convicted of aiding and abetting the commission of this offence upon such a finding. In this case the appellant gave his certificate, one is bound to assume, quite honestly, and therefore it seems to me he ought not to be convicted under s 5 of aiding and abetting the exposing of the meat for sale.

Appeal allowed. Conviction quashed

Questions

1. It is clear that it would have been no defence for the butcher to show that he was exercising all proper care reasonably relying on the skill and judgement of the vet, and had no means of knowing that the meat was unsound: *Hobbs v Winchester Corpn* [1910] 2 KB 471, CA (a decision to which Kennedy LJ was a party). In such a case, what is the justification for convicting the butcher who is blameless while acquitting the veterinary surgeon who is the cause of the commission of the offence?

2. If the policy of strict liability requires the conviction of a blameless principal, why does it not equally require the conviction of a blameless secondary party?—let alone a negligent secondary party?

(8) ABETTING BY INACTIVITY

Clause 27 of the Draft Criminal Code provides:

27(1) A person is guilty of an offence as an accessory if:

(a) he intentionally procures, assists or encourages the act which constitutes or results in the commission of the offence by the principal; and....

(3) Assistance or encouragement includes assistance or encouragement arising from a failure by a person to take reasonable steps to exercise any authority or to discharge any duty he has to control the relevant acts of the principal in order to prevent the commission of the offence.

The Law Commission comment as follows:

9.22 *Passive assistance or encouragement.* Sub-section (3) states a more controversial principle, which is, however, well supported by authority. A person does not ordinarily become an accessory to an offence merely by omitting to take steps to prevent it. But he may incur accessory liability through failure to exercise some special authority or duty that he has to control the act of another that constitutes an offence. Having such an authority, for example, by virtue of his management of premises or his ownership of a chattel, he may fail to take steps to prevent an offence taking place on those premises or through use of the chattel. This failure to act may in the circumstances constitute assistance, or be a source of encouragement, to the principal. This seems to be the effect of the case law, although the language of the judgments is not always easy to interpret.

9.23 The principle has been criticised by the Working Party, who proposed its abolition [Working Paper No 43, Proposition 6(4)], by Professor Glanville Williams [187 LS 92] and by the Society of Public Teachers of Law in its submission to us on the Code team's Bill. But most commentators on the Working Paper and on the Bill found nothing objectionable in the principle, although some concern was expressed about the width of what is now clause 27(3). As that provision is an attempt to state a principle of the common law which we are satisfied does exist, its inclusion is consistent with our general restatement aim. As regards the statement of the principle, we believe, first, that on the authorities it is rightly stated in terms of a person's having either an authority or a duty to control the conduct of the principal; and, secondly, that it is not possible to express it more narrowly by any formula limiting the range of cases in which a relevant authority or duty arises.

The authorities referred to are *Du Cros v Lambourne* [1907] 1 KB 40; *Rubie v Faulkner* [1940] 1 KB 571; *Harris* [1964] Crim LR 54; *Tuck v Robson* [1970] 1 All ER 1171, [1970] 1 WLR 741; *Bland* [1988] Crim LR 41.

In *Du Cros v Lambourne* D was charged with driving his Mercedes motor car at a speed dangerous to the public (about 50 mph), contrary to s 8 of the Motor Car Act 1903. A number of witnesses testified that D was driving the car but D and three other persons gave evidence that it was being driven by Miss Victoria Godwin, a 'certified expert motor-car driver'. The court of Quarter Sessions were satisfied that, whether D or Godwin was driving, he must have known that the speed at which the car was being driven was very dangerous to the public, having regard to the locality and all the circumstances of the case. If Godwin was driving, she was doing so with the consent and approval of D, who was the owner and in control of the car and was sitting by her side, and he could and ought to have prevented her driving at such excessive and dangerous speed, but instead he allowed her to do so and did not interfere in any way. They held that it was therefore unnecessary to decide whether D was himself driving or not. The Divisional Court (Alverstone LCJ, Ridley and Darling JJ) agreed. Alverstone LCJ said:

It is impossible to come to any other conclusion than that the court was satisfied that the appellant was doing acts which would amount to aiding, abetting, counselling or procuring.

Darling J said (1906) 21 Cox CC 311 at 316, that allowing Godwin to drive:

... was precisely the same thing as if he did it himself. He had authority and power to interfere but he did not do so although he knew the car was being driven at excessive speed. It seems to me that it is a misuse of language to say that he was not driving the motor-car.

But Darling J evidently had second thoughts because this passage does not appear in his revised judgment in [1907] 1 KB 40, 46. Were second thoughts best?

Note that under cl 27(1) of the Draft Code the court or jury must be satisfied that D in fact assisted or encouraged, and intended to assist or encourage, the relevant act. Subsection (3) provides only that actual and intended assistance or encouragement by failure to take reasonable steps is enough.

R v Allan

[1963] 2 All ER 897, Court of Criminal Appeal

(Edmund Davies, Marshall and Lawton JJ)

The appellants were convicted of making an affray at common law (see now Public Order Act 1986) and appealed on the ground of misdirection.

Edmund Davies J. In effect, it amounts to this: that the learned judge ... directed the jury that they were in duty bound to convict an accused who was proved to have been present and witnessing an affray if it was also proved that he nursed an intention to join in if help was needed by the side which he favoured, and this notwithstanding that he did nothing by words or deeds to evince his intention and outwardly played the role of a purely passive spectator. It was said that, if that direction is right, where A and B behave themselves to all outward appearances in an exactly similar manner, but it be proved that A had the intention to participate if needs be, whereas B had no such intention, then A must be convicted of being a principal in the second degree to the affray, whereas B should be acquitted. To do that, it is objected, would be to convict A on his thoughts, even though they found no reflection in his actions. For the Crown, on the other hand, it is contended that the direction was unimpeachable, and that, in the given circumstances, a jury doing its duty would be bound to convict A of aiding and abetting in an affray, even though he uttered no word of encouragement and acted throughout in exactly the same manner as all the other spectators of what was happening.

Applying [passages in *Coney*] to the direction in the present case, we have come to the conclusion that, in effect, the trial judge here dealt with facts which, at most, might provide some evidence of encouragement as amounting to conclusive proof of guilt. The jury were in terms told that a man who chooses to remain at a fight, nursing the secret intention to help if the need arose, but doing nothing to evince that intention, *must* in law be held to be a principal in the second degree and that, on these facts being proved, the jury would have no alternative but to convict him. In our judgment, that was a misdirection. As Cave J said in *Coney* [(1882) 8 QBD 534 at 540], 'Where presence is prima facie not accidental it is evidence, but no more than evidence, for the jury', and it remains no more than evidence for the jury even when one adds to presence at an affray a secret intention to help. No authority in support of the direction given in the present case has been cited to us. The passage in *Young* [(1838) 8 C & P 644 at 652] cited in *Coney* [(1882) 8 QBD 534 at 541], is incomplete, and reference to the report itself makes clear that Vaughan J was there dealing with presence at a fight as the result of a previous arrangement. The only other case cited by the Crown, *Wilcox v Jeffery* [below, p 314] turned on special facts very different from the present, and is one from which we think no general principle can be deduced. In the present case, the trial judge dealt with matters of evidence from which encouragement (and, therefore, guilty participation) might be inferred if—but only if—the jury thought fit to do so as necessarily amounting in law to proof that guilt was established. In our judgment, this amounted to a misdirection, and one, unfortunately, of a basic kind.

Appeals allowed

R v Clarkson and Carroll

[1971] 3 All ER 344, Courts-Martial Appeal Court

(Megaw LJ, Geoffrey Lane and Kilner Brown JJ)

The appellants, soldiers, entered a room in their barracks in which a girl was being raped by other soldiers. They were charged with aiding and abetting the rape. There was no evidence that either had done any act or uttered any word which involved direct physical participation or verbal encouragement. They appealed on the ground of misdirection by the judge-advocate.

[**Megaw LJ** delivered the judgment of the court:]

Coney [(1882) 8 QBD 534] decided that non-accidental presence at the scene of the crime is not conclusive of aiding and abetting. The jury has to be told by the judge, or as in this case the court-martial has to be told by the judge-advocate, in clear terms what it is that has to be proved before they can convict of aiding and abetting; what it is of which the jury or the court-martial, as the case may be, must be sure as matters of inference before they can convict of aiding and abetting in such a case where the evidence adduced by the prosecution is limited to non-accidental presence (His Lordship quoted from *Coney* [(1882) 8 QBD 534 at 557, 558]). It is not enough, then, that the presence of the accused has, in fact, given encouragement. It must be proved that he *wilfully* encouraged. In such a case as the present, more than in many other cases where aiding and abetting is alleged, it was essential that that element should be stressed; for there was here at least the possibility that a drunken man with his self-discipline loosened by drink, being aware that a woman was being raped, might be attracted to the scene and might stay on the scene in the capacity of what is known as a voyeur; and, while his presence and the presence of others might in fact encourage the rapers or discourage the victim, he himself, enjoying the scene or at least standing by assenting, might not intend that his presence should offer encouragement to rapers and would-be rapers or discouragement to the victim; he might not realise that he was giving encouragement; so that, while encouragement there might be, it would not be a case in which, to use the words of Hawkins J [(1882) 8 QBD 534 at 558] the accused person wilfully encouraged. [His Lordship quoted *Allan*, p **312**, above.]

From that it follows that mere intention is not in itself enough. There must be an intention to encourage; and there must also be encouragement in fact, in cases such as the present case.

Appeals allowed

Wilcox v Jeffery
[1951] 1 All ER 464, King's Bench Division

(Lord Goddard CJ, Humphreys and Devlin JJ)

Lord Goddard CJ. This is a case stated by the metropolitan magistrate at Bow Street Magistrates' Court before whom the appellant, Herbert William Wilcox, the proprietor of a periodical called *Jazz Illustrated*, was charged on an information that 'on 11 December 1949, he did unlawfully aid and abet one Coleman Hawkins in contravening art 1(4) of the Aliens Order 1920, by failing to comply with a condition attached to a grant of leave to land, to wit, that the said Coleman Hawkins should take no employment paid or unpaid while in the United Kingdom, contrary to art 18(2) of the Aliens Order 1920'. Under the Aliens Order, art 1(1), it is provided that

'... an alien coming ... by sea to a place in the United Kingdom—(a) shall not land in the United Kingdom without the leave of an immigration officer ...'

It is provided by art 1(4) that:

'An immigration officer, in accordance with general or special directions of the Secretary of State, may, by general order or notice or otherwise, attach such conditions as he may think fit to the grant of leave to land, and the Secretary of State may at any time vary such conditions in such manner as he thinks fit, and the alien shall comply with the conditions so attached or varied ...'

If the alien fails to comply, he is to be in the same position as if he has landed without permission, ie he commits an offence.

The case is concerned with the visit of a celebrated professor of the saxophone, a gentleman by the name of Hawkins who was a citizen of the United States. He came here at the invitation of two gentlemen of the name of Curtis and Hughes, connected with a jazz club which enlivens the neighbourhood of Willesden. They, apparently, had applied for permission for Mr Hawkins to land and it was refused, but, nevertheless, this professor of the saxophone arrived with four French musicians. When they came to the airport, among the people who were there to greet them was the appellant. He had not arranged their visit, but he knew they were coming and he was there to report the arrival of these important musicians for his magazine. So, evidently, he was regarding the visit of Mr Hawkins as a matter which would be of interest to himself and the magazine which he was editing and selling for profit. Messrs Curtis and Hughes arranged a concert at the Princes Theatre, London. The appellant attended that concert as a spectator. He paid for his ticket. Mr Hawkins went on the stage and delighted the audience by playing the saxophone. The appellant did not get up and protest in the name of the musicians of England that Mr Hawkins ought not to be here competing with them and taking the bread out of their mouths or the wind out of their instruments. It is not found that he actually applauded, but he was there having paid to go in, and, no doubt, enjoying the performance, and then, lo and behold, out comes his magazine with a most laudatory description, fully illustrated, of this concert. On those facts the magistrate has found that he aided and abetted.

Reliance is placed by the prosecution on *Coney* [see p 313, above].

There was not accidental presence in this case. The appellant paid to go to the concert and he went there because he wanted to report it. He must, therefore, be held to have been present, taking part, concurring, or encouraging, whichever word you like to use for expressing this conception. It was an illegal act on the part of Hawkins to play the saxophone or any other instrument at this concert. The appellant clearly knew that it was an unlawful act for him to play. He had gone there to hear him, and his presence and his payment to go there was an encouragement. He went there to make use of the performance, because he went there, as the magistrate finds and was justified in finding, to get 'copy' for his newspaper. It might have been entirely different, as I say, if he had gone there and protested, saying: 'The musicians' union do not like you foreigners coming here and playing and you ought to get off the stage'. If he had booed, it might have been some evidence that he was not aiding and abetting. If he had gone as a member of a *claque* to try to drown the noise of the saxophone, he might very likely be found not guilty of aiding and abetting. In this case it seems clear that he was there, not only to approve and encourage what was done, but to take advantage of it by getting 'copy' for his paper. In those circumstances there was evidence on which the magistrate could find that the appellant aided and abetted, and for these reasons I am of opinion that the appeal fails.

Humphreys J. I agree that there was evidence sufficient to justify the finding of the magistrate.

Devlin J. I agree, and I wish to add only a word on the application of *Coney*. Counsel for the appellant sought to distinguish that case on the facts inasmuch as in *Coney* the performance, which was a prize fight, was illegal from beginning to end, whereas in the case we are considering the bulk of the concert was quite legal, the only part of the performance which was illegal being that which involved Mr Hawkins. That, however, is not, in my judgment, a distinction which affects the application to this case of the principle in *Coney*. It may well be that if a spectator goes to a concert he may explain his presence during an illegal item by saying that he hardly felt it necessary to get up and go out and then return when the performance resumed its legality, if I may so call it. It is conceivable that in such circumstances (and I should wish to consider it further if it ever arose) the presence of a person during one item might fall within the accidental or casual class was envisaged by Cave J. Here there was abundant evidence, apart from the mere fact of the appellant's presence, that he was making use of this item in the performance and that his attendance at that item was, therefore, deliberate. In those circumstances I think the principle in *R v Coney* applies, and that the magistrate was justified in drawing the inference which he did draw.

Appeal dismissed with costs

Questions

1. Fred and George go to a public house on Saturday night. They know that during the evening an obscene performance lasting half an hour will be given. Fred, who only drinks lemonade, goes because he relishes an obscene show. George, who is not interested in the show, is only there for the beer. The licensee is convicted of keeping a disorderly house. Are Fred and George guilty of abetting him?

2. Cf Law Commission Working Paper No 43, Proposition 8:

A person does not become an accessory to an offence if the offence is so defined that his conduct in it is inevitably incidental to its commission and such conduct is not expressly penalised.

If this were law, would *Wilcox v Jeffery* be overruled?

(9) JOINT ENTERPRISE

R v Powell; R v English

[1997] 4 All ER 545, House of Lords

(Lords Goff, Jauncey, Mustill, Steyn and Hutton)

P and D went with another man to the house of a drug dealer for the purpose of buying drugs but the drug dealer was shot dead at the door. It was not clear who had shot the drug dealer but P and D were convicted of murder on the basis of the Crown's case that if the third man had fired the gun, they knew that he was armed with a gun and realized that he might use it to kill or cause really serious injury to the drug dealer. P and D appealed against their convictions to the Court of Appeal, which dismissed the appeals and P and D appealed to the House of Lords.

In the second appeal, E and W took part in a joint attack on a police officer in which they both caused injury with wooden posts but the police officer died from fatal stab wounds inflicted by W. E was convicted of murder, the judge having directed the jury to do so if they found that he had joined in an unlawful attack realizing at the time that there was a substantial risk that W might kill the police officer during the attack or at least cause some really serious injury to him. E and W appealed to the Court of Appeal, which dismissed the appeals and E appealed to the House of Lords.

Lord Goff and **Lord Jauncey** agreed with the speech of **Lord Hutton**.

Lord Mustill concurred in the reasoning of **Lord Steyn** and **Lord Hutton**.

Lord Steyn agreed with the speech of **Lord Hutton** and continued:

There are two separate but complementary legal concepts at stake. The first is the mental element sufficient for murder, ie an intention to kill or to cause really serious bodily injury. Only if this element is proved in respect of the primary offender, and if the other ingredients of murder are proved, does the second concept arise for consideration, viz the criminal liability of accessories to a joint criminal enterprise. Under the accessory principle criminal liability is dependent on proof of subjective foresight on the part of a participant in the criminal enterprise that the primary offender might commit a greater offence, that being in these cases foresight that the primary offender might commit murder as defined in law.

The thrust of both appeals was to challenge the existing law and practice regarding the second concept. The appeals under consideration relate to charges of murder. But there is no special rule regarding the criminal liability of accessories in cases of murder. The principle governing the criminal liability of accessories applies across the spectrum of most criminal offences. Any alteration in the accessory principle, as presently understood, would have to apply to most criminal offences. That does not mean that the arguments advanced on behalf of the appellants are unsound. But it under-lines the sweeping impact of the changes to the existing law and practice necessarily involved in an acceptance of the submissions made on behalf of the appellants in these appeals.

The established principle is that a secondary party to a criminal enterprise may be criminally liable for a greater criminal offence committed by the primary offender of a type which the former foresaw but did not necessarily intend. The criminal culpability lies in participating in the criminal enterprise with that foresight. Foresight and intention are not synonymous terms. But foresight is a necessary and sufficient ground of the liability of accessories. That is how the law has been stated in two carefully reasoned decisions of the Privy Council (see *Chan Wing-siu v R* [1984] 3 All ER 877, [1985] AC 168 and *Hui Chi-ming v R* [1991] 3 All ER 897, [1992] 1 AC 34). In a valuable article Professor Sir John Smith has recently concluded that there is no doubt that this represents English law (see 'Criminal Liability of Accessories: Law and Law Reform' (1997) 113 LQR 453 at 455). And Lord Hutton has demonstrated in his comprehensive review of the case law that the law is as stated in the two Privy Council decisions. That does not mean that the established principle cannot be re-examined and, if found to be flawed, reformulated. But the existing law and practice forms the starting point.

Counsel for the appellants argued that the secondary party to a criminal enterprise should only be guilty of a murder committed by the primary offender if the secondary party has the full mens rea sufficient for murder, ie an intent to kill or to cause really serious bodily harm. Their arguments fell into three parts, namely: (1) that there is a disharmony between two streams of authority; (2) that the accessory principle involves a form of constructive criminal liability; and (3) that it is anomalous that a lesser form of culpability is sufficient for a secondary party than for the primary offender. The first part of the argument centred on the scope of decisions of the House of Lords in *R v Moloney*, above, p **120** and *R v Hancock*, above, p **124**. Those decisions distinguish between foresight and intention and require in the case of murder proof of intention to kill or cause serious bodily injury. But those decisions were intended to apply to a primary offender only. The liability of accessories was not in issue. Plainly the House did not intend in those decisions to examine or pronounce on the accessory principle. The resort to authority must therefore fail.

That brings me to the second argument. If the application of the accessory principle results in a form of constructive liability that would be contrary to principle and it would be a defect in our criminal law. But subject to a qualification about the definition of the mens rea required for murder to which I will turn later, I would reject the argument that the accessory principle *as such* imposes a form of constructive liability. The accessory principle requires proof of a subjective state of mind on the part of a participant in a criminal enterprise, viz foresight that the primary offender might commit a different and more serious offence. Professor Sir John Smith explained how the principle applies in the case of murder ((1997) 113 LQR 453 at 464):

> 'Nevertheless, as the critics point out it is enough that the accessory is reckless, whereas, in the case of the principal, intention must be proved. Recklessness whether death be caused is a sufficient *mens rea* for a principal offender in manslaughter, but not murder. The accessory to murder, however, must be proved to have been reckless, not merely whether death might be caused, but whether murder might be committed; *he must have been aware, not merely that death or grievous bodily harm might be caused, but that it might be caused intentionally, by a person whom he was assisting or encouraging to commit a crime*. Recklessness whether murder be committed is different from, and more serious than, recklessness whether death be caused by an accident.' (My emphasis.)

The foresight of the secondary party must be directed to a real possibility of the commission by the primary offender in the course of the criminal enterprise of the greater offence. The liability is imposed because the secondary party is assisting in and encouraging a criminal enterprise which he is aware might result in the commission of a greater offence. The liability of an accessory is predicted on his culpability in respect of the greater offence as defined in law. It is undoubtedly a lesser form of mens rea. But it is unrealistic to say that the accessory principle as such imposes constructive criminal liability.

At first glance, there is substance in the third argument that it is anomalous that a lesser form of culpability is required in the case of a secondary party, viz foresight of the possible commission of the greater offence, whereas in the case of the primary offender the law insists on proof of the specific intention which is an ingredient of the offence. This general argument leads, in the present case, to the particular argument that it is anomalous that the secondary party can be guilty of murder if he foresees the possibility of such a crime being committed while the primary can only be guilty if he has an intent to kill or cause really serious injury. Recklessness may suffice in the case of the secondary party but it does not in the case of the primary offender. The answer to this supposed anomaly, and other similar cases across the spectrum of criminal law, is to be found in practical and policy considerations. If the law required proof of the specific intention on the part of a secondary party, the utility of the accessory principle would be gravely undermined. It is just that a secondary party who foresees that the primary offender might kill with the intent sufficient for murder, and assists and encourages the primary offender in the criminal enterprise on this basis, should be guilty of murder. He ought to be criminally liable for harm which he foresaw and which in fact resulted from the crime he assisted and encouraged. But it would in practice almost invariably be impossible for a jury to say that the secondary party wanted death to be caused or that he regarded it as virtually certain. In the real world proof of an intention sufficient for murder would be well nigh impossible in the vast major-ity of joint enterprise cases. Moreover, the proposed change in the law must be put in context. The criminal justice system exists to control crime. A prime function of that system must be to deal justly but effectively with those who join with others in criminal enterprises. Experience has shown that joint criminal enterprises only too readily escalate into the commission of greater offences. In order to deal with this important social problem the accessory principle is needed and cannot be abolished or relaxed. For these reasons, I would reject the arguments advanced in favour of the revision of the accessory principle.

Lord Hutton, having comprehensively reviewed the authorities, concluded that it is sufficient to found a conviction for murder for a secondary party to have realised that in the course of the joint enterprise the primary party might kill with intent to do so or with intent to cause grievous bodily harm and that, accordingly, the appeals of Powell and Daniels must be dismissed:

Mr Sallon QC, for the appellant, advanced to your Lordships' House the submission (which does not appear to have been advanced in the Court of Appeal) that in a case such as the present one where the primary party kills with a deadly weapon, which the secondary party did not know that he had and therefore did not foresee his use of it, the secondary party should not be guilty of murder. He sub-mitted that to be guilty under the principle stated in *Chan Wing-siu v R* the secondary party must foresee an act of the type which the principal party committed, and that in the present case the use of a knife was fundamentally different to the use of a wooden post.

My Lords, I consider that this submission is correct. It finds strong support in the passage of the judgment of Lord Parker CJ in *R v Anderson and Morris* [1966] 2 All ER 644 at 648, [1966] 2 QB 110 at 120 which I have set out earlier, but which it is convenient to set out again in this portion of the judgment:

> 'It seems to this court that to say that adventurers are guilty of manslaughter when one of them has departed completely from the concerted action of the common design and has suddenly formed an intent to kill and has used a weapon and acted in a way which no party to that common design could suspect is something which would revolt the conscience of people today.'

The judgment in *Chan Wing-siu v R* [1984] 3 All ER 877 at 880, [1985] AC 168 at 175 also supports the argument advanced on behalf of the appellant because Sir Robin Cooke stated: 'The case must depend rather on the wider principle whereby a secondary party is criminally liable for *acts by the primary offender of a type* which the former foresees but does not necessarily intend.' (My emphasis).

There is also strong support for the appellant's submission in the decision of Carswell J (as he then was), sitting without a jury in the Crown Court in Northern Ireland, in *R v Gamble* [1989] NI 268. In that case, the four accused were all members of a terrorist organisation, the Ulster Volun-teer Force, who had a grievance against a man named Patton. The four accused entered upon a joint venture to inflict punishment upon him, two of them, Douglas and McKee, contemplating that Patton would be subjected to a severe beating or to 'kneecapping' (firing a bullet into his kneecap). In the course of the attack upon him Patton was brutally murdered by the other two accused. His throat was cut with a knife with great force which rapidly caused his death. In addition he was shot with four bullets, and two of the bullet wounds would have been fatal had his death not been caused by the cutting of his throat. Douglas and McKee had not foreseen killing with a knife or firing of bullets into a vital part of the body. It was argued, however, on behalf of the prosecution that the joint enterprise of committing grievous bodily harm, combined with the rule that an intent to cause such harm grounded a conviction for murder in respect of a resulting death, was sufficient to make the two accused liable for murder notwithstanding that they had not foreseen the actions which actually caused death. After citing the relevant authorities Carswell J rejected this argument and stated (at 283–284):

'When an assailant "kneecaps" his victim, ie discharges a weapon into one of his limbs, most commonly into the knee joint, there must always be the risk that it will go wrong and that an artery may be severed or the limb may be so damaged that gangrene sets in, both potentially fatal complications. It has to be said, however, that such cases must be very rare among victims of what is an abhorrent and disturbingly frequent crime. Persons who take a part in inflicting injuries of this nature no doubt do not generally expect that they will endanger life, and I should be willing to believe that in most cases they believe that they are engaged in a lesser offence than murder. The infliction of grievous bodily harm came within the contemplation of Douglas and McKee, and they might therefore be regarded as having placed themselves within the ambit of life-threatening conduct. It may further be said that they must be taken to have had within their contemplation the possibility that might be put at risk. The issue is whether it follows as a consequence that they cannot be heard to say that the murder was a different crime from the attack which they contemplated, and so cannot escape liability for the murder on the ground that it was outside the common design. To accept this type of reasoning would be to fix an accessory with consequences of his acts which he did not foresee and did not desire or intend. The modern development of the criminal law has been away from such an approach and towards a greater emphasis on subjective tests of criminal guilt, as Sir Robin Cooke pointed out in *Chan Wing-Siu*. Although the rule remains well entrenched that an intention to inflict grievous bodily harm qualifies as the mens rea of murder, it is not in my opinion necessary to apply it in such a way as to fix an accessory with liability for a consequence which he did not intend and which stems from an act which he did not have within his contemplation. I do not think that the state of the law compels me to reach such a conclusion, and it would not in my judgment accord with the public sense of what is just and fitting.'

In my opinion, this decision was correct in that a secondary party who foresees grievous bodily harm caused by kneecapping with a gun should not be guilty of murder where, in an action unforeseen by the secondary party, another party to the criminal enterprise kills the victim by cutting his throat with a knife. The issue (which is one of fact after the tribunal of fact has directed itself, or has been directed, in accordance with the statement of Lord Parker CJ in *R v Anderson and Morris* [1966] 2 All ER 644 at 648, [1966] 2 QB 110 at 120) whether a secondary party who foresees the use of a gun to kneecap, and death is then caused by the deliberate firing of the gun into the head or body of the victim, is guilty of murder is more debatable although, with respect, I agree with the decision of Carswell J on the facts of that case.

Accordingly, in the appeal of English, I consider that the direction of the learned trial judge was defective (although this does not constitute a criticism of the judge...

Powell and Daniels' appeals dismissed

English's appeal allowed

R v Uddin
[1998] 2 All ER 744, Court of Appeal, Criminal Division

(Beldam LJ, Johnson and Wright JJ)

The appellant, U, was one of six men who, with poles and bars, attacked another man, V. V died of a stab wound inflicted in the course of the attack by one of the men, T. T and U were convicted of murder and three others of manslaughter. U appealed on the ground that the judge had failed to direct the jury that U was guilty of murder only if he foresaw the possibility that a knife would be used.

Beldam LJ, having discussed *English* and *Chan Wing-siu*: Such an analysis of the assessment of risk, whilst appropriate in the case of criminals who agree together in advance to commit an offence such as armed robbery, does not readily fit the spontaneous behaviour of a group of irrational individuals who jointly attack a common victim, each intending severally to inflict serious harm by any means at their disposal and giving no thought to the means by which the others will individually commit similar offences on the same person. In truth each in committing his individual offence assists and encourages the others in committing their individual offences. They are at the same time principals and secondary parties. Because it is often a matter of chance whether one or other of them inflicts a fatal injury, the law attributes responsibility for the acts done by one to all of them, unless one of the attackers completely departs from the concerted actions of the others and in so doing causes the victim's death. An example found in the observations of Lord Parker CJ in *R v Anderson and Morris* [1966] 2 All ER 644 at 648, [1966] 2 QB 110 at 120 is when one of the participants suddenly forms an intent to kill using a weapon in a way in which no other party could suspect.

In this example the party departing from the common enterprise has not only formed a different intent but has acted in a way which no other party could suspect. In short he has not merely brought about the death of the victim with a different intent but has used a weapon which the others did not know or suspect he had with him. The essential ingredients of his offence are different and the actions of the others coincided with, but did not contribute to or assist, the commission of his offence. The difficulty in applying these principles to a case such as the present led to the expression in the speeches of Lord Mustill and Lord Steyn in *R v Powell* [above, p **316**] of the difficulties in the concepts of joint enterprise and accessory liability and their calls for urgent review of the law of homicide. Notwithstanding these difficulties, we think that the principles applicable to a case such as the present are as follows.

(i) Where several persons join to attack a victim in circumstances which show that they intend to inflict serious harm and as a result of the attack the victim sustains fatal injury, they are jointly liable for murder; but if such injury inflicted with that intent is shown to have been caused solely by the actions of one participant of a type entirely different from actions which the others foresaw as part of the attack, only that participant is guilty of murder.

(ii) In deciding whether the actions are of such a different type the use by that party of a weapon is a significant factor. If the character of the weapon, eg its propensity to cause death is different from any weapon used or contemplated by the others and if it is used with a specific intent to kill, the others are not responsible for the death unless it is proved that they knew or foresaw the likelihood of the use of such a weapon.

(iii) If some or all of the others are using weapons which could be regarded as equally likely to inflict fatal injury, the mere fact that a different weapon was used is immaterial.

(iv) If the jury conclude that the death of the victim was caused by the actions of one participant which can be said to be of a completely different type to those contemplated by the others, they are not to be regarded as parties to the death whether it amounts to murder or manslaughter. They may nevertheless be guilty of offences of wounding or inflicting grievous bodily harm with intent which they individually commit.

(v) If in the course of the concerted attack a weapon is produced by one of the participants and the others knowing that he has it in circumstances where he may use it in the course of the attack participate or continue to participate in the attack, they will be guilty of murder if the weapon is used to inflict a fatal wound.

(vi) In a case in which after a concerted attack it is proved that the victim died as a result of a wound with a lethal weapon, eg a stab wound, but the evidence does not establish which of the participants used the weapon, then if its use was foreseen by the participants in the attack they will all be guilty of murder notwithstanding that the particular participant who administered the fatal blow cannot be identified (see *R v Powell*). If, however, the circumstances do not show that the participants foresaw the use of a weapon of this type, none of them will be guilty of murder though they may individually have committed offences in the course of the attack.

(vii) The mere fact that by attacking the victim together each of them had the intention to inflict serious harm on the victim is insufficient to make them responsible for the death of the victim caused by the use of a lethal weapon used by one of the participants with the same or shared intention.

As we have said, in the present case there was no evidence upon which the jury could find that before the attack began the others involved knew that [T] was carrying a flick-knife....

We are further troubled by the distinction apparently drawn by the jury between the parts played by the three accused convicted of manslaughter and the part played by the appellant. If the actions of Tahid did in fact go outside the common purpose of the attack then those who took part aware that a knife might be used were guilty of murder as secondary parties; if they were not aware that a knife might be used they were entitled to be acquitted. (See the observations of Lord Hutton in *R v English*)....

[The court quashed U's conviction and ordered a retrial and directed that the judgment should be brought to the attention of the co-accused who had been convicted of manslaughter to consider whether they wished to make a renewed application for leave to appeal.]

In the similar case of *Greatrex* [1999] 1 Cr App R 126, [1998] Crim LR 733, it was held that it should have been left to the jury to decide whether kicking with 'a shod foot' which was contemplated by B, was fundamentally different from striking with a bar or spanner, which was not contemplated by him.

The application of the principles can involve the courts in some fine factual distinctions. In *O'Flaherty and others* [2004] EWCA Crim 526, the deceased had been subjected to attack; on one possible view this amounted to a single prolonged incident, but on another possible view it involved two closely related incidents. All three appellants (F, R and T) had been involved in the first incident (or the first part of the incident), but R and T had not taken part in the second incident (or second part). The deceased has suffered a number of serious injuries, including stab wounds inflicted by a fourth defendant, but the exact cause of death was not clear. It was therefore possible that the fatal injuries had been inflicted only after R and T had ceased to play an active role in the attack. On these facts it was held that the jury should have been directed that they had to be satisfied: (i) that the fatal injuries were sustained when the joint enterprise was continuing and that the defendant was still acting within that joint enterprise and (ii) that the acts which caused death were within the scope of that joint enterprise. Even if the jury concluded that there was only one extended incident, they had to be satisfied that the fatal injuries were sustained when the joint enterprise was continuing and that a particular defendant was still acting within that joint enterprise. In F's case there was cogent evidence of his involvement throughout (armed with a cricket bat) but there was no such evidence against R and T, whose convictions were accordingly quashed as unsafe. The court held that:

A defendant who effectively disengages or withdraws before the fatal injury is or injuries are inflicted is not guilty of murder because he was not party to and did not participate in any unlawful violence which caused the fatal injury or injuries.... The question whether or not the violence formed one evolving incident or was two separate and discreet incidents is only relevant in helping to decide whether a particular defendant disengaged before the fatal injury or injuries were caused or joined in after they had been caused.

On the subject of weapons the court considered the authorities (including *Powell and English* (above) and *Uddin*) and observed:

The statements in *Powell and English* and *Uddin* about types of weapons should not be seen as reflecting principles of law as opposed to questions of evidence. The Judicial Studies Board specimen direction in relation to the scenario in *English* treats the question whether use of a knife is fundamentally different from any act which the defendant realised the principal might do as a question of fact for the jury. The principles set out in *Uddin* are not stated to be principles of law as opposed to matters of evidence, and it would be unfortunate if they crystallised as such. The result would be the creation of a complex body of doctrine as to whether one weapon (for instance a knife) differs in character from another (for example a claw hammer) and which weapons are morelikely to inflict fatal injury.

Notes and questions

1. A good earlier illustration of the principle in *English* is *Mahmood* [1994] Crim LR 368. A and B took a car. There was a police chase. A, the driver, abandoned the car in gear so that it ran on and killed a baby. It was held that this was manslaughter by A but not B. Although the jury, having been properly directed, had found as a fact that B *did* foresee that A might do such an act, the Court of Appeal held there was no evidence on which they could so find. It would perhaps have been otherwise if A had killed by excessive speed, going through a red light, etc, acts which a jury might properly find B did foresee. The reckless act which did occur was of an exceptional nature, not one of those acts commonly associated with 'joyriding'.

2. *Use of weapons.* A great many of the joint enterprise cases, as in *English, Uddin* and *Greatrex*, turn on the question whether B knew that A was carrying the weapon he used to cause injury or death. If B did know, that is cogent evidence that he knew that there was a risk that A might commit the crime charged. If B did not know, that is evidence in his favour. When discussing *Gamble* (above, p **318**) Lord Hutton agreed with Carswell J that B, who contemplated the use of a shotgun by A to kneecap V, would not be liable when A produced a knife which B did not know he had, and cut V's throat; but he left open the possibility that B might have been liable if A, unforeseen by B, had used the shotgun to blow V's brains out. Would that make any sense? And is it compatible with Beldam LJ's later dicta in *Uddin*? Is the right view to be found in *Roberts* [1993] 1 All ER 583, where the court said 'True, it will be easier for the Crown to prove that B participated in the venture realising that A might wound with murderous intent if weapons are carried or if the object is to attack the victim or both. But that is purely an evidential difference, not a difference in principle.' See also *Carberry* [1994] Crim LR 446.

3. *Unforeseen consequences of foreseen acts done in the course of a joint enterprise.* It is apparent from the above cases that where B is liable for *an act* done by A in the course of a joint enterprise, he is liable for the unforeseen consequences of that act to the same extent as A. B foresees that A may do an act with intent to cause gbh—A does so and, unforeseen by either, the act causes death—both are guilty of murder. If B foresees that A may do an act with intent to cause abh and A does so, both are guilty of manslaughter if, unforeseen and unforeseeably, the act causes death. What of A who instructs B to carry a shotgun to frighten V, but B uses it to shoot V dead at point blank range. Is A liable for murder? For

manslaughter? What is the act that A must have foreseen—the firing of a shotgun in V's presence or the shooting at V?

4. *Where there is no common purpose and no intention to assist or encourage.* If A and B independently intend the same result, but it is not proved that each intends to assist or encourage the other, neither is liable for acts done by the other which, though he might be pleased by the result, he did not assist or encourage the other to commit: *Petters and Parfitt* [1995] Crim LR 501. If, in such a case, it is not possible to prove which caused the injury or death, neither can be convicted. If, however, B intentionally assists A, even without A's knowledge, it seems that B will be liable for any crime committed by A which B foresaw A might commit while doing the act assisted.

5. *Where there is no common purpose.* In the cases considered above the parties had a common purpose, whether planned or formed on the spur of the moment. Most accessories probably have a common purpose with the principal, but not all. B may give assistance or encouragement to A to commit an offence without in any way sharing his purpose to commit it. He may sell A equipment, knowing that A intends to use it to commit burglary, or a gun, knowing that A intends to use it to kill, being completely indifferent what A does and interested only in the profit to be made on the sale: *National Coal Board v Gamble*, above, p **303**, per Devlin J. Or B may give assistance to A of which A is unaware. Coming by chance upon A assaulting a constable, B trips up a second constable who was running to the aid of the first. Or, being told by A that he is going to commit a certain crime, B encourages him: 'Good. Do that.' This is enough, according to *Giannetto* [1997] 1 Cr App R 1, 13, to make B liable. In these cases, B is liable for the crime which he knows A intends to, and does, commit. What if he knows that there is a real risk that, in the course of committing the intended crime, A will commit—and he does commit—some other more serious offence? In *Reardon* [1999] Crim LR 392 A shot two men, X and Y, in the bar of a public house and carried them, both dying, into the garden. He returned to the bar, said to B that one of them was still alive and asked B for the loan of his knife. B handed A a knife with a six-inch blade which A took into the garden. Medical evidence established that both men would have died from the gunshot wounds but both in fact died from stab wounds inflicted with B's knife. B appealed against his conviction on two counts of murder. He argued that he had loaned the knife to kill only the one person whom he believed to be still alive. He relied on a passage in *Smith and Hogan* (8th edn, 142):

If [B] aids, abets, counsels or procures [A] to commit a crime against a particular person, . . . [B] is not liable if A intentionally commits an offence of the same type against some other person . . .

The court did not dispute this proposition but held there was a further question (the *Chan Wing-siu/English* question):

Did [B] foresee at least the strong possibility that if [A] found that the other deceased was still breathing and alive, he might use the knife in the same way, and if he did so was that an act by [A] of a type which this appellant foresaw but did not necessarily intend?

This was a jury question which, in the court's opinion, had been answered in the affirmative. If the jury had answered the question, no, then there would have been great force in B's submission that he could be convicted of neither murder. Certainly it was a case of both or neither, for there was no way of distinguishing between the victims. B did not know which murder he was aiding. If A had said, 'X is still alive,' B would certainly have been guilty of the murder of X, but not guilty of the murder of Y, unless the *Chan Wing-siu* question were answered in the affirmative. There is no suggestion of common *purpose* between A and B to kill either X or Y. So the case decides that 'parasitic' liability applies to the aider, even where there is no common purpose. The 'parasitic' offence here was of the same gravity as the intended offence, but is not the principle the same? If B had loaned A the knife for the purpose of threatening V, knowing there was a real risk that A would use it intentionally to kill V, and he did, must it not follow logically that B would be guilty of murder?

If, in the example given above, B, when he trips up the officer coming to the aid of his colleague, A, knows that A habitually carries a knife which he is likely to use against a policeman, B would seem to be liable for the wounding which follows—and for murder if he knew there was risk that A would intentionally cause serious injury with the knife. There is a strongly held view that, even before *Reardon*, the law relating to the liability of the accessory stretched too far. What do you think?

6. *Are parties to a joint enterprise all 'principals' in the first degree*? Recently a theory has emerged that all parties to a joint enterprise who are present at the commission of the crime are, in the old terminology of felonies, all principals in the first degree, not secondary parties or accessories. This notion probably lies at the root of a Law Commission recommendation that the whole law of aiding, abetting, counselling and procuring be abolished—s 8 of the 1861 Act, above p 273, would be repealed and replaced by two substantive offences of assisting and encouraging crime, while—possibly, at least—leaving the common law of joint enterprise intact. See Law Com Consultation Paper No 131, 'Assisting and Encouraging Crime', criticized in (1994) 144 NLJ 679. Joint enterprise liability, according to this view, is something different from secondary liability. The Commission's opinion has been impliedly endorsed by Lord Hobhouse, and accords with a decision of High Court of Australia in *Osland v R* (1998) 73 ALJR 173.

In *Osland* a woman and her son, D, agreed to kill V, her husband, D's stepfather, when V was asleep. D, in O's presence, killed him by a blow with an iron pipe. The jury convicted her of murder but disagreed about D. There was therefore no proven murder for the woman to aid and abet. The conviction was upheld by a majority of five to two, relying inter alia on a casebook, *Brett, Waller and Williams*, which states that all parties acting in concert to commit a crime are principals *in the first degree*. It appears to be similar to *Stewart and Schofield* [1995] 3 All ER 159. The appellants and L set out to rob a shopkeeper. L was armed with a scaffolding bar. He and Stewart went into the shop while Schofield kept watch outside. L killed the shopkeeper by blows with the bar. He was convicted of murder and the appellants foresaw that L might cause *some* injury but did *not* foresee that the bar would, or might, be used with intent to cause *serious* injury. The appellants relied, inter alia, on *Dunbar* [1988] Crim LR 693. There, the prosecution's case (which was not accepted by the jury) was that Dunbar hired X to kill Y. X killed Y and the jury convicted X of murder, but acquitted Dunbar of murder and convicted her of manslaughter. As the Court of Appeal said, the jury must have found that Dunbar contemplated the use by X of violence short of gbh but that X went beyond that, and acted with intent to cause at least gbh. Dunbar's conviction of manslaughter was quashed. If she was a party only to an agreement to inflict some harm less than gbh, the killing with intent to do *grievous* bodily harm was not within the ambit of the agreement and she was guilty of neither murder nor manslaughter. She was not responsible for that unforeseen act. In *Stewart and Schofield* Hobhouse LJ, dismissing the appeals, said that *Dunbar* probably should not be categorized as a case of joint enterprise at all. He distinguished a party to a joint enterprise from, as he put it, a 'mere aider and abettor, etc', or secondary party.

In contrast where the allegation is joint enterprise, the allegation is that one party participated in the criminal act of another.

How do you 'participate in the criminal act of another' except by assisting or encouraging that act?—that is, by aiding, abetting, counselling or procuring it. A, B and C agree, and set out, to rape V. A and B hold her down while C has intercourse with her. How can they participate in the act of penile penetration except by assisting or encouraging C to do it? Is it any different in principle if A, B and C set out to kill and C fires the fatal shot?

One possible ground of distinction between *Dunbar* and *Stewart* is that Dunbar was not present, Stewart was. But the Court of Appeal had already decided in *Rook* [1993] 2 All ER 955, [1993] 1 WLR 1005 that the same principles apply to an absent secondary party as to one who is present. *Rook* was not cited to the court in *Stewart and Schofield*; but it seems it would have made no difference to Hobhouse LJ's decision. In a civil action, *Generale Bank Nederland NV v Export Credits Guarantee Department* [1998] 1 Lloyd's Rep at pp 42–44 he relied particularly on *Macklin* (1838) 2 Lew CC 225 where a group of persons attacked a constable, some with sticks, some by throwing stones and some with their fists. Alderson B directed the jury that it is a principle of law that '. . . if several persons act together in pursuance of a common intent, every act in furtherance of such intent by each of them is, in law done by all.'

This formulation of the law goes back at least to the early seventeenth century. Hale, *Pleas of the Crown*, I, 463 refers to a case where one of a number of rioters killed a constable's assistant and it was unanimously agreed at the King's Bench, 'That, altho the indictment were, that B gave the stroke, and the rest were present aiding and abetting, tho in truth C gave the stroke, or that it did not appear on the evidence which of them gave the stroke, but only that it was given by one of the rioters, yet the evidence was sufficient to maintain the indictment, for in law it was the stroke of all that party according to the resolution in Mackally's case. 9 Co Rep 67 b.' Hobhouse LJ went on,

Thus persons who participate in a criminal joint enterprise are, through *the attribution to them of the actus reus,* in reality joint principals with the primary actor. However since the primary actor has himself committed a criminal offence, there is a tendency to treat him alone as the principal and all the others as mere accessories. [Italics added.]

This is not merely 'a tendency'. It is ancient law. Aiders and abettors who were present were traditionally called 'accessories at the fact'. Principals were those who 'actually and with their own hands committed the fact': Foster, *Crown Law* ((1792) 3rd edn 1809), 347–350, analysing the earliest authorities and Stephen, *Digest of the Criminal Law* (1886), Art 38, 'Common Purpose'. Cf the analysis by Beldam LJ in *Uddin*, above, p 320.

Do we 'attribute the actus reus' to the secondary party—or merely *responsibility* for it? Cf *DPP for Northern Ireland v Maxwell*, above, p 295. Does it matter whether the act, or only responsibility for the act, is attributed to a party in a joint enterprise? Consider *Murtagh and Kennedy* (1955) 39 Cr App R 72, [1955] Crim LR 315. M and K, engaged in a feud with another gang, were charged with murder by running down X in a car in which M was the driver and K the passenger. The jury were directed that driving a car at a person with intent to kill him or cause him serious injury would be murder but that, if the intent was to drive near to X, so as to terrorize him, it would be manslaughter. The jury convicted M of murder and

K of manslaughter. Both convictions were quashed on other grounds which are irrelevant for present purposes. The verdicts, however, implied that M, the driver, intended to run X down but that K intended only that the car be driven close so as to frighten him. Surely these are fundamentally different acts. M and K were clearly engaged in an unlawful joint enterprise in a feud with V; but how can we attribute M's act of running V down to K in view of the implicit finding that K did not intend—and no finding that he foresaw—any such act? Compare the South African case of *S v Robinson*, above, p 297.

R v Gilmour

[2000] 2 Cr App R 407, Court of Appeal of Northern Ireland

[Carswell LCJ, Nicholson LJ and Coghlin J]

According to G, whose admissions were the only evidence of his part in the incident, he was roused from his bed by M and P ('the principals'), whom he knew to be members of the UVF, who told him to drive them to what turned out to be the scene of the crime, 'which he did not do willingly'. There, a one-litre whisky bottle containing petrol was thrown by M or P through the ground floor window of a house in which six people were asleep. A fierce fire quickly developed with thick smoke. Three adults escaped but three young boys were killed by carbon monoxide poisoning. The judge (sitting in a Diplock court without a jury) was satisfied, having regard to the nature of the bottle from which the bomb was constituted, that those who made and threw it had an actual intention to kill. He was satisfied that G knew that M intended to use a petrol bomb and to cause really serious injury. He convicted all three of murder. G appealed.

[**Carswell LCJ** rejected an attack on the judge's conclusion as to the intention of M and P and continued]:

There is, however, more substance in the next submission, that the proof is insufficient that the appellant realised that those who threw the petrol bomb intended at least grievous bodily harm to the occupants of the house. Throwing petrol bombs at dwelling houses is regrettably common and always contains an element of potential danger to the occupants. It is right to say, however, that it has fortunately been only a rare consequence that occupants have been injured in such attacks, and the majority of them appear, so far as judicial notice can take us, to cause only minor fires. There is not in our view sufficient evidence to conclude that the appellant was aware that the petrol was contained in an unusually large bottle, which might be expected to cause a larger conflagration and result in greater danger to the occupants. On the evidence he realised at a late stage that a petrol bomb attack was about to take place, and his intention was formed in that short period before he co-operated in driving the principals away from the scene. It would be difficult to attribute to him with any degree of certainty an intention that the attack should result in more than a blaze which might do some damage, put the occupants in fear and intimidate them into moving from the house. The principals and the appellant did have a grudge against Colm Quinn, but there is not sufficient evidence to establish that they expected him to be sleeping in the house that night. Nor do we think that the talk that Colm Quinn was 'going to be used as a Guy Fawkes' is enough to establish beyond reasonable doubt that the appellant intended that those who were in occupation should suffer injuries in the fire. We therefore do not consider that the judge's finding that he appreciated that the principals intended to inflict grievous bodily harm can be supported as a safe conclusion of fact.

We conclude accordingly that the appellant's conviction for murder cannot be sustained. Nor can his conviction on counts 4, 5 and 6, each of which involves an intention to commit grievous bodily harm. The issue then is whether he can be found guilty of manslaughter on the first three counts, on the basis that if the principals had thrown the petrol bomb into the house without the intention of killing or inflicting grievous bodily harm on any person they would have properly been convicted of that offence. It was argued on behalf of the appellant that if he did not share the intention of the principals he should not be found guilty of either murder or manslaughter, in the same way as if the principals go outside the contemplated acts involved in the joint enterprise the accessory cannot be convicted of either offence: see our recent decision in *Crooks* [1999] NI 226, following the principles laid down in *R v Powell and English* [1998] 1 Cr App R 261, [1999] AC 1.

The issue is discussed in Blackstone's *Criminal Practice*, 2000 ed, para A5.5 at p 75, in which the example is posed where the principal and accessory agree that the principal will post an incendiary device to the victim, the accessory contemplating only superficial injuries but the principal foreseeing and hoping that the injuries will be serious or fatal. The principal will be guilty of murder and the accessory will not. The editors conclude that the accessory should in such a case be convicted of manslaughter, because the act done by the principal is precisely what was envisaged.

In our opinion this is the correct principle to apply in the present case. The appellant foresaw that the principals would carry out the act of throwing a petrol bomb into the house, but did not realise that in so doing they intended to kill or do grievous bodily harm to the occupants. To establish that a person charged as an accessory to a crime of specific intent is guilty as an accessory it is necessary to prove that he realised the principal's intention: see *Hyde* (1991) 92 Cr App R 131, 135, [1991] 1 QB 134, 139, *per* Lord Lane CJ, approved by Lord Hutton in *R v Powell and English* [1998] 1 Cr App R 261, 283, [1999] AC 1, 27–28. The line of authority represented by such cases as *Anderson and Morris* (1966) 50 Cr App R 216, [1966] 2 QB 110, approved in *R v Powell and English*, deals with situations where the principal departs from the contemplated joint enterprise and perpetrates a more serious act of a different kind unforeseen by the accessory. In such cases it is established that the accessory is not liable at all for such unforeseen acts. It does not follow that the same result should follow where the principal carries out the very act contemplated by the accessory, though the latter does not realise that the principal intends a more serious consequence from the act.

We do not consider that we are obliged by authority to hold that the accessory in such a case must be acquitted of manslaughter as well as murder. The cases in which an accessory has been found not guilty both of murder and manslaughter all concern a departure by the principal from the *actus reus* contemplated by the accessory, not a difference between the parties in respect of the *mens rea* of each. In such cases the view has prevailed that it would be wrong to hold the accessory liable when the principal committed an act which the accessory did not contemplate or authorise. We do not, however, see any convincing policy reason why a person acting as an accessory to a principal who carries out the very deed contemplated by both should not be guilty of the degree of offence appropriate to the intent with which he so acted. It is of course conceivable, as is suggested in *Blackstone, loc cit*, that in some cases the nature of the principal's *mens rea* may change the nature of the act committed by him and take it outside the type of act contemplated by the accessory, but it does not seem to us that the existence of such a possibility affects the validity of the basic principle which we have propounded. A verdict of guilty of manslaughter on this basis was upheld by the Court of Appeal in *Stewart and Schofield* [1995] 1 Cr App R 441, [1995] 3 All ER 159. The judgment has been strongly criticised by Sir John Smith in [1995] Crim LR 296 and [1995] Crim LR 422 and in Smith & Hogan, *Criminal Law*, 9th edn, 1999 p 145. Even if there may be ground for criticism of some of the propositions enunciated in the Court's judgment, the principle accepted as its basis is in our view sustainable.

We accordingly allow the appeal, substitute a verdict of not guilty of murder but guilty of manslaughter on counts 1 to 3 and set aside the verdicts of guilty on counts 4 to 6.

Appeal allowed

Questions

1. Was there any evidence that G shared the common purpose of M and P to throw a petrol bomb? Was his purpose in 'unwillingly' driving the car to and from the scene proved to be other than that of avoiding unpleasant consequences to himself or his family? Was he properly regarded as a party to a joint enterprise? Does it—should it—make any difference? Did he not know he was aiding and abetting a joint enterprise?

2. Was the throwing of the unusually large bottle fundamentally different from the throwing of an ordinary bottle which, it appears, is unlikely to cause any injury? Should not the judge have asked himself this question? In an English court, would not a judge have been obliged to leave it to the jury?—*Powell and English*, above, p **316.**

3. Was this a case where 'the very deed' contemplated by G was carried out by M and P?

4. E administers to V a particular drug, XYZ, which E knows is certain to kill, and is assisted or encouraged by D who knows the drug is XYZ but believes the only effect of XYZ will be to give V a headache. V is killed. Is D guilty of manslaughter? Was the administration by E the 'very deed' contemplated by P? Cf commentary at [2000] Crim LR 763, discussion of *Gilmour* at [2001] Crim LR 333–335 and *Day* [2001] Crim LR 984.

(10) WITHDRAWAL

How, if at all, can a person who is about to become a secondary party to an offence withdraw so as to avoid liability when the crime is committed?

R v Becerra and Cooper

(1975) 62 Cr App R 212, Court of Appeal, Criminal Division

(Roskill and Bridge LJJ and Kilner Brown J)

B, C and G broke into a house with intent to steal from the householder, an old lady, F. While G was holding a pillow over F's face, B cut the telephone wires with a knife with a 3½ inch blade. B then gave the knife to C. The burglars were surprised by the appearance of a man, V, the tenant of a flat in the house. B called out 'Come on, let's go' and, followed by G, climbed out of a window and ran away. C tried the back door but it was locked and, being confronted by V, stabbed and killed him. B and C were convicted of murder and appealed.

[**Roskill LJ**, having held that there was evidence to support the jury's finding of a common design to cause death or serious bodily harm if it was necessary to do so in order to carry out the theft, turned to the argument that B had effectively withdrawn from any common design:]

It is necessary, before dealing with that argument in more detail, to say a word or two about the relevant law. It is a curious fact, considering the number of times in which this point arises where two or more people are charged with criminal offences, particularly murder or manslaughter, how relatively little authority there is in this country upon the point. But the principle is undoubtedly of long standing.

Perhaps it is best first stated in *Saunders and Archer* (1573) 2 Plowd 473 (in the eighteenth year of the first Queen Elizabeth) at p 476, in a note by *Plowden*, thus: '...for if I command one to kill JS and before the Fact done I go to him and tell him that I have repented, and expressly charge him not to kill JS and he afterwards kills him, there I shall not be Accessory to this Murder, because I have countermanded my first Command, which in all Reason shall discharge me, for the malicious Mind of the Accessory ought to continue to do ill until the Time of the Act done, or else he shall not be charged; but if he had killed JS before the Time of my Discharge or Countermand given, I should have been Accessory to the Death, notwithstanding my private Repentance'.

The next case to which I may usefully refer is some 250 years later, but over 150 years ago. *Edmeads* (1828) 3 C & P 390, where there is a ruling of Vaughan B at a trial at Berkshire Assizes, upon an indictment charging Edmeads and others with unlawfully shooting at game keepers. At the end of his ruling the learned Baron said on the question of common intent, at p 392, 'that is rather a question for the jury; but still, on this evidence, it is quite clear what the common purpose was. They all draw up in lines, and point their guns at the game keepers, and they are all giving their countenance and assistance to the one of them who actually fires the gun. If it could be shewn that either of them separated himself from the rest, and showed distinctly that he would have no hand in what they were doing, the objection would have much weight in it.'

I can go forward over 100 years. Mr Owen (to whose juniors we are indebted for their research into the relevant Canadian and United States cases) referred us to several Canadian cases, to only one of which it is necessary to refer in detail, a decision of the Court of Appeal in British Columbia in *Whitehouse* (alias *Savage*) [1941] 1 WWR 112. I need not read the headnote. The Court of Appeal held that the trial judge concerned in that case, which was one of murder, had been guilty of misdirection in his direction to the jury on this question of 'withdrawal'. The matter is, if I may most respectfully say so, so well put in the leading judgment of Sloan JA, that I read the whole of the passage at pp 115 and 116:

> 'Can it be said on the facts of this case that a mere change of mental intention and a quitting of the scene of the crime just immediately prior to the striking of the fatal blow will absolve those who participate in the commission of the crime by overt acts up to that moment from all the consequences of its accomplishment by the one who strikes in ignorance of his companions' change of heart? I think not. After a crime has been committed and before a prior abandonment of the common enterprise may be found by a jury there must be, in my view, in the absence of exceptional circumstances, something more than a mere mental change of intention and physical change of place by those associates who wish to dissociate themselves from the consequences attendant upon their willing assistance up to the moment of the actual commission of that crime. I would not attempt to define too closely what must be done in criminal matters involving participation in a common unlawful purpose to break the chain of causation and responsibility. That must depend upon the circumstances of each case but it seems to me that one essential element ought to be established in a case of this kind: Where practicable and reasonable there must be timely communication of the intention to abandon the common purpose from those who wish to dissociate themselves from the contemplated crime to those who desire to continue in it. What is "timely communication" must be determined by the facts of each case but where practicable and reasonable it ought to be such communication, verbal or otherwise, that will serve unequivocal notice upon the other party to the common unlawful cause that if he proceeds upon it he does so without the further aid and assistance of those who withdraw. The unlawful purpose of him who continues alone is then his own and not one in common with those who are no longer parties to it nor liable to its full and final consequences.'

The learned judge then went on to cite a passage from 1 Hale's *Pleas of the Crown* 618 and the passage from *Saunders and Archer* (supra) to which I have already referred.

In the view of each member of this court, that passage, if we may respectfully say so, could not be improved upon and we venture to adopt it in its entirety as a correct statement of the law which is to be applied in this case.

The last case, an English one, is *Croft* (1944) 29 Cr App R 169, [1944] 1 KB 295; a well known case of a suicide pact where, under the old law, the survivor of a suicide pact was charged with and convicted of murder. It was sought to argue that he had withdrawn from the pact in time to avoid liability (as the law then was) for conviction for murder.

The Court of Criminal Appeal, comprising Lawrence J (as he then was), Lewis and Wrottesley JJ dismissed the appeal and upheld the direction given by Humphreys J to the jury at the trial. Towards the end of the judgment Lawrence J said, at p 173 (pp 297 and 298): '... counsel for the appellant complains—although I do not understand that the point had ever been taken in the court below—that the summing-up does not contain any reference to the possibility of the agreement to commit suicide having been determined or countermanded. It is true that the learned judge does not deal expressly with that matter except in a passage where he says: "Even if you accept his statement in the witness-box that the vital and second shot was fired when he had gone through that window, he would still be guilty of murder if she was then committing suicide as the result of an agreement which they had mutually arrived at that should be the fate of both of them, and it is no answer for him that he altered his mind after she was dead and did not commit suicide himself."…the authorities, such as they are, show in our opinion, that where a person has acted as an accessory before the fact, in order that he should not be held guilty as an accessory before the fact, he must give express and actual countermand or revocation of the advising, counselling, procuring, or abetting which he had given before.'

It seems to us that those authorities make plain what the law is which has to be applied in the present case.

We therefore turn back to consider the direction which the learned judge gave in the present case to the jury and what was the suggested evidence that Becerra had withdrawn from the common agreement. The suggested evidence is the use by Becerra of the words 'Come on let's go,' coupled, as I said a few moments ago, with his act in going out through the window. The evidence, as the judge pointed out, was that Cooper never heard that nor did the third man. But let it be supposed that that was said and the jury took the view that it was said.

On the facts of this case, in the circumstances then prevailing, the knife having already been used and being contemplated for further use when it was handed over by Becerra to Cooper for the purpose of avoiding (if necessary) by violent means the hazards of identification, if Becerra wanted to withdraw at that stage, he would have to 'countermand', to use the word that is used in some of the cases or 'repent' to use another word so used, in some manner vastly different and vastly more effective than merely to say 'Come on, let's go' and go out through the window.

It is not necessary, on this application, to decide whether the point of time had arrived at which the only way in which he could effectively withdraw, so as to free himself from joint responsibility for any act Cooper thereafter did in furtherance of the common design, would be physically to intervene so as to stop Cooper attacking Lewis, as the judge suggested, by interposing his own body between them or somehow getting in between them or whether some other action might suffice. That does not arise for decision here. Nor is it necessary to decide whether or not the learned judge was right or wrong, on the facts of this case, in that passage which appears at the bottom of p 206, which Mr Owen criticised: 'and at least take all reasonable steps to prevent the commission of the crime which he had agreed the others should commit.' It is enough for the purposes of deciding this application to say that under the law of this country as it stands, and on the facts (taking them at their highest in favour of Becerra), that which was urged as amounting to withdrawal from the common design was not capable of amounting to such withdrawal. Accordingly Becerra remains responsible, in the eyes of the law, for everything that Cooper did and continued to do after Becerra's disappearance through the window as much as if he had done them himself.

Cooper being unquestionably guilty of murder, Becerra is equally guilty of murder. Mr Owen's careful argument must therefore be rejected and the application by Becerra for leave to appeal against conviction fails.

Appeal dismissed

Notes and questions

1. In *Mitchell and King* [1999] Crim LR 496 an unplanned fight broke out in and around a restaurant. One person was killed. The appellants were convicted of murder, alleged to have

been committed in the course of a joint enterprise. M claimed that if there was such an enterprise, he had withdrawn from it before the fatal act. The judge directed the jury by reading the passage from *Whitehouse*, above. Quashing M's conviction, Otton LJ said:

The case from which this passage is taken concerned pre-planned violence. It is not necessary when the violence is spontaneous. Although absent any communication, it may, as a matter of evidence, be easier to persuade a jury that a defendant, who had previously participated, had not in fact withdrawn. Such considerations are clearly relevant in such cases, but less so when violence has erupted spontaneously.

Secondary participation consists in assisting or encouraging the principal offender in the commission of the crime. A party who withdraws from an enterprise, spontaneous or not, usually ceases to assist but he does not necessarily cease to encourage. Suppose that A is encouraged in the fight because he knows B is in there with him. Cf *Uddin*, above, p **319**. If B decides he has had enough and quietly slopes off without attracting A's attention, the external element of secondary participation still continues. B's encouragement of A is still operative. Does mere withdrawal then relieve B of responsibility? A person who had done an act which makes him potentially liable for a crime cannot relieve himself of responsibility by a mere change of mind. Once the arrow is in the air, it is no use, wishing to have never let it go. The archer is guilty of homicide when the arrow gets the victim through the heart. Cf *Jakeman*, above, p **45**. The withdrawer, it is true, does not merely change his mind: he withdraws—but is that relevant if the withdrawal has no more effect on subsequent events than the archer's repentance?

Commenting on *O'Flaherty*, above, p **321** Professor Ashworth observes:

Why should withdrawal be a defence? The main reason must be that a person who aids, abets, counsels or procures at first but then has a voluntary change of mind, before the full offence is completed, is significantly less culpable than an accomplice who continued to support the commission of the offence throughout. The withdrawing accomplice remains liable for what was done up to that point, but not for what was done thereafter. This desert-based rationale must be linked to the nature of the accomplice's contribution to the principal offence, and the requirements of withdrawal should similarly depend on that contribution. In other words, the further D has gone in supporting the commission of the offence, the more it is right to expect by way of withdrawal (*cf.* K.J.M. Smith, 'Withdrawal in Complicity: A Restatement of Principles' [2001] Crim.L.R. 769). On this approach, then, the law should 'reward' the withdrawing accomplice by providing the possibility of a defence, though strictly circumscribed (mitigation of sentence will provide for those whose purported withdrawal is insufficiently definite). Others prefer to say that the defence is necessary to provide an incentive for accomplices to withdraw, although the language of incentives is really only apposite if people in that situation are aware of the legal rule. But much also depends on whether the rationale for accessorial liability lies primarily in the culpability of the accomplice or in the causal contribution to the principal offence, since withdrawal may negative culpability for subsequent acts but not (in some instances) sever the causal contribution to subsequent acts. Judicial discussion of complicity is suffused with references to 'joint enterprise' and 'common enterprise', and the significance of this decision is to demonstrate the shortcomings of expressing cases of complicity in that way. The language of joint enterprise assumes some kind of plan to commit an offence, however hastily or informally conceived. One then moves from the idea of a plan to the notion of withdrawing from the plan. However, many of the cases coming before the courts concern violence erupting outside a pub, club or sporting venue, where some people join in, some stay on the fringes, and others walk away. Thus, in *Mitchell and King* [1999] Crim.L.R. 496, Otton L.J. said (at para.6): 'Communication of withdrawal is a necessary condition for dissociation from preplanned violence. It is not necessary when the violence is spontaneous. Although absent any communication it may, as a matter of evidence, be easier to persuade a jury that a defendant, who had previously participated, had not in fact withdrawn. Such considerations are clearly relevant in such cases, but less so when the violence has erupted spontaneously.' Otton L.J. drew this distinction between planned and spontaneous offences without reliance on any authority. In this case, Mantell L.J. followed the *Mitchell and King* approach, but translated it into the language of joint enterprise. Thus, the jury must be satisfied 'that the fatal injuries were sustained when the joint enterprise was continuing and that the defendant was still acting within that joint enterprise' (at [64]); and 'in a case of spontaneous violence such as this where there has been no prior agreement, the jury will usually have to make inferences as to the scope of the joint enterprise from the knowledge and actions of individual participants' (at [65]). It is doubtful whether it is helpful to translate the events into a joint enterprise and then, as it were, translate them back in order to make sense of the roles of individual participants. This was a spontaneous chain of events. Sir John Smith doubted whether the fact that an attack arose spontaneously should lead to an alteration of the requirements for withdrawal: is it right to allow withdrawal without communication, he asked, 'if A was encouraged by B's participation and was unaware that B had withdrawn?' (Smith and Hogan, *Criminal Law* (10th ed., 2002), p.177). The answer depends, surely, on the rationale. If the foundations of complicity and of withdrawal lie chiefly in B's culpability, a definite withdrawal from spontaneous violence (even if not accompanied by communication) should suffice. But if the foundations lie chiefly in B's contribution to A's offence, B's withdrawal in those circumstances may (as Sir John hinted) be no more effective than an uncommunicated withdrawal from a non-spontaneous offence. On the facts of this case, two of the men (R and T) participated in the initial attack but then broke off from the group and did not accompany them into the next street. They did not 'communicate' their withdrawal to anyone. But it was a spontaneous attack, and they had probably not signalled their arrival either, other than by physical participation. Should we speculate on whether the group of attackers who went into the next street were still being encouraged by the belief that the two men were with them, when they were not? Surely the two men's act of leaving should be sufficient to dissociate them from subsequent events, in the absence of any kind of plan to which they had all assented. They were culpable for what they had done up to that point, but not in respect of anything thereafter. The attackers had eyes and ears, and had no reason to believe that the two were still supporting them. But O'Flaherty's position was held to be different because he did follow the attackers into the next street and he was present, holding a cricket bat, when the fatal attack took place. He did not participate actively in the fatal attack, but neither he did he do anything amounting to withdrawal. It is then a question of fact whether his series of actions amounted to aiding and abetting murder, resulting in the mandatory sentence of life imprisonment.

2. In *Grundy* [1977] Crim LR 543 D had supplied E, a burglar, with information which was presumably valuable to E in committing the burglary in question; but, for two weeks before E did so, D had been trying to stop him breaking in. It was held that there was evidence of an effective withdrawal which should have been left to the jury. In *Whitefield* (1984) 79 Cr App R 36, [1984] Crim LR 97 there was evidence that D had served unequivocal notice on E that, if he proceeded with a burglary they had planned together, he would do so without D's aid or assistance. It was held that the jury should have been told that, if they accepted this evidence, there was a defence. Cf *McPhillips*, below, p **502**, where an uncommunicated intention to frustrate an agreement to commit murder, to which D was a party, was a defence to a charge of conspiracy to murder and *Rook* [1993] 2 All ER 955, [1993] Crim LR 698.

3. Is withdrawal (i) a defence that operates only where D brings to an end the *actus reus* of assisting or encouraging P; (ii) a defence that operates because D's withdrawal negates his mens rea of intention to assist or encourage; (iii) a defence operating despite the presence of D's continuing actus reus and mens rea as a secondary party? Which should it be?

Bryce

[2004] EWCA Crim 1, [2004] 2 Cr App R 592, [2004] Crim LR 936, Court of Criminal Appeal, Criminal Division

(Potter LJ, Hooper and Astill JJ)

The facts appear above, p **285**.

[75] ..... if the secondary party is to avoid liability for assistance rendered to the perpetrator in respect of steps taken by the perpetrator towards the commission of the crime, only an act taken by him which amounts to countermanding of his earlier assistance and a withdrawal from the common purpose will suffice. Repentance alone, unsupported by action taken to demonstrate withdrawal will be insufficient. Thus, if the secondary party had the necessary mens rea at the time of the act of rendering his advice or assistance, the fact that his mind is 'innocent' at the time when the crime is committed is no defence: see *R v Becerra* (1975) 62 Crim App R 212. In that case it was stated that any communication of withdrawal by the secondary party to the perpetrator must be such as to serve "unequivocal notice" upon the other party to the common unlawful cause that, if he proceeds upon it, he does so without the further aid and assistance of the withdrawing party: c.f. the position in *R v Whitefield* (1984) 79 Crim App R 36, [1984] Crim LR 97.

See further, D. Lanham, 'Accomplices and Withdrawal' (1981) 97 LQR 575; K. J. M. Smith, 'Withdrawal in Complicity: A Restatement of Principles' [2001] Crim LR 769.

(11) VICTIMS ALLEGED TO BE PARTIES

Where an offence is created for the protection of a class of persons, a member of the class who is the victim of such an offence cannot be convicted either of inciting or aiding, abetting, counselling or procuring its commission, even though he has done acts which would usually amount to such an offence. See *Whitehouse* and *Pickford*, below, pp **481–483**.

FURTHER READING

P. ALLDRIDGE, 'The Doctrine of Innocent Agency' (1990) 2 Criminal Law Forum 45

I. H. DENNIS, 'The Mental Element for Accessories' in P. Smith (ed) *Essays in Honour of J. C. Smith* (1987)

I. H. DENNIS, 'Intent and Complicity—A Reply' [1988] Crim LR 649

G. SULLIVAN, 'Intent, Purpose and Complicity' [1988] Crim LR 638

G. WILLIAMS, 'Innocent Agency and Causation' (1992) Criminal Law Forum 289

10

Vicarious liability and liability of corporations

1. VICARIOUS LIABILITY

Vicarious liability means liability for the acts of another. It is common in the civil law. Employers are generally liable for the tortious acts of their employees committed in the course of their employment. An employee will rarely have the means adequately to compensate a person to whom he has caused a serious injury, so the loss will lie with the innocent victim unless the employer can be required to pay. As between the victim and the employer, it is thought right that the employer should bear the loss, even though he may personally be blameless. The primary function of the criminal law, however, is not the compensation of the victim but the punishment of the wrongdoer—and there are no grounds for punishing the blameless employer. The employee's wrongful act is sometimes a crime as well as a tort. It may be theft, criminal deception, assault, or even manslaughter and the employee is of course liable to conviction of the crime. The employer, even though responsible for the act in the civil law and liable to pay compensation is not criminally liable. Criminal liability is of a personal nature. That is the general rule and, with the exception of the anomalous offence of public nuisance, now the universal rule at common law; but, in statutory offences, there are exceptions, or apparent exceptions, to it. They fall into two main groups.

In the first group, the only physical act is that of the employee but it is construed in law to be the act of the employer; so in legal theory it is not a case of vicarious liability at all. For example there are many offences of selling, such as selling goods with a false trade description. In law, a sale is the transfer of the ownership in goods from A to B. When goods are sold by a shop assistant, 'the seller' is the owner of the goods, the employer. If the goods have been sold with a false trade description, it is the owner of the shop who has so sold them, even if he is on holiday on the Costa Brava at the time. If he is unaware of the circumstances of the sale, of course he has no mens rea; but, if the offence is one of strict liability, that will not help him. He is taken to have committed the offence. Sale is the most conspicuous example, but it by no means stands alone. An employer is, in law, in possession of goods even though they are under the physical control of his employee; and there are many offences of possessing various articles. An employer has been held to 'keep' and to 'use' a vehicle when it is in the keeping of, or used by, his employee in circumstances which the law forbids. Whether a particular verb is apt to include the inactive employer is a question of statutory interpretation. It should be noted that the law often has it both ways: the statute may be so construed that the shop assistant has also 'sold' the goods belonging to her employer and to be guilty, as a principal, of the same offence. In the case of a sale of intoxicating liquor, it seems that the owner of the liquor, the licensee and the barmaid may, all three, be guilty as principals of the same offence. Each has, in law, 'sold': *Allied Domecq Leisure Ltd v Cooper* [1999] Crim LR 230 and commentary. See also *Nottingham City Council v Wolverhampton and Dudley Breweries* [2004] 2 WLR 820.

The first group is confined to offences of strict liability but the second applies to a limited category of offences requiring mens rea. Where statute imposes a duty on a particular person—for example, the holder of a justices' licence—and that person delegates the performance of the statutory duty to another, he may be held liable for breaches of it committed by the delegate, even though mens rea is required. The mens rea of the delegate is sufficient to impose liability on the delegator for breach of the duty which is imposed on him and him alone. This principle has been applied only to licensees and similar functionaries; and it involves the question of what is a sufficient delegation.

The operation of these principles is illustrated in the following cases.

(1) DOING AN ACT THROUGH ANOTHER

Coppen v Moore (No 2)
[1898] 2 QB 306, Divisional Court

(Lord Russell CJ, Sir F. H. Jeune P, Chitty LJ, Wright, Darling and Channell JJ)

Under s 2(2) of the Merchandise Marks Act 1887 it was an offence to sell goods to which a false trade description had been applied. The appellant who owned six shops sent the following instruction to each shop:

Most important.

Please instruct your assistants most explicitly that the hams described in list as breakfast hams must not be sold under any specific name of place or origin. That is to say, they must not be described as 'Bristol,' 'Bath,' 'Wiltshire,' or any such title, but simply as breakfast hams. Please sign and return.

An assistant in one of the shops sold one of the hams (an American ham) as 'a Scotch ham'. The appellant appealed from his conviction of the offence.

[**Lord Russell CJ**, having accepted that the general principle is 'Nemo reus est nisi mens sit rea', said that it was subject to exceptions:]

But by far the greater number of exceptions engrafted upon the general rule are cases in which it has been decided that by various statutes criminal responsibility has been put upon masters for the acts of their servants. Amongst such cases is *Mullins v Collins* [(1874) LR 9 QB 292], where a licensed victualler was convicted of an offence under s 16 of the Licensing Act 1872, for supplying liquor to a constable on duty, although this was done by his servant without the knowledge of the master. Again, in *Bond v Evans* [(1888) 21 QBD 249], a licensed victualler was convicted of an offence against s 17 of the same Act, where gaming had been allowed in the licensed premises by the servant in charge of the premises although without the knowledge of his master. The decisions in these and in other like cases were based upon the construction of the statute in question. The Court in fact came to the conclusion that, having regard to the language, scope, and object of those Acts, the Legislature intended to fix criminal responsibility upon the master for acts done by his servant in the course of his employment, although such acts were not authorised by the master, and might even have been expressly prohibited by him.

The question, then, in this case, comes to be narrowed to the simple point, whether upon the true construction of the statute here in question the master was intended to be made criminally responsible for acts done by his servants in contravention of the Act, where such acts were done, as in this case, within the scope or in the course of their employment. In our judgment it was clearly the intention of the Legislature to make the master criminally liable for such acts, unless he was able to rebut the prima facie presumption of guilt by one or other of the methods pointed out in the Act. Take the facts here, and apply the Act to them. To begin with, it cannot be doubted that the appellant sold the ham in question, although the transaction was carried out by his servants. In other words, he was the seller, although not the actual salesman. . . .

In answer, then, to the question which alone is put to us, namely, whether upon the facts stated the decision of the magistrates convicting the appellant was in point of law correct, our answer is that in our judgment it was. When the scope and object of the Act are borne in mind, any other conclusion would to a large extent render the Act ineffective for its avowed purposes. The circumstances of the present case afford a convenient illustration of this. The appellant, under the style of the 'London Supply Stores', carries on an extensive business as grocer and provision dealer, having, it appears, six shops or branch establishments, and having also a wholesale warehouse. It is obvious that, if sales with false trade descriptions could be carried out in these establishments with impunity so far as the principal is concerned, the Act would to a large extent be nugatory. We conceive the effect of the Act to be to make the master or principal liable criminally (as he is already, by law, civilly) for the acts of his agents and servants in all cases within the sections with which we are dealing where the conduct constituting the offence was pursued by such servants and agents within the scope or in the course of their employment, subject to this: that the master or principal may be relieved from criminal respons-ibility where he can prove that he had acted in good faith and had done all that it was reasonably possible to do to prevent the commission by his agents and servants of offences against the Act.

Appeal dismissed

In *Tesco Stores Ltd v Brent London Borough Council* [1993] 2 All ER 718, [1993] Crim LR 624, DC, the company was held to have 'supplied' a video to a person, P, under the age stated in the classification certificate, contrary to the Video Recordings Act 1984. The video was sold to the child by an assistant, Miss J. It is defence under the Act to prove that 'the accused neither knew nor had reasonable grounds to believe that [the buyer] had not attained [the specified age] . . .' The magistrates found that Miss J had reasonable grounds to know that P was under age and it followed that the defence was not available to the company. The Divisional Court agreed. The company, not Miss J, was 'the accused'. Were they rightly denied the defence?

In *Harrow London Borough Council v Shah and Shah*, above, p 232 the court observed that the ticket was sold, not by either of the defendants, but by their employee, H (who was not charged), and held, 'Unfortunately, but inevitably, his offence was, at once, their offence, given the principles of vicarious liability as explained in *Mousell Bros Ltd v London and North-Western Rly* [1917] 2 KB 836, DC. These principles were applied in *St Helens Metro-politan Police Borough Council v Hill* (1992) 156 JP 602'. (It is not clear whether Mitchell J meant merely that it was unfortunate for the Shahs—which it certainly was—or unfortunate as a matter of principle.) *St Helens Metropolitan Borough Council v Hill* (1992) 156 JP 602 (sale of cigarettes to child under 16) was a straightforward application of the attributed act principle—once it was decided that the offence was one of strict liability, it followed that the owner of the shop was liable. But the only reason given for imposing strict liability was that the offence was for the protection of children. That may not be enough in future. The offences in *B (a minor) v DPP* and *K* were both for the protection of children but mens rea was emphatically required. The attributed act principle does not apply to offences requiring mens rea (which the offence in *Moussell* appeared to do). If the offence under s 13 had been held to require mens rea, the Shahs would not have been liable, even if their employee had known he was selling to an under-age child. The *Mousell Bros* case is one to which undue importance seems to have been attributed. It is discussed in the commentary on *Harrow London Borough Council v Shah* [2000] Crim LR 693. Glanville Williams, CLGP 274, wrote that, apart from the licensee [that is, 'delegation'] cases there is no instance of a master being convicted of a crime requiring mens rea merely on account of the mens rea of his servant—but he then acknowledged *Mousell* as 'the solitary exception' and went on:

The best explanation of this decision seems to be that it belongs to an intermediate stage in the development of corporate criminal responsibility. At the present day the company would be held responsible in such circumstances not on the ground of vicarious responsibility but because the act or state of mind of a director or manager would be imputed to the company as its personal wrong.

However, Reading CJ said in *Moussell* 'there is nothing to distinguish a limited company from any other principal. . . .' Subsequently Williams was content to observe (TBCL (2nd edn) 967, n 3) that 'it seems from the speech of Lord Evershed in *Vane v Yiannopolous* that *Mousell Bros Ltd* is to be restrictively interpreted, and is no authority for saying that every employer is vicariously for his employee's offences involving mens rea.' *Mousell* is, to say the least, an obscure decision and not clear authority for anything.

(2) THE DELEGATION PRINCIPLE

Allen v Whitehead
[1929] All ER Rep 13, King's Bench Division

(Lord Hewart CJ, Avory and Branson JJ)

The Metropolitan Police Act 1839, s 44, provided that—

. . . every person who shall have or keep any house, shop, room or place of public resort within the metropolitan police district, wherein provisions, liquors or refreshments of any kind shall be sold or consumed (whether the same shall be kept or retailed therein or procured elsewhere) . . . and who shall knowingly permit or suffer prostitutes or persons of notoriously bad character to meet together and remain therein, shall, for every such offence, be liable to a penalty . . .

D, the occupier and licensee of a cafe, while receiving the profits, did not himself manage the premises. He visited the cafe once or twice a week. Having been warned by the police about the harbouring of prostitutes on the premises, he instructed his manager not to allow prostitutes to congregate and caused a notice to be displayed forbidding prostitutes to enter the cafe after midnight. Subsequently on eight consecutive days a number of women known by the manager to be prostitutes met and remained on the premises between 8 pm and 4 am, indulging in obscene language. The magistrates dismissed an information against D for knowingly suffering prostitutes to meet on the premises, contrary to s 44, above, on the ground that D did not know that this was happening. The prosecutor appealed by way of case stated.

[**Lord Hewart CJ**, having held that it was plain that there was knowledge on the part of the manager, went on:]

The question is whether, upon the proper construction of this section, that knowledge in the servant is to be imputed to the employer, so as to make the employer liable.

In my opinion, the answer to that question is in the affirmative. The principle seems to me to be that which was explained, for example, in *Mousell Bros Ltd v London and North-Western Rly Co* ([1917] 2 KB 836 at 845), where Atkin J said:

> 'I think that the authorities cited by my Lord make it plain that while prima facie a principal is not to be made criminally responsible for the acts of his servants, yet the legislature may prohibit an act or enforce a duty in such words as to make the prohibition or the duty absolute; in which case the principal is liable if the act is in fact done by his servants. To ascertain whether a particular Act of Parliament has that effect or not, regard must be had to the object of the statute, the words used, the nature of the duty laid down, the person upon whom it is imposed, the person by whom it would in ordinary circumstances be performed, and the person upon whom the penalty is imposed.'

Applying that canon to the present case, I think that this provision in this statute would be rendered nugatory, if the contention raised on behalf of this respondent were held to prevail. That contention was that, as the respondent did not himself manage the refreshment house, had no personal knowledge that prostitutes met together and remained therein, had not been negligent in failing to notice these facts, and had not wilfully closed his eyes to the facts, he could not, in law, be held responsible. There is a whole chain of cases on the lines of the passage which I have just read from *Mousell Bros Ltd v London and North Western Rail Co*. Reference has been made to *Mullins v Collins* (1874) LR 9 QB 292; *Coppen v Moore (No 2)* [1898] 2 QB 306; *Bond v Evans* (1888) 21 QBD 249, and other cases. This seems to me to be a case where the proprietor, the keeper of the house, had delegated his position to a manager, so far as the conduct of the house was concerned; he had transferred to the manager the exercise of discretion in the conduct of the business, and it seems to me the only reasonable conclusion is, regard being had to the purpose of this Act, that knowledge in the manager was knowledge in the keeper of the house. I think, therefore, that this case ought to go back to the learned magistrate, with a direction to convict.

[**Avory** and **Branson JJ** gave judgment, agreeing that the appeal should be allowed.]

Appeal allowed

Question

Was the construction of the section in *Allen v Whitehead* justifiable? See the remarks of Lord Donovan, below, p **341**.

Vane v Yiannopoullos
[1964] 3 All ER 820, House of Lords

(Lords Reid, Evershed, Morris of Borth-y-Gest, Hodson and Donovan)

The respondent was the holder of a restaurant licence. A condition of the licence was that liquor should not be sold except to persons taking meals. The restaurant was on two floors. While the respondent was on one floor, conducting the business of the restaurant, a waitress on the other floor sold liquor to customers who had not ordered a meal. The waitress had been instructed to serve liquor only to customers ordering a meal. The respondent did not know of these sales.

A charge of knowingly selling intoxicating liquor to persons to whom he was not entitled to sell, contrary to s 22 of the Licensing Act 1961, was dismissed by the justices. The prosecutor's appeal was dismissed by the Divisional Court on the ground that the respondent had not delegated to the waitress the management of the business. The prosecutor appealed.

Lord Reid. . . . The appellant maintains that under this section there is vicarious responsibility, so that the licence holder must be held guilty if a servant employed to sell liquor sells knowingly to a person to whom the licence holder is not permitted to sell, and that it is no defence that the accused had forbidden the servant so to sell and did not know of or connive at the sale. The appellant does not dispute that it is the general rule in criminal cases that an accused person cannot be convicted unless he has mens rea; but he maintains that the authorities have established a principle of interpretation of the provisions of the Licensing Acts that, where a licence holder is prohibited from doing or suffering certain things, vicarious responsibility must be inferred, so that the knowledge of the servant must be imputed to the licence holder whatever be the terms of the section under which he is prosecuted. His counsel frankly agreed that, but for this principle, a man charged with knowingly selling could not be convicted unless it was shown that he knew what his servant was doing or at least connived or shut his eyes to facts indicating that the servant was doing wrong or disobeying his orders.

The offence charged in this case is a new offence created for the first time by s 22 of the Act of 1961 and it must be observed that in the immediately preceding section, s 21(1), it is enacted that 'the holder of the licence or his servant shall not knowingly sell intoxicating liquor to a person under eighteen...'. The appellant denies that the contrast between this provision and that in s 22, 'If the holder of a justices' on-licence knowingly sells or supplies intoxicating liquor to persons...', has any relevance. Section 21(1) enables the servant himself to be prosecuted if he is the guilty person, but, to be consistent, the appellant must and does argue that if a servant does this without the knowledge of the licence holder then the prosecutor can prosecute under s 21 both the servant and the innocent licence holder—the servant because he has directly infringed the section, and the licence holder because he is vicariously responsible for the servant's acts. I doubt whether any authority however strong would justify your lordships reaching a result so contrary to the ordinary principles of construction and to the fundamental principle that an accused person cannot be convicted without proof of mens rea, unless from a consideration of the terms of the statute and other relevant circumstances it clearly appears that that must have been the intention of Parliament.

I shall not deal in detail with the cases on which the appellant has to rely. They are all more than 60 years old and with one exception they dealt with provisions in which the word 'knowingly' did not occur. The courts relied on the fact that it must have been known to Parliament that the things prohibited would frequently be done by servants of the licence holder and that in many cases the licence holder would have no knowledge of what his servant had done or at least that it would be very difficult to prove his knowledge or connivance. As there was no provision making the servant himself liable to prosecution, it would be impossible to enforce the law adequately if it was necessary in every case to prove mens rea in the licence holder. Those were strong arguments, and, as there was nothing in the wording of the relevant sections to exclude vicarious responsibility, I think that the courts were well justified in construing the sections as they did. The only case in which the word 'knowingly' occurred in the relevant section was *Avards v Dance* [(1862) 26 JP 437], where the offence was knowingly suffering gaming to take place, and it was suggested—it was no more than a suggestion—that, if the licence holder left someone else in charge, he might be answerable.

There are four cases *Emary v Nolloth* [[1903] 2 KB 264, [1900–03] All ER Rep 606; *McKenna v Harding* (1905) 69 JP 354; *Allen v Whitehead* [1930] 1 KB 211, [1929] All ER Rep 13; and *Linnett v Metropolitan Police Comr* [1946] KB 290, [1946] 1 All ER 380], since 1903 where the word 'knowingly' did occur in the relevant section, but they do not support the contention of the appellant in this case. There the courts adopted a construction which on any view I find it hard to justify. They drew a distinction between acts done by a servant without the knowledge of the licence holder while the licence holder was on the premises and giving general supervision to his business, and acts done without the knowledge of the licence holder but with the knowledge of a person whom the licence holder had left in charge of the premises. In the latter case they held that the knowledge of the person left in charge must be imputed to the licence holder. If that distinction is valid then I agree with the Divisional Court [[1964] 2 All ER at 823] that, on the facts of this case, there was not that 'delegation' by the accused necessary to make him answerable for the servant having acted against the orders of the accused.

Counsel for the appellant strenuously argued that this distinction is illogical and not warranted by any statutory provision. He maintained that if a licence holder entrusts to his wine waiter the duty of selling intoxicating liquor that is sufficient delegation and that, if the wine waiter disobeys his orders and sells to persons to whom he ought not to sell, there is nothing to justify the licence holder being acquitted, if he happens to have gone out leaving the wine waiter in charge. If this were a new distinction recently introduced by the courts I would think it necessary to consider whether a provision that the licence holder shall not knowingly sell can ever make him vicariously liable by reason of the knowledge of some other person; but this distinction has now been recognised and acted on by the courts for over half a century. It may have been unwarranted in the first instance, but I would think it now too late to upset so long-standing a practice.

It is, however, quite another matter to extend a long-standing anomaly particularly because there may in this matter be good practical reasons for requiring a licence holder to be specially careful about the person whom he chooses to leave in charge in his absence. One might have expected to find in the Licensing Acts some provisions regulating the position in the common case of a licence holder being absent from the licensed premises during the permitted hours, but there appears to be none. So, if the courts have in effect legislated to fill the gap, I think that we should leave matters as they are....

I can find nothing to require your lordships to give to the recent enactment with which we are concerned in the present case such an unusual meaning as would be necessary to support the appellant's case. This appeal must, therefore, be dismissed. In accordance with the terms imposed when giving leave to appeal the appellant must pay the respondent's costs.

[**Lord Evershed** having stated the facts and the issues, continued:]

It is, of course, a well-established proposition of the English criminal law that as a general rule the existence of mens rea is an essential requisite to a finding of guilt on the part of one accused of a criminal offence. None-the-less it appears to have now been established in the course of the numerous cases decided during the past century, to which counsel for the appellant alluded in his careful and elaborate argument, that where offences are charged under legislation such as that involved in the present case—eg licensing legislation—an exception to the general rule has been accepted, so that persons holding licences or exercising powers or duties under legislation of the character to which I have alluded have been held guilty of the statutory offences formulated in the legislation in the absence of any mens rea on their part. I have used the word 'accepted': and though it may be difficult to assert complete coherence in all the cases—particularly having regard to the considerable variation in the terminology of the numerous statutes which have been involved—yet it seems to me now impossible to reject the general conclusion which I have formulated, namely, that in statutes of the kind with which your lordships are here concerned an exception to the general common law rule will (for better or worse) be accepted if, on the general terms of the statute, liability on the part of the licensee is required to give practical effect to the legislative intention. [Lord Evershed went on to hold that no 'knowledge was proved against the licensee and that there was no sufficient evidence of such delegation as would render him liable on that ground'.]

[**Lord Morris of Borth-y-Gest** found it unnecessary to express any opinion on the delegation cases and held that, as a matter of construction, in the context of s 22(1), the presence of the word 'knowingly' requires knowledge in the licensee. The interpretation urged by the appellant involved reading words into the sub-section which were not there.]

[**Lord Hodson**, having stated the arguments continued:]

In this case the Divisional Court held [[1964] 2 All ER at 823] that there had been no delegation of authority in the sense in which the word has been used in *Emary v Nolloth* [[1903] 2 KB 264 at 269, [1900–03] All ER Rep 606 at 608] and in succeeding cases which have followed, because here the licensee was himself controlling the premises and had given direct instructions to the persons in his employment (including the waitress who served the liquor in contravention of the terms of the licence) that these terms had to be strictly observed. The distinction is a narrow one and the extent of the delegation may raise difficult questions, but it has never so far been extended so as to cover the case where the whole of the authority of the licensee has not been transferred to another: contrast this case where no more than a partial delegation has occurred. I agree with your lordships that, even if the 'delegation cases' are to remain undisturbed, so as to give the word 'knowingly' as applied to the licensee a meaning which embraces the licensee or his substitute, there is no justification for enlarging the ambit of the section so as to embrace the activities of any servant who is in breach of the provisions of a licence or of a statutory requirement....

The charge ... was laid under s 22(1)(a) of the Act of 1961 which creates the following offence:

> 'If (a) the holder of a justices' on licence knowingly sells or supplies intoxicating liquor to persons to whom he is not permitted by the conditions of the licence to sell or supply it ... he shall be guilty of an offence under this section.'

One must compare and contrast the language of the preceding section, s 21, which provides that 'the holder of the licence *or his servant* shall not knowingly sell intoxicating liquor to a person under eighteen...'. It would be strange if the words 'or his servant' which appear in s 21 but do not appear in s22 were to be implied in the latter section from which they would seem to have been deliberately excluded.

Your lordships are not I think driven to such a conclusion, and I would dismiss the appeal.

Lord Donovan. ... The rule that there may be liability in certain cases on an otherwise innocent licensee, if he has delegated sufficient control of the premises to the person who actually commits the offence, but no liability if he has delegated insufficient control, is a rule which so far I have failed to spell out of any Act of Parliament cited to us. In the present case it is, fortunately, not necessary to pronounce on its validity. Like my noble and learned friends, I think that the case can and should be decided on the language of s 22(1)(a) alone: since it is sufficiently clear by itself not to need elucidation by reference to the outside aids to which the appellant has been obliged to resort. If a decision that 'knowingly' means 'knowingly' will make the provision difficult to enforce, the remedy lies with the legislature.

Appeal dismissed

R v Winson

[1968] 1 All ER 197, Court of Appeal, Criminal Division

(Lord Parker CJ, Salmon LJ and Widgery J)

The appellant was a director of a company which owned a club and the holder of a justices' on-licence in respect of the club. It was a term of the licence that liquor should not be sold to anyone who had been a member for less than 48 hours. Liquor was sold in breach of this term. At the material times the club was run by a manager appointed by the managing director. The appellant, who also held licences in respect of three other premises, visited the club only occasionally. He was charged under s 161(1) of the Licensing Act 1964, which reproduced s 22 of the Licensing Act 1961 (above).

[**Lord Parker CJ**, having stated the facts, referred to *Vane v Yiannopoullos* [p **338**, above] and the fact that the Lords Morris and Donovan thought that, if the doctrine of delegation was part of the law, it could not apply to s 22 of the 1961 Act: but that Lords Reid and Evershed thought that, if there had been delegation, it would have applied to s 22. His Lordship continued:]

Accordingly, it seems to the court that their lordships in *Vane v Yiannopoullos* were equally divided on this point. It is, therefore, necessary to look a little further back into the inception of this doctrine.

It is to be observed in the first instance that this doctrine is something quite independent of the principles which come into play when Parliament has created an absolute offence. When an absolute offence has been created by Parliament, then the person on whom a duty is thrown is responsible, whether he has delegated or whether he has acted through a servant; he is absolutely liable regardless of any intent or knowledge or mens rea. The principle of delegation comes into play, and only comes into play, in cases where, though the statute uses words which import knowledge, or intent such as in this case 'knowingly' or in some other cases 'permitting' or 'suffering' and the like, cases to which knowledge is inherent, nevertheless it has been held that a man cannot get out of the responsibilities which have been put on him by delegating those responsibilities to another.

[His Lordship discussed *Allen v Whitehead*, above, p **337**.]

It is just worth referring to *Somerset v Hart* itself, if only because that was decided on the basis that there had been no valid delegation. The offence there concerned gaming, that the licensee of premises had suffered gaming to take place on the premises. In fact he had not delegated the management to anybody else, but a servant of his employed on the premises, without any connivance or wilful blindness on the part of the licensee, had suffered gaming to take place. In the course of the argument, Lord Coleridge CJ said [(1884) 12 QBD at 362]:

> 'How can a man suffer a thing done when he does not know of it? It is true that a man may put another in his position so as to represent him for the purpose of knowledge, but there is no evidence of such delegation here.'

In his judgment, Lord Coleridge CJ said [(1884) 12 QBD at 364]:

> 'I quite agree that the provisions of an Act which is passed in the interests of public morality and order should receive a reasonably liberal construction. I do not say that proof of actual knowledge on the part of the landlord is necessary. Slight evidence might be sufficient to satisfy the magistrates that the landlord might have known what was taking place if he had pleased, but where no actual knowledge is shown there must, as it seems to me, be something to show either that the gaming took place with the knowledge of some person clothed with the landlord's authority, or that there was something like connivance on his part, that he might have known but purposely abstained from knowing.'

Finally, of the more important authorities on this point, there is *Linnett v Metropolitan Police Comr* [[1946] KB 290, [1946] 1 All ER 380]. The offence there was 'knowingly permitting disorderly conduct, contrary to s 44 of the Metropolitan Police Act 1839'. In fact the licensee of the premises had absented himself from the premises and left the control to another man. It was held that, although he, the licensee, had no knowledge, the man he had appointed manager or controller did have knowledge and that, on the principle of delegation, he the licensee, was liable. Lord Goddard CJ said [[1946] KB 290 at 294, 295, [1946] 1 All ER 380 at 382]:

> 'The point does not, as I say, depend merely on the fact that the relationship of master and servant exists; it depends on the fact that the person who is responsible in law as the keeper of the house, or the licensee of the house if the offence is under the Licensing Act, has chosen to delegate his duties, powers and authority to somebody else.'

He went on to refer to *Somerset v Hart* and pointed out that in that case there had been no delegation of control, but that it was merely a case, as indeed was *Vane v Yiannopoullos*, of a servant acting behind the back of the licensee. He ended up by saying [[1946] KB 290 at 295, 296, [1946] 1 All ER 380 at 382, 383]:

> 'Where there is such delegation [that is true delegation] then the knowledge of the servant or agent becomes that of the master or principal. In this case there was no relationship of master and servant between the appellant and Baker. They were joint licensees. If one licensee chooses to say to his co-licensee, although not his servant: "We are both licensees and both keepers of this house, but I am

not going to take any part in the management of this house, I leave the management to you", he is putting his co-licensee into his own place to exercise his own powers and duties and he must, therefore, accept responsibility for what is done or known by his co-licensee in that exercise. That is the principle which underlies all the cases to which I have referred. I am far from saying, and I do not wish it to be thought that I am saying, that where a statute provides that in any business a certain act permitted by the manager shall be an offence on the part of the manager if it is done with his knowledge, that if that act takes place whilst the manager himself is carrying on that business and is in charge of that business but without his knowledge, so that he was powerless to prevent it, that person necessarily commits the offence. But if the manager chooses to delegate the carrying on of the business to another, whether or not that other is his servant, then what that other does or what he knows must be imputed to the person who put the other into that position.'

That is the doctrine of delegation which does form part of our law, and no one in the House of Lords has said that it does not. I should add that reference was made to a Scottish case since the decision of the House of Lords in *Vane's* case, that of *Noble v Heatly* [1967 SLT 26]. The court can get no assistance from that case, if only because it was a decision that this doctrine of delegation, though as I said part of the law of England, formed no part of the law of Scotland.

Accordingly, one comes back to the question whether this well established doctrine applies to s 161 of the Licensing Act 1964—a matter on which their lordships in *Vane's* case were divided. This court can see no valid distinction between the earlier cases, whether they concern prostitutes, drunkenness or gaming, and the provisions in this section. Parliament must be taken, when this section was originally introduced in 1961 [in s 22 of the Licensing Act 1961] and continued in 1964, to know that the doctrine of delegation had been applied in a number of licensing cases, and that the principle of those cases was that a man cannot get out of the responsibilities and duties attached to a licence by absenting himself. The position of course is quite different if he remains in control. It would be only right that he should not be liable if a servant behind his back did something which contravened the terms of the licence. If, however, he wholly absents himself leaving somebody else in control, he cannot claim that what has happened has happened without his knowledge if the delegate has knowingly carried on in contravention of the licence. Indeed, with all respect to Lord Morris and Lord Donovan, it is difficult to see how s 22 of the Act of 1961 differs in essential respects from the sections in other Acts dealt with in the earlier cases. The general principle in the opinion of this court must be applicable to a licensing case under this section as it is applicable in the other cases.

Finally, in a recent case since *Vane's* case, namely, *Ross v Moss* [[1965] 2 QB 396, [1965] 3 All ER 145], while intimating that the matter remained open for argument and decision in the future, I did venture to suggest [[1965] QB at 407, 408, [1965] 3 All ER at 149] that in the present state of authority the principle of delegation would seem to apply to an offence against this section.

Accordingly, for the reasons that I have endeavoured to state, this court has come to the conclusion that this appeal fails and must be dismissed.

Appeal dismissed

Question

While Dan, the licensee of The Bell, is answering the telephone, Bess, the barmaid, sells liquor (a) to Plod, a constable on duty; and (b) to Scott, a drunken person. Bess knows that Plod is on duty, but is quite reasonably unaware that Scott is drunk. See Licensing Act 1964, ss 172(3) ('The holder of a justices' licence shall not sell intoxicating liquor to a drunken person') and 178 (the holder of a justices' licence commits an offence if he 'supplies any liquor . . . to any constable on duty'); and *Sherras v De Rutzen* and *Cundy v Le Cocq*, pp 233–236, above. Consider the liability of Bess and Dan.

2. LIABILITY OF A CORPORATION

A corporation is a legal person, for example, a limited company or the University of Leeds, a person distinct from the persons who are members of it. The corporation, as distinct from its members, has no physical existence. It exists only in law. It cannot therefore act or form an intention except through its members. But a corporation can incur legal liabilities, both civil and criminal. This liability is always in a sense vicarious because it is necessarily incurred through the acts of its members. In criminal law, however, the corporation is held to be *personally* liable because the acts in the course of the corporation's business of those officers who control its affairs (in the draft Code called 'controlling officers'), and the intentions with which those acts are done, are deemed to be the acts and intentions of the corporation. This is so in respect of common law as well as statutory offences. A corporation may be a party to a common law conspiracy and may commit manslaughter. A corporation is not criminally liable for the acts of its members or employees who are not controlling officers, unless it is an offence to which the rules of vicarious liability considered above apply—for example, it is a case of selling in breach of a statutory provision. In the case of other offences, the question often is whether the status of the individual perpetrator is that of a controlling officer.

(1) CRIMES A CORPORATION CANNOT COMMIT

A corporation cannot commit a crime for which it cannot be sentenced. So it cannot commit murder, as a principal or an accessory, because the mandatory sentence is life imprisonment and a corporation is incapable of being imprisoned. Nearly all crimes are punishable by a fine so this is not a serious limitation on the scope of criminal liability. There are other offences which it is extremely unlikely that an official of a corporation could commit within the scope of his employment; for example, bigamy, rape, incest and perjury (cf *Re Odyssey (London) Ltd v OIC Run Off Ltd* (2000) The Times, 3 March, Court of Appeal (Civ Div)).

The fact that a corporation cannot commit the offence as a principal does not mean however that it is incapable of committing it as an accessory. It is difficult to imagine a case in which a company could be held liable as a principal for dangerous driving but it may certainly be convicted as a secondary party. In *Robert Millar (Contractors) Ltd* [1970] 1 All ER 577, [1970] 2 QB 54, M, the managing director of a company in Scotland, sent a heavy lorry on a journey to England. The court found that he must have known that the lorry had a seriously defective tyre. The tyre burst in England and the lorry crashed causing six deaths. H, the driver, was convicted on six counts of causing death by dangerous driving and M and the company were convicted of counselling and procuring those offences. The judge imposed a modest fine and disqualification upon H but he sentenced M to nine months' imprisonment and fined the company £750. An appeal by M and the company was dismissed. Similarly, though a corporation could not commit bigamy as a principal, it might do so if the managing director of an incorporated marriage advisory bureau were to arrange a marriage which he knew to be bigamous.

(2) THE LIABILITY OF CORPORATE AND UNINCORPORATED BODIES FOR STATUTORY OFFENCES

When Parliament creates an offence the statute usually provides that it is an offence for 'a person' to do or omit to do the act in question; and the Interpretation Act 1978, s 5, provides: 'In any Act, unless the contrary intention appears, words and expressions listed in Schedule 1 to this Act are to be construed according to that Schedule.'

Schedule 1 provides: ' "Person" includes a body of persons corporate or unincorporate. [1889].'

By Schedule 2, para 4(1)(a), the date, '[1889]', means that the definition of 'person' applies to Acts passed after 1889. Schedule 2, para 4(5) provides:

The definition of 'person', so far as it includes bodies corporate, applies to any provision of an Act whenever passed relating to an offence punishable on indictment or on summary conviction.

The effect is that, where it is a statutory offence for 'a person' to do or not do something, that offence may (unless the contrary intention appears) be committed by a corporation, whatever the date of the statute, and by an unincorporate body if the statute was passed after 1889. A contrary intention may appear because, for example, the actus reus is incapable of being committed by a corporation.

(3) WHOSE ACTS ARE THE ACTS OF THE CORPORATION?

Where a corporation is charged with an offence which can be committed only personally and not vicariously, a crucial question is whether the person who did the relevant acts was 'the directing mind and will of the company'. If he is, the company has done those acts. If he is not, there may be a question whether the company should nevertheless be held liable for them. The case which follows is, like many of the leading cases on this question, a civil action. The same principles apply in criminal law. The Board discusses the precedents in both civil and criminal law.

Meridian Global Funds Management Asia Ltd v Securities Commission
[1995] 3 WLR 413, Privy Council

(Lords Keith, Jauncey, Mustill, Lloyd and Hoffmann)

Koo, the chief investment officer, and Ng, the senior portfolio manager of an investment management company, unknown to the board of directors or managing director, used funds managed by the company to acquire shares in a public issuer and failed to give the notice required by s 20 of the New Zealand Securities Amendment Act 1988. Heron J held that the company was in breach, holding that, for the purposes of the section, the knowledge of Koo and Ng was to be attributed to the company. The Court of Appeal upheld that decision on the basis that Koo was the directing mind and will of the company. The company appealed to the Privy Council.

[**Lord Hoffmann**, delivering the judgment of the Board:]

The phrase 'directing mind and will' comes of course from the celebrated speech of Viscount Haldane LC in *Lennard's Carrying Co Ltd v Asiatic Petroleum Co Ltd* [1915] AC 705, 713. But their Lordships think that there has been some misunderstanding of the true principle upon which that case was decided. It may be helpful to start by stating the nature of the problem in a case like this and then come back to *Lennard's* case later.

Any proposition about a company necessarily involves a reference to a set of rules. A company exists because there is a rule (usually in a statute) which says that a persona ficta shall be deemed to exist and to have certain of the powers, rights and duties of a natural person. But there would be little sense in deeming such a persona ficta to exist unless there were also rules to tell one what acts were to count as acts of the company. It is therefore a necessary part of corporate personality that there should be rules by which acts are attributed to the company. These may be called 'the rules of attribution'.

The company's primary rules of attribution will generally be found in its constitution, typically the articles of association, and will say things such as 'for the purpose of appointing members of the board, a majority vote of the shareholders shall be a decision of the company' or 'the decisions of the board in managing the company's business shall be the decisions of the company.' There are also primary rules of attribution which are not expressly stated in the articles but implied by company law, such as

> 'the unanimous decision of all the shareholders in a solvent company about anything which the company under its memorandum of association has power to do shall be the decision of the company;' see *Multinational Gas and Petrochemical Co v Multinational Gas and Petrochemical Services Ltd* [1983] Ch 258....

The company's primary rules of attribution together with the general principles of agency, vicarious liability and so forth are usually sufficient to enable one to determine its rights and obligations. In exceptional cases, however, they will not provide an answer. This will be the case when a rule of law, either expressly or by implication, excludes attribution on the basis of the general principles of agency or vicarious liability. For example, a rule may be stated in language primarily applicable to a natural person and require some act or state of mind on the part of that person 'himself', as opposed to his servants or agents. This is generally true of rules of the criminal law, which ordinarily impose liability only for the actus reus and mens rea of the defendant himself. How is such a rule to be applied to a company?

One possibility is that the court may come to the conclusion that the rule was not intended to apply to companies at all; for example, a law which created an offence for which the only penalty was community service. Another possibility is that the court might interpret the law as meaning that it could apply to a company only on the basis of its primary rules of attribution, ie if the act giving rise to liability was specifically authorised by a resolution of the board or a unanimous agreement of the shareholders. But there will be many cases in which neither of these solutions is satisfactory; in which the court considers that the law was intended to apply to companies and that, although it excludes ordinary vicarious liability, insistence on the primary rules of attribution would in practice defeat that intention. In such a case, the court must fashion a special rule of attribution for the particular substantive rule. This is always a matter of interpretation: given that it was intended to apply to a company, how was it intended to apply? Whose act (or knowledge, or state of mind) was *for this purpose* intended to count as the act etc of the company? One finds the answer to this question by applying the usual canons of interpretation, taking into account the language of the rule (if it is a statute) and its content and policy.

The fact that the rule of attribution is a matter of interpretation or construction of the relevant substantive rule is shown by the contrast between two decisions of the House of Lords, *Tesco Supermarkets Ltd v Nattrass* [1971] 2 All ER 127, [1972] AC 153 and *In Re Supply of Ready Mixed Concrete (No 2)* [1995] 1 AC 456. In the *Tesco* case [1972] AC 153 the question involved the construction of a provision of the Trade Descriptions Act 1968. Tesco were prosecuted under section 11(2) for displaying a notice that goods were being 'offered at a price less than that at which they were in fact being offered . . .'. Its supermarket in Northwich had advertised that it was selling certain packets of washing powder at the reduced price of 2s 11d, but a customer who asked for one was told he would have to pay the normal price of 3s 11d. This happened because the shop manager had negligently failed to notice that he had run out of the specially marked low-price packets. Section 24(1) provided a defence for a shopowner who could prove that the commission of the offence was caused by 'another person' and that: 'He took all reasonable precautions and exercised all due diligence to avoid the commission of such an offence by himself or any person under his control.' The company was able to show that it owned hundreds of shops and that the board had instituted systems of supervision and training which amounted, on its part, to taking reasonable precautions and exercising all due diligence to avoid the commission of such offences in its shops. The question was: whose precautions counted as those of the company? If it was the board, then the defence was made out. If they had to include those of the manager, then it failed.

The House of Lords held that the precautions taken by the board were sufficient for the purposes of section 24(1) to count as precautions taken by the company and that the manager's negligence was not attributable to the company. It did so by examining the purpose of section 24(1) in providing a defence to what would otherwise have been an absolute offence: it was intended to give effect to 'a policy of consumer protection which does have a rational and moral justification': per Lord Diplock, at pp194–195. This led to the conclusion that the acts and defaults of the manager were not intended to be attributed to the company. . . .

On the other hand, in *In Re Supply of Ready Mixed Concrete (No 2)* [1995] 1 AC 456, a restrictive arrangement in breach of an undertaking by a company to the Restrictive Practices Court was made by executives of the company acting within the scope of their employment. The board knew nothing of the arrangement; it had in fact given instructions to the company's employees that they were not to make such arrangements. But the House of Lords held that for the purposes of deciding whether the company was in contempt, the act and state of mind of an employee who entered into an arrangement in the course of his employment should be attributed to the company. This attribution rule was derived from a construction of the undertaking against the background of the Restrictive Trade Practices Act 1976: such undertakings by corporations would be worth little if the company could avoid liability for what its employees had actually done on the ground that the board did not know about it. As Lord Templeman said, at p465, an uncritical transposition of the construction in *Tesco Supermarkets Ltd v Nattrass* [1972] AC 153:

> 'would allow a company to enjoy the benefit of restrictions outlawed by Parliament and the benefit of arrangements prohibited by the courts provided that the restrictions were accepted and implemented and the arrangements were negotiated by one or more employees who had been forbidden to do so by some superior employee identified in argument as the "higher management" of the company or by one or more directors of the company identified in argument as "the guiding will" of the company.'

[His Lordship returned to *Lennard's* case and continued:]

Because Lennard's Carrying Co Ltd does not seem to have done anything except own ships, there was no need to distinguish between the person who fulfilled the function of running the company's business in general and the person whose functions corresponded, in relation to the cause of the casualty, to those of an individual owner of a ship. They were one and the same person. It was this coincidence which left Viscount Haldane LC's speech open to the interpretation that he was expounding a general metaphysic of companies. In *H L Bolton (Engineering) Co Ltd v T J Graham & Sons Ltd* [1956] 3 All ER 624, [1957] 1 QB 159 Denning LJ certainly regarded it as a generalisation about companies 'as such' when, in an equally well known passage, at p172, he likened a company to a human body: 'It has a brain and nerve centre which controls what it does. It also has hands which hold the tools and act in accordance with directions from the centre.'

But this anthropomorphism, by the very power of the image, distracts attention from the purpose for which Viscount Haldane LC said, at p713, he was using the notion of directing mind and will, namely to apply the attribution rule derived from section 502 [of the Merchant Shipping Act 1894] to the particular defendant in the case:

> 'For if Mr. Lennard was the directing mind of the company, then his action must, unless a corporation is not to be liable at all, have been an action which was the action of the company itself *within the meaning of section 502*.' (Emphasis supplied.)

[His Lordship discussed *The Truculent* [1952] P 1 and *The Lady Gwendolen* [1965] P 294.]

Once it is appreciated that the question is one of construction rather than metaphysics, the answer in this case seems to their Lordships to be as straightforward as it did to Heron J. The policy of section 20 of the Securities Amendment Act 1988 is to compel, in fast-moving markets, the immediate disclosure of the identity of persons who become substantial security holders in public issuers. Notice must be given as soon as that person knows that he has become a substantial security holder. In the case of a corporate security holder, what rule should be implied as to the person whose knowledge for this purpose is to count as the knowledge of the company? Surely the person who, with the authority of the company, acquired the relevant interest. Otherwise the policy of the Act would be defeated. Companies would be able to allow employees to acquire interests on their behalf which made them substantial security holders but would not have to report them until the board or someone else in senior management got to know about it. This would put a premium on the board paying as little attention as possible to what its investment managers were doing.Their Lordships would therefore hold that upon the true construction of section 20(4)(e), the company knows that it has become a substantial security holder when that is known to the person who had authority to do the deal. It is then obliged to give notice under section 20(3). The fact that Koo did the deal for a corrupt purpose and did not give such notice because he did not want his employers to find out cannot in their Lordships' view affect the attribution of knowledge and the consequent duty to notify.

It was therefore not necessary in this case to inquire into whether Koo could have been described in some more general sense as the 'directing mind and will' of the company. But their Lordships would wish to guard themselves against being understood to mean that whenever a servant of a company has authority to do an act on its behalf, knowledge of that act will for all purposes be attributed to the company. It is a question of construction in each case as to whether the particular rule requires that the knowledge that an act has been done, or the state of mind with which it was done, should be attributed to the company. Sometimes, as in *In Re Supply of Ready Mixed Concrete (No 2)* [1995] 1 AC 456 and this case, it will be appropriate. Likewise in a case in which a company was required to make a return for revenue purposes and the statute made it an offence to make a false return with intent to deceive, the Divisional Court held that the mens rea of the servant authorised to discharge the duty to make the return should be attributed to the company: see *Moore v I Bresler Ltd* [1944] 2 All ER 515. On the other hand, the fact that a company's employee is authorised to drive a lorry does not in itself lead to the conclusion that if he kills someone by reckless driving, the company will be guilty of manslaughter. There is no inconsistency. Each is an example of an attribution rule for a particular purpose, tailored as it always must be to the terms and policies of the substantive rule.

Appeal dismissed

Notes and questions

1. Do *Meridian* and *Ready Mixed Concrete* demonstrate anything more than that a statute imposes vicarious liability if that appears to have been the intention of the legislature?

2. How, if at all, does *Meridian* affect cases in which a corporation is charged with a common law offence, such as conspiracy to defraud, perversion of the course of justice, or manslaughter, where there is no statute to construe?

3. The arrangement made by the employee in *Ready Mixed Concrete* was a contract binding the company (Lord Nolan at pp 150–151). So the company had given an undertaking that it would make no such arrangement and it had made such an arrangement. Was the decision any different in principle, then, from that in *Coppen v Moore* (above, p 335)?

4. The Draft Code, cl 30(6), would reverse *Moore v Bresler Ltd* by providing that a corporation is not liable for the act of a controlling officer when it is done with intention of doing harm, or concealing harm done, to the corporation. In the light of the Privy Council's apparent approval of the decision, is this a good recommendation? Cf question 2, p 763, below.

R v P & O European Ferries (Dover) Ltd
(1990) 93 Cr App R 72, Central Criminal Court

(Turner J)

The vessel, 'Herald of Free Enterprise', met with a catastrophe in Zeebrugge harbour on 6 March 1987, causing many deaths. Seven individual defendants and P & O Ltd, the owners of the 'Herald', were charged with manslaughter. It was argued that an indictment for manslaughter would not lie against a corporation. Reliance was placed on the proposition that manslaughter is the killing of a human being *by a human being* which is to be found in the books from *Coke* (1601) to *Halsbury's Laws of England* (4th edn, re-issue, 1990), in Stephen J's draft Code Bill of 1880 and in statutes in the United States and New Zealand which followed Stephen.

[*Ruling* by **Turner J**:]

The main thrust of the argument for the company in support of the submission that the four counts of manslaughter in this indictment should be quashed was not merely that English law does not recognise the offence of corporate manslaughter but that, as a matter of positive English law, manslaughter can only be committed when one natural person kills another natural person. Hence it was no accident that there is no record of any corporation or non-natural person having been successfully prosecuted for manslaughter in any English court. It was, however, accepted that there is no conceptual difficulty in attributing a criminal state of mind to a corporation. The broad argument advanced on behalf of the prosecution was that, there being no all embracing statutory definition of murder or manslaughter, there is, in principle, no reason why a corporation, or other non-natural person, cannot be found guilty of most offences in the criminal calendar. The exceptions to such a broad proposition could be found either in the form of punishment, which would be inappropriate for a corporation, or in the very personal nature of individual crimes or categories of crime such as offences under the Sexual Offences Act, bigamy and, arguably, perjury. It was further argued that the definitions of homicide to be found in the works of such as *Coke*, *Hale*, *Blackstone* and *Stephen*, and which were strongly relied upon by the company, were and were not intended to be exclusive, but reflected the historical fact that, at the dates when these definitions originated, the concept of criminal liability of a corporation, just as their very existence, was not within the contemplation of the courts or the writers of the legal treatises referred to. Before the days when corporate crime was in contemplation, it can be a matter of no surprise to find that the definition of homicide did not include the possibility of a corporation committing such a crime. As recently as 1701 Sir John Holt CJ is reported as having said: 'A corporation is not indictable but the particular members of it are.' Reported in 12 Mod 559. History does not, however, relate what was the subject matter of the litigation which provoked the above *dictum*.

The prosecution advanced an alternative argument to the effect that, if it were necessary that the death be, in fact, caused by a human being, then given the modern doctrine of 'identification', as to which see below, if the perpetrator of the act who was a human being which caused death could be treated as the embodiment of the corporation, then to that extent the test would be satisfied. It is obvious, however, that this alternative argument detracts from the force of the main argument.

[The judge examined the history of corporate liability.]

Since the nineteenth century there has been a huge increase in the numbers and activities of corporations whether nationalised, municipal or commercial, which enter the private lives of all or most of 'men and subjects' in a diversity of ways. A clear case can be made for imputing to such corporations social duties including the duty not to offend all relevant parts of the criminal law. By tracing the history of the cases decided by the English Courts over the period of the last 150 years, it can be seen how first tentatively and, finally, confidently the Courts have been able to ascribe to corporations a 'mind' which is generally one of the essential ingredients of common law and statutory offences. Indeed, it can be seen that in many Acts of Parliament the same concept has been embraced. The parliamentary approach is, perhaps, exemplified by section 18 of the Theft Act 1968 which provides for directors and managers of a limited company to be rendered liable to conviction if an offence under section 15, 16 or 17 of the Act is proved to have been committed—and I quote: 'with the consent, connivance of any director, manager, secretary... purporting to act in such capacity, then such director, manager or secretary shall be guilty of the offence.' Once a state of mind could be effectively attributed to a corporation, all that remained was to determine the means by which that state of mind could be ascertained and imputed to a non-natural person. That done, the obstacle to the acceptance of general criminal liability of a corporation was overcome. *Cessante ratione legis, cessat ipsa lex.* As some of the decisions in other common law countries indicate, there is nothing essentially incongruous in the notion that a corporation should be guilty of an offence of unlawful killing. I find unpersuasive the argument of the company that the old definitions of homicide positively exclude the liability of a non-natural person to conviction of an offence of manslaughter. Any crime, in order to be justiciable must have been committed by or through the agency of a human being. Consequently, the inclusion in the definition of the expression 'human being' as the author of the killing was either tautologous or, as I think more probable, intended to differentiate those cases of death in which a human being played no direct part and which would have led to forfeiture of the inanimate, or if animate non-human, object which caused the death (*deodand*) from those in which the cause of death was initiated by human activity albeit the instrument of death was inanimate or if animate non-human. I am confident that the expression 'human being' in the definition of homicide was not intended to have the effect of words of limitation as might have been the case had it been found in some Act of Parliament or legal deed. It is not for me to attempt to set the limits of corporate liability for criminal offences in English law. Examples of other crimes which may or may not be committed by corporations will, no doubt, be decided on a case by case basis in conformity with the manner in which the common law has adapted itself in the past. Suffice it that where a corporation, through the controlling mind of one of its agents, does an act which fulfils the prerequisites of the crime of manslaughter, it is properly indictable for the crime of manslaughter....

In conclusion, if my primary reason for this ruling were incorrect in law, I would be minded to follow a route close to that adopted by Henry J in *Murray Wright's* case [1969] NZLR 1069, in New Zealand who ruled that if it be accepted that manslaughter in English law is the unlawful killing of one human being by another human being (which must include both direct and indirect acts) and that a person who is the embodiment of a corporation and acting for the purposes of the corporation is doing the act or omission which caused the death, the corporation as well as the person may also be found guilty of manslaughter.

Ruling accordingly

Turner J's ruling in *P & O* that a corporation may be convicted of manslaughter was followed by Ognall J in *Kite and OLL Ltd* (1994) unreported, when the defendant company was convicted of that offence. But that was a case of a one-man company and the one man directed the fatal operation so there was no problem of identification.

In *Great Western Trains Co (GWT)* (30 June 1999, unreported), Scott Baker J ruled that the only basis on which a case for manslaughter could be established against the company was by identifying some one person within the company whose gross negligence was that of GWT itself. As no such person was identified he directed a verdict of not guilty. (Note that the company was subsequently convicted of an offence under s 33 of the Health and Safety at Work etc Act (which is punishable, like manslaughter, by an unlimited fine) and was fined.) He held that the *Meridian* case had made no difference in this respect and was unimpressed by the argument that GWR owed a personal duty to establish a safe system of work, of which they had committed a gross breach. He held that the negligence of individual officers of the company could not be aggregated so as to amount to gross negligence. He did not accept that, following *Adomako*, manslaughter by gross negligence is an entirely objective crime, requiring no proof of a state of mind. The Attorney-General referred the case to the Court of Appeal.

Attorney-General's Reference (No 2 of 1999)
[2000] 2 Cr App R 207, Court of Appeal

(Lord Justice Rose (Vice-President), Potts and Curtis JJ)

Rose LJ (Vice-President): The Court's opinion is sought in relation to two questions referred by the Attorney-General under section 36 of the Criminal Justice Act 1972:

1. Can a defendant be properly convicted of manslaughter by gross negligence in the absence of evidence as to that defendant's state of mind? 2. Can a non-human defendant be convicted of the crime of manslaughter by gross negligence in the absence of evidence establishing the guilt of an identified human individual for the same crime?

[His lordship referred to the ruling of Scott Baker J at the Central Criminal Court on 30 June 1999].

... The case for the prosecution was that the cause of the collision was, first, the driver's failure to see or heed the double yellow and single yellow signals warning of impending red and, secondly, the defendant's manner of operating the HST. The case against the defendant was that it owed a duty to take reasonable care for the safety of its passengers, of which it was in grossly negligent breach. Three signals were passed because the AWS and ATP were switched off and there was only one man in the cab. The defendant should not have permitted such a train to operate in such circumstances. Following the judge's ruling, the defendant pleaded guilty to count 8 on the indictment, which alleged failure to conduct an undertaking, namely the provision of transport by rail to members of the public, in such a way as to ensure that they were not exposed to risks to their health and safety, contrary to sections 3(1) and 33(1)(a) of the Health and Safety at Work Act 1974. The defendant was fined GBP1.5 million for what the judge described as 'a serious fault of senior management'. No employee of the defendant, apart from the driver, was prosecuted....

[Having dealt with the question of gross negligence manslaughter, his lordship considered the argument for aggregating the states of mind of those at fault in the company.]

Mr Lissack [Counsel for the Attorney] ... suggested that aggregation has a role to play, i.e. where a series of venial management failures are aggregated and cumulatively amount to gross negligence, a company may be convicted. There is a tentatively expressed passage in *Smith and Hogan on Criminal Law* (9th ed, 1999) at p. 186, based on an analogy with civil negligence, which supports this suggestion. But there is no supporting and clear contrary judicial authority—see per Bingham L.J. in *R. v. H.M. Coroner for East Kent, ex p. Spooner* (1989) 88 Cr.App.R. 10 at p. 16:

> 'A case against a personal defendant cannot be fortified by evidence against another defendant. The case against a corporation can only be made by evidence properly addressed to showing guilt on the part of the corporation as such'.

The Law Commission Report No. 237 at paragraph 7.33 is against introducing the concept of aggregation. We reject the suggestion that aggregation has any proper role to play......

There is, as it seems to us, no sound basis for suggesting that, by their recent decisions, the courts have started a process of moving from identification to personal liablity as a basis for corporate liability for manslaughter. In *Adomako* the House of Lords were, as it seems to us, seeking to escape from the unnecessarily complex accretions in relation to recklessness arising from *Lawrence (Stephen)* (1981) 73 Cr.App.R. 1, [1982] A.C. 510 and *Caldwell* (1981) 73 Cr.App.R. 13, [1982] A.C. 341 [above, p **146**]. To do so, they simplified the ingredients of gross negligence manslaughter by restating them in line with *Bateman*. But corporate liability was not mentioned anywhere in the submissions of counsel or their Lordship's speeches. In any event, the identification principle is in our judgment just as relevant to the actus reus as to mens rea. In *Tesco v. Nattrass* at p. 173D Lord Reid said:

> 'The judge must direct the jury that if they find certain facts proved then, as a matter of law, they must find that the criminal act of the officer, servant or agent, including his state of mind, intention, knowledge or belief is the act of the Company.'

In *R. v. H.M. Coroner for East Kent, ex p. Spooner* (1989) 88 Cr.App.R. 10, Bingham L.J. said at p. 16:

> 'For a company to be criminally liable for manslaughter... it is required that the mens rea and the actus reus of manslaughter should be established... against those who were to be identified as the embodiment of the company itself.'

In *P. & O. European Ferries (Dover) Ltd* (1990) 93 Cr.App.R. 72 Turner J., in his classic analysis of the relevant principles, said at p. 83:

> 'Where a corporation through the controlling mind of one of its agents, does an act which fulfils the prerequisite of the crime of manslaughter, it is properly indictable for the crime of manslaughter.'

In our judgment, unless an identified individual's conduct, characterisable as gross criminal negligence, can be attributed to the company the company is not, in the present state of the common law, liable for manslaughter. Civil negligence rules, e.g. as enunciated in *Wilsons & Clyde Coal Co. Ltd v. English* [1938] A.C. 57, are not apt to confer criminal liability on a company. None of the authorities relied on by Mr Lissack as pointing to personal liability for manslaughter by a company supports that contention. In each, the decision was dependent on the purposive construction that the particular statute imposed, subject to a defence of reasonable practicability, liability on a company for conducting its undertaking in a manner exposing employees or the public to health and safety risk. In each case there was an identified employee whose conduct was held to be that of the company. In each case it was held that the concept of directing mind and will had no application when construing the statute. But it was not suggested or implied that the concept of identification is dead or moribund in relation to common law offences. Indeed, if that were so, it might have been expected that Lord Hoffmann, in *Associated Octel*, would have referred to the ill health of the doctrine in the light of his own speech, less than a year before, in *Meridian*. He made no such reference, nor was *Meridian* cited in *Associated Octel*. It therefore seems safe to conclude that Lord Hoffmann (and, similarly, the members of the Court of Appeal (Criminal Division) in *British Steel* and in *Gateway Food Market*) did not think that the common law principles as to the need for identification have changed. Indeed, Lord Hoffmann's speech in *Meridian*, in fashioning an additional special rule of attribution geared to the purpose of the statute, proceeded on the basis that the primary 'directing mind and will' rule still applies, although it is not determinative in all cases. In other words, he was not departing from the identification theory but reaffirming its existence.

This approach is entirely consonant with the Law Commission's analysis of the present state of the law and the terms of their proposals for reform in their Report No. 237 published in March 1996. In this report, both the House of Lords' decision in *Adomako* and the Privy Council's decision in *Meridian* were discussed. In the light of their analysis, the Law Commission concluded, (paragraph 6.27 and following and paragraph 7.5), that in the present state of the law, a corporation's liability for manslaughter is based solely on the principle of identification and they drafted a Bill to confer liability based on management failure not involving the principle of identification (see clause 4 of the Draft Bill annexed to their Report). If Mr Lissack's submissions are correct, there is no need for such a Bill and, as Scott Baker J. put it, the Law Commission have missed the point. We agree with the judge that the Law Commission have not missed the point and Mr Lissack's submissions are not correct: the identification principle remains the only basis in common law for corporate liability for gross negligence manslaughter....

Determination accordingly

(4) WHY CONVICT CORPORATIONS AT ALL?

What is the purpose of imposing criminal liability upon a corporation? It is a creature of the law with no physical existence. It cannot suffer imprisonment or any kind of physical punishment. It can be fined but the fine does not have the effects it does upon a human being. The corporation cannot go cold or hungry or feel the loss of the luxuries of life. It cannot feel shame, remorse or repentance. It is as devoid of moral as of physical sensations. Of course, its officers can suffer like other persons, but the penalties of the criminal law can be imposed on them without making the corporation liable. The imposition of a fine may affect a company's shareholders by reducing their dividends, but in the case of large companies this is likely to be imperceptible, except in the case of a quite exceptionally large fine. (See for a full discussion of fines: M. Jefferson, 'Corporate Criminal Liability: The Problem of Sanctions' (2001) J Crim L 235.) In any case, the shareholders rarely have any effective control over the day-to-day operation of the company's business and so, morally, may well be thought to have no responsibility for the company's transgressions. Moreover, many corporations do not have shareholders. A heavy fine on the University of Barchester could adversely affect only the staff and students and the research and other activities of the University.

On the other hand it is clear that the officers of corporations do care about a criminal conviction of the corporation. It is something they are anxious to avoid. The expensive efforts of Alphacell Ltd to get the company's conviction quashed have already been remarked on. Obviously the directors were worried, not about the trivial amount of the fine, but about the effect of the conviction on the standing and reputation of the company. The conviction of the company has an effect on the public mind that the conviction of individual officers does not. If directors are so very concerned about the effect of a conviction, is it not likely that they will make strenuous efforts to avoid contravention of the criminal law? And if they do, has not the law achieved its purpose? Do we need to look for any further justification?

But there is another aspect. The victims of corporate wrongdoing may have a powerful urge to punish the corporation. Press reports suggest that the indignation of many of those bereaved by the Zeebrugge disaster was directed not so much at individual officers as at the shipping company itself. It is perhaps significant that the corporation was prosecuted not merely for regulatory offences but for the common law crime of manslaughter, punishable in the case of a human being with life imprisonment. When the prosecution of the company failed, the prosecution of individual officers was discontinued—though the grounds for dismissal of the charge against the company did not necessarily remove the basis of the case against some of the officers. Similar reactions against corporations have been observed to other disasters, such as the King's Cross fire. Although GWR was fined as much for its offence under the Health and Safety at Work Act as it would have been on conviction for manslaughter, public disquiet at its acquittal of homicide was unabated. The satisfaction of the demand for retribution by those injured by crime has long been recognized as a proper ground for the imposition of punishment. Is it a sufficient ground for the imposition of criminal liability on a corporation that strong public feeling demands that corporate wrongdoing should be publicly condemned by the courts? If that feeling exists, does it matter whether it is rational or irrational?

To what extent is our decision whether to criminalize corporate wrongs conditioned by how that can be done within the existing legal framework? Wells questions this in the context of manslaughter.

C. Wells, 'The Decline and Rise of English Murder: Corporate Crime and Individual Responsibility' [1988] Crim LR 788

... The ... assumption, that corporations do not act intentionally or recklessly, is I think connected with the conceptual difficulties caused by the phenomenon of corporate harms. Part of the reason they are not perceived as crimes is that they do not fit the socially constructed image of criminal behaviour. But the other part of the reason is that crime is subject to a form of legal construction which excludes corporate or collective harm. The analysis of crime into an 'act' and a 'state of mind' immediately marginalises corporate behaviour which is typically much more diverse in its activities and more diffuse in its chains of decision making. This makes the ascription of responsibility more difficult, but we should be wary of being caught by traps which reflect more the mode of legal analysis favoured by criminal lawyers and less the substance of the issue itself. Someone at Ford did know that there was a risk attached to the design of the Pinto's fuel tank; someone in Townsend's management knew that roll on-off ferries were potentially unstable; someone in the United States' blood bank industry knew that AIDS was probably infectious, and so on. One task for criminal lawyers is to question critically how such knowledge within corporations can be related to familiar notions of individual culpability. Another is to consider, as I suggest below, whether corporate crime demands the deployment of completely different indices of fault.

...

It is not of course true that criminal liability is conditional on a subjective mental element. The requirements of many conventional crimes are satisfied by a mental element less demanding than intention; ... Why argue then that this rotten system should embrace yet more offenders in the form of corporate criminals? At the risk of counter-argument three reasons can be articulated for continuing to explore corporate crime.

(i) The existence of objective fault elements should not be allowed to detract or distract from their differential application to individuals and corporations. We are not dealing here with obsolete laws which are merely waiting for formal repeal. Objective recklessness is part of the everyday currency of the criminal process; there are clearly many circumstances where law enforcement officials regard it as appropriate. It does not seem therefore a good argument against corporate liability to say that conventional crime is or ought to be based on subjective intention or recklessness.

(ii) The argument in (i) above might lead us to question what instrumental effect would result from narrowing the definition of manslaughter. An underlying theme of this article is that public perceptions of harm and crime do have impact on trial and inquest verdicts. There are occasions when juries rebel, or attempt to rebel, against strict legal definitions of crime. This can work both ways. Sometimes 'societal conceptions' indicate an unwillingness to convict. At others, juries seem less keen to show leniency as the Zeebrugge inquest demonstrated. Clearly what is at stake here is how we view the respective roles of formal legal definition and those of the legal and lay actors in the criminal justice drama. It is not possible to explore the extent and nuances of that particular script here but suffice it to say that the relationships are probably symbiotic and certainly complex.

(iii) A different response altogether would be to consider whether corporate harm presents such peculiar problems to the criminal law that the concept of individual culpability is unsuitable for corporate conglomerates. In other words, we may want to consider imposing a different, though not necessarily lesser, standard on corporations whose technology, as we see tragically only too often, has the potential to cause injury and death on a quite devastating scale. This anticipates the argument below that the nature and scope of corporate liability can itself present obstacles to the enforcement of corporate criminal harms. To compare the 'intending' individual with the 'negligent' corporation does not necessarily impose too great a responsibility on the latter given the nature of much corporate enterprise. Although not developed here there is clearly room for an argument that culpability is relative not just to the state of mind of the criminal actor but also to the risk inherent in the enterprise in which she is engaged. This is familiar as one rationale for the imposition of strict liability. It should not be lightly dismissed.

A paradox has, however, to be confronted. The obstacle to a pursuit of criminal charges against Townsend Thoresen, now P&O, after the Zeebrugge capsize, seemed to be related to the difficulty of perceiving crime as more than a matter of individual responsibility. Some of the relatives were concerned that the blame should not be borne by the officers who operated the ship but by the company who managed both them and the ship. But the experience of the Health and Safety Executive suggests that corporate liability allows companies to evade rather than to take responsibility. The Executive itself has recently begun to question the effectiveness of corporate prosecution. In a report on safety (or lack of it) in the construction industry, it argued that safety inspectors should prosecute individuals instead of companies for breaches of regulations. Most people, the report said, were killed from lack of simple planning and precautions. Some 70 per cent. of the 739 deaths investigated over four years could have been saved by appropriate management action. A senior director of the Executive's London South area was reported to have said:

> 'If construction companies try to wriggle out of health and safety regulations by trying to blame it on subcontractors, we will then go for the individuals such as middle managers and foremen who are supposed to supervise safety matters.'

The paradox is not as great as might at first seem. The question in both parts of the paradox is concerned with the allocation of responsibility. The relatives at Zeebrugge did not want ship level operatives to take the blame for management failure, while the Health and Safety Executive is concerned that management do not hide behind the corporation. The niceties of corporate versus individual responsibility may not have mattered to the Zeebrugge relatives so long as the right individuals were pursued. This echoes the *Film Recovery Systems* case in Illinois. After a worker died from cyanide poisoning, the company was fined $4855 for 20 safety violations under the Occupational Safety and Health Act. Dissatisfied with this, the local District Attorney successfully filed criminal homicide charges and three executives were given prison sentences while the company was fined $24,000.

In the report of the Zeebrugge inquiry held under the Merchant Shipping Act 1950, Sheen J. criticised a number of the individuals who had failed to perform their duty, in particular those responsible for failing to close the bow doors, failing to see that the doors were closed and sailing without knowing that the doors were closed.

> 'At first sight the faults which led to this disaster were the aforesaid errors of omission on the part of the Master, the Chief Officer and the assistant bosun, and also the failure by Captain Kirby to issue and enforce clear orders. But a full investigation into the circumstances of the disaster leads inexorably to the conclusion that the underlying or cardinal faults lay higher up in the company. The Board of Directors did not appreciate their responsibility for the safe management of their ships. They did not apply their minds to the question: What orders should be given for the safety of our ships? The directors did not have any proper comprehension of what their duties were. There appears to have been a lack of thought about the way in which The Herald ought to have been organised for the Dover/Zeebrugge

run. All concerned in management, from the members of the Board of Directors down to the junior superintendents, were guilty of fault in that all must be regarded as sharing responsibility for the failure of management. From top to bottom the body corporate was infected with the disease of sloppiness...The failure on the part of shore management to give proper and clear directions was a contributory cause of the disaster...[M.V. Herald of Free Enterprise, Report of the [Sheen] Court, No. 8074. Dept of Transport, 1987, para. 14]'

A stronger official statement of blame would be difficult to imagine, yet the inquest coroner clearly felt that he was not dealing with deaths caused by unlawful homicide. There was a fundamental difference between his view and that of the applicant relatives. They saw the sinking of the ship both as a crime and one for which responsibility should be taken by management, not in a vicarious sense but directly. Fisse and Braithwaite have argued that formal criminal law is in a state of crisis. Because it is rooted in the 'ideology of Individualism,' it is unable to deal with the responsibility of collectivities [Brent Fisse and John Braithwaite, 'Accountability and the Control of Corporate Crime' in *Understanding Crime and Criminal Justice*, by Mark Findlay and Russell Hogg (eds.), (Sydney, The Law Book Co. Ltd., 1988)]. There is something ironic in this since it is part of received wisdom that socialist systems tend to pin blame on individuals when things go wrong. After the Chernobyl nuclear plant disaster three of its directors were sentenced to 10 years' hard labour. But this is not confined to collectively based economies. It seems to be a feature of Japanese capitalism that there is often an individual response to corporate failure.

Individuals within corporations

There has been a shift in perceptions of corporate responsibilities since the Zeebrugge and King's Cross disasters. The extent of the shift is difficult to assess. If, however, there is more willingness to use conventional crime classification in these situations, it is worthwhile considering Fisse and Braithwaite's arguments about how best to make corporations criminally accountable. There are currently (at least) two obstacles to making corporations criminally responsible. One is the nature of corporate liability itself which is dependent on the anthropomorphic view of company structure [see above p **347**]. This required the coroner at the Zeebrugge inquest to look for evidence that those who represented the directing mind and will of the company and controlled what it did had been guilty of conduct amounting to manslaughter. The relatives argued that the coroner should have aggregated the individual instances of neglect of safety matters by different management officials and directors. The Divisional court summarily dismissed this:

'I do not think the aggregation argument assists the applicants...The case against a corporation can only be made by evidence properly addressed to showing guilt on the part of the corporation as such.' [See also *A-G's Ref (No 2 of 1999)* above p **351**]

The emphasis on the need to find an individual, or a number of individuals acting together, who could be identified as the embodiment of the company itself confirms Clark's observation:

'In the West decision-making is presented as individual until adversity proves it collective. [R. Clark, *The Japanese Company* (Yale University Press, 1979), p **130**]'

The second obstacle is really the same problem in reverse. If corporate liability is based on a form of collective responsibility for an individual's wrongdoing, what and against whom is the appropriate sanction? Corporations are faceless bureaucracies not human beings writ large. Fisse and Braithwaite favour a strategy which would ensure that enforcement was structured 'so as to activate and monitor the private justice systems of corporate defendants. [op cit p.110]' It is a deterrent based argument involving both corporate and individual responsibility. They argue that corporate criminal liability already has as an underlying aim, that of stimulating internal discipline, the problem is in ensuring that such discipline is effectively carried out. Their solution is to make corporate liability to punishment conditional on a failure to achieve internal accountability. The punishment they envisage if the company fails to fulfill the condition would involve both individual and corporate sanctions which would include 'court-ordered adverse publicity, community service, and punitive injunctions. [op cit p 111]' This latter would be an injunction which would put pressure on a company by requiring it to take some form of preventative action. It is not clear how far this proposal overcomes the problems of scapegoating or of ensuring compliance. [Fisse and Braithwaite acknowledge the first of these.]

Although sharing many of Fisse and Braithwaite's concerns about the enforcement of corporate crime, Box showed less sympathy with the notion of individual accountability.

> '[T]he essence of corporate crime is not the behaviour of individuals, but the "behaviour" of corporations…In order to be effective, the level of intervention to regulate corporate crime has to be organizational rather than individual (original italics). [*Power, Crime and Mystification* (1983) 70.]'

His preferred solution was for encarceration through temporary nationalisation with the appointment of public directors. In a continuation of his analogy with forms of punishment conventionally applied to individuals, Box suggested that probation, community service, and compensation orders could be effectively adapted to apply to corporations.

There is much similarity of approach between these writers in trying to grapple with the contradictions of corporate liability which has to acknowledge that, although they are not like individuals, corporations are ultimately entities made up of human parts. Box emphasises the corporate nature of their liability but insists that a far more imaginative use of traditionally individual penal sanctions can be made against them. Fisse and Braithwaite confront the individual within the corporation at a much earlier stage in the analysis. And certainly what they share is a willingness, rarely found amongst criminal theorists, to confront the issues posed by corporate crime. As Box concluded.

> 'If there is no way of implementing justice for the largest and worst offending corporations then it is surely unjust to pursue with such ruthless and cruel tenacity the majority of those eventually condemned to prison. [op cit p 79]'

It is thought somehow unseemly for criminal lawyers to defend or argue for the widening of the parameters of criminal liability. There is much unjustifiable control through the criminal law of behaviour which is neither harmful nor threatening to others. There is also differential enforcement of activities which do threaten and do cause harm. The issues I have raised here need to be seen in that context. Ideas derived from individual culpability are not effective in their response to some of the harms which reliance on modern, and not so modern, technology brings in its wake. An extension or rethinking of corporate liability may or may not reduce those harms. But at the very least it would demonstrate a commitment to a critical approach to the symbolic message which is carried by the criminal law…

Different approaches are advocated by others. For example, J. Gobert, 'A Corporate Criminality: New Crimes for the Times' [1994] Crim LR 722 writes:

The subject of corporate criminality is ripe for systematic review by Parliament. Liability should not depend upon the identification of those persons responsible for the crime in question, a task which is difficult at best; let alone on the determination of the perpetrators' status within the company, as required under *Nattrass*. Instead, a model of 'corporate fault' should be adopted [Gobert, 'Corporate Criminality: Four Models of Fault' (1994) 14 LS]. A company should be criminally liable where a crime is authorised, permitted or tolerated as a matter of company policy or de facto practice. In this situation liability should be for the substantive offence which has occurred.

The difficulty with formulating liability in these terms is one of proof. A prosecutor may search in vain for a company policy which authorises, permits, or tolerates criminal behaviour. Far more likely to be found is a pro forma resolution which prohibits crimes by company personnel or which exhorts employees to conduct themselves in accord with the highest ethical standards. To pierce this different type of corporate veil, another form of criminal liability is needed. The focus would be on the creation of risks likely to lead to the occurrence of serious harm. If the harm in fact materialised, the company's liability would be for the failure to prevent the harm rather than for the substantive crime itself. Penalties would not necessarily be identical to those for the substantive offence, although some overlap might be desirable to cover cases where it was both foreseeable and virtually inevitable that the corporate failure would lead to the actual harm which occurred.

...

The crux of the liability proposed in this article ... is a failing on the company's part, but it is that failing in and of itself which would constitute the offence. That the risk created did not eventuate would not necessarily be fatal to a prosecution, although it might be of evidentiary significance as to whether there actually was a danger. The proposed liability is predicated on an implied duty on the part of a company to prevent crime. From where might such a duty arise? The state allows companies to carry on a business for profit under the protective umbrella of its laws. Its courts provide relief from the unfair practices of competitors, and a mechanism for securing debts owed to the company. In exchange for being able to operate within this legal structure, created and enforced by the state, comes a corresponding duty not to conduct its business in a way which exposes innocent individuals to the dangers of harms proscribed by that same state's criminal laws [Leigh, 'The Criminal Liability of Corporations and other Groups' (1977) 9 Ottawa L Rev 247 at 287].

Furthermore, a company is free to choose the business which it enters into, and the methods by which it conducts that business. From these choices it derives its profit. Often the nature of a company's activities engenders risks to the public. A company that creates a situation of danger, or places an employee in a better position to perpetrate a crime than he or she would otherwise have been in, has an obligation to take steps to prevent criminal harm from occurring. What this means in practical terms is that companies have a duty to promulgate and adopt policies directed towards the prevention of crime and, more intangibly but no less importantly, to establish a corporate ethos which gives appropriate place to protecting the public from crimes which might occur in the course of the company's business.

As for mens rea in the corporate context, this construct may confound rather than promote reasoned analysis. Again it may prove helpful to return to basics, and ask what function mens rea is designed to serve. In instrumental terms mens rea provides a useful tool for identifying defendants who have acted in a blameworthy manner and for assessing the degree of their culpability. Without a concept of mens rea, it might be argued, companies that have done their best to prevent harm might be convicted of crime. Not so. Mens rea is one way, but not the only way, of getting at the issue of blameworthiness.

An alternative, arguably more apropos in the corporate context, is to ask whether the company could have taken steps to identify and avoid the occurrence of harm, whether it was reasonable for it to do so, and whether it in fact did so. In other words, instead of requiring the Crown to prove mens rea, it should be a defence for the company to prove due diligence. Such a defence is not unknown in English law. On occasion Parliament has incorporated it into a statute (Weights and Measures Act 1985, s. 34). What is envisaged here, however, is more broadly conceived, across-the-board defence which would protect a corporate defendant from liability where the company has made a conscientious and reasonable effort to prevent the substantive crime which has occurred (American Law Institute, Model Penal Code, s. 2.07(5). [See also Note, 'Developments in the Law— Corporate Crime: Regulating Corporate Behaviour Through Criminal Sanctions' (1979) 92 Harv LR 1127 at 1257–59).]

As the company is in the best position to know what it has done to protect against the commission of a crime, the burden of establishing due diligence should be on it. The burden should not be simply that of presenting evidence in the first instance but should extend to convincing the trier of fact by a balance of probabilities that it acted with due diligence. More severe a burden would be too onerous, and any less a burden would put the Crown in the position of having to disprove due diligence when records and other relevant evidence lay buried within a mountain of files controlled by the defendant. The burden should not be subject to discharge by mere proof of an unawareness of the dangers on the part of management without also a showing that it was not reasonable to expect the company to have been aware of the risks [Wells, 'Corporations: Culture, Risk and Criminal Liability' [1993] Crim LR 551).] Nor should it be enough for the company to establish that its mode of operation conformed to that which was prevalent in the industry. Although compliance with an industry wide standard may be evidence of due diligence, the possibility must nonetheless be entertained that the entire industry has acted in a culpable manner.

How much must a company do in order to satisfy the demands of due diligence? No simple answer is possible or even desirable. The likelihood of harm and the extent of harm, should the risk which has been created eventuate, will need to be balanced against the social utility of the activity in question and the practicability and cost of eliminating risk. A company will have to demonstrate that it took reasonable and appropriate steps under the circumstances to prevent harm from occurring. ...

At some point the question of corporate criminality becomes one of political will. There is an understandable legislative ambivalence about addressing corporate crime that is not present when the offender is an individual. The typical murder or theft has no social redeeming value, and there are few compunctions about imprisoning the perpetrator of such a crime. A company, on the other hand, often contributes to the public welfare through the products it manufactures. Through the taxes it pays and its employment of workers it promotes the economic well-being of the nation. It is not so obviously in the government's interest to jeopardise its own financial position by discouraging corporate activity that might border on the criminal. ...

A fair yet firm approach to corporate crime is called for. Regulatory offences lack the muscle to provide a sufficient disincentive from activities which are profitable but which may entail the commission of criminal offences, and the *Nattrass* approach to conventional criminal law may simply encourage devolved decision-making as a means of avoiding liability. The role of corporate policy (or absence thereof) in the bringing about of the crime warrants close examination, and the Crown should not be satisfied with the scapegoat prosecutions of individuals. The law needs to be restructured so that companies that do not take seriously their responsibilities to society are sanctioned, and those which do are not inadvertently drawn into the net of the criminal law. Much more than it has to date, the law must grapple with the questions of when it can be said that a company has acted in a blameworthy manner and what consequences attach to a showing of such blameworthiness.

REFORM OF THE LAW

The Law Commission Report No 237 (1996) observe that the Sheen Report (MV Herald of Free Enterprise: Report of the Court No 8074, Dept of Transport, 1987) concluded that the P&O company was 'infected with the disease of sloppiness' from top to bottom, yet the company was subsequently acquitted of manslaughter. The Commission consider that this provides an 'overpowering argument' that, on the ground of public policy, a corporation should be liable for a fatal accident caused by gross negligence in the management or organisation of its activities. They recommend the creation of an offence of corporate killing based on whether there had been a management failure. Subsequently, in 2005, the government produced a document—*Corporate Manslaughter: The Government's Draft Bill for Reform* (2005) Cm 6497—including a Bill which it is proposed to introduce into Parliament. The principal clauses of the Bill provide:

[Corporate manslaughter]

1 The offence

(1) An organisation to which this section applies is guilty of the offence of corporate manslaughter if the way in which any of the organisation's activities are managed or organised by its senior managers—

(a) causes a person's death, and

(b) amounts to a gross breach of a relevant duty of care owed by the organisation to the deceased.

(2) The organisations to which this section applies are—

(a) a corporation;

(b) a government department or other body listed in the Schedule.

(3) The Secretary of State may amend the Schedule by order.

(4) An organisation that is guilty of corporate manslaughter is liable on conviction on indictment to a fine.

(5) An individual cannot be guilty of aiding, abetting, counselling or procuring an offence of corporate manslaughter.

(6) Proceedings for an offence under this section may not be instituted without the consent of the Director of Public Prosecutions.

(7) In this Act 'senior manager', 'gross breach', 'relevant duty of care' and 'corporation' have the meaning given by sections 2 to 5.

2 Senior manager

A person is a 'senior manager' of an organisation if he plays a significant role in—

(a) the making of decisions about how the whole or a substantial part of its activities are to be managed or organised, or

(b) the actual managing or organising of the whole or a substantial part of those activities.

3 Gross breach

(1) A breach of a duty of care by an organization is a 'gross' breach if the failure in question constitutes conduct falling far below what can reasonably be expected of the organisation in the circumstances.

(2) In deciding that question the jury must consider whether the evidence shows that the organisation failed to comply with any relevant health and safety legislation or guidance, and if so—

(a) how serious was the failure to comply;

(b) whether or not senior managers of the organisation—

(i) knew, or ought to have known, that the organisation was failing to comply with that legislation or guidance;

(ii) were aware, or ought to have been aware, of the risk of death or serious harm posed by the failure to comply;

      (iii) sought to cause the organisation to profit from that failure.

(3) In subsection (2) 'health and safety legislation or guidance' means—

    (a) any enactment dealing with health and safety matters, including in particular the Health and Safety at Work etc. Act 1974 (c. 37), or any legislation made under such an enactment;

    (b) any code, guidance, manual or similar publication that is concerned with health and safety matters and is made or issued (under an enactment or otherwise) by an authority responsible for the enforcement of any enactment or legislation of the kind mentioned in paragraph (a).

(4) Subsection (2) does not prevent the jury from having regard to any other matters they consider relevant to the question.

4 Relevant duty of care

(1) A 'relevant duty of care', in relation to an organisation, means a duty owed under the law of negligence by the organisation—

    (a) to its employees as such,

    (b) in its capacity as occupier of land, or

    (c) in connection with—

      (i) the supply by the organisation of goods or services (whether for consideration or not), or

      (ii) the carrying on by the organisation of any other activity on a commercial basis, otherwise than in the exercise of an exclusively public function.

(2) An organisation that is a public authority does not owe a duty of care for the purposes of this Act in respect of a decision as to matters of public policy (including in particular the allocation of public resources or the weighing of competing public interests).

(3) Whether for the purposes of this Act a particular organisation owes a duty of care to a particular individual is a question of law.

    The judge must make any findings of fact necessary to decide that question.

(4) In this section—

'exclusively public function' means a function that falls within the prerogative of the Crown or is, by its nature, exercisable only with authority conferred—

    (a) by the exercise of that prerogative, or

    (b) by or under an enactment;

'the law of negligence' includes the Occupiers' Liability Act 1957 (c. 31), the Defective Premises Act 1972 (c. 35) and the Occupiers' Liability Act 1984 (c. 3);

'public authority' has the same meaning as in section 6 of the Human Rights Act 1998 (c. 42) (disregarding subsections (3)(a) and (4) of that section).

5 Corporation

'Corporation' does not include a corporation sole but includes any body corporate wherever incorporated.

[Remedial orders]

6 Power to order breach etc to be remedied

(1) A court before which an organisation is convicted of corporate manslaughter may order it to take specified steps to remedy—

   (a) the breach mentioned in section 1(1);

   (b) any matter that appears to the court to have resulted from that breach and to have been a cause of the death.

(2) The order must specify a period within which the steps are to be taken.

(3) The period so specified may be extended or further extended by order of the court on an application made before the end of that period or extended period.

(4) An organisation that fails to comply with an order under this section is guilty of an offence and liable—

   (a) on conviction on indictment, to a fine;

   (b) on summary conviction, to a fine not exceeding £20,000.

Notes

For comment on the proposals see C. Clarkson, 'Corporate Manslaughter: Yet More Government Proposals' [2005] Crim LR 677. He concludes:

The proposal to introduce an offence of corporate manslaughter (or corporate killing) is to be welcomed as is the requirement that the company exhibit more fault than is required for a mere breach of a health and safety offence. . . . The focus of the new offence should be on the culpability or failings of the company as a whole. While this is a notoriously difficult matter when dealing with a pure legal entity such as a company, the present proposal with its emphasis on the 'senior managers' seems to have lost sight of the real issue of how best to lay blame on the company as a whole. The Law Commission's 'management failure' test came closer to identifying the real issue: whether the activities and organisational practices of the company were seriously deficient. If they were and if such grave shortcomings caused a death, there is no need to specify that the company must be under a duty of care. All companies surely owe a duty not to kill people through their bad practices. While these central recommendations have much to commend them [with some qualifications discussed], it is regrettable that a separate new offence covering the causing of serious injury (at least) has not been introduced. And, finally and perhaps most significant of all, the fact that individuals cannot be liable under the proposals represents a grave shortcoming.

FURTHER READING

D. BERGMAN, *The Case for Corporate Responsibility* (2000)

C. CLARKSON, 'Corporate Culpability' [1998] 2 Web JCLI

C. CLARKSON, 'Kicking Corporate Bodies and Damning their Souls' (1996) 59 MLR 557

S. FIELD and N. JORG, 'Corporate Liability and Manslaughter: should we be going Dutch?' [1991] Crim LR 156

P. R. GLAZEBROOK, 'A Better Way of Convicting Businesses of Avoidable Deaths and Injuries' (2002) CLJ 405

J. Gobert, 'Corporate Criminality: four models of fault' (1994) 14 Legal Studies 393

J. Gobert, 'Corporate Killing at Home and Abroad: Reflections on the Government Proposals' (2002) 118 LQR 72

J. Gobert and M. Punch, *Rethinking Corporate Crime* (2003)

R. Grantham, 'Corporate Knowledge: Identification or Attribution?' (1996) 59 MLR 732

H. Keating, 'The Law Commission Report on Involuntary Manslaughter: (1) The Restoration of a Serious Crime' [1998] Crim LR 535

Law Commission Report No 237, *Involuntary Manslaughter* (1996)

L. H. Leigh, *Strict and Vicarious Liability*, Chs 2 and 3

A. McGolgan, 'Heralding Corporate Liability' [1994] Crim LR 547

P. J. Pace, 'Delegation—a Doctrine in Search of a Definition' [1982] Crim LR 627

G. Richardson, 'Strict Liability for Regulatory Crime: the Empirical Research' [1987] Crim LR 295

G. R. Sullivan, 'Expressing Corporate Guilt (1995) 15 OJLS 281

G. R. Sullivan 'Corporate Killing—Some Government Proposals' [2001] Crim LR 31

C. Wells, *Corporations and Criminal Responsibility* (1993)

C. Wells, *Corporations and Criminal Responsibility* (2nd edn, 2001)

C. Wells, 'The Law Commission Report on Involuntary Manslaughter: (2) The Corporate Manslaughter Proposals: Pragmatism, Paradox and Peninsularity' (1996) Crim LR 545

11

Mental abnormality

1. INTRODUCTION

The mental abnormality of a person (D) accused of crime may be relevant at three stages of criminal proceedings, two of them before trial.

(1) When D has been remanded in custody for trial it may appear that his condition is so bad that it would not be practicable to bring him before a court, or to do so would have an injurious effect on his mental state. If the Home Secretary is satisfied by reports from at least two medical practitioners that:

> that person is suffering from mental illness or severe mental impairment of a nature or degree which makes it appropriate for him to be detained in a hospital for medical treatment and that he is in urgent need of such treatment

—he may exercise his power under the Mental Health Act 1983, s 48, to order that D be detained in a hospital. The Home Secretary exercises this power only when it is necessary to do so. It is thought that the issue of an accused person's mental fitness to be tried and his responsibility for his actions should be determined by a jury whenever it is possible. So when a person who has been detained under s 48 recovers sufficiently to be triable, the prosecution will proceed. Cf the statistics revealed by Mackay and Machin, *Transfers from Prison to Hospital—the operation of s 48 of the Mental Health Act 1983* (Home Office Research Directorate) No 84. To what extent is this compatible with the guarantee of liberty in Article 5 of the ECHR, above, p 9.

(2) The second stage is when D is brought up for trial. It may then be asserted by D, or the prosecution, or the judge, that he is 'unfit to plead'—that is, incapable, because of mental disability, of being properly tried. In *M* [2003] EWCA Crim 3452 the trial judge ruled that the defendant had to have sufficient ability in relation to six things: (i) to understand the charges, (ii) to understand the plea, (iii) to challenge jurors, (iv) to instruct counsel and his solicitor, (v) to understand the course of the trial, and (vi) to give evidence if he chooses. Are these the most pertinent questions? Is it appropriate to try D when he is suffering from some impairment that inhibits his competence to run the best trial in his defence?

The issue of fitness to plead was formerly determined by a jury, usually specially empanelled for that purpose, but since the Domestic Violence, Crime and Victims Act 2004, s 22, the issue is now to be determined by a court without a jury. The procedure is set out in the Criminal Procedure (Insanity) Act 1964 as amended (below, p 367). If D is found to be fit to plead the trial proceeds. If he is found unfit but not to have done the act or made the omission charged he is simply acquitted: and if he is found unfit and to have done the act or made the omission charged he may be dealt with under the powers in s 5 of the 1964 Act (below, p 381).

(3) If D is found fit to plead, or that issue is not raised, he may raise the defence that he was so insane at the time of the act or omission alleged as not to be responsible for his actions. This is the subject of the M'Naghten Rules below, p 374.

2. FITNESS TO PLEAD

R v Podola

[1959] 3 All ER 418, Court of Criminal Appeal

(Lord Parker CJ, Hilbery, Donovan, Ashworth and Paull JJ)

Podola, being indicted for capital murder, raised a preliminary issue that he was unfit to plead owing to loss of memory of events prior to and including the time of the alleged homicide. Edmund Davies J ruled that there was an onus of proof on a balance of probabilities on the defendant to establish his unfitness. The jury found that the defendant was not suffering from a genuine loss of memory. The trial proceeded and Podola was found guilty of capital murder. The Home Secretary, being of the opinion that the question of onus of proof on the preliminary issue ought to be considered by the Court of Criminal Appeal, referred the whole case to the court under s 19(a) of the Criminal Appeal Act 1907.

[**Lord Parker CJ**, having ruled that the question specifically referred to the court involved by necessary implication the question whether the alleged amnesia could in law bring the accused within the scope of s 2 of the Criminal Lunatics Act 1800, continued:]

We deal first with the matter specifically referred to us, namely the question as to onus of proof. The relevant words in s 2 of the Criminal Lunatics Act 1800, are as follows:

> '... if any person indicted for any offence shall be insane, and shall upon arraignment be found so to be by a jury lawfully empanelled for that purpose, so that such person cannot be tried upon such indictment...'

Those words do not indicate how or by whom the question of the accused person's sanity is to be raised. But it is now well established that the question may be raised either by the prosecution or by the defence or by the court itself. Indeed, if a court becomes aware, either before or during a trial, that the accused person's sanity is doubtful, it is the duty of the court to have the doubt resolved before beginning or continuing the trial. For the purpose of deciding whether a person is 'insane ... so that he cannot be tried upon the indictment' a jury is empanelled and as counsel for the appellant emphasised, the procedure before that jury is an inquiry and not a trial. In most cases in which this course is taken, there is no contest between the prosecution and the defence as to the accused person's insanity, and the evidence to that effect is unchallenged. In such cases, although the jury must be satisfied of the accused person's insanity before so finding, the question of onus of proof is not a live issue. But cases have arisen of which the present one is an example, where either the prosecution or the defence has challenged the alleged insanity, and in a case in Scotland (*Russell v H M Advocate* [1946 JC 37]) ... the court itself refused to give effect to a plea in bar of trial put forward on behalf of the defence and not contested by the prosecution.

It was contended by counsel for the appellant that, inasmuch as the proceedings on the issue of insanity are an inquiry and not a trial, it is wrong to introduce any principle as to onus of proof, derived from proceedings properly regarded as trials. We do not agree with this contention. In our judgment the right principles may be stated as follows:

1. In all cases in which a preliminary issue as to the accused person's sanity is raised, whether that issue is contested or not, the jury [see now above, p **364**] should be directed to consider the whole of the evidence and to answer the question 'Are you satisfied on that evidence that the accused person is insane so that he cannot be tried on the indictment?' If authority were needed for the principle, it is to be found in the very words of the section itself, quoted above.

2. If the contention that the accused is insane is put forward by the defence and contested by the prosecution, there is in our judgment a burden on the defence of satisfying the jury of the accused's insanity. In such a case, as in other criminal cases in which the onus of proof rests on the defence, the onus is discharged if the jury are satisfied on the balance of probabilities that the accused's insanity has been made out.

3. Conversely, if the prosecution alleges and the defence disputes insanity, there is a burden on the prosecution of establishing it. . . .

It is not suggested in this case that the appellant could not plead to the indictment, or that he did not know that he had the right of challenge, or that he could not follow the evidence given, but counsel for the appellant submitted strongly that, where there was the partial obliteration of memory alleged in this case, a prisoner could not make a proper defence and could not 'comprehend' the details of the evidence within the meaning of the words used in *Pritchard* [(1836) 7 C & P 303 at 304]. So far as 'making a proper defence' is concerned, it is important to note that the words do not stand alone, but form part of a sentence the whole of which is 'whether he is of sufficient intellect to comprehend the course of proceedings on the trial, so as to make a proper defence'. In other words this passage itself defines what Alderson B meant by 'making a proper defence'. As to the word 'comprehend' we do not think that this word goes further in meaning than the word 'understand'. In our judgment the direction given by Alderson B is not intended to cover and does not cover a case where the prisoner can plead to the indictment and has the physical and mental capacity to know that he has the right of challenge and to understand the case as it proceeds.

[His Lordship then referred to two Scottish cases and concluded:]

It is true that in the case of a deaf mute the word 'insane' does not strictly apply, but . . . the practice of including as coming within the word the case of persons who, from mental or physical infirmity cannot follow what is happening in a case is in accordance with reason and common sense. We cannot see that it is in accordance either with reason or common sense to extend the meaning of the word to include persons who are mentally normal at the time of the hearing of the proceedings against them and are perfectly capable of instructing their solicitors as to what submission their counsel is to put forward with regard to the commission of the crime . . .

Appeal dismissed

Questions

1. Is a person fit to be tried if he is perfectly intelligent and aware at the time of trial but, because of mental disability, is unable to remember anything at all about the period of the alleged crime? Is he capable of instructing counsel as to any defence which may in fact exist?

2. Is the effect of *Podola*'s case that a person may be convicted although a court was not satisfied that he was capable of making out a proper defence at his trial?

Until 1964 any person who was found unfit to plead was ordered to be detained in a mental hospital for an indefinite period, the power to discharge him being exercisable only with the Home Secretary's consent. In grave cases detention might be lifelong. Yet a person who was found unfit to plead was not proved to have done anything wrong. The 1964 Act went some way towards remedying this situation and the provisions substituted by the 1991 Act carry the process further.

Criminal Procedure (Insanity) Act 1964

(Sections substituted by the Criminal Procedure (Insanity and Unfitness to Plead) Act 1991 as amended)

4. Finding of unfitness to plead

(1) This section applies where on the trial of a person the question arises (at the instance of the defence or otherwise) whether the accused is under a disability, that is to say, under any disability such that apart from this Act it would constitute a bar to his being tried.

(2) If, having regard to the nature of the supposed disability, the court are of opinion that it is expedient to do so and in the interests of the accused, they may postpone consideration of the question of fitness to be tried until any time up to the opening of the case for the defence.

(3) If, before the question of fitness to be tried falls to be determined, the jury return a verdict of acquittal on the count or each of the counts on which the accused is being tried, that question shall not be determined.

(4) Subject to sub-sections (2) and (3) above, the question of fitness to be tried shall be determined as soon as it arises.

(5) The question of fitness to be tried shall be determined by [the court without a jury].

(6) The Court shall not make a determination under sub-section (5) above except on the written or oral evidence of two or more registered medical practitioners at least one of whom is duly approved.

4A. Finding that the accused did the act or made the omission charged against him

(1) This section applies where in accordance with section 4(5) above it is determined by the court without a jury that the accused is under a disability.

(2) The trial shall not proceed or further proceed but it shall be determined by a jury -
    (a) on the evidence (if any) already given in the trial; and
    (b) on such evidence as may be adduced or further adduced by the prosecution, or adduced by a person appointed by the court under this section to put the case for the defence,

whether they are satisfied, as respects the count or each of the counts on which the accused was to be or was being tried, that he did the act or made the omission charged against him as the offence.

(3) If as respects that count or any of those counts the jury are satisfied as mentioned in sub-section (2) above, they shall make a finding that the accused did the act or made the omission charged against him.

(4) If as respects that count or any of those counts the jury are not so satisfied, they shall return a verdict of acquittal as if on the count in question the trial had proceeded to a conclusion.

(5) Where the question of disability was determined after arraignment of the accused, the determination under sub-section (2) is to be made by the jury by whom he was being tried.

In *Egan* (1996) 35 BMLR 103, [1997] Crim LR 225, Ognall J said of s 4(2)(b) above: 'we are satisfied, and indeed both counsel agree, that although the words "the act" are used in the relevant legislation, the phrase means neither more or less than proof of all the necessary ingredients of what otherwise would be an offence, in this case theft.' There is no doubt that this was the meaning intended by the Butler Committee on Mentally Abnormal Offenders on whose recommendation the section was based: Cmnd 6244, 1975, para 1024, 'Trial of the facts'. But it is certainly not the natural meaning of the words 'the act' and it is not the meaning intended by the Home Office minister who introduced the Bill in the House of Commons—and therefore probably not the meaning intended by Parliament. See R. D. Mackay and G. Kearns, 'The Trial of the Facts and Unfairness to Plead' [1997] Crim LR 644. In *A-G's Reference (No 3 of 1998)* [1999] 3 All ER 40, [2000] QB 401 the court noted that the same words 'did the act or made the omission charged' are used in the Trial of Lunatics Act 1883 (below, p 376) and were held in *Felstead* [1914] AC 534, HL, to refer only to the actus reus. The court said that *Egan* appears to have been decided per incuriam.

R v Antoine
[2000] 2 All ER 208, House of Lords

(Lords Nicholls, Mackay, Nolan, Hope and Hutton)

A was charged with murder and found unfit to plead by reason of disability. A different jury was empanelled to determine whether A 'had done the act . . . charged against him as an offence'. The judge rejected a submission that A was entitled to rely on diminished responsibility as a defence and the jury found that A had done the act of murder. The Court of Appeal dismissed A's appeal. In the House of Lords all their Lordships agreed with the speech of Lord Hutton.

Lord Hutton. The purpose of s 4A, in my opinion, is to strike a fair balance between the need to protect a defendant who has, in fact, done nothing wrong and is unfit to plead at his trial and the need to protect the public from a defendant who has committed an injurious act which would constitute a crime if done with the requisite mens rea. The need to protect the public is particularly important where the act done has been one which caused death or physical injury to another person and there is a risk that the defendant may carry out a similar act in the future. I consider that the section strikes this balance by distinguishing between a person who has not carried out the actus reus of the crime charged against him and a person who has carried out an act (or made an omission) which would constitute a crime if done (or made) with the requisite mens rea. As Judge LJ stated:

> 'Where on an indictment for rape it is proved that sexual intercourse has taken place without the consent of the woman, and the defendant has established insanity, he should not be entitled to an acquittal on the basis that he mistakenly, but insanely, understood or believed that she was consenting'. (See *A-G's Reference (No 3 of 1998)* [1999] 3 All ER 40 at 48, [1999] 3 WLR 1194 at 1202.)

A number of learned authors have commented that it is difficult in some cases to distinguish precisely between the actus reus and the mens rea and that the actus reus can include a mental element. In Smith and Hogan *Criminal Law* p 28, Professor Sir John Smith states: 'It is not always possible to separate actus reus from mens rea. Sometimes a word which describes the actus reus, or part of it, implies a mental element.'

In his speech in *DPP for Northern Ireland v Lynch* [1975] 1 All ER 913 at 933, [1975] AC 653 at 688 Lord Simon of Glaisdale recognised the difficulties arising from what he termed 'the chaotic terminology' relating to the mental element in crime. Nevertheless, he recognised that actus reus and mens rea are useful terms and said:

> 'Both terms have, however, justified themselves by their usefulness; and I shall myself employ them in their traditional senses—namely, actus reus to mean such conduct as constitutes a crime if the mental element involved in the definition of the crime is also present (or, more shortly, conduct prohibited by law); and mens rea to mean such mental element, over and above volition, as is involved in the definition of the crime.' (See [1975] 1 All ER 913 at 934, [1975] AC 653 at 690.)

Therefore, I consider that the ruling of the Court of Appeal in *A-G's Reference (No 3 of 1998)* was correct.

In their full and helpful submissions counsel raised a further issue on which they invited the guidance of your Lordships. The issue is this. If, on a determination under s 4A(2), the jury are only concerned to decide whether the defendant did the 'act' and are not required to consider whether the defendant had the requisite mens rea for the offence, should the jury nevertheless decide that the defendant did not do the 'act' if the defendant would have had an arguable defence of accident or mistake or self-defence which he could have raised if he had not been under a disability and the trial had proceeded in the normal way. The difficulty inherent in this issue is that such defences almost invariably involve some consideration of the mental state of the defendant. Thus in *Palmer v R* [1971] 1 All ER 1077 at 1088, [1971] AC 814 at 832 when considering self-defence, Lord Morris of Borth-y-Gest referred to the defendant doing 'what he honestly and instinctively thought was necessary' to defend himself. But on the determination under s 4A(2) the defendant's state of mind is not to be considered. How then is this difficulty to be resolved? I would hold that it should be resolved in this way. If there is objective evidence which raises the issue of mistake or accident or self-defence, then the jury should not find that the defendant did the 'act' unless it is satisfied beyond reasonable doubt on all the evidence that the prosecution has negatived that defence. For example, if the defendant had struck another person with his fist and the blow had caused death, it would be open to the jury under s 4(A)(4) to acquit the defendant charged with manslaughter if a witness gave evidence that the victim had attacked the defendant with a knife before the defendant struck him. Again, if a woman was charged with theft of a handbag and a witness gave evidence that on sitting down at a table in a restaurant the defendant had placed her own handbag on the floor and, on getting up to leave, picked up the handbag placed beside her by a woman at the next table, it would be open to the jury to acquit.

But what the defence cannot do, in the absence of a witness whose evidence raises the defence, is to suggest to the jury that the defendant may have acted under a mistake, or by accident, or in self-defence, and to submit that the jury should acquit unless the prosecution satisfies them that there is no reasonable possibility that that suggestion is correct. I consider that the same approach is to be taken if defence counsel wishes to advance the defence that the defendant, in law, did not do the 'act' because his action was involuntary, as when a man kicks out and strikes another in the course of an uncontrollable fit brought about by a medical condition. In such a case there would have to be evidence that the defendant suffered from the condition.

The defence of provocation to a charge of murder is only relevant when the jury are satisfied that the defendant had the requisite mens rea for murder, and I wish to reserve my opinion on the question whether, on a determination under s 4A(2), it would be open to the defence to call witnesses to raise the issue of provocation.

As I have observed at the commencement of this judgment, it was the co-accused of the appellant who killed the victim by stabbing him and it appears that the appellant was charged as a principal in the second degree. No issue was raised before the Crown Court judge or before the Court of Appeal or your Lordships in relation to the fact that the appellant was the secondary party, no doubt because it was clear that by his own actions in preventing the victim from leaving and in striking him the appellant had played a part in the killing. However, on a determination under s 4A(2) where the defendant had been charged with participation in a murder as a secondary party and another person had carried out the actual killing, difficult questions could arise as to the meaning of the word 'act' in such a situation and as to the matters which the jury would have to consider, and I express no opinion on such questions in this judgment.

Therefore, for the reasons which I have given, I would dismiss the appeal. I would answer the certified question in the negative, and I would answer the wider question formulated by counsel in the negative, subject to the right of defence counsel to raise the defence of mistake, accident, self-defence or involuntariness in the way which I have stated.

Appeal dismissed

Notes and questions

1. Are not the 'defences' of mistake and accident simply pleas that mens rea has not been proved? If those 'defences' are allowed, what has become of the ruling that 'the act' means the actus reus?

2. Can the defences of diminished responsibility and provocation, which reduce murder to manslaughter, be equated for the purpose of this issue, with complete defences? In *Grant* [2002] Crim LR 404 it was held that provocation which was intimately bound up with the defendant's state of mind could not sensibly be considered in the context of s 4A. Provocation pre-supposed that all the elements of murder, including the intent to kill or cause grievous bodily harm were present. See commentary by D.C.O. at 406.

3. For a case where D's own intentions were a part of the act, see *R (on the application of Young) v Central Criminal Court* [2001] Crim LR 588, DC. D was alleged to have concealed his intention to do X, Y and Z, contrary to s 47 of the Financial Services Act 1986.

4. Concerns were raised as to the compatibility of the procedure under s 4A of the Act with Article 6 of the ECHR (above, p 10). Consider the next case and the House of Lords' avoidance of the problem.

R v H
[2003] 2 Cr App R 2

(Lords Bingham of Cornhill, Nicholls of Birkenhead, Hutton, Hobhouse of Woodborough and Walker of Gestingthorpe)

H was charged with two offences of indecent assault against a girl aged 14. H was 13 at the time. Two psychiatrists who examined H before his trial agreed that he was unfit to stand trial. A jury found that H was under a disability and so unfit to stand trial. At a subsequent hearing a different jury found that H had done the acts alleged. He was absolutely discharged, but his father was directed to cause him to be registered as a sex offender. H appealed against the finding of the second jury, contending that the procedure followed was incompatible with Article 6 of the European Convention on Human

Rights. The Court of Appeal rejected that appeal but certified a question for the House of Lords:

Is the procedure defined by section 4A of the Criminal Procedure (Insanity) Act 1964 compatible with an accused person's rights arising under Article 6(1), 6(2) and 6(3)(d) of the European Convention for the Protection of Human Rights and Fundamental Freedoms? In particular:

(i) Does the procedure in so far as:

(a) it provides for an acquittal of the accused person in the circumstances defined by the Act;

(b) it provides for a finding that the accused 'did the act' which constitutes the actus reus of the crime;

amount to the 'determination' of a criminal charge for the purposes of Article 6(1)?

(ii) Does a finding that an accused person 'did the act' which constitutes the actus reus of the crime of indecent assault, being a crime of basic intent, violate the presumption of innocence afforded by Article 6(2)?

Lord Bingham. [His lordship set out the facts, quoted the relevant statutory provisions and outlined their operation.]

12 The issue on which the parties locked horns was the categorisation of the procedure provided under s. 4A, following a finding of unfitness, namely the procedure followed to enable the jury to decide whether the accused had done the act or made the omission charged against him as the offence. In an able argument for the appellant, Mr Robert Smith QC contended that, viewed as a matter of substance, this was to all intents and purposes a procedure to determine a criminal charge against the appellant. It therefore attracted the guarantees provided in Article 6 of the Convention. But these guarantees were not met since the appellant, being ex hypothesi unfit to plead, could not give instructions and participate fully in his own defence. Therefore he should not be tried at all, but should (if appropriate) be detained, in the same way as a person not accused of a criminal offence, under the Mental Health Act 1983. In contending that the procedure involved, in substance, the determination of a criminal charge, Mr Smith relied in particular on the nature of the crimes of indecent assault charged against the appellant, which were crimes of basic intent, requiring proof of no more than non-accidental touching of the victim in circumstances of indecency. The procedure could lead to an acquittal. The finding that the appellant had done the acts charged against him amounted in substance to conviction of the offences. In the eyes of the public the findings carried the stigma which attaches to the commission of such offences. The Rehabilitation of Offenders Act 1974 and the Sex Offenders Act 1997 applied to findings adverse to the accused as they applied to convictions.

13 Mr Paul Worsley QC for the prosecution and Mr David Perry for the Secretary of State made common cause. They did not contend that the s. 4A procedure met the requirements of Article 6(2) and (3) if those provisions were applicable to it. But they strongly argued that this procedure did not involve the determination of a criminal charge and that the Article 6 guarantees did not apply. To the extent that the appellant was deprived of his liberty, this was justified under Article 5(1)(e) of the Convention. If the procedure involved determination of the appellant's civil rights and obligations, it satisfied Article 6(1) of the Convention and provided every reasonable safeguard of his rights.

14 It was not suggested by the appellant that the s. 4A procedure was incompatible with the Convention even if it did not involve the determination of a criminal charge. His argument depended on making good his premise that the procedure did involve the determination of a criminal charge. Thus the crucial issue dividing the parties was whether the procedure did or did not involve the determination of a criminal charge.

The Determination Of A Criminal Charge

15 In a passage cited and applied on very many occasions, the European Court of Human Rights in para 82 of its judgment in *Engel v The Netherlands (No. 1)* (1976) 1 EHRR 647 at 678–679 gave authoritative guidance on the tests to be applied in deciding whether an issue is to be regarded as criminal on the one hand or disciplinary or civil on the other. The parties were rightly agreed that these tests fell to be applied in the present case.

16 It is first necessary to know how the issue is classified in domestic law. This test is far from decisive and rightly so, since the Convention seeks the achievement of broadly equivalent standards among the member states of the Council of Europe and such aim would be defeated if domestic rules were determinative. But this is the starting point, and it is clear that the domestic law of England and Wales does not treat the s. 4A procedure as involving the determination of a criminal charge. When a finding of unfitness is made it is provided that the trial (meaning the criminal trial) 'shall not proceed or further proceed'. Section 4A(2) is expressed in terms which make clear that the task of the jury is not that carried out by a jury in a criminal trial: for reasons already given, the jury have power to acquit but they have none to convict. The jury take an oath different from that in a criminal trial. There can be no verdict of guilty. There can be no punishment. In a case such as the present, as the legislation has been amended to make clear, an order of absolute discharge may be made in the absence of any conviction and without consideration of the expediency of punishment. It is true that by virtue of s. 1(4)(b) of the Rehabilitation of Offenders Act 1974 references in that Act to a conviction are expressed to include reference to a finding that a person has done the act or made the omission charged, but this was an Act designed to promote the rehabilitation of offenders by enabling them to live down past convictions and the obvious purpose of this provision was to give persons subject to adverse findings under s. 4A the benefit of that protection. It is also true that a person found to have done the act or made the omission charged is subject, by virtue of s. 1(1)(b) of the Sex Offenders Act 1997, to the notification requirements of that Act. But I regard it as clear, as a matter of domestic law, that this provision is designed to protect the public and not to punish the subject of the order. The non-punitive nature of the order was recognised by the Commission in *Ibbotson v United Kingdom* (1998) 27 EHRR CD 332. The registration order is analogous to a sex offender order or an anti-social behaviour order such as were considered in *B v Chief Constable of Avon and Somerset Constabulary* [2001] 1 WLR 340 and *R (McCann) v Crown Court at Manchester* [2003] 1 Cr App R 27, [2002] 3 WLR 1313 respectively. Mr Smith came very close to accepting that, in domestic law, the s. 4A procedure was not criminal.

17 The second *Engel* test, and that on which the appellant's argument depended, directed attention to the very nature of the offence. The points, briefly mentioned above, concerning the nature of an offence of basic intent such as indecent assault, the similarity between an adverse finding under s. 4A and a verdict of guilty by a trial jury and the stigma attaching to an adverse finding under s. 4A were relied on as showing that the appellant was in substance being tried by the jury for offences of indecent assault.

18 It would be highly anomalous if s. 4A, introduced by amendment for the protection of those unable through mental unfitness to defend themselves at trial, were itself to be held incompatible with the Convention. It is very much in the interest of such persons that the basic facts relied on against them (shorn of issues concerning intent) should be formally and publicly investigated in open court with counsel appointed to represent the interests of the person accused so far as possible in the circumstances. The position of accused persons would certainly not be improved if s. 4A were abrogated. In my opinion, however, the argument is plainly bad in law. Whether one views the matter through domestic or European spectacles, the answer is the same: the purpose and function of the s. 4A procedure is not to decide whether the accused person has committed a criminal offence. The procedure can result in a final acquittal, but it cannot result in a conviction and it cannot

result in punishment. Even an adverse finding may lead, as here, to an absolute discharge. But if an adverse finding leads to the making of a hospital order, there is no bar to a full criminal trial if the accused person recovers, an obviously objectionable outcome if the person has already been convicted. The s. 4A procedure lacks the essential features of criminal process as identified in *Customs and Excise Commissioners v City of London Magistrates' Court* [2000] 2 Cr App R 348, 353.

19 The third *Engel* test was expressed by the European Court in this way ((1976) 1 EHRR 647 at 678–679, para 82):

'However, supervision by the court does not stop there. Such supervision would generally prove to be illusory if it did not also take into consideration the degree of severity of the penalty that the person concerned risks incurring. In a society subscribing to the rule of law, there belong to the "criminal" sphere deprivations of liberty liable to be imposed as a punishment, except those which by their nature, duration or manner of execution cannot be appreciably detrimental. The seriousness of what is at stake, the traditions of the Contracting States and the importance attached by the Convention to respect for the physical liberty of the person all require that this should be so.'

Mr Smith for the appellant accepted that he could not rely on this test, because he accepted that the orders which the court could make on a finding by the jury adverse to the accused under s. 4A were none of them punitive. But the fact that the procedure cannot culminate in any penalty is not neutral. The House was referred to no case in which the European Court has held a proceeding to be criminal even though an adverse outcome for the defendant cannot result in any penalty. It is, indeed, difficult if not impossible to conceive of a criminal proceeding which cannot in any circumstances culminate in the imposition of any penalty, since it is the purpose of the criminal law to proscribe, and by punishing to deter, conduct regarded as sufficiently damaging to the interests of society to merit the imposition of penal sanctions.

…

I am in complete agreement with the reasons given by the Court of Appeal for dismissing the appellant's appeal, and I would dismiss it for those reasons as well as those I have given. The procedure under s. 4A must always, of course, be conducted with scrupulous regard for the interests of the accused person, but the procedure if properly conducted is fair and it was not suggested that the procedure was not properly conducted in this case.

21 I would answer the general opening question posed by the Court of Appeal by ruling that the s. 4A procedure laid down by the 1964 Act as amended is compatible with the rights of an accused person under article 6(1), (2) and (3) of the Convention. I would answer each of the particular questions (i) and (ii) in the negative.

[The other Law Lords concurred.]

Appeal dismissed

Notes and questions

1. Does not the outcome for *H* look very much like a criminal sanction?

2. On ECHR concerns with the operation of the procedure see E. Baker, 'Human Rights and McNaughten and the 1991 Act' [1994] Crim LR 84; R. D. Mackay, 'On Being Insane in Jersey Part Three—the Case of the *Attorney General v O'Driscoll*' [2004] Crim LR 219; 'On Being Insane in Jersey Part Two' [2002] Crim LR 728.

3. THE M'NAGHTEN RULES

M'Naghten's Case
(1843)10 Cl & Fin 200

M'Naghten was charged with the murder by shooting of Edward Drummond. He pleaded not guilty. Medical evidence was called on behalf of the prisoner to prove that he was not, at the time of committing the act, in a sound state of mind. The evidence was to the effect that persons of otherwise sound mind might be affected by morbid delusions and that the prisoner was in that condition; that a person labouring under a morbid delusion might have a moral perception of right and wrong, but that in the case of the prisoner it was a delusion which carried him away beyond the power of his own control, and left him with no such perception; and that he was not capable of exercising any control over acts which had connection with his delusion: that it was the nature of the disease with which the prisoner was affected to go on gradually until it had reached a climax, when it burst forth with irresistible intensity: that a man might go on for years quietly, though at the same time under its influence, but would all at once break out into the most extravagant and violent paroxysms.

Some of the witnesses who gave this evidence had previously examined the prisoner, others had never seen him till he appeared in court, and they formed their opinions on hearing the evidence given by other witnesses.

[**Tindal CJ** directed the jury:]

The question to be determined is whether at the time the act in question was committed, the prisoner had or had not the use of his understanding, so as to know that he was doing a wrong or wicked act. If the jurors should be of opinion that the prisoner was not sensible, at the time he committed it, that he was violating the laws of both God and man, then he would be entitled to a verdict in his favour: but if, on the contrary, they were of opinion that when he committed the act he was in a sound state of mind, then their verdict must be against him.

Verdict, Not guilty, on the ground of insanity

This verdict was made the subject of debate in the House of Lords and it was determined to take the opinion of all the judges on the law governing such cases. The judges attended on two occasions and, on the second occasion, five questions were put to them.

[**Maule J** having referred to the difficulty which he felt about answering hypothetical questions on which he had heard no argument and his fear that the answers might embarrass the administration of criminal justice, stated that he would have been glad if his learned brethren would have joined him in praying their Lordships to excuse them from answering the questions. Maule J then offered his own answers.]

Tindal CJ. The first question proposed by your Lordships is this: 'What is the law respecting alleged crimes committed by persons afflicted with insane delusion in respect of one or more particular subjects or persons: as, for instance, where at the time of the commission of the alleged crime the accused knew he was acting contrary to law, but did the act complained of with a view, under the influence of insane delusion, of redressing or revenging some supposed grievance or injury, or of producing some supposed public benefit?'

In answer to which question, assuming that your Lordships' inquiries are confined to those persons who labour under such partial delusions only, and are not in other respects insane, we are of opinion that, notwithstanding the party accused did the act complained of with a view, under the influence of insane delusion, of redressing or revenging some supposed grievance or injury, or of producing some public benefit, he is nevertheless punishable according to the nature of the crime committed, if he knew at the time of committing such crime that he was acting contrary to law; by which expression we understand your Lordships to mean the law of the land.

Your Lordships are pleased to inquire of us, secondly, 'What are the proper questions to be submitted to the jury, where a person alleged to be afflicted with insane delusion respecting one or more particular subjects or persons, is charged with the commission of a crime (murder, for example), and insanity is set up as a defence?' And, thirdly, 'In what terms ought the question to be left to the jury as to the prisoner's state of mind at the time when the act was committed?' And as these two questions appear to us to be more conveniently answered together, we have to submit our opinion to be, that the jurors ought to be told in all cases that every man is to be presumed to be sane, and to possess a sufficient degree of reason to be responsible for his crimes, until the contrary be proved to their satisfaction; and that to establish a defence on the ground of insanity, it must be clearly proved that, at the time of the committing of the act, the party accused was labouring under such a defect of reason, from disease of the mind, as not to know the nature and quality of the act he was doing; or, if he did know it, that he did not know he was doing what was wrong. The mode of putting the latter part of the question to the jury on these occasions has generally been, whether the accused at the time of doing the act knew the difference between right and wrong: which mode, though rarely, if ever, leading to any mistake with the jury, is not, as we conceive, so accurate when put generally and in the abstract, as when put with reference to the party's knowledge of right and wrong in respect to the very act with which he is charged. If the question were to be put as to the knowledge of the accused solely and exclusively with reference to the law of the land, it might tend to confound the jury, by inducing them to believe that an actual knowledge of the law of the land was essential in order to lead to a conviction; whereas the law is administered upon the principle that everyone must be taken conclusively to know it, without proof that he does know it. If the accused was conscious that the act was one which he ought not to do, and if that act was at the same time contrary to the law of the land, he is punishable; and the usual course therefore has been to leave the question to the jury, whether the party accused had a sufficient degree of reason to know that he was doing an act that was wrong: and this course we think is correct, accompanied with such observations and explanations as the circumstances of each particular case may require.

The fourth question which your Lordships have proposed to us is this: 'If a person under an insane delusion as to existing facts, commits an offence in consequence thereof, is he thereby excused?' To which question the answer must of course depend on the nature of the delusion: but, making the same assumption as we did before, namely, that he labours under such partial delusion only, and is not in other respects insane, we think he must be considered in the same situation as to responsibility as if the facts with respect to which the delusion exists were real. For example, if under the influence of his delusion he supposes another man to be in the act of attempting to take away his life, and he kills that man, as he supposes, in self-defence, he would be exempt from punishment. If his delusion was that the deceased had inflicted a serious injury to his character and fortune, and he killed him in revenge for such supposed injury, he would be liable to punishment.

The question lastly proposed by your Lordships is: 'Can a medical man conversant with the disease of insanity, who never saw the prisoner previously to the trial, but who was present during the whole trial and the examination of all the witnesses, be asked his opinion as to the state of the prisoner's mind at the time of the commission of the alleged crime, or his opinion whether the prisoner was conscious at the time of doing the act that he was acting contrary to law, or whether he was labouring under any and what delusion at the time?' In answer thereto, we state to your Lordships, that we think the medical man, under the circumstances supposed, cannot in strictness be asked his opinion in the terms above stated, because each of those questions involves the determination of the truth of the facts deposed to, which it is for the jury to decide, and the questions are not mere questions upon a matter of science, in which such evidence is admissible. But where the facts are admitted or not disputed, and the question becomes substantially one of science only, it may be convenient to allow the question to be put in that general form, though the same cannot be insisted on as a matter of right.

Trial of Lunatics Act 1883, s 2 (as amended)

2. *Special verdict where accused found guilty, but insane at date of act or omission charged, and orders thereupon*

    (1) Where in any indictment or information any act or omission is charged against any person as an offence, and it is given in evidence on the trial of such person for that offence that he was insane, so as not to be responsible, according to law, for his action at the time when the act was done or omission made, then, if it appears to the jury before whom such person is tried that he did the act or made the omission charged, but was insane as aforesaid at the time when he did or made the same, the jury shall return a special verdict that the accused is not guilty by reason of insanity.

(2)–(4) [Repealed.]

Criminal Procedure (Insanity and Unfitness to Plead) Act 1991

1. *Acquittals on grounds of insanity*

    (1) A jury shall not return a special verdict under section 2 of the Trial of Lunatics Act 1883 (acquittal on ground of insanity) except on the written or oral evidence of two or more registered medical practitioners at least one of whom is duly approved.

[Section 1(2) contains provisions respecting proof of an offender's mental condition.]

R v Clarke

[1972] 1 All ER 219, Court of Appeal, Criminal Division

(Lord Widgery CJ, Sachs LJ and Ackner J)

The applicant selected various items in a supermarket and put them into the wire basket provided. Before she went to the checkout, she transferred three items into her own bag so that, when she presented the basket, these items were not in it and were not paid for. She was charged with stealing them. Her defence was that she had no intent to steal. She suffered from diabetes and had various domestic problems. There was evidence that, prior to the alleged theft, she had behaved absent-mindedly in the home. She said that she must have put the articles in her bag in a moment of absent-mindedness. Her doctor and a consultant psychiatrist were called and testified that she was suffering from depression which one of them accepted to be a minor mental illness which could produce absent-mindedness consistent with her story.

Ackner J. Unfortunately the medical witnesses were pressed to, what it seems to us, an unreasonable degree to explain the workings of this particular illness. The psychiatrist stated that what happens in these cases is 'that there is a patchy state of affairs, and the consciousness, if you like, goes off at times and comes on again, changing every few minutes and not in proper control of the patient'.

The effect of this evidence on the assistant recorder was to convince him that the defence was in truth a defence of 'not guilty by reason of insanity' under the *M'Naghten* rules [p **374**, above]. He was undoubtedly influenced to this decision by the evidence that the depression was an illness which he translated as meaning also a disease and by the fact that on the medical evidence, as he understood it, a possible explanation was that there had been a total lack of consciousness at the moment when the offence was committed. In order to sustain a defence under the *M'Naghten* rules it is necessary to show that the party accused was labouring under *such a defect of reason from the disease of the mind as not to know the nature and quality of the act he was doing* or if he did know, that he did not know that what he was doing was wrong.

It may be that on the evidence in this case the assistant recorder was entitled to the view that the appellant suffered from a disease of the mind but we express no concluded view on that. However, in our judgment the evidence fell very far short either of showing that she suffered from a defect of reason or that the consequences of that defect in reason, if any, were that she was unable to know the nature and quality of the act she was doing. The *M'Naghten* rules relate to accused persons who by reason of a disease of the mind are deprived of the power of reasoning. They do not apply and never have applied to those who retain the power of reasoning but who in moments of confusion or absent-mindedness fail to use their powers to the full. The picture painted by the evidence was wholly inconsistent [sic] with this being a woman who retained her ordinary powers of reason but who was momentarily absent-minded or confused and acted as she did by failing to concentrate properly on what she was doing and by failing adequately to use her mental powers.

Because the assistant recorder ruled that the defence put forward had to be put forward as a defence of insanity, although the medical evidence was to the effect that it was absurd to call anyone in the appellant's condition insane, defending counsel felt constrained to advise the appellant to alter her plea from not guilty to guilty so as to avoid the disastrous consequences of her defence, as wrongly defined by the assistant recorder, succeeding. Thus the appellant in this case ultimately pleaded guilty solely by reason of the assistant recorder's ruling.... The conviction is accordingly quashed.

Appeal allowed

R v Windle

[1952] 2 All ER 1, Court of Criminal Appeal

(Lord Goddard CJ, Jones and Parker JJ)

[**Lord Goddard CJ** delivered the following judgment of the court:]

The appellant was convicted before Devlin J at Birmingham Assizes of the murder of his wife. He is a man of little resolution and weak character who was married to a woman 18 years older than himself. His married life was very unhappy. His wife, in the opinion of the doctors, though they never saw her, must have been certifiable, and was always talking about committing suicide. The appellant became obsessed with this and discussed it with his workmates until they were tired of hearing him, and on one occasion, just before this crime was committed, one of them said 'Give her a dozen aspirins'. On the day of the crime the appellant seems to have given the woman 100 aspirin tablets, which was a fatal dose. Later, he told the police that he supposed he would be hanged for it.

The defence at the trial was that he was insane and that the jury should return a special verdict to that effect, but Devlin J ruled that there was no issue of insanity to be left to the jury. There was some evidence that the prisoner suffered from some defect of reason or disease of the mind. The doctor called for the defence said it was a form of communicated insanity known as *folie à deux* which arises when a person is in constant attendance on a person of unsound mind. [His Lordship quoted the M'Naghten Rules.]

The argument in this appeal really has been concerned with what is meant by the word 'wrong'. The evidence that was given on the issue of insanity was that of the doctor called by the appellant and that of the prison doctor who was called by the prosecution. Both doctors expressed without hesitation the view that when the appellant was administering this poison to his wife he knew he was doing an act which the law forbade. I need not put it higher than that. It may well be that in the misery in which he had been living with this nagging and tiresome wife who constantly expressed the desire to commit suicide, he thought she was better out of the world than in it. He may have thought it was a kindly act to put her out of her sufferings or imagined sufferings, but the law does not permit such an act as that. There was some exceedingly vague evidence that the appellant was suffering from a defect of his reason owing to his communicated insanity, and, if the only question in the case had been whether the appellant was suffering from a disease of the mind, that question must have been left to the jury because there was some evidence of it, but that was not the question. The question, as I endeavoured to point out in giving judgment in *Rivett* [(1950) 34 Cr App Rep 87], in all these cases is one of responsibility. A man may be suffering from a defect of reason, but, if he knows that what he is doing is wrong—and by 'wrong' is meant contrary to law—he is responsible. Counsel for the appellant suggested that the word 'wrong' as it is used in the M'Naghten rules did not mean contrary to law, but had some qualified meaning—morally wrong—and that, if a person was in a state of mind through a defect of reason that he thought that what he was doing, although he knew it was wrong in law, was really beneficial, or kind, or praiseworthy, that would excuse him.

Courts of law, however, can only distinguish between that which is in accordance with the law and that which is contrary to law. There are many acts which, we all know, to use an expression to be found in some of the old cases, are contrary to the law of God and man. In the Decalogue are the commandments: 'Thou shall not kill' and 'Thou shall not steal'. Such acts are contrary to the law of man and they are contrary to the law of God. In regard to the Seventh Commandment: 'Thou shall not commit adultery', it will be found that, so far as the criminal law is concerned, though that act is contrary to the law of God, it is not contrary to the law of man.

The test must be whether an act is contrary to law. In *Rivett* I referred to the Trial of Lunatics Act 1883, s 2(1) of which provides:

> 'Where in any indictment or information any act or omission is charged against any person as an offence, and it is given in evidence on the trial of such person for that offence that he was insane, so as not to be responsible, according to law, for his actions at the time when the act was done or omission made, then if it appears to the jury before whom such person is tried that he did the act or made the omission charged, but was insane as aforesaid at the time when he did or made the same, the jury shall return a special verdict . . .'

I emphasise again that the test is responsibility 'according to law'. . . . Devlin J was right to withdraw the case from jury. This appeal fails.

Appeal dismissed

(1) 'DISEASE OF THE MIND' AND NON-INSANE AUTOMATISM

Most of the modern reported cases concerning the M'Naghten Rules have been concerned with the question whether the accused's alleged condition was the result of a 'disease of the mind' or some other cause, see above, pp **20–34**. The focus on the definition *in legal terms* with no direct correlation with medical definitions renders this aspect of the test potentially incompatible with Article 5(1)(e) of the ECHR where it results in D's loss of liberty.

P. Sutherland and C. Gearty, 'Insanity and the ECHR'
[1992] Crim LR 418, 422

A European challenge?
Article 5 of the European Convention on Human Rights has already been the impetus behind many changes in our mental health law, and the key provision for present purposes is paragraph 1, and in particular sub-paragraph (e) (emphasis added):

> '(1) Everyone has the right to liberty and security of person. No one shall be deprived of his liberty save in the following cases and in accordance with a procedure prescribed by law: . . . (e) the the lawful

detention of persons for the prevention of the spreading of infectious diseases, of persons of unsound mind, alcoholics or drug addicts or vagrants...'

The basic guarantee here is to 'liberty and security of person.' Every deprivation of liberty must be 'in accordance with a procedure prescribed by law.' While the discretionary procedure is probably within the terms of the Convention, with the exercise of judicial discretion likely to be given the benefit of the doubt in Strasbourg [*X v United Kingdom* (1981) 4 EHRR 188, para. 41], it may be that the mandatory referral may in certain circumstances violate the Convention. Mandatory incarceration in a hospital after an acquittal on a murder charge can only be justified, if at all, under the relevant portion of (e), namely it must be a 'lawful detention' of a person 'of unsound mind.' Since the committal is manifestly 'prescribed by law,' these are the two key phrases which determine the validity of the process.

Four decisions of the European Court of Human Rights are relevant. The leading case is *Winterwerp v. The Netherlands* [(1979) 2 E.H.R.R. 387.], which concerned the compulsory detention of mentally ill persons, and in which the court remarked that the 'Convention does not state what is to be understood by the words "persons of unsound mind." [para. 37.]' It went on:

> 'This term is not one that can be given a definitive interpretation: as was pointed out by the Commission, the Government and the applicant, it is a term whose meaning is continually evolving as research in psychiatry progresses, an increasing flexibility in treatment is developing and society's attitudes to mental illness change, in particular so that a greater understanding of the problems of mental patients is becoming more widespread.' [ibid]

In the case before it, this part of article 5(1) was satisfied on account of the close connection between the legal and the psychiatric definitions of mental illness in the relevant Dutch law.

As regards the requirement that the detention be 'lawful,' the Court 'fully' agreed with the Commission's view that this meant that 'no one may be confined as "a person of unsound mind" in the absence of medical evidence establishing that his mental state is such as to justify his compulsory hospitalisation. [para 39]' (Under the United Kingdom 1991 Act, medical evidence is required but is not determinative of the issue of legal insanity.) Except in emergency cases, he must be 'reliably shown to be of "unsound mind," ' and the 'very nature of what has to be established before the competent national authority—that is, a true mental disorder—calls for objective medical expertise. [ibid]' Furthermore, 'the mental disorder must be of a kind or degree warranting compulsory confinement.' The Court's task was to review decisions about detention, recognising that the local authorities must be given some leeway, 'since it is in the first place for [them] to evaluate the evidence adduced before them in a particular case [para 40.] In the applicant's case, his emergency detention was "lawful" in accordance with these criteria.'

The remaining three decisions do not depart from the approach set down in this first case on these issues. [*X v United Kingdom* (1981) 4 EHRR 188.] involved the recall of a patient to Broadmoor Hospital, a special secure mental hospital for the criminally insane. The court followed Winterwerp but emphasised the need for local discretion, particularly where an emergency case was involved, and applied this reasoning in favour of the Government on the article 5(1) issue. In *Ashingdane v. United Kingdom* [(1985) 7 E.H.R.R. 528], the issue of unsoundness of mind was not controverted by the applicant [para 39] and the Court had no difficulty in upholding the lawfulness of his detention on the medical and psychiatric facts of the case. Finally, in *Luberti v. Italy* [(1984) 6 E.H.R.R. 440], the applicant was acquitted on appeal against a murder conviction on the ground of mental incapacity. Two psychiatric experts appointed by Rome's Appeal Court reported that at the date of the killing the applicant was suffering from a paranoiac syndrome depriving him of the capacity to form an intention. He was ordered to be confined in a psychiatric hospital for two years and the European Court refused to find a violation of article 5(1) in these circumstances. The court emphasised the reliance by the Italian Appeal Court on the psychiatric finding before it and recognised 'the national authorities . . . as having a certain margin of appreciation' on these matters [para. 27].

Conclusion

Even allowing for a circumspect European jurisdiction in this area, the mandatory committal of acquitted persons who are found insane under the M'Naghten rules is surely open to doubt. The key factor in the British approach—and what distinguishes it from *Luberti*—is that the legal definition of insanity differs so radically from the psychiatric and medical versions. The 'objective medical expertise' repeatedly stressed by the European Court is never conclusive and is relevant only in so far as it tends to prove or rebut the state of insanity in law. Furthermore, because committal is mandatory where the acquittal follows a murder charge, the element of medical judgment in this decision which is also insisted on by the Court is wholly absent: detention follows as a matter of course after the establishment of a state of mind, legal insanity, which may have no connection with its psychiatric counterpart.

While it remains open for the prosecution to force the defence of insanity upon defendants falling within the outmoded M'Naghten Rules, eventually one of our sleep-walking, epileptic or diabetic 'insane' charged with murder will find him- or herself facing mandatory commitment, notwithstanding the 1991 Act. If so, the chance of an application to Strasbourg would present itself. An adverse judgment by the European Court may eventually be the final straw that compels the Government to rid itself and us of the M'Naghten Rules.

See also R.D. Mackay and C. Gearty, 'On being Insane in Jersey—the case of Attorney General v Jason Prior'
[2001] Crim LR 560

1. The M'Naghten Rules and the Human Rights Act

. . . .the way in which the English courts have interpreted 'disease of the mind' to include conditions such as diabetic hyperglycaemia and epilepsy does seem to run counter to the *Winterwerp* requirement that there must be objective medical expertise supporting the fact that the accused is of unsound mind. In this connection it is of particular importance to note that the objective medical evidence that is required, relates not to whether the accused suffered from hyperglycaemia or epilepsy, but to the fact of mental disorder. A lack of such objective medical expertise supporting the fact that the accused is suffering from a true mental disorder in these diabetes and epilepsy cases seems to present an insuperable problem from a Convention perspective. Further, in the recent decision of the European Court of Human Rights in *Varbanov v. Bulgaria* [5 October 2000, application no. 00031365/96], it was stated in a case dealing with the lawfulness of detention under article 5(1)(e), that 'the medical assessment must be based on the actual state of mental health of the person concerned and not solely on past events. A medical opinion cannot be seen as sufficient to justify deprivation of liberty if a significant period of time has elapsed'. This additional requirement presents a further problem in so far as the defence of insanity relates to the accused's state of mind at the time of the commission of the offence.

As far as English law is concerned there is nothing in the relevant statutory provisions under the 1964 and 1991 Acts to prevent the detention in hospital of a defendant based solely on the fact that he was legally insane at the time of the commission of the offence rather than on his present mental state. It appears that the same is true of the law in Jersey. The fact that English law has introduced flexibility of disposal under the Criminal Procedure (Insanity and Unfitness to Plead) Act 1991 fails to answer this point for two reasons. First, the 1991 Act retains compulsory detention in cases where the sentence is fixed by law, which means a court has no opportunity, but to hospitalise the defendant even in cases where this may not be appropriate. Secondly, in those cases where a court is able to choose how to dispose of a defendant found not guilty by reason of insanity, although in exercising a choice between guardianship, a supervision and treatment order or absolute discharge the court must decide which one 'is most suitable in all the circumstances of the case (see below)' the same requirement does not apply to the making of an admission order to hospital. This means that there is nothing in the statute to prevent a court making such an admission order although by the time of the trial the accused is mentally well and does not require in-patient treatment....

See further R. D. Mackay, 'On Being Insane in Jersey Part Three—the Case of the *Attorney General v O'Driscoll*' [2004] Crim LR 219; 'On Being Insane in Jersey Part Two' [2002] Crim LR 728.

4. DISPOSAL OF PERSONS UNFIT TO PLEAD OR NOT GUILTY BY REASON OF INSANITY

Until 1991 a person found not guilty by reason of insanity, like a person found unfit to plead, had to be ordered to be detained indefinitely in a mental hospital. Defendants who may in truth have been not guilty by reason of insanity sometimes preferred to plead guilty rather than incur the stigma of the insanity label and indefinite detention. Cf *Sullivan*, above, p **28**. The stigma remains but indefinite detention is no longer the necessary result of a finding either of unfitness to plead or a verdict of not guilty by reason of insanity, except in a case where the sentence is fixed by law—in practice, murder. Defendants may be more ready to raise the defence of insanity in future.

Criminal Procedure (Insanity) Act 1964

(Sections substituted by the Criminal Procedure (Insanity and Unfitness to Plead) Act 1991)

5 Powers to deal with persons not guilty by reason of insanity or unfit to plead etc

(1) This section applies where—
   (a) a special verdict is returned that the accused is not guilty by reason of insanity; or
   (b) findings have been made that the accused is under a disability and that he did the act or made the omission charged against him.

(2) The court shall make in respect of the accused—
   (a) a hospital order (with or without a restriction order);
   (b) a supervision order; or
   (c) an order for his absolute discharge.

(3) Where—
   (a) the offence to which the special verdict or the findings relate is an offence the sentence for which is fixed by law, and
   (b) the court have power to make a hospital order,

the court shall make a hospital order with a restriction order (whether or not they would have power to make a restriction order apart from this subsection).

5. REFORM OF THE LAW

See E. J. Griew, 'Let's Implement Butler on Mental Disorder and Crime' [1984] CLP 47 and
the Butler Report on *Mentally Abnormal Offenders* (Cmnd 6244, 1975).
   The Draft Criminal Code Bill provides:

35. Case for mental disorder verdict: defence of severe disorder

   (1) A mental disorder verdict shall be returned if the defendant is proved to have committed an
       offence but it is proved on the balance of probabilities (whether by the prosecution or by
       the defendant) that he was at the time suffering from severe mental illness or severe mental
       handicap.

   (2) Sub-section (1) does not apply if the court or jury is satisfied beyond reasonable doubt that the
       offence was not attributable to the severe mental illness or severe mental handicap.

   (3) A court or jury shall not, for the purposes of a verdict under sub-section (1), find that the
       defendant was suffering from severe mental illness or severe mental handicap unless two
       medical practitioners approved for the purposes of section 12 of the Mental Health Act 1983
       as having special experience in the diagnosis or treatment of mental disorder have given evid-
       ence that he was so suffering.

   (4) Sub-section (1), so far as it relates to severe mental handicap, does not apply to an offence
       under section 106(1), 107 or 108 (sexual relations with the mentally handicapped).

36. Case for mental disorder verdict: evidence of disorder
A mental disorder verdict shall be returned if:

   (a) the defendant is acquitted of an offence only because, by reason of evidence of mental dis-
       order or a combination of mental disorder and intoxication, it is found that he acted or may
       have acted in a state of automatism, or without the fault required for the offence, or believ-
       ing that an exempting circumstance existed; and

   (b) it is proved on the balance of probabilities (whether by the prosecution or by the defendant)
       that he was suffering from mental disorder at the time of the act.

The Commentary on the draft Bill, having referred to the M'Naghten 'nature and quality'
rule ('case (i)') and 'right and wrong' rule ('case (ii)'), continues (footnotes omitted):

   11. *Structure of the proposed provisions.* Clauses 35 and 36, following the structure proposed by
the Butler Committee, are similarly concerned with two kinds of case, in each of which there is to be
a verdict of acquittal in special form ('not guilty on evidence of mental disorder'). On the return of a
mental disorder verdict the court would have flexible disposal powers, the availability of which
would undoubtedly give clauses 35 and 36 greater practical importance than the insanity defence
now has.
   (a) *Clause 35(1).* In one case all the elements of the offence are proved but severe mental
       disorder operates as a true defence. This is equivalent to case (ii) above.
   (b) *Clause 36.* In the other case an acquittal is inevitable because the prosecution has failed
       to prove that the defendant acted with the required fault (or to disprove his defence of
       automatism or mistake); but the reason for that failure is evidence of mental disorder, and
       it is proved that the defendant was indeed suffering from mental disorder at the time of
       the act. This differs from case (i) above in casting no burden on the defendant of proving
       his innocence....

Clause 35: Case for mental disorder verdict: defence of severe disorder

11.15 Sub-section (1) provides that even though he has done the act specified for the offence with the fault required, a defendant is entitled to an acquittal, in the form of a mental disorder verdict, if he was suffering from severe mental illness or severe mental handicap at the time. This implements the Butler Committee's conception with some modifications.

11.16 *Attributability of offence to disorder; a rebuttable presumption.* One aspect of the Committee's recommendation has proved controversial. The Committee acknowledged that:

> 'it is theoretically possible for a person to be suffering from a severe mental disorder which has in a causal sense nothing to do with the act or omission for which he is being tried';

but they found it 'very difficult to imagine a case in which one could be sure of the absence of any such connection'. They therefore proposed, in effect, an irrebuttable presumption that there was a sufficient connection between the severe disorder and the offence. This proposal is understandable in view of the limitation of the defence to a narrow range of very serious disorders; and its adoption would certainly simplify the tasks of psychiatric witnesses and the court. Some people, however, take the view that it would be wrong in principle that a person should escape conviction if, although severely mentally ill, he has committed a rational crime which was uninfluenced by his illness and for which he ought to be liable to be punished. They believe that the prosecution should be allowed to persuade the jury (if it can) that the offence was not attributable to the disorder. We agree. Sub-section (2) provides accordingly. We believe that it must improve the acceptability of the Butler Committee's generally admirable scheme as the basis of legislation.

Clause 34 of the Draft Bill provides:
Mental disorder: definitions

In this Act:

'mental disorder' means:

  (a) severe mental illness; or

  (b) a state of arrested or incomplete development of mind; or

  (c) a state of automatism (not resulting only from intoxication) which is a feature of a disorder, whether organic or functional and whether continuing or recurring, that may cause a similar state on another occasion;

'return a mental disorder verdict' means:

  (a) in relation to trial on indictment, return a verdict that the defendant is not guilty on evidence of mental disorder; and

  (b) in relation to summary trial, dismiss the information on evidence of mental disorder;

'severe mental illness' means a mental illness which has one or more of the following characteristics:

  (a) lasting impairment of intellectual functions shown by failure of memory, orientation, comprehension and learning capacity;

  (b) lasting alteration of mood of such degree as to give rise to delusional appraisal of the defendant's situation, his past or his future, or that of others, or lack of any appraisal;

  (c) delusional beliefs, persecutory, jealous or grandiose;

  (d) abnormal perceptions associated with delusional misinterpretation of events;

  (e) thinking so disordered as to prevent reasonable appraisal of the defendant's situation or reasonable communication with others;

'severe mental handicap' means a state of arrested or incomplete development of mind which includes severe impairment of intelligence and social functioning.

(1) DIMINISHED RESPONSIBILITY

For the purposes of the law of murder only, a much broader category of mental abnormality may, since the Homicide Act 1957, afford a defence. See below, p 577.

FURTHER READING

A. DUFF, 'Fitness to Plead and Fair Trials' [1994] Crim LR 419

P. FENNELL, 'The Criminal Procedure (Insanity and Unfitness to Plead) Act 1991' (1992) 55 MLR 547

D. GRUBIN, 'What Constitutes Unfitness to Plead' [1993] Crim LR 748

R. D. MACKAY, *Mental Condition Defences in Criminal Law* (1998)

R. D. MACKAY, 'Fact and Fiction About the Insanity Defence' [1990] Crim LR 247

R. D. MACKAY and G. KEARNS, 'The Continued Underuse of Unfitness to Plead and the Insanity Defence' [1994] Crim LR 546

R. D. MACKAY and G. KEARNS, 'The Trial of the Facts and Unfitness to Plead' [1997] Crim LR 644

R. D. MACKAY and G. KEARNS, 'More Facts(s) about the Insanity Defence' [1999] Crim LR 714

S. WHITE, 'The Criminal Procedure (Insanity and Unfitness to Plead) Act 1991' [1992] Crim LR 4

12

General defences

In this chapter we are concerned with defences in the strictest sense of the word. The defendant is not denying that he committed the actus reus with mens rea. He is asserting the existence of other facts which, he claims, justify or excuse his doing what would otherwise be a crime. Following *Woolmington*, above, p 172, he does not have to prove the existence of those facts. If there is some evidence of them, the onus is on the prosecution to disprove one or more of them. The defence succeeds if, on consideration of the whole of the evidence, the jury think it reasonably possible that all the elements of the defence were present. If so, the prosecution has not proved beyond reasonable doubt that the defendant is guilty.

1. THE INCAPACITY OF CHILDREN

(1) CHILDREN UNDER 10 YEARS

Children and Young Persons Act 1933, s 50

Age of criminal responsibility. It shall be conclusively presumed that no child under the age of ten years can be guilty of any offence.

There may be the clearest evidence that a young child intentionally killed another person—the actus reus and mens rea of murder; but once it is shown that he was, or may have been, under the age of 10 at the time of the act, no criminal proceedings may follow.

(2) CHILDREN OVER NINE AND UNDER 14 YEARS

At common law there was a rebuttable presumption that these children were *doli incapax*, incapable of forming a criminal state of mind. The presumption was rebutted only if the prosecution proved beyond reasonable doubt, not only that the child caused the actus reus with mens rea, but also that he knew that the particular act was not merely naughty or mischievous but 'seriously wrong'. If there was no evidence of such knowledge other than that implicit in the act itself, there was no case to answer. In *C v DPP* the Divisional Court held that this ancient rule was outdated and no longer represented the common law but the House of Lords ruled that it was not open to the courts so to hold: [1996] AC 1, [1995] 2 All ER 43. The consequence of the decision appears to have been a much more rigorous application of the rule and a series of unmeritorious acquittals caused such disquiet that Parliament intervened.

Crime and Disorder Act 1998, s 34

The rebuttable presumption of criminal law that a child aged ten or over is incapable of committing an offence is hereby abolished.

It seems to have been generally thought that this section would abolish the defence as well as the presumption and put children aged 10 and above on the same footing as adults so far as liability to conviction is concerned. Another view, however, is that the substantive law is unaffected so that it is still open to a child to argue, and to introduce evidence, that he did not know that what he did was seriously wrong, whereupon it would be for the prosecution to prove that he did know that. See Nigel Walker (1999) 149 NLJ 64. Even this less far-reaching construction would probably remove most of the problems previously encountered by the prosecution. Any normal 13-year-old boy would know that it was seriously wrong to rape his mother. But it was not formerly open to the jury to infer that it followed that this apparently normal boy knew. Judges were warned against applying a presumption of normality. Now, it would be for the defence to introduce evidence of abnormality. Raising a doubt in the minds of the jury in the case posed would seem to call for evidence of something like insanity within the M'Naghten rules. In other, less blatant, cases, however, it might be quite feasible to make out the defence.

2. DURESS—THREATS AND CIRCUMSTANCES

It is now established that two forms of duress are recognized by the criminal law. The first, duress by threats, has existed for centuries but, until modern times, made very rare appearances in the law reports. In the last 40 years the law has developed relatively quickly and is now reasonably well-defined though still with several areas of uncertainty. Much more recent is the recognition of the existence of the related defence of duress of circumstances, the first case *Willer*, below, p 427, appearing in the law reports in 1986, the first use of the phrase by the courts in 1988 (*Conway*, below, p 425) and its recognition as a general defence in 1995 (*Pommel*, below, p 428).

The typical case of duress by threats is that where D is told, 'Do this (the crime charged) or else...' D yields to the threat and does the act which is a crime—unless the defence applies. Duress of circumstances also may arise from the threatening acts of others. The difference here is that no one is telling the accused to commit the crime. The effect of the threat, however, may be the same. D, who is disqualified from driving—

(i) is told by a menacing gang of youths, 'Drive the car or we will kill you';

(ii) sees the same gang bearing down on him with shouts of 'Kill him' and the only way he can escape is to drive the car.

In both cases D intentionally commits the actus reus of the offence of driving while disqualified and in both cases he does so in order to save his life from the same menace. If he has a defence in the one case, he ought to have a defence in the other. The close relationship is witnessed by the fact that in *Willer* the court was concerned with a case of type (ii) (circumstances) but it showed no awareness of this and relied on the law relating to duress by threats; whereas in *Martin*, below, p 431, the court decided the case as one of duress by circumstances, whereas closer inspection would have revealed that it was duress by threats. It appears probable then that the principles applicable to the two types of duress are the same and that the cases below, though mainly concerned with duress by threats, state the law for duress of circumstances.

R v Hasan

[2005] UKHL 22, [2005] All ER (D) 299 (Mar), [2005] 2 WLR 709

(Lord Bingham of Cornhill, Lords Steyn, Rodger of Earlsferry, Brown of Eaton-Under-Heywood and Baroness Hale of Richmond)

H was charged with aggravated burglary and pleaded duress. H claimed that he had been coerced into committing the burglary by S, a drug dealer with a reputation for violence, who had threatened that H and his family would be harmed if H did not commit the crime. H claimed that he had had no chance to escape and go to the police.

Lord Bingham of Cornhill: [His Lordship dealt with the facts of the case and other unrelated issues]

17. The common sense starting point of the common law is that adults of sound mind are ordinarily to be held responsible for the crimes which they commit. To this general principle there has, since the 14th century, been a recognised but limited exception in favour of those who commit crimes because they are forced or compelled to do so against their will by the threats of another. Such persons are said, in the language of the criminal law, to act as they do because they are subject to duress.

18. Where duress is established, it does not ordinarily operate to negative any legal ingredient of the crime which the defendant has committed. Nor is it now regarded as justifying the conduct of the defendant, as has in the past been suggested: *Attorney-General v Whelan* [1934] IR 518, 526; Glanville Williams, *Criminal Law, The General Part* (2nd edn, 1961), p 755. Duress is now properly to be regarded as a defence which, if established, excuses what would otherwise be criminal conduct: *Director of Public Prosecutions for Northern Ireland v Lynch* [1975] AC 653, 671, 680, 710–711; *Hibbert v The Queen* (1995) 99 CCC (3d) 193, paras 21, 38, 47, per Lamer CJC.

19. Duress affords a defence which, if raised and not disproved, exonerates the defendant altogether. It does not, like the defence of provocation to a charge of murder, serve merely to reduce the seriousness of the crime which the defendant has committed. And the victim of a crime committed under duress is not, like a person against whom a defendant uses force to defend himself, a person who has threatened the defendant or been perceived by the defendant as doing so. The victim of a crime committed under duress may be assumed to be morally innocent, having shown no hostility or aggression towards the defendant. The only criminal defences which have any close affinity with duress are necessity, where the force or compulsion is exerted not by human threats but by extraneous circumstances, and, perhaps, marital coercion under section 47 of the Criminal Justice Act 1925.

20. Where the evidence in the proceedings is sufficient to raise an issue of duress, the burden is on the prosecution to establish to the criminal standard that the defendant did not commit the crime with which he is charged under duress: *R v Lynch*, above, p 668. In its Report 'Legislating the Criminal Code. Offences against the Person and General Principles' (1993, Law Com. No 218, Cm 2370, paras 33–34), the Law Commission recommended that a legal burden of proof, on the balance of probabilities, be placed on a defendant to establish a defence of duress. It was not suggested in argument that this was a change which should be made, and there must be real doubt whether it is a change which the House in its judicial capacity could properly make even if persuaded of the merits of doing so. Imposition of a reverse legal burden on the defendant would in any event require very careful consideration. But it must be accepted, as the Law Commission pointed out in para 33 of this

Report, that the defence of duress is peculiarly difficult for the prosecution to investigate and disprove beyond reasonable doubt. As Professor Sir John Smith QC observed in his commentary on *R v Cole* [1994] Crim LR 582, 584, with reference to the Law Commission proposal,

> 'duress is a unique defence in that it is so much more likely than any other to depend on assertions which are peculiarly difficult for the prosecution to investigate or subsequently to disprove.'

The prosecution's difficulty is of course the greater when, as is all too often the case, little detail of the alleged compulsion is vouchsafed by the defence until the trial is under way.

21. Having regard to these features of duress, I find it unsurprising that the law in this and other jurisdictions should have been developed so as to confine the defence of duress within narrowly defined limits. Most of these are not in issue in this appeal, but it seems to me important that the issues the House is asked to resolve should be approached with understanding of how the defence has developed, and to that end I shall briefly identify the most important limitations:

(1) Duress does not afford a defence to charges of murder (*R v Howe* [1987] AC 417), attempted murder (*R v Gotts* [1992] 2 AC 412) and, perhaps, some forms of treason (Smith & Hogan, *Criminal Law*, 10th edn, 2002, p 254). The Law Commission has in the past (eg. in 'Criminal Law. Report on Defences of General Application' (Law Com No 83, Cm 556, 1977, paras 2.44–2.46)) recommended that the defence should be available as a defence to all offences, including murder, and the logic of this argument is irresistible. But their recommendation has not been adopted, no doubt because it is felt that in the case of the gravest crimes no threat to the defendant, however extreme, should excuse commission of the crime. It is noteworthy that under some other criminal codes the defence is not available to a much wider range of offences: see, for example, section 20(1) of the Tasmanian Criminal Code, section 40(2) of the Criminal Code Act of the Northern Territory of Australia, section 31(4) of the Criminal Code Act Compilation Act 1913 of Western Australia, section 17 of the Canadian Criminal Code and section 24 of the Crimes Act 1961 of New Zealand.

(2) To found a plea of duress the threat relied on must be to cause death or serious injury. In *Alexander MacGrowther's Case* (1746) Fost. 13, 14, 168 ER 8, Lee CJ held:

> 'The only force that doth excuse, is a force upon the person, and present fear of death.'

But the Criminal Law Commissioners in their Seventh Report of 1843 (p 31, article 6) understood the defence to apply where there was a just and well-grounded fear of death or grievous bodily harm, and it is now accepted that threats of death or serious injury will suffice: *R v Lynch*, above, p 679; *R v Abdul-Hussain* (Court of Appeal (Criminal Division), 17 December 1998, unreported).

(3) The threat must be directed against the defendant or his immediate family or someone close to him: Smith & Hogan, above, p 258. In the light of recent Court of Appeal decisions such as *R v Conway* [1989] QB 290 and *R v Wright* [2000] Crim LR 510, the current (April 2003) specimen direction of the Judicial Studies Board suggests that the threat must be directed, if not to the defendant or a member of his immediate family, to a person for whose safety the defendant would reasonably regard himself as responsible. The correctness of such a direction was not, and on the facts could not be, in issue on this appeal, but it appears to me, if strictly applied, to be consistent with the rationale of the duress exception.

(4) The relevant tests pertaining to duress have been largely stated objectively, with reference to the reasonableness of the defendant's perceptions and conduct and not, as is usual in many other areas of the criminal law, with primary reference to his subjective perceptions. It is necessary to

return to this aspect, but in passing one may note the general observation of Lord Morris of Borth-y-Gest in *R v Lynch*, above at p 670:

> '....it is proper that any rational system of law should take fully into account the standards of honest and reasonable men. By those standards it is fair that actions and reactions may be tested.'

(5) The defence of duress is available only where the criminal conduct which it is sought to excuse has been directly caused by the threats which are relied upon.

(6) The defendant may excuse his criminal conduct on grounds of duress only if, placed as he was, there was no evasive action he could reasonably have been expected to take. It is necessary to return to this aspect also, but this is an important limitation of the duress defence and in recent years it has, as I shall suggest, been unduly weakened.

(7) The defendant may not rely on duress to which he has voluntarily laid himself open. The scope of this limitation raises the most significant issue on this part of this appeal, and I must return to it. [see below p **392**]

22. For many years it was possible to regard the defence of duress as something of an antiquarian curiosity, with little practical application. Sir James Stephen, with his immense experience, never knew or heard of the defence being advanced, save in the case of married women, and could find only two reported cases: *A History of the Criminal Law of England* (1883), vol II, p 106. Edwards, drawing attention to the absence of satisfactory modern authority, inferred that the defence must be very rare: 'Compulsion, Coercion and Criminal Responsibility' (1951) 14 MLR 297. Professor Hart described duress as a defence of which little is heard: *Punishment and Responsibility* (1960), p 16. This has changed. As Dennis correctly observed in 'Duress, Murder and Criminal Responsibility' (1980) 96 LQR 208,

> 'In recent years duress has become a popular plea in answer to a criminal charge.'

This is borne out by the steady flow of cases reaching the appellate courts over the past 30 years or so, and by the daily experience of prosecutors. As already acknowledged, the House is not invited in this appeal to recast the law on duress. It can only address, piecemeal, the issues which fall for decision. That duress is now regularly relied on as a complete defence to serious criminal charges does not alter the essential task which the House must undertake, but does give it additional practical importance. I must acknowledge that the features of duress to which I have referred in paras 18 to 20 above incline me, where policy choices are to be made, towards tightening rather than relaxing the conditions to be met before duress may be successfully relied on. In doing so, I bear in mind in particular two observations of Lord Simon of Glaisdale in *R v Lynch* above (dissenting on the main ruling, which was reversed in *R v Howe*, above):

> '.... your Lordships should hesitate long lest you may be inscribing a charter for terrorists, gang-leaders and kidnappers.' (p 688).

> 'A sane system of criminal justice does not permit a subject to set up a countervailing system of sanctions or by terrorism to confer criminal immunity on his gang.'(p 696).

The restriction on pleading duress to charges of murder and attempted murder is considered below, p **416.**

(1) THE NATURE OF THE THREAT

There are eight issues to consider in relation to the threat and its sufficiency to found the defence of duress or duress of circumstances.

1. A threat of death or serious injury. In *DPP for N Ireland v Lynch* [1975] AC 653 D was charged with helping others to murder a police officer in Northern Ireland. D drove the gunmen to and from the crime. D pleaded duress as he was ordered to drive the car by a gunman known for his ruthlessness. The House of Lords concluded (on the issue of what constitutes a sufficient threat) per Lord Simon at p 686:

The type of threat which affords a defence must be one of human physical harm, (including possibly, imprisonment) so that threat of injury [sic] to property is not enough...

Threats of a non-violent nature, no matter how overwhelming will not suffice. In *Singh* [1973] 1 All ER 122 D was trafficking in illegal immigrants and pleaded duress based on the threats of blackmail against him. The Court of Appeal held, per Lawton LJ, at p 126:

the submission on duress which counsel for the appellant... made was old but wrong. He asked us to say that a man who commits a crime at the request of a blackmailer whom he fears can plead duress. He cannot. Duress arises from threats of violence not exposure.

This strict limitation is adopted in most jurisdictions See LCCP 122, para 18.5:

the overwhelming tendency of the authorities as of modern codes, is to limit the defence to cases where death or serious injury is threatened.... Consultation strongly supported that limitation on the defence of duress, which is imposed by clause 25(2)(a) of the Criminal Law Bill.

Is a threat of damage to property, or of blackmail, sometimes as effective on D's will as a threat of violence? Should the law, in each case, balance the harm threatened against the seriousness of the crime committed? If the harm D caused by submitting to the threat was clearly less than that which would have been inflicted had he defied it, should he be allowed a defence? But what of D who commits a serious crime when faced with a threat of serious injury? What is 'serious injury' for these purposes? Can it depend on the crime D has committed when faced with the threat?

2. Against whom must the threat be made? The Law Commission recommended (Law Com No 218, paras 28.1 et seq) that there should be no formal limitation to any class of persons against whom the threat must be directed. The relationship between D and the person threatened should be only one of the circumstances to be taken into account in determining whether the threat was one which D could reasonably be expected to resist. In *Shayler* [2001] 1 WLR 2206, the Lord Chief Justice at para 49, approving a statement of Rose LJ in *Abdul-Hussain*, stated that:

the evil must be directed towards the defendant or a person or persons for whom he has responsibility or, we would add, persons for whom the situation makes him responsible; ... [this extends], by way of example, [to] the situation where the threat is made to set off a bomb unless the defendant performs the unlawful act. The defendant may have not have had any previous connection with those who would be injured by the bomb but the threat itself creates the defendant's responsibility for those who will be at risk if he does not give way to the threat.

If a bank robber threatens to shoot a customer in the bank unless D, the clerk, hands him the keys, does D have a defence to a charge of abetting the robbery?

3. The threat must be an extraneous one. The threat must have some source extraneous to the defendant himself. In *Rodger and Rose* [1998] 1 Cr App R 143, D who was serving a life sentence was informed that his tariff had been substantially increased. He broke out of prison and raised duress as a defence to the charge of prison-breaking. It was conceded for the purpose of the appeal that he broke out because he had become suicidal and would have committed suicide had he not done so. So there was a threat to his life, but since the threat did not come from an extraneous source, it was no defence. To allow it, said the court, 'could amount to a licence to commit crime dependent on the personal characteristics and vulnerability of the offender'. See also *R v Quayle* (below, p **444** in relation to necessity).

4. *Duress and mixed motives.* There may be several threats, one capable of amounting to duress, the others not: 'Do it or you will be made bankrupt, your adultery will be revealed to your wife and you will be maimed'; or there may be a threat capable of amounting to duress coupled with a promise: 'Do it and there is £100,000 for you; don't do it and you will be shot.' Is duress a defence and, if so, in what circumstances? Under the Criminal Law Bill the question would be simply whether D did it 'because' of the threat, as he saw it.

In *Valderrama-Vega* [1985] Crim LR 220 D was charged with being knowingly concerned in the fraudulent evasion of the prohibition on the importation of cocaine from Colombia. His defence was (i) that he and his family had been subjected to threats of death or injury by a Mafia-type organization in Colombia; (ii) that he was heavily indebted and under severe financial pressure; and (iii) that he had been threatened with disclosure of his homosexual inclinations. Neither (ii) nor (iii) could amount to duress. The jury were directed that duress was a defence only if D acted *solely* as the result of threats of death or serious injury. Though D's conviction was upheld, it was held that the use of the word 'solely' was wrong: it 'might have led the jury to convict even though they believed that [D] would not have acted as he did in the absence of threats to his life, if there were other motives or reasons for his actions . . . '.

Ortiz (1986) 83 Cr App R 173 also concerned a Colombian importer of cocaine who apparently had substantial financial inducements to commit the crime: he had been provided with a flat in Chelsea, he had paid £50,000 into a Swiss bank account and had £39,000 on his person when arrested. The judge told the jury to write down the elements of the defence: 'Did he act solely as a result of threats [of death or serious injury]. . . . The important word is "solely" so you can underline that.' The Court of Appeal, dismissing his appeal, held that, while the word 'solely' is best omitted in a summing up, this was a correct direction 'within the context of the trial'—'the case was never run on the basis that the appellant was influenced partly by the threats and partly from the attraction of the material benefits which were made available to him.' The court said:

The essence of the defence is that the will of the subject of the threats is no longer under his own control because of the fear engendered by those threats. There is no room for other motives for his acts.

What if D would not have done it for the money alone; he would have resisted the threats but for the offer of the money; but the combination of the money and the threats was irresistible?

What if D would have done it for the money alone but was terrified by the threat and would have yielded to it even if no money had been on offer? Consider:

DPP v Bell [1992] RTR 335, [1992] Crim LR 176, DC. Bell had been drinking and had excess alcohol in his breath. He admitted that he intended to drive home. A fracas occurred and, fearing serious personal injury, he ran to his car pursued by others and drove off. The Crown Court allowed his appeal against conviction for driving with an excess of alcohol on the ground of duress [sc of circumstances] and an appeal by way of case stated was dismissed. It had been found as a fact that he drove because of terror and whether he would have driven if there had been no threats was a hypothetical question. He might have changed his mind or been persuaded by his passengers not to drive. What if the Crown Court had found as a fact that Bell would have driven home with an excess of alcohol anyway?

5. *The (risk of the) threat must not be one D has knowingly 'courted'.* This operates as a further important limitation on the defence, and one that has become increasingly important as the courts have sought to prevent the defence being too readily available to those involved in drug-related and terrorist crime in particular where their involvement demonstrates a degree of prior culpability. The problem commonly arises where D has joined a criminal organization and, having committed a crime as part of that organiza-tion or on behalf of it, D pleads that members of the organization threatened death or serious injury to him/others unless he committed the crime. What limitations might be placed on the defence to meet these concerns? What if D has not voluntarily joined the organization? Perhaps he was under duress to join. Of what types of organization will membership prevent D relying on a defence? Must D be an active member of the organization at the time of the commission of the crime? To what type of risk must D be exposing himself? Must D be aware of the risk that he is exposing himself to or is it sufficient that he ought to have been aware? Must D be aware of the type of crime he might be compelled to commit?

Hasan
[2005] UKHL 22, [2005] All ER (D) 299 (Mar), [2005] 2 WLR 709

(Lord Bingham of Cornhill, Lords Steyn, Roger of Earlsferry, Brown of Eaton-Under-Heywood and Baroness Hale of Richmond)

Lord Bingham: 29. . . . [T]he Court of Appeal ruled that the [trials judge's direction] was a misdirection because the judge had not directed the jury to consider whether the defendant knew that he was likely to be subjected to threats to commit a crime of the type of which he was charged. It is this rul-ing which gives rise to the certified question on this part of the case, which is:

'Whether the defence of duress is excluded when as a result of the accused's voluntary association with others:
  (i) he foresaw (or possibly should have foreseen) the risk of being subjected to any compulsion by threats of violence, or
  (ii) only when he foresaw (or should have foreseen) the risk of being subjected to compulsion to commit criminal offences, and, if the latter,
  (iii) only if the offences foreseen (or which should have been foreseen) were of the same type (or possibly of the same type and gravity) as that ultimately committed.'

The Crown contend for answer (i) in its objective form. The defendant commends the third answer, omitting the first parenthesis.

30. In their definition of duress the Criminal Law Commissioners of 1879 included a proviso:

'Provided also, that he [the defendant] was not a party to any association or conspiracy the being party to which rendered him subject to such compulsion.'

A qualification to very similar effect is to be found in the criminal codes of Queensland (section 67(3)(b) and (c)), Tasmania (section 20(1)), the Northern Territory of Australia (section 41(2)), Western Australia (section 31(4)), the Commonwealth of Australia (section 10.2(3)), the Australian

Capital Territory (section 40(3)), Canada (section 17), New Zealand (section 24(1)) and no doubt others. But its implications were not for many years examined in the British courts.

31. The issue might have been raised in *R v Lynch* [above], where the appellant claimed to have been press-ganged by the IRA, but the argument in that case was largely directed to the question whether the defence of duress was open to a defendant charged as a secondary party to murder. It was in *R v Fitzpatrick* [1977] NI 20, another IRA case, that the Court of Criminal Appeal in Northern Ireland had occasion to consider the matter in depth. The ratio of the decision is found in the judgment of the court delivered by Lowry LCJ at p 33:

'A person may become associated with a sinister group of men with criminal objectives and coercive methods of ensuring that their lawless enterprises are carried out and thereby voluntarily expose himself to illegal compulsion, whether or not the group is or becomes a proscribed organization. . . .

 . . . . if a person voluntarily exposes and submits himself, as the appellant did, to illegal compulsion, he cannot rely on the duress to which he has voluntarily exposed himself as an excuse either in respect of the crimes he commits against his will or in respect of his continued but unwilling association with those capable of exercising upon him the duress which he calls in aid.'

32. That statement was no doubt drafted with the peculiar character of the IRA in mind. *R v Sharp* [1987] QB 853 arose from criminal activity of a more routine kind committed by a gang of robbers. The trial judge's direction which was challenged on appeal is fully quoted in *R v Shepherd* (1987) 86 Cr App R 47, 51, and was to this effect:

'. . . . but in my judgment the defence of duress is not available to an accused who voluntarily exposes and submits himself to illegal compulsion.

 It is not merely a matter of joining in a criminal enterprise; it is a matter of joining in a criminal enterprise of such a nature that the defendant appreciated the nature of the enterprise itself and the attitudes of those in charge of it, so that when he was in fact subjected to compulsion he could fairly be said by a jury to have voluntarily exposed himself and submitted himself to such compulsion.'

The Court of Appeal (Lord Lane CJ, Farquharson and Gatehouse JJ) upheld that direction in *R v Sharp*, expressing the principle at p 861:

'. . . . where a person has voluntarily, and with knowledge of its nature, joined a criminal organisation or gang which he knew might bring pressure on him to commit an offence and was an active member when he was put under such pressure, he cannot avail himself of the defence of duress.'

In *R v Shepherd*, above, the criminal activity was of a less serious kind: the question which the jury should have been (but were not) directed to consider (p 51) was 'whether the appellant could be said to have taken the risk of P's violence simply by joining a shoplifting gang of which he [P] was a member'.

33. *R v Ali* is summarised at [1995] Crim LR 303, but the ratio of the decision more clearly appears from the transcript of the judgment given by the Court of Appeal (Lord Taylor of Gosforth CJ, Alliott and Rix JJ) on 14 November 1994. The appellant claimed to have become involved in drug dealing and to have become indebted to his supplier, X, who (he said) had given him a gun and told him to obtain the money from a bank or building society the following day, failing which he would be killed. The appellant accordingly committed the robbery of which he was convicted. In directing the jury on the defence of duress advanced by the defendant the trial judge had said:

'The final question is this: did he, in obtaining heroin from Mr X and supplying it to others for gain, after he knew of Mr X's reputation for violence, voluntarily put himself in a position where he knew that he was likely to be forced by Mr X to commit a crime?'

It was argued by the appellant that the judge should have said 'forced by Mr X to commit armed robbery', but this was rejected, and the court held that by 'a crime' the jury could only have understood the judge to be referring to a crime other than drug dealing. The principle stated by the court on p 7 of the transcript was this:

'The crux of the matter, as it seems to us, is knowledge in the defendant of either a violent nature to the gang or the enterprise which he has joined, or a violent disposition in the person or persons involved with him in the criminal activity he voluntarily joined. In our judgment, if a defendant voluntarily participates in criminal offences with a man "X", whom he knows to be of a violent disposition and likely to require him to perform other criminal acts, he cannot rely upon duress if "X" does so.'

(In this case, as in *R v Cole*, above, it would seem that the defence of duress should in any event have failed, for lack of immediacy, since the threat was not to be executed until the following day, and therefore the defendant had the opportunity to take evasive action).

34. In its Working Paper No 55 of 1974, the Law Commission in para 26 favoured

'a limitation upon the defence [of duress] which would exclude its availability where the defendant had joined an association or conspiracy which was of such a character that he was aware that he might be compelled to participate in offences of the type with which he is charged.'

This reference to 'offences of the type with which he is charged' was, in substance, repeated in the Law Commission's 'Report on Defences of General Application' (Law Com No 83) of 1977, paras 2.38 and 2.46(8), in clause 1(5) of the draft bill appended to that report, in clause 45(4) of the draft bill appended to the Law Commission's Report on 'Codification of the Criminal Law' (Law Com No 143) of 1985, as explained in para 13.19 of the Report, and in clause 42(5) of the Law Commission's draft 'Criminal Code Bill' (Law Com No 177) published in 1989. But there was no warrant for this gloss in any reported British authority until the Court of Appeal (Roch LJ, Richards J and Judge Colston QC) gave judgment in *R v Baker and Ward* [1999] 2 Cr App R 335. The facts were very similar to these in *R v Ali*, above, save that the appellants claimed that they had been specifically instructed to rob the particular store which they were convicted of robbing. The trial judge had directed the jury (p 341):

'A person cannot rely on the defence of duress if he has voluntarily and with full knowledge of its nature joined a criminal group which he was aware might bring pressure on him of a violent kind or require him if necessary to commit offences to obtain money where he himself had defaulted to the criminal group in payment to the criminal group.'

This was held to be a misdirection (p 344):

'What a defendant has to be aware of is the risk that the group might try to coerce him into committing criminal offences of the type for which he is being tried by the use of violence or threats of violence.'

At p 346 this ruling was repeated:

'The purpose of the pressure has to be to coerce the accused into committing a criminal offence of the type for which he is being tried.'

The appeals were accordingly allowed and the convictions quashed.

35. Counsel for the defendant in the present case contends (as the Court of Appeal accepted) that this ruling was correct and that the trial judge in the present case misdirected the jury because he did not insist on the need for the defendant to foresee pressure to commit the offence of robbery of which he was convicted.

36. In *R v Heath* (Court of Appeal: Kennedy LJ, Turner and Smedley JJ, 7 October 1999, [2000] Crim LR 109) the appellant again claimed that he had become indebted to a drug supplier, and

claimed that he had been compelled by threats of physical violence to collect the consignment of drugs which gave rise to his conviction. His defence of duress failed at trial, rightly as the Court of Appeal held. In its judgment, Kennedy LJ said:

> 'The appellant in evidence conceded that he had put himself in the position where he was likely to be subjected to threats. He was therefore, in our judgment, not entitled to rely on those same threats as duress to excuse him from liability for subsequent criminal conduct.'

The court found it possible to distinguish *R v Baker and Ward*, observing:

> 'It is the awareness of the risk of compulsion which matters. Prior awareness of what criminal activity those exercising compulsion may offer as a possible alternative to violence is irrelevant.'

The facts in *R v Harmer* (Court of Appeal: May LJ, Goldring and Gross JJ, 12 December 2001, [2002] Crim LR 401) were very similar to those in *R v Heath*, which the court followed. It does not appear from the court's judgment given by Goldring J whether *R v Baker and Ward* was directly cited, but it would seem that counsel for the appellant did not rely on it. He argued that the appellant did not foresee that he might be required to commit crimes for the supplier. But the court did not accept this argument:

> 'We cannot accept that where a man voluntarily exposes himself to unlawful violence, duress may run if he does not foresee that under the threat of such violence he may be required to commit crimes. There is no reason in principle why that should be so.'

37. The principal issue between the Crown on one side and the appellant and the Court of Appeal on the other is whether *R v Baker and Ward* correctly stated the law. To resolve that issue one must remind oneself of the considerations outlined in paras 18–22 [extracted at p **387**] above. The defendant is seeking to be wholly exonerated from the consequences of a crime deliberately committed. The prosecution must negative his defence of duress, if raised by the evidence, beyond reasonable doubt. The defendant is, ex hypothesi, a person who has voluntarily surrendered his will to the domination of another. Nothing should turn on foresight of the manner in which, in the event, the dominant party chooses to exploit the defendant's subservience. There need not be foresight of coercion to commit crimes, although it is not easy to envisage circumstances in which a party might be coerced to act lawfully. In holding that there must be foresight of coercion to commit crimes of the kind with which the defendant is charged, *R v Baker and Ward* mis-stated the law.

38. There remains the question, which the Court of Appeal left open in para 75 of their judgment, whether the defendant's foresight must be judged by a subjective or an objective test: i.e. does the defendant lose the benefit of a defence based on duress only if he actually foresaw the risk of coercion or does he lose it if he ought reasonably to have foreseen the risk of coercion, whether he actually foresaw the risk or not? I do not think any decided case has addressed this question, and I am conscious that application of an objective reasonableness test to other ingredients of duress has attracted criticism: see, for example, Elliott, 'Necessity, Duress and Self-Defence' [1989] Crim LR 611, 614–615, and the commentary by Professor Ashworth on *R v Safi* [2003] Crim LR 721, 723. The practical importance of the distinction in this context may not be very great, since if a jury concluded that a person voluntarily associating with known criminals ought reasonably to have foreseen the risk of future coercion they would not, I think, be very likely to accept that he did not in fact do so. But since there is a choice to be made, policy in my view points towards an objective test of what the defendant, placed as he was and knowing what he did, ought reasonably to have foreseen. I am not persuaded otherwise by analogies based on self-defence or provocation for reasons I have already given. The policy of the law must be to discourage association with known criminals, and it should be slow to excuse the criminal conduct of those who do so. If a person

voluntarily becomes or remains associated with others engaged in criminal activity in a situation where he knows or ought reasonably to know that he may be the subject of compulsion by them or their associates, he cannot rely on the defence of duress to excuse any act which he is thereafter compelled to do by them. It is not necessary in this case to decide whether or to what extent that principle applies if an undercover agent penetrates a criminal gang for bona fide law enforcement purposes and is compelled by the gang to commit criminal acts.

39. I would answer this certified question by saying that the defence of duress is excluded when as a result of the accused's voluntary association with others engaged in criminal activity he foresaw or ought reasonably to have foreseen the risk of being subjected to any compulsion by threats of violence. I would answer the other certified question as proposed by Lord Steyn.

Baroness Hale: [Her ladyship referred to the Law Commission's Report, *Legislating the Criminal Code: Offences against the Person and General Principles* (Law Com No 218, 1993) (published when her Ladyship was a Law Commissioner).]

69. The Commission adhered to the view that duress should be a complete defence to all crimes, not simply a matter of mitigation:

> '31.4 We believe that if it is wrong even in respect of murder to condemn the defendant for not acting heroically rather than reasonably, it would be even more unjust to condemn defendants for lesser acts done under the same conditions. To censure and punish defendants who found themselves in such circumstances would bring the law into disrepute. To take a recent example, it was confirmed in *Lewis* [The Times, 19 November 1992] that a threat of a reprisal that it is unreasonable to expect the witness to resist is a defence to a charge of contempt in respect of a refusal to give evidence. It would, in our view, be intolerable if, for instance, a wife whose husband threatened her with serious injury or death, and who as a result reasonably refused to give evidence against him, had nonetheless to be convicted of the offence of contempt.'

The Commission also saw practical difficulties in the way of treating duress as mitigation:

> '31.7 ... If duress is rejected as a defence, that must be either because the defendant who acts under duress is at some way at fault, albeit it only by not behaving heroically; or because there is some public policy reason for convicting him even though he is not at fault. If he is at fault, the law should mark his fault by a penalty, or at least should not assume that in no case will an effective penalty be imposed. If the reasons for rejecting duress as a defence are ones of public policy, it is hard to see that that policy is forwarded by a regime that assumes that convictions are to be purely nominal in nature; or, even more, that assumes that in some cases the law will not be enforced at all.'

70. As Professor Andrew Ashworth (in *Principles of Criminal Law*, 4th edition 2003, p 228) points out, there are other policy problems with relying on duress as a mitigating factor:

> 'Mitigation may be right if "desert" is the basis for sentence, but supporters of deterrent sentencing have a particular problem. Their general approach is to maintain that the stronger the temptation or pressure to commit a crime, the stronger the law's threat should be in order to counter-balance it. The law and its penalties should be used to strengthen the resolve of those under pressure.'

That is, indeed, a common approach to sentencing: in drug smuggling cases, for example, the 'mule' may well have been subjected to intense pressure to carry the goods into the United Kingdom, but heavy sentences are imposed, not only to deter others from succumbing to such pressures, but also to deter the barons from using them. Mr Perry, for the Crown, argued that it was doing the vulnerable no favours to expand the scope of duress for their benefit, as this would merely encourage their duressors to exploit them. As Professor Ashworth continues:

'The difficulty with this analysis is that it suggests heavy deterrent sentences for all cases except the most egregious, where it prescribes no penalty at all—a distinction with momentous effects but no clear reference point.'

71. The Commission was, of course, thoroughly aware of the practical difficulties caused by the fact that duress is most likely to arise in terrorist, gang or other organised crime offences and that, particularly in such circumstances, 'the defence of duress is so easy to raise and may be so difficult for the prosecution to disprove beyond reasonable doubt, the facts of necessity being as a rule known only to the defendant himself' (Law Com No 218, para 30.15, quoting Lord Lane CJ in *R v Howe* [1986] QB 626, 641, to which Lords Bridge and Griffiths attached particular weight in the House of Lords [1987] AC 417, 438 and 444).

72. The Commission's solution, strongly supported by the judiciary and most practitioners, was to place the persuasive burden of proving duress, on the balance of probabilities, on the defence (paras 30.16, 33.1 to 33.16). Duress, in their view, was different from other defences, in that the facts on which it is founded are not part and parcel of the incident during which the offence was committed. They will characteristically have happened well before, and quite separately from, the actual commission of the offence that the prosecution must know about and must prove. The difficulty of the prosecution disproving the unilateral claims of the defendant made it 'hardly surprising that…judges and others should express lack of enthusiasm about the defence of duress as a whole.'

73. This solution, coupled with the Commission's 'sell-out to subjectivism', has been strongly criticised: see Jeremy Horder, 'Occupying the moral high ground? The Law Commission on duress' [1994] Crim LR 334. The moral basis of the defence remains a hot topic of debate: see, for example, Professor William Wilson, 'The Structure of Criminal Defences' [2005] Crim LR 108. I accept that even the person with a knife at her back has a choice whether or not to do as the knifeman says. The question is whether she should have resisted the threat. But, perhaps because I am a reasonable but comparatively weak and fearful grandmother, I do not understand why the defendant's beliefs and personal characteristics are not morally relevant to whether she could reasonably have been expected to resist. No doubt unduly influenced by Professors Sir John Smith, Edward Griew and Ian Dennis, therefore, I remain attracted by the Law Commission's proposals. The real reasons for the unpopularity of the defence are those given by Lord Lane CJ in Howe: that it is readily raised by the least deserving of people but difficult for the prosecution to disprove. We are told by Mr Perry that, perhaps because of advances in forensic science which have made crimes easier to detect and more difficult to defend, duress is now very frequently raised, often late in the day, by defendants up and down the country.

74. If we are not to have legislation to alter the burden of proof, and I agree that it is not open to us to do it ourselves, then I understand your lordships' desire to maintain the objective standards set by Lord Lane in *Graham*. But it seems to me that the best counter to Lord Lane's concerns is the *Fitzpatrick* doctrine which is the issue in this case. Logically, if it applies, it comes before all the other questions raised by the defence: irrespective of whether there was a threat which he could not reasonably be expected to resist, had the defendant so exposed himself to the risk of such threats that he cannot now rely on them as an excuse? If even on his own story he had done so, then the defence can be withdrawn from the jury without more ado; if that issue has to be left to the jury, but they resolve it against him, there is no need for them to consider the other questions.

75. But how far does this principle go? The 1985 draft code (Law Com No 143, clause 45(4)) and the 1989 draft (Law Com 177, volume 1, clause 42(5) as both provided that the defence of duress

'does not apply to a person who has knowingly and without reasonable excuse exposed himself to the risk of such a threat.' The code team believed that this was to the same effect as the 1977 draft (Law Com No 83, draft Criminal Liability (Duress) Bill, clause 1(5)) which had referred to someone who 'knew he would or might be called upon to commit the offence with which he is charged or any offence of the same or a similar character'. They must therefore have thought that the words 'such a threat' encompassed not only the harm threatened but also the reasons why the threat was made. Similarly, the draft Criminal Law Bill (annexed to Law Com No 218) provided in clause 25(4):

> 'This section does not apply to a person who knowingly and without reasonable excuse exposed himself to the risk of the threat made or believed to have been made.'

76. I agree, of course, that there was nothing in the case law before *R v Baker and Ward* to limit the kinds of crime which the defendant should have foreseen that he might be compelled to commit. I also agree that the limitation is unworkable in practice and difficult to justify in principle. The principle is that someone who voluntarily accepts the risk of being placed in the 'do it or else' dilemma should not be allowed to use that dilemma as an excuse (even if in some circumstances it might amount to mitigation). There are, however, two other questions.

77. The first is that the cases tend to talk about exposing oneself to the risk of 'unlawful violence'. That, it seems to me, is not enough. The foreseeable risk should be one of duress: that is, of threats of such severity, plausibility and immediacy that one might be compelled to do that which one would otherwise have chosen not to do. The battered wife knows that she is exposing herself to a risk of unlawful violence if she stays, but she may have no reason to believe that her husband will eventually use her broken will to force her to commit crimes. For the same reason, I would say that it must be foreseeable that duress will be used to compel the person to commit crimes of some sort. I have no difficulty envisaging circumstances in which a person may be coerced to act lawfully. The battered wife knows very well that she may be compelled to cook the dinner, wash the dishes, iron the shirts and submit to sexual intercourse. That should not deprive her of the defence of duress if she is obliged by the same threats to herself or her children to commit perjury or shoplift for food.

78. But this brings me to a concern which I have had throughout this case. It is one thing to deny the defence to people who choose to become members of illegal organisations, join criminal gangs, or engage with others in drug-related criminality. It is another thing to deny it to someone who has a quite different reason for becoming associated with the duressor and then finds it difficult to escape. I do not believe that this limitation on the defence is aimed at battered wives at all, or at others in close personal or family relationships with their duressors and their associates, such as their mothers, brothers or children. The Law Commission's Bills all refer to a person who exposes himself to the risk 'without reasonable excuse'. The words were there to cater for the police infiltrator (see Law Com No 83, para 2.37) but they are also applicable to the sort of association I have in mind. The other elements of the defence, narrowly construed in accordance with existing authority, are more than adequate to keep it within bounds in such cases.

79. The certified question on this part of the appeal was:

> 'Whether the defence of duress is excluded when as a result of the accused's voluntary association with others: (i) he foresaw (or possibly should have foreseen) the risk of being subjected to any compulsion by threats of violence; or (ii) only when he foresaw (or should have foreseen) the risk of being subjected to compulsion to commit criminal offences, and, if the latter, (iii) only if the offences foreseen (or which should have been foreseen) were of the same type (or possibly of the same type and gravity) as that ultimately committed.'

As will be apparent, I would have chosen option (ii), together with the further explanation of the concept of 'voluntary association with others' given in paragraph 78 above. It follows that I too would allow the Crown's appeal on this part of the case.

6. *How immediate must the threat be?*

R v Hudson and Taylor

[1971] 2 All ER 244, Court of Appeal, Criminal Division

(Lord Parker CJ, Widgery LJ and Cooke J)

The accused, girls aged 17 and 19 respectively, were the principal prosecution witnesses at the trial of one Wright, on a charge of wounding. They both failed to identify Wright and testified that they did not know him. Wright was acquitted. At their trial for perjury the accused admitted that their evidence was false and set up the defence of duress. Hudson said that she had been approached before the trial of Wright by men, including one, Farrell, who had a reputation for violence and warned that they would 'cut her up' if she 'told on' Wright. Hudson passed this on to Taylor, who had also been warned by other girls. The accused were frightened and decided to tell lies to avoid the consequences. Their decision was confirmed when, on arriving in court, they saw Farrell in the gallery.

The recorder directed that the defence of duress was not open because there was no present immediate threat capable of being carried out there and then, since the accused were in court in the presence of the judge and the police. On appeal the Crown argued that the ruling could be upheld on the additional ground that the accused should have neutralised the threat by seeking police protection when they came to court or beforehand.

[Lord Widgery CJ, having stated the facts, continued:]

…We have been referred to a large number of authorities and to the views of writers of text books. Despite the concern expressed in 2 Stephen's *History of the Criminal Law in England* [Vol 2, p 107], that it would be:

> '…a much greater misfortune for society at large if criminals could confer impunity upon their agents by threatening them with death or violence if they refused to execute their commands…'

it is clearly established that duress provides a defence in all offences including perjury (except possibly treason or murder as a principal) if the will of the accused has been overborne by threats of death or serious personal injury so that the commission of the alleged offence was no longer the voluntary act of the accused. This appeal raises two main questions; first, as to the nature of the necessary threat and, in particular, whether it must be 'present and immediate'; secondly, as to the extent to which a right to plead duress may be lost if the accused has failed to take steps to remove the threat as, for example, by seeking police protection.

It is essential to the defence of duress that the threat shall be effective at the moment when the crime is committed. The threat must be a 'present' threat in the sense that it is effective to neutralise the will of the accused at that time. Hence an accused who joins a rebellion under the compulsion of threats cannot plead duress if he remains with the rebels after the threats have lost their effect and his own will has had a chance to re-assert itself (*McGrowther's case* [(1746) Fost 13] and *A-G v Whelan* [[1934] IR 518]). Similarly a threat of future violence may be so remote as to be insufficient to overpower the will at the moment when the offence was committed, or the accused may have elected to commit the offence in order to rid himself of a threat hanging over him and not because he was driven to act by immediate and unavoidable pressure. In none of these cases is the defence of duress available because a person cannot justify the commission of a crime merely to secure his own peace of mind.

When, however, there is no opportunity for delaying tactics, and the person threatened must make up his mind whether he is to commit the criminal act or not, the existence at that moment of threats sufficient to destroy his will ought to provide him with a defence even though the threatened injury may not follow instantly, but after an interval. This principle is illustrated by *Subramaniam v Public Prosecutor* [[1956] 1 WLR 965], when the appellant was charged in Malaya with unlawful possession of ammunition and was held by the Privy Council to have a defence of duress, fit to go to the jury, on his plea that he had been compelled by terrorists to accept the ammunition and feared for his safety if the terrorists returned.

In the present case the threats of Farrell were likely to be no less compelling, because their execution could not be effected in the court room, if they could be carried out in the streets of Salford the same night. Insofar, therefore, as the recorder ruled as a matter of law that the threats were not sufficiently present and immediate to support the defence of duress we think that he was in error. He should have left the jury to decide whether the threats had overborne the will of the appellants at the time when they gave the false evidence.

Counsel for the Crown, however, contends that the recorder's ruling can be supported on another ground, namely, that the appellants should have taken steps to neutralise the threats by seeking police protection either when they came to court to give evidence, or beforehand. He submits on grounds of public policy that an accused should not be able to plead duress if he had the opportunity to ask for protection from the police before committing the offence and failed to do so. The argument does not distinguish cases in which the police would be able to provide effective protection, from those when they would not, and it would, in effect, restrict the defence of duress to cases where the person threatened had been kept in custody by the maker of the threats, or where the time interval between the making of the threats and the commission of the offence had made recourse to the police impossible. We recognise the need to keep the defence of duress within reasonable bounds but cannot accept so severe a restriction on it. The duty, of the person threatened, to take steps to remove the threat does not seem to have arisen in an English case but in a full review of the defence of duress in the Supreme Court of Victoria (*Hurley and Murray* [[1967] VR 526]), a condition of raising the defence was said to be that the accused 'had no means, with safety to himself, of preventing the execution of the threat'.

In the opinion of this court it is always open to the Crown to prove that the accused failed to avail himself of some opportunity which was reasonably open to him to render the threat ineffective, and that on this being established the threat in question can no longer be relied on by the defence. In deciding whether such an opportunity was reasonably open to the accused the jury should have regard to his age and circumstances, and to any risks to him which may be involved in the course of action relied on.

In our judgment the defence of duress should have been left to the jury in the present case, as should any issue raised by the Crown and arising out of the appellants' failure to seek police protection. The appeals will, therefore, be allowed and the convictions quashed.

Appeals allowed

What does Lord Widgery mean when he says 'the will of the accused has been overborne by threats . . . so that the commission of the alleged offence was no longer the voluntary act of the accused'? In what sense was the act not voluntary? Duress is a defence to causing gbh with intent but not to murder. Suppose D is acquitted of gbh on the ground of duress but the victim then dies of the gbh inflicted by D and he is charged (as he could be) with murder. Can we sensibly say, at the first trial, that D's act was involuntary and at the second that it was voluntary? A person whose act is involuntary in the sense of the automatism cases (above, p 20) cannot be convicted of any crime, including murder. Does 'not voluntary' here mean 'He would not have done it but for the threat and the threat was one he could not be expected to resist'?—or what?

In *Abdul-Hussain* [1999] Crim LR 570 the appellants were convicted of hijacking, contrary to s 1(1) of the Aviation Security Act 1982. They were Shiite Muslims from southern Iraq, living in Sudan and they feared return by the Sudanese authorities to Iraq, followed by torture and probable death. Using imitation hand grenades and plastic knives, they hijacked an aircraft bound for Amman and eventually landed in England. The judge withdrew the defence of duress from the jury. Citing *Cole* [1994] Crim LR 582 and *Loughnan* [1981] VR 443, he ruled:

The established limits of the defence of necessity involve…a connection between the threat and criminal act so close and immediate as will give rise to what is virtually a spontaneous reaction to the physical risk arising.…

I am quite clear that the situation in which these defendants found themselves falls short of that very strict requirement. The connection relied upon on behalf of the defendants requires, as it seems to me, a series of contingent and consequential steps. First, detection. Secondly, a decision by the Sudanese authorities to arrest.… Third, having been arrested, a decision to deport…Fourthly, the actual act of deportation itself.…

Following *Hudson and Taylor*, above, p **399**, the Court of Appeal held that the defence should have been left to the jury. While the threat must be 'imminent', it need not be 'immediate'; nor need the reaction be 'spontaneous'. The appellants were in no immediate danger of death or serious bodily harm, but there was evidence that the threat was hanging over them, that it was 'imminent'. In *Cole* the court spoke of immediacy as a requirement; but the present court thought that the court in *Cole* might have taken a different view had the argument exposed the difference between imminence and immediacy. If *Cole* was inconsistent with *Hudson and Taylor*, the court preferred, and, in any event, was bound by, *Hudson and Taylor*. *Cole*, a case of duress by threats, is, however, by no means the only case in which reference is made to a requirement of immediacy.

The Draft Code, cl 42 (Duress by threats), states that the defendant must believe 'that the threat will be carried out immediately if he does not do the act or, if not immediately, before he … can obtain official protection' and the law was stated in the same terms in *A-G v Whelan* [1934] IR 518 (Irish CCA) and *Hurst* [1995] 1 Cr App R 82 at 93.

Clause 43 of the Code (Duress of circumstances) requires a belief that the relevant act is 'immediately necessary'. *Abdul Hussain* is a case of duress of circumstances. The court gave a vivid and persuasive example to support its decision.

If Anne Frank had stolen a car to escape from Amsterdam and been charged with theft, the tenets of English law would not, in our judgment, have denied her a defence of duress of circumstances, on the ground that she should have waited for the Gestapo's knock on the door.

In *Hasan*, (above p **387**) the trial judge had directed the jury that, 'The third question is: Could the defendant have avoided acting as he did without harm coming to his family?… If you are sure that he could have avoided acting as he did without harm coming to his family, again the defence fails and he is guilty.'

Lord Bingham:

24. As recorded…above, the Court of Appeal held that the judge had misdirected the jury on question 3 because, it was held, there was no suggestion that the defendant could have taken evasive action. This may, or may not, on the facts, be so, and this suggested misdirection does not feature in the question on duress certified for the opinion of the House.…..the third question put by the judge, and regularly put in such cases, whether or not correctly put on the facts of this case, in my opinion focuses attention on a cardinal feature of the defence of duress, and I would wish to warn against any

general notion that question 3 'collapses' into [the question about whether D has responded reasonably to the threat as he reasonably perceives it to be see below, p **404**].

25. In the draft Criminal Code prepared by the Criminal Law Commissioners in 1879, section 23, a defence was provided in the case of 'Compulsion by threats of immediate death or grievous bodily harm from a person actually present at the commission of the offence'. The requirement of immediacy is reflected in the criminal codes of several other jurisdictions. Section 67(1) of the Queensland Criminal Code refers to 'immediate death or grievous bodily harm threatened by someone else able to carry out the threat'. Section 20(1) of the Tasmanian Code refers to 'compulsion by threats of immediate death or grievous bodily harm, from a person actually present at the commission of the offence'. Section 31(4) of the Western Australian Code, section 17 of the Canadian Code and section 24(1) of the New Zealand Code use very much the same language. In Scotland where, as in England and Wales, the defence of coercion has recently enjoyed something of a vogue after a long period of dormancy, the law is clear that a threat, to found the defence, must be of immediate and not future death or serious injury: Hume's Commentaries, vol i, p 53; *Thomson v HM Advocate* 1983 JC 69, 72–73, 75, 80; *Cochrane v H M Advocate* 2001 SCCR 655, 656, 659–661. In *Perka v The Queen* [1984] 2 SCR 232, 251, 259, a decision directed to the analogous defence of necessity, Dickson J identified the necessary conditions as including 'urgent situations of clear and imminent peril' in which 'compliance with the law [would be] demonstrably impossible'. In *Hibbert v The Queen* (1995) 99 CCC (3d) 193, para 49, Lamer CJC quoted with approval the reference by Horder ('Autonomy, Provocation and Duress' [1992] Crim LR 706, 709) to taking 'the necessary evasive action'.

26. The recent English authorities have tended to lay stress on the requirement that a defendant should not have been able, without reasonably fearing execution of the threat, to avoid compliance. Thus Lord Morris of Borth-y-Gest in *R v Lynch*, above, at p 670, emphasised that duress

> 'must never be allowed to be the easy answer of those who can devise no other explanation of their conduct nor of those who readily could have avoided the dominance of threats nor of those who allow themselves to be at the disposal and under the sway of some gangster-tyrant.'

Lord Simon of Glaisdale gave as his first example of a situation in which a defence of duress should be available (p 687):

> 'A person, honestly and reasonably believing that a loaded pistol is at his back which will in all probability be used if he disobeys.....'

In the view of Lord Edmund-Davies (p 708) there had been

> 'for some years an unquestionable tendency towards progressive latitude in relation to the plea of duress.'

27. In making that observation Lord Edmund-Davies did not directly criticise the reasoning of the Court of Appeal in its then recent judgment in *R v Hudson and Taylor* [1971] 2 QB 202, but that was described by Professor Glanville Williams as 'an indulgent decision' (*Textbook of Criminal Law*, 2nd edn, 1983, p 636), and it has in my opinion had the unfortunate effect of weakening the requirement that execution of a threat must be reasonably believed to be imminent and immediate if it is to support a plea of duress. [His lordship referred to the decision in *Hudson and Taylor* extracted above].

The Court of Appeal placed reliance on the decision of the Privy Council in *Subramaniam v Public Prosecutor* [1956] 1 WLR 965. That case, however, involved a defendant who sought at trial to advance a defence of duress under a section of the Penal Code of the Federated Malay States which provided that, with certain exceptions,

> 'nothing is an offence which is done by a person who is compelled to do it by threats, which, at the time of doing it, reasonably cause the apprehension that instant death to that person will otherwise be the consequence.....'

The appeal was allowed because evidence relied on by the appellant to show that he had had a reasonable apprehension of instant death was wrongly excluded. It is hard to read that decision as authority for the Court of Appeal's conclusion. I can understand that the Court of Appeal in *R v Hudson and Taylor* had sympathy with the predicament of the young appellants but I cannot, consistently with principle, accept that a witness testifying in the Crown Court at Manchester has no opportunity to avoid complying with a threat incapable of execution then or there. When considering necessity in *R v Cole* [1994] Crim LR 582, 583, Simon Brown LJ, giving the judgment of the court, held that the peril relied on to support the plea of necessity lacked imminence and the degree of directness and immediacy required of the link between the suggested peril and the offence charged, but in *R v Abdul-Hussain*, above, the Court of Appeal declined to follow these observations to the extent that they were inconsistent with *R v Hudson and Taylor*, by which the court regarded itself as bound.

28. The judge's direction on question 3 was modelled on the JSB specimen direction current at the time, and is not in my opinion open to criticism. It should however be made clear to juries that if the retribution threatened against the defendant or his family or a person for whom he reasonably feels responsible is not such as he reasonably expects to follow immediately or almost immediately on his failure to comply with the threat, there may be little if any room for doubt that he could have taken evasive action, whether by going to the police or in some other way, to avoid committing the crime with which he is charged.

Following *Hasan*, would Anne Frank have been best advised to wait until the Gestapo knocked at the door to be able to plead duress when charged with stealing a car to escape to freedom?

Should the defence be available where D has not taken the opportunity to seek official protection? The draft Criminal Law Bill, cl 25(2) provides, as one of the conditions of the defence, that D does the act 'because he knows or believes . . . (c) that there is no other way of preventing the threat being carried out.'

Is that a satisfactory solution?

7. Must the threat be backed by a demand to commit a nominated crime? In the paradigmatic case of duress, the defendant will have been told by the threatening party 'perform this crime or else'. The question has arisen how specific the nomination of the crime must be for D to be able to rely on the threats.

In *Cole* [1994] Crim LR 582 D was convicted of robbing two building societies and pleaded duress on the basis that he had been threatened by money lenders to whom he was in debt. The Court of Appeal held that a plea of duress was not available as the money lenders had not stipulated that he commit robbery to meet their demands. There was not the degree of immediacy and directness required between the peril threatened and the offence charged.

Subsequently in *Ali* [1995] Crim LR 303, D, a heroin addict, was convicted of robbing a building society and claimed that his supplier, X, who had a reputation for violence, had demanded repayment of money D owed him. Further, that X had provided D with a gun and told D to get the money by the following day from a bank or a building society. The Court of Appeal upheld his conviction but appeared to accept that a threat is capable of amounting to duress when the duressee is charged with robbing a particular building society not specified by the duressor.

In view of the strict approach taken to the issue of immediacy in *Hasan*, doubt must be cast on both authorities.

8. The threat need not exist in fact. There is no requirement for there to be a threat in fact. It is sufficient that D believes that there is a threat of the relevant gravity. If the defence was only available where there was a threat in fact, D could not plead duress where threatened with an unloaded gun, nor where D escaped from prison erroneously believing it to be on fire. This would be unduly restrictive. The existence of a threat in fact is wholly irrelevant if D was unaware of it. It becomes relevant only if, and to the extent that, D is aware of it. Is the existence of the threat any more relevant when D knows of it than when he mistakenly believes in it? Is not his culpability determined exclusively by his state of mind? Is there a case for requiring D's belief to be reasonable in order to deny the defence to those suffering from irrational fear?

Safi and others

[2003] EWCA Crim 1809; [2003] Crim LR 721, Court of Appeal (Criminal Division)

(Longmore LJ, Hooper and Cox JJ)

Afghan members of the Organization of Young Intellectuals of Afghanistan (the 'Organization') hijacked a plane which ultimately landed at Stansted. The defence said that the Taliban had discovered that the Organization was its political opponent, and had arrested and tortured four of its members who between them knew the names of the appellants and most of the other members of the Organization. The defendants claimed that their fear of persecution at the hands of the Taliban constituted a defence of duress of circumstances. The trial judge directed that the defence failed unless there was evidence that there was in fact, or might in fact have been, an imminent peril to the defendants or their families. S appealed on the basis that the defence should be available if he *reasonably* believed that if he had not acted in the way he had, he (and/or the family) would have been killed or seriously injured.

Lord Justice Longmore: [His lordship stated the facts and the grounds of appeal and discussed the inconsistent directions given at the first trial and on the retrial]

The question of law that arises in this appeal can thus be framed as follows, subject always to further consideration if an application is made for a certificate that a point of law of general public importance is involved in our decision:—

> 'Is it sufficient, once a defence of duress is raised, for the Crown to prove in relation to the first element of that defence, that there was no threat or circumstance giving rise to duress in fact or must the Crown prove that the defendants had no belief in the existence of such threat or circumstances.
>
> There may be a further question whether, if the Crown has to prove the latter, the defendant's belief has to be merely a genuine belief or whether it must not only be a genuine but also a reasonable belief. But that does not arise for decision in this case.'

The basis of the directions of Butterfield J [at the first trial]

As we have already indicated, these directions were modelled on the authority of *R v Graham* [see below, p **407**]

The court... doubted whether the Crown were right to concede that the question of duress ever arose on the facts, since... 'the words and deeds of King relied on by the defence were far short of those needed to raise a threat of the requisite gravity.' This is not surprising since, on the facts as reported, there was no evidence of an express threat nor was there evidence that Graham believed that any threat of death or serious physical injury to him existed if he did not take hold of the flex as ordered.

The issue for the Court of Appeal in the *Graham* case did not, in fact, turn on the first (subjective) part of the direction but raised the question whether the second (objective) part of the direction was required at all. The court held that it was and held that the defences of duress and provocation were analogous. In cases of provocation the law required the defendant to have the self-control reasonably to be expected of the ordinary citizen in his situation; so also should cases of duress. Similarly in cases of self-defence, the law only permitted the use of reasonable force. The judge had given a two-fold direction incorporating both the subjective and the objective question, so the appeal was dismissed. But at the end of his judgment Lord Lane CJ, delivering the judgment of the court set out how a jury should be directed:—

> 'The Crown having conceded that the issue of duress was open to the appellant and was raised on the evidence, the correct approach on the facts of this case would have been as follows: (1) Was the defendant, or may he have been, impelled to act as he did because, *as a result of what he reasonably believed King had said or done*, he had good cause to fear that if he did not so act King would kill him or (if this is to be added) cause him serious physical injury? (2) If so, have the prosecution made the jury sure that a sober person of reasonable firmness, sharing the characteristics of the defendant, would not have responded *to whatever he reasonably believed King said or did* by taking part in the killing? The fact that a defendant's will to resist has been eroded by the voluntary consumption of drink or drugs or both is not relevant to this test.' (Emphasis added.)

The passages we have underlined show that the defendant's conduct is to be judged by what he reasonably believed King had said or done both in the first and second questions. It can, no doubt, be said that Lord Lane CJ's formulation of the first part of the direction was *obiter*, but on any view it was carefully considered and must have been intended as a guide for judges who had to direct juries on the defence of duress in future. Moreover, the directions which Lord Lane CJ stated should be given to the jury were approved by Lord Mackay in the House of Lords in *R v Howe* [1987] AC 417, 459 as 'entirely correct'. They have subsequently been followed more than once by the Court of Appeal. In *R v Conway* [1989] QB 290, 298C Lord Woolf giving the judgment of the court said that 'the approach must be that indicated by Lord Lane CJ in *Graham*'. *Conway* was itself approved and followed in *R v Martin* (1989) 88 Cr App R 343.

Reasons for Sir Edwin's ruling [on the retrial]

7. Sir Edwin held that a threat must exist in fact before the defence of duress could be raised because:-

(1) *Graham* did not decide to the contrary, since the Crown had there conceded that duress did arise on the facts;

(2) provocation, with which duress was said to be analogous, required actual words or conduct before the defence could be relied on;

(3) the approval of Graham in *Howe* was irrelevant to the 'threshold' issue for duress;

(4) *Conway* and *Martin* required an actual, rather than a perceived, threat to exist;

(5) the more recent case of *Abdul-Hussain* 17th December 1998, unreported but noted in [1999] Crim L Rev 570, required an imminent peril to exist in fact before duress could be relied on;

(6) the cases of *Cairns* [1999] 2 Crim App Rep 137 and *Martin (David)* [2000] 2 Crim App Rep 42 proceeded on a concession by the Crown, and were decided *per incuriam*.

We have reached the conclusion that the suggested direction in *Graham* continues to be the law in relation to duress and that Sir Edwin was, with respect, incorrect to hold that there must be a threat in fact, rather than something the defendant reasonably believed to be a threat, before the defence of duress can be invoked....

Although it is true that the Crown in *Graham* conceded that duress did arise on the facts and although it is true that the court was critical of that concession, that criticism does not, in our view, undermine the considered direction which Lord Lane CJ thought it right to formulate. It is clear that it is the defendant's reasonable belief in relation to the words or conduct said to constitute the threat for the purpose of the defence of duress that is critical; that is separate from the fact that the defendant must also have 'good cause' to fear death or physical injury. Mr Houlder QC for the Crown submitted that what Lord Lane CJ meant to convey was that there had to be an actual threat *and* the defendant had, reasonably, to believe that there was such a threat. But we cannot so read Lord Lane's words; indeed, if there was a threat in fact, it would be superfluous to superimpose a further requirement that the defendant must reasonably believe there to be a threat. It cannot, moreover, be right to disregard a considered decision as to the appropriate direction to be given to a jury, even if there is, in the background, a dubious concession on the facts by the Crown. The decision was intended to be a guide for future cases and should be so regarded.

Mr Houlder's submission is, in any event, not without its practical difficulties. If a defendant commits a crime as a result of a gun being pointed at him, would it be open to the Crown to prove there was no threat in fact, because the gun was not loaded? If a prisoner escapes from prison thinking there is a fire and he does not intend to 'stay to be burnt' (to adopt the Tudor example cited in *Southwark LBC v Williams* [1971] 1 Ch 734, 746), can the Crown prove there was no fire in fact so that, however reasonable the prisoner's belief may be, he is guilty of the offence of escape from lawful custody? In the present case itself, the judge's ruling led to the Crown calling evidence from the Home Office to prove that there was, in fact, no risk of the defendants' return to Afghanistan from England. The defence, by way of riposte, called evidence from Mr Ian Macdonald QC to show that such risk did, in fact, exist. None of this evidence was necessary in the first trial.

If, moreover, Mr Houlder's submission were correct, hearsay evidence of the existence of a threat would, strictly, be inadmissible. Yet in cases of duress it is routinely admissible as evidence of the defendant's state of mind. In *Subramaniam v Public Prosecutor* [1956] 1 WLR 965 the Privy Council held that what was said to the defendant was admissible to show that he had good reason to fear death or personal injury; there can be no reason to suppose that such evidence could not also be admissible to show the defendant's state of mind in relation to the existence of a threat or other circumstance giving rise to a defence of duress. To adopt Rose LJ V-P's example [In *Abdul-Hussain* [1999] Crim LR 570 above, p **401**], if Anne Frank would have been entitled to invoke the defence of duress before the Gestapo knocked on her door, it might very well be because a sympathiser had informed her that the Gestapo were on their way.

Appeals allowed

The court was clearly concerned by the anxiety that its judgment created a terrorists' or hijackers' charter. It stated:

In the light of some of the newspaper comments on the announcement of our decision, we think it right to add that we do not for a moment accept that the success of this appeal is a charter for future hi-jackers. The only reason why this appeal has succeeded is that there was a misdirection in relation to the law as explained to the jury. An earlier jury was given a direction that, in one respect may have been too generous to the defendants, and was unable to agree. We have every confidence that future juries given a correct direction, in accordance with the law set out in *R v Graham* in 1982, will convict in appropriate cases and acquit, if it is right to do so.

The decision clearly does not give carte-blanche to hijackers. It decides only that the defence of duress was wrongly explained to the jury. If the defence is left to the jury, they would have had to consider whether the hijacking was a reasonable and proportionate response to the threat—an objective question. The onus would of course have been on the prosecution to prove that it was not; but is not hijacking such a dangerous and terrifying operation that the prosecution might well have succeeded? It is to this objective element of the defence that we must turn.

(2) EVALUATING D'S RESPONSE TO THE PERCEIVED THREAT

R v Graham

[1982] 1 All ER 801, Court of Appeal, Criminal Division

(Lord Lane CJ, Taylor and McCullough JJ)

The appellant (G) was a practising homosexual living in 'a bizarre ménage à trois' with his wife (W) and another homosexual, King (K). G suffered from an anxiety state. He was taking valium which, according to medical evidence, would make him more susceptible to bullying. K was a violent man and had in 1978 tipped G and W off a settee because they were embracing and he was jealous. G knew K had been guilty of other acts of violence. On 27 June 1980 K attacked W with a knife. W then went to G's mother's home. G and K stayed drinking heavily while G also took valium. K suggested getting rid of the wife once and for all. G induced her to return by pretending that he had cut his wrists. She knelt beside him, as he lay face down on the floor pretending to be seriously hurt. K put a percolator flex round her neck, saying, 'What's it like to know you are going to die?' She put up her hands to the flex. K told G to pull on one end of the flex. He did so, he said, only because he was afraid of K. The plug which he was pulling came off the flex, leaving it in doubt whether his act made any contribution to W's death. G was convicted of murder.

Lord Lane CJ. . . . The Crown at the trial conceded that, on those facts, it was open to the defence to raise the issue of duress. In other words, they were not prepared to take the point that the defence of duress is not available to a principal in the first degree to murder. Consequently, the interesting question raised by the decisions in *Lynch v DPP for Northern Ireland* [1975] 1 All ER 913, [1975] AC 653, and *Abbott v R* [1976] 3 All ER 140, [1977] AC 755 was not argued before us. We do not have to decide it. We pause only to observe that the jury would no doubt have been puzzled to learn that whether the appellant was to be convicted of murder or acquitted altogether might depend on whether the plug came off the end of the percolator flex when he began to pull it. . . .

The judge then went on to direct the jury that if the answer to that first question [Did G act because he had a well-grounded fear of death?] was 'Yes', or 'He may have been', the jury should then go on to consider a second question importing an objective test of reasonableness. This is the issue which arises in this appeal. Counsel for the appellant contends that no second question arises at all; the test is purely subjective. He argues that if the appellant's will was in fact overborne by threats of the requisite cogency, he is entitled to be acquitted and no question arises as to whether a reasonable man, with or without his characteristics, would have reacted similarly.

Counsel for the Crown, on the other hand, submits that such dicta as can be found on the point are in favour of a second test; this time an objective test. He argues that public policy requires this and draws an analogy with provocation. . . .

[Having considered the authorities and the Law Commission Report (1977, Law Com No 83) para 2.28] As a matter of public policy, it seems to us essential to limit the defence of duress by means of an objective criterion formulated in terms of reasonableness. Consistency of approach in defences to criminal liability is obviously desirable. Provocation and duress are analogous. In provocation the words or actions of one person break the self-control of another. In duress the words or actions of one person break the will of another. The law requires a defendant to have the self-control reasonably to be expected of the ordinary citizen in his situation. It should likewise require him to have the steadfastness reasonably to be expected of the ordinary citizen in his situation. So too with self-defence, in which the law permits the use of no more force than is reasonable in the circumstances. And, in general, if a mistake is to excuse what would otherwise be criminal, the mistake must be a reasonable one.

It follows that we accept counsel for the Crown's submission that the direction in this case was too favourable to the appellant. The Crown having conceded that the issue of duress was open to the appellant and was raised on the evidence, the correct approach on the facts of this case would have been as follows: (1) was the defendant, or may he have been, impelled to act as he did because, as a result of what he reasonably believed King had said or done, he had good cause to fear that if he did not so act King would kill him or (if this is to be added) cause him serious physical injury? (2) if so, have the prosecution made the jury sure that a sober person of reasonable firmness, sharing the characteristics of the defendant, would not have responded to whatever he reasonably believed King said or did by taking part in the killing? The fact that a defendant's will to resist has been eroded by the voluntary consumption of drink or drugs or both is not relevant to this test.

Appeal dismissed

Note

Note that Lord Lane, equating duress with self-defence in this respect, thought that in self-defence the law permits only force that is reasonable in the circumstances and that only a reasonable mistake would excuse. But less than two years later in *Gladstone Williams*, below, p **454**, Lord Lane took a different view regarding self-defence, holding that an unreasonable belief might excuse if it was honestly held. In *Williams* Lord Lane followed *Kimber* [1983] 3 All ER 316, [1983] 1 WLR 1118, a case of indecent assault, where Lawton LJ appreciated the general effect of *DPP v Morgan*, above, p **181**. Should this have required a change of mind by Lord Lane regarding duress as well? In *DPP v Rogers* [1998] Crim LR 202, DC, the court seems to have mistakenly assumed that the Law Commission recommendation for reform of the law (Law Com No 218, 49–51) had been implemented. *Abdul Hussain*, however, confirms that it is still the law that a defendant cannot rely on an unreasonable mistake of fact in order to found a defence of duress of either variety. See also *Safi* (above).

R v David Paul Martin

[2000] 2 Cr App R 42, Court of Appeal, Criminal Division

(Mantell LJ, Turner J and Judge Richard Gibbs)

M was charged with, and admitted that he had carried out, two robberies. He claimed that he was acting under duress by two men. A consultant psychiatrist gave evidence that he was suffering from a psychiatric condition known as a schizoid-affective state which would make him more likely than others to regard things said to him as threatening and to believe that such threats would be carried out. He was convicted and appealed on the ground that the judge had directed the jury that his belief was to be judged against the concept of a reasonable man not afflicted with a schizoid affective disorder.

Mantell LJ: The classic definition of duress is to be found in the speech of Lord Simon of Glaisdale in *DPP v Lynch* (1975) 61 Cr App Rep 6, [1975] AC 653 at pp 23 and 686:

> 'I take it for present purposes to denote such [well-grounded] fear, produced by threats, of death or grievous bodily harm [or unjustified imprisonment] if a certain act is not done, as overbears the actor's wish not to perform the act, and is effective, at the time of the act, in constraining him to perform it. I am quite uncertain whether the words which I have put in square brackets should be included in any such definition. It is arguable that the test should be purely subjective, and that it is contrary to principle to require the fear to be a reasonable one.'

The definition was approved in *R v Howe* (1987) 85 Cr App Rep 32, [1987] AC 417, HL. In the same case Lord MacKay of Clashfern cited with approval the judgment of Lord Lane CJ in *Graham* (1982) 74 Cr App R 235, [1982] 1 WLR 294 at pp 241 and 300…

[**Mantell LJ** quoted from Lord Lane's judgment, above, pp **407–408**]

It is to be observed that Lord Simon left open the question whether or not the fear had to be well grounded and whether the words 'reasonable belief' should be tested subjectively or objectively. The passage cited from *Graham* might suggest the latter. However, Lord Lane considered that duress and self-defence were analogous. It is now accepted that 'the test to be applied for self-defence is that a person may use such force as is reasonable in the circumstances as he honestly believes them to be in the defence of himself or another' (see *Beckford v R* (1987) 85 Cr App Rep 378, [1988] AC 130 *per* Lord Griffiths at 387 and 145). The same subjective approach has been approved by this Court in cases of duress of circumstances or duress of necessity (see *Cairns* (1999) 2 Cr App Rep 137, [1999] Crim LR 826). We cannot see that any distinction should be made in a case of straightforward duress by threat. It follows that in our view the learned judge was in error in directing the jury as he did with regard to the appellant's understanding or perception of the words alleged to have been used. We ought also to say that we have every sympathy for him. *Cairns* had not been decided, let alone reported. Other than *Graham* there was no authority directly in point. However that may be, we are satisfied that there was a misdirection.

[Mantell LJ went on to hold that, notwithstanding the misdirection, the conviction was safe.]

Appeal dismissed

Notes and questions

1. In *Cairns*, in which Mantell LJ also gave the judgment, there was nothing to suggest a departure from the objective test stated in *Graham*, requiring that the accused must have been 'impelled to act as he did because as a result of what he *reasonably believed* to be the situation he had *good cause* to fear…'

The difference between the tests for duress and self-defence may be simply the result of the historical accident that Lord Lane came to appreciate the effects of *Morgan* after his decision in *Graham* and before his decision in *Gladstone Williams*, but the difference certainly seems to exist. However, in *Anthony Martin*, below, p 455, a case of self-defence, the court decline to admit evidence of the kind held admissible in *David Paul Martin*, thus applying a more objective test for self-defence. But *Martin DP* was not cited in *Martin A*.

2. If D strikes V causing him grievous bodily harm, because he believes, honestly but unreasonably, that this is the only way to prevent V from killing or causing serious injury, he may have a defence of self-defence but he cannot invoke duress. The Law Commission found, on consultation, that there was almost no support for the view that D's belief must be reasonable and recommended that the law of duress be assimilated in this respect to that of self-defence. Their draft Bill so provides. Jeremy Horder has argued ('Occupying the

Moral High Ground? The Law Commission on Duress' [1994] Crim LR 334 at 341) that this would be a mistake, criticizing the Commission's 'slavish adherence to subjectivism' and arguing the recommendation (i) overlooks the extent to which the requirement of reasonableness can be sensitive to the fact that people may make mistakes under the pressure of circumstances; and (ii) would permit defendants to indulge prejudice and act without proper regard for the interests of victims who are then harmed or killed by them. He puts the following example:

Suppose D, a racist who considers all Afro-Caribbean people to be by nature violent had only one ground for fearing that the threatener—X, say—would carry out the threat, namely that he was Afro-Caribbean. Under the Commission's proposals, a jury must be told to take the belief at face value without regard to its unreasonableness.

We have to envisage an Afro-Caribbean who has made a threat of death or serious bodily harm, since those are the only threats that are relevant. This threat would not be taken sufficiently seriously by a reasonable 'non-racist' to overcome his fortitude. It would be for the jury to decide whether the alleged belief was, or may have been, truly held; but if D really did believe that death or serious injury was imminent, is his moral blameworthiness in responding to the threat any greater than that of a person who shares the same fear on any other ground—for example, he believes, mistakenly and unreasonably, that X is an inmate of a unit whose members are all offenders disposed to uncontrollable violence? Or he is a notorious paedophile who fears for his life in circumstances where others would not, because he is aware of the hostility of the community. In these cases, if D were to strike the threatener and to rely on self-defence, it is clear that the jury would be required to have regard to his actual belief. Should it be different where his defence is duress?

3. If the jury think that D may reasonably have held the belief alleged and that that belief may have given him good cause to fear, the next question is whether 'a sober person of reasonable firmness sharing the characteristics of the defendant' would have responded as he did. What characteristics are relevant? *Ex hypothesi*, a weak will and irresolution are not. In *Bowen* [1996] 2 Cr App R 157, [1996] Crim LR 577, CA, it was held that a low IQ was not a relevant characteristic:

We do not see how low IQ, short of mental impairment or mental defectiveness, can be said to be a characteristic that makes those who have it less courageous and less able to withstand threats and pressure.

The Court of Appeal reviewed the cases and confirmed the following principles:

(1) The mere fact that the accused is more pliable, vulnerable, timid or susceptible to threats than a normal person are not characteristics with which it is legitimate to invest the reasonable/ ordinary person for the purpose of considering the objective test.

(2) The defendant may be in a category of persons who the jury may think less able to resist pressure than people not within that category. Obvious examples are age, where a young person may well not be so robust as a mature one; possibly sex, though many woman would doubtless consider they had as much moral courage to resist pressure as men; pregnancy, where there is added fear for the unborn child; serious physical disability, which may inhibit self protection; recognised mental illness or psychiatric condition, such as post traumatic stress disorder leading to learned helplessness.

(3) Characteristics which may be relevant in considering provocation, because they relate to the nature of the provocation, itself will not necessarily be relevant in cases of duress. Thus homosexuality may be relevant to provocation if the provocative words or conduct are related to this

characteristic; it cannot be relevant in duress, since there is no reason to think that homosexuals are less robust in resisting threats of the kind that are relevant in duress cases.

(4) Characteristics due to self-induced abuse, such as alcohol, drugs or glue-sniffing cannot be relevant.

(5) Psychiatric evidence may be admissible to show that the accused is suffering from some mental illness, mental impairment or recognised psychiatric condition provided persons generally suffering from such condition may be more susceptible to pressure and threats and thus to assist the jury in deciding whether a reasonable person suffering from such a condition might have been impelled to act as the defendant did. It is not admissible simply to show that in the doctor's opinion an accused, who is not suffering from such illness or condition, is especially timid, suggestible or vulnerable to pressure and threats. Nor is medical opinion admissible to bolster or support the credibility of the accused.

(6) Where counsel wishes to submit that the accused has some characteristic which falls within (2) above, this must be made plain to the judge.......

(7) In the absence of some direction from the judge as to what characteristics are capable of being regarded as relevant, we think that the direction approved in *Graham* without more will not be as help-ful as it might be, since the jury may be tempted, especially if there is evidence, as there was in this case, relating to suggestibility and vulnerability, to think that these are relevant. In most cases it is probably only the age and sex of the accused that is capable of being relevant. If so, the judge should, as he did in this case, confine the characteristics in question to these. [per Stuart Smith LJ at p 166–7.]

If the defendant with low IQ is no less able to resist pressure than a person with average IQ, there is no need to afford him any special treatment. But the court said that persons suffering from a 'recognised mental illness or psychiatric condition, such as post traumatic stress disorder leading to learned helplessness [see *Emery*, below, **412**]' are a category whose condition should be taken into account. Certainly this is so on the subjective issue, that is, whether D's will was in fact 'overborne'; but the question is whether they can be taken into account in applying the objective test. In *Hurst* [1995] 1 Cr App R 82, 90, Beldam LJ said, 'we find it hard to see how the person of reasonable firmness can be invested with the characteristics of a person who lacks reasonable firmness.'

There is an analogous problem in provocation (below, pp **589–614**). One view, now rejected, was that only characteristics which affect the gravity of the provocation are relevant. Those affecting D's level of self-control are not. By analogy, only characteristics affecting the gravity of the threat would be relevant. These, depending on the circum-stances, might include age, sex, pregnancy, physical disability—anything which made the threat more frightening. Characteristics which made it harder for D to resist it, making him a person of less than reasonable firmness—and that would seem to include 'recognized psychiatric conditions'—would not be relevant. Though this was not what the Law Commission intended, their recommendation, if enacted, might be construed to reach this result: The threat must be one which—

in all the circumstances (including any of his personal characteristics *which affect its gravity*) he cannot reasonably be expected to resist. [Italics added]

A further difficulty is that, according to one expert opinion, there are no recognized criteria identifying a group whose ability to withstand threats is reduced and that the test in *Bowen* is unworkable: A. Buchanan and G. Virgo, 'Duress and Mental Abnormality' [1999] Crim LR 517 at 529. However, the courts continue to apply it. In *Rogers* [1999] 9 *Archbold News* 1,

CA, it was held that the appellant's history of 'Asperger Syndrome and other co-morbid conditions which would have made him peculiarly amenable [to threats]' should have been taken into account. On the other hand in *Hegarty* [1994] Crim LR 353 evidence that the defendant was 'emotionally unstable' and 'in a grossly elevated neurotic state' was not to be taken into account in applying the objective test. In *Hurst* (above) the judge refused to admit the evidence of a psychiatrist of the effect of sexual abuse upon the defendant as a child. It was held that he was right to do so, even if it indicated that D, due to her experiences, suffered from a personality defect which made her lack the firmness and resolution to be expected of someone of her age and sex.

Horder is also critical of this aspect of the Law Commission's proposal. He puts the case of a practising paedophile who has been threatened with serious injury unless he has intercourse with a child. 'The fact that he is inured to intercourse with children might well be something that made it less reasonable to expect him to resist the threat.' But does the fact that D is a paedophile affect the 'gravity of the threat'? The threat to beat him up might be more terrifying because D is small, or a haemophiliac, or otherwise physically vulnerable; but is it any more terrifying because he happens to be a paedophile? The fact that D is a 'racist' may cause him more readily to succumb to a demand that he assault a person of a different race; but does it affect the gravity of a threat to slash his face if he does not do so? Are not paedophilia and racism irrelevant by any test?

4. A simple threat to twist an arm is one thing. A threat to twist an arm after 24 hours of continuous arm-twisting is quite another. The man of reasonable fortitude who would certainly resist the former may well succumb to the latter. Attention cannot reasonably be confined to the final act which caused the defendant to give way. In *Emery* (1992) 14 Cr App R (S) 394, discussed in the commentary on *Hegarty*, above, D relied unsuccessfully on duress to a charge of cruelty to a child. The Court of Appeal held that expert medical evidence admitted at the trial was allowed to go too far but that it would have been properly admitted if it had been confined to 'an expert account of the cause of the condition of dependent helplessness, the circumstances in which it might arise and what level of abuse would be required to produce it.' Lord Taylor CJ said:

The question for the doctors was whether a woman of reasonable firmness with the characteristics of Miss Emery, if abused in the same manner which she said, would have had her will crushed so that she could not have protected the child.

Obviously a woman of reasonable firmness suffering from a condition of dependent helplessness would be a contradiction in terms. Is the point that the alleged history of violence said to have produced that condition is all part of the duress? Does the jury have to envisage an ordinary woman who is of reasonable firmness before the history of violence begins and consider whether, by the time of the alleged offence, her will would have been so overborne that she would be unable to resist the threat? In *Emery* the ill-treatment of the child was an ongoing state of affairs. If the defendant was a person of reasonable firmness when she began to commit the crime she was presumably then liable and continued to be liable for acts done up to the point when it became unreasonable to expect her to escape from or resist the threat. After that point, she had the defence but only in respect of acts done to the child thereafter. If she had a defence to the cruelty offences would she not, once reduced to 'dependent helplessness' also have had a defence to any other crimes committed in response to her oppressor's threats—for example, to rob a bank or to inflict grievous bodily harm?

(3) TO WHICH CRIMES IS DURESS AVAILABLE?

Lynch v Director of Public Prosecutions for Northern Ireland
[1975] 1 All ER 913, House of Lords

(Lords Morris of Borth-y-Gest, Wilberforce, Simon of Glaisdale, Kilbrandon, Edmund-Davies)

The appellant was summoned by Meehan, a well-known and ruthless gunman, and ordered to drive Meehan and his accomplices to a place where they intended to kill, and did kill, a policeman. The appellant remained in the car while the shooting took place and drove the gunmen away afterwards. There was evidence that it would be perilous to disobey Meehan and, on the occasion in question, he gave his instructions in a manner which indicated that he would tolerate no disobedience. The appellant testified that he believed that, if he had disobeyed the instructions, he would have been shot. He was convicted of murder and appealed. His appeal was dismissed by the Court of Criminal Appeal for Northern Ireland.

[**Lord Morris of Borth-y-Gest** made a speech allowing the appeal.]

[**Lord Wilberforce,** having held that duress is in general a defence to crime, including crimes requiring proof of intention, continued:]

What reason then can there be for excepting murder? One may say—as some authorities do (cf *A-G v Whelan* per Murnaghan J [[1934] IR 518 at 526], *Hurley and Murray* per Smith J [[1967] VR 526 at 543]) that murder is the most heinous of crimes: so it may be, and in some circumstances, a defence of duress in relation to it should be correspondingly hard to establish. Indeed, to justify the deliberate killing by one's own hand of another human being may be something that no pressure or threat even to one's own life which can be imagined can justify—no such case ever seems to have reached the courts. But if one accepts the test of heinousness, this does not, in my opinion, involve that all cases of what is murder in law must be treated in the same way. Heinousness is a word of degree, and that there are lesser degrees of heinousness, even of involvement in homicide, seems beyond doubt. An accessory before the fact, or an aider or abettor, may (not necessarily must) bear a less degree than the actual killer: and even if the rule of exclusion is absolute, or nearly so in relation to the latter, it need not be so in lesser cases. Nobody would dispute that the greater the degree of heinousness of the crime, the greater and less resistable must be the degree of pressure, if pressure is to excuse. Questions of this kind where it is necessary to weigh the pressures acting on a man against the gravity of the act he commits are common enough in the criminal law, for example with regard to provocation and self-defence: their difficulty is not a reason for a total rejection of the defence. To say that the defence may be admitted in relation to some degrees of murder, but that its admission in cases of direct killing by a first degree principal is likely to be attended by such great difficulty as almost to justify a ruling that the defence is not available, is not illogical. It simply involves the recognition that by sufficiently adding to the degrees, one may approach an absolute position.

So I find no convincing reason, on principle, why, if a defence of duress in the criminal law exists at all, it should be absolutely excluded in murder charges whatever the nature of the charge; hard to establish, yes, in case of direct killing so hard that perhaps it will never be proved; but in other cases to be judged, strictly indeed, on the totality of facts. Exclusion, if not arbitrary, must be based either on authority or policy. I shall deal with each.

[His Lordship examined the authorities and continued:] The conclusion which I deduce is that although, in a case of actual killing by a first degree principal the balance of judicial authority at the present time is against the admission of the defence of duress, in the case of lesser degrees of participation, the balance is, if anything, the other way. At the very least, to admit the defence in such cases involves no departure from established decisions....

The broad question remains how this House, clearly not bound by any precedent, should now state the law with regard to this defence in relation to the facts of the present case. I have no doubt that it is open to us, on normal judicial principles, to hold the defence admissible. We are here in the domain of the common law; our task is to fit what we can see as principle and authority to the facts before us, and it is no obstacle that these facts are new. The judges have always assumed responsibility for deciding questions of principle relating to criminal liability and guilt and particularly for setting the standards by which the law expects normal men to act. In all such matters as capacity, sanity, drunkenness, coercion, necessity, provocation, self-defence, the common law, through the judges, accepts and sets the standards of right-thinking men of normal firmness and humanity at a level which people can accept and respect. The House is not inventing a new defence; on the contrary, it would not discharge its judicial duty if it failed to define the law's attitude to this particular defence in particular circumstances. I would decide that the defence is in law admissible in a case of aiding and abetting murder, and so in the present case. I would leave cases of direct killing by a principal in the first degree to be dealt with as they arise.

It is said that such persons as the appellant can always be safeguarded by action of the executive which can order an imprisoned person to be released. I firmly reject any such argument. A law, which requires innocent victims of terrorist threats to be tried for murder and convicted as murderers, is an unjust law even if the executive, resisting political pressures, may decide, after it all, and within the permissible limits of the prerogative to release them. Moreover, if the defence is excluded in law, much of the evidence which would prove the duress would be inadmissible at the trial, not brought out in court, and not tested by cross-examination. The validity of the defence is far better judged by a jury, after proper direction and a fair trial, than by executive officials; and if it is said that to allow the defence will be to encourage fictitious claims of pressure I have enough confidence in our legal system to believe that the process of law is a better safeguard against this than enquiry by a Government department.

I would allow the appeal...

[**Lord Simon of Glaisdale** and **Lord Kilbrandon** made speeches in favour of dismissing the appeal.]

[**Lord Edmund-Davies** made a speech allowing the appeal.]

Appeal allowed: new trial ordered

Abbott v R
[1976] 3 All ER 140, Privy Council

(Lords Wilberforce, Hailsham of St Marylebone, Kilbrandon, Salmon and Edmund-Davies)

The appellant was induced to take part in the murder of Gale Benson as a result of threats against his own and his mother's life made by one Malik, who was subsequently hanged for murder. In the appellant's view Malik's 'respectability' made complaint to the police futile. He dug a hole for the body, and held the victim as she was stabbed by another man. She was left dying in the hole, which was then filled in by the appellant and three other men while the deceased was still alive. Death was caused by (1) the stab wound and (2) the inhalation of dirt. Lord Salmon said it was 'clearly hopeless' to argue that the appellant was only a principal in the second degree. The appellant argued unsuccessfully that duress was available as a defence to a principal in the first degree.

Lord Salmon. . . . Whilst their Lordships feel bound to accept the decision of the House of Lords in *Lynch v DPP for Northern Ireland* [p **413**, above] they find themselves constrained to say that had they considered (which they do not) that that decision was an authority which required the extension of the doctrine to cover cases like the present, they would not have accepted it. . . .

Prior to the present case it has never even been argued in England or any other part of the Commonwealth that duress is a defence to a charge of murder by a principal in the first degree. The only case in which such a view was canvassed is *S v Goliath* [1972 (3) SA 1]; this was a case decided under a mixture of Roman-Dutch and English law after South Africa had left the Commonwealth. From time immemorial it has been accepted by the common law of England that duress is no defence to murder, certainly not to murder by a principal in the first degree.

Counsel for the appellant has argued that the law presupposes a degree of heroism of which the ordinary man is incapable and which therefore should not be expected of him and that modern conditions and concepts of humanity have rendered obsolete the rule that the actual killer cannot rely on duress as a defence. Their Lordships do not agree. In the trials of those responsible for wartime atrocities such as mass killings of men, women or children, inhuman experiments on human beings, often resulting in death, and like crimes, it was invariably argued for the defence that these atrocities should be excused on the ground that they resulted from superior orders and duress: if the accused had refused to do these dreadful things, they would have been shot and therefore they should be acquitted and allowed to go free. This argument has always been universally rejected. Their Lordships would be sorry indeed to see it accepted by the common law of England.

It seems incredible to their Lordships that in any civilised society, acts such as the appellant's, whatever threats may have been made to him, could be regarded as excusable or within the law. We are not living in a dream world in which the mounting wave of violence and terrorism can be contained by strict logic and intellectual niceties alone. Common sense surely reveals the added dangers to which in this modern world the public would be exposed, if the change in the law proposed on behalf of the appellant were effected. It might well, as Lord Simon of Glaisdale said in *Lynch v DPP for Northern Ireland*, prove to be a charter for terrorists, gang leaders and kidnappers. A terrorist of notorious violence might, eg threaten death to A and his family unless A obeys his instructions to put a bomb with a time fuse set by A in a certain passenger aircraft and/or in a thronged market, railway station or the like. A, under duress, does obey his instructions and as a result, hundreds of men, women and children are killed or mangled. Should the contentions made on behalf of the appellant be correct, A would have a complete defence and, if charged, would be bound to be acquitted and set at liberty. Having now gained some real experience and expertise, he might again be approached by the terrorist who would make the same threats and exercise the same duress under which A would then give a repeat performance, killing even more men, women and children. Is there any limit to the number of people you may kill to save your own life and that of your family?

We have been reminded that it is an important part of the judge's role to adapt and develop the principles of the common law to meet the changing needs of time. Their Lordships, however, are firmly of the opinion that the invitation extended to them on behalf of the appellant goes far beyond adapting and developing the principles of the common law. What has been suggested is the destruction of a fundamental doctrine of our law which might well have far-reaching and disastrous consequences for public safety, to say nothing of its important social, ethical and maybe political implications. Such a decision would be far beyond their Lordships' powers even if they approved—as they certainly do not—of this revolutionary change in the law proposed on behalf of the appellant. Judges have no power to create new criminal offences nor, in their Lordships' opinion, for the reasons already stated, have they the power to invent a new defence to murder which is entirely contrary to fundamental legal doctrine, accepted for hundreds of years without question. If a policy change of such fundamental nature were to be made it could, in their Lordships' view, be made only by Parliament.

[**Lord Wilberforce** and **Lord Edmund-Davies** gave a dissenting judgment.]

Appeal dismissed

R v Howe and Bannister; R v Burke and Clarkson
[1987] 1 All ER 771, House of Lords

(Lord Hailsham LC, Lords Bridge, Brandon, Griffiths and Mackay)

There were two separate cases.

(1) The appellants, Howe and Bannister, were charged with murder together with Murray and Bailey who pleaded guilty. The four of them drove Elgar, whom Murray had offered a job, to a remote spot. Murray told the appellants that Elgar was a 'grass' and they were going to kill him. Both appellants kicked and punched Elgar and he was finally strangled by Bailey. The appellants said they attacked Elgar only because they believed they would receive the same treatment if they did not. Very similar events resulted in the death of another man, Pollitt. The appellants appealed against their conviction for murder on the ground, inter alia, that the judge had misdirected the jury that the defence of duress was not available to a person charged as a principal in the first degree to murder.

(2) Burke shot a criminal, Botton, on the doorstep of Botton's house. The prosecution alleged that he had done this at the request of Clarkson who was anxious to prevent Botton giving evidence against him. Clarkson's defence was that he had nothing to do with the shooting. Burke's defence was that he had agreed to shoot Botton only out of fear of Clarkson; but that, in the event, the gun went off accidentally and the killing was unintentional and therefore only manslaughter. See below, p 622.

Burke appealed on the ground, inter alia, that the judge had misdirected the jury in not leaving the defence of duress to them on the murder charge. The appeals were dismissed by the Court of Appeal.

One of the questions certified for the House of Lords was: 'Is duress available to a person charged with murder as principal in the first degree (the actual killer)?' The House dismissed the appeal, holding that the defence of duress is not available to a person charged with murder whether as principal or as accessory and overruling *Lynch*'s case.

[**Lord Hailsham** and **Lord Bridge** made speeches dismissing the appeal.]

Lord Brandon. My Lords, I have had the advantage of reading in draft the speech prepared by my noble and learned friend Lord Mackay. I agree with it, and for the reasons which he gives I would dismiss the appeal.

I cannot pretend, however, that I regard the outcome as satisfactory. It is not logical, and I do not think it can be just, that duress should afford a complete defence to charges of all crimes less grave than murder, but not even a partial defence to a charge of that crime. I say nothing as to treason, for that is not here in issue. I am persuaded, nevertheless, to agree with my noble and learned friend by three considerations. Firstly, it seems to me that, so far as the defence of duress is concerned, no valid distinction can be drawn between the commission of murder by one who is a principal in the first degree and one who is a principal in the second degree. Secondly, I am satisfied that the common law of England has developed over several centuries in such a way as to produce the illogical, and as I think unjust, situation to which I have referred. Thirdly, I am convinced that, if there is to be any alteration in the law on such an important and controversial subject, that alteration should be made by legislation and not by judicial decision.

[**Lord Griffiths** made a speech dismissing the appeal.]

Lord Mackay. The question whether duress is available as a defence in law to a person charged with murder as a principal in the first degree (the actual killer) has not been the subject of a previous decision of this House. The matter received consideration in this House in *Lynch v DPP for Northern Ireland* ...

It was accepted by the majority of the House in *Lynch's* case that at that time the balance of such judicial authority as existed was against the admission of the defence of duress in cases of first degree murder. The writers were generally agreed in saying that the defence was not available in murder although later writers appear to have said so following Hale. The references are *Hale's Pleas of the Crown* (I Hale PC (1736) 51, 434); *East's Pleas of the Crown* (I East PC (1803) 294); *Blackstone's Commentaries on the Laws of England* (4 Bl Com (1809 edn) 30); Glanville Williams *Criminal Law: The General Part* (2nd edn, 1961) p 759, para 247; *Russell on Crime* (12th edn, 1964) vol 1, pp 90–91; Smith and Hogan *Criminal Law* (3rd edn, 1973) pp 166–167....

Counsel for Burke, Bannister and Howe in his very detailed and careful submission accepted this position as reflecting the law up to the time of *Lynch's* case. Since that time, on this question there has been the decision of the Privy Council in *Abbott v R* [1976] 3 All ER 140, [1977] AC 755, a majority decision in which the minority consisted of Lord Wilberforce and Lord Edmund-Davies, who, along with Lord Morris, had constituted the majority in *Lynch's* case. Counsel for these appellants submitted that your Lordships should hold that the reasoning of the majority in *Lynch's* case should be applied and extended to cover the present cases. He recognised that this would involve a change in the law on this matter but argued that the change was one which your Lordships should properly decide to make as the consequence of the decision of the House in *Lynch's* case....

In the present appeal, as I have said, the reason advanced on behalf of the appellants to allow the defence of duress to persons in the appellants' position as the actual killers is based on the assertion that this House in *Lynch's* case allowed it to a person who was charged with murder as a principal in the second degree otherwise described as an aider and abettor and that there was no relevant distinction between that case and the case of the actual killer. He submitted that the reasoning of the majority in *Lynch's* case when logically applied to the circumstances of the present case led to the result that the defence of duress should have been admitted here and that the appeal should accordingly be allowed.

Counsel for the Crown submitted that the appeal should be refused, that the existing law did not allow the defence of duress to an actual killer or principal in the first degree and that if no proper distinction could be made between this and *Lynch's* case the House should decline to follow *Lynch's* case because in his submission the reasoning in *Lynch's* case was flawed.

The first question, accordingly, that arises in this appeal is whether any distinction can be made between this case and *Lynch's* case.

[His Lordship quoted from the speeches in *Lynch's* case.]

In my opinion, it is plain from these quotations that the majority of this House in Lynch's case, and particularly Lord Morris, were reaching a decision without committing themselves to the view that the reasoning which they had used would apply to an actual killer.

While therefore *Lynch's* case was decided by reasoning which does not extend to the present case, the question remains whether there is a potential distinction between this case and *Lynch's* case by which to determine whether or not the defence of duress should be available. I consider that *Smith and Hogan* were perfectly right in the passage cited from that work by Lord Edmund-Davies to which I have already referred. ['The difficulty about adopting a distinction between the principal and secondary parties as a rule of law is that the contribution of the secondary party to the death may be no less than that of the principal': 3rd edn, 1973, p 166.] I have not been able to find any writer of authority that is able to give rational support for the view that the distinction between principals in the first degree and those in the second degree is relevant to determine whether or not duress should be available in a particular case of murder. Whatever may have divided Lord Wilberforce and Lord Edmund-Davies on the one hand from Lord Simon and Lord Kilbrandon on the other, it is apparent that all agree that this is not a distinction which should receive practical effect in the law.

I believe that the discussions of this matter have shown that at one extreme, namely that of the person who actually kills by a deliberate assault on a person who is then present, there is a fair body of support for the view either that the defence of duress should not be allowed or that the practical result will be, even if it is allowed, that it will never be established, while there is also strong support for the view that at the other extreme minor participation which the law regards as sufficient to impute criminal guilt should be capable of being excused by the defence of duress.

So far, I have not found any satisfactory formulation of a distinction which would be sufficiently precise to be given practical effect in law and at the same time differentiate between levels of culpability so as to produce a satisfactory demarcation between those accused of murder who should be entitled to resort to the defence of duress and those who were not.

The House is therefore, in my opinion, faced with the unenviable decision of either departing altogether from the doctrine that duress is not available in murder or departing from the decision of this House in *Lynch's* case. While a variety of minor attacks on the reasoning of the majority were mounted by counsel for the Crown in the present case, I do not find any of these sufficiently important to merit departing from *Lynch's* case on these grounds. I do, however, consider that, having regard to the balance of authority on the question of duress as a defence to murder prior to *Lynch's* case, for this House now to allow the defence of duress generally in response to a charge of murder would be to effect an important and substantial change in the law. In my opinion too, it would involve a departure from the decision in the famous case of *R v Dudley and Stephens* (1884) 14 QBD 273, [1881–5] All ER Rep 61. The justification for allowing a defence of duress to a charge of murder is that a defendant should be excused who killed as the only way of avoiding death himself or preventing the death of some close relation such as his own well-loved child. This essentially was the dilemma which Dudley and Stephens faced and in denying their defence the court refused to allow this consideration to be used in a defence to murder. If that refusal was right in the case of *Dudley and Stephens* it cannot be wrong in the present appeals. Although the result of recognising the defence advanced in that case would be that no crime was committed and in the case with which we are concerned that a murder was committed and a particular individual was not guilty of it (subject to the consideration of the second certified question) that does not distinguish the two cases from the point of view now being considered.

To change the law in the manner suggested by counsel for the appellants in the present case would, in my opinion, introduce uncertainty over a field of considerable importance.

So far I have referred to the defence of duress as if it were a precisely defined concept, but it is apparent from the decisions that it is not so and I cannot do better in this connection than refer to what Lord Simon said on this point in *Lynch's* case [1975] AC 653 at 686, [1975] 1 All ER 913 at 931:

> 'Before turning to examine these considerations, it is convenient to have a working definition of duress—even though it is actually an extremely vague and elusive juristic concept. I take it for present purposes to denote such [well-grounded] fear, produced by threats, of death or grievous bodily harm [or unjustified imprisonment] if a certain act is not done, as overbears the actor's wish not to perform the act, and is effective, at the time of the act, in constraining him to perform it. I am quite uncertain whether the words which I have put in square brackets should be included in any such definition. It is

arguable that the test should be purely subjective, and that it is contrary to principle to require the fear to be a reasonable one. Moreover, I have assumed, on the basis of *R v Hudson* [1971] 2 All ER 244, [1971] 2 QB 202, that threat of future injury may suffice, although Stephen *Digest of the Criminal Law* (1877) note to art 10 is to the contrary. Then the law leaves it also quite uncertain whether the fear induced by threats must be of death or grievous bodily harm, or whether threatened loss of liberty suffices: cases of duress in the law of contract suggest that duress may extend to fear of unjustified imprisonment; but the criminal law returns no clear answer. It also leaves entirely unanswered whether, to constitute such a general criminal defence, the threat must be of harm to the person required to perform the act, or extends to the immediate family of the actor (and how immediate?), or to any person. Such questions are not academic, in these days when hostages are so frequently seized.'

To say that a defence in respect of which so many questions remain unsettled should be introduced in respect of the whole field of murder is not to promote certainty in the law. In this connection it is worth observing that, when in their Report on Defences of General Application (Law Com no 83) the Law Commission recommended that the defence of duress should be available in murder, they suggested a definition of duress which is, I believe, considerably narrower than that generally thought to be available in the present law in respect of other offences. In particular, they required that the defendant must believe that 'the threat will be carried out immediately, before he can have any real opportunity of seeking official protection' and they suggested that the fact that any official protection which might have been available in the circumstances would or might not have been effective to prevent the harm threatened should be immaterial in this context. It is of interest and importance to notice that this point figured long before in Hale's statement which I have quoted. It is to be noted that it was of this very part of Hale's statement that Lord Wilberforce said in *Lynch's* case [1975] AC 653 at 682, [1975] 1 All ER 913 at 928:

'Even if this argument was ever realistic, he would surely have recognised that reconsideration of it must be required in troubled times.'

I notice that in the Law Commission report dated 28 March 1985 (Law Com no 143), which contains a report to the Law Commission in respect of the codification of the criminal law by a team from the Society of Public Teachers of Law, doubt is expressed on the soundness of this recommendation in Law Com no 83. This particular matter does not arise in the circumstances of the present case, but the great difficulty that has been found in obtaining a consensus of informed opinion on it is just one illustration of the uncertain nature of what would be introduced into this most important area of the criminal law if the defence of duress were to be available.

Since the decision in *Lynch's* case the Law Commission have published in their report (Law Com no 83), to which I have referred, the result of an extensive survey of the law relating to duress and have made recommendations on it which have been laid before Parliament. In my opinion the problems which have been evident in relation to the law of murder and the availability of particular defences is not susceptible of what Lord Reid described as a solution by a policy of make do and mend (see *Myers v DPP* [1965] AC 1001 at 1002, [1964] 2 All ER 881 at 886). While I appreciate fully the gradual development that has taken place in the law relating to the defence of duress, I question whether the law has reached a sufficiently precise definition of that defence to make it right for us sitting in our judicial capacity to introduce it as a defence for an actual killer for the first time in the law of England. Parliament, in its legislative capacity, although recommended to do so by the report of the Law Commission, has not taken any steps to make the defence of duress available generally to a charge of murder even where it has the power to define with precision the circumstances in which such a defence would be available.

It has also been suggested for consideration whether, if the defence of duress is to be allowed in relation to murder by the actual killer, the defence should have the effect, if sustained, of reducing the crime to that of manslaughter by analogy with the defence of provocation. Provocation itself was introduced into the law by judicial decision in recognition of human frailty, although it is now the subject of a statutory provision (see the Homicide Act 1957, s 3) and it was suggested that the same approach might be taken now with regard to duress....

In my opinion we would not be justified in the present state of the law in introducing for the first time into our law the concept of duress acting to reduce the charge to one of manslaughter even if there were grounds on which it might be right to do so. On that aspect of the matter the Law Commission took the view that where the defence of duress had been made out it would be unjust to stigmatise the person accused with a conviction and there is clearly much force in that view.

The argument for the appellants essentially is that, *Lynch's* case having been decided as it was and there being no practical distinction available between *Lynch's* case and the present case, this case should be decided in the same way. The opposite point of view is that, since *Lynch's* case was concerned not with the actual killer but with a person who was made guilty of his act by the doctrine of accession, the correct starting point for this matter is the case of the actual killer. In my opinion this latter is the correct approach. The law has extended the liability to trial and punishment faced by the actual killer to those who are participants with him in the crime and it seems to me, therefore, that, where a question as important as this is in issue, the correct starting point is the case of the actual killer. It seems to me plain that the reason that it was for so long stated by writers of authority that the defence of duress was not available in a charge of murder was because of the supreme importance that the law afforded to the protection of human life and that it seemed repugnant that the law should recognise in any individual in any circumstance, however extreme, the right to choose that one innocent person should be killed rather than another. In my opinion that is the question which we still must face. Is it right that the law should confer this right in any circumstances, however extreme? While I recognise fully the force of the reasoning which persuaded the majority of this House in *Lynch's* case to reach the decision to which they came in relation to a person not the actual killer, it does not address directly this question in relation to the actual killer. I am not persuaded that there is good reason to alter the answer which Hale gave to this question. No development of the law or progress in legal thinking which has taken place since his day has, to my mind, demonstrated a reason to change this fundamental answer. In the circumstances which I have narrated of a report to Parliament from the Law Commission concerned, inter alia, with this very question, it would seem particularly inappropriate to make such a change now. For these reasons, in my opinion, the first certified question should be answered in the negative.

It follows that, in my opinion, the House should decline to follow the decision in *Lynch's* case.

Appeals dismissed

Questions

1. Lord Hailsham criticized what he took to be the view of the majority in *Lynch* and the minority in *Abbott* that 'the ordinary man of reasonable fortitude is not to be supposed to be capable of heroism if he is asked to take an innocent life rather than sacrifice his own'. But should a person be liable to conviction for murder for failing to be a hero? Are there no circumstances in which a person of reasonable fortitude would submit to threats? If duress were a defence to murder, would a person have a defence if he submitted to threats which would not prevail upon a person of reasonable fortitude? See K. J. M. Smith, 'Must Heroes Behave Heroically?' [1989] Crim LR 622 and 'Duress and Steadfastness: In Pursuit of the Unintelligible' [1999] Crim LR 363.

2. Lord Hailsham also thought that a man who takes the life of another to save his own cannot claim that he is choosing the lesser of two evils. Suppose that D is told, 'Kneecap

X'—that is, cause him serious bodily harm—'or you, your wife and family will all be killed.' If D does as he is told, and X dies, could not D, being charged with murder, claim that he chose the lesser of two evils?

3. Is it a good argument that Parliament had not acted on the recommendation of the Law Commission some years earlier that the defence of duress should be extended to murder? Does this fact reveal anything about the opinion of Parliament? In *Hasan*, Lord Bingham referred to the Law Commission's view:

The Law Commission has in the past (eg. in 'Criminal Law. Report on Defences of General Application' (Law Com No 83, Cm 556, 1977, paras 2.44–2.46)) recommended that the defence should be available as a defence to all offences, including murder, and the logic of this argument is irresistible.

4. Is it a good argument against allowing the defence that in 'hard cases' no prosecution will be brought (the 'duressee' may be a prosecution witness on the trial of the duressor) or that, if he is prosecuted and convicted of murder (and sentenced to life imprisonment) he will soon be let out (on licence for the rest of his life, of course)?

5. Can it be justifiable that a person who is acquitted, because of duress, of an offence under s 18 of the Offences Against the Person Act 1861 (below, p **698**) should become guilty of murder if his victim dies? How can it be that the act which was excusable as long as the victim lived became inexcusable when he died?

6. The Select Committee of the House of Lords on Murder and Life Imprisonment (1989, HL Paper 78–1, paras 90–92) agreed with the opinion of the Lord Chief Justice giving the judgment of the Court of Appeal in *Howe* [1986] QB 626 at 641:

It seems to us that it would be a highly dangerous relaxation in the law to allow a person who has deliberately killed, maybe a number of innocent people, to escape conviction and punishment altogether because of a fear that his own life or those of his family might be in danger if he did not, particularly when the defence of duress is so easy to raise and may be so difficult for the prosecution to disprove beyond reasonable doubt, the facts of necessity being as a rule known only to the defendant himself.

The Committee thought it would not be appropriate to provide for a defence of duress reducing murder to manslaughter. If, as the Committee recommend, the mandatory sentence of life imprisonment were to be abolished, the judge would be able to take into account any evidence of duress in fixing the appropriate sentence.

Is this a convincing argument? Should the judge take account in sentencing of evidence of duress where he thinks it is just possible, but is not satisfied, that there was duress? Is the refusal of a defence of duress of murder an instance of a 'bad effect' of *Woolmington*, above, p 172.

R v Gotts
[1992] 1 All ER 832, House of Lords

(Lords Keith, Templeman, Jauncey, Lowry and Browne-Wilkinson)

Gotts, aged 16, seriously injured his mother with a knife. He pleaded not guilty to a charge of attempted murder. He sought to adduce evidence that he was acting under duress because his father had threatened to shoot him unless he killed her. The judge ruled that the evidence was inadmissible since duress was not a defence to a charge of attempted murder.

Gotts then pleaded guilty and was put on probation for three years. His appeal against conviction, on the ground that the judge's ruling was wrong, was dismissed by the Court of Appeal, [1991] 1 QB 660, [1991] 2 All ER 1. He appealed to the House of Lords.

[**Lord Keith** (dissenting) said that he agreed with Lord Lowry and would allow the appeal. (1) There was much to be said in favour of the view that the defence was withheld only in the case of murder and treason. (2) Murder is a crime in a category of its own. (3) He found it difficult to accept that a person acting under duress had a truly evil intent. (4) It was unsatisfactory that a defence should be available on a charge of wounding with intent to cause gbh and not on a charge of attempted murder—there being in many cases a nice question whether an offence was the one or the other. The issue was much better left to Parliament.]

[**Lord Templeman** agreed with Lord Keith that the matter would be best decided by Parliament but he would dismiss the appeal for the reasons given by Lord Jauncey.]

[**Lord Jauncey,** having reviewed the authorities and arguments:]

As the question is still open for decision by your Lordships it becomes a matter of policy how it should be answered. It is interesting to note that there is no uniformity of practice in other common law countries. The industry of Mr Miskin who appeared with Mr Farrer disclosed that in Queensland, Tasmania, Western Australia, New Zealand and Canada duress is not available as a defence to attempted murder but that it is available in almost all the states of the United States of America. The reason why duress has for so long been stated not to be available as a defence to a murder charge is that the law regards the sanctity of human life and the protection thereof as of paramount importance. Does that reason apply to attempted murder as well as to murder? As Lord Griffiths pointed out in the passage to which I have just referred—an intent to kill must be proved in the case of attempted murder but not necessarily in the case of murder. Is there logic in affording the defence to one who intends to kill but fails and denying it to one who mistakenly kills intending only to injure? If I may give two examples. (1a) A stabs B in the chest intending to kill him and leaves him for dead. By good luck B is found whilst still alive and rushed to hospital where surgical skill saves his life. (1b) C stabs D intending only to injure him and inflicts a near identical wound. Unfortunately D is not found until it is too late to save his life. I see no justification or logic or morality for affording a defence of duress to A who intended to kill when it is denied to C who did not so intend. (2a) E plants in a passenger aircraft a bomb timed to go off in mid-flight. Owing to bungling it explodes while the aircraft is still on the ground with the result that some 200 passengers suffer physical and mental injuries of which many are permanently disabling, but no one is killed. (2b) F plants a bomb in a light aircraft intending to disable the pilot before it takes off but in fact it goes off in mid-air killing the pilot who is the sole occupant of the airplane. It would in my view be both offensive to common sense and decency that E if he established duress should be acquitted and walk free without a stain on his character notwithstanding the appalling results which he has achieved, whereas F who never intended to kill should, if convicted in the absence of the defence, be sentenced to life imprisonment as a murderer.

It is of course true that withholding the defence in any circumstances will create some anomalies but I would agree with Lord Griffiths that nothing should be done to undermine in any way the highest duty of the law to protect the freedom and lives of those that live under it (see [1987] 1 All ER 771 at 789, [1987] AC 417 at 444). I can therefore see no justification in logic, morality or law in affording to an attempted murderer the defence which is withheld from a murderer. The intent required of an attempted murderer is more evil than that required of a murderer and the line which divides the two offences is seldom, if ever, of the deliberate making of the criminal. A man shooting to kill but missing a vital organ by a hair's breadth can justify his action no more than can the man who hits that organ. It is pure chance that the attempted murderer is not a murderer and I entirely agree with what Lord Lane CJ said ([1991] 2 All ER 1 at 8, [1991] 1QB 660 at 667): '. . . the fact that the attempt failed to kill should not make any difference.'

For the foregoing reasons I have no doubt that the Court of Appeal reached the correct conclusion and that the appeal should be dismissed.

[**Lord Lowry**, having reviewed the authorities and arguments:]

If the common law has had a policy towards duress heretofore, it seems to have been to go by the result and not primarily by the intent and, if a change of policy is needed with regard to criminal liability, it must be made prospectively by Parliament and not retrospectively by a court.

I am not influenced in favour of the appellant by the supposed illogicality of distinguishing between attempted murder on the one hand and conspiracy and incitement to murder on the other and I agree on this point with the view of Lord Lane CJ: short of murder itself, attempted murder is a special crime. But I am not swayed in favour of the Crown by the various examples of the anomalies which are said to result from holding that the duress defence applies to attempted murder. As Lord Lane CJ said, it would be possible to suggest anomalies wherever the line is drawn (see [1991] 2 All ER 1 at 8, [1991] 1QB 660 at 667). The real logic would be to grant or withhold the duress defence universally.

Attempted murder, however heinous we consider it, was a misdemeanour. Until 1861 someone who shot and missed could suffer no more than two years' imprisonment and I submit that, when attempted murder became a felony, that crime, like many other serious felonies, continued to have available the defence of duress.

My Lords, having considered all the arguments on either side, I am of the opinion that your Lordships *are* constrained by a common law rule (though not by judicial authority) from holding that the defence of duress does not apply to attempted murder. Accordingly, I would allow the appeal, quash the conviction and set aside the probation order but, in the special circumstances of this case, I would not propose that a new trial be ordered.

[**Lord Browne-Wilkinson** said that the speeches of Lord Jauncey and Lord Lowry both demonstrated that it was uncertain whether duress is a defence to attempted murder. Their Lordships had to clarify the position. He could see no logical or policy ground for distinguishing between the case of the successful and unsuccessful would-be murderer and would dismiss the appeal. He hoped that Parliament would consider the whole question of duress as a defence to all crimes with particular reference to the question whether duress is not better regarded as a mitigating factor than as a defence.]

Appeal dismissed

Notes

It would certainly be illogical to allow duress as a defence to attempted murder when it is not a defence to murder; but, as Lord Lowry shows, it is equally illogical to allow duress to be a defence to a charge of causing gbh with intent when it is not a defence to the murder which might be charged if the victim were to die of the gbh. So long as duress is not a defence to murder, the only question is, where is the illogical line to be drawn? As far as logic goes, it might as well be under murder as under attempted murder. In Lord Lowry's view, under murder would be the appropriate place, the reason for the exclusion of the defence being 'the stark fact of death'.

Should the defence be reformed so as to be available to murder and attempted murder? The judges in *Howe* and in *Gotts* and more recently in *Hasan* seem generally to accept that the time is ripe for Parliament to consider the defence of duress and to decide whether it should exist at all and, if so, what its extent should be. Lord Lowry says, 'The real logic would be to grant or withhold the duress defence universally.' There appears to be strong judicial support for abolishing the defence altogether, leaving duress to be taken into account as a matter of mitigation. This was the opinion of Stephen J in the nineteenth century. But duress is accepted as a general defence (though not, usually, to murder) throughout the common law world.

If Parliament were to abolish the defence of duress by threats, what would become of duress of circumstances? Since the latter has developed by analogy to the former, it would be logical to decide that they stand or fall together. It would certainly be very strange if the main growth were cut down and the offshoot left standing. It is not clear what effect this would have on the defence of necessity, which certainly exists though its limits are uncertain. It would be absurd to provide that threats, or the imminence of, death or serious bodily harm should never be a defence if other less serious threats or dangers might; so the logical implication might be the abolition of any existing defence of necessity as well. This was at one time proposed by the Law Commission but the proposal attracted such powerful criticism that it was soon withdrawn and the draft Code recognizes that there is such a defence.

Could the problem be solved by providing that the abolition should not extend to any separate defence of necessity existing at common law? If that were done, it would surely allow a defence in some cases which are at present regarded as examples of duress. These are cases where the evil threatened by the duressor materially outweighs that sought to be prevented by the law defining the offence charged. How do we expect a man to behave if he is threatened that his wife and family will be killed unless he drives his car when disqualified from driving? Do our lawmakers wish him to say, 'No, it's against the law. They will have to die?' Rather more realistically, is the bank manager to respond in those words when bank robbers make the same threat to compel him to accompany them to the bank in the middle of the night to open the safe? To exempt such a man from liability would not be merely making 'a concession to human frailty' which is often said to be the basis of the duress defence. It would be to recognize that there are some circumstances in which the most stout-hearted and right-thinking man would break the letter of the law.

Is it a satisfactory answer that the hypothetical bank manager, though in law guilty of the offence, would never be prosecuted for aiding and abetting the robbery of the bank? If he is guilty, is it not the law that it was his duty to leave his family to their fate? Is that a stand that a reasonable and civilized system of law should take?

Does the theory of justification and excuse shed light on the correct way forward? The discussion above supports the view that duress sometimes excuses conduct which would otherwise be a crime and sometimes justifies it. When the duressee's conduct springs from human frailty, duress is an excuse; when it is the natural reaction of a strong but prudent man, it is a justification. This would be significant if the defence of duress was abolished leaving the defence of necessity intact; but, as the law stands, such a distinction has no significance. In either case the defendant is acquitted. As we have seen (above, p 16) it has been suggested that if an act is justified, it is immaterial that the actor is unaware of the justifying facts. But could the bank manager who dishonestly assisted the robber whilst unaware of an existing threat to kill his family or himself claim that his action was justified even if they would in fact have been killed if he had not assisted?

Could the burden of proof be reversed where D pleads duress to murder? It took many years and many cases to establish the generality of the principle in *Woolmington*, above, p 172, that the burden of disproving defences which have been properly raised is, with the anomalous exception of insanity, on the prosecution. The case for shifting the onus of proof of duress (whether by threats or of circumstances) to the defendant is very fully argued by the Law Commission in Law Com No 218, 59–62. In the Commission's opinion, duress is a unique defence in that it is so much more likely than any other to depend on assertions which are peculiarly difficult for the prosecution to investigate and disprove. They distinguish self-defence and related defences on the ground that the circumstances founding such defences are part and parcel of the incident during which the offence was committed. But the difficulties of disproof by the prosecution may be no less in cases of self-defence—as where only the defendant and the person he is alleged to have murdered were present. The Commission cite *Dudley and Stephens*, below, p 437, as an example justifying the shifting of the burden in a case of duress of circumstances; but the difficulties for the prosecution would be no less if shipwrecked mariners claimed they had killed one of their number in self-defence before eating him.

The recommendation would not affect any separate defence of necessity which may exist. If there is such a defence it would surely include duress which would justify, as distinct from merely excuse, D's act. The difficulty of directing a jury if a defence is raised which might amount to one or the other is obvious.

The Commission satisfied themselves that (para 31.1–31.15) the proposal does not contravene Article 6.2 of the European Convention on Human Rights which requires only that there be reasonable grounds for imposing a burden on the accused, that the burden can be fairly discharged and that 'at the end of the process any doubt is resolved in favour of the accused'. That seems to justify only an evidential burden. If the burden *of proof* is shifted, as the Commission intend, any doubt must be resolved in favour of the prosecution. (Cf the doubts expressed by the House of Lords in *Hasan*.)

The proposed shift is, in effect the price to be paid for extending the defence to murder. Is it worth the price?

(4) DURESS OF CIRCUMSTANCES

Curiously, all the early cases on duress of circumstances related to driving offences but *Pommel*, below, p 428, acknowledged the generality of the defence which is confirmed by *Abdul-Hussain*. It applies to all offences except murder, attempted murder and some forms of treason. There is a tentative suggestion in *Abdul-Hussain* that it does not apply to conspiracy; but the defence of duress by threats was held applicable (though not made out on the facts) to a charge of conspiracy to defraud in *Verrier* [1965] Crim LR 732. If duress is a defence to doing something, must it not also be defence to agreeing to do it? Otherwise, might not two duressees find themselves effectively deprived of the defence, whereas, in exactly similar circumstances, one would not?

R v Conway
[1988] 3 All ER 1025, Court of Appeal, Criminal Division

(Woolf LJ, McCullough and Auld JJ)

A passenger in the appellant's car, Tonna, had been the target of an attack on another vehicle a few weeks earlier when another man was shot and Tonna was chased and narrowly escaped.

On the occasion which was the subject of the present appeal, two young men in civilian clothes came running towards the appellant's parked car and Tonna shouted hysterically, 'Drive off.' The appellant drove off because he said he feared a fatal attack on Tonna. His car was chased by the two men in an unmarked vehicle and he drove in a manner which would undoubtedly be normally regarded as reckless. He was convicted of reckless driving. The two young men were police officers who knew Tonna was the subject of a bench warrant but the appellant said he did not know this until after the incident. It was accepted at the trial that the case could not be distinguished from *Denton* (1987) 85 Cr App R 246 where the trial judge refused to leave the defence of necessity to the jury and an appeal was dismissed.

Woolf J:

In *R v Denton* the court went on to comment on another recent decision of this court, *R v Willer* (1986) 83 Cr App Rep 225. In *R v Willer* the appellant had been convicted of reckless driving. As he drove up a narrow road he was confronted with a gang of shouting and bawling youths, 20 to 30 strong. He heard one of them shouting, 'I'll kill you, Willer,' and another threatening to kill his passenger. He stopped and tried to turn the car around. The youths surrounded him. They banged on the car. One of the youths dived on the passenger who was sitting in the back and, in the words of Watkins LJ (at 226):

> 'The appellant realised that the only conceivable way he could somehow escape from this formidable gang of youths, who were obviously bent on doing further violence, was to mount the pavement on the right-hand side [of the road] and on the pavement to drive through a small gap into the front of the shopping precinct (which he did at about 10 miles per hour).'

Subsequently he returned, driving back very slowly, because he realised one of his passengers was missing from the car. Throughout this period there was still a youth fighting with one of his rear passengers in the car, so the appellant drove to the local police station and reported the matter. During the course of the trial Willer changed his plea after a ruling that he was not entitled to rely on the defence of necessity. In dealing with this change of plea, Watkins LJ said (at 227):

> 'Returning to how the appellant came to change his plea, one begins with the reasons advanced by the assistant recorder for declaring that the defence of necessity was not available to the appellant. He seems to have based himself upon the proposition, though saying that necessity was a defence known to English law, that it was not, albeit available to the appellant in respect of the journey through the gap into the car park in front of the shopping precinct, available to him upon the return journey because he was not at that stage being besieged by the gang of youths. We feel bound to say that it would have been for the jury to decide, if necessity could have been a defence at all in those circumstances, whether the whole incident should be regarded as one, or could properly be regarded as two separate incidents so as to enable them to say that necessity applied in one instance but not in the other. For that reason alone the course adopted by the assistant recorder was we think seriously at fault. Beyond that upon the issue of necessity we see no need to go for what we deem to have been appropriate in these circumstances to raise as a defence by the appellant was duress. The appellant in effect said: "I could do no other in the face of this hostility than to take the right turn as I did, to mount the pavement and to drive through the gap out of further harm's way, harm to person and harm to my property." Thus the defence of duress, it seems to us, arose but was not pursued. What ought to have happened therefore was that the assistant recorder upon those facts should have directed that he would leave to the jury the question as to whether or not upon the outward or the return journey, or both, the appellant was wholly driven by force of circumstance into doing what he did and did not drive the car otherwise than under that form of compulsion, ie under duress.'

It will be noted from the passage in Watkins LJ's judgment that in *R v Willer* it was apparently accepted by the assistant recorder and counsel that there could be a defence of necessity to reckless driving. This may explain why the report does not suggest that any authorities were cited to the Court of Appeal, although apparently authorities, including American and Australian authorities, were cited to the assistant recorder.

It is convenient to refer to the 'duress' of which Watkins LJ spoke as 'duress of circumstances'. In *R v Denton* (1987) 85 Cr App Rep 246 at 248, in relation to *R v Willer*, the court said:

'This authority might be taken to suggest that the court assumed that on the facts of the case the defence of necessity could have been raised to a charge of reckless driving. We do not think this authority goes so far. We think it shows that the court doubted whether necessity as a defence could have been raised on the facts of that case but the court saw no need to decide whether such a defence existed as a matter of law. The court said a very different defence was available, which was duress, which should have been left to the jury. It should be observed that where the head-note says ((1986) 83 Cr App Rep 225) "Further the judge erred in ruling that the defence of necessity was not available to the defendant" it is referring to the argument advanced by the appellant and not to the decision of the appellate court.'

The judgment in *R v Denton*, while making this reservation on the decision in *R v Willer* so far as the defence of necessity is concerned, made no similar reservation with regard to what was said in *R v Willer* as to duress. In *R v Willer* there were a number of grounds on which this court disapproved of the way in which the case had been dealt with in the Crown Court. However, in relation to duress we regard the decision as binding on this court.

We have, in addition, had the advantage of having been referred to such other authorities as there are on the subject. In particular, we have been referred to the views of Professor Glanville Williams in his *Textbook of Criminal Law* (2nd edn, 1983) p 517 and Smith and Hogan *Criminal Law* (6th edn, 1988) p 224. We have also been referred to the Law Commission's Report on Defences of General Application (Law Com no 83 (1977)), which recommended that 'there should be no general defence of necessity and if any such general defence exists at common law, it should be abolished'. This conclusion was in striking contrast to the commission's provisional proposals in its Working Paper no 55 (1974), to which we were also referred. We have also seen the Law Commission's report on the Codification of the Criminal Law (Law Com no 143 (1985)), which took the view that necessity should remain as a defence at common law, in so far as it is one already. It appears that it is still not clear whether there is a general defence of necessity or, if there is, what are the circumstances in which it is available.

We conclude that necessity can only be a defence to a charge of reckless driving where the facts establish 'duress of circumstances', as in *R v Willer*, ie where the defendant was constrained by circumstances to drive as he did to avoid death or serious bodily harm to himself or some other person.

As the learned editors point out in Smith and Hogan *Criminal Law* (6th edn, 1988) p 225, to admit a defence of 'duress of circumstances' is a logical consequence of the existence of the defence of duress as that term is ordinarily understood, ie 'do this or else'. This approach does no more than recognise that duress is an example of necessity. Whether 'duress of circumstances' is called 'duress' or 'necessity' does not matter. What is important is that, whatever it is called, it is subject to the same limitations as the 'do this or else' species of duress. As Lord Hailsham LC said in his speech in *R v Howe* [1987] AC 417 at 429, [1987] 1 All ER 771 at 777:

'There is, of course, an obvious distinction between duress and necessity as potential defences: duress arises from the wrongful threats or violence of another human being and necessity arises from any other objective dangers threatening the accused. This, however, is, in my view a distinction without a relevant difference, since on this view duress is only that species of the genus of necessity which is caused by wrongful threats. I cannot see that there is any way in which a person of ordinary fortitude can be excused from the one type of pressure on his will rather than the other.'

No wider defence to reckless driving is recognised. Bearing in mind that reckless driving can kill, we cannot accept that Parliament intended otherwise. When Parliament intended a wider defence it made express provision. Section 36(3) of the Road Traffic Act 1972, in relation to the lesser offence of driving motor vehicles elsewhere than on roads, provides:

> 'A person shall not be convicted of an offence under this section with respect to a vehicle if he proves to the satisfaction of the court that it was driven in contravention of this section for purposes of saving life or extinguishing a fire or meeting any other like emergency.'

It follows that a defence of 'duress of circumstances' is available only if from an objective stand-point the defendant can be said to be acting in order to avoid a threat of death or serious injury. The approach must be that indicated by Lord Lane CJ in *R v Graham* [1982] 1 All ER 801. Lord Lane CJ, in a passage of his judgment approved by the House of Lords in *R v Howe*, said... [The passage is set out above, p **416**].

Adopting the approach indicated by Lord Lane CJ, and not that argued by counsel, which involved a subjective element, we ask ourselves whether the judge in the Crown Court should have left the defence of 'duress of circumstances' to the jury, notwithstanding the submission made by his counsel that it was 'impossible to run the defence of necessity... or indeed leave it to the jury.'

On the facts alleged by the appellant we are constrained to hold that the judge was obliged to do so, notwithstanding the appellant's counsel's submission at the hearing. The judge was referred to both *R v Denton* and *R v Willer*, and it appears that the explanation for counsel not relying on *R v Willer* is that he was wrongly of the view that the facts of this case are indistinguishable from those in *R v Denton*. However, in fact, as indicated by the judge, his client's defence was that he drove as he did because he was in fear for his life and that of Tonna. Although it is unlikely that the outcome of the jury's deliberations would have been any different, they should have been directed as to the possibility that they could find the appellant not guilty because of duress of circumstances, although they were otherwise satisfied that he had driven recklessly.

The jury not having received this direction, this is not a case in which we can properly apply the proviso. On the facts the non-direction related in reality to the appellant's only conceivable defence, and, although unlikely, it is just possible that the jury, if properly directed, would have found the appellant not guilty because of this defence.

Accordingly, we allow this appeal and quash the conviction.

R v Pommell
[1995] 2 Cr App R 607 Court of Appeal, Criminal Division

(Kennedy LJ, Steel and Hooper JJ)

Pommell was found by police at 8.00 am lying in bed with a loaded sub-machine gun against his leg. He said that between 12.30 and 1.00 am, 'I took it off a geezer who was going to do some people some damage with it.' He said that he removed the loaded gun but put it back when he decided to wait until morning to get his brother to hand the gun in to the police. He kept the gun in bed because he did not want his girlfriend to see it. The trial judge ruled that his failure to go to the police immediately deprived him of any defence of necessity that might otherwise have been available. He appealed against conviction for possessing a prohibited weapon and ammunition without a licence, arguing that this ruling was wrong.

Kennedy LJ: There is an obvious attraction in the argument that if A finds B in possession of a gun which he is about to use to commit a crime, and if A is then able to persuade B to hand over the gun so that A may hand it to the police, A should not immediately upon taking possession of the gun become guilty of a criminal offence. However, if that is right, then in 1974, at least in the result, the case of *Woodage v Moss* [1974] 1 All ER 584, DC, was wrongly decided.

The strength of the argument that a person ought to be permitted to breach the letter of the criminal law in order to prevent a greater evil befalling himself or others has long been recognised (see, for example, *Stephen's Digest of Criminal Law*), but it has, in English law, not given rise to a recognised general defence of necessity, and in relation to the charge of murder, the defence has been specifically held not to exist (see *Dudley and Stephens* (1884) 14 QBD 273). Even in relation to other offences, there are powerful arguments against recognising the general defence. As Dickson J said in the Supreme Court of Canada in *Perka v R* (1984) 13 DLR (4th) 1, at p14:

'"... no system of positive law can recognise any principle which would entitle a person to violate the law because on his view the law conflicted with some higher social value". The Criminal Code has specified a number of identifiable situations in which an actor is justified in committing what would otherwise be a criminal offence. To go beyond that and hold that ostensibly illegal acts can be validated on the basis of their expediency, would import an undue subjectivity into the criminal law. It would invite the courts to second-guess the Legislature and to assess the relative merits of social policies underlying criminal prohibitions.'

However, that does not really deal with the situation where someone commendably infringes a regulation in order to prevent another person from committing what everyone would accept as being a greater evil with a gun. In that situation it cannot be satisfactory to leave it to the prosecuting authority not to prosecute, or to individual courts to grant an absolute discharge. The authority may, as in the present case, prosecute because it is not satisfied that the defendant is telling the truth, and then, even if he is vindicated and given an absolute discharge, he is left with a criminal conviction which, for some purposes, would be recognised as such.

It was, as it seems to us, to meet this difficulty that the limited defence of duress of circumstances has been developed in English law in relation to road traffic offences.

[**Kennedy LJ** discussed the cases, including *DPP v Jones* [1990] RTR 33, and continued:]

Commenting on the case of *Bell* [above, p **391**], Professor Sir John Smith has written:

'All the cases so far have concerned road traffic offences but there are no grounds for supposing that the defence is limited to that kind of case. On the contrary, the defence, being closely related to the defence of duress by threats, appears to be general, applying to all crimes except murder, attempted murder and some forms of treason,...': see [1992] Crim LR 176.

We agree.

7. Conclusion

That leads us to the conclusion that in the present case the defence was open to the appellant in respect of his acquisition of the gun.... That leaves the question as to his continued possession of the gun thereafter. In our judgment, the test laid down in *Martin*, [below, p **431**], is not necessarily the appropriate test for determining whether a person continues to have a defence available to him. For example, a person takes a gun off another in the circumstances in which this appellant says he did and then locks it away in a safe with a view to safeguarding it while the police are informed. When the gun is in the safe, the test laid down in *Martin* may not be satisfied: there would then be no immediate fear of death or serious injury. In our judgment, a person who has taken possession of a gun in circumstances where he has the defence of duress by circumstances must 'desist from committing the crime as soon as he reasonably can' (Smith and Hogan, *Criminal Law* (7th edn) p239). This test is similar to the test in *Jones*, to which we have already referred. In deciding whether a defendant acted reasonably, regard would be had to the circumstances in which he finds himself. Can it be said, in this case, that there was no evidence upon which a jury could have reached the conclusion that the appellant did desist, or may have desisted, as soon as he reasonably could? In answering this question, the jury would have to have regard to the delay that had occurred between, on the appellant's account, his acquisition of the gun and ammunition at 12.30 to 1 am, and the arrival of the police some hours later. The appellant has offered an explanation for that delay but, as it seems to us, the defence of duress of circumstances could not avail him once a reasonable person in his position would have known that the duress, in this case the need to obtain and retain the firearm, had ceased. In the present case the judge said that the failure of the appellant to go immediately to the police 'robs him of a defence'. We accept that in some cases a delay, especially if unexplained, may be such as to make it clear that any duress must have ceased to operate, in which case the judge would be entitled to conclude that even on the defendant's own account of the facts, the defence was not open to him. There would then be no reason to leave the issue to the jury. However, the situation does not seem to us to have been sufficiently clear cut to make that an appropriate step in the present case. In the first place, the delay of a few hours overnight might not be regarded as being unduly long and, secondly, the defendant did offer an explanation for it, therefore, in our judgment, the proposed defence should have been left to the jury.

We have considered whether the reloading of the gun and the fact that the appellant had the gun in his bed deprived him of the defence. Must a person who has acquired a gun in circumstances in which he has the defence of duress of circumstances not only desist from committing the offence as soon as he reasonably can but, in the meanwhile, act in a reasonable manner with the gun? The answer is that if he does not do so, it will be difficult for the court to accept that he desisted from committing the offence as soon as he reasonably could. Therefore, in our judgment, the acts of reloading and putting the gun in the bed do not of themselves deprive him of the defence, but are matters which may be taken into account by the jury in deciding the issues to which we have already made reference.

Appeal against conviction allowed

Retrial ordered

J. C. Smith, *Justification and Excuse in the Criminal Law* (Hamlyn Lectures, 1988), discussing *Conway*

It seems probable, therefore, that duress of circumstances, like duress by threats, is a defence to crimes generally, but not a defence to murder, or perhaps attempted murder. It applies not only to an act done for the preservation of one's own life and safety but also to an act done to protect another—probably any other person who is in peril. It does not appear that there was any relationship between Conway and Tonna, other than that of driver and passenger. The case is therefore of considerable importance. Consider the following hypothetical case put by Lord Denning in *Buckoke v Greater London Council* [1971] 2 All ER 254, CA:

> 'A driver of a fire engine with ladders approaches the traffic lights. He sees 200 yards down the road a blazing house with a man at an upstairs window in extreme peril. The road is clear in all directions. At that moment the lights turn red. Is the driver to wait for 60 seconds or more, for the lights to turn green? If the driver waits for that time, the man's life will be lost.'

Lord Denning accepted the opinion of both counsel in that case that the driver would commit an offence if he crossed the red light. Necessity would be no answer to a charge of breaking the Road Traffic Regulations. But would it be the same now that the courts have discovered the defence of duress of circumstances? The threat to the fictional man at the upstairs window seems to be no less than the threat to the passenger in Conway's car. The necessity for immediate action is no less. If we have to look for some relationship between the defendant and the person rescued, that between a fireman and a person imperilled by a fire is surely enough—the fireman probably has a duty to do all that he lawfully and reasonably can to rescue any member of the public. But it is thought that the better view is that no special relationship is necessary. Suppose that Mr Tonna had leapt into the car of a perfect stranger, screaming that he was about to be shot. Would not the stranger be excused, no less than Mr Conway, for any infringement of the letter of the law which reasonably appeared to him to be necessary to save a man from being murdered? Should a private citizen, driving a van with a long ladder, be less deserving of excuse than a fireman because he crossed the red light to make a rescue? I submit, not.

Perhaps Lord Denning would not be displeased by this result. He was applying the law as he believed it then to be; but he said of his hypothetical fire engine driver who crossed the red light: he 'should not be prosecuted. He should be congratulated.' It has always seemed to me very odd that the great Master of the Rolls should find that this conduct was both a breach of the criminal law and a case for congratulation. Plainly, he thought that, from a moral point of view, the driver's conduct was not only excusable but justifiable.

Question

In *Willer*, *Conway* and *Martin* (below) the threat came from the actions of human beings. In *Buckoke* it came from a fire. Is that a material difference? Should it have been different in *Willer* or *Conway* if the threat had come from a wall of floodwater, a runaway lorry or a herd of charging bulls?

R v Martin (CM)

[1989] 1 All ER 652, Court of Appeal, Criminal Division

(Lord Lane CJ, Simon Brown and Roch JJ)

M was convicted of driving while disqualified. He alleged that his stepson overslept so that he was bound to be late for work and at risk of losing his job unless driven there. M's wife, who had suicidal tendencies, was in a distraught state and threatened to commit suicide if M did not drive the boy to work. A doctor had made a statement that it was likely that she would have carried out her threat. M said he drove because he genuinely and reasonably believed she would carry out her threat if he did not. The judge ruled that these facts, if proved, would constitute no defence to the charge, whereupon M pleaded guilty and appealed.

[**Simon Brown J**, having referred to *Conway*, above, p **425**:]

The principles may be summarised thus: first, English law does, in extreme circumstances, recognise a defence of necessity. Most commonly this defence arises as duress, that is pressure on the accused's will from the wrongful threats or violence of another. Equally however it can arise from other objective dangers threatening the accused or others. Arising thus it is conveniently called 'duress of circumstances'.

Second, the defence is available only if, from an objective standpoint, the accused can be said to be acting reasonably and proportionately in order to avoid a threat of death or serious injury.

Third, assuming the defence to be open to the accused on his account of the facts, the issue should be left to the jury, who should be directed to determine these two questions: first, was the accused, or may he have been, impelled to act as he did because as a result of what he reasonably believed to be the situation he had good cause to fear that otherwise death or serious physical injury would result; second, if so, would a sober person of reasonable firmness, sharing the characteristics of the accused, have responded to that situation by acting as the accused acted? If the answer to both those questions was Yes, then the jury would acquit; the defence of necessity would have been established.

That the defence is available in cases of reckless driving is established by *R v Conway* itself and indeed by an earlier decision of the court in *R v Willer*. *R v Conway* is authority also for the proposition that the scope of the defence is no wider for reckless driving than for other serious offences. As was pointed out in the judgment, 'reckless driving can kill'.

We see no material distinction between offences of reckless driving and driving whilst disqualified so far as the application and scope of this defence is concerned. Equally we can see no distinction in principle between various threats of death; it matters not whether the risk of death is by murder or by suicide or indeed by accident. One can illustrate the latter by considering a disqualified driver being driven by his wife, she suffering a heart attack in remote countryside and he needing instantly to get her to hospital.

It follows from this that the judge quite clearly did come to a wrong decision on the question of law, and the appellant should have been permitted to raise this defence for what it was worth before the jury.

Appeal allowed

Threats alleged to be unlawful in international law

In *Jones and others [2004] EWCA Crim 1981*, Ds were charged with conspiracy to commit criminal damage at an RAF base, their defences were duress/necessity, lawful excuse, under s 5(2)(b) of the Act and the prevention of crime, under s 3 of the Criminal Law Act 1967. Each of these defences was predicated on the argument that the UK was engaged in an unlawful act of war against Iraq. At a preliminary hearing, Grigson J ruled that the issue of the legality of the war was not justiciable in domestic courts as the UK government was exercising its prerogative powers relating to foreign policy. (If there is no international consensus on what amounts to a crime of aggression, it is surely undesirable for it to form a part of domestic law.) His lordship made further rulings in relation to the defences. The Court of Appeal held that the defence of duress of circumstances was potentially a domestic law (that is, not international law) defence to a domestic law offence, but no domestic crime was engaged. The executive's action in declaring and waging war was, in itself, a lawful exercise of its powers under the prerogative. The trial court would therefore have to consider the extent to which necessity might afford a defence to the defendants in the light of their beliefs on that basis.

The commentary in the Criminal Law Review [2005] Crim LR 122 observes:

The court's reasoning on necessity is, it is submitted, oversimplified. The conclusion is that no 'domestic crime' is involved by the UK's act of war on Iraq. From that the court concludes that the defences of duress and necessity are unavailable. With respect, it is not clear that this follows. Taking first the defence of duress of circumstances, the requirement is that D (or those he acts to protect) faces an imminent threat of death or serious injury. That does not require that the death or serious injury threatened against him/them is criminal in origin. D might plead the defence where he steals V's car to take to safety his family when they are faced with a threat of death from a looming cloud of noxious gas that has escaped from a factory without criminal fault. The jury, in evaluating the reasonableness of D's response must surely have regard to the type of threat D faces? How can the jury assess the proportionality of D's actions in ignorance of the lawfulness of the action D is responding to?

Turning to necessity, there is no requirement that there is a threat of death or serious injury, nor even a criminal act facing D or those he seeks to protect. The court's suggestion that necessity is only a 'domestic defence to a domestic crime is', it is submitted, far too narrow. Clearly it is its operation as a domestic defence that matters, but since there is no requirement that D's acts are in response to an offence, let alone a domestic one, how can it be limited to acts against domestic crimes? Admittedly, even on a more liberal interpretation of the defence of necessity, it is not clear that the defence would be available to Ds in the present case since the jury would have to be convinced that the actions were reasonable and proportionate to protect people for whom Ds could reasonably regard themselves as being responsible.

3. NECESSITY

Duress of circumstances is treated by the courts in *Conway* and *Martin* as a defence of necessity. As noted above, the effect, logically, should be to extend the defence to some cases where it was previously thought not to apply, as in the conduct of Lord Denning's hypothetical fireman in *Buckoke's* case. It could also have the effect of limiting the defence by importing the restrictions which seem to have become established on the defence of duress by threats—the limitation to threats of death or grievous bodily harm and the objective tests of *reasonable* belief in facts creating the necessity, *good* cause for fear and the response of a person of *reasonable* firmness. Consider whether the following case does not show that necessity is a wider defence than duress of circumstances.

F v West Berkshire Authority
[1989] 2 All ER 545, House of Lords

(Lords Bridge, Brandon, Griffiths, Goff and Jauncey)

F, aged 36, a female patient in a mental hospital, suffered from a very serious mental disability. She had formed a sexual relationship with a male patient. Medical evidence was that, from a psychiatric point of view, it would be disastrous if she became pregnant. There were serious objections to all ordinary methods of contraception. She was incapable of giving consent to a sterilization operation. Her mother, acting as her next friend, obtained a declaration that the absence of her consent would not make sterilization an unlawful act. The Court of Appeal dismissed an appeal by the Official Solicitor who appealed to the House of Lords. The appeal was dismissed. The operation was lawful because it was in the best interests of the patient.

Lord Brandon. At common law a doctor cannot lawfully operate on adult patients of sound mind, or give them any other treatment involving the application of physical force however small (which I shall refer to as 'other treatment'), without their consent. If a doctor were to operate on such patients, or give them other treatment, without their consent, he would commit the actionable tort of trespass to the person. There are, however, cases where adult patients cannot give or refuse their consent to an operation or other treatment. One case is where, as a result of an accident or otherwise, an adult patient is unconscious and an operation or other treatment cannot be safely delayed until he or she recovers consciousness. Another case is where a patient, though adult, cannot by reason of mental disability understand the nature or purpose of an operation or other treatment. The common law would be seriously defective if it failed to provide a solution to the problem created by such inability to consent. In my opinion, however, the common law does not fail. In my opinion, the solution to the problem which the common law provides is that a doctor can lawfully operate on, or give other treatment to, adult patients who are incapable, for one reason or another, of consenting to his doing so, provided that the operation or other treatment concerned is in the best interests of such patients.

The operation or other treatment will be in their best interests if, but only if, it is carried out in order either to save their lives or to ensure improvement or prevent deterioration in their physical or mental health.

Different views have been put forward with regard to the principle which makes it lawful for a doctor to operate on or give other treatment to adult patients without their consent in the two cases to which I have referred above. The Court of Appeal in the present case regarded the matter as depending on the public interest. I would not disagree with that as a broad proposition, but I think that it is helpful to consider the principle in accordance with which the public interest leads to this result. In my opinion, the principle is that, when persons lack the capacity, for whatever reason, to take decisions about the performance of operations on them, or the giving of other medical treatment to them, it is necessary that some other person or persons, with the appropriate qualifications, should take such decisions for them. Otherwise they would be deprived of medical care which they need and to which they are entitled.

In many cases, however, it will not only be lawful for doctors, on the ground of necessity, to operate on or give other medical treatment to adult patients disabled from giving their consent: it will also be their common law duty to do so.

Lord Goff. On what principle can medical treatment be justified when given without consent? We are searching for a principle on which, in limited circumstances, recognition may be given to a need, in the interests of the patient, that treatment should be given to him in circumstances where he is (temporarily or permanently) disabled from consenting to it. It is this criterion of a need which points to the principle of necessity as providing justification.

That there exists in the common law a principle of necessity which may justify action which would otherwise be unlawful is not in doubt. But historically the principle has been seen to be restricted to two groups of cases, which have been called cases of public necessity and cases of private necessity. The former occurred when a man interfered with another man's property in the public interest, for example (in the days before we could dial 999 for the fire brigade) the destruction of another man's house to prevent the spread of a catastrophic fire, as indeed occurred in the Great Fire of London in 1666. The latter cases occurred when a man interfered with another's property to save his own person or property from imminent danger, for example when he entered on his neighbour's land without his consent in order to prevent the spread of fire onto his own land.

There is, however, a third group of cases, which is also properly described as founded on the principle of necessity and which is more pertinent to the resolution of the problem in the present case. These cases are concerned with action taken as a matter of necessity to assist another person without his consent. To give a simple example, a man who seizes another and forcibly drags him from the path of an oncoming vehicle, thereby saving him from injury or even death, commits no wrong. But there are many emanations of this principle, to be found scattered through the books. These are concerned not only with the preservation of the life or health of the assisted person, but also with the preservation of his property (sometimes an animal, sometimes an ordinary chattel) and even to certain conduct on his behalf in the administration of his affairs. Where there is a pre-existing relationship between the parties, the intervener is usually said to act as an agent of necessity on behalf of the principal in whose interests he acts, and his action can often, with not too much artificiality, be referred to the pre-existing relationship between them. Whether the intervener may be entitled either to reimbursement or to remuneration raises separate questions which are not relevant to the present case.

We are concerned here with action taken to preserve the life, health or well-being of another who is unable to consent to it. Such action is sometimes said to be justified as arising from an emergency; in Prosser and Keeton *Torts* (5th edn, 1984) p 117 the action is said to be privileged by the emergency. Doubtless, in the case of a person of sound mind, there will ordinarily have to be an emergency before such action taken without consent can be lawful; for otherwise there would be an opportunity to communicate with the assisted person and to seek his consent. But this is not always so; and indeed the historical origins of the principle of necessity do not point to emergency as such as providing the criterion of lawful intervention without consent. The old Roman doctrine of negotiorum gestio presupposed not so much an emergency as a prolonged absence of the dominus from home as justifying intervention by the gestor to administer his affairs. The most ancient group of cases in the common law, concerned with action taken by the master of a ship in distant parts in the interests of the ship-owner, likewise found its origin in the difficulty of communication with the owner over a prolonged period of time, a difficulty overcome today by modern means of communication. In those cases, it was said that there had to be an emergency before the master could act as agent of necessity; though the emergency could well be of some duration. But, when a person is rendered incapable of communication either permanently or over a considerable period of time (through illness or accident or mental disorder), it would be an unusual use of language to describe the case as one of 'permanent emergency', if indeed such a state of affairs can properly be said to exist. In truth, the relevance of an emergency is that it may give rise to a necessity to act in the interests of the assisted person without first obtaining his consent. Emergency is however not the criterion or even a prerequisite; it is simply a frequent origin of the necessity which impels intervention. The principle is one of necessity, not of emergency.

Appeal dismissed

In *F*'s case the doctor performing the operation would have been guilty of criminal offences of assault and wounding in the absence of some defence. The majority of their Lordships were content that the operation was in the best interests of the patient and in the public interest. But there is no authority for any such general defence to crime and tort. Lords Brandon and Goff searched for a principle underlying the conclusion reached by all their Lordships and found it in the defence of necessity. No such search was undertaken in *Gillick v West Norfolk and Wisbech Area Health Authority* [1985] 1 All ER 553, [1986] AC 112 by any of their Lordships who found to be lawful conduct which, prima facie, amounted to aiding and abetting an offence. The question was: 'whether a doctor may ever, in any circumstances, lawfully give contraceptive advice or treatment to a girl under the age of sixteen without her parent's consent.'

Under the Sexual Offences Act 1956, a man who had intercourse with a girl under 16 committed an offence, but the girl was guilty of no offence, even though she may have incited, aided, abetted, counselled and procured the man to commit it. The provision of contraceptive advice or treatment encourages or facilitates the commission of the offence by removing the inhibition of the risk of an unwanted pregnancy (see now the defence in s 73 of the Sexual Offences Act 2003, below, p 735). The doctor therefore appeared to be a party to the offence, no less than one who supplies equipment to a burglar, knowing that it will facilitate the commission by him of burglaries. The House, Lords Brandon and Templeman dissenting, nevertheless held the question should be answered in the affirmative. According to Lord Fraser the doctor acts lawfully if he is satisfied:

(1) that the girl (although under 16 years of age) will understand his advice; (2) that he cannot persuade her to inform her parents or to allow him to inform the parents that she is seeking contraceptive advice; (3) that she is very likely to begin or to continue having sexual intercourse with or without contraceptive treatment; (4) that unless she receives contraceptive advice or treatment her physical or mental health or both are likely to suffer; (5) that her best interests require him to give her contraceptive advice, treatment or both without the parental consent.

Lord Scarman said:

He may prescribe only if she has the capacity to consent or if exceptional circumstances exist which justify him in exercising his clinical judgment without parental consent. The adjective "clinical" emphasises that it must be a medical judgment based on what he honestly believes to be necessary for the physical, mental and emotional health of his patient. The bona fide exercise by a doctor of his clinical judgment must be a complete negation of the guilty mind which is an essential ingredient of the criminal offence of aiding and abetting the commission of unlawful sexual intercourse.

Lord Templeman dissented only on the ground that the treatment or advice must be given with the concurrence of the girl's parents. He said:

Section 6 of the Sexual Offences Act 1956 does not, however, in my view, prevent parent and doctor from deciding that contraceptive facilities shall be made available to an unmarried girl under the age of 16 whose sexual activities are recognised to be uncontrolled and uncontrollable. Section 6 is designed to protect the girl from sexual intercourse. But if the girl cannot be deterred then contraceptive facilities may be provided, not for the purpose of aiding and abetting an offence under s 6 but for the purpose of avoiding the consequences, principally pregnancy, which the girl may suffer from illegal sexual intercourse where sexual intercourse cannot be prevented.

Lord Brandon thought the contraceptive advice was always unlawful, whether the parents concurred in it or not, because it necessarily encouraged the commission of the offence.

Notwithstanding dicta in the case, the basis for the doctor's immunity does not appear to be lack of the necessary intention because he knows that he is encouraging the commission of the offence and it is no answer for an alleged aider and abettor to say 'It would have happened anyway'. What is the basis of the immunity if not necessity? (See commentary at [1986] Crim LR 114.)

What if the doctor prescribed contraception after the girl told him that she would not have intercourse without it (see Lord Fraser above) but she says that abstinence is making her ill, and he honestly believed that it was necessary for her physical, mental and emotional health (see Lord Scarman above)?

There may be other cases in the medical field where a defence of necessity is the underlying but unexpressed justification or excuse for certain practices. It is possible that a defence of necessity would be available in cases such as the search of a psychiatric patient, for which there was no statutory authority, where there are grounds for believing that the patient may be armed with an offensive weapon which he might use to cause injury or even death if he were allowed to retain it. See M. J. Gunn, 'Personal Searches of Psychiatric Patients' [1992] Crim LR 767, 775.

A more dramatic example is the case of *Mrs S* [1994] 4 All ER 671, where, on 13 October 1992, Stephen Brown P granted a declaration that it was lawful for surgeons to carry out a caesarean operation upon a woman without her consent in an attempt to save the life of her unborn child. The woman, who was competent to make the decision and who was supported by her husband, had refused to submit to the operation because of the nature of her religious beliefs. The evidence of the surgeon was that it was a matter of life and death for both the mother and child and a matter of minutes rather than hours. The operation was carried out but the child died. The life of the mother was saved.

Professor Ian Kennedy is reported in *The Times* to have said of the 'epoch-making' decision:

It has massive implications for the status of women in regarding them as chattels and ambulatory wombs. It is so potentially intrusive as to reduce women back to the status of slaves.

Do you agree? Suppose that the surgeon had decided there was no time to go to court and that, if the child was to have a chance of survival, the operation must be carried out immediately. If he had done so and been prosecuted for assault or wounding, should he have had a defence of duress of circumstances?

R v Dudley and Stephens
[1881–5] All ER Rep 61, Queen's Bench Division

(Lord Coleridge CJ, Grove and Denman JJ, Pollock and Huddleston BB)

The two accused, with a third man and the deceased, a 17-year-old boy, were cast away in an open boat, 1,600 miles from land. When they had been eight days without food and six days without water, the accused killed the boy, who was weak and unable to resist but did not assent to being killed. The men fed upon his body and blood for four days when they were picked up by a passing vessel. At the trial for murder, the jury found by a special verdict that if the men had not fed upon the boy they would probably not have survived the four days; that the boy was likely to have died first; that at the time of the act there was no reasonable prospect of relief; that it appeared to the accused that there was every probability that they would die of starvation unless one of the castaways was killed; that there was no appreciable chance of saving life except by killing; but that there was no greater necessity for killing the boy than any of the three men. The finding of the jury was referred to the Queen's Bench Division for its decision.

[**Lord Coleridge CJ**, having referred to the special verdict, continued:]

…this is clear, that the prisoners put to death a weak and unoffending boy upon the chance of preserving their own lives by feeding upon his flesh and blood after he was killed, and with a certainty of depriving him of any possible chance of survival. The verdict finds in terms that: 'if the men had not fed upon the body of the boy, they would probably not have survived…' and that 'the boy, being in a much weaker condition, was likely to have died before them'. They might possibly have been picked up next day by a passing ship; they might possibly not have been picked up at all; in either case it is obvious that the killing of the boy would have been an unnecessary and profitless act. It is found by the verdict that the boy was incapable of resistance, and, in fact, made none; and it is not even suggested that his death was due to any violence on his part attempted against, or even so much as feared by, them who killed him.…

[His Lordship dealt with objections taken by counsel for the prisoners which do not call for report, and continued:]

First, it is said that it follows, from various definitions of murder in books of authority—which definitions imply, if they do not state, the doctrine—that, in order to save your own life you may lawfully take away the life of another, when the other is neither attempting nor threatening yours, nor is guilty of any illegal act whatever towards you or anyone else. But, if these definitions be looked at, they will not be found to sustain the contention. The earliest in point of date is the passage cited to us from Bracton, who wrote in the reign of Henry III.…But in the very passage as to necessity, on which reliance has been placed, it is clear that Bracton is speaking of necessity in the ordinary sense, the repelling by violence—violence justified so far as it was necessary for the object—any illegal violence used towards oneself. If, says Bracton (Lib iii, Art De Corona, cap 4, fol 120), the necessity be 'evitabilis et evadere posset absque occisione, tunc erit reus homicidii'—words which show clearly that he is thinking of physical danger, from which escape may be possible, and that 'inevitabilis necessitas', of which he speaks as justifying homicide, is a necessity of the same nature.

It is, if possible, yet clearer that the doctrine contended for receives no support from the great authority of Lord Hale. It is plain that in his view the necessity which justifies homicide is that only which has always been, and is now, considered a justification. He says (I Hale, PC 491):

'In all these cases of homicide by necessity, as in pursuit of a felon, in killing him that assaults to rob, or comes to burn or break a house, or the like, which are in themselves no felony.'

Again, he says that the necessity which justifies homicide is of two kinds:

'(1) That necessity which is of private nature; (2) That necessity which relates to the public justice and safety. The former is that necessity which obligeth a man to his own defence and safeguard; and this takes in these inquiries: 1. What may be done for the safeguard of a man's own life;'

and then follow three other heads not necessary to pursue. Lord Hale proceeds (I Hale PC 478):

'1. As touching the first of these, viz, homicide in defence of a man's own life, which is usually styled se defendendo.'

It is not possible to use words more clear to show that Lord Hale regarded the private necessity which justified, and alone justified, the taking the life of another for the safeguard of one's own to be what is commonly called self-defence. But if this could be even doubtful upon Lord Hale's words, Lord Hale himself has made it clear, for, in the chapter in which he deals with the exemption created by compulsion or necessity, he thus expresses himself (I Hale PC 51):

'If a man be desperately assaulted, and in peril of death, and cannot otherwise escape, unless to satisfy his assailant's fury he will kill an innocent person then present, the fear and actual force will not acquit him of the crime and punishment of murder if he commit the fact, for he ought rather to die himself than to kill an innocent; but if he cannot otherwise save his own life, the law permits him in his own defence to kill the assailant, for, by the violence of the assault and the offence committed upon him by the assailant himself, the law of nature and necessity hath made him his own protector *cum debito moderamine inculpatae tutelae.*'

But, further still, Lord Hale, in the following chapter (I Hale PC 54), deals with the position asserted by the casuists, and sanctioned, as he says by Grotius and Puffendorf, that in a case of extreme necessity, either of hunger or clothing,

'theft is no theft, or at least not punishable as theft, and some even of our own lawyers have asserted the same; but I take it that here in England that rule, at least by the laws of England, is false, and, therefore, if a person, being under necessity for want of victuals or clothes, shall upon the account clandestinely and *animo furandi* steal another man's goods, it is a felony and a crime by the laws of England punishable with death.'

If, therefore, Lord Hale is clear, as he is, that extreme necessity of hunger does not justify larceny, what would he have said to the doctrine that it justified murder?

It is satisfactory to find that another great authority, second probably only to Lord Hale, speaks with the same unhesitating clearness on this matter. [His Lordship referred to *Foster's Discourse on Homicide*, chapter 3, and other authorities.]

There remains the authority of Stephen J who both in his *Digest* (art 32) and in his *History of the Criminal Law* (vol 2, p 108) uses language perhaps wide enough to cover this case. The language is somewhat vague in both places, but it does not in either place cover this case of necessity, and we have the best authority for saying that it was not meant to cover it. If it had been necessary we must with true deference have differed from him; but it is satisfactory to know that we have, probably at least, arrived at no conclusion in which, if he had been a member of the court, he would have been unable to agree. Neither are we in conflict with any opinion expressed upon this subject by the learned persons who formed the commission for preparing the Criminal Code. They say on this subject:

'We are not prepared to suggest that necessity should in every case be a justification; we are equally unprepared to suggest that necessity should in no case be a defence. We judge it better to leave such questions to be dealt with when, if ever, they arise in practice by applying the principles of law to the circumstances of the particular case.'

It would have been satisfactory to us if these eminent persons could have told us whether the received definitions of legal necessity were, in their judgment, correct and exhaustive, and, if not, in what way they should be amended; but as it is we have, as they say, 'to apply the principles of law to the circumstances of this particular case.'

It is admitted that the deliberate killing of this unoffending and unresisting boy was clearly murder, unless the killing can be justified by some well-recognised excuse admitted by the law. It is further admitted that there was in this case no such excuse, unless the killing was justified by what has been called necessity. But the temptation to the act which existed here was not what the law has ever called necessity. Nor is this to be regretted. Though law and morality are not the same, and though many things may be immoral which are not necessarily illegal, yet the absolute divorce of law from morality would be of fatal consequence, and such divorce would follow if the temptation to murder in this case were to be held by law an absolute defence of it. It is not so.

To preserve one's life is generally speaking, a duty, but it may be the plainest and the highest duty to sacrifice it. War is full of instances in which it is a man's duty not to live, but to die.... It is not correct, therefore, to say that there is any absolute and unqualified necessity to preserve one's life.... It is enough in a Christian country to remind ourselves of the Great Example which we profess to follow.

It is not needful to point out the awful danger of admitting the principle which has been contended for. Who is to be the judge of this sort of necessity? By what measure is the comparative value of lives to be measured? Is it to be strength, or intellect, or what? It is plain that the principle leaves to him who is to profit by it to determine the necessity which will justify him in deliberately taking another's life to save his own. In this case the weakest, the youngest, the most unresisting was chosen. Was it more necessary to kill *him* than one of the grown men? The answer be, No....

There is no path safe for judges to tread but to ascertain the law to the best of their ability, and to declare it according to their judgment, and if in any case the law appears to be too severe on individuals, to leave it to the Sovereign to exercise that prerogative of mercy which the Constitution has entrusted to the hands fittest to dispense it. It must not be supposed that, in refusing to admit temptation to be an excuse for crime, it is forgotten how terrible the temptation was, how awful the suffering, how hard in such trials to keep the judgment straight and the conduct pure. We are often compelled to set up standards we cannot reach ourselves, and to lay down rules which we could not ourselves satisfy. But a man has no right to declare temptation to be an excuse, though he might himself have yielded to it, nor allow compassion for the criminal to change or weaken in any manner the legal definition of the crime....

[The Lord Chief Justice thereupon passed sentence of death in the usual form. The prisoners were afterwards respited and their sentence commuted to one of six months' imprisonment without hard labour.]

Judgment for the Crown

Questions

1. Should it have been a defence if the boy had consented to die? Andanaes (GPCL of Norway, 171): 'Even though consent generally has no impunitive effect in murder

([Norwegian] Penal Code, s 236, para 2), the situation is different when there is both a necessity situation *and* consent.'

2. Should it be a defence that many lives would be saved by the sacrifice of one? Andanaes (GPCL of Norway, 169) thinks not: 'It would conflict with the general attitude towards the inviolability of human life to interfere in this way with the course of events.'

3. A is injured and needs an immediate blood transfusion to save his life. B is the only person who can be found with the same rare blood group. He refuses to give any blood. May B be overpowered and the blood taken without his consent?

4. Should the criminal law 'set up standards we [reasonable people] cannot reach ourselves'?

See, on *Dudley and Stephens*, A. W. B. Simpson, *Cannibalism and the Common Law* (1984).

Re A (children) (conjoined twins) (above, p 107)

Brooke LJ:

Necessity: modern academic writers

Those who prepared that report [Law Com No 218, 1993] would have been familiar with a modern update of the 'two men on a plank dilemma (which dates back to Cicero *De officiis*) and the 'two mountaineers on a rope' dilemma which was mentioned by Professor John Smith in his 1989 Hamlyn Lectures (published under the title *Justification and Excuse in the Criminal Law* (1989)). At the coroner's inquest conducted in October 1987 into the Zeebrugge disaster, an army corporal gave evidence that he and dozens of other people were near the foot of a rope ladder. They were all in the water and in danger of drowning. Their route to safety, however, was blocked for at least ten minutes by a young man who was petrified by cold or fear (or both) and was unable to move up or down. Eventually the corporal gave instructions that the man should be pushed off the ladder, and he was never seen again. The corporal and many others were then able to climb up the ladder to safety.

In his third lecture, 'Necessity and Duress', Professor Smith evinced the belief at pp 77–78 that if such a case ever did come to court it would not be too difficult for a judge to distinguish *R v Dudley and Stephens*. He gave two reasons for this belief. The first was that there was no question of choosing who had to die (the problem which Lord Coleridge had found unanswerable in *R v Dudley and Stephens* because the unfortunate young man on the ladder had chosen himself by his immobility there. The second was that unlike the ship's boy on the Mignonette, the young man, although in no way at fault, was preventing others from going where they had a right, and a most urgent need, to go, and was thereby unwittingly imperilling their lives.

I would add that the same considerations would apply if a pilotless aircraft, out of control and running out of fuel, was heading for a densely populated town. Those inside the aircraft were in any event 'destined to die'. There would be no question of human choice in selecting the candidates for death, and if their inevitable deaths were accelerated by the plane being brought down on waste ground, the lives of countless other innocent people in the town they were approaching would be saved.

It was an argument along these lines that led the rabbinical scholars involved in the 1977 case of conjoined twins to advise the worried parents that the sacrifice of one of their children in order to save the other could be morally justified. George J Annas *Siamese Twins: Killing One to Save the Other* (Hastings Center Report, April 1987) p 27, described how they—

> 'reportedly relied primarily on two analogies. In the first, two men jump from a burning aeroplane. The parachute of the second man does not open, and as he falls past the first man, he grabs his legs. If the parachute cannot support them both, is the first man morally justified in kicking the second man away

to save himself? Yes, said the rabbis, since the man whose parachute didn't open was "designated for death". The second analogy involves a caravan surrounded by bandits. The bandits demand a particular member of the caravan be turned over for execution; the rest will go free. Assuming that the named individual has been "designated for death", the rabbis concluded it was acceptable to surrender him to save everyone else. Accordingly, they concluded that if a twin A was "designated for death" and could not survive in any event, but twin B could, surgery that would kill twin A to help improve the chance of twin B was acceptable.'

There is, however, no indication in the submission we received from the Archbishop of Westminster that such a solution was acceptable as part of the philosophy he espoused. The judge's dilemma in a case where he or she is confronted by a choice between conflicting philosophies was thoughtfully discussed by Simon Gardner in his article 'Necessity's Newest Inventions' (1991) 11 OJLS 125. He explored the possibility of rights-based justifications based on a principle that otherwise unlawful actions might be justified where the infraction was calculated to vindicate a right superior to the interest protected by the rule, but he was perplexed by the idea that judges in a democracy could make their own decisions as to what was right and what was wrong in the face of established law prohibiting the conduct in question. The whole article requires careful study, but its author concluded that in jurisdictions where rights were guaranteed, the judicial vindication of a guaranteed right would be seen as protecting democracy rather than contravening it. This consideration does not, however, assist us in a case where there are conflicting rights of apparently equal status and conflicting philosophies as to the priority, if any, to be given to either.

Before I leave the treatment afforded to the topic of necessity by modern academic writers of great distinction (there is a valuable contemporary summary of the issues in Smith and Hogan's *Criminal Law* (9th edn, 1999) pp 245–252 [11th edn, 2005, pp 315–325]), I must mention the section entitled 'Justifications, Necessity and the Choice of Evils' in *Principles of Criminal Law* (3rd edn, 1999) by Professor Andrew Ashworth. After referring to the facts of the Zeebrugge incident he said at pp 153–154:

'No English court has had to consider this situation, and it is clear that only the strongest prohibition on the taking of an innocent life would prevent a finding of justification here: in an urgent situation involving a decision between n lives and $n + 1$ lives, is there not a strong social interest in preserving the greater number of lives? Any residual principle of this kind must be carefully circumscribed; it involves the sanctity of life, and therefore the highest value with which the criminal law is concerned. Although there is a provision in the Model Penal Code allowing for a defence of "lesser evil", it fails to restrict the application of the defence to cases of imminent threat, opening up the danger of citizens trying to justify all manner of conduct by reference to overall good effects. The moral issues are acute: "not just anything is permissible on the ground that it would yield a net saving of lives". Closely connected with this is the moral problem of "choosing one's victim", a problem which arises when, for example, a lifeboat is in danger of sinking, necessitating the throwing overboard of some passengers, or when two people have to kill and eat another if any of the three is to survive. To countenance a legal justification in such cases would be to regard the victim's rights as morally and politically less worthy than the rights of those protected lives saved and deaths avoided in the aggregate but must somehow attempt to come to grips with the nature of the rights and duties being assessed. This would seem to be consistent with Lord Coleridge's conclusion that necessity can provide no justification for the taking of a life, such an act representing the most extreme form of rights violation. As discussed above, if any defence for such a homicidal act is to succeed, it would have to be framed as an excuse grounded on self-preservation. It could not possibly be declared by the court to be rightful.'

Questions

1. Was the corporal guilty of murder under the law as stated in *Dudley and Stephens*?

2. According to a report in *The Times*, 5 May 1998, the commander of an Australian naval ship 'took the decision to save the rest of his crew by sealing four sailors in the blazing engine room, consigning them to certain death, after rescuers were beaten back by the flames'. Was the officer guilty of murder of the four sailors? If he had refused to seal the engine room and the four had escaped but the ship had been lost with most of the crew would he have been guilty of any offences? Can it be the law that both of the alternative courses amount to crimes? If the officer's belief that the only way to save the ship and crew was to sacrifice the four men was reasonable, is it conceivable that he would be convicted of murder?—or any crime?

3. Consider the case of conjoined twins who have only one heart. The heart cannot be divided, as some other organs can. It cannot support both twins and, if nothing is done, both will soon die. Should that be allowed to happen if one can be saved by being given the heart? Will the inevitable death of the other be murder? Should it make any difference that one is (a) slightly stronger, (b) very much stronger, than the other? Or that one is a boy and the other a girl and the parents dearly want a boy and are not interested in a girl (or vice versa)? See Richard Huxtable, 'Separation of Conjoined Twins: What Next for English law?' [2002] Crim LR 459.

(1) NECESSITY AND KILLING TO SAVE FROM PAIN

In the case of *Bodkin Adams* ([1957] Crim LR 365, (1957) Times, 9 April) Devlin J directed the jury that there is no special defence justifying a doctor in giving drugs which shorten life in the case of severe pain: 'If life were cut short by weeks or months it was just as much murder as if it were cut short by years.' He went on:

But that does not mean that a doctor aiding the sick or dying has to calculate in minutes or hours, or perhaps in days or weeks, the effect on a patient's life of the medicines which he administers. If the first purpose of medicine—the restoration of health—can no longer be achieved, there is still much for the doctor to do, and he is entitled to do all that is proper and necessary to relieve pain and suffering even if measures he takes may incidentally shorten life.

In September 1992 Dr Nigel Cox was convicted of attempted murder and sentenced to 12 months' imprisonment suspended for a year after he had administered potassium chloride to a patient, B, a 70-year-old woman in order to terminate the great pain from which she was suffering. B died within five minutes of the injection. She had pleaded with Dr Cox to end her life. He was not charged with murder because it was no longer possible to prove the actual cause of death.

In this case, pain-killing drugs were no longer effective to relieve B's suffering. Dr Cox decided to give the injection of potassium chloride which had the effect of stopping her heart. He said: 'I seemed to have no more options left. She was going to die very soon in any case. I was faced with a choice of several evils. I chose what seemed to me the least evil with respect to [B] at that time.' An expert medical witness at a subsequent General Medical Council hearing said that Dr Cox's mistake was to give potassium chloride; a large dose of sedative, causing B to lapse into a coma, would have fallen on the right side of the law ((1992) The Times, 18 November).

What is the difference between administering potassium chloride in order to end pain and administering the sedative to do so, if the doctor knows that the sedative will also shorten life? Is it that the purpose of the doctor in the former case is to kill in order to relieve pain whereas in the latter his purpose is to relieve pain? Is this a valid distinction?

Dr Moor's Case (Hooper J) ('The Trial of Dr David Moor' by Anthony Arlidge QC [2000] Crim LR 31 and comment by J. C. Smith at p 41) seems to confirm that there is a special doctor's defence: although satisfied that he knew his act would accelerate death significantly, the jury is not entitled to convict him of murder if they think his purpose was, or may have been, to give treatment which, in the circumstances as he understood them, he believed to be proper treatment to relieve pain. This seems to be, in substance, an application of the doctrine of double effect.

The doctrine of double effect

This is a philosophical or theological rather than a legal doctrine which applies where a person knows that his act will inevitably have two immediate consequences, one good and one bad. If he acts with the sole purpose of bringing about the good consequence, he is not to be blamed for bringing about the bad one. According to Glanville Williams, *The Sanctity of Life in the Criminal Law*, 184, 'it is allowed to be used only when both effects are the immediate result of the act.' The doctrine is not applied if the good effect is the result of the bad one for this would be to admit the unacceptable proposition that the end justifies the means.

Ward LJ in *Re A* readily accepted that the doctrine could apply to the doctor administering drugs to a patient for the sole purpose of relieving pain, knowing that the effect would be to accelerate the patient's death, but thought it could not apply in the case before him where the good effect was on one patient and the bad effect on another. Brooke LJ also thought that:

> ...the doctrine of double effect could have no possible application in this case because...by no stretch of the imagination it could be said that the surgeons would be acting in Mary's best interests when they prepared an operation which benefit Jodie but kill Mary.

This is difficult to follow since the doctrine presupposes one bad as well as one good consequence. Although Robert Walker LJ thought the operation would be in the best interests of both twins, he recognized that to kill Mary, merely because it was in her best interests to die, would have been murder, and, if it was murder, it could hardly be regarded, in law, as other than an evil consequence, an evil consequence, however, which would not be unlawful because it was not 'the purpose or intention of the surgery'.

Did not Ward and Brooke LJJ in substance apply the doctrine of double effect (at least as it is described by Glanville Williams) in *Re A*? Their purpose was to bring about the good result—the healthy survival of Jodie while simultaneously causing the (as they acknowledged) bad result, killing Mary?

Sequel to the conjoined twins case

The operation was performed successfully and, as expected, Mary died shortly afterwards. Jodie, after further treatment, was discharged from hospital and returned with her parents to their island home. A television programme showed Jodie to be a remarkably beautiful, healthy child, obviously alert, intelligent and happy. Her parents were naturally delighted with her. So, it seemed, was everyone on the island, where the family received a rapturous reception. The parish priest was equally delighted with the new member of his flock. Yet the parents still said that the operation should not have taken place. So too did the priest. They apparently believed that this beautiful child, who had brought them so much joy and who now had the prospect of a full and happy life, should have been allowed to die after a short and harrowing struggle to maintain the life of her sister who would die with her. Their belief was that the will of God should have been allowed to prevail and that, if the will of God was that both should die, then so be it.

Was it right for the law to override the wishes of the parents?

Necessity—a new formulation of the elements of the defence?

R v Quayle and Other Appeals; Attorney-General's Reference (No 2 of 2004), Re Ditchfield
[2005] EWCA Crim 1415, Court of Appeal, Criminal Division

(Mance LJ, Newman and Fulford JJ)

The court heard a number of appeals against conviction and a reference by the Attorney-General because they raised similar issues, in particular whether the common law defence of 'necessity by circumstance' (sic) should be left to the jury in respect of offences of: (1) possession, cultivation or production of cannabis where the accused had genuinely and reasonably believed that the activities were *necessary* to avoid him suffering pain arising from a pre-existing medical condition or from conventional medicine to which he or she would otherwise resort to reduce the pain; and (2) importation or possession with intent to supply of cannabis for the purpose of alleviating the same type of pain suffered by others in such a predicament.

In rejecting the availability of a defence of necessity to each case, the Court of Appeal summarized a number of principles relating to that defence.

Lord Justice Mance: [His Lordship dealt with the introduction and summary of facts in the relevant cases]

The Attorney General now seeks the opinion of this Court on the following question of law: 'May the defence of necessity be available to a defendant in respect of an offence of possession of cannabis or cannabis resin with intent to supply, contrary to section 5(3) of the Misuse of Drugs Act 1971, if his case is that he was in possession of the controlled drug intending to supply it to another for the purpose of alleviating pain arising from a pre-existing illness such as multiple sclerosis?'

[His lordship referred to the legislative framework under the Misuse of Drugs Act 1971 for prescription of drugs and licensing of production, cultivation supply and possession. His lordship also set out in detail a reply to a report dated 4 November 1998 of the House of Lords Select Committee on Science and Technology, 'Cannabis, the Scientific and Medical Evidence' (9th Report, 1997–98, HL Paper 151, Session 1997–98).]

… The primary case advanced on behalf of Messrs Quayle, Wales [who were cultivating the drug for personal use to ease their pain with various illnesses] and Kenny [who was in possession and was supplying to those who preferred to use cannabis rather than conventional medicines to ease pain] is that their cultivation or preparation (and use and possession) of cannabis were all excusable in law since they genuinely and reasonably believed that these activities were necessary to avoid them suffering serious injury or pain, and that the charges against them should have been left to the jury on that basis; alternatively, that, if such activities were only excusable in law if necessary to avoid serious injury (as distinct from pain), the judge should also have left the jury to consider the charges on that basis. In this context, Mr Fitzgerald submits that, on the evidence, it was open to the jury to conclude that pain may involve or lead to psychological injury and/or that the alternative analgesic drugs may themselves cause 'serious injury'. In the case of *Wales* the judge is further criticised for his direction that the defence of necessity could only be available if the defendant believed that he would (i) imminently and (ii) inevitably suffer serious injury.

In the cases of Messrs Taylor and Lee [who were importing with a view to distributing to those who would use the drug as a pain killer], the contention is that the judge's ruling in each case wrongly prevented the jury considering a defence of necessity, to the effect that they acted as they did in the interests of others towards whom they reasonably regarded themselves as responsible and who they genuinely and reasonably feared would suffer serious pain and/or (if required) serious injury if they did not receive the cannabis being imported or supplied. The successful defence of Mr Ditchfield was to that effect.

The appellants and Mr Ditchfield buttress their submissions by a contention that, if the law does not provide potential defences in the terms which the appellants submit should have been (and which were in the case of *Ditchfield*) left to the jury, this country would be in breach of the European Convention on Human Rights [Article 8]....

The Crown's case before us operates at two levels. At a detailed level, Mr Chawla's submits that, whatever view might be taken regarding the avoidance of serious pain, the cases of *Quayle*, *Wales* and *Kenny* lack at least one fundamental and essential ingredient, namely that the allegedly causative feature of the commission of the offence must be extraneous to the defendant; while the cases of *Taylor* and *Lee* concern persons who could not in reality be regarded as anything other than volunteers, operating maybe for reasons of altruism but also in the context of a commercial enterprise and not in any circumstances where they could reasonably be said to have a responsibility towards those for whose benefit they say they were acting. The Attorney General pursues the further submission that the defence of necessity does not embrace the avoidance of serious pain, and should not be extended (in this context at least) to do so.

....

In *Brown* [2003] EWCA Crim 2637 this court (Kay LJ, Silber and Levesen JJ)...the proposed defence [to producing cannabis] was necessity arising from chronic pain. At the start of the trial, the judge had been invited by counsel to rule whether, as a matter of law on the defendant's own factual and medical evidence, there was any defence properly to be left to the jury; and, after his negative ruling, the defendant pleaded guilty and sought to appeal. Levesen J giving the judgment upholding the judge's ruling, said:

> 'In this case the choice facing the applicant was not severe pain without cannabis or absence of pain with cannabis, rather it was absence of pain with adverse side effects without cannabis, and, on his account, absence of pain with minimal side effects with cannabis. The difference is restricted to the adverse side effects which, however unpleasant, could not sensibly be said to raise a prime facie possibility of serious injury, let alone one such as would overwhelm the will of the defendant.
>
> Quite apart from this point, there has to be material from which a jury could come to a conclusion that they were not sure from an objective stand point that the applicant was not acting reasonably and proportionately. The evidence makes it clear that it was possible for the applicant to control pain by conventional and legal means. These arguments are sufficient to demonstrate that the learned judge was correct to conclude that the evidence, even at its highest, was not sufficient to raise a defence to be left to the jury.
>
> Finally, the Crown argued that in order to provide prima facie evidence of a defence fit to be left to the jury there had to be material from which the jury could conclude that the causative feature of the applicant's commission of the offence was, or may have been, extraneous to the applicant on the basis

that the defence does not extend to include the subjective thought processes and emotions of the defendant: see *R v Roger* [1998] 1 Cr App R 142,....'

With regard to the references in the authorities to a need for a threat to life or of serious injury, the appellants submit that the avoidance of severe pain should be equated with the avoidance of serious injury, Mr Fitzgerald QC for Mr Quayle and Mr Wales invokes in this connection case-law concerning medical treatment and general considerations of principle. The case-law include *Bourne* [1939] 1 KB 687, *Gillick v. West Norfolk and Wisbech Area H.A.* [1986] 1 AC 142, *In re F (Mental Patient: Sterilisation)* [1990] 2 AC 1 and *In re A* [considered above, p 40].... In both *Gillick* and *In re F* the issue was whether doctors could act in the best interests of persons for whose treatment they were medically responsible, in circumstances where those persons could not decide for themselves. That is a very different situation from the present.

In *Bourne* the issue could also be viewed as involving competing interests of the parent and an as yet unborn child. In *In re A* doctors owing duties to both conjoined twins faced the clinical dilemma that any chance of saving the life of the one (Jodie) over a longer period involved an operation which would positively invade the bodies of both and necessarily end the life of the other (Mary) at once. Brooke LJ's comprehensive discussion described the 'species of the genus of necessity which is caused by wrongful threats' in terms tending to equate it with 'the newly identified defence of "duress of circumstances"', which he exemplified by reference to, inter alia, *Martin*. He distinguished both from 'cases of pure necessity where the actor's mind is not irresistibly overborne by external pressures' but 'the claim is that his or her conduct was not harmful because on a choice between two evils the choice of avoiding the greater harm was justified' (pages 232C–236B). Brooke LJ treated this situation, at least, as one where the law might speak of conduct as justified (compare Lord Bingham's statement in *Hasan* at paragraph 18 that, in the context of duress by threats, the law is concerned with no more than a potential excuse). Robert Walker LJ at p.253H-255E also found in the previous cases concerning duress of circumstances no real assistance or clear principle or analogy applicable to the situation of clinical dilemma faced by the doctors in *re A*. Recognising that, in the absence of parliamentary intervention, the law had to develop on a case by case basis, as indicated by Rose LJ in *Abdul-Hussain*, he concluded that, on the particular facts, where Mary was on the evidence bound to die soon in any event, the doctors' fundamental duty to protect the life of Jodie justified the medical operation to separate the twins, despite its inevitably fatal effect for Mary. This reasoning in our view underlines the danger of Mr Fitzgerald's approach in so far as that seeks to extract from cases from the very different area of medical intervention general principles to be applied across the whole area of duress by threats or necessity by circumstances.

In the light of these authorities, we are not persuaded by Mr Fitzgerald's attempts to derive from individual authorities in different areas a coherent over-arching principle applicable in all cases of necessity. Such an attempt appears to us to pay too little attention to the particular context of individual decisions, and not to correspond with the case by case approach suggested by the authorities. However, there is a recognised defence of duress by threats, to which it is clear that the defence of necessity by circumstances bears a close affinity. Save that, in the present cases at least, the offences in question are not readily seen as involving any individual victim, the arguments which Lord Bingham mentioned in *Hasan* in favour of a confined definition appear to us applicable to any defence of necessity by circumstances.

Apart from the general considerations addressed ... above, there are also detailed requirements of any defence of necessity which are indicated by the common law authorities and which the present cases in our view lack.

Extraneous circumstances. Lord Bingham spoke in *Hasan* of the need for 'a just and well-founded fear', while accepting that threats of death or serious injury will suffice. He noted that the relevant requirements had been defined objectively, and went on (with the majority of the House) to apply the same approach when he decided that the defence was not available if the defendant ought reasonably to have foreseen the risk of coercion. It is by 'the standards of honest and reasonable men' therefore that the existence or otherwise of such a fear or such threats falls to be decided. We have observed that Lord Bingham did not address or comment on the case of *Safi*, in which this court held that what matters is not whether there was actually a threat of torture, but whether there was a reasonable perception of such a threat. But that still involves an objective test based on external events, conduct or words about which evidence would have to be produced or given. It is also notable that Lord Bingham described the criminal defence which he thought had a close affinity with duress by threats as 'necessity.... by extraneous circumstances'.

There is therefore considerable authority pointing towards a need for extraneous circumstances capable of objective scrutiny by judge and jury and as such, it may be added, more likely to be capable of being checked and, where appropriate, met by other evidence. Lord Bingham's dictum fits in this regard with dicta in *Abdul-Hussain*, the decision in *Rodger & Rose* and Lord Woolf's dicta in *Shayler* speaking of a 'fundamental ingredient' of 'some external agency' as well as with the non-counsel decision in *Brown*.

The appellants' objection to any such distinction is that it means, for example, that the commission of an offence could be excused if it was to avoid the realisation of a danger of one's wife committing suicide (cf *Martin*), but not if in that case it had been the wife herself who, realising that she would commit suicide unless she drove her son to school, had driven while disqualified (cf *Rodger & Rose*). Likewise, they suggest, the distinction could deny a defence of necessity to a person at risk of serious injury or perhaps pain, but allow it potentially to a parent or carer responsible for the well-being of such a person; and in circumstances like those in *Rodger & Rose*, a compassionate warder with responsibility for the prisoner, could release the prisoner, if he was able to detect the risk of suicide in time; while in cases such as the present, a person in or at risk of serious injury or pain could not himself engage in cultivation, possession or use of cannabis for medical purposes, but a parent or carer responsible for his upkeep could cultivate or obtain and administer cannabis to him or her for such purposes. The appellants suggest that none of these distinctions can stand scrutiny, so that *Rodger & Rose* must be regarded as a special case based on policy considerations.

We accept that it is right to remember the context of the decision in *Rodger & Rose*. Any court was, we think, bound to recognise the incongruous penal results and the risk of abuse that would result from recognising a defence of necessitous escape from prison based on danger that the prisoner escaping would commit suicide if he remained in custody. But, on that basis, the suggestion that a prison officer in a situation like that in *Rodger & Rose* might legitimately free a prisoner is we think likely to run into problems at a more basic level of legislative policy, which in our view the cases before us also present. … Nevertheless, although the court in *Rodger & Rose* adverted to considerations of policy when it said that the suggested defence was undesirable, it did so not to justify a particular exception in this context to the defence, but in support of a generally expressed common law exception, based on the undesirability of introducing 'an entirely subjective element divorced from any extraneous influence' into the defence. On the authorities …, the requirement of an objectively ascertainable extraneous cause has a considerable, and in our view understandable, basis. It rests on the pragmatic consideration that the defence of necessity, which the Crown would carry the onus to disprove, must be confined within narrowly defined limits or it will become an opportunity for almost untriable and certainly peculiarly difficult issues, not to mention abusive defences. On that basis, we consider that the Crown's first narrow point, namely that, for the defence of necessity of circumstances to be potentially available, there must be extraneous circumstances capable of objective scrutiny by judge and jury, is valid.

Pain. It is, however, submitted on behalf of Messrs. Quayle, Wales and Kenny that any such test is satisfied in all their cases both because of the objectively ascertainable facts giving rise to the pain they suffer actually, or would suffer if they were not to use cannabis, whether from their afflictions or from taking alternative lawful medicaments, and because pain is capable of some degree of objective scrutiny and is not wholly subjective. In addressing this submission, we do not gain any real assistance from cases from other areas of the law, where distinctions may or may not have been drawn between injury and harm or pain.

The reason why we would not accept the submission is that the law has to draw a line at some point in the criteria which it accepts as sufficient to satisfy any defence of duress or necessity. Courts and juries have to work on evidence. If such defences were to be expanded in theory to cover every possible case in which it might be felt that it would be hard if the law treated the conduct in question as criminal, there would be likely to be arguments in considerable numbers of cases, where there was no clear objective basis by reference to which to test or determine such arguments. It is unlikely that this would lead overall to a more coherent result, or even necessarily to a more just disposition of any individual case. There is, on any view, a large element of subjectivity in the assessment of pain not directly associated with some current physical injury. The legal defences of duress by threats and necessity by circumstances should in our view be confined to cases where there is an imminent danger of physical injury. In reaching these conclusions, we recognise that hard cases can be postulated, but these, as Lord Bingham said, can and should commonly be capable of being dealt with in other ways. The nature of the sentences passed in the cases before us is consistent with this.

It is also submitted that the present cases involve not merely pain, but a risk of serious physical or psychological injury as a result of pain, or as a result of the alternative medicines which would have to be taken if cannabis was not. We have in the case of *Quayle* already given our reasons for rejecting on the facts Mr Fitzgerald's submission that there was any relevant risk of suicide in that case. In the case of *Wales*, the judge is criticised for failing to explain that serious pain could amount to serious injury because of its psychological consequences, but there does not appear to have been any evidence which could have justified such a case. Mr Wales did describe the pain he suffered as 'life-threatening' and the judge reminded the jury of this, although it does not appear to have been Mr Wales's case that there was an actual risk of suicide. His case on the facts was that cannabis helped him cope with the pain, without side effects, while the prescribed medicines had side-effects (stopping him eating) and, on the expert evidence that he called, also involved medical risks such as a general risk of peritonitis. We do not see in the evidence any basis on which a jury could be asked to conclude that Mr Wales faced any imminent risk of serious injury sufficient to justify him taking cannabis on a regular basis. Further, if there was such a case, it was left to the jury. Finally, in the case of *Kenny*, the evidence did not suggest any risk other than that of pain, and the criticism is that that risk should have been left to the jury.

Imminence and immediacy. We consider that these requirements represent another reason why, even at the detailed level, it is difficult to accept that there could be any successful defence of necessity in the cases of *Quayle, Wales* and *Kenny*. Their defences amount to saying that it is open to defendants on a continuous basis to plan for and justify breaches of the law. However, we need not express a view whether that would have alone justified a judge in refusing to leave their defences to a jury. The requirements of imminence and immediacy mean, in any event, in our view that the judge was right to refuse to leave any defence of necessity to the jury in *Taylor* and *Lee*, and that the defence should not have been left to the jury in *Ditchfield*. In each of these three cases, the defendant was taking a deliberately considered course of conduct over a substantial period of time, involving continuous or regular breaches of the law. In each case, the defendant was not the immediate sufferer and had every opportunity to reflect and to desist. The compassionate grounds which may well have motivated Mr Taylor and Ms Lee and which the jury evidently accepted did motivate Mr Ditchfield cannot avoid the fact that they deliberately chose to act contrary to the law on a continuous basis.

We note in passing that the court in *Southwark L.B.C. v. Williams* refused to recognise a defence of necessity raised by squatters in answer to a claim to recover possession of properties owned by the council. The evidence was that there were no homes for the squatters, they had been living in 'quite deplorable conditions' and the empty council properties in which they then squatted had been vandalised by the council to make them unfit for habitation, but that they had entered and lived there in an orderly way and repaired them after entry. Nevertheless, the court upheld summary possession orders, 'for the sake of law and order', as Lord Denning put it, and because the circumstances 'do not…constitute the sort of emergency to which the plea [of necessity] applies', as Edmund Davies LJ said. Megaw LJ agreed with both judgments on this aspect. The case is an old one, and the law has developed, so that we need not consider it further. But the underlying theme, that a continuous and deliberate course of otherwise unlawful self-help is unlikely to give rise to the defence has itself, in our view, continuing relevance.

The point made [above]…may also be viewed in another way. Where there is no imminent or immediate threat or peril, but only a general assertion of an internal motivation to engage in prohibited activities in order to prevent or alleviate pain, it is also difficult to identify any extraneous or objective factors by reference to which a jury could be expected to measure whether the motivation was such as to override the defendant's will or to force him to act as he did. If the response is that the defendant was not forced, but chose to act as he did, then the considerations mentioned in the previous paragraph apply.

Conclusions

….None of the defendants in any of the cases before us was in our view able to rely at trial on any facts which could at common law give him or her any defence of necessity. The judicial rulings to that effect in the cases of *Quayle*, *Taylor*, *Lee* and *Kenny* were correct in the result, even though not in every case in their reasoning. The judges in *Wales* and in the *Attorney General's Reference* in *Ditchfield* were wrong to leave the defence of necessity to the jury. In the case of *Wales*, the jury anyway convicted, but in the case of *Ditchfield* the jury acquitted. It follows that all the appeals will be dismissed, and the question of law on which this court's opinion is sought by the Attorney General in the reference will be answered in the negative.

Have the courts now merged the defences of duress and necessity completely? Were these individuals compelled to claim to be under a threat of death or serious injury simply to attempt to fit into the duress of circumstances defence?

The court's language is in terms of necessity, but does it not narrow that defence by the requirements of duress of circumstances?

4. RELATIONSHIP BETWEEN DURESS AND NECESSITY

In *Shayler* the Court of Appeal (Woolf LCJ, Wright and Levenson JJ) (reported sub nom *R v S (D)* in [2001] Crim LR 986) discussed the relationship between duress of circumstances and necessity.

The House of Lords [2002] 2 All ER 477 held that no question of duress or necessity arose and that it was 'a little unfortunate' that these topics had been discussed by the trial judge and the Court of Appeal. Lord Bingham (para 15) and Lord Hutton (para 117) made it clear that they did not necessarily agree with all that was said about these defences. The Court of Appeal's remarks are therefore obiter but, coming from a strong court, of some weight.

Woolf LCJ said that *Abdul-Hussain* (above, p **400**) reflected other decisions 'which have treated the defences of duress and necessity as being part of the same defence and the extended form of the defence [that is, duress of circumstances] as being different labels for essentially the same thing.' But is this so?

(i) It seems to be settled that duress cannot be a defence to murder or attempted murder (*Howe and Bannister*, above, p **416**, *Gotts*, above, p **421**) but is it not now reasonably clear that, following *Re A (children (conjoined twins)*, necessity may in some circumstances be a defence?

(ii) The only occasion for a defence of duress of either variety are imminent threats of death or gbh. But is necessity so limited? Should it not be a defence to a charge of battery that D was pushing a child to save him from some quite minor injury or even damage to his clothing?

(iii) Necessity is a defence only if the evil which D seeks to avoid is greater than that which he knows he is causing. But if D yields to torture which no ordinary person could be expected to resist, should he not be excused, however grave the consequences of his capitulation?

(iv) It seems that necessity may create a duty to act—cf *Re A* and *F v West Berkshire Health Authority*, above, p **433**—but can duress ever do so?

5. THE USE OF FORCE IN PUBLIC OR PRIVATE DEFENCE

A person may lawfully use force in defence of certain public or private interests. If he has used only such force as he may lawfully use, then he will have a defence to any charge which may be brought against him of homicide, or other offence against the person or of criminal damage. The purposes for which a person may use such force are conveniently summarised in the draft Code Bill and the Non-Fatal Offences Bill as follows:

(a) preventing or terminating crime, or affecting or assisting in the lawful arrest of an offender or suspected offender or of a person unlawfully at large;

(b) preventing or terminating a breach of the peace;

(c) protecting himself or another from unlawful force or unlawful injury;

(d) preventing or terminating the unlawful detention of himself or another;

(e) protecting property (whether belonging to himself or another) from unlawful appropriation, destruction, damage or infringement; or

(f) preventing or terminating a trespass to his person or property or, with the authority of another, of preventing or terminating a trespass to the person or property of that other.

Under these draft provisions, the right to use force for the specified purposes would be governed by the common principles stated in the clause. This would be a great simplification because, as the law stands, the principles are found in a variety of sources and are not uniform. Purpose (a) is regulated by the Criminal Law Act 1967, s 3 and

PACE 1984, ss 24, 25 and 28; purposes (b), (c), (d) and (f) are regulated by the common law. Purpose (e) is complex. If the charge is simply one of damage to property, the use of force is regulated by the Criminal Damage Act 1971, s 5; but if the charge is one of causing damage to property, intending to endanger life, or being reckless whether life is endangered, or if it is a charge of causing injury to the person, it is regulated by the common law.

It is convenient to begin with the common law.

Beckford v R
[1987] 3 All ER 425, Privy Council

(Lords Keith, Elwyn-Jones, Templeman, Griffiths and Oliver)

The appellant, a police officer, while investigating a report that a man was terrorizing his family, shot and killed a man who ran out of the back of the house. There was a conflict of evidence as to the circumstances. At the trial of the appellant for murder the judge directed the jury that he was entitled to be acquitted on the ground of self-defence if he had a reasonable belief that his life was in danger or that he was in danger of serious bodily harm. He appealed to the Court of Appeal in Jamaica on the ground that the jury should have been told that he had a defence if he had an honest belief in the danger, even if it was unreasonable. The appeal was dismissed. He appealed to the Privy Council.

Lord Griffiths. . . . It is accepted by the Crown that there is no difference on the law of self-defence between the law of Jamaica and the English common law and it therefore falls to be decided whether it was correctly decided by the Court of Appeal in *R v Williams* [above, p **408**] that the defence of self-defence depends on what the accused 'honestly' believed the circumstances to be and not on the reasonableness of that belief, what the Court of Appeal in Jamaica referred to as the 'honest belief' and 'reasonable belief' schools of thought.

There can be no doubt that prior to the decision of the House of Lords in *DPP v Morgan* [above, p **181**], the whole weight of authority supported the view that it was an essential element of self-defence not only that the accused believe that he was being attacked or in imminent danger of being attacked but also that such belief was based on reasonable grounds. No elaborate citation of authority is necessary but counsel for the Crown rightly drew attention to such nineteenth century authorities as *R v Forster* (1825) 1 Lew CC 187, 168 ER 1007; *R v Weston* (1879) 14 Cox CC 346 and *R v Rose* (1884) 15 Cox CC 540, in which the judges charged the jury that self-defence provided a defence to a charge of murder if the accused honestly and on reasonable grounds believed that his or another's life was in peril. It is, however, to be remembered that it was not until 1898 that an accused was able to give evidence in his own defence and it is natural that the judges, in the absence of any direct statement of his belief from the accused, should have focused attention on the inference that could be drawn from the surrounding circumstances. Nevertheless, even after 1898 the law of self-defence continued to be stated as propounded by the judges in the nineteenth century: see *R v Chisam* (1963) 47 Cr App Rep 130, in which Lord Parker CJ approved the following statement of the law in 10 Halsbury's Laws (3rd edn) p721, para 1382:

'Where a forcible and violent felony is attempted upon the person of another, the party assaulted, or his servant, or any other person present, is entitled to repel force by force, and, if necessary, to kill the aggressor. There must be a reasonable necessity for the killing, or at least an honest belief based upon reasonable grounds that there is such a necessity . . .'

In *R v Fennell* [1971] 1 QB 428 at 431, [1970] 3 All ER 215 at 217 Widgery LJ, who was soon to succeed Lord Parker CJ as Lord Chief Justice, said:

> 'Where a person honestly and reasonably believes that he or his child is in imminent danger of injury, it would be unjust if he were deprived of the right to use reasonable force by way of defence merely because he had made some genuine mistake of fact.'

The question then is whether the present Lord Chief Justice, Lord Lane CJ, in *R v Williams* was right to depart from the law as declared by his predecessors in the light of the decision of the House of Lords in *DPP v Morgan*.

DPP v Morgan was a case of rape, and counsel for the prosecution has submitted that the decision of the majority turns solely on their view of the specific intention required for the commission of that crime and accordingly had no relevance to the law of self-defence. It was further submitted that the question now before their Lordships was settled by an earlier decision of the Privy Council in *Palmer v R* [below, p **457**]. This submission is founded on the fact that Lord Morris in giving the judgment of the Board set out a very lengthy passage from the summing up of the judge and commented ([1971] AC 814 at 824, [1971] 1 All ER 1077 at 1082):

> 'Their Lordships conclude that there is no room for criticism of the summing-up or of the conduct of the trial unless there is a rule that in every case where the issue of self-defence is left to the jury they must be directed that if they consider that excessive force was used in defence then they should return a verdict of guilty of manslaughter. For the reasons which they will set out their Lordships consider that there is no such rule.'

The only question raised for the determination of the Board was that stated by Lord Morris. It is true that, in the passage quoted from the summing up the judge had stated the ingredients of self-defence in the then conventional form of reasonable belief; but it was not this part of his summing up that was under attack nor did it receive any particular consideration by the Board. Their Lordships are unable to attach greater weight to the approval of the summing up than as indicating that it was in conformity with the practice of directing juries that the accused must have reasonable grounds for believing that self-defence was necessary.

In *DPP v Morgan* each member of the House of Lords held that the mens rea required to commit rape [under the Sexual Offences Act 1956 was] the knowledge that the woman [was] not consenting or recklessness whether she [was] consenting or not. From this premise the majority held that unless the prosecution proved that the man did not believe the woman was consenting or was at least reckless as to her consent they had failed to prove the necessary mens rea which is an essential ingredient of the crime. Lord Edmund-Davies in his dissent referred to the large body of distinguished academic support for the view that it is morally indefensible to convict a person of a crime when owing to a genuine mistake as to the facts he believes that he is acting lawfully and has no intention to commit the crime and therefore has no guilty mind. He expressed his preference for this moral approach but felt constrained by the weight of authority, including the cases on self-defence, to hold that the law required that the accused's belief should not only be genuine but also based on reasonable grounds.

In *R v Kimber* [1983] 3 All ER 316, [1983] 1 WLR 1118, the Court of Appeal applied the decision in *DPP v Morgan* to a case of indecent assault and held that a failure to direct the jury that the prosecution had to make them sure that the accused had never believed that the woman was consenting was a misdirection. Lawton LJ, in the course of his judgment, rejected the submission that the decision in *DPP v Morgan* was confined to rape and clearly regarded it as of far wider significance. Commenting on an obiter dictum in *R v Phekoo* [1981] 3 All ER 84, he said:

> '... the court went on, after referring to *DPP v Morgan*, to say, clearly obiter ([1981] 3 All ER 84 at 93, [1981] 1 WLR 1117 at 1127): "... it seems to us clear that this decision was confined and intended to

be confined to the offence of rape." We do not accept that this was the intention of their Lordships in *Morgan's* case. Lord Hailsham started his speech by saying that the issue of belief was a question of great academic importance in the theory of English criminal law.'

[See [1983] 3 All ER 316 at 320, [1983] 1 WLR 1118 at 1123.]

In *R v Williams* the decision in *DPP v Morgan* was carried a step further and, in their Lordships' view, to its logical conclusion. The facts and the grounds of the decision are adequately summarised in the headnote (see (1987) 78 Cr App Rep 276):

'One M saw a black youth rob a woman in a street. He caught the youth and held him, but the latter broke from M's grasp. M caught the youth again and knocked him to the ground. The appellant, who had only seen the later stages of the incident was told by M that he, M, was arresting the youth for mugging a woman. M said that he was a police officer, which was untrue, so when asked by the appellant for his warrant card, he could not produce one. A struggle followed and the appellant assaulted M by punching him in the face and was charged with assault occasioning actual bodily harm contrary to section 47 of the Offences against the Person Act 1861. His defence was that he honestly believed that the youth was being unlawfully assaulted by M. The jury was directed that, on the assumption that M was acting lawfully, the appellant's state of mind on the issue of defence of another was to be determined by whether the appellant had an honest belief based on reasonable grounds that reasonable force was necessary to prevent a crime. The appellant was convicted and appealed on the ground that the judge had misdirected the jury. Held, that the jury should have been directed that, first, the prosecution had the burden of proving the unlawfulness of the appellant's actions; secondly, if the appellant might have been labouring under a mistake as to facts, he was to be judged according to his mistaken view of the facts, whether or not the mistake was, on an objective view, reasonable or not. The reasonableness or unreasonableness of the appellant's belief was material to the question whether the belief was held by him at all. If the belief was held, its unreasonableness, so far as guilt or innocence was concerned, was irrelevant. Accordingly, the appeal must be allowed and the conviction quashed.'

In the course of his judgment Lord Lane CJ, discussing the offence of assault, said ([1987] 3 All ER 411 at 414):

'The mental element necessary to constitute guilt is the intent to apply unlawful force to the victim. We do not believe that the mental element can be substantiated by simply showing an intent to apply force and no more.'

And later in the judgment he expressly disapproved the decision of the Divisional Court in *Albert v Lavin* [1981] 1 All ER 628, [1982] AC 546, in which it was said that the word 'unlawful' was tautologous and not part of the definitional element of assaulting a police officer in the course of his duty. In so doing Lord Lane CJ was expressing the same view of *Albert v Lavin* that had been previously expressed by Lawton LJ in *R v Kimber*.

The common law recognises that there are many circumstances in which one person may inflict violence on another without committing a crime, as for instance in sporting contests, surgical operations or, in the most extreme example, judicial execution. The common law has always recognised as one of these circumstances the right of a person to protect himself from attack and to act in the defence of others and if necessary to inflict violence on another in so doing. If no more force is used than is reasonable to repel the attack such force is not unlawful and no crime is committed. Furthermore, a man about to be attacked does not have to wait for his assailant to strike the first blow or fire the first shot: circumstances may justify a pre-emptive strike.

It is because it is an essential element of all crimes of violence that the violence or the threat of violence should be unlawful that self-defence, if raised as an issue in a criminal trial, must be disproved by the prosecution. If the prosecution fail to do so the accused is entitled to be acquitted because the prosecution will have failed to prove an essential element of the crime, namely that the violence used by the accused was unlawful.

If then a genuine belief, albeit without reasonable grounds, is a defence to rape because it negatives the necessary intention, so also must a genuine belief in facts which if true would justify self-defence be a defence to a crime of personal violence because the belief negatives the intent to act unlawfully. Their Lordships therefore approve the following passage from the judgment of Lord Lane CJ in *R v Williams* [1987] 3 All ER 411 at 415 as correctly stating the law of self-defence:

> 'The reasonableness or unreasonableness of the defendant's belief is material to the question of whether the belief was held by the defendant at all. If the belief was in fact held, its unreasonableness, so far as guilt or innocence is concerned, is neither here nor there. It is irrelevant. Were it otherwise, the defendant would be convicted because he was negligent in failing to recognise that the victim was not consenting or that a crime was not being committed and so on. In other words the jury should be directed, first of all, that the prosecution have the burden or duty of proving the unlawfulness of the defendant's actions, second, that if the defendant may have been labouring under a mistake as to the facts he must be judged according to his mistaken view of the facts and, third, that that is so whether the mistake was, on an objective view, a reasonable mistake or not. In a case of self-defence, where self-defence or the prevention of crime is concerned, if the jury come to the conclusion that the defendant believed, or may have believed, that he was being attacked or that a crime was being committed, and that force was necessary to protect himself or to prevent the crime, then the prosecution have not proved their case. If, however, the defendant's alleged belief was mistaken and if the mistaken belief was an unreasonable one, that may be a powerful reason for coming to the conclusion that the belief was not honestly held and should be rejected. Even if the jury come to the conclusion that the mistake was an unreasonable one, if the defendant may genuinely have been labouring under it, he is entitled to rely on it.'

Looking back, *DPP v Morgan* can now be seen as a landmark decision in the development of the common law, returning the law to the path on which it might have developed but for the inability of an accused to give evidence on his own behalf. Their Lordships note that not only has this development the approval of such distinguished criminal lawyers as Professor Glanville Williams and Professor Smith (see *Textbook of Criminal Law* (2nd edn, 1983) pp 137–138 and Smith and Hogan *Criminal Law* (5th edn, 1983) pp 329–330) but it also has the support of the Criminal Law Revision Committee (see 14th Report on Offences Against the Person (1980) (Cmnd 7844) and of the Law Commission (see Codification of the Criminal Law (1985) (Law Com no 143)).

There may be a fear that the abandonment of the objective standard demanded by the existence of reasonable grounds for belief will result in the success of too many spurious claims of self-defence. The English experience has not shown this to be the case. The Judicial Studies Board, with the approval of the Lord Chief Justice, has produced a model direction on self-defence which is now widely used by judges when summing up to juries. The direction contains the following guidance:

> 'Whether the plea is self-defence or defence of another, if the defendant may have been labouring under a mistake as to the facts, he must be judged according to his mistaken belief of the facts: that is so whether the mistake was, on an objective view a reasonable mistake or not.'

Their Lordships have heard no suggestion that this form of summing up has resulted in a disquieting number of acquittals. This is hardly surprising, for no jury is going to accept a man's assertion that he believed that he was about to be attacked without testing it against all the surrounding circumstances. In assisting the jury to determine whether or not the accused had a genuine belief the judge will of course direct their attention to those features of the evidence that make such a belief more or less probable. Where there are no reasonable grounds to hold a belief it will surely only be in exceptional circumstances that a jury will conclude that such a belief was or might have been held.

Their Lordships therefore conclude that the summing up in this case contained a material misdirection and they answer question 1(a) by saying that the test to be applied for self-defence is that a person may use such force as is reasonable in the circumstances as he honestly believes them to be in the defence of himself or another.

Appeal allowed. Conviction quashed

A passage in *Scarlett* [1993] 4 All ER 629, 636 ('provided [D] believed the circumstances called for the degree of force used, he is not to be convicted even if his belief was unreasonable') appeared significantly to qualify the objective element in the defence; but *Owino* [1996] 2 Cr App R 128, [1995] Crim LR 743 tells us that, 'properly understood and read in context', *Scarlett* was merely applying the established law: a person may use such force as is (objectively) reasonable in the circumstances as he (subjectively) believes them to be. See also *DPP v Armstrong-Braun* [1999] Crim LR 416. *Scarlett*, on this issue, is best ignored.

R v Martin (Anthony)

[2002] 1 Cr App R 323, Court of Appeal

(Lord Woolf CJ, Wright and Grigson JJ)

M lived alone in an isolated farmhouse ('Bleak House'). Two men, evidently burglars, broke a window and entered the house at night. M shot them both with a pump-action shotgun and one died. M's defence of self-defence was rejected by the jury who convicted him of murder. He appealed on various grounds. It was held that he was not entitled to rely on the evidence of two psychiatrists, not called at the trial, to the effect that he was suffering from an abnormality of mind, a long-standing personality disorder; and that the breaking into his house would be perceived by him as being a greater threat to his safety than it would in the case of a normal person.

Lord Woolf CJ. Mr Wolkind [for the appellant] relied on the recent decision of the House of Lords in *R v Smith (Morgan)* [[2001] 1 Cr App Rep 31 [2001] 1 AC 146, below, p **600**.] This was also a provocation case that Mr Wolkind contended could be applied to the similar issues which arise when a defendant relies on self-defence. In that case Smith was relying upon evidence that he suffered from clinical depression. There was no dispute that the evidence was admissible and relevant on the issue as to whether he was provoked, the subjective issue. The problem was whether the evidence was admissible as being relevant on the objective issue of loss of self-control. As to this the majority of their Lordships came to the conclusion that the jury were entitled to take into account some characteristic, whether temporary or permanent, which affected the degree of control which society could reasonably expect of a defendant and which it would be unjust not to take into account.

Is the same approach appropriate in the case of self-defence? There are policy reasons for distinguishing provocation from self-defence. Provocation only applies to murder, but self-defence applies to all assaults. In addition, provocation does not provide a complete defence; it only reduces the offence from murder to manslaughter. There is also the undoubted fact that self-defence is raised in a great many cases resulting from minor assaults and it would be wholly disproportionate to encourage medical disputes in cases of that sort. Lord Hobhouse in his dissenting speech in *Smith* recognised that in relation to self-defence, too generous an approach as to what is reasonable could result in an 'exorbitant defence' (para. 186). Lord Hoffmann also appeared conscious of this. As a matter of principle we would reject the suggestion that the approach of the majority in *Smith* in relation to provocation should be applied directly to the different issue of self-defence.

We would accept that the jury are entitled to take into account in relation to self-defence the physical characteristics of the defendant. However, we would not agree that it is appropriate, except in exceptional circumstances which would make the evidence especially probative, in deciding whether excessive force has been used to take into account whether the defendant is suffering from some psychiatric condition....

[Having rejected the defence of self-defence, the court quashed the conviction for murder and substituted a conviction for manslaughter on the ground of diminished responsibility.]

Notes and questions

1. The defendant is to be judged on the facts as he honestly believed them to be, whether reasonably or not. But he may use only such force as *is* reasonable in those supposed circumstances. It is for the jury to decide whether the force used was reasonable in the circumstances as the defendant believed them to be. But the law thus stated perhaps leaves a hiatus. Awareness of facts is one thing. An assessment of the danger to which those facts give rise is another. The former is a matter of observation, the latter a matter of judgement. If there is, or may be, a difference between the degree of danger which the defendant believed to arise and that which, in the opinion of the jury, actually arose, which is to be applied in determining whether the force used was reasonable? There does not seem to be any previous English authority directly in point which, perhaps, is why counsel fell back on the analogy of provocation. The court rejected this because provocation applies only to murder and is not a complete defence. But what about duress which applies to virtually all crimes except murder and is a complete defence? See *Martin (DP)* [2000] 2 Cr App R 42, [2000] Crim LR 615, above, p **408**. This decision may be controversial but it is a recent decision of the Court of Appeal and, if it is right, why does not the same principle apply to private defence? What policy could justify the admission of this evidence for a defendant relying on duress but not for one relying on self-defence? Is it not equally relevant to both? The courts have never assumed a discretion to exclude relevant evidence tendered by the defendant.

2. In *Shaw v R* [2002] 1 Cr App R 77, [2002] Crim LR 140, PC, D appealed against his conviction for murder in Belize, having unsuccessfully raised the defence of self-defence. It was common ground that the applicable law was as stated in Smith and Hogan, *Criminal Law* (9th edn) 253, and as it was put by the appellant's counsel—'. . . you will judge him as he saw it and only as he saw it.' The Board (Lords Bingham, Hoffmann, Cooke and Scott and Sir Patrick Russell), applying the common law—common to England and Belize—framed the two essential questions for the jury:
   (1) Did the appellant honestly believe or may he have believed that it was necessary to defend himself?
   (2) If so, and taking the circumstances and the danger as the appellant honestly believed them to be, was the amount of force which he used reasonable?

Note the words, '*the danger* as the appellant honestly believed it to be'. If that is right, was the expert evidence properly excluded on the issue of self-defence in *Martin (Anthony)*?

R v Clegg
[1995] 1 All ER 334, House of Lords

(Lords Keith, Browne-Wilkinson, Slynn, Lloyd and Nicholls)

C was a soldier on patrol in the course of his duties in Northern Ireland in 1990. A car approached the patrol at speed. C fired three shots at the windscreen and a fourth after the car had passed him. The last shot killed the passenger. C was charged with murder. His defence was that he fired in defence of himself and a fellow soldier. C was convicted of murder and his appeal was dismissed by the Court of Appeal of Northern Ireland. He appealed to the House of Lords.

[**Lord Lloyd** said that the first question, whether, when force used in self-defence is excessive, the law allows a verdict of manslaughter instead of murder, did not arise since the danger had passed when C fired the fourth and fatal shot; but that it was convenient to deal with it. Having discussed the Report of the Royal Commission of 1879, he continued:]

There does not appear to have been any development in the law until *R v Howe* (1958) 100 CLR 448, decided by the High Court of Australia in 1958. There was an extensive citation of all the authorities in this corner of the law going back to *Cook's* Case (1639) Cro Car 537, 79 ER 1063. The decision of the court is well summarised in the following paragraph of the headnote:

'Where a plea of self-defence to a charge of murder fails only because the death of the deceased was occasioned by the use of force going beyond what was necessary in the circumstances for the protection of the accused or what might reasonably be regarded by him as necessary in the circumstances, it is, in the absence of clear and definite decision, reasonable in principle to regard such a homicide as reduced to manslaughter.'

Twelve years later the same point came before the Privy Council on appeal from the Supreme Court of Jamaica (see *Palmer v R* [1971] 1 All ER 1077, [1971] AC 814). Lord Morris of Borth-y-Gest, giving the opinion of the Privy Council, declined to follow *R v Howe* (1958) 100 CLR 448, preferring the decision of the West Indian Federal Supreme Court in *De Freitas v R* (1960) 2 WIR 523.

After setting out the elements of the defence of self-defence, he said ([1971] 1 All ER 1077 at 1088, [1971] AC 814 at 832):

'...if the prosecution have shown that what was done was not done in self-defence then that issue is eliminated from the case. If the jury consider that an accused acted in self-defence or if the jury are in doubt as to this then they will acquit. The defence of self-defence either succeeds so as to result in an acquittal or it is disproved in which case as a defence it is rejected.'

In other words, there is no half-way house. There is no rule that a defendant who has used a greater degree of force than was necessary in the circumstances should be found guilty of manslaughter rather than murder.

In 1971 a Court of Appeal consisting of Edmund Davies LJ and Lawton and Forbes JJ approved and followed *Palmer v R* in *R v McInnes* [1971] 3 All ER 295 at 301:

'But where self-defence fails on the ground that the force used went clearly beyond that which was reasonable in the light of the circumstances as they reasonably appeared to the accused, is it the law that the inevitable result must be that he can be convicted of manslaughter only, and not of murder? It seems that in Australia that question is answered in the affirmative...but not, we think, in this country. On the contrary, if self-defence fails for the reason stated, it affords the accused no protection at all.'

Of course, as the court pointed out, the verdict may be reduced from murder to manslaughter on other grounds, for example, if the prosecution fail to negative provocation, where it arises, or fail to prove the requisite intent for murder. But so far as self-defence is concerned, it is all or nothing. The defence either succeeds or it fails. If it succeeds, the defendant is acquitted. If it fails, he is guilty of murder.

In a subsequent case in Australia, *Viro v R* (1978) 141 CLR 88, the High Court decided by a bare majority over a strong dissent by Barwick CJ to follow *R v Howe* (1958) 100 CLR 448 in preference to *Palmer v R*. Mason J suggested that in self-defence cases juries should be directed in accordance with six propositions which he formulated at the end of his judgment, and which, in his view, best accorded 'with acceptable standards of culpability'. But the propositions proved to be unworkable in practice. Juries found difficulty in applying, or perhaps even understanding them. As a result, a Full Court of seven judges was convened to reconsider the position in *Zecevic v DPP (Victoria)* (1987) 162 CLR 645. The High Court decided by a majority of five to two to revert to the law as stated in *Palmer v R* and *R v McInnes*, and declined to follow *R v Howe* and *Viro v R*. Wilson, Dawson and Toohey JJ said (at 665):

> 'Believing, as we do, that the law as we have set it out is dictated by basic principle upon a matter of fundamental importance, it is unthinkable that the Court should abdicate its responsibility by declining to declare it accordingly. It has the virtue of being readily understandable by a jury. It restores consistency to the law relating to self-defence whether raised in a case of homicide or otherwise. Finally, it has the effect of expressing the common law in terms which are in accord with the views expressed in *Palmer* (adopted in England in *McInnes*) and which are generally consonant with the law in the code States.'

[**Lord Lloyd** went to hold that the degree of permissible force, and the consequence of the use of excessive force, is the same, whether the force be used in self-defence or in the prevention of crime; and in the circumstances of this case, it made no difference that C was a member of the security forces, acting in the course of his duty. There is no defence of superior orders.]

Appeal dismissed

Lord Lloyd said that the question whether the law should be changed to allow a conviction of manslaughter was, in truth, part of the wider question whether the mandatory sentence for murder should still be maintained. But is not that a different question? Members of the Criminal Law Revision Committee who were in favour of the abolition of the mandatory life sentence nevertheless thought that the defences of diminished responsibility and provocation reducing murder to manslaughter should be maintained: Fourteenth Report (Cmnd 7844, (1980)) para 56. Similarly, the recommendations of the Committee that killing by excessive force in self-defence should be manslaughter and not murder was quite independent of the question of the mandatory life sentence. The Select Committee of the House of Lords on Murder and Life Imprisonment (HL Paper 78–1, session 1988–89, para 83) agreed with the CLRC's opinion; and the Select Committee's own recommendation for a defence to murder of excessive self-defence was coupled with its principal recommendation that the mandatory life sentence should be abolished: 'If murder is to be reserved for those homicides most deserving of stigma this does not seem to be one of them', para 88.

Noting that the House had, by a majority, extended the defence of duress to a charge of aiding and abetting murder in *Lynch v DPP for Northern Ireland*, above, p **413**, Lord Lloyd remarked that the difference is that duress is a matter of common law, whereas in the use of force to prevent crime 'Parliament has already taken a hand by enacting section 3 of the 1967 [Criminal Law] Act. Parliament did not, in doing so, see fit to create a qualified defence in cases where the defendant uses excessive force in preventing crime.' Does not this overlook the fact that, notwithstanding the title of the Act, the law stated in s 3 is primarily civil law? It states when force may be used—when its use is lawful, so that it is neither a tort nor a crime. It says nothing at all about defences to crime, which is a different question as is demonstrated by *Gladstone Williams*, above, p **454** and its successors. A person who uses force which is *unreasonable* in the circumstances to prevent crime and who cannot therefore justify his actions under s 3 nevertheless has a defence to a criminal charge if the force would have been unreasonable if the circumstances had been as he mistakenly (and even unreasonably) believed them to be. Parliament did not see fit to enact the *Gladstone Williams* defence either, but the courts have held that it exists and rightly so. The questions whether the use of force is justified under s 3 and whether the user has a defence to a criminal charge are not the same. See generally, J. C. Smith, 'Using Force in Self-Defence and the Prevention of Crime' (1994) 47 Current Legal Problems 101. A holding that the user of excessive force is guilty only of manslaughter and not of murder would have been in no sense inconsistent with s 3. See further J. Rogers, 'Justifying the use of firearms by policemen and soldiers: a response to the Home Office's review of the law on the use of lethal force' (1998) 18(4) LS 486 and S. Skinner, 'Citizens in Uniform: Public Defence, Reasonablenss and Human Rights' [2000] PL 266.

Defence against non-criminal acts

The draft Criminal Code, cl 44, having provided that a person does not commit an offence by using necessary and reasonable force to protect himself or another from unlawful force or unlawful personal harm, gocs on:

(3) For the purpose of this section, an act is 'unlawful' although a person charged with an offence in respect of it would be acquitted on the ground only that—

  (a) he was under 10 years of age; or
  (b) he lacked the fault required for the offence or believed that an exempting circumstance existed; or
  (c) he acted in pursuance of a reasonable suspicion; or
  (d) he acted under duress, whether by threats or circumstances; or
  (e) he was in a state of automatism or suffering from severe mental illness or severe mental handicap.

There appears to be no judicial authority for these propositions but they probably represent informed legal opinion about the common law. In A *(children) (conjoined twins)*, above, p **440**, Ward LJ said:

The reality here—harsh as it is to state it, and unnatural as it is that it should be happening—is that Mary is killing Jodie. That is the effect of the incontrovertible medical evidence and it is common ground in the case. Mary uses Jodie's heart and lungs to receive and use Jodie's oxygenated blood. This will cause Jodie's heart to fail and cause Jodie's death as surely as a slow drip of poison. How can it be just that Jodie should be required to tolerate that state of affairs? One does not need to label Mary with the American terminology which would paint her to be 'an unjust aggressor', which I feel is wholly inappropriate language for the sad and helpless position in which Mary finds herself. I have no difficulty in agreeing that this unique happening cannot be said to be unlawful. But it does not have to be unlawful. The six-year-old boy indiscriminately shooting all and sundry in the school playground is not acting unlawfully for he is too young for his acts to be so classified. But is he 'innocent' within the moral meaning of that word as used by the Archbishop? I am not qualified to answer that moral question because, despite an assertion—or was it an aspersion—by a member of the Bar in a letter to *The Times* that we, the judges, are proclaiming some moral superiority in this case, I for my part would defer any opinion as to a child's innocence to the Archbishop [of Westminster] for that is his territory. If I had to hazard a guess, I would venture the tentative view that the child is not morally innocent. What I am, however, competent to say is that *in law* killing that six-year-old boy in self-defence of others would be fully justified and the killing would not be unlawful. I can see no difference in essence between that resort to legitimate self-defence and the doctors coming to Jodie's defence and removing the threat of fatal harm to her presented by Mary's draining her life-blood. The availability of such a plea of quasi self-defence, modified to meet the quite exceptional circumstances nature has inflicted on the twins, makes intervention by the doctors lawful.'

R v Hussey

(1924) 18 Cr App R 160, Court of Criminal Appeal

(Lord Hewart CJ, Avory and Salter JJ)

Appeal against conviction and sentence.

Appellant was convicted on 13 November 1924, before Acton J at the Central Criminal Court of unlawful wounding, and was sentenced to twelve months' imprisonment with hard labour.

Marston Garsia for the appellant (under s 10 of the Criminal Appeal Act 1907), who was present. In June 1924, appellant rented a room at Brixton from a Mrs West. In July Mrs West purported to give him an oral notice to quit, which he contended was not a valid notice. Because he refused to vacate the room Mrs West, a woman named Mrs Gould, and a man named Crook, armed with a hammer, a spanner, a poker and a chisel, tried to force their way into the room, the door of which the appellant had barricaded. A panel of the door was broken, and appellant thereupon fired through the opening and Mrs Gould and Crook were wounded. At no place in the summing-up was the attention of the jury drawn to the distinction in law between what is permissible in self-defence and what is permissible in defence of one's house: Archbold's *Criminal Pleading, Evidence and Practice*, 26th edn, p 887. On the contrary, the matter was treated throughout as if only the law of self-defence was applicable.

Eustace Fulton for the Crown. The question now raised was never urged at the trial, where the defence was that the violence used by appellant was necessary to protect his life and that of his wife and children. The rule of law referred to in Archbold (above) is a very ancient one, and belonged to the days when persons went out with armed retainers to seize other persons' lands. It is no longer to be observed. Appellant made no attempt to use lesser methods. With a proper direction the jury would have come to the same conclusion.

The Lord Chief Justice. No sufficient notice had been given to appellant to quit his room, and therefore he was in the position of a man defending his house. In *Archbold's Criminal Pleading, Evidence and Practice*, 26th edn, p 887, it appears that:

> 'In defence of a man's house, the owner or his family may kill a trespasser who would forcibly dispossess him of it, in the same manner as he might, by law, kill in self-defence a man who attacks him personally; with this distinction, however, that in defending his home he need not retreat, as in other cases of self-defence, for that would be giving up his house to his adversary.'

That is still the law, but not one word was said about that distinction in the summing-up, which proceeded on the foundation that the defence was the ordinary one of self-defence. The jury, by their verdict, negatived felonious intent, and with a proper direction they might have come to a different conclusion. This appeal must therefore be allowed.

Conviction quashed

Questions

1. Hussey was acting in the defence of his home. Was he also acting in the prevention of crime? Should it make any difference to the amount of force he might lawfully use?

2. Would it have been different if the assailants had intended, not to dispossess Hussey, but to gate-crash a party he was giving?

3. Would it be reasonable to stand and fight in defence of the home when it would be unreasonable not to retreat if the attack was directed at the defendant's person?

4. Al and Ben try to burst open the door of Dan's ground floor room, intending to tar-and-feather him. Dan could easily escape through the window. He fires a shotgun through the door and wounds Al. Is he guilty of unlawful wounding?

Director of Public Prosecutions v Bayer
[2003] EWHC Admin 2567, Divisional Court

(Brooke LJ and Silber J)

The respondents had trespassed on land and sought to disrupt the planting of GM maize seeds by attaching themselves to a tractor. Section 68(1) of the Criminal Justice and Public Order Act 1994 provides that:

(1) A person commits the offence of aggravated trespass if he trespasses on land in the open air, and, in relation to any lawful activity which persons are engaging in or are about to engage in on that or adjoining land in the open air, does there anything which is intended by him to have the effect— ... (c) of disrupting that activity.

Lord Justice Brooke considered the facts and the decision at first instance.

22. One matter needs to be made clear at the outset. In 1967 Parliament reformed and codified that part of the common law that is concerned with the use of force in arresting offenders or suspected offenders. In 1971 Parliament reformed and codified that part of the common law that identifies the ingredients of a lawful excuse for what would otherwise be an act of criminal damage (Criminal Damage Act 1972 s 5(2)). But Parliament has neither reformed nor codified that part of the common law that is concerned with force used in private defence, so that it is to caselaw alone that we must look when exploring the scope of a defence of lawful justification in a case like this.

23. It is a principle of the common law that a person may use a proportionate degree of force to defend himself, or others, from attack or the threat of imminent attack, or to defend his property or the property of others in the same circumstances. It is sufficient to refer, without express citation, to Hale, *Pleas of the Crown*, Vol 1 Chapter 8; Blackstone, *Laws of England*, Book 3, Chapter 1; Stephen, *Digest of the Criminal Law*, Article 306; *Hanway v Boultbee* 1 M and Rob 15; *R v Rose* (1847) 2 Cox 329. So far as the defence of property is concerned, when Sir James Stephen codified the law he did so in these terms:

> 'The intentional infliction of ... bodily harm is not a crime when it is inflicted by any person in order to defend his property or the property of another from a felony involving the use of force towards such property ... provided the person inflicting it inflicts no greater injury than he in good faith believed to be necessary when he inflicts it.'

24. A hundred years later, in the second edition of his *Textbook of Criminal Law* (1983) Professor Glanville Williams said pithily at p 501 that 'protective force' can be used to ward off unlawful force, to prevent unlawful force, to avoid unlawful detention and to escape from such detention. At p 503 he says of the defence of 'private defence' that the act of defence must be immediately necessary (there must be no milder way of achieving the end) and proportional to the harm feared.

25. These concepts are reflected in the modern authorities. In *Evans v Hughes* [1972] 3 All ER 412 the Divisional Court considered that for a defendant to justify his possession of a metal bar on a public highway he had to show that there was an imminent particular threat affecting the particular

circumstances in which the weapon was carried. In *Taylor v Mucklow* [1973] Crim LR 750 the same court upheld a decision of magistrates who considered that a building owner was deploying an unreasonable use of force in equipping himself with a loaded airgun against a builder who was demolishing a new extension because his bills were unpaid. In *Attorney-General's Reference No 2 of 1983* [1984] 1 All ER 988 the Court of Appeal held that a defendant could set up the statutory defence of showing that he possessed an explosive substance 'for a lawful purpose' if he could establish on the balance of probabilities that his purpose was to protect himself or his family or property by way of self-defence against an imminent and apprehended attack by means which he believed to be no more than reasonably necessary to meet the attack.

26. This line of authority is concerned with the defence of 'private defence' or 'protective force' when unlawful force is used or imminently threatened against a person who may use proportionate force to defend persons or property. It is to be distinguished from the line of authority which is concerned with a similar defence against trespassers. In the Law Commission's most recent attempt, following very widespread consultation, to articulate the relevant principles of law in a simple codified form (see *Offences Against the Person and General Principles* (1993) Law Com No 218, pp 106–110), these defences are set out (so far as they relate to defence of property) in the following terms:

> '27(i) The use of force by a person for any of the following purposes, if only such as is reasonable in the circumstances as he believes them to be, does not constitute an offence—
>> (c) to protect his property...from trespass;
>> (d) to protect property belonging to another from...damage caused by a criminal act or (with the authority of the other) from trespass...
>
> '29(i) For the purposes of section...27...
>> (a) a person uses force in relation to...property not only where he applies force to, but also where he causes an impact on,...that property;'

27. Although no authority directly in point was quoted to us, we are prepared to assume for the purposes of this judgment that when the respondents tied themselves to the tractors in Horselynch Plantation they were using force within the meaning of this line of authority. If in the circumstances as they believed them to be they thought that unlawful damage was being inflicted or was about to be inflicted on the property of another, then it is hard to understand why the defence should not be available if they prevented the damage by tying themselves to the tractors rather than by attacking the tractor drivers.

28. However, it has always been a requisite ingredient of this element of the common law defence that what is being experienced or feared is an unlawful or criminal act, and this is not a topic the district judge addressed at all. In the present case it is clear that the respondents knew quite well that there was nothing unlawful about the drilling of GM maize seed on Mr Jones's land, even if the seed might blow about or be transferred by one means or another to neighbouring land. They acted as they did because they believed so strongly that the seed represented a danger to neighbouring property and they knew that the law would not help them because what was going on was not unlawful or criminal. This is a far cry from the reasoning behind the need for the common law defence which was identified by Hale (op cit) when he referred to the need for 'an imminent and inevitable danger for [a man's] own life; for the law hath provided...recourse to the civil magistrate for protection'.

29. In our judgment, the district judge ought to have directed himself as a matter of law that the defence of private defence or protective force simply was not available to the respondents on these facts. He moved directly to considering their subjective beliefs and fears without first considering the ingredients of the defence. The answer to the question he posed is therefore: 'No, because the defence of "defence of property" was not available to the respondents on the facts set out in the case stated'. The case must therefore be remitted to him with a direction to convict, since

all the ingredients of the offence were established and no defence of lawful excuse is available to the defendants.

30. It may be that the district judge was led into error because of the way the statutory defence contained in section 5(2)(b) of the Criminal Damage Act is drafted. In that statutory scheme a person who commits what would otherwise be regarded as criminal damage is given a statutory defence of 'lawful excuse'

> 'if he damaged...the property in question...in order to protect property belonging to... another...and at the time of the...acts alleged to constitute the offence he believed—
> (i) that the property...was in immediate need of protection;
> (ii) that the means of protection adopted...were...reasonable having regard to all the circumstances.'

31. The common law defence of 'defence of property' has different ingredients. We note that in its 1993 report the Law Commission recommended (at para 37.6) that the ingredients of these two defences should be brought into line when any statutory restatement of the law was undertaken.

32. If the common law defence is raised in circumstances similar to those that arose in this case a court should first ask itself:

> 'Are the defendants contending that they used reasonable force in order to defend property from actual or imminent damage which constituted or would constitute an unlawful or criminal act?'

If the answer to this question is 'no', as in the present case, the defence is not available. If the answer is 'yes', then the court must go on to consider the facts as the defendants honestly believed them to be, and should then determine objectively whether the force they used was no more than was reasonable in all the circumstances, given their beliefs.

Question

If D is attacked by someone who is insane or under 10, surely D can use reasonable force to protect himself?

ECHR concerns

The Human Rights Act has prompted many to ask whether the protection English law affords to a victim of a defendant acting in 'self defence'/ 'private defence' is compatible with Article 2. The fact that D is entitled to an acquittal if he held a genuine though unreasonable belief in the need for violence is argued to be too generous to D, and results in the UK providing inadequate protection for its citizens' lives under Article 2. See A. Ashworth, 'Human Rights: Case Commentary on *Andronicou and Constantinou v. Cyprus*' [1998] Crim LR 823–825. See also A. Ashworth, 'The European Convention and criminal law' chapter in J. Beatson, *The Human Rights Act and the Criminal Justice and Regulatory Process* (1999).

Article 2 of the ECHR provides that:

Everyone's right to life shall be protected by law. No-one shall be deprived of his life intentionally save in the execution of a sentence of a court following his conviction of a crime for which this penalty is provided by law.

F. Leverick, 'Is English Self-Defence Law Incompatible With Article 2 of the ECHR'
[2002] Crim LR 347

concludes that:
English law is contrary to Article 2 of the ECHR. The reason for this claim is that, in allowing the unreasonably mistaken defendant to escape punishment in this way, English law fails to respect the

right to life of the person who, through no fault of their own, is mistaken for an attacker. An examination of relevant case law leads to the conclusion that the substance of English law does indeed contravene Article 2. It had been suggested that because killing in self-defence is not an intentional killing, Article 2 does not apply. Regardless of the theoretical merits of this suggestion, it can be dismissed as it has consistently been held that self-defensive killing does fall to be assessed under Article 2. Further, an examination of relevant cases shows that the court has consistently required that a mistaken belief in the need to use self-defensive force be based on good reasons. It is also clear, from cases such as *A v. United Kingdom* and *X and Y v. Netherlands*, that a violation of the Convention can take place when there has been a failure on the part of the State to provide a criminal law sanction that protects its citizens from the violent acts of other individuals, regardless of whether these individuals were State officials or private citizens. This is not to say that the Convention would necessarily require English law to convict the unreasonably mistaken self-defender of murder. It may be that a conviction for a lesser offence, such as manslaughter, is sufficient. Consideration of the degree of punishment appropriate in such circumstances is outside the scope of this paper. The point is that English law as it stands at present contains no sanctions whatsoever for the defendant who deprives another of her life in the unreasonable belief that she was an attacker.

Sir John Smith responded [2002] Crim LR 952:

The established English law is that, where a person is charged with a crime requiring mens rea and alleged to be committed by the use of force when acting in public or private defence, he is to be judged on the facts as he honestly believed them to be, whether reasonably or not. If, in light of the supposed circumstances, it was reasonable to use that degree of force, he is not guilty of such a criminal offence. It has been suggested by no less an authority than Professor Andrew Ashworth [Commentary on *Andronicou and Constantinou v. Cyprus* [1998] Crim L R 823–825] that this may be incompatible with Article 2 (Right to Life) of the ECHR—that the Article requires a criminal sanction where a person kills on the basis of an erroneous and unreasonable belief. I have argued otherwise and have recently written [[2001] Crim L R 400 at 402–403] that the point appears to be settled for English law by the decision in *Re A (children) (conjoined twins): surgical separation.* [above]…Article [2] proscribes only intentional killing, which means by an act done with the purpose of killing. The doctors in that case intended to kill within the meaning of the common law of murder because they knew that death was certain to result from their act but they did not act with the purpose of killing, so the Article was inapplicable.

Fiona Leverick criticises my argument and states that I cite no authority for my view. If that were so, I would indeed by remiss, but I thought, and think, it is obvious that my authority was the very decision for the Court of Appeal on which I was commenting. The judgments of the three Lords Justices, though arriving at the same result, differ in some important respects. But they appear to be unanimously of the opinion that 'intentionally' in the Article means 'with the purpose of' [Brooke L.J. at 1050 a-e and Robert Walker L.J. at 1067–1068]; and this ruling is the ratio decidendi of the court on this issue. For the purposes of the English law of murder, the doctors intended to kill baby Mary but, as their only purpose was to save the life of twin Jodie, they were not killing Mary intentionally within the meaning of the Article.

Ms Leverick states that my argument 'can be fairly easily dismissed' from an examination of the case law on Article 2 and goes on to discuss a series of decisions of the European Court of Human Rights ('ECtHR'). But, while an English court must 'take into account' any judgment of the ECtHR, such a judgment is not binding but only persuasive—as, of course, Ms Leverick knows. I was, and am, discussing English law and, if there is an inconsistency between the interpretation put on the Convention by the English courts and that which appears to be put on it by the ECtHR, it is the English court's ruling which prevails and represents the law of England.

It appears that the court in *Re A* received extensive written and oral argument on the issue of Article 2 and that relevant decisions of the ECtHR were cited. I do not venture into this arena, but, if the court's interpretation of those decisions differs from that of Ms Leverick, it is the court's interpretation which must prevail. She cites some European decisions delivered after *Re A* but, however persuasive they might be, they cannot affect the authority of *Re A* unless and until an English court decides otherwise.

…So I adhere firmly to my view that, until the House of Lords or Parliament decide otherwise, *Re A* decides that Article 2 has no application to a person acting bona fide in self-defence and that is the law of England.

What if the Article does require a criminal sanction?

Ms Leverick concedes that the Convention would not necessarily require English law to convict the unreasonably mistaken self-defender of murder:

> 'It may be that a conviction for a lesser offence, such as manslaughter, is sufficient… The point is that English law as it stands at present contains no sanction whatsoever for the defendant who deprives another of her life in the unreasonable belief that she was an attacker.'

This is an understandable view because there is no direct authority that the unreasonably mistaken killer in self-defence is guilty of a crime. However, I do not believe it is the law and I have so argued long before the question of compatibility with the ECHR arose.…

Where the force used was reasonable in the circumstances which the defendant believed to exist. The defendant is not guilty of murder but the question whether he may be guilty of manslaughter at common law does not appear to have been raised in any case.… Where the evidence suggests that the defendant was acting under a mistaken belief, a jury should be directed that, if the force used was reasonable in the circumstances as he honestly believed them to be, then they must acquit him of murder. But, if they do so acquit him, they must go on to consider whether (i) in the actual circumstances, the force used was unreasonable and, if it was, (ii) whether the defendant, in making the mistake, was guilty of gross negligence, so bad as in their judgment to amount to a crime. If they are sure that he was, then they should convict him of manslaughter.…

Ms Leverick concentrates on private defence but suggests that the incompatibility argument may be 'especially compelling' where force is used in the prevention of crime and section 3 of the Criminal Law Act 1967 is in issue because 'section 3 of the Human Rights Act 1998 requires primary legislation to be read and given effect in a way which is compatible with Convention rights'. But a person who uses more than reasonable force in the prevention of crime is in breach of section 3. He is acting unlawfully, whatever his honest belief. Section 3 can hardly be said to be incompatible with the Convention but, notwithstanding the title of the Act, this section does not say anything about the criminal law. When the defendant is charged with a criminal offence, it is the criminal law which is in issue. The court is not construing section 3. The requirements of mens rea are the same, whether it is public or private defence which is in issue.

See Fiona Leverick's further response at [2002] Crim LR 963.

The Law Commission, Report No 290, *Partial Defences to Murder* (2004), recently concluded that no new partial defence to murder should be created for the defendant who kills by using excessive force. A defendant will, in appropriate circumstances, be able to advance a 'pure' self defence plea and the new broader provocation based plea. Under the proposed scheme, if the jury rejects the self defence plea, they might still return a manslaughter verdict on the application of the new defence.

1) Unlawful homicide that would otherwise be murder should instead be manslaughter if the defendant acted in response to (a) gross provocation (meaning words or conduct or a combination of words

and conduct which caused the defendant to have a justifiable sense of being seriously wronged); or (b) fear of serious violence towards the defendant or another; or (c) a combination of (a) and (b); and a person of the defendant's age and of ordinary temperament, i.e. ordinary tolerance and self-restraint, in the circumstances of the defendant might have reacted in the same or a similar way.

2) In deciding whether a person of ordinary temperament in the circumstances of the defendant might have acted in the same or a similar way, the court should take into account the defendant's age and all the circumstances of the defendant other than matters whose only relevance to the defendant's conduct is that they bear simply on his or her general capacity for self-control.

3) The partial defence should not apply where (a) the provocation was incited by the defendant for the purpose of providing an excuse to use violence, or (b) the defendant acted in considered desire for revenge.

4) A person should not be treated as having acted in considered desire for revenge if he or she acted in fear of serious violence, merely because he or she was also angry towards the deceased for the conduct which engendered that fear.

5) The partial defence should not apply to a defendant who kills or takes part in the killing of another person under duress of threats by a third person. (pending a wider review of the law of murder)

6) A judge should not be required to leave the defence to the jury unless there is evidence on which a reasonable jury, properly directed, could conclude that it might apply.

Criminal Damage Act 1971, s 5

5. 'Without lawful excuse'

(1) This section applies to any offence under section 1(1) above and any offence under section 2 or 3 above [see below, p **946**] other than one involving a threat by the person charged to destroy or damage property in a way which he knows is likely to endanger the life of another or involving an intent by the person charged to use or cause to permit the use of something in his custody or under his control so to destroy or damage property.

(2) A person charged with an offence to which this section applies shall, whether or not he would be treated for the purposes of this Act as having a lawful excuse apart from this sub-section, be treated for those purposes as having a lawful excuse:

...

(b) if he destroyed or damaged or threatened to destroy or damage the property in question or, in the case of a charge of an offence under section 3 above, intended to use or cause or permit the use of something to destroy or damage it, in order to protect property belonging to himself or another or a right or interest in property which was or which he believed to be vested in himself or another, and at the time of the act or acts alleged to constitute the offence he believed:

(i) that the property, right or interest was in immediate need of protection; and

(ii) that the means of protection adopted or proposed to be adopted were or would be reasonable having regard to all the circumstances.

(3) For the purposes of this section it is immaterial whether a belief is justified or not if it is honestly held.

It will be noted that, under this provision, the question is whether *the defendant* believed that the force he used was or would be reasonable; whereas at common law the test is objective—it is for the jury or magistrates to say whether the force used was, in the circumstances which the defendant believed to exist, reasonable. Consider the following case.

D, whose flocks have suffered grievously from predatory dogs, sees that his sheep are being attacked by a large, savage dog and are in imminent danger of being killed. D waits for an opportunity to shoot at the dog. As he gets it in his sights, he realizes that the dog's owner, V, is standing some distance behind it. He pulls the trigger, kills the dog and wounds V. D asserts that, in his opinion, it was entirely reasonable to shoot, even though he knew there was a slight risk of injuring V. A jury or magistrates may think that D is, or may be, telling the truth but be satisfied that in fact it was not reasonable to shoot. How should the case be decided if D is charged with:

(i) damage to property (the dog) contrary to s 1(1) of the Criminal Damage Act 1971; or

(ii) damage to property being reckless whether the life of another be endangered contrary to s 1(2) of the 1971 Act; or

(iii) unlawfully and maliciously wounding V contrary to OAPA 1861, s 20?

Can these distinctions be justified in principle?

Criminal Law Act 1967, s 3

3. Use of force in making arrest, etc

(1) A person may use such force as is reasonable in the circumstances in the prevention of crime, or in effecting or assisting in the lawful arrest of offenders or suspected offenders or of persons unlawfully at large.

(2) Sub-section (1) above shall replace the rules of the common law on the question when force used for a purpose mentioned in the sub-section is justified by that purpose.

Section 3 operates only where D responds to prevent a 'crime'. In *Jones and others* [2005] Crim LR 122 (above), the Court of Appeal concluded that the concept of 'crime' in this context can only have been intended to mean a 'domestic' crime (that is, not a crime only in international law). The Criminal Law Revision Committee explained the proposed s 3 in very broad terms:

the court, in considering what was reasonable force, would take into account all the circumstances, including in particular the nature and degree of force used, the seriousness of the evil to be prevented and the possibility of preventing it by other means; but there is no need to specify in the clause the criteria for deciding the question. Since the clause is framed in general terms, it is not limited to arrestable or any other class of offences, though in the case of very trivial offences it would very likely be held that it would not be reasonable to use even the slightest force to prevent them. (Cmnd 2659, para 23.)

Despite the breadth of this statement the Court of Appeal's limitation in *Jones* seems warranted if the defence is to retain the degree of certainty desirable.

Section 3 excuses only the use of force. In *Blake v DPP* [1993] Crim LR 586 D, demonstrating against the Iraqi war, wrote with a felt pen on a concrete pillar near the Houses of Parliament. He was charged with criminal damage and argued that his act was justified by (inter alia) s 3. The court held that his act was 'insufficient to amount to the use of force within the section'. This suggests that the defence might not have been ruled out on this ground (though, in this particular case, it almost certainly would on other grounds) if D had used a hammer and chisel. It is odd that force should be excused when less serious acts might not be. Is that the effect of the section?

6. UNKNOWN CIRCUMSTANCES OF JUSTIFICATION OR EXCUSE

In *Dadson* (above, p 18) we saw that circumstances, which would have justified or excused D's conduct in shooting at V if he had been aware of them, were no defence because D was unaware that those circumstances existed. The majority of the CLRC were satisfied that the principle of that case was correct and it was embodied in their recommendation in their Fourteenth Report as to the law of private defence.

In *Williams (Gladstone)*, discussed above, pp 453, the Court of Appeal held that the recommendation was a true statement of the common law and therefore it now is the law, being persuasively confirmed by *Beckford* (above, p 451). An arrest can be lawful only if the arrestor is in a position to state a valid ground for arrest. Dadson was not in that position. 'I arrest you on the ground that you have stolen wood from the copse' would not satisfy the common law or s 28 of PACE. Stealing the wood was not a felony but an offence punishable only on summary conviction by a fine of £5 with no power to arrest the offender. Accordingly, the latest proposal to emerge from the Law Commission, cl 27(1) of the Non-Fatal Offences Bill (Law Com No 218) (1993), begins:

(1) The use of force by a person for any of the following purposes, if only such as is reasonable in *the circumstances as he believes them to be*, does not constitute an offence.

7. BELIEF, OR BELIEF ON REASONABLE GROUNDS?

For many years the courts stated that a defendant could rely on public or private defence only if he believed *on reasonable grounds* in the circumstances which entitled him to take the defensive action—for example, that a belief that he faced certain death at the hands of an aggressor unless he took the action in question was no defence to a charge of murder unless the belief was based on reasonable grounds. As we have seen, in *Williams (Gladstone)*, above, p 453, the Court of Appeal held that this was an incorrect statement of the common law and that the only question was whether the belief was honestly held. The view that only reasonable mistakes of fact can excuse has now been comprehensively repudiated by the House of Lords: *B (a minor) v DPP* and *K*, above, p 216 and 221.

On the other hand, we have also seen that in the common law of duress the courts still insist that the defence is open only to one who believes on reasonable grounds in the threat of death or grievous bodily harm: *Graham*, approved in *Howe*, above, p 416.

Can this distinction be justified? The Code Team and the Law Commission thought not and the Draft Code, cl 41(1) provides:

Belief in circumstances affording a defence. Unless otherwise provided, a person who acts in the belief that a circumstance exists has any defence that he would have if the circumstances existed.

The draft Non-Fatal Offences Bill does not restate this general provision but the definitions in the Bill of the particular defences require only a belief, not a reasonable belief, in the circumstances founding the defence. The Law Commission could see no ground for distinguishing between duress and self-defence or other defences in this respect. Reasonableness, according to this view, is only a matter of evidence—the more unreasonable the alleged belief, the less likely is the court or jury to find that it may have been honestly held.

Not everyone agrees with this 'subjective' approach. The Australian courts continue to require reasonable grounds for a defence of self-defence, an approach which is defended by Yeo, *Compulsion in the Criminal Law*, 200–219. A distinction is taken between elements of offences (as to which a subjective test is appropriate) and defence elements, where the test is objective. The distinction is related to the theory of justification and excuse. On a practical point Yeo puts the case of 'a person who is unnaturally apprehensive or cowardly which leads her to honestly but unreasonably believe that she is being attacked. Without the limitation of reasonable belief, such a person can react violently with impunity. And she can do so time and again if that is her inclination.' Is this a valid objection to the subjective test?

Unreasonable mistakes as to defence elements in crimes of negligence

A person who believes that the only way in which he can save his own life is by killing an aggressor has a defence to a charge of murder even though his belief is grossly unreasonable. Self-defence, unlike provocation which reduces murder to manslaughter, is generally a complete defence resulting in an outright acquittal. Does this mean that the grossly mistaken killer will be completely acquitted? Not necessarily. Gross negligence is now acknowledged to be a sufficient fault for manslaughter (below, p **638**) so why should not the grossly negligent mistake, resulting as it does in death, be a ground of liability in itself? See also *O'Grady*, above, p **206**, and Question 2 above, p **208**. In the case of non-fatal offences, the grossly negligent mistake would exempt the defendant entirely; but this is consistent with the present law, that causing non-fatal injuries by gross negligence is not an offence.

8. JUDICIAL DEVELOPMENT OF DEFENCES

Glanville Williams, 'Necessity'
[1978] Crim LR 128

[Having pointed out that a purpose of codification is to enable the citizen to know what conduct is penalized, the writer continues:]

It by no means follows that it should be any part of the purpose of a code to get rid of open-ended defences, or to fetter the power of the courts to create new defences in the name of the common law. That the courts have power to enlarge defences is sometimes denied by the judges, just as they deny in terms their power to enlarge offences; but history records some examples of the former activity as well as innumerable examples of the latter.

The Draft Code of 1879 recognised this distinction of policy. It contained two sections (5 and 19), one removing the power of the judges to create new crimes and the other preserving judicial creativity in respect of justifications and excuses. The proposal was immediately criticised by Cockburn LCJ on the ground that the arguments for exhaustive codification of offences applied equally to defences. Stephen, the architect of the code, replied to this criticism in a notable article. [See the Nineteenth Century for January 1880, pp 152–157. I am indebted to Sir Rupert Cross for calling my attention to this article.] He first distinguished two meanings of the term 'common law': a body of relatively fixed principles resulting from judicial decisions, and the qualified power of the judges to make new law under the fiction of declaring existing law, or in other words 'not a part of the law actually existing, but law which has only a potential existence—that which, if the case should ever occur, the judges would declare to be the law.' Stephen thought it justifiable to save the common law in the second sense in respect of defences, though not in respect of offences. The central passage of his argument is worth quoting rather fully.

'It appears to me that the two proposed enactments stand on entirely different principles. After the experience of centuries, and with a Parliament sitting every year, and keenly alive to all matters likely to endanger the public interest, we are surely in a position to say the power of declaring new offences shall henceforth be vested in Parliament only. The power which has at times been claimed for the judges of declaring new offences cannot be useful now, whatever may have been its value in earlier times.

On the other hand it is hardly possible to foresee all the circumstances which might possibly justify or excuse acts which might otherwise be crimes. A long series of authorities have settled certain rules which can be put into a distinct and convenient form, and it is of course desirable to take the opportunity of deciding by the way minor points which an examination of the authorities shows to be still open. In this manner rules can be laid down as to the effect of infancy, insanity, compulsion, and ignorance of law, and also as to the cases in which force may lawfully be employed against the person of another; but is it therefore wise or safe to go so far as to say that no other circumstances than those expressly enumerated shall operate by way of excuse or justification for what would otherwise be a crime? To do so would be to run a risk, the extent of which it is difficult to estimate, of producing a conflict between the Code, and the moral feelings of the public. Such a conflict is upon all possible grounds to be avoided. It would, if it occurred, do more to discredit codification than anything which could possibly happen, and it might cause serious evils of another kind. Cases sometimes occur in which public opinion is at once violently excited and greatly divided, so that conduct is regarded as criminal or praiseworthy according to the sympathies of excited partisans. If the Code provided that nothing should amount to an excuse or justification which was not within the express words of the Code, it would, in such a case, be vain to allege that the conduct of the accused person was justifiable; that, but for the Code, it would have been legally justifiable; that every legal analogy was in its favour; and that the omission of an express provision about it was probably an oversight. I think such a result would be eminently unsatisfactory. I think the public would feel that the allegations referred to ought to have been carefully examined and duly decided upon.

To put the whole matter very shortly, the reason why the common law definitions of offences should be taken away, whilst the common law principles as to justification and excuses are kept alive, is like the reason why the benefit of a doubt should be given to a prisoner. The worst result that could arise from the abolition of the common law offences would be the occasional escape of a person morally guilty. The only result which can follow from preserving the common law as to justification and excuse is, that a man morally innocent, not otherwise protected, may avoid punishment. In the one case you remove rusty spring-guns and man-traps from unfrequented plantations, in the other you decline to issue an order for the destruction of every old-fashioned drag or lifebuoy which may be found on the banks of a dangerous river, but is not in the inventory of the Royal Humane Society. This indeed does not put the matter strongly enough. The continued existence of the undefined common law offences is not only dangerous to individuals, but may be dangerous to the administration of justice itself. By allowing them to remain, we run the risk of tempting the judges to express their disapproval of conduct which, upon political, moral, or social grounds, they consider deserving of punishment, by declaring upon slender authority that it constitutes an offence at common law; nothing, I think, could place the bench in a more invidious position, or go further to shake its authority....

Besides the well-known matters dealt with by the Code, there are a variety of speculative questions which have been discussed by ingenious persons for centuries, but which could be raised only by such rare occurrences that it may be thought pedantic to legislate for them expressly beforehand, and rash to do so without materials which the course of events has not provided. Such cases are the case of necessity (two shipwrecked men on one plank), the case of a choice of evils (my horses are running away, and I can avoid running over A only by running over B), and some others which might be suggested.

Any ingenious person may divert himself, as Hecato did, by playing with such questions. The Commission acted on the view that in practice the wisest answer to all of them is to say, "When the case actually happens it shall be decided"; and this is effected by the preservation of such parts of the common law as to justification and excuse as are not embodied in the Code. Fiction apart, there is at present no law at all upon the subject, but the judges shall make one under the fiction of declaring it, if the occasion for doing so should ever arise.'

The Code Team and the Law Commission found Stephen's argument persuasive and the following provisions of the Code are intended to preserve the power of the courts at common law to develop existing and new defences. The most likely area for new development is necessity but the provisions do not limit the court in any way.

In *Kingston*, above, p **188**, although counsel was not disposed to argue the point, Lord Mustill considered ([1994] 3 All ER at 370) whether the House might take the 'bold step' of recognising a new defence of involuntary intoxication. He suspected that no new general defence had been created in modern times (but what about duress of circumstances, and *Janaway's* case (below)), adding:

'Nevertheless, the criminal law must not stand still, and if it is both practical and just to take this step, and if judicial decision rather than legislation is the proper medium, then the courts should not be deterred simply by the novelty of it.'

Having examined the nature of the proposed defence, Lord Mustill found that it ran into difficulties at every turn. Involuntary intoxication was best left to be taken into account in sentencing; but the question of a new defence was one which the Law Commission might usefully consider.

Criminal Code Bill

4. (1) …

(2) Rules of the common law corresponding to or inconsistent with the provisions of this Act are abrogated for all purposes not relating to acts done before the commencement of this Act.

(3) …

(4) This Act does not affect any rule of the common law not abrogated by sub-section (2) or limit any power of the courts to determine the existence, extent or application of any such rule.

…

45. A person does not commit an offence by doing an act which is justified or excused by:

(a) …

(b) …

(c) any rule of the common law continuing to apply by virtue of section 4(4).

F v West Berkshire Health Authority, above, p **433**, *Gillick's* case, above, p **435** and *Re A (children) (conjoined Twins)*, above, p **440**, may perhaps be regarded as applications of the common law power in relation to necessity.

Consider also *R v Salford Health Authority, ex p Janaway* [1989] AC 537, CA (Civil Division) (affirmed on other grounds [1989] AC 537, HL). The question in this civil action was whether a secretary employed by the Health Authority who had refused to type a letter arranging an abortion was in breach of her contract of employment. She argued that she was not because of s 4(1) of the Abortion Act 1967, which provides that no person is under a duty to participate in any treatment authorized by the Act to which he has conscientious objection. She said that she had a conscientious objection to abortion and therefore was under no duty to write the letter. The contemplated abortion was not illegal because it was authorized by the Act but it would have been illegal before 1967. The Court of Appeal held that she could rely on the conscientious objection clause only if she was being asked to do something that it would have been illegal for her to do before 1967—that is, the question was, would a secretary, instructed by her employer to write a letter arranging a criminal abortion, be guilty of aiding and abetting the crime if she wrote the letter? It was held that she would not. Slade LJ said:

> Whatever might be said of the doctor whose letter she was being asked to type, she herself in typing it would have been merely intending to carry out the obligations of her employment and not endeavouring to produce a result consisting of an abortion. Thus she would…not have had the necessary intent to render her a procurer.

The use of the word 'procure' in this context is ambiguous. The word is used to describe one of the activities amounting to secondary participation in a crime (above, Ch 9); but 'procuring an abortion' is the offence and the procurer is the principal offender. So the question was whether the secretary would have been aiding and abetting, shall we say, the *commission* of the abortion. If she wrote the letter, she would be doing an act which she knew would, and was intended, to further the commission of the offence. If a secretary typed a letter dictated by her boss arranging a 'contract killing' of his wife, what would the court have said to an argument that she was 'merely intending to carry out the obligations of her employment and not endeavouring to' cause a murder? So far as the requisite intention for secondary participation is concerned, the case is indistinguishable.

It is generally accepted that 'superior orders' is not a defence to crime. It is no answer for an employee accused of crime to say that he was only obeying the instructions of his employer. Is this a case where the court, in substance, recognized a defence of superior orders—the role of the typist being relatively insignificant and the letter she was asked to type being of the same general character as the letters she was properly employed to type? Or was the case (so far as this ground is concerned) wrongly decided? Consider the following case.

An abortion is lawful under the Abortion Act only if two registered medical practitioners have formed the opinion in good faith that one of the specified conditions is satisfied. Quack, having been unable to find any practitioner willing to agree that any of the conditions are satisfied in respect of Mabel, dictates to his secretary, Fred, a letter to Mabel, explaining the situation and arranging for the abortion to be carried out secretly. Fred types and posts the letter. Quack carries out the abortion as agreed and is convicted of the offence under s 58 of OAPA 1861. Is Fred liable? Can he plead (a) lack of the necessary intent or (b) that he was only carrying out the obligations of his employment?

FURTHER READING

P. ALLDRIDGE, 'Developing the Defence of Duress' [1986] Crim LR 433

A. ASHWORTH, 'Criminal Liability in a Medical Context: the Treatment of Good Intentions' in Simester and Smith (eds) *Harm and Culpability* (1996)

R. CHRISTOPHER, 'Unknowing Justification and the logical necessity of the *Dadson* principle in self defence' (1995) 15 OJLS 229

C. CLARKSON, 'Necessary Action: A New Defence' [2004] Crim LR 81

I. H. Dennis, 'Duress Murder and Criminal Responsibility' [1980] 106 LQR 208

D. W. Elliott, 'Necessity, Duress and Self-Defence' [1989] Crim LR 611

S. Gardner, 'Necessity's Newest Invention' (1991) 11 OJLS 125

P. R. Glazebrook, 'The Necessity Plea in English Criminal Law' [1972A] CLJ 87

J. Rogers, 'Necessity, private defence and the killing of Mary' [2001] Crim LR 515

W. Wilson, 'The Structure of Defences' [2005] Crim LR 125

13

Incitement

1. INCITEMENT

We have already noticed (above, p 272) that the mere incitement of another to commit a crime is itself a crime, committed as soon as the act of incitement is done; so that if Donna tells Edward that she wants him to kill her husband, Victor, she commits an offence. It is immaterial that Edward immediately declines; Donna has already committed incitement.

Incitement is a common law offence, a misdemeanour. This is so whether the offence incited is a common law offence such as murder or a statutory offence such as theft. Like common law misdemeanours generally, at common law it was triable only on indictment and was punishable by imprisonment or fine without limit at the discretion of the court. This was so even if the offence incited was triable only summarily. Now, however, the Magistrates' Courts Act 1980, s 45 provides:

Incitement

(1) Any offence consisting in the incitement to commit a summary offence shall be triable summarily.

(2) Subsection (1) above is without prejudice to any other enactment by virtue of which any offence is triable only summarily.

(3) On conviction of an offence consisting in the incitement to commit a summary offence a person shall be liable to the same penalties as he would be liable to on conviction of the last-mentioned offence.

Incitement to commit an indictable offence is triable on indictment and the penalty is still at the discretion of the court; so that incitement to commit an offence punishable by a maximum of, for example, two years' imprisonment is, in law, punishable by life imprisonment. In practice, of course, the sentencing judge will have regard to the penalty for the full offence and is unlikely to impose a greater sentence for inciting it. As a matter of principle, it would be desirable if incitement were put on a statutory footing with prescribed maximum sentences.

The examination of incitement requires consideration of three further issues:

(i) What is incitement, that is, the actus reus of the offence?

(ii) What mens rea is required?

(iii) Which activities can be incited?

(1) WHAT IS INCITEMENT?

The actus reus of incitement is extremely broad, including pressure of a hostile or non-hostile manner, implied or express, irrespective of whether it persuades the incitee to commit the substantive crime. When Iago said to Othello, 'Do it not with poison, strangle her in her bed', he was undoubtedly guilty of incitement to murder, even if Othello had already made up his mind to do away with his unfortunate wife. But things are not always as straightforward as that. Consider this controversial case.

Invicta Plastics Ltd v Clare
[1976] RTR 251, Queen's Bench Division

(Lord Widgery CJ, Park and May JJ)

The defendant company manufactured a device called 'Radatec' which emitted a high-pitched whine when within 800 yards of wireless telegraphy transmissions, including those used for police radar traps. The company advertised the device in a motoring magazine. The advertisement stated, 'You ought to know more about Radatec. Ask at your accessory shop or write for name of nearest stockist...' It depicted a view of a road and a speed limit sign through a car windscreen with the device attached. In response to a request by the prosecutor, the company sent him a stockist's name and a leaflet which included the words: 'The majority of [such] transmissions are not intended for public use and therefore their deliberate reception is illegal unless licensed by the Post Office.... However, no licence is required to receive [other such] transmissions. It is illegal to employ the Radatec specifically for the reception of, for instance, police radar transmissions.' The defendants were convicted by justices of inciting readers of the magazine and of the leaflet to contravene s 1(1) of the Wireless Telegraphy Act 1949 which forbade the use of any wireless telegraphy apparatus except under a licence.

[**Park J**, having held that the justices had rightly decided that a person using Radatec in his car would be using wireless telegraphy apparatus and, having no licence, would commit an offence under s 1(1) of the Act:]

When summing up to the jury on a case of incitement, judges sometimes use such words as 'incitement involves the suggestion to commit the offence' or 'a proposal to commit the offence' or 'persuasion or inducement to commit the offence' which the defendant is alleged to have incited. But Lord Denning MR considered the meaning of 'incitement' in *Race Relations Board v Applin* [1973] QB 815, 825G, where he said:

> 'Mr Vinelott suggested that to "incite" means to urge or spur on by advice, encouragement, and persuasion, and not otherwise. I do not think the word is so limited, at any rate in this context. A person may "incite" another to do an act by threatening or by pressure, as well as persuasion.'

Accordingly, the justices had to decide whether, in the context, the advertisement amounted to an incitement to the readers of the magazine to commit the offence.

It is submitted on behalf of the company that, before the offence of incitement could be committed by means of the advertisement, there had to be in it an incitement to use the device which was advertised; that, if not, any matter in the advertisement would not constitute incitement, as it would not be sufficiently proximate to the offence alleged to have been incited; and that, as the advertisement merely encouraged readers to find out more about the device, it did not amount to incitement in fact or in law.

I think that it is necessary to look at the advertisement as a whole. Approaching it in this way, I have come to the conclusion that the company did incite a breach of the Act by means of the advertisement. I think, therefore, that the justices were right to convict the company of this offence.

It is conceded that on the other summons against the company the case is much stronger because it depends upon the view taken by the justices of the pamphlet. Mr Crawford, in the course of his argument, conceded that this pamphlet would amount to incitement except for two sentences, which I have read, which he submits amount to 'disclaimers'. Those two sentences are those where the pamphlet states that the majority of X band transmissions are not intended for public use and, therefore, their deliberate reception is illegal unless licensed by the Post Office, and where it states that it is illegal to employ Radatec specifically for the reception of, for instance, police radar transmissions.

Again, looking at the pamphlet as a whole, as the justices did, it is plain that from the words used readers were being persuaded and incited to use the Radatec device. In my view, therefore, the justices were also right to convict the company on that charge.

Appeal dismissed

Questions

1. The defendants were obviously trying to persuade readers to buy Radatec, but as buying the device did not constitute an offence, so incitement to buy it was not an offence. Was there evidence that the defendants intended to persuade, and were trying to persuade, readers to *use* Radatec in contravention of the Act? (Note that the requirement of a licence has since been removed by legislation.)

2. Could the defendants have been convicted of inciting motorists to exceed the speed limit? If they were inciting motorists to use Radatec, what did they expect them to use it for, except to exceed the speed limit with impunity? They wanted to sell Radatec, but did they care what was done with it afterwards?

3. A news item in The Times, 6 August 1998, reports that a student was fined for 'selling speed trap jammers' to motorists. The conviction was for 'inciting motorists to exceed the speed limit'. Would D have any liability if he published a map identifying the position of all the speed cameras in London? Is he encouraging motorists to abide by the speed limit?

Notes

1. In *Marlow* [1997] Crim LR 897 M, under a pseudonym, wrote a book on the cultivation and production of cannabis which was advertised in *Private Eye* and sold some 500 copies. He was convicted of a specific statutory incitement contrary to s 19 of the Misuse of Drugs Act 1971 ('It is an offence to incite or attempt to incite another person to commit [an offence under any other provision of this Act']). The prosecution alleged that the book was an incitement of those who bought it to cultivate cannabis, contrary to s 4(2) of the Act. The defence was that the book was no more than a scientific exposition of the subject and was not reasonably capable of being regarded as incitement. The judge directed the jury that they had to be 'sure that this is a book which may encourage or persuade or ... is capable of encouraging and persuading other people to produce the drug ...'. M appealed on the ground that this put the test for the actus reus too low. The court held, that in the overall context, the conviction was safe, but agreed with the criticism, saying that the judge should have adhered to the formula, 'a book which encourages or persuades'.

Is that correct? As the court recognizes, the offence is committed when the inciting words are communicated and it cannot then be known whether it will in fact encourage or persuade anyone. If the book is capable of persuading, and is published with purpose of persuading, is not that incitement? Is the appropriate test for the actus reus whether the reasonable reader (the juror or magistrate) would think he was being persuaded to do it?

Marlow pursued his case to the ECtHR in Strasbourg claiming that his Article 10 rights of freedom of expression had been infringed. The Court declared the application inadmissible ([2001] EHRLR 444). Is the English law of incitement compatible with Article 10? (See above, p **12**.)

2. If there can be an incitement by advertisements and publications of this nature, consider the implications for email advertisements sent across many jurisdictions to millions of potential purchasers of a product.

3. In *Goldman* [2001] Crim LR 822, ESV, a company in Amsterdam advertised pornographic videos for sale. G wrote requesting a tape of young girls, aged 7 to 13. He was charged with attempting to incite ESV to distribute indecent photographs of children under 16 (then an offence under the Protection of Children Act 1978, s 1(b)), contrary to s 1 of the Criminal Attempts Act 1981 (below, p **519**). The trial judge ruled that it was no answer to the charge that G was responding to an offer to supply indecent photographs. G was convicted and his appeal was dismissed. The court said this was not a mere response to an offer but amounted to a suggestion, proposal, persuasion or inducement of ESV by G to commit the offence. Should it be the offence of incitement to act on the invitation of one who declares himself ready, willing and able to commit the offence? It does not appear why only an attempt and not the full offence was charged. Consider the benefits this case offers for undercover policing.

4. In *O'Shea* [2004] EWHC 905 (Admin) (The Times, 22 April) the Administrative Court held that there was a prima facie case that by subscribing to a website with indecent images of children D had incited or encouraged E, the supply business, to continue even though that computer system was wholly automated. Cf the discussion in Ch 22 below on deception. The fact that the owners produced bi-weekly updates to their website provides evidence that they were actively responding to the communications, maintaining the service and thus that there was a person who was receiving D's communication. It is important to note that this is merely evidence to support the charge of incitement because there is of course no need to prove that the website owners were actually encouraged: incitement is committed as soon as D has communicated his encouragement, etc irrespective of whether the incitee ignores it. Again, it is submitted that this deserves further judicial examination. The actus reus of the offence requires that D has performed acts capable of encouraging or inciting a person (presumably any legal person including a company). The much misunderstood mens rea requirement is that D intends to encourage a person to engage in conduct that constitutes a crime. In some cases therefore D might deny mens rea, claiming that he was sufficiently well informed of the workings of the system of the website to believe that he was not communicating with any person, but only with a machine.

5. Since the offence is committed at the time when D communicates with E, there is no scope for a defence of withdrawal. Should there be?

6. In *James and Ashford* (1985) 82 Cr App R 226, [1986] Crim LR 118 the defendants were convicted of conspiring to incite others to commit the offence of abstracting electricity (Theft Act 1968, s 13, below, p **766**). They manufactured 'black boxes' which may be used to reverse electricity meters and there was evidence that they intended to sell the boxes to a 'middleman', Kenny Williams, who would sell them to others who would use them on their electricity meters. The court allowed the appeal. Having dealt with matters relating to conspiracy, they said:

Furthermore, it is right, on our judgment, as the appellants argued in this case, that there are other substantial problems as to the convictions on count 3. First, the sale or proposed sale of these particular boxes was to a middleman. There was no evidence that the appellants conspired to incite Kenny Williams to use a box or boxes personally. And even if it is possible (as it may be) for there to exist a conspiracy to incite one person (Williams) to incite ultimate users, that was certainly neither the thrust nor the factual position proved in the present case.

Secondly, this was not the sort of case which could be within the decision in the case of *Invicta Plastics Ltd v Clare* [1976] RTR 251. There was here no advertisement or open persuasion to others to use these devices, and indeed no evidence of the intention other than an intention to make the devices and sell them 'wholesale' to Williams.

Question

1. What if Kenny Williams had been, not a 'middleman', but the defendants' agent to sell the black boxes to householders for use on their meters?

(2) THE MENS REA OF INCITEMENT

In *DPP v Armstrong* [2000] Crim LR 379, DC, the court stated that the common law offence is accurately defined in cl 47 of the Draft Criminal Code as follows:

A person is guilty of incitement to commit an offence or offences if—

  (a) he incites another to do or cause to be done an act or acts which, if done, will involve the commission of the offence or offences by the other; and—

  (b) he intends or believes that the other, if he acts as incited, shall or will do so with the fault end required for the offence or offences.

In that case, D phoned E asking for pornography of girls 'not younger than say 12 years'. Unknown to D, E was a police officer, concerned with detecting offences of paedophilia. D was charged with inciting E to commit the offence of distributing indecent photographs of children contrary to the Protection of Children Act 1978. The magistrate dismissed the charge on the ground that the person incited must have 'parity of *mens rea*' with the inciter. Applying the above definition, the court held that this was wrong and allowed the appeal. Cf *Shaw*, below, p **480**.

Questions

1. Towards what consequence must D have an intention? Is it enough that he intends to communicate the message? Must D intend that the message be understood? Must D intend that the message be acted on?

2. What does intention mean in this context? D, a bank official, informs E, whom he knows to be an experienced burglar, that the bank's alarm system has been playing up. Is it sufficient that D intends to communicate with E and knows that once E receives the message E will be virtually certain to commit the crime? Must D have the commission of the crime by E as his 'purpose'? Could it be argued that D's conduct is sufficiently blameworthy because he is reckless in providing E with an opportunity over which he (D) then has no control?

3. D tells E that E's wife, V, has been committing adultery. D is aware that E will be virtually certain to kill V when he hears this. Has D incited murder? V. Tadros (2002) LS 448, 454 argues that since D takes no responsibility for the action or potential action of E if he has not identified with it, D ought not to be convicted of the incitement. Do you agree?

Note

It is important to keep separate the requirement of D's mens rea from any mens rea that E might have if he went on to commit the substantive crime.

R v Curr

[1967] 1 All ER 478, Court of Appeal, Criminal Division

(Lord Parker CJ, Salmon LJ and Fenton Atkinson J)

The appellant was a trafficker in family allowance books. He advanced money to married women with large families on the security of their books and got them to sign some of the vouchers. He employed a team of women agents to cash the vouchers, pocketed the proceeds in repayment of the loan and returned the books. He handled about 40 to 80 books a week and made about 800 per cent per annum on the transactions. He admitted that he knew that he was not entitled to receive the family allowance payments. He appealed from his convictions for inciting to commit offences contrary to s 9(b) of the Family Allowances Act 1945 (incitement to commit a summary offence is now triable only summarily: Magistrates' Courts Act 1980, s 45) and of conspiring to commit offences contrary to that section. Section 9(b) provides:

If any person—...(b) obtains or receives any sum as on account of an allowance, either as in that person's own right or as on behalf of another, knowing that it was not properly payable, or not properly receivable by him or her; that person shall be liable on summary conviction to imprisonment for a term not exceeding three months or to a fine not exceeding £50 or both such imprisonment and such fine.

Fenton Atkinson J. Counsel for the appellant's argument was that, if the woman agent in fact has no guilty knowledge, knowing perhaps nothing of the assignment, or supposing that the appellant was merely collecting for the use and benefit of the woman concerned, then she would be an innocent agent, and, by using her services in that way, the appellant would be committing the summary offence himself, but would not be inciting her to receive money knowing that it was not receivable by her. He contends that it was essential to prove, to support this charge, that the woman agent in question in this transaction affecting a Mrs Currie, knew that the allowances were not properly receivable by her. Counsel for the Crown's answer to that submission was that the woman agent must be presumed to know the law, and, if she knew the law, she must have known, he contends, that the allowance was not receivable by her. [His Lordship referred to regulations providing that the allowance was receivable only by the wife or husband except during a short period of illness.]

In our view, the argument for the Crown here gives no effect to the word 'knowing' in the section, and in our view the appellant could be guilty on count 3 only if the woman agent sent to collect the allowance knew that the action which she was asked to carry out amounted to an offence. As has already been said, the appellant himself clearly knew that his conduct in the matter was illegal and contrary to s 9(b), but it was essential in our view for the jury to consider the knowledge, if any, of the woman agent. When the assistant recorder dealt with this count, he referred to soliciting in this way:

> 'Solicited means encouraged or incited another person to go and draw that money which should have been paid, you may think, to Mrs Currie.'

He then dealt with ignorance of the law being no excuse. He went on to deal with statutory offences, and read s4 of the Family Allowances Act 1945, telling the jury in effect that, apart from the case of sickness, nobody else could legally receive these allowances, and then he went on to consider the position of the appellant, asking the rhetorical question whether he could be heard to say with his knowledge of this matter and his trafficking in these books that it was not known to be wrong to employ an agent to go and collect the family allowances. He never followed that, however, with the question of the knowledge of the women agents, and in the whole of the summing-up dealing with this matter he proceeded on the assumption that either guilty knowledge in the woman was irrelevant, or alternatively, that any woman agent must be taken to have known that she was committing an offence under s9(b). If the matter had been left on a proper direction for the jury's consideration, they might well have thought that the women agents, other than Mrs Nicholson, whom they acquitted, must have known very well that they were doing something wrong; some of them were apparently collecting as many as ten of these weekly payments. The matter, however, was never left to them for their consideration, and here again, so it seems to this court, there was a vital matter where the defence was not left to the jury at all and there was no sufficient direction; it would be quite impossible to say that, on a proper direction, the jury must have convicted on this count.

[His Lordship held that the convictions for conspiracy must also be quashed as the jury had not been told that both parties to the alleged conspiracy must have known that the money was not properly payable.]

Appeal allowed. Convictions quashed

Notes and questions

1. The Criminal Code team criticized *Curr* on the ground that 'it is not necessary that any offence should be committed or even intended by the person incited.' Do you agree? Suppose that D has stolen a necklace and he presses E to accept it as a gift. Should D, in the following alternative circumstances, be guilty of inciting E to handle stolen goods?

(a) D believes that E thinks he acquired the necklace honestly. Actually, E knows he stole it.

(b) D believes that E knows he stole the necklace. In fact, E believes that D bought the necklace from a well-known, reputable jeweller.

If E receives the necklace, in (a) she will be guilty, in (b) she will be not guilty, of handling stolen goods; but in (b) D intends that E shall commit an offence, in (a) he does not.

2. In *Shaw* [1994] Crim LR 365 D, an employee of a car-leasing company, persuaded K, another employee of the company, to obtain cheques from the company by falsely accepting bogus invoices, supplied by D as real invoices for real work done by real garages. He was charged with inciting K to obtain property by deception. His defence was that his purpose was not to make a profit but to demonstrate to his employers how easy it was to circumvent

their security arrangements. He did not tell K his purpose, but eventually he would have done so. D's appeal was allowed. The court said that the mens rea of both D and K, including the intention permanently to deprive, had to be considered, and that the jury should have been told that if they thought it possible that D's purpose was to demonstrate the insecurity of the system, they must acquit. If D intended K to carry out the scheme with the dishonest intention of permanently depriving the company of money, should it have been a defence to the charge of incitement that D intended to disclose his purpose and prevent any loss to the company? It was certainly necessary to prove that D intended K to act with the dishonest intention of permanently depriving the company, but was it necessary to show that D had any such dishonest intention? See cl 47(1) of the Criminal Code Bill above, p 478 and *DPP v Armstrong*, above, p 478.

(3) WHAT CAN BE INCITED?

The act incited must be one which, when done, would involve the commission of the crime by the person incited or through his innocent agent.

R v Whitehouse

[1977] 3 All ER 737, Court of Appeal, Criminal Division

(Scarman and Geoffrey Lane LJJ and Donaldson J)

The defendant pleaded guilty to a charge of incitement of his 15-year-old daughter to commit incest with him. Under s 11 of the Sexual Offences Act 1956 [see now the Sexual Offences Act 2003, below Ch 20) it is an offence for a woman of 16 or over to permit (*inter alios*) her father to have intercourse with her but a girl aged 15 cannot commit incest. The court held that it had jurisdiction to entertain an appeal against conviction and continued:

Scarman LJ. It is of course accepted by the Crown that at common law the crime of incitement consists of inciting another person to commit a crime. When one looks at this indictment in the light of the particulars of the offence pleaded, one sees that it is charging the accused man with inciting a girl to commit a crime which in fact by statute she is incapable of committing. If therefore the girl was incapable of committing the crime alleged, how can the accused be guilty of the common law crime of incitement? The Crown accepts the logic of that position and does not seek in this court to rely on s 11 of the 1956 Act or to suggest that this man could be guilty of inciting his daughter to commit incest, to use the old phrase, as a principal in the first degree. But the Crown says that it is open to them on this indictment to submit that it covers the offence of inciting the girl to aid and abet the man to commit the crime of incest on her. Section 10 of the 1956 Act makes it an offence for a man to have sexual intercourse with a woman whom he knows to be his daughter, and the Crown says that on this indictment it is possible to say that the accused has committed an offence known to the law, the offence being that of inciting his daughter under the age of 16 to aid and abet him to have sexual intercourse with her...

There is no doubt of the general principle, namely that a person, provided always he or she is of the age of criminal responsibility, can be guilty of aiding or abetting a crime even though it be a crime which he or she cannot commit as a principal in the first degree. There are two famous illustrations in the books of this principle. A woman can aid and abet a rape so as herself to be guilty of rape, and a boy at an age where he is presumed impotent can nevertheless aid and abet a rape. The cases, which are very well known, are first in time *R v Eldershaw* [(1828) 3 C & P 396]. In that case Vaughan B, in the course of a six line judgment, the brevity of which I wish I could emulate, says: 'This boy being under fourteen, he cannot, by law, be found guilty of a rape, except as a principal in the second degree.' So much for the boy. The position in regard to a woman is stated by Bowen LJ [*R v Ram and Ram* (1893) 17 Cox CC 609] in one line and a half, where two prisoners, a Mr and Mrs Ram, were indicted jointly for rape on Annie Edkins of the age of 13. It was submitted that the woman could not be indicted for rape. Bowen LJ declined to quash the indictment for rape as against the female prisoner. Those cases clearly establish, and have been regarded for a very long time as establishing, the general principle to which I have referred.

But what if the person alleged to be aiding and abetting the crime is herself the victim of the crime? …

The question in our judgment is determined by authority. It is, strictly speaking, persuasive authority only because it deals with a different Act of Parliament, but it is a decision by a strong court which has declared a principle which is as applicable to the statutory provision with which we are concerned as to that with which that case was concerned. The case is *R v Tyrrell* [[1894] 1QB 710, [1891–4] All ER Rep 1215]. It was a decision of the Court for Crown Cases Reserved and it was a five judge court, consisting of Lord Coleridge CJ, Mathew, Grantham, Lawrence and Collins JJ. The headnote reads as follows [[1894] 1QB 710]:

> 'It is not a criminal offence for a girl between the ages of thirteen and sixteen to aid and abet a male person in committing, or to incite him to commit, the misdemeanour of having unlawful carnal knowledge of her contrary to s5 of the Criminal Law Amendment Act 1885'.

It is necessary to look at the facts. I take them from the report. The defendant was tried and convicted on an indictment charging her with having unlawfully aided and abetted, counselled and procured the commission by one Thomas Ford of the misdemeanour of having unlawful carnal knowledge of her while she was between the ages of 13 and 16, and it was proved at the trial that the girl did aid and abet, solicit or incite the man to commit the misdemeanour made punishable by s 5 of the 1885 Act. Lord Coleridge CJ in giving judgment said [[1894] 1QB 710 at 712, cf [1891–4] All ER Rep 1215 at 1215, 1216]:

> '[The Act] was passed for the purpose of protecting women and girls against themselves. At the time it was passed there was a discussion as to what point should be fixed as the age of consent. That discussion ended in a compromise, and the age of consent was fixed at sixteen. With the object of protecting women and girls against themselves the Act of Parliament has made illicit connection with a girl under that age unlawful; if a man wishes to have such illicit connection he must wait until the girl is sixteen otherwise he breaks the law; but it is impossible to say that the Act, which is absolutely silent about aiding or abetting, or soliciting or inciting, can have intended that the girls for whose protection it was passed should be punishable under it of the offences committed upon themselves'.

The other four judges agreed with Lord Coleridge CJ.

In our judgment it is impossible, as a matter of principle, to distinguish *R v Tyrrell* from the present case. Clearly the relevant provisions of the Sexual Offences Act 1956 are intended to protect women and girls. Most certainly s 11 is intended to protect girls under the age of 16 from criminal liability, and the Act as a whole exists, insofar as it deals with women and girls exposed to sexual threat, to protect them. The very fact that girls under the age of 16 are protected from criminal liability for what would otherwise be incest demonstrates that this girl who is said to have been the subject of incitement was being incited to do something which, if she did it, could not be a crime by her.

I refer to s 1 of the Indecency with Children Act 1960. By that section any person, and I leave out the immaterial words, who incites a child under the age of 14 to an act of gross indecency shall be liable on conviction on indictment to imprisonment for a term not exceeding two years. Had his daughter been under the age of 14, the accused would have been guilty of this statutory incitement, and on a plea of guilty that would have been the end of the matter. It is noted that in the earlier 1975 indictment there was included a count under s 1 of the 1960 Act to which he did in fact plead guilty. But the gap remains between the age of 14 and the age of 16. It may be that the legislature will consider it desirable to stop that gap....

Appeals against conviction allowed. Appeal against sentence allowed; sentence varied

Notes

1. Parliament responded quickly to the suggestion for legislation with the Criminal Law Act 1977, s 54 and the Sexual Offences Act 2003 replaces this with a number of broad offences including s 26:

A person (A) commits an offence if,

(a) he intentionally incites another person (B) to touch, or allow himself to be touched by, A,

(b) the touching is sexual,

(c) the relation of A to B is [as very extensively defined in section 27 to include blood relationships, foster parent/child and relationships involving cohabitation or care for the child],

(d) A knows or could reasonably be expected to know that his relation to B is of a description falling within that section, and

(e) either—

(i) B is under 18 and A does not reasonably believe that B is 18 or over, or

(ii) B is under 13.

Whitehouse's plea of guilty could now be sustained.

Questions

1. Who is a 'victim' for the purposes of the law of incitement? Consider D, a masochist who incites E, a sadist, to beat him (cause him actual bodily harm). Is D guilty of incitement? Cf *Brown*, p **687**, below)

2. In *Pickford* [1995] 1 Cr App R 420 D pleaded guilty to inciting his son, L, to commit incest with his mother between 1 January and 31 December 1975. L's fourteenth birthday occurred during this period. At the time, the rule that a boy under the age of 14 could not commit offences involving sexual intercourse (abolished by the Sexual Offences Act 1993) still applied. The Court of Appeal held that if L was, as he may have been, under 14 at the time of the intercourse, D had pleaded guilty to an offence unknown to the law. (The court nevertheless upheld D's conviction under the proviso under s 2 of the Criminal Appeal Act 1968 on the ground that no miscarriage of justice had occurred because D could have been charged with inciting his wife to commit incest with L and he was clearly guilty of that offence; but the proviso has now been abolished by the Criminal Appeal Act 1995—see [1995] Crim LR 920.) The court, referring to *Tyrrell*, above, p **482**, held that the because Parliament had enacted an offence for a woman to commit incest with her son it must have intended to protect the son from the sexual advances of his mother. Do you find that reasoning convincing? Cf s 65 of the Sexual Offences Act 2003.

3. To what extent is it necessary that D incites a 'full' crime by E? Is it sufficient that D incites an actus reus? Consider D who incites E to damage property by falsely informing E that it is his (D's) property. E will act without mens rea if he damaged the property. Should D be liable for inciting such conduct? Recall *DPP v Armstrong* (above, p **478**).

4. Consider the case of D who incites E to inflict harm on V, believing that for E to do so would be an act of legitimate self-defence? Cf *El Faisal* [2004] EWCA Crim 456 where D had incited his audiences to kill Americans, Jews, Hindus and 'unbelievers'. His unsuccessful defence was that the encouragement was for the incitees to kill 'on the battlefield' and as such did not amount to solicitation to murder, only to commit lawful killings. Does it matter whether E thought he had such a defence?

(4) INCITING SECONDARY PARTICIPATION OR OTHER INCHOATE OFFENCES

Inciting secondary participation

D incites E to do an act which is not itself a crime but which, if a crime contemplated by D and E were committed, would render E liable as a secondary party. For example, intending to commit burglary in Bigshot Manor, D incites E, Lord Bigshot's butler, to leave open a window in the Manor. Leaving a window open, even with the intention of assisting a burglary, is not an offence known to the law; but if D enters through the open window, E will be guilty as a secondary party of the burglary thereby committed by D. If, however, D abandons the plan and no burglary is committed, is he guilty of incitement? The only possible charge seems to be incitement to commit burglary; but burglary is entering a building as a trespasser with intent to steal, and D has not incited E to do that. Cf *Bodin and Bodin* [1979] Crim LR 176 where D paid E £50 to find someone to assault V. It was held that there was no case to answer on an indictment alleging that D incited E to assault V. He incited E to become a secondary party to an assault on V but Judge Geoffrey Jones said that it is not an offence to incite another to become 'an accessory before the fact'. But if this is right, why did not the court in *Whitehouse*, above, quash the conviction on the short ground that there is no offence of incitement to abet an offence? Is it simply that the point was overlooked? Is D's conduct in these cases any less blameworthy than where D incites E to commit the 'full' substantive offence?

Incitement of other inchoate offences

It will have been noted that in *James and Ashford*, above, p **478**, the court thought that there may be a conspiracy to incite A to incite B to commit a crime; so at common law one inchoate offence may be built upon another. The difference from the examples considered in the preceding paragraph is that the aiding, abetting, counselling or procuring of the Accessories and Abettors Act is not an offence, but only a variety of ways of participating in an offence; whereas incitement, conspiracy and attempt are offences in themselves. The common law has been modified by the Criminal Law Act 1977, s 5(7), which provides:

Incitement…to commit the offence of conspiracy (whether the conspiracy incited…would be an offence at common law or under section 1 above, or any other enactment) shall cease to be an offence.

The Court of Appeal has twice held (*Sirat* (1985) 83 Cr App R 41; *Evans* [1986] Crim LR 470) that there is an offence of incitement to incite unless the second incitement would amount to an agreement to commit the contemplated offence. In that case the second incitement would result in a conspiracy and the opinion of the courts appears to be that to allow this incitement to conspire to be charged as an incitement to incite would be an illegitimate evasion of the abolition of the former offence. If D says to E, 'Here is £1,000—hire a killer to do away with my wife, V', incitement to incite will not lie because the hiring clearly involves an agreement, a conspiracy, to kill V. D has incited E to conspire and Parliament has said that is not to be an offence. But if D says to E, 'Don't meet or speak to F but get a message to him that, if he kills V, £1,000 will be paid into his bank account', D may be convicted of inciting E to incite F because any agreement between E and F is ruled out. The Law Commission were primarily responsible for this state of affairs because it was on their recommendation that s 5(7) was enacted; but now they have appreciated the consequences of that provision, they have had second thoughts and state, 'Such an absurd distinction cannot be stated in the Code'. Section 5(7) would be repealed by cl 47(5)(b), below.

The Criminal Code Bill

47. Incitement to commit an offence

(1) A person is guilty of incitement to commit an offence or offences if:

    (a) he incites another to do or cause to be done an act or acts which, if done, will involve the commission of the offence or offences by the other; and

    (b) he intends or believes that the other, if he acts as incited, shall or will do so with the fault required for the offence or offences.

(2) Subject to section 52(1), 'offences' in this section means any offence triable in England and Wales.

(3) Where the purpose of an enactment creating an offence is the protection of a class of persons, no member of that class who is the intended victim of such an offence can be guilty of incitement to commit that offence.

(4) A person may be convicted of incitement to commit an offence although the identity of the person incited is unknown.

(5) It is not an offence under this section, or under any enactment referred to in section 51, to incite another to procure, assist or encourage as an accessory the commission of an offence by a third person; but:

    (a) a person may be guilty as an accessory to the incitement by another of a third person to commit an offence; and

    (b) this subsection does not preclude a charge of incitement to incite (under this section or any other enactment), or of incitement to conspire (under section 8 or any other enactment), or of incitement to attempt (under section 9 or any other enactment), to commit an offence.

FURTHER READING

Law Commission Consultation Paper No 131, *Assisting and Encouraging Crime* (1993)

R. Leng, 'Incitement—An objective approach to the definition of crime?' (1978) 41 MLR 725

J. C. Smith, in P. R. Glazebrook (ed) *Crime Proof and Punishment* (1978) 21

V. Tadros, 'The system of the criminal law' (2002) LS 448

14

Conspiracy

1. INTRODUCTION

The second inchoate offence is conspiracy which is committed as soon as A and B agree to cause the forbidden result, as for example where A and B agree to burgle a house next week. The crime is committed and is not undone even if they immediately repent and abandon the plan. Their repentance would mitigate the sentence but would have no effect on liability to conviction. If the result intended by A and B was a crime, even a summary offence, the indictable offence of conspiracy was committed and at common law was punishable by fine and imprisonment at the discretion of the court.

At common law, unlike incitement and attempt, conspiracy was not limited to cases where the defendants had in view the commission of a crime. Conspiracy was defined at common law as an agreement to do an unlawful act or to do a lawful act by unlawful means; and the word 'unlawful' included not only all crimes but also some torts, fraud, the corruption of public morals and the outraging of public decency, whether or not the acts in question amounted to crimes when done by an individual. The scope of criminal liability was excessive.

2. RATIONALE OF OFFENCE

Where D1 and D2 agree to graffiti V's house, a conspiracy to commit criminal damage is complete even though they have never been near the house and have taken no further steps to perpetrate that crime. Although it is accepted that the substantive offence of criminal damage should exist, the question is whether the mere agreement to do so ought also to be subject to the criminal sanction. Some argue that the conduct represents a different 'wrong' or 'harm' from the commission of criminal damage itself, but is it a sufficiently serious wrong to warrant criminalization? See the discussion I. Dennis, 'The Rationale of Criminal Conspiracy' (1977) 93 LQR 39, and in the USA, P. Marcus, 'Conspiracy: The Criminal Agreement in Theory and in Practice' (1977) 65 Geo LJ 925, 950; P. E. Johnson, 'The Unnecessary Crime of Conspiracy' (1973) 61 Cal L Rev 1137, 1141. These are not mere 'ivory towered' anxieties: when the Law Commission began its study of the subject in 1970, one of the first questions posed to Glanville Williams was 'Do we need an offence of Conspiracy at all?'(D. Hodgson, 'Law Commission No 76: A Case Study in Criminal Law Reform' in P. R. Glazebrook (ed), *Reshaping Criminal law: Essays in Honour of Glanville Williams* (1978)).

There are numerous arguments, many of considerable merit, which cannot be dealt with in full here, however, it is possible to give a flavour of the diversity and ingenuity of the objections to what is an offence of considerable pedigree, and significant practical value:

- It criminalizes conduct before it has been confirmed to constitute a harm or real threat of harm—even earlier than an attempt in which an overt act of more than mere preparation is required.

- It allows for the punishment of conduct by two which would not be criminal if performed by a sole actor.

- Procedurally, it allows the Crown to avoid specificity in the case and carries with it the disadvantages inherent in joint trials.

There are equally respectable counter arguments defending the need for conspiracy:

- The offence allows for the intervention of the police authorities at an early stage of the enterprise and this better protects society against the commission of the substantive crime.

- There is a unique and distinct harm involved in the preparedness to collaborate in criminal activity.

- Conspiracy is important in deterring not only the commission of the substantive crime but the planning and collaboration in crime generally. This differs from attempt where no distinct harm, and hence no distinct deterrence, is involved in the performance of an act more than merely preparatory to the offence.

- As the US Supreme Court has observed:

  > For two or more to…combine together to commit…a breach of the criminal laws is an offense of the gravest character, sometimes quite outweighing, in injury to the public, the mere commission of the contemplated crime. It involves deliberate plotting to subvert the laws, educating and preparing the conspirators for further and habitual criminal practices. And it is characterized by secrecy, rendering it difficult of detection, requiring more time for its discovery and adding to the importance of punishing it when discovered. (*US v Rabinowich* 238 US 78, 88 (1915).)

- This same view has been expressed in the English literature from the middle of the nineteenth century:

  > The general principle on which the crime of conspiracy is founded is this, that the confederacy of several persons to effect any injurious object creates such a new and additional power to cause injury as requires criminal restraint; although none would be necessary were the same thing proposed, or even attempted to be done, by any person singly. (Criminal Law Commission, *Seventh Report* (1843), p 90.)

- Collaboration may increase the likelihood of commission of the offence and perhaps even an increased level of harm if committed. (This must surely depend on the type of crime. Counter arguments are that the collaboration may also render conspiracies weaker since they are more susceptible to a disclosure of information or one party reneging. On the psychological and economic strengths of conspiracies see N. Katyal, 'Conspiracy Theory' (2003) 112 Yale LJ 1307).)

- Conspiracy allows the true nature of the criminality of a group of individuals to be the focus of a prosecution.

- Arguably, conspiracy better respects the principle of fair labelling since the description of D's conduct accurately reflects his personal behaviour.

Questions

1. Is a crime of conspiracy necessary when a defendant can be charged with attempt as soon as he goes beyond acts of mere preparation towards the commission of the offence?

2. To what extent is it desirable and/or possible to have an offence of conspiracy focused on the mere fact of agreement and collaboration? To what extent must the offence depend on the detail of the substantive offence that is the object of the conspiracy?

3. STATUTORY AND COMMON LAW CONSPIRACY

The common law of conspiracy has been greatly modified by statute. The Criminal Law Act 1977 created a new offence of statutory conspiracy. Section 1 of that Act (as amended) provides:

1. The offence of conspiracy

  (1) Subject to the following provisions of this Part of this Act, if a person agrees with any other person or persons that a course of conduct shall be pursued which, if the agreement is carried out in accordance with their intentions, either:
    (a) will necessarily amount to or involve the commission of any offence or offences by one or more of the parties to the agreement, or
    (b) would do so but for the existence of facts which render the commission of the offence or any of the offences impossible, he is guilty of conspiracy to commit the offence or offences in question.

  (2) Where liability for any offence may be incurred without knowledge on the part of the person committing it of any particular fact or circumstance necessary for the commission of the offence, a person shall not be guilty of conspiracy to commit that offence by virtue of subsection (1) above unless he and at least one other party to the agreement intend or know that that fact or circumstance shall or will exist at the time when the conduct constituting the offence is to take place.

  (3) [*Repealed.*]

  (4) In this Part of this Act 'offence' means an offence triable in England and Wales.

  [Section 1A, Conspiracies to commit offences outside the United Kingdom, is omitted.]

Statutory conspiracy is not limited to agreements to commit a statutory crime—agreements to commit the common law offence of murder are charged under this offence—rather the term 'statutory conspiracy' is used to distinguish it from common law conspiracies. An agreement to commit a crime is now a statutory conspiracy, regulated by the 1977 Act instead of the common law. The penalty for statutory conspiracy is provided by s 3 of the Act—broadly the conspiracy is punishable in the same manner as the crime the offenders have conspired to commit.

(1) PENALTIES FOR CONSPIRACY

3. Penalties for conspiracy

  (1) A person guilty by virtue of section 1 above of conspiracy to commit any offence or offences shall be liable on conviction on indictment—
    (a) in a case falling within subsection (2) or (3) below, to imprisonment for a term related in accordance with that subsection to the gravity of the offence or offences in question (referred to below in this section as the relevant offence or offences); and
    (b) in any other case, to a fine.

Paragraph (b) above shall not be taken as prejudicing the application of [s 127 of the Powers of Criminal Courts (Sentencing) Act 2000] [s 163 of the Criminal Justice Act 2003] (general power of court to fine offender convicted on indictment) in a case falling within subsection (2) or (3) below.

(2) Where the relevant offence or any of the relevant offences is an offence of any of the following descriptions, that is to say—

(a) murder, or any other offence the sentence for which is fixed by law;

(b) an offence for which a sentence extending to imprisonment for life is provided; or

(c) an indictable offence punishable with imprisonment for which no maximum term of imprisonment is provided,

the person convicted shall be liable to imprisonment for life.

(3) Where in a case other than one to which subsection (2) above applies the relevant offence or any of the relevant offences is punishable with imprisonment, the person convicted shall be liable to imprisonment for a term not exceeding the maximum term provided for that offence or (where more than one such offence is in question) for any one of those offences (taking the longer or the longest term as the limit for the purposes of this section where the terms provided differ).

In the case of an offence triable either way the references above in this subsection to the maximum term provided for that offence are references to the maximum term so provided on conviction on indictment.

Section 3(3) seems to leave no room for the application of the principle of *Courtie* [1984] 1 All ER 740, [1984] AC 463, above, p 44. If an indictment alleges a conspiracy to (i) sexually assault (10 years) and (ii) murder (life), the maximum is life. Section 3(1) and (3) makes it clear that this is a single offence of conspiracy. Suppose the jury are satisfied that the parties agreed to commit sexual assault but not murder. Clearly the single offence of conspiracy alleged is not proved. Likewise if they are satisfied as to the agreement to murder but not as to the agreement to assault. Does this mean that the accused goes free? Section 6(3) of the Criminal Law Act 1967 provides that, where the jury acquit of the offence specifically charged in the indictment, but the allegations in the indictment amount to or include another offence, they may find the accused guilty of that offence. It ought therefore to be possible to convict D of conspiracy to sexually assault in the first contingency and of conspiracy to murder in the second.

This demonstrates the good sense of the *Courtie* principle. In substance, two conspiracies are alleged and it would be much more satisfactory, for the purposes both of the judge's direction to the jury and the taking of the verdict, if there were two counts of conspiracy. But, since the 1977 Act treats the agreement as a single offence, the taint of duplicity is absent. An indictment charging a conspiracy to sexually assault a child under 13, in effect, inevitably alleges a second offence—sexual assault of a child under 16; and, if a jury was sure that the parties knew the girl was under 16 but were not sure that they knew she was under 13, they could convict of the included lesser offence: Criminal Law Act 1967, s 6(3).

(2) COMMON LAW CONSPIRACIES

It is an offence triable only on indictment to agree:

(i) to defraud, whether or not the fraud amounts to a crime or even a tort;

(ii) to do an act which tends to corrupt public morals or outrage public decency, whether or not the act amounts to a crime.

The 1977 Act has no part to play in the prosecution of such offences.

It is the ultimate aim of the Law Commission to limit conspiracy to agreements to commit crimes. If that aim is achieved, s 1 above will represent the whole law of conspiracy. It was thought, however, that the complete abolition of common law conspiracy would leave some unacceptable gaps in the law and that, pending the enactment of some new but undefined substantive offences, it was necessary to ensure that conspiracies to defraud, to corrupt public morals and to outrage public decency continue to be punishable even if the conduct agreed upon does not amount to an offence.

(3) RELATIONSHIP BETWEEN COMMON LAW AND STATUTORY CONSPIRACIES

Section 5(1) to (3), as originally enacted, provided:

5. Abolitions, savings, transitional provisions, consequential amendment and repeals

(1) Subject to the following provisions of this section, the offence of conspiracy at common law is hereby abolished.

(2) Subsection (1) above shall not affect the offence of conspiracy at common law so far as relates to conspiracy to defraud [and section 1 above shall not apply in any case where the agreement in question amounts to a conspiracy to defraud at common law].

(3) Subsection (1) above shall not affect the offence of conspiracy at common law if and in so far as it may be committed by entering into an agreement to engage in conduct which:
    (a) tends to corrupt public morals or outrages public decency; but
    (b) would not amount to or involve the commission of an offence if carried out by a single person otherwise than in pursuance of an agreement.

So far as the corruption of public morals and outrage of public decency are concerned, the relationship between common law and statutory conspiracy is clearly defined by s 5(3)(b). The agreement is a conspiracy at common law only if it 'would not amount to or involve the commission of an offence if carried out by a single person otherwise than in pursuance of an agreement.' If it would amount to or involve the commission of an offence then it is a statutory conspiracy to commit that offence, contrary to s 1 of the 1977 Act.

There is no corresponding provision for conspiracy to defraud. On the contrary, if s 5(2) is given its natural meaning it preserves the whole of the common law of conspiracy to defraud and makes it clear that an agreement which is a conspiracy to defraud cannot be a statutory conspiracy. After much controversy, however, the House of Lords in *Ayres* [1984] 1 All ER 619, [1984] AC 447 took a different view, holding that statutory conspiracy and conspiracy to defraud are indeed mutually exclusive but that it is the statutory, not the common law, conspiracy which prevails: any agreement to defraud, the performance of which would involve the commission of an offence, must be indicted as a statutory conspiracy to commit that offence and not as a conspiracy to defraud. This decision caused great difficulties for prosecutors. Indictments and convictions for conspiracy to defraud had to be quashed because it was discovered that the carrying out of the agreement necessarily involved the commission of some offence, however trivial.

In *Cooke* [1986] 2 All ER 985, [1986] AC 909 British Rail stewards plotted to sell their own food on trains and to keep the proceeds, thus defrauding British Rail of the profit they should have made. This agreement probably did not involve the commission of any offence against BR. Though the stewards would be bound to account for their ill-gotten gains, BR had (or it was generally understood at that time that they had) no proprietary interest in them; so it was not a conspiracy to steal the profits. See below, p 782, note 5. But the Court of Appeal held that the carrying out of the agreement would necessarily involve an offence of going equipped to cheat the passengers, contrary to s 25 of the Theft Act 1968, below, p 915, and therefore the conviction for conspiracy to defraud must be quashed. The House of Lords allowed the prosecution's appeal. They confirmed that common law and statutory conspiracy are mutually exclusive but recognized that a single agreement may involve more than one conspiracy. A conspiracy to defraud was ruled out only if its constituents coincided exactly with a conspiracy to commit a specific offence. The conspiracy to defraud BR involved fraudulent conduct going substantially beyond the commission of offences under s 25 (and s 15) of the Theft Act 1968. It appears that it was immaterial that the carrying out of the conspiracy to defraud *involved* the commission of a specific offence, so long as it did not *amount* to the commission of such an offence.

The Criminal Justice Act 1987, s 12, repealing the words in brackets in s 5(2), above, restored the full scope of conspiracy to defraud at common law:

12. Charges of and penalty for conspiracy to defraud

(1) If:
  (a) a person agrees with any other person or persons that a course of conduct shall be pursued; and
  (b) that course of conduct will necessarily amount to or involve the commission of any offence or offences by one or more of the parties to the agreement if the agreement is carried out in accordance with their intentions,

the fact that it will do so shall not preclude a charge of conspiracy to defraud being brought against any of them in respect of the agreement.

(2) In section 5(2) of the Criminal Law Act 1977, the words from 'and' to the end are hereby repealed.

(3) A person guilty of conspiracy to defraud is liable on conviction on indictment to imprisonment for a term not exceeding 10 years or a fine or both.

It is now immaterial on a charge of conspiracy to defraud that the course of conduct agreed upon will necessarily amount to or involve the commission of an offence. The prosecutor has now a choice between indicting for conspiracy to defraud and statutory conspiracy—a discretion which should be exercised in accordance with the guidance in the Code for Crown Prosecutors issued by the DPP under s 10(1) of the Prosecution of Offences Act 1985. See www.cps.gov.uk.

However, the law as stated in *Cooke* continues to apply to conspiracies committed between 1 December 1977 when s 1 of the Criminal Law Act 1977 came into force and 20 July 1987 when s 12 of the Criminal Justice Act 1987 took effect: *Levitz* (1989) 90 Cr App R 33, [1989] Crim LR 714 shows such conspiracies are now unlikely to come before the courts. A conspiracy entered into before 20 July 1987 but continuing after that date may be charged as a conspiracy to defraud as well as a statutory conspiracy: *Boyle and Mears* (1991) 94 Cr App R 158.

4. THE ELEMENTS OF STATUTORY CONSPIRACY

  (1) an agreement

  (2) a course of conduct

  (3) necessarily involving the commission of a criminal offence

  (4) the crime to be committed by one of the parties to the conspiracy

  (5) intention

    (a) intention to carry out the agreement

    (b) conspiracy as an agreement without intent to carry out the agreement

    (c) playing some part in the agreed course of conduct

  (6) knowledge as to circumstances

(1) AN AGREEMENT

The offence is complete once a concluded agreement (going beyond mere negotiation) exists. Once there is an agreement it (and therefore the criminal conspiracy) subsists until the agreement is performed or abandoned: *DPP* v *Doot* [1973] AC 807. During this time anyone joining the enterprise, knowing of the criminal purpose, becomes a party to the conspiracy. It is not necessary for all the parties to know each other or even to know what other parties exist: *Meyrick* (1929) 21 Cr App R 94. In that case Ds had each been involved in the bribery of a police officer in Soho. Their individual agreements with the police officer enabled them to contravene the licensing laws. A number of the defendants appealed against their conviction on the ground that all those involved in the conspiracy had never even met each other. Their appeals were dismissed.

Lord Hewart CJ:

It seems to us that it was clearly put to the jury that in order to find these persons, or any of them, guilty of the conspiracy charged…it was necessary that the prosecution should establish, not indeed that the individuals were in direct communication with each other, or directly consulting together, but that they entered into an agreement with a common design. Such agreements may be made in various ways. There may be one person, to adopt the metaphor of counsel, round whom the rest revolve. The metaphor is the metaphor of the centre of the circle and the circumference. There may be a conspiracy of another kind, where the metaphor would be rather that of a chain; A communicates with B, B with C, C with D, and so on to the end of the list of conspirators. What has to be ascertained is always the same matter: is it true to say, in the words already quoted, that the acts of the accused were done in pursuance of a criminal purpose held in common between them?

But there must be a criminal purpose that the parties share as their common purpose: *Griffiths* [1966] 1 QB 589: D conspired with each of a number of farmers to defraud the Ministry of Agriculture; but it was not shown to be one conspiracy and therefore was not chargeable as such.

Notes and Questions

1. How realistic is it to say that D1 and D2 are in agreement on something if they have never met or communicated together?

2. The conspiracy may revolve around some third party, X, who is in touch with each of D1, D2, D3, though they are not in touch with one another (a 'wheel conspiracy'). Provided that the result is that they have a common design—for example, to rob a particular bank—D1, D2 and D3 may properly be indicted for conspiring together though they have never been in touch with one another until they meet in the dock. The same is true of a chain conspiracy where D1 communicates with D2, D2 with D3 etc.

(2) COURSE OF CONDUCT

The parties must agree 'that a course of conduct shall be pursued which . . . will necessarily amount to or involve the commission of any offence . . . by one or more parties to the agreement'. A 'course of conduct' is an ambiguous phrase. It might mean that A and B need only have agreed on (a) the actual physical acts which they propose shall be done; or (b) that they have agreed on the act and consequences which they intend to follow from their conduct and the relevant circumstances which they know, or believe, or intend, to exist.

'Course of conduct' must include the contemplated result. If A and B agree to kill V by shooting him, this is surely conspiracy to murder even though B knows that he is a rotten shot and may well miss his target. Is this too philosophical? They agree *and* intend to kill. Their objective *is* the intended result, and the agreed course of conduct is merely the means (however flawed) towards that intended end.

As for relevant circumstances, it would again seem absurd not to include these as requirements of the 'course of conduct'. If D1 and D2 agree to have intercourse with a person, V, their liability for conspiracy to rape a child under 13 must depend on their agreed course of conduct including the circumstance of the child's age.

Not only are relevant circumstances part of the 'course of conduct', but to work, further words arguably need to be read into the statute to provide that the circumstances that DD *believe will exist* are material. Thus, if D1 agrees to marry D2 next week, knowing that D1 is married. There ought to be a conspiracy to commit bigamy. But if 'course of conduct' means only physical acts, that is, that D goes through the ceremony, it cannot be said that there was an agreement as to a course of conduct that will necessarily involve the commission of a criminal offence: D1's wife may die before the week is out. The circumstance of D1's married status may on one view be held to be intended because D1 *believes* it will persist at the time of the wedding to D2.

(3) 'NECESSARILY AMOUNT TO OR INVOLVE THE COMMISSION OF ANY OFFENCE . . . BY ONE OR MORE PARTIES TO THE AGREEMENT'

Consider the following two examples provided by the Court of Appeal in *Reed* [1982] Crim LR 819:

In the first, A and B agree to drive from London to Edinburgh in a time which can be achieved without exceeding the speed limits, but only if the traffic they encounter is exceptionally light. Their agreement will not necessarily involve the commission of any offence even if it is carried out in accordance with their intentions, and they do arrive from London to Edinburgh within the agreed time. Accordingly the agreement does not constitute the offence of statutory conspiracy or indeed of any offence. In the second example, A and B agree to rob a bank, if when they arrive at the bank it seems safe to do so. Their agreement will necessarily involve the commission of an offence of robbery if it is carried out in accordance with their intentions. Accordingly, they are guilty of the statutory offence of conspiracy.

In *Reed* A and B were held guilty of conspiring to aid and abet suicide where they agreed that A would visit individuals contemplating suicide and either discourage them or actively help them, depending on his assessment of the appropriate course of action. In *Jackson* [1985] Crim LR 442, CA D and E agreed to shoot their friend V in the leg if he was convicted of the burglary for which he was on trial. (They believed he would thereby receive a lighter sentence.) V was shot and disabled. D and E were convicted of conspiring to pervert the course of justice. They appealed on the ground that their agreement did not necessarily involve the commission of a crime, as everything depended on a contingency— V being convicted. The court held:

Planning was taking place for a contingency and if that contingency occurred the conspiracy would necessarily involve the commission of an offence. `Necessarily' is not to be held to mean that there must inevitably be the carrying out of an offence. It means, if the agreement is carried out in accordance with the plan, there must be the commission of the offence referred to in the conspiracy count.

Questions

1. Is the distinction to be drawn on the basis of whether the commission of the crime is the direct object or incidental to the agreement? Is that a workable solution in practice?

2. Can these cases be better dealt with as each involving two agreements? An agreement to drive to Edinburgh and an agreement to speed if traffic is heavy? The latter necessarily involves the commission of a crime subject to a condition, but that does not preclude a conspiracy. (D1 and D2 agree to burgle 20 Lyddon Terrace unless there are police outside when they arrive to do so—this is a completed conspiracy, their reservation does not preclude liability.)

3. In *O'Hadhmaill*, [1996] Crim LR 509 it was held that an agreement by members of the IRA during the period of the IRA ceasefire to make bombs with a view to causing explosions, if, but only if, the ceasefire came to an end was a conspiracy to cause an explosion. Is this an agreement subject to a reservation, or contingency?

4. Are burglars guilty of conspiracy to murder if they set out to commit burglary, having agreed that, if it is necessary to do so in order to complete the burglary or to escape, they will shoot to kill? Will the agreement 'necessarily' involve murder? The courts have concluded that if conspirators agree that they will steal a particular item and that they will, if necessary, either commit burglary or robbery to obtain that item, that will amount to an agreement to commit the offences of theft, burglary *and* robbery: *A-G's Reference (No 4 of 2003)* [2004] EWCA Crim 1944, para 14.

5. What of D1 and D2 agreeing that if the next person who walks around the corner is a man they will rob him and if it is a woman they will rape her. Can this be an agreement to rob or rape? It is two conditional agreements: one to rob *and* one to rape? It is possible to enter an agreement to commit offence A *or* offence B, but such an agreement in law constitutes a conspiracy to commit offence A *and* offence B. An agreement to rob the first person who comes around the corner if it is a man constitutes a conspiracy to rob. Similarly

an agreement to rape the first person to come around the corner if it is a woman constitutes a conspiracy to rape. Thus, an agreement to rob the first person who comes around the corner if it is a man, but to rape if it is a woman, is an agreement to commit only one of two offences, but it is an agreement which in law amounts to a conspiracy to do both. The condition precedent of the one offence excludes the commission of the other, but at the time of the agreement the relevant facts are unknown and it seems that the parties therefore agree to commit robbery or rape as the prevailing circumstances permit.

(4) CRIME TO BE COMMITTED BY ONE OR MORE OF THE PARTIES TO THE CONSPIRACY

An agreement will amount to a statutory conspiracy only if carrying it out will necessarily amount to or involve the commission of an offence *by one or more of the parties to the conspiracy*. In *Hollinshead*, below, the Court of Appeal held that, in this respect, the Act did no more than restate the common law; so that there could be no conspiracy to defraud where the fraud contemplated was to be carried out, not by any party to the agreement, but by a third party: [1985] 1 All ER 850 at 857. The defendants had agreed to supply 'black boxes' to a man (in fact an undercover policeman) who was expected to resell them to persons unknown who would use them to defraud electricity boards. (The black box reverses the flow of current so as to make it appear that less electricity has been used. It has no other use.) The Court of Appeal also refused leave to proceed on another count (count 1) alleging a statutory conspiracy to aid, abet, counsel or procure an offence under s 1 of the Theft Act 1968, p **749**, below, following Smith and Hogan, *Criminal Law* (5th edn), pp 234–235 and holding that an agreement to aid, etc is not a conspiracy under the 1977 Act. (Cf Draft Code, cl 48(7), p **517**, below.) The prosecution obtained leave to appeal to the House of Lords.

R v Hollinshead

[1985] 2 All ER 769, House of Lords

(Lords Fraser, Diplock, Roskill, Bridge and Brandon)

Lord Roskill. The real question, as already stated, is whether in order to secure conviction on count 2 it was necessary to aver and prove a dishonest agreement by the respondents actually to use the black boxes, the submission being that it was not enough to show only an intention that such a dishonest use should follow their dishonest manufacture and sale.

My Lords, in my view, with all respect to those who have taken a different view, this submission is contrary to authority. I start with the decision of this House in *Scott v Comr of Police for the Metropolis* [1974] 3 All ER 1032, [1975] AC 819. It is to be observed that that case was decided before the passing of the 1977 Act. Scott was charged with two offences. First, he was charged with conspiracy to defraud and, second, with conspiracy to infringe s 21(1)(a) of the Copyright Act 1956. He ultimately pleaded guilty to both and was sentenced on both counts (see [1974] 3 All ER 1032 at 1033, [1975] AC 819 at 822). In this connection I have the permission of my noble and learned friend Lord Bridge to say that he was in error in saying in his speech in *R v Ayres* that the conspiracy under consideration in *Scott v Comr of Police for the Metropolis* did not involve the commission of any identifiable offence (see [1984] 1 All ER 619 at 622, [1984] AC 447 at 454). But the House was not there concerned with what would now be called a statutory conspiracy. Indeed, since *R v Ayres* the two counts would be mutually exclusive and Scott could not have been convicted on both. That is, however, of no importance in the present case. The importance of the decision in *Scott v Comr of Police for the Metropolis* lies in the conclusion summarised in the headnote ([1975] AC 819 at 820):

> '(3) That the common law offence of conspiracy to defraud was not limited to an agreement between two or more persons to deceive the intended victim and by such deceit to defraud him; and accordingly, as deceit was not an essential ingredient of the offence, the count was not bad in law and the appellant had been rightly convicted.'

Viscount Dilhorne said ([1974] 3 All ER 1032 at 1038, [1975] AC 819 at 839): 'One must not confuse the object of a conspiracy with the means by which it is intended to be carried out.' Lord Diplock said ([1974] 3 All ER 1032 at 1040, [1975] AC 819 at 841):

> '(2) Where the intended victim of a "conspiracy to defraud" is a private individual the purpose of the conspirators must be to cause the victim economic loss by depriving him of some property or right, corporeal or incorporeal, to which he is or would or might become entitled. The intended means by which the purpose is to be achieved must be dishonest. They need not involve fraudulent misrepresentation such as is needed to constitute the civil tort of deceit. Dishonesty of any kind is enough.'

In *A-G's Reference (No 1 of 1982)* [1983] 2 All ER 721, [1983] QB 751 (the whisky label case) the Court of Appeal (Lord Lane CJ, Taylor and McCowan JJ) was primarily concerned with the question of jurisdiction to try persons for conspiracy which had been entered into in England but which was to be carried out abroad though that conspiracy would cause economic damage to persons in England. The court held that there was no such jurisdiction. But it is apparent from a passage in the judgment of that court delivered by Lord Lane CJ that but for the question of jurisdiction the former defendants would have been guilty of conspiracy to defraud. Lord Lane CJ said ([1983] 2 All ER 721 at 724, [1983] QB 751 at 757):

> 'In each case, to determine the object of the conspiracy, the court must see what the defendants actually agreed to do. Had it not been for the jurisdictional problem we have no doubt that the charge against these conspirators would have been conspiracy to defraud potential purchasers of the whisky, for that was the true object of the agreement.'

The dishonest agreement there under consideration was to produce, label and distribute bottles of whisky so as to represent them as containing whisky of a well-known brand which in fact they did not contain. The object, as Lord Lane CJ said, was to defraud potential purchasers of the whisky outside this country.

In my view the respondents were liable to be convicted of conspiracy to defraud because they agreed to manufacture and sell and thus put into circulation dishonest devices, the sole purpose of which was to cause loss, just as the former defendants in the case just referred to would, apart from the jurisdictional problem, have been liable to be convicted of conspiracy to defraud because they agreed dishonestly to produce, label and distribute bottles of whisky, the sole purpose of the sale of which was to defraud potential purchasers of those bottles....

I can deal with the question raised in connection with count 1 more briefly. As was pointed out in *R v Ayres* [1984] 1 All ER 619 at 622, [1984] AC 447 at 455 in the passage, to which I have already referred, offences of statutory conspiracy and of common law conspiracy to defraud are mutually exclusive. It follows that, if your Lordships agree with me that the respondents were properly convicted on count 2 of conspiracy to defraud, this conclusion presupposes that the respondents could not properly have been convicted on count 1 of the statutory conspiracy there charged. The Court of Appeal was of the opinion that they could not have been so convicted for the reason that s 1(1) of the 1977 Act did not, on its true construction, make a charge of conspiracy to aid, abet, counsel or procure possible in law. The foundation for this view is a passage in Smith and Hogan *Criminal Law* (5th edn, 1983) pp 234–235, which is quoted in full in the judgment by Hodgson J and with which the

Court of Appeal expressed complete agreement (see [1985] 1 All ER 850 at 857–858, [1985] 2 WLR 761 at 770–771).

My Lords, I do not find it necessary to consider whether or not this view is correct for this reason. Even if such a charge of conspiracy to aid, abet, counsel or procure were possible in law, I can see no evidence whatever that the respondents ever agreed so to aid, abet, counsel or procure or indeed did aid, abet, counsel or procure those who as the ultimate purchasers or possessors of the black boxes were destined to be the actual perpetrators of the intended frauds on electricity boards. It follows that on no view could the respondents have been convicted on count 1 even if that count were sustainable in law. This last question is obviously one of some difficulty and a case in which that question arose for direct decision is likely to be a rarity. I suggest that in any future case in which that question does arise it should be treated as open for consideration de novo, as much may depend on the particular facts of the case in question.

[**Lords Fraser, Diplock, Bridge** and **Brandon** agreed.]

Appeal allowed

Questions

1. Was it true to say that it was the *purpose* of the alleged conspirators to cause economic loss to the electricity boards? Suppose that the buyer (not being a policeman or other entrapper) having bought and paid for the boxes, were to see the error of his ways and destroy them, would the defendants have considered the enterprise a failure? Would it be more realistic to say that it was their *intention* that the boards should be defrauded because this was a natural and expected consequence of what they did? Cf *Moloney*, p **120**, above. In conspiracy cases the courts frequently refer to a requirement of 'purpose' but their actions seem to belie their words. See commentaries on *A-G's Reference (No 1 of 1982)* [1983] Crim LR 534 and *McPherson and Watts* [1985] Crim LR 508.

2. Lord Roskill said that he could see no evidence whatever of an agreement to aid, abet, etc. Yet he also held that 'the manufacture and sale was for the dishonest purposes of enabling those black boxes to be used by persons other than the respondents to the detriment of the intended victim.' If that is not aiding, etc, what is?

3. If an agreement to aid and abet is a statutory conspiracy it could not, under the law prevailing at the time, be a common law conspiracy: *Ayres*, p **490**, above. Does the decision (as distinct from the dicta) suggest that an agreement to aid and abet is not a statutory conspiracy? See Draft Code Bill, cl 48(7), p **517**, below.

(5) INTENTION AND CONSPIRACY

The Law Commission Report on Conspiracy and Criminal Law Reform (Law Com No 76, 1976), on which Part I of the Criminal Law Act 1977 was based, includes a full discussion of the mental element to be required for conspiracy (paras 1.25–1.41). The Law Commission's conclusion on the common law was that:

… it is reasonably clear from such authority as there is that what the law requires before a charge of conspiracy can be proved against a defendant is that *he should intend to bring about any consequences prohibited by the offence* and should have full knowledge of all the circumstances or facts which need to be known to enable him to know that the agreed course of conduct will result in a crime. (Italics added.)

The Commission thought that this was what the law ought to be: 'We think that the law should require full intention and knowledge before a conspiracy can be established.' Their recommendation (5), para 7.2 reads:

A person should be guilty of conspiracy if he agrees with another person that an offence shall be committed. *Both must intend that any consequence in the definition of the offence will result* and both must know of the existence of any state of affairs which it is necessary for them to know in order to be aware that the course of conduct agreed upon will amount to the offence. (Italics added.)

The Report included a draft Bill, implementing the Commission's intentions. Clause 1, which became s 1 of the 1977 Act, included the phrase, 'in accordance with their intentions', which was discussed by the House of Lords in the next case.

(a) *Intention to carry out the agreement*

R v Anderson
[1985] 2 All ER 961, House of Lords

(Lords Scarman, Diplock, Keith, Bridge and Brightman)

The appellant was remanded in custody with Ahmed Andaloussi. He confidently expected to be released on bail but Andaloussi was awaiting trial for very serious drug offences. The appellant agreed with Andaloussi's brother Mohamed and Mohamed Assou to participate in a scheme to effect Andaloussi's escape from prison. The appellant was to supply diamond wire capable of cutting through metal bars to be smuggled into prison. He received £2,000 on account and admitted that he intended to supply the wire on payment of a further £10,000 but said that he would then have left for Spain and taken no further part in the scheme, which he believed could not possibly succeed. His submission that he lacked the mental element for conspiracy to commit the crime of escape was rejected by the trial judge and the Court of Appeal. That court held (1) that a person who agrees with two or more others, who do intend to carry out the agreement, but who has a secret intention himself to participate only in part, is guilty of an offence under s 1(1) of the Criminal Law Act 1977; and (2) if he is not guilty as a principal offender, then he may be convicted of aiding and abetting the conspiracy. He appealed to the House of Lords and both points of law were certified for decision.

Lord Bridge. The 1977 Act, subject to exceptions not presently material, abolished the offence of conspiracy at common law. It follows that the elements of the new statutory offence of conspiracy must be ascertained purely by interpretation of the language of s 1(1) of the 1977 Act. For purposes of analysis it is perhaps convenient to isolate the three clauses each of which must be taken as indicating an essential ingredient of the offence as follows: (1) 'if a person agrees with any other person or persons that a course of conduct shall be pursued' (2) 'which will necessarily amount to or involve the commission of any offence or offences by one or more of the parties to the agreement' (3) 'if the agreement is carried out in accordance with their intentions'.

Clause (1) presents, as it seems to me, no difficulty. It means exactly what it says and what it says is crystal clear. To be convicted, the party charged must have agreed with one or more others that 'a course of conduct shall be pursued'. What is important is to resist the temptation to introduce into this simple concept ideas derived from the civil law of contract. Any number of persons may agree that a course of conduct shall be pursued without undertaking any contractual liability. The agreed course of conduct may be a simple or an elaborate one and may involve the participation of two or any larger number of persons who may have agreed to play a variety of roles in the course of conduct agreed.

Again, clause (2) could hardly use simpler language. Here what is important to note is that it is not necessary that more than one of the participants in the agreed course of conduct shall commit a substantive offence. It is, of course, necessary that any party to the agreement shall have assented to play his part in the agreed course of conduct, however innocent in itself, knowing that the part to be played by one or more of the others will amount to or involve the commission of an offence.

It is only clause (3) which presents any possible ambiguity. The heart of the submission for the appellant is that in order to be convicted of conspiracy to commit a given offence the language of clause (3) requires that the party charged should not only have agreed that a course of conduct shall be pursued which will necessarily amount to or involve the commission of that offence by himself or one or more other parties to the agreement, but must also be proved himself to have intended that the offence should be committed. Thus, it is submitted here that the appellant's case that he never intended that Andaloussi should be enabled to escape from prison raised an issue to be left to the jury, who should have been directed to convict him only if satisfied that he did so intend. I do not find it altogether easy to understand why the draftsman of this provision chose to use the phrase 'in accordance with their intentions'. But I suspect the answer may be that this seemed a desirable alternative to the phrase 'in accordance with its terms' or any similar expression, because it is a matter of common experience in the criminal courts that the 'terms' of a criminal conspiracy are hardly ever susceptible of proof. The evidence from which a jury may infer a criminal conspiracy is almost invariably to be found in the conduct of the parties. This was so at common law and remains so under the statute. If the evidence in a given case justifies the inference of an agreement that a course of conduct should be pursued, it is a not inappropriate formulation of the test of the criminality of the inferred agreement to ask whether the further inference can be drawn that a crime would necessarily have been committed if the agreed course of conduct had been pursued in accordance with the several intentions of the parties. Whether that is an accurate analysis or not, I am clearly driven by consideration of the diversity of roles which parties may agree to play in criminal conspiracies to reject any construction of the statutory language which would require the prosecution to prove an intention on the part of each conspirator that the criminal offence or offences which will necessarily be committed by one or more of the conspirators if the agreed course of conduct is fully carried out should in fact be committed. A simple example will illustrate the absurdity to which this construction would lead. The proprietor of a car hire firm agrees for a substantial payment to make available a hire car to a gang for use in a robbery and to make false entries in his books relating to the hiring to which he can point if the number of the car is traced back to him in connection with the robbery. Being fully aware of the circumstances of the robbery in which the car is proposed to be used he is plainly a party to the conspiracy to rob. Making his car available for use in the robbery is as much a part of the relevant agreed course of conduct as the robbery itself. Yet, once he has been paid, it will be a matter of complete indifference to him whether the robbery is in fact committed or not. In these days of highly organised crime the most serious statutory conspiracies will frequently involve an elaborate and complex agreed course of conduct in which many will consent to play necessary but subordinate roles, not involving them in any direct participation in the commission of the offence or offences at the centre of the conspiracy. Parliament cannot have intended that such parties should escape conviction of conspiracy on the basis that it cannot be proved against them that they intended that the relevant offence or offences should be committed.

There remains the important question whether a person who has agreed that a course of conduct will be pursued which, if pursued as agreed, will necessarily amount to or involve the commission of an offence is guilty of statutory conspiracy irrespective of his intention, and, if not, what is the mens rea of the offence. I have no hesitation in answering the first part of the question in the negative. There may be many situations in which perfectly respectable citizens, more particularly those concerned with law enforcement, may enter into agreements that a course of conduct shall be pursued which will involve commission of a crime without the least intention of playing any part in furtherance of the ostensibly agreed criminal objective, but rather with the purpose of exposing and frustrating the criminal purpose of the other parties to the agreement. To say this is in no way to encourage schemes by which police act, directly or through the agency of informers, as agents provocateurs for the purpose of entrapment. That is conduct of which the courts have always strongly disapproved. But it may sometimes happen, as most of us with experience in criminal trials well know, that a criminal enterprise is well advanced in the course of preparation when it comes to the notice either of the police or of some honest citizen in such circumstances that the only prospect of exposing and frustrating the criminals is that some innocent person should play the part of an intending collaborator in the course of criminal conduct proposed to be pursued. The mens rea implicit in the offence of statutory conspiracy must clearly be such as to recognise the innocence of such a person, notwithstanding that he will, in literal terms, be obliged to agree that a course of conduct be pursued involving the commission of an offence.

I have said already, but I repeat to emphasise its importance, that an essential ingredient in the crime of conspiring to commit a specific offence or offences under s1(1) of the 1977 Act is that the accused should agree that a course of conduct be pursued which he knows must involve the commission by one or more of the parties to the agreement of that offence or those offences. But, beyond the mere fact of agreement, the necessary mens rea of the crime is, in my opinion, established if, and only if, it is shown that the accused, when he entered into the agreement, intended to play some part in the agreed course of conduct in furtherance of the criminal purpose which the agreed course of conduct was intended to achieve. Nothing less will suffice; nothing more is required.

Applying this test to the facts which, for the purposes of the appeal, we must assume, the appellant, in agreeing that a course of conduct be pursued that would, if successful, necessarily involve the offence of effecting Andaloussi's escape from lawful custody, clearly intended, by providing diamond wire to be smuggled into the prison, to play a part in the agreed course of conduct in furtherance of that criminal objective. Neither the fact that he intended to play no further part in attempting to effect the escape, nor that he believed the escape to be impossible, would, if the jury had supposed they might be true, have afforded him any defence.

[**Lords Scarman**, **Diplock**, **Keith** and **Brightman** agreed.]

Appeal dismissed

Questions

1. Unlike the Court of Appeal, the House did not insist that there must be two parties who do intend to carry out the agreement. What if only one intends to do so? Or none?

2. Was there a valid reason for not giving the words 'in accordance with their intentions' their natural meaning? Does the decision carry out the intention of Parliament (who must be taken to have read the Report presented to them by the Law Commission)? Cf Lord Griffiths in *Yip Chiu-cheung*, above, p 118.

3. Is there any warrant in the words of the Act for the opinion that a person is guilty of conspiracy only if he intended to play some part in the furtherance of the criminal purpose? A incites B to murder C and B agrees to do so. A intends to do nothing more. Is this not a conspiracy to murder?

4. Cf the Draft Code Bill, cl 48(1)(b) and (7), below, p 517. Would these provisions (a) implement the proposals of the Law Commission regarding intention and (b) make adequate provision for cases such as *Anderson* and Lord Bridge's example of the car-hire firm?

(b) Conspiracy as an agreement without intent to carry out the agreement?

R v Edwards

[1991] Crim LR 45, Court of Appeal, Criminal Division

(Russell LJ, Drake and Morland JJ)

The prosecution evidence was that on 19 April 1989, undercover agents, C and A, investigating the source and supply of amphetamine in Cambridgeshire called at E's house and indicated that they wanted one pound of amphetamine and might be interested in purchasing, ultimately, a kilogram of that drug. E said there would be no problem and the price of a pound would be £1,600. C said that would be acceptable but he would expect a discount on future purchases. E said that delivery would be at his house in a week's time. On 26 April C and A returned to take delivery but E told them they would have to go to Huntingdon, saying, 'It's all set up.' They all went to Huntingdon and E went into the house of E's sister, N, the co-accused. After 20 minutes, E returned to say, 'I'm sorry, she hasn't got it all.' He was then arrested. There was evidence that what was available at the Huntingdon house was not amphetamine but a milder drug, not controlled in the same way as amphetamine, namely ephedrine.

E and N were charged in count 1 with conspiring between 18 and 22 April 1989 to supply amphetamine to persons unknown; and in an alternative count, 3, with conspiring dishonestly to obtain money by falsely representing to any purchaser that the substance they were supplying was amphetamine when in fact it was ephedrine. The jury convicted on count 1 and were discharged from giving a verdict on count 3.

E appealed, arguing that C and A were agents provocateurs (defined by the Royal Commission on Police Powers as 'a person who entices another to commit an express breach of the law which he would not otherwise have committed and then proceeds to inform against him in respect of such an offence') and that consequently the evidence of the officers should have been excluded under s 78 of PACE 1984 (evidence, the admission of which 'would have such an adverse effect on the fairness of the proceedings that the court ought not to admit it'). It was submitted that, but for the enticement, the offence charged would not have occurred.

Russell LJ. The contrary argument to that is of course to this effect. The whole scenario demonstrated that this was not, on the part of this appellant, an isolated incident into which he was enticed by the invitations of the police officers. Because of the way in which the appellant behaved, because of his reaction to the police officer's request, because of his familiarity with what might be termed as the drugs scene, evidenced by his acknowledgment of drug slang, because of his agreement to accept a discount upon the price in respect of future supplies, it is manifestly plain that this appellant, at the time he was approached by the police officers was already an established drug dealer and what happened involving the police officers was simply an isolated manifestation of a much wider conspiracy involving his co-defendants to which the appellant was a party....

[Having discussed and approved the summing up:]

We are abundantly satisfied that it would be an abuse of language to say here that these officers in the circumstances of this case were enticing the appellant to commit an isolated offence. We are abundantly satisfied that when the officers came on the scene there was ample evidence to demonstrate that he was already established in the type of conspiracy which formed the subject-matter of count 1 in this indictment. Accordingly we take the view that there is no merit in the submission, however admirably it has been made by Mr Gold, that there was here evidence that the undercover officers were agents provocateurs.…

Mr Gold [for the appellant]… points out accurately that it was important that the jury should understand the distinction between count 1 and count 3 and that they should convict on count 1 only if they were sure that the appellant intended to supply amphetamine. If the reality of the situation was that they were sure that the appellant knew full well that the drug involved was not amphetamine but ephedrine and was seeking to cheat those who were to be its recipients by pretending that the substance was one form of drug when in fact it was another, only in this situation would count 3 arise.

Appeal dismissed

Questions

1. What if E and N had been charged with conspiring to supply C and A with one pound of amphetamine? Would C and A then have been agents provocateurs? Would the same evidence then have had an adverse effect on the fairness of the proceedings which it did not have when the charge was of a conspiracy to supply goods to persons unknown—that is, a continuing conspiracy to supply any suitable customers who presented themselves? Cf commentary at [1991] Crim LR 46.

2. E had agreed to supply amphetamine. According to Lord Bridge in *Anderson*, did it matter if he never intended to supply amphetamine? Ought it to matter?

3. What if the jury had been uncertain whether E intended to supply amphetamine or ephedrine? If they could (as the court says) convict of conspiracy to supply amphetamine only if they were sure that E intended to supply amphetamine, and of conspiracy to obtain by deception only if they were sure he did *not* intend to supply amphetamine (as must be the case), could they have convicted on either count? Would they be bound to acquit although they were quite sure he was guilty on the one count or the other? Cf *Bellman* [1989] 1 All ER 22, [1989] Crim LR 301 and commentary.

R v McPhillips
[1990] 6 BNIL, Court of Appeal of Northern Ireland (unreported)

(Lord Lowry CJ, O'Donnell and Kelly LJJ)

About 11 pm on 10 October 1985 the police in Portadown stopped a car driven by one, Drumm, going towards the Seagoe Hotel. McPhillips was in the front passenger seat. Behind the driver's seat was a bomb containing four kilograms of explosive. It was a device of considerable power, capable of causing a significant explosion. In a statement McPhillips admitted that the bomb was to be placed on the flat roof of the Seagoe Hotel where a disco was taking place. He said that it had been decided by Drumm and other accomplices that the best time for the bomb to go off would be 1 am as the disco was going on until 1.30 am. McPhillips and Drumm were charged with (1) conspiracy to murder, (2) conspiracy to cause an explosion, and (3) offences under the Explosive Substances Act 1883. At the trial McPhillips accepted that he was a party to the plan to cause the explosion and pleaded guilty to counts (2) and (3). He pleaded not guilty to conspiracy to murder. He said, and the trial judge believed him, that he intended to give a warning to the police in time for the dance hall to be cleared. The judge held that, notwithstanding McPhillips' intention to give a warning, he was guilty as an aider and abettor of conspiracy to murder. He appealed on the ground that this ruling was wrong.

Lord Lowry CJ. To be guilty at common law of conspiracy to murder the accused must agree with another that murder will be committed and must intend that this will happen. The guilty act is the agreement that the crime contemplated will be committed; the guilty mind is the intention that that crime will be committed.... In regard to the offence of statutory conspiracy section 1(1) 'assumes the existence of an intention of the parties to carry out the agreement': Smith and Hogan, *Criminal Law*, 6th edition, p 259. The wording of the identical Article 9(1) makes this clear: the agreed course of conduct was the planting of a 'no warning' bomb at the Seagoe Hotel and persons who had agreed to that course of conduct intending it to be carried out would be guilty of conspiracy to murder because, if the agreement had been carried out in accordance with their intentions it would (unless all the patrons of the disco had gone home or had a miraculous escape) necessarily involve the commission of murder. But, on the facts found here, this result would not have been in accordance with the intention of the appellant. Therefore he was not guilty of conspiracy to murder. So, although by going to the Seagoe in Drumm's car, the appellant up to a point acted in accordance with the agreed course of conduct (and was thereby guilty of conspiracy to cause an explosion), he was not guilty as an alleged conspirator in respect to count 1. This result is consistent with the doctrine that, if a joint enterprise goes beyond the agreed or authorised act, a party to that enterprise is not guilty beyond the acts which he agreed to or authorised. To put the matter simply, there must be a common criminal design and, in order to be guilty of a conspiracy to carry out that design, the accused must be a party to the design. That condition is not satisfied in this case.

The Crown's alternative proposition is that the appellant was guilty of aiding and abetting a conspiracy to murder on the part of the conspirators and was therefore liable to be tried, indicted and punished (as happened in the instant case) as a principal offender. The need, and the ability, to rely on this proposition must stem from the hypothesis that the appellant was not a party to the conspiracy to murder, and that hypothesis (having regard to the appellant's ostensible acquiescence in the murder plan) must be based on the fact that the appellant did not intend or authorise the commission of murder. But how then, say the appellant's counsel, did he aid and abet a conspiracy to murder? The Crown's answer is that the appellant assisted the conspirators by his presence when the murder plan was devised and by accompanying Drumm in the car which was conveying the bomb to the intended scene of the crime, and counsel relies on the following passage in the judgment of the learned trial judge.

[Lord Lowry quoted and discussed the passage and continued:]

The common law offence of aiding and abetting involves an act of assisting the principal (actus reus) and a guilty intention (mens rea) that the crime will be committed. This intention is not to be confused with purpose, motive or desire (although those elements may be and often are present) but can be inferred from, and has been in the recent past wrongly identified with, the probability, overwhelming probability or certainty (known to the aider and abettor) that the crime will be committed. Conspiracy is a crime which it is possible to aid and abet and thus the ingredients of aiding and abetting a conspiracy remain as we have described them: a person aids and abets a conspiracy to commit a crime when, not being a party to the conspiracy (otherwise he would be a principal offender) and knowing of the agreement and at least its general object, he assists the principal offenders (by an actus reus, such as supplying a vehicle or a weapon) with the guilty intention (mens rea) that the object of the conspiracy should be achieved.... the decisive point here is that, whether the test is based on *Hyam* or on *Hancock*, the fact that the appellant had the intention, which he could reasonably have expected to implement, that murder would not take place destroys the possibility of finding the necessary mens rea on his part.

The appellant's acts and intentions were sufficient to render him guilty of conspiracy to cause an explosion, and the same acts are relied on to prove him guilty of aiding and abetting the conspiracy to murder. This overlooks the fact that his intentions differed between causing an explosion and aiding the commission of a murder. The law relating to joint criminal enterprises, which was reviewed at length by Sir Robin Cooke in *Chan Wing-Siu v R* [1985] AC 168, [1984] 3 All ER 877, provides a ready answer. The action proposed by the conspirators, namely, to plant a bomb with no warning (and thereby to extend a property damaging explosion into a murder) was something which the appellant did not authorise and had actually made up his mind to prevent. And the fact that the extension of the crime involved a negative, that is, a failure to warn, cannot obscure the reality that this proposed failure was to be an aggravation of the crime, since the distinction between a warning bomb and a no warning bomb is well understood.

[Lord Lowry discussed the decision of the Court of Appeal in *Anderson*, above, p **498**, and continued:]

So far as concerns the hearing before the House of Lords, we find it necessary only to recall what Lord Bridge of Harwich, who delivered the leading speech, said in *R v Anderson* [1986] AC 27, [1985] 2 All ER 961, at p 39D of the former report:

> 'I have said already, but I repeat to emphasise its importance, that an essential ingredient in the crime of conspiring to commit a specific offence or offences under section 1(1) of the Act of 1977 is that the accused should agree that a course of conduct be pursued which he knows must involve the commission by one or more of the parties to the agreement of that offence or those offences.'

It is obvious, for the reasons already given, that, so far as count 1 is concerned, the conduct of the appellant does not satisfy that test. It is equally clear that *R v Anderson* [1986] AC 27, [1985] 2 All ER 961, is not an authority for the proposition that someone who at all times intends to frustrate the commission of the crime 'agreed upon' is guilty of conspiracy to commit that crime or of aiding and abetting such a conspiracy.

[Lord Lowry referred to Lord Bridge's dictum in *Anderson* concerning the person who joins a criminal conspiracy with the object of frustrating it and continued:]

In the different circumstances of this case, the same principle applies: the appellant was not guilty of conspiracy to murder either as a principal offender or as an accomplice because his mind did not go with his acts, but on the contrary was directed towards frustrating the conspiracy to murder. The mere fact that the appellant had already committed terrorist offences and was a member of a terrorist organisation does not disable him from relying on the absence of the necessary intent and the principle enunciated in *R v Fitzpatrick* [1977] NI 20, is not in point.

While the conviction on counts 2 and 3 will stand, the conviction appealed against in relation to count 1 must therefore be quashed.

Questions

1. Is Lord Lowry's judgment consistent with Lord Bridge's opinion that it is not necessary to prove that a principal conspirator intended that the criminal offence be committed?

2. Does Lord Lowry confuse (a) intention that the murder be committed with (b) intention to aid and abet the conspiracy to murder? Which is necessary in order to convict a person of aiding and abetting a conspiracy to murder?

3. When McPhillips joined in the agreement to plant a 'no-warning bomb' and helped to carry out the initial stages of the plan, did he not intentionally aid and abet the continuance of the on-going conspiracy to murder?

4. Does *Chan Wing-siu* (above, p **318**) support Lord Lowry's conclusion? Lord Lowry said that McPhillips did not 'authorize' a no-warning bomb. Did he not authorize it when, by words or conduct, he joined in what he knew to be a conspiracy by others to plant a no-warning bomb? In any event, in *Hui Chi-ming* [1991] 3 All ER 897, PC, Lord Lowry said

that their Lordships considered that Sir Robin used the word 'authorize' 'to emphasize the fact that mere foresight is not enough: the accessory in order to be guilty, must have foreseen the relevant offence which the principal may commit *as a possible incident of the common unlawful enterprise* and must, with such foresight, have participated in the enterprise.'

5. If Drumm and McPhillips had planted the bomb and if, because McPhillips was unable to get away from Drumm to make the telephone call, it had gone off at 1 am, killing the dancers below, would McPhillips have been guilty of murder? Assuming he was not a principal (because he did not intend to kill) must he not have foreseen the commission of murder 'as a possible incident of the joint enterprise and . . ., with such foresight, have participated in the enterprise'?

6. Does McPhillips fit Lord Bridge's dictum (above, p **499**) about the perfectly respectable citizens who enter into agreements to commit crime with the purpose of exposing and frustrating the criminal purpose? Cf *Yip Chiu-cheung*, above, p **118**.

7. Is *Anderson* distinguishable on the ground that McPhillips intended, so far as murder was concerned, to frustrate the enterprise?

(c) Playing some part in the agreed course of conduct?

R v Siracusa

[1989] Crim LR 712, Court of Appeal, Criminal Division

(O'Connor LJ, Boreham and Ian Kennedy JJ)

The appellants were convicted of conspiracies to commit offences against the Customs and Excise Management Act 1979, s170(2)(b), above, p **498**. The judge directed the jury as follows:

What matters is whether you are satisfied that he agreed with any other defendant or any other named conspirator that a course of conduct should be pursued which, if carried out in accordance with their intentions, would amount to this offence by any of those other persons, because if it does, then he is guilty of conspiracy, whether he himself has actively done anything in order to bring about the objects of that conspiracy, because the reason, as you will appreciate, is that the nub of the offence of conspiracy consists of the agreement to do the unlawful act, and that may mean that you are doing it yourself actively or that you are agreeing that somebody else should do it actively. In either event, you are guilty of the conspiracy.

The appeals were dismissed.

[**O'Connor LJ**, referring to *Anderson*, above, p **498**, said:] We think it obvious that Lord Bridge cannot have been intending that the organiser of a crime who recruited others to carry it out would not himself be guilty of conspiracy unless it could be proved that he intended to play some active part himself thereafter. Lord Bridge had pointed out [p **499**, above] that 'in these days of highly organised crime the most serious statutory conspiracies will frequently involve an elaborate and complex agreed course of conduct in which many will consent to play necessary but subordinate roles not involving them in any direct participation in the commission of the offence or offences at the centre of the conspiracy'.

The present case is a classic example of such a conspiracy. It is the hallmark of such crimes that the organisers try to remain in the background and more often than not are not apprehended. Secondly, the origins of all conspiracies are concealed and it is usually quite impossible to establish when or where the initial agreement was made, or when or where other conspirators were recruited. The very existence of the agreement can only be inferred from overt acts. Participation in a conspiracy is infinitely variable: it can be active or passive. If the majority shareholder and director of a company consents to the company being used for drug smuggling carried out in the company's name by a fellow director and minority shareholder, he is guilty of conspiracy. Consent, that is the agreement or adherence to the agreement, can be inferred if it is proved that he knew what was going on and the intention to participate in the furtherance of the criminal purpose is also established by his failure to stop the unlawful activity. Lord Bridge's dictum does not require anything more.

Appeal dismissed

Question

1. What *did* Lord Bridge mean?

(6) KNOWLEDGE AS TO CIRCUMSTANCES

Section 1(2) of the Criminal Law Act 1977 provides:

Where liability for any offence may be incurred without knowledge on part of the person committing it of any particular fact or circumstance necessary for the commission of the offence, a person shall nevertheless not be guilty of conspiracy to commit that offence by virtue of subsection (1) above unless he and at least one other party to the agreement intend or know that that fact or circumstance shall or will exist at the time when the conduct constituting the offence is to take place.

This deals with the case where the parties are charged with conspiracy to commit an offence which imposes strict liability, or is satisfied by recklessness as to some fact or circumstance. The subsection makes clear that a party to the agreement is not guilty of conspiracy unless he, and at least one other party, 'intend or know that the fact or circumstance shall or will exist.' It appears then that the prosecution must prove intention or knowledge as to every fact or circumstance in the actus reus. This is an exceptionally strict requirement since mens rea at common law was generally satisfied by proof of recklessness. It is stricter than is required by the related offence of attempt; see below, p 524.

Consider D1 who agrees to help D2 move out of his flat. D2 is unsure whether the cabling he has installed for his hi-fi now belongs to him or to his landlord. D1 and D2 confer together and are uncertain, but agree, nevertheless, to remove it knowing their actions will result in damage to the cabling in the process. They therefore have an intention to cause damage, and are reckless as to whether the property belongs to another. The substantive offence of criminal damage requires that D intends or is reckless as to the causing of damage (the result), *and* that D knows or is reckless as to whether the property belongs to another (circumstance). If D1 and D2 went ahead, they would have sufficient mens rea to be convicted of the substantive offence. As for the conspiracy, in the *actual* circumstances that exist, the carrying out of the agreement 'will necessarily amount' to criminal damage; but on an orthodox reading of s 1(2) it is not a conspiracy to commit criminal damage. It would not be criminal damage in the circumstances which the parties *intend, or know, shall or will exist*. Ds are reckless as to the circumstance. Recklessness as to the circumstance of the actus reus (property belonging to another) is not a sufficient mens rea on a charge of conspiracy to commit a crime (criminal damage) even where it is a sufficient mens rea for the crime itself.

A further example of its operation is that if A and B, in order to acquire property, agree to make a representation, being reckless whether it is true or false, they will be guilty of an offence under s 15 of the Theft Act 1968 if they succeed in obtaining the property and the representation is in fact false; but they are not guilty of conspiracy.

Conspiracy to commit offences under the Misuse of Drugs Act 1971 to which s 28 of the Act (above, p 252) applies, clearly falls within this provision. If D is charged with possession of a particular drug, say heroin, the fact that the substance was heroin must be proved by the prosecution, but s 28(3)(a) makes it quite clear that the prosecution do not have to prove that D knew, or suspected, or even had reason to suspect, that it was heroin. If he thought the substance in his possession was cannabis, he may be convicted of possessing heroin. But if he is charged with conspiracy to produce or supply or possess heroin, it must be proved that he intended or knew that the substance he was dealing with should be or was heroin. The same applies to offences of importation of drugs under the Customs and Excise Management Act 1979, above p **498**.

The problem has become acute where persons agree to launder money which they know has been or will be illicitly obtained. D1 and D2 might agree to commit crime A (laundering the proceeds of drug trafficking) or crime B (laundering the proceeds of crime other than drug trafficking) with the prosecution being unsure whether the illicit source is (a) drugs or (b) other criminality. How can the defendants have the requisite mens rea within s 1(2)? The requirement is that D (and one other party) *knows* the relevant circumstances for the commission of the offence (the provenance of the money). They know that the money will be the proceeds of drug trafficking or of some other criminal activity. If it is the former they will commit an offence under s 49(2) of the Drug Trafficking Act 1994. If it is the latter they will commit a different offence under s 93C(2) of the Criminal Justice Act 1988. Can it be said that the parties 'intend or know' that the money will be the proceeds of drug trafficking? Or that they 'intend or know' that it will be the proceeds of criminal conduct other than drug trafficking? If it is one or the other, they cannot know both, so they cannot know either. A person who believes that there is a 50/50 chance that something is so can hardly be said to 'know' that it is so; and 'intend' appears to be irrelevant where the parties know they have no control over the existence of the fact or circumstance—as here. See Smith and Hogan, *Criminal Law* (11th edn, 2005) pp **379–382** and [1977] Crim LR 598 at 602–605. It is difficult to see how the decision in *Hussain, Bhatti and Bhatti* [2002] Crim LR 408 that an indictment charging a conspiracy to commit crime A or crime B is lawful can be justified in the light of s 1(2) of the Criminal Law Act 1977, which was not cited.

Harmer
[2005] EWCA Crim 01, [2005] Crim LR 482

(May LJ, Beatson J and Sir Charles Martell)

H was convicted of conspiracy to convert or transfer currency which he had reasonable grounds to suspect represented another person's proceeds of criminal conduct and/or drug trafficking (Criminal Justice Act 1988, s 93C(2)(b); Drug Trafficking Act 1994, s 49(2)(b)). The judge did not direct the jury that the Crown had to prove that the relevant money was the proceeds of crime (a direction in accordance with the law as understood before *Montilla* [2004] UKHL 50). The Crown were unable to show the criminal provenance of the money (or the person or persons whose proceeds of crime it was; or whether it was drug trafficking or criminal conduct). The appeals were allowed.

25. There is a further answer to [the Crown's] submission, which, in our judgment, is fatal to it. It derives from the late Professor Sir John Smith QC's commentary on *Hussain* in [2002] Crim. L.R. 407 at 409 where he said:

'Agreement to commit crime A or B as circumstances dictate. The parties agree to launder money illicitly obtained—i.e. obtained contrary to section 49(2) of the 1994 Act or (a different crime) contrary to section 93C(2) of the 1977 Act. The difficulty here lies in the very strict mens rea requirements of statutory conspiracy. Recklessness is not enough. The effect of section 1(2) (not mentioned in *Siracusa*, *El Kurd* or the judgment in the present case) is that D is not guilty of conspiracy to commit an offence by virtue of section 1(1)—

> "unless [D] and at least one other party to the agreement intend or know that [all the facts and circumstances necessary for the commission of the offence] shall or will exist at the time when the conduct constituting the offence is to take place".

Can it be said that the parties "intend or know" that the money will be the proceeds of drug trafficking? Or that they "intend or know" that it will be the proceeds of criminal conduct other than drug trafficking? If it is one or the other, they cannot know both, so they cannot know either. A person who believes that there is a 50/50 chance that something is so can hardly be said to "know" that it is so; and "intend" appears to be irrelevant where the parties know they have no control over the existence of fact or circumstances—as here.'

26. This commentary addresses the more complicated problem, alluded to earlier in this judgment and discussed in *El Kurd* and *Hussain*, when the prosecution cannot establish that the provenance of obviously illicit money is criminal conduct on the one hand or drug trafficking on the other. But the commentary emphasises the statutory requirement that, where, as in the present case, the substantive charge would only be that the defendant had reasonable grounds to suspect that the money was the proceeds of crime (i.e. the offence would be incurred without knowledge on the part of the person committing it), he is not to be guilty of conspiracy unless he and at least one other party to the agreement intend or know that the money will be the proceeds of crime when the agreed conduct takes place. This intention or knowledge is precisely what the prosecution in the present case accepted they could not prove when the words 'knew or' were omitted from the particulars of count 2. If the prosecution cannot prove that the money was the proceeds of crime, they cannot prove that the appellant knew that it was. So section 1(2) of the 1977 Act applies and is not satisfied.

Appeal allowed

Question

Why should the mens rea for conspiracy be so much stricter than the mens rea for the substantive offence?

5. COMMON LAW CONSPIRACIES

(1) CONSPIRACY TO DEFRAUD

Until recently it was generally accepted that there are two categories of conspiracy to defraud. The first relates to injury to economic interests, the second to inducing a person to act contrary to his duty. The second category, as well as the first, is relevant to commercial fraud because its most likely application is to inducing acts which will lead to economic gain, such as obtaining an export licence. The nearest approach to a definition of the first category of conspiracy to defraud is the statement by Lord Dilhorne with which all their Lordships agreed in *Scott v Metropolitan Police Comr* [1975] AC 819 at 840, HL:

...it is clearly the law that an agreement by two or more by dishonesty to deprive a person of something which is his or to which he is or would be or might be entitled and an agreement by two or more by dishonesty to injure some proprietary right of his, suffices to constitute the offence of conspiracy to defraud.

(At p 839 Lord Dilhorne put it slightly differently—'might *but for the perpetration of the fraud* be entitled' (italics added).)

A person is also defrauded if he is deceived into acting contrary to his duty. An agreement by deception to induce a public official to issue an export licence (*Board of Trade v Owen* [1957] AC 602, HL) or a national insurance number to a person not entitled to one (*Moses* [1991] Crim LR 617) is a conspiracy to defraud the official. These examples are all concerned with public officials performing public duties. Lord Diplock, in *Scott*, said that the offence was limited to such cases.

In *Wai Yu-tsang v R* [1991] 4 All ER 664 at 670, however, the Privy Council disapproved of Lord Diplock's dictum in *Scott*, pointing out that he alone took this point in that case. But no reference was made in *Wai* to *Withers* [1975] AC 842, HL, where Lords Simon and Kilbrandon seem to have been of the same mind as Lord Diplock. However that may be, the Privy Council considered that:

...the cases concerned with persons performing public duties are not to be regarded as a special category...but rather as exemplifying the general principle that conspiracies to defraud are not restricted to cases of intention to cause the victim economic loss. On the contrary they are to be understood in the broad sense described by Lord Radcliffe and Lord Denning in *Welham's* case [1961] AC 103.

Lord Denning said in *Welham*: 'If anyone may be prejudiced in any way by the fraud, that is enough'; and Lord Radcliffe said 'What it [the law] has looked for in considering the effect of cheating on another person and so in defining the criminal intent is the prejudice of that person; what *Blackstone's Commentaries* (4 Bl Com (18th ed) 247 called "to the prejudice of another man's right".'

So it appears that conspiracy to defraud is an agreement dishonestly to do *any* act prejudicial to another. Dishonesty is the concept formulated in *Ghosh*, below, p **787**. The House in *Withers* rid the law of an offence of public mischief (an act prejudicial to the public) and conspiracy to effect a public mischief; but are we not left with something like an offence of conspiracy to effect a private mischief which is little, if any less, objectionable?

Everything depends on whether the jury consider the agreement to be dishonest. Consider the case exemplified by a newspaper report (*The Independent on Sunday*, 17 April 1994, by David Hellier and Patrick Hosking) according to which the finance director of a large company boasted of its success in delaying payment to its suppliers for as long as 67 days and 'as a direct result... contributing £8/9m to the funding position at the end of the year.'

This seems to have all the elements of a conspiracy by the officers of the company to defraud the company's suppliers, with the possible exception of dishonesty. Failure to pay on the due day is a breach of contract so they were agreeing on unlawful, though not criminal, conduct. Their view to gain is manifest. The creditors are deprived unlawfully, if only temporarily, of the price due to them, and they are deprived permanently of the interest which they could have earned on the money between the due date and the actual date of payment—something to which a creditor 'would be or might be entitled'. The prejudice is obvious and, indeed, it is said that it is often late payment that drives small companies to insolvency.

A director could hardly allege that he has a 'claim of right' to do this because he must know that he is acting in breach of contract. But does not the fact that the director regards his achievement as something to boast about suggest that, even if a jury considered this to be dishonest according to the ordinary standards of reasonable and honest people, it would be very difficult to prove, as *Ghosh* requires, that the directors realized that reasonable and honest people regard what they did as dishonest? According to Hosking, 'the culture of feet-dragging is deeply embedded in companies' and 'the reality is that the brownie points go to the finance director who can find the most reasons for delaying payment to suppliers'. Is this different in principle (only much more damaging to the 'defrauded' persons and the public interest) from the belief in some sections of the community that shop lifting from large companies is a legitimate sport?

The Law Commission has been struggling for over 20 years with the problem of replacing common law conspiracy to defraud either with a series of specific offences of dishonesty or a general fraud offence.

Law Commission Report No 276, Fraud (2002)

Part III.

Defects of the present law [references omitted]

....

CONSPIRACY TO DEFRAUD

An anomalous crime

3.2 The concept of fraud, for the purposes of conspiracy to defraud, is wider than the range of conduct caught by any of the individual statutory offences involving dishonest behaviour. Thus it can be criminal for two people to *agree* to do something which it would not be unlawful for one person to do.

3.3 This anomaly has an historical basis. Before the Criminal Law Act 1977, a criminal conspiracy could be based on an agreement to commit an unlawful but non-criminal act, such as a tort or breach of contract. It appears that the justification for this was that there was a greater danger from people acting in concert than alone. As Professor Andrew Ashworth has explained:

> In legal terms, the reasoning seemed to be that acts which were insufficiently antisocial to justify criminal liability when done by one person could become sufficiently antisocial to justify criminal liability when done by two or more people acting in agreement. Such a combination of malefactors might increase the probability of harm resulting, might in some cases increase public alarm, and might in other cases facilitate the perpetration and concealment of the wrong.

3.4 The 1977 Act was the implementation of our Report on Conspiracy and Criminal Law Reform, which 'emphatically' concluded that the object of a conspiracy should be limited to the commission of a substantive offence and that there should be no place in a criminal code for a law of conspiracy extending beyond this ambit. An agreement should not be criminal where that which it was agreed should be done would not amount to a criminal offence if committed by one person.

3.5 This Commission has repeated its adherence to this principle in subsequent reports and we believe it commands very wide support. *Either* conspiracy to defraud is too wide in its scope (in that it catches agreements to do things which are rightly not criminal) *or* the statutory offences are too narrow (in that they fail to catch certain conduct which *should* be criminal)—or, which is our view, the problem is a combination of the two. On any view, the present position is anomalous and has no place in a coherent criminal law.

The definition of 'to defraud'

3.6 As we stated in paragraphs 2.4 to 2.6, the cases on the meaning of 'to defraud' have given it a broad meaning, so that any dishonest agreement to make a gain at another's expense could form the basis of conspiracy to defraud. We take the view that this definition is *too* broad. In a capitalist society, commercial life revolves around the pursuit of gain for oneself and, as a corollary, others may lose out, whether directly or indirectly. Such behaviour is perfectly legitimate. It is only the element of 'dishonesty' which renders it a criminal fraud. In other words, that element 'does all the work' in assessing whether particular facts fall within the definition of the crime.

3.7 In most cases it will be self-evident that the conduct alleged, if proved, would be dishonest, and the question will be whether that conduct has been proved. Nonetheless, in some cases, the defence will argue that the alleged conduct was not dishonest. There is no statutory definition of dishonesty, so the issue is determined with reference to *Ghosh*. In that case it was held that the fact-finders must be satisfied (a) that the defendant's conduct was dishonest according to the ordinary standards of reasonable and honest people, *and* (b) that the defendant must have realised that it was dishonest according to those standards (as opposed to his or her own standards).

3.8 Activities which would otherwise be legitimate can therefore become fraudulent if a jury is prepared to characterise them as dishonest. Not only does this delegate to the jury the responsibility for defining what conduct is to be regarded as fraudulent, but it leaves prosecutors with an uncommonly broad discretion when they are deciding whether to pursue a conspiracy to defraud case. If, for example, the directors of a company enter into 'industrial espionage' in order to gain the edge over a competitor, they could potentially be prosecuted for conspiracy to defraud, despite the absence of any statutory offence governing such activities. As *Smith and Hogan* states, the offence opens 'a very broad vista of potential criminal liability'.

3.9 In effect, conspiracy to defraud is a 'general dishonesty offence', subject only to the irrational requirement of conspiracy.

Note

The Home Office has concluded that alongside its three proposed offences of fraud, the common law offence of conspiracy to defraud should remain in place, as a safeguard against any unforeseen gaps in the protection offered by the new scheme. See www.homeoffice.gov.uk/docs3/fraud_law_reform.pdf.

6. CORRUPTION OF PUBLIC MORALS AND OUTRAGING PUBLIC DECENCY

Shaw v Director of Public Prosecutions
[1961] 2 All ER 446, House of Lords

(Viscount Simonds, Lords Reid, Tucker, Morris of Borth-y-Gest and Hodson)

The appellant published a booklet entitled 'The Ladies' Directory' with the object of enabling prostitutes to ply their trade. The booklet contained names and addresses and sometimes photographs of prostitutes and in some cases abbreviations indicating the type of conduct in which the woman would indulge. The women paid for the advertisements to be inserted. He was convicted on three counts: (i) conspiracy to corrupt public morals; (ii) living wholly or in part on the earnings of prostitution, contrary to s 30(1) of the Sexual Offences Act 1956 and (iii) publishing an obscene article contrary to s 2(1) of the Obscene Publications Act 1959. His appeal to the Court of Criminal Appeal was dismissed. That court held that conduct calculated and intended to corrupt public morals was an indictable misdemeanour at common law and that it followed that an agreement to do so was a conspiracy; s 2(4) of the Obscene Publications Act 1959 did not prohibit the prosecution of the appellant for conspiracy because that offence consisted in an agreement to corrupt, and did not 'consist of the publication' of the booklets. The appellant appealed against his conviction on the first and second counts.

The following extracts from the speeches of their Lordships relate only to the conspiracy charge.

[**Viscount Simonds**, having asserted that, contrary to the appellant's submission conspiracy to corrupt public morals is an offence known to the common law, continued:]

Need I say, my Lords, that I am no advocate of the right of the judges to create new criminal offences?...

But I am at a loss to understand how it can be said either that the law does not recognise a conspiracy to corrupt public morals or that, though there may not be an exact precedent for such a conspiracy as this case reveals, it does not fall fairly within the general words by which it is described. I do not propose to examine all the relevant authorities. That will be done by my noble and learned friend. The fallacy in the argument that was addressed to us lay in the attempt to exclude from the scope of general words acts well calculated to corrupt public morals just because they had not been committed or had not been brought to the notice of the court before. It is not thus that the common law has developed. We are, perhaps, more accustomed to hear this matter discussed on the question whether such and such a transaction is contrary to public policy. At once the controversy arises. On the one hand it is said that it is not possible in the twentieth century for the court to create a new head of public policy, on the other it is said that this is but a new example of a well-established head. In the sphere of criminal law, I entertain no doubt that there remains in the courts of law a residual power to enforce the supreme and fundamental purpose of the law, to conserve not only the safety and order but also the moral welfare of the state, and that it is their duty to guard it against attacks which may be the more insidious because they are novel and unprepared for. That is the broad head (call it public policy if you wish) within which the present indictment falls. It matters little what label is given to the offending act. To one of your Lordships it may appear an affront to public decency, to another, considering that it may succeed in its obvious intention of provoking libidinous desires, it will seem a corruption of public morals. Yet others may deem it aptly described as the creation of a public mischief or the undermining of moral conduct. The same act will not in all ages be regarded in the same way. The law must be related to the changing standards of life, not yielding to every shifting impulse of the popular will but having regard to fundamental assessments of human values and the purposes of society. Today a denial of the fundamental Christian doctrine, which in past centuries would have been regarded by the ecclesiastical courts as heresy and by the common law as blasphemy, will no longer be an offence if the decencies of controversy are observed. When Lord Mansfield, speaking long after the Star Chamber had been abolished, said [in *Delaval* (1763) 3 Burr 1434 at 1438] that the Court of King's Bench was the *custos morum* of the people and had the superintendency of offences *contra bonos mores*, he was asserting, as I now assert, that there is in that court a residual power, where no statute has yet intervened to supersede the common law, to superintend those offences which are prejudicial to the public welfare. Such occasions will be rare, for Parliament has not been slow to legislate when attention has been sufficiently aroused. But gaps remain and will always remain since no one can foresee every way in which the wickedness of man may disrupt the order of society. Let me take a single instance to which my noble and learned friend, Lord Tucker, refers. Let it be supposed that, at some future, perhaps, early, date homosexual practices between adult consenting males are no longer a crime. Would it not be an offence if, even without obscenity, such practices were publicly advocated and encouraged by pamphlet and advertisement? Or must we wait until Parliament finds time to deal with such conduct? I say, my Lords, that, if the common law is powerless in such an event, then we should no longer do her reverence. But I say that her hand is still powerful and that it is for Her Majesty's judges to play the part which Lord Mansfield pointed out to them.

The appeal on both counts should, in my opinion, be dismissed.

[**Lord Reid** made a dissenting speech.]

[**Lord Tucker**, **Lord Morris** and **Lord Hodson** made speeches dismissing the appeal.]

Appeal dismissed

Knuller Ltd v Director of Public Prosecutions
[1972] 2 All ER 898, House of Lords

(Lords Reid, Morris of Borth-y-Gest, Diplock, Simon of Glaisdale and Kilbrandon)

The appellants published a magazine, the 'International Times', which contained on inner pages columns of advertisements headed 'Males'. Most of the advertisements were inserted by homosexuals for the purpose of attracting persons who would indulge in homosexual activities. The magazine had a circulation of over 30,000 copies. It was not disputed that a great many copies found their way into the hands of young students and schoolboys, but the prosecution did not make any point of the fact that it was likely that males under 21, the age of consent to homosexual activity at that time, would reply to the advertisements.

The appellants were charged in two counts. The first count alleged a conspiracy to corrupt public morals. The particulars were that the appellants conspired by means of the advertisements:

to induce readers thereof to meet those persons inserting such advertisements for the purpose of sexual practices taking place between such male persons and to encourage readers thereof to indulge in such practices, with intent thereby to debauch and corrupt the morals as well of youth as divers other liege subjects of Our Lady the Queen.

The second count alleged a conspiracy to outrage public decency by the publication of the 'lewd, disgusting and offensive' advertisements.

The appellants were convicted on both counts and their appeals to the Court of Appeal were dismissed.

[**Lord Reid**, having said that it was technically correct that s 2(4) of the Obscene Publications Act does not exclude prosecution for the offence of corrupting morals but that the distinction seemed to him to offend against the policy of the Act; and that, if the draftsman had foreseen *Shaw's* case, he might well have drafted the subsection differently, continued:]... The matter was raised in the House of Commons on 3 June 1964 when the Solicitor-General gave an assurance, repeating an earlier assurance, that a conspiracy to corrupt public morals would not be charged so as to circumvent the statutory defence in s4. That does at least show that Parliament has not been entirely satisfied with *Shaw's* case [[1962] AC 220, [1961] 2 All ER 446, p **480**, above]. It is not for me to comment on the undesirability of seeking to alter the law by undertakings or otherwise than by legislation. But I am bound to say that I was surprised to learn that nothing effective had been done to bring this undertaking to the notice of the legal profession. Very experienced senior counsel in this case had never heard of it. It was not said that the course of the present case would have been different if counsel had known of the undertaking. But I cannot avoid an uneasy suspicion that ignorance of it may have affected the conduct of some other prosecution for this crime.

Although I would not support reconsidering *Shaw's* case I think that we ought to clarify one or two matters. In the first place conspiracy to corrupt public morals is something of a misnomer. It really means to corrupt the morals of such members of the public as may be influenced by the matter published by the accused.

Next I think that the meaning of the word 'corrupt' requires some clarification. One of my objections to the *Shaw* decision is that it leaves too much to the jury. I recognise that in the end it must be for the jury to say whether the matter published is likely to lead to corruption. But juries, unlike judges, are not expected to be experts in the use of the English language and I think that they ought to be given some assistance. In *Shaw's* case a direction was upheld in which the trial judge said [[1962] AC 220 at 290, [1961] 2 All ER at 466]:

> 'And, really, the meaning of debauched and corrupt is again, just as the meaning of the word induce is, essentially a matter for you. After all the arguments, I wonder really whether it means in this case and in this context much more than lead astray morally.'

I cannot agree that that is right. 'Corrupt' is a strong word and the jury ought to be reminded of that, as they were in the present case. The Obscene Publications Act 1959 appears to use the words 'deprave' and 'corrupt' as synonymous, as I think they are. We may regret that we live in a permissive society but I doubt whether even the most staunch defender of a better age would maintain that all or even most of those who have at one time or in one way or another been led astray morally have thereby become depraved or corrupt. I think that the jury should be told in one way or another that although in the end the question whether matter is corrupting is for them, they should keep in mind the current standards of ordinary decent people.

I can now turn to the appellants' second argument. They say that homosexual acts between adult males in private are now lawful so it is unreasonable and cannot be the law that other persons are guilty of an offence if they merely put in touch with one another two males who wish to indulge in such acts. But there is a material difference between merely exempting certain conduct from criminal penalties and making it lawful in the full sense. Prostitution and gaming afford examples of this difference. So we must examine the provisions of the Sexual Offences Act 1967 to see just how far it altered the old law. It enacts subject to limitation that a homosexual act in private shall not be an offence but it goes no further than that. Section 4 shows that procuring is still a serious offence and it would seem that some of the facts in this case might have supported a charge under that section.

I find nothing in the Act to indicate that Parliament thought or intended to lay down that indulgence in these practices is not corrupting. I read the Act as saying that, even though it may be corrupting, if people choose to corrupt themselves in this way that is their affair and the law will not interfere. But no licence is given to others to encourage the practice. So if one accepts *Shaw's* case as rightly decided it must be left to each jury to decide in the circumstances of each case whether people were likely to be corrupted. In this case the jury were properly directed and it is impossible to say that they reached a wrong conclusion. It is not for us to say whether or not we agree with it. So I would dismiss the appeal as regards the first count.

The second count is conspiracy to outrage public decency, the particulars based on the same facts being that the appellants conspired with persons inserting lewd, disgusting and offensive advertisements in the magazine 'by means of the publication of the said magazine containing the said advertisements to outrage public decency'.

The crucial question here is whether in this generalised form this is an offence known to the law. There are a number of particular offences well known to the law which involve indecency in various ways but none of them covers the facts of this case. We were informed that a charge of this character has never been brought with regard to printed matter on sale to the public. The recognised offences with regard to such matter are based on its being obscene, ie likely to corrupt or deprave. The basis of the new offence if it is one is quite different. It is that ordinary decent-minded people who are not likely to become corrupted or depraved will be outraged or utterly disgusted by what they read. To my mind questions of public policy of the utmost importance are at stake here.

I think that the objections to the creation of this generalised offence are similar in character to but even greater than the objections to the generalised offence of conspiracy to corrupt public morals. In upholding the decision in *Shaw's* case [[1962] AC 220, [1961] 2 All ER 446] we are, in my view, in no way affirming or lending any support to the doctrine that the courts still have some general or residual power either to create or so to widen existing offences as to make punishable conduct of a type hitherto not subject to punishment. Apart from some statutory offences of limited application, there appears to be neither precedent nor authority of any kind for punishing the publication of written or printed matter on the ground that it is indecent as distinct from being obscene. To say that published matter offends against public decency adds nothing to saying that it is indecent. To say, as is said in this charge, that it outrages public decency adds no new factor; it seems to me to mean no more than that the degree of indecency is such that decent members of the public who read the material will not merely feel shocked or disgusted but will feel outraged. If this charge is an attempt to introduce something new into the criminal law it cannot be saved because it is limited to what a jury might think to be a high degree of indecency.

There are at present three well-known offences of general application which involve indecency: indecent exposure of the person, keeping a disorderly house, and exposure or exhibition in public of indecent things or acts. The first two are far removed from sale of indecent literature and I can see no real analogy with the third.

Indecent exhibitions in public have been widely interpreted. Indecency is not confined to sexual indecency; indeed it is difficult to find any limit short of saying that it includes anything which an ordinary decent man or woman would find to be shocking, disgusting and revolting. And 'in public' also has a wide meaning. It appears to cover exhibitions in all places to which the public have access either as of right or gratis or on payment. There is authority to the effect that two or more members of the public must be able to see the exhibition at the same time, but I doubt whether that applies in all cases. We were not referred to any case where the exhibition consisted of written or printed matter but it may well be that public exhibition of an indecent notice or advertisement would be punishable.

But to say that an inside page of a book or magazine exposed for sale is exhibited in public seems to me to be going far beyond both the general purpose and intendment of this offence and any decision or even dictum in any case. I need not go farther because this offence is not charged and it was not argued that it could have been charged in this case.

I must now consider what the effect would be if this new generalised crime were held to exist. If there were in any book, new or old, a few pages or even a few sentences which any jury could find to be outrageously indecent, those who took part in its publication and sale would risk conviction. I can see no way of denying to juries the free hand which *Shaw's* case gives them in cases of conspiracy to corrupt public morals. There would be no defence based on literary, artistic or scientific merit. The undertaking given in Parliament with regard to obscene publications would not apply to this quite different crime. Notoriously many old works, commonly regarded as classics of the highest merit, contain passages which many a juryman might regard as outrageously indecent. It has been generally supposed that the days for Bowdlerising the classics were long past, but the introduction of this new crime might make publishers of such works think twice. It may be said that no prosecution would ever be brought except in a very bad case. But I have expressed on previous occasions my opinion that a bad law is not defensible on the ground that it will be judiciously administered. To recognise this new crime would go contrary to the whole trend of public policy followed by Parliament in recent times. I have no hesitation in saying that in my opinion the conviction of the appellants on the second count must be quashed.

[**Lords Morris**, **Simon** and **Kilbrandon** agreed that the conviction on count 1 should be upheld. **Lord Diplock**, dissenting, thought it should be quashed.]

Lords Diplock, **Simon** and **Kilbrandon** agreed that the conviction on count 2 should be quashed. Lord Diplock agreed with **Lord Reid** that there was no such offence as a conspiracy to outrage public decency. Lords Simon, Kilbrandon and **Morris** held that the authorities established an offence of outraging public decency and it followed that it was a conspiracy to agree to commit it; but Lords Simon and Kilbrandon held that 'outrage' was a very strong word, going considerably beyond offending the susceptibilities of, or even shocking, reasonable people; and the jury had not been adequately directed to that effect, so the conviction must be quashed. Lord Morris thought the jury had been fairly and sufficiently directed and would have dismissed the appeal.

Appeal dismissed on count 1

Appeal allowed on count 2

Note

As the Court of Appeal confirmed in *Gibson* [1991] 1 All ER 439 that there is a common law offence of outraging public decency, any conspiracies ought to be charged as statutory conspiracies.

7. EXEMPTIONS FROM LIABILITY FOR CONSPIRACY

Section 2 of the Criminal Law Act 1977 provides:

2. Exemptions from liability for conspiracy

(1) A person shall not by virtue of section 1 above be guilty of conspiracy to commit any offence if he is an intended victim of that offence.

(2) A person shall not by virtue of section 1 above be guilty of conspiracy to commit any offence or offences if the only other person or persons with whom he agrees are (both initially and at all times during the currency of the agreement) persons of any one or more of the following descriptions, that is to say:
   (a) his spouse [or civil partner];
   (b) a person under the age of criminal responsibility; and
   (c) an intended victim of that offence or of each of those offences.

(3) A person is under the age of criminal responsibility for the purposes of subsection (2)(b) above so long as it is conclusively presumed, by virtue of section 50 of the Children and Young Persons Act 1933, that he cannot be guilty of any offence.

In relation to sub-s (1) and sub-s (2)(c), see *Tyrrell*, discussed above, p **482**.

Questions

1. Is D guilty of conspiracy if he agrees:
   (a) with Poppy, a 15-year-old girl, to have sexual intercourse with her?

(b) with Poppy to take her out of the possession of her parents? Is Poppy or are her parents 'the victim'? Cf *Prince* (1875) 2 CCR 154.

2. D and his fiancée, Penny, carry on a business as suppliers of prohibited drugs. On 1 April 2002, they get married. On 5 April, Al, an undercover officer, inquires about drugs and they agree to supply him. Is Al an 'agent provocateur'? (See *Edwards*, above, p **501**.)

8. THE DRAFT CRIMINAL CODE BILL AND CONSPIRACY

The authors of the Draft Code assumed that common law conspiracies will have been abolished and the gap filled by the creation of suitable substantive offences by the time a codification Bill is presented to Parliament. The Draft Bill therefore avoids some of the troubles which plague the present law. It provides:

48. Conspiracy to commit an offence

(1) A person is guilty of conspiracy to commit an offence or offences if:
   (a) he agrees with another or others that an act or acts shall be done which, if done, will involve the commission of the offence or offences by one or more of the parties to the agreement; and
   (b) he and at least one other party to the agreement intend that the offence or offences shall be committed.

(2) For the purposes of subsection (1) an intention that an offence shall be committed is an intention with respect to all the elements of the offence (other than fault elements), except that recklessness with respect to a circumstance suffices where it suffices for the offence itself.

(3) Subject to section 52, 'offence' in this section means any offence triable in England and Wales; and
   (a) it extends to an offence of murder which would not be so triable; but
   (b) it does not include a summary offence, not punishable with imprisonment, constituted by an act or acts agreed to be done in contemplation of a trade dispute.

(4) Where the purpose of an enactment creating an offence is the protection of a class of persons, no member of that class who is the intended victim of such an offence can be guilty of conspiracy to commit that offence.

(5) A conspiracy continues until the agreed act or acts is or are done, or until all or all save one of the parties to the agreement have abandoned the intention that such act or acts shall be done.

(6) A person may become a party to a continuing conspiracy by joining the agreement constituting the offence.

(7) It is not an offence under this section, or under any enactment referred to in section 51, to agree to procure, assist or encourage as an accessory the commission of an offence by a person who is not a party to such an agreement; but:
   (a) a person may be guilty as an accessory to a conspiracy by others; and
   (b) this subsection does not preclude a charge of conspiracy to incite (under section 47 or any other enactment) to commit an offence.

(8) A person may be convicted of conspiracy to commit an offence although:
   (a) no other person has been or is charged with such conspiracy;

(b) the identity of any other party to the agreement is unknown;

(c) any other party appearing from the indictment to have been a party to the agreement has been or is acquitted of such conspiracy, unless in all the circumstances his conviction is inconsistent with the acquittal of the other; or

(d) the only other party to the agreement cannot be convicted of such conspiracy (for example, because he was acting under duress by threats (section 42), or he was a child under ten years of age (section 32(1)) or he is immune from prosecution).

FURTHER READING

I. Dennis, 'The Rationale of Criminal Conspiracy' (1977) 93 LQR 39

D. Hodgson, 'Law Commission No 76: A Case Study in Criminal Law Reform' in P. R. Glazebrook (ed) *Reshaping Criminal Law: Essays in Honour of Glanville Williams* (1978)

P. E. Johnson, 'The Unnecessary Crime of Conspiracy', 61 Cal L Rev 1137 (1973)

N. Katyal 'Conspiracy Theory' (2003) 112 Yale LJ 1307

P. Marcus, 'Conspiracy: The Criminal Agreement in Theory and in Practice', 65 Geo LJ 925 (1977)

15

Attempt

The third inchoate offence is attempt. The common law of attempts to commit crime has been abolished for all purposes not relating to acts done before the commencement of the Criminal Attempts Act 1981 by s 6 of that Act. The present law of attempts to commit crime is to be found entirely in the 1981 Act. Section 1 provides:

1. Attempting to commit an offence

(1) If, with intent to commit an offence to which this section applies, a person does an act which is more than merely preparatory to the commission of the offence, he is guilty of attempting to commit the offence.

[Subsections (1A) and (1B) which relate to attempts to commit an offence under the Computer Misuse Act 1990 are omitted.]

(2) A person may be guilty of attempting to commit an offence to which this section applies even though the facts are such that the commission of the offence is impossible.

(3) In any case where:
   (a) apart from this subsection a person's intention would not be regarded as having amounted to an intent to commit an offence; but
   (b) if the facts of the case had been as he believed them to be, his intention would be so regarded,
   then, for the purposes of subsection (1) above, he shall be regarded as having had an intent to commit that offence.

(4) This section applies to any offence which, if it were completed, would be triable in England and Wales as an indictable offence, other than:
   (a) conspiracy (at common law or under section 1 of the Criminal Law Act 1977 or any other enactment);
   (b) aiding, abetting, counselling, procuring or suborning the commission of an offence:
   (c) offences under section 4(1) (assisting offenders) or 5(1) (accepting or agreeing to accept consideration for not disclosing information about an arrestable offence) of the Criminal Law Act 1967.

Section 1A, which extends jurisdiction to certain attempts to commit offences which, if completed, would not be triable in England and Wales, is omitted. The method of trial of, and the penalties for, offences of attempt are provided by s 4:

4. Trial and penalties

(1) A person guilty by virtue of section 1 above of attempting to commit an offence shall:
   (a) if the offence attempted is murder or any other offence the sentence for which is fixed by law, be liable on conviction on indictment to imprisonment for life; and

(b) if the offence attempted is indictable but does not fall within paragraph (a) above, be liable on conviction on indictment to any penalty to which he would have been liable on conviction on indictment of that offence; and

(c) if the offence attempted is triable either way, be liable on summary conviction to any penalty to which he would have been liable on summary conviction of that offence.

(2) In any case in which a court may proceed to summary trial of an information charging a person with an offence and an information charging him with an offence under section 1 above of attempting to commit it or an attempt under a special statutory provision, the court may, without his consent, try the informations together.

(3) Where, in proceedings against a person for an offence under section 1 above, there is evidence sufficient in law to support a finding that he did an act falling within subsection (1) of that section, the question whether or not his act fell within that subsection is a question of fact.

(4) Where, in proceedings against a person for an attempt under a special statutory provision, there is evidence sufficient in law to support a finding that he did an act falling within subsection (3) of section 3 above, the question whether or not his act fell within that subsection is a question of fact.

(5) Subsection (1) above shall have effect—

(a) …

(b) notwithstanding anything—

(i) in section 32(1) (no limit to fine on conviction on indictment) of the Criminal Law Act 1977; or

(ii) in [s 78(1) and (2)] (maximum of six months' imprisonment on summary conviction unless express provision made to the contrary) of [the Powers of Criminal Courts (Sentencing) Act 2000].

[(ii) in s 154(1) and (2) (general limit on magistrates' court's powers to impose imprisonment) of the Criminal Justice Act 2003.]

1. MENS REA

It will be noted that s 1(1) of the Act begins with the words, 'If, with intent to commit an offence to which this section applies . . . '. The next case, *Whybrow*, states that, in attempt, the intent is 'the principal ingredient of the crime.' It is convenient then to begin with a consideration of the mens rea of attempt. The Act offers no definition of 'intent' (cf the draft Code, cl 1(a), p **133**, above and cl 49(2), p **539**, below) but in *Pearman* (1984) 80 Cr App R 259, [1984] Crim LR 675 the Court of Appeal could see no reason why the Act should have altered the common law in this respect and applied *Mohan*, p **521**, below and it is clear that *Whybrow* also represents the present law.

R v Whybrow

(1951) 35 Cr App R 141, Court of Criminal Appeal

(Lord Goddard CJ, Hilbery, Finnemore, Slade and Devlin JJ)

The appellant was convicted of attempted murder of his wife. The case for the prosecution was that he had administered an electric shock to her while she was in a bath, by means of an apparatus connecting a soap dish with the mains power supply. The appellant's explanation of the apparatus was that it was to provide an earth for a wireless set in his bedroom and that, if she did get an electric shock, it was an accident. He appealed against his conviction on the ground of misdirection.

Goddard LCJ.... The case lasted two days and the learned Judge's summing-up, so far as the facts were concerned, was meticulously careful and meticulously accurate, but unfortunately he did, in charging the jury, confuse in his mind for a moment the direction given to a jury in a case of murder with the direction given to a jury in a case of attempted murder. In murder the jury is told—and it has always been the law—that if a person wounds another or attacks another either intending to kill or intending to do grievous bodily harm, and the person attacked dies, that is murder, the reason being that the requisite malice aforethought, which is a term of art, is satisfied if the attacker intends to do grievous bodily harm. Therefore, if one person attacks another, inflicting a wound in such a way that an ordinary, reasonable person must know that at least grievous bodily harm will result, and death results, there is the malice aforethought sufficient to support the charge of murder. But, if the charge is one of attempted murder, the intent becomes the principal ingredient of the crime. It may be said that the law, which is not always logical, is somewhat illogical in saying that, if one attacks a person intending to do grievous bodily harm and death results, that is murder, but that if one attacks a person and only intends to do grievous bodily harm, and death does not result, it is not attempted murder, but wounding with intent to do grievous bodily harm. It is not really illogical because, in that particular case, the intent is the essence of the crime while, where the death of another is caused, the necessity is to prove malice aforethought, which is supplied in law by proving intent to do grievous bodily harm....

The learned Judge, as I say, had in his mind the charge which is given to a jury in a case of murder.... There is no question that that was a misdirection, and the jury should have been told that the essence of the offence was the intent to murder...

[The court concluded that there had been no substantial miscarriage of justice and dismissed the appeal under the proviso to s 4 of the Criminal Appeal Act 1907 (a power no longer available).]

R v Mohan

[1975] 2 All ER 193, Court of Appeal, Criminal Division

(James LJ, Talbot and Michael Davies JJ)

The appellant was convicted on count 2 of an indictment of attempting by wanton driving to cause bodily harm to be done to a police constable. The judge directed the jury that it must be proved that the appellant 'must have realised at the time that he was driving that such driving ... was likely to cause bodily harm if he went on, or he was reckless as to whether bodily harm was caused. It is not necessary to prove an intention actually to cause bodily harm.'

[**James LJ**, giving the judgment of the court, said:]

The first question we have to answer is: what is the meaning of 'intention' when that word is used to describe the mens rea in attempt? It is to be distinguished from 'motive' in the sense of an emotion leading to action: it has never been suggested that such a meaning is appropriate to 'intention' in this context. It is equally clear that the word means what is often referred to as 'specific intent' and can be defined as 'a decision to bring about a certain consequence' or as the 'aim'. In *Hyam* [p **562**, below] Lord Hailsham cited with approval the judicial interpretation of 'intention' or 'intent' applied by Asquith LJ in *Cunliffe v Goodman* [1950] 2 KB 237 at 253. 'An "intention" to my mind connotes a state of affairs which the party intending—I will call him X—does more than merely contemplate: it connotes a state of affairs which, on the contrary, he decides so far as in him lies to bring about and which, in point of possibility, he has a reasonable prospect of being able to bring about by his own act of volition.'

If that interpretation of 'intent' is adopted as the meaning of mens rea in the offence of attempt it is not wide enough to justify the direction in the present case. The direction, taken as a whole, can be supported as accurate only if the necessary mens rea includes not only specific intent but also the state of mind of one who realises that, if his conduct continues, the likely consequence is the commission of the complete offence and who continues his conduct in that realisation, or the state of mind of one who, knowing that continuation of his conduct is likely to result in the commission of the complete offence, is reckless as to whether or not that is the result. [His Lordship considered *Hyam* (p **562**, below) and continued:]

We do not find in the speeches of their Lordships in the case of *Hyam* anything which binds us to hold that mens rea in the offence of attempt is proved by establishing beyond reasonable doubt that the accused knew or correctly foresaw that the consequences of his act unless interrupted would 'as a high degree of probability', or would be 'likely' to, be the commission of the complete offence. Nor do we find authority in that case for the proposition that a reckless state of mind is sufficient to constitute the mens rea in the offence of attempt.

Prior to the enactment of the Criminal Justice Act 1967, s 8, the standard test in English Law of a man's state of mind in the commission of an act was the foreseeable or natural consequence of the act. Therefore it could be said that when a person applied his mind to the consequences that did happen and foresaw that they would probably happen he intended them to happen, whether he wanted them to happen or not. So knowledge of the foreseeable consequence could be said to be a form of 'intent'. [His Lordship read s 8 (above, p **179**).]

Thus, upon the question whether or not the accused had the necessary intent in relation to a charge of attempt, evidence tending to establish directly, or by inference, that the accused knew or foresaw that the likely consequence, and, even more so, the highly probable consequence, of his act—unless interrupted—would be the commission of the completed offence, is relevant material for the consideration of the jury. In our judgment, evidence of knowledge of likely consequences, or from what knowledge of likely consequences can be inferred, is evidence by which intent may be established but it is not, in relation to the offence of attempt, to be equated with intent. If the jury find such knowledge established they may and, using common sense, they probably will find intent proved, but it is not the case that they must do so.

An attempt to commit crime is itself an offence. Often it is a grave offence. Often it is as morally culpable as the completed offence which is attempted but not in fact committed. Nevertheless it falls within the class of conduct which is preparatory to the commission of a crime and is one step removed from the offence which is attempted. The Court must not strain to bring within the offence of attempt conduct which does not fall within the well established bounds of the offence. On the contrary, the Court must safeguard against extension of those bounds save by the authority of Parliament. The bounds are presently set requiring proof of specific intent, a decision to bring about, in so far as it lies within the accused's power, the commission of the offence which it is alleged the accused attempted to commit, no matter whether the accused desired that consequence of his act or not.

In the present case the final direction was bad in law. Not only did the judge maintain the exclusion of 'intent' as an ingredient of the offence in Count 2 but he introduced an alternative basis for a conviction which did not and could not constitute the necessary mens rea…

Appeal on count 2 allowed

Questions

1. '…P and D are walking at the edge of a cliff; they both see a watch lying on the path in front of them, and both plunge forward to get it. P is the more powerful and swifter man

and will inevitably reach the watch first unless D takes extreme measures. D therefore gives P a sudden and treacherous push which he intends to result in P's falling over the cliff. He knows full well that if he is successful in his plan, P will certainly be killed.... There is no reason why D should not be guilty of attempted murder':Glanville Williams, *The Mental Element in Crime*, p 24. Do you agree?

2. In *Walker and Hayles* (1989) 90 Cr App R 226, [1990] Crim LR 44 it was held on a charge of attempted murder that it was not a misdirection for the judge to direct that it was sufficient that the defendant foresaw that there was 'a very high degree of probability' that he would cause death. The Court of Appeal, when upholding the conviction for murder in *Woollin*, above, p **126**, said they were 'fortified' by that decision. The House of Lords quashed Woollin's conviction, insisting that nothing less than foresight of virtual certainty would suffice. If that is so for murder, should it not be so, *a fortiori*, for attempted murder—and attempts generally? But should even foresight of virtual certainty be enough? Does not attempting mean *trying* to achieve a result—having the *purpose* of doing so?

3. In many instances intention in attempt is equated with the defendant 'trying' to commit the substantive offence. Is this an accurate description of the mens rea? Is there a difference between (i) trying to do something and (ii) trying to succeed? See J. Hornby, 'On What's Intentionally Done' in S. Shute, J. Gardner and J. Horder, *Action and Value in Criminal Law* (1993) 60 and J. Horder, 'Varieties of Intention, Criminal Attempts and Endangerment' (1994) 14 LS 335.

2. INTENTION AND CIRCUMSTANCES

It is clear that, on a charge of attempt, intention is required as to any result in the definition of the actus reus even though it is not required on a charge of committing the complete crime. In *Whybrow* it was necessary to prove that the defendant intended to kill and in *Mohan* that he intended to cause bodily harm. But there has been much controversy over the question whether, on a charge of attempt, intention is required as to a circumstance in the actus reus, where, on a charge of committing the complete crime, recklessness as to that circumstance would suffice. The Law Commission's Working Party thought that recklessness should be enough but the Commission at first took a different view. They thought that a distinction between consequences and circumstances would be unworkable and recommended that intention should be required as to all the elements in the definition of the offence. The Criminal Attempts Act 1981, above, p **519**, does not deal with the matter expressly. It simply requires 'intent to commit [the] offence'. The Code Team's draft (Law Com No 143, cl 53(2)) would have implemented the Commission's recommendation by providing that 'An "intention of committing an offence" means an intention in respect of all the elements of the offence.' This proposal was criticized and the Law Commission changed their minds. Their Draft Code, cl 49(2), below, p **539**, now provides that, on a charge of attempt, 'recklessness as to a circumstance suffices where it suffices for the offence itself'.

In the meantime, the question is as to the proper construction of s 1 of the Criminal Attempts Act 1981. See the next case.

R v Khan
[1990] 2 All ER 783, Court of Appeal

(Russell LJ, Rose and Morland JJ)

After a disco a 16-year-old girl accompanied five youths in a car to a house where they were joined by other youths. Three youths succeeded in having sexual intercourse with her. Four others, the appellants, tried to do so but failed. The girl did not consent to any sexual activity. The appellants were convicted of attempted rape and appealed. It was argued that the judge had misdirected the jury by telling them that, even if a defendant did not know the girl was not consenting, he was guilty of attempted rape if he tried unsuccessfully to have sexual intercourse, being reckless whether she consented or not—that is, it was sufficient that he could not care less whether she consented or not.

Russell LJ. The impact of the words of s 1 of the 1981 Act [above, p **519**] and in particular the words 'with intent to commit an offence' has been the subject matter of much debate amongst distinguished academic writers. We were referred to and we have read and considered an article by Professor Glanville Williams entitled 'The Problem of Reckless Attempts' [1983] Crim LR 365. The argument there advanced is that recklessness can exist within the concept of attempt and support is derived from *R v Pigg* [1982] 2 All ER 591, [1982] 1 WLR 762 [S. White, 'Three points on *Pigg*' [1989] Crim LR 539, 541] albeit that authority was concerned with the law prior to the 1981 Act. This approach also receives approval from Smith and Hogan *Criminal Law* (6th edn, 1988) pp 287–289.

Contrary views, however, have been expressed by Professor Griew [Current Law Statutes, 1981] and Mr Richard Buxton QC, [1984] Crim LR 25 who have both contended that the words 'with intent to commit an offence' involves an intent as to every element constituting the crime....

[**Russell LJ** quoted from the judgment of Mustill LJ in *Millard and Vernon* [1987] Crim LR 393 and continued:]

In our judgment an acceptable analysis of the offence of rape [as defined under the 1956 Act see now the definition in s 1 of the Sexual Offences Act 2003, below] as is as follows: (1) the intention of the offender is to have sexual intercourse with a woman; (2) the offence is committed if, but only if, the circumstances are that (a) the woman does not consent *and* (b) the defendant knows that she is not consenting or is reckless as to whether she consents.

Precisely the same analysis can be made of the offence of attempted rape: (1) the intention of the offender is to have sexual intercourse with a woman; (2) the offence is committed if, but only if, the circumstances are that (a) the woman does not consent *and* (b) the defendant knows that she is not consenting or is reckless as to whether she consents.

The only difference between the two offences is that in rape sexual intercourse takes place whereas in attempted rape it does not, although there has to be some act which is more than preparatory to sexual intercourse. Considered in that way, the intent of the defendant is precisely the same in rape and in attempted rape and the mens rea is identical, namely an intention to have intercourse plus a knowledge of or recklessness as to the woman's absence of consent. No question of attempting to achieve a reckless state of mind arises; the attempt relates to the physical activity; the mental state of the defendant is the same. A man does not recklessly have sexual intercourse, nor does he recklessly attempt it. Recklessness in rape and attempted rape arises not in relation to the physical act of the accused but only in his state of mind when engaged in the activity of having or attempting to have sexual intercourse.

If this is the true analysis, as we believe it is, the attempt does not require any different intention on the part of the accused from that for the full offence of rape. We believe this to be a desirable result which in the instant case did not require the jury to be burdened with different directions as to the accused's state of mind, dependent on whether the individual achieved or failed to achieve sexual intercourse.

We recognise, of course, that our reasoning cannot apply to all offences and all attempts. Where, for example as in causing death by reckless driving or reckless arson, no state of mind other than recklessness is involved in the offence, there can be no attempt to commit it.

In our judgment, however, the words 'with intent to commit an offence' to be found in s 1 of the 1981 Act mean, when applied to rape, 'with intent to have sexual intercourse with a woman in circumstances where she does not consent and the defendant knows or could not care less about her absence of consent'. The only 'intent', giving that word its natural and ordinary meaning, of the rapist is to have sexual intercourse. He commits the offence because of the circumstances in which he manifests that intent, ie when the woman is not consenting and he either knows it or could not care less about the absence of consent.

Accordingly, we take the view that in relation to the four appellants the judge was right to give the directions that he did when inviting the jury to consider the charges of attempted rape.

Appeals against conviction dismissed

Thus, recklessness as to the circumstance of consent is a sufficient mens rea for the attempt. The decision in *Khan* was limited to rape but it was followed in *A-G's Reference (No 3 of 1992)* (1993) 98 Cr App R 383, [1994] Crim LR 348, below, p **960**, where the offence charged was attempted arson, being reckless whether life be endangered, contrary to s 1(2) of the Criminal Damage Act 1971 (below, p **955**). The court stated a general principle:

...a defendant, in order to be guilty of an attempt, must be in one of the states of mind required for the commission of the full offence, and did [sic] his best, so far as he could, to supply what was missing from the completion of the offence. It is the policy of the law that such people should be punished notwithstanding that in fact the intentions of such a defendant have not been fulfilled.

Four issues arise from the decision and the dictum.

(i) The decision goes beyond *Khan* and the Draft Code (below, p **539**) in that the recklessness related not to a circumstance but to a result. This perhaps reveals a deficiency in the Draft Code: where the definition of the full offence is satisfied by recklessness whether the *result* occurs *even if it does not in fact do so*, is not this right? The result which must occur for the full offence is arson and D did intend that. Section 1(2) of the Criminal Damage Act is exceptional in this respect.

(ii) Secondly, the statement is overbroad. Read literally this approach would lead to the conviction for attempt of D who is merely reckless as to a consequence element of the offence provided he had an intention as to the relevant missing circumstance element(s). This is clearly not what the Act was intended to mean.

(iii) The principle stated in *A-G's Reference* would introduce strict liability into the law of attempts. If D tries to touch sexually a girl, V, whom he believes on reasonable grounds to be aged 16 but who is in fact only 12, he would be guilty of an attempt to commit the offence under s 7 of the Sexual Offences Act 2003. He has the state of mind required for the commission of the full offence (an intention to touch a person, who is in fact, whether he knows it or not, under the age of 13); and he has done his best 'to supply [in the quaint language of the court] what was missing from the commission of the full offence'—sexual touching. There is a logical argument in favour of such an extension of inchoate liability: J. C. Smith (1957) 70 Harv LR 422 at 433 and [1962] Crim LR 135, but it goes beyond anything actually decided and beyond any recommendation of the Law Commission.

(iv) Finally, at the time of the *A-G's Reference*, it was settled that *Caldwell* recklessness was sufficient for the full offence under the Criminal Damage Act and the court held that this was also the right test on the attempt charge. Advertent recklessness (*Cunningham/G* recklessness) has long been thought to be an acceptable mens rea as to circumstances in attempt because it is a true state of mind. However, a person may be *Caldwell* reckless even if the possibility of the relevant risk (danger to life), never enters his head. Arguably, this is an unacceptable extension of liability for an inchoate offence. The point does not appear to have been considered explicitly by the court. Given the overruling of *Caldwell* in *G* (above p **140**) the issue assumes less significance in relation to criminal damage, but if it is interpreted more broadly so that recklessness, negligence or even strict liability as to a circumstance suffice, it remains of fundamental importance.

3. THE ACTUS REUS OF ATTEMPT

In deciding whether there was an actus reus, the first step should be to determine precisely the nature of the crime alleged to be attempted. In *Nash* [1999] Crim LR 308 D, who had left notes for paper boys inviting them to meet him and perform indecent acts with him, was held to be guilty of attempting to procure acts of gross indecency. What the court seems to have overlooked is that an act is not 'procured' until it is done. The charge was in substance, one of attempting to commit an act of gross indecency. D's conduct fell far short of that. Cf P. R. Glazebrook [1959] Crim LR 774, commenting on *Miskell* (1954) 37 Cr App R 214.

The actus reus of attempt cannot be defined with the same precision as the actus reus of a substantive offence. It can take as many forms as there are substantive offences. It may, moreover, be an objectively innocent act. D puts sugar in V's tea. There is nothing wrong with that—V likes sweet tea. But D believes, mistakenly, that the sugar is arsenic and intends to kill V. He is guilty of attempted murder, the actus reus of the attempt being that objectively innocent act.

It will be recalled that Lord Goddard in *Whybrow*, p **520**, above, described the intent as the principal ingredient of the offence of attempt. It is not however the only ingredient. Something must be done to put the intent into execution. The question is, how much? The law has always distinguished mere acts of preparation from attempts. It was said at common law that the act had to be sufficiently proximate to the complete offence. The doctrine of proximity excluded from liability acts which some thought should entail guilt. A conspicuous example is *Robinson*, below. The 1981 Act, above, p **519**, following the recommendations of the Law Commission, makes no attempt to state a test of proximity. It merely requires that the act done by the defendant should be 'more than merely preparatory to the commission of the offence'.

R. A. Duff, *Criminal Attempts* (1996), p **386** observes:

What relates an agent's conduct to the commission of an offence is partly her intention to commit that offence, but it also matters how close she has come to fully actualizing that intent. The conduct of someone who has so far only reconnoitered a building from which he plans to steal, for example, or only obtained a poison with which he intends to kill someone, is still 'remote' from the commission of theft (or burglary) or murder. We could not yet count her actions as essentially larcenous or murderous, or as attacks on property or life; there is still too wide a gap between what she has actually done and the commission, of the intended offence.

This is not to say that we should see her conduct simply as, for instance, 'walking round a building', or 'buying arsenic', which are indeed remote from the commission of the theft or murder that she intends to commit; we understand it, and respond to it, as by her intention, and her commission of the crime has so far only a shadowy existence in the public world: it exists in thought (in her intention), but has yet to acquire any very concrete existence in her actions. As her criminal enterprise advances, and her criminal intention is further actualized in action, her prospective commission of the crime becomes less shadowy, more concrete as an active engagement in the world. Her actions connect her more closely to the commission of the crime, and in the end that crime becomes something she is doing, rather than merely something she is intending or preparing to do.

Why should this matter? Why should we demand not merely conduct undertaken with intent to commit an offence (and perhaps corroborative of that intent), but conduct which comes close to the actual commission of the offence? An initial answer is that the law should leave intending criminals a *locus poenitentiae*: the chance to decide for themselves to abandon their criminal enterprises. This matters, because the law should treat and address its citizens as responsible agents. The central value to which this answer appeals is that of individual freedom to determine one's own actions.

The only well-settled rule of common law was that if D had done the last act which, as he knew, was necessary to achieve the consequence alleged to be attempted, he was guilty. Every act preceding the last one might quite properly be described as 'preparatory'. The assassin crooks his finger round the trigger *preparatory* to pulling it. If every preparatory act were to be regarded as outside the scope of the offence the effect of the Act would be to narrow the offence. It was well recognized at common law that some prior acts were sufficiently proximate: see *White*, p **533**, below but cf *Ilyas*, p **530**, below. Though it has been argued that the word 'merely' does no more than add emphasis (E. Griew, annotations to *Current Law Statutes*), it seems that it has a key role. Not all preparatory acts are excluded; only those that are *merely* preparatory; and it is thought that the assassin's crooking of the finger, though preparatory, would not be regarded as *merely* preparatory. The reason, it appears, is that he is now engaged in the commission of the offence—as Rowlatt J put it in *Osborn* (1919) 84 JP 63, he is 'on the job'.

Whether the act is more than merely preparatory is a question of fact: s 4(4). In a jury trial it is for the judge to decide whether there is sufficient evidence to support such a finding. In *A-G's Reference (No 1 of 1992)* [1993] 2 All ER 190, [1993] Crim LR 274 the point of law referred was 'Whether, on a charge of attempted rape, it is incumbent on the prosecution, as a matter of law, to prove that the defendant physically attempted to penetrate the woman's vagina with his penis.' The court answered, No. It is sufficient that there is evidence of intent to rape and of acts which a jury could properly regard as more than merely preparatory to the commission of the offence—for example, in the present case, the respondent's acts of dragging V up some steps, lowering his trousers and interfering with her private parts. [Note that under the Sexual Offences Act 2003, s 1 the offence is extended to include penile penetration of the vagina, anus or mouth of the complainant.]

As rape consists in the physical penetration of a person's vagina, anus or mouth by a man's penis, how can there be an attempt to commit rape if there is no attempt by the man to penetrate the orifice? Is it not a contradiction in terms to say:

(a) he did not attempt to penetrate her, but

(b) he did attempt to rape her?

To take an analogous case, can there be an attempt to commit murder if there is no attempt to kill? Can we properly say:

(a) D did not attempt to kill V, but

(b) he did attempt to murder him?

Is the solution that there may be an 'attempt' within the meaning of the Criminal Attempts Act when there is no attempt in the ordinary meaning of the word? Or is it that the ordinary meaning is wider than the court appears to allow? For example, *was* the respondent, lowering his trousers and interfering with V's private parts with intent to penetrate her, attempting to do so in the ordinary meaning of the word? Cf commentary, [1993] Crim LR 276.

R v Robinson
[1915] 2 KB 342, Court of Criminal Appeal

(Lord Reading CJ, Bray and Lush JJ)

The appellant was a jeweller. A policeman passing his shop heard someone inside shout, 'I am bound and gagged. Open the door.' The policeman whistled for assistance and then broke in. The appellant was found with his legs and one hand tied with cords. He said that after locking the door of the shop the previous evening he had been knocked on the head. The safe was open and empty. He said, 'They have cleared me out.' The police not being satisfied, took him to the station and searched his premises. They found the jewellery concealed in a recess at the back of the safe. The appellant admitted that he had insured his stock for £1,200 and that he had staged the burglary with a view to making a claim. He was convicted of attempting to obtain the money by false pretences and appealed.

Lord Reading CJ. On those facts it was not disputed that the appellant had arranged a fraudulent scheme with the object of its being used to obtain money on the policy from the underwriters, and the only question was whether, the police having intervened and prevented its execution, the offence of attempting to obtain the money had been committed. If he had made a claim of the money from the underwriters, or had communicated to them the facts of the pretended burglary upon which a claim was to be subsequently based, he clearly could have been convicted of an attempt to obtain the money. It seems to the Court upon consideration of the authorities that there is no real difficulty in formulating the principle of law which is applicable to cases of this kind. A safe guide is to be found in the statement of the law which is laid down by Parke B in *R v Eagleton* [(1855) Dears CC 376, 515 at p 538]:

> 'The mere intention to commit a misdemeanour is not criminal. Some act is required, and we do not think that all acts towards committing a misdemeanour are indictable. Acts remotely leading towards the commission of the offence are not to be considered as attempts to commit it, but acts immediately connected with it are.'

The difficulty lies in the application of that principle to the facts of the particular case. In some cases it is a difficult matter to determine whether an act is immediately or remotely connected with the offence of which it is alleged to be an attempt. In other cases the question is easier of solution, as for instance in *R v Button* [[1900] 2 QB 597]. There upon the evidence there was a false pretence made directly to the race authorities with the intent to make them part with the prize, and one which, but for the fact of the fraud being discovered, would necessarily have had that effect. In the present case the real difficulty lies in the fact that there is no evidence of any act done by the appellant in the nature of a false pretence which ever reached the minds of the underwriters, though they were the persons who were to be induced to part with the money. The evidence falls short of any communication of such a pretence to the underwriters or to any agent of theirs. The police were not acting on behalf of the underwriters. In truth what the appellant did was preparation for the commission of a crime, not a step in the commission of it. It consisted in the preparation of evidence which might indirectly induce the underwriters to pay; for if the police had made a report that a burglary had taken place,— and that was presumably what the appellant intended,—it may very well be that the underwriters would have paid without further inquiry. But there must be some act beyond mere preparation if a person is to be charged with an attempt. Applying the rule laid down by Parke B, we think that the appellant's act was only remotely connected with the commission of the full offence, and not imme-diately connected with it. If we were to hold otherwise we should be going further than any case has ever yet gone, and should be opening the door to convictions for acts which are not at present criminal offences. We think the conviction must be quashed, not on the technical ground that no infor-mation or evidence as to the property lost was given to the underwriters as required by the policy, but upon the broad ground that no communication of any kind of the false pretence was made to them.

Appeal allowed

Had Robinson done an act which was 'more than merely preparatory' to obtaining money by false pretences (or deception)? (Cf p **839**, below.) If he had not, what of the defendant in *Comer v Bloomfield* (1970) 55 Cr App R 305, [1971] Crim LR 230? He owned a van worth about £35 and insured only in respect of third party risks. He crashed the van and pushed the wrecked vehicle into some woods so as to conceal it. The following day, he reported to the police that the van had been stolen the night before. A week after the crash, the respondent gave a circumstantial story to the police of how the van had been stolen. The same day he wrote to his insurers: 'I have had my van stolen . . . I would be pleased to know if I could make a claim for stolen van. . . .' Later the respondent admitted the truth and on being asked why he had falsely reported the van to be stolen, said: 'Well, it was a write-off. I thought I would have a few bob off the insurance.' He was charged with attempting to obtain money by decep-tion but the justices were of opinion that the letter amounted only to an inquiry and was therefore not sufficiently proximate to the offence to amount to an attempt. The prosecutor appealed by way of case stated. The Divisional Court held that the justices were entitled to conclude that the respondent's acts were not sufficiently proximate and dismissed the appeal. The letter was 'no more than a preliminary inquiry to sound the position and see if a claim could effectively be put forward at all.' Was this more than 'merely preparatory'? Would it have been if the letter had said (i) 'I wish to make a claim for my stolen van. Please send me a claim form'? or (ii) 'My van has been stolen. I claim its value (£35) under my insurance'?

R v Gullefer (1986)
[1990] 3 All ER 882, Court of Appeal

(Lord Lane CJ, Kennedy and Owen JJ)

Gullefer jumped on to the track at a greyhound racing stadium and waved his arms in order to distract the dogs during the running of a race. He later admitted that he hoped that the stew-ards would declare 'no race' so that he would recover from a bookmaker the stake he had placed on a dog that was losing. He was convicted of attempted theft of his stake from the bookmaker under s 1(1) of the Criminal Attempts Act 1981 and appealed to the Court of Appeal.

[**Lord Lane CJ**, having cited ss 1(1) and 4(3) of the 1981 Act:]

Thus the judge's task is to decide whether there is evidence on which a jury could reasonably come to the conclusion that the defendant had gone beyond the realm of mere preparation and had embarked on the actual commission of the offence. If not, he must withdraw the case from the jury. If there is such evidence, it is then for the jury to decide whether the defendant did in fact go beyond mere preparation. That is the way in which the judge approached this case. He ruled that there was sufficient evidence. Counsel for the appellant submits that he was wrong in so ruling.

The first task of the court is to apply the words of the 1981 Act to the facts of the case. Was the appellant still in the stage of preparation to commit the substantive offence, or was there a basis of fact which would entitle the jury to say that he had embarked on the theft itself? Might it properly be said that when he jumped on to the track he was trying to steal £18 from the bookmaker?

Our view is that it could not properly be said that at that stage he was in the process of committing theft. What he was doing was jumping onto the track in an effort to distract the dogs, which in its turn, he hoped, would have the effect of forcing the stewards to declare 'no race', which would in its turn give him the opportunity to go back to the bookmaker and demand the £18 he had staked. In our view there was insufficient evidence for it to be said that he had, when he jumped onto the track, gone beyond mere preparation.

So far at least as the present case is concerned, we do not think that it is necessary to examine the authorities which preceded the 1981 Act, save to say that the sections we have already quoted in this judgment seem to be a blend of various decisions, some of which were not easy to reconcile with others.

However, in deference to the arguments of counsel, we venture to make the following observations. Since the passing of the 1981 Act, a division of this court in *R v Ilyas* (1983) 78 Cr App R 17 has helpfully collated the authorities. As appears from the judgment in that case, there seem to have been two lines of authority. The first was exemplified by the decision in *R v Eagleton* (1855) Dears CC 376, 515, [1843–60] All ER Rep 363. That was a case where the defendant was alleged to have attempted to obtain money from the guardians of a parish by falsely pretending to the relieving officer that he had delivered loaves of bread of the proper weight to the outdoor poor, when in fact the loaves were deficient in weight.

Parke B, delivering the judgment of the court of nine judges, said ((1855) Dears CC 376, 515 at 538, [1843–60] All ER Rep 363 at 367):

> 'Acts remotely leading towards the commission of the offence are not to be considered as attempts to commit it, but acts immediately connected with it are; and if, in this case, after the credit with the relieving officer for the fraudulent overcharge, any *further step* on the part of the defendant had been necessary to obtain payment, as the making out a further account or producing the vouchers to the Board, we should have thought that the obtaining credit in account with the relieving officer would not have been sufficiently proximate to the obtaining the money. But, on the statement in this case, no other act on the part of the defendant would have been required. It was the last act, *depending on himself*, towards the payment of the money, and therefore it ought to be considered as an attempt.' (Parke B's emphasis.)

Lord Diplock in *DPP v Stonehouse* [1977] 2 All ER 909 at 917, [1978] AC 55 at 68, having cited part of that passage from *R v Eagleton* (1855) Dears CC 376, 515, [1843–60] All ER Rep 363, added: 'In other words the offender must have crossed the Rubicon and burnt his boats.'

The other line of authority is based on a passage in *Stephen's Digest of the Criminal Law* (5th edn, 1894) art 50:

> 'An attempt to commit a crime is an act done with intent to commit that crime, and forming part of a series of acts which would constitute its actual commission if it were not interrupted.'

As Lord Edmund-Davies points out in *DPP v Stonehouse* [1977] 2 All ER 909 at 933, [1978] AC 55 at 85–86, that definition has been repeatedly cited with judicial approval: see Byrne J in *Hope v Brown* [1954] 1 All ER 330 at 332, [1954] 1 WLR 250 at 253 and Lord Parker CJ in *Davey v Lee* [1967] 2 All ER 423 at 425, [1968] 1 QB 366 at 370. However, as Lord Parker CJ in the latter case points out, *Stephen's* definition falls short of defining the exact point of time at which the series of acts can be said to begin.

It seems to us that the words of the 1981 Act seek to steer a midway course. They do not provide, as they might have done, that the *R v Eagleton* test is to be followed, or that, as Lord Diplock suggested, the defendant must have reached a point from which it was impossible for him to retreat before the actus reus of an attempt is proved. On the other hand the words give perhaps as clear a guidance as is possible in the circumstances on the point at which *Stephen's* 'series of acts' begins. It begins when the merely preparatory acts come to an end and the defendant embarks on the crime proper. When that is will depend of course on the facts in any particular case.

Appeal allowed

Questions

1. In *Jones*, below, it was held that there was an attempt although Jones may have had as many as three more acts to do. How many acts had Gullefer still to do? Is it helpful to count the acts to be done? Or are *time* and *place* more important? Is it significant that Jones (i) was in the place where the crime was to be committed (see also *Campbell*, below) and (ii) would have committed it within seconds if the victim had not escaped?

2. What if the declaration of 'no race' would have led (or the defendant believed it would have led) to the automatic refund of his stake?

3. It was not necessary to decide whether the successful completion of Gullefer's plan would have amounted to theft; but would it? Cf commentary, [1987] Crim LR 196.

R v Jones (Kenneth)
[1990] 3 All ER 886, Court of Appeal

(Taylor LJ, Mars-Jones and Waite JJ)

Jones got into a car driven by his ex-mistress's new lover, Foreman. He was wearing overalls and a crash helmet with the visor down and carrying a bag containing a loaded sawn-off shotgun. He had bought the gun and sawn off the barrel a few days earlier. Jones pointed the gun at Foreman at a range of 10 to 12 inches and said, 'You are not going to like this', or similar words. Foreman grabbed the end of the gun and, after a struggle, escaped unharmed. The safety catch on the gun was on and it was unclear whether Jones's finger was ever on the trigger. Jones was charged with attempted murder. It was submitted that there was no case to go to the jury because Jones had at least three acts to do before murder could be committed—(i) to remove the safety catch, (ii) to put his finger on the trigger, and (iii) to pull it. The judge rejected the submission, the jury convicted of attempted murder and Jones appealed to the Court of Appeal on the ground that the case should have been withdrawn.

[**Taylor LJ**, having cited the last paragraph of the extract from Lord Lane CJ's judgment in *Gullefer*, above:]

We respectfully adopt those words. We do not accept counsel's contention that s 1(1) of the 1981 Act in effect embodies the 'last act' test derived from *R v Eagleton*. Had Parliament intended to adopt that test, a quite different form of words could and would have been used.

It is of interest to note that the 1981 Act followed a report from the Law Commission on *Attempt, and Impossibility in Relation to Attempt, Conspiracy and Incitement* (Law Com No 102). At para 2.47 the report states:

> 'The definition of sufficient proximity must be wide enough to cover two varieties of cases; first, those in which a person has taken all the steps towards the commission of a crime which he believes to be necessary as far as he is concerned for that crime to result, such as firing a gun at another and missing. Normally such cases cause no difficulty. Secondly, however, the definition must cover those instances where a person has to take some further step to complete the crime, assuming that there is evidence of the necessary mental element on his part to commit it; for example, when the defendant has raised the gun to take aim at another but has not yet squeezed the trigger. We have reached the conclusion that, in regard to these cases, it is undesirable to recommend anything more complex than a rationalisation of the present law.'

In para 2.48 the report states:

> 'The literal meaning of "proximate" is "nearest, next before or after (in place, order, time, connection of thought, causation, etc)". Thus, were this term part of a statutory description of the actus reus of attempt, it would clearly be capable of being interpreted to exclude all but the "final act"; this would not be in accordance with the policy outlined above.'

Clearly, the draftsman of s 1(1) must be taken to have been aware of the two lines of earlier authority and of the Law Commission's report. The words 'an act which is more than merely preparatory to the commission of the offence' would be inapt if they were intended to mean 'the last act which lay in his power towards the commission of the offence'.

Looking at the plain natural meaning of s 1(1) in the way indicated by Lord Lane CJ, the question for the judge in the present case was whether there was evidence from which a reasonable jury, properly directed, could conclude that the appellant had done acts which were more than merely preparatory. Clearly his actions in obtaining the gun, in shortening it, in loading it, in putting on his disguise and in going to the school could only be regarded as preparatory acts. But, in our judgment, once he had got into the car, taken out the loaded gun and pointed it at the victim with the intention of killing him there was sufficient evidence for the consideration of the jury on the charge of attempted murder. It was a matter for them to decide whether they were sure that those acts were more than merely preparatory. In our judgment, therefore, the judge was right to allow the case to go to the jury, and the appeal against conviction must be dismissed....

Appeal dismissed

Notes and questions

1. In *Boyle and Boyle* (1986) 84 Cr App R 270, [1987] Crim LR 111, CA, persons who damaged a house door with a view to entering premises were held to have done an act more than merely preparatory to burglary. The court said that in deciding whether an act is more than merely preparatory it was entitled to look at the law before 1981. In *Jones* the court thought that counsel's invitation to them to construe the Act 'by reference to previous conflicting case law' was misconceived. Taylor LJ referred to Lord Herschell's well-known statement in *Bank of England v Vagliano Bros* [1891] AC 107 at 144–145 that the proper course in construing a codifying Act is 'to examine the language of the statute and to ask what is its natural meaning, uninfluenced by any considerations derived from the previous state of the law...'; but he was not asserting that 'resort may never be had to the previous state of the law for the purpose of aiding in the construction of the provisions of the code. If, for example, a provision be of doubtful import, such resort would be perfectly legitimate.'

Is s 1(1) of the Criminal Attempts Act 'of doubtful import'? See K. J. M. Smith, 'Proximity in Attempt: Lord Lane's "midway course" ' [1991] Crim LR 576.

2. In *Campbell* (1990) 93 Cr App R 350, [1991] Crim LR 268, C was arrested within a yard of the door of a post office. He was wearing a crash helmet and gloves and carrying an imitation gun and a threatening note. He admitted that he intended to use the note to frighten the person behind the counter in the post office to hand over money. He claimed he had changed his mind and decided not to carry out the robbery but was arrested before he could leave. His conviction for attempted robbery was quashed: a number of acts remained undone and he had not even gained the place where he could be in a position to perform an act which could properly be said to be an attempt. He was convicted of the offence of carrying an imitation firearm.

How should the police deal with a man whom they believe to be armed and about to enter and rob a post office? Should they arrest him on the ground that he is, or they have reasonable grounds for suspecting that he is, about to commit an offence? Or should they wait until he demands money at the counter of the post office, so that they are sure he has committed attempted robbery?

3. In *Geddes* [1996] Crim LR 894 D was found in the boys' toilet of a school, equipped in such a way as to suggest strongly that his purpose was kidnapping. His conviction for attempted false imprisonment was quashed. Even clear evidence of what D had in mind 'did not throw light on whether he had begun to carry out the commission of the offence'. The offence would now be one of trespass with intent to commit a sex offence contrary to the Sexual Offences Act 2003, s 63. *Tosti* [1997] Crim LR 746 where the accused were examining a door to decide how best to break in was held to fall on the other side of the line: there was sufficient evidence of attempted burglary—that is, of an attempt to enter. In *R v Bowles and Bowles* [2004] EWCA Crim 1608 the Court of Appeal held that there was no case to answer in respect of a count of attempting to make a false instrument (a last will and testament) with intent, where DDs' acts of drafting the document and placing it is a drawer for safe keeping were no more than preparatory acts within the Criminal Attempts Act 1981, s 1(1).

R v White

[1908–10] All ER Rep 340, Court of Criminal Appeal

(Lord Alverstone CJ, Bray and Pickford JJ)

The appellant's mother was found dead sitting on a sofa. Beside her was a glass three parts filled with a drink called nectar. The glass also contained two grains of cyanide of potassium. Her death was due to heart failure due to fright or some external cause. There was no evidence to show that she had taken any of the liquid and the quantity of poison in the glass was, even if she had taken the whole, insufficient to cause her death.

The appellant was indicted for murder and convicted of attempted murder. He appealed.

[**Bray J** (delivering the judgment of the court), having held that there was evidence on which the jury could find that the appellant had put the poison in the glass and reviewed the evidence of his intent, continued:]

He, therefore, perfectly well knew the deadly character of this poison, and supposed that a very small quantity would produce an instant effect. Upon consideration of all the evidence, including the denial of the prisoner that he had put anything into the wine glass at all, we are of opinion that there was sufficient evidence to warrant the jury also in coming to the conclusion that the appellant put the cyanide in the glass with intent to murder his mother.

The next point made was that, if he put it there with that intent, there was no attempt at murder; that the jury must have acted upon a suggestion of the learned judge in his summing up that this was one, the first or some later, of a series of doses which he intended to administer and so cause her death by slow poisoning, and if they did act on that suggestion there was no attempt at murder, because the act of which he was guilty—viz, the putting of poison in the wine glass—was a completed act and could not be and was not intended by the appellant to have the effect of killing her at once. It could not kill unless it were followed by other acts which he might never have done. There seems no doubt that the learned judge in effect did tell the jury that, if this was a case of slow poisoning, the appellant would be guilty of the attempt to murder. We are of opinion that this direction was right, and that the completion or attempted completion of one of a series of acts intended by a man to result in killing is an attempt to murder even although this completed act would not, unless followed by the other acts, result in killing. It might be the beginning of the attempt, but would none the less be an attempt. While saying this, we must say also that we do not think it likely the jury acted on this suggestion, because there was nothing to show that the administration of small doses of cyanide of potassium would have a cumulative effect; we think it much more likely, having regard to the statement made by the prisoner to the witness Carden, that the appellant supposed he had put sufficient poison in the glass to kill her. This, of course, would be an attempt to murder....

Appeal dismissed

Director of Public Prosecutions v Stonehouse
[1977] 2 All ER 909, House of Lords

(Lord Diplock, Viscount Dilhorne, Lords Salmon, Edmund-Davies and Keith of Kinkel)

The appellant, a well-known public figure, was convicted of 13 offences of dishonesty and on five charges of attempting by deception to enable another to obtain property contrary to s 15 of the Theft Act 1968. The appellant had insured his life for £125,000 with five different life insurance companies. On 20 November 1974 he faked his death by drowning in Miami so that his wife, who was not a party to the plan, could claim the policy moneys. The news of his 'death' was, as he intended, quickly transmitted to England by the media, but his wife made no claim on any of the policies. Five weeks later the appellant was discovered in Australia and extradited. His appeal was dismissed by the Court of Appeal which certified that the following point of law of public importance was involved in the decision:

Whether the offence of attempting on 20 November 1974 to obtain property in England by deception, the final act alleged to constitute the offence of attempt having occurred outside the jurisdiction of the English courts is triable in an English court, all the remaining acts necessary to constitute the complete offence being intended to take place in England.

Lord Diplock.... So I start by considering the territorial element in [the jurisdiction of the English courts] to try the complete crime; for on this and on the corresponding offence under s 32 of the Larceny Act 1916, which has been replaced by s 15 of the Theft Act 1968, there is long-standing authority to the effect that in a 'result-crime' the English courts have jurisdiction to try the offence if the described consequence of the conduct of the accused which is part of the definition of the crime took place in England....

Once it is appreciated that territorial jurisdiction over a 'result-crime' does not depend on acts done by the offender in England but on consequences which he causes to occur in England, I see no ground for holding that an attempt to commit a crime which, if the attempt succeeded, would be justiciable in England does not fall within the jurisdiction of the English courts, notwithstanding that the physical acts intended to produce the proscribed consequences in England were all of them done abroad....

If in order to found jurisdiction it were necessary to prove that something had been actually caused to happen in England by the acts done by the offender abroad a qualified answer to the certified question would be called for. I do not think that it is necessary. So I would answer with an unqualified Yes.

I can deal much more briefly with the two other points of law relied on on behalf of the accused. The constituent elements of the inchoate crime of an attempt are a physical act by the offender sufficiently proximate to the complete offence and an intention on the part of the offender to commit the complete offence. Acts that are merely preparatory to the commission of the offence, such as, in the instant case, the taking out of the insurance policies, are not sufficiently proximate to constitute an attempt. They do not indicate a fixed irrevocable intention to go on to commit the complete offence unless involuntarily prevented from doing so. As it was put in the locus classicus *Eagleton* (1855) Dears CC 376, 515 at 538:

> 'The mere intention to commit a misdemeanour is not criminal, some act is required; and we do not think that all acts towards committing a misdemeanour are indictable. Acts remotely leading towards the commission of the offence are not to be considered as attempts to commit it; but acts immediately connected with it are....'

In other words the offender must have crossed the Rubicon and burnt his boats.

In the instant case, as I have pointed out, the accused by 20 November 1974 had done all the physical acts lying within his power that were needed to enable Mrs Stonehouse to obtain the policy moneys if all had gone as he had intended. There was nothing left for him to do thereafter except to avoid detection of his real identity. That was the day on which he crossed his Rubicon and burnt his boats.

In my opinion it is quite unarguable that, given the necessary intention, those acts were not sufficiently proximate to the complete offence of obtaining property by deception to be capable in law of constituting an attempt to commit the offence. On the contrary they clearly do constitute such an attempt in law. At the trial indeed the judge so regarded the matter. He directed the jury in the following terms:...[His Lordship quoted from the direction and continued:] So he did not leave it to the jury to decide whether the acts of the accused in Florida on 20 November 1974 were sufficiently 'proximate' to constitute an attempt.

The Court of Appeal took the view, which I understand is shared by all your Lordships, that what the accused did on 20 November 1974 was so obviously sufficiently proximate to constitute an attempt that no reasonable jury could have any doubt about it; a contrary finding could only be perverse. The Court of Appeal held that in those circumstances it was proper for the judge to tell the jury that if the facts alleged were proved they should find the accused guilty of the attempt charged. With this I agree...

In directing the jury that the only acts of the accused of which there is evidence are outside the range of proximity which any reasonable person could regard as conforming to that concept as a constituent element in the common law offence of attempt, the judge is exercising his responsibility as controller of the trial to prevent its resulting in a perverse verdict which would call for correction by the Court of Appeal under s 2(1)(a) of the Criminal Appeal Act 1968. If the acts of the accused lay beyond the other extreme of the range of proximity within which any reasonable person could doubt that they conformed to that concept as a constituent element in the offence of attempt, a verdict of acquittal on the ground that the acts of the accused were not sufficiently proximate would also be perverse.

When in either case any opinion to the contrary would be equally perverse, why, if the judge is bound to tell the jury that particular acts of the accused are so remotely connected with the intended offence that they do not amount in law to an attempt to commit it, should the judge be forbidden to tell the jury that particular acts of the accused, if established, are so closely connected with the offence that they do amount in law to an attempt to commit it?

It has been suggested by counsel for the prosecution that the difference lies in the accused being entitled to be protected against being *convicted* on a verdict that is perverse but is entitled to his chance of a perverse verdict of *acquittal*. This cynical view of justice and the jury system is inconsistent with the test applied by the Court of Appeal under the proviso to s 2(1) of the Criminal Appeal Act 1968 in deciding to uphold a conviction, notwithstanding that the trial judge has made an error in summing-up, on the ground that no substantial miscarriage of justice has actually occurred as a result of his error.

[**Viscount Dilhorne** agreed with Lord Diplock that the judge had not misdirected the jury by instructing them that the facts proved constituted an attempt.]

[**Lord Salmon** held that the judge had misdirected the jury by not leaving it to them to decide whether the facts proved amounted to an attempt, but since no reasonable jury could have failed so to find, the proviso to s 2(1) of the Criminal Appeal Act 1968 should be applied.]

[**Lord Edmund-Davies** having reviewed the authorities, continued:]

But what, for my part, I am not prepared to adopt is the view sometimes advanced (eg Glanville Williams, *Criminal Law (The General Part)* p 622 and Smith and Hogan, *Criminal Law* (3rd edn, p 198)) that a man *must* be guilty of an attempt if he has done the last act which he expects to do and which it is necessary for him to do to achieve the consequence aimed at. That is probably based on the observation of Parke B in *Eagleton* at p 538, regarding a charge of attempting to obtain money from guardians of the poor by false pretences, that:

'no other act on the part of the defendant would have been required. It was the last act *depending on himself*, towards the payment of the money, and therefore it ought to be considered as an attempt'. (Italics supplied.)

But even so, the wrongdoer may not have progressed a sufficient distance along the intended path, and his actions may still amount (as in *Hope v Brown*) to no more than mere 'preparation'. As Lord Widgery CJ pointed out in the instant case, he may have been given merely 'jobs of a kind which were obviously preparatory and not proximate'. What has always to be borne in mind, as I think, is the nature of the *full* offence alleged to have been attempted. In the instant case, it would not have been that by deception the appellant dishonestly obtained a cheque from an insurance company by falsely pretending that he had died, for such a charge would be manifestly ridiculous; and, even if it were not, one can well imagine it being argued, on the lines of *Robinson* (above, p **528**), that what the appellant did in Miami did not go beyond mere preparation. But the charge actually laid was based on one of the extended meanings of 'obtain' contained in s 15(2) of the Theft Act 1968, viz 'enabling another to obtain'. So, had it been carried through to completion and not been interrupted by his being recognised and arrested in Australia, the full offence charged would have been that the appellant dishonestly and by deception enabled his wife to obtain insurance money by the false pretence that he had drowned. Towards the commission of *that* offence, the faking of his death (a) was intended to produce that result; (b) was the final act that he could perform, and (c) went a substantial distance towards the attainment of his goal. In short, in my judgment it was sufficiently proximate thereto to constitute the attempts charged in counts 17 to 21....

[His Lordship held that the judge ought to have left it to the jury to say whether the facts constituted an attempt but, since no reasonable jury could have decided otherwise, the proviso should be applied.]

My Lords, the erroneous direction in the instant case is but one example of a prevalent (though fortunately not universal) tendency in our courts in these days to withdraw from the jury issues which are solely theirs to determine. The tendency has been deplored, notably by Lord Devlin in commenting on *Larkin* [1943] KB 174, [1943] 1 All ER 217: see his *Trial by Jury* (revised edn, 1966, p 186, appendix II). It has been markedly evinced in cases arising under the Road Traffic Acts, and this despite the earlier warning of Lord Parker CJ in *Waters* (1963) 47 Cr App Rep 149, [1963] Crim LR 437. Whether this tendency springs from distrust of the jury's capacity or from excessive zeal in seeking to simplify their task, it needs careful watching, and there are welcome signs that judges are awakening to that fact... And it has to be said that, while the possibility of a perverse verdict cannot be wholly eliminated, the risk that directions to convict may lead to quashings can be obviated by clarity in identifying the contested issue, by commenting on the evidence (maybe even in strong terms, provided that they fall short of a direction, as Lord Devlin stressed in *Chandler v DPP* [1964] AC 763 at 804, [1962] 3 All ER 142 at 154), and by then trusting the jury to play their constitutional part in the criminal process...

[**Lord Keith of Kinkel**, having quoted from the judgment of the Court of Appeal in *Baxter* [1971] 2 All ER 359 at 362, continued:]

...I would myself prefer to rest the matter not so much on the proposition that the offence is a continuing one, or on the alternative proposition, also favoured by Sachs LJ, that part of the offence is committed within the jurisdiction, as on the principle that an offence is committed if the effects of the act intentionally operate or exist within the jurisdiction. This would be the situation if a bomb or a letter sent from abroad were found anywhere within the jurisdiction. Its presence at that spot would be an intended effect of the act of despatching it. In my opinion it is not the present law of England that an offence is committed if no effect of an act done abroad is felt here, even though it was the intention that it should be. Thus if a person on the Scottish bank of the Tweed, where it forms the border between Scotland and England, were to fire a rifle at someone on the English bank, with intent to kill him, and actually did so, he would be guilty of murder under English law. If he fired with similar intent but missed his intended victim, he would be guilty of attempted murder under English law, because the presence of the bullet in England would be an intended effect of his act. But if he pressed the trigger and his weapon misfired, he would be guilty of no offence under the law of England, provided at least that the intended victim was unaware of the attempt, since no effect would have been felt there. If, however, the intended victim were aware of the rifle being pointed at him, and was thus put into a state of alarm, an effect would have been felt in England and a crime would have been committed there. The result may seem illogical, and there would appear to be nothing contrary to international comity in holding that an act done abroad intended to result in damage in England, but which for some reason independent of the actor's volition had no effect there, was justiciable in England. But if that were to be the law, I consider that it would require to be enacted by Parliament...

[His Lordship held that the jury had been misdirected but that the proviso should be applied.]

Appeal dismissed

Questions

1. If Mrs Stonehouse had been (she was not) a party to the fraud, would the answer to the question whether Stonehouse's acts were sufficiently proximate have been the same? (Cf commentary, below.)

2. D overhears E and F plotting to steal from the office where he works. In order to facilitate their plan he leaves open the window through which he believes they intend to enter and leaves the keys to the strong room in an unlocked drawer. E and F change their minds and do not carry out the plan. Is D guilty of an attempt to commit any crime? Cf Code Bill, cl 49(6), below, p 539. What if G finds the window open, enters, takes the keys and steals from the strong room? Cf *Davis* [1977] Crim LR 542.

3. Is the criticism by Lord Edmund-Davies of the 'last act' doctrine valid?

4. Should the judge be able to direct the jury that particular facts, if proved, amount to an attempt to commit a crime?

Commentary by J. C.Smith on *DPP v Stonehouse*, [1977] Crim LR 544 at 547

In the present case, the scheme had advanced no farther than in *Comer v Bloomfield* [above, p **529**]. It does not necessarily follow that that case is wrongly decided. There is an important difference between the facts of the two cases. Stonehouse's plan involved the use of an innocent agent, his wife. Bloomfield's plan did not. All that Stonehouse had to do, having staged his death, was to remain concealed; the claim would be made by his wife. Bloomfield had to fill in and despatch a claim form. Stonehouse was much nearer to the end of his part in the enterprise than Bloomfield and nearer still than Robinson. It is argued below that, where the alleged principal offender has done, or attempted to do, the last act which it is intended that he should do and which it is necessary for him to do in order to achieve the consequence alleged to be attempted, this must be sufficiently proximate. Having disappeared, Stonehouse had to stay out of the way long enough for it to be inferred that he was dead and for his wife to make a claim. If she had in fact made a claim, the case would have been clear, but she did not. This, however, was, in the nature of the scheme, a matter over which he could exercise no control—he was supposed to be dead. He had done all he could do up to the moment of his discovery—and was continuing to do so. That must surely be sufficiently proximate.

It is interesting to note that it would have been quite different if his wife had been a party to the fraudulent scheme. On this hypothesis, she would have been the principal in the first degree in the proposed fraud and she had done nothing to further it. As an aider and abettor the defendant could have been guilty of an offence only if the principal had committed the actus reus, at least of attempt. It is possible to be guilty of aiding and abetting an attempt, but there is no such offence as an attempt to aid and abet, except where aiding and abetting is the principal offence, as in the Suicide Act 1961—cf *McShane* (1977) 66 Cr App Rep 97, [1977] Crim LR 737. Therefore, even though the defendant had completely performed his part of the scheme, he would have been guilty of no offence...if the defendant's wife had been an accomplice, his part would have consisted only in doing preparatory acts. The attempt, on this hypothesis, was to be committed by the wife. Since however, the wife was in fact innocent, the defendant himself was the principal in the first degree in the proposed crime. It appears that an act which is insufficiently proximate when done as an abettor may be an attempt when done as the intending principal acting through an innocent agent....

Where the defendant is to be the principal offender, it must surely be true to say that his last act is sufficiently proximate. It is now or never. If there is no attempt at this point, then it seems that the crime is one which cannot be attempted. There may be a few such crimes but they are rare. See Smith and Hogan, *Criminal Law* (3rd edn), p 206 [see 11th edn, p **416**]. It is submitted that there could be no serious doubt that the accused's last act was sufficiently proximate where, if his intention had been effectuated, he would have been the direct cause of the actus reus. It might be argued that it is different where the accused is acting through an innocent agent: that the accused is guilty of an attempt only when *the agent* has done a sufficiently proximate act. If that is right, either the present case or *Comer v Bloomfield* is wrongly decided; but it is submitted that it is not right. If D hands poison to his *accomplice*, telling him to administer it tomorrow night to P, that might well be thought too remote to be an attempt to murder; but if D hands poison to an *innocent agent*, telling him that it is a medicine which he must administer to P tomorrow, it is submitted that D is guilty of an attempt to murder.

Eagleton was a case of innocent agency. The defendant made false statements as to the weight of loaves he had supplied to poor persons, thereby causing the relieving officer to enter a credit in his favour which would have led, without further action on the defendant's part, to his being paid money to which he was not entitled. If the relieving officer had been an accomplice whose entries would have deceived the paying officer, the defendant's statement would probably not have been an attempt.

Lord Edmund-Davies also referred to *Hope v Brown* [1954] 1 All ER 330, [1954] 1 WLR 250. This case, which is criticised by Professor Glanville Williams at [1956] Crim LR 66 and 68, is a questionable decision, particularly in the light of the present case. In a shop managed by the defendant were found packages of meat bearing tickets marked with the correct price. In a drawer was found another set of tickets, marked with higher prices, prices above the maximum then permitted by law. The defendant had prepared this second set of tickets and instructed a girl to change them before delivering the meat. The Divisional Court held that this was not an attempt to sell meat at an excessive price. It would have been different, they thought, if the offending tickets had been affixed to the meat. The girl was apparently not charged and presumably she was an innocent agent. Even if she was a party to the illegality, the defendant was probably the principal offender because the girl was not a 'seller'. It appears that the defendant had done the last act intended to be done, and necessary to be done, by him. If the girl had been uninterrupted and had done as he told her, the offence would have been completed, at the latest, when she delivered the meat. At least as much, probably more, had to happen in the present case before the crime was complete. The defendant had to stay out of the way, his wife had to make a claim, the claim had to be scrutinised by the insurance company's officials, the company had to satisfy itself that the defendant was dead, payment had to be authorised and made. A possible distinction is that the girl in *Hope v Brown* was under the immediate supervision of the defendant who could have intervened at any moment. But Mr Stonehouse could also have intervened at any moment, simply by announcing that he was alive. It is thought that *Hope v Brown* is difficult to reconcile with the present case and is probably wrongly decided.

4. THE CODE BILL ON ATTEMPTS

Clause 49 of the Code Bill is substantially a restatement of the Criminal Attempts Act 1981 in the style and language of the Code. It provides:

49. Attempt to commit an offence

(1) A person who, intending to commit an indictable offence, does an act that is more than merely preparatory to the commission of the offence is guilty of attempt to commit the offence.

(2) For the purposes of subsection (1), an intention to commit an offence is an intention with respect to all the elements of the offence other than fault elements, except that recklessness with respect to a circumstance suffices where it suffices for the offence itself.

(3) 'Act' in this section includes an omission only where the offence intended is capable of being committed by an omission.

(4) Where there is evidence to support a finding that an act was more than merely preparatory to the commission of the offence intended, the question whether that act was more than merely preparatory is a question of fact.

(5) Subject to section 52(1), this section applies to any offence which, if it was completed, would be triable in England and Wales as an indictable offence, other than an offence under section 4(1) (assisting offenders) or 5(1) (accepting or agreeing to accept consideration for not disclosing information about an arrestable offence) of the Criminal Law Act 1967.

(6) It is not an offence under this section, or under any enactment referred to in section 51, to attempt to procure, assist or encourage as an accessory the commission of an offence by another, but:

  (a) a person may be guilty as an accessory to an attempt by another to commit an offence; and

  (b) this subsection does not preclude a charge of attempt to incite (under section 47 or any other enactment), or of attempt to conspire (under section 48 or any other enactment), to commit an offence.

Recklessness

It will be seen that sub-s (2) restates the effect of *Khan*, above, p **524**, as a general principle but does not go so far as the decision in *A-G's Reference (No 3 of 1992)* above, p **525**.

Omission

It is generally thought that s 1(1) of the Criminal Attempts Act 1981, above, p **519** ('does an act'), rules out attempts by omission, although it was in fact the intention of the government that in some cases attempt by omission should be an offence. Clause 49(3) would make it clear that where a substantive offence like murder (above, p **88**) can be committed by omission, there may be an attempt by omission to perform a duty to act.

Abetting an attempt is, but attempting to abet is not, an offence

Section 1(4)(b) of the Criminal Attempts Act is unsatisfactorily worded but its effect, as interpreted in *Dunnington* [1984] 1 All ER 676, [1984] QB 472, is stated by sub-s (6). Attempting to commit a crime is itself a crime, so it can be abetted like any other crime; but abetting is not, as such, an offence, so there can be no attempt to 'commit' it. Paragraph (b) would reverse s 4(1)(a) of the 1981 Act and restore the common law that there may be an attempt to conspire.

5. WHY HAVE A CRIME OF ATTEMPT?

Does the criminal law need a crime of attempt:

  (1) To allow the investigating agency to intervene before the harm involved in the substantive offence is caused? If so, is the law defined with sufficient clarity to optimise the opportunity for the police to act in a preventative role?

  (2) To reflect the moral wrongdoing of one who has tried to commit a crime? Is that moral wrongdoing any less than one who succeeds in the commission of the substantive crime?

Andrew Ashworth, 'Belief and intent in Criminal Liability' in J. Eekelaar and J. Bell (eds) *Oxford Essays in Jurisprudence* (1987) p 16 asks:

Is A, who shoots at X intending to kill him but misses because X unexpectedly moves, any less culpable than B who shoots at Y intending to kill him and does so? An external description of both sets of events would probably not suggest that they have 'done' the same thing, whereas an account which paid more attention to the actor's point of view and to matters which lay within the actor's control would suggest that they both intended and tried, to the same extent, to do the same thing.

The argument here is that, because of the element of uncertainty in the outcome of things which we try to do, it would be wrong for assessments of culpability to depend on the occurrence or non-occurrence of the intended consequences. 'Success or failure…makes no difference at all to [an agent's] moral status in relation to his original act. His original act, strictly considered, was simply his trying and that is what moral assessment must concern itself with' (Winch, *Ethics and Action*, 1972, p.139)…Moral blame and criminal liability should be based so far as possible on choice and control, on the trying and not what actually happened thereafter. What are the reasons for wishing to reduce the influence of chance upon criminal liability? It cannot be doubted that luck plays a considerable part. Actual results also play a considerable part in judgments of others, and tend to dominate assessments in such fields as business, sport, and education. Those who try hard but are unsuccessful often receive less recognition than those who achieve goals (no matter how little effort they put into it). But these are not moral assessments of the individual and their characters. If one turns to moral and social judgments, it is doubtful whether outcomes should be proper criteria. It may be desirable overall to have fewer bad outcomes and more good outcomes in society, but that does not lead to the conclusion that moral praise and blame should be allocated solely according to result. Indeed, a bad outcome stemming from a good intent may be a better predictor of good outcomes than a good outcome born of a bad intent. From time to time we may praise someone for producing a good result, even though it was not what he was trying to do, but this is more a reflection of our pleasure at the outcome than an assessment of his conduct and character. If we turn to blaming, is it not unacceptable to blame people for causing results irrespective of whether they were caused intentionally, negligently, or purely accidentally? Blaming is a moral activity which is surely only appropriate where the individual had some choice or control over the matter. For this reason the criminal law should seek to minimize the effect of luck upon the incidence and scale of criminal liability.

Compare the view of J. C. Smith, 'The Element of Chance in Criminal Liability' [1971] Crim LR 63

…great significance is still attached to the harm done, as distinct from the harm intended or foreseen. Perhaps the significance of the harm done derives from our emotional reaction to the acts of others. If one of my small boys, not looking what he is doing, throws a stone which just misses the dining room window, I shall be very cross with him; but if the stone breaks the dining room window, I shall be absolutely furious. His behaviour is just as bad and just as dangerous in the one case as in the other; but my indignation is much greater in the case where he has caused the harm than in that where he has not.

It might fairly be answered that the criminal law should be rational and not based on emotional reactions. Is not this naked retribution—and a very crude form of retribution, the degree of punishment being based not on the moral culpability but on the harm done?

On the other hand, it is certain that the legislator cannot afford to ignore altogether the reactions—even the irrational reactions—of ordinary people, in the interests of logic and consistency. Stephen J., the great criminal law judge of the nineteenth century thought that the gratification of public sentiment was a proper purpose of the criminal law.…He thought there was nothing irrational in basing liability on the harm done:

'If two persons are guilty of the very same act of negligence, and if one of them causes thereby a railway accident, involving the death and mutilation of many persons, whereas the other does no injury to anyone, it seems to me that it would be rather pedantic than rational to say that each had committed the same offence, and should be subjected to the same punishment. In one sense, each has committed an offence, but the one has had the bad luck to cause a horrible misfortune, and to attract public attention to it, and the other the good fortune to do no harm. Both certainly deserve punishment, (*History of the Criminal Law*, Vol. III, pp. 311 et seq.)'

Would a crime of endangerment offer a partial solution to this problem?

FURTHER READING

R. A. Duff, *Criminal Attempts* (1996)

J. Horder, 'Varieties of Intention, Criminal Attempts and Endangerment' (1994) 14 LS 335

J. Hornby, 'On What's Intentionally Done' in S. Shute, J. Gardner and J. Horder (eds) *Action and Value in Criminal Law* (1993) 60

K. J. M. Smith, 'Proximity in Attempt: Lord Lane's "midway course" ' [1991] Crim LR 576

J. Stannard, 'Making Up for the Missing Element: A Sideways Look at Attempts' (1987) 7 LS 194

G. Sullivan, 'Intent, Subjective Recklessness and Culpability' (1992) 12 OJLS 380

16

Impossibility and preliminary offences

If it is impossible to commit a crime, no one can be convicted of committing it, but it does not follow that no one can be convicted of inciting another, or conspiring, or attempting to commit it. As a matter of fact, people do from time to time incite, conspire and attempt to do what is impossible. It might naturally be expected that the same general principles would apply to solve the problem in all three of these closely related offences. As will appear, this is not so. The problem is most conveniently analysed in relation to attempts because it is here that it most commonly arises. The analysis which follows is derived from an article by J. C. Smith, 'Attempts, Impossibility and the Test of Rational Motivation' in *Auckland Law School Centenary Lectures* (1983) 25:

The principal characteristic of an attempt is that the attempter is trying, striving, to achieve some result. He has an objective which he wishes to attain. We cannot conceive of an attempt where the actor does not have some objective in view. Secondly, the concept of attempt involves failure or, if not failure, incompleteness of some kind. Naturally enough, charges of attempt to commit a crime are usually brought only when the accused has failed, or is believed to have failed, to achieve his objective. If he has succeeded, he will naturally be charged with the full offence. It is often said that attempt involves failure. Hall, GPCL, 557, writes 'attempt implies failure', and Fletcher, *Rethinking*, 131, 'Attempts are cases of failure'. But this is not necessarily so. It is well established that it is no defence to a charge of attempt for the defendant to show that he went on to complete the crime: *Smith & Hogan*, [11th edn, p **415**]. This is perfectly logical, for the greater includes the less. In the great majority of successful crimes there was a point at which the defendant had committed an attempt and the complete crime includes this, even though it was completed only a matter of seconds later. An attempt may, then, be a failure to commit, or a proximate step towards the successful commission of, an offence.

Since sane men do not attempt what they know to be impossible, it follows that, in all cases of attempts to do the impossible, the defendant was labouring under a mistake of some kind. The cases may conveniently be divided into three categories according to the kind of mistake that the defendant was making.

(1) Where the defendant is making a mistake about the criminal law

He is making no mistake about any material fact, but he believes his objective to be criminal when it is not. The objective is not impossible of attainment and, when it is attained, no crime will have been committed. His conduct is in no sense a failure nor is it a proximate step towards the commission of an offence. For example:

D is living in a jurisdiction where it was formerly illegal for a man of any age to have homosexual relations. It is now permissible for adult males to have homosexual relations in private. D (aged 21), being unaware that the law has been changed, engages in homosexual relations in private. He believes he is committing a criminal offence. He accomplishes his objective. The enterprise is in no sense a failure. It was not his purpose to commit crime.

D has sexual intercourse with a 17-year-old girl, believing that the criminal law forbids sexual intercourse with girls under the age of 18. He is wrong. The age is 16. The accomplished objective is not criminal.

D, believing that it is unlawful to shoot rabbits in May, shoots a rabbit on 1 May. The law allows rabbits to be shot in May. There is nothing unlawful in what he has done.

It is generally agreed that these examples do not amount to attempts to commit crimes in law. This is surely right. [Cf *Taafe*, above, p **43**.] There is no *actus reus* for the act done is lawful. If *mens rea* means (or includes) an intention to cause, or to take the risk of causing, a result which the law forbids, there is no *mens rea*, for the result intended by the defendant is not one which the law forbids. A belief that an act is a criminal offence is not *mens rea* or part of it. Only one writer, so far as is known, has argued that these cases should amount to attempts. Professor Brett argued that, because the defendant has shown that he is prepared to defy the law, he should be liable to conviction, provided that there is some crime to which his conduct can be related: *An Inquiry into Criminal Guilt* (1963) 128–129.

(2) Where the defendant, because he is making a mistake of fact, believes his objective to be criminal when it is not

The prototype of this case is that posed by Bramwell B, in *Collins* (1864) 9 Cox CC 497 at 498. D takes an umbrella, intending to steal it. It turns out to be his own. D, we will suppose, has lost his umbrella. He believes it has been stolen. On leaving his Club one rainy day he decides to help himself to an umbrella left in the stand at the Club entrance. He intends to steal the umbrella from the owner, whoever he may be. When he gets home he finds that there is a mark inside the umbrella which proves conclusively that it is his own umbrella, the one he had thought to be stolen. It had, all along, been in the Club where he absent-mindedly left it six months ago. He has the intention to steal, but he does nothing wrong. Many similar cases may be put.

> D has sexual intercourse with a girl believing her to be 13—a criminal intention. In fact she is 18. He commits no offence against the criminal law. Or, he believes the girl of 18 to be a mental defective. If that were true, the intercourse would be criminal. But it is not true. She is quite normal. D goes through a ceremony of marriage, having no doubt that his wife is alive. He intends to commit bigamy. But, five minutes before the ceremony, she was run down and killed. The marriage ceremony is perfectly lawful.
>
> D buys a valuable painting in a junk shop for an absurdly low price. He has no doubt that it is stolen goods, but he is wrong. The shopkeeper acquired it lawfully and had no idea of its value. D intended to receive stolen goods but he has done nothing wrong.

There is a much stronger case for conviction in these cases than in the first group.

(a) These persons do have the *mens rea* of the various offences—dishonestly to appropriate an umbrella belonging to another; to have sexual intercourse with a girl under the age of 16; to have sexual intercourse with a mental defective; to marry during the life of a spouse; to receive stolen goods. It follows from this that:

(b) morally, the actor is just as bad as the person who actually commits the offence and;

(c) he is as dangerous as the person who actually commits the offence to whatever interest it is that the particular law is designed to protect.

On the other hand, in these cases the actor succeeds in doing the precise thing that he sets out to do. He accomplishes his objective. The transaction is complete—and it is not a crime. These are cases neither of failure nor of a proximate step towards the successful commission of a crime. The umbrellaless defendant decided to acquire that umbrella and did so. It was no part of his purpose that the umbrella should belong to another—he had no umbrella and he wanted to, and did, acquire one. He wanted to have sexual intercourse with that girl and did so. It would be very surprising if the man who actually had sexual intercourse with the woman whom he mistakenly believed to be a defective (*DPP v Head* [1958] 1 All ER 679, [1959] AC 83) said, when he learned that, after all, she was not a defective, 'Dammit, I've failed.' The intending bigamist would hardly be disappointed to discover that he had lawfully married the object of his desire instead, as he thought, of committing an offence. Certainly the receiver of the painting will not be disappointed to learn that his bargain is a lawful one.

Because the defendant achieves (or would, if not interrupted, achieve) his objective without committing a crime, it is argued that he should not be guilty of an indictable attempt. Since the deed is done and is not a crime, the defendant should not be liable to conviction merely for his criminal intention. Fletcher (*Rethinking*, 163) argues in favour of his test of rational motivation,

> 'first, that the test appears to be in tune with judicial intuitions that still reign in Anglo-American case-law; and secondly, that this analysis of attempting, based upon the ordinary usage of the words "trying" and "attempting", carries out the objectivist programme of grounding liability in an act of attempting that is conceptually separable from the actor's intent.'

(3) Where the defendant's objective, if it could be attained, would be a crime and, because he is making a mistake of fact, he believes it to be possible when it is not

These are cases of failure, where, if the defendant had succeeded, he would have committed a crime. Because of the decision of the House of Lords in *Haughton v Smith* [1973] 3 All ER 1109, [1975] AC 476 this third group must be divided into two sub-categories, though it may be thought that no rational distinction can be made between them.

Sub-category (a) is that where the defendant has used inadequate means to achieve his objective.

With intent to kill, he administers a dose of poison (or what he believes to be poison) which could not possibly kill anyone. With intent to steal, he uses a jemmy to break into a safe which could never be opened with such an implement. With intent to obtain money by deception, he writes a letter containing a false pretence to a person who knows the truth in the matter and could not possibly be deceived by it. The defendant in these cases intends to murder, to steal, to obtain by deception. His objective is the result constituting the commission of the crime. He will, inevitably, fail to attain his objective.

Sub-category (b) includes all other cases where it is in fact impossible to attain the defendant's criminal objective.

They are principally cases where the alleged subject-matter does not exist or lacks some essential characteristic. Defendant, intending to steal money, puts his hand into a pocket, or searches a wallet, which contains no money. His objective is the commission of theft but, inevitably, he will fail to do so. With intent to kill P, he fires a hail of bullets into P's bed. The bed is empty. It should make no difference whether P is lying under the bed, having taken evasive action in the nick of time, or is downstairs making himself a cup of cocoa, or is enjoying a good night's sleep 50 miles away. Indistinguishable is the case where D shoots at a tree stump, believing it to be his deadly enemy. The only difference is that, in the latter case, it is more difficult to prove the intention to kill. There is no such difficulty, however, if it is proved that he is hunting his enemy through swirling mist on a moor. Into the same category falls the case of the man who, with intent to kill, shoots at a person who is already dead. His purpose is to kill and he fails. Similarly with the American case of *Guffey*. Defendant shot at what he believed to be a deer. In fact it was not a living animal, but a stuffed one. His conviction for attempting to kill a protected animal out of season was quashed. But if, as seems certain, he was seeking venison for dinner or for sale, he certainly failed in his objective—and it would have been a crime had he succeeded. On the other hand, the theory fits perfectly with *People v Siu* 126 Cal

App 2d 41 (1945) where D initiated negotiations to get possession of heroin. A sheriff's deputy handed him a package containing talcum powder. Undeniably this was a failure to achieve a criminal objective. Siu did not get what he wanted. Similarly with the New Zealand case of *Jay* [1974] 2 NZLR 204 where the would-be purchaser of cannabis was handed a bag containing hedge-clippings. A variation of the 'umbrella case' would fall within the third category. Defendant sees a celebrity, P, leave his umbrella in the umbrella stand of a club. He has an overwhelming desire to possess something belonging to P and resolves to steal his umbrella. When an opportunity occurs, he surreptitiously takes from the stand the umbrella which he believes to be that left by P, but P's umbrella has already been removed. It is a second, different, umbrella and, when he gets it home, D finds that it is his own, lost, umbrella. Here he has plainly failed to achieve his objective. If he had succeeded, he would have been guilty of theft.

According to *Haughton v Smith*, only cases in category 3(a) constituted indictable attempts at common law. Cases in categories 1, 2 and 3(b) were not offences. The House of Lords held that the same principles applied to common law conspiracy in *DPP v Nock* [1978] 2 All ER 654, [1978] AC 979; and the Court of Appeal held that they were also applicable to incitement in *Fitzmaurice* [1983] 1 All ER 189, [1983] QB 1083; so it appears that *Haughton v Smith* continues to apply to these offences at the present day. Attempts are, however, now governed by the Criminal Attempts Act 1981, above, p **519**, as interpreted in *Shivpuri* below; and statutory conspiracies (see p **488**, above) are probably governed by the same principles as attempts.

1. IMPOSSIBILITY IN INCITEMENT AND COMMON LAW CONSPIRACIES

The result of the decisions in *Haughton v Smith* and for conspiracy, in *DPP v Nock* is that impossibility *is* a general defence for common law conspiracies and incitement. Thus, D will *not* be guilty of incitement where—

(i) The subject matter of the offence does not exist. D incites E to steal from V's safe. V's safe is empty.

(ii) The victim of the offence does not exist. D incites E to murder V. V is already dead.

(iii) The subject matter of the offence lacks some quality which is an element of the offence. D and E believe a certain diamond to have been stolen. D incites E to receive it. It had not been stolen.

(iv) The victim of the offence lacks some quality which is an element of the offence. D and E believe V to be aged 15. In fact she is 16. D incites E to have consensual sexual intercourse with her.

The only exception is that D may be convicted where the impossibility results merely from the inadequacy of the means used, or to be used, to commit the offence. Thus D *may be* guilty of incitement where—

(i) He gives E a jemmy and urges him to use it to break into V's safe and steal a diamond. The diamond is in the safe, but it is impossible to break in with the jemmy.

(ii) He gives E some poison and tells him to administer it to V so as to kill him. The dose is inadequate to kill anyone.

Question

In *DPP v Armstrong* [2000] Crim LR 379, DC, above, p **478**, the magistrate gave as a second reason for dismissing the case that the offence was impossible because J would not have supplied the pornographic material. The Divisional Court held that the offence was not impossible because J in fact had a supply of pornographic material. The court relied on *Fitzmaurice* (1982) 76 Cr App R 17, [1982] Crim LR 677, CA, where a conviction of inciting robbery of 'a woman at Bow' was upheld. The inciter had been tricked into believing that a woman would be carrying money from a factory to a bank at Bow. No such woman existed but the court thought that 'By no stretch of the imagination was that an impossible offence to carry out.' How does it differ from inciting to steal from an empty safe or pocket which, according to *Haughton v Smith*, is not an offence?

2. IMPOSSIBILITY IN ATTEMPTS AND STATUTORY CONSPIRACY

R v Shivpuri
[1986] 2 All ER 334, House of Lords

(Lord Hailsham LC, Lords Elwyn-Jones, Scarman, Bridge and Mackay)

The appellant was arrested by customs officials while in possession of a suitcase. He admitted that he knew that it contained prohibited drugs. Analysis showed that the material in the suitcase was not a prohibited drug but vegetable matter akin to snuff. The appellant was convicted under the Criminal Attempts Act 1981, s 1(1), above, p **519**, of attempting to commit the offence of being knowingly concerned in dealing with and harbouring prohibited drugs contrary to s 170(1)(b) of the Customs and Excise Management Act 1979. He appealed on the ground that because the substance was not a prohibited drug he had not done an act which was 'more than merely preparatory to the commission of the offence' as required by the 1981 Act. The Court of Appeal dismissed his appeal.

[**Lord Hailsham LC**, having stated that save for one relatively minor point, he agreed with Lord Bridge, continued:]

I must add, however, that, even had I not been able to follow my noble and learned friend in interring *Anderton v Ryan* [below] by using the 1966 Practice Statement, I would still have dismissed the instant appeal by distinguishing its facts from that case. Shortly, my reasoning would have been that the appellant was guilty on the clear wording of s 1(1) and (2) of the 1981 Act and that no recourse was therefore necessary to the wording of s 1(3), which if so would be irrelevant.

[The Criminal Attempts Act 1981, s 1(2) and (3) provide:

'(2) A person may be guilty of attempting to commit an offence to which this section applies even though the facts are such that the commission of the offence is impossible.

(3) In any case where—

   (a) apart from this subsection a person's intention would not be regarded as having amounted to an intent to commit an offence; but

   (b) if the facts of the case had been as he believed them to be, his intention would be so regarded, then for the purposes of subsection (1) above he shall be regarded as having an intent to commit that offence'.]

I would have arrived at this conclusion by asking myself three simple questions to which the answers could only be made in one form. They are: *Question 1*. What was the intention of the appellant throughout? *Answer*. His intention throughout was to evade and defeat the customs authorities of the United Kingdom. He had no other intention. His motive was gain (the bribe of £1,000). But as I pointed out in *Hyam v DPP* [1974] 2 All ER 41 at 5, [1975] AC 55 at 73 motive is not the same thing as intention. *Question 2*. Is the knowing evasion of the United Kingdom customs in the manner envisaged in the appellant's intent an offence to which s 1 of the 1981 Act applies? *Answer*. Yes: see s 1(4). *Question 3*. Did the appellant do an act which was more than preparatory to the commission of the offence? *Answer*. Yes, for the reasons stated in the relevant paragraphs of my noble and learned friend Lord Bridge's speech.

In this connection I do not feel it would have been necessary to invoke the doctrine of dominant and subordinate intention referred to by my noble and learned friend. The *sole* intent of the instant appellant from start to finish was to defeat the customs prohibition. In *Anderton v Ryan* the only intention of Mrs Ryan was to buy a particular video cassette recorder at a knock-down price, and the fact that she believed it to be stolen formed no part of that intention. It was a belief, assumed to be false and not an intention at all. It was a false belief as to a state of fact, and, if it became an intention, it was only the result of the deeming provisions of s 1(3). Whether or not *Anderton v Ryan* was correctly decided, one has to go to s 1(3) to decide whether Mrs Ryan had committed a criminal attempt under the Act as the result of her belief, assumed to be false, that the video cassette recorder had in fact been stolen. Similarly, to my mind, the only intention of the lustful youth postulated by my noble and learned friends Lord Roskill and Lord Bridge by way of example in *Anderton v Ryan* was to have carnal connection with a particular girl. One has to go to s 1(3) to discover whether or not a criminal attempt had been committed as the result of his false belief that she was under age.

[**Lord Elwyn-Jones** said that he would have been content to dismiss the appeal by distinguishing *Anderton v Ryan*, as Lord Hailsham had done; but he agreed with Lord Bridge and would dismiss the appeal for the reasons given by him.]

[**Lord Scarman** agreed with Lord Bridge.]

[**Lord Bridge**, having cited the Criminal Attempts Act 1981, s 1 (above, p **519**) continued:]

Applying this language to the facts of the case, the first question to be asked is whether the appellant intended to commit the offences of being knowingly concerned in dealing with and harbouring drugs of class A or class B with intent to evade the prohibition on their importation. Translated into more homely language the question may be rephrased, without in any way altering its legal significance, in the following terms: did the appellant intend to receive and store (harbour) and in due course pass on to third parties (deal with) packages of heroin or cannabis which he knew had been smuggled into England from India? The answer is plainly Yes, he did. Next, did he, in relation to each offence, do an act which was more than merely preparatory to the commission of the offence? The act relied on in relation to harbouring was the receipt and retention of the packages found in the lining of the suitcase. The act relied on in relation to dealing was the meeting at Southall station with the intended recipient of one of the packages. In each case the act was clearly more than preparatory to the commission of the intended offence; it was not and could not be more than merely preparatory to the commission of the actual offence, because the facts were such that the commission of the actual offence was impossible. Here then is the nub of the matter. Does the 'act which is more than merely preparatory to the commission of the offence' in s 1(1) of the 1981 Act (the *actus reus* of the statutory offence of attempt) require any more than an act which is more than merely preparatory to the commission of the offence which the defendant intended to commit? Section 1(2) must surely indicate a negative answer; if it were otherwise, whenever the facts were such that the commission of the actual offence was impossible, it would be impossible to prove an act more than merely preparatory to the commission of that offence and sub-ss (1) and (2) would contradict each other.

This very simple, perhaps over-simple, analysis leads me to the provisional conclusion that the appellant was rightly convicted of the two offences of attempt with which he was charged. But can this conclusion stand with *Anderton v Ryan*? The appellant in that case was charged with an attempt to handle stolen goods. She bought a video recorder believing it to be stolen. On the facts as they were to be assumed it was not stolen. By a majority the House decided that she was entitled to be acquitted. I have re-examined the case with care. If I could extract from the speech of Lord Roskill or from my own speech a clear and coherent principle distinguishing those cases of attempting the impossible which amount to offences under the statute from those which do not, I should have to consider carefully on which side of the line the instant case fell. But I have to confess that I can find no such principle.

Running through Lord Roskill's speech and my own in *Anderton v Ryan* is the concept of 'objectively innocent' acts which, in my speech certainly, are contrasted with 'guilty acts'. A few citations will make this clear. Lord Roskill said ([1985] 2 All ER 355 at 364, [1985] AC 560 at 580):

> 'My Lords, it has been strenuously and ably argued for the respondent that these provisions involved that a defendant is liable to conviction for an attempt even where his actions are innocent but he erroneously believes facts which, if true, would make those actions criminal, and further, that he is liable to such a conviction whether or not in the event his intended course of action is completed.'

He proceeded to reject the argument. I referred to the appellant's purchase of the video recorder and said ([1985] 2 All ER 355 at 366, [1985] AC 560 at 582): 'Objectively considered, therefore, her purchase of the recorder was a perfectly proper commercial transaction.'

A further passage from my speech stated ([1985] 2 All ER 355 at 366, [1985] AC 560 at 582–583):

> 'The question may be stated in abstract terms as follows. Does s 1 of the 1981 Act create a new offence of attempt where a person embarks on and completes a course of conduct, which is objectively innocent, solely on the ground that the person mistakenly believes facts which, if true, would make that course of conduct a complete crime? If the question must be answered affirmatively it requires convictions in a number of surprising cases: the classic case, put by Bramwell B in *R v Collins* (1864) 9 Cox CC 497 at 498, of the man who takes away his own umbrella from a stand, believing it not to be his own and with intent to steal it; the case of the man who has consensual intercourse with a girl over 16 believing her to be under that age; the case of the art dealer who sells a picture which he represents to be and which is in fact a genuine Picasso, but which the dealer mistakenly believes to be a fake. The common feature of all these cases, including that under appeal, is that the mind alone is guilty, the act is innocent.'

I then contrasted the case of the man who attempts to pick the empty pocket, saying ([1985] 2 All ER 355 at 367, [1985] AC 560 at 583):

> 'Putting the hand in the pocket is the guilty act, the intent to steal is the guilty mind, the offence is appropriately dealt with as an attempt, and the impossibility of committing the full offence for want of anything in the pocket to steal is declared by [sub-s (2)] to be no obstacle to conviction.'

If we fell into error, it is clear that our concern was to avoid convictions in situations which most people, as a matter of common sense, would not regard as involving criminality. In this connection it is to be regretted that we did not take due note of para 2.97 of the Law Commission Report, Criminal

Law: Attempt and Impossibility in Relation to Attempt, Conspiracy and Incitement (1980) (Law Com no 102) which preceded the enactment of the 1981 Act, which reads:

> 'If it is right in principle that an attempt should be chargeable even though the crime which it is sought to commit could not possibly be committed, we do not think that we should be deterred by the consideration that such a change in our law would also cover some extreme and exceptional cases in which a prosecution would be theoretically possible. An example would be where a person is offered goods at such a low price that he believes that they are stolen, when in fact they are not; if he actually purchases them, upon the principles which we have discussed he would be liable for an attempt to handle stolen goods. Another case which has been much debated is that raised in argument by Bramwell B in *Reg v Collins*. If A takes his own umbrella, mistaking it for one belonging to B and intending to steal B's umbrella, is he guilty of attempted theft? Again, on the principles which we have discussed he would in theory be guilty, but in neither case would it be realistic to suppose that a complaint would be made or that a prosecution would ensue.'

The prosecution in *Anderton v Ryan* itself falsified the Commission's prognosis in one of the 'extreme and exceptional cases'. It nevertheless probably holds good for other such cases, particularly that of the young man having sexual intercourse with a girl over 16, mistakenly believing her to be under that age, by which both Lord Roskill and I were much troubled.

However that may be, the distinction between acts which are 'objectively innocent' and those which are not is an essential element in the reasoning in *Anderton v Ryan* and the decision, unless it can be supported on some other ground, must stand or fall by the validity of this distinction. I am satisfied on further consideration that the concept of 'objective innocence' is incapable of sensible application in relation to the law of criminal attempts. The reason for this is that any attempt to commit an offence which involves 'an act which is more than merely preparatory to the commission of the offence' but which for any reason fails, so that in the event no offence is committed, must ex hypothesi, from the point view of the criminal law, be 'objectively innocent'. What turns what would otherwise, from the point of view of the criminal law, be an innocent act into a crime is the intent of the actor to commit an offence. I say 'from the point of view of the criminal law' because the law of tort must surely here be quite irrelevant. A puts his hand into B's pocket. Whether or not there is anything in the pocket capable of being stolen, if A intends to steal his act is a criminal attempt; if he does not so intend his act is innocent. A plunges a knife into a bolster in a bed. To avoid the complication of an offence of criminal damage, assume it to be A's bolster. If A believes the bolster to be his enemy B and intends to kill him, his act is an attempt to murder B; if he knows the bolster is only a bolster, his act is innocent. These considerations lead me to the conclusion that the distinction sought to be drawn in *Anderton v Ryan* between innocent and guilty acts considered 'objectively' and independently of the state of mind of the actor cannot be sensibly maintained.

Another conceivable ground of distinction which was to some extent canvassed in argument, both in *Anderton v Ryan* and in the instant case, though no trace of it appears in the speeches in *Anderton v Ryan*, is a distinction which would make guilt or innocence of the crime of attempt in a case of mistaken belief dependent on what, for want of a better phrase, I will call the defendant's dominant intention. According to the theory necessary to sustain this distinction, the appellant's dominant intention in *Anderton v Ryan* was to buy a cheap video recorder; her belief that it was stolen was merely incidental. Likewise in the hypothetical case of attempted unlawful sexual intercourse, the young man's dominant intention was to have intercourse with the particular girl; his mistaken belief that she was under 16 was merely incidental. By contrast, in the instant case the appellant's dominant intention was to receive and distribute illegally imported heroin or cannabis.

While I see the superficial attraction of this suggested ground of distinction, I also see formidable practical difficulties in its application. By what test is a jury to be told that a defendant's dominant intention is to be recognised and distinguished from his incidental but mistaken belief? But there is perhaps a more formidable theoretical difficulty. If this ground of distinction is relied on to support the acquittal of the appellant in *Anderton v Ryan*, it can only do so on the basis that her mistaken belief that the video recorder was stolen played no significant part in her decision to buy it and therefore she may be acquitted of the intent to handle stolen goods. But this line of reasoning runs into head-on collision with s 1(3) of the 1981 Act. The theory produces a situation where, apart from the subsection, her intention would not be regarded as having amounted to any intent to commit an offence. Section 1(3)(b) then requires one to ask whether, if the video recorder had in fact been stolen, her intention would have been regarded as an intent to handle stolen goods. The answer must clearly be Yes, it would. If she had bought the video recorder knowing it to be stolen, when in fact it was, it would have availed her nothing to say that her dominant intention was to buy a video recorder because it was cheap and that her knowledge that it was stolen was merely incidental. This seems to me fatal to the dominant intention theory.

I am thus led to the conclusion that there is no valid ground on which *Anderton v Ryan* can be distinguished. I have made clear my own conviction, which as a party to the decision (and craving the indulgence of my noble and learned friends who agreed in it) I am the readier to express, that the decision was wrong. What then is to be done? If the case is indistinguishable, the application of the strict doctrine of precedent would require that the present appeal be allowed. Is it permissible to depart from precedent under the 1966 *Practice Note* ([1966] 3 All ER 77) notwithstanding the especial need for certainty in the criminal law? The following considerations lead me to answer that question affirmatively. Firstly, I am undeterred by the consideration that the decision in *Anderton v Ryan* was so recent. The 1966 Practice Statement is an effective abandonment of our pretention to infallibility. If a serious error embodied in a decision of this House has distorted the law, the sooner it is corrected the better. Secondly, I cannot see how, in the very nature of the case, anyone could have acted in reliance on the law as propounded in *Anderton v Ryan* in the belief that he was acting innocently and now find that, after all, he is to be held to have committed a criminal offence. Thirdly, to hold the House bound to follow *Anderton v Ryan* because it cannot be distinguished and to allow the appeal in this case would, it seems to me, be tantamount to a declaration that the 1981 Act left the law of criminal attempts unchanged following the decision in *Haughton v Smith* [1975] AC 476. Finally, if, contrary to my present view, there is a valid ground on which it would be proper to distinguish cases similar to that considered in *Anderton v Ryan*, my present opinion on that point would not foreclose the option of making such a distinction in some future case.

I cannot conclude this opinion without disclosing that I have had the advantage, since the conclusion of the argument in this appeal, of reading an article by Professor Glanville Williams entitled 'The Lords and Impossible Attempts, or Quis Custodiet Ipsos Custodes?' [1986] CLJ 33. The language in which he criticises the decision in *Anderton v Ryan* is not conspicuous for its moderation, but it would be foolish, on that account, not to recognise the force of the criticism and churlish not to acknowledge the assistance I have derived from it.

I would answer the certified question in the affirmative and dismiss the appeal.

[**Lord Mackay** agreed with disposal of the appeal proposed by Lord Bridge; but agreed with Lord Hailsham on the 'relatively minor point' referred to by him.]

[A second ground of appeal, that is, that the judge was wrong to direct the jury that it was immaterial that the appellant did not know precisely what the prohibited goods were, was also rejected: although s 170(1)(b) created a number of separate offences, the only mens rea necessary was the knowledge that the thing was a controlled drug. See above, p **45**.]

Appeal dismissed

Questions

1. If *Anderton v Ryan* is distinguishable was it right (or possible) to overrule it? How should a case similar to *Anderton v Ryan* be decided today?

2. Is *Anderton v Ryan* really distinguishable? Mrs Ryan was convinced that the recorder was stolen ('I may as well be honest. It was a stolen one I bought.' 'Yes, I knew it was stolen.'). How can it possibly be said that she did not intend to handle stolen goods? Cf Commentary at [1986] Crim LR 539. See attempts to reconcile the two decisions see R. A. Duff, 'Regarding Intention: The Criminal Attempts Act 1981 s 1(3)' [1990] XII(2) Liverpool Law Review 161.

3. Does the decision in *Shivpuri* offend the principle of legality (no one shall be convicted of doing something which has not been declared by the law to be an offence)? Cf [1984] Crim LR 584 and [1985] Crim LR 504, 505 and B. Hogan, 'The Principle of Legality' (1986) NLJ 267. (Note also Art 7 of the ECHR, above, p 3).

4. D and E agree that they will use D's tools to break into V's safe and steal a diamond. D tries to do so. It is quite impossible to break into the safe with that jemmy. Of what offences are D and E guilty? Does it matter whether the diamond exists? What if D attempts to break open the safe, but it is empty?

5. D tells the police, falsely, that he was the victim of a sexual assault perpetrated by Mr Bloggs. Unbeknown to D Mr Bloggs is now dead. Attempting to pervert the course of justice? See *Brown* [2004] Crim LR 665.

6. D, 16, has sex with V. She consents. He thinks she is only 12, she is in fact 16. Attempted rape of a child under 13?

7. D sticks pins in a wax effigy of V, his worst enemy, believing they will cause V's death. Attempted murder?

3. REFORM

The Draft Criminal Code provides:

50. Impossibility and preliminary offences

> (1) A person may be guilty of incitement, conspiracy or attempt to commit an offence although the commission of the offence is impossible, if it would be possible in the circumstances which he believes or hopes exist or will exist at the relevant time.
>
> (2) Subsection (1) applies:
>   (a) to offences under section 47 [incitement], 48 [conspiracy] and 49 [attempt]:
>   (b) to any offence referred to in section 51(1) [preliminary offences under other enactments].
>
> (3) Subsection (1) does not render a person guilty of incitement, conspiracy or attempt to commit an offence of which he is not guilty because circumstances exist which, under section 45 or any other provision of this or any other Act, justify or excuse the act he does.

FURTHER READING

M. COHEN, 'Inciting the Impossible' [1979] Crim LR 239

H. L. A. HART, 'The House of Lords on Attempting the Impossible' in Tapper (ed) *Crime Proof and Punishment: Essays in Honour of Sir Rupert Cross* (1981), 1

J. TEMKIN, 'Impossible Attempts: Another View' (1976) 39 MLR 55

G. WILLIAMS, 'Attempting the Impossible—the Last Round?' (1985) 135 NLJ 337

G. WILLIAMS, 'The Lords and Impossible Attempts' [1986] CLJ 33

17

Murder

Attorney-General's Reference (No 3 of 1994)
[1997] 3 All ER 936

My Lords, murder is widely thought to be the gravest of crimes. One could expect a developed system to embody a law of murder clear enough to yield an unequivocal result on a given set of facts, a result which conforms with apparent justice and has a sound intellectual base. This is not so in England, where the law of homicide is permeated by anomaly, fiction, misnomer and obsolete reasoning. (Per Lord Mustill at p 938.)

1. HOMICIDE

The actus reus of murder and manslaughter is generally the same. It is the unlawful killing of any person 'under the Queen's Peace'.

(1) CAUSING DEATH

It must be proved that the defendant caused the death of the deceased person. The most common source of problems of causation in the criminal law is homicide. The leading cases have been considered, above, Ch 3, and reference may be made to these.

(2) YEAR AND A DAY RULE

At common law homicide was committed only if the death occurred within a year and a day of the act causing death (see D. Yale, 'A Year and A Day in Homicide' [1989] CLJ 202, and on the reform see LCCP No 136, *The Year and a Day Rule in Homicide* (1994). That rule was abolished by the Law Reform (Year and a Day Rule) Act 1996. If an act can be shown to be the cause of death, it may now be murder, or any other homicide offence, or suicide, however much time has elapsed between the act and the death. The Act, however, requires the consent of the Attorney-General to the prosecution of any person for murder, manslaughter, infanticide, or any other offence of which one of the elements is causing a person's death, or aiding and abetting suicide, (i) where the injury alleged to have caused the death was sustained more than three years before the death occurred or (ii) where the accused has previously been convicted of an offence committed in circumstances alleged to be connected with the death. So, if D has been convicted of wounding V who has subsequently died of the wound within three years of D's causing it, consent is required for a prosecution of D for murder or manslaughter. Similarly, it would seem, if D has been convicted of a robbery, burglary or driving offence in the course of which V sustained an injury of which he subsequently died. The year-and-a-day rule continues to apply where any act or omission causing death was committed before 17 June 1996.

(3) A PERSON 'IN BEING'

The victim of homicide must have been born and not have died before the defendant's act took effect. Although this principle is discussed exclusively in connection with homicide, it is probably applicable to offences against the person generally. As to birth:

CLRC (14th Report)

35. The common law definition of birth (for the purposes of offences against the person) has not been the subject of judicial review or comment for a long time. The last reported case on the subject that we can trace occurred in 1874. We have examined not only the common law test of birth but also the statutory formulation in the Infant Life (Preservation) Act 1929 which provides that the offence of child destruction may apply only to the killing of a child 'before it has an existence independent of its mother'. In our opinion the test of independent existence should be adopted. It also seems to us right that there should be an ascertainable point up to which the killing of a child would be child destruction under the Infant Life (Preservation) Act 1929 after which the law of homicide would apply. We therefore recommend that for a killing to constitute murder (or manslaughter or infanticide) the victim should have been born and have an existence independent of its mother.

In *Re A (children) (conjoined twins)*, above, p **440**, the court was satisfied that Mary was 'a reasonable creature in being', having an existence independent of her mother, although she was wholly dependent on Jodie for her continued existence. Mary thus came under the protection of the law of murder.

Brooke LJ: Advances in medical treatment of deformed neonates suggest that the criminal law's protection should be as wide as possible, and a conclusion that a creature in being was not reasonable would be confined only to the most extreme cases of which this is not an example. Whatever might have been thought of as monstrous by Bracton, Coke, Blackstone, Locke and Hobbes, different considerations would apply today. This proposition might be tested in this way: suppose an intruder broke into the hospital and stabbed twin M causing her death. Clearly it could not be said that his actions would be outside the limit of the law of homicide.

Modern English statute law has mitigated the prospective burden that might otherwise fall on the parents of severely handicapped children and their families if they are willing to avail themselves of its protection at any time up to the time the child (or children) is born. [His Lordship considered section 1(1)(d) of the Abortion Act 1997, as substituted by section 37(1) of the Human Fertilisation and Embryology Act 1990, and continued] Once a seriously handicapped child is born alive, the position changes, and it is as much entitled to the protection of the criminal law as any other human being.

Killing or injuring the foetus

In *A-G's Reference (No 3 of 1994)* [1997] 3 All ER 936, [1998] AC 245, above, p **35**, D stabbed his pregnant girlfriend. At that point in time it was not appreciated that the stab wound had penetrated the abdomen of the foetus. D pleaded guilty to the offence of wounding. The girlfriend gave birth to a 'grossly premature' daughter. The stabbing had in fact injured the foetus. The daughter survived for 120 days; her death attributed to her being grossly premature. The defendant was charged with murder. The trial judge ruled that there could be no conviction for either murder or manslaughter. The Attorney-General referred the issue to the Court of Appeal which held that the since the foetus was a part of the mother, the defendant's intent to cause at least serious injury to the mother was sufficient to found liability for murder in respect of the child. On appeal to the House of Lords, **Lord Mustill** perceived the following as established rules.

1. It is sufficient to raise a prima facie case of murder (subject to entire or partial excuses such as self-defence or provocation) for it to be proved that the defendant did the act which caused the death intending to kill the victim or to cause him at least grievous bodily harm. Although it will be necessary to look at the reasoning which founded this rule, it is undeniably a part of English law: see *R v Vickers* [1957] 2 All ER 741, [1957] 2 QB 664; *Hyam v DPP* [1974] 2 All ER 41, [1975] AC 55 and *R v Cunningham* [1981] 2 All ER 863, [1982] AC 566. Thus, if M had died as a result of the injuries received B would have been guilty of murdering her, even though in the everyday sense he did not intend her death.

2. If the defendant does an act with the intention of causing a particular kind of harm to X, and unintentionally does that kind of harm to Y, then the intent to harm X may be added to the harm actually done to Y in deciding whether the defendant has committed a crime towards Y. This rule is usually referred to as the doctrine of 'transferred malice', a misleading label but one which is too firmly entrenched to be discarded. Nor would it be possible now to question the rule itself, for although the same handful of authorities are called up repeatedly in the texts they are constantly cited without disapproval.... [See above, p **34**].

3. Except under statute an embryo or foetus *in utero* cannot be the victim of a crime of violence. In particular, violence to the foetus which causes its death *in utero* is not a murder. The foundation authority is the definition by Sir Edward Coke of murder by reference to the killing of 'a reasonable creature, *in rerum natura*' (see 3 Co Inst (1680) 50). The proposition was developed by the same writer into examples of prenatal injuries as follows:

> 'If a woman be quick with childe, and by a potion or otherwise killeth it in her wombe; or if a man beat her, whereby the child dieth in her body, and she is delivered of a dead childe; this is a great misprision, and no murder ...'

It is unnecessary to look behind this statement to the earlier authorities, for its correctness as a general principle, as distinct from its application to babies expiring in the course of delivery or very shortly thereafter, has never been controverted. It can, for example, be found in 4 Bl Com (1830) 198, *Stephen Digest of the Criminal Law* (1877) p 138, *Smith and Hogan Criminal Law* (8th edn, 1996) p 338 and in many other places over the years.

4. The existence of an interval of time between the doing of an act by the defendant with the necessary wrongful intent and its impact on the victim in a manner which leads to death does not in itself prevent the intent, the act and the death from together amounting to murder, so long as there is an unbroken causal connection between the act and the death.

5. Violence towards a foetus which results in harm suffered after the baby has been born alive can give rise to criminal responsibility even if the harm would not have been criminal (apart from statute) if it had been suffered *in utero*. Once again, the rule founds on a statement of Coke, following immediately after the passage above quoted:

> '... if the childe be born alive, and dieth of the potion, battery, or other cause, this is murder: for in law it is accounted a reasonable creature, *in rerum natura*, when it is born alive.' (See 3 Co Inst 50.)

This view did not at first command universal acceptance, largely on the practical ground that medical science did not then permit a clear proof of causal connection, but it was adopted in early Victorian times by the *Fourth Report of the Commissioners on Criminal Law* (1839), British Parliamentary

Papers (1839) vol 19, pp 235, 266 and the Second Report of the Commissioners for Revising and Consolidating Criminal Law (1846), British Parliamentary Papers (1846) vol 24, pp 107, 127 and never substantially doubted since. In *R v West* (1848) 2 Car & Kir 784, 175 ER 329, a case to which I must briefly return, the rule was extended to a situation such as the present where the assault caused the death, not through injury to the child, but by causing the child to be born prematurely. In *R v Senior* (1832) 1 Mood CC 346, 168 ER 1298 the principle was applied to manslaughter, where death resulted from gross negligence by a midwife before the child had been fully born. Since the principle is not disputed I will not cite the numerous references to it by institutional writers during the past three centuries....

Article 2 and the right to life

The European Court of Human Rights has declined to decide directly whether the foetus is protected by the right to life in Article 2. In *Vo v France* [2004] 2 FCR 577 a doctor negligently caused fatal injury to a viable foetus after mistaking the mother's identity for that of another patient. The French Criminal Court acquitted him on the basis that the foetus was not a human being for the purposes of the offence. On application to the ECtHR, the Court ruled that the issue of life's commencement and its protection by criminal law was within the margin of appreciation extended to the Member States. The Court acknowledged that in:

the circumstances examined to date by the Convention institutions—that is, in the various laws on abortion—the unborn child is not regarded as a 'person' directly protected by Article 2 of the Convention and that if the unborn do have a 'right' to 'life', it is implicitly limited by the mother's rights and interests. The Convention institutions have not, however, ruled out the possibility that in certain circumstances safeguards may be extended to the unborn child ... It is also clear from an examination of these cases that the issue has always been determined by weighing up various, and sometimes conflicting, rights or freedoms claimed by a woman, a mother or a father in relation to one another or *vis-à-vis* an unborn child. [para 80]

Death

CLRC (14th Report)

37. We have considered whether there should be a statutory definition of death. A memorandum issued by the honorary secretary of the Conference of Medical Royal Colleges and Faculties in the United Kingdom on 15 January 1979 refers to an earlier report of the Conference which expressed their unanimous opinion that 'brain death' could be diagnosed with certainty. The memorandum states that the report published by the Conference has been widely accepted and says that the identification of brain death means that a patient is truly dead, whether or not the function of some organs, such as a heart beat, is still maintained by artificial means. Brain death is said to be when all the functions of the brain have permanently and irreversibly ceased. We are however extremely hesitant about embodying in a statute (which is not always susceptible of speedy amendment) an expression of present medical opinion and knowledge derived from a field of science which is continually progressing and inevitably altering its opinions in the light of new information. If a statutory definition of death were to be enacted there would, in our opinion, be a risk that further knowledge would cause it to lose the assent of the majority of the medical profession. In that event, far from assisting the medical profession, for example in cases of organ transplants, the definition might be a hindrance to them. Moreover, while there might be agreement that the statutory definition was defective, there might be differences of view about the proper content of any new definition.

An additional reason for not recommending a definition of death is that such definition would have wide repercussions outside offences against the person and the criminal law. A legal definition of death would also have to be applicable in the civil law. It would be undesirable to have a statutory definition confined only to offences against the person, which is the extent of our present remit. For these reasons therefore we are not recommending the enactment of a definition of death.

See also *Malcherek*, p 71, above.

Airedale NHS Trust v Bland
[1993] 2 WLR 316, House of Lords

(Lords Keith of Kinkel, Goff of Chievdey, Lowry, Browne-Wilkinson and Mustill)

B was very seriously injured in the Hillsborough disaster. He suffered irreversible brain damage which left him in a persistent vegetative state. All medical opinion was that there was no hope of recovery or improvement. The Health Authority sought a declaration that it would be lawful to discontinue all life sustaining treatment including all medical and nutritional support except so as to allow B to die peacefully with the least pain. The House of Lords held that it would be lawful to discontinue the treatment even though in this case there was no consent by B. As the time had come when B had no further interest in being kept alive, the necessity for the treatment had gone and it would not be unlawful to omit to perform what had previously been a duty.

Lord Keith of Kinkel (at p 362). Where one individual has assumed responsibility for the care of another who cannot look after himself or herself, whether as a medical practitioner or otherwise, that responsibility cannot lawfully be shed unless arrangements are made for the responsibility to be taken over by someone else.... [I]t is of course true that in general it would not be lawful for a medical practitioner who assumed responsibility for the care of the unconscious patient simply to give up treatment in circumstances where continuance of it would confer some benefit on the patient.

The ECHR and death

In *R (Burke) v GMC* [2004] EWHC 1879 (Admin), the court recognized that a withdrawal of artificial feeding and hydration (ANH) which a competent patient wishes to continue or which an incompetent person has previously, when competent, directed to continue would infringe Article 8 of the ECHR. (On the GMC Guidelines see J. Keown, 'Beyond Bland: A critique of the BMA Guidance on Withholding and Withdrawing Medical Treatment' (2000) 20 LS 66; cf D. Price, 'Fairly Bland: An Alternative View of a Supposed New 'Death Ethic' and the BMA Guidelines' (2001) 21 LS 618.) The court declined to decide whether there would be such a breach of Article 8 once the patient was in a coma, but suggested that withdrawal once the patient was in a coma and being treated with dignity might be legitimate if it was in the final stages of life and serving no purpose.

Munby J: 213. In relation to matters generally I can summarise my conclusions as follows:

(h) The personal autonomy which is protected by Article 8 embraces such matters as how one chooses to pass the closing days and moments of one's life and how one manages one's death.

(i) The dignity interests protected by the Convention include, under Article 8, the preservation of mental stability and, under Article 3, the right to die with dignity and the right to be protected from treatment, or from a lack of treatment, which will result in one dying in avoidably distressing circumstances....

(p) Reference to Article 2 does not add anything in this type of case. Article 2 does not entitle anyone to force life-prolonging treatment on a competent patient who refuses to accept it. Article 2 does not entitle anyone to continue with life-prolonging treatment where to do so would expose the patient to "inhuman or degrading treatment" breaching Article 3. On the other hand, a withdrawal of life-prolonging treatment which satisfies the exacting requirements of the common law, including a proper application of the intolerability test, and in a manner which is in all other respects compatible with the patient's rights under Article 3 and Article 8, will not give rise to any breach of Article 2....

(r) Accepting for present purposes that the court will not grant a mandatory order requiring an individual doctor to treat a patient, this does not mean that a doctor can simply decline to go on treating his patient merely because his views as to what is in his patient's best interests differ from those of the patient or the court. A competent patient, properly advised by a doctor, may elect to choose a form of treatment which is not the one that the doctor would recommend. But this does not release the doctor from his continuing duty to care for his patient, unless perhaps, that is, he finds himself conscientiously unable to do so. In any event, if a doctor is for any reason unable to carry out the wishes of his patient, his duty is to find another doctor who will do so.

(s) The fact that the court will not make a mandatory order against a doctor is no reason why in principle it should not in an appropriate case grant declaratory relief against him. Nor is it any reason why the court should not in an appropriate case grant both declaratory and mandatory relief against a NHS trust or other health authority. Thus the court can by appropriate orders ensure that a patient who ought to be treated is, if need be, transferred to the care of doctors who are willing to do so.

214. In relation to the withdrawal of ANH I can summarise my conclusions as follows:

(a) Under the Convention, as at common law, if the patient is competent (or, although incompetent, has made an advance directive which is both valid and relevant to the treatment in question) his refusal to accept ANH—his decision that ANH not be started or, if started, that it be stopped—is determinative.

(b) If the patient is competent (or, although incompetent, has made an advance directive which is both valid and relevant to the treatment in question) his decision to require the provision of ANH which he believes is necessary to protect him from what he sees as acute mental and physical suffering is likewise in principle determinative. There are two separate reasons why this is so. The first is based on the competent patient's rights under Article 8. The second is based on his rights, whether competent or incompetent, under Article 3....

(f) ....once the claimant has entered into the final stage and has finally lapsed into a coma. Assuming that the patient is otherwise being treated with dignity, and in a manner which is in all other respects compatible with his rights under Article 3 and Article 8, there will not be any breach either of Article 3 or of Article 8 or of Article 2 if ANH is withdrawn in circumstances where it is serving absolutely no purpose other than the very short prolongation of the life of a dying patient who has slipped into his final coma and lacks all awareness of what is happening. For it can then properly be said that the continuation of ANH would be bereft of any benefit at all to the patient and that it would indeed be futile.

(g) Where it is proposed to withhold or withdraw ANH the prior authorisation of the court is required as a matter of law (and thus ANH cannot be withheld or withdrawn without prior judicial authorisation): (i) where there is any doubt or disagreement as to the capacity (competence) of the patient; or (ii) where there is a lack of unanimity amongst the medical professionals as to either (1) the patient's condition or prognosis or (2) the patient's best interests or (3) the likely outcome of

ANH being either withheld or withdrawn or (4) otherwise as to whether or not ANH should be withheld or withdrawn; or (iii) where there is evidence that the patient when competent would have wanted ANH to continue in the relevant circumstances; or (iv) where there is evidence that the patient (even if a child or incompetent) resists or disputes the proposed withdrawal of ANH; or (v) where persons having a reasonable claim to have their views or evidence taken into account (such as parents or close relatives, partners, close friends, long-term carers) assert that withdrawal of ANH is contrary to the patient's wishes or not in the patient's best interests.

(4) THE QUEEN'S PEACE

'Alien enemies' who are actually engaged in hostile operations against the Crown will not be within the Queen's Peace. Their killing will not, therefore, amount to murder. *R v Page* [1954] 1 QB 170. Killings by armed forces personnel of enemy forces will be criminal if the enemy agents have already surrendered. Note that murder committed by a British citizen outside England can still be tried by English courts: Offences Against the Person Act 1861, s 9. (See further P. Rowe, 'Murder and the Law of War' (1991) NILQ 216.) Note that the civilian criminal law applies to police and armed forces using lethal force on citizens. (See cases discussed on self-defence, in particular see *R v Clegg* [1995] 1 AC 482.)

Notes and questions

1. The CLRC is apparently content to endorse a statutory definition of birth based on nineteenth-century cases which held that the child should have been born and have an existence independent of its mother. These cases require that the child should be wholly extruded from the body of the mother but do not require that the umbilical cord should have been severed or that the child should have breathed because, it had been observed, children sometimes do not breathe until they receive vigorous treatment. It was suggested to the Broderick Committee (Death Certification and Coroners, 1971, Cmnd 4810) that live birth should be determined by the allegedly scientifically verifiable test of whether the child had breathed and that consequently the requirement for complete extrusion from the womb could be deleted as irrelevant and arbitrary. The Committee rejected the suggestion on the grounds (a) that this would imply that other signs of life were unimportant; and (b) that any alteration in the definition 'would ruin the continuity of statistics which were first collected in 1926'. Are these convincing arguments in favour of the status quo?

2. As to death the CLRC was unwilling to recommend any definition because, to put the matter simply, medical advances cause the goalposts to be shifted. This is, perhaps, a convincing argument against a statutory definition of death. But who defines death in a case where it is relevant?

2. MURDER: THE MENTAL ELEMENT

The starting point is that we are concerned with proof of a real state of mind. The prosecution have to satisfy the jury so as to make them sure that the person in the dock had the requisite state of mind, whatever it is, when he did the fatal act. This was not always clear.

In *DPP v Smith* ([1960] 3 All ER 161, [1961] AC 290), D, fearing that V, a police officer, was about to discover stolen goods in his car, drove off at high speed with V clinging on to the bonnet. D drove at increasing speed for 130 yards, during which time his car struck three oncoming vehicles, until V was finally thrown off into the path of another vehicle and killed. Restoring D's conviction for murder, Viscount Kilmuir LC, with whom all their Lordships concurred, said (at p 167):

The jury must, of course, in such a case as the present make up their minds on the evidence whether the accused was unlawfully and voluntarily doing something to someone. The unlawful and voluntary act must clearly be aimed at someone in order to eliminate cases of negligence or of careless or dangerous driving. Once, however, the jury are satisfied as to that, it matters not what the accused in fact contemplated as the probable result or whether he ever contemplated at all, provided he was in law responsible and accountable for his actions, that is, was a man capable of forming an intent, not insane within the M'Naghten Rules and not suffering from diminished responsibility. On the assumption that he is so accountable for his actions, the sole question is whether the unlawful and voluntary act was of such a kind that grievous bodily harm was the natural and probable result. The only test available for this is what the ordinary responsible man would, in all the circumstances of the case, have contemplated as the natural and probable result.

Few cases can have attracted such a barrage of hostile criticism from the commentators. It was considered in, though not formally overruled by, *Hyam*, *Moloney* and *Hancock*. Lord Diplock did say in *Hyam* that it was wrongly decided, and Lord Bridge in *Moloney* and Lord Ackner in *Hancock* said that insofar as it laid down an objective test it did not represent the common law. Another view expressed (by Lord Hailsham in *Hyam* among others) was that there was no need to overrule it because its effect had been modified by s 8 of the Criminal Justice Act 1967 (above, p 179). As we have seen, however, s 8, properly construed, does not affect the mens rea required for any crime. The section is concerned with how intention or foresight must be proved, not when they must be proved.

The issue had to be met, as it were, head on, in *Frankland and Moore* ([1987] AC 576, PC). The appellants had been convicted on a *Smith* direction on the Isle of Man at a time when the Isle of Man had no provision equivalent to s 8. Since the common law is the same in this matter as the common law of England, it was necessary to decide whether *Smith* correctly stated the common law. It was forthrightly held by five Law Lords that it did not. While decisions of the Privy Council cannot overrule decisions of the House of Lords, it seems safe to assume that the decision in *Smith* is not, and never was, the law of England.

The mental element required for the crime of murder, as for the crime of manslaughter, has varied over the centuries. From Coke's time (when the judges were prepared to treat killing by any unlawful act as murder) there has been a steady contraction of the definition of murder but for the unfortunate decision in *DPP v Smith* (above). Reporting in 1953 the Royal Commission on Capital Punishment (Cmd 8932) found it 'impractical' to frame a satisfactory definition of murder but it did recommend that the reach of murder be curtailed by the abolition of the doctrine of 'constructive' murder. Under this doctrine a person was guilty of murder if he caused death during the commission of a felony involving violence (for example, rape, robbery) or if he caused death while resisting an officer of justice. The RCCP's recommendation was embodied in s 1 of the Homicide Act 1957. This must be the starting point of a discussion of the mental element in murder though it tells us much more of what the mental element is not and tells us precious little about what it is. Section 1 provides—

1. Abolition of 'constructive malice'

(1) Where a person kills another in the course or furtherance of some other offence, the killing shall not amount to murder unless done with the same malice aforethought (express or implied) as is required for a killing to amount to murder when not done in the course or furtherance of another offence.

(2) For the purposes of the foregoing subsection, a killing done in the course or for the purpose of resisting an officer of justice, or of resisting or avoiding or preventing a lawful arrest, or of effecting or assisting an escape or rescue from legal custody, shall be treated as a killing in the course or furtherance of an offence.

The section uses the expression 'malice aforethought' to describe the mens rea of murder. Traditionally the mens rea of murder was described as malice aforethought but the term is unhelpful: 'malice' does not mean ill will and 'aforethought' tells us no more than that the mens rea must not come as an afterthought. It is simply a label used to refer to those mental states (whatever they are) that suffice for murder.

(1) INTENTION TO KILL

The section refers to two kinds of malice aforethought: 'express' and 'implied'. 'Express' malice must be a reference to whatever was considered as express malice at common law. What that was has nowhere been judicially defined nor has there been any explanation of it in the case law since the Homicide Act. What did Parliament (or the draftsman) have in mind when it was enacted that express malice sufficed for murder? The term was used by the institutional writers to denote those whose conduct was intentional. The earlier writers (Hale, Hawkins) did not restrict the term to those who intentionally caused death, but it now appears that the term 'express malice' means 'with intent to kill', and 'implied malice' means 'with intent to do serious bodily harm'.

The leading cases on intention are now *Moloney*, *Hancock* and particularly, *Woollin*, above pp **120**, **124**, and **126** but the earlier decision of the House of Lords in *Hyam* may still require consideration.

Hyam v Director of Public Prosecutions
[1974] 2 All ER 41, House of Lords

(Lord Hailsham of St Marylebone LC, Viscount Dilhorne, Lords Diplock, Cross of Chelsea and Kilbrandon)

The facts appear in the speech of Lord Hailsham.

Lord Hailsham LC: ... The facts are simple, and not in dispute. In the early hours of Saturday, 15 July 1972, the appellant set fire to a dwelling-house in Coventry by deliberately pouring about a half gallon of petrol through the letterbox and igniting it by means of a newspaper and a match. The house contained four persons, presumably asleep. They were a Mrs Booth and her three children, a boy and the two young girls who were the subjects of the charges. Mrs Booth and the boy escaped alive through a window. The two girls died as the result of asphyxia by the fumes generated by the fire. The appellant's motive (in the sense in which I shall use the word 'motive') was jealousy of Mrs Booth whom the appellant believed was likely to marry a Mr Jones of whom the appellant herself was the discarded, or partly discarded, mistress. Her account of her actions, and her defence, was that she had started the fire only with the intention of frightening Mrs Booth into leaving the neighbourhood, and that she did not intend to cause death or grievous bodily harm. The judge directed the jury:

'The prosecution must prove, beyond all reasonable doubt, that the accused intended to (kill or) do serious bodily harm to Mrs Booth, the mother of the deceased girls. If you are satisfied that when the accused set fire to the house she knew that it was highly probable that this would cause (death or) serious bodily harm then the prosecution will have established . . . the necessary intent. It matters not if her motive was, as she says, to frighten Mrs Booth.'

The judge explained that he had put brackets round the words 'kill or' and 'death or' because he advised the jury to concentrate on the intent to do serious bodily harm rather than the intent to kill.

There were other passages in the summing-up to the same effect, but this was the vital passage, and the judge reduced it to writing and caused the jury to retire with it into the jury room. As the case proceeded, it is the only passage in the judge's summing-up to which I need draw attention, and gives rise to the only point which was argued before your Lordships' House. The Court of Appeal [[1973] 3 All ER 842, [1974] QB 99] dismissed the appeal 'not without some reluctance', and, in giving leave to appeal to the House of Lords, certified that it involved the following point of law of general public importance, namely, the question:

'Is malice aforethought in the crime of murder established by proof beyond reasonable doubt that when doing the act which led to the death of another the accused knew that it was highly probable that that act would result in death or serious bodily harm?'

[Having rejected the argument that a consequence foreseen as highly probable is intended, Lord Hailsham continued:]

But this, again, does not dispose of the matter. Another way of putting the case for the Crown was that, even if it be conceded that foresight of the probable consequences is not the same thing as intention, it can, nevertheless, be an alternative type of malice aforethought, equally effective as intention to convert an unlawful killing into murder. This view, which is inconsistent with the view that foresight of a high degree of probability is only another way of describing intention, derives some support from the way in which the proposition is put in Stephen's *Digest* where it is said that malice aforethought for the purpose of the law of murder includes a state of mind in which there is:

'knowledge that the act which causes death will probably cause the death of, or grievous bodily harm to, some person, whether such person is the person actually killed or not, although such knowledge is accompanied by indifference whether death or grievous bodily harm is caused or not, or by a wish that it may not be caused'.

If this is right, Ackner J's direction can be justified on the grounds that such knowledge is itself a separate species of malice aforethought, and not simply another way of describing intention. . . .

But what are we to say of the state of mind of a defendant who knows that a proposed course of conduct exposes a third party to a serious risk of death or grievous bodily harm, without actually intending those consequences, but nevertheless and without lawful excuse deliberately pursues that course of conduct regardless whether the consequences to his potential victim take place or not? In that case, if my analysis be correct, there is not merely actual foresight of the probable consequences, but actual intention to expose his victim to the risk of those consequences whether they in fact occur or not. Is that intention sufficient to reduce the crime to manslaughter notwithstanding a jury's finding that they are sure that it was the intention with which the act was done? In my opinion, it is not . . . It is the man's actual state of knowledge and intent which, as in all other cases, determines his criminal responsibility. Nor, for the like reason, does this set up an irrebuttable presumption. It simply proclaims the moral truth that if a man, in full knowledge of the danger involved, and without lawful excuse, deliberately does that which exposes a victim to the risk of the probable grievous bodily harm (in the sense explained) or death, and the victim dies, the perpetrator of the crime is guilty of murder and not manslaughter to the same extent as if he had actually intended the consequence to follow, and irrespective of whether he wishes it. That is because the two types of intention are morally indistinguishable, although factually and logically distinct, and because it is therefore just that they should bear the same consequences to the perpetrator as they have the same consequences for the victim if death ensues. . . . for the reasons I have given in my opinion the appeal fails and should be dismissed.

[**Viscount Dilhorne** said that whether or not knowledge that certain consequences are highly probable is to be treated as intent (he was inclined to think it was), it had been established for at least 100 years that such knowledge amounted to malice aforethought. The jury had not been misdirected. **Lord Cross** took a similar view but was not prepared to decide without further argument whether intention to cause, or foresight of the probability of, serious bodily harm was sufficient. On the footing that *Vickers*, infra, was rightly decided, he would dismiss the appeal. **Lord Diplock**, with whom **Lord Kilbrandon** agreed, dissenting, held that an intention to do serious bodily harm was not enough. There must be an intention to do an act likely to endanger life (see below, p **569**).]

Appeal dismissed

Notes and questions

1. Is there any life left in *Hyam* in the absence of a reversal of *Woollin* and, indeed, of *Moloney*?

A. Norrie, 'After *Woollin*'
[1999] Crim LR 532

There has always been a deep-seated problem in the murder cases because what they have given with one hand, a narrow foresight of virtual certainty test, they have taken back with the other, through a broader foresight of probability approach in the guidelines. The guidelines in *Moloney* proved a Trojan Horse by virtue of which *Hyam* recklessness remained a part of the mens rea of murder. While declaring an orthodox subjectivist principle to be at the core of the law, the appeal courts undercut it by what they said judges should tell juries. It is not surprising, given the passage quoted [in *Woollin*] from *Nedrick*, that the trial judge in *Woollin* instructed his jury according to foresight of virtual certainty one day and according to foresight of substantial risk the next, because *Hancock* and *Shankland* and *Nedrick* sanction both approaches. . . . .

In *Woollin*, Lord Steyn declares that the words 'entitled to infer' in the model *Nedrick* direction should be replaced with the clearer 'entitled to find'. Professor Smith applauds the move, but wonders if the change in wording will remove one problem with the original formulation. If indirect intention is a species of intention, then to identify foresight of a virtual certainty in the accused's mind is to identify that she intended the crime. The use of the word 'entitled' however suggests that the jury may so identify intention, but, alternatively may not do so. 'Entitled' is permissive rather than obligatory, so that the formulation 'involves some ambiguity with the hint of the existence of some ineffable, undefinable, notion of intent, locked in the breasts of the jurors'. . .

I have previously argued that the idea of a mysterious gap between the law of intention and a factual finding of foresight of a virtual certainty owed its initial existence to some loose talk in *Moloney* about the place of foresight in the law of indirect intention. Lord Bridge wanted to distinguish recklessness from indirect intention, but he did so by suggesting that 'intend' and 'foresee' 'connote two different states of mind'. What he should have said, to be consistent with his analysis of indirect intention, was that the relevant distinction was between the mental states of 'foresight of a moral certainty' and 'foresight of a consequence within the range of probability'. Having said what he said, however, he then had to deal with the question of how the accused's foresight could be relevant to the law of (indirect) intention. His answer was that it played an evidential role so that indirect intention could be inferred from it. How this was logically possible given Lord Bridge's initial premise was never made clear, but the result of his argument was the idea of a gap between evidence of foresight of moral certainty and the law of indirect intention such that the former may, but need not, lead to a finding (previously an inference) of intention. This idea has remained an *idée fixe* of the law ever since, despite Professor Smith's best efforts to disabuse the judges of it....

A narrow account of th[e] law makes *Woollin* and *Moloney* manslaughterers, a broad account makes them murderers, but neither the broad nor the narrow account actually captures the moral essence of the judgment that lies behind, but is mediated through, the law....

In *Hyam*, the judges opted for the broad approach, but while the test of foresight of probable or highly probable consequence covered Mrs Hyam, it did not catch the essence of her moral wrong doing. While 'foresight of a probable consequence of death or serious injury' carries moral information, it is still a relatively neutral way of describing the reckless animus with which Mrs Hyam addressed her victims. Still, unlike 'foresight of moral certainty', the lesser degree of risk enables her conviction. Again the test reflects the desired moral conclusion, but does not embody it....

[T]he broader spirit of *Hyam* has always lurked within the indirect intention cases even when they have denied it, and this is as true of *Woollin* as the others. The case law contains both foresight of virtual certainty and foresight of (high) probability elements precisely because neither approach adequately embodies the moral judgments required by the murder label. For the same reason mutatis mutandis, the cases also leave the door ajar to a narrower, direct intention only, interpretation of the law in the manner of *Steane*.

2. Lords Steyn, Nolan and Hope constitute a majority in favour of the reasons given by Lord Steyn in *Woollin*, whatever unspoken reservations the other two judges (who, while concurring in the result, did not express agreement with Lord Steyn's reasons) may have had. Foresight of virtual certainty, even if it is not 'intention', is a condition precedent to liability; and foreseeing that the result was highly probable is materially different from foreseeing that it was virtually certain. But Professor Norrie's article suggests that the present formula leaves open the possibility of the addition of a further ingredient in the mens rea. What is the judge to say if the jury tell him they are unanimous that D foresaw that the result was virtually certain, but are divided as to whether he intended it, and seek guidance as to how they should decide? The best practical advice to the judge probably is to fudge the issue: 'Members of the jury, intention is an ordinary word of the English language. It is a matter for you, applying your common sense and knowledge of the world.' This tells the jury nothing but it may result in a verdict. Would a more honest instruction to the jury be: 'If, in the light of all the evidence you have heard, you are satisfied D deserves to be convicted of murder call his state of mind intention and convict. Otherwise acquit him of murder and convict him of manslaughter.' It may be that is how the jury do it anyway. And Professor Norrie's article suggests—in effect—that this may be the right answer.

It is already the law (below, p 641) in gross negligence that the test is whether the negligence is 'bad enough' to be condemned as criminal. This direction makes sense if it is treated as bad enough to be manslaughter (below, p 647). That approach has long been heavily criticized on the ground that it leaves a question of law to be determined by the jury (cf *Misra* below, p 651). But if we are to have a law of manslaughter by gross negligence— and we do—there is probably no other way. There is no logical compulsion for a similar principle in murder; but should it be adopted as a matter of policy where it is not alleged that it was D's purpose to cause death or gbh? Should the judge be required to tell the jury in all such cases—not waiting to be asked: 'If you are sure that D knew the result was virtually certain, then, and only then, are you entitled to convict him of [murder]. But you will do so only if you are sure that, in the light of all the evidence, his conduct in causing death was bad enough to deserve condemnation as murder'?

This would explain the judges' strange reluctance to treat foresight of virtual certainty as intention in murder cases and insist that it is only evidence; but would it be fair to allow this escape route for hard cases where it is not D's purpose to kill, while excluding that route where death or gbh is his purpose? The mercy killer acts with the purpose of causing death, and his is perhaps the hardest case of all. The surgeons in *Re A (children) (conjoined twins)* were not guilty of murder, not simply because of their impeccable motives, but because the killing of Mary was necessary to defend the life of Jodie or was justified by a more general defence of necessity.

(2) INTENTION TO CAUSE GRIEVOUS BODILY HARM

Section 1 of the Homicide Act 1957 tells us not only that express malice suffices for murder but also that implied malice suffices. As with express malice the reference to implied malice is simply a reference, and an unhelpful one, to whatever was understood to be meant by 'implied malice'. The term was again one frequently used by the institutional writers who gave various interpretations of it.

It is quite clear that s 1(1) abolished the rule that death caused in the course or furtherance of committing a felony—typically, robbery, burglary or rape—was murder. The section also clearly abolished the rule that a killing was murder simply because the death was caused in the circumstances described in s 1(2). Beyond that, the section told us nothing about the meaning of 'malice aforethought'—it remained a question of common law.

R v Vickers
[1957] 2 All ER 741, Court of Criminal Appeal

(Lord Goddard CJ, Hilbery, Byrne, Slade and Devlin JJ)

The appellant broke into the cellar of a shop which was occupied by an old woman of 73, a Miss Duckett, intending to steal money. At the shop Miss Duckett carried on a prosperous business of grocer and tobacconist, and she lived alone on the same premises in two rooms above the shop; she was a small woman and the appellant, who lived in lodgings a short distance away, knew that she was deaf. While the appellant was in the cellar Miss Duckett came down the stairs leading to it and saw the appellant. She asked him what he was doing and came towards him, whereupon the appellant attacked her with his fists and struck her several blows; she fell down. The medical evidence was that Miss Duckett was struck by 10 to 15 blows and was kicked in the face by the appellant, and that death was caused by shock due to general injuries; the medical evidence was also that the degree of force necessary to inflict the injuries sustained by Miss Duckett would be moderately severe to quite slight force.

The appellant now appealed against his conviction inter alia on the ground that the judge misdirected the jury when he told them that malice aforethought could be implied if the victim was killed by a voluntary act done with the intention of causing grievous bodily harm.

[**Lord Goddard CJ** delivering the judgment of the court:]

... The point that is raised is this: s 1(1) of the Act of 1957 says: [His Lordship quoted the subsection.] The marginal note of s 1, which of course is not part of the section, but may be looked at as some indication of the purpose, is: 'Abolition of "constructive malice" '.

'Constructive malice' is an expression that has crept into the law—I do not think that it will be found in any particular decision but it is to be found in the text-books—and is something different from implied malice. The expression 'constructive malice' is generally used and the best illustration of constructive malice which is generally given is that if a person caused death during the course of his carrying out a felony which involved violence, that always amounted to murder. There were cases in which a man was not intending to cause death, as for instance where a mere push was given which would never have been considered in the ordinary way as one which would cause death, but the person pushed fell down and most unfortunately struck his head or fell down the stairs and broke his neck, yet if the act were done, for example, in the course of burglary, it amounted to murder. Take the case of rape. If a man raped a woman and in order to overcome her resistance proceeded to strangle her, the fact that he might only have used a moderate degree of violence in the strangling, in holding her throat, would have been no defence. If he did cause death it would have been murder because he caused death during the commission of the offence of rape. Another instance of constructive malice which was always held sufficient to amount to murder was the killing of a police officer in the execution of his duty. If a prisoner was resisting arrest, although he might use only a moderate degree of violence on a police officer, yet if he caused the death of the officer from some unusual or perhaps extraordinary reason, he was, before the Act of 1957, guilty of murder. Murder is, of course, killing with malice aforethought and 'malice aforethought' is a term of art. Malice aforethought has always been defined in English law as either an express intention to kill such as could be inferred when a person, having uttered threats against another, produced a lethal weapon and used it on him, or an implied intention to kill, as where the prisoner inflicted grievous bodily harm, that is to say, harmed the victim by a voluntary act intended to harm him and the victim died as the result of that grievous bodily harm. If a person does an act on another which amounts to the infliction of grievous bodily harm he cannot say that he did not intend to go so far. It is put as *malum in se* in the old cases and he must take the consequences. If he intends to inflict grievous bodily harm and that person dies, that has always been held in English law, and was at the time when the Act of 1957 was passed, sufficient to imply the malice aforethought which is a necessary constituent of murder.

It will be observed that s 1 preserves the implied malice as well as express malice and the words 'where a person kills another in the course or furtherance of some other offence' cannot in our opinion refer to the infliction of the grievous bodily harm, if the case which is made against the prisoner is that he killed a person by having assaulted the person with intent to do grievous bodily harm and from the bodily harm which he inflicted that person dies. The furtherance of some other offence must refer to the offence that he was committing or endeavouring to commit other than the killing, otherwise there would be no sense in it. It was always the English law that if death were caused by a person in the course of committing a felony involving violence, that was murder. Therefore, in this particular case it is perfectly clear that the words 'where a person kills another in the course or furtherance of some other offence' must be attributed to the burglary which the appellant was committing. The killing was in the course or furtherance of that burglary. He killed that person in the course of the burglary because he realised that the victim recognised him and he therefore inflicted grievous bodily harm on her, perhaps only intending to render her unconscious, but he did intend to inflict grievous bodily harm by the blows he inflicted on her and by kicking her in the face, of which there was evidence.

Section 1(1) of the Act of 1957 then goes on:

'the killing shall not amount to murder unless done with the same malice aforethought (express or implied) as is required for a killing to amount to murder when not done in the course or furtherance of another offence.'

It would seem clear, therefore, that what the legislature is providing is that where there is a killing, though it may be done in the course or furtherance of another offence, that other offence must be ignored. The other offence is not taken into consideration. What has to be considered are the circumstances of the killing; and if the killing would amount to murder by reason of the express or implied malice then that person is guilty of capital murder. It is not enough that he killed in the course of the felony unless the killing is done in a manner which would amount to murder ignoring the felony which is committed. It seems to the court, therefore, that here you have a case of a burglar attacking a householder to prevent recognition. The householder died as the result of blows inflicted on her— blows or kicks or both—and if s 1 of the Act of 1957 had not been passed there could be no doubt that the man would have been guilty of murder. He is guilty of murder because he has killed a person with the necessary malice aforethought being implied from the fact that he intended to do grievous bodily harm.

I will now briefly refer to the summing-up of Hinchcliffe J, which the court thinks is quite impeccable....

The court desires to say quite firmly that in considering the construction of s 1(1), it is impossible to say that the doing of grievous bodily harm is the other offence which is referred to in the first line and a half of the sub-section. It must be shown that independently of the fact that the accused is committing another offence, that the act which caused the death was done with malice aforethought as implied by law. The existence of express or implied malice is expressly preserved by the Act of 1957 and, in our opinion, a perfectly proper direction was given by Hinchcliffe J, to the jury, and accordingly this appeal fails and is dismissed.

Appeal dismissed

Notes and questions

1. There were those who took the view that the rule that intent to cause gbh was the mens rea of murder was a form of constructive malice and that it had been abolished. The argument to this effect was 'dismissed out of hand'—per Lord Mustill in *A-G's Reference (No 3 of 1994)* [1997] 3 All ER 936 at 946, above, pp 35 and 555—in *Vickers*. The reasoning in *Vickers* was promptly criticized by J. W. C. Turner who pointed out ([1958] Crim LR 15) that causing grievous bodily harm with intent was a felony under s 18 of the Offences Against the Person Act 1861; so s 1(1) could, and he argued, should, be read to say that it is not murder merely because D caused death in the course of causing grievous bodily harm with intent.

2. The correctness of *Vickers* was doubted by Lord Diplock, with whom Lord Kilbrandon agreed, in *Hyam*. In an elaborate argument Lord Diplock concluded that D could not be convicted of murder on proof that he had caused death with intent to cause grievous bodily harm, and, of course, still less if D had merely foreseen grievous bodily harm as probable or highly probable. He thought that the grievous bodily harm doctrine in murder was subsumed within constructive malice which had been abolished by s 1 of the Homicide Act. He saw the grievous bodily harm doctrine as originating with Lord Ellenborough's Act of 1803 which made it a felony to cause grievous bodily harm done by any means 'with intent to maim, disfigure or disable . . . or to do some other grievous bodily harm.'

Lord Diplock admitted that before 1803 an intention to cause a harm less than death would suffice for murder (it has been pointed out above, p 562, that Hale and Hawkins were prepared to consider an intent to cause harm less than death as falling within express malice) but he concluded that their thinking, and that of the judges, was that an intention to cause a harm less than death sufficed only where that harm created a risk of death which D foresaw. He indicated that a harm inflicted in earlier times which would have been foreseen as creating a risk of death would not now, given the advances in medical science, be seen as so doing.

Lord Diplock was thus able to conclude that the mens rea of murder was either (a) an intention to kill; or (b) an intention to cause bodily injury knowing that it is likely to cause death.

Looked at as a matter of principle the views expressed by Lord Diplock in *Hyam* have much to commend them (cf the redefinition of the mens rea of murder in the Draft Criminal Code Bill, below, p **661**).

Lord Hailsham LC and Viscount Dilhorne, however, said that *Vickers* had been correctly decided. That left Lord Cross with a casting vote which he declined to cast, reaching his decision '*on the footing that R v Vickers was rightly decided*' (his Lordship's italics).

R v Cunningham
[1981] 2 All ER 863, House of Lords

(Lord Hailsham LC, and Lords Wilberforce, Simon, Edmund-Davies and Bridge)

The appellant attacked the deceased in a pub and hit him repeatedly with a chair. The deceased died from his injuries. The judge directed the jury that the appellant was guilty of murder if he intended to cause really serious harm. The Court of Appeal dismissed his appeal and he appealed to the House of Lords, relying on the speeches of Lords Diplock and Kilbrandon in *Hyam*, p 562, above.

Lord Hailsham LC. ... The real nerve of Lord Diplock's argument, however, does, as it seems to me, depend on the importance to be attached to the passing in 1803 of Lord Ellenborough's Act (43 Geo 3 c 58) by which, for the first time, wounding with the intent to inflict grievous bodily harm became a felony. This, Lord Diplock believes, rendered it possible to apply the doctrine of 'felony murder' as defined in Stephen's category (c), abolished in 1957, to all cases of felonious wounding, where death actually ensued from the wound. The abolition of 'felony murder' in 1957 was thus seen to enable the judiciary to pursue the mental element in murder behind the curtain imposed on it by the combined effect of the statutory crime of felonious wounding and the doctrine of constructive malice, and so to arrive at a position in which the mental element could be redefined in terms either of an intention to kill, or an intention actually to endanger human life, to correspond with the recommendations of the Fourth Report of Her Majesty's Commissioners on Criminal Law (8th March 1839).

It seems to me, however, that this highly ingenious argument meets with two insuperable difficulties. I accept that it appears to be established that the actual phrase 'grievous bodily harm', if not an actual coinage by Lord Ellenborough's Act, can never be found to have appeared in print before it, though it has subsequently become current coin, and has passed into the general legal jargon of statute law, and the cases decided thereon. But counsel, having diligently carried us through the institutional writers on homicide, starting with Coke, and ending with East, with several citations from the meagre reports available, only succeeded in persuading me at least that, even prior to Lord Ellenborough's Act of 1803, and without the precise label 'grievous bodily harm', the authors and the courts had consistently treated as murder, and therefore unclergiable, any killing with intent to do serious harm, however described, to which the label 'grievous bodily harm', as defined by Viscount Kilmuir LC in *DPP v Smith* [1960] 3 All ER 161 at 171, [1961] AC 290 at 334, reversing the 'murder by pinprick' doctrine arising from *R v Ashman* (1858) 1 F & F 88, 175 ER 638, could properly have been applied. It would be tedious to pursue the citations all in detail. We were referred successively to 3 Co Inst 47–52, 1 Hale PC 424–477, 1 Hawk PC 85–88, 4Bl Com 191–201, Foster's Discourse on Homicide (Crown Law) 255–267 and 1 East PC 103, 214–233. But the further we went into these passages the more hopeless appeared to be the view that, irrespective of constructive malice, malice aforethought had ever been limited to the intention to kill or endanger life. On the contrary, these authorities reinforced the conclusion arrived at by Stephen's original Note XIV (in the Sturge edition Note VIII). This is the more striking in that the last few lines of the note demonstrate clearly that the possible combined effect of the felony-murder rule and the existence of a statutory crime of felonious wounding was consciously present to the author's mind.

There is a second difficulty in the way of treating Lord Ellenborough's Act as providing the kind of historical watershed demanded by Lord Diplock's speech and contended for in the instant appeal by the appellant's counsel. This consists in the fact that, though the nineteenth century judges might in theory have employed the felony-murder rule to apply to cases where death ensued in the course of a felonious wounding, they do not appear to have done so in fact. No case was cited where they did so. On the contrary, there appears to be no historical discontinuity between criminal jurisprudence before and after 1803. Stephen never so treated the matter (either in his text, or, except in the last few lines, in his Note XIV). It was not so treated in the Australian case of *La Fontaine v R* (1976) 136 CLR 62 (after *Hyam*, but in a jurisdiction in which the constructive malice rule still applied). It was pointed out by counsel for the Crown that the relevant felony created by Lord Ellenborough's Act was limited to cutting or stabbing and did not extend, for example, to beating, which would effectively have excluded the felony-murder doctrine from many cases where death ensued from an act intended to inflict grievous bodily harm. For myself, I think that there is a logical difficulty not based on this narrow point of construction, which prevented the judges from adopting the principle. Felonious wounding intrinsically involves proof by the prosecution of the requisite intention and therefore gives no added force to the earlier law, if I have correctly interpreted the learning before 1803. The way is thus clear on any view to accept as decisive what I myself had always understood to be the law prior to 1957. This is contained in the statement of Lord Goddard CJ representing the court of five judges in *Vickers* [1957] 2 QB 664 at 670; cf [1957] All ER 741 at 743 [p **566**, above].

Appeal dismissed

Notes and questions

1. In *A-G's Reference (No 3 of 1994)* [1997] 3 All ER 936 at 946, [1997] Crim LR 829, HL, in *Powell & Daniels and English* [1997] 4 All ER 545 at 551–552, 549, HL, and in *Woollin* [1998] 4 All ER 103 at 107, [1998] Crim LR 890, HL, Lords Mustill and Steyn criticized what Lord Mustill called the 'conspicuous anomaly', that an intention to cause grievous bodily harm is the mens rea of murder, as an instance of 'constructive crime'—that is, where the mens rea of a lesser offence is sufficient to ground liability for a greater: 'The fault element does not correspond to the conduct leading to the charge, ie the causing of death. A person is liable to conviction for a more serious crime than he foresaw . . . .'. . . . a defendant may be convicted of murder who is in no ordinary sense a murderer.'

'Anomaly' implies something irregular or exceptional. In the context of offences against the person, the murder rule is hardly an anomaly. The law of offences against the person abounds in constructive crime—it appears to be the general rule. Under s 20 of the OAPA 1861, unlawfully and maliciously inflicting gbh, it is enough that D foresaw some harm, not necessarily grievous harm: *DPP v Parmenter*, above, at p **160**. Under s 47, assault occasioning abh, it is not necessary to prove that D foresaw any harm—the mens rea of common assault, a mere summary offence, is enough. Is it correct to describe the murder rule, as Lord Mustill does, as 'a fiction'? Do we pretend that an intention to cause gbh is an intention to kill? Or is this, and the related rules, simply a matter of policy? But is the policy a sound one? Does it allow the conviction of murder of a person 'who is in no ordinary sense a murderer'?

2. The Select Committee of the House of Lords on Murder and Life Imprisonment (1989, HL Paper 78–1) stated:

52. Two main criticisms have been made of the present definition of murder. The first is that it is too broad in so far as it requires the conviction of murder of a person who kills, intending to cause serious bodily harm but not to kill and who may not even foresee the possibility of death occurring...

53. The second criticism is that the definition is too narrow in that it does not cover the killer who displays outrageous recklessness; for example the terrorist who kills by an act done with intent to cause fear of death or injury, but does not intend to cause death or serious, or indeed any, bodily harm.

The Committee recommended that the first criticism be met by implementing the definition of murder proposed by the Law Commission (following the CLRC) in the Draft Code below, p **661**. After considering much evidence, including the argument by Lord Goff of Chieveley in favour of the Scottish concept of 'wicked recklessness' ('The Mental Element in the Crime of Murder' (1988) 104 LQR 30, below) and the reply by Glanville Williams ('The Mens Rea for Murder: Leave it Alone' (1989) 105 LQR 387), the Committee concluded that the proper place for reckless killings in English law was in the law of manslaughter. The principle of the Code definition should not be distorted to deal with the reckless terrorist and other wickedly reckless killers, who will in any event be liable to imprisonment for life (para 76).

Robert Goff, 'The Mental Element in the Crime of Murder'
(1988) 104 LQR 30

.... I turn from intention to kill to intention to cause grievous bodily harm. In *Hyam* Lord Diplock, in a dissenting speech, suggested that the historical basis for the existence of this alternative form of the mental element in murder was unsound; he considered that, if the defendant did not intend to kill, he 'must have intended or foreseen as a likely consequence of his act that human life would be endangered.' But Lord Diplock's historical interpretation was emphatically rejected by the House of Lords in the later case of *Cunningham*. It is now settled by that case, for the time being at least, that this alternative form of the mental element, i.e. intention to cause grievous bodily harm, does indeed exist in English law, and further that (following a statement to the like effect by Viscount Kilmuir in *Smith*) grievous bodily harm means, quite simply, really serious bodily harm.

But the most serious objections exist to this as a form of the mental element in the crime of murder. The most fundamental objection is that the crime of murder is concerned with unlawful killing of a particularly serious kind; and it seems very strange that a man should be called a murderer even though not only did he not intend to kill the victim, but he may even have intended that he should not die. There are cases known to occur where the defendant does indeed intend not to kill but only to cause serious injury—as, for example, in the case of terrorists who punish traitors from their ranks by 'knee-capping' them—shooting them in the knee with a gun. This they do with a positive intent not to kill but to leave the victim maimed, pour encourager les autres. If a man so injured were to die in consequence, perhaps because he contracted an infection from his wound, the man who 'kneecapped' him would, in English law, be held to have murdered him, even though he positively intended not to kill him.

In case the point may be thought to be fanciful, let me give an example from my own practical experience. In certain areas of England there is a horrible practice called 'glassing.' A man takes a pint-size beer glass, knocks the top off on the edge of a table leaving a jagged edge, and then rams the jagged edge into the face of his victim—obviously causing dreadful cuts and scarring to his face. I found myself trying a young man for murder at Nottingham. He had gone out to a local public house with his uncle. They both had too much to drink. Another young man was there, who was regarded as an enemy. 'Glass him!' said the uncle to his nephew, and the boy proceeded to do so. But for some reason—perhaps the victim moved slightly—he caught not his face but the side of his neck, and severed his jugular vein. The victim staggered outside, covered with blood, and died shortly afterwards. The assailant and his uncle were both charged with murder. The facts were beyond dispute. The two defendants were ready to plead guilty to manslaughter; but the prosecution was not prepared to accept the plea, and the trial proceeded on the charge of murder. I summed up to the jury, as was my duty, on the basis that, if the jury were sure that the assailant had intended to kill his victim, or to cause him really serious bodily harm, then they should convict him of murder. The jury acquitted the defendants of murder but convicted them of manslaughter, and I sentenced them accordingly. Now it was plain to me, and must have been plain to the jury, that the assailant did indeed intend to cause the victim really serious bodily harm; yet they could not bring themselves to call him a murderer. This was a feeling with which I entirely sympathised, for the simple reason that, not merely could it never have crossed the assailant's mind that there was any risk of causing death to his victim, but he was horrified when he died. It may interest you to know that a colleague of mine on the English Bench had exactly the same experience in another case involving glassing.

The truth is that, for the reasons I have given, an intent to cause really serious harm should not be of itself sufficient to constitute the mental element in the crime of murder. Considerations such as these have led some law reformers to propose that a gloss should be placed upon this form of mental element. Such was the recommendation of the Criminal Law Revision Committee in its 14th Report (1980), to which I have already referred. I think it right that I should at this stage set out their recommendation in full:

> 'We therefore conclude that it should be murder:
>   (a) if a person, with intent to kill, causes death and
>   (b) if a person causes death by an unlawful act intended to cause serious injury and known by him
>   to involve a risk of causing death.'

In addition, the Committee proposed a third possible category (to meet fears expressed about terrorism) as follows:

> 'That it should be murder if a person causes death by an unlawful act intended to cause fear (of death
> or serious injury) and known to the defendant to involve a risk of causing death.'

It is of course with recommendation (b) that we are at present concerned. To me there are two serious objections to this formulation. The first is that it is restricted to cases where there is an intention to cause serious injury. But why is it so limited? If a defendant does an unlawful act known by him to involve the risk of causing death, it would appear that (on this formulation) it is the knowledge of that risk which renders him a murderer. So what of the case where he only intends to cause a slight injury, or indeed no injury at all, but knows that his action involves a risk of causing death? Why should that be any different? For example, a nick in the skin of a haemophiliac could be as dangerous to life as a more serious wound to a normal man. Again, a man may project some missile in the vicinity of another, not intending harm but realising that there is a risk that, if it strikes some vital part, the other man may die; on the Committee's approach, if the victim was so struck, and died, that could not be murder. The formulation reeks, therefore, of a gloss upon an old but objectionable formula, rather than being a reformulation of the requisite intent. But there is a second objection, that as well as being too narrow (in the sense I have indicated) it is also, in another sense, too wide. The criterion chosen is that the defendant's act is known by him to involve a risk of causing death. But is that enough? For one may recognise a risk, and discount it as unrealistic; one may recognise a risk, and hope to avoid it. If a man does so, should he be called a murderer? For myself, I doubt it. Something more is, I think, required.

The additional suggestion, chosen to meet fears about terrorism, appears to me to be subject to the same objections. Indeed, it leads to the startling consequence that if a terrorist, not intending to cause fear of death or serious injury, but realising that his action involves a risk of causing death, blows up a national monument in order to publicise his cause and thereby kills the night watchman, then that cannot be murder. But I feel that this proposed category should not in any event constitute a separate category; and I also feel that, if one could look deep under the skin of category (b), it might be possible to discern a reformulation which would, on a more satisfactory basis, embrace both category (b) and the additional category designed to deal with terrorist.

[In Scots Law] 'when death results from the perpetration of any serious or dangerous crime, murder may have been committed, although the specific intent to kill be absent. This is so where the crime perpetrated involves either wilful intent to do grave personal injury, or the wilful use of dangerous means implying wicked disregard of consequences to life.'

If this approach is right, then both English and Scots law should abandon intention to cause grievous bodily harm or grave personal injury as constituting of itself a sufficient mental element for the crime of murder, if indeed this be Scots law.

Question

Can the gbh rule be defended as reflecting a general principle that the law imposes an obligation on an attacker to take the unforeseen consequences of his actions (J. Horder, 'Two Histories and Four Hidden Principles of Mens Rea' [1997] 113 LQR 9)? Or as an appropriate response in cases of death caused by an 'attack'? (W. Wilson, 'Murder and the Structure of Homicide' in A. Ashworth and B. Mitchell (eds) *Rethinking English Homicide Law* (2000), at pp 44–46.)

3. REFORM

The Law Commission, in its Report No 290, *Partial Defences to Murder* (2004) urged the government to permit a review of the law of murder. Chapter 2 of that Report provides a useful summary of the defects in the present law: www.lawcom.gov.uk/files/lc290.pdf. The Commission concluded that:

2.74 The present law of murder in England and Wales is a mess. There is both a great need to review the law of murder and every reason to believe that a comprehensive consideration of the offence and the sentencing regime could yield rational and sensible conclusions about a number of issues. These could include the elements which should comprise the substantive offence; what elements, if any, should elevate or reduce the level of culpability; and what should be the appropriate sentencing regime. We recommend that the Law Commission be asked to conduct a review of the law of murder with a view to:

(1) considering the definition of the offence, together with any specific complete or partial defences which may seem appropriate.

(2) considering whether the offence of murder should be further categorised on grounds of aggravation and/or mitigation and if so what those categories should comprise.

(3) in the light of (1) and (2), considering the application of a mandatory life sentence to the offence of murder or to any specific categories of murder.

(4) Examining how each of (1), (2) and (3) may differently be addressed where the offender is a child.

It is anticipated that a review will be completed in the next year.

Consider the Law Commission's summaries of the law of murder in other European jurisdictions below. Which do you consider to offer the most desirable scheme of homicide offences? Why? Which features of the definitions of murder would you like to see adopted in English law?

2.54…

(1) Cyprus distinguishes between premeditated murder and homicide. Premeditation differs from 'malice aforethought'. It is essential to show an intention to cause death, which was formed, and continued to exist, before the time of the act and at the time of acting, despite the opportunity to reflect and desist. There is a mandatory life sentence for premeditated murder.

(2) In Denmark there is a fundamental distinction between intentional homicide and causing another person's death because of negligence. Intentional killing is divided into four categories: a general category, paedocide, homicide committed on request (euthanasia or mercy killing) and genocide. The sentence is between 5 years and life, though a lesser sentence than 5 years can be imposed in extenuating circumstances. The average sentence falls within the 8 to 16 year bracket but there is a small number of life sentences passed each year.

(3) France…*Meurtre* is limited to homicide carried out with the intention of causing death. It does not carry a mandatory life sentence. Intention for this purpose carries broadly the same meaning as intention now carries in English law. There are aggravated forms of murder which carry a mandatory life penalty. They are where the murder is connected with another crime or wrong, or where it is carried out with premeditation, or where the victim falls within a range of specified victims such as relatives, minors, public officials or where the killing was a 'hate crime' based on racism or homophobia.

(4) Germany… The basic homicide offence is killing intentionally (with an intention to kill or cause grievous bodily harm). It carries a sentence ranging from 5 years to life. Murder is defined very narrowly as an intended killing (where there is an intention to cause death) 'out of a lust for killing, [or] in order to satisfy his sexual desires, [or] motivated by greed or other despicable reasons, [or] deviously or cruelly or with means capable of causing widespread mayhem or in order to enable or to cover-up the commission of another crime.' This offence carries a mandatory life sentence.

(5) Italy has an offence of simple intentional homicide supplemented by certain identified aggravating circumstances. The difference between the basic and the aggravated offence is the different minimum lengths of a fixed term of imprisonment. In every case the term is a maximum of 30 years.

(6) In Luxembourg there is a distinction between voluntary and involuntary homicide. Within voluntary homicide, *meurtre* requires an intention to kill whereas *homicide voluntaire* does not. Where there is both an intention to kill and premeditation the offence is *assassination*. There are also distinctions based on the means of killing, the circumstances of the killing and the status of the victim. The sentencing structure operates by specifying a particular sentence for a type of crime but it can be reduced either compulsorily, where certain extenuating circumstances are established, or at the judge's discretion for other extenuating circumstances.

(7) In Malta there is a distinction between wilful, justifiable and involuntary homicide. 'Wilful' homicide requires malice and an intent to kill or to put the life of the other in manifest jeopardy. It carries a mandatory life sentence.

(8) In the Netherlands there is a distinction between intentionally taking a person's life and causing the death of another. Within each of these divisions there are subcategories. Within the former there are distinctions between: (a) a person who acts with full knowledge; (b) a person who must have foreseen that the primary though undesired result (death) was inevitable; and (c) a person who is indifferent whether the primary, though undesired, result (death) will follow or not. The sentence is at large.

(9) In Norway the main criterion for distinguishing is between negligence, intent or premeditation. The main use of this distinction is for sentencing. The sentence for murder ranges from a minimum of 6 months to 21 years. Sentences for premeditated killing are on average 15.2 years and for intentional killings, 7.3 years.

(10) In Spain there are three categories of intentional homicide: Parricide, where the victim is a blood or marriage relative, carries a penalty of between 20 and 30 years. Murder, where the death of the person falls within one of the following circumstances (1) by treachery, (2) for a price, (3) by means of inundation, fire, poison or explosive, (4) with proved premeditation, (5) by aggravated brutality, deliberately and cruelly increasing the pain of the victim, carries a penalty between 26 and 30 years. Homicide where none of these elements are present, carries a penalty between 12 and 20 years. There are also three levels of non-intentional homicide which range from recklessness (penalty six months to six years), to negligence without breaking any rules, for which the penalty is a fine or reprimand.

(11) In Sweden there is a distinction between murder and manslaughter. The distinction seems to be a matter for the judge in each case, depending on intentions, motives and the way the defendant acted. The sentence is at large including a discretionary life sentence.

(12) In Switzerland the basic offence of *meurtre* is for intentional killing and carries a sentence of at least 5 years, up to a maximum of 20. There is an aggravated offence of *assassination* which is *meurtre* plus one of a number of aggravating features: premeditation, depravity, where the defendant is particularly dangerous by reference to the means used, the level of cruelty or treachery, the motives, relationship with the deceased, or the presence or absence of remorse. This offence carries a presumptive life sentence subject to extenuating circumstances.

(13) In Turkey homicide requires intent to kill, defined as a willing and conscious desire to commit homicide and to expect its consequences. The penalty for the basic offence is 24–30 years. The offence can be aggravated based on the identity of the victim: family, or member of the National Assembly or civil servant on duty and the motive (premeditation in pursuit of or avoiding detection of crime). Matters such as provocation are taken into account in deciding punishment.

FURTHER READING

H. BRIGGS, *Euthanasia, Death with Dignity and the Law* (2002)

I. M. KENNEDY, 'Alive or Dead?' (1969) 22 CLP 102

I. M. KENNEDY, 'Switching Off Life Support Machines' [1977] Crim LR 443

I. M. KENNEDY and A. GRUBB, *Medical Law Text with Materials* (2000), chs 16, 17, 18 and references therein

B. MITCHELL, 'Culpably Indifferent Murder' (1996) 25 Anglo Am LR 64

B. MITCHELL, 'Public Perceptions of Homicide and Criminal Justice' (1998) 38 Cr J Crim 453

B. MITCHELL, 'Further Evidence of the Relationship Between Legal and Public Opinion on the Homicide Law' [2000] Crim LR 814

J. TEMKIN, 'Pre-natal Injury, Homicide and the Draft Criminal Code' [1986] CLJ 414

W. WILSON, 'Murder and the Structure of Homicide' in A. Ashworth and B. Mitchell (eds) *Rethinking English Homicide Law* (2000)

18

Manslaughter

Manslaughter is a complex crime of no fewer than six varieties. It covers three cases where the defendant kills with the fault required for murder but, because of the presence of a particular extenuating circumstance recognized by law, the offence is reduced to manslaughter. These cases are traditionally known as 'voluntary manslaughter'. The other cases—'involuntary manslaughter'—consist of homicides committed with a fault element less than that required for murder but recognized by the common law as sufficient to found liability for homicide. It should be emphasized that there is only one offence. Whether the defendant is guilty of the voluntary or the involuntary variety, he is convicted simply of manslaughter. The only qualification to this is that, where diminished responsibility has been left to the jury, it is the practice for the judge to invite the jury to inform him when giving their verdict of guilty of manslaughter whether it is on that ground. A life sentence is mandatory for murder but for manslaughter the maximum is life and there is no minimum. It is an offence which may be committed with a wide variety of culpability and sometimes may be properly dealt with by a fine or a conditional or absolute discharge.

The law might be summarized as follows:

A person is guilty of manslaughter where:

(a) he kills or is a party to the killing of another with the fault required for murder (p **560**, above) but he acted:
 (i) under diminished responsibility (Homicide Act 1957, s 2, below); or
 (ii) under provocation (Homicide Act 1957, s 3, p **585**, below); or
 (iii) in pursuance of a suicide pact (Homicide Act 1957, s 4, p **618**, below); or

(b) he is not guilty of murder by reason only of the fact that, because of voluntary intoxication, he lacked the fault required (p **190**, above); or

(c) he kills another:
 (i) by an unlawful and dangerous act (p **622**, below); or
 (ii) being grossly negligent as to death; or
 (iii) being reckless (in the *Cunningham* sense) as to death or serious bodily harm (p **659**, below).

1. DIMINISHED RESPONSIBILITY

Homicide Act 1957, s 2

(1) Where a person kills or is a party to the killing of another, he shall not he convicted of murder if he was suffering from such abnormality of mind (whether arising from a condition of

arrested or retarded development of mind or any inherent causes or induced by disease or injury) as substantially impaired his mental responsibility for his acts and omissions in doing or being a party to the killing.

(2) On a charge of murder, it shall be for the defence to prove that the person charged is by virtue of this section not liable to be convicted of murder.

(3) A person who but for this section would be liable, whether as principal or as accessory, to be convicted of murder shall be liable instead to be convicted of manslaughter.

(4) The fact that one party to a killing is by virtue of this section not liable to be convicted of murder shall not affect the question whether the killing amounted to murder in the case of any other party to it.

R v Byrne

[1960] 3 All ER 1, Court of Criminal Appeal

(Lord Parker CJ, Hilbery and Diplock JJ)

[**Lord Parker CJ** read the following judgment of the court:]

The appellant was convicted of murder before Stable J at Birmingham Assizes and sentenced to imprisonment for life. The victim was a young woman whom he strangled in the YWCA hostel, and after her death he committed horrifying mutilations on her dead body. The facts as to the killing were not disputed, and were admitted in a long statement made by the appellant. The only defence was that in killing his victim the appellant was suffering from diminished responsibility as defined by s2 of the Homicide Act 1957, and was accordingly guilty, not of murder, but of manslaughter.

Three medical witnesses were called by the defence, the senior medical officer at Birmingham prison and two specialists in psychological medicine. Their uncontradicted evidence was that the appellant was a sexual psychopath, that he suffered from abnormality of mind, as, indeed, was abundantly clear from the other evidence in the case, and that such abnormality of mind arose from a condition of arrested or retarded development of mind or inherent causes. The nature of the abnormality of mind of a sexual psychopath, according to the medical evidence, is that he suffers from violent perverted sexual desires which he finds it difficult or impossible to control. Save when under the influence of his perverted sexual desires, he may be normal. All three doctors were of opinion that the killing was done under the influence of his perverted sexual desires, and, although all three were of opinion that he was not insane in the technical sense of insanity laid down in the rules in *M'Naghten's Case* [see p **374** above], it was their view that his sexual psychopathy could properly be described as partial insanity.

In his summing-up the learned judge, after summarising the medical evidence, gave to the jury a direction of law, on the correctness of which this appeal turns. He told the jury that, if on the evidence they came to the conclusion that the facts could be fairly summarised as follows:

'(i) from an early age [the appellant] has been subject to these perverted, violent desires and in some cases has indulged his desires; (ii) the impulse or urge of these desires is stronger than normal impulse or urge of sex to such an extent that the subject finds it very difficult or perhaps impossible in some cases to resist putting the desire into practice; (iii) the act of killing this girl was done under such impulse or urge; and (iv) setting aside these sexual addictions and practices, [the appellant] was normal in every other respect'

—those facts, with nothing more, would not bring a case within the section and 'do not constitute such abnormality of mind as substantially to impair a man's mental responsibility for his acts'. He went on to say:

'In other words, mental affliction is one thing. The section is there to protect them. The section is not there to give protection where there is nothing else than what is vicious and depraved.'

Taken by themselves those last words are unobjectionable, but it is contended on behalf of the appellant that the direction, taken as a whole, involves a misconstruction of the section, and had the effect of withdrawing from the jury an issue of fact which it was peculiarly their province to decide.

Section 2 of the Homicide Act 1957, is dealing with the crime of murder in which there are, at common law, two essential elements: (i) the physical act of killing another person, and (ii) the state of mind of the person who kills or is a party to the killing, namely, his intention to kill or to cause grievous bodily harm. Section 2(1) does not deal with the first element. It modified the existing law as respects the second element, that is, the state of mind of the person who kills or is a party to a killing. Before the passing of the Homicide Act 1957, a person who killed or was party to a killing could escape liability for murder—as for any other crime requiring mens rea—if he showed that at the time of the killing he was insane within the meaning of the M'Naghten Rules [see p **374**, above], that is,

> '... that ... [he] was labouring under such a defect of reason, from disease of the mind, as not to know the nature and quality of the act he was doing; or, if he did know it, that he did not know he was doing what was wrong.'

If established, this defence negatives mens rea and the accused was, and still is, entitled to a special verdict of 'guilty of the act but insane' at the time of doing the act, which is an acquittal of any crime. The test is a rigid one: it relates solely to a person's intellectual ability to appreciate (a) the physical act that he is doing, and (b) whether it is wrong. If he has such intellectual ability, his power to control his physical acts by exercise of his will is irrelevant.

The ability of the accused to control his physical acts by exercise of his will was relevant before the passing of the Homicide Act 1957, in one case only: that of provocation. Loss of self-control on the part of the accused so as to make him for the moment not master of his mind had the effect of reducing murder to manslaughter if (i) it was induced by an act or series of acts done by the deceased to the accused, and (ii) such act or series of acts would have induced a reasonable man to lose his self-control and act in the same manner as the accused acted (see *Duffy* [[1949] 1 All ER 932n]). Whether loss of self-control induced by provocation negatived the ordinary presumption that a man intended the natural ordinary consequences of his physical acts so that in such a case the prosecution had failed to prove the essential mental element in murder (namely, that the accused intended to kill or to inflict grievous bodily harm) is academic for the purposes of our consideration. What is relevant is that loss of self-control has always been recognised as capable of reducing murder to manslaughter, but that the criterion has always been the degree of self-control which would be exercised by a reasonable man, that is to say, a man with a normal mind.

It is against that background of the existing law that s 2(1) of the Homicide Act 1957, falls to be construed. To satisfy the requirements of the subsection the accused must show (a) that he was suffering from an abnormality of mind, and (b) that such abnormality of mind (i) arose from a condition of arrested or retarded development of mind or any inherent causes or was induced by disease or injury, and (ii) was such as substantially impaired his mental responsibility for his acts in doing or being a party to the killing. 'Abnormality of mind', which has to be contrasted with the time-honoured expression in the M'Naghten Rules 'defect of reason', means a state of mind so different from that of ordinary human beings that the reasonable man would term it abnormal. It appears to us to be wide enough to cover the mind's activities in all its aspects, not only the perception of physical acts and matters and the ability to form a rational judgment whether an act is right or wrong, but also the ability to exercise will-power to control physical acts in accordance with that rational judgment. The expression 'mental responsibility for his acts' points to a consideration of the extent to which the accused's mind is answerable for his physical acts which must include a consideration of the extent of his ability to exercise will-power to control his physical acts.

Whether the accused was at the time of the killing suffering from any 'abnormality of mind' in the broad sense which we have indicated above is a question for the jury. On this question medical evidence is, no doubt, of importance, but the jury are entitled to take into consideration all the evidence including the acts or statements of the accused and his demeanour. They are not bound to accept the medical evidence if there is other material before them which, in their good judgment, conflicts with it and outweighs it. The aetiology of the abnormality of mind (namely, whether it arose from a condition of arrested or retarded development of mind or any inherent causes or was induced by disease or injury) does, however, seem to be a matter to be determined on expert evidence. Assuming that the jury are satisfied on the balance of probabilities that the accused was suffering from 'abnormality of mind' from one of the causes specified in the parenthesis of the subsection, the crucial question nevertheless arises: Was the abnormality such as substantially impaired his mental responsibility for his acts in doing or being a party to the killing? This is a question of degree and essentially one for the jury. Medical evidence is, of course, relevant but the question involves a decision, not merely whether there was some impairment of the mental responsibility of the accused for his acts, but whether such impairment can properly be called 'substantial', a matter on which juries may quite legitimately differ from doctors.

Furthermore, in a case where the abnormality of mind is one which affects the accused's self-control, the step between 'he did not resist his impulse' and 'he could not resist his impulse' is, as the evidence in this case shows, one which is incapable of scientific proof. A fortiori, there is no scientific measurement of the degree of difficulty which an abnormal person finds in controlling his impulses. These problems, which in the present state of medical knowledge are scientifically insoluble, the jury can only approach in a broad, common sense way. This court has repeatedly approved directions to the jury which have followed directions given in Scots cases where the doctrine of diminished responsibility forms part of the common law. We need not repeat them. They are quoted in *Spriggs* [[1958] 1 QB 270, [1958] 1 All ER 300]. They indicate that such abnormality as 'substantially impairs his mental responsibility' involves a mental state which in popular language (not that of M'Naghten Rules) a jury would regard as amounting to partial insanity or being on the borderline of insanity.

It appears to us that the learned judge's direction to the jury that the defence under s2 of the Act was not available, even though they found the facts set out in No (ii) and No (iii) of the learned judge's summary [see p **578**, above], amounted to a direction that difficulty or even inability of an accused person to exercise will-power to control his physical acts could not amount to such abnormality of mind as substantially impaired his mental responsibility. For the reasons which we have already expressed, we think that this construction of the Act is wrong. Inability to exercise will-power to control physical acts, provided that it is due to abnormality of mind from one of the causes specified in the parenthesis in the subsection, is, in our view, sufficient to entitle the accused to the benefit of the section; difficulty in controlling his physical acts, depending on the degree of difficulty, may be. It is for the jury to decide on the whole of the evidence whether such inability or difficulty has, not as a matter of scientific certainty but on the balance of probabilities, been established and, in the case of difficulty, whether the difficulty is so great as to amount in their view to a substantial impairment of the accused's mental responsibility for his acts. The direction in the present case thus withdrew from the jury the essential determination of fact which it was their province to decide.

As already indicated, the medical evidence as to the appellant's ability to control his physical acts at the time of the killing was all one way. The evidence of the revolting circumstances of the killing and the subsequent mutilations, as of the previous sexual history of the appellant, pointed, we think, plainly, to the conclusion that the appellant was what would be described in ordinary language as on the border-line of insanity or partially insane. Properly directed, we do not think that the jury could have come to any other conclusion than that the defence under s 2 of the Homicide Act 1957, was made out. The appeal will be allowed and a verdict of manslaughter substituted for the verdict of murder. The only possible sentence, having regard to the tendencies of the appellant, is imprisonment for life. The sentence will, accordingly, not be disturbed.

Appeal allowed
Sentence confirmed

R. Mackay, 'The Abnormality of Mind Factor in Diminished Responsibility'
[1999] Crim LR 117
writes:

This dictum [in *Byrne*] has had a profound effect on the development of diminished responsibility, for by permitting psychiatric evidence of sexual psychopathy to be admitted as a form of abnormality of mind, irresistible Impulse was introduced into English law. Further, since the decision in *Byrne*, the courts have been willing in many cases to accept a whole range of less serious mental conditions as falling within 'abnormality of mind' in order to ensure a lenient sentence or disposal. Indeed, in his assessment of such cases, particularly those relating to mercy-killing, Glanville Williams remarked that while 'One may question whether leniency has not sometimes gone too far ... there can be no doubt of the beneficial effect of the defence in [such] cases. Here it is invariably accepted by the jury on the flimsiest medical evidence, and thankfully used by the judge as a reason for leniency'. (Williams, *Textbook of Criminal Law* (2nd edn, 1983), p.693.)

Barbara Wootton, *Crime and the Criminal Law*, p 74, comments on *Byrne*

Apart from admiration of the optimism which expects common sense to make good the deficiencies of science, it is only necessary to add that the problem would seem to be insoluble, not merely in the present, but indeed in any, state of medical knowledge. Improved medical knowledge may certainly be expected to give better insight into the origins of mental abnormalities, and better predictions as to the probability that particular types of individuals will in fact 'control their physical acts' or make 'rational judgments'; but neither medical nor any other science can ever hope to prove whether a man who does not resist his impulses does not do so because he cannot or because he will not. The propositions of science are by definition subject to empirical validation; but since it is not possible to get inside another man's skin, no objective criterion which can distinguish between 'he did not' and 'he could not' is conceivable.

Logic, experience and the Lord Chief Justice [ie *Parker*] thus all appear to lead to the same conclusion—that is to say, to the impossibility of establishing any reliable measure of responsibility in the sense of a man's ability to have acted otherwise than as he did. After all, every one of us can say with St Paul (who, as far as I am aware, is not generally suspected of diminished responsibility) 'the good that I would I do not: but the evil which I would not, that I do'.

Questions

1. Is it true that we can never be satisfied beyond reasonable doubt that a person could have resisted an impulse to commit crime? Is it a good reason for not acting on such a belief that it cannot be scientifically validated?

2. Are all people who commit murder suffering from some degree of abnormality of mind?

3. In dealing with a person who is not alleged to be mentally abnormal, a jury can draw on its own experience in deciding what he must have known or foreseen, and whether he could have chosen to act differently. Is this so in the case of a person alleged to be mentally abnormal? Is it justifiable to draw conclusions as to the validity of theories of

criminal responsibility generally from an analysis of cases concerned with diminished responsibility?

4. If an accused person proves that he did not merely find it difficult, but that he was *unable* to control his acts, is his responsibility merely 'diminished'? Should such a person be convicted of manslaughter?

5. What do the bracketed words 'whether arising from a condition of arrested or retarded development of mind or any inherent causes or induced by disease or injury' mean? In *Sanderson* (1994) 98 Cr App R 325, S killed his girlfriend during a violent argument by hitting her around 100 times with a cricket bat and a hockey stick. The prosecution psychiatrist suggested that any paranoia suffered by the accused resulted from the effect of drug abuse; the defence psychiatrist testified that S suffered from mental illness, in the form of a paranoid psychosis arising from inherent causes, namely his upbringing and amounted to an abnormality of mind. The Court of Appeal substituted a verdict of manslaughter. Roch LJ stated that:

Cases of diminished responsibility can become difficult and confusing for a jury, and it is important that the judge in directing the jury should tailor his directions to suit the facts of the particular case. We think it will rarely be helpful to the jury to read to them section 2(1) in its entirety.

Notes

Intoxication and mental abnormality. Cases where D was suffering from a mental abnormality and was to some degree intoxicated when he killed have caused particular difficulty. In *Dietschmann* [2003] 1 AC 1209, [2003] Crim LR 550, D killed the victim while he (D) was heavily intoxicated. He was also suffering from a mental abnormality which all the medical witnesses described as an adjustment disorder arising from a 'depressed grief reaction' to the death of his aunt with whom he had a close physical and emotional relationship. D was convicted of murder on a jury direction that D had to satisfy them that if he had not taken the drink he would have killed as he did and that he would have been under diminished responsibility when he did so. The House of Lords held that this was misdirection.

Lord Hutton, stressed that this case did not involve alcohol dependence syndrome. As such, his lordship was confident that:

the meaning to be given to the subsection would appear on first consideration to be reasonably clear .... [I]f the defendant satisfies the jury that, notwithstanding the alcohol he had consumed and its effect on him, his abnormality of mind substantially impaired his mental responsibility for his acts in doing the killing, the jury should find him ... guilty of manslaughter. I take this view because I think that in referring to substantial impairment of mental responsibility, the subsection does not require the abnormality of mind to be the sole cause of the defendant's acts in doing the killing. In my opinion, even if the defendant would not have killed if he had not taken drink, the causative effect of the drink does not necessarily prevent an abnormality of mind suffered by the defendant from substantially impairing his mental responsibility for his fatal acts.

Lord Hutton addressed the policy arguments against this interpretation, and concluded that a brain-damaged person who is intoxicated and who commits a killing is not in the same position as a person who is intoxicated, but not brain-damaged, and who commits a killing. The test is now appropriately focused on the overriding question whether the defendant would have killed and had a substantial impairment of his mental responsibility at that time. The jury will need help from expert evidence on the defendant's abnormality of mind when sober. See also J. Tolmie, 'Alcoholism and Criminal Liability' (2001) MLR 688; F. Bowland, 'Intoxication and Criminal Liability' (1986) J Crim Law 100.

(1) THE USE OF THE DEFENCE

Professor Mackay conducted empirical research for the Law Commission (Report No 290, *Partial Defences to Murder* (2004)), in which of the 157 cases studied, the prosecution accepted a diminished responsibility plea in 77.1 per cent of cases (para 5.4). In 2001/2002 there were 15 successful pleas.

(2) REFORM OF THE LAW

The Law Commission Report No 290, *Partial Defences to Murder* (2004)

The Commission found that there was, on consultation, 'overwhelming support from those consultees who addressed the issue for the retention of a partial defence of diminished responsibility for as long as there is the mandatory life sentence for murder'

Arguments in favour of retention of the defence of diminished responsibility

5.18 The main rationale which underlies the body of opinion favouring retention of diminished responsibility, even if the mandatory life sentence were to be abolished, can be summed up in the phrase 'fair and just labelling'. Consultees frequently expressed the view that it is unjust to label as murderers those not fully responsible for their actions. Some consultees referred to the stigma which attaches to a conviction for murder, the most serious of all crimes. According to those consultees, the reason why it is unjust is that their *culpability* is diminished.

Reduced culpability should be reflected in 'fair and just labelling' and not just by mitigation of sentence.

5.19 This rationale merits two comments. First, the frequent reference to culpability is problematic because, traditionally, English law has employed the concept of mens rea (in conjunction with actus reus), and in particular the distinction between intention and subjective recklessness, as a means of assessing culpability and labelling conduct. Murder stands at the apex of offences of physical violence because of the requirement of intent attached to the actus reus of unlawful killing. The partial defences represent an exception to the general approach precisely because they only come into play if the jury is satisfied beyond reasonable doubt that the defendant committed the conduct element and had the mens rea of murder. Further, they are not a complete defence exculpating the defendant from all liability. Some would maintain that, for this reason, these partial defences are anomalous and owe their existence solely to the respective mandatory sentencing regimes, which have always existed for murder.

5.20 Professor Ronnie Mackay recognised the contradiction, namely that diminished responsibility allows a defendant to be convicted of one offence when he has the mens rea, and, on the traditional analysis, the culpability of another and more serious offence but stated:

> 'There is, in my view, a clear moral distinction between murder and a diminished responsibility killing despite the presence of the mens rea of the former offence ... what is needed is a newly crafted plea which more appropriately reflects this moral distinction.'

5.21 Second, if the defence is necessary and desirable for labelling purposes, why should it be confined to the offence of murder? If the person who kills with the mens rea of murder can and should be labelled as somebody other than a murderer because of reduced responsibility, then why not the person who is guilty of attempted murder (with its stricter mens rea requirement) or who inflicts grievous bodily harm with intent . . .

5.22 Apart from the need to ensure fair and just labelling, a number of other factors were mentioned in individual responses:
- the out-dated nature of the insanity defence as contained in the M'Naghten Rules. The narrowness of the Rules, in the sense of their preoccupation with cognitive understanding, is seen as reinforcing the need for a partial defence of diminished responsibility. In addition, the stigma which attaches to being labelled 'insane' makes defendants reluctant to plead insanity;
- the need to enable jurors to convict a defendant of a homicide offence in cases where, if the only conviction open to them was for murder, they might otherwise (perversely) acquit altogether;
- the importance of ensuring that the issue, which goes to the culpability of the defendant, is determined by a jury and not by the judge as part of the sentencing process;
- the need to ensure public confidence in sentencing. Sentences passed by judges following a finding by a jury that the defendant is guilty of manslaughter by reason of diminished responsibility are more likely to find public acceptance than sentences passed following a conviction for murder;
- the need in a disputed case for a jury, rather than a judge, to determine between experts whether responsibility is diminished;
- the fact that diminished responsibility is presently often the only defence to murder available to abused women 'driven to kill';
- the fact that the defence may enable a merciful but just disposition of certain types of case where all parties consider it meets the justice of the case.

. . . .

Arguments against retention of the defence of diminished responsibility
5.43 A significant minority of consultees, particularly amongst the judiciary, favoured the abolition of the defence provided that the mandatory life sentence was abolished. The arguments for adopting this view were not entirely uniform but can be summarised as follows:

- *logically*, as diminished responsibility reduces the defendant's *responsibility* for the killing, it ought to be viewed as a mitigating factor rather than a partial defence in a case where, by definition, the defendant's level of *culpability* is established by reference to the traditional concepts of conduct and mens rea.
- the issues addressed by the defence are matters of mitigation, which go to sentence. Instead, they have been, in the words of Buxton LJ, 'artificially forced into the straightjacket of substantive liability'. The defence was introduced to 'sanitise the worst aspects of capital punishment';
- there are insuperable definitional problems. The definition contained in section 2 is 'disastrous' and 'beyond redemption';
- the 'chaos of the present law' which has enabled the smuggling in of mercy is a very poor substitute for the rational sentencing exercise that could be undertaken, as in any other case of mental illness or social dislocation, once the mandatory sentence goes;
- the defence is 'grossly abused' and whether a defendant finds a psychiatrist who will be prepared to testify that, for example, depression was responsible for his behaviour is 'a lottery';

. . .

Conclusion

5.47 We are not persuaded that it is desirable to come to a final view about diminished responsibility in advance of a comprehensive review of the law of murder and the sentencing regime. A decision on the need for a partial defence of diminished responsibility can only sensibly be taken as a part of that review.

...

The Law Commission's final recommendation was for a defence drafted as follows:

A person, who would otherwise be guilty of murder, is not guilty of murder but of manslaughter if, at the time of the act or omission causing death,

(1) that person's capacity to:
  (a) understand events; or
  (b) judge whether his actions were right or wrong; or
  (c) control himself,

was substantially impaired by an abnormality of mental functioning arising from an underlying condition and

(2) the abnormality was a significant cause of the defendant's conduct in carrying out or taking part in the killing.

'Underlying condition' means a pre-existing mental or physiological condition other than of a transitory kind.

Question

Is this test any more specific than s 2? Is it any less likely to be relied upon and applied as a general and flexible defence to murder for those suffering some abnormality of mind?

2. PROVOCATION

Homicide Act 1957, s 3

Where on a charge of murder there is evidence on which the jury can find that the person charged was provoked (whether by things done or by things said or by both together) to lose his self-control, the question whether the provocation was enough to make a reasonable man do as he did shall be left to be determined by the jury; and in determining that question the jury shall take into account everything both done and said according to the effect which, in their opinion, it would have on a reasonable man.

Where the issue of provocation is raised, the jury should first be asked to consider whether D was in fact provoked to lose his self-control (the subjective condition); and, if so, then to consider whether the provocation was enough to make a reasonable man do as he did (the objective condition). The issue is raised whenever evidence is admitted which might lead a jury to think it is possible that D was provoked to lose his self-control, whether D has relied on the defence of provocation or not. Where there is such evidence, counsel on both sides have a duty to point it out to the judge: *Cox* [1995] 2 Cr App R 513, [1995] Crim LR 741.

(1) PROVOCATIVE ACTS OR WORDS

Any acts or words may be provocation: *R v Doughty* (1986) 83 Cr App R 319, CA. D's wife gave birth to her child. On being discharged from hospital, she remained in bed on medical advice. D looked after W, baby and the house. He was a conscientious father, but became fatigued. Some 17 days after its birth, the baby was found dead. It seems that on the night of its death the baby had cried consistently, despite being fed, changed and cared for. D lost his temper and tried to silence the child by covering its head with cushions and kneeling on them. The baby died. The trial judge refused to allow the jury to consider the provocation of the baby's persistent crying. The Court of Appeal allowed the appeal: s 3 is mandatory in its requirement that if there is a causal link between 'something', such as the baby crying, and the response of D, the jury must be left that 'something' in considering the objective question. The court rejected an argument that the decision would open the floodgates: the decision did not mean that baby-killers would easily be able to avoid conviction for murder on the basis of provocation '. . . because reliance can be placed upon the common sense of juries upon who the task of deciding the issue is imposed by section 3 and that common sense will ensure that only in cases where the facts fully justified it would their verdict be likely to be that they would hold a defendant's act in killing a crying child would be the response of a reasonable man within the section' per Stocker LJ at p 326.

There must be some acts or words that may have provoked the accused: *Acott* [1997] 2 Cr App R 94. The Court of Appeal (Criminal Division) in *Acott* certified that there was a point of law of public importance involved in the decision to dismiss the appeal namely: 'In a prosecution for murder, before the judge is obliged to leave the issue of provocation to the jury, must there be some evidence, either direct or inferential as to what was either done or said to provoke the alleged loss of self-control?' The House of Lords observed:

Strictly, the certified question need not be answered in order to dispose of the appeal. But it seems possible to summarise the legal position in terms which might be helpful. Section 3 is only applicable if there is evidence . . . that the person charged was provoked (whether by things done or things said or by both together) to lose his self-control. A loss of self-control caused by fear, panic, sheer bad temper or circumstances (e.g. a slow down of traffic due to snow) would not be enough. There must be some evidence tending to show that the killing might have been an uncontrolled reaction to provoking conduct rather than an act of revenge. Moreover, although there is no longer a rule of proportionality as between provocation and retaliation, the concept of proportionality is nevertheless still an important factual element in the objective inquiry. It necessarily requires of the jury an assessment of the seriousness of the provocation. It follows that there can only be an issue of provocation to be considered by the jury if the judge considers that there is some evidence of a specific act or words of provocation resulting in a loss of self-control. (Per Lord Steyn at p 312.)

Questions

1. D arrives at work and is so angered by the bad weather and the fact that he has no holiday entitlement left, that he loses his temper and pushes the first person he sees down the stairs to his death. Can he plead provocation? Is he any more blameworthy than a person in the same position who responds in like fashion to a colleague's pompous email?

2. What is the law seeking to do by providing the defence of provocation? Protect against the harshness of murder? Label correctly a distinct category of killer?

(2) A SUDDEN AND TEMPORARY LOSS OF SELF-CONTROL

In *Duffy* [1949] 1 All ER 932n, Devlin J as he then was gave an explanation of this first limb of the defence which has subsequently been approved by the Court of Criminal Appeal:

Provocation is some act or series of acts done by the dead man to the accused which would cause in any reasonable person and actually causes in the accused, a sudden and temporary loss of self-control, rendering the accused so subject to passion as to make him for the moment not master of his mind.

That passage refers to 'a sudden and temporary loss of self-control', which has to be of such a kind as to make the accused for the moment not master of his mind. Later in the same summing up, in another passage which was also approved by the Court of Criminal Appeal in *Duffy* Devlin J stated that:

Indeed, circumstances which induce a desire for revenge are inconsistent with provocation, since the conscious formulation of a desire for revenge means that a person has had time to think, to reflect, and that would negative a sudden temporary loss of self-control, which is of the essence of provocation.

Notes and questions

1. The court was seeking to distinguish revenge killings (planned, premeditated and deserving of punishment) from spontaneous killings by someone out of control (less blameworthy). The test provided by Devlin suggests that the longer the period to cool off and calm down the more likely the killing is not a revenge killing. But is this assumption borne out by psychological/physiological evidence? See P. Brett, 'The Physiology of Provocation' [1970] Crim LR 634. Do some people get gradually more angry over time? This slow burn is apparently more likely in cases of battered women who kill their abusive spouse (see below).

2. In *Cocker* [1989] Crim LR 740, CA, H for 11 years had looked after W, his wife, who was suffering from an incapacitating and incurable disease. Repeatedly W requested H to kill her. Eventually, during one sleepless night she continually scratched him and kept saying, 'You promised me, you bastard.' Finally H put a pillow over W's face and asphyxiated her. He surrendered to the police and kept saying, 'It was the last straw.' It was held that there was no evidence that H had been provoked to lose his self-control. Cf P. R. Taylor 'Provocation and Mercy Killing' [1991] Crim LR 111.

3. In *Ibrams and Gregory* (1981) 74 Cr App R 154, CA, the appellants and a young woman, A, had been bullied and terrorized by Monk over a period up to and including Sunday 7 October. They had been unable to obtain effective police protection. Anticipating that there would be a repetition of Monk's behaviour on Sunday 14 October, on Wednesday 10 October the three made a plan. On Sunday Monk was to be got drunk and encouraged to take A to his bed. She would slip the catch on the door and leave a signal for the appellants who would attack him and break his arms and legs. The plan was carried out meticulously and Monk was killed. The appellants were convicted of murder. They appealed on the ground that the judge had wrongly withdrawn the defence of provocation from the jury.

Delivering the judgment of the court dismissing the appeal, Lawton LJ said (at p 159):

Here the last act of provocation was on Sunday, 7 October. It was not in any way suggested that the dead man had provoked anybody on the night of his death. In fact, when Gregory and Ibrams went into the bedroom he was asleep. The first blow he received was inflicted on him by Gregory, and it dazed him but did not knock him unconscious. He was able to sit up in bed, and he was then attacked by Ibrams. Nothing happened on the night of the killing which caused Ibrams to lose his self-control. There having been a plan to kill Monk, his evidence that when he saw him all the past came to his mind does not, in our judgment, provide any evidence of loss of self-control.

In our judgment, the matter is really concluded by the summing-up to the jury of Devlin J (as he then was) [his lordship quoted from *Duffy* above].

4. In the passage cited Lawton LJ says, 'Nothing happened on the night of the killing which caused Ibrams to lose self-control.' This may suggest that the provocative conduct must immediately precede the loss of self-control but s 3 says the jury must take account of 'everything' (that is, all the provocative conduct) and in *Ahluwalia* [1992] 4 All ER 889, CA, the court said,

We accept that the subjective element in the defence of provocation would not as a matter of law be negatived simply because of the delayed reaction in such cases, provided that there was at the time of the killing a 'sudden and temporary loss of self-control' caused by the alleged provocation. However, the longer the delay and the stronger the evidence of deliberation on the part of the defendant, the more likely it will be that the prosecution will negative provocation.

(See D. Nicholson and R. Sanghvi, 'Battered Women and Provocation: The Implications of R v Ahluwalia' [1993] Crim LR 728.)

5. In *Thornton* [1992] 1 All ER 306, D was convicted of murder of her husband, a heavy drinker and a possessive and jealous man. During their marriage of some 10 months he had behaved violently towards her. Following a row about his drinking, during which he called D a whore, she went to the kitchen and sharpened a carving knife with which she returned, she said, for her protection. After further abusive exchanges she stabbed him. She called an ambulance and the police. She told the police she wanted to kill him and said 'Let him die.' It was unsuccessfully argued that the judge had misdirected the jury by telling them there must have been a 'sudden' loss of self-control and that Devlin J's words in *Duffy*, above, were no longer appropriate where a person had been subjected to a long course of provocative violence.

In every such case the question for the jury is whether at the moment the fatal blow was struck the accused had been deprived for that moment of the self-control which previously he or she had been able to exercise.

Thornton's conviction was quashed on receipt of fresh evidence: *Thornton (No 2)* [1996] 2 Cr App R 108.

6. What has to be 'sudden and temporary' is the loss of self-control, *not* the provocation which may, in point of theory, precede the loss of self-control by any length of time so long as, at the time of the killing, it precipitates the loss of self-control. All s 3 appears to require is a loss of self-control at the time of the killing. It may accordingly be a misdirection to confine the jury's attention to events immediately surrounding the killing. The jury should be directed to consider relevant anterior conduct of the deceased (for example, his physical abuse of D) because this may make credible the loss of self-control at the time of the killing on a 'last straw' basis; the significance of the final act of provocation can be properly assessed only in light of the anterior conduct: *Humphreys* [1995] 4 All ER 1008, CA. Nor, in point of theory, is there a limit to the 'temporary' period during which D has lost his self-control. D may lose his self-control for seconds, minutes or even hours. In *Baillie* [1995] 2 Cr App R 31, [1995] Crim LR 739, CA, D, on learning that V, a drugs dealer who had been supplying D's son, had threatened the son would 'get a slap' if the son sought to get his drugs from any other dealer, took a shotgun and a razor and drove to V's house. There D inflicted serious injuries on V with the razor and, as V fled, D fired at him and V was killed by particles blasted from a wire fence by the shots. It was held that the trial judge had taken 'too austere' an approach in withdrawing provocation from the jury because in his view the sudden and temporary loss of self-control must have ceased by the time of the killing. The trial judge must withdraw the issue of provocation from the jury if there is no credible evidence that D was in fact provoked to lose his self-control; but it seems he must leave the issue to the jury if there is any evidence that at the time of the killing D was no longer in possession of his self-control.

7. In *Davies* (1975) 60 Cr App R 253 at 259 the court said, obiter, that a direction that the jury could 'take account of the "whole course of [the deceased's] conduct right through the turbulent year of 1972" was too generous'. But the Act requires the jury to take account of '*everything* both done and said'. If the jury thought that course of conduct through the whole year had an effect on D at the flashpoint, were they not entitled—and bound—to take account of it? Unless of course no reasonable jury could have thought it relevant to the loss of self-control.

8. The Law Commission (Report No 290) recently stated that:

3.29 The courts have responded to the criticism that the law of provocation treats an angry strong person more favourably than a frightened weak person by extending the concept of loss of self-control to include 'slow-burn' cases but in so doing they have made the concept of loss of self-control still more unclear.

3.30 In summary, the requirement of loss of self-control was a judicially invented concept, lacking sharpness or a clear foundation in psychology. It was a valiant but flawed attempt to encapsulate a key limitation to the defence—that it should not be available to those who kill in considered revenge.

The objective condition

The objective question requires a comparison between what the accused did and what the reasonable person would have done.

(a) would the reasonable person have lost his control?

(b) would the reasonable person have reacted as did the accused?

The courts have been troubled by the extent to which it is necessary or desirable to take into account the characteristics of the particular defendant when assessing the likely response of the reasonable man.

Director of Public Prosecutions v Camplin
[1978] 2 All ER 168, House of Lords

(Lords Diplock, Morris of Borth-y-Gest, Simon of Glaisdale, Fraser of Tullybelton and Scarman)

The facts appear in the speech of Lord Diplock with whom Lords Fraser and Scarman agreed. Lords Simon and Morris made speeches dismissing the appeal.

Lord Diplock. My Lords, for the purpose of answering the question of law on which this appeal will turn only a brief account is needed of the facts that have given rise to it. The respondent, Camplin, who was 15 years of age, killed a middle-aged Pakistani, Mohammed Lal Khan, by splitting his skull with a chapatti pan, a heavy kitchen utensil like a rimless frying pan. At the time the two of them were alone together in Khan's flat. At Camplin's trial for murder before Boreham J his only defence was that of provocation so as to reduce the offence to manslaughter. According to the story that he told in the witness box but which differed materially from that which he had told to the police, Khan had buggered him in spite of his resistance and had then laughed at him, whereupon Camplin had lost his self-control and attacked Khan fatally with the chapatti pan.

In his address to the jury on the defence of provocation, counsel for Camplin had suggested to them that when they addressed their minds to the question whether the provocation relied on was enough to make a reasonable man do as Camplin had done, what they ought to consider was not the reaction of a reasonable adult but the reaction of a reasonable boy of Camplin's age. The judge thought that this was wrong in law. So in his summing-up he took pains to instruct the jury that they must consider whether:

> 'the provocation was sufficient to make a reasonable man in like circumstances act as the defendant did. Not a reasonable boy, as [counsel for Camplin] would have it, or a reasonable lad; it is an objective test—a reasonable man.'

The jury found Camplin guilty of murder. On appeal the Court of Appeal, Criminal Division [[1978] QB 254, [1978] 1 All ER 1236], allowed the appeal and substituted a conviction for manslaughter on the ground that the passage I have cited from the summing-up was a misdirection. The court held that [[1978] 1 All ER 1236]:

> 'the proper direction to the jury is to invite the jury to consider whether the provocation was enough to have made a reasonable person of the same age as the appellant in the same circumstances do as he did.'

The point of law of general public importance involved in the case has been certified as being:

> 'Whether, on the prosecution for murder of a boy of 15, where the issue of provocation arises, the jury should be directed to consider the question, under s3 of the Homicide Act 1957, whether the provocation was enough to make a reasonable man do as he did by reference to a "reasonable adult" or by reference to a "reasonable boy of 15".' ...

For my part I find it instructive to approach this question by a brief survey of the historical development of the doctrine of provocation at common law. Its origin at a period when the penalty for murder was death is to be found, as Tindal CJ, echoing Sir Michael Foster [see *Broadfoot's Case* (1743) Fost 154], put it in *Hayward* [(1833) 6 C & P 157 at 159], in 'the law's compassion to human infirmity'. The human infirmity on which the law first took compassion in a violent age when men bore weapons for their own protection when going about their business appears to have been chance medley or a sudden falling out at which both parties had recourse to their weapons and fought on equal terms. Chance medley as a ground of provocation was extended to assault and battery committed by the deceased on the accused in circumstances other than sudden falling out. But with two exceptions actual violence offered by the deceased to the accused remained the badge of provocation right up to the passing of the 1957 Act. The two exceptions were the discovery by a husband of a wife in the act of committing adultery and the discovery by a father of someone committing sodomy on his son; but these apart, insulting words or gestures unaccompanied by physical attack did not in law amount to provocation.

The 'reasonable man' was a comparatively late arrival in the law of provocation. As the law of negligence emerged in the first half of the 19th century he became the anthropomorphic embodiment of the standard of care required by the law. It would appear that Keating J in *Welsh* [(1869) 11 Cox CC 336] was the first to make use of the reasonable man as the embodiment of the standard of self-control required by the criminal law of persons exposed to provocation, and not merely as a criterion by which to check the credibility of a claim to have been provoked to lose his self-control made by an accused who at that time was not permitted to give evidence himself. This had not been so previously and did not at once become the orthodox view. In his *Digest of the Criminal Law* [(1877)] and his *History of the Criminal Law* [(1883)] Sir James Fitzjames Stephen makes no reference to the reasonable man as providing a standard of self-control by which the question whether the facts relied on as provocation are sufficient to reduce the subsequent killing to manslaughter is to be decided. He classifies and defines the kinds of conduct of the deceased that alone are capable in law of amounting to provocation and appears to treat the questions for the jury as being limited to (1) whether the evidence establishes conduct by the deceased that falls within one of the defined classes and, if so, (2) whether the accused was thereby actually deprived of his self-control.

The reasonable man referred to by Keating J [(1869) 11 Cox CC 336 at 338] was not then a term of legal art nor has it since become one in criminal law. He (or she) has established his (or her) role in the law of provocation under a variety of different sobriquets in which the noun 'man' is frequently replaced by 'person' and the adjective 'reasonable' by 'ordinary', 'average' or 'normal'. At least from as early as 1914 (see *R v Lesbini* [[1914] 3 KB 1116]), the test of whether the defence of provocation is entitled to succeed has been a dual one: the conduct of the deceased to the accused must be such as (1) might cause in any reasonable or ordinary person and (2) actually causes in the accused a sudden and temporary loss of self-control as the result of which he commits the unlawful act that kills the deceased. But until the 1957 Act was passed there was a condition precedent which had to be satisfied before any question of applying this dual test could arise. The conduct of the deceased had to be of such a kind as was capable in law of constituting provocation; and whether it was or was not a question for the judge, not for the jury. This House so held in *Mancini* where it also laid down a rule of law that the mode of resentment, as for instance the weapon used in the act that caused the death, must bear a reasonable relation to the kind of violence that constituted the provocation.

It is unnecessary for the purposes of the present appeal to spend time on a detailed account of what conduct was or was not capable in law of giving rise to a defence of provocation immediately before the passing of the 1957 Act. It had remained much the same as when Stephen was writing in the last quarter of the 19th century. What, however, is important to note is that this House in *Holmes* had recently confirmed that words alone, save perhaps in circumstances of a most extreme and exceptional nature, were incapable in law of constituting provocation.

My Lords, this was the state of law when *Bedder* fell to be considered by this House. The accused had killed a prostitute. He was sexually impotent. According to his evidence he had tried to have sexual intercourse with her and failed. She taunted him with his failure and tried to get away from his grasp. In the course of her attempts to do so she slapped him in the face, punched him in the stomach and kicked him in the groin, whereupon he took a knife out of his pocket and stabbed her twice and caused her death. The struggle that led to her death thus started because the deceased taunted the accused with his physical infirmity; but in the state of the law as it then was, taunts unaccompanied by any physical violence did not constitute provocation. The taunts were followed by violence on the part of the deceased in the course of her attempt to get away from the accused, and it may be that this subsequent violence would have a greater effect on the self-control of an impotent man already enraged by the taunts than it would have had on a person conscious of possessing normal physical attributes. So there might be some justification for the judge to instruct the jury to ignore the fact that the accused was impotent when they were considering whether the deceased's conduct amounted to such provocation as would cause a reasonable or ordinary person to lose his self-control. This indeed appears to have been the ground on which the Court of Criminal Appeal [[1954] 2 All ER 801 at 803] had approved the summing-up when they said:

> '...no distinction is to be made in the case of a person who, though it may not be a matter of temperament is physically impotent, is conscious of that impotence, *and therefore mentally liable to be more excited unduly* if he is "twitted" or attacked on the subject of that particular infirmity.'

This statement, for which I have myself supplied the emphasis, was approved by Lord Simonds LC speaking on behalf of all the members of this House who sat on the appeal; but he also went on to lay down the broader proposition that [[1954] 2 All ER 801 at 803, 804]:

> 'It would be plainly illogical not to recognise an unusually excitable or pugnacious temperament in the accused as a matter to be taken into account but yet to recognise for that purpose some unusual physical characteristic, be it impotence or another.'

Section 3 of the 1957 Act is in the following terms [His Lordship read s 3, above, p **585**]:

My Lords, this section was intended to mitigate in some degree the harshness of the common law of provocation as it had been developed by recent decisions in this House. It recognises and retains the dual test: the provocation must not only have caused the accused to lose his self-control but also be such as might cause a reasonable man to react to it as the accused did. Nevertheless it brings about two important changes in the law. The first is it abolishes all previous rules of law as to what can or cannot amount to provocation and in particular the rule of law that, save in the two exceptional cases I have mentioned, words unaccompanied by violence could not do so. Secondly it makes it clear that if there was any evidence that the accused himself at the time of the act which caused the death in fact lost his self-control in consequence of some provocation however slight it might appear to the judge, he was bound to leave to the jury the question, which is one of opinion not of law, whether a reasonable man might have reacted to that provocation as the accused did.

I agree with my noble and learned friend, Lord Simon of Glaisdale, that since this question is one for the opinion of the jury the evidence of witnesses as to how they think a reasonable man would react to the provocation is not admissible.

The public policy that underlay the adoption of the 'reasonable man' test in the common law doctrine of provocation was to reduce the incidence of fatal violence by preventing a person relying on his own exceptional pugnacity or excitability as an excuse for loss of self-control. The rationale of the test may not be easy to reconcile in logic with more universal propositions as to the mental element in crime. Nevertheless it has been preserved by the 1957 Act but falls to be applied now in the context of a law of provocation that is significantly different from what it was before the Act was passed.

Although it is now for the jury to apply the 'reasonable man' test, it still remains for the judge to direct them what, in the new context of the section, is the meaning of this apparently inapt expression, since powers of ratiocination bear no obvious relationship to powers of self-control. Apart from this the judge is entitled, if he thinks it helpful, to suggest considerations which may influence the jury in forming their own opinions as to whether the test is satisfied; but he should make it clear that these are not instructions which they are required to follow: it is for them and no one else to decide what weight, if any, ought to be given to them.

As I have already pointed out, for the purposes of the law of provocation the 'reasonable man' has never been confined to the adult male. It means an ordinary person of either sex, not exceptionally excitable or pugnacious, but possessed of such powers of self-control as everyone is entitled to expect that his fellow citizens will exercise in society as it is today. A crucial factor in the defence of provocation from earliest times has been the relationship between the gravity of provocation and the way in which the accused retaliated, both being judged by the social standards of the day. When Hale was writing in the 17th century pulling a man's nose was thought to justify retaliation with a sword; when *Mancini* was decided by this House, a blow with a fist would not justify retaliation with a deadly weapon. But so long as words unaccompanied by violence could not in common law amount to provocation the relevant proportionality between provocation and retaliation was primarily one of degrees of violence. Words spoken to the accused before the violence started were not normally to be included in the proportion sum. But now that the law has been changed so as to permit of words being treated as provocation, even though unaccompanied by any other acts, the gravity of verbal provocation may well depend on the particular characteristics or circumstances of the person to whom a taunt or insult is addressed. To taunt a person because of his race, his physical infirmities or some shameful incident in his past may well be considered by the jury to be more offensive to the person addressed, however equable his temperament, if the facts on which the taunt is founded are true than it would be if they were not. It would stultify much of the mitigation of the previous harshness of the common law in ruling out verbal provocation as capable of reducing murder to manslaughter if the jury could not take into consideration all those factors which in their opinion would affect the gravity of taunts and insults when applied to the person to whom they are addressed. So to this extent at any rate the unqualified proposition accepted by this House in *Bedder* that for the purposes of the 'reasonable man' test any unusual physical characteristics of the accused must be ignored requires revision as a result of the passing of the 1957 Act.

That he was only 15 years of age at the time of the killing is the relevant characteristic of the accused in the instant case. It is a characteristic which may have its effects on temperament as well as physique. If the jury think that the same power of self-control is not to be expected in an ordinary, average or normal boy of 15 as in an older person, are they to treat the lesser powers of self-control possessed by an ordinary, average or normal boy of 15 as the standard of self-control with which the conduct of the accused is to be compared?

It may be conceded that in strict logic there is a transition between treating age as a characteristic that may be taken into account in assessing the gravity of the provocation addressed to the accused and treating it as a characteristic to be taken into account in determining what is the degree of self-control to be expected of the ordinary person with whom the accused's conduct is to be compared. But to require old heads on young shoulders is inconsistent with the law's compassion of human infirmity to which Sir Michael Foster ascribed the doctrine of provocation more than two centuries ago. The distinction as to the purpose for which it is legitimate to take the age of the accused into account involves considerations of too great nicety to warrant a place in deciding a matter of opinion, which is no longer one to be decided by a judge trained in logical reasoning but by a jury drawing on their experience of how ordinary human beings behave in real life.

There is no direct authority prior to the Act that states expressly that the age of the accused could not be taken into account in determining the standard of self-control for the purposes of the reasonable man test, unless this is implicit in the reasoning of Lord Simonds LC in *Bedder*. The Court of Appeal distinguished the instant case from that of *Bedder* on the ground that what it was there said must be ignored was an unusual characteristic that distinguished the accused from ordinary normal persons, whereas nothing could be more ordinary or normal than to be aged 15. The reasoning in *Bedder* would, I think, permit of this distinction between normal and abnormal characteristics, which may affect the powers of self-control of the accused; but for reasons that I have already mentioned the proposition stated in *Bedder* requires qualification as a consequence of changes in the law effected by the 1957 Act. To try to salve what can remain of it without conflict with the Act could in my view only lead to unnecessary and unsatisfactory complexity in a question which has now become a question for the jury alone. In my view *Bedder*, like *Mancini* and *Holmes*, ought no longer to be treated as an authority on the law of provocation.

In my opinion a proper direction to a jury on the question left to their exclusive determination by s 3 of the 1957 Act would be on the following lines. The judge should state what the question is, using the very terms of the section. He should then explain to them that the reasonable man referred to in the question is a person having the power of self-control to be expected of an ordinary person of the sex and age of the accused, but in other respects sharing such of the accused's characteristics as they think would affect the gravity of the provocation to him, and that the question is not merely whether such a person would in like circumstances be provoked to lose his self-control but also would react to the provocation as the accused did.

I accordingly agree with the Court of Appeal that the judge ought not to have instructed the jury to pay no account to the age of the accused even though they themselves might be of opinion that the degree of self-control to be expected in a boy of that age was less than in an adult. So to direct them was to impose a fetter on the right and duty of the jury which the 1957 Act accords to them to act on their own opinion on the matter.

I would dismiss this appeal.

Appeal dismissed

R v Morhall
[1995] 3 All ER 659, House of Lords

(Lords Goff of Chieveley, Browne-Wilkinson, Slynn of Hadley, Nicholls of Birkenhead, and Steyn)

Lord Goff of Chieveley. My Lords, this case raises once more the question of the proper direction to be given to a jury on provocation.... Alan Paul Morhall, was convicted, after a trial before Alliott J and a jury, of the murder of Stephen Denton. The circumstances in which the appellant killed the deceased are set out in the judgment of the Court of Appeal ([1993] 4 All ER 888 at 889), delivered by Lord Taylor of Gosforth CJ whose account I gratefully adopt:

'During the daytime on 7 June 1991 the deceased and one Donnellan had been taking the appellant to task over his glue sniffing. At about 5 pm they were at his flat during an argument between the deceased and his girlfriend, also over his glue sniffing of which she disapproved. She left. Later, the deceased and Donnellan went out a couple of times. The appellant was sniffing glue when they left and when they returned. By 10 pm, when they came back with some cider and beer, the appellant was "high". He was unsteady and his speech was affected. The deceased resumed nagging him about his glue sniffing. At about 2 am the deceased went out and brought in some food. Whilst the other two ate, the appellant carried on glue sniffing. The deceased chided him again and then head-butted him. The appellant picked up a hammer and hit the deceased on the head. A fight ensued. It was broken up by Donnellan, who got the appellant to go to his bedroom. However, the deceased would not stop. He said, "I am not having that, I am going to do him". He went to the appellant's bedroom and Donnellan heard crashing and banging. When he went in the appellant was holding the Commando dagger and the deceased said, "The bastard has stabbed me." Donnellan wrestled with the appellant. Meanwhile, the deceased had gone down to the next landing where he fell to the floor. He had been fatally stabbed.'

Before the Court of Appeal, the sole ground of appeal related to the judge's direction to the jury on provocation. He directed the jury as follows:

'Provocation is some act or series of acts done, and/or words spoken, which causes in the defendant a sudden and temporary loss of control and which would cause a reasonable person to lose his self-control and to behave as the defendant did. You therefore have to consider two questions. One, did the allegedly provoking conduct cause the defendant to lose his self-control? Two, might that conduct have caused a reasonable person to lose his self-control and to behave as the defendant did? As to the second question, take into account everything said and done that you find happened on that occasion in the defendant's flat and you take that into account according to the effect which in your opinion it would have on a reasonable man. A reasonable man is a person having the powers of control to be expected of an ordinary person of the age of the defendant ...'

However, in the absence of the jury, Mr Henderson QC for the appellant drew the attention of the judge to the fact that he had not referred to the characteristic of the appellant that he was addicted to glue sniffing, and submitted that was a matter which had to be 'taken into account in deciding what a reasonable man would do . . .' As a result, when the jury returned, the judge added the following passage to his direction to the jury on provocation:

'So far as the addiction to glue is concerned, the matter that Mr Henderson wished to raise, and which is why I sent the remainder of you out, after others for more compelling reasons, so we could discuss this in your absence was this. Going to provocation, he invites me to say to you that the addiction—as opposed to the short-term consequences of that addiction—but the addiction is something you should take into account, not least because it was the very topic on which, as he contends and for you to decide, provocative words were uttered.'

Before the Court of Appeal, it was submitted that the judge's direction was inadequate because it failed to bring home to the jury that the appellant's addiction to glue sniffing was a characteristic to be taken into account by them when considering the gravity of the provocation. The Court of Appeal however rejected that submission. They preferred the submission of the Crown, which was that characteristics repugnant to the concept of a reasonable man do not qualify for consideration. Lord Taylor of Gosforth CJ, delivering the judgment of the court, stated that otherwise some remarkable results would follow. He continued (at 893):

'Not only would a defendant, who habitually abuses himself by sniffing glue to the point of addiction, be entitled to have that characteristic taken into account in his favour by the jury; logic would demand similar indulgence towards an alcoholic, or a defendant who had illegally abused heroin, cocaine, or crack to the point of addiction. Similarly, a paedophile, upbraided for molesting children, would be entitled to have his characteristic weighed in his favour on the issue of provocation. Yet none of these addictions or propensities could sensibly be regarded as consistent with the reasonable man. It is to be noted, and we emphasise, that s3 [of the Homicide Act 1957] refers to "a reasonable man", not just to a person with the self-control of a reasonable man. Whilst *DPP v Camplin* ([1978] 2 All ER 168, [1978] AC 705) decided that the "reasonable man" should be invested with the defendant's characteristics, they surely cannot include characteristics repugnant to the concept of the reasonable man. Quite apart from the incongruity of regarding glue, or drug addiction, or paedophilia, as characteristics of a reasonable man, the problem of getting a jury to understand how possession of any of those characteristics, and being bated about it, would affect the self-control of a reasonable man who ex hypothesi would not have such a characteristic, seems to us insuperable.'

He expressed the conclusion of the court as follows (at 894):

'In our judgment, however, a self-induced addiction to glue sniffing brought on by voluntary and persistent abuse of solvents is wholly inconsistent with the concept of a reasonable man. In effect, Mr Worsley's argument [for the appellant] would stultify the test. It would result in the so-called reasonable man being a reincarnation of the appellant with his peculiar characteristics whether capable of being possessed by a reasonable man or not and whether acquired by nature or by his own abuse.'

The Court of Appeal gave leave to appeal to your Lordships' House, certifying that the following point of law of general public importance was involved in the decision:

'When directing a jury on provocation under s3 of the Homicide Act 1957, and explaining to them in accordance with the model direction of Lord Diplock in *DPP v Camplin* [1978] 2 All ER 168 at 175, [1978] AC 705 at 718 that "the reasonable man referred to in the question is a person having the power of self-control to be expected of an ordinary person of the sex and age of the accused, but in other respects sharing such of the accused's characteristics as they think would affect the gravity of the provocation to him", should the judge exclude from the jury's consideration characteristics and past behaviour of the defendant at which the taunts are directed, which in the judge's view are inconsistent with the concept of a reasonable man?'

Provocation is, of course, a defence to a charge of murder. It is essentially a defence at common law; but the common law defence was modified in significant respects by s3 of the Homicide Act 1957, and the impact of that section on the common law was examined in depth by your Lordships' House in *DPP v Camplin* [1978] 2 All ER 168, [1978] AC 705.

In his leading speech in that case (with which both Lord Fraser of Tullybelton and Lord Scarman agreed) Lord Diplock described the historical development of the law on this subject. Historically, actual violence offered by the deceased to the defendant was necessary to establish provocation, subject to two well-established exceptions (discovery by a husband of his wife in the act of adultery, and by a father of a man committing sodomy on his son). Words alone were not capable of amounting in law to provocation, as was confirmed (subject to a possible exception in the most extreme circumstances) by your Lordships' House in *Holmes v DPP* [1946] 2 All ER 124, [1946] AC 588.

However, an important qualification was engrafted onto the common law principle. By the early twentieth century it had become established that it was not enough that the accused himself should have been provoked to act as he did. At least after *R v Lesbini* [1914] 3 KB 1116 a dual test had to be complied with, under which the conduct of the deceased towards the accused had to be such as (1) might cause in a reasonable person and (2) actually caused in the accused, a sudden and temporary loss of self-control as a result of which he committed the unlawful act which killed the deceased. The introduction of this 'reasonable person' test, which appears to have been an act of policy designed to set a standard of self-control which must be complied with before the accused is able to rely on the defence of provocation, has given rise to problems which have been discussed by judges in a number of common law jurisdictions, notably in Australia and New Zealand as well as in this country. It is this test which forms the main subject of s3 of the 1957 Act. Section 3 provides [His Lordship read s 3, p **585** above, and continued:]

As has been pointed out (for example, by Smith and Hogan *Criminal Law* (7th edn, 1992) p351), the section does not purport to codify the law of provocation. On the contrary, it assumes the existence of the common law offence, and amends it. In particular, it assumes the existence of the dual test. The principal amendment introduced by the section is that it is now recognised that words alone (or words together with acts) may constitute provocation in law. This in itself has led to the important consequence that, as Lord Diplock pointed out in *DPP v Camplin* [1978] 2 All ER 168 at 174, [1978] AC 705 at 717—

> 'the gravity of verbal provocation may well depend on the particular characteristics or circumstances of the person to whom a taunt or insult is addressed ... It would stultify much of the mitigation of the previous harshness of the common law in ruling out verbal provocation as capable of reducing murder to manslaughter if the jury could not take into consideration all those factors which in their opinion would affect the gravity of taunts or insults when applied to the person to whom they are addressed.'

This in turn led their Lordships to reconsider a proposition accepted by this House in *Bedder v DPP* [1954] 2 All ER 801, [1954] 1 WLR 1119, viz that, for the purposes of the reasonable person test, any unusual physical characteristics of the accused must be ignored. It is now recognised that such characteristics should be taken into account for that purpose, in so far as they affect the gravity of the provocation in question.

It is against the background of the decision in *DPP v Camplin*, and the speeches of their Lordships in that case, that I now turn to consider the problem in the present case, which is whether the appellant's addiction to glue sniffing should have been taken into account as affecting the gravity of the provocation.

Judging from the speeches in *DPP v Camplin*, it should indeed have been taken into account. Indeed, it was a characteristic of particular relevance, since the words of the deceased which were said to constitute provocation were directed towards the appellant's shameful addiction to glue sniffing and his inability to break himself of it. Furthermore, there is nothing in the speeches in *DPP v Camplin* to suggest that a characteristic of this kind should be excluded from consideration. On the contrary, in the passage which I have already quoted from his speech Lord Diplock spoke of the jury taking into consideration 'all those factors' which would affect the gravity of the taunts or insults when applied to the defendant. Likewise, Lord Simon of Glaisdale said that—

'in determining whether a person of reasonable self-control would lose it in the circumstances, the entire factual situation, which includes the characteristics of the accused, must be considered.' (See [1978] 2 All ER 168 at 182, [1978] AC 705 at 727.)

Even so, the Court of Appeal felt that the appellant's addiction to glue sniffing should be excluded because it was a characteristic which was repugnant to the concept of a reasonable man. It seems to me, with all respect, that this conclusion flows from a misunderstanding of the function of the so-called 'reasonable person test' in this context. In truth the expression 'reasonable man' or 'reasonable person' in this context can lead to misunderstanding. Lord Diplock described it in *DPP v Camplin* [1978] 2 All ER 168 at 173, [1978] AC 705 at 716 as an 'apparently inapt expression'. This is because the 'reasonable person test' is concerned not with ratiocination, nor with the reasonable man whom we know so well in the law of negligence (where we are concerned with reasonable foresight and reasonable care), nor with reasonable conduct generally. The function of the test is only to introduce, as a matter of policy, a standard of self-control which has to be complied with if provocation is to be established in law: see *DPP v Camplin* [1978] 2 All ER 168 at 173, 181–182, [1978] AC 705 at 716, 726 per Lord Diplock and Lord Simon of Glaisdale. Lord Diplock himself spoke of 'the reasonable or ordinary person', and indeed to speak of the degree of self-control attributable to the ordinary person is (despite the express words of the statute) perhaps more apt, and certainly less likely to mislead, than to do so with reference to the reasonable person. The word 'ordinary' is in fact the adjective used in criminal codes applicable in some other common law jurisdictions (as in New Zealand, as to which see *R v McGregor* [1962] NZLR 1069 and *R v McCarthy* [1992] 2 NZLR 550, and in Tasmania, as to which see *Stingel v R* (1990) 171 CLR 312). Indeed, by exploiting the adjective 'reasonable' it is easy to caricature the law as stated in s3 of the 1957 Act by talking of the test of, for example, the reasonable blackmailer or, nowadays perhaps, the reasonable glue sniffer; indeed, the sting of the caricature is derived from the implication that the adjective 'reasonable' refers to a person who is guided by reason or who acts in a reasonable manner. This is however misleading. In my opinion it would be entirely consistent with the law as stated in s3 of the 1957 Act, as properly understood, to direct the jury simply with reference to a hypothetical person having the power of self-control to be expected of an *ordinary* person of the age and sex of the defendant, but in other respects sharing such of the defendant's characteristics as they think would affect the gravity of the provocation to him: see *DPP v Camplin* [1978] 2 All ER 168 at 175, [1978] AC 705 at 718 per Lord Diplock.

I wish however to stress two things. First, it is plain that, in the passage from his speech to which I have just referred, Lord Diplock was not attempting to dictate to judges how they should formulate their directions to juries on provocation. This appears from his statement that 'a' proper direction to a jury would be 'on the following lines…' Provided that trial judges direct juries in accordance with the law, they may do so as they think right, tailoring their direction to the facts of the particular case before them. Second, in an appropriate case it may be necessary to refer to other circumstances affecting the gravity of the provocation to the defendant which do not strictly fall within the description 'characteristics', as for example the defendant's history or the circumstances in which he is placed at the relevant time (see *DPP v Camplin* [1978] 2 All ER 168 at 174, 182, [1978] AC 705 at 717, 727 per Lord Diplock, where he referred to 'the particular characteristics or circumstances' of the defendant, and per Lord Simon of Glaisdale, who referred to 'the entire factual situation', including the characteristics of the defendant). At all events in the present case, when the judge turned to the second and objective inquiry, he was entitled to direct the jury that they must take into account the entire factual situation (and in particular the fact that the provocation was directed at a habitual glue sniffer taunted with his habit) when considering the question whether the provocation was enough to cause a man possessed of an ordinary man's power of self-control to act as the defendant did.

However, the point can be taken further. Among the characteristics stated to be excluded from consideration on the approach favoured by the Court of Appeal is that of being a paedophile. But suppose that a man who has been in prison for a sexual offence, for example rape, has after his release been taunted by another man with reference to that offence. It is difficult to see why, on ordinary principles, his characteristic or history as an offender of that kind should not be taken into account as going to the gravity of the provocation. The point is well made by Professor Smith in his commentary on the present case ([1993] Crim LR 957 at 958):

> 'Suppose that an old lag, now trying to go straight, is taunted with being "a jailbird." This might be extremely provoking, especially if it reveals his murky past to new friends or employers unaware of it. It really would not make much sense to ask the jury to consider the effect of such provocation on a man of good character.'

In truth, the mere fact that a characteristic of the defendant is discreditable does not exclude it from consideration, as was made plain by Lord Diplock in *DPP v Camplin* [1978] 2 All ER 168 at 174, [1978] AC 705 at 717 when he referred to a shameful incident in a man's past as a relevant characteristic for present purposes. Indeed, even if the defendant's discreditable conduct causes a reaction in another, which in turn causes the defendant to lose his self-control, the reaction may amount to provocation: see *Edwards v R* [1973] 1 All ER 152, [1973] AC 648, a case concerned with a hostile reaction to his blackmailer by a man whom he was trying to blackmail, and *R v Johnson* [1989] 2 All ER 839, [1989] 1 WLR 740, in which *Edwards v R* was followed and applied by the Court of Appeal. These cases are, in my opinion, inconsistent with the decision of the Court of Appeal in the present case.

Of course glue sniffing (or solvent abuse), like indulgence in alcohol or the taking of drugs, can give rise to a special problem in the present context, because it may arise in more than one way. First, it is well established that, in considering whether a person having the power of self-control to be expected of an ordinary person would have reacted to the provocation as the defendant did, the fact (if it be the case) that the defendant was the worse for drink at the time should not be taken into account, even though the drink would, if taken by him, have the effect of reducing an ordinary person's power of self-control. It is sometimes suggested that the reason for this exclusion is that drunkenness is transitory and cannot therefore amount to a characteristic. But I doubt whether that is right. Indeed some physical conditions (such as eczema) may be transitory in nature and yet can surely be taken into account if the subject of taunts. In *DPP v Camplin* [1978] 2 All ER 168 at 182, [1978] AC 705 at 726 Lord Simon of Glaisdale considered that drunkenness should be excluded as inconsistent with the concept of the reasonable man in the sense of a man of ordinary self-control; but it has to be recognised that, in our society, ordinary people do sometimes have too much to drink. I incline therefore to the opinion that the exclusion of drunkenness in this context flows from the established principle that, at common law, intoxication does not of itself excuse a man from committing a criminal offence, but on one or other of these bases it is plainly excluded.

At all events it follows that, in a case such as the present, a distinction may have to be drawn between two different situations. The first occurs where the defendant is taunted with his addiction (for example, that he is an alcoholic, or a drug addict, or a glue sniffer), or even with having been intoxicated (from any cause) on some previous occasion. In such a case, however discreditable such a condition may be, it may where relevant be taken into account as going to the gravity of the provocation. The second is the simple fact of the defendant being intoxicated—being drunk, or high with drugs or glue—at the relevant time, which may not be so taken into account, because that, like displaying a lack of ordinary self-control, is excluded as a matter of policy. Although the distinction is a fine one, it will, I suspect, very rarely be necessary to explain it to a jury. Drunkenness itself may be a not unusual feature of cases raising the issue of provocation, as occurred, for example, in *R v Newell* (1980) 71 Cr App Rep 331, where the drunkenness of the defendant was rightly excluded as irrelevant. But none of the counsel in the present case had any experience, or indeed knowledge, of a case other than the present in which addiction as such was the subject of verbal taunts or insults said to constitute provocation, with the effect that the addiction was therefore relevant as going to the gravity of the provocation. The present case may therefore be compared with *R v Newell*, in which the defendant's chronic alcoholism was excluded from consideration because 'it had nothing to do with the words by which it is said that he was provoked' (see (1980) 71 Cr App Rep 331 at 340 per Lord Lane CJ). I only wish to add a warning that the court's strong reliance in that case on the judgment of North J in *R v McGregor* [1962] NZLR 1069 must be regarded with caution, having regard to the reservations expressed with regard to that judgment by the Court of Appeal of New Zealand in *R v McCarthy* [1992] 2 NZLR 550 at 557–558 per Cooke P delivering the judgment of the court, part of which is quoted by Professor Smith in his commentary on the present case ([1993] Crim LR 957 at 958). In particular, I wish to record my concern that the Court of Appeal in *R v Newell* may have placed too exclusive an emphasis on the word 'characteristic', as a result of relying on the judgment of North J in *R v McGregor*, where North J was construing a statute in which that word was used.

It follows from what I have said that I am, with all respect, unable to accept the reasoning or the conclusion of the Court of Appeal. The answer to the question of law posed for consideration by your Lordships' House is apparent from what I have said earlier in this speech. In my opinion, the judge should have directed the jury to take into account the fact of the appellant's addiction to glue sniffing when considering whether a person with the ordinary person's power of self-control would have reacted to the provocation as the appellant did. The judge failed so to direct the jury in the first passage which I have quoted from the summing up. Furthermore, in my opinion his reference to the appellant's addiction in the second passage was ambiguous. This was because it did not make clear whether the appellant's addiction to glue sniffing was a characteristic which went to the gravity of the provocation to be taken into account when considering whether a person having the power of self-control to be expected of an ordinary person would have reacted to the provocation as the appellant did, or whether it was only to be taken into account when considering whether, as the judge put it, the allegedly provoking conduct caused the appellant to lose his self-control. It follows that, since it is accepted that no question of the exercise of the proviso arises in the present case, the conviction of the appellant for murder must be quashed and a conviction of manslaughter substituted. The matter must however be remitted to the Court of Appeal to consider the question of sentence.

[**Lords Browne-Wilkinson, Slynn of Hadley, Nicholls of Birkenhead** and **Steyn** agreed.]

Appeal allowed

Questions

1. Is it possible to maintain a workable distinction between characteristics which affect the gravity of the provocation experienced by D and D's characteristics which affect his ability

to exercise self-control? See in particular Professor Ashworth's influential article 'The Doctrine of Provocation' [1976] CLJ 292, cf A. Norrie, 'From Criminal Law to Legal Theory: The Mysterious Case of the Reasonable Glue Sniffer' (2002) 65 MLR 538.

2. V taunts D, a small man of fiery temper, who is suffering from sunburn by saying 'You bad tempered, little lobster'. D responds by killing V. Following *Morhall,* how should a jury be directed on the issue of provocation?

R v Smith
[2000] 4 All ER 289, House of Lords

(Lords Slynn, Hoffmann, Clyde, Hobhouse and Millett)

Smith and his friend, V, both alcoholics, had a petty row. Smith, who was suffering from a serious clinical depression, took a kitchen knife and stabbed V to death. Defences of no mens rea, diminished responsibility and provocation were all rejected by the jury. The judge directed the jury that, for the purposes of the defence of provocation, the fact that the depressive illness may have reduced Smith's powers of self-control was 'neither here nor there' and should not be taken into account. The Court of Appeal allowed Smith's appeal and certified the following point of law of general public importance:

Are characteristics other than age and sex, attributable to a reasonable man for the purpose of section 3 of the Homicide Act 1957, relevant not only to the gravity of the provocation to him but also to the standard of self-control to be expected?

[**Lord Slynn** made a speech dismissing the appeal.]

[**Lord Hoffmann** referring to *Camplin:*] It was ... decided that, at least for the purpose of considering the gravity of the provocation, the reasonable man should normally be assumed to share the relevant characteristics of the accused. Whether the decision went further and allowed the jury to take into account characteristics of the accused which affected his powers of self-control is the chief question in this appeal and, in order to answer it, I shall have to analyse the case later in more detail. It can however be said that *Camplin*'s case allowed at least one such characteristic to be taken into account, namely. the youth of the accused. The actual decision was that the jury should have been told to consider what the effect of the provocation would have been upon a person with the powers of self-control of a reasonable boy of 15 and not those of a grown-up.

The extent to which matters affecting the power of self-control should be taken into account divided the Judicial Committee of the Privy Council in *Luc Thiet Thuan v R* [1996] 2 All ER 1033, [1997] AC 131. The majority, in an opinion given by Lord Goff of Chieveley, decided that in principle the actual characteristics of the accused were relevant only to the gravity of the provocation. The only characteristics of the accused which could be attributed to the reasonable person for the purpose of expressing a standard of self-control were his or her age and sex. There had been evidence that the accused suffered from brain damage which made it difficult for him to control his impulses in response to minor provocation. But this was held irrelevant to the question of whether the objective element in the defence had been satisfied. The majority said that the English cases after *Camplin*'s case (to some of which I shall later refer) which had held that the jury should be directed that they could take such matters into account had been wrongly decided. Lord Steyn, in a minority opinion, said that the later cases were not inconsistent with *Camplin*'s case, constituted a logical extension of its reasoning and were in accordance with justice and common sense.

[After analysing Lord Diplock's speech in *Camplin,* Lord Hoffmann continued:] I invite your Lordships' attention to the following points.

(1) Lord Diplock says that youth may be taken into account because the principle of compassion to human infirmity, as a jury drawing on their experience may apply it, requires one to do so. He does not say that the same principle of compassion is incapable of applying to any other characteristics which a jury might on similar grounds think should be taken into account. It would have been easy for him to have said that youth was for this purpose unique.

(2) Lord Diplock expressly rejects the distinction between the effect of age on the gravity of the provocation and on the power of self-control on the grounds that it is 'of too great nicety' for application by a jury. Again, there is nothing to suggest that this comment is not equally true of other characteristics. Since *Camplin*'s case, there is a great deal of material which demonstrates that Lord Diplock's scepticism about whether the distinction could be made to work in practice was well founded.

(3) If age were to be the only case in which a particular characteristic could be taken into account as relevant to the expected power of self-control, it would be necessary to explain why it should be so singled out. The High Court of Australia, in *Stingel v R* (1990) 171 CLR 312 at 330, said that it was because age is a normal characteristic 'the process of development from childhood to maturity is something which, being common to us all, is an aspect of ordinariness'. This explanation was embraced by Lord Goff of Chieveley in *Luc Thiet Thuan v R* [1996] 2 All ER 1033 at 1041, [1997] AC 131 at 140. It had, as I have said, been relied upon in *Camplin*'s case by the Court of Appeal to distinguish *Bedder*'s case. But the distinction between normal and abnormal characteristics was expressly rejected by Lord Diplock. He said that:

> 'The reasoning in *Bedder* would, I think, permit of this distinction between normal and abnormal characteristics, which may affect the powers of self-control of the accused; but for reasons that I have already mentioned the proposition stated in *Bedder* requires qualification as a consequence of the changes in the law effected by the 1957 Act. To try to salve what can remain of it without conflict with the Act could in my view only lead to unnecessary and unsatisfactory complexity in a question which has now become a question for the jury alone.' (See [1978] 2 All ER 168 at 175, [1978] AC 705 at 718.)

My Lords, the important passage which I have cited from Lord Diplock's speech provides in my view no support for the theory, widely advanced in the literature, that he was making a clear distinction between characteristics relevant to the gravity of the provocation and characteristics relevant to the power of self-control, with age (and possibly sex) as arbitrary exceptions which could be taken into account for the latter purpose. This interpretation depends principally upon what Lord Diplock described as 'a proper direction to the jury' which he gave at the end of his speech (above, p **594**).

8. The gravity of provocation/self-control distinction

Although *Camplin*'s case does not in my opinion provide authoritative support for the distinction between gravity of provocation and powers of self-control, it has been adopted in Australia (*Stingel v R* (1990) 171 CLR 312), New Zealand (*R v Campbell* [1997] 1 NZLR 16 and *R v Rongonui* [2000] 2 NZLR 385), Canada (*R v Hill* [1986] 1 SCR 313) and by the Privy Council for Hong Kong (*Luc Thiet Thuan v R* [1996] 2 All ER 1033, [1997] AC 131). It also has a good deal of academic support: see in particular Professor Ashworth's influential article 'The Doctrine of Provocation' [1986] CLJ 292, Jeremy Horder 'Between Provocation and Diminished Responsibility' (1999) 2 KCLJ 143 and Professor MJ Allen 'Provocation's Reasonable Man: A Plea for Self-Control' [2000] J Crim L 216. It must therefore be considered on its own merits.

The theoretical basis for the distinction is that provocation is a defence for people who are, as Professor Ashworth put it, 'in a broad sense mentally normal' ([1976] CLJ 292 at 312). If they claim that they had abnormal characteristics which reduced their powers of self-control, they should plead diminished responsibility. There is a clear philosophical distinction between a claim that an act was at least partially excused as normal behaviour in response to external circumstances and a claim that the actor had mental characteristics which prevented him from behaving normally: see Sir Peter Strawson 'Freedom and Resentment' in Watson *Free Will* (1982) pp 64–67.

The difficulty about the practical application of this distinction in the law of provocation is that in many cases the two forms of claim are inextricably muddled up with each other.....

There is however one really serious argument in favour of the distinction between characteristics affecting the gravity of the provocation and characteristics affecting the power of self-control. This is the claim that, despite all its difficulties of application, it is the only way to hold the line against complete erosion of the objective element in provocation. The purpose of the objective element in provocation is to mark the distinction between (partially) excusable and inexcusable loss of self-control. As Lord Diplock said in *Camplin*'s case [1978] 2 All ER 168 at 174, [1978] AC 705 at 717, the conduct of the accused should be measured against 'such powers of self-control as everyone is entitled to expect that his fellow citizens will exercise in society as it is today'. If there is no limit to the characteristics which can be taken into account, the fact that the accused lost self-control will show that he is a person liable in such circumstances to lose his self-control. The objective element will have disappeared completely.

My Lords, I share the concern that this should not happen. For the protection of the public, the law should continue to insist that people must exercise self-control. A person who flies into a murderous rage when he is crossed, thwarted or disappointed in the vicissitudes of life should not be able to rely upon his anti-social propensity as even a partial excuse for killing. In *Stingel v R* (1990) 171 CLR 312, for example, the accused was obsessively infatuated with a woman who had terminated their relationship. He became a stalker, following her about. She obtained a court order restraining him from approaching her. One evening after a party he found the woman in a car with another man. According to his own account, they were having sex. He went back to his own car, fetched a butcher's knife and came back and killed the man. His evidence conformed to the standard narrative which the legal requirement of 'loss of control' imposes on such defences:

> 'I was all worked up and feeling funny. It was like I was in a rage, almost to the stage where I felt dazed. It was like I really didn't know what happened until the knife went into him.'

The High Court of Australia held that the judge was right to withdraw the issue of provocation from the jury on the ground that such conduct could not raise even a reasonable doubt as to whether the objective element in the defence had been satisfied. I respectfully agree. Male possessiveness and jealousy should not today be an acceptable reason for loss of self-control leading to homicide, whether inflicted upon the woman herself or her new lover. In Australia the judge was able to give effect to this policy by withdrawing issue from the jury. But s 3 prevents an English judge from doing so. So, it is suggested, a direction that characteristics such as jealousy and obsession should be ignored in relation to the objective element is the best way to ensure that people like Stingel cannot rely upon the defence. . . . I would dismiss the appeal.

[**Lord Clyde** made a speech dismissing the appeal.]

Lord Hobhouse: The striking thing about the present and similar cases is that the defendant is either unwilling to rely upon s 2 or, having done so, fails to satisfy the jury and wishes then to adopt a strained construction of s 3 in order to escape the burden of proof and introduce vaguer concepts not contemplated by either section. The present case has only come before the Court of Appeal and your Lordships' House because the jury, having heard the evidence and having been properly directed upon the law, rejected the defence under s 2. They were not satisfied that whatever degree of depressive illness the respondent was suffering from was such as substantially to impair his mental responsibility for the killing, that is to say, the actual killing with which he was charged taking into account the circumstances in which it occurred.

This is important because there seems in some quarters to be an implicit assumption that the assessment by a jury under s 2 is inadequate properly to allow for the defendant's abnormality of mind in relation to any killing which was contributed to by provocation. There is no reason to make this assumption. Further, it is contrary to the drafting of s 2 and to ss 2 and 3 read together. The brain-damaged man has an abnormality of the mind. If it is of sufficient severity, in the opinion of the jury, to impair substantially his mental responsibility for killing his provoker, he will be found guilty of manslaughter, not murder, even if his action was not that of a reasonable man (indeed, one could say, *because* his action was not that of a reasonable man).

If the defendant is merely someone with a personality disorder, for example an exceptionally violent or immoral disposition, he will not be able to rely on s 2, nor will he be able to rely on s 3 if his response to the provocation was disproportionate. This is all in accord with the specific policy of the 1957 Act and the ordinary principles of criminal responsibility. Similarly, if the defendant suffered from an abnormality but the jury do not consider it to be sufficient substantially to impair his responsibility, he will not have a defence under s 2. This simply reflects the policy of the statute and it would be contrary to that policy to extend s 3 to give him the defence advisedly denied him by s 2.

One of the errors that have bedevilled some of the recent judicial statements in this part of the English law of homicide is the failure to take account of the interaction of ss 2 and 3 and appreciate that they not only show that the strained construction of s 3 is wrong but also that the perceived injustice which the strained construction is designed to avoid is in fact covered by an application of s 2 in accordance with its ordinary meaning. Section 2 is of course capable of applying in any situation and those situations include a killing by a defendant who has killed after losing his self-control. A defendant in this situation can contend that his conduct was not abnormal and require the prosecution to satisfy the jury that his loss of self-control was not the result of provocation or his response to it was not that of a reasonable man. Or, he can contend and seek to satisfy the jury on the balance of probabilities that he had an abnormality of the mind which in the circumstances substantially reduced his mental responsibility for what he did. A defendant can of course place both contentions before the jury, as the respondent did in this case. The jury can then return a verdict of manslaughter on the one or the other basis. But it is always open to the jury to conclude (as no doubt the jury did in the present case) that the defendant's response was objectively disproportionate and that his abnormality of mind did not suffice to impair his mental responsibility for what he had done.

This point was made by the Criminal Law Revision Committee and by Lord Simon of Glaisdale, by quotation, in *DPP v Camplin* [1978] 2 All ER 168 at 182, [1978] AC 705 at 726–727:

> 'In this country the law on this matter [provocation] has been indirectly affected by the introduction of the defence of diminished responsibility. It is now possible for a defendant to set up a combined defence of provocation and diminished responsibility, the practical effect being that the jury may return a verdict of manslaughter if they take the view that the defendant suffered from an abnormality of the mind *and* was provoked. In practice this may mean that a conviction of murder will be ruled out although the provocation was not such as would have moved a person of normal mentality to kill.' (Lord Simon's emphasis.)

This very point had also been made by Lord Parker LCJ when giving the judgment of the Court of Appeal (which included Hilbery and Diplock JJ) in *R v Byrne* [1960] 3 All ER 1 at 4, [1960] 2 QB 396 at 402, recognising that the criterion of the reasonable man, 'that is to say, a man with a normal mind', ruled out the defence of provocation for a sexual psychopath with 'violent perverted sexual desires which he finds it difficult or impossible to control'. His *only* available defence was accordingly diminished responsibility under s 2. The judgment of Lord Parker and the decision in *R v Byrne* are strongly contradictory of the respondent's argument in the present case and the thesis that it is necessary and permitted to introduce abnormalities of mind into s 3....

Conclusion

The law, as provided in s 3 of the 1957 Act had held in the authorities down to *Luc Thiet Thuan v R*, establishes that the constituents of provocation are the following. (a) The defendant must have been provoked (whether by things done or by things said or by both together) to lose his self-control and kill or do whatever other act is alleged to render him guilty of murder. (b) This is a factual question upon which all relevant evidence is admissible including any evidence which tends to support the conclusion that the defendant either may have or did not lose his self-control. (c) If the jury conclude that the defendant may have been provoked to lose his self-control and do as he did, the jury should, as an exercise of judgment, but taking into account all the evidence, form a view as to the gravity of the provocation for the defendant in all the circumstances. (d) Finally, the jury should decide whether in their opinion, having regard to the actual provocation ((a) and (b) above) and their view as to its gravity ((c) above), a person having ordinary powers of self-control would have done what the defendant did.

If some elaboration of the word 'ordinary' is thought necessary, it should be along the lines advised by Lord Diplock and used by Judge Coombe in the present case. The phrase 'reasonable man' although used in the section is better avoided as not assisting the understanding of the criterion 'ordinary powers of self-control'. The word 'characteristics' should be avoided altogether in relation to (d). It is not used in the section. It is alien to the objective standard of ordinariness and experience has shown that it is a persistent source of confusion. Where relevant the age or gender of the defendant should be referred to since they are not factors which qualify the criterion of ordinariness. But language which qualifies or contradicts such ordinariness must be avoided. But language which qualifies or contradicts such ordinariness must be avoided. It is the standard of ordinary not an abnormal self-control that has to be used. It is the standard which conforms to what everyone is entitled to expect of their fellow citizens in society as it is.

If the scheme which I have set out above is followed, there should be no difficulty in directing the jury using simple and clearly understandable language. No artificialities are involved and the contradictions involved in the approach contended for by the defendant are avoided. Judge Coombe did this successfully in the present case as have many judges before him. It does less than justice to juries to suggest that they are incapable of understanding directions as simple as the four which I have set out above. If, as will usually be the case where the defence rely upon a mental element, diminished responsibility is also raised, s 2 and the concept of abnormality and mind provides the judge with an opportunity, if he thinks it helpful, to make an illustrative point of contrast with the objective test in s 3....

The appeal should be allowed. The direction of the judge was appropriate to the issues at the trial. The conviction was not unsafe.

[**Lord Millett** made a speech, concluding that he would dismiss the appeal and restore the conviction for murder.]

Appealed dismissed

Notes and questions

1. Can it be said that Smith, whose ability to control his actions was substantially impaired, who was 'disinhibited' and who lost his self-control and inflicted fatal wounds with a knife simply because his friend would not admit to an accusation of theft was not 'exceptionally excitable or pugnacious' or that he exercised such powers of self-control as everyone is entitled to expect?—as required by Lord Diplock's speech, above, p 592.

2. Should age and sex be the only characteristics which are (or may be) relevant to the objective limb of the test? Why should they be? Is it because they are not abnormalities?

Are mental abnormalities leading to violence to be taken into account only when they amount to diminished responsibility?

3. See further T. Macklem and J. Gardner, 'Compassion without Respect: Nine Fallacies in *R v Smith*' [2001] Crim LR 623; and, Provocation and Pluralism' [2001] MLR 815.

R v Weller [2003]
EWCA Crim 815, [2004] 1 Cr App R 1, [2003] Crim LR 724

(Mantell LJ, Jack and Hedley JJ)

Mantell LJ delivered the judgment:

1. ... David Weller, was convicted of the murder of his girlfriend, [ZF] ... The sole issue for the jury at the trial was whether the appellant was guilty of murder as charged or guilty of manslaughter by reason of provocation. There was no dispute that he had strangled [ZF]. The appeal turns on the directions given by the judge to the jury with regard to provocation ...

2. It is unnecessary to refer to the facts in any detail. The appellant and ZF had been lovers for about 12 months. She was 18 years old; he was 34. On Friday, 27 October 2000 after they had been living together for about five months there was a heated argument because she wished to end the relationship. It appears that this was because he was unduly possessive and jealous as to which there was considerable evidence. She spent the night with a friend and over the weekend attempted to collect her belongings from the flat they shared in Bridgwater. On Monday 30 October they met up and went back to the flat. Another heated argument occurred over her conduct with other men. The appellant grabbed her by the throat and strangled her. He hid her body. He gave himself up to the police on Wednesday, 1 November 2001.

The law of provocation

3. The issue raised by the appeal is whether the judge's directions to the jury on the issue of provocation were adequate. We do not intend any wider review of the law relating to provocation than is necessary to set the legal context and to deal with the matters that arise on this appeal.

... [his lordship referred to Smith (above)]

16. In our view it is to be concluded from the majority speeches in *Smith* that the question whether the defendant should reasonably have controlled himself is to be answered by the jury taking all matters into account. That includes matters relating to the defendant, the kind of man he is and his mental state, as well as the circumstances in which the death occurred. The judge should not tell the jury that they should, as a matter of law, ignore any aspect. He may give them some guidance as to the weight to be given to some aspects, provided he makes it clear that the question is one which, as the law provides, they are to answer, and not him.

17. This approach has the considerable advantage that it is unnecessary to determine whether what has been called a "characteristic" of the accused is an eligible characteristic for the purposes of the second element in provocation, the objective element, or is one of which no account should be taken. It avoids categorising human defects into one category or the other, which would otherwise be necessary and is surely artificial. We refer in particular to the difficulties which arose in *R v Dryden* [1995] 4 All ER 987 and to *R v Humphreys* [1995] 4 All E.R. 1008. It is all a matter for the jury. ...

The present case

19. The complaint is that the judge did not direct the jury that, in considering whether the defendant should reasonably have controlled himself, they could take into account his jealousy and possessiveness. ...

26. It is plain from the majority speeches in *Smith* that characteristics such as jealousy remain with the jury as matters which fall for consideration in connection with the second, objective element of provocation and section 3. Plainly the jury must not be directed that they should take no account of them and it is essential that it is made clear that such matters may form part of their deliberations. In this case we have concluded that the direction given was sufficient. In many cases, however, it might well prove the better course to identify the particular characteristics relied upon whether or not accompanied by further guidance.

27. In *Lowe*, unreported 21 February 2003 a decision of this Court, the practice was commended by which the judge places the proposed direction on provocation in writing before counsel for their consideration. In that case, as in this, the jury came back with a question showing that they were having difficulty in understanding the direction. It seems to us that there may also be considerable advantages in giving the direction to the jury in writing at the appropriate moment in the summing up before taking them through it. It is asking a lot of a jury to absorb the direction as they listen to it and to carry it in their minds with them into the jury room.

The appeal was dismissed.

In *Rowland* [2003] EWCA Crim 3636 the Court of Appeal referred to *Weller* [2003] EWCA Crim 815 and to Professor Ashworth's commentary [2003] Crim LR 724, at pp 725–727 raising concern at the 'evaluative free-for-all' whereby everything was left for the jury to determine resulting from the speeches of the majority in *Smith (Morgan)*. The court recognized that the 'reasonable man' was now to be regarded as 'an archetype best left lurking in the statutory undergrowth' [41].

61. Before speeches, the trial judge should discuss with counsel the terms of the appropriate direction. The Judicial Studies Board specimen direction should be taken as the appropriate starting point and be suitably tailored to the circumstances of the case. In particular the judge should discuss with counsel (1) the things allegedly said and/or done to constitute the provocation and, unless it is obvious, the evidence pointing to the loss of self-control ... and (2) any factors which may have a bearing on the second question ... with a view to determining what should be put before the jury in the summing-up.

62. In this connection, the judge should bear in mind ... that, in addition to cases where particular factors clearly have a bearing on the issue, there may be difficult borderline cases, particularly as between mere bad temper or excitability on the one hand and identifiable mental conditions and personality traits on the other. In such cases, after prior discussion with counsel, the trial judge should be careful to include all potentially relevant factors at the appropriate point in his summing-up to the jury.

Is it conceivable that Parliament intended that the same characteristic should be relevant to both diminished and provocation, and that the onus of proving it should be on the defendant for diminished and onus of disproving it on the prosecution for provocation. Is such a law workable when both defences are raised?

Lord Millett, in *Smith*, said that the decision of the Court of Appeal was 'inconsistent with the English authorities and an understanding of the law shared by three successive Lords Chief Justice, Lord Parker, Lord Lane and Lord Taylor CJJ'. He added, 'We cannot adopt it without department from *R v Morhall*, a unanimous decision of your Lordship's House not yet five years old and preferring Lord Steyn's dissenting opinion in *Luc Thiet Thuan* to that of the majority.' Lord Hobhouse said that *Morhall* is 'a binding authority in English law. It distinguishes between matters going to the gravity of the provocation and the required degree of control.' Does it appear that these judges do not regard themselves as bound by *Smith*?

Her Majesty's Attorney-General for Jersey Appellant v Dennis Peter Holley Respondent
[2005] UKPC 23

(Lords Bingham of Cornhill, Nicholls of Birkenhead, Hoffmann, Hope of Craighead, Scott of Foscote, Rodger of Earlsferry, Walker of Gestingthorpe, Baroness Hale of Richmond and Lord Carswell)

Lord Nicholls.

1. .... This appeal, being heard by an enlarged Board of nine members, is concerned to resolve this conflict [between *Morhall* and *Smith*] and clarify definitively the present state of English law, and hence Jersey law, on this important subject.

2. Following a re-trial held at the Royal Court on 12 July 2002 Mr Dennis Peter Holley was convicted of murder. He was a chronic alcoholic. He admitted killing his longstanding girl friend with an axe while under the influence of alcohol. The sole issue at the trial was provocation. On 17 January 2003 the Court of Appeal, comprising Southwell JA, Carey (Bailiff of Guernsey) and Hodge JA, allowed an appeal by Holley and set aside the conviction of murder, on the ground that the Deputy Bailiff had misdirected the jury on the issue of provocation: see 2003 JLR 22. The Court of Appeal later substituted a conviction of manslaughter. From that decision the Attorney General appealed to their Lordships' Board.....

[His lordship recited section 3.]

5. Thus, in line with the common law, section 3 envisages that the defence of provocation has two ingredients. The first ingredient, known as the subjective or factual ingredient, is that the defendant was provoked into losing his self-control. This concept is not without its own difficulties, but it is not necessary to pursue them on this occasion. Suffice to say, in deciding whether this ingredient exists in a particular case all evidence which is probative is admissible. This includes evidence of any mental or other abnormality making it more or less likely that the defendant lost his self-control.

6. The second ingredient, often called the objective or evaluative ingredient, raises, in the language of the statute, 'the question whether the provocation was enough to make a reasonable man do as he did ... [taking] into account everything both done and said according to the effect ... it would have on a reasonable man'. Broken down, this objective ingredient has two elements. The first element calls for an assessment of the gravity of the provocation. The second element calls for application of an external standard of self-control: 'whether the provocation was enough to make a reasonable man do as he did'.

7. The statutory reference to a 'reasonable man' in this context is, by common accord, not the best choice of words. It is difficult to conceive of circumstances where it would be 'reasonable' for a person to respond to a taunt by killing his tormentor. Rather, the phrase is intended to refer to an ordinary person, that is, a person of ordinary self-control.

[His lordship referred to *Camplin* [1978] AC 705, above and *Morhall* [1996] AC 90.]

11. Hence if a homosexual man is taunted for his homosexuality it is for the jury to consider whether a homosexual man having ordinary powers of self-control might, in comparable circumstances, be provoked to lose his self-control and react to the provocation as the defendant did. Authority for this proposition, if needed, is the 'glue-sniffer' case of *R v Morhall* [1996] AC 90. There the deceased nagged the defendant about his addiction to glue-sniffing. The problem before the

House of Lords was whether this addiction should have been taken into account at the defendant's trial as affecting the gravity of the provocation: see page 97D. Lord Goff of Chieveley, with whose speech all members of the House agreed, said it should. The thrust of his reasoning was that, for this purpose, 'the entire factual situation' was to be taken into account. This includes matters not falling strictly within the description 'characteristics'. It also includes matters which are discreditable to the defendant. Lord Goff said, at page 99:

> 'suppose that a man who has been in prison for a sexual offence, for example rape, has after his release been taunted by another man with reference to that offence. It is difficult to see why, on ordinary principles, his characteristic or history as an offender of that kind should not be taken into account as going to the gravity of the provocation.'

12. Of course, assessing the conduct of a glue-sniffing defendant against the standard of a glue-sniffing man having ordinary powers of self-control may mean the defendant is assessed against a standard of self-control he cannot attain. He may be exceptionally excitable or pugnacious. But this is so with every defendant who seeks to rely upon provocation as a defence. The objective standard of self-control is the standard set by the common law and, since 1957, by the statutory reference to a 'reasonable man'. It is of general application. Inherent in the use of this prescribed standard as a uniform standard applicable to all defendants is the possibility that an individual defendant may be temperamentally unable to achieve this standard.

13. Taking into account the age and sex of a defendant, as mentioned in *Camplin*, is not an exception to this uniform approach. The powers of self-control possessed by ordinary people vary according to their age and, more doubtfully, their sex. These features are to be contrasted with abnormalities, that is, features not found in a person having ordinary powers of self-control. The former are relevant when identifying and applying the objective standard of self-control, the latter are not.

14. That Lord Diplock intended to draw this distinction in *Camplin* is plain from the terms of his suggested direction to a jury, quoted above. The statutory reasonable man has the power of self-control to be expected of an ordinary person of like sex and age. In other respects, that is, in respects other than power of self-control, the reasonable man shares such of the defendant's characteristics as the jury think would affect the gravity of the provocation to the defendant. This direction, approved by the other members of the House, was clearly intended to be a model direction, of general application in cases of provocation.

Persons of diminished responsibility

15. Before proceeding further it is important to pause and note that when adopting the 'reasonable man' standard in section 3 of the Homicide Act 1957 Parliament recognised that, standing alone, this provision might work harshly on defendants suffering from mental abnormality. Accordingly, cheek by jowl with section 3 Parliament introduced into English law the partial defence of diminished responsibility. In short, under section 2 a person is not to be convicted of murder if he shows he was suffering from such abnormality of mind, whether arising from a condition of arrested or retarded development of mind or any inherent causes or induced by disease or injury, as 'substantially impaired' his mental responsibility for his acts and omissions in killing or being a party to the killing. In such a case the defendant is liable to be convicted of manslaughter. The burden of proof rests on the defendant who seeks to rely on this defence.

16. This provision, which is reproduced in article 3 of the Jersey law, is apt to embrace some cases where it is inappropriate to apply to the defendant the standard of self-control of an ordinary person. Section 3, with its objective standard, is to be read with this in mind. The statutory provision regarding diminished responsibility in section 2 represents the legislature's view on how cases of mental abnormality are to be accommodated in the law of homicide. *R v Raven* [1982] Crim LR 51 appears to be an instance of a case where this defence would have been relevant. There a 22-year old

defendant had a mental age of 9 years. Similarly in *R v Ahluwalia* [1992] 4 All ER 889, where a defence of provocation failed, the Court of Appeal ordered a retrial on the issue of diminished responsibility. Section 2 should not be distorted to accommodate the types of case for which section 3 was specifically enacted.

The two views

17. Against this background their Lordships turn to consider the point where the substantial difference in judicial views has emerged. Exceptional excitability or pugnacity is one thing. But what if the defendant is suffering from serious mental abnormality, as in the *Morgan Smith* case where the defendant suffered from severe clinical depression? Is he, for the purposes of the defence of provocation, to be judged by the standard of a person having ordinary powers of self-control?

18. The view of the minority in the case of *Morgan Smith* is that he is. The standard is a constant, objective standard in all cases. The jury should assess the gravity of the provocation to the defendant. In that respect, as when considering the subjective ingredient of provocation (did the defendant lose his self-control?), the jury must take the defendant as they find him, 'warts and all', as Lord Millett observed. But having assessed the gravity of the provocation to the defendant, the standard of self-control by which his conduct is to be evaluated for the purpose of the defence of provocation is the external standard of a person having and exercising ordinary powers of self-control. That is the standard the jury should apply when considering whether or not the provocation should be regarded as sufficient to bring about the defendant's response to it: see Lord Millett, at page 211.

19. This view accords with the approach applied by their Lordships' Board in *Luc Thiet Thuan v The Queen* [1997] AC 131, an appeal from Hong Kong. On a trial for murder the defendant relied on the defences of diminished responsibility and provocation. Medical evidence showed the defendant suffered from brain damage and was prone to respond to minor provocation by losing his self-control and acting explosively. The trial judge directed the jury that this medical evidence was not relevant on the defence of provocation. The jury rejected both defences. The correctness of the judge's direction on provocation was the issue on the appeal. The Board, Lord Steyn dissenting, upheld the judge's direction. Lord Goff of Chieveley noted that mental infirmity of the defendant, if itself the subject of taunts by the deceased, may be taken into account as going to the gravity of the provocation. He continued, at page 146:

> 'But this is a far cry from the defendant's submission that the mental infirmity of a defendant impairing his power of self-control should as such be attributed to the reasonable man for the purposes of the objective test.'

The majority view expressed in *Morgan Smith* rejects this approach. According to this view, the standard of self-control required by the common law and by the statute is not the constant standard of a person having and exercising ordinary self-control. The required standard is more flexible. The jury should apply the standard of control to be expected of the particular individual. The jury must ask themselves whether the defendant 'exercised the degree of self-control to be expected of someone in his situation' (emphasis added): see Lord Slynn of Hadley, at page 155. Lord Hoffmann expressed the view, at page 163, that the effect of the change in the law made by section 3 of the Homicide Act was that in future the jury 'were to determine not merely whether the behaviour of the accused complied with some legal standard but could determine for themselves what the standard in the particular case should be'. . . .

[His lordship referred to the speeches of Lord Hoffmann and Clyde above.]

22. This majority view, if their Lordships may respectfully say so, is one model which could be adopted in framing a law relating to provocation. But their Lordships consider there is one compelling, overriding reason why this view cannot be regarded as an accurate statement of English law. It is this. The law of homicide is a highly sensitive and highly controversial area of the criminal law.

In 1957 Parliament altered the common law relating to provocation and declared what the law on this subject should thenceforth be. In these circumstances it is not open to judges now to change ('develop') the common law and thereby depart from the law as declared by Parliament. However much the contrary is asserted, the majority view does represent a departure from the law as declared in section 3 of the Homicide Act 1957. It involves a significant relaxation of the uniform, objective standard adopted by Parliament. Under the statute the sufficiency of the provocation ('whether the provocation was enough to make a reasonable man do as [the defendant] did') is to be judged by one standard, not a standard which varies from defendant to defendant. Whether the provocative act or words and the defendant's response met the 'ordinary person' standard prescribed by the statute is the question the jury must consider, not the altogether looser question of whether, having regard to all the circumstances, the jury consider the loss of self-control was sufficiently excusable. The statute does not leave each jury free to set whatever standard they consider appropriate in the circumstances by which to judge whether the defendant's conduct is 'excusable'.

23. On this short ground their Lordships, respectfully but firmly, consider the majority view expressed in the *Morgan Smith* case is erroneous.

Points arising

24. Their Lordships mention some ancillary points. The first is relevant to the facts in the present case. It concerns application of the principles discussed above in circumstances where the defendant acted under the influence of alcohol or drugs and, therefore, at a time when his level of self-control may have been reduced. If the defendant was taunted on account of his intoxication, that may be a relevant matter for the jury to take into account when assessing the gravity of the taunt to the defendant. But the defendant's intoxicated state is not a matter to be taken into account by the jury when considering whether the defendant exercised ordinary self-control. The position is the same, so far as provocation is concerned, if the defendant's addiction to alcohol has reached the stage that he is suffering from the disease of alcoholism.

25. The second point their Lordships wish to mention concerns the three examples given by Lord Steyn in his dissenting opinion in *Luc Thiet Thuan v The Queen* [1997] AC 131, 149. Lord Steyn instanced cases of women who are more prone to lose their self-control because they are suffering from postnatal depression, or 'battered woman syndrome', or a personality disorder. Lord Steyn suggested that, on the majority view of the law expressed in that case, in those three instances the judge would have to direct the jury that on the defence of provocation the evidence of the woman's condition was admissible on the 'first and subjective inquiry' but not on the 'second and objective inquiry'. Their Lordships respectfully differ. This is not wholly correct. As explained above, the evidence of the woman's condition may be relevant on two issues: whether she lost her self-control, and the gravity of the provocation for her. The jury will then decide whether in their opinion, having regard to the actual provocation and their view of its gravity for the defendant, a woman of her age having ordinary power of self-control might have done what the defendant did. More importantly, in each of these three cases the defendant will in principle have available to her the defence of diminished responsibility. The potential availability of this defence in these cases underlines the importance of not viewing the defence of provocation in isolation from the defence of diminished responsibility. These two defences must be read together to obtain an overall, balanced view of the law in this field.

26. Next, in recent years much play has been made of the 'mental gymnastics' required of jurors in having regard to a defendant's 'characteristics' for one purpose of the law of provocation but not another. Their Lordships consider that any difficulties in this regard have been exaggerated. The question is largely one of presentation. It will be noted that their Lordships have eschewed use of the expression 'characteristics', accompanied as that expression now is with much confusing baggage. The better approach is summarised by Lord Hobhouse of Woodborough in the *Morgan Smith* case at page 205C–H.

27. The final point is this. In expressing their conclusion above their Lordships are not to be taken as accepting that the present state of the law is satisfactory. It is not. The widely held view is that the law relating to provocation is flawed to an extent beyond reform by the courts: see the Law Commission report 'Partial Defences to Murder', (Law Com no 290) (2004 Cm 6301), para 2.10. Their Lordships share this view. But the law on provocation cannot be reformulated in isolation from a review of the law of homicide as a whole. In October 2004 the Home Secretary announced the government's intention to review the law of murder. Given the importance of this area of the criminal law it is imperative that a review, of all aspects of the law of murder, should be undertaken as soon as possible.

…

Dissenting judgment by **Lord Bingham of Cornhill** and **Lord Hoffmann.**

42. We regret that we cannot concur in the opinion of the majority of the Board.

43. The common law of England has for some centuries recognised that there may be circumstances in which a defendant is not justified in killing another but in which the culpability of the defendant is to some extent mitigated because he was provoked to kill that other and would not otherwise have done so. The unjustifiability of such a killing has been reflected in condemning and punishing the defendant for the very serious crime of manslaughter. The element of mitigation is reflected in the reduction of the crime committed from murder to that lesser crime, even where the mental elements necessary for proof of murder have been established.

44. The reason why provocation was accepted by the judges as a partial defence to a charge of murder has been stated on many occasions over many years. It was a humane concession to human infirmity and imperfection, acknowledgement 'that by reason of the frailty of our nature we cannot always stand upright': see, for example, *R v Hayward* (1833) 6 C&P 157, 159, per Tindal CJ; *R v Thomas* (1837) 7 C&P 817, 819, per Parke B; *R v Kirkham* (1837) 8 C&P 115, 117, 119, per Coleridge J; *Holmes v Director of Public Prosecutions* [1946] AC 588, 601, per Viscount Simon; *Director of Public Prosecutions v Camplin* [1978] AC 705, per Lord Diplock at 713, 717, per Lord Morris of Borth-y-Gest at 719, 722, per Lord Simon of Glaisdale at 725; *R v Baillie* [1995] 2 Cr App R 31, 37, per Henry LJ. As was said by Coleridge J in *R v Kirkham*, above, p 117,

> 'The law requires from him [the defendant] and will allow him to show that there were some mitigating circumstances, which alter the presumed character of the act, because it has at once a sacred regard for human life and also a respect for man's failings, and will not require more from an imperfect creature than he can perform.'

We share the opinion, widely expressed, that the law of homicide stands in urgent need of comprehensive and radical reform. But so long as provocation continues to be recognised as a partial defence to a charge of murder it should be applied consistently with its underlying rationale.

45. The partial defence of provocation has always, as Lord Diplock pointed out in *Camplin*, above, at p 713, represented an anomaly in English law, for the reason which he gave, that if it expressed a general principle of criminal law it could not logically be recognised (as it is) as a defence only to a charge of murder (although it is, in that respect, no more anomalous than the statutory defence of diminished responsibility, to which the same restriction applies). It seems clear that the provocation defence was developed by the judges to mitigate the harshness of the ancient law requiring sentence of death to be passed on every defendant convicted of murder. But for the undiscriminating inflexibility of that rule, it may well be that a provocation defence would not have been recognised. But the abolition of capital punishment in Jersey, as in the United Kingdom, does not mean that the true scope of the provocation defence has become a matter of academic interest and no practical importance. In those jurisdictions which continue to follow English authority and which retain the death penalty, the distinction between

conviction of murder and conviction of manslaughter on grounds of provocation may continue to make the difference between life and death. In other jurisdictions, such as Jersey and England and Wales, the penal consequences of conviction of the one crime rather than the other are different, and may be very different. And the rationale of the provocation defence is still the consideration of justice which gave rise to it, that the law should 'not require more from an imperfect creature than he can perform'.

  ...

47. The concept of the reasonable man in this context has been recognised as 'inapt' by Lord Diplock in *Camplin*, [above, at p 716] and by Lord Goff of Chieveley, for the House of Lords, in *R v Morhall* [1996] AC 90, 97–98, for the reason which they gave, that powers of ratiocination bear no obvious relationship to powers of self-control. It may no doubt have been recognition of this inaptness which led Viscount Simon LC to refer in *Mancini*, above, p 9, to 'an ordinary person' and Lord Goddard CJ in *R v McCarthy* [1954] 2 QB 105, 112, to 'an average person'. The public policy underlying adoption of the reasonable man test in the common law doctrine of provocation was to reduce the incidence of fatal violence by preventing a person relying on his own exceptional pugnacity or excitability as an excuse for loss of self-control: see *Camplin*, above, p 716, per Lord Diplock, p 726, per Lord Simon of Glaisdale; *Morhall*, above, p 98, per Lord Goff of Chieveley. But the reasonable man test, literally applied, is in our opinion subject to an even more fundamental objection. Whatever the position in earlier days, when hot blood and a violent response to perceived injury could be more readily excused, few judges or jurors could now conceive of any circumstances in which a reasonable or ordinary or average person would be provoked to take the life of another with the intent necessary for murder.

... [His lordship referred to *Camplin* and reviewed extensively the authorities since that case.]

65. The decisions to which we have referred in *Newell, Raven, Ahluwalia, Dryden, Humphreys, Morhall* and *Thornton (No 2)* were, in our respectful opinion, faithful to the principles laid down by the House in *Camplin*. Importantly, they reflected the rationale of the provocation defence, both in its recognition of the sanctity of human life and its allowance for human imperfection. The effect of the decisions was not to abrogate the important safeguard provided by the objective comparison, and there is nothing in these cases to suggest that short temper or undue pugnacity or excitability could begin to excuse the deliberate taking of a human life. The cases do, however, make clear that the objective comparison is a matter for the opinion of the jury, as Parliament had enacted, with such properly expressed judicial guidance as might be appropriate in the particular case. And they make clear, as *Camplin* had done, that the question is not whether the defendant showed such self-control as an abstract hypothetical person would have done but such self-control as would reasonably be expected of a person having such of his attributes as the jury thought relevant in the factual situation in which the defendant actually found himself at the relevant time.

[His lordship considered the case of *Luc Thiet Than* above.]

  67 ...

  '(2) We cannot reconcile the majority's reading of the speeches in *Camplin* with what their Lordships said in that case, discussed at some length above. The majority [in *Luc*] (pp 140–141) attribute to the House in *Camplin* acceptance of Professor Ashworth's observation ('The Doctrine of Provocation' [1976] CLJ 292, 300) that

    "The proper distinction ... is that individual peculiarities which bear on the gravity of the provocation should be taken into account, whereas individual peculiarities bearing on the accused's level of self-control should not",

  leading the majority to conclude (p 144) that

    "There is no basis upon which mental infirmity on the part of the defendant which has the effect of reducing his powers of self-control below that to be expected of an ordinary person can, as such, be attributed to the ordinary person for the purposes of the objective test in provocation".

> "There is, however, nothing in the report of argument or the speeches to suggest that the House in *Camplin* was referred to the article of Professor Ashworth, and consideration of the gravity of the provocation cannot rationally and fairly be divorced from consideration of the effect of the provocation on the particular defendant in relation to both limbs of the defence. Otherwise one is not comparing like with like, and is losing sight of the essential question whether, in all the circumstances, the defendant's conduct was to some degree excusable."

> (3) We would not accept that the defences of diminished responsibility and provocation are as sharply demarcated as the majority (pp 146–147) suggest....'

[**Lord Carswell** delivered a dissenting opinion agreeing with the reasons given and the conclusions reached in the dissenting opinion of Lords Bingham and Hoffmann.]

71. In developing the criminal law the courts should strive to meet three important criteria: its principles should fit a logical pattern; it should be capable of explanation to a jury; and, above all, it should achieve justice. My concern is that the law of provocation accepted as correct by the majority of the Board fails to meet these criteria.

72. The dichotomy expressed by the Board in *Luc Thiet Thuan v The Queen* [1997] AC 131, and approved by the majority in the present appeal, was neatly expressed by Professor AJ Ashworth in his influential article 'The Doctrine of Provocation' [1976] CLJ 292 at 300:

> 'The proper distinction...is that individual peculiarities which bear on the gravity of the provocation should be taken into account, whereas individual peculiarities bearing on the accused's level of self-control should not.'

I cannot myself see any convincing logical ground for this distinction. It is, however, always as well to remember the famous remark of Oliver Wendell Holmes Jr about logic and the law, the full version of which bears repetition, for it could have been written about this very topic (*The Common Law* (1881), p 1):

> 'The life of the law has not been logic: it has been experience. The felt necessities of the time, the prevalent moral and political theories, intuitions of public policy, avowed or unconscious, even the prejudices which judges share with their fellow-men, have had a good deal more to do than the syllogism in determining the rules by which men should be governed.'

That said, I regard the dichotomy as an unsatisfactory compromise, which should be maintained only if one is compelled to do so by necessary interpretation of the governing legislation or if there are good practical grounds to support it ...

Notes and questions

1. Should the English Court of Appeal follow the decision in *Morgan Smith* which is binding on it, or the decision of the majority in *Holley* which is of persuasive weight only? In *Mohammed* [2005] EWCA Crim 1880 the Court of Appeal applied *Holley*.

2. Has the hearing by a nine-member Board created the clarity and certainty that the law requires when dealing with such an important defence?

Andrew Ashworth, commenting on the case at [2005] Crim LR 970, states that: 'Lords Bingham and Hoffmann invoke what they regard as the true rationale of the partial defence of provocation—"a human concession to human infirmity and imperfection" (at [44]), ensuring that the law "will not require more from an imperfect creature than he can perform" (at [45]), and thus asking "whether, in all the circumstances, the defendant's conduct was to some degree excusable" (at [66]). The difficulty with these statements of the rationale is that they are wide and unspecific, saying nothing about provocation in particular.

They are couched solely in the language of excuse, and without any clear boundaries.' Do you agree? Do they provide an opportunity for a more humane response to the mandatory sentence?

Phillips v R

(1968) 53 Cr App R 132, Privy Council

(Lords Hodson, Guest and Diplock)

At the appellant's trial for murder in Jamaica, the judge directed the jury as follows:

If you are satisfied, if you find that the accused did commit the act as a result of provocation you will have to consider the retaliation as against the type of provocation that he received. You have to determine whether the provocation under which the accused was labouring was enough to make a reasonable person do as the accused did. In deciding this question you must consider the provocation received and the manner of the retaliation, and ask whether a reasonable person provoked in the way that the accused was provoked would retaliate in the way that the accused retaliated. If a reasonable person would not retaliate in the way that the accused retaliated, the defence of provocation cannot avail the accused because the standard fixed by law is that of the reasonable man, and you, the jury, must be satisfied not only that the accused was so provoked that he lost his self-control and retaliated, but that a reasonable person would have lost his self-control in the same circumstances and do as the accused did....

On appeal to the Privy Council:

Lord Diplock.... The test of provocation in the law of homicide is two-fold. The first, which has always been a question of fact for the jury, assuming that there is any evidence upon which they can so find, is: 'Was the defendant provoked into losing his self-control?' The second, which is one not of fact but of opinion, 'Would a reasonable man have reacted to the same provocation in the same way as the defendant did?'

Before their Lordships, counsel for the appellant contended, not as a matter of construction but as one of logic, that once a reasonable man had lost his self-control his actions ceased to be those of a reasonable man and that accordingly he was no longer fully responsible in law for them whatever he did. This argument is based on the premise that loss of self-control is not a matter of degree but is absolute: there is no intermediate stage between icy detachment and going berserk. This premise, unless the argument is purely semantic, must be based upon human experience and is, in their Lordships' view, false. The average man reacts to provocation according to its degree with angry words, with a blow of the hand, possibly, if the provocation is gross and there is a dangerous weapon to hand, with that weapon. It is not insignificant that the appellant himself described his own instantaneous reaction to the victim's provocation in spitting on his mother as: 'I spin around quickly was to punch her with my hand.'

In that part of his direction which the Court of Appeal held to be objectionable, the learned judge followed closely the actual words of the section and made it clear to the jury that it was their responsibility, not his, to decide whether a reasonable man would have reacted to the provocation in the way that the appellant did. In their Lordships' view this was an impeccable direction.

Since the passing of the legislation, it may be prudent to avoid the use of the precise words of Viscount Simon's in *Mancini v DPP* ([1942] AC 1) 'the mode of resentment must bear a reasonable relationship to the provocation' unless they are used in a context which makes it clear to the jury that this is not a rule of law which they are bound to follow, but merely a consideration which may or may not commend itself to them. But their Lordships would repeat that it is the effect of the summing-up as a whole that matters and not any stated verbal formula used in the course of it.

As already pointed out, the learned judge in the instant case did not use the *Mancini* (supra) formula at all. He made it abundantly clear to the jury that it was their function and theirs alone to decide whether or not a reasonable man would have reacted to the provocation in the way the appellant did. In their Lordships' view the Court of Appeal of Jamaica should have dismissed the appeal on the ground that there was no error in the summing-up on provocation. The question of the application of the proviso to s 16(1) of the Jamaica Judicature (Court of Appeal) Law, does not therefore arise.

For these reasons their Lordships humbly advised Her Majesty that this appeal should be dismissed.

Appeal dismissed

Question

How is the view that the 'reasonable relationship' principle is not a rule of law but merely a consideration which may or may not commend itself to the jury to be reconciled with the words of the section, 'enough to make a reasonable man do as he did'?

R v Johnson

(1989) 89 Cr App R 148, Court of Appeal, Criminal Division

(Watkins LJ, McCowan and Judge JJ)

J and R had been drinking at a night club. J made threats of violence to R's female friend and to R himself. A struggle developed between J and R. J was carrying a flick knife. He stabbed R and killed him. He was convicted of murder and appealed on the ground that the judge ought to have, but did not, direct the jury on provocation.

Watkins LJ. There was undoubtedly evidence to suggest that, if the appellant had lost his self-control, it was his own behaviour which caused others to react towards him in the way we have described.

We were referred to the decision of the Privy Council in *Edwards v R* [1973] AC 648. In that case the trial Judge had directed the jury thus:

> 'In my view the defence of provocation cannot be of any avail to the accused in this case … it ill befits the accused, having gone there with the deliberate purpose of blackmailing this man—you may well think it ill befits him to say out of his own mouth that he was provoked by any attack. In my view the defence of provocation is not one which you need consider in this case.'

The full Court in Hong Kong held that this direction was erroneous. The Privy Council agreed with the full Court. On the particular facts of the case Lord Pearson, giving the judgment of the Board, said (page 658): 'On principle it seems reasonable to say that (1) a blackmailer cannot rely on the predictable results of his own blackmailing conduct as constituting provocation … and the predictable results may include a considerable degree of hostile reaction by the person sought to be blackmailed; (2) but if the hostile reaction by the person sought to be blackmailed goes to extreme lengths it might constitute sufficient provocation even for the blackmailer; (3) there would in many cases be a question of degree to be decided by the jury.' Those words cannot, we think, be understood to mean, as was suggested to us, that provocation which is 'self-induced' ceases to be provocation for the purposes of section 3.

The relevant statutory provision being considered by the Privy Council was in similar terms to section 3. In view of the express wording of section 3, as interpreted in *Camplin*, which was decided after *Edwards*, we find it impossible to accept that the mere fact that a defendant caused a reaction in others, which in turn led him to lose his self-control, should result in the issue of provocation being kept outside a jury's consideration. Section 3 clearly provides that the question is whether things done or said or both provoked the defendant to lose his self-control. If there is any evidence that it may have done, the issue must be left to the jury. The jury would then have to consider all the circumstances of the incident, including all the relevant behaviour of the defendant, in deciding (a) whether he was in fact provoked and (b) whether the provocation was enough to make a reasonable man do what the defendant did.

Accordingly, whether or not there were elements in the appellant's conduct which justified the conclusion that he had started the trouble and induced others, including the deceased, to react in the way they did, we are firmly of the view that the defence of provocation should have been left to the jury.

Conviction for murder quashed. Conviction for manslaughter substituted

See, generally, A. J. Ashworth, 'Self-induced Provocation and the Homicide Act' [1973] Crim LR 483.

(3) REFORM

The Law Commission's Report No 290, 'Partial Defences to Murder' (2004) made radical proposals for reform. Note, this was before *Holley*. (On Consultation Paper No 173, see J. Chalmers, 'Merging Provocation and Diminished Responsibility: Some Reasons for Scepticism' [2004] Crim LR 198; R. D. Mackay and B. Mitchell, 'Replacing Provocation: More on A Combined Plea' [2004] Crim LR 219; J. Gardner and T. Macklem, 'No Provocation without Responsibility: A Reply to Mackay and Mitchell' [2004] Crim LR 213.)

The major problems with provocation

3.20 There was widespread dissatisfaction among consultees both with the theoretical underpinning of the defence of provocation and with its various component parts. It is not underpinned by any clear rationale. There is widespread agreement that the concept of provocation has become far too loose, so that a judge may be obliged to leave the issue to the jury when the conduct and/or the words in question are trivial. The concept of loss of self-control has proved to be very troublesome. The supposed requirement of a sudden and temporary loss of self-control has given rise to serious problems, especially in the 'slow burn' type of case. There is much controversy about the supposed objective test (that the provocation was enough to make a reasonable person do as the defendant did), which has been interpreted by the majority of the House of Lords in *Smith (Morgan)* in a way that may enable a defendant to rely on personal idiosyncrasies which make him or her more short tempered than other people. . . .

3.36 Powerful arguments can be advanced for and against the abolition of provocation as a defence. Abolitionists argue that a person who is sane and who kills another person unlawfully, with the intent required for murder, ought to be guilty of murder however great the provocation may have been. Provocation may be a mitigating circumstance which should be taken into account in passing sentence, but not in defining the offence. Assessing sentence requires a balanced appraisal of all the circumstances of the case (aggravating as well as mitigating), and this is a judicial rather than a jury function. Not only is it inappropriate that provocation should be singled out among other possible mitigating circumstances as providing a special partial defence, but there are great difficulties in trying to define what may amount to provocation and how serious it has to be in order to amount to a partial defence.

3.37 Those who argue for the retention of some form of provocation defence, whether or not the mandatory sentence is retained, say that there are moral and practical reasons for doing so. Where the defendant's conduct was precipitated by really serious provocation, it is morally right that this should be reflected in the way that society labels and sentences the defendant; and it is desirable that the factual and evaluative question whether the defendant was provoked in that sense should be taken by the jury. A short sentence (or even in some circumstances a non-custodial sentence) for a provoked killing will be more understandable by, and acceptable to, the public if it results from a conviction by a jury of an offence not carrying the title of murder, than a decision by a judge after a conviction for murder. The existence of such a partial defence is justifiable in the law of murder, although there is no similar partial defence to non-fatal offences of violence, not only because the sentence for murder is fixed by law but also because of the unique gravity and stigma attached to murder. The real problem with provocation is not the underlying concept, but the way it has developed. It needs to be reshaped.

The Law Commission's final proposal in Report No 290 is:

(1) Unlawful homicide that would otherwise be murder should instead be manslaughter if the defendant acted in response to:
    (a) gross provocation (meaning words or conduct or a combination of words and conduct which caused the defendant to have a justi.able sense of being seriously wronged);
    or
    (b) fear of serious violence towards the defendant or another; or
    (c) combination of (a) and (b).

(2) A person of the defendant's age and of ordinary temperament, that is, ordinary tolerance and self-restraint, in the circumstances of the defendant might have reacted in the same or a similar way.

(3) In deciding whether a person of ordinary temperament in the circumstances of the defendant might have acted in the same or a similar way, the court should take into account the defendant's age and all the circumstances of the defendant other than matters whose only relevance to the defendant's conduct is that they bear simply on his or her general capacity for self-control.

(3) The partial defence should not apply where:
    (a) the provocation was incited by the defendant for the purpose of providing an excuse to use violence, or
    (b) the defendant acted in considered desire for revenge.

(4) A person should not be treated as having acted in considered desire for revenge if he or she acted in fear of serious violence merely because he or she was also angry towards the deceased for the conduct which engendered that fear.

(5) The partial defence should not apply to a defendant who kills or takes part in the killing of another person under duress of threats by a third person.

(6) A judge should not be required to leave the defence to the jury unless there is evidence on which a reasonable jury, properly directed, could conclude that it might apply.

For criticism see R. D. Mackay and B. Mitchell, 'But is this Provocation? Some Thoughts on Law Commission Report No 290' [2005] Crim LR 44.

3. SUICIDE PACTS AND COMPLICITY IN SUICIDE

Homicide Act 1957, s 4

(1) It shall be manslaughter, and shall not be murder, for a person acting in pursuance of a suicide pact between him and another to kill the other or be a party to the other ... being killed by a third person.

(2) Where it is shown that a person charged with the murder of another killed the other or was a party to his ... being killed, it shall be for the defence to prove that the person charged was acting in pursuance of a suicide pact between him and the other.

(3) For the purposes of this section 'suicide pact' means a common agreement between two or more persons having for its object the death of all of them, whether or not each is to take his own life, but nothing done by a person who enters into a suicide pact shall be treated as done by him in pursuance of the pact unless it is done while he has the settled intention of dying in pursuance of the pact.

Suicide Act 1961, s 1

The rule of law whereby it is a crime for a person to commit suicide is hereby abrogated.

Suicide Act 1961, s 2

(1) A person who aids, abets, counsels or procures the suicide of another, or an attempt by another to commit suicide, shall be liable on conviction on indictment to imprisonment for a term not exceeding fourteen years.

(2) If on the trial of an indictment for murder or manslaughter it is proved that the accused aided, abetted, counselled or procured the suicide of the person in question, the jury may find him guilty of that offence.

See *R (on the application of Pretty) v DPP* [2002] 1 All ER 1, HL, above, p 112.

Questions

1. Don decides to commit suicide. He closes his eyes and throws himself from a fifth floor window into the street below. He lands on Paul. Paul's neck is broken and he dies. Don breaks both his legs but, after six months in hospital, is now fully recovered. Is Don guilty of any offence?

2. Dick and Dora agree that they will die together. They are found in a gas-filled room. Dora is dead, but Dick recovers. Dick cannot remember who turned on the gas-tap and there is no evidence on the point. Can Dick be convicted of an offence under the Suicide Act or under s 4 of the Homicide Act? Might it be different if Dora had been shot and it was impossible to prove whether she shot herself or was shot by Dick?

3. Eric and Ernie, who belong to a strange religious sect, agree that they will inflict mutilations on each other, amounting to grievous bodily harm. They believe that this will put them in a state of grace. They carry out their agreement. Are they guilty of an offence? (See Ch 19 below.) If Ernie dies of the injuries inflicted by Eric, is Eric guilty of homicide?

4. Kevin, a prisoner, announces that he will neither eat nor drink until he is released or he dies. Leo, the prison governor, tells the prison staff that Kevin's wishes are to be respected, that he is to be offered neither food nor drink unless he asks for it. Kevin asks for nothing and dies. Is Leo guilty of an offence? See *Secretary of State for Home Department v Robb* [1995] 1 All ER 677 and *Reeves v Metropolitan Police Comr* [1999] 3 All ER 897, HL.

R v McShane

(1977) 66 Cr App R 97, Court of Appeal, Criminal Division

(Orr, Browne LJJ and Willis J)

The appellant was in some financial difficulty. Her grandmother had left a large part of her estate in trust for the appellant, but provided that the appellant's mother should receive the income from that estate for her life. The appellant's mother was elderly and ill, and had often talked of committing suicide. On at least three occasions the appellant had left fatal doses of pills with her mother, and on the last was heard to advise her that 'Whisky with barbiturates is fatal.' The appellant was convicted of an attempt to counsel or procure her mother's suicide. She argued that this was not an offence known to the law.

[**Orr LJ** read the judgment of the court:]

... The answer to that ground is, in our judgment, that every attempt to commit an offence is an offence at common law, whether the crime attempted is one by statute or at common law (see *Archbold* (39th edn) paragraph 4100 and the authorities there cited). It follows in our judgment that the appellant was properly charged under count 1 with an offence of attempting to aid or abet, counsel or procure the suicide of Mrs Mott and none the less so because the crime defined in section 2(1) of the Act 1961 is itself of the nature of an attempt ...

Appeal dismissed

Questions

1. Why was the defendant charged with an attempt and not with the full offence of counselling suicide?

2. *Is* the crime defined in s 2(1) in the nature of an attempt? Can there be an attempt to attempt?

3. Does the case establish a general principle that there can be an attempt to aid and abet? Cf *Stonehouse*, p **534**, above and [1977] Crim LR 542, 544 and 738.

R v S

[2005] EWCA Crim 819, Court of Appeal, Criminal Division

(Rix LJ, Holman J and Sir Michael Wright)

Lord Justice Rix:
4. ... On the afternoon of 29th January 2002 the appellant's 15 year old girlfriend was discovered lying on rocks below a stone jetty at St David's Quay near Aberystwyth. She was taken to hospital and found to be suffering from serious injuries which would have resulted in her asphyxiation from her own blood had she not received prompt medical attention. Moreover, if she had not been recovered from where she lay at the foot of the stone jetty she would within a short further period of time in all probability have been drowned by the incoming tide.

5. It was the prosecution case that her then 14 year old boyfriend, the appellant, had intended that she should kill herself and had aided and abetted her to do so. It was not ultimately alleged that he had counselled or procured her to do so.

6. It was submitted that as they had walked home on 29th January of that year he had encouraged her to jump off a bridge, said that her life was 'crap' and that he wanted her to be free. Further, that at his house he had plied her with alcohol and dictated her suicide note before taking her up to the jetty where he had pushed her to the edge and encouraged her to jump. After she had gone over the edge the appellant left the scene and did not call the emergency services until an hour and a half later. His girlfriend maintained that she never intended to jump. The Crown alleged that he had a fascination and unhealthy interest in death, Satanism, suicide, serial killers and necrophilia and that he had got a sexual thrill from the thought of death and infliction of pain . . . .

7. It was the defence case that the appellant had neither done nor said anything to encourage or assist his girlfriend to commit suicide and that he had not seen her fall. She had spoken of suicide on previous occasions and was unhappy at home, but he did not know that she had intended to jump off the jetty. He had not dictated or helped her with the note and thought it just referred to their plan to run away . . . .

[His lordship dealt with the facts and recited s 2(1) of the Suicide Act 1961 (above).]

28. Mr Jennings [counsel for the appellant] submitted that in concentrating solely upon the appellant's intention the learned judge had failed to direct the jury that it was necessary to the commission of the offence that the appellant should know, or at least believe, that the girlfriend was intending to or contemplating suicide, Mr Jennings pointed out that on the girlfriend's own evidence she had denied any such intention or contemplation.

29. Before developing that submission, we should refer to the manner in which the judge had summed up the ingredients of the offence. At 9C to E of the transcript he said this: 'Now there are two separate ingredients to this offence, both of which must be proved by the prosecution. First, it must be proved that at the time—in other words immediately leading up to and during [her] fall off the stone jetty—the defendant intended that she should kill herself. Now it is his intent with which you are concerned and not [her] intent. Whether [she] did or did not want to commit suicide is immaterial to this offence. And, secondly, it must be proved that [the appellant] did some act—whether it was a physical act or whether it consisted of words of encouragement—which constituted an attempt to aid, abet, counsel or procure her to do so.' . . .

31. The judge went on a little later on the same page (at 12G to 13A): 'But in this case [she] told you that she didn't want to commit suicide and that she didn't do so or attempt to do so. She wasn't saying that the defendant persuaded her at all and that that led her to deliberately jump off. And so whilst the attributed comments, advice and encouragement prior to their arrival at the jetty are important for you to assess in determining the defendant's state of mind and therefore his intent, you should only convict if sure that at the end of the jetty he did or said something to her which he intended would cause her to try and take her life.'

32. Then at 13D to 14B he said:

'Now you will note that the offence particularises "an attempt" to aid and abet and that is because on [her] evidence, as I referred to it a moment go, she did not in fact try to commit suicide at all. We do not know why on the evidence she fell. We know that she had had a lot to drink; we know that she was sitting on the edge of the jetty in very stormy weather conditions. She cannot specifically recall how she came to fall on to the rocks. She cannot say if she was pushed and therefore there is no evidence to support such a contention or even possibility of that.

Accordingly, on this evidence the Crown can only allege that the defendant attempted to aid and abet her suicide. Now before you can convict the defendant, therefore, you must be sure that he intended that she commit suicide, as I have explained already, and that with that intention he did something which was more than mere preparation towards encouraging or assisting her to do so. If you accept [her] evidence that he was physically pushing her to the edge and that he removed her shoes and told her to fetch one that he'd thrown into sea, then you may think that that does go beyond mere preparation for encouraging or assisting her to commit suicide but ultimately it's for you to decide. You may think that the real issue here is whether you believe [her] or not. If you are sure that her evidence was correct in respect of those events, then you may think that this charge is made out but if you are not sure of that, then you should acquit and that is for you to decide.'

[His lordship referred to *McShane* and *Attorney-General v Able* [1984] QB 795 where the Attorney-General had sought, unsuccessfully, a declaration against defendants who were members of the Executive Committee of the Voluntary Euthanasia Society and who had published a booklet entitled 'A guide to self-deliverance' for distribution to members of the society with the express aim of overcoming the fear of the process of dying.]

39. ... The words of the statute make it clear that there has to be the aiding, abetting, or attempting to aid and abet, the suicide or attempted suicide 'of another' (those are words in section 2 (1).... In the present case the 'another' which was relevant to the facts here was the appellant's girlfriend.

40. The question, it seems to us, that the jury here were properly directed to keep their close attention to was the appellant's intention and nothing else. The fact that that intention to aid and abet the suicide or attempted suicide of another would be impossible in circumstances where that another had no intention herself to commit suicide or even attempt to commit suicide, merely means that on the facts of such a case the attempt would merely be the attempt of an impossibility. But it is clear from the House of Lords decision in *R v Shivpuri* [1987] AC 1 [above p **547**] that it is no impediment to the offence of an attempted crime that the actual crime would have been impossible on the facts of the case, such as attempting to pick an empty pocket or attempting to handle goods which have not been stolen, or attempting to murder not a person but a bolster in a bed. So, at pages 19 to 20 of Lord Bridge of Harwich's speech in *Shivpuri* the critical ingredients of an attempted crime under section 1 of the 1981 [Criminal Attempts] Act are focused on as being the defendant's intent, and, with that intent, the doing of an act more than merely preparatory to the commission of the offence.

41. Similarly it is in those terms that the offence of an attempt is defined by the learned editors of *Smith and Hogan* at page 346 in this passage: 'In the case of an attempt it must be proved that D had an intention to commit the crime in question. Once that is established the only question is whether with that intent he has done an act which is "more than merely preparatory" to the commission of the offence.'

42. Of course it may in many circumstances be implicit in an intention to aid and abet a suicide or suicide attempt, that the defendant has a belief in the other person's intention or willingness to attempt suicide or, at any rate, in that other person's contemplation of suicide. But in certain circumstances such a belief may fade into almost nothing, or into nothing itself, as where a defendant attempts to aid and abet a person to commit suicide merely on the whim that if he, the defendant, can provide enough assistance, then any person at all, even someone who would never have contemplated suicide could be brought to the point of taking the final step.

43. In our judgment, therefore, the judge directed the jury, in the passages to which we have referred, entirely accurately. We dismiss this ground of appeal.

4. INVOLUNTARY MANSLAUGHTER

The difficulties of defining involuntary manslaughter were described by Lord Atkin in the leading case of *Andrews v DPP* [1937] AC 576, [1937] 2 All ER 552, p **638**, below.

My Lords, of all crimes manslaughter appears to afford most difficulties of definition, for it concerns homicide in so many and so varying conditions. From the early days, when any homicide involved penalty, the law has gradually evolved 'through successive differentiations and integrations' until it recognises murder on the one hand, based mainly, though not exclusively, on an intention to kill, and manslaughter on the other hand, based mainly, though not exclusively, on the absence of intention to kill, but the presence of an element of 'unlawfulness' which is the elusive factor.

There appear now to be three categories of involuntary manslaughter:

(1) killing by an 'unlawful and dangerous' act;

(2) killing by gross negligence;

(3) killing by subjective recklessness.

These categories overlap to a considerable degree.

(1) 'UNLAWFUL ACT' MANSLAUGHTER

Parallel to the doctrine of constructive murder (above, pp **561–562**) there existed a doctrine of constructive manslaughter. While death caused during the commission of a felony was murder, death caused during the commission of an 'unlawful' act was manslaughter. As appears above the doctrine of constructive murder had been narrowed down by the judges before it was finally abolished by the Homicide Act 1957. Somewhat similarly the doctrine of constructive manslaughter has been narrowed down but, despite recommendations of the CLRC and the Law Commission (below, p **663**), has not been abolished.

The doctrine in its extreme form may be illustrated by *Fenton* (1830) 1 Lew CC 179 where Tindal CJ directed the jury that throwing stones down a mine shaft was a trespass and therefore it followed that the defendant was guilty of manslaughter where a stone broke some scaffolding with the result that a corf overturned and miners were killed.

R v Franklin
(1883) 15 Cox CC 163, Sussex Assizes

The defendant on the West Pier at Brighton, took up 'a good sized box' from a refreshment stall and wantonly threw it into the sea. It struck T who was swimming underneath and caused his death. The prosecution, citing *Fenton*, above, urged that throwing the refreshment stall-keeper's box into the sea was an unlawful act and it followed that, if it caused death, that was manslaughter.

[Field J, having consulted Mathew J:]

I am of opinion that the case must go to the jury upon the broad ground of negligence and not upon the narrow ground proposed by the learned counsel, because it seems to me—and I may say that in this view my brother Mathew agrees—that the mere fact of a civil wrong committed by one person against another ought not to be used as an incident which is a necessary step in a criminal case. I have a great abhorrence of constructive crime. We do not think the case cited by the counsel for the prosecution is binding upon us in the facts of this case, and, therefore, the civil wrong against the refreshment-stall keeper is immaterial to this charge of manslaughter. I do not think that the facts of this case bring it clearly within the principle laid down by Tindal CJ in *R v Fenton*. If I thought this case was in principle like that case I would, if requested, state a case for the opinion of the Court of Criminal Appeal. But I do not think so.

It was not disputed that the prisoner threw the box over the pier, that the box fell upon the boy, and the death of the boy was caused by the box falling upon him.

[*Gill*, for the prisoner, relied upon the point that there was not proved such negligence as was criminal negligence on the part of the prisoner.

Field J, in summing up the case to the jury, went carefully through the evidence, pointing out how the facts as admitted and proved affected the prisoner upon the legal question as he had explained it to them.

The jury returned a verdict of guilty of manslaughter.]

R v Larkin

[1943] 1 All ER 217, Court of Criminal Appeal

(Viscount Caldecote CJ, Humphreys and Asquith JJ)

The woman with whom the appellant was living died from a throat wound inflicted by the appellant. He found her at a drinking party with a man, Nielsen, with whom she had been committing what would have been adultery if she had in fact been married to the appellant. He went away, brooded on the matter and returned with a razor. He stated in evidence that his only intention was to terrify Nielsen with the razor but the woman, groggy with drink, swayed against him and her throat was cut by accident.

[At the trial for murder, **Oliver J** directed the jury:]

'A man who rushes into a house flourishing a naked razor and wounds someone, even accidentally, is still guilty of manslaughter if that person dies ... I have told you ... the law is for me, and I will tell you on my responsibility that in threatening a man with a naked razor because you wanted to scare him, however good reason you may have for disliking him, you are doing an unlawful act.'

Humphreys J. Perhaps it is as well that once more the proposition of law should be stated which has been stated for generations by judges and, so far as we are aware, never disputed or doubted. If a person is engaged in doing a lawful act, and in the course of doing that lawful act behaves so negligently as to cause the death of some other person, then it is for the jury to say, upon a consideration of the whole of the facts of the case, whether the negligence proved against the accused person amounts to manslaughter, and it is the duty of the presiding judge to tell them that it will not amount to manslaughter unless the negligence is of a very high degree; the expression most commonly used is unless it shows the accused to have been reckless as to the consequences of the act. That is where the act is lawful. Where the act which a person is engaged in performing is unlawful, then, if at the same time it is a dangerous act, that is, an act which is likely to injure another person, and quite inadvertently he causes the death of that other person by that act, then he is guilty of manslaughter. If, in doing that dangerous and unlawful act, he is doing an act which amounts to a felony he is guilty of murder, and he is equally guilty of murder if he does the act with the intention of causing grievous bodily harm to the person whom, in fact, he kills ...

Appeal dismissed

R v Church
[1965] 2 All ER 72, Court of Criminal Appeal

(Edmund Davies, Marshall and Widgery JJ)

The appellant, according to his account, took a woman, Mrs Nott, to his van for sexual purposes. He was unable to satisfy her. She reproached him and slapped his face. They had a fight and he knocked her out. He tried unsuccessfully for about half an hour to wake her, panicked, dragged her out of the van and put her in the river. Mrs Nott was drowned.

At the trial, for the first time, the appellant said that he thought she was dead when he put her in the water. The judge directed the jury that if Nott in fact was alive when thrown into the river, whether the appellant knew it or not, that was manslaughter. The jury convicted him of manslaughter.

[**Edmund Davies J** having cited the judge's direction on this issue:]
Such a direction is not lacking in authority; see, for example, *Shoukatallie v R* [[1962] AC 81, [1961] 3 All ER 996], in Lord Denning's opinion [[1962] AC 81 at 86, 92, [1961] 3 All ER 996 at 998, 1001], and Dr Glanville Williams' *Criminal Law* (2nd edn) at p 173. Nevertheless, in the judgment of this court it was misdirection. It amounted to telling the jury that, whenever any unlawful act is committed in relation to a human being which resulted in death there must be, at least, a conviction for manslaughter. This might at one time have been regarded as good law: see, for example, *Fenton* [(1830) 1 Lew CC 179]. It appears to this court, however, that the passage of years has achieved a transformation in this branch of the law and, even in relation to manslaughter, a degree of mens rea has become recognised as essential. To define it is a difficult task, and in *Andrews v DPP* [[1937] AC 576 at 582, [1937] 2 All ER 552 at 555; p **638**, below] Lord Atkin spoke of the element of '"unlawfulness" which is the elusive factor'. Stressing that we are here leaving entirely out of account those ingredients of homicide which might justify a verdict of manslaughter on the grounds of (a) criminal negligence, or (b) provocation or (c) diminished responsibility, the conclusion of this court is that an unlawful act causing the death of another cannot, simply because it is an unlawful act, render a manslaughter verdict inevitable. For such a verdict inexorably to follow, the unlawful act must be such as all sober and reasonable people would inevitably recognise must subject the other person to, at least, the risk of some harm resulting therefrom, albeit not serious harm....

If such be the test, as we adjudge it to be, then it follows that, in our view, it was a misdirection to tell the jury simpliciter that it mattered nothing for manslaughter whether or not the appellant believed Mrs Nott to be dead when he threw her in the river....

[The court dismissed the appeal on the ground that judge's direction on criminal negligence was an adequate one and, quite apart from that, the principle of *Thabo Meli*, p **47**, above, applied to manslaughter (following Glanville Williams, *Criminal Law* (2nd edn), p 174) and the jury were entitled to regard the appellant's conduct as a series of acts which culminated in her death.]

Appeal dismissed

R v Lamb
[1967] 2 All ER 1282, Court of Appeal, Criminal Division

(Sachs LJ, Lyell and Geoffrey Lane JJ)

The appellant, in jest, pointed at his best friend a revolver with five chambers. It had bullets in two of the chambers but neither of these was opposite the barrel. He thought it was safe to pull the trigger. His friend was also treating the matter as a joke. Lamb pulled the trigger and shot his friend dead. The revolver functioned in such a way that, when the trigger was pulled, the chambers rotated, bringing the loaded chamber opposite the barrel, before the firing pin struck. The appellant was charged with manslaughter and set up the defence of accident. The judge directed that the pointing of the revolver and pulling of the trigger was an unlawful act even if there was no intent to injure or alarm and that the jury did not need to consider whether the pointing of the gun was an assault.

[**Sachs LJ**, reading the judgment of the court:]

Counsel for the Crown, however, had at all times put forward the correct view that for the act to be unlawful it must constitute at least what he then termed 'a technical assault'. In this court, moreover, he rightly conceded that there was no evidence to go to the jury of any assault of any kind. Nor did he feel able to submit that the acts of the appellant were on any other ground unlawful in the criminal sense of that word. Indeed no such submission could in law be made: if, for instance, the pulling of the trigger had had no effect because the striking mechanism or the ammunition had been defective no offence would have been committed by the appellant. Another way of putting it is that mens rea being now an essential ingredient in manslaughter (compare *Andrews v DPP* [[1937] AC 576 at 582, [1937] 2 All ER 552 at 555, 556; p **638**, below] and *Church* [[1965] 2 All ER 72 at 76, [1966] 1QB 59 at 70; p **624** above] this could not in the present case be established in relation to the first ground except by proving that element of intent without which there can be no assault. It is perhaps as well to mention that when using the phrase 'unlawful in the criminal sense of that word' the court has in mind that it is long settled that it is not in point to consider whether an act is unlawful merely from the angle of civil liabilities. That was first made clear in *Franklin* [(1883) 15 Cox CC 163]. The relevant extracts from this and from later judgments are collected in *Russell on Crime* (11th edn, 1958), pp 651–658. The whole of that part of the summing-up which concerned the first ground was thus vitiated by misdirections based on an erroneous concept of the law; and the strength with which that ground was put to the jury no doubt stemmed from the firm view of the trial judge, expressed more than once in the course of the discussion on law in relation to the undisputed facts: 'How can there be a defence to the charge of manslaughter? Manslaughter requires no intent.' . . . [His Lordship discussed the judge's direction on criminal negligence.] The general effect of the summing-up was thus to withdraw from the jury the defence put forward on behalf of the appellant. When the gravamen of a charge is criminal negligence—often referred to as recklessness—of an accused, the jury have to consider amongst other matters the state of his mind, and that includes the question of whether or not he thought that that which he was doing was safe. In the present case it would, of course, have been fully open to a jury, if properly directed, to find the accused guilty because they considered his view as to there being no danger was formed in a criminally negligent way. But he was entitled to a direction that the jury should take into account the fact that he had indisputably formed this view and that there was expert evidence as to this being an understandable view. Strong though the evidence of criminal negligence was, the appellant was entitled as of right to have his defence considered but he was not accorded this right and the jury was left without a direction on an essential matter. Those defects of themselves are such that the verdict cannot stand. . . .

Appeal allowed

Notes and questions

1. What would have been the position if:
   (i) the accused had intended to alarm his friend by pointing the gun but the friend was not alarmed?
   (ii) the accused did not intend to alarm his friend, or foresee that he might be alarmed, but the friend was in fact alarmed?

2. Did the court consider that proof of criminal negligence requires proof of a state of mind? Could the defendant, in the view of the court, be guilty though he believed his conduct was perfectly safe?

3. Why was it necessary for the jury to consider, on the negligence ground, what the accused himself thought?

4. Do the foregoing cases establish either of the following propositions: (i) a mere civil wrong does not suffice as an 'unlawful' act; (ii) an act is not 'unlawful' unless it is criminal? (iii) all crimes are 'unlawful' acts?

5. For a conviction for unlawful act manslaughter do the foregoing cases require that D intended or foresaw at least some harm to the victim? If not, what is it that D must intend or foresee?

6. In *Scarlett* [1993] 4 All ER 629, D, a licensee, caused death by using excessive force while lawfully expelling a trespasser from his pub. His conviction for manslaughter was quashed because the judge had directed that D was guilty if he had used unnecessary and unreasonable force—which would have been the tort of battery. It was necessary to prove that the force used was excessive in the circumstances *which D believed to exist—Gladstone Williams*, above p 453—that is, not merely that he had committed the tort but that he had the *mens rea* of the *crime* of battery.

7. In *Slingsby* [1995] Crim LR 570 S had vaginal and anal sex with V with her consent. Then, also with her consent, he penetrated her vagina and rectum with his hand. V suffered cuts caused by a signet ring on S's hand. She did not realize for some time that the injuries were potentially very serious. Eventually she was admitted to hospital but died of septicaemia. S was charged with manslaughter by an unlawful and dangerous act. Judge J ruled that, putting the Crown's case at its highest, the charge could not be sustained. The injuries were suffered as a result of vigorous sexual activity with V's consent. It would, in Judge J's judgment be contrary to principle to treat as criminal activity which would not otherwise amount to an assault merely because in the course of that activity an injury occurred. The Crown offered no evidence and a verdict of not guilty was returned.

There are, however, difficulties with a dictum of Lord Lane in *A-G's Reference (No 6 of 1980)* [1981] QB 715 at 719, and *Boyea* (1992) 156 JP 505, [1992] Crim LR 574. Lord Lane, discussing when there is an assault notwithstanding consent, said:

> ... it is not in the public interest that people should try to cause *or should cause* each other bodily harm for no good reason. ... it is an assault if actual bodily harm is intended *and/or* caused. [Italics added.]

—and this passage was quoted by all three of the majority of the House of Lords in *Brown*, below, p **687**. The problem is with the words 'or should cause' and 'and/or'. These seem plainly to mean that an act done to another with the other's consent is an assault although it is not intended to cause harm if it in fact does so. The acts done by S to V in *Slingsby* would plainly have been assaults if V had not consented to them. When we turn to the *A-G's Reference* and *Brown* (in both of which injury was intentionally inflicted) to find out whether consent negatives assault, the dictum appears to say that it does not. Was Judge J right to withdraw the case from the jury?

Director of Public Prosecutions v Newbury and Jones
[1976] 2 All ER 365, House of Lords

(Lords Diplock, Simon of Glaisdale, Kilbrandon, Salmon and Edmund-Davies)

The facts appear in the speech of Lord Salmon, with which all their Lordships agreed.

Lord Salmon. My Lords, on 11 October 1974 the train travelling from Pontypridd to Cardiff was approaching a bridge which crossed the railway line. The guard was sitting next to the driver of the train in the front cab. The driver noticed the heads of three boys above the parapet of the bridge. He saw one of the boys push something off the parapet towards the oncoming train. This proved to be part of a paving stone which some workmen had left on the parapet. It came through the glass window of the cab in which the driver and the guard were sitting, struck the guard and killed him. There was ample evidence that just as the train was about to reach the bridge the two appellants, who were each about 15 years of age, were jointly concerned in pushing over the parapet the piece of paving stone which killed the guard. They were jointly charged with manslaughter and after a very fair and lucid summing-up, each was found guilty. Both of them appealed against conviction and sentence and their appeals against conviction were dismissed. The appellants now appeal to this House. The point of law certified to be of general public importance is:

> 'Can a defendant be properly convicted of manslaughter, when his mind is not affected by drink or drugs, if he did not foresee that his act might cause harm to another?'

The learned trial judge did not direct the jury that they should acquit the appellants unless they were satisfied beyond a reasonable doubt that the appellants had foreseen that they might cause harm to someone by pushing the piece of paving stone off the parapet into the path of the approaching train. In my view the learned trial judge was quite right not to give such a direction to the jury. The direction which he gave is completely in accordance with established law, which, possibly with one exception to which I shall presently refer, has never been challenged. In *Larkin* [[1943] 1 All ER 217 at 219] Humphreys J said:

> 'Where the act which a person is engaged in performing is unlawful, then if at the same time it is a dangerous act, that is, an act which is likely to injure another person, and quite inadvertently he causes the death of that other person by that act, then he is guilty of manslaughter.'

I agree entirely with Lawton LJ that that is an admirably clear statement of the law which has been applied many times. It makes it plain (a) that an accused is guilty of manslaughter if it is proved that he intentionally did an act which was unlawful and dangerous and that that act inadvertently caused death and (b) that it is unnecessary to prove that the accused knew that the act was unlawful or dangerous. This is one of the reasons why cases of manslaughter vary so infinitely in their gravity. They may amount to little more than pure inadvertence and sometimes to little less than murder.

I am sure that in *Church* Edmund Davies J, in giving the judgment of the court, did not intend to differ from or qualify anything which had been said in *Larkin*. Indeed he was restating the principle laid down in that case by illustrating the sense in which the word 'dangerous' should be understood. Edmund Davies J said [[1966] 1QB 59 at 70, [1965] 2 All ER 72 at 76]:

> 'For such a verdict [guilty of manslaughter] inexorably to follow, the unlawful act must be such as all sober and reasonable people would inevitably recognise must subject the other person to, at least, the risk of some harm resulting therefrom, albeit not serious harm.'

The test is still the objective test. In judging whether the act was dangerous, the test is not did the accused recognise that it was dangerous but would all sober and reasonable people recognise its danger. . . .

Appeal dismissed

Questions

1. Since the judge did not direct the jury that it must be proved that the defendant foresaw harm to anyone, the question for the House was whether a person doing what the defendants did but not foreseeing harm to anyone could properly be convicted. What is the 'unlawful act' which such a person commits?

2. Is *Lamb* reconcilable with *Newbury and Jones*? Why is foresight of injury to or alarm of P necessary if D points a revolver at P but not necessary if he throws a paving stone from a parapet? Was the court in *Scarlett*, above, p 626 right to quash the conviction?

R v Cato
[1976] 1 All ER 260, 270n, Court of Appeal, Criminal Division

(Lord Widgery CJ, O'Connor and Jupp JJ)

The appellant was convicted of manslaughter and of administering a noxious thing contrary to s 23 of the Offences Against the Person Act 1861. The appellant had injected the deceased with a mixture of heroin and water from a syringe several times throughout the night. The intoxication eventually caused his respiratory system to cease to function. The deceased himself prepared the strength of the mixture of each 'fix', just as the appellant prepared those fixes which the deceased was to give him. An appeal to the Court of Appeal was dismissed.

Lord Widgery CJ. . . . The trial judge left the manslaughter charge to the jury on the two alternative bases which the Crown had suggested, and it will be appreciated at once what they were. The first alternative was that the death was caused by the injection and the consequent intrusion of morphine into the body, and that was an unlawful act so that the killing was the result of an unlawful act and manslaughter on that footing.

The next matter, I think, is the unlawful act. Of course on the approach to manslaughter in this case it was necessary for the prosecution to prove that Farmer had been killed in the course of an unlawful act. Strangely enough, or it may seem strange to most of us, although the possession or supply of heroin is an offence, it is not an offence to take it, and although supplying it is an offence, it is not an offence to administer it. At least it is not made to be an offence, and so counsel for Cato says there was no unlawful act here. That which Cato did—taking Farmer's syringe already charged and injecting the mixture into Farmer as directed—is not an unlawful act, says counsel for Cato because there is nothing there which is an offence against the Misuse of Drugs Act 1971, and when he shows us the terms of the section it seems that that is absolutely right.

Of course if the conviction on count 2 remains (that is the charge under s23 of the Offences Against the Person Act 1861, of administering a noxious thing), then that in itself would be an unlawful act. The prohibition in that Act would be enough in itself, and it is probably right to say that as we are going to uphold the conviction on count 2, as will appear presently, that really answers the problem and destroys the basis of counsel for Cato's argument.

But since he went to such trouble with the argument, and in respect for it, we think we ought to say that had it not been possible to rely on the charge under s23 of the 1861 Act, we think there would have been an unlawful act here, and we think the unlawful act would be described as injecting the deceased Farmer with a mixture of heroin and water which at the time of the injection Cato had unlawfully taken into his possession. As I say, it is not really necessary to rely on that because of our views on the other count, but we would not wish it to be thought that we had felt counsel for Cato's argument on this point would have succeeded had it been effectively open to him. So much then for the unlawful act.

[His Lordship considered the judge's direction on recklessness and held that it was satisfactory. See further, below.]

Appeal dismissed

Questions

1. In what sense was the injection of Farmer with the mixture of heroin and water an 'unlawful act'? Was it a crime? Was it dangerous? Is an act 'unlawful' simply because it is dangerous?

2. What was the unlawful act in *Lipman*, above, p **200**?

3. What of crimes of strict liability? Suppose that in *Alphacell v Woodward*, above, p **241**, a swimmer in the river had ingested some of the effluent and died as a result. Manslaughter?

R v Dalby

[1982] 1 All ER 916, Court of Appeal, Criminal Division

(Waller LJ, Jupp and Waterhouse JJ)

[**Waller LJ** read the judgment of the court:]

The appellant and O'Such were both drug addicts and had been friends for some years. On Friday, 2 May 1980, after he had been staying with O'Such and his wife in their flat in Bournemouth for about a week, the appellant lawfully obtained, on prescription, 32 tablets of diconal. They were to be taken two every four hours, ie 8 per day. During his journey back to the flat, the appellant swallowed a number of tablets. At 8 pm shortly after his return, he supplied O'Such with some tablets: the evidence was unclear as to how many but probably four at that time and four or eight more later. The appellant and O'Such each injected himself intravenously and they then went out shortly after 9.30 pm to a discotheque where they parted company. The evidence was that O'Such met another friend at the discotheque who helped him administer an intravenous injection, of an unspecified substance, shortly before midnight and later a second intravenous injection.

When the appellant returned to the flat at about 2 am O'Such was already asleep on a settee in the living room and the appellant went to sleep himself. He was woken by Mrs O'Such at 8 am and both of them attempted to wake O'Such but without success. Mrs O'Such asked the appellant whether an ambulance should be called but he said No. When the appellant went out at 1.30pm, O'Such was still asleep. At 3 pm Mrs O'Such called an ambulance and when the ambulance attendants arrived some five minutes later they found O'Such was dead.

The Crown case was that the appellant was guilty of manslaughter because he had supplied diconal unlawfully, that it was a dangerous act and caused O'Such's death, or alternatively that the appellant owed a duty of care to O'Such and was grossly negligent in not calling an ambulance at an earlier stage.

Before this court, the argument proceeded on the former of those two alternatives because it was agreed that if the direction concerning an unlawful act that was dangerous, causing the death of O'Such was in error, then the appeal must succeed.

The judge directed the jury that there were five questions which they had to consider: first, did the appellant supply the diconal; second, did he intend to supply the diconal; third, was the supply of diconal to O'Such an unlawful act? No question arises about those three questions because the answer was clearly Yes in each case. The fourth and fifth questions were dealt with by the judge as follows: 'Was the supply of the diconal a dangerous act, because manslaughter is by a dangerous and unlawful act. By a dangerous act, we mean any act which subjects the victim to the risk of some harm, not necessarily serious harm. The test for whether the act was dangerous or not is an objective one.' Then the fifth question was posed: 'The fifth and last question you will ask yourself is whether the supply of the diconal was a substantial cause of the victim's death. It does not have to be the only cause of death, but it has to be a substantial cause of death, by which we mean a cause which is not merely trivial.' The judge then went on to discuss with the jury the question of whether or not it could be a substantial cause of death when it was O'Such who administered the diconal to himself.

The argument before this court has not centred on the precise words of the judge. It was submitted on behalf of the appellant: (1) that the unlawful act must be one directed at the victim; the supply of drugs in this case was not such a direct act; (2) that the supply of drugs can be harmless or extremely harmful according to the manner in which the victim deals with them; (3) that the drugs in this case were taken voluntarily by the victim in a form, ie intravenously, and in a quantity which together made them extremely dangerous and resulted in death; the line of causation was therefore broken between the unlawful act of supplying drugs and the death resulting from intravenous injection of too great a quantity of them.

Clearly there may be circumstances which would justify a finding of criminal negligence resulting in death which would found a case of manslaughter but this part of the argument is not concerned with negligence.

The earlier authorities show that any unlawful act resulting in death would justify a verdict of manslaughter but modern authorities have restricted this form of manslaughter to unlawful acts which are dangerous.

[His Lordship referred to *Larkin*, p **623**, above, *Church*, p **624**, above and *Newbury*, p **627**, above.]

There are several reported cases of manslaughter where the conduct which led to the death of the victim was not a direct act but these have been cases of manslaughter by negligence. In *R v Markuss* (1864) 4 F & F 356, 176 ER 598 a herbalist prescribed a cure for a cold which killed the patient and in *R v Benge* (1865) 4 F & F 504, 176 ER 665 a foreman platelayer placed his flagman at too short a distance from the approaching train with the result that somebody was killed. In such cases, it is necessary to prove gross negligence. In the well-known words of Lord Hewart CJ in *R v Bateman* (1925) 94 LJKB 791 at 793–794, [1925] All ER Rep 45 at 48, he said:

> '...in order to establish criminal liability the facts must be such that, in the opinion of the jury, the negligence of the accused went beyond a mere matter of compensation between subjects and showed such disregard for the life and safety of others as to amount to a crime against the State and conduct deserving punishment.'

But in all the reported cases of manslaughter by an unlawful and dangerous act, the researches of counsel have failed to find any case where the act was not a direct act.

The difficulty in the present case is that the act of supplying a controlled drug was not an act which caused direct harm. It was an act which made it possible, or even likely, that harm would occur subsequently, particularly if the drug was supplied to somebody who was on drugs. In all the reported cases, the physical act has been one which inevitably would subject the other person to the risk of some harm from the act itself. In this case, the supply of drugs would itself have caused no harm unless the deceased had subsequently used the drugs in a form and quantity which was dangerous.

It is interesting to note that in Smith and Hogan *Criminal Law* (4th edn, 1978) p274, when discussing intervening causes, a number of examples are cited, but the whole discussion is based on an original injury followed by some other intervening act.

In the judgment of this court, the unlawful act of supplying drugs was not an act directed against the person of O'Such and the supply did not cause any direct injury to him. The kind of harm envisaged in all the reported cases of involuntary manslaughter was physical injury of some kind as an immediate and inevitable result of the unlawful act, eg a blow on the chin which knocks the victim against a wall causing a fractured skull and death, or threatening with a loaded gun which accidentally fires, or dropping a large stone on a train (see *DPP v Newbury*) or threatening another with an open razor and stumbling with death resulting (see *R v Larkin*).

In the judgment of this court, where the charge of manslaughter is based on an unlawful and dangerous act, it must be an act directed at the victim and likely to cause immediate injury, however slight.

In his certificate giving leave to appeal, the judge posed this question:

> 'In the circumstances in which the intravenous consumption of a dangerous drug is a substantial cause of the death of the deceased, does the unlawful act of supply of the dangerous drug by the defendant to the deceased per se constitute the actus reus of the offence of manslaughter?'

For the reasons given, the answer to that question is No. . . ,

Appeal allowed. Conviction of manslaughter quashed

Questions

1. Did Dalby cause O'Such's death? Does the case decide he did not?

2. *If* Dalby caused the death for the purposes of 'reckless' or 'gross negligence manslaughter', must he not also have done so for the purposes of 'unlawful act' manslaughter?

3. Can the 'directed at' requirement be reconciled with *Newbury* where it was held that the defendant need not know that his act was dangerous? Is the requirement affected by *Moloney* (p **120**, above)?

4. Is *Markuss* distinguishable? Presumably the patient did not know the dangerous nature of 'the cure' he took.

5. Cf *Pagett*, p **61**, above. Was it not just as likely that O'Such would take the drug and suffer harm as that the police would shoot Gail when Pagett used her as a shield? If the latter result was caused by D, why not the former?

Notes

1. In *Goodfellow* (1986) 83 Cr App R 23, [1986] Crim LR 468, G, wanting to move from his council house but having no chance of exchanging it, set fire to the house, attempting to make it appear that the fire was caused by a petrol bomb. His wife, another woman and his son died in the fire. He appealed from conviction of manslaughter on the ground that the jury had been misdirected as to '*Lawrence* recklessness' (above, p **148**). The Court of Appeal, having held that there had been no such misdirection, said there was also a case for an 'unlawful and dangerous act' direction. The appellant argued that the acts were not 'directed at' the victim, as required by *Dalby*. The court responded:

However we do not think that [Waller LJ] was suggesting that there must be an intention on the part of the defendant to harm or frighten or a realisation that his acts were likely to harm or frighten. Indeed it would have been contrary to the dicta of Lord Salmon in *DPP v Newbury* if he was. What he was, we believe, intending to say was that there must be no fresh intervening cause between the act and the death. Indeed at p351 he said this: '. . . the supply of drugs would itself have caused no harm unless the deceased had subsequently used the drugs in a form and quantity which was dangerous.'

The court added that its interpretation of *Dalby* seemed to be supported by *Pagett*, above, p **61**, and *Mitchell* [1983] 2 All ER 427, [1983] QB 741 and dismissed the appeal. Did the court interpret *Dalby* correctly? Does *Pagett* support the view that there must be 'no fresh intervening cause between the act and death'? Was not the act of the police officer a fresh intervening cause? It was certainly a cause and it certainly intervened.

2. In *Kennedy No 1* [1999] Crim LR 65, the court said that *Dalby* was factually distinguishable in at least one material respect: K prepared a syringe and handed it to B for the latter immediately to inject himself. It followed that his conduct would not be limited to supplying but would also be unlawful as assisting or encouraging B to inject himself (referring to *Cato*, above, p **628**). Do you agree that this is a material distinction? Did not Dalby also assist and encourage O'Such by supplying him and participating in the 'injection party'?

R v Dias

[2001] All ER (D) 198 (Dec), Court of Appeal, Criminal Division

(Keene LJ, Sir Richard Tucker and Judge Maddision)

Dias and Escott were vagrants. Together they bought a £10 bag of heroin. Dias prepared the heroin and drew it into a syringe which he handed to Escott who injected himself and, consequently, died. Dias was convicted of manslaughter by an unlawful and dangerous act. The trial judge granted a certificate asking, 'Was I correct as a matter of law to direct the jury that it is unlawful for a man to inject heroin into himself?' He ruled, following *Kennedy No 1*, above, that it followed that aiding and abetting such an offence would make Dias liable for the unlawful act which had caused Escott's death.

Keene LJ, [having considered the arguments of counsel:]

19. We begin with the authorities which have been cited to us. The earliest in time, *Cato*, undoubtedly arrived at the right result since to inject someone with heroin and water would normally be an offence under section 23 of the 1861 Act. That was the basis of the decision, and both the passages relied on (one by each side) from page 47 of the report were strictly obiter. The case was in any event concerned with the injection by one person of another with heroin and water, not with self-injection. The statement that injecting the deceased with that mixture was an unlawful act, irrespective of section 23, is not explained at any length. It may be that it was based on the fact that the appellant was thereby supplying heroin to the deceased—a criminal offence.

20. In *Dalby* the appellant had supplied the deceased with a class A drug (Diconal) in tablet form and both had then injected themselves intravenously. It was not contended that the act of self-injection was unlawful. The supply of the tablets clearly was, and the case turned on the issue of causation. But the end result was that the conviction for manslaughter was quashed.

21. The facts of *Kennedy* have already been set out earlier in this judgment. However, it is not easy to see on what basis the court concluded that the act of self-injection was unlawful because there is no real elaboration of this point. It is not surprising that the Crown in this present appeal finds it difficult to uphold that particular sentence in the report. The decision on this aspect has been criticised in both *Archbold* 2002 at paragraph 19–100 and in *Smith and Hogan* (9th edn) page 432. If *Kennedy* is rightly decided on this aspect, then it would seem that *Dalby* should have had a different result since on the facts there seems to have been a comparable degree of assistance and encouragement by the appellant in the latter case to that which took place in *Kennedy*. There is no offence under the Misuse of Drugs Act 1971, or other statute, or at common law, of injecting oneself with a prohibited drug.

22. There is the offence of possession of such a drug, and that offence was committed by Escott, the deceased. We have considered, therefore, whether that renders the act of injection unlawful for these purposes, but we find it difficult to see that it can do so. The causative act (the act causing death) was essentially the injection of the heroin rather than the possession of it. Self-injection undoubtedly requires unlawful possession in a case such as this, but it is not in itself a separate offence. No one could be charged with injecting himself with heroin, only with the possession of it. The deceased was in possession of the heroin before he injected it and also after he had injected it. Such possession amounted to an offence, but the act of injecting was not itself part of the offence. It was merely made possible by the unlawful possession of the heroin.

23. It seems therefore to this court that the dictum of Lord Widgery CJ in *Cato*, namely that it is not an offence to take heroin, was soundly based. To inject another person with heroin, as in *Cato*, is likely to be unlawful, not merely because of section 23 but also because it would amount to a supply of a prohibited drug. But that is not this case.

24. There is a further problem about the basis of the present conviction, given the direction by the trial judge. The case was not left to the jury on the footing that the appellant might have caused the death of Escott, and that is perhaps understandable since the act of self-injection was seen by the judge as a voluntary act of an adult not labouring under any mistake as to what he was doing. The judge seems to have taken the view that the chain of causation would have been broken by Escott's own action. It follows from that that the appellant could only have been guilty of manslaughter as a secondary party and not as a principal. But in that case who is the principal guilty of manslaughter? As there is no offence of self-manslaughter, it is difficult to see how the appellant could be guilty of that offence as a secondary party because of his encouragement or assistance to Escott over the injection of the drug.

25. We accept that there may be situations where a jury could find manslaughter in cases such as this, so long as they were satisfied so as to be sure that the chain of causation was not broken. That is not this case because causation here was not left to the jury. The argument advanced by Mr Coker that the jury found assistance and encouragement on the part of the appellant will not, in our judgment, suffice. Assistance and encouragement is not to be automatically equated with causation. Causation raises questions of fact and degree. The recipient does not have to inject the drug which he is encouraged and assisted to take. He has a choice. It may be that in some circumstances the causative chain will still remain. That is a matter for the jury to decide. The Crown's current approach as argued on this appeal hearing, namely that the supply of heroin is unlawful and can be a dangerous act causing death, is sound. The most obvious case is where the supply takes the form of one person injecting the other who then dies. The position is more difficult where the victim injects himself, but there may possibly be situations where the chain of causation could be established. It is, however, important that that issue be left to the jury to determine, as happened at the trial in *Kennedy*.

26. The trial judge in a case such as this, after identifying the unlawful act on the part of the defendant relied upon, must direct the jury to ask whether they are sure that that act was at least a substantive cause of the victim's death, as well as being dangerous. That did not happen here, and we cannot see that the jury's finding can be seen as establishing causation between unlawful supply on the one hand and death on the other. That is not how the matter was left to them. It may seem to some that there is morally not a great deal between this situation where A hands B a syringe containing a drug such as heroin, with death resulting, and that where A injects B with his consent with the contents of the syringe. But the vital difference (and this is why causation cannot be assumed) is that the former situation involves an act of B's taken voluntarily and leading to his death. We do not wish to suggest that there may not sometimes be cases where, on somewhat different facts, manslaughter by way of gross negligence may arise if a duty of care can be established, or where section 23 may be relied on so long as the chain of causation is not broken.

Appeal allowed

Notes and questions

1. Did Cato or Dias 'supply' the drug to the deceased? In *Harris* (1968) 52 Cr App R 277, CCA, it was held that A does not supply heroin to B if he injects B with B's own heroin. It was said obiter that it would be different if A injected B with A's own heroin. In *Cato* the drug was produced by the deceased and in *Dias* it was jointly owned—they each contributed £5.

2. These niceties are necessary because of the requirement in this type of manslaughter of an unlawful—that is, criminal—act. But is there any good reason in principle why liability for homicide should turn on whether drugs legislation has made it an offence to inject another, or oneself, with a prohibited drug?

3. Was Widgery LCJ right to conclude that the injection of the drug was an unlawful act, independently of s 23? Or was it an erroneous obiter dictum?

R v Kennedy
[2005] EWCA Crim 685, Court of Appeal, Criminal Division

(Lord Woolf CJ, Davis, Field JJ)

Lord Woolf CJ [recited the facts (see above, p **63**) and referred to the first appeal and to *Dias*:]

[26] The next case was *Rogers* [2003] EWCA Crim 945, [2003] 1 WLR 1374. The important point in *Rogers* was that the defendant applied a tourniquet to the deceased's arm while the deceased injected himself with heroin. Rose VP agreed with Keene LJ in *Dias* and accepted that Waller LJ (Junior)'s reasoning in the first appeal was incorrect 'insofar as the reasoning was based on self-injection being an unlawful act'. . . .

[27] In giving the judgment of the court in *Rogers*, Rose VP focused on the question of whether the defendant's conduct in that case was that of a principal or a secondary party. He stressed that the application of the tourniquet should not be considered in isolation. He added:

> 'It is artificial and unreal to separate the tourniquet from the injection. The purpose and effect of the tourniquet, plainly, was to raise a vein in which the deceased could insert the syringe. Accordingly, by applying and holding the tourniquet, the defendant was playing a part in the mechanics of the injection which caused death. It is therefore, as it seems to us, immaterial whether the deceased was committing a criminal offence.
>   . . . A fortiori, as it seems to us, a person who actively participates in the injection process commits the actus reus and can have no answer to an offence under section 23 or a charge of manslaughter if death results. Once the [defendant] is categorised as such a participant, it being common ground that death resulted from the injection, no question arises in relation to causation.' (Paragraphs 7 and 8)

Rose VP regarded his approach as not being in conflict with that of Keene LJ in *Dias* (paragraph 8).

[28] Pausing, before turning to the final case in the series, it is important to point out where the authorities that we have already cited take us;

i) That a person who kills himself is not committing a crime.

ii) Contrary to part of the judgment of Waller LJ (Junior) on the first appeal, even though a person may encourage another to take his own life, he is not an accessory to manslaughter on this ground alone as there is no principal of whom he is the accessory.

iii) If, however, the role played by the defendant, in concert with the deceased, amounts to administering or causing the drug to be administered, then that person will have committed an offence under s.23 of the 1861 Act and he will be guilty of an unlawful act. The fact that the deceased may die does not affect that situation. Furthermore, if the defendant participates in an offence involving the administration of the drug, there could be no question of difficulties in relation to causation.

iv) On the first appeal, Waller LJ (Junior) was right when he regarded 'the critical question to which the jury must direct its mind, where (as in the instance case) there is an act causative of death performed by, in this case the deceased himself, is whether the Appellant can be said to be jointly responsible for the carrying out of that act.' (emphasis added)

...

[51] In view of the conclusions that we have come to as a result of our examination of the authorities, it appears to us that it was open to the jury to convict the Appellant of manslaughter. To convict, the jury had to be satisfied that, when the heroin was handed to the deceased 'for immediate injection', he and the deceased were both engaged in the one activity of administering the heroin. These were not necessarily to be regarded as two separate activities; and the question that remains is whether the jury were satisfied that this was the situation. If the jury were satisfied of this then the Appellant was responsible for taking the action in concert with the deceased to enable the deceased to inject himself with the syringe of heroin which had been made ready for his immediate use.

[52] In our view, the jury would have been entitled to find (and indeed it is an appropriate finding) that in these circumstances the Appellant and the deceased were jointly engaged in administering the heroin. This was the conclusion of this Court on the first appeal, as we understand Waller LJ's judgment, and we do not feel it necessary to take a different view, though we do accept that the issue could have been left by the trial judge to the jury in more clear terms than it was.

[53] The point in this case is that the Appellant and the deceased were carrying out a 'combined operation' for which they were jointly responsible. Their actions were similar to what happens frequently when carrying out lawful injections: one nurse may carry out certain preparatory actions (including preparing the syringe) and hand it to a colleague who inserts the needle and administers the injection, after which the other nurse may apply a plaster. In such a situation, both nurses can be regarded as administering the drug. They are working as a team. Both their actions are necessary. They are interlinked but separate parts in the overall process of administering the drug. In these circumstances, as Waller LJ stated on the first appeal, they 'can be said to be jointly responsible for carrying out that act.'

[54] Whether the necessary linkage existed between the actions of the Appellant and the deceased was very much a matter for the jury to determine. The question then arises as to whether the trial judge in the summing up expressed the issue in sufficiently clear terms for the jury? As to this, we share similar reservations to those expressed by Waller LJ in his judgment on the first appeal. There was no need for the jury to find the encouragement that Waller LJ thought was necessary. However, the jury did have to find that the Appellant and the deceased were acting in concert in administering the heroin.

Appeal dismissed

Questions

1. What is D's unlawful act? The offence under s 23 of the OAPA requires administration to another. D has not administered anything to 'another'; V has administered it to himself. See D. C. Ormerod and R. Fortson [2005] Crim LR 819.

2. Could D be liable for gross negligence manslaughter if, for example, he became aware of V's difficulties once he had taken the heroin?

R v Ball

[1989] Crim LR 730, Court of Appeal, Criminal Division

(Stuart-Smith LJ, Hobhouse and Leggatt JJ)

After an altercation between the appellant and Mrs G, the appellant shot and killed her as she was climbing over a wall. Mrs G had called on him accompanied by two young men and his case was that he was frightened by them, that he kept live and blank cartridges together in the pocket of his overall in the house, that he grabbed a handful of cartridges when he picked up the gun, that he intended only to frighten by using a blank cartridge, not a live one, and believed that a blank was in the gun. He was acquitted of murder but convicted of manslaughter by doing an unlawful and dangerous act. Chadwin QC, for the appellant, argued that the judge had misdirected the jury by withdrawing from their consideration the appellant's belief that the cartridge was only a blank. The court accepted that the acquittal of murder showed that the jury was not satisfied that he knew the cartridge in the gun was a live one. It was admitted that firing the gun was an assault but submitted that the objective assessment of danger must be based on the appellant's belief that he was firing a blank.

Stuart-Smith LJ. In support of his argument Mr Chadwin instanced a number of cases where an accused might be guilty of a criminally unlawful act but by reason of a mistaken belief as to the facts ought not, in his submission, to be considered to have done a dangerous act or to be held guilty of manslaughter if death results. A publican serving an under age customer commits an unlawful act; is he guilty of manslaughter if unknown to the publican someone adds poison to the drink? Someone who injects a child or unconscious person may commit an assault even if he believes the dose is therapeutic; if unknown to him someone had substituted a lethal dose is he guilty of manslaughter? Or, he gave the example of a person storing goods known to be stolen; if unknown to him the goods contain unstable explosive which explodes killing another, is that manslaughter?

Each of these examples raises the question considered by the Court of Appeal in *Goodfellow*. It may be thought that that case decided that death resulting from an unlawful injection was manslaughter. How the first and third examples would be determined is not a question which arises in the present case. The act of the appellant in firing a gun at Mrs Green was, in the phrase of Waller LJ in *Dalby*, 'an act directed at the victim'. In the present case there was 'no fresh intervening cause between the act and the death', to adopt the formulation of Lord Lane CJ in *Goodfellow*. The appellant used his own cartridges and loaded his gun himself; no agency other than himself was involved.

Mr Chadwin relied in support of his submission on a passage in the judgment of Watkins LJ in *R v Dawson* (1985) 81 Cr App Rep 150. In that case masked robbers carrying an imitation firearm and pickaxe handle robbed a 60-year-old filling station attendant, threatening him with both weapons. After pressing the alarm the robbers fled. Unhappily the attendant suffered from a severe heart condition and he died of a heart attack shortly after the police arrived. The appellants' convictions for manslaughter were quashed. At page 157 the learned judge said:

> 'We look finally at the direction, "That is to say all reasonable people who knew the facts that you know." What the jury knew included, of course, the undisputed fact that the deceased had a very bad heart which at any moment could have ceased to function. It may be the judge did not intend that this fact should be included in the phrase "the facts that you know". If that was so, it is regrettable that he did not make it clear. By saying as he did, it is argued "including the fact that the gun was a replica" and so on, the jury must have taken him to be telling them that all facts known to them, including the heart

condition, should be taken into account in performing what is undoubtedly an objective test. We think there was a grave danger of that. This test can only be undertaken upon the basis of the knowledge gained by a sober and reasonable man as though he were present at the scene of and watched the unlawful act being performed and who knows that, as in the present case, an unloaded replica gun was in use, but that the victim may have thought it was a loaded gun in working order. In other words, he has the same knowledge as the man attempting to rob and no more. It was never suggested that any of these appellants knew that their victim had a bad heart. They knew nothing about him.'

Mr Chadwin submits that the reference to the sober and reasonable man having the same knowledge as the man committing the robbery and no more, involves the proposition that if that person has a mistaken belief, albeit brought about by his own carelessness, the sober and reasonable man must share that mistaken belief. But in our judgment *Dawson's* case goes no further than showing that the sober and reasonable man must look at the unlawful act to see if it is dangerous and not at peculiarities of the victim.

Once these matters are established, namely, that the act was both unlawful and that he intended to commit the assault, the question whether the act is a dangerous one is to be judged not by the appellant's appreciation but by that of the sober and reasonable man, and it is impossible to impute into his appreciation the mistaken belief of the appellant that what he was doing was not dangerous because he thought he had a blank cartridge in the chamber. At that stage the appellant's intention, foresight or knowledge is irrelevant.

Appeal dismissed

Questions

1. In dealing with Chadwin QC's hypothetical cases, does the court apply the *Goodfellow* interpretation of *Dalby* or apply the phrase 'directed at' in its literal sense? In the case of the publican, assuming the drink was poisoned before it was served, is *Dalby* relevant if all it requires is that there be no fresh intervening cause? What about the stolen goods case where there is clearly no fresh intervening cause?

2. In *Dawson* was the deceased's heart condition properly ignored in deciding whether the act was dangerous because it was a 'peculiarity of the victim'? Or because it would not have been known to the sober and reasonable bystander at the robbery? *Dawson* was again distinguished in *Watson* (1989) 89 Cr App R 211, [1989] Crim LR 733, CA, where V, an 87-year-old man, died of a heart attack following a burglary by D. V's frailty and great age had become apparent to D in the course of his burglarious intrusion. His conviction was quashed only because it was not proved that the intrusion caused the death. What if V had sustained a fatal shock (causation being proved) on D's entry and before D had the opportunity to observe V's frailty?

Notes

1. *Can there be manslaughter by an unlawful and dangerous omission?* In *Khan and Khan* [1998] Crim LR 830 the court said that manslaughter by omission is no more than an example of manslaughter arising from a grossly negligent breach of duty. Certainly the fault alleged in omission cases will usually be gross negligence. But we have seen that an omission in breach of a duty to act, with intent to cause grievous bodily harm, will be murder if death results: *Gibbins and Proctor* (1918) 13 Cr App R 134, above, p 105, and it seems logical that, if the intent was to cause some lesser degree of harm, the offence should

be manslaughter. This falls into the 'constructive' category rather than that of gross negligence. Glanville Williams thought (TBCL 276) that *Lowe* [1973] 1 All ER 805, [1973] QB 702 was authority that a criminal omission can never be an 'unlawful act' for the purposes of constructive manslaughter; but that case was forcefully and cogently criticized by the editor (Ashworth) in [1976] Crim LR 529. ('In the absence of strong and clear arguments in favour of treating homicide by neglect as less serious than other forms of homicide, the distinction set out in *Lowe* can only be based on superstition.')

2. *Does the* Church *direction necessarily include a gross negligence direction?* In *Watts* [1998] Crim LR 833 there was evidence that D, a nurse and devoted mother of a severely handicapped child, had removed a tracheotomy tube from the child's throat after an operation. She was charged with murder and convicted of manslaughter. The judge directed the jury as to the ingredients of unlawful and dangerous act manslaughter. Defending counsel had raised the issue of manslaughter by gross negligence in his speech to the jury and the judge referred to that point in his summing up but did not direct as to the ingredients of that form of the offence. D appealed on the ground that the jury might have convicted of that offence without being aware of, or satisfied about, its constituents. The Crown argued unsuccessfully that the unlawful and dangerous act direction, as in *Church*, was a sufficient basis for the jury to convict of gross negligence manslaughter. *Church* does indeed require gross negligence. Since an element is that 'all sober and reasonable people would inevitably recognise the risk' it must surely be grossly negligent not to recognize it; but, (i) in unlawful act manslaughter it need be a risk of only some slight harm, whereas grossly negligent manslaughter requires foreseeability of death and, (ii)— the crucial point in *Watts*—the negligence must be considered bad enough by the jury to justify conviction of manslaughter. Such badness is not an ingredient of unlawful act manslaughter. A properly instructed jury which is sure that D is guilty of unlawful act manslaughter is not by any means necessarily sure that he is guilty of manslaughter by gross negligence.

(2) MANSLAUGHTER BY GROSS NEGLIGENCE

Andrews v Director of Public Prosecutions
[1937] AC 576, [1937] 2 All ER 552, House of Lords

(Lords Atkin, Thankerton, Wright, Viscount Finlay and Lord Roche)

The appellant, an employee of Leeds corporation, was sent to assist a corporation bus which had broken down about three or four miles away at 10.30 pm on a Saturday night. Driving fast, over 30 mph, in a van, he overtook a car and, driving well over on the off-side of the road, struck a man, Craven, who was crossing the road. Craven was carried forward on the bonnet, thrown off and run over. The appellant did not stop. He was convicted of manslaughter and appealed on the ground of misdirection in that the judge had told the jury that they must convict if the appellant caused death by driving recklessly or in a dangerous manner, contrary to the Road Traffic Act 1930, s 11.

[*Note* that there is no longer an offence of reckless driving which is replaced by a new offence of dangerous driving (see above, p **168**) but this does not affect the authority of this decision.]

[**Lord Atkin**, having stated the facts, continued:]

...of all crimes manslaughter appears to afford most difficulties of definition, for it concerns homicide in so many and so varying conditions. From the early days, when any homicide involved penalty, the law has gradually evolved 'through successive differentiations and integrations' until it recognises murder on the one hand, based mainly, though not exclusively, on an intention to kill, and manslaughter on the other hand, based mainly, though not exclusively, on the absence of intention to kill, but with the presence of an element of 'unlawfulness' which is the elusive factor. In the present case it is necessary to consider manslaughter only from the point of view of an unintentional killing caused by negligence, ie the omission of a duty to take care. I do not propose to discuss the development of this branch of the subject as treated in the successive treatises of Coke, Hale, Foster and East, and in the judgments of the courts to be found either in directions to juries by individual judges, or in the more considered pronouncements of the body of judges which preceded the formal Court of Crown Cases Reserved. Expressions will be found which indicate that to cause death by lack of due care will amount to manslaughter; but, as manners softened and the law became more humane, a narrower criterion appeared. After all, manslaughter is a felony, and was capital, and men shrank from attaching the serious consequences of a conviction for felony to results produced by mere inadvertence. The stricter view became apparent in prosecutions of medical men, or men who professed medical or surgical skill, for manslaughter by reason of negligence. As an instance I will cite *Williamson* [(1807) 3 C & P 635], where a man who practised as an accoucheur, owing to a mistake in his observation of the actual symptoms, inflicted on a patient terrible injuries from which she died. Lord Ellenborough said:

'To substantiate that charge [of manslaughter] the prisoner must have been guilty of criminal misconduct, arising either from the grossest ignorance or the most criminal inattention.'

The word 'criminal' in any attempt to define a crime is perhaps not the most helpful, but it is plain that Lord Ellenborough meant to indicate to the jury a high degree of negligence. So at a much later date in *Bateman* [(1925) 94 LJKB 791], a charge of manslaughter was made against a qualified medical practitioner in circumstances similar to those of *Williamson's* case. In a considered judgment of the court, Lord Hewart LCJ, after pointing out that, in a civil case, once negligence is proved the degree of negligence is irrelevant, said, at p 793:

'In a criminal court, on the contrary, the amount and degree of negligence are the determining question. There must be mens rea.'

After citing *Cashill v Wright*, a civil case, Lord Hewart LCJ proceeds:

'In explaining to juries the test which they should apply to determine whether the negligence, in the particular case, amounted or did not amount to a crime, judges have used many epithets, such as "culpable", "gross", "wicked", "clear", "complete". But, whatever epithet be used and whether an epithet be used or not, in order to establish criminal liability the facts must be such that, in the opinion of the jury, the negligence of the accused went beyond a mere matter of compensation between subjects and showed such disregard for the life and safety of others, as to amount to a crime against the State and conduct deserving punishment.'

Here, again, I think, with respect, that the expressions used are not, indeed they probably were not intended to be, a precise definition of the crime. I do not myself find the connotations of mens rea helpful in distinguishing between degrees of negligence, nor do the ideas of crime and punishment in themselves carry a jury much further in deciding whether, in a particular case, the degree of negligence shown is a crime, and deserves punishment. But the substance of the judgment is most valuable, and, in my opinion, is correct. In practice, it has generally been adopted by judges in charging juries in all cases of manslaughter by negligence, whether in driving vehicles or otherwise.

The principle to be observed is that cases of manslaughter in driving motor cars are but instances of a general rule applicable to all charges of homicide by negligence. Simple lack of care such as will constitute civil liability is not enough. For the purpose of the criminal law there are degrees of negligence, and a very high degree of negligence is required to be proved before the felony is established. Probably of all the epithets that can be applied 'reckless' most nearly covers the case. It is difficult to visualise a case of death caused by 'reckless' driving, in the connotation of that term in ordinary speech, which would not justify a conviction for manslaughter, but it is probably not all-embracing, for 'reckless' suggests an indifference to risk, whereas the accused may have appreciated the risk, and intended to avoid it, and yet shown in the means adopted to avoid the risk such a degree of negligence as would justify a conviction. If the principle of *Bateman's* case is observed, it will appear that the law of manslaughter has not changed by the introduction of motor vehicles on the road. Death caused by their negligent driving, though unhappily much more frequent, is to be treated in law as death caused by any other form of negligence, and juries should be directed accordingly.

If this view be adopted, it will be easier for judges to disentangle themselves from the meshes of the Road Traffic Acts. Those Acts have provisions which regulate the degree of care to be taken in driving motor vehicles. They have no direct reference to causing death by negligence. Their prohibitions, while directed, no doubt, to cases of negligent driving, which, if death be caused, would justify convictions for manslaughter, extend to degrees of negligence of less gravity. Section 12 of the Road Traffic Act imposes a penalty for driving without due care or attention. This would apparently cover all degrees of negligence. Section 11 imposes a penalty for driving recklessly, or at a speed or in a manner which is dangerous to the public. There can be no doubt that this section covers driving with such a high degree of negligence as that, if death were caused, the offender would have committed manslaughter. But the converse is not true, and it is perfectly possible that a man may drive at a speed or in a manner dangerous to the public, and cause death, and yet not be guilty of manslaughter. The legislature appears to recognise this by the provision in the Road Traffic Act 1934, s34, that, on an indictment for manslaughter, a man may be convicted of dangerous driving. But, apart altogether from any inference to be drawn from s34, I entertain no doubt that the statutory offence of dangerous driving may be committed, though the negligence is not of such a degree as would amount to manslaughter if death ensued. As an instance, in the course of argument it was suggested that a man might execute the dangerous manoeuvre of drawing out to pass a vehicle in front with another vehicle meeting him, and be able to show that he would have succeeded in his calculated intention but for some increase of speed in the vehicle in front: a case very doubtfully of manslaughter, but very probably of dangerous driving. I cannot think of anything worse for users of the road than the conception that no one could be convicted of dangerous driving unless his negligence was so great that, if he had caused death, he must have been convicted of manslaughter. It therefore would appear that, in directing the jury in a case of manslaughter, the judge should in the first instance charge them substantially in accordance with the general law, ie requiring the high degree of negligence indicated in *Bateman's* case, and then explain that such degree of negligence is not necessarily the same as that which is required for the offence of dangerous driving, and then indicate to them the conditions under which they might acquit of manslaughter and convict of dangerous driving. A direction that all they had to consider was whether death was caused by dangerous driving within the Road Traffic Act 1930, s11, and no more, would, in my opinion, be a misdirection.

In dealing with the summing-up in the present case, I feel bound to say, with every respect to the learned and very careful judge, that there are passages which are open to criticism. In particular, at the beginning of his charge to the jury, he began with the statement that, if a man kills another in the course of doing an unlawful act, he is guilty of manslaughter, and then proceeded to ascertain what the unlawful act was by considering the Road Traffic Act 1930, s 11. If the summing-up rested there,

there would have been misdirection. There is an obvious difference in the law of manslaughter between doing an unlawful act and doing a lawful act with a degree of carelessness which the legislature makes criminal. If it were otherwise, a man who, while driving without due care and attention, killed another, would *ex necessitate* commit manslaughter. But as the summing-up proceeded the learned judge reverted to, and I think rested the case on, the principles which have been just stated. On many occasions he directed the attention of the jury to the recklessness and high degree of negligence which the prosecution alleged to have been proved, and which would justify them in convicting the accused. On consideration of the summing-up as a whole, I am satisfied that the true question was ultimately left to the jury.

[**Lords Thankerton**, **Wright**, **Finlay** and **Roche** concurred.]

Appeal dismissed

Questions

1. Is there 'an obvious difference in the law of manslaughter between doing an unlawful act and doing a lawful act with a degree of carelessness which the legislature makes criminal'? What is it?

2. In attempting to define 'gross negligence' Lord Atkin says that of all the epithets that can be applied 'reckless' 'most nearly' covers the case. Why only 'most nearly'? When, in Lord Atkin's view, would a conviction for manslaughter be justified when the defendant is not 'reckless' in the sense that he uses that term? Is the test laid down by Lord Atkin subjective or objective?

Note

Before turning to the decision of the House of Lords in *Adomako* it is helpful to consider the decision of the Court of Appeal in *Prentice, Adomako, Holloway* [1993] 4 All ER 935, [1994] QB 302, and the cases leading up to it.

At the time there were two tests of 'recklessness' in the criminal law. There was the subjective (*Cunningham*) test which requires foresight of consequences and which applies now throughout the law, and there was the objective (*Caldwell/Lawrence*) test, p 146, above, which applied until 2003, at the least, to offences of criminal damage. Following *Caldwell* and *Lawrence* there was a move, spearheaded by the House of Lords (there was less enthusiasm for it in lower courts), to adopt the single *Caldwell/Lawrence* test for recklessness and, in particular, to replace gross negligence manslaughter by reckless (that is, *Caldwell/Lawrence* recklessness) manslaughter. This development came to a head in the House of Lords decision in *Seymour* [1983] 2 All ER 1058, [1983] 2 AC 493, a case of so-called motor manslaughter (on which see the observations of Lord Mackay, LC, in *Adomako*, below) and in the Privy Council decision in *Kong Cheuk Kwan v R* (1985) 82 Cr App R 18, [1985] Crim LR 787.

This development placed the Court of Appeal in a dilemma in considering the appeals in *Prentice, Adomako, Holloway*.

In *Adomako*, next considered, the trial judge had given a 'traditional' direction on gross negligence on which the defendant was convicted and his appeal was dismissed. In *Prentice* and in *Holloway*, however, the jury had convicted of manslaughter following a *Caldwell/Lawrence/Seymour* direction.

In *Prentice*, D, under the supervision of E, administered an injection to a patient. Owing to a series of errors and misunderstandings between D and E, D administered the wrong drug with fatal results. Quashing the convictions of D and E the court said:

In effect, therefore, once the jury found 'that the defendant gave no thought to the possibility of there being any such risk', on the learned judge's directions they had no option but to convict. [Counsel's] point is that if the jury had been given gross negligence as the test, they could properly have taken into account 'excuses' or mitigating circumstances in deciding whether the necessary high degree of gross negligence had been established. The question for the jury should have been whether, in the case of each doctor, they were sure that the failure to ascertain the correct mode of administering the drug and to ensure that only that mode was adopted was grossly negligent to the point of criminality having regard to all the excuses and mitigating circumstances in the case.

In *Holloway*, D, an electrician, who had done the electrical work on a central-heating system in a house, returned to check the system after complaints that contact with the radiators caused electric shocks. His checks failed to reveal, as they should have done, that there was a fault in the wiring. V was subsequently electrocuted and died. It was held by the Court of Appeal, quashing D's conviction, that the proper issue for the jury's consideration was not whether D had given no thought to the serious risk but whether he was grossly negligent in forming the view that the installation was safe.

The Court of Appeal appears to have taken the view in these cases that the *Caldwell/Lawrence* test was too strict for manslaughter. But is this right? Given that there is a risk of death or serious harm (that is, a risk to which any sensible person would have adverted) why should not a failure to advert to such a risk be accounted gross negligence?

R v Adomako

[1994] 3 All ER 79, House of Lords

(Lord Mackay of Clashfern LC, Lords Keith of Kinkel, Goff of Chieveley, Browne-Wilkinson, and Woolf)

During an operation at which the appellant was assisting as anaesthetist the tube carrying oxygen from the ventilator to the patient became disconnected. The appellant failed to notice the disconnection and some six minutes later the patient suffered a cardiac arrest from which, despite efforts at resuscitation, he died. At no stage did the appellant check the integrity of the equipment. The case against the appellant was that he had been grossly negligent in failing to notice or respond appropriately to obvious signs that a disconnection had occurred and that the patient had ceased to breathe.

Lord Mackay of Clashfern, LC . . . On behalf of the appellant it was conceded at his trial that he had been negligent. The issue was therefore whether his conduct was criminal. . . .

The jury convicted the appellant of manslaughter by a majority of 11 to 1. The Court of Appeal, Criminal Division dismissed the appellant's appeal against conviction but certified that a point of law of general public importance was involved in the decision to dismiss the appeal, namely:

'In cases of manslaughter by criminal negligence not involving driving but involving a breach of duty is it a sufficient direction to the jury to adopt the gross negligence test set out by the Court of Appeal in the present case following *R v Bateman* (1925) 19 Cr App Rep 8 and *Andrews v DPP* [1937] 2 All ER 552, [1937] AC 576 without reference to the test of recklessness as defined in *R v Lawrence* [1981] 1 All ER 974, [1982] AC 510 or as adapted to the circumstances of the case?'

The decision of the Court of Appeal is reported at [1993] 4 All ER 935, [1994] QB 302 along with a number of other cases involving similar questions of law. The Court of Appeal held that except in cases of motor manslaughter the ingredients which had to be proved to establish an offence of involuntary manslaughter by breach of duty were the existence of the duty, a breach of the duty which had caused death and gross negligence which the jury considered to justify a criminal conviction; the jury might properly find gross negligence on proof of indifference to an obvious risk of injury to health or of actual foresight of the risk coupled either with a determination nevertheless to run it or with an intention to avoid it but involving such a high degree of negligence in the attempted avoidance as the jury considered justified conviction or of inattention or failure to advert to a serious risk of going beyond mere inadvertence in respect of an obvious and important matter which the defendant's duty demanded he should address; and that, in the circumstances, the appeals of the two junior doctors and the electrician would be allowed and the appeal of the anaesthetist, namely Dr Adomako, would be dismissed. The reason that the Court of Appeal excepted the cases of motor manslaughter and their formulation of the law was the decision of this House in *R v Seymour* [1983] 2 All ER 1058, [1983] 2 AC 493 in which it was held that where manslaughter was charged and the circumstances were that the victim was killed as a result of the reckless driving of the defendant on a public highway, the trial judge should give the jury the direction which had been suggested in *R v Lawrence* [1981] 1 All ER 974, [1982] AC 510 but that it was appropriate also to point out that in order to constitute the offence of manslaughter the risk of death being caused by the manner of the defendant's driving must be very high.

In opening his very cogent argument for the appellant before your Lordships, counsel submitted that the law in this area should have the characteristics of clarity, certainty, intellectual coherence and general applicability and acceptability. For these reasons he said the law applying to involuntary manslaughter generally should involve a universal test and that test should be the test already applied in this House to motor manslaughter. He criticised the concept of gross negligence which was the basis of the judgment of the Court of Appeal submitting that its formulation involved circularity, the jury being told in effect to convict of a crime if they thought a crime had been committed and that accordingly using gross negligence as the conceptual basis for the crime of involuntary manslaughter was unsatisfactory and the court should apply the law laid down in *R v Seymour* [1983] 2 All ER 1058, [1983] 2 AC 493 generally to all cases of involuntary manslaughter or at least use this as the basis for providing general applicability and acceptability.

Like the Court of Appeal your Lordships were treated to a considerable review of authority. I begin with *R v Bateman* (1925) 19 Cr App Rep 8 and the opinion of Lord Hewart CJ, where he said (at 10–12):

[**Lord Mackay** quoted extensively from **Lord Hewart's** judgment, pp 10–13, concluding:]

> 'The foregoing observations deal with civil liability. To support an indictment for manslaughter the prosecution must prove the matters necessary to establish civil liability (except pecuniary loss), and, in addition, must satisfy the jury that the negligence or incompetence of the accused went beyond a mere matter of compensation and showed such disregard for the life and safety of others as to amount to a crime against the State and conduct deserving punishment.'

Next I turn to *Andrews v DPP*, [above, p **638**] which was a case of manslaughter through the dangerous driving of a motor car. In a speech with which all the other members of this House who sat agreed, Lord Atkin said . . .

[His Lordship quoted the passage beginning 'After citing *Cashill*' on p **639**, above, ending 'directed accordingly.']

In my opinion the law as stated in these two authorities is satisfactory as providing a proper basis for describing the crime of involuntary manslaughter. Since the decision in *Andrews v DPP* [1937] 2 All ER 552, [1937] AC 576 was a decision of your Lordships' House, it remains the most authoritative statement of the present law which I have been able to find and although its relationship to *R v Seymour* [1983] 2 All ER 1058, [1983] 2 AC 493 is a matter to which I shall have to return, it is a decision which has not been departed from. On this basis in my opinion the ordinary principles of the law of negligence apply to ascertain whether or not the defendant has been in breach of a duty of care towards the victim who has died. If such breach of duty is established the next question is whether that breach of duty caused the death of the victim. If so, the jury must go on to consider whether that breach of duty should be characterised as gross negligence and therefore as a crime. This will depend on the seriousness of the breach of duty committed by the defendant in all the circumstances in which the defendant was placed when it occurred. The jury will have to consider whether the extent to which the defendant's conduct departed from the proper standard of care incumbent upon him, involving as it must have done a risk of death to the patient, was such that it should be judged criminal.

It is true that to a certain extent this involves an element of circularity, but in this branch of the law I do not believe that is fatal to its being correct as a test of how far conduct must depart from accepted standards to be characterised as criminal. This is necessarily a question of degree and an attempt to specify that degree more closely is I think likely to achieve only a spurious precision. The essence of the matter, which is supremely a jury question, is whether, having regard to the risk of death involved, the conduct of the defendant was so bad in all the circumstances as to amount in their judgment to a criminal act or omission.

My Lords the view which I have stated of the correct basis in law for the crime of involuntary manslaughter accords I consider with the criteria stated by counsel although I have not reached the degree of precision in definition which he required, but in my opinion it has been reached so far as practicable and with a result which leaves the matter properly stated for a jury's determination.

My Lords in my view the law as stated in *R v Seymour* [1983] 2 All ER 1058, [1983] 2 AC 493 should no longer apply since the underlying statutory provisions on which it rested have now been repealed by the Road Traffic Act 1991. It may be that cases of involuntary motor manslaughter will as a result become rare but I consider it unsatisfactory that there should be any exception to the generality of the statement which I have made, since such exception, in my view, gives rise to unnecessary complexity. For example, in *Kong Cheuk Kwan v R* (1985) 82 Cr App Rep 18, it would give rise to unnecessary differences between the law applicable to those navigating vessels and the lookouts on the vessels.

I consider it perfectly appropriate that the word 'reckless' should be used in cases of involuntary manslaughter, but as Lord Atkin put it 'in the ordinary connotation of that word'. Examples in which this was done, to my mind, with complete accuracy are *R v Stone*, *R v Dobinson* [1977] 2 All ER 341, [1977] QB 354 and *R v West London Coroner, ex p Gray* [1987] 2 All ER 129, [1988] QB 467.

In my opinion it is quite unnecessary in the context of gross negligence to give the detailed directions with regard to the meaning of the word 'reckless' associated with *R v Lawrence* [1981] 1 All ER 974, [1982] AC 510. The decision of the Court of Appeal, Criminal Division in the other cases with which they were concerned at the same time as they heard the appeal in this case indicates that the circumstances in which involuntary manslaughter has to be considered may make the somewhat elaborate and rather rigid directions inappropriate. I entirely agree with the view that the circumstances to which a charge of involuntary manslaughter may apply are so various that it is unwise to attempt to categorise or detail specimen directions. For my part I would not wish to go beyond the description of the basis in law which I have already given.

In my view the summing up of the learned judge in the present case was a model of clarity in analysis of the facts and in setting out the law in a manner which was readily comprehensible by the jury. The summing up was criticised in respect of the inclusion of the following passage:

> 'Of course you will understand it is not for every humble man of the profession to have all that great skill of the great men in Harley Street but, on the other hand, they are not allowed to practise medicine in this country unless they have acquired a certain amount of skill. They are bound to show a reasonable amount of skill according to the circumstances of the case, and you have to judge them on the basis that they are skilled men, but not necessarily so skilled as more skilful men in the profession, and you can only convict them criminally if, in your judgment, they fall below the standard of skill which is the least qualification which any doctor should have. You should only convict a doctor of causing a death by negligence if you think he did something which no reasonably skilled doctor should have done.'

The criticism was particularly of the latter part of this quotation in that it was open to the meaning that if the defendant did what no reasonably skilled doctor should have done it was open to the jury to convict him of causing death by negligence. Strictly speaking this passage is concerned with the statement of a necessary condition for a conviction by preventing a conviction unless that condition is satisfied. It is incorrect to treat it as stating a sufficient condition for conviction. In any event I consider that this passage in the context was making the point forcefully that the defendant in this case was not to be judged by the standard of more skilled doctors but by the standard of a reasonably competent doctor. There were many other passages in the summing up which emphasised the need for a high degree of negligence if the jury were to convict and read in that context I consider that the summing up cannot be faulted.

For these reasons I am of the opinion that this appeal should be dismissed and that the certified question should be answered by saying:

> 'In cases of manslaughter by criminal negligence involving a breach of duty, it is a sufficient direction to the jury to adopt the gross negligence test set out by the Court of Appeal in the present case following R v Bateman (1925) 19 Cr App Rep 8 and Andrews v DPP [1937] 2 All ER 552, [1937] AC 576 and it is not necessary to refer to the definition of recklessness in R v Lawrence [1981] 1 All ER 974, [1982] AC 510, although it is perfectly open to the trial judge to use the word "reckless" in its ordinary meaning as part of his exposition of the law if he deems it appropriate in the circumstances of the particular case.'

We have been referred to the consultation paper by the Law Commission, *Criminal Law, Involuntary Manslaughter An Overview* (Law Com no 135), and we have also been referred to a number of standard textbooks. I have also had the opportunity of considering the note by Sir John Smith in [1994] Crim LR 292 since the hearing was completed. While I have not referred to these in detail I have derived considerable help in seeking to formulate my view as a result of studying them.

I have reached the same conclusion on the basic law to be applied in this case as did the Court of Appeal. Personally I would not wish to state the law more elaborately than I have done. In particular I think it is difficult to take expressions used in particular cases out of the context of the cases in which they were used and enunciate them as if applying generally. This can I think lead to ambiguity and perhaps unnecessary complexity. The task of trial judges in setting out for the jury the issues of fact and the relevant law in cases of this class is a difficult and demanding one. I believe that the supreme test that should be satisfied in such directions is that they are comprehensible to an ordinary member of the public who is called to sit on a jury and who has no particular prior acquaintance with the law. To make it obligatory on trial judges to give directions in law which are so elaborate that the ordinary member of the jury will have great difficulty in following them, and even greater difficulty in retaining them in his memory for the purpose of application in the jury room, is no service to the cause of justice. The experienced counsel who assisted your Lordships in this appeal indicated that as a practical matter there was a danger in over-elaboration of definition of the word 'reckless'. While therefore I have said in my view it is perfectly open to a trial judge to use the word 'reckless' if it appears appropriate in the circumstances of a particular case as indicating the extent to which a defendant's conduct must deviate from that of a proper standard of care, I do not think it right to require that this should be done and certainly not right that it should incorporate the full detail required in *R v Lawrence* [1981] 1 All ER 974, [1982] AC 510.

[Lords Keith of Kinkel, Goff of Chieveley, Browne-Wilkinson and Woolf agreed.]

Appeal dismissed

Notes and questions

1. *The Bateman test.* The question is whether the negligence was bad enough to amount to a crime and conduct deserving of punishment. But every instance of driving without due care and attention is a crime and it can scarcely be the law that every such case would be manslaughter if the driving happened to cause death. As *Andrews* decided, even causing death by dangerous driving is not necessarily manslaughter. In *Litchfield* [1998] Crim LR 507 the master of a square-rigged schooner which foundered off the Cornish coast was convicted of manslaughter by gross negligence (but see below) by steering an unsafe course, knowing that he might need to rely on the vessel's engines and that they might fail through contaminated fuel. The judge, in the time-honoured fashion, directed the jury that negligence must have been 'so bad that it could properly amount to a criminal act . . .'

Section 27(2) of the Merchant Shipping Act 1970 makes it an offence, punishable by two years' imprisonment, for a master of a ship to do or omit to do anything which causes or is likely to cause, inter alia, loss or destruction of or serious damage to his ship, or the death of or serious injury to any person, if the act or omission amounts to a breach or neglect of duty. Two counts under this section were included in the original indictment but the prosecution decided not to lay them before the jury. In so deciding the prosecution were apparently making a judgement that the negligence alleged went beyond, not merely a matter of compensation between parties, but beyond anything which could be adequately dealt with by conviction and sentence under the 1970 Act. It was argued on appeal that—

. . . if the facts proved do indeed amount to a statutory crime it is illogical and contrary to public policy to ask a jury to determine whether the conduct found is so bad that it *ought* to be judged a crime.

So it was said that 'there is no room (or virtually no room) in the law for a shipping manslaughter case'. The court dismissed this argument as 'impossible'.

For a start it makes nonsense of *Adomako* . . . Secondly, of course, it would quite inappropriately benefit those who are made subject to a statutory criminal liability. Why, one wonders, should mariners be advantaged over doctors?

Everyone will agree that there is no reason why mariners (or dangerous drivers) should be immune from prosecution of manslaughter; but does not the argument suggest that it is absurd to ask a jury to decide whether the negligence goes beyond a mere matter of compensation between parties? The negligence may go well beyond that while falling well short of what is required for manslaughter. Is not the real quesiton, not whether the negligence is bad enough to deserve punishment but *whether it is bad enough to be condemned as the very grave crime of manslaughter and punished accordingly.* (In *Litchfield* the judge did say 'way above' and 'so bad, so obviously wrong ... that it can properly be condemned as criminal, not in some technical sense of the word, like somebody might be regarded as criminal if they did not have light on the back of their bicycle, but in the ordinary language of men and women of the world.') If the statutory offence and manslaughter were charged in the same indictment how could the judge explain their task to the jury but by telling them that the manslaughter charge required a higher degree of fault?

2. *Negligence—a civil standard?*

R v Wacker

[2002] EWCA Crim 1944, [2003] 4 All ER 295, Court of Appeal, Criminal Division

(Kay LJ, Colman, Ouseley JJ)

The defendant used his HGV to transport 60 illegal immigrants into the UK via Dover. The only ventilation to the container on the HGV was a small vent. The vent was shut and remained closed for over five hours. Fifty-eight of the people hidden in the container suffocated. The defendant was convicted of 58 offences of manslaughter. At his trial the Crown accepted the general proposition that the principle of *ex turpi causa non oritur action* applied in determining whether there was a duty of care in considering a charge of manslaughter by gross negligence just as it did in determining whether a civil claim for damages for negligence could succeed.

The judge held that a proper distinction could be drawn between those criminal activities for which the passengers were solely responsible, those for which there was a shared responsibility, and those for which the defendant and others were solely responsible. He ruled that the defendant's failure to ensure that the concealed illegal immigrants had sufficient air was incidental to their role but critical to the defendant's own role so that, in establishing the necessary duty of care, since the immigrants would be 'relying' on a matter incidental to their criminality, they would not be 'relying' upon their own unlawful conduct. The defendant appealed against the manslaughter convictions contending that no duty of care could be said to have been owed by him to the illegal immigrants because they shared the same joint illegal purpose; and that the judge had been wrong in his directions to the jury as to the circumstances in which a duty of care would arise. He also appealed against sentence. The Attorney-General referred to the court the sentences for manslaughter as being unduly lenient, although he did not contend that the total sentence should be increased but only to the way in which the total of 14 years had been made up.

Held—(1) As a matter of public policy there was no justification for concluding that the criminal law should decline to hold a person as criminally responsible for the death of another simply because the two were engaged in some joint unlawful activity at the time or because there might have been an element of acceptance of a degree of risk by the victim in order to further the joint unlawful enterprise. Nor could the duty to take care be permitted to be affected by the countervailing demands of the criminal enterprise. It was not necessary to examine whether the distinction between matters for which the immigrants were responsible and those incidental to their illegality was a proper one; how matters might have been characterized in a civil claim had no relevance to the issue that the jury had to decide. Accordingly, the approach taken in the court below had been too favourable to the defendant. In every other respect the necessary ingredients of the offences of manslaughter had been properly left to the jury and there were no reasons to doubt the safety of those convictions.

Kay LJ: [his lordship stated the facts.]

[11] At the conclusion of the prosecution case, Mr Michael Lawson QC on behalf of the defendant submitted to the trial judge that there was no case for the defendant to answer on each of the manslaughter charges. He took as the foundation for his submission, the observation of Lord Mackay of Clashfern LC in *R v Adomako* [1994] 3 All ER 79 at 86–87, [1995] 1 AC 171 at 187:

> '... in my opinion the ordinary principles of the law of negligence apply to ascertain whether or not the defendant has been in breach of a duty of care towards the victim who has died. If such breach of duty is established the next question is whether that breach of duty caused the death of the victim. If so, the jury must go on to consider whether that breach of duty should be characterised as gross negligence and therefore as a crime.'

[12] Mr Lawson therefore submitted that the first question to be decided was whether applying 'the ordinary principles of the law of negligence', the defendant owed to those in the container a duty of care. He submitted that one of the general principles of the law of negligence, known by the Latin maxim of *ex turpi causa non oritur actio*, was that the law of negligence did not recognise the relationship between those involved in a criminal enterprise as giving rise to a duty of care owed by one participant to another. In his ruling Moses J summarised Mr Lawson's submission on the facts of the case:

> 'Mr Lawson contends that a failure to produce sufficient air or ventilation stems directly from the criminal activity in which both driver and passengers were engaged. It was essential to the criminal activity of all that secrecy be maintained. The closure of the vent, and the failure to reopen it during the course of the journey on board the ferry, which caused the death by suffocation of the 58 occupants, arose directly, he contends, from an enterprise the very essence of which was that secrecy was maintained. Secrecy could only be maintained by keeping the vent closed, since if it was open voices might be heard and, as the evidence of at least one of the survivor's revealed, the occupants had been told only to speak when the vent was open. Moreover, it is not possible for the court to determine the appropriate standard of care to be exercised by the driver. What is the appropriate standard of care to be applied in the case of a driver seeking, as part of a joint criminal exercise, to conceal the presence of 60 occupants of his lorry? In other words, the criminal activity on which all were engaged does, so he submits, have a bearing upon the appropriate standard of care. That standard cannot be ascertained without regard to the clandestine nature of the joint criminal activity. It was the driver's job to increase the chance of entry without detection, the very object which the passengers themselves sought to achieve.'

...

[35] [L]ooked at as a matter of pure public policy, we can see no justification for concluding that the criminal law should decline to hold a person as criminally responsible for the death of another simply because the two were engaged in some joint unlawful activity at the time or, indeed, because there may have been an element of acceptance of a degree of risk by the victim in order to further the joint unlawful enterprise. Public policy, in our judgment, manifestly points in totally the opposite direction.

[36] The next question that we are bound to ask ourselves is whether in any way we are required by authority to take a different view. The foundation for the contention that ex turpi causa is as much a part of the law of manslaughter as it is a part of the law of negligence is the passage from the speech of Lord Mackay of Clashfern LC in *R v Adomako* [1994] 3 All ER 79, [1995] 1 AC 171 set out at [11], above. In particular it is Lord Mackay's reference to 'the ordinary principles of the law of negligence'.

[37] *R v Adomako* was a case where an anaesthetist had negligently brought about the death of a patient. It, therefore, involved no element of unlawful activity on the part of either the anaesthetist or the victim. We have no doubt that issues raised in the case we are considering would never have crossed the minds of those deciding that case in the House of Lords. In so far as Lord Mackay referred to 'ordinary principles of the law of negligence' we do not accept for one moment that he was intending to decide that the rules relating to ex turpi causa were part of those ordinary principles. He was doing no more than holding that in an 'ordinary' case of negligence, the question whether there was a duty of care was to be judged by the same legal criteria as governed whether there was a duty of care in the law of negligence. That was the only issue relevant to that case and to give the passage the more extensive meaning accepted in the court below was in our judgment wrong.

Appeals dismissed

3. *Duty: who decides?* There was confusion over who decides whether the defendant owed a duty of care to the deceased? See *Khan and Khan* [1998] Crim LR 830 and *Gurphal Singh* [1999] Crim LR 582, above, p **98**. The matter is now settled by the Court of Appeal in *Willoughby*.

R v Willoughby
[2004] EWCA Crim 3365, Court of Appeal, Criminal Division

(Rose LJ, Douglas Brown and Mackay JJ)

It was alleged that W had employed D to assist in burning down a disused pub owned by W, because he was unable to pay the mortgages on it. D died in the fire. W was charged with arson which recklessly endangered life and manslaughter. The charge of manslaughter was put as either gross negligence manslaughter or manslaughter by an illegal and dangerous act, and the judge found a duty of care could arise, on the basis that W owed D a duty to safeguard his health and safety while on his premises. The judge left it to the jury to decide whether there was indeed a duty of care. They convicted on both charges and the defendant appealed on the manslaughter charge only.

Rose LJ:
[21] It is convenient to say something about a conflict which there is in the present authorities as to whether the judge should decide whether a duty of care exists, or whether he should give appropriate directions to the jury, in a case where there is evidence capable of establishing a duty, so that they may determine whether a duty exists.

[22] As it seems to us, the clear implication from the words used by Lord Mackay of Clashfern, Lord Chancellor in *R v Adomako* [1995] 1 AC 171, [1994] 3 All ER 79, in the well-known passage at 187B to 187C, particularly the words 'the jury must go on' is that existence of duty, breach causing death and judgment of criminality are all three usually matters for the jury. That is the way in which this Court interpreted that speech in *R v Khan & Khan* [1998] Crim LR 83 (transcript 18 March 1998) followed in *R v Sinclair* 148 NLJ 1353 (transcript 21 August 1998). In *R v Singh* [1999] Crim LR 582 (transcript 19 February 1999), where the court apparently approved the trial judge's direction to the jury that a duty of care was owed, neither *Khan* nor *Sinclair* appear to have been cited and *Adomako* is not referred to in the judgment. *Archbold* 2005 edition, para 19–111 prefers the approach in Khan. A footnote in *Smith & Hogan* 10th edn, p 387 prefers *Singh*. *Khan*, *Sinclair* and *Singh* were all cited in *Wacker*. The trial judge in that case (see paras 19 and 22 of the Court of Appeal's judgment) directed the jury that they had to be sure that a duty of care was owed and there is no criticism by the Court of Appeal in that case of that approach. Similarly, in *Mark and Nationwide*

Heating Services [2004] EWCA Crim 2490, the trial judge had directed the jury (see para 18 of the Court of Appeal's judgment) that they must be sure that the defendant owed a duty of care. On an application for leave to appeal, that direction attracted no criticism from highly experienced leading counsel or from the Court of Appeal, in which Scott Baker LJ presided.

[23] We add that there may be exceptional cases, for example where a duty of care obviously exists, such as that arising between doctor and patient, or where Parliament has imposed a particular type of statutory duty, in which the judge can properly direct the jury that a duty exists. But, for the reasons which we have sought to explain, that is a question normally for the jury's determination.

4. *Risk of death*. Though Lord Mackay refers to a risk of death, it was not completely clear that a risk of causing serious bodily harm was not enough, since the law of murder equates the two. But in *Gurphal Singh*, above, the judge directed: 'The circumstances must be such that a reasonably prudent person would have foreseen a serious and obvious risk not merely of injury or even serious injury but of death.' The Court of Appeal has now confirmed in *Misra* (the next case extracted below) that a risk of death is required.

[49] No issue arises whether both appellants owed a duty of care to the deceased, or were negligently in breach of it. There was however helpful argument about the nature of the relevant risk. Was it, as the judge directed the jury in the present case 'serious risk to life', or was it much broader, extending to serious risk to safety as well as life? In its original formulation in *Bateman*, Lord Hewitt CJ referred to 'disregard to the life and safety of others' in the sense of serious injury. In *Seymour*, the risk was confined to the risk of death. In *Stone* [1977] QB 554 and *West London Coroner, ex parte Grey* [1988] QB 467, [1987] 2 All ER 129 reference was made to risks in broader terms, extending to health and welfare. Although Lord Mackay spoke in approving terms of these decisions in a different context, it is clear that his approval was directed to the deployment of the word 'reckless'. He was not addressing, and it would have been inconsistent with his own analysis of the legal principles if he were approving, the wider basis for identifying risk described in *Stone* and *West London Coroner ex parte Grey*. It is also striking that Lord Mackay did not expressly adopt or approve the broader formulation of risk made by Lord Taylor CJ in *Prentice*. Since *Adomako*, this issue has been addressed in this court, in *R (on the application of Gurphal) v Singh* [1999] CLR 582 and the Divisional Court in *Lewin v CPS*, unreported, 24 May 2002. In *Gurphal Singh*, this court strongly approved the trial judge's direction in a case of manslaughter by gross negligence that 'the circumstances must be such that a reasonably prudent person would have foreseen a serious and obvious risk not merely of injury, even serious injury, but of death'. In *Lewin*, the Divisional Court applied that direction.

[50] Mr David Perry, on behalf of the Attorney General, informed us that, as a matter of policy, when making a decision whether to prosecute for this offence in cases like the present, the Director of Public Prosecutions looks for evidence of an obvious risk of death, and that, if the extent of the risk were limited to the obvious risk of serious injury, and no more, prosecution would not follow.

[51] The editors of *Blackstone's Criminal Practice* suggest that the law needs clarification, and that, if it were clarified, some 'degree of symmetry' between murder and manslaughter would be achieved if, for the purposes of gross negligence manslaughter, the risk should extend to grievous bodily harm. Professor Smith took the contrary view, suggesting that 'if we are to have an offence of homicide by gross negligence at all, it seems right that it should be... limited. The circumstances must be such that a reasonably prudent person would have foreseen a serious risk, not merely of injury, even serious injury, but of death.'

[52] There will, of course, be numerous occasions when these distinctions are entirely theoretical. From time to time, however, they will be of great significance, not only to the decision whether to

prosecute, but also to the risk of conviction of manslaughter. In our judgment, where the issue of risk is engaged, *Adomako* demonstrates, and it is now clearly established, that it relates to the risk of death, and is not sufficiently satisfied by the risk of bodily injury or injury to health. In short, the offence requires gross negligence in circumstances where what is at risk is the life of an individual to whom the defendant owes a duty of care. As such it serves to protect his or her right to life.

5. *Is the gross negligence test too uncertain?*

Misra and Srivastava
[2004] EWCA Crim 2375, Court of Appeal, Criminal Division

(Judge LJ, Deputy Chief Justice of England and Wales, Treacy, Bean JJ)

M and S were doctors who, on duty in a hospital, failed to recognize that a knee surgery patient had developed toxic shock syndrome. The poison built up in his body and he died. The prosecution relied not on M and S's failure to diagnose the precise condition, since that was a rare one and failure to identify it may well not have amounted to negligence at all. The Crown relied on their failure to appreciate that the patient was seriously ill, despite his showing persistent signs of infection and, notwithstanding suggestions by other members of the medical team. M and S did not obtain the blood results that someone had ordered nor did either make any enquiry about the results. They did not seek help from senior colleagues. An expert for the prosecution testified that if he were examining a third or fourth year medical student, and the student failed to diagnose infection in such circumstances, he would have thought of failing the student on that basis alone.

Judge LJ: [reading the judgment of the court:]
[His Lordship reviewed the facts].

[28] Mr Michael Gledhill QC on behalf of Dr Misra submitted that manslaughter by gross negligence is an offence which lacks certainty. As presently understood, it requires the trial judge to direct the jury that the defendant should be convicted of manslaughter by gross negligence if they are satisfied that his conduct was 'criminal'. Indeed, the effect of his argument was that it is a separate additional ingredient of this offence that the jury has to decide whether the defendant's conduct amounted to a crime. Relying in particular on the Law Commission paper on Involuntary Manslaughter (Law Com. No. 237) as a convenient summary of a good deal of the debate by distinguished academic commentators, he suggested that the current test is 'circular'. It is this circularity which leads to uncertainty. Mr Gledhill drew attention to, and adopted for the purposes for his argument, the way in which the Law Commission identified the potential problems arising from linking the civil and the criminal law concepts of negligence where the allegation against the defendant arose from omission. This was such a case. 'It is by no means certain that the scope of liability for negligent omissions is the same in criminal law as it is in tort.' The principles were 'so unclear' that it is difficult to tell whether 'the law as currently understood represents a change, and if so, what the implications might be.' The relevant part of the Law Commission paper ends, 'It is possible that the law in this area fails to meet the standard of certainty required by the European Convention on Human Rights (ECHR).' In Mr Gledhill's submission this is an understatement: the standard of certainty is not met.

[29] To develop his argument on uncertainty, Mr Gledhill focussed our attention on art 7 of the ECHR, entitled 'No punishment without law', which provides:

'7(1) No-one shall be held guilty of any criminal offence on account of any act or omission which did not constitute a criminal offence under national or international law at the time when it was committed nor shall a heavier penalty be imposed than the one that was applicable at the time the criminal offence was committed.'

In our view the essential thrust of this Article is to prohibit the creation of offences, whether by legislation or the incremental development of the common law, which have retrospective application. It reflects a well-understood principle of domestic law, that conduct which did not contravene the criminal law at the time when it took place should not retrospectively be stigmatised as criminal, or expose the perpetrator to punishment. As Lord Reid explained in *Waddington v Miah* [1974] 2 All ER 377, [1974] 59 Cr App R 149 at p. 150 and 151,

> 'There has for a very long time been a strong feeling against making legislation, and particularly criminal legislation, retrospective.... I use retrospective in the sense of authorising people being punished for what they did before the Act came into force.'

[His lordship reviewed English common law authorities for the principle of legality.]

[34] ... In summary, it is not to be supposed that prior to the implementation of the Human Rights Act 1998, either this Court, or the House of Lords, would have been indifferent to or unaware of the need for the criminal law in particular to be predictable and certain. Vague laws which purport to create criminal liability are undesirable, and in extreme cases, where it occurs, their very vagueness may make it impossible to identify the conduct which is prohibited by a criminal sanction. If the court is forced to guess at the ingredients of a purported crime any conviction for it would be unsafe. That said, however, the requirement is for sufficient rather than absolute certainty.

[35] The ambit of the principle, as well as its limitations, were clearly described in the *Sunday Times v United Kingdom* [1979] 2 EHRR 245. The law must be formulated:

> '...with sufficient precision to enable the citizen to regulate his conduct: he must be able—if need be with appropriate advice—to foresee to a degree that is reasonable in the circumstances, the consequences which any given action may entail. Those consequences need not be foreseeable with absolute certainty: experience shows this to be unobtainable. Again, whilst certainty is highly desirable, it may bring in its train excessive rigidity, and the law must be able to keep pace with changing circumstances. Accordingly, many laws are inevitably couched in terms which, to a greater or lesser extent, are vague, and whose interpretation and application are questions of practice.'

Moreover, there is a distinction to be drawn between undesirable, and in extreme cases, unacceptable uncertainty about the necessary ingredients of a criminal offence, and uncertainty in the process by which it is decided whether the required ingredients of the offence have been established in an individual case. The point was highlighted in *Wingrove v United Kingdom* [1996] 24 EHRR 1:

> 'It was a feature common to most laws and legal systems that tribunals may reach different conclusions, even when applying the same laws to the same facts. This did not necessarily make the laws inaccessible or unforeseeable.'

[36] We can see the practical application of these comments in *Handyside v United Kingdom* [1974] 17 YB 228, where the Commission considered the definition of obscenity in the Obscene Publications Acts, 1959–1964. This offence is concerned with items which have a tendency to deprave and corrupt, a very general definition, certainly capable on forensic analysis of being criticised on the basis of uncertainty. The Commission nevertheless concluded that the offence was adequately described. In *Wingrove* itself, the court rejected the argument that blasphemous libel—that is, libel defined in very broad terms as 'likely to shock and outrage the feelings of the general body of Christian believers'—was insufficiently accessible or certain.

[37] Since the implementation of the Human Rights Act, the issue of uncertainty has also been addressed on a number of occasions in this court. It has been decided that the offence of making indecent photographs of children was sufficiently certain to satisfy arts 8 and 10 of the Convention (*R v Smethurst* [2001] EWCA Crim 772, [2002] 1 Cr App Rep 50, 165 JP 377); that the offence of publishing an obscene article satisfies the requirements of art 7 of the Convention (*R v Perrin* [2002]

EWCA Crim 747); and that the offence of causing a public nuisance, by sending an envelope through the post containing salt, which was suspected to be anthrax, contrary to common law, was also sufficiently certain to satisfy the requirements of art 7, 8 and 10 of the Convention (*R v Goldstein* [2003] EWCA Crim 3450, [2004] 1 Cr App R 388). In each case the uncertainty argument was rejected. In *Goldstein* itself, at p. 395, Latham LJ commented:

> 'The elements of the offence are sufficiently clear to enable a person, with appropriate legal advice if necessary, to regulate his behaviour.... A citizen, appropriately advised, could foresee that the conduct identified was capable of amounting to a public nuisance.'

In our judgment, the incorporation of the ECHR, while providing a salutary reminder, has not effected any significant extension of or change to the 'certainty' principle as long understood at common law.

[His lordship dealt with the issues of recklessness and gross negligence discussed below.]

[58] We can now return to the argument based on circularity and uncertainty, and the application of arts 6 and 7 of the ECHR. The most important passages in the speech of Lord Mackay on the issue of circularity read:

> '... The jury must go on to consider whether that breach of duty should be characterised as gross negligence and therefore as a crime. This will depend on the seriousness of the breach of duty committed by the defendant in all the circumstances in which the defendant was placed when it occurred. The jury will have to consider whether the extent to which the defendant's conduct departed from the proper standard of care incumbent upon him, involving as it must have done a risk of death to the patient, was such that it should be judged criminal.
>
> It is true that, to a certain extent, this involves an element of circularity, but in this branch of the law I do not believe that is fatal to its being correct as a test of how far conduct must depart from accepted standards to be characterised as criminal ... The essence of the matter which is supremely a jury question is whether, having regard to the risk of death involved, the conduct of the defendant was so bad in all the circumstances as to amount in their judgment to a criminal act or omission.'

[59] Mr Gledhill suggested that this passage demonstrated that an additional specific ingredient of this offence was that the jury had to decide whether the defendant's conduct amounted to a crime. If the jury could, or was required to, define the offence for itself, and accordingly might do so on some unaccountable or unprincipled or unexplained basis, to adopt Bacon, the sound given by the law would indeed be uncertain, and would then strike without warning. Mr Gledhill's argument then would be compelling.

[60] Looking at the authorities since *Bateman*, the purpose of referring to the differences between civil and criminal liability, whether in the passage in Lord Mackay's speech to which we have just referred, or in directions to the jury, is to highlight that the burden on the prosecution goes beyond proof of negligence for which compensation would be payable. Negligence of that degree could not lead to a conviction for manslaughter. The negligence must be so bad, 'gross', that if all the other ingredients of the offence are proved, then it amounts to a crime and is punishable as such.

[61] This point was addressed by Lord Atkin in *Andrews* at p. 582, when he referred to *Williamson* (1807) 3 C&P 635:

> '... where a man who practiced as an accoucheur, owing to a mistake in his observation of the actual symptoms, inflicted on a patient terrible injuries from which she died.' To substantiate that charge— namely, manslaughter—Lord Ellenborough said, 'The prisoner must have been guilty of criminal misconduct, arising either from the grossest ignorance or the most criminal inattention.' The word 'criminal' in any attempt to define a crime is perhaps not the most helpful: but it is plain that the Lord Chief Justice meant to indicate to the jury a high degree of negligence. So at a much later date in

Bateman [1925] 18 Cr. App. R 8 a charge of manslaughter was made against a qualified medical practitioner in similar circumstances to those of *Williamson's* case ... I think with respect that the expressions used are not, indeed they were probably not intended to be, a precise definition of the crime.

[62] Accordingly, the value of references to the criminal law in this context is that they avoid
the danger that the jury may equate what we may describe as 'simple' negligence, which in relation to manslaughter would not be a crime at all, with negligence which involves a criminal offence.
In short, by bringing home to the jury the extent of the burden on the prosecution, they ensure that
the defendant whose negligence does not fall within the ambit of the criminal law is not convicted
of a crime. They do not alter the essential ingredients of this offence. A conviction cannot be
returned if the negligent conduct is or may be less than gross. If however the defendant is found
by the jury to have been grossly negligent, then, if the jury is to act in accordance with its duty, he
must be convicted. This is precisely what Lord Mackay indicated when, in the passage already
cited, he said, '... The jury must go on to consider whether that breach of duty should be characterised as gross negligence and therefore as a crime' (our emphasis). The decision whether the
conduct was criminal is described not as 'the' test, but as 'a' test as to how far the conduct in question must depart from accepted standards to be 'characterised as criminal'. On proper analysis,
therefore, the jury is not deciding whether the particular defendant ought to be convicted on
some unprincipled basis. The question for the jury is not whether the defendant's negligence was
gross, and whether, additionally, it was a crime, but whether his behaviour was grossly negligent
and consequently criminal. This is not a question of law, but one of fact, for decision in the
individual case.

[63] On examination, this represents one example, among many, of problems which juries are
expected to address on a daily basis. They include equally difficult questions, such as whether a
defendant has acted dishonestly, by reference to contemporary standards, or whether he has acted
in reasonable self-defence, or, when charged with causing death by dangerous driving, whether the
standards of his driving fell far below what should be expected of a competent and careful driver.
These examples represent the commonplace for juries. Each of these questions could be said to be
vague and uncertain. If he made enquiries in advance, at most an individual would be told the principle of law which the jury would be directed to apply: he could not be advised what a jury would
think of the individual case, and how it would be decided. That involves an element of uncertainty
about the outcome of the decision-making process, but not unacceptable uncertainty about the
offence itself.

[64] In our judgment the law is clear. The ingredients of the offence have been clearly defined, and
the principles decided in the House of Lords in *Adomako*. They involve no uncertainty. The hypothetical
citizen, seeking to know his position, would be advised that, assuming he owed a duty of care to the
deceased which he had negligently broken, and that death resulted, he would be liable to conviction
for manslaughter if, on the available evidence, the jury was satisfied that his negligence was gross.
A doctor would be told that grossly negligent treatment of a patient which exposed him or her to the
risk of death, and caused it, would constitute manslaughter.

[65] After Lord Williams' sustained criticism of the offence of manslaughter by gross negligence,
the House of Lords in *Adomako* clarified the relevant principles and the ingredients of this offence.
Although, to a limited extent, Lord Mackay accepted that there was an element of circularity in
the process by which the jury would arrive at its verdict, the element of circularity which he identified
did not then and does not now result in uncertainty which offends against Article 7, nor if we may say
so, any principle of common law. Gross negligence manslaughter is not incompatible with the ECHR.
Accordingly the appeal arising from the question certified by the trial judge must be dismissed.

Appeals dismissed

Question

The court explains that 'a doctor would be told that grossly negligent treatment of a patient which exposed him or her to the risk of death, and caused it, would constitute manslaughter' (para 64). What should the response be when the doctor then asks how gross his negligent conduct has to be in order to be convicted? How can the relevant standard be described to the doctor otherwise than by reference to whether the jury thinks that it is criminal?

6. *Gross negligence and mens reas.* In *Misra*, the appellants also argued that in the light of the decision of the House of Lords in *G* (above, p **140**), the gross negligence manslaughter formulation should be abandoned in favour of a test of subjective reckless manslaughter. The Court of Appeal rejected this ground of appeal.

[39] After he had fully considered the recent decision of the House of Lords in *R v G and Another* [2003] UKHL 50, [2004] 1 AC 1034, Mr Gledhill deployed an additional argument which was not before Langley J. In essence, he submitted that with the exception of causing death by dangerous driving, no serious criminal offence could be committed without mens rea. He relied on what Lord Bingham, at para 32, described as a 'salutary principle that conviction of serious crime should depend on proof not simply that the defendant caused (by act or omission) an injurious result to another but that his state of mind when so acting was culpable'. Unless some element of mens rea, such, for example, as recklessness, was a necessary ingredient of manslaughter by gross negligence, this essential principle was contravened. . . .

[55] It is convenient now to address the argument that the decision in *R v G and Another* should lead us to reassess whether gross negligence manslaughter should now be replaced by and confined to reckless manslaughter. As we have shown, precisely this argument by Lord Williams of Mostyn was rejected in *Adomako*. We also note, first, that Parliament has not given effect to possible reforms on this topic discussed by the Law Commission and, second, notwithstanding that *Adomako* was cited in argument in *R v G and Another*, it was not subjected to any reservations or criticisms. Indeed in his speech Lord Bingham of Cornhill emphasised that in *R v G* he was not addressing the meaning of 'reckless' in any other statutory or common law context than s 1(1) and (2) of the Criminal Damage Act 1971. In these circumstances, although we gave leave to Mr Gledhill to amend his grounds of appeal to enable him to deploy the argument, we reject it.

[56] We can now reflect on Mr Gledhill's associated contention that if recklessness is not a necessary ingredient of this offence, the decision in *Attorney General's Reference (No. 2 of 1999)* [2000] QB 796, [2000] 3 All ER 182 led to the unacceptable conclusion that manslaughter by gross negligence did not require proof of any specific state of mind, and that the defendant's state of mind was irrelevant. In our judgment the submission is based on a narrow reading of the decision that a defendant may properly be convicted of gross negligence manslaughter in the absence of evidence as to his state of mind. However when it is available, such evidence is not irrelevant to the issue of gross negligence. It will often be a critical factor in the decision (see *R (on the application of Rowley) v DPP* [2003] EWHC 693). In *Adomako* itself, Lord Mackay directed attention to 'all' of the circumstances in which the defendant was placed: he did not adopt, or endorse, or attempt to redefine the list of states of mind to which Lord Taylor CJ referred in *Prentice*, which was not in any event 'exhaustive' of possible relevant states of mind. It is therefore clear that the defendant is not to be convicted without fair consideration of all the relevant circumstances in which his breach of duty occurred. In each case, of course, the circumstances are fact-specific.

[57] Mr Gledhill nevertheless contended that even so, the problem of mens rea remains. This, he argued was a necessary, but absent ingredient of the offence. We have reflected, of course, that if the defendant intends death or really serious harm, and acts in such a way to cause either, and death results, he would be guilty of murder. If he intends limited injury, and causes death, he would be guilty of manslaughter in any event. We are here concerned with the defendant who does not intend injury, but who in all the contemporaneous circumstances is grossly negligent. As a matter of strict language, 'mens rea' is concerned with an individual defendant's state of mind. Speaking generally, negligence is concerned with his failure to behave in accordance with the standards required of the reasonable man. Looked at in this way, the two concepts are distinct. However the term 'mens rea' is also used to describe the ingredient of fault or culpability required before criminal liability for the defendant's actions may be established. In *Sweet v Parsley* [1970] AC 132, [1969] 1 All ER 347, Lord Reid explained that there were occasions when gross negligence provided the 'necessary mental element' for a serious crime. Manslaughter by gross negligence is not an absolute offence. The requirement for gross negligence provides the necessary element of culpability.

Questions

1. Is the gross negligence formula more favourable to the defendant than the *Caldwell* recklessness form of mens rea? The difference is that that recklessness test did not include the requirement that the jury must be satisfied that the defendant's conduct was bad enough to be a crime. A direction in *Caldwell* terms deprived D of the chance of acquittal on that ground. In *Prentice*, for example, there were many strongly mitigating factors in the doctors' conduct, which were irrelevant if the jury were concerned only with what was foreseeable, but highly relevant to question whether their behaviour was bad enough to deserve condemnation as manslaughter.

2. Like Lord Atkin, Lord Mackay in *Adomako* considers it 'perfectly appropriate' that the word 'reckless' should be used in cases of manslaughter but, again agreeing with Lord Atkin, 'in the ordinary connotation of that word'. But what is the 'ordinary connotation of that word' which Lord Atkin and Lord Mackay had in mind?

3. Lord Mackay in *Adomako* gives as an example of where recklessness was used 'with complete accuracy' the case of *Stone and Dobinson* [1977] 2 All ER 341, [1977] QB 354, CA. There S and D, S's mistress, allowed S's sister to lodge with them. The sister became infirm while lodging with them and died of toxaemia from infected bed sores and prolonged immobilisation. S and D had made only half-hearted and wholly ineffectual attempts to secure medical attention for the sister. Upholding the convictions of S and D for manslaughter, the court said (at p 347):

The duty which a defendant has undertaken is a duty of caring for the health and welfare of the infirm person. What the Crown has to prove is a breach of that duty in such circumstances that the jury feel convinced that the defendant's conduct can properly be described as reckless. That is to say a reckless disregard of danger to the health and welfare of the infirm person. Mere inadvertence is not enough. The defendant must be proved to have been indifferent to an obvious risk of injury to health, or actually to have foreseen the risk but to have determined nevertheless to run it.

But:

(i) Is this statement entirely clear? Does it suggest, with its contrasting tests of indifference *or* foresight, that D may be accounted indifferent without actual foresight of the risk?

(ii) The risk as to which it is stated D must be reckless is a risk, not of death, but merely of 'health and welfare'. What does that mean? Is it now the law that if on a charge of manslaughter the case against D proceeds on the basis of gross negligence the prosecution must prove that the reasonable man would have foreseen that the conduct in question involved a risk of death, but if it proceeds on recklessness it is enough to prove that D was indifferent to or foresaw some risk much less than death? If so, if this defensible?

4. In *R v DPP, ex p Jones* [2000] Crim LR 858, DC, below, p **658**, it was acknowledged that experience shows that a jury is more likely to convict of manslaughter when there is evidence of subjective recklessness than when there is not. This seems to be common sense. Where the prosecution case is expressly based on gross negligence, which does not require proof of any subjective element, should such evidence be admissible or is it precluded by the principle of *Sandhu* (above, p **229**)? See commentary on *Ex p Jones*.

R (on the application of Rowley) v Director of Public Prosecutions
[2003] EWHC 693 (Admin), Queen's Bench Division, Divisional Court

(Kennedy LJ and Hooper J)

R's profoundly disabled son died when in a care home run by a local authority. The carer responsible for bathing him left him unattended in the bath and he drowned. R sought a review of the decision not to prosecute. The DPP considered that a factor favouring prosecution was that a severely disabled person was left unsupervised in the bath posing an obvious risk of death, but the lack of awareness of risk on the part of the carer was treated as a factor weighing against that finding. The DPP maintained the decision not to prosecute, and R applied for judicial review. One issue for the court was whether the carer's state of mind was a factor that the jury might take into account in the carer's favour when considering whether her conduct was so bad as to amount to gross negligence.

Kennedy LJ
[his lordship set out the facts:]

28. It is clear from what Lord Mackay said [in *Adomako*] that there is a fifth ingredient: 'criminality' (albeit defining the ingredient in this way 'involves an element of circularity') or 'badness'. Using the word 'badness', the jury must be sure that the defendant's conduct was so bad as in all the circumstances to amount 'to a criminal act or omission'. Lord Hewart C.J. in *Bateman* used the words: 'to amount to a crime against the state and conduct deserving punishment' that is, conduct which does not merely call for compensation but for criminal punishment.

29. It is clear that subjective recklessness (actual foresight of risk) is not a pre-requisite for a conviction for gross negligence manslaughter. The thrust of the case against Dr Adomako was that he had failed to notice or respond to the obvious signs. If he had noticed that a disconnection had occurred or that breathing had stopped he would have taken action- but he had not. It is also clear that the presence of subjective recklessness may be taken into account by the jury as a strong factor demonstrating that the defendant's negligence was criminal. This was confirmed in *Attorney-General's Reference (No 2 of 1999)* [2000] QB 796 and in *R v DPP ex parte Jones* [2000] IRLR 373, a decision on which Mr Hunt places considerable reliance.

30. In the first of those cases the Attorney-General asked the Court of Appeal Criminal Division to consider two questions arising out of the ruling of a trial judge in relation to the prosecution of a

railway company for gross negligence manslaughter which was said to have been a cause of a train crash. The questions were—

'(1) Can a defendant be properly convicted of manslaughter by gross negligence in the absence of evidence as to that defendant's state of mind?

(2) Can a non-human defendant be convicted of the crime of manslaughter by gross negligence in the absence of evidence establishing the guilt of an identified human individual for the same crime?'

31. The court answered the first question in the affirmative, and the second question in the negative. At 809 Rose LJ said in relation to question 1—

'Although there may be cases where the defendant's state of mind is relevant to the jury's consideration when assessing the grossness and criminality of his conduct, evidence of his state of mind is not a pre-requisite to a conviction for manslaughter by gross negligence. The *Adomako* test is objective but a defendant who is reckless as defined in *R v Stone* may be the more readily found to be grossly negligent to a criminal degree.'

In the case of *Stone* Geoffrey Lane LJ had said at 363 that where a defendant had undertaken a duty of care for the health and safety of an infirm person the prosecution had to prove—

'A reckless disregard of danger to the health and welfare of the infirm person. Mere inadvertence is not enough. The defendant must be proved to have been indifferent to an obvious risk of injury to health, or actually to have foreseen the risk but to have determined nevertheless to run it.'

32. In *R v DPP ex parte Jones* the facts were as follows. Mr Martell, the Managing Director of a company called Euromin, had arranged for a dockside crane to be adapted, so that with the jaws of the grab bucket open bags could be attached to hooks fitted within the bucket. Jones was in the hold of a ship loading bags onto the hooks when the jaws of the bucket closed and he was decapitated. In deciding not to prosecute the managing director and the company for gross negligence, the lack of subjective recklessness on the part of Mr Mantell was 'dispositive' (see paragraph 36 of the judgment of Buxton LJ). In paragraph 23 of his judgment Buxton LJ referred to *Adomako* and the passage at page 809 of the *Attorney-General's Reference* case which we have already set out, and at paragraph 24 he continued—

'The law is, therefore, quite clear. If the accused is subjectively reckless, then that may be taken into account by the jury as a strong factor demonstrating that his negligence was criminal, but negligence will still be criminal in the absence of any recklessness if on an objective basis the defendant demonstrated what, for instance, Lord Mackay quoted the Court of Appeal in *Adomako* as describing as:

"failure to advert to a serious risk going beyond mere inadvertence in respect of an obvious and important matter which the defendant's duty demanded that he should address."

That is a test in objective terms.'

33. The issue raised in the present case by Mr Hunt is whether the state of mind of the defendant is a factor which the jury may take into account in the defendant's favour when considering whether his conduct is so bad as to amount to a criminal offence. Mr Hunt submitted that subjective reckless-ness may help to establish a prosecution case, but that otherwise the state of mind of the proposed defendant is irrelevant.

34. That seems to us to be an unrealistic approach which the authorities do not require, which no judge would enforce, and which no jury would adopt. Once it can be shown that there was ordinary common law negligence causative of death and a serious risk of death, what remains to be estab-lished is criminality or badness. In considering whether there is criminality or badness, Lord Mackay makes it clear that all the circumstances are to be taken into account.

35. An examination of the Court of Appeal decision in *Prentice* also shows that Mr Hunt's submission is not supported by authority. . . .

[His lordship referred to the decision in *Prentice* (above, p 641).]

38. The fact that Dr Prentice was 'inexperienced, reluctant to give the treatment and wholly unaware . . . of the likely fatal consequences' were all factors which the jury were entitled to take into account in the defendant's favour. Likewise in Dr Sullman's favour, his belief and his understanding could be taken into account.

39. There is further authority for the proposition that the state of mind of the defendant is a factor which the jury may take into account in the defendant's favour in the passage which we have cited from the *Attorney-General's Reference* case and which was cited by Buxton LJ in *Jones*. Rose LJ makes it clear that the defendant's state of mind is relevant to the jury's consideration when assessing the grossness and criminality of his conduct.

40. It follows that it is relevant to look at all of the circumstances, many of which may cast light upon the defendant's state of mind . . .

The application was dismissed

Question

Is the decision consistent with that in *R v DPP, ex p Jones?*

(3) RECKLESS MANSLAUGHTER

Manslaughter by advertent recklessness, that is, conscious risk-taking still survives as a separate head of manslaughter. As we have seen, where D killed by an act (not unlawful apart from the fact that it is done recklessly) knowing that it was highly probable that he would cause serious bodily harm, this was murder (*Hyam*) before the decision in *Moloney*. It must still be manslaughter. Where death is so caused, the jury do not have to decide whether it is 'bad enough' to amount to a crime. That question is appropriate only when we are concerned with degrees of negligence. The jury are not asked this question in non-fatal offences against the person which may be committed recklessly so it would be quite inconsistent if it applied when death is caused. What is uncertain is whether there is a sufficient fault:

(i) when D's awareness of an unreasonable risk is of less than high probability; or

(ii) where the risk he foresees is of bodily harm, less than serious bodily harm.

It is submitted that the better view is that the offence includes (i) but not (ii). Arguably, it should include (i) because a distinction based solely on the degree of probability is unsatisfactory since that is only one of many factors which may determine whether conduct is properly characterised as reckless. It should not include (ii) because, by analogy with murder, manslaughter should be limited to cases where the known risk is of serious bodily harm.

There is a great difference with subjective recklessness from a case of inadvertent negligence, like *Adomako*. Adomako was quite unaware of the risk his failure was causing to the life of the patient but the prosecution's case against Litchfield (above) was that 'With his vast experience of sailing, he must have appreciated the obvious and serious risk of death to his crew'; and 'he knew the risk he was running in using contaminated fuel . . . and chose to run the obvious and serious risk of death by doing so.' The fault involved—subjective recklessness—is different, not merely in degree, but in kind, from the neglect which satisfies the Merchant Shipping Act, so the question of reconciling the two does not, or should not, arise.

R v Lidar (Narinder Singh)

(1999) Court of Appeal, Criminal Division (unreported)

(Evans LJ, Alliott J, Jackson J)

The deceased, Kully, was killed when he was hanging onto a car, with half his body through the car window fighting with the appellant who was driving. He was carried about 225 m when his feet caught in the near side rear wheel and he fell to the ground and was run over, suffering fatal crush injuries.

Lord Justice Evans [his lordship reviewed the facts and the evidence:]

The relevant direction of law as regards manslaughter was this:

> 'In order for manslaughter to be proved in this case, the Crown have to prove that the defendant acted recklessly. Recklessly in this context means that the defendant foresaw that some physical harm, however slight, might result to Kully from driving the car as he did and yet ignoring that risk he nevertheless went on to drive as he did. Mere inadvertence is not enough. The defendant must have been proved to have been indifferent to an obvious risk of injury to health or actually to have foreseen the risk but to have determined nevertheless to run it. If you are sure that the defendant acted recklessly you find him guilty of manslaughter. If you are not sure you find him not guilty'.

[His lordship reviewed the grounds of appeal.]

Mr Beckman applied for leave to add a further ground, which is to the effect that the judge ought to have directed the jury that this was a case of 'gross negligence' manslaughter which they should approach in accordance with the House of Lords' judgment in *Adomako* [1995] 1 AC 171. Whether the submission was that the 'gross negligence' direction should be given in addition to or in substitution for the 'recklessness' direction in fact given was not made entirely clear, but there was no complaint about the terms in which the direction was given, if 'recklessness' was appropriate. The application to add this ground of appeal was not opposed by Mr Milmo QC for the prosecution, and we gave leave because of the connection which must exist between the proper definition of the offence of manslaughter and the relevance of the suggested defences of self-defence and necessity to it . . .

[His lordship dealt with the issue of self defence.] . . .

In *Adomako* the House of Lords affirmed the characteristics of 'gross negligence' manslaughter and further held that there is no distinction in principle between motor manslaughter and other cases where gross negligence is the basis of criminal liability. The House of Lords also held that juries might properly be directed in terms of recklessness although the precise definition derived from *Seymour* [1983] 2 AC 493 should no longer be used (188A). Lord Mackay LC said this:

> 'I consider it perfectly appropriate that the word "reckless" be used in cases of involuntary manslaughter, but as Lord Atkin put it "in the ordinary connotation of that word." Examples in which this was done, in my mind with complete accuracy are *Reg v Stone* [1977] QB 354 and *Reg v West London Coroner ex parte Gray* [1988] QB 467 . . . . I entirely agree with the view that the circumstances to which a charge of involuntary manslaughter may apply are so various that it is unwise to attempt to categorise or detail specimen directions. For my part I would not wish to go beyond the description of the basis in law which I have already given' (187H–188B).

Nothing here suggests that for the future 'recklessness' could no longer be a basis for proving the offence of manslaughter: rather, the opposite. *Smith & Hogan* records that 'For many years the courts have used the terms "recklessness" and "gross negligence" to describe the fault required for involuntary manslaughter.... without any clear definition of either term. It was not clear whether these terms were merely two ways of describing the same thing, or whether they represented two distinct conditions of fault' (page 375). After referring to *Adomako*, the learned author continues

'*Reckless manslaughter*. Gross negligence is a sufficient, but not necessarily the only fault for manslaughter. To some extent manslaughter by overt recklessness, conscious risk-taking still survives' (p.377).

He goes on to ask whether it is necessary for the offence of reckless manslaughter that the risk foreseen is of serious, rather than non-serious, bodily harm.

In our judgment, the judge was correct in his view that this was a case of 'reckless' manslaughter and to direct the jury accordingly. We reject the alternative submission that he was wrong not to direct the jury as to gross negligence manslaughter, whether in place of or in substitution for the direction as to recklessness. Indeed, in a case such as the present, we find it difficult to understand how the point of criminal liability can be reached, where gross negligence is alleged, without identifying the point by reference to the concept of recklessness as it is commonly understood: that is to say, whether the driver of the motor vehicle was aware of the necessary degree of risk of serious injury to the victim and nevertheless chose to disregard it, or was indifferent to it. If the gross negligence direction had been given, the recklessness direction would still have been necessary. The recklessness direction in fact given made the gross negligence direction superfluous and unnecessary.

...

Recklessness

The direction given by the judge might be said to be open to criticism for failing to specify, first, that there had to be a high probability of physical harm to Kully, and secondly, that the risk was of serious injury rather than, as the judge put it, 'injury to health' and 'some physical harm, however slight'. This criticism was not advanced as a ground of appeal, but we should nevertheless consider what force there might be in it. In our judgment, there is none, because in the circumstances of this case both requirements undoubtedly were satisfied. The risk of harm to Kully, of which the jury has found that the appellant was aware, was clearly and unarguably a high degree of risk of serious injury to him. In the circumstances, therefore, we are satisfied that the verdict could not be considered unsafe if there was a mis-direction in this respect.

Appeal dismissed

5. REFORM

(1) HOMICIDE UNDER THE DRAFT CODE

The Draft Code incorporates, with some modification, the reforms proposed by the Criminal Law Revision Committee in their Fourteenth Report (Cmnd 7844). The clauses relating to homicide are as follows:

Homicide

54(1) A person is guilty of murder if he causes the death of another:
    (a) intending to cause death; or
    (b) intending to cause serious personal harm and being aware that he may cause death, unless section 56, 58, 59, 62 or 64 applies.

(2) A person convicted of murder shall be sentenced to life imprisonment, except that, where he appears to the court to have been under the age of eighteen years at the time the offence was committed, he shall be sentenced to detention in such place and for such period and subject to such conditions as to release as the Secretary of State may determine.

55 A person is guilty of manslaughter if:
  (a) he is not guilty of murder by reason only of the fact that a defence provided by section 56 (diminished responsibility), 58 (provocation) or 59 (use of excessive force) applies; or
  (b) he is not guilty of murder by reason only of the fact that, because of voluntary intoxication, he is not aware that death may be caused or believes that an exempting circumstance exists; or
  (c) he causes the death of another:
    (i) intending to cause serious personal harm; or
    (ii) being reckless whether death or serious personal harm will be caused.

[Clause 56 relates to diminished responsibility.]

58 A person who, but for this section, would be guilty of murder is not guilty of murder if:
  (a) he acts when provoked (whether by things done or by things said or by both and whether by the deceased person or by another) to lose his self-control; and
  (b) the provocation is, in all the circumstances (including any of his personal characteristics that affect its gravity), sufficient ground for the loss of self-control.

59 A person who, but for this section, would be guilty of murder is not guilty of murder if, at the time of his act, he believes the use of the force which causes death to be necessary and reasonable to effect a purpose referred to in section 44 (use of force in public or private defence), but the force exceeds that which is necessary and reasonable in the circumstances which exist or (where there is a difference) in those which he believes to exist.

60 A person is guilty of murder or manslaughter (where section 54 or 55 applies) if:
  (a) he causes a fatal injury to another to occur within the ordinary limits of criminal jurisdiction, whether his act is done within or outside and whether the death occurs within or outside those limits;
  (b) he causes the death of another anywhere in the world by an act done within the ordinary limits of criminal jurisdiction; or
  (c) being a British citizen, he causes the death of another anywhere in the world by an act done anywhere in the world.

61 A person who attempts to cause the death of another, where section 56, 58 or 59 would apply if death were caused, is not guilty of attempted murder but is guilty of attempted manslaughter.

62(1) A person who, but for this section, would be guilty of murder is not guilty of murder but is guilty of suicide pact killing if his act is done in pursuance of a suicide pact between himself and the person killed.

  (2) 'Suicide pact' means an agreement between two or more persons having for its object the death of all of them, whether or not each is to take his own life, but nothing done by a person who enters into a suicide pact shall be treated as done by him in pursuance of the pact unless it is done while he has the settled intention of dying in pursuance of the pact.

  (3) A person acting in pursuance of a suicide pact between himself and another is not guilty of attempted murder but is guilty of attempted suicide pact killing if he attempts to cause the death of the other.

63 A person is guilty of an offence if he procures, assists or encourages suicide or attempted suicide committed by another.

64(1) A woman who, but for this section, would be guilty of murder or manslaughter of her child is not guilty of murder or manslaughter, but is guilty of infanticide, if her act is done when the child is under the age of twelve months and when the balance of her mind is disturbed by reason of the effect of giving birth or of circumstances consequent upon the birth.

(2) A woman who in the circumstances specified in subsection (1) attempts to cause the death of her child is not guilty of attempted murder but is guilty of attempted infanticide.

(3) A woman may be convicted of infanticide (or attempted infanticide) although the jury is uncertain whether the child had been born or whether it had an existence independent of her when its death occurred (or, in the case of an attempt, when the act was done).

Notes

So far as murder is concerned the draft Code would restrict the operation of the grievous bodily harm doctrine (see *Cunningham*, above). Under the Code *Cunningham* would be guilty of murder only if in intentionally inflicting serious bodily harm he was aware that he might cause death; otherwise he would be guilty of manslaughter.

The Law Commission (Law Com No 237, Involuntary Manslaughter (1996)) has now proposed the abolition of the common law of involuntary manslaughter and its replacement by two offences as follows:

1.—(1) A person who by his conduct causes the death of another is guilty of reckless killing if—
  (a) he is aware of a risk that his conduct will cause death or serious injury; and
  (b) it is unreasonable for him to take that risk having regard to the circumstances as he knows or believes them to be.

(2) A person guilty of reckless killing is liable on conviction on indictment to imprisonment for life.

2.—(1) A person who by his conduct causes the death of another is guilty of killing by gross carelessness if—
  (a) a risk that his conduct will cause death or serious injury would be obvious to a reasonable person in his position;
  (b) he is capable of appreciating that risk at the material time; and
  (c) either—
    (i) his conduct falls far below what can reasonably be expected of him in the circumstances; or
    (ii) he intends by his conduct to cause some injury or is aware of, and unreasonably takes, the risk that it may do so.

(2) There shall be attributed to the person referred to in subsection (1)(a) above—
  (a) knowledge of any relevant facts which the accused is shown to have at the material time; and
  (b) any skill or experience professed by him.

(3) In determining for the purposes of subsection (1)(c)(i) above what can reasonably be expected of the accused regard shall be had to the circumstances of which he can be expected to be aware, to any circumstances shown to be within his knowledge and to any other matter relevant for assessing his conduct at the material time.

(4) Subsection (1)(c)(ii) above applies only if the conduct causing, or intended to cause, the injury constitutes an offence.

(5) A person guilty of killing by gross carelessness is liable on conviction on indictment to imprisonment for a term not exceeding [ ] years.

For the proposed additional liability of corporations for homicide, see above, Ch 10.

FURTHER READING

Diminished responsibility

S. Dell, *Murder into Manslaughter: the Diminished Responsibility Defence in Practice* (1984)

E. J. Griew, 'The Future of Diminished Responsibility' [1988] Crim LR 75

R. D. Mackay, 'Diminished Responsibility and Mentally Disordered Killers' in A. Ashworth and B. Mitchell (eds) *Rethinking English Homicide Law* (2000)

E. Tennant, *The Future of the Diminished Responsibility Defence to Murder'* (2001)

Provocation

A. Ashworth, 'The Doctrine of Provocation', [1976] CLJ 292

J. Horder, *Provocation and Responsibility* (1992)

J. Horder, 'Reshaping the Subjective Element in the Provocation Defence' (2005) OJLS 123

Law Commission's Report No 290, *Partial Defences to Murder* (2004)

Unlawful act manslaughter

See C. Clarkson, 'Context and Culpability in Involuntary Manslaughter: Principle or Instinct' in A. Ashworth and B. Mitchell (eds) *Rethinking English Homicide Law* (2000)

Gross negligence

Law Commission Report No 237, *Involuntary Manslaughter* (1996) Part III

J. Stannard, 'From Andrews to Seymour and Back Again' [1996] 47 NILQ 1

Reform

H. Keating, 'The Restoration of a Serious Crime' [1996] Crim LR 535

M. Wasik, 'Form and Function in the Law of Involuntary Manslaughter' [1994] Crim LR 883

19

Non-fatal offences against the person

The Home Office Consultation Document, 'Violence: Reforming the Offences Against the Person Act 1861', of February 1998 acknowledged that, 'That Act was itself not a coherent statement of the law but a consolidation of much older law. It is therefore not surprising that the law has been widely criticised as archaic and unclear and that it is now in urgent need of reform.' Lord Ackner has agreed with the blunter criticism that the Act is a rag-bag of offences brought together from a wide variety of sources with no attempt, as the draftsman frankly acknowledged, to introduce consistency as to substance or as to form: *Savage* [1991] 4 All ER 698, at 721, above, p **160**. But, notwithstanding the admitted urgency, nothing more has been heard (as at May 2005) from the Home Office since February 1998, so lawyers and students must continue to grapple with the archaic and unclear law.

1. ASSAULT AND BATTERY

Criminal Justice Act 1988, s 39

Common assault and battery shall be summary offences and a person guilty of either of them shall be liable to a fine not exceeding level 5 on the standard scale, to imprisonment for a term not exceeding six months, or to both.

The CPS charging standards advise that the appropriate charge is assault or battery (rather than aggravated assaults) where the injuries sustained amount to no more than: grazes; scratches; abrasions; minor bruising; swellings; reddening of the skin; superficial cuts; or a 'black eye'.

(1) THE ELEMENTS OF ASSAULT AND BATTERY

Collins v Wilcock
[1984] 3 All ER 374, Queen's Bench Division

(Robert Goff LJ and Mann J)

The respondent and another police officer saw the appellant and another woman apparently soliciting for the purposes of prostitution. The appellant was not a known prostitute and when asked to get into the police car for questioning she refused and walked away. The respondent walked after the appellant with a view to ascertaining her identity and, if in fact she was suspected of being a prostitute, to cautioning her in accordance with police practice before charging her with being a prostitute contrary to s 1 of the Street Offences Act 1959. The appellant refused to speak to the respondent and again walked away. The respondent then took hold of her by the arm to restrain her whereupon the appellant became abusive and scratched the respondent's arm with her fingernails.

The appellant appealed against her conviction for assaulting a police officer acting in the execution of her duty. The judgment of the court was delivered by:

Robert Goff LJ, having quoted from the case stated, continued:

The magistrate then stated the following question for the opinion of the court:

> 'The question for the consideration of the High Court is whether a Police Constable is acting in the execution of her duty when detaining a woman against her will for the purpose of questioning her regarding her identity and her conduct which was such as to lead the Constable to believe she may have been soliciting men.'

In considering this question, which is drawn in wide terms, we think it important to observe that in this case it is found as a fact that the respondent took hold of the appellant by the left arm to restrain her. Before considering the question as drawn, we think it right to consider whether, on the facts found in the case, the magistrate could properly hold that the respondent was acting in the execution of her duty. In order to consider this question, it is desirable that we should expose the underlying principles.

The law draws a distinction, in terms more easily understood by philologists than by ordinary citizens, between an assault and a battery. An assault is an act which causes another person to apprehend the infliction of immediate, unlawful, force on his person; a battery is the actual infliction of unlawful force on another person. Both assault and battery are forms of trespass to the person. Another form of trespass to the person is false imprisonment, which is the unlawful imposition of constraint on another's freedom of movement from a particular place. The requisite mental element is of no relevance in the present case.

We are here concerned primarily with battery. The fundamental principle, plain and incontestable, is that every person's body is inviolate. It has long been established that any touching of another person, however slight, may amount to a battery. So Holt CJ held in 1704 that 'the least touching of another in anger is a battery': see *Cole v Turner* (1704) 6 Mod Rep 149, 90 ER 958. The breadth of the principle reflects the fundamental nature of the interest so protected; as Blackstone wrote in his Commentaries, 'the law cannot draw the line between different degrees of violence, and therefore totally prohibits the first and lowest stage of it; every man's person being sacred, and no other having a right to meddle with it, in any the slightest manner' (see 3 B1 Com 120). The effect is that everybody is protected not only against physical injury but against any form of physical molestation.

But so widely drawn a principle must inevitably be subject to exceptions. For example, children may be subjected to reasonable punishment; people may be subjected to the lawful exercise of the power of arrest; and reasonable force may be used in self-defence or for the prevention of crime. But, apart from these special instances where the control or constraint is lawful, a broader exception has been created to allow for the exigencies of everyday life. Generally speaking, consent is a defence to battery; and most of the physical contacts of ordinary life are not actionable because they are impliedly consented to by all who move in society and so expose themselves to the risk of bodily contact. So nobody can complain of the jostling which is inevitable from his presence in, for example, a supermarket, an underground station or a busy street; nor can a person who attends a party complain if his hand is seized in friendship, or even if his back is (within reason) slapped (see *Tubervell v Savage* (1669) 1 Mod Rep 3, 86 ER 684). Although such cases are regarded as examples of implied consent, it is more common nowadays to treat them as falling within a general exception embracing all physical contact which is generally acceptable in the ordinary conduct of daily life. We observe that, although in the past it has sometimes been stated that a battery is only committed where the action is 'angry, or revengeful, or rude, or insolent' (see 1 Hawk PC c 62, s 2), we think that nowadays it is more realistic, and indeed more accurate, to state the broad underlying principle, subject to the broad exception.

Among such forms of conduct, long held to be acceptable, is touching a person for the purpose of engaging his attention, though of course using no greater degree of physical contact than is reasonably necessary in the circumstances for that purpose. So, for example, it was held by the Court of Common Pleas in 1807 that a touch by a constable's staff on the shoulder of a man who had climbed on a gentleman's railing to gain a better view of a mad ox, the touch being only to engage the man's attention, did not amount to a battery (see *Wiffin v Kincard* (1807) 2 Bos & PNR 471, 127 ER 713; for another example, see *Coward v Baddeley* (1859) 4 H & N 478, 157 ER 927). But a distinction is drawn between a touch to draw a man's attention, which is generally acceptable, and a physical restraint, which is not. So we find Parke B observing in *Rawlings v Till* (1837) 3 M & W 28 at 29, 150 ER 1042, with reference to *Wiffin v Kincard*, that 'There the touch was merely to engage a man's attention, not to put a restraint on his person.' Furthermore, persistent touching to gain attention in the face of obvious disregard may transcend the norms of acceptable behaviour, and so be outside the exception. We do not say that more than one touch is never permitted; for example, the lost or distressed may surely be permitted a second touch, or possibly even more, on a reluctant or impervious sleeve or shoulder, as may a person who is acting reasonably in the exercise of a duty. In each case, the test must be whether the physical contact so persisted in has in the circumstances gone beyond generally acceptable standards of conduct; and the answer to that question will depend on the facts of the particular case.

The distinction drawn by Parke B in *Rawlings v Till* is of importance in the case of police officers. Of course, a police officer may subject another to restraint when he lawfully exercises his power of arrest; and he has other statutory powers, for example, his power to stop, search and detain persons under s66 of the Metropolitan Police Act 1839, with which we are not concerned. But, putting such cases aside, police officers have for present purposes no greater rights than ordinary citizens. It follows that, subject to such cases, physical contact by a police officer with another person may be unlawful as a battery, just as it might be if he was an ordinary member of the public. But a police officer has his rights as a citizen, as well as his duties as a policeman. A police officer may wish to engage a man's attention, for example if he wishes to question him. If he lays his hand on the man's sleeve or taps his shoulder for that purpose, he commits no wrong. He may even do so more than once; for he is under a duty to prevent and investigate crime, and so his seeking further, in the exercise of that duty, to engage a man's attention in order to speak to him may in the circumstances be regarded as acceptable (see *Donnelly v Jackman* [1970] 1 All ER 987, [1970] 1 WLR 562). But if, taking into account the nature of his duty, his use of physical contact in the face of non-co-operation persists beyond generally acceptable standards of conduct, his action will become unlawful; and if a police officer restrains a man, for example by gripping his arm or his shoulder, then his action will also be unlawful, unless he is lawfully exercising his power of arrest. A police officer has no power to require a man to answer him, though he has the advantages of authority, enhanced as it is by the uniform which the state provides and requires him to wear, in seeking a response to his inquiry. What is not permitted, however, is the unlawful use of force or the unlawful threat (actual or implicit) to use force; and, excepting the lawful exercise of his power of arrest, the lawfulness of a police officer's conduct is judged by the same criteria as are applied to the conduct of any ordinary citizen of this country.

We have been referred by counsel to certain cases directly concerned with charges of assaulting a police officer in the execution of his duty, the crucial question in each case being whether the police officer, by using physical force on the accused in response to which the accused assaulted the police officer, was acting unlawfully and so not acting in the execution of his duty. In *Kenlin v Gardiner* [1966] 3 All ER 931, [1967] 2 QB 510 it was held that action by police officers in catching hold of two schoolboys was performed not in the course of arresting them but for the purpose of detaining them for questioning and so was unlawful (see [1967] 2 QB 510 at 519, [1966] 3 All ER 931 at 934, per Winn LJ). Similarly, in *Ludlow v Burgess* (1971) 75 Cr App Rep 227n at 228 per Lord Parker CJ it was held that 'this was not a mere case of putting a hand on [the defendant's] shoulder, but it resulted in the detention of [the defendant] against his will', so that the police officer's act was 'unlawful and a serious interference with the citizen's liberty' and could not be an act performed by him in the execution of his duty.

In *Donnelly v Jackman* the police officer wished to question the defendant about an offence which he had cause to believe that the defendant had committed. Repeated requests by the police officer to the defendant to stop and speak to him were ignored. The officer tapped him on the shoulder; he made it plain that he had no intention of stopping to speak to him. The officer persisted and again tapped the defendant on the shoulder, whereupon the defendant turned and struck him with some force. The justices convicted the defendant of assaulting the officer in the execution of his duty, and this court dismissed an appeal from that conviction by way of case stated. The court was satisfied that the officer had not detained the defendant, distinguishing *Kenlin v Gardiner* as a case where the officers had in fact detained the boys (see [1970] 1 All ER 987 at 989, [1970] 1 WLR 562 at 565). It appears that they must have considered that the justices were entitled to conclude that the action of the officer, in persistently tapping the defendant on the shoulder, did not in the circumstances of the case exceed the bounds of acceptable conduct, despite the fact that the defendant had made it clear that he did not intend to respond to the officer's request to stop and speak to him; we cannot help feeling that this is an extreme case.

Finally, in *Bentley v Brudzinski* (1982) 75 Cr App Rep 217, [1982] Crim LR 825 it was found by the justices that the police officer, having caught up with the defendant, said, 'Just a minute'; then, not in any hostile way, but merely to attract attention, he placed his right hand on the defendant's left shoulder. The defendant then swore at the police officer and punched him in the face; and a struggle ensued. The justices considered that the act of the police officer amounted to an unlawful attempt to stop and detain the defendant, and so dismissed an information against the defendant alleging that he assaulted the police officer in the execution of his duty. This court dismissed the prosecutor's appeal by way of case stated; it appears that they considered that, having regard to all the facts of the case as found by the justices, they were entitled to hold that the police officer's act was performed not merely to engage the attention of the defendant, but as part of a course of conduct in which the officer was attempting unlawfully to detain the defendant.

We now return to the facts of the present case. Before us, counsel for the respondent police officer sought to justify her conduct, first by submitting that, since the practice of cautioning women found loitering or soliciting in public places for the purposes of prostitution is recognised by s2 of the 1959 Act, therefore it is implicit in the statute that police officers have a power to caution, and for that purpose they must have the power to stop and detain women in order to find out their names and addresses and, if appropriate, caution them. This submission, which accords with the opinion expressed by the magistrate, we are unable to accept. The fact that the statute recognises the practice of cautioning by providing a review procedure does not, in our judgment, carry with it an implication that police officers have the power to stop and detain women for the purpose of implementing the system of cautioning. If it had been intended to confer any such power on police officers that power could and should, in our judgment, have been expressly conferred by the statute.

Next, counsel for the respondent submitted that the purpose of the police officer was simply to carry out the cautioning procedure and that, having regard to her purpose, her action could not be regarded as unlawful. Again, we cannot accept that submission. If the physical contact went beyond what is allowed by law, the mere fact that the police officer has the laudable intention of carrying out the cautioning procedure in accordance with established practice cannot, we think, have the effect of rendering her action lawful. Finally, counsel for the respondent submitted that the question whether the respondent was or was not acting in the execution of her duty was a question of fact for the magistrate to decide; and that he was entitled, on the facts found by him, to conclude that the respondent had been acting lawfully. We cannot agree. The fact is that the respondent took hold of the appellant; and since her action went beyond the generally acceptable conduct of touching a person to engage his or her attention, it must follow, in our judgment, that her action constituted a battery on the appellant, and was therefore unlawful. It follows that the appellant's appeal must be allowed, and her conviction quashed.

We turn finally to the question posed by the magistrate for our consideration. As we have already observed, this question is in wide general terms. Furthermore, the word 'detaining' can be used in more than one sense. For example, it is a commonplace of ordinary life that one person may request another to stop and speak to him; if the latter complies with the request, he may be said to do so willingly or unwillingly, and in either event the first person may be said to be 'stopping and detaining' the latter. There is nothing unlawful in such an act. If a police officer so 'stops and detains' another person, he in our opinion commits no unlawful act, despite the fact that his uniform may give his request a certain authority and so render it more likely to be complied with. But if a police officer, not exercising his power of arrest, nevertheless reinforces his request with the actual use of force, or with the threat (actual or implicit) to use force if the other person does not comply, then his act in thereby detaining the other person will be unlawful. In the former event, his action will constitute a battery; in the latter event, detention of the other person will amount to false imprisonment. Whether the action of a police officer in any particular case is to be regarded as lawful or unlawful must be a question to be decided on the facts of the case.

Having regard to the facts of the present case, we have no doubt that the magistrate framed his question having in mind the act of the respondent in taking hold of the appellant's arm to restrain her, which we have held to be a battery and so unlawful. But, having regard to the distinctions we have drawn, we consider the question itself to be so widely drafted as not to be susceptible of a simple answer. We therefore prefer not to answer it; and we shall exercise our power to amend the case by adding the following further question which arises on the facts of the case, viz whether, on the facts found by the magistrate, the respondent was acting in the course of her duty when she detained the appellant. That question we shall, for the reasons we have already given, answer in the negative.

Appeal allowed; conviction quashed

Notes and questions

1. Robert Goff LJ said in delivering the judgment of the court (above, p **666**) that, 'The law draws a distinction, in terms more easily understood by philologists than by ordinary citizens, between assault and battery.' However difficult it may be for the ordinary citizen to understand the distinction, it is essential for lawyers to do so. Assault and battery are distinct crimes with distinctive features. The distinction between the two has become blurred partly because the word 'assault' is commonly used (the *OED* so uses it) to include a battery, and partly because one and the same act (a punch on the nose, a kick on the shin) commonly amounts to both an assault and a battery. But, as Robert Goff LJ goes on to explain, a battery involves an unlawful and unwanted contact with the body of another while assault involves causing another to apprehend an unlawful unwanted contact.

Since assault and battery are separate offences (see CJA 1988, s 39, above, p **665**) it was held in *DPP v Taylor*; *DPP v Little* [1992] 1 All ER 299, [1992] QB 645, DC, that an information alleging that 'L . . . did unlawfully assault and batter J' was bad for duplicity (that is, for charging more than one offence in the same information). In *Lynsey* [1995] 3 All ER 654, 656, CA the court found it unnecessary to express any opinion on the criticisms that have been made of that decision (*Archbold*, 18–178, J. C. Smith [1991] Crim LR 900). Comparing s 39, above, with the next section, 40 (where 'common assault' is used in a context in which the only sensible meaning is 'common assault or battery'), Henry LJ observed: 'At this point angels prepare to dance on needles and legal pedants sharpen their quill pens.'

2. What offences does D commit in the following circumstances:
    (i)   he strikes V on the back of the head with a blunt instrument;
    (ii) he aims to strike V on the back of the head but misses;
    (iii) he aims at V a gun which he knows to be unloaded and threatens to shoot V and V believes the gun is loaded;
    (iv) he aims a gun at V which he knows to be unloaded and threatens to shoot V and V also knows the gun to be unloaded;
    (v)   he aims a gun at V which he believes to be unloaded and threatens to shoot V and V also believes the gun to be unloaded but, unknown to both, the gun is in fact loaded and when D pulls the trigger V is shot and injured?

R v Ireland; R v Burstow
[1997] 4 All ER 225, House of Lords

(Lords Goff, Slynn, Steyn, Hope and Hutton)

Ireland made repeated silent telephone calls, mostly at night, to three women who consequently suffered psychiatric illness. His conviction on three counts of assault occasioning actual bodily harm was upheld by the Court of Appeal, holding that psychiatric injury could amount to actual bodily harm and that, since repeated telephone calls could cause the victim to apprehend immediate and unlawful violence, his conduct was capable of amounting to assault.

Burstow had conducted an eight-month campaign of harassment against a woman, including both silent and abusive telephone calls. She was fearful of personal violence and a psychiatrist testified that she was suffering from a severe depressive illness. B's appeal against conviction on one count of unlawfully and maliciously inflicting grievous bodily harm contrary to s 20 of the 1861 Act was dismissed by the Court of Appeal on the ground that psychiatric injury could amount to grievous bodily harm under s 20. At the time the Protection from Harassment Act 1997 had not been enacted.

Lord Goff and Lord Slynn said they agreed with the speech of Lord Steyn.

Lord Steyn. My Lords, it is easy to understand the terrifying effect of a campaign of telephone calls at night by a silent caller to a woman living on her own. It would be natural for the victim to regard the calls as menacing. What may heighten her fear is that she will not know what the caller may do next. The spectre of the caller arriving at her doorstep bent on inflicting personal violence on her may come to dominate her thinking. After all, as a matter of common sense, what else would she be terrified about? The victim may suffer psychiatric illness such as anxiety neurosis or acute depression. Harassment of women by repeated silent telephone calls, accompanied on occasions by heavy breathing, is apparently a significant social problem. That the criminal law should be able to deal with this problem, and so far as is practicable, afford effective protection to victims is self-evident.

From the point of view, however, of the general policy of our law towards the imposition of criminal responsibility, three specific features of the problem must be faced squarely. First, the medium used by the caller is the telephone: arguably it differs qualitatively from a face-to-face offer of violence to a sufficient extent to make a difference. Secondly, ex hypothesi the caller remains silent: arguably a caller may avoid the reach of the criminal law by remaining silent however menacing the context may be. Thirdly, it is arguable that the criminal law does not take into account 'mere' psychiatric illnesses.

At first glance it may seem that the legislature has satisfactorily dealt with such objections by s 43(1) of the Telecommunications Act 1984, which makes it an offence persistently to make use of a public telecommunications system for the purpose of causing annoyance, inconvenience or needless anxiety to another. The maximum custodial penalty is six months' imprisonment. This penalty may be inadequate to reflect a culpability of a persistent offender who causes serious psychiatric illness to another. For the future there will be for consideration the provisions of ss 1 and 2 of the Protection from Harassment Act 1997, not yet in force, which creates the offence of pursuing a course of conduct which amounts to harassment of another and which he knows or ought to know amounts to harassment of the other. The maximum custodial penalty is six months' imprisonment. This penalty may also be inadequate to deal with persistent offenders who cause serious psychiatric injury to victims. Section 4(1) of the 1997 Act, which creates the offence of putting people in fear of violence, seems more appropriate. It provides for maximum custodial penalty upon conviction on indictment of five years' imprisonment. On the other hand, s 4 only applies when as a result of a course of conduct the victim has cause to fear, on at least two occasions, that violence *will* be used against her. It may be difficult to secure a conviction in respect of a silent caller: the victim in such cases may have cause to fear that violence *may* be used against her but no more. In my view, therefore, the provisions of these two statutes are not ideally suited to deal with the significant problem which I have described. One must therefore look elsewhere…

It is now necessary to consider whether the making of silent telephone calls causing psychiatric injury is capable of constituting an assault under s 47. The Court of Appeal, as constituted in *R v Ireland*, answered that question in the affirmative. There has been substantial academic criticism of the conclusion and reasoning in *R v Ireland* (see *Archbold News*, Issue 6, 12 July 1996, *Archbold's Criminal Pleading, Evidence and Practice* (1995), Supplement No 4 (1996) pp 345–347, Smith and Hogan *Criminal Law* p 413, Jonathan Herring 'Assault by Telephone' [1997] CLJ 11, and 'Assault' [1997] Crim LR 134 at 435–436). Counsel's arguments, broadly speaking, challenged the decision in *R v Ireland* on very similar lines. Having carefully considered the literature and counsel's arguments, I have come to the conclusion that the appeal ought to be dismissed.

The starting point must be that an assault is an ingredient of the offence under s 47. It is necessary to consider the two forms which an assault may take. The first is battery, which involves the unlawful application of force by the defendant upon the victim. Usually, s 47 is used to prosecute in cases of this kind. The second form of assault is an act causing the victim to apprehend an imminent application of force upon her (see *Fagan v Metropolitan Police Comr* [1968] 3 All ER 442 at 445, [1969] 1 QB 439 at 444).

One point can be disposed of, quite briefly. The Court of Appeal was not asked to consider whether silent telephone calls resulting in psychiatric injury is capable of constituting a battery. But encouraged by some academic comment it was raised before your Lordships' House. Counsel for Ireland was most economical in his argument on the point. I will try to match his economy of words. In my view it is not feasible to enlarge the generally accepted legal meaning of what is a battery to include the circumstances of a silent caller who causes psychiatric injury.

It is to assault in the form of an act causing the victim to fear an immediate application of force to her that I must turn. Counsel argued that as a matter of law an assault can never be committed by words alone and therefore it cannot be committed by silence. The premise depends on the slenderest authority, namely an observation by Holroyd J to a jury that 'no words or singing are equivalent to an assault' (see *Meade's and Belt's Case* (1823) 1 Lew CC 184 at 185, 168 ER 1006). The proposition that a gesture may amount to an assault, but that words can never suffice, is unrealistic and indefensible. A thing said is also a thing done. There is no reason why something said should be incapable of causing an apprehension of immediate personal violence, eg a man accosting a woman in a dark alley saying 'come with me or I will stab you'. I would, therefore, reject the proposition that an assault can never be committed by words.

That brings me to the critical question whether a silent caller may be guilty of an assault. The answer to this question seems to me to be 'Yes, depending on the facts'. It involves questions of fact within the province of the jury. After all, there is no reason why a telephone caller who says to a woman in a menacing way 'I will be at your door in a minute or two' may not be guilty of an assault if he causes his victim to apprehend immediate personal violence. Take now the case of the silent caller. He intends by his silence to cause fear and he is so understood. The victim is assailed by uncertainty about his intentions. Fear may dominate her emotions, and it may be the fear that the caller's arrival at her door may be imminent. She may fear the *possibility* of immediate personal violence. As a matter of law the caller may be guilty of an assault: whether he is or not will depend on the circumstance and in particular on the impact of the caller's potentially menacing call or calls on the victim. Such a prosecution case under s 47 may be fit to leave to the jury. And a trial judge may, depending on the circumstances, put a commonsense consideration before jury, namely what, if not the possibility of imminent personal violence, was the victim terrified about?

I conclude that an assault may be committed in the particular factual circumstances which I have envisaged. For this reason I reject the submission that as a matter of law a silent telephone caller cannot ever be guilty of an offence under s 47. In these circumstances no useful purpose would be served by answering the vague certified question in *R v Ireland*.

Having concluded that the legal arguments advanced on behalf of Ireland on s 47 must fail, I nevertheless accept that the concept of an assault involving immediate personal violence as an ingredient of the s 47 offence is a considerable complicating factor in bringing prosecutions under it in respect of silent telephone callers and stalkers. That the least serious of the ladder of offences is difficult to apply in such cases is unfortunate. At the hearing of the appeal of *R v Ireland* attention was drawn to the Bill which is annexed to Law Commission report, *Legislating the Criminal Code: Offences Against the Person and General Principles* (Law Com Consultation Paper No 218) (1993). Clause 4 of that Bill is intended to replace s 47. Clause 4 provides: 'A person is guilty of an offence if he intentionally or recklessly causes injury to another.' This simple and readily comprehensible provision would eliminate the problems inherent in s 47. In expressing this view I do not, however, wish to comment on the appropriateness of the definition of 'injury' in cl 18 of the Bill, and in particular the provision that 'injury' means 'impairment of a person's mental health'.

Notes and questions

1. The House of Lords again confirmed the definition of assault (as distinct from battery): 'Any act by which a person intentionally or recklessly causes another to apprehend immediate and unlawful personal violence.'

2. *Immediacy*. The House did no more than reject the submission that a silent telephone caller can *never* be guilty of assault. Lords Slynn and Hutton made it clear that the House was not deciding how the concept of immediacy should be applied or whether it was satisfied in *Ireland*. If the caller says, 'There's a bomb under your house which I am about to detonate' there would seem to be a clear case of assault. What about Lord Steyn's suggestion of the caller who says, 'I will be at your door in a minute or two'? Notice that it is not enough that the victim is immediately alarmed. He must fear that something is going to happen

immediately. In *Constanza* [1997] 2 Cr App R 492, [1997] Crim LR 576 D made numerous silent telephone calls, sent over 800 letters to V, repeatedly drove past her home and on three occasions wrote offensive words on her front door. She received two letters on 4 and 12 June which she interpreted as clear threats. D's conviction of assault occasioning actual bodily harm was upheld. It is easy to accept that V was immediately put in fear but did she really apprehend *immediate* violence when she read letters at the breakfast table? If she did was this two assaults (in which case the indictment would be bad for duplicity) or one continuing assault? See also *Cox* [1998] Crim LR 810 and commentary. Is the offence of assault fitted to deal with an ongoing campaign of this kind?

3. Lord Hope says that, in the case of a telephone call, the silence conveys a message to V and that it is perhaps otherwise where the parties are in the same room. The caller does something more than remain silent; he rings up. What if he is present and merely gives a hard stare, or glowers?

4. Is the question for the jury simply 'Are you sure that D's conduct caused V to apprehend immediate violence and that D intended that it should, or knew that it might?' Is there any difference in principle between a gesture (which can certainly be an assault) and a glare?

5. D aims a blow at V who is asleep. V awakes and dodges the blow. Since battery is triable only summarily, there is no offence of attempted battery. Is D guilty of an assault?

6. Earlier cases showed a tendency to take a generous view of 'immediacy'. In *Lewis* [1970] Crim LR 647 D was uttering threats from another room. In *Logdon v DPP* [1976] Crim LR 121 it was held that D committed an assault by showing V a pistol in a drawer and declaring that he would hold her hostage. In *Smith v Chief Superintendent of Woking Police Station* (1983) 76 Cr App R 234, [1983] Crim LR 323 (assault by looking through the window of a bed-sitting room at V in her night clothes with intent to frighten her) Kerr LJ limited his decision to a case where D 'is immediately adjacent, albeit on the other side of a window' and distinguished, without dissenting from, the opinion in the fourth edition of *Smith and Hogan* that 'there can be no assault if it is obvious to V that D is unable to carry out his threat, as where D shakes his fist at V who is safely locked inside his car.' There may be an assault although D has no means of carrying out the threat. The question is whether he intends to cause V to believe that he can and will carry it out and whether V does so believe.

R v Venna

[1975] 3 All ER 788, Court of Appeal, Criminal Division

(James and Ormrod LJJ and Cusack J)

The appellant and others were creating a disturbance in a public street. The police were sent for and during a scuffle which ensued as the police sought to arrest him, the appellant kicked out with his feet. In so doing he struck the hand of an officer and caused a fracture which resulted in his being convicted of an assault occasioning actual bodily harm.

James LJ read the following judgment of the court:

… The second substantial ground of appeal relates to the conviction of assault occasioning actual bodily harm. …

On the evidence of the appellant himself, one would have thought that the inescapable inference was that the appellant intended to make physical contact with whoever might try to restrain him. Be that as it may, in the light of the direction given, the verdict may have been arrived at on the basis of 'recklessness'. Counsel for the appellant cited *Ackroyd v Barett* [(1894) 11 TLR 115] in support of his argument that recklessness, which falls short of intention, is not enough to support a charge of battery, and argued that, there being no authority to the contrary, it is now too late to extend the law by a decision of the courts and that any extension must be by the decision of Parliament.

Counsel for the appellant sought support from the distinction between the offences which are assaults and offences which by statute include the element contained in the word 'maliciously', eg unlawful and malicious wounding contrary to s20 of the Offences against the Person Act 1861, in which recklessness will suffice to support the charge: see *Cunningham* [[1957] 2 QB 396, [1957] 2 All ER 412]. Insofar as the editors of textbooks commit themselves to an opinion on this branch of the law, they are favourable to the view that recklessness is or should logically be sufficient to support the charge of assault or battery: see Glanville Williams [*Criminal Law* (2nd edn, 1961), p 65, para 27]; Kenny [*Outlines of Criminal Law* (19th edn, 1966), p 218, para 164]; Russell [*Russell on Crime* (12th edn, 1964), vol 1, p656] and Smith and Hogan [*Criminal Law* (3rd edn, 1973), pp 283, 286]....

We see no reason in logic or in law why a person who recklessly applies physical force to the person of another should be outside the criminal law of assault. In many cases the dividing line between intention and recklessness is barely distinguishable. This is such a case. In our judgment the direction was right in law; this ground of appeal fails....

For these reasons we dismiss the appeal.

Appeal dismissed

Notes and questions

1. The reference to recklessness in *Venna* is clearly a reference to *Cunningham* recklessness, that is, requiring foresight by the defendant of the risk of the physical contact to another which occurs (battery) or the apprehension by another of physical contact (assault). Post *Caldwell, DPP v K (a minor)* [1990] 1 All ER 331, [1990] 1 WLR 1067, DC, applied *Caldwell* recklessness to assault. *DPP v K (a minor)* was thought by the CA in *Spratt* [1991] 2 All ER 210, [1990] 1 WLR 1073 to have been wrongly decided. Although *Spratt* was overruled in *Savage, Parmenter* [1991] 4 All ER 698, above, p **160**, this was in relation to the CA's ruling as to the mens rea of an assault occasioning actual bodily harm. *Venna* and *Cunningham* were expressly approved by the HL in *Savage, Parmenter*. Since *G* (above, p **160**) there can be no suggestion that *Caldwell*-type recklessness has any part to play in offences against the person.

2. May the touching of another amount to an assault though it is not done in anger? If one touches another in anger is that necessarily an assault?

3. Robert Goff LJ addresses the issue of hostility in *Collins v Wilcock*, p **667**, above, and appears to conclude that hostility is not an ingredient of assault and battery. His Lordship says that nobody can complain of the jostling which is inevitable in a supermarket, underground station or a busy street. It is not unknown (at least in Leeds) for (admittedly small) numbers of football supporters returning from a game to dash through shopping precincts, shouting obscenities and rudely pushing shoppers aside. Do they commit a battery? If so, is this because their jostling is accompanied by rudeness or hostility or for some other reason?

4. In *Brown*, below, p **687**, Lord Jauncey appears to accept that hostility is an ingredient of assault but concludes, 'If the appellants' activities in relation to the receivers were unlawful they were also hostile and a necessary ingredient of assault was present.' But if the act is unlawful, as it must be to constitute an assault or battery, does it add anything to the ingredients of the crimes to say that it is therefore hostile?

Blackburn v Bowering
[1994] 3 All ER 380, Court of Appeal, Civil Division

(Sir Thomas Bingham MR, Leggatt and Roch LJJ)

D was convicted of assaulting V, an officer of the court, contrary to s 14(1)(b) of the County Courts Act 1984. His defence was that he did not believe V was a bailiff—he thought he was using reasonable force against a trespasser. The judge ruled that s 14, like s 51 of the Police Act 1964 (now replaced by s 89 of the Police Act 1996), creates an offence of strict liability, following *Forbes and Webb* (above) and that D's mistaken belief was no defence. He remarked on the extraordinary situation that if D had been charged with 'an ordinary assault simpliciter' he would have had a defence.

Sir Thomas Bingham MR, referring to the ruling in *Forbes and Webb*: (above) and in other cases up to the present day: *R v Maxwell and Clanchy* (1909) 2 Cr App Rep 26 and *McBride v Turnock* [1964] Crim LR 456. It has sometimes led to surprising results (as in *McBride v Tunnock*), and has not been immune from academic criticism (see, for example, Smith and Hogan *Criminal Law* (7th edn, 1992) p 417) but a similar view (despite very powerful dissents) has prevailed in Australia (see *R v Reynhoudt* (1962) 107 CLR 381) and there is no directly contrary authority. It is therefore clear that in a prosecution under s 51 of the Police Act 1964 [see now s 89 of the Police Act 1996] or a prosecution or complaint under s 14 of the County Courts Act 1984 it is not incumbent on the prosecutor or complainant to establish as part of his case that the defendant knew or believed that the victim of the alleged assault was (as the case may be) a police or court officer. This makes good sense, given the public policy of giving such officers special protection when carrying out their difficult and sometimes dangerous duties.

Counsel for the defendants did not make any frontal challenge to this line of authority. His argument was more indirect, and I think involved these steps.

(1) It is not every contact between one person and another which amounts to an assault or battery. To be criminal, the show or application of force must be unlawful. It is not tautologous to define assault as an unlawful offer or application of force.

(2) In deciding whether a defendant exerted reasonable force in defending himself, a court must judge him on the basis of what (reasonably or unreasonably) he believed to be the facts and not on the basis of what the facts actually were.

(3) If a defendant applies force to a police or court officer which would be reasonable if that person were not a police or court officer, and the defendant believes that he is not, then even if his belief is unreasonable he has a good plea of self-defence.

(4) Since the state of belief of these defendants was, accordingly, relevant to their liability, the judge was wrong to rule as he did.

The first of these steps is, in my judgment, established in *R v Kimber* [1983] 3 All ER 316, [1983] 1 WLR 1118 and *R v Williams* [1987] 3 All ER 411. The second and third steps are made good by *R v Williams* and *Beckford v R* above, [p **453**]. It accordingly seems to me that the fourth step follows, subject to the important qualification that the mistake must be one of fact (particularly as to the victim's capacity) and not a mistake of law as to the authority of a person acting in that capacity (*R v Fennell* [1970] 3 All ER 215, [1971] 1 QB 428).

Leggatt and **Roch JJ** delivered concurring judgments.

Appeal allowed

Note and questions

1. The appeal came before the Civil Division of the court because the offence was in the nature of a contempt, but the case is an authority on the criminal law.

2. What does the case tell us about the common proposition that an offence of strict liability requires no mens rea? *Is* the offence one of strict liability? Or is it a 'constructive crime' (above, p 570, Question 1).

3. D throws a pebble at V, a tramp. The pebble misses V and, unforeseen by D and unforeseeably hits X, a constable on duty. Is D guilty of assaulting a constable in the execution of his duty? Should he be?

(2) CONSENT AND ASSAULT

It is necessary to address two different problems:

> (i) situations in which V cannot be said to have given true consent—where, for example, V has been deceived or acts under threats or duress; and

> (ii) cases where V gives factual consent but this is treated as a matter of policy as being ineffective in the eyes of the law.

(i) The effectiveness in fact of the purported consent

R v Diana Richardson
[1998] 2 Cr App R 200, Court of Appeal

(Otton LJ, Turner and Dyson JJ)

Otton LJ: In the Crown Court at Nottingham, before HHJ Matthewman QC, following a ruling by the judge the appellant changed her pleas to guilty on six counts of assault occasioning actual bodily harm. She now appeals against conviction by leave of the single judge.

The facts can be briefly stated: The appellant was a registered dental practitioner until 30 August 1996 but was suspended from practice by the General Dental Council. Whilst still suspended, she carried out dentistry on a number of patients in September 1996. The mother of two of those patients complained to the police, not because of the suspension, but because she thought that the appellant appeared to be under the influence of drink or drugs. The appellant denied having taken drink, and said that the only drugs that she had taken had been prescribed by a doctor for psychiatric reasons. The police discovered that the appellant had been practising whilst disqualified, resulting in the charges.

Before the trial judge, defence counsel submitted:

> (1) [omitted]
> (2) The hostile intent requisite for assault was not present.
> (3) The patients consented to the treatment, even though they did not know that the appellant was disqualified from practice.

The judge ruled against the appellant on each ground. This appeal is concerned only with the last two grounds. On the third ground the judge accepted the argument for the Crown that there was fraud here which vitiated the apparent consent. He said:

'It would not be unlawful if there was consent to the act, that is real consent, not one induced by fraud relating to a fundamental fact, that is, as put here, the identity of the person who claims to have acted by consent. The prosecution say here there was such fraud because the apparent consent was on the basis of the identity of a person who was qualified to act and, indeed, a person who was not qualified to act. In my judgment, identity in those circumstances means not merely facial features or other features, bodily features and dress or whatever of a person, identity encompasses other matters, the whole identity and that includes, in this particular case a qualification to practice. The identity presented to the patients—'Mrs Diane Richardson able and presently lawfully dealing with your teeth' which was, in fact, a fraudulent claim and, in my judgment, a fundamental one, it was not merely not having a piece of paper it was a fraudulent total identity.'

Following these rulings the defendant pleaded guilty to all offences in the indictment.

The agreed basis upon which the plea of guilty was tendered was that the appellant had practised while suspended, that the treatment was of a reasonable standard and was carried out on willing patients who had presented themselves for such treatment, and that all of the complainants had been treated by her before her suspension, without complaint.

Miss Caroline Bradley on behalf of the appellant now concentrates her argument on the issue of consent. She acknowledges that without consent the surgical procedures carried out were capable of amounting to an assault in law.

The general proposition which underlies this area of the law is that the human body is inviolate but there are circumstances which the law recognises where consent may operate to prevent conduct which would otherwise be classified as an assault from being so treated. Reasonable surgical interference is clearly such an exception. Counsel relies upon the *dicta* of Lord Lane CJ in *A-G's Reference (No 6 of 1980)* (1981) 73 Cr App Rep 63, [1981] QB 715 where it was held that an assailant was not guilty of assault if the victim consented to it but that an exception to that principle existed where the public interest required. Lord Lane said at p 66 and p 719:

'Nothing which we have said is intended to cast doubt upon the accepted legality of…lawful chastisement…reasonable surgical interference…etc. The apparent exceptions can be justified as involving the exercise of a legal right, in the case, of chastisement…or as needed in the public interest, in other cases.'

Thus it can be accepted that a person may give lawful consent to the infliction of actual bodily harm upon himself and is justifiable as being in the public interest where reasonable surgical treatment is concerned. But the question then arises, what is the effect on the validity of consent, if any, if the complainant has had concealed from them the true nature of the status of the person who, in the guise of performing a reasonable surgical procedure, subsequently inflicts bodily harm.

Professor J C Smith QC, in Smith and Hogan *Criminal Law* (8th ed), at p 420 states:

'Fraud does not necessarily negative consent. It does so only if it deceives P as to the identity of the person or the nature of the act.'

This statement of principle is derived from *Clarence* (1888) 22 QBD 23 where the victim [D's wife] consented to sexual intercourse with the accused and although she would not have consented had she been aware of the disease from which D knew he was suffering, this was no assault. Wills J stated at p 7:

'That consent obtained by fraud is no consent at all is not true as a general proposition either in fact or in law.'

Stephen J stated at p 44:

'… The only sorts of fraud that so far destroy the effect of a woman's consent as to convert a connection consented to in fact into a rape are frauds as to the nature of the act itself, or as to the identity of the person who does the act.'

There is a clear line of authority concerning fraud and the nature of the act. In *Williams* [1923] 1 KB 340 the appellant, a choir master, had sexual intercourse with a girl of sixteen years of age under the pretence that her breathing was not quite right and that he had to perform an operation to enable her to produce her voice properly. The girl submitted to what was done under the belief, wilfully and fraudulently induced by the appellant, that she was being medically and surgically treated by the appellant and not with any intention that she should have intercourse with him. The Court of Criminal Appeal held that the appellant was properly convicted of rape. Lord Hewart CJ referred to *Case* (1850) 4 Cox CC 220 where a medical practitioner had sexual connection with a girl of fourteen years of age upon the pretence that he was treating her medically and the girl made no resistance owing to a bona fide belief that she was being medically treated. It was held that he was properly convicted of an assault and might have been convicted of rape. The Lord Chief Justice also referred with approval to the *dicta* of Branson J in *Dicken* (1877) 14 Cox CC 8:

'The law has laid it down that where a girl's consent is procured by the means which the girl says this prisoner adopted, that is to say, where she is persuaded that what is being done to her is not the ordinary act of sexual intercourse but is some medical or surgical operation in order to give her relief from some disability from which she is suffering, then that is rape although the actual thing that is done was done with her consent, because she never consented to the act of sexual intercourse. She was persuaded to consent to what he did because she thought it was not sexual intercourse and because she thought it was a surgical operation.'

In *Harms* (1944) 2 DLR 61 the Supreme Court of Canada considered s 298 of the Canadian Criminal Code which established that in order to vitiate consent the false or fraudulent misrepresentation had to be as to the nature and quality of the act. Harms had falsely represented himself to be a medical doctor. Although the complainant knew that he was proposing sexual intercourse she consented thereto because of his representations that the intercourse was in the nature of a medical treatment necessitated by a condition which he said he had diagnosed. Harms was not a medical man at all. The court held that a jury was entitled to conclude that the nature and quality of the act as far as the complainant was concerned was therapeutic and not carnal. In other words, the complainant had consented to a therapeutic act, which it was not, and had not consented to a carnal act which it was. The consent induced by the fraudulent representation was held to have been vitiated.

The later case of *Bolduc and Bird v R* (1967) 63 DLR (2d) 82 was held to be on the other side of the line. The Supreme Court of Canada considered the case of a doctor who falsely represented that his colleague was a medical student and obtained the complainant's consent to the colleague's presence at a vaginal examination. It was held that there was no indecent assault because the fraud was not as to the nature and quality of what was to be done. It was observed that the defendant's conduct was 'unethical and reprehensible', but did not have the effect of vitiating the consent.

In *Papadimitropoulos* (1957) 98 CLR 249 the High Court of Australia considered the case of a complainant who had sexual relations with a man whom she believed to be her husband. Unknown to her no valid marriage ceremony had ever taken place. The complainant had consented to sexual intercourse under the belief, fraudulently induced, that she had contracted a valid marriage to the man whom she believed to be her husband. It was held that in these circumstances this did not support a conviction for rape. The Court stated at p 261:

'Rape, as a capital felony, was defined with exactness, and although there has been some extension over the centuries in the ambit of the crime, it is quite wrong to bring within its operation forms of evil conduct because they wear some analogy to aspects of the crime deserved of punishment... The key to such a case as the present lies in remembering that it is the penetration of the woman's body without her consent to such penetration that makes the felony. The capital felony was not directed to fraudulent conduct inducing the consent. Frauds under that head must be punished under other heads of the criminal law or not at all; they are not rape... To return to the central point; rape is carnal knowledge of a woman without her consent; carnal knowledge is the physical fact of penetration; it is the consent to that which is in question; such a consent demands a perception as to what is about to take place, as to the identity of the man and the character of what he is doing. But once the consent is comprehending and actual the inducing causes cannot destroy its reality and leave the man guilty of rape.'

And earlier at p 260:

'It must be noted that in considering whether an apparent consent is unreal it is the mistake or misapprehension that makes it so. It is not the fraud producing the mistake which is material so much as the mistake itself... tends to distract the attention from the essential inquiry, namely whether the consent is no consent because it is not directed to the nature and character of the act. The identity of the man and the character of the physical act that is done or proposed seem now clearly to be regarded as forming part of the nature and character of the act to which the woman's consent is directed. That accords with the principles governing mistake vitiating apparent manifestations within other chapters of the law.'

This result is not altogether surprising, for otherwise every bigamist would be guilty of rape.

The Law Commission in their Consultation Paper No 139 'Consent in the Criminal Law', having considered fraud and consent generally proposed a lesser offence of obtaining consent by deception and stated (at para 6.27) that:

'consent should not in general be *nullified* by deception as to any circumstances other than the nature of the act and the identity of the person doing it, but that deception as to other circumstances should give rise to liability for a lesser offence than that of non-consensual conduct. Where the defendant is aware that the other person is or may be mistaken about the nature of the act or the defendant's identity, we think that the other person's consent should be nullified as if the mistake by fraud... If a deception as to circumstances in question would give rise to liability *only* for our proposed offence of obtaining consent by deception, as distinct from the more serious offence of acting without any consent at all, liability for taking advantage of a self-induced mistake as to that circumstance could *at most* be for the lesser offence.'

It is, thus, unremarkable that neither counsel has been able to cite any authority in which the complainant in a sexual case has been deceived as to the identity of the assailant and her apparent consent has held to have been vitiated by fraud. It is to be noted that section 1(3) Sexual Offences Act 1956 provides that a man can be guilty of rape if he induces a married woman to have sexual intercourse with him by impersonating her husband. However this only covers the type of case where the woman is legally married and for some reason believes that the person with whom she is having sexual relations is her husband when in fact he is not. [This provision has now been repealed and replaced by s 76 of the Sexual Offences Act 2003, on which see below, p **721**].

Miss Bradley who argued the case ably contends that the complainants were deceived neither as to the nature or quality of the act nor as to the identity of the person carrying out the act. The statutory offence was created to punish such conduct as took place here.

Both before the judge and before this Court the respondent expressly disavowed reliance upon the nature or quality of the act. Mr Peter Walmsley succinctly submitted that the patients were deceived into consenting to treatment by the representation that the defendant was a qualified and practising dentist and not one who had been disqualified. He further submitted that the evidence of the patients was unequivocal: had they known that the defendant had been suspended they would not have consented to any treatment. If the treatment had been given by a person impersonating a dentist it would have been an assault. There was no distinction to be drawn between the unqualified dentist and one who is suspended. On this basis there was a mistake as to the true identity of the defendant.

We are unable to accept that argument. There is no basis for the proposition that the rules which determine the circumstances in which consent is vitiated can be different according to whether the case is one of sexual assault or one where the assault is non-sexual. The common element in both these cases is that they involve an assault, and the question is whether consent has been negatived. It is nowhere suggested that the common law draws such a distinction. The common law is not concerned with the question whether the mistaken consent has been induced by fraud on the part of the accused or has been self induced. It is the nature of the mistake that is relevant, and not the reason why the mistake has been made. In summary, either there is consent to actions on the part of a person in the mistaken belief that he or they are other than they truly are, in which case it is assault or, short of this, there is no assault.

In essence the Crown contended that the concept of the 'identity of the person' should be extended to cover the qualifications or attributes of the dentist on the basis that the patients consented to treatment by a qualified dentist and not a suspended one. We must reject that submission. In all the charges brought against the appellant the complainants were fully aware of the identity of the appellant. To accede to the submission would be to strain or distort the every day meaning of the word identity, the dictionary definition of which is 'the condition of being the same'.

It was suggested in argument that we might be assisted by the civil law of consent, where such expressions as 'real' or 'informed' consent prevail. In this regard the criminal and the civil law do not run along the same track. The concept of informed consent has no place in the criminal law. It would also be a mistake, in our view, to introduce the concept of a duty to communicate information to a patient about the risk of an activity before consent to an act can be treated as valid. The gravamen of the appellant's conduct in the instant case was that the complainants consented to treatment from her although their consent had been procured by her failure to inform them that she was no longer qualified to practice. This was clearly reprehensible and may well found the basis of a civil claim for damages. But we are quite satisfied that it is not a basis for finding criminal liability in the field of offences against the person.

We have arrived at this conclusion without any real difficulty. It is our considered view that the common law has developed as far as it can without the intervention of the legislature. For the better part of a century, the common law concept of consent in the criminal law has been certain and clearly delineated. It is not for this Court to attempt to unwrite the law which has been settled for so long. This is an area in which it is to be hoped that the proposals of the Law Commission will be given an early opportunity for implementation.

Finally, we feel obliged to observe that we are left with a state of unease at the procedure which was adopted in this case. We are concerned about the wisdom of the Crown being prepared to accept 'reasonable surgical intervention' as the factual basis of the plea. If the allegations of assault occasioning actual bodily harm had been persisted in and proved in accordance with the committal statements there would have been little or no room for the defence of consent. The nature of the dental treatment (if proved) would have gone far beyond the treatment that was either contemplated or consented to by the patients or their parents.

Accordingly, we must allow the appeal and quash the convictions.

Appeal allowed

Convictions quashed

Notes and questions

1. How could the prosecution both (i) agree that the treatment was of a reasonable standard and (ii) allege that it constituted actual bodily harm? Is a dentist properly drilling a

diseased tooth (or a surgeon properly amputating a limb to save life) causing 'harm'? If consent had been vitiated—for example, there had been a misrepresentation of identity—there would have been an assault but, if the treatment was necessary and competently done, would it have been an assault occasioning actual bodily harm?

2. In the circumstances of *Richardson* would it have been an assault occasioning actual bodily harm if the treatment had been harmful? Does consent to proper treatment negative assault if the treatment is improper? What if the treatment amounts to *grievous* bodily harm?

3. Consistently with the decisions in *Kimber*, above, p **408**, and *Gladstone Williams*, above, p **453**, it was held in *Jones* (1986) 83 Cr App R 375, [1987] Crim LR 123, CA, that there is no assault where D genuinely believes in the other's consent, and it is irrelevant whether that belief is reasonably held or not.

4. The Sexual Offences Act 2003, s 76 provides that it shall be conclusively presumed that V was not consenting where D has deceived V as to the nature or purpose of his acts or as to his identity. In relation to non-sexual offences, the question remains whether a deception as to the quality or purpose of the act, as opposed to its nature, will vitiate consent.

R v Tabassum
[2000] 2 Cr App R 328, Court of Appeal, Criminal Division

(Rose LJ, Kennedy and Hallett JJ)

Tabassum, who had no medical qualifications or training, persuaded women to allow him to measure their breasts by representing, perhaps truthfully, that he was doing so for the purpose of preparing a database for sale to doctors, concerned with breast cancer. The women were fully aware of the nature of the acts he proposed to do, but said that they consented only because they thought T had either medical qualifications or medical training. The trial judge ruled that 'what they consented to was a medical examination by a person with medical qualifications and not a sexual act.' He quoted from the judgment of Stephen J in *Clarence*: (above, p **677**):

'There is abundant authority to show that such frauds as these [that is, "frauds as to the nature of the act itself, or as to the identity of the person who does the act" p **678**, above] vitiate consent both in the case of rape and in the case of indecent assault. I should prefer myself to say that consent in such cases does not exist at all, because the act consented to is not the act done. Consent to a surgical operation or examination is not consent to sexual connection or indecent behaviour.'

T appealed from his conviction of indecent assault.

Rose LJ. Mr Macdonald [for the appellant] referred the Court to *Kimber* (1983) 77 Cr App Rep 225, [1983] 1 WLR 1118. There, it was held that the prosecution has to prove that the defendant intended to lay hands on the victim without her consent and, if he did not intend to do this, he is entitled to be found not guilty. If he did not so intend because he believed she was consenting, the prosecution would have failed to prove the charge, see pp 229 and 1122:

'It is the defendant's belief, not the grounds on which it was based, which goes to negative consent.'

Mr Macdonald submits, in his written submission, that the judge failed to give the jury any direction as to the reasonableness of the defendant's belief in the complainant's consent.

In our judgment, the pertinent authorities, in relation to Mr Macdonald's first submission, can properly be analysed in this way. The wife in *Clarence*, and the prostitute in *Linekar* [below, p **721**], each consented to sexual intercourse knowing both the nature and the quality of that act. The additional unexpected consequences, of infection in the one case and non-payment in the other, were irrelevant to and did not detract from the women's consent to sexual intercourse.

In *Richardson*, the case proceeded solely by reference to the point on identity. As is apparent from pp 205F and 449 of the judgment, the prosecution in that case did not at trial or on appeal rely on the nature or quality of the act. In our judgment, the learned judge was entitled to follow the passage in the judgment of Stephen J in *Clarence*, which he cited in the course of his ruling. In the present case the motive and intent of the defendant were irrelevant (see *C* [1994] Crim LR 642, to which reference has already been made). The nature and quality of the defendant's acts in touching the breasts of women to whom, in sexual terms he was a stranger, was unlawful and an indecent assault unless the complainants consented to that touching.

On the evidence, if the jury accepted it, consent was given because they mistakenly believed that the defendant was medically qualified or, in the case of the third complainant, trained at Christie's and that, in consequence, the touching was for a medical purpose. As this was not so, there was no true consent. They were consenting to touching for medical purposes not to indecent behaviour, that is, there was consent to the nature of the act but not its quality. *Flattery* and *Harms*, which we have earlier cited, are entirely consistent with that view because, in each of those cases, the woman's consent to sexual intercourse was to a therapeutic, not a carnal, act. A similar principle underlies the decision in *Rosinski* (1824) 1 Mood 18, 168 Eng Rep 1168. It follows that, in our judgment, the judge's ruling was correct.

As to the criticisms of the judge's directions on *mens rea*, there was, as it seems to us, no need for the judge to direct the jury as to the absence of evidence that the defendant's conduct was intended to be sexual. The touching was prima facie indecent, as we have said. Whether the defendant had any sexual motive or intent was irrelevant. The only issues were consent and whether the defendant may have believed that the complainants were consenting.

As to that, the directions which we have quoted were, as it seems to us, entirely adequate. The reasonableness or otherwise of any such behaviour on the defendant's part called for no direction, in our judgment: for the issue was not whether any belief which the defendant had was reasonable, but whether there may have been, on his part, any belief at all that the victims were consenting. Unlike the trial judge in *Kimber*, this trial judge gave, as it seems to us, an appropriate direction on this aspect of the matter. It follows that the appeal against conviction is dismissed.

Notes and questions

1. Do any of the authorities cited support the proposition that consent is vitiated where V is aware of the 'nature' of the act but mistaken as to its 'quality'? Is it supported by *Clarence*?

2. Can this case be reconciled with *Richardson*?

3. Is intercourse with a man suffering from a 'loathsome' contagious disease an act of the same quality as intercourse with a healthy man? If *Tabassum* is right, would not *Clarence* today be guilty of rape of his wife? See *Dica* (below).

4. In cases charged as offences against the person (for example, *Clarence*) rather than sexual offences, what matters is surely whether V has been deceived as to the risk of the harm proscribed by the offence against the person with which he is charged?

R v Dica
[2004] EWCA Crim 1103, Court of Appeal, Criminal Division

(Lord Woolf CJ, Judge LJ and Forbes J)

D was charged with two offences under s 20 of the Offences Against the Person Act 1861 where, knowing that he was HIV+, he had unprotected intercourse with two sexual partners causing each to be infected with the virus. He did not disclose his HIV status to either partner. He was convicted and appealed on the basis that (i) the trial judge had, notwithstanding *R v Clarence* (1889) 22 QB 23, held that it was open to the jury to convict D, and (ii) the trial judge had ruled that whether or not the complainants knew of D's condition, their consent, if any, was irrelevant and provided no defence (this issue is dealt with below, p **694**).

Lord Justice Judge:

[His lordship stated the facts.]

10. It is perhaps important to emphasise at the outset that the prosecution did not allege that the appellant had either raped or deliberately set out to infect the complainants with disease. Rather, it was alleged that when he had consensual sexual intercourse with them, knowing that he himself was suffering from HIV, he was reckless whether they might become infected. Thus, in the language of the counts in the indictment, he 'inflicted grievous bodily harm' on them both.

11. It was not in dispute that at least on the majority of occasions, and with both complainants, sexual intercourse was unprotected. Recklessness, as such, was not in issue. If protective measures had been taken by the appellant that would have provided material relevant to the jury's decision whether, in all the circumstances, recklessness was proved.

12. Although both women were willing to have sexual intercourse with the appellant, the prosecution's case was that their agreement would never have been given if they had known of the appellant's condition. The appellant would have contended that he told both women of his condition, and that they were nonetheless willing to have sexual intercourse with him, a case which in the light of the judge's ruling, he did not support in evidence. The suggestion would have been strongly disputed by them both.

. . .

(a) The Crown's case   ·

Concealment of the truth by the appellant

33. The judgments of the majority in *Clarence* included considerable discussion about the issue of fraud (in the sense of concealment), and the consequences if consent were vitiated. Again, however, the observations have to be put into the context of the perceived requirement that in the absence of an assault Clarence could not be guilty of the s.20 offence, and the deemed consent of the wife to have sexual intercourse with her husband....

36. Clarence did not face a charge of rape or indecent assault, yet the concept of his wife's notional consent to the act of sexual intercourse was inextricably linked with the quashing of his convictions for offences of violence. He was not charged with an offence under s 3(2) of the Criminal Law Amendment Act 1885, until recently, s. 3 of the Sexual Offences Act 1956, and now in slightly different terms, s.4 of the Sexual Offences Act 2003.

    . . . .

37. The present case is concerned with and confined to s.20 offences alone, without the burdensome fiction of deemed consent to sexual intercourse. The question for decision is whether the victims' consent to sexual intercourse, which as a result of his alleged concealment was given in ignorance of the facts of the appellant's condition, *necessarily amounted to consent to the risk of being infected by him* (emphasis added). If that question must be answered 'Yes', the concept of consent in relation to s.20 is devoid of real meaning.

38. The position here is analogous to that considered in *R v Tabassum* [2000] 2 CAR 328. The appellant was convicted of indecently assaulting women who allowed him to examine their breasts

in the mistaken belief that he was medically qualified. Rose LJ considered *Clarence*, and pointed out that in relation to the infection suffered by the wife, this was an additional, unexpected, consequence of sexual intercourse, which was irrelevant to her consent to sexual intercourse with her husband. Rejecting the argument that an 'undoubted consent' could only be negatived if the victim had been deceived or mistaken about the nature and quality of the act, and that consent was not negatived 'merely because the victim would not have agreed to the act if he or she had known all the facts', Rose LJ observed, in forthright terms, 'there was no true consent'. Again, in *R v Cort* [2003] 3 WLR 1300, a case of kidnapping, the complainants had consented to taking a ride in a motor car, but not to being kidnapped. They wanted transport, not kidnapping. Kidnapping may be established by carrying away by fraud.

> 'It is difficult to see how one could ever consent to that once fraud was indeed established. The "nature" of the act here is therefore taking the complainant away by fraud. The complainant did not consent to that event. All that she consented to was a ride in the car, which in itself is irrelevant to the offence and a different thing from that with which Mr Cort is charged.'

39. In our view, on the assumed fact now being considered, the answer is entirely straightforward. These victims consented to sexual intercourse. Accordingly, the appellant was not guilty of rape. Given the long-term nature of the relationships, if the appellant concealed the truth about his condition from them, and therefore kept them in ignorance of it, there was no reason for them to think that they were running any risk of infection, and they were not consenting to it. On this basis, there would be no consent sufficient in law to provide the appellant with a defence to the charge under s.20.

Notes and questions

1. The Court of Appeal finally lays to rest that aspect of *Clarence* relating to implied consent. Thus, where V is unaware of D's infected state, by consenting to the act of unprotected sexual intercourse she cannot be said to have impliedly consented to the risk of infection from that intercourse. In principle, this aspect of the decision is welcome. True consent is based on an informed choice being made by the 'victim', and the decision respects that principle.

2. In *Dica*, the victims had been defrauded as to the risk of infection (and hence had not consented to bodily harm), but had not been defrauded as to the nature of the act of sexual intercourse (and hence had not been raped). HIV infected intercourse is still intercourse.

3. To what extent is D obliged to inform his sexual partners where D merely suspects that he is HIV+? John Spencer has written that:

To infect an unsuspecting person with a grave disease you know you have, *or may have*, by behaviour that you know involves a risk of transmission, and that you know you could easily modify to reduce or eliminate the risk, is to harm another in a way that is both needless and callous. For that reason, criminal liability is justified unless there are strong countervailing reasons. In my view there are not.

(J. Spencer, 'Liability for Reckless Infection: Part 2' (2004) 154 NLJ 385, 448.)

In contrast, M. Weait ('Criminal Law and the Sexual Transmission of HIV: R v Dica' [2005] MLR 121) writes:

While it may be right and proper to affirm that consent to intercourse itself should not be taken to imply consent to the risk of resultant harm, it is arguable that *Dica* does not—at least so far as its interpretation of *Clarence* is concerned—mean that consent to intercourse will necessarily imply an absence of consent to harm where other conditions are met—i.e. where the defendant is ignorant of his HIV positive status or where he knows and his partner is aware of the fact. If it were otherwise, *Dica* would mean that a person who was ignorant of his HIV positive status could not lawfully have unprotected consensual intercourse with anyone, nor could a person who knew of a partner's HIV positive status give a legally recognised consent to intercourse with them. If such a couple were to have sexual intercourse it seems counter-intuitive to suggest that they are not having consensual intercourse, but are instead having non-consensual intercourse in respect of which there has been consent to the risk of HIV transmission. Such an interpretation would render the distinction between conduct of this kind and rape so fine as to be unsustainable—a conclusion which the Court of Appeal was keen to preclude.

4. Is D taking a risk of transmission where he knows that he is HIV+ and uses a condom being aware that even so there is 'a' risk of transmission and infection? Is this a *justified* risk for him to take? Irrespective of disclosing his status to V?

5. To what extent is V's consent dependent on accurate information?

R v Konzani [2005]
EWCA Crim 706 , Court of Appeal, Criminal Division

(Judge LJ, Grigson J and Judge Radford)

K had been informed that he was HIV+, and he subsequently had unprotected sexual intercourse with three complainants, having not revealed to any of them that he was HIV+. Each of the three contracted the HIV virus. K was charged with inflicting grievous bodily harm on each of them contrary to s 20 of the OAPA 1861. K argued that by consenting to the intercourse, each consented to the risks associated with sexual intercourse. The judge directed the jury that before the consent of the complainant might provide the defendant with a defence that consent had to be an informed and willing consent to the risk of contracting HIV. The jury convicted. The defendant appealed on the basis that (i) the judge had failed to leave to the jury the issue whether the defendant might honestly, even if unreasonably, have believed that the complainants had consented to the risk of contracting the HIV virus; and (ii) that the judge had misdirected the jury on the issue of consent.

Judge LJ ... 5. Notwithstanding their evidence that he withheld vital information about his condition from them, and that each complainant expressly denied that she consented to the risk of catching the HIV virus from him, counsel on his behalf addressed the jury on the basis that by consenting to unprotected sexual intercourse with him, they were impliedly consenting to all the risks associated with sexual intercourse. He argued that as infection with the HIV virus may be one possible consequence of unprotected sexual intercourse, the complainants had consented to the risk of contracting the HIV virus from him. Accordingly he should be acquitted. By their verdicts, the jury found that none of the complainants consented to the risk of contracting the HIV virus.

...

Consent

34. Referring to HIV, the judge directed the jury that they had to be sure that the complainant in each individual case:

> '... did not willingly consent to the risk of suffering that infection. Note that I use the phrase "to the risk of suffering that infection" and not merely just "to suffering it". That is an important point which Mr Roberts

rightly drew to your attention in his speech to you this morning. He put it this way, it is whether she consented to that risk, not consented to being given the disease which is, as he put it graphically, a mile away from the former. That is right, but note that I use the word "willingly" in the phrase "willingly consent", and I did that to highlight that the sort of consent I am talking about means consciously.'

He returned to the clear and important distinction between 'running a risk on one hand and consenting to run that risk on the other', pointing out that the prosecution had to establish that the complainant 'did not willingly consent to the risk of suffering the infection in the sense of her having consciously thought about it at the time and decided to run it'. He added that the appellant should be acquitted, if, in relation to any complainant, she had thought of the risk of getting HIV, and nevertheless decided to take the risk. In answer to a question from the jury, he returned to emphasise that before the appellant could be convicted, the prosecution had to prove that she 'did not willingly consent to the risk of suffering that infection', and he repeated that for the purposes of his direction, 'willingly' meant 'consciously'. He again repeated the distinction between 'running a risk on the one hand and consenting to run that risk on the other', adding that the 'willing' consent involved knowing the implications of infection with the HIV virus.

35. In short, the judge explained that before the consent of the complainant could provide the appellant with a defence, it was required to be an informed and willing consent to the risk of contracting HIV.

....

42. The recognition in *R v Dica* of informed consent as a defence was based on 'but limited by' potentially conflicting public policy considerations. In the public interest, so far as possible, the spread of catastrophic illness must be avoided or prevented. On the other hand, the public interest also requires that the principle of personal autonomy in the context of adult non-violent sexual relationships should be maintained. If an individual who knows that he is suffering from the HIV virus conceals this stark fact from his sexual partner, the principle of her personal autonomy is not enhanced if he is exculpated when he recklessly transmits the HIV virus to her through consensual sexual intercourse. On any view, the concealment of this fact from her almost inevitably means that she is deceived. Her consent is not properly informed, and she cannot give an informed consent to something of which she is ignorant. Equally, her personal autonomy is not normally protected by allowing a defendant who knows that he is suffering from the HIV virus which he deliberately conceals, to assert an honest belief in his partner's informed consent to the risk of the transmission of the HIV virus. Silence in these circumstances is incongruous with honesty, or with a genuine belief that there is an informed consent. Accordingly, in such circumstances the issue either of informed consent, or honest belief in it will only rarely arise: in reality, in most cases, the contention would be wholly artificial.

43. This is not unduly burdensome. The defendant is not to be convicted of this offence unless it is proved that he was reckless. If so, the necessary *mens rea* will be established. Recklessness is a question of fact, to be proved by the prosecution. Equally the defendant is not to be convicted if there was, or may have been an informed consent by his sexual partner to the risk that he would transfer the HIV virus to her. In many cases, as in *Dica* itself, provided recklessness is established, the critical factual area of dispute will address what, if anything, was said between the two individuals involved, one of whom knows, and the other of whom does not know, that one of them is suffering the HIV virus. In the final analysis, the question of consent, like the issue of recklessness is fact-specific.

44. In deference to Mr Roberts' submission, we accept that there may be circumstances in which it would be open to the jury to infer that, notwithstanding that the defendant was reckless and concealed his condition from the complainant, she may nevertheless have given an informed consent to the risk of contracting the HIV virus. By way of example, an individual with HIV may develop a sexual relationship with someone who knew him while he was in hospital, receiving treatment for the

condition. If so, her informed consent, if it were indeed informed, would remain a defence, to be disproved by the prosecution, even if the defendant had not personally informed her of his condition. Even if she did not in fact consent, this example would illustrate the basis for an argument that he honestly believed in her informed consent. Alternatively, he may honestly believe that his new sexual partner was told of his condition by someone known to them both. Cases like these, not too remote to be fanciful, may arise. If they do, no doubt they will be explored with the complainant in cross-examination. Her answers may demonstrate an informed consent. Nothing remotely like that was suggested here. In a different case, perhaps supported by the defendant's own evidence, material like this may provide a basis for suggesting that he honestly believed that she was giving an informed consent. He may provide an account of the incident, or the affair, which leads the jury to conclude that even if she did not give an informed consent, he may honestly have believed that she did. Acknowledging these possibilities in different cases does not, we believe, conflict with the public policy considerations identified in *R v Dica*. That said, they did not arise in the present case.

45. Why not? In essence because the jury found that the complainants did not give a willing or informed consent to the risks of contracting the HIV virus from the appellant. We recognise that where consent does provide a defence to an offence against the person, it is generally speaking correct that the defendant's honest belief in the alleged victim's consent would also provide a defence. However for this purpose, the defendant's honest belief must be concomitant with the consent which provides a defence. Unless the consent would provide a defence, an honest belief in it would not assist the defendant. This follows logically from *R v Brown* [see below]. For it to do so here, what was required was some evidence of an honest belief that the complainants, or any one of them, were consenting to the risk that they might be infected with the HIV virus by him. There is not the slightest evidence, direct or indirect, from which a jury could begin to infer that the appellant honestly believed that any complainant consented to that specific risk. As there was no such evidence, the judge's ruling about 'honest belief' was correct. In fact, the honest truth was that the appellant deceived them.

46. In our judgment, the judge's directions to the jury sufficiently explained the proper implications to the case of the consensual participation by each of the complainants to sexual intercourse with the appellant. The jury concluded, in the case of each complainant, that she did not willingly or consciously consent to the risk of suffering the HIV virus.

Appeal against conviction dismissed.

(ii) In what circumstances is a person permitted in law to consent to harm and to what level of harm may they consent?

R v Brown
[1993] 2 All ER 75, House of Lords

(Lords Templeman, Jauncey of Tullichettle, Lowry, Mustill and Slynn of Hadley)

The appellants belonged to a group of sado-masochistic homosexuals who willingly co-operated in the commission of acts of violence against each other for sexual pleasure. Their activities included whipping and caning, branding, the application of stinging nettles to the genital area, and inserting map pins or fish hooks into the penis. There was no permanent injury done, no infection of the wounds and no evidence that any of the men had sought medical treatment. Their actions were carried out in private and there was no complaint made to the police who found out about these activities by chance when they were investigating other matters. The appellants were convicted of assault occasioning actual bodily harm contrary to s 47, and, in three cases, of malicious wounding contrary to s 20 of the Offences Against the Person Act 1861.

These convictions were upheld by the Court of Appeal which certified the following point of law of general public importance:

'Where A wounds or assaults B occasioning him actual bodily harm in the course of a sado-masochistic encounter, does the prosecution have to prove lack of consent on the part of B before they can establish A's guilt under section 20 and section 47 of the 1861, Offences against the Person Act?'

Lord Templeman...In the present case each of the appellants intentionally inflicted violence upon another (to whom I refer as 'the victim') with the consent of the victim and thereby occasioned actual bodily harm or in some cases wounding or grievous bodily harm. Each appellant was therefore guilty of an offence under section 47 or section 20 of the Act of 1861 unless the consent of the victim was effective to prevent the commission of the offence or effective to constitute a defence to the charge.

In some circumstances violence is not punishable under the criminal law. When no actual bodily harm is caused, the consent of the person affected precludes him from complaining. There can be no conviction for the summary offence of common assault if the victim has consented to the assault. Even when violence is intentionally inflicted and results in actual bodily harm, wounding or serious bodily harm the accused is entitled to be acquitted if the injury was a foreseeable incident of a lawful activity in which the person injured was participating. Surgery involves intentional violence resulting in actual or sometimes serious bodily harm but surgery is a lawful activity. Other activities carried on with consent by or on behalf of the injured person have been accepted as lawful notwithstanding that they involve actual bodily harm or may cause serious bodily harm. Ritual circumcision, tattooing, ear-piercing and violent sports including boxing are lawful activities.

In earlier days some other forms of violence were lawful and when they ceased to be lawful they were tolerated until well into the 19th century. Duelling and fighting were at first lawful and then tolerated provided the protagonists were voluntary participants. But where the results of these activities was the maiming of one of the participants, the defence of consent never availed the aggressor; see *Hawkins Pleas of the Crown* (1824), 8th edn, chapter 15. A maim was bodily harm whereby a man was deprived of the use of any member of his body which he needed to use in order to fight but a bodily injury was not a maim merely because it was a disfigurement. The act of maim was unlawful because the King was deprived of the services of an able-bodied citizen for the defence of the realm. Violence which maimed was unlawful despite consent to the activity which produced the maiming. In these days there is no difference between maiming on the one hand and wounding or causing grievous bodily harm on the other hand except with regard to sentence.

When duelling became unlawful, juries remained unwilling to convict but the judges insisted that persons guilty of causing death or bodily injury should be convicted despite the consent of the victim.

Similarly, in the old days, fighting was lawful provided the protagonists consented because it was thought that fighting inculcated bravery and skill and physical fitness. The brutality of knuckle fighting however caused the courts to declare that such fights were unlawful even if the protagonists consented. Rightly or wrongly the courts accepted that boxing is a lawful activity.

In *R v Coney* (1882) 8 QBD 534, the court held that a prize-fight in public was unlawful...

The conclusion is that a prize-fight being unlawful, actual bodily harm or serious bodily harm inflicted in the course of a prize-fight is unlawful notwithstanding the consent of the protagonists.

In *R v Donovan* [1934] 2 KB 498 the appellant in private beat a girl of seventeen for purposes of sexual gratification, it was said with her consent. Swift J said, at 507 that:

'It is an unlawful act to beat another person with such a degree of violence that the infliction of bodily harm is a probable consequence, and when such an act is proved, consent is immaterial.'

In *A-G's Reference (No 6 of 1980)* [1981] 2 All ER 1057, [1981] QB 715 where two men quarrelled and fought with bare fists Lord Lane CJ, delivering the judgment of the Court of Appeal, said at 719:

'...It is not in the public interest that people should try to cause, or should cause, each other bodily harm for no good reason. Minor struggles are another matter. So, in our judgment, it is immaterial whether the act occurs in private or in public; it is an assault if actual bodily harm is intended and/or caused. This means that most fights will be unlawful regardless of consent. Nothing which we have said is intended to cast doubt upon the accepted legality of properly conducted games and sports, lawful chastisement or correction, reasonable surgical interference, dangerous exhibitions, etc. These apparent exceptions can be justified as involving the exercise of a legal right, in the case of chastisement or correction, or as needed in the public interest, in the other cases.' [Cf *Slingsby*, above, p **626**]

Duelling and fighting are both unlawful and the consent of the protagonists affords no defence to charges of causing actual bodily harm, wounding or grievous bodily harm in the course of an unlawful activity.

The appellants and their victims in the present case were engaged in consensual homosexual activities. The attitude of the public towards homosexual practices changed in the second half of this century. Change in public attitudes led to a change in the law....[Lord Templeman referred to the Wolfenden Report and subsequent legislation.]

My Lords, the authorities dealing with the intentional infliction of bodily harm do not establish that consent is a defence to a charge under the Act of 1861. They establish that the courts have accepted that consent is a defence to the infliction of bodily harm in the course of some lawful activities. The question is whether the defence should be extended to the infliction of bodily harm in the course of sado-masochistic encounters. The Wolfenden Committee did not make any recommendations about sado-masochism and Parliament did not deal with violence in 1967. The Act of 1967 is of no assistance for present purposes because the present problem was not under consideration.

The question whether the defence of consent should be extended to the consequences of sado-masochistic encounters can only be decided by consideration of policy and public interest. Parliament can call on the advice of doctors, psychiatrists, criminologists, sociologists and other experts and can also sound and take into account public opinion. But the question must at this stage be decided by this House in its judicial capacity in order to determine whether the convictions of the appellants should be upheld or quashed.

Counsel for some of the appellants argued that the defence of consent should be extended to the offence of occasioning actual bodily harm under section 47 of the Act of 1861 but should not be available to charges of serious wounding and the inflicting of serious bodily harm under section 20. I do not consider that this solution is practicable. Sado-masochistic participants have no way of foretelling the degree of bodily harm which will result from their encounters. The differences between actual bodily harm and serious bodily harm cannot be satisfactorily applied by a jury in order to determine acquittal or conviction.

Counsel for the appellants argued that consent should provide a defence to charges under both section 20 and section 47 because, it was said, every person has a right to deal with his body as he pleases. I do not consider that this slogan provides a sufficient guide to the policy decision which must now be made. It is an offence for a person to abuse his own body and mind by taking drugs. Although the law is often broken, the criminal law restrains a practice which is regarded as dangerous and injurious to individuals and which if allowed and extended is harmful to society generally. In any event the appellants in this case did not mutilate their own bodies. They inflicted bodily harm on willing victims. Suicide is no longer an offence but a person who assists another to commit suicide is guilty of murder or manslaughter. [This is wrong. See p **618** above: DCO.]

The assertion was made on behalf of the appellants that the sexual appetites of sadists and masochists can only be satisfied by the infliction of bodily harm and that the law should not punish the consensual achievement of sexual satisfaction. There was no evidence to support the assertion that sado-masochist activities are essential to the happiness of the appellants or any other particip-ants but the argument would be acceptable if sado-masochism were only concerned with sex, as the appellants contend. In my opinion sado-masochism is not only concerned with sex. Sado-masochism is also concerned with violence. The evidence discloses that the practices of the appellants were unpredictably dangerous and degrading to body and mind and were developed with increasing barbarity and taught to persons whose consents were dubious or worthless.

A sadist draws pleasure from inflicting or watching cruelty. A masochist derives pleasure from his own pain or humiliation. The appellants are middle-aged men. The victims were youths some of whom were introduced to sado-masochism before they attained the age of 21. In his judgment in the Court of Appeal, Lord Lane CJ said that two members of the group of which the appellants formed part, namely one Cadman and the appellant Laskey:

> '…were responsible in part for the corruption of a youth K…It is some comfort at least to be told, as we were, that K has now it seems settled into a normal heterosexual relationship. Cadman had befriended K when the boy was 15 years old. He met him in a cafeteria and, so he says, found out that the boy was interested in homosexual activities. He introduced and encouraged K in "bondage affairs". He was interested in viewing and recording on videotape K and other teenage boys in homosexual scenes…One cannot overlook the danger that the gravity of the assaults and injuries in this type of case may escalate to even more unacceptable heights.'

[His Lordship referred to various of the sado-masochistic acts which had been performed, that while the appellants had not contracted AIDS two members of the group had died from AIDS, that the assertion that the instruments were sterile could not remove the risk of infection, that cruelty to humans had been supplemented by cruelty to animals in the form of bestiality, and that, given the nature of the acts, it was not surprising there had been no complaint to the police.]

In principle there is a difference between violence which is incidental and violence which is inflicted for the indulgence of cruelty. The violence of sado-masochistic encounters involves the indulgence of cruelty by sadists and the degradation of victims. Such violence is injurious to the participants and unpredictably dangerous. I am not prepared to invent a defence of consent for sado-masochistic encounters which breed and glorify cruelty and result in offences under sections 47 and 20 of the Act of 1861…

Lord Jauncey of Tullichettle…

It was accepted by all the appellants that a line had to be drawn somewhere between those injuries to which a person could consent to infliction upon himself and those which were so serious that con-sent was immaterial. They all agreed that assaults occasioning actual bodily harm should be below the line but there was disagreement as to whether all offences against section 20 of the Act of 1861 should be above the line or only those resulting in grievous bodily harm. The four English cases to which I have referred were not concerned with the distinction between the various types of assault and did not therefore have to address the problem raised in these appeals. However it does appear that in *Donovan; A-G's Reference (No 6 of 1980)*, and *Boyea* (1992) 156 JP 505, [1992] Crim LR 574, the infliction of actual bodily harm was considered to be sufficient to negative any consent. Indeed in *Donovan* and *Boyea* such injuries as were sustained by the two women could not have been described as in any way serious. Cave J in *Coney* also appeared to take the same view. On the other hand, Stephen J in *Coney* appeared to consider that it required serious danger to life and limb to negative consent, a view which broadly accords with the passage in his digest to which I have already referred. A similar view was expressed by McInerney J in the Supreme Court of Victoria in *Pallante v Stadiums Property Ltd* [1976] VR 331.

I prefer the reasoning of Cave J in *Coney* and of the Court of Appeal in the later three English cases which I consider to have been correctly decided. In my view the line properly falls to be drawn between assault at common law and the offence of assault occasioning actual bodily harm created by section 47 of the Offences Against the Person Act 1861, with the result that consent of the victim is no answer to anyone charged with the latter offence or with a contravention of section 20 unless the circumstances fall within one of the well known exceptions such as organised sporting contests and games, parental chastisement or reasonable surgery. There is nothing in sections 20 and 47 of the Act of 1861 to suggest that consent is either an essential ingredient of the offences or a defence thereto....

[I]n considering the public interest it would be wrong to look only at the activities of the appellants alone, there being no suggestion that they and their associates are the only practitioners of homosexual sado-masochism in England and Wales. This House must therefore consider the possibility that these activities are practised by others and by others who are not so controlled or responsible as the appellants are claimed to be. Without going into details of all the rather curious activities in which the appellants engaged it would appear to be good luck rather than good judgment which has prevented serious injury from occurring. Wounds can easily become septic if not properly treated, the free flow of blood from a person who is HIV positive or who has AIDS can infect another and an inflicter who is carried away by sexual excitement or by drink or drugs could very easily inflict pain and injury beyond the level to which the receiver had consented. Your Lordships have no information as to whether such situations have occurred in relation to other sado-masochistic practitioners. It was no doubt these dangers which caused Lady Mallalieu to restrict her propositions in relation to the public interest to the actual rather than the potential result of the activity. In my view such a restriction is quite unjustified. When considering the public interest potential for harm is just as relevant as actual harm. As Mathew J said in *Coney* (1882) 8 QBD 534, 547:

> 'There is however abundant authority for saying that no consent can render that innocent which is in fact dangerous.'

Furthermore, the possibility of proselytisation and corruption of young men is a real danger even in the case of these appellants and the taking of video recordings of such activities suggest that secrecy may not be as strict as the appellants claimed to your Lordships. If the only purpose of the activity is the sexual gratification of one or both of the participants what then is the need of a video recording?

My Lords I have no doubt that it would not be in the public interest that deliberate infliction of actual bodily harm during the course of homosexual sado-masochistic activities should be held to be lawful. In reaching this conclusion I have regard to the information available in these appeals and of such inferences as may be drawn therefrom. I appreciate that there may be a great deal of information relevant to these activities which is not available to your Lordships. When Parliament passed the Sexual Offences Act 1967 which made buggery and acts of gross indecency between consenting males lawful it had available the Wolfenden Report (1957) (Cmnd 247) which was the product of an exhaustive research into the problem. If it is to be decided that such activities as the nailing by A of B's foreskin or scrotum to a board or the insertion of hot wax into C's urethra followed by the burning of his penis with a candle or the incising of D's scrotum with a scalpel to the effusion of blood are injurious neither to B, C and D nor to the public interest then it is for Parliament with its accumulated wisdom and sources of information to declare them to be lawful....

There was argument as to whether consent, where available, was a necessary ingredient of the offence of assault or merely a defence. There are conflicting data as to its effect. In *Coney* Stephen J referred to consent as 'being no defence', whereas in *A-G's Reference (No 6 of 1980)* [1981] 2 All ER 1057, [1981] QB 715 Lord Lane CJ referred to the onus being on the prosecution to negative consent. In *Collins v Wilcock* [1984] 1 WLR 1172, 1177F Goff LJ referred to consent being a defence to a battery. If it were necessary, which it is not, in this appeal to decide which argument was correct I would hold that consent was a defence to but not a necessary ingredient in assault....

I would...dismiss the appeals.

[**Lord Lowry** made a speech dismissing the appeals.]

Lord Mustill...I ask myself not whether as a result of the decision in this appeal, activities such as those of the appellants should *cease* to be criminal, but rather whether the Act of 1861 (a statute which I venture to repeat once again was clearly intended to penalise conduct of a quite different nature) should in this new situation be interpreted so as to *make* it criminal. Why should this step be taken? Leaving aside repugnance and moral objection, both of which are entirely natural but neither of which are in my opinion grounds upon which the court could properly create a new crime, I can visualise only the following reasons:

1. Some of the practices obviously created a risk of genito-urinary infection, and others of septi-caemia. These might indeed have been grave in former times, but the risk of serious harm must surely have been greatly reduced by modern medical science.

2. The possibility that matters might get out of hand, with grave results....If this happened, those responsible would be punished according to the ordinary law, in the same way as those who kill or injure in the course of more ordinary sexual activities are regularly punished. But to penalise the appellants' conduct even if the extreme consequences do not ensue, just because they might have done so would require an assessment of the degree of risk, and the balance of this risk against the interests of individual freedom. Such a balancing is in my opinion for Parliament, not the courts....

3. I would give the same answer to the suggestion that these activities involved a risk of acceler-ating the spread of auto-immune deficiency syndrome, and that they should be brought within the Act of 1861 in the interests of public health. The consequence would be strange, since what is currently the principal cause for the transmission of this scourge, namely consenting buggery between males, is now legal. Nevertheless, I would have been compelled to give this proposition the most anxious consideration if there had been any evidence to support it. But there is none, since the case for the respondent was advanced on an entirely different ground.

4. There remains an argument to which I have given much greater weight. As the evidence in the pre-sent case has shown, there is a risk that strangers (and especially young strangers) may be drawn into these activities at an early age and will then become established in them for life. This is indeed a disturb-ing prospect, but I have come to the conclusion that it is not a sufficient ground for declaring these activ-ities to be criminal under the Act of 1861. The element of the corruption of youth is already catered for by the existing legislation; and if there is a gap in it which needs to be filled the remedy surely lies in the hands of Parliament, not in the application of a statute which is aimed at other forms of wrong-doing.

Leaving aside the logic of this answer, which seems to me impregnable, plain humanity demands that a court addressing the criminality of conduct such as that of the present should recognise and respond to the profound dismay which all members of the community share about the apparent increase of cruel and senseless crimes against the defenceless. Whilst doing so I must repeat for the last time that in the answer which I propose I do not advocate the decriminalisation of conduct which has hitherto been a crime: nor do I rebut a submission that a new crime should be created, penalising this conduct, for Mr Purnell has rightly not invited the House to take this course. The only question is whether these consensual private acts are offences against the existing law of violence. To this question I return a negative response. I would allow these appeals.

Lord Slynn made a speech and said that he would allow the appeals.

Appeals dismissed

Notes and questions

1. The rules seem to be that one cannot consent to the infliction of harm which amounts to (or is likely to amount to?) actual bodily harm or worse *unless* the infliction occurs in the course of conduct which is regarded as falling within a recognized exceptional category: surgery, tattooing, boxing, manly sports, male circumcision, horseplay, etc.

2. Is the level of harm to which one is permitted to consent clearly defined? The judges in *Brown* seem to agree that consent is a complete defence to common assault and (except for persons under 16 and defectives) that it would have been a defence to the charge of inde-cent assault (now repealed, see Sexual Offences Act 2003); yet in *Donovan*, where V con-sented it was held that, but for misdirection, D's convictions for common and indecent assault would have been upheld; and that view seems to have been generally accepted. Lord Lowry however, [1993] 2 All ER at 97, finds this aspect of *Donovan* hard to follow: 'If the jury, properly directed, had found that consent was not disproved, they must have acquitted the appellant of the only charges brought against him. How, then, could they have con-victed the appellant of either of those charges or of the offence of assault, occasioning actual bodily harm, with which he was *not* charged?' Is the answer that it is the law that con-sent is not a defence, even to common assault, if bodily harm, though not charged, is likely or intended? Should that be the law?

3. D (an adult) spanks V (an adult) with her consent. Is D guilty of an offence if (i) he intended to inflict bodily harm, as V desired, but was too timid in his delivery and inflicted only a battery; (ii) he intended to cause only a minor battery (as V desired), but he mis-judged his strength and inflicted actual bodily harm?

4. Are the categories of exceptional conduct clearly defined? Does this list of exceptions based on policy grounds reflect a coherent and desirable approach to the limits of consent? See Law Commission Consultation Paper No 139, *Consent in the Criminal Law* (1995).

5. Counsel for some of the appellants in *Brown* argued that consent should be a defence to a charge under s 47 but not to serious wounding or serious bodily harm under s 20. Lord Templeman rejected this because 'differences between actual bodily harm and serious bodily harm cannot be satisfactorily applied by a jury in order to determine acquittal or convic-tion.' But is this not a distinction which juries are regularly called upon to make?

6. In *Wilson* [1996] 2 Cr App R 241, [1996] Crim LR 573, D branded his initials with a hot knife on his wife's buttocks. She had wanted his initials to be tattooed thereon, but, as he did not know how to do that, she had agreed to the branding instead. D was charged with assault occasioning actual bodily harm, contrary to s 47. The judge held that he was bound by *Brown* to direct the jury to convict. The Court of Appeal quashed D's conviction, saying that they shared the trial judge's disquiet that the proceedings should have been brought. *Brown* was not authority for the proposition that consent was no defence to a charge under s 47 in all circumstances. *Brown* concerned sado-masochism involving torture, danger of serious physical injury and blood infection. The act in *Donovan* was done for the purposes of sexual gratification and had an aggressive element. There was no aggressive element on D's part. D was assisting W to acquire a physical adornment, not logically different from a tattoo. The court asked itself, did public policy and the public interest demand that D's activity should be visited by the sanctions of the criminal law—that is, should the *offence* be extended? and

answered, no. In *Brown*, Lord Templeman thought that the question was whether the *defence* of consent should be extended to the consequences of sado-masochistic activity; and answered, no. Compare the approach of Lord Mustill in *Brown*. May the result then depend on how the court poses the question? Is the effect of *Wilson* that bottom-branding is to be added to a list of exceptions—manly sports, male circumcision, ear-piercing, tattooing, etc—where consent is a defence to a charge under s 47 or s 20? Or does it mean that consent is, after all, a defence to those charges—*except* where public policy demands it should not be? Would the result have been different if Wilson had admitted that he derived sexual gratification from the performance of the operation? Should it be different?

7. In *Emmett* (1999) The Times, 15 October, E participated in sado-masochistic practices with his partner, which included igniting lighter fuel poured over her breasts, and applying ligatures to her neck. E was convicted under s 47 of the OAPA. The Court of Appeal, upheld the conviction, distinguishing *Wilson* on the basis that a s 47 offence had not been committed, there was no evidence of significant harm in that case, and the parties had been married (in the present case the parties had only married since the incident). Is this a convincing basis for distinction? Is it a distinction that would withstand challenge under Article 8 and Article 14 of the ECHR? (see above, p 11)

8. To what extent is the court's decision on whether an activity is to be regarded as an exceptional one in which consent is permitted, based on whether it has a sexual element?

R v Dica

[2004] EWCA Crim 1103, Court of Appeal, Criminal Division

(Lord Woolf CJ, Judge LJ and Forbes J)

[The facts are set out above, p **682**. The court referred to the cases of *Brown*, *Boyea*, *Donovan* etc.]

46. These authorities demonstrate that violent conduct involving the deliberate and intentional infliction of bodily harm is and remains unlawful notwithstanding that its purpose is the sexual gratification of one or both participants. Notwithstanding their sexual overtones, these cases were concerned with violent crime, and the sexual overtones did not alter the fact that both parties were consenting to the deliberate infliction of serious harm or bodily injury on one participant by the other. To date, as a matter of public policy, it has not been thought appropriate for such violent conduct to be excused merely because there is a private consensual sexual element to it. The same public policy reason would prohibit the deliberate spreading of disease, including sexual disease.

47. In our judgement the impact of the authorities dealing with sexual gratification can too readily be misunderstood. It does not follow from them, and they do not suggest, that consensual acts of sexual intercourse are unlawful merely because there may be a known risk to the health of one or other participant. These participants are not intent on spreading or becoming infected with disease through sexual intercourse. They are not indulging in serious violence for the purposes of sexual gratification. They are simply prepared, knowingly, to run the risk—not the certainty—of infection, as well as all the other risks inherent in and possible consequences of sexual intercourse, such as, and despite the most careful precautions, an unintended pregnancy. At one extreme there is casual sex between complete strangers, sometimes protected, sometimes not, when the attendant risks are known to be higher, and at the other, there is sexual intercourse between couples in a long-term and loving, and trusting relationship, which may from time to time also carry risks.

48. The first of these categories is self-explanatory and needs no amplification. By way of illustration we shall provide two examples of cases which would fall within the second.

49. In the first, one of a couple suffers from HIV. It may be the man: it may be the woman. The circumstances in which HIV was contracted are irrelevant. They could result from a contaminated blood transfusion, or an earlier relationship with a previous sexual partner, who unknown to the sufferer with whom we are concerned, was himself or herself infected with HIV. The parties are Roman Catholics. They are conscientiously unable to use artificial contraception. They both know of the risk that the healthy partner may become infected with HIV. Our second example is that of a young couple, desperate for a family, who are advised that if the wife were to become pregnant and give birth, her long-term health, indeed her life itself, would be at risk. Together the couple decide to run that risk, and she becomes pregnant. She may be advised that the foetus should be aborted, on the grounds of her health, yet, nevertheless, decide to bring her baby to term. If she does, and suffers ill health, is the male partner to be criminally liable for having sexual intercourse with her, notwith-standing that he knew of the risk to her health? If he is liable to be prosecuted, was she not a party to whatever crime was committed? And should the law interfere with the Roman Catholic couple, and require them, at the peril of criminal sanctions, to choose between bringing their sexual relation-ship to an end or violating their consciences by using contraception?

50. These, and similar risks, have always been taken by adults consenting to sexual intercourse. Different situations, no less potentially fraught, have to be addressed by them. Modern society has not thought to criminalise those who have willingly accepted the risks, and we know of no cases where one or other of the consenting adults has been prosecuted, let alone convicted, for the consequences of doing so.

51. The problems of criminalising the consensual taking of risks like these include the sheer imprac-ticability of enforcement and the haphazard nature of its impact. The process would undermine the general understanding of the community that sexual relationships are pre-eminently private and essentially personal to the individuals involved in them. And if adults were to be liable to prosecution for the consequences of taking known risks with their health, it would seem odd that this should be confined to risks taken in the context of sexual intercourse, while they are nevertheless permitted to take the risks inherent in so many other aspects of everyday life, including, again for example, the mother or father of a child suffering a serious contagious illness, who holds the child's hand, and comforts or kisses him or her goodnight.

52. In our judgement, interference of this kind with personal autonomy, and its level and extent, may only be made by Parliament....

60. In view of our conclusion that the trial judge should not have withdrawn the issue of consent from the jury, the appeal is allowed....

R v Konzani

[2005] EWCA Crim 706, Court of Appeal, Criminal Division

(Judge LJ, Grigson J and Judge Radford)

[The facts appear above, p 685.]

Judge LJ ...

35. In short, the judge explained that before the consent of the complainant could provide the appellant with a defence, it was required to be an informed and willing consent to the risk of contracting HIV.

...

40. *R v Dica* represented what Lord Mustill in *R v Brown* described as a 'new challenge', and confirmed that in specific circumstances the ambit of the criminal law extended to consensual sexual intercourse between adults which involved a risk of the most extreme kind to the physical health of one participant. In the context of direct physical injury, he pointed out that cases involving the '... consensual infliction of violence are special. They have been in the past, and will continue to be in the future, the subject of special treatment by the law'. In his subsequent detailed examination of the 'situations in which the recipient consents or is deemed to consent to the infliction of violence upon him', activity of the kind currently under consideration did not remotely fall within any of the ten categories which he was able to identify. *Brown* itself emphatically established the clear principle that the consent of the injured person does not form a kind of all purpose species of defence to an offence of violence contrary to s 20 of the 1861 Act.

41. We are concerned with the risk of and the actual transmission of a potentially fatal disease through or in the course of consensual sexual relations which did not in themselves involve unlawful violence of the kind prohibited in *R v Brown*. The prosecution did not seek to prove that the disease was deliberately transmitted, with the intention required by s 18 of the 1861 Act. The allegation was that the appellant behaved recklessly on the basis that knowing that he was suffering from the HIV virus, and its consequences, and knowing the risks of its transmission to a sexual partner, he concealed his condition from the complainants, leaving them ignorant of it. When sexual intercourse occurred these complainants were ignorant of his condition. So although they consented to sexual intercourse, they did not consent to the transmission of the HIV virus.

Notes and questions

1. Why should V be permitted to consent to the risk of a potentially fatal infection of HIV by sex, but not to the risk of infection from the use of implements in genital torture?

2. How should Parliament define the limits of consent to injury or physical harm (or the risk thereof) in criminal law? P. Roberts, 'The Philosophical Foundations of Consent in the Criminal Law' (1997) 17 OJLS 389.

Consent and the ECHR

In *Laskey v UK* (1997) the European Court heard an application made by the defendants in *Brown* alleging breaches of Article 8—the right to respect for private life. The European Court held unanimously there was no violation.

36. The Court observes that not every sexual activity carried out behind closed doors necessarily falls within the scope of Article 8. In the present case, the applicants were involved in consensual sadomasochistic activities for purposes of sexual gratification. There can be no doubt that sexual orientation and activity concern an intimate aspect of private life (see, *mutatis mutandis*, the *Dudgeon v the United Kingdom* judgment of 22 October 1981, Series A no. 45, p. 21, § 52). However, a considerable number of people were involved in the activities in question which included, *inter alia*, the recruitment of new 'members', the provision of several specially-equipped 'chambers', and the shooting of many video-tapes which were distributed among the 'members' ... It may thus be open to question whether the sexual activities of the applicants fell entirely within the notion of 'private life' in the particular circumstances of the case.

However, since this point has not been disputed by those appearing before it, the Court sees no reason to examine it of its own motion in the present case. Assuming, therefore, that the prosecution and conviction of the applicants amounted to an interference with their private life, the question arises whether such an interference was 'necessary in a democratic society' within the meaning of the second paragraph of Article 8....

38. In support of their submission, the applicants alleged that all those involved in the sado-masochistic encounters were willing adult participants; that participation in the acts complained of was carefully restricted and controlled and was limited to persons with like-minded sado-masochistic proclivities; that the acts were not witnessed by the public at large and that there was no danger or likelihood that they would ever be so witnessed; that no serious or permanent injury had been sustained, no infection had been caused to the wounds, and that no medical treatment had been required. Furthermore, no complaint was ever made to the police—who learnt about the applicants' activities by chance....

39. The applicants submitted that their case should be viewed as one involving matters of sexual expression, rather than violence. With due regard to this consideration, the line beyond which consent is no defence to physical injury should only be drawn at the level of intentional or reckless causing of serious disabling injury.

40. For the Government, the State was entitled to punish acts of violence, such as those for which the applicants were convicted, that could not be considered of a trifling or transient nature, irrespective of the consent of the victim. In fact, in the present case, some of these acts could well be compared to 'genital torture' and a Contracting State could not be said to have an obligation to tolerate acts of torture because they are committed in the context of a consenting sexual relationship. The State was moreover entitled to prohibit activities because of their potential danger.

The Government further contended that the criminal law should seek to deter certain forms of behaviour on public health grounds but also for broader moral reasons. In this respect, acts of torture—such as those at issue in the present case—may be banned also on the ground that they undermine the respect which human beings should confer upon each other. In any event, the whole issue of the role of consent in the criminal law is of great complexity and the Contracting States should enjoy a wide margin of appreciation to consider all the public policy options....

43. The Court considers that one of the roles which the State is unquestionably entitled to undertake is to seek to regulate, through the operation of the criminal law, activities which involve the infliction of physical harm. This is so whether the activities in question occur in the course of sexual conduct or otherwise.

44. The determination of the level of harm that should be tolerated by the law in situations where the victim consents is in the first instance a matter for the State concerned since what is at stake is related, on the one hand, to public health considerations and to the general deterrent effect of the criminal law, and, on the other, to the personal autonomy of the individual.

45. The applicants have contended that, in the circumstances of the case, the behaviour in question formed part of private morality which is not the State's business to regulate. In their submission the matters for which they were prosecuted and convicted concerned only private sexual behaviour.

The Court is not persuaded by this submission. It is evident from the facts established by the national courts that the applicants, 'sado-masochistic activities involved a significant degree of injury or wounding which could not be characterised as trifling or transient. This, in itself, suffices to distinguish the present case from those applications which have previously been examined by the Court concerning consensual homosexual behaviour in private between adults where no such feature was present (see the *Dudgeon v the United Kingdom* judgment cited above, the *Norris v Ireland* judgment of 26 October 1988, Series A no. 142, and the *Modinos v Cyprus* judgment of 22 April 1993, Series A no. 259).

46. Nor does the Court accept the applicants 'submission that no prosecution should have been brought against them since their injuries were not severe and since no medical treatment had been required.

In deciding whether or not to prosecute, the State authorities were entitled to have regard not only to the actual seriousness of the harm caused—which as noted above was considered to be significant—but also, as stated by Lord Jauncey of Tullichettle …, to the potential for harm inherent in the acts in question. In this respect it is recalled that the activities were considered by Lord Templeman to be 'unpredictably dangerous'…

Question

Do you agree that the English law is sufficiently certain? And that criminalization is necessary and proportionate within Article 8(2)?

2. WOUNDING AND CAUSING OR INFLICTING GRIEVOUS BODILY HARM, AND CAUSING ACTUAL BODILY HARM

Three closely related offences under the Offences Against the Person Act 1861 require consideration. They are, in descending order of gravity:

Section 18:
Whosoever shall unlawfully and maliciously by any means whatsoever wound or cause any grievous bodily harm to any person…with intent…to do some grievous bodily harm to any person, or with intent to resist or prevent the lawful apprehension of any person, shall be guilty…[of an offence and liable to imprisonment for life].

Section 20:
Whoever shall unlawfully and maliciously wound or inflict any grievous bodily harm upon any other person either with or without any weapon or instrument, shall be guilty…[of an offence and liable to imprisonment for five years].

Section 47:
Whoever shall be convicted upon an indictment of any assault occasioning actual bodily harm shall be liable [to imprisonment for five years]…

CPS charging standards recommend charging s 47 where there is a loss or breakage of teeth, loss of consciousness, extensive or multiple bruising, displaced broken nose, minor fractures, minor non-superficial cuts or psychiatric injury. By comparison, examples of what would usually amount to s 20 include: injury resulting in permanent disability or permanent loss of sensory function; injury which results in more than minor permanent, visible disfigurement; broken or displaced limbs or bones, including fractured skull; compound fractures, broken cheek bone, jaw, ribs, etc; injuries which cause substantial loss of blood, usually necessitating a transfusion; injuries resulting in lengthy treatment or incapacity; psychiatric injury (CPS Charging Standard www.cps.gov.uk/legal/section5/chapter_c.html#10.)

Wounding

In order to constitute a wound, the continuity of the whole skin must be broken. Where a pellet fired by an air pistol hit V in the eye but caused only an internal rupturing of blood vessels and not a break in the skin, there was no wound: *C (a minor) v Eisenhower* [1984]

QB 331. It is not enough that the cuticle or outer skin be broken if the inner skin remains intact. Where V was treated with such violence that his collarbone was broken, it was held that there was no wound if his skin was intact: *Wood* (1830) 1 Mood CC 278. It was held to be a wound, however, where the lining membrane of the urethra was ruptured and bled, evidence being given that the membrane is precisely the same in character as that which lines the cheek and the external skin of the lip.

Question

Why should the criminal law provide a specific offence labelled as 'wounding' rather than treat such cases as grievous or actual bodily harm as necessary? See on the significance of appropriate labelling to reflect the moral differences in harms caused, J. Gardner, 'Rationality and the Rule of Law in Offences Against the Person' [1994] CLJ 520.

Actual and grievous bodily harm: 'cause' and 'inflict'

'Grievous bodily harm' was formerly interpreted to include any harm which seriously interferes with health or comfort; but in *DPP v Smith* the House of Lords said that there was no warrant for giving the words a meaning other than that which they convey in their ordinary and natural meaning. Grievous bodily harm may cover cases where there is no wounding as, for instance, the broken collarbone in *Wood*. Conversely, there might be a technical 'wounding' which could not be said to amount to grievous bodily harm. Whereas s 18 uses the word 'cause', s 20 uses 'inflict'. In a series of cases from 1861 to 1983 it was held or assumed that the words 'inflict' and 'wound' both imply an 'assault'. The effect was that D could be convicted of an offence under s 20 only if it was proved that he wounded or caused grievous bodily harm by committing an assault. The House of Lords in *Wilson* [1984] AC 242, 260, resolved the matter by deciding, following the Australian case of *Salisbury* [1976] VR 452, 461, that 'inflict' does not, after all, imply an assault. Arguably, the case decided no more than that; but Lord Roskill cited the opinion of the Australian court that 'inflict' has a narrower meaning than 'cause' and requires 'force being violently applied to the body of the victim'. The leading case was *Clarence*, above, p 677. These concepts must be considered in the light of the next case.

R v Ireland; R v Burstow
[1997] 4 All ER 225, House of Lords

(Lords Goff, Slynn, Steyn, Hope and Hutton)

[For other aspects of the case, see above, p 670]

Lord Steyn. It will now be convenient to consider the question which is common to the two appeals, namely whether psychiatric illness is capable of amounting to bodily harm in terms of ss 18, 20 and 47 of the 1861 Act. The answer must be the same for the three sections....

  Courts of law can only act on the best scientific understanding of the day. Some elementary distinctions can be made. The appeals under consideration do not involve structural injuries to the brain such as might require the intervention of a neurologist. One is also not considering either psychotic illness or personality disorders. The victims in the two appeals suffered from no such conditions. As a result of the behaviour of the appellants they did not develop psychotic or psychoneurotic conditions. The case was that they developed mental disturbances of a lesser order, namely neurotic disorders. For present purposes the relevant forms of neurosis are anxiety disorders and depressive disorders.

Neuroses must be distinguished from simple states of fear, or problems in coping with everyday life. Where the line is to be drawn must be a matter of psychiatric judgment. But for present purposes it is important to note that modern psychiatry treats neuroses as recognisable psychiatric illnesses (see *Liability for Psychiatric Illness* (Law Com Consultation Paper No 137) (1995) Pt III (The Medical Background) and Mullany and Handford *Tort Liability for Psychiatric Damage* (1993), discussion on 'A medical perspective' pp 24–42, esp p 30, footnote 88). Moreover, it is essential to bear in mind that neurotic illnesses affect the central nervous system of the body, because emotions such as fear and anxiety are brain functions....

[His Lordship referred to developments in the Civil Law.]

The criminal law has been slow to follow this path. But in *R v Chan-Fook* [1994] 2 All ER 552, [1994] 1 WLR 689 the Court of Appeal squarely addressed the question whether psychiatric injury may amount to bodily harm under s 47 of the 1861 Act. The issue arose in a case where the defendant had aggressively questioned and locked in a suspected thief. There was a dispute as to whether the defendant had physically assaulted the victim. But the prosecution also alleged that even if the victim had suffered no physical injury, he had been reduced to a mental state which amounted to actual bodily harm under s 47. No psychiatric evidence was given. The judge directed the jury that an assault which caused a hysterical and nervous condition was an assault occasioning actual bodily harm. The defendant was convicted. Upon appeal the conviction was quashed on the ground of misdirections in the summing up and the absence of psychiatric evidence to support the prosecution's alternative case. The interest of the decision lies in the reasoning on psychiatric injury in the context of s 47. In a detailed and careful judgment given on behalf of the court Hobhouse LJ said ([1994] 2 All ER 552 at 558–559, [1994] 1 WLR 689 at 695, 696):

> 'The first question on the present appeal is whether the inclusion of the word "bodily" in the phrase "actual bodily harm" limits harm to harm to the skin, flesh and bones of the victim...The body of the victim includes all parts of his body, including his organs, his nervous system and his brain. Bodily injury therefore may include injury to any of those parts of his body responsible for his mental and other faculties.'

In concluding that 'actual bodily harm' is capable of including psychiatric injury Hobhouse LJ emphasised that—

> 'it does not include mere emotions such as fear or distress or panic nor does it include, as such, states of mind that are not themselves evidence of some identifiable clinical condition.'

He observed that in the absence of psychiatric evidence a question whether or not an assault occasioned psychiatric injury should not be left to the jury....

The proposition that the Victorian legislator when enacting ss 18, 20 and 47 of the 1861 Act, would not have had in mind psychiatric illness is no doubt correct. Psychiatry was in its infancy in 1861. But the subjective intention of the draftsman is immaterial. The only relevant inquiry is as to the sense of the words in the context in which they are used. Moreover the 1861 Act is a statute of the 'always speaking' type: the statute must be interpreted in the light of the best current scientific appreciation of the link between the body and psychiatric injury.

For these reasons I would, therefore, reject the challenge to the correctness of *R v Chan-Fook* [1994] 2 All ER 552, [1994] 1 WLR 689. In my view the ruling in that case was based on principled and cogent reasoning and it marked a sound and essential clarification of the law. I would hold that 'bodily harm' in ss 18, 20 and 47 must be interpreted so as to include recognisable psychiatric illness....

R v Burstow: the meaning of 'inflict' in s 20

The decision in *R v Chan-Fook* opened up the possibility of applying ss 18, 20 and 47 in new circumstances. The appeal of Burstow lies in respect of his conviction under s 20. It was conceded that in principle the wording of s 18, and in particular the words 'cause any grievous bodily harm to any person', do not preclude a prosecution in cases where the actus reus is the causing of psychiatric injury. But counsel laid stress on the difference in legislative intent: inflict is a narrower concept than cause. This argument loses sight of the genesis of ss 18 and 20. In his commentary on the 1861 Act Greaves, the draftsman, explained the position in *The Criminal Law Consolidation and Amendment Acts* (2nd edn, 1862) pp 3–4:

> 'If any question should arise in which any comparison may be instituted between different sections of any one or several of these Acts, it must be carefully borne in mind in what manner these Acts were framed. None of them was re-written; on the contrary, each contains enactments taken from different Acts passed at different times and with different views, and frequently varying from each other in phraseology, and... these enactments, for the most part, stand in these Acts with little or no variation in their phraseology, and, consequently, their differences in that respect will be found generally to remain in these Acts. It follows, therefore, from hence, that any argument as to a difference in the intention of the legislature, which may be drawn from a difference in the terms of one clause from those in another, will be entitled to no weight in the construction of such clauses; for that argument can only apply with force where an Act is framed from beginning to end with one and the same view, and with the intention of making it thoroughly consistent throughout.'

The difference in language is therefore not a significant factor.

Counsel for Burstow then advanced a sustained argument that an assault is an ingredient of an offence under s 20. He referred your Lordships to cases which in my judgment simply do not yield what he sought to extract from them. In any event, the tour of the cases revealed conflicting dicta, no authority binding on the House of Lords, and no settled practice holding expressly that assault was an ingredient of s 20. And, needless to say, none of the cases focused on the infliction of psychiatric injury. In these circumstances I do not propose to embark on a general review of the cases cited: compare the review in Smith and Hogan *Criminal Law* (8th edn, 1996) pp 440–441. Instead I turn to the words of the section. Counsel's argument can only prevail if one may supplement the section by reading it as providing 'inflict *by assault* any grievous bodily harm'. Such an implication is, however, not necessary. On the contrary, s 20, like s 18, works perfectly satisfactorily without such an implication. I would reject this part of counsel's argument.

But counsel had a stronger argument when he submitted that it is inherent in the word 'inflict' that there must be a direct or indirect application of force to the body. Counsel cited the speech of Lord Roskill in *R v Wilson (Clarence); R v Jenkins (Edward John)* [1983] 3 All ER 448 at 454–455m [1984] AC 242 at 259–260, in which Lord Roskill quoted with approval from the judgment of the full court of the Supreme Court of Victoria in *R v Salisbury* [1976] VR 452. There are passages that give assistance to counsel's argument. But Lord Roskill expressly stated that he was 'content to accept, as did the [court in *Salisbury*], that there can be an infliction of grievous bodily harm contrary to s 20 without an assault being committed' (see [1983] 3 All ER 448 at 455, [1984] AC 242 at 260). In the result the effect of the decisions in *R v Wilson* and *R v Salisbury* is neutral in respect of the issue as to the meaning of 'inflict'. Moreover, in *R v Burstow* [1997] 1 Cr App Rep 144 at 149 Lord Bingham of Cornhill CJ pointed out that in *R v Mandair* [1994] 2 All ER 715 at 719, [1995] 1 AC 208 at 215 Lord Mackay of Clashfern LC observed with the agreement of the majority of the House of Lords: 'In my opinion... the word "cause" is wider or at least not narrower than the word "inflict". Like Lord Bingham of Cornhill CJ I regard this observation as making clear that in the context of the 1861 Act there is no radical divergence between the meaning of the two words'.

That leaves the troublesome authority of the decision of the Court for Crown Cases Reserved in *R v Clarence* (1888) 22 QBD 23, [1886–90] All ER Rep 133. At a time when the defendant knew that he was suffering from a venereal disease, and his wife was ignorant of his condition, he had sexual intercourse with her. He communicated the disease to her. The defendant was charged and convicted of inflicting grievous bodily harm under s 20. There was an appeal. By a majority of nine to four the court quashed the conviction. The case was complicated by an issue of consent. But it must be accepted that in a case where there was direct physical contact the majority ruled that the require-ment of infliction was not satisfied. This decision has never been overruled. It assists counsel's argu-ment. But it seems to me that what detracts from the weight to be given to the dicta in *R v Clarence* is that none of the judges in that case had before them the possibility of the inflicting, or causing, of psychiatric injury. The criminal law has moved on in the light of a developing understanding of the link between the body and psychiatric injury. In my judgment *R v Clarence* no longer assists.

Notes and questions

1. Expert evidence is required to prove a 'recognizable psychiatric illness'. Even where V can give evidence of headaches and physical pain, capable of being ABH and occurring after the assault (*stricto sensu*—not a battery), there must be expert evidence to prove that these were caused by psychiatric injury: *Morris* [1998] 1 Cr App R 386. Serious psychiatric injury is GBH. Does the expert or the jury decide whether it is 'serious'?

2. Is it really feasible to prove that the defendant foresaw that he would or might cause a condition that the expert witness subsequently diagnoses as a recognizable psychiatric injury?—a condition which a judge and jury is not competent to recognize?

3. *Cause and inflict.* We are told that 'cause' and 'inflict' are not synonymous but there is no 'radical divergence' of meaning. Is there *any* difference of meaning? Lord Hope suggests: 'the word "inflict" implies that the consequence of the act is something which the victim is likely to find unpleasant or harmful.' But what about *Brown* [1993] 2 All ER 75, [1994] 1 AC 212, HL, above, p **687**? Everyone was having a jolly good time. If grievous bodily harm had been proved (it was not) would the House really have held that, though there was an unlaw-ful wounding contrary to s 20, there was no unlawful 'inflicting' contrary to that section?

4. In *Dica* (above), the Court of Appeal held:

29. In *R v Ireland: R v Burstow*, ... Lord Steyn recognised that the two words, 'inflict' and 'cause', are not synonymous. In relation to '*Clarence*', he acknowledged that the possibility of inflicting or causing psychiatric injury would not then have been in contemplation, whereas nowadays it is. In his view the infliction of psychiatric injury without violence could fall within the ambit of s.20. Lord Steyn described *Clarence* as a 'troublesome authority', and in the specific context of the meaning of 'inflict' in s.20 said expressly that *Clarence* 'no longer assists'. Lord Hope similarly examined the con-sequences of the use of the word 'inflict' in s.20 and 'cause' in s 18. He concluded that for practical purposes, and in the context of a criminal act, the words might be regarded as interchangeable, pro-vided it was understood that 'inflict' implies that the consequence to the victim involved something detrimental or adverse.

30. Such differences as may be discerned in the language used by Lord Steyn and Lord Hope respectively do not obscure the fact that this decision confirmed that even when no physical violence has been applied, directly or indirectly to the victim's body, an offence under s.20 may be committed. Putting it another way, if the remaining ingredients of s.20 are established, the charge is not answered simply because the grievous bodily harm suffered by the victim did not result from direct or indirect physical violence. Whether the consequences suffered by the victim are physical injuries or psychiatric injuries, or a combination of the two, the ingredients of the offence prescribed by s.20 are identical. If psychiatric injury can be inflicted without direct or indirect violence, or an assault, for

the purposes of s.20 physical injury may be similarly inflicted. It is no longer possible to discern the critical difference identified by the majority in *Clarence*, and encapsulated by Stephen J in his judgment, between an 'immediate and necessary connection' between the relevant blow and the consequent injury, and the 'uncertain and delayed' effect of the act which led to the eventual development of infection. The erosion process is now complete.

31. In our judgment, the reasoning which led the majority in *Clarence* to decide that the conviction under s.20 should be quashed has no continuing application. If that case were decided today, the conviction under s.20 would be upheld. Clarence knew, but his wife did not know, and he knew that she did not know that he was suffering from gonorrhoea. Nevertheless he had sexual intercourse with her, not intending deliberately to infect her, but reckless whether she might become infected, and thus suffer grievous bodily harm. Accordingly we agree with Judge Philpot's first ruling, that notwithstanding the decision in *Clarence*, it was open to the jury to convict the appellant of the offences alleged in the indictment.

5. In *Santana-Bermudez* [2003] EWHC 2908 (Admin) S-B, a drug user, had assured a police officer about to search him that he was carrying no 'sharps'. The officer stabbed her finger on a syringe needle in his pocket during the search. Applying *Miller*, Maurice Kay J said:

… where someone (by act or word or a combination of the two) creates a danger and thereby exposes another to a reasonably foreseeable risk of injury which materialises, there is an evidential basis for the *actus reus* of an assault occasioning actual bodily harm. It remains necessary for the prosecution to prove an intention to assault or appropriate recklessness.

3. RACIALLY AGGRAVATED ASSAULTS

The Crime and Disorder Act 1998 created a new category of racially aggravated crimes and in the wake of 9/11, the Anti-Terrorism, Crime and Security Act 2001 extended these to include religiously aggravated offences. (See E. Burney, 'Using the Law of Racially Aggravated Offences' [2003] Crim LR 28. See generally, M. Malik, 'Racist Crime: Racially Aggravated Offences in the Crime and Disorder Act 1998' (1999) 62 MLR 409; M. Idriss, 'Religion and the Anti-Terrorism, Crime and Security Act 2001' [2002] Crim LR 890.)

Crime and Disorder Act 1998, s 28

28 Meaning of 'racially or religiously aggravated'

(1) An offence is racially or religiously aggravated for the purposes of sections 29 to 32 below if—
   (a) at the time of committing the offence, or immediately before or after doing so, the offender demonstrates towards the victim of the offence hostility based on the victims membership (or presumed membership) of a racial or religious group; or
   (b) the offence is motivated (wholly or partly) by hostility towards members of a racial or religious group based on their membership of that group.

(2) In subsection (1)(a) above—

'membership', in relation to a racial or religious group, includes association with members of that group;
'presumed' means presumed by the offender.

(3) It is immaterial for the purposes of paragraph (a) or (b) of subsection (1) above whether or not the offenders hostility is also based, to any extent, on any other factor not mentioned in that paragraph.

(4) In this section 'racial group' means a group of persons defined by reference to race, colour, nationality (including citizenship) or ethnic or national origins.

(5) In this section 'religious group' means a group of persons defined by reference to religious belief or lack of religious belief.

A person commits an offence under s 29 of the 1998 Act if he commits an offence:

(i)   under s 20 of the OAPA 1861 (malicious wounding or grievous bodily harm, above, p **698**); or

(ii) s 47 of that Act (above, p **698**); or

(iii) a common assault (above p **665**)

which is 'racially or religiously aggravated' for the purposes of s 29.

Offences (i) and (ii), above, are punishable on indictment with seven years' imprisonment (compared with five years for the basic, non-aggravated offence) and offence (iii) with two years, the basic offence being triable only summarily. In cases where offences (i) or (ii) are charged, a jury could convict of the basic offence if they were satisfied that it had been committed, but were not satisfied that aggravation was proved. A jury could not, however, convict of a common assault because that is triable only summarily.

'Race' is widely defined to include colour, nationality (including citizenship) or ethnic or national origins. It has been held that 'African' does not denote an ethnic, but does denote a racial group (*White* [2001] Crim LR 576). The courts have taken an extremely wide view of what constitutes a race and racial group. It has been accepted that the terms are satisfied by non-inclusive expressions as where D demonstrates hostility to V by calling him 'non white' or 'foreign'. It has been said, obiter, that a racially aggravated assault might be committed by one white person on another if the former were, for example, to call the latter 'nigger lover': *DPP v Pal* [2000] Crim LR 756.

'Religious group' means a group of persons defined by reference to religious belief or lack of religious belief. The Act gives no further guidance. Given the broad interpretation in Article 9 of the ECHR, it would seem likely that the domestic courts will interpret the offence as affording protection to a religion as widely understood. By analogy with the interpretation of race, non-inclusive terms will suffice, for example, 'gentile': *DPP v M* [2004] EWHC 1453 (Admin).

Director of Public Prosecutions v Green, Queen's Bench Division, Divisional Court
[2004] EWHC 1225 (Admin)

(Maurice Kay LJ, Rafferty J)

[The facts appear in the judgment.]

Rafferty J. On 24 December 2002 PCs M, C and S attended a Smethwick address so as to arrest the respondent because of a complaint of assault and criminal damage. Upon their arrival she was drunk. Constables M and C, attempting to arrest her, were abused, as she swore and kicked out at them. Once she had been arrested and handcuffed, PC Q and WPC R joined them.

3. The respondent began her abuse of PC Q with 'paki cunt.' Inside the police vehicle she said to him, 'and you can fuck off, you paki', and called him 'a black bastard paki'. He arrested her for a racially aggravated offence. She called him 'a paki' and a 'black bastard' several more times. At the police station she said, 'you paki black bastard'; 'fuck off you black cunt'; 'paki bastard', and 'I fucking hate you, you black bastard'. On one occasion, shortly after arrival at the police station, she called WPC R, 'a white cunt.'

4. The magistrates found that PC Q was of Asian appearance. For reasons not quite clear to us the respondent's best friend, a woman described as 'black', gave evidence that she, the friend, felt that the respondent had no racist tendencies. The respondent herself has children of mixed ethnic origin. She did not give evidence.

[Her ladyship recited the sections of the Act.]

. . .

6. The magistrates considered the incident and the respondent's conduct in totality, reminding themselves of what happened before and during the remarks. They found that she assaulted the officers verbally and physically to make plain her disinclination to be arrested. She abused three officers, apparently of a racial group similar to her own, swearing and shouting.

7. Because of the comment to WPC R, the magistrates concluded that the respondent did not display any hostility to PC Q which she did not also display to WPC R. The abuse was a continuation of her opposition to arrest rather than what they described as 'deliberately engaging in racial hostility' towards PC Q. Her attitude was not, they found, based on his membership of the Asian race, but wholly based on the fact that he was a police officer.

8. They felt unable to conclude that the respondent was anti-Asian or, for that matter, anti-White, and found this to be a one-off incident, motivated by hostility towards the police, aggravated by her drunken state, rather than by PC Q's ethnic origin pursuant to s 28(1)(b).

9. On the evidence as a whole, they were not satisfied that the respondent was racially hostile. From the moment she was handcuffed she would have abused any police officer in whatever way possible. Their reasons for dismissing the case, so far as we can see, were given at the time as follows, at least in part:

'The defendant did say those remarks but she was clearly drunk. She called one PC a racial name and a different PC of different racial origin a different racial name. Bearing this in mind, and the evidence of Jeena Harewood, we do not think that she showed racial hostility. She did not mean to insult the officer in the way the Crown suggest.'

They explain in their case stated that one should read 'intend' for 'mean'.

10. Whilst, ordinarily, using the terms 'paki bastard' et cetera, et cetera, might indicate racial hostility, they found that in context and within the entirety of the incident, excluding her voluntary intoxication when considering racial insult, they were unable to conclude that her undoubtedly abusive words had been motivated by racial hostility. Hence they acquitted her.

11. [One of the questions posed for the court was:]

'(a) Was the court wrong in law on the evidence before it, to conclude that the respondent did not demonstrate racial hostility towards PC Q?'

12. For the respondent the argument is that s 28(1)(a) requires particular concentration on one phrase: the offender must demonstrate towards the victim hostility 'based on' the victim's membership of a racial group. This can be seen either as meaning simple hostility with an element of racism, or hostility wholly or in part due to the victim's race. The respondent prays in aid s 28(3) . . .

Thus, so runs the argument, (s 28(3)) contemplates the basis for hostility as relevant both to sub-ss (a) and (b).

13. In *DPP v Pal* [2000] CLR 756 an Asian-looking male said to another such, 'white man's arse-licker' and 'brown Englishman.' Simon Brown LJ (as he then was) said at para 14:

'...I would wish to make it perfectly plain that I will reject also an argument put before us...to the effect that section 28(1)(a) has no application to:
    "...street arguments when insults may be thrown without thought being given to whether the same are racially abusive, which conduct is already covered by other offences..."

'Were it otherwise, this argument runs:

"..as soon as one racial word is uttered—whatever the motivation—then there is no defence to the charge." '

Finally, at para 16:

'That, of course, is not so. It will always be necessary for the prosecution to prove the demonstration of racial hostility, although the use of racially abusive insults will ordinarily, no doubt, be found sufficient for that purpose.'

14. The appellant on the other hand contends that were s 28(1)(a) by a construction of the words 'based on' (to incorporate motivation) the two subsections would become the same. 'Based on' in s 28(1)(a) means hostility must be directed against the victim and no more than that. This submission is supported in *RG and LT v DPP* [2004] EWHC 183 (Admin), where May LJ at paras 13 and 14, albeit strictly obiter, said of s 28(1)(a):

'That is not so much to indicate the offender's state of mind as to prove what he did or said so as to demonstrate racial hostility towards the victim. Often the demonstration will be by words or shouting.'

Later, at para 14:

'By contrast, section 28(1)(b) is concerned with the defendant's motivation. The offence has to be wholly, or in part, motivated by racial hostility...motive is necessarily a state of mind...to establish [it] will often, perhaps usually, involve the kind of demonstration of racial hostility to which I have referred in relation to section 28(1)(a). The difference, however, is that section 28(1)(a) essentially requires proof of what the offender did, and what he or she did at the time of committing the offence or at a time closely related to it. Motive, in my judgment, is at least capable of being established by evidence relating to what the defendant may have said or done on another or other occasions.'

15. Thus Mr Green for the appellant argues that what the magistrates succeeded in achieving was incorporation into s 28(1)(a) elements additional to the offence: first, motivation based on racial hostility, and second motivation by racial hostility standing proud, absent any other factors, when the remarks were made.

16. Section 28(1)(a), as distinct from (b), creates a racially aggravated offence without the requirement to prove a racist motive. Disposition at the time is irrelevant. Whether or not the respondent generally resented police activity is also, suggests the appellant, irrelevant, as a reading of s 28(3) makes plain. An offender might be minded to offer abuse consequent upon a range of factors, but that cannot diminish or undermine what is contemplated and expressed as 'the additional wrong' of demonstrated racial hostility.

17. Section 28(3) addresses situations in which there has been shown hostility not only as to race but also other factors. Those who sit regularly in criminal courts are sadly accustomed to hearing some police officers addressed as, for example, 'a paki pig bastard', or 'a fat paki motherfucker'. There are present in both those unwelcome epithets more than one factor, but is it to be suggested, the appellant asks rhetorically that such plurality protects from guilt?

18. The appellant relies on the words of Simon Brown LJ in *Pal*, whilst pointing out that there the factual matrix was quite distinct from that before this court. In *Pal* the object, and the object achieved, was to manipulate the race of the victim so as to label him a racial traitor.

19. For my part, I derive considerable assistance from the words of Maurice Kay LJ in *R v Woods* [2002] EWHC 85 (Admin). Having rehearsed the brief factual basis, which was that the accused said, moments before he committed an assault, 'you black bastard', my Lord said:

> 'In my judgment, if the Justices had had regard to that provision [he refers to section 28(3)], it is inevitable that a conviction would have followed. Section 28(1)(a) was not intended to apply only to those cases in which the offender is motivated solely, or even mainly, by racial malevolence. It is designed to extend to cases which may have a racially neutral gravamen but in the course of which there is demonstrated towards the victim hostility based on the victim's membership of a racial group. Any contrary constriction would emasculate section 28(1)(a).'

...

22. In my judgment, the respondent shouted, swore, and kicked at PCs M, C and S, but it was only upon the subsequent arrival and involvement of PC Q that she uttered phrases capable of amounting to racism. Towards the end of her time with him and WPC R she made one remark, 'white cunt', to the latter. That she directed a single foul-mouth comment towards a white woman whose race she mentioned seems to me in no sense to weaken the strength of the appellant's case. It was a brief remark at the conclusion of a chronicle of abuse of PC Q. I can find nothing in statute or in authority to preclude the respondent's behaviour from attracting more than one epithet.

...**25.** For my part, to both questions I would answer in the affirmative. I would quash the acquittal and remit with a direction to convict.

Maurice Kay LJ. 26. I agree. At the heart of Mr Puzey's submission is the proposition that the words 'based on' in s 28(1)(a) import a requirement of a motive based on the victim's race. I do not accept that submission. In my judgment it sits uneasily with what May LJ said in the recent case of *RG and LT* at paras 13 and 14, and with what I said on a previous occasion in the case of *Woods* at para 12.

27. If Mr Puzey were correct, two undesirable consequences would follow: the section would be deprived of much of its impact because a defendant would be able to deflect the emphasis from what he said to some underlying grievance or perceived grievance which caused him to say it; secondly, it would encourage an investigation of motive which, on the face of it, the provision does not require. An investigation of motive is unavoidable under s 28(1)(b), the statute so provides. However, it would be unusual to import a similar requirement where the statute does not expressly call for it. The search for a specific motive can be elusive and complex. That is why the establishment of criminal liability does not generally require it.

28. In my judgment, it would be wholly inappropriate to require it when, as we find, the words of s 28(1)(a), properly construed, does not call for it.

Judgment accordingly

Notes and questions

1. Lord Monson in the debates on the Crime and Disorder Act anticipated this problem and described the section as Orwellian in that it seeks to police people's emotions (Hansard,

HL, 12 February 1998, col 1266). Do you agree? At present, only insults relating to religion and race are criminalized in this way. This highlights the arbitrariness of the legislation—calling someone a 'fat/gay/stupid so and so' is not yet criminal. Should it be?

2. In terms of broader social objective of the legislation, the section may well be regarded as a success if it deters individuals from using racist language in *any* context. Whether this will be the effect or whether those convicted will bear such resentment at the stigma as to become more racist is debatable. See generally E. Burney and G. Rose, 'Racially Aggravated Offences: How is the Law Working?' (2002) HORS 244, and E. Burney, 'Using the Law on Racially Aggravated Offences' [2003] Crim LR 28.

4. ADMINISTERING POISON, ETC

Offences Against the Person Act 1861, s 23:

Whosoever shall unlawfully and maliciously administer to or cause to be administered to or taken by any other person any poison or other destructive or noxious thing, so as thereby to endanger the life of such person, or so as thereby to inflict upon such person any grievous bodily harm shall be guilty of [an offence], and being convicted thereof shall be liable...to [imprisonment] for any term not exceeding ten years...

Offences Against the Person Act 1861, s 24:

Whosoever shall unlawfully and maliciously administer to or cause to be administered to or taken by any other person any poison or other destructive or noxious thing, with intent to injure, aggrieve, or annoy such person, shall be guilty of [an offence], and being...convicted thereof shall be liable to [imprisonment for a term not exceeding five years].

Sections 23 and 24 both speak of 'any poison or other destructive or noxious thing' which suggests a common definition. But the definition appears to have reference, under s 23, to the effect it is required to have and, under s 24, to the intentions of D. Thus if D, intending to kill, places a small amount of cyanide in his victim's glass of milk (cf *White*, above, p **533**) he is guilty of attempted murder but not of the offence under s 23 if the amount was so small that the victim was in no danger of suffering death or grievous bodily harm. D would, however, commit the offence under s 24 because he has administered a noxious thing and his intent to kill is more than enough to satisfy an intent to injure, aggrieve or annoy. Cyanide remains a noxious thing though administered in an amount too small to cause harm. It was held in *Marcus* [1981] 2 All ER 833, [1981] 1 WLR 774, CA, that a thing which would not ordinarily be described as noxious (in that case it was a sedative but it would embrace many proprietary medicines) was noxious if administered in a sufficient amount to injure, aggrieve or annoy.

To complete the offence D must 'administer or cause to be administered to or taken by' the victim the poison or other destructive or noxious thing. In *Gillard* (1988) 87 Cr App R 189, [1988] Crim LR 531, CA, D was convicted of conspiring to commit an offence (the offence being that of administering a noxious thing contrary to s 24) contrary to s 1(1) of the Criminal Law Act 1977 in agreeing with others to spray CS gas (a potent eye, throat and skin irritant) into the faces of P and others. Delivering the judgment of the court, McNeill J said:

Where...the learned recorder was in error was in holding that 'administering' and 'taking' were to be treated effectively as synonymous or as conjunctive words in the section: on the contrary, the repeated use of the word 'or' makes it clear that they are disjunctive. The word 'takes' postulates some 'ingestion' by the victim: 'administer' must have some other meaning and there is no difficulty in including in that meaning such conduct as spraying the victim with noxious fluid or vapour, whether from a device such as a gas canister or, for example, hosing down with effluent. There is no necessity when the word 'administer' is used to postulate any form of entry into the victim's body, whether through any orifice or by absorption.... [T]he proper construction of 'administer' in s24 includes conduct which not being the application of direct force to the victim nevertheless brings the noxious thing into contact with his body.

In *Kennedy*, above, p 63, where D, at V's request supplied him with a heroin-filled syringe with which V injected himself, the court could see no reason why D should not have been convicted under s 23.

There is some authority that a poison or noxious thing is 'administered' by D to V if D secretly puts it into V's drink and V consumes it. This was the opinion, obiter, of the court in *Harley* (1830) 4 C & P 369, and, in *Dale* (1852) 6 Cox CC 14, Wightman J was of the same opinion when directing a jury on a charge of attempting to administer. But, in these cases, the consumption of the *poison* by V was not a voluntary act—V intended to drink nothing but coffee. Where the consumption or injection of the thing is a fully voluntary act by an adult who knows exactly what he is doing (cf *Hill*, below, p 714), it is administered by the person taking it, and by him alone. It is not an offence under s 23 for a person to administer a noxious thing to himself, so the supplier cannot be guilty as a secondary party either. It is perhaps more feasible to argue that D *caused* V to take the drug; but this argument too seems to founder on the point that V's fully voluntary act breaks the chain of causation. Do the tobacco companies *cause* the smokers (who ignore the government health warnings) to smoke? Or are the smokers, now fully aware of the risks, the sole authors of their own misfortune, if it strikes?

Following decisions of the Court of Appeal casting doubt on the decision in *Kennedy*, the Criminal Cases Review Commission referred the case to the Court of Appeal.

R v Kennedy (No 2)
[2005] EWCA Crim 685, Court of Appeal, Criminal Division

(Woolf LCJ, Davis and Field JJ)

The Lord Chief Justice. 31. The last case in the series is the case of *Finlay* [2003] EWCA Crim 3868. Initially there was an issue as to whether Finlay had personally injected the deceased or whether he had merely cooked and prepared the heroin, loaded the syringe and handed it to the deceased who had injected herself. The problem with the defendant's case at the trial was that, even if 'the appellant had not himself wielded the syringe, he would have committed an offence under s.23 if he had caused the administration of the heroin even though he did not himself physically administer it.' As Buxton LJ said in the judgment in *Finlay*:

'Effectively, the only matter in issue was whether it was open to the judge to leave to the jury the possibility that there was a version of events that caused Mr Finlay to be guilty of an offence under Section 23 of the 1861 Act even though he had not himself held the syringe.'

32. This was because the trial judge, anticipating the judgment of this court in *Rogers*, gave a ruling stating:

'So it seems to me that subject to one further point, to which I will turn almost immediately, cooking up heroin, loading it into a syringe, and then giving the syringe to someone who is clearly going to inject themselves almost immediately, is capable of coming within the terms of section 23. Whether or not it does so in any given case is a question of fact which falls for the jury and not the court to decide.'

The last remaining point in relation to section 23 is this. In order to establish limb two of their case, the prosecution would have to prove that the defendant caused the heroin to be administered to, or be taken by, the deceased. In my view it is not necessary for the Crown to prove that the defendant's actions were the sole cause of the deceased injecting heroin. Here, by cooking up, loading the syringe, and handing it to the deceased, the defendant produced a situation in which the deceased could inject and in which an injection by her into herself was entirely foreseeable. It was not a situation in which injection could be regarded as something extraordinary. That being the case, it seems to me that on the authority of *Environment Agency v Empress Car Company Limited, [1999] 2 AC 22* that it would be open to the jury to conclude that the defendants action caused heroin to be administered to, or to be taken by, the deceased.

At the end of the day this is a question of fact for the jury to decide.'

33. Of this part of the ruling on the appeal, Buxton LJ said:

'That clearly sets out the law as it was understood by this court in the case of *R v Rogers*. The test is one of causation. In this case, could it be said that the act of the deceased in taking up the syringe and using it on herself, which are to be assumed to be the facts, prevented Mr Finlays previous acts being causative of the injection. The judge rightly referred to *Environment Agency v Empress Car Company*. In that case Lord Hoffmann said that the prosecution need not prove that the defendant did something which was the immediate cause of death. When the prosecution had identified an act done by the defendant, the court had to decide, particularly when a necessary condition of the event complained of was the act of a third party, whether that act should be regarded as a matter of ordinary occurrence which would not negative the effect of the defendants act; or something extraordinary, on the other hand which would leave open a finding that the defendant did not cause the criminal act or event. That, said Lord Hoffmann, with the agreement of the rest of the House of Lords, was a question of fact and degree to which, in the case before him, the justices had to apply their common sense, as in a jury trial the jury has to apply its common sense. That was exactly the way in which the judge directed himself in his observations on the application that count 2 should be removed from the jury....

Whether or not the defendant caused heroin to be administered to or taken by the deceased is a question of fact and degree which you have to decide, and you should decide it by applying your common sense and knowledge of the world to the facts that you find to be proved by the evidence. The prosecution do not have to show that what the defendant did or said was a sole cause of the injection of heroin into the deceased. Where the defendant has produced the situation in which there is the possibility for heroin to be administered to or taken by Jasmine Grosvenor, but the actual injection of heroin involves an act on part of another—in this case Jasmine herself—then if the injection of heroin is to be regarded in your view as a normal fact of life, in the situation proved by the evidence, then the act of the other person will not prevent the defendants deeds or words being a cause, or one of the causes, of that injection. On the other hand, if in the situation proved by the evidence, injection is to be regarded as an extraordinary event, then it would be open to you to conclude that the defendant did not cause heroin to be administered to or taken by the deceased....

Mr Gibson-Lee really advances two reasons why the judge should not have taken that view, and why he should have considered that count 2 should not have gone to the jury. The first is that on the assumption that it was the deceased who injected herself, that act of itself breaks the chain of causation between whatever it was that the accused did and the actual event of injection. That is a view that is also taken in a critical commentary on the decision in *Rogers* in the Criminal Law Review. We have to say that that approach is not correct. It seeks to make the existence of what used to be called a *novus actus interveniens*, and can now more simply be regarded as an act of another person, as something that as a matter of *law* [emphasis added] breaks the chain of causation. It was that view or assumption that was rejected by the House of Lords in the *Empress Car* case. Intervening acts are only a factor to be taken into account by the jury in looking at all the circumstances, as the judge told them to do.

Secondly, Mr Gibson-Lee says that in any event the facts of this case were such that it simply was not open to the jury to conclude that Mr Finlay had caused the injection. He had done no more than form part of the background, or provide the opportunity of which the deceased availed herself:—in other words, that the case was so extreme or so clear that it was not appropriate for the jury to look at it as a case of causation at all. The judge did not take that view, nor do we. The unhappy circumstances of this case, and in particular the unhappy circumstances of this lady's life and condition, in our view indicate that it was certainly open to a jury to conclude in *Empress Car* terms that in those circumstances, and we emphasise that, it was what Lord Hoffmann described as an 'ordinary' occurrence for the purpose of the law of causation that she should have taken advantage of whatever it was that Mr Finlay did towards her or with her. It is not necessary for that conclusion to decide, as Mr Gibson-Lee suggested it was that she was incapable of knowing what she was doing or had ceased entirely to be a rational being. All that is necessary, in our judgment, is that the circumstances should be such that it could properly be said to fall within the ambit of possible and ordinary events that she will take the opportunity given her. We quite accept that, on facts different from these, there might be more difficulty in coming to that conclusion'

34. It was because of his view that the test to be applied was 'one of causation' that Buxton LJ, like the judge, referred to Lord Hoffmann's speech in *Environment Agency v Empress Car Company Limited*. By focusing on the issue of causation, and by proceeding on the footing that the issue under s.23 was whether the defendant had caused to be administered the drug, Buxton LJ was departing somewhat from the approach of Rose VP in *Rogers*. If Finlay's actions were part and parcel of the administering of the drug or the causing the drug to be administered for the purposes of s.23 of the 1861 Act, then there really could be no problem as to causation as Rose VP indicated in *Rogers*. Of course, if the jury had taken the view that the activities of Finlay formed no more than 'part of the background' to the drug taking or simply 'provide[d] the opportunity of which the deceased availed herself', then the position would be different. Questions of causation would be determined otherwise.

35. The reliance by Buxton LJ on what Lord Hoffmann said in the *Empress* case as to causation is criticised by the Commission and the appellant and in academic articles (see for example, Criminal Law Review 2004 pp 463–7). This raises the question, as the Commission and Mr Bentley point out on behalf of the appellant, whether the *Empress* approach is intended to be of general application, or confined to situations similar to that which was being considered in the *Empress* case.

. . .

40. In *Finlay*, Buxton LJ was suggesting that the approach the House of Lords appropriately applied in the *Empress* case to a statute dealing with pollution could be applied equally here to the issues of causation where the statutory context is very different. It is, however, to be noted that the question of causation can arise on a charge of manslaughter when s.23 of the 1861 Act is not relied upon, and in two different circumstances when s.23 is relied upon. It can arise on the general question of whether the defendant's unlawful action caused the deceased's death. It can also arise on the question of whether the defendant caused to be administered 'any poison or other destructive or noxious thing contrary to s.23'. These are distinct situations.

41. In his summing-up in *Finlay*, the trial judge referred to the need for the prosecution, in relation to the s.23 offence, to prove that the defendant caused the heroin to be administered to, or to be taken by, the deceased. In that context he referred to the *Empress* case. As we understand the position, it was to this context that Buxton LJ was addressing himself when he referred with approval to the approach of the judge to establishing causation in accordance with Lord Hoffmann's speech in the *Empress* case. In that context, this appears to us to be, with respect, an unnecessary sophistication. All the jury had to decide as to causation was whether Finlay's actions were as a matter of fact causative of the deceased taking the action to administer the drug. If it was, his conduct contravened s.23 and was unlawful. Otherwise it was not.

42. It has to be remembered that when considering whether the defendant's act has caused death, what amounts to causation in a case of this nature is not dependent upon a particular

statutory context. Accordingly if a defendant is acting in concert with the deceased, what the deceased does in concert with the defendant will not break the chain of causation, even though the general principles as to causation have to be applied. This was recognised by Lord Steyn when he qualified the general position when saying in *R v Latif & Others* [1996] 2 Cr. App. R. 92 at p 104:

> 'The free, deliberate and informed intervention of a second person, who intends to exploit the situation created by the first, *but is not acting in concert with him* is held to relieve the first actor of criminal responsibility.' (Emphasis added)

43. Kennedy either caused the deceased to administer the drug or was acting jointly with the deceased in administering the drug, Kennedy would be acting in concert with the deceased and there would be no breach in the chain of causation.

44. The exception made for the person 'acting in concert' is of considerable importance. The fact that a person who takes his own life does not commit an unlawful act by so doing, does not mean that a person who helps him to commit that act, if that helping act is contrary to s.23, does not commit an unlawful act. On the contrary, the helper does commit an unlawful act and could be charged under s.23 and convicted. He could also be convicted of manslaughter if the person he was helping dies in consequence. The requirement of an unlawful act is fulfilled. There should, in the appropriate case, be no difficulty in establishing foreseeability of risk. Nor should there be difficulty in establishing causation because the participants were acting in concert.

45. The Commission, in their Statement of Reasons, suggest that if the defendant cannot be an accessory, then nor can he be a joint principal. However, this approach ignores the significance of the independent unlawful act under s.23. If the defendant is guilty of an unlawful act under s.23 of the 1861 Act, this in turn can result in his being guilty of the different offence of manslaughter. So if the defendant is properly proved to have committed an offence under one or other of the limbs of s.23, then, subject to the other requirements of establishing manslaughter, he will be guilty of manslaughter. Insofar as the Commission and Mr Bentley submitted otherwise, we reject their contentions, which are, in any event, inconsistent with previous decisions of this Court which are binding upon us. Keene LJ in *Dias* also recognised that an approach based on s.23 may result in the offence of manslaughter being established 'so long as the chain of causation was not broken'.

46. The Commission argue that taking the reasoning in *Finlay* to its logical conclusion, the outcome would be that a person who assists another to commit suicide by providing a loaded syringe of heroin to another, in order that that person can take his own life, would now become a principal to murder. It is suggested by the Commission that such 'assisted suicide' type situations are analogous to the *Finlay/Kennedy* type situation, save that in the former instance there is a joint intention to kill.

47. In the *Finlay/Kennedy* type situation, the Commission argue that the 'helper' would have the necessary mens rea (intent to cause death or really serious bodily harm, foresight of such consequences providing evidence of the necessary intent; quite different from motive or desire) and, by virtue of the reasoning in *Finlay*, they would also be committing the actus reus of murder (performing an act that was a substantial cause of death) even though the 'helper' may not himself have administered the fatal dose or injection.

48. The Commission add that a logical extension of the *Finlay* reasoning in this way in the present case would effectively drive a 'coach and horses' through the offence of 'assisted suicide' created by s.2 of the Suicide Act 1961. It is also suggested by the Commission that the creation by Parliament of a separate offence of 'assisted suicide,' whereby the 'helper' is treated as the principal to this

separate offence, is demonstrative of the fact that the law, as Parliament understood it prior to 1961, cannot have been that a 'helper' commits the actus reus of manslaughter as principal. The Commission submit that, invoking the doctrine of joint principalship in the *Kennedy/Finlay* type situation would lead to there being a direct and irreconcilable overlap between the s.2 offence and the offence of murder.

49. We recognise the force of these arguments made by the Commission but we reject them. They ignore the consequences created by the existence of the s.23 offence. In addition, Parliament, by enacting the Suicide Act 1961, must be taken to have provided a statutory code for offences, in situations involving an individual deliberately taking his own life. In view of s.2 of the 1961 Act, it would be an abuse to prosecute someone assisting another to commit suicide for murder. Furthermore, in practice, it would not happen. So we do not see this as a dangerous consequence of the views expressed on this appeal and in *Rogers* and *Finlay*.

...

52. In our view, the jury would have been entitled to find (and indeed it is an appropriate finding) that in these circumstances the appellant and the deceased were jointly engaged in administering the heroin. This was the conclusion of this Court on the first appeal, as we understand Waller LJ's judgment, and we do not feel it necessary to take a different view, though we do accept that the issue could have been left by the trial judge to the jury in more clear terms than it was.

53. The point in this case is that the appellant and the deceased were carrying out a 'combined operation' for which they were jointly responsible. Their actions were similar to what happens frequently when carrying out lawful injections: one nurse may carry out certain preparatory actions (including preparing the syringe) and hand it to a colleague who inserts the needle and administers the injection, after which the other nurse may apply a plaster. In such a situation, both nurses can be regarded as administering the drug. They are working as a team. Both their actions are necessary. They are interlinked but separate parts in the overall process of administering the drug. In these circumstances, as Waller LJ stated on the first appeal, they 'can be said to be jointly responsible for carrying out that act'.

54. Whether the necessary linkage existed between the actions of the appellant and the deceased was very much a matter for the jury to determine. The question then arises as to whether the trial judge in the summing up expressed the issue in sufficiently clear terms for the jury? As to this, we share similar reservations to those expressed by Waller LJ in his judgment on the first appeal. There was no need for the jury to find the encouragement that Waller LJ thought was necessary. However, the jury did have to find that the appellant and the deceased were acting in concert in administering the heroin.

Appeal dismissed

Question

Section 23 requires that the administration is 'to another'. Where D has assisted V in the 'combined effort' of administration, who is the 'other' to whom administration has occurred?

R v Cunningham
[1957] 2 All ER 412, Court of Criminal Appeal

The case is set out in the speech by Lord Ackner in *Savage, Parmenter*, above, p **160** at 163.

R v Cato

[1976] 1 All ER 260, 270n, Court of Appeal, Criminal Division

(Lord Widgery CJ, O'Connor and Jupp JJ)

The appellant, with V's consent, administered heroin to him with a syringe causing his death. He was convicted of manslaughter and of an offence under s 23.

Lord Widgery CJ [delivering the judgment of the court, dealt with the conviction for manslaughter, p **628**, above, and continued:]

Thus, a number of things have to be proved in order to establish the offence [under s 23] and the two which are relevant to the argument of counsel for Cato are 'maliciously' and 'noxious'. The thing must be a 'noxious thing' and it must be administered 'maliciously'.

What is a noxious thing, and in particular is heroin a noxious thing? The authorities show that an article is not to be described as noxious for present purposes merely because it has a potentiality for harm if taken in an overdose. There are many articles of value in common use which may be harmful in overdose, and it is clear on the authorities when looking at them that one cannot describe an article as noxious merely because it has that aptitude. On the other hand, if an article is liable to injure in common use, not when an overdose in the sense of an accidental excess is used but is liable to cause injury in common use, should it then not be regarded as a noxious thing for present purposes?

When one has regard to the potentiality of heroin in the circumstances which we read about and hear about in our courts today we have no hesitation in saying that heroin is a noxious thing and we do not think that arguments are open to an accused person in a case such as the present, whereby he may say: 'Well the deceased was experienced in taking heroin: his tolerance was high', and generally to indicate that the heroin was unlikely to do any particular harm in a particular circumstance. We think there can be no doubt, and it should be said clearly, that heroin is a noxious thing for the purposes of s 23.

[The court considered *Cunningham* [1957] 2 All ER 412 at 413 in a passage which is set out above, p **143**, and continued:]

No doubt this is correct in the *Cunningham* type of case where the injury to the victim was done indirectly; done, as it was in that case, by the escape of gas making itself felt in the wholly different part of the house. No doubt if the injury to the victim is indirect, then the element of foresight arises and the element of foresight will be taken from the words of Byrne J in *Cunningham*. But these problems do not arise when the act complained of is done directly to the person of the victim, as it was in this case. We think in this case where the act was entirely a direct one that the requirement of malice is satisfied if the syringe was deliberately inserted into the body of Farmer, as it undoubtedly was, and if Cato at a time when he so inserted the syringe knew that the syringe contained a noxious substance. That is enough, we think, in this type of direct injury case to satisfy the requirement of maliciousness.

Appeal dismissed

Notes and questions

1. In *Hill* (1985) 81 Cr App R 206, CA; revsd (1986) 83 Cr App R 386, HL, D, who admitted he was a homosexual who was attracted to young boys, gave Tenuate Dospan tablets to boys of 11 and 13. He told them they were 'speed' tablets which would make them feel cheerful. These tablets were available only on prescription (D got them on the black market) as slimming tablets and a side effect of them, of which D was aware, was that if taken at the wrong time or in excess of the appropriate dose they could cause sleeplessness. The prosecution's case was that D's intention in giving the tablets was to disinhibit the boys so as to cause them to lose their natural reserve and be more inclined to do things that otherwise they would not do. One of the boys who stayed with D spent a sleepless night but D made no sexual advances. Both boys suffered from diarrhoea and vomiting. The CA quashed D's convictions under s 24 on the ground that the trial judge's direction to the jury left it open to them to convict if D's intention had been only to keep the boys awake. The following question was then certified: 'whether the offence of administering a noxious thing contrary to s 24 . . . is capable of being committed when a noxious thing is administered to a person without lawful excuse with the intention only of keeping that person awake.' In the result the House, restoring D's convictions, held that the trial judge's direction did not leave it open to the jury to convict if they found that D's intention was only to keep the boys awake and accordingly found it unnecessary to answer the certified question. 'It is,' said Lord Griffiths (at 390), 'in any event, a question which it is not sensible to attempt to answer without knowing the factual background against which it is asked. If the noxious thing is administered for a purely benevolent purpose such as keeping a pilot of an aircraft awake the answer will almost certainly be no, but if administered for a malevolent purpose such as a prolonged interrogation the answer will almost certainly be yes.' This appears to have been the view of the Court of Appeal. 'We have no doubt,' said Robert Goff LJ (at 210):

that, in considering whether in any particular case the accused acted 'with intent to injure', it is necessary to have regard not merely to his intent with regard to the effect which the noxious thing will have upon the person to whom it is administered, but to his whole object in acting as he has done. The accused may, in one case, administer the noxious thing with the intent that it would itself injure the person in question; but in another case he may have an ulterior motive, as for example when he administers a sleeping pill to a woman with an intent to rape her when she is comatose. In either case he will, in our judgment, have an intent to injure the person in question, within the words in the section. By way of contrast, if a husband puts a sleeping draught in his wife's nightcap, without her knowledge, because he is worried that she has been sleeping badly and wishes to give her a decent night's sleep, he will commit no offence. So, in each case it is necessary to ask the question: Did the accused have the intention, in administering the noxious thing, to injure the person in question? And in each case it is necessary to look, not just at his intention as regards the immediate effect of the noxious thing upon that person, but at the whole object of the accused. If his intention, so understood, is that the noxious thing should itself injure the person in question, then that is enough; but it will also be enough if he has an ulterior motive that the person should, as a result of taking the noxious thing, suffer injury. Within this latter category there will, in our judgment, fall those cases where the accused intends, in administering the noxious thing, thereby to achieve or facilitate an act of unlawful sexual interference with the person in question—unlawful, either because it is not consented to (as, for example, in the case of rape), or because the law forbids it (as, for example, in the case of sexual intercourse with girls under the age of 16, or of unlawful homosexual activity). In such cases the accused does, we consider, have an intent to injure the person in question within the meaning of those words in the section.

While holding that such an intent falls within the words 'intent to injure' in the section, we do not think it necessary or right to attempt to attach a definitive meaning to those words in this judgment. It may very well be that if, for example, the accused administers a sleeping pill to a person with a view to stealing his property while he is asleep, he will have an intent to injure that person, for the purposes of the section, in the sense of an intent to deprive him of his property. Such an attempt appears to us, at first sight, to fall more naturally within the words 'intent to injure' than the words 'intent to aggrieve'; for, on their natural meaning, the words 'intent to aggrieve' appear to be directed to cases where the intention is to cause distress, and to deprive another person of his property is, we incline to think, not merely distressing, but also injurious to the victim. But we need express no final opinion on the point, which does not arise in the present case, and on which we have heard no argument. We mention it only to show that our decision is intended to indicate that certain categories of case fall within the words 'intent to injure', rather than to provide a complete definition of those words.

2. In *Weatherall* [1968] Crim LR 115 (Judge Brodrick), D administered Tuinal to his wife to make her sleep more soundly so that he could search her handbag for letters which he thought might prove her guilty of adultery. The judge ruled that there was no evidence of an intent to annoy or aggrieve. Do you agree?

3. Suppose that when Cunningham (above) pulled the gas meter from the wall he had realized that the gas would escape into the adjoining house but had thought that the occupants would be no more than mildly discomfited. Could he be convicted of the offences under s 23 and s 24?

4. Does it make sense for the purposes of s 23 to draw, as was done in *Cato*, a distinction between injuries directly and indirectly done? Where the injury is directly done, in what precise respect does Lord Widgery see the mens rea as differing from a case where the injury is caused indirectly?

5. REFORM OF THE LAW

The Home Office Consultation Document referred to above, p **665**, included a draft Bill. The Bill is based on the recommendations first made by the CLRC, 14th Report, *Offences Against the Person*, Cmnd 7844 (1980), adopted in the Law Commission Draft Code and then, in a modified form, in Law Commission Report, Law Com No 218 (1993).

The law in this area is far from satisfactory, for a variety of reasons. The Law Commission recently commented that it 'was defective on grounds both of effectiveness and of justice'. (Consultation Paper No 122, Legislating the Criminal Code: Offences Against the Person and General Principles 1992). It is an area of law which is very clearly in need of reform. The Law Commission Report No 218 contained recommendations, but these have been superseded by those in the Home Office *Consultation Paper on Violence* (1998) on which see J. C. Smith, 'Offences Against The Person: The Home Office Consultation Paper' [1998] Crim LR 317. Relevant clauses provide as follows:

    1. **Intentional serious injury.**—(1) A person is guilty of an offence if he intentionally causes serious injury to another.

        (2) A person is guilty of an offence if he omits to do an act which he has a duty to do at common law, the omission results in serious injury to another, and he intends the omission to have that result.

        (3) An offence under this section is committed notwithstanding that the injury occurs outside England and Wales if the act causing injury is done in England and Wales or the omission resulting in injury is made there.

        (4) A person guilty of an offence under this section is liable on conviction on indictment to imprisonment for life.

2. **Reckless serious injury.**—(1) A person is guilty of an offence if he recklessly causes serious injury to another.

    (2) An offence under this section is committed notwithstanding that the injury occurs outside England and Wales if the act causing injury is done in England and Wales.

    (3) A person guilty of an offence under this section is liable—

        (a) on conviction on indictment, to imprisonment for a term not exceeding 7 years;

        (b) on summary conviction, to imprisonment for a term not exceeding 6 months or a fine not exceeding the statutory maximum or both.

3. **Intentional or reckless injury.**—(1) A person is guilty of an offence if he intentionally or recklessly causes injury to another.

    (2) An offence under this section is committed notwithstanding that the injury occurs outside England and Wales if the act causing injury is done in England and Wales.

    (3) A person guilty of an offence under this section is liable—

        (a) on conviction on indictment, to imprisonment for a term not exceeding 5 years;

        (b) on summary conviction, to imprisonment for a term not exceeding 6 months or a fine not exceeding the statutory maximum or both.

4. **Assault.**—(1) A person is guilty of an offence if—

        (a) he intentionally or recklessly applies force to or causes an impact on the body of another, or

        (b) he intentionally or recklessly causes the other to believe that any such force or impact is imminent.

    (2) No such offence is committed if the force or impact, not being intended or likely to cause injury, is in the circumstances such as is generally acceptable in the ordinary conduct of daily life and the defendant does not know or believe that it is in fact unacceptable to the other person.

    (3) A person guilty of an offence under this section is liable on summary conviction to imprisonment for a term not exceeding 6 months or a fine not exceeding level 5 on the standard scale or both.

5. **Assault on a constable.**—(1) A person is guilty of an offence if he assaults—

        (a) a constable acting in the execution of his duty, or

        (b) a person assisting a constable acting in the execution of his duty.

    (2) For the purposes of this section a person assaults if he commits the offence under section 4.

    (3) A reference in this section to a constable acting in the execution of his duty includes a reference to a constable who is a member of a police force maintained in Scotland or Northern Ireland when he is executing a warrant, or otherwise acting in England or Wales, by virtue of an enactment conferring powers on him in England and Wales.

    (4) For the purposes of subsection (3) each of the following is a police force—

        (a) a police force within the meaning given by section 50 of the Police (Scotland) Act 1967;

        (b) the Royal Ulster Constabulary and the Royal Ulster Constabulary Reserve.

    (5) A person guilty of an offence under this section is liable on summary conviction to imprisonment for a term not exceeding 6 months or a fine not exceeding level 5 on the standard scale or both.

6. **Causing serious injury to resist arrest etc.**—(1) A person is guilty of an offence if he causes serious injury to another intending to resist, prevent or terminate the lawful arrest or detention of himself or a third person.

    (2) The question whether the defendant believes the arrest or detention is lawful must be determined according to the circumstances as he believes them to be.

(3) A person guilty of an offence under this section is liable on conviction on indictment to imprisonment for life.

7. Assault to resist arrest etc.—(1) A person is guilty of an offence if he assaults another intending to resist, prevent or terminate the lawful arrest or detention of himself or a third person.

(2) The question whether the defendant believes the arrest or detention is lawful must be determined according to the circumstances as he believes them to be.

(3) For the purposes of this section a person assaults if he commits the offence under section 4.

(4) A person guilty of an offence under this section is liable—

   (a) on conviction on indictment, to imprisonment for a term not exceeding 2 years;

   (b) on summary conviction, to imprisonment for a term not exceeding 6 months or a fine not exceeding the statutory maximum or both.

FURTHER READING

On assault and battery

M. Hirst, 'Assault, Battery and Indirect Violence' [1999] Crim LR 557

J. Horder, 'Reconsidering Psychic Assault' [1998] Crim LR 392

On consent

M. Allen, 'Consent and Assault' (1994) 58 J Crim Law 183

N. Bamforth, 'Sadomasochism and Consent' [1994] Crim LR 661.

M. Giles, 'Consensual Harm and the Public Interest' (1994) 57 MLR 101

D. Kell, 'Social Disutility and Consent' (1994) OJLS 121

Law Commission, LCCP No 134, 'Consent and Offences against the Person' (1994)

Law Commission, LCCP No 139, 'Consent in Criminal Law' (1995)

D. C. Ormerod, 'Consent and Offences Against the Person: Law Commission Consultation Paper No 134' (1994) 57 MLR 928

D. C. Ormerod and M. J. Gunn, 'Consent—A Second Bash' [1996] Crim LR 694

P. Roberts, 'The Philosophical Foundations of Consent in the Criminal Law' (1997) 17 OJLS 389

S. Shute, 'Something Old, Something New, Something Borrowed—Three Aspects of the Consent Project' [1996] Crim LR 684

On HIV transmission

S. H. Bronitt, 'Spreading Disease and the Criminal Law' [1994], Crim LR 21

J. Dine and B. Watt, 'The Transmission of Disease During Consensual Sexual Activity and the Concept of Associative Autonomy', 4 *Web Journal of Current Legal Issues* (1998)

D. C. Ormerod and M. J. Gunn, 'Criminal Liability for the Transmission of HIV', 1 *Web Journal of Current Legal Issues* (1996)

K. J. M. Smith, 'Sexual Etiquette, Public Interest and the Criminal Law', 42 *Northern Ireland Legal Quarterly* [1991] 309

20

Sexual offences

1. THE BACKGROUND TO THE SEXUAL OFFENCES ACT 2003

The CLRC's Fifteenth Report, *Sexual Offences* (Cmnd 9213, 1984) made numerous recommendations for the reform of the law of sexual offences. They were incorporated in the Law Commission's Draft Criminal Code, Chapter II, but were never implemented. Many of those recommendations were overtaken by events, both in case law and statute. The need for reform became more urgent particularly as attrition rates (that is, the proportion of those cases reported as sexual assaults which did not lead to a successful conviction) rose dramatically in the 1980s and 1990s. See the *Report of the Joint Investigation into the Investigation and Prosecution of Cases Involving Allegations of Rape* (2002) HMCPSI. In July 2000 the Home Office published a consultation paper, *Setting the Boundaries, Reforming the law on sexual offences* Home Office, seeking opinions on proposals for the reform of the whole law of sexual offences (see N. Lacey, 'Beset by Boundaries' [2001] Crim LR 3). That report is the foundation for the Sexual Offences Act 2003 and is worthy of further consideration from those researching into the new offences, see also *Protecting the Public: strengthening protection against sex offenders and reforming the law on sexual offences*. Cm 5668 2002, and the range of guides available at www.homeoffice.gov.uk/justice/sentencing/sexualoffencesbill/index.html.

For detailed criticism of the old law see J. Temkin, *Rape and the Legal Process* (2nd edn, 2002). Most of the relevant law was contained in the Sexual Offences Act 1956, but that was itself merely a consolidation of various statutes dating back to the late nineteenth century. The law was widely regarded as: incoherent; discriminatory; failing to reflect the morality and prevalent sexual attitudes and practices of the twenty-first century; providing inadequate protection for the vulnerable, but failing also to respect the sexual autonomy of those capable of making informed choices about their sexual behaviour. Many aspects of the old law were so discriminatory as to be incompatible with ECHR obligations: for example, offences such as gross indecency between males breached Article 8: *ADT v UK* (2000) 31 EHRR 803. The Government review in *Setting the Boundaries* set out to produce coherent and clear offences which protect individuals, especially children and the more vulnerable, from abuse and exploitation; to enable abusers to be more appropriately punished and to be fair and non-discriminatory in accordance with the ECHR and Human Rights Act 1998.

The 2003 Act redefines many of the offences found in the old legislation, but introduces a great number of new offences. It is not however a complete codification of sexual offences. It has been subjected to stringent and cogent criticism: see especially J. Temkin and A. Ashworth,

'Rape, Sexual Assaults and the Problems of Consent' [2004] Crim LR 328; J. R. Spencer, 'Child and Family Offences' [2004] Crim LR 347. It is impossible to deal with all of the offences in this chapter. The focus is on the non-consensual and child offences.

2. NON-CONSENSUAL OFFENCES

(1) RAPE

Sexual Offences Act 2003, s 1

(1) A person (A) commits an offence if—

    (a) he intentionally penetrates the vagina, anus or mouth of another person (B) with his penis,

    (b) B does not consent to the penetration, and

    (c) A does not reasonably believe that B consents.

(2) Whether a belief is reasonable is to be determined having regard to all the circumstances, including any steps A has taken to ascertain whether B consents.

The actus reus

For the first time in England and Wales, rape includes non-consensual fellatio. It was argued by some that this devalues 'real' rape. The Court of Appeal has emphasized that in sentencing terms there is no distinction based on which orifice is penetrated: *Ismail* [2005] EWCA Crim 397. Indictments should specify which orifice is penetrated. The offence can be committed as a principal offender only by a man. Note that s 2 below provides a new offence of sexual penetration by objects other than the penis. Section 79(3) makes clear that surgically reconstructed body parts are included as parts of the 'body'. A, with his surgically reconstructed penis, can rape B with her surgically reconstructed vagina. This was something that had posed a problem under the old law: see M. Hicks and G. Branston, 'Transsexual Rape—A Loophole Closed?' [1997] Crim LR 565. Under the 1956 Act, it was held that sexual intercourse was a continuing act, and if B withdrew consent at any time during the act, A would commit the actus reus of rape: *Kaitamaki v R* [1985] AC 147, PC. Rape is now defined in terms of 'penetration' rather than 'sexual intercourse', and s 79(2) provides that penetration is a continuing act. Section 44 of the 1956 Sexual Offences Act (now repealed) provided that it was not necessary to prove the completion of intercourse by the 'emission of seed'. There is no such provision in the 2003 Act.

Consent

The crucial element of rape remains the absence of consent. Without that, penile penetration is not merely not criminal, it is an explicit expression of intimacy. Sections 74–76 of the 2003 Act seek to provide a clear definition of consent that can be applied consistently. These sections create three separate routes by which the prosecution may seek to establish absence of consent:

- s 76: conclusive (irrebuttable) presumptions;
- s 75: rebuttable presumptions;
- s 74: general definition of consent.

Section 76—Conclusive presumptions

If A performed the relevant act (in the case of rape that is penetration, it will differ as between the other non-consensual offences) and any one of the circumstances specified in s 76 (2) existed, it is to be *conclusively presumed* that the complainant did not consent to the relevant act, and that A did not believe that the complainant consented. The circumstances in s 76(2) are:

(a) the defendant intentionally deceived the complainant as to the nature or purpose of the relevant act;

(b) the defendant intentionally induced the complainant to consent to the relevant act by impersonating a person known personally to the complainant.

Notes and questions

1. Under the 1956 Act, frauds by A as to the nature of the act would vitiate B's consent. In *R v Flattery* (1877) 2 QBD 410 (approved in *R v Williams* [1923] 1 KB 340) A told B, aged 19, that he could cure her of her fits by performing a surgical operation upon her. She allowed him to have intercourse with her, believing that the act was a surgical one. This would be a fraud as to the nature of the act under s 76(2)(a).

2. How would *R v Linekar* [1995] 2 WLR 237, [1995] Crim LR 321 be decided under s 76(2)? A was charged with raping a prostitute, B. A approached B and she agreed to have intercourse with him for £25. Having had intercourse D left without paying.

3. A tells B that he will use a condom when he has sex with her. He does not do so. Rape?

4. Why are these frauds under s 76(2) conclusive of anything beyond A's absence of a belief in consent?

5. Note that there is no replacement for s 3 of the 1956 Act—procuring sexual intercourse by false pretences. This is lamentable. It means that the jury are left with the stark alternative of rape or nothing—there is no alternative offence where they believe that the fraud was not so significant as to vitiate consent.

6. The provisions apply to the non-consensual offences that do not involve penile penetration, and as a matter of common sense it is more likely that frauds as to the nature or purpose of those acts will succeed. What of A who tells B, accurately, that an intimate medical examination is necessary. She allows this to happen. X, A's friend derives sexual gratification from watching (cf *Bolduc & Bird* (1967) 63 DLR 2d 82). Is there a deception as to 'the purpose'?

7. In *Tabassum* [2000] 2 Cr App R 328, [2000] Crim LR 686, CA, A, who was not medically qualified, persuaded women to allow him to measure their breasts by representing (perhaps truthfully) that he was doing so for the purpose of a database he was preparing for doctors. His convictions for indecent assault were upheld, although the women were fully aware of the nature of the acts to be done because (i) they would not have consented to these acts if they had not believed that he had medical qualifications and (ii) the defendant knew that this was so. How would the case be decided under s 76?

8. In s 76(2)(b) are all people B has ever met 'known personally to' B? Is it only those with whom B has had some greater degree of intimacy? Can B be known personally to a person by

email correspondence? Consider the couple who arrange to meet after internet dating. A gets cold feet and decides he cannot face meeting B. X, his friend steps in and assumes D's name. Is there a conclusive presumption that B was not consenting to any subsequent sexual activity?

9. If B visits a surgery and is told that the doctor on duty is Dr A, and B allows A to perform an intimate examination, which frauds by Dr A should negative B's apparent consent? That 'A' is really called 'X'? That A is not medically qualified? Which frauds are caught by s 76? See *Richardson* [1999] Crim LR 62, above, p 676.

Section 75—Evidential presumptions

If A is proved to have performed the relevant act to which s 75 applies (in the case of rape that is penile penetration), and it is proved that any of the circumstances listed in sub-s (2) exists and A knows it exists, the complainant is taken not to have consented and A not to have a reasonable belief in her consent unless sufficient evidence is adduced to raise the issue.

The circumstances in sub-s (2) are:

(a) any person was, at the time of the relevant act or immediately before it began, using violence against the complainant or causing the complainant to fear that immediate violence would be used against him;

(b) any person was, at the time of the relevant act or immediately before it began, causing the complainant to fear that violence was being used, or that immediate violence would be used, against another person;

(c) the complainant was, and the defendant was not, unlawfully detained at the time of the relevant act;

(d) the complainant was asleep or otherwise unconscious at the time of the relevant act;

(e) because of the complainant's physical disability, the complainant would not have been able at the time of the relevant act to communicate to the defendant whether the complainant consented;

(f) any person had administered to or caused to be taken by the complainant, without the complainant's consent, a substance which, having regard to when it was administered or taken, was capable of causing or enabling the complainant to be stupefied or overpowered at the time of the relevant act.

(3) In subsection (2)(a) and (b), the reference to the time immediately before the relevant act began is, in the case of an act which is one of a continuous series of sexual activities, a reference to the time immediately before the first sexual activity began.

Notes and questions

1. In Parliament, Baroness Scotland of Asthal stated:

In order for these presumptions not to apply, the defendant will need to satisfy the judge from the evidence that there is a real issue about consent that is worth putting to the jury. The evidence relied on may be, for example, evidence that the defendant himself gives in the witness box, or evidence given on his behalf by a defence witness, or evidence given by the complainant during cross-examination. If the judge is satisfied that there is sufficient evidence to justify putting the issue of consent to the jury, then the issues will have to be proved by the prosecution in the normal way. If the judge does not think the evidence relied on by the defendant meets the threshold, he will direct the jury to find the defendant guilty. Hansard, HL col 670 (17 June 2003).

2. Any one of the circumstances must be 'proved' before the presumption bites. A has to *know* that 'those circumstances existed' (s 75(1)(c)). But the requirement is only that any *one* circumstance is proved (s 75(1)(b)). The presumption only bites in the first place if three issues are proved by the prosecution—the sexual act (in rape that is penile penetration), the specified circumstance, and A's awareness of it.

3. Why do these presumptions apply to the issue of consent rather than merely to A's belief? There is no requirement that the existence of the circumstances listed in (a)–(f) *caused* B's lack of consent. The absence of consent is simply presumed.

4. The section places an obligation on A to raise sufficient evidence to raise an issue, and is more likely to withstand ECtHR challenge than original versions of the Bill which had reverse burdens of proof. A problem stems from the fact that there is no direct match between the issues proved by the prosecution in s 75(1) and the issues A is obliged to raise evidence about. The prosecution are establishing the act, the circumstance and the awareness of the circumstance. A is not required to rebut those directly. He has to rebut the presumed legal consequences of the elements proved by the prosecution—A rebuts consent/reasonable belief in consent. For example, the prosecution prove that A had sex and that the circumstance existed—B was physically disabled and produce some evidence that A was aware of that circumstance. A then raises an issue that although he was aware of the disability, he reasonably believed in B's consent but does not challenge that sex occurred nor that she was disabled. It seems that the presumption still bites in relation to the absence of consent. The prosecution might prove absence of consent merely by proving the three initial elements of the presumption in sub-s (1). Is it for the judge to decide whether or not A's evidential burden is discharged. If sufficient evidence is adduced to raise an issue, can the prosecution still get home by satisfying the jury of the circumstance and A's knowledge of it? Surely not. If A satisfies the evidential burden in relation to the reasonable belief in consent, section 75 has no further part to play, even in proving that V was not in fact consenting.

Threats of violence

5. The threat of/actual violence in (a) and (b) need not emanate from A. This is welcomed. Why is the element in (a) one of immediate violence? What if A threatens B that he will get her 'one day' unless she has sex with him now? Will the court interpret this as flexibly as in offences against the person? What of threats less than those of force/violence? These can also vitiate consent, but the presumption will not apply. There is no section to replace s 2 of the Sexual Offences Act 1956 (procuring sexual intercourse by threats).

6. Has the new law dealt adequately with the need to criminalize sexual conduct where B claims that she was not consenting although she offered no physical resistance and was not threatened with violence by A? Is English law compatible with the obligation to protect complainants from sexual attack (amounting to inhuman and degrading treatment contrary to Article 3 of the ECHR)? Cf *M C v Bulgaria* [2003] ECHR 39272/98.

Unconscious victims

7. There is no stipulation as to the cause of the lack of consciousness; it could arise from self-induced intoxication. The presumption will deal with cases such as *Malone* [1998] 2 Cr App R 447 where A was alleged to have had intercourse with a 16-year-old who was so drunk she could not walk. In *Protecting the Public*, the Government rejected a broader suggestion for a provision that 'someone who is inebriated could claim they were unable to give consent—as opposed to someone who was unconscious for whatever reason, including because of alcohol' on the ground that it would give rise to 'mischievous accusations'. Is the new law too narrow? Under the 1956 Act, if a complainant, through alcohol or drugs, was not capable of exercising a judgement on consent, she was not consenting—now there is merely a presumption of non-consent. Is the new law too wide? A, who performs a relevant sexual act (note that the presumption applies to offences of touching and not just penetrative acts) on his sleeping partner as a gesture of intimacy to wake her is presumed to have acted without her consent.

Stupefying complainants

8. This provision was introduced late in the Bill's progress as a response to the growing concern over 'drug assisted rape'. See E. Finch and V. Munro, 'Intoxicated Consent and the Boundaries of Drug Assisted Rape' [2003] Crim LR 773; 'The Sexual Offences Act 2003: Intoxicated Consent and Drug Assisted Rape Revisited' [2004] Crim LR 789. Under the old law there was a much narrower offence under s 4(1) of 1956 Act applicable to administering drugs to women with intent to stupefy or overpower in order only to facilitate intercourse. The new presumption of non-consent applies to complainants of both sexes and to sexual acts other than vaginal intercourse.

9. Although targeted at drugs which induce states of incapacity such as Rohypnol and GHB, (gamma hydroxyl butyrate acid) there is no statutory limitation on the type of substance which will trigger the presumption. Alcohol is certainly capable of satisfying the definition, so A who surreptitiously laces B's soft drink with spirits will be caught. If B's consumption is purely voluntary and fully informed the presumption does not bite. What if B indicates at the beginning of the date that she would not have sex with A, and A surreptitiously laces B's drink with potent alcohol, it may be that B later willingly engages in sexual activity with A (not being unconscious nor stupefied); her inhibitions having been lowered. Is A nevertheless presumed to be acting without consent?

10. Section 61 introduces an offence of intentional administration of a substance/causing it to be taken by B without consent with intent to stupefy/overpower to enable any person to engage in sex with B. This is a further response to the growing problem of drug assisted rape. This covers A spiking B's drinks as well as administering drugs such as Rohypnol. It does not extend to A encouraging B to drink alcohol so that A may more readily persuade B to have sex. It applies where A himself administers the substance to B, and where A causes the substance to be taken by B, with administering it. There is no requirement that B actually is involved in any sexual activity.

Section 74

Section 74 provides that:

a person consents if he agrees by choice, and has the freedom and capacity to make that choice.

This definition, based on 'free agreement', is intended to emphasize that the absence of the complainant's protest, resistance or injury does not necessarily signify his consent.

Notes and questions

1. Although the Act is silent as to the precise moment at which B's consent or agreement must be present, it is clear that the relevant time is that of the alleged sexual wrongdoing. What if B has indicated to A his willingness to engage in sexual activity later that evening, but then becomes so heavily intoxicated that at the time of the sexual act B is incapable of making any coherent decision? Or where B initially indicates his *dis*inclination to engage in sexual activity but later does so when voluntarily intoxicated?

2. J. Temkin and A. Ashworth ([2004] Crim LR 328) point out that freedom is only used to rule out the suggestion of some or all of its antitheses, (see p 336, citing J. Austin, 'A Plea for Excuses' in H. Morris (ed) *Freedom and Responsibility* (1961) p 8). From what must B be free to be consenting? Fear? Fear of what? Is freedom, a sufficiently clear concept to use to define such an important aspect of these grave offences?

3. Is the jury to apply a proportionality test? The greater the pressure facing B the less 'freedom' he has to make his choice to engage in sexual activity. In which of the following cases has B freely agreed? A threatens to divorce B unless B has sex? A threatens to blackmail B by disclosing pornographic images of her unless she has sex? (In *Harold* (1984) 6 Cr App R (S) 30, CA, A was convicted of attempting to procure intercourse with B where he threatened to disclose to B's employers that she had once been a prostitute.) A threatens to dismiss B from employment unless she has sex? A threatens never to speak to B unless she has sex?

4. What of a police officer who secures the woman's submission by threatening to report her for an offence if she does not? Winn J once ruled that the police officer had no case to answer on a charge of rape but in *Wellard* (1978) 67 Cr App R 364 at 368, the court noted, without comment, that W had previously been convicted of rape where he had pretended to be a security officer and had secured the victim's submission to sexual intercourse by saying that otherwise he would inform the police and her parents that she had been having intercourse in a public place. Does the victim in such cases as these any more consent than the victim who submits to avoid personal violence? If not, what of the actress who submits to sexual intercourse by a film producer who tells her that otherwise she will not get a part in the film? Is it a possible distinction that the actress gets what she wants (the part in the film) whereas in the *Wellard* situation she merely avoids what she does not want (disclosure to police and parents)? Do the actress and the girl in *Wellard* consent? Is there a difference between offers and threats in this context?

5. Under the 1956 Act, the leading authority on consent was *R v Olugboja* (1981) 73 Cr App R 344 in which O had sex with V. She did not scream or struggle because she was too frightened, having been raped earlier and witnessed her friend being raped. O claimed that V's lack of protest meant that she was consenting. The Court of Appeal confirmed that rape was an offence against consent, not one requiring proof of violence. 'It is wrong to assume that the woman must show signs of injury or that she must always physically resist before there can be a conviction for rape.' This aspect of the decision was of critical importance given that the majority of rapes are not stranger rapes committed by sudden attacks, but by those known to the victim. The court held that 'It is for the jury in distinguishing between real consent and mere submission to use their good sense experience and knowledge of

human nature and modern behaviour in deciding the issue of consent. . . . [The jury should be] directed to concentrate on the state of mind of the victim immediately before the act of sexual intercourse, having regard to all the relevant circumstances, and in particular the events leading up to the act, and her reaction to them showing their impact on her mind. Apparent acquiescence after penetration does not necessarily involve consent . . .' per Dunn LJ at p 351. (See S. Gardner, 'Appreciating Olugboja' (1996) 16 LS 275 arguing that this respects the autonomy of the victim; cf Glanville Williams suggesting it was 'one more manifestation of the deplorable tendency of the criminal courts to leave important questions of legal policy to the jury', TBCL (2nd edn, 1983) at 551. How would the jury be directed now? Is the result any more certain?

6. 'Choice' presupposes that B has options from which to choose and that in turn surely presupposes B is possessed of adequate information about each to make an 'informed' choice between them. Note that the Court of Appeal has confirmed that a complainant's consent to the risk of contracting HIV has to be an informed consent: *Konzani* [2005] EWCA Crim 706 (above p **685**).

7. 'Capacity' is not further defined. Is what matters whether B has the *mental* capacity to choose to perform the specified act with A on the occasion in question? It is unclear to what extent B must have the capacity to understand the consequences of the action as well as its nature. For example, must B understand the risks of disease and pregnancy from unprotected intercourse in case of penile penetration? No further clarification, indeed only obfuscation is generated by cross-referring to the offences protecting those with a mental disorder in s 30 whereby: B is unable to refuse if (a) he lacks the capacity to choose whether to agree to the [activity] (whether because he lacks sufficient understanding of the nature or reasonably foreseeable consequences of what is being done, or for any other reason), or (b) he is unable to communicate such a choice to A.

Mens rea of rape

Director of Public Prosecutions v Morgan
[1975] 2 All ER 347, House of Lords

The case is set out at p **181**, above.

After *Morgan* and following the Heilbron Report (Cmnd 6352, 1975) rape was redefined in s 1(1) of the Sexual Offences (Amendment) Act 1976 to include the case where the defendant was reckless as to whether the victim consents. The mens rea became accepted to be a state where A was reckless in the sense that he 'couldn't care less' whether B consented. The test was subjective. Someone cannot be said not to care less about something unless he has realized that there is a risk of it, and carried on. It might be that he has not in fact thought about it and if he had he would not have cared less, but that was not the test. It remained the case that A's unreasonable beliefs that B was consenting, if believed by the jury, would lead to an acquittal. There was little categorical evidence that *Morgan* defences were successfully run, so jurors were presumably not readily believing defendants' spurious claims. Nevertheless, the plea was easy to run and difficult to disprove, and sent an undesirable message—that it is acceptable to take unreasonable risks as to your partner's consent to sexual conduct. See J. Horder, 'Cognition, Emotion and Criminal Culpability' (1990) 106 LQR 469, 477; T. Pickard, 'Culpable Mistakes' (1980) 30 U Toronto LJ 75; C. Wells, 'Swatting the Subjectivist Bug' [1982] Crim LR 209.

One of the most significant effects of the 2003 Act is to reverse *Morgan:* a genuine but unreasonable belief in consent will be a sufficient mens rea for the offences in ss 1–4.

The *mens rea* in rape and the other non-consensual offences (ss 1–4) comprises two elements:

(i) A does not reasonably believe B consents.

(ii) Whether a belief is reasonable is to be determined having regard to all the circumstances, including any steps A has taken to ascertain whether B consents.

Notes and questions

1. The possibility of a purely objective test—whether the reasonable person would have believed B was consenting—was considered, but rejected in favour of this test which pays some heed to A's physical and mental capabilities. See for discussion of alternatives H. Power, 'Towards a redefinition of the *Mens rea* of Rape' (2003) 23 OJLS 379.

2. There are in effect two reasonableness requirements. D's belief must be reasonable, and the process by which he came to that belief must be reasonable.

3. The question is whether A has a reasonable belief in consent. This must relate to A's personal capacity to evaluate whether B is consenting. A who does not think about B's consent is guilty, as is A who considers and wrongly concludes that B is consenting—unless that mistake is reasonable. Under s 1(2) is the correct question as to (a) A's purely subjective belief about consent measured against a standard of reasonableness applied by the jury or magistrate, or (b) A's assessment that his own belief as to consent was reasonable? Is *Morgan* successfully abolished? Can A who is of limited mental capacity, who genuinely but unreasonably holds the belief that B is consenting, still run the defence that *he* made such efforts as *he* considered reasonable?

4. Which of A's characteristics are to be considered when assessing whether it was reasonable for him to hold that belief in B's consent? The Government's view was that 'it is for the jury to decide whether any of the attributes of the defendant are relevant to their deliberations, subject to directions from the judge where necessary'. 'All the circumstances' would appear to include all circumstances that might be relevant to whether a belief is reasonable. Ministerial statements in Parliament have made it clear that 'circumstances' are not limited to surrounding facts. Lord Falconer of Thoroton Hansard, HL, 2 June 2003, vol 648, col 1076; Furthermore, in response to concerns expressed in Parliament that the New Zealand wholly objective approach might be adopted, Baroness Scotland of Asthal provided reassurance, ibid, vol 649, col 678 (June 17, 2003):

We fully expect that characteristics such as mental incapacity and extreme youth will be taken into account in line with existing case law in such issues. We would not expect our courts to follow the New Zealand approach. We believe we can rely principally on case law as regards reasonableness.

5. Will A's lack of sexual experience be relevant? His learning disability? His extreme youth and lack of understanding of sexual mores? Surely not his voluntarily intoxication through alcohol or drugs? What of A's knowledge of B's previous sexual history?

A note on marital rape

It was for centuries the law that a husband could not be found guilty of raping his wife during the subsistence of marital cohabitation. This rule was based on the view, first authoritatively expressed by Hale in 1736 (I PC 629), that the wife, having given her consent upon marriage, could not retract it. Inevitably the tide of opinion turned against this antiquated and indefensible view. The Law Commission recommended its abolition in 1990, a recommendation widely supported, and it seemed to be only a matter of time before Parliament would abolish it.

In *R* [1991] 4 All ER 481, [1992] 1 AC 599, however, the House of Lords, in effect, preempted legislative change by holding that the rule was no longer appropriate in the modern law which recognized husband and wife as equal partners in marriage and that accordingly a husband could now be guilty of the rape of his wife.

Note that the House of Lords did not hold that Hale has misstated the law—he had correctly stated the law as it stood in 1736 and this remained the law for many years thereafter—but that (this must have been on some unspecified day before R had forcible intercourse with his wife in October 1989) the law had changed as no longer compatible with modern conditions.

The case is open to criticism (see [1992] Crim LR 207) not least because of the then statutory requirement in the law of rape that the sexual intercourse be 'unlawful' which was understood to mean 'outside the bounds of marriage'.

The European Court of Human Rights subsequently (*CR v United Kingdom* [1996] 1 FLR 434 declined to find that the decision violated Article 7 of the European Convention on Human Rights which provides that no one may be convicted of a crime which was not a crime at the time of its commission (see Ch 2 above). In *C* [2005] Crim LR 238 and commentary by Ashworth, the Court of Appeal upheld the defendant's 2002 conviction for raping his wife in 1970. Was it an offence to rape your wife in 1970? Could C have known that if no law book said so until 1991?

See further G. Williams, 'Rape is Rape' (1992) 142 NLJ p 11; M. Giles, 'Judicial Law Making in the Criminal Courts: the case of marital rape' [1992] Crim LR 407; V. Laird, 'Reflections on *R v R*' [1992] 55 MLR 386; J. Barton, 'The story of marital rape' (1992) 108 LQR 260.

(2) ASSAULT BY PENETRATION

Sexual Offences Act 2003, s 2

(1) A person (A) commits an offence if—

    (a) he intentionally penetrates the vagina or anus of another person (B) with a part of his body or anything else,

    (b) the penetration is sexual,

    (c) B does not consent to the penetration, and

    (d) A does not reasonably believe that B consents.

(2) Whether a belief is reasonable is to be determined having regard to all the circumstances, including any steps A has taken to ascertain whether B consents.

Notes and questions

1. This is an entirely new offence. Penetration with fingers and inanimate objects such as knives and bottles are covered. Such acts would have only been charged as indecent

assault under the old law. The new offence provides a more suitable label and sentencing powers.

2. The issues of consent and mens rea are as discussed above in relation to rape. It remains unclear whether there is an element of mens rea as to the 'sexual' nature of the penetration. As a matter of principle, each element of the actus reus ought to have a corresponding element of mens rea.

3. Penetration must be 'sexual' as defined above. Thus, the intention is that medical examinations, intimate body searches, etc are not caught by this offence. What of A who forcibly penetrates B with an object as an act of violence and humiliation?

'Sexual' is defined in section 78:

Penetration, touching or any other activity is sexual if a reasonable person would consider that—

    (a) whatever its circumstances or any person's purpose in relation to it, it is because of its nature sexual, or

    (b) because of its nature it may be sexual and because of its circumstances or the purpose of any person in relation to it (or both) it is sexual.

4. See *H* (below p 730).

(3) SEXUAL ASSAULT

Sexual Offences Act 2003, s 3

    (1) A person (A) commits an offence if—

        (a) he intentionally touches another person (B),

        (b) the touching is sexual,

        (c) B does not consent to the touching, and

        (d) A does not reasonably believe that B consents.

    (2) Whether a belief is reasonable is to be determined having regard to all the circumstances, including any steps A has taken to ascertain whether B consents.

Sexual is defined as above.

Touching is defined in section 79(8)

Touching includes touching—

    (a) with any part of the body,

    (b) with anything else,

    (c) through anything,

and in particular includes touching amounting to penetration.

Notes

1. The shift from 'assault' to 'touching' may be significant. No hostility is required. Sexual words do not constitute a touching (but might have been assaults). Similarly, D who walks towards someone with his penis exposed commits no touching, but this would have been indecent assault—*Rolfe* (1952) 36 Cr App R 4.

R v H [2005]
EWCA Crim 732, Court of Appeal, Criminal Division

(Lord Woolf CJ, Davis and Field JJ)

A approached B at 10 pm one evening as she walked across a field and said to her 'Do you fancy a shag?' B ignored him whereon A grabbed B's tracksuit bottoms by the fabric, attempted to pull her towards him and, attempted unsuccessfully to put his hand over her mouth. B escaped. A was convicted of sexual assault, contrary to s 3 of the Sexual Offences Act 2003. Two issues had arisen at trial:

   (i) whether the touching of the B's tracksuit bottoms alone amounted to the 'touching' of another person within the meaning of s 79(8) of the 2003 Act; and

  (ii) whether anything which had occurred amounted to what a reasonable person might regard as being 'sexual' within the meaning of s 78 of the Act, which provides:

   Penetration, touching or any other activity is sexual if a reasonable person would consider that—
      (a) whatever its circumstances or any person's purpose in relation to it, it is because of its nature sexual, or
      (b) because of its nature it may be sexual and because of its circumstances or the purpose of any person in relation to it (or both) it is sexual.

The Lord Chief Justice:
[His lordship referred to Temkin and Ashworth [2004] Crim LR 328 and to the relevant statutory provisions:]

   8. In this case we are concerned with section 78(b). Miss Egerton who appears on behalf of the Crown accepts that (a) has no application. The nature of the touching with which we are concerned was not inevitably sexual. It is important to note that there are two requirements in section 78(b). First, there is the requirement that the touching because of its nature *may* be sexual; and secondly, there is the requirement that the touching because of its circumstances or the purpose of any person in relation to it (or both) *is* sexual.

   9. Miss Egerton agreed with the view of the court expressed in argument that if there were not two requirements in (b), the opening words 'because of its nature it may be sexual' would be surplus. If it was not intended by the legislature that effect should be given to those opening words, it would be sufficient to create an offence by looking at the touching and deciding whether because of its circumstances it was sexual. In other words, there is not one comprehensive test. It is necessary for both halves of section 78(b) to be complied with.

   10. It is no doubt because of this aspect of section 78(b) and the article in the Criminal Law Review that Mr West who appears on behalf of the appellant referred to *R v Court*. That case dealt with an alleged indecent assault. An assistant in a shop struck a 12 year old girl visitor twelve times, for no apparent reason, outside her shorts on her buttocks. The assistant was convicted. Both this court and the House of Lords dismissed the assistant's appeal. At pages 42B–43E of his speech Lord Ackner set out his general approach. On reading that passage it is understandable why the article should have made the comment to which we referred. It is quite clear to the court that the staged approach which we have observed in section 78 is reflected in Lord Ackner's speech. The only difficulty that we have with applying Lord Ackner's approach is that he referred to *R v George* [1956] Crim LR 52. In that case the prosecution relied on the fact that on a number of occasions the defendant had removed a shoe from a girl's foot. He had done so, as he admitted, because it gave him a perverted

sexual gratification. Streatfeild J ruled that an assault became indecent only if it was accompanied by circumstances of indecency towards the person alleged to have been assaulted and that none of the assaults in that case (namely the removal or attempted removal of the shoes) could possibly amount to an indecent assault.

11. We would express reservations as to whether or not it would be possible for the removal of shoes in that way, because of the nature of the act that took place, to be sexual as sexual is defined now in section 78. That in our judgment may well be a question that it would be necessary for a jury to determine.

12. The fact that in section 78(b) there are two different questions which we have sought to identify complicates the task of the judge and that of the jury. If there is a submission of "no case" the judge may have to ask himself whether there is a case to be left to the jury. He will answer that question by determining whether it would be appropriate for a reasonable person to consider that the touching because of its nature may be sexual. Equally, the judge will have to consider whether it would be possible for a reasonable person to conclude, because of the circumstances of the touching or the purpose of any person in relation to the touching (or both), that it is sexual. If he comes to the conclusion that a reasonable person could possibly answer those questions adversely to the defendant, then the matter would have to be left to the jury.

13. We would suggest that in that situation the judge would regard it as desirable to identify two distinct questions for the jury. First, would they, as twelve reasonable people (as the section requires), consider that because of its nature the touching that took place in the particular case before them could be sexual? If the answer to that question was 'No', the jury would find the defendant not guilty. If 'Yes', they would have to go on to ask themselves (again as twelve reasonable people) whether in view of the circumstances and/or the purpose of any person in relation to the touching (or both), the touching was in fact sexual. If they were satisfied that it was, then they would find the defendant guilty. If they were not satisfied, they would find the defendant not guilty.

14. In that suggested approach the reference to the nature of the touching in the first half refers to the actual touching that took place in that case. In answering the first question, the jury would not be concerned with the circumstances before or after the touching took place, or any evidence as to the purpose of any person in relation to the touching.

[His lordship referred to section 62 'Committing an offence with intent to commit a sexual offence' and outlined the facts revealed by the evidence in the present case.]

24. ... Where a person is wearing clothing we consider that touching of the clothing constitutes touching for the purpose of the section 3 offence.

25. As against that approach Mr West relied on section 79(8) (set out above). He submits that under section 79(8)(c) touching through anything (through clothing), if pressure in some form is not brought against the body of the person concerned, there cannot be touching; there has to be some form of touching of the body of the individual who is alleged to have been assaulted, even if it be through clothing. Mr West submits that, having regard to the complainant's evidence in this case, there was no such touching.

26. It is important to note that the opening words of section 79(8) are 'touching includes touching' and in particular 'through anything'. Subsection (8) is not a definition section. We have no doubt that it was not Parliament's intention by the use of that language to make it impossible to regard as a sexual assault touching which took place by touching what the victim was wearing at the time.

27. The second unsuccessful submission made by Mr West for the case to be withdrawn from the jury was as to whether anything occurred which a reasonable person could regard as sexual within the meaning of the Act. The judge's view was that there were here clearly circumstances in which the

offence was alleged to have occurred, including the words alleged to have been spoken beforehand, which could make the actions which took place properly to be regarded as being sexual. In his approach at that time, and indeed in his summing-up, the judge did not take a two stage approach to section 78(b). He looked at the matter as a whole. The problem about that approach is that in a borderline case a person's intention or other circumstances may appear to show that what happened was sexual, although their nature might not have been sexual. For the reasons we have already given that approach is not one which we regard as appropriate, although we recognise that in the great majority of cases the answer will be the same whether the two stage approach is adopted or the position is looked at as a whole.

[His Lordship dealt with other grounds of appeal.]

Appeal dismissed

Notes and questions

1. In *Court*, A, an assistant in a shop, pulled a girl, aged 12, who was in the shop across his knee and spanked her on her clothed bottom. When asked why he did it, he said 'Buttock fetish'. The House held (Lord Goff dissenting) that because it was ambiguous whether the act was indecent it was legitimate to refer to A's motive. In circumstances where the act was unambiguously indecent there was no need to refer to A's motive. In cases where the act was unambiguously not indecent, A's indecent motive could not make it such.

2. Lord Woolf CJ referred to the Temkin and Ashworth article which states that:

. . . as under the *Court* test, conduct, which on the face of it is not sexual, cannot be brought within that description by pointing to its circumstances and/or purpose. The *Court* test and its application have been criticised as 'vague' and unclear, but a superior alternative remains to be found. In practice, in most cases, it will not be difficult to apply the test in section 78(a). It will be in unusual cases only that section 78(b) will be brought into play. Whilst section 78 might require some fine-tuning, it was wise to have included a provision of this kind. In Canada a decision to exclude any such provision from the legislation has led to a costly proliferation of cases in which courts have been called upon to rule in what circumstances a particular assault may be described as sexual.

His lordship stated that 'the expectation indicated in that part of the article that it will only be in unusual cases that section 78(b) will be brought into play is probably over-optimistic, as the facts of this case indicate.'

3. Is there any conduct that a reasonable person would conclude may *not* be sexual?

4. In *H*, the defendant touched only B's clothes. How can that be a touching of the 'person' as s 3 requires? What if A touches only the hem of B's skirt? Is that distinguishable from touching B's bikini-clad buttock?

5. Would soaking B's flimsy T-shirt be a sexual touching? Does A have to be holding the implement that touches B?

6. The touching must be intentional. What then of A, who is drunk at the office party, and who gropes B and claims that any contact was 'accidental'?

7. Sexual touching is an offence under s 3, if it involves penetration, it is indictable only and carries a different sentence and as such, following *Courtie* [1984] AC 463 represents a separate offence.

(4) INTENTIONALLY CAUSING SOMEONE TO ENGAGE IN SEXUAL ACTIVITY

Sexual Offences Act 2003, s 4

(1) A person (A) commits an offence if—
   (a) he intentionally causes another person (B) to engage in an activity,
   (b) the activity is sexual,
   (c) B does not consent to engaging in the activity, and
   (d) A does not reasonably believe that B consents.

(2) Whether a belief is reasonable is to be determined having regard to all the circumstances, including any steps A has taken to ascertain whether B consents.

Notes and questions

1. This is an entirely new and potentially very useful offence, which has as one of its purposes criminalizing the actions of women who force men to penetrate them. Other examples of the offence would include A requiring B to masturbate A, or to masturbate B, or A requiring B to masturbate C, etc. The offence can be committed by words alone.

2. Sexual is as defined above; touching is as defined above, p 729. Sections 74–76 (consent and presumptions discussed above, pp 721–726) apply.

3. Subsection (4) elevates the crime to an indictable offence with a maximum sentence of life imprisonment if it involves: penetration of B's anus or vagina; penetration of B's mouth with a person's penis; penetration of a person's anus or vagina by B with his body or otherwise; penetration of a person's mouth with B's penis.

4. Since A must 'cause' the action, it can be assumed that it is sufficient for A to be *a* cause without being the sole cause (see p 56, Ch 3).

3. OFFENCES AGAINST CHILDREN

These provisions (ss 5–16) are some of the most heavily criticized, in particular for their overcriminalization and undue reliance on prosecutorial discretion. The legislation makes no attempt to distinguish between exploitative sexual activity against a child under 16 (whether by older individuals or not) and that of informed consensual sexual experimentation between children under that age.

The use of strict liability as to age in these offences reverses the effect of *B v DPP* and *K* (above, p 216). Although there is a clear and legitimate objective in providing protection to young people, the use of strict liability, such that an offender's belief that the victim is older is immaterial, *may* be problematic both as a matter of justice, and as an issue under Article 6 of the ECHR. These problems may be exacerbated by the failure in the Act to distinguish, in the context of those offences, between young and other offenders.

As for the retention of 16 as the age of consent, Lord Millett's observations in *R v K* go unheeded: 'the age of consent has long ceased to reflect ordinary life, and in this respect Parliament has signally failed to discharge its responsibility for keeping the criminal law in touch with the needs of society': [2001] UKHL 41, [44].

The Government defended its position by claiming that there was no significant change in the law. Is this true? Under the old law under 16s were protected against indecent assault and intercourse—but the law now criminalizes a broader range of consensual sexual activities between under 16s than previously. The Act is supposed to modernize the law and to reflect the sexual mores of the twenty-first century. Does it?

J. Spencer, 'The Sexual Offences Act 2003 (2) Child and Family Offences'
[2004] Crim LR 347

The new child sex offences are open to two obvious criticisms: complexity and obscurity, and 'legislative overkill'....

The 'legislative overkill' point is that the child sex offences cover not only consensual sexual acts between children and adults, but all forms of sexual behaviour between consenting children. The result is to render criminal a range of sexual acts, some of which are usually thought to be normal and proper, and others at least not seriously wrong. They include mouth-to-mouth kissing or minor acts of sexual exploration between consenting 14 or 15-year-olds (five years); two boys giving themselves a sexual thrill by looking at a dirty book (five years); and 'rude games' between two 10-year-olds (14 years, or maybe life). In 1994 a widely respected study reported that the average age of young people's first sexual experiences (kissing, cuddling, petting, etc) then stood at 14 for women and 13 for men. This also showed that 18.7 per cent of women and 27.6 per cent of men had full sexual intercourse before they were 16—figures which a follow-up study shows now stand at 24.8 per cent and 30.7 per cent. So far are these provisions of the Act out of line with the sexual behaviour of the young that, unless they provoke a sexual counter-revolution, they will eventually make indictable offenders of the whole population.

There was no need for this, because behind the specific crimes of consensual sex with children the Act provides a range of crimes that punish every form of nonconsensual sex. So it would be have been safe as well as simple to exclude from the offences of consensual sex with minors, any consensual act between persons of the same or similar age....

The concern about the potential overcriminalization was countered with the responses that the CPS would exercise appropriate discretion. But, as the Joint Parliamentary Committee on Human Rights observed:

Creating catch all offences and then relying on the prosecutor's discretion to sort things out satisfactorily undermines [the rule of law]. It leaves prosecutors to do the job that Parliament should be doing, and gives them discretion to prosecute (or not to prosecute) people who ought never to have been within the scope of criminal liability in the first place. (12th Report 2002–3 *Scrutiny of Bills: Further Progress Report 2003* (HL 119; HC 765).)

The Code for Crown Prosecutors now provides that:

The 2003 Act protects all children from engaging in sexual activity at an early age, irrespective of whether or not a person under 13 may have the necessary understanding of sexual matters to give ostensible consent. The intention behind sections 5–8 is to provide maximum protection to very young children.

CPS Charging Practice provides:

In summary, where a defendant, for example, is exploitative, or coercive, or much older than the victim, the balance may be in favour of prosecution, whereas if the sexual activity is truly of the victim's own free will the balance may not be in the public interest to prosecute.

In addition, it is **not** in the public interest to prosecute children who are of the same or similar age and understanding that engage in sexual activity, where the activity is truly consensual for both parties and there are no aggravating features, such as coercion or corruption. In such cases, protection will normally be best achieved by providing education for the children and young people and providing them and their families with access to advisory and counselling services. This is the intention of Parliament.

(1) OFFENCES AGAINST CHILDREN UNDER 13

Rape of a child under 13

Sexual Offences Act 2003, s 5

(1) A person commits an offence if—
  (a) he intentionally penetrates the vagina, anus or mouth of another person with his penis, and
  (b) the other person is under 13.

Notes and questions

1. There is no issue of consent—A is guilty even if B is a consenting party. Liability as to age and consent is strict. B, 12 years old, who willingly performs fellatio on A, her 12-year-old boyfriend, thereby renders him a rapist. Is X, A's friend, who tells A that he should ask B to perform oral sex guilty of inciting rape?

2. The clear intention is that liability is strict as to age (cf *B v DPP and R v K* (above, Ch 8). There is no opportunity for a plea of mistaken belief as to consent or as to the age of the complainant, even if mistake is reasonable. J. Spencer above, argues that because ss 9 and 10 (below) specify that liability in relation to age under 13 is strict, but ss 5–8 do not state this explicitly, there is a mens rea requirement as to age in ss 5–8. Is the argument likely to succeed?

3. Will there be scope for an Article 8 challenge by A and or B? Is a right to respect for private life infringed by legislation that is not necessary and proportionate to a legitimate aim such as the protection of health or morals, or the protection of the rights and freedoms of others? Necessity is a strict requirement, based on whether there is a pressing social need. See Ch 1 above.

4. Note that there is no liability for aiding and abetting or counselling rape of a child under 13 if the actor's purpose is to protect the child from STD/pregnancy or to protect his or her physical safety or promote his or her emotional well being, unless the actor's purpose is to gain sexual gratification or to cause or encourage the relevant sexual act: s 73. The doctor who provides contraceptives to the 12-year-old girl to protect her in her consensual sexual acts with her partner will not be aiding and abetting her 'rape'. What of the parent who takes the view that he would rather his daughter had sex with her boyfriend in the safety of her bedroom than, say, the local bus shelter?

5. Is prosecutorial discretion enough to prevent this offence being misused? This is an offence of *rape*. Can the CPS be seen not to be prosecuting child rapes?

Assault of a child under 13 by penetration

Sexual Offences Act 2003, s 6

> (1) A person commits an offence if—
>> (a) he intentionally penetrates the vagina or anus of another person with a part
>>   of his body or anything else,
>> (b) the penetration is sexual, and
>> (c) the other person is under 13.

The s 73 defence for aiding and abetting applies as discussed above.

Notes

1. Consent is irrelevant. Liability is strict as to the age of the victim. The maximum sentence is life imprisonment.

2. The penetration must be sexual. The intimate examination of a child under 13 performed by a medical professional is not caught by the offence.

Sexual assault of a child

Sexual Offences Act 2003, s 7

> (1) A person commits an offence if—
>> (a) he intentionally touches another person,
>> (b) the touching is sexual, and
>> (c) the other person is under 13.

The s 73 defence for aiding and abetting applies as discussed above.

Notes and questions

1. The section criminalizes consensual kissing by 12-year-olds. The maximum sentence is 14 years on indictment; 6 months summarily.

2. 'Touching' and 'sexual' are defined as above, p 729.

3. Is liability as to the 'sexual' nature of the touching strict?

4. Does not the law's denial of the factual consent of the under 13-year-old to engage in sexual touching clash with the laws willingness to accept such a child's capacity to consent to, for example, invasive medical procedures?

5. The Home Secretary has stated in a press release on the Act receiving Royal Assent that there would be no prosecution for sexual activity between children under the age of 16 where the activity is genuinely consensual. This rather begs the question why the Act is not drafted so as to include a requirement of an absence of consent.

6. The CPS Guidelines for Prosecution state that 'In deciding whether or not to prosecute [children] prosecutors should have careful regard to the factors below. The weight to be attached to a particular factor will vary depending on the circumstances of each case. The factors are: The age and understanding of the offender. This may include whether the

offender has been subjected to any exploitation, coercion, threat, deception, grooming or manipulation by another which has lead him or her to commit the offence; The relevant ages of the parties, i.e. the same or no significant disparity in age; Whether the complainant entered into sexual activity willingly, i.e. did the complainant understand the nature of his or her actions and that (s)he was able to communicate his or her willingness freely; Parity between the parties in regard to sexual, physical, emotional and educational development; The relationship between the parties, its nature and duration and whether this represents a genuine transitory phase of adolescent development; Whether there is any element of exploitation, coercion, threat, deception, grooming or manipulation in the relationship; The nature of the activity e.g. penetrative or non-penetrative activity; What is in the best interests and welfare of the complainant; and What is in the best interests and welfare of the defendant.'

Causing or inciting a child under 13 to engage in sexual activity

Sexual Offences Act 2003, s 8

(1) A person commits an offence if—
   (a) he intentionally causes or incites another person (B) to engage in an activity,
   (b) the activity is sexual, and
   (c) B is under 13.

Notes and questions

1. A who persuades his 12-year-old girlfriend to masturbate herself commits the actus reus of this offence. If she agrees, he has caused it, if not, he has incited it. It covers the case where A, the 12-year-old friend of B, also aged 12, encourages B to have oral sex with B's boyfriend C.

2. T, a school teacher, is approached by B, 12, who asks whether she, B, should engage in full sex with her boyfriend, A, as A would like. T suggests that since they are both only 12 they should stick to other intimate activities short of sex (even perhaps just kissing). Does T commit the offence under s 8?

3. Andrew, 14, asks Britney, 12, to give him a 'shiner' (see *B v DPP* (above, p 216)), meaning for her to perform oral sex on him. In her naivety Britney mistakenly believes that Andrew wants her to give him a black eye, so she hits Andrew and causes him severe facial bruising. Consider the criminal liability of Andrew and Britney.

4. Note that the offence is indictable only and carries a maximum sentence of life imprisonment if the activity involves (a) penetration of B's anus or vagina, (b) penetration of B's mouth with a person's penis, (c) penetration of a person's anus or vagina by B, or (d) penetration of a person's mouth with B's penis.

(2) SEXUAL OFFENCES WITH A CHILD AGED 13–16

The group of offences dealing with conduct towards children between 13 and 16 demonstrates the unnecessary complexity and overlapping nature of the provisions in the 2003 Act. In short, ss 9–13 deal with cases where B is between 13 and 16. Each section creates offences for A aged over 18. All charges under ss 9–12 against under 18-year-olds are either way and have a maximum five years on indictment/six months summarily. Section 13 also makes these offences available (with different sentences) where A is under 18, in which case the sentence is one of six months summarily, five years on indictment: s 13. Section 13 does not distinguish between cases where the offence involves penetration or not.

J. Spencer, 'The Sexual Offences Act 2003 (2) Child and Family Offences'
[2004] Crim LR 347

... this part of the new law replaces the previous law, which consisted of three specific offences of sex with children plus four child related adaptations of more general offences, with a new list of no less than 11 specific offences. Why so many new offences?

The number might be justified if all of them covered different ground. But this is not the case, because a number of the offences seriously overlap: in particular ss.5–8 (sexual acts committed upon children under 13) and ss.9 and 10 (sexual acts with children under 16, including those under 13). This overlap might be justified if the offences overlapped at the edges only and the general arrangement showed a clear hierarchy of gravity, with maximum penalties to match: but this is not the case...

It is hard to see any advantage in this multiplication of offences, and on the negative side it gives rise to serious difficulties about what the relationship between them is—and in particular, which ones (if any) are offences of strict liability, and ... how far they apply to defendants who are also minors.

....

The fact that ss.9 and 10 now cover all sexual acts with children under 13 makes it questionable whether there is any need for ss.5–8 at all, given that ss.9 and 10 are punishable with no less than 14 years' imprisonment. And the way in which ss.9 and 10 are now drafted has certainly undermined the Home Office's aim of making ss.5–8 offences carry strict liability. As ss.9 and 10 are now drafted .... it is plain that here the defendant is liable only if negligent where the child is older, but where the victim is under 13 liability is strict. But the fact that these sections impose strict liability as regards victims under 13 gives rise to a plausible argument that, for ss.5–8—which are in principle more serious and in two cases more heavily punishable—the defendant is by contrast liable only where he acted with mens rea ...

Sexual activity with a child

Sexual Offences Act 2003, s 9

    (1) A person aged 18 or over (A) commits an offence if—
        (a) he intentionally touches another person (B),
        (b) the touching is sexual, and
        (c) either—
            (i) B is under 16 and A does not reasonably believe that B is 16 or over, or
            (ii) B is under 13.

The s 73 defence for aiding and abetting applies as discussed above.

The offence is indictable only and carries a maximum sentence of 14 years' imprisonment if the activity involves (a) penetration of B's anus or vagina, (b) penetration of B's mouth with a person's penis, (c) penetration of a person's anus or vagina by B, or (d) penetration of a person's mouth with B's penis.

Notes and questions

1. Consent is irrelevant. A, 18, kissing/touching his consenting 15-year-old girlfriend is guilty if that is a 'sexual touching'—of course that falls to be decided by the jury. A, 18, kissing his 12-year-old, consenting girlfriend is guilty, even if she said she was 16. There is no defence for couples under 16, lawfully married in another country and visiting England.

2. Alan is 19, he has sex with Bronwyn who is 12 but Alan thinks she is 16 as she told him so. Alice, who is 15 fondles Brian, who is 14 but whom she thinks is 16. Which offences have been committed and what sentences are available?

3. Does this offence adequately respect the Article 8 rights of the 15-year-olds?

4. Does the offence reflect the reality of sexual conduct of under 16-year-olds in the twenty-first century? During the debates in Parliament the Home Secretary offered champagne to anyone who could provide a more suitable code of offences. How might a better form of offences have been drafted?

Causing or inciting a child to engage in sexual activity

Sexual Offences Act 2003, s 10

(1) A person aged 18 or over (A) commits an offence if—
　　(a) he intentionally causes or incites another person (B) to engage in an activity,
　　(b) the activity is sexual, and
　　(c) either—
　　　　a. B is under 16 and A does not reasonably believe that B is 16 or over, or
　　　　b. B is under 13.

Note that the offence is indictable only and carries a maximum sentence of 14 years' imprisonment if the activity involves (a) penetration of B's anus or vagina, (b) penetration of B's mouth with a person's penis, (c) penetration of a person's anus or vagina by B, or (d) penetration of a person's mouth with B's penis.

Non-penetrative activities are triable either way and carry a maximum 14 years on indictment/six months summarily.

Notes and questions

1. The dual use of cause or incite suggests the offence is very broad and can be committed by the mere act of encouragement without any activity subsequently occurring. A, 18, begs his 15-year-old girlfriend to strip for him. She declines. A, 18, asks his 15-year-old girlfriend to strip for him. She does so willingly. A commits the offence on both occasions.

2. The offence can also be committed by a person under 18, if so the sentence is one of six months summarily, five years on indictment: s 13.

3. Bearing in mind that the offence can be committed by (a) causing or (b) inciting, and applies to (c) over 18s and (b) under 18s, and differs for victims aged (d) under 13 and (e) between 13 and 16 and attracts different sentences for (f) penetrative acts and (g) non penetrative acts (unless A is under 18), can it really be said that this is a satisfactorily clear method of drafting for such a serious offence?

Engaging in sexual activity in the presence of a child

Sexual Offences Act 2003, s 11

1. A person aged 18 or over (A) commits an offence if—
    (a) he intentionally engages in an activity,
    (b) the activity is sexual,
    (c) for the purpose of obtaining sexual gratification, he engages in it
        (i) when another person (B) is present or is in a place from which A can be observed, and
        (ii) knowing or believing that B is aware, or intending that B should be aware that he is engaging in it, and
    (d) either—
        (i) B is under 16 and A does not reasonably believe that B is 16 or over, or
        (ii) B is under 13.

The maximum sentence is 10 years on indictment/six months summarily. The offence can also be committed by a person under 18, if so the sentence is one of six months summarily, five years on indictment: s 13.

Notes and questions

1. This is a completely new offence. It is designed to tackle the paedophile who performs sexual acts in a child's presence to gain sexual gratification.

2. Must A's sole purpose be to derive sexual pleasure from B's watching? A has consensual sex with C, aware that B, 15, is watching. What if A derives sexual pleasure from the sex and the watching?

3. Presumably this can be an offence committed on a webcam? Observation includes viewing an image (s 79(4)). Does the observation have to be in real time?

4. What of A and C who become rather intimate in the corner of the school disco, aware that B is watching? Or the thrill seekers ('doggers' as they are called) who have sex in the park visible from the nearby school playground?

5. There is no requirement that B is actually aware of A's acts. Note that there must be a person under 16 who is able to see the act. An undercover officer alone witnessing the event will not suffice.

Causing a child to watch a sexual act

Sexual Offences Act 2003, s 12

(1) A person aged 18 or over (A) commits an offence if—
    (a) for the purpose of obtaining sexual gratification, he intentionally causes another person (B) to watch a third person engaging in an activity, or to look at an image of any person engaging in an activity,
    (b) the activity is sexual, and
    (c) either—
        (i) B is under 16 and A does not reasonably believe that B is 16 or over, or
        (ii) B is under 13.

The maximum sentence is 10 years on indictment six months summarily. The offence can also be committed by a person under 18, if so the sentence is one of six months summarily, five years on indictment: s 13.

Notes and questions

1. The offence was included to deal with paedophiles who use pornography as part of their grooming process. They show pornographic images to children in an attempt to break down the child's inhibitions about engaging in sexual conduct.

2. Is the offence too wide? Consider A, 17, and B, 15, lawfully married abroad and visiting England on honeymoon, who watch the hotel's 'adult movie'? What of Alan, 16, who lends Beatrice, 15, his collection of pornographic magazines at her request, but who derives sexual gratification from knowing that she will read them?

3. Since what is 'sexual' is defined by the jury, can A claim that he did not realize the images were sexual when he caused B to watch them?

Arranging or facilitating commission of a child sex offence

Sexual Offences Act 2003, s 14

(1) A person commits an offence if—
   (a) he intentionally arranges or facilitates something that he intends to do, intends another person to do, or believes that another person will do, in any part of the world, and
   (b) doing it will involve the commission of an offence under any of sections 9 to 13.

(2) A person does not commit an offence under this section if—
   (a) he arranges or facilitates something that he believes another person will do, but that he does not intend to do or intend another person to do, and
   (b) any offence within subsection (1)(b) would be an offence against a child for whose protection he acts.

(3) For the purposes of subsection (2), a person acts for the protection of a child if he acts for the purpose of—
   (a) protecting the child from sexually transmitted infection,
   (b) protecting the physical safety of the child,
   (c) preventing the child from becoming pregnant, or
   (d) promoting the child's emotional well-being by the giving of advice, and not for the purpose of obtaining sexual gratification or for the purpose of causing or encouraging the activity constituting the offence within subsection (1)(b) or the child's participation in it.

The maximum sentences are 14 years on indictment/six months summarily.

Notes and questions

1. Consider Alfie, father of Britney, a 15-year-old, who would rather she had sex with her boyfriend at home than elsewhere. Is Alfie covered by s 14(3)(b)?

2. The parents of brothers Alan, 21, and Ben, 15, are on holiday. Alan drives to pick up Ben's girlfriend Christine, 15, so that she can stay at the house and during her stay she has sex with Ben. Does Alan commit an offence?

3. Alice is the mother of Beatrice, 15. She arranges a holiday in Spain for Beatrice and some of her school friends to celebrate the end of their GCSEs. The group will be sharing bedrooms. The group includes Dan, 16, who is Beatrice's long-standing boyfriend. What must the prosecution prove for Alice to commit the offence?

Meeting a child following sexual grooming, etc

Sexual Offences Act 2003, s 15

(1) A person aged 18 or over (A) commits an offence if—
  (a) having met or communicated with another person (B) on at least two earlier occasions, he—
    i. intentionally meets B, or
    ii. travels with the intention of meeting B in any part of the world,
  (b) at the time, he intends to do anything to or in respect of B, during or after the meeting and in any part of the world, which if done will involve the commission by A of a relevant offence,
  (c) B is under 16, and
  (b) A does not reasonably believe that B is 16 or over.

(2) In subsection (1)—
  (a) the reference to A having met or communicated with B is a reference to A having met B in any part of the world or having communicated with B by any means from, to or in any part of the world;
  (b) 'relevant offence' means—
    (i) an offence under this Part,
    (ii) an offence within any of paragraphs 61 to 92 of Schedule 3,
    (iii) anything done outside England and Wales and Northern Ireland which is not an offence within sub-paragraph (i) or (ii) but would be an offence within sub-paragraph (i) if done in England and Wales.

The maximum sentence is 10 years on indictment/six months summarily.

Notes and questions

1. This is the much publicized 'grooming' offence.

2. Is it too broad? A, 18, writes two love letters to B, 15, arranging to meet at the local club. A hopes that the evening will end in sexual activity. Is A guilty of the offence? When? Is there any limit on the period of time between the previous meeting/communication and the planned meeting? At what 'time' must the sexual motive be apparent? When the communication occurs or when the meeting is to take place?

3. Is the offence too narrow? A, 58, is a paedophile. He posts internet messages to B, believing her to be 15. She is an undercover woman police officer, aged 32. Is A guilty?

4. OTHER GROUPS OF OFFENCES

(1) ABUSE OF TRUST

The Sexual Offences (Amendment) Act 2000 created new offences of abuse of a position of trust. The 2003 Act replaces them with four offences where A (aged over 18) who is in a position of trust to B (under 18):

- sexually touches B (s 16);
- causes or incites B to engage in sexual activity (s 17);
- engages in sexual activity in B's presence for the purpose of sexual gratification (s 18);
- causes B to watch a sexual image or activity for the purpose of obtaining sexual gratification.

The most notable feature of the sections is that the offences criminalize consensual conduct with those under 18. Although 16–18-year-olds may consent to sexual activity in other circumstances, they cannot do so with those who 'look after' them (see ss 21 and 22). The category of those in trust includes, for example, pupils and students. The offences place a burden on A where his position of trust arises in an institutional setting, to present evidence that he did not know nor could he reasonably be expected to know that he was in a position of trust towards B. This may well be difficult to raise unless A is working in a large institution.

No offence is committed where A has a reasonable belief that B is aged over 18 (unless B is under 13). There is a defence for A to prove that he was lawfully married to B (aged 16+) or that immediately before the position of trust arose there existed a lawful sexual relationship between them. This covers cases where for example, A and B had a sexual relationship before A became a trainee teacher at B's school.

(2) FAMILY OFFENCES

The 2003 Act creates two sets of offences to deal with offences within the family. In relation to children, ss 25 and 26 criminalize the same forms of activity as ss 9 and 12 (above):

- sexual touching and
- causing a child to engage in sexual activity.

Sections 25 and 26 differ from ss 9 and 12 in two important respects: B must be under 18 and A must be a family member. Family membership is defined in very broad terms in the Act, extending well beyond blood relationships to reflect the diverse structures of modern life. Family members, include:

- blood and adoptive relationships (parents, current or former foster parents, grandparents, brothers, sisters, half-brothers, half-sisters, aunts and uncles);
- wider family members who live, or have lived, in the same household as the child or who are, or have been, regularly involved in caring for, training or supervising or being in sole charge of the child (step-parents, cousins, step-siblings, current or former foster siblings);

- others who are living in the same household as the child and who hold a position of trust or authority in relation to the child at the time of the alleged offence. This offence will not be committed if A has a lawful sexual relationship with the child after the familial relationship has ceased, even where the child is under 18.

The breadth of the extended family caught by the Act reflects the shift in emphasis in the legislation from a blood relationship based offence of heterosexual intercourse (incest based on eugenics arguments) to one based on gender neutral exploitation of sexual vulnerability in the home environment.

There are defences in s 28 where A is lawfully married to B at the time of engaging in the sexual activity, and under s 29 where A proves that a lawful sexual relationship existed between A and B immediately before the familial relationship arose.

(3) OFFENCES INVOLVING MENTAL DISORDER

The Act provides three specific groups of offences to protect those with a mental disorder. In each category the types of behaviour criminalized are roughly the same as those in relation to children. In short the activities prohibited are:

- sexual touching of B;
- causing or inciting sexual activity by B;
- engaging in sexual activity in B's presence;
- causing B to watch sexual activity.

When these activities arise in an exploitative context are they criminalized. The three contexts are:

- ss 30–33 where B is mentally disordered and 'unable to refuse';
- ss 34–37 where B is mentally disordered and the activity is caused by 'threats or deception or inducement' (which need not vitiate consent under s 74);
- ss 38–41 where B is mentally disordered and A is 'in a relationship as a carer'.

There are numerous general improvements in the new scheme. Creating specific offences produces much fairer labelling—defendants are convicted of offences that better describe their actions. The language has been modernized, and gender specificity has been removed. This is not mere window dressing: for example, one result is that mentally disordered men are protected against heterosexual abuse. The offensive terminology of the 1956 Act has been replaced by the appropriate (but technical) language of the Mental Health Acts. 'Mental disorder' is defined as: 'a state of arrested or incomplete development of mind, psychopathic disorder ['psychopathic disorder' is itself defined in s 1(2) of the MHA 1983—'persistent disorder or disability of mind (whether or not including significant impairment of intelligence) which results in abnormally aggressive or seriously irresponsible conduct.' Note that s 1(3) provides that this definition shall not be construed as implying that a person may be dealt with under the Act as suffering from a mental disorder by reason of 'promiscuity or other immoral conduct, sexual deviancy or dependence on alcohol or drugs'] and any other disease or disability of the mind.' This produces greater coherence, and extends protection beyond those with severe mental disorder, to those with a learning disability. (Estimates are of 200,000 people with learning disability in this country: *Setting the Boundaries*, para 4.1.5.)

As with the Act in general, there is tremendous complexity. Many of the definitions are internally complex and their interrelationship with other provisions in the Act exacerbates this problem. As elsewhere, there is the potential for significant overlap with other offences. If the activity is seemingly non-consensual (or at least B is unable to refuse), and involves a child complainant and a carer who is in a family relationship with B, the possible range of offences committed is vast. It is arguable that too much discretion lies in the hands of the CPS who will face an especially difficult task in deciding whether to prosecute in cases where for example A and B are both mentally disordered, or, for example, where a carer claims that the actions were performed for the appropriate sex education of an individual. Symbolically it was very important for the Act to criminalize exploitative behaviour, but the message is confused when it overcriminalizes and potentially inhibits the appropriate sexual behaviour of those with learning disability.

(4) PROSTITUTION AND PORNOGRAPHY

The Act provides specific protection against the sexual exploitation of children in pornography and prostitution. Section 47 provides an offence of paying (as widely defined) for the sexual services of a child and s 48 provides wider supporting offences of causing or inciting child prostitution or pornography, being designed to catch those who recruit vulnerable children into such activities.

Further broadly defined offences provide protection against controlling a child prostitute or a child involved in pornography (s 49) and arranging or facilitating child prostitution or pornography (s 50).

Provisions to deal with adult sexual exploitation are strengthened with a range of offences introduced to deal with causing or inciting (s 52) or controlling prostitution for gain (s 53). The rise in trafficking for prostitution is combated by offences of trafficking into, within and outwith the UK (ss 57, 58, 59). Section 56 and Schedule 1 also extend the offences under the Street Offences Act 1959, rendering them gender neutral in effect.

(5) INDECENT PHOTOGRAPHS OF CHILDREN

There are offences of taking, making, permitting to take, distributing, showing, possessing with intent to distribute, and advertising indecent photographs or pseudo-photographs of children under 18. There is a defence if the child is aged over 16 and A proves that he and the child were married or living together as partners in an enduring family relationship, that the child consented to the image being taken and that the image shows no one other than B (and A). See A. Gillespie [2004] Crim LR 361.

(6) PRELIMINARY AND OTHER OFFENCES

Section 61 introduces an offence of intentional administration of a substance/causing it to be taken by B without consent with intent to stupefy/overpower to enable any person to engage in sex with B. This is a further response to the growing problem of drug-assisted rape (see also s 75(2)(f)). The offence is wider than that in s 4 of the 1956 Act, being gender-neutral and relating to all sexual activity. Section 61 covers A spiking B's drinks as well as administering drugs such as Rohypnol. It does not extend to A encouraging B to drink alcohol so that A may more readily persuade B to have sex. It applies where A himself administers the substance to B, and where A causes the substance to be taken by B, with C administering it. There is no requirement that B is actually involved in any sexual activity.

Section 62 introduces an offence of 'committing an offence with intent to commit a sexual offence.' The offence is designed for cases where A kidnaps B so that he can rape her or assaulted B to subdue her. There is no requirement that the preliminary offence is directed at B, the person against whom the substantive sexual offence is committed.

Section 63: 'trespass with intent to commit a sexual offence'. This is committed where A, commits a sexual offence whilst he is on any premises as a trespasser, either knowing, or being reckless as to whether, he is trespassing. A person is a trespasser if he is on any premises without the owner's or occupier's consent, or other lawful excuse. This replaces the offence under the Theft Act 1968, s 9 in relation to burglary with intent to rape. It is clearly wider since it involves any trespass and includes sexual offences beyond rape.

Exposure—s 66 creates an offence for A intentionally exposing his or her genitals with the intention that another person will see them and be caused alarm or distress. This extends the previous law to include female exposure. It is not necessary that anyone should have seen the genitals or have been caused alarm or distress. As finally enacted, the offence would not apply to a naturist unless the exposure is with intention to cause alarm or distress. Similarly, 'streakers' at sports events will be unlikely to be prosecuted. The distress they cause will be by holding up play not (usually) by their genitals.

Voyeurism—s 67 creates an offence where A, for the purposes of sexual gratification, observes another person doing a 'private act' in the knowledge that the other person does not consent to being observed for that purpose. The offence extends beyond simple 'peeping toms' looking through keyholes. Section 67 (2) creates an offence of A 'operating equipment' with the intention of enabling another person, C, for their sexual gratification, to observe B doing a 'private act' in the knowledge that B has not consented to this being done for another person's sexual gratification. Similarly, s 67(3) makes it an offence for a person A to record B doing a 'private act' with the intention that A or a third person will, for the purposes of sexual gratification look at the recorded image, when it is known that B does not consent to being recorded for that purpose. Finally, s 67(4) creates an offence for a person to install equipment, or to construct or adapt a structure ('structure' includes 'a tent, vehicle or vessel or other temporary or movable structure') with the intention of enabling himself, or another person, to commit an offence under s 67 (1). Section 68 defines 'Private act' as 'an act done in a place and in circumstances where the person would reasonably expect privacy and either the person's genitals, buttocks or breasts are exposed or covered only by underwear, or the person is using a lavatory or the person is doing a sexual act that is not of a kind ordinarily done in public.' There is already one reported sentencing case— *P* [2004] 3 All ER (D) 31 (Oct), D surreptitiously videoing his 24-year-old stepdaughter in the shower.

Bestiality—s 69 creates an offence for A intentionally to penetrate the vagina or anus of a living animal with his penis where he knows or is reckless as to whether that is what he is penetrating. It also creates an offence for A intentionally to cause or allow her vagina or his or her anus to be penetrated by the penis of a living animal where he or she knows or is reckless as to whether it is the penis of a live animal that is penetrating him/her.

Necrophilia—s 70 creates an offence for A intentionally to penetrate sexually any part of the body of a corpse with A's penis, any other body part or any other object, knowing or being reckless as to whether he is penetrating any part of a corpse. A commits no offence if B dies during intercourse unless A realizes and continues to penetrate her/him!

Sexual activity in a public lavatory—s 71 creates a summary only offence for A to engage in sexual activity in a public lavatory. There is no requirement that any person is alarmed or distressed by the activity. There is no need for the act to have shocked, disgusted or revolted a member of the public.

FURTHER READING

R. CARD, *Sexual Offences: The New Law* (2004)

P. ROOK and R. WARD, *Sexual Offences: Law and Practice* (2004)

A useful website for updates is:
www.homeoffice.gov.uk/justice/sentencing/
sexualoffencesbill/index.html

The Sexual Offences Act is available at:
www.legislation.hmso.gov.uk/acts/acts2003/
20030042.htm

The Home Office Explanatory Notes:
www.legislation.hmso.gov.uk/acts/en2003/
2003en42.htm

Sentencing Advisory Panel:
www.sentencing-guidelines.gov.uk/about/sap

CPS guidance:
www.cps.gov.uk/legal/section7/
sexoffencesact2003.htm

21

Theft and robbery

The law relating to theft and related offences is to be found in the Theft Acts 1968, 1978 and the Theft (Amendment) Act 1996. These Acts were largely based on the recommendations of the Criminal Law Revision Committee (*Eighth Report, Theft and Related Offences*, Cmnd 2977 (1966); and *Thirteenth Report, Section 16 of the Theft Act 1968*, Cmnd 6733 (1977)) which had decided (Cmnd 2977, para 7) that the time had come 'for a new law of theft and related offences, based on a fundamental reconsideration of the principles underlying this branch of the law and embodied in a modern statute.'

Interpreting the Act

So far as the law of *theft* is concerned these Acts constitute the authoritative, comprehensive and exclusive source of the law. But, of course, a law of theft assumes laws relating to property and ownership. A person cannot steal property of which he is the sole owner. He can steal only property that belongs, or is deemed by statute to belong, in part at least, to another. While s 5 of the Theft Act 1968 states when property is to be treated as belonging to another for the purposes of theft, it is immediately apparent that in order fully to determine key terms under that section such as whether there is another with a 'proprietary right or interest' or whether property is 'subject to a trust' or whether a person is 'under an obligation to make restoration' reference must be made to civil cases, whether decided before or after the coming into force of the Theft Acts which provide authoritative explanations of these concepts. Hence whether D is guilty of theft may involve a consideration of the law of contract, the Sale of Goods Acts, or principles of equity.

In the early years of the interpretation of the legislation courts often showed impatience with arguments based on what Sachs LJ in *Baxter* [1971] 2 All ER 359, 363 referred to as 'the finer distinctions in civil law', but crucial issues such as whether property 'belongs to another' for the purposes of theft, as Bingham LJ said in *Dobson v General Accident Fire and Life Assurance Corpn plc* [1989] 3 All ER 927, 937 'is a question to which the criminal law offers no answer and can only be answered by reference to civil law principles.' And in *Shadrokh-Cigari* [1988] Crim LR 465, CA whether property belonged to V was determined by reference to principles of equity. All this remains true notwithstanding the decision in *Hinks*, below, p 750, that D may commit theft where he dishonestly acquires title to property, even where that title is indefeasible in the civil law, that is, the property is his exclusively.

Aside from necessary reference to definitions of general application and to civil law concepts, the Theft Acts represent a clean break with the past. In their interpretation the courts have aimed to give words and expressions their ordinary meaning so as to avoid undue technicality and subtlety. There is nothing wrong with that of course as a general precept of statutory interpretation but it led to a practice, endorsed by the House of Lords in *Brutus v Cozens* [1972] 2 All ER 1297, [1973] AC 854 of leaving the interpretation, at least of 'ordinary' words and expressions to be determined by a jury or magistrates as a matter of fact. This was a less desirable (and indeed a questionable) development and the courts have retreated from it somewhat (see D. W. Elliott, '*Brutus v Cozens*: Decline and Fall' [1989] Crim LR 323).

Consider throughout the chapter the extent to which the appellate courts are content to uphold the conviction of those who have been found to have acted dishonestly, even if the conviction for the offence charged is technically flawed. This prompts the question to what extent theft is treated as a 'dishonesty', rather than a 'property', based offence.

In examining the courts' interpretation of the offence, which was designed as part of a new code, consider the extent to which a more radical approach would be desirable in any new codification of the law. Consider Robinson's proposal in his Draft Code: 'You may not damage, take, use, dispose of, or transfer another's property without the other's consent. Property is anything of value, including services offered for payment and access to recorded information.' (Note that the Code would have a qualification that no prosecution should take place in any case too trivial to warrant the condemnation of a criminal conviction.) See P. H. Robinson, *Structure and Function in Criminal Law* (1997) pp 211–225.

1. THEFT

Basic definition of theft

(1) A person is guilty of theft if he dishonestly appropriates property belonging to another with the intention of permanently depriving the other of it; and 'thief' and 'steal' shall be construed accordingly.

Theft Act 1968, s 7

7. Theft
A person guilty of theft shall on conviction on indictment be liable to imprisonment for a term not exceeding seven years.

(1) APPROPRIATION

Theft Act 1968, s 3

3. 'Appropriates'
   (1) Any assumption by a person of the rights of an owner amounts to an appropriation, and this includes, where he has come by the property (innocently or not) without stealing it, any later assumption of a right to it by keeping or dealing with it as owner.
   (2) Where property or a right or interest in property is or purports to be transferred for value to a person acting in good faith, no later assumption by him of rights which he believed himself to be acquiring shall, by reason of any defect in the transferor's title, amount to theft of the property.

The meaning of 'appropriation' is fundamental in the law of theft and has been the subject of extensive litigation. All the leading cases are examined in the controversial case of *Hinks* which follows.

R v Hinks

[2000] 4 All ER 833, House of Lords

(Lords Slynn, Jauncey, Steyn, Hutton and Hobhouse)

Hinks (H), a 38-year-old woman, was friendly with John Dolphin (D). She described herself as D's main carer. There was evidence that D was extremely naive and gullible. It would be easy to take advantage of him. But he understood the concept of ownership and was quite capable of making a gift. In a period of a few months he withdrew about £60,000 from his building society account. The money was deposited in H's account. D also gave H a television set. H was convicted of theft in four counts covering moneys and one count covering the television. The question left to the jury was 'Was [D] so mentally incapable that the defendant herself realised that ordinary and decent people would regard it as dishonest to accept a gift from him?' On appeal it was argued that, if the gift was valid, the acceptance of it could not be theft. Rose LJ, dismissing the appeal, ruled:

. . . in relation to theft, one of the ingredients for a jury to consider is not whether there has been a gift, valid or otherwise, but whether there has been an appropriation. A gift may be clear evidence of appropriation. But a jury should not, in our view, be asked to consider whether a gift has been validly made.

H appealed.

[**Lord Jauncey** said he would dismiss the appeal for the reasons given by Lord Steyn.]

Lord Steyn. Since the enactment of the Theft Act 1968 the House of Lords has on three occasions considered the meaning of the word 'appropriates' in s 1(1) of the 1968 Act, namely in *Lawrence v Comr of Police for the Metropolis* [1971] 2 All ER 1253, [1972] AC 626; in *R v Morris; Anderton v Burnside* [1983] 3 All ER 288, [1984] AC 320; and in *R v Gomez* [1993] 1 All ER 1, [1993] AC 442. The law as explained in *Lawrence*'s case and *R v Gomez*, and applied by the Court of Appeal in the present case ([2000] 1 Cr App Rep 1) has attracted strong criticism from distinguished academic lawyers: see for example, JC Smith [1993] Crim LR 304 and [1998] Crim LR 904; Edward Griew *The Theft Acts* (7th edn, 1995) pp 41–59; ATH Smith 'Gifts and the Law of Theft' [1999] CLJ 10. These views have however been challenged by equally distinguished academic writers: PR Glazebrook 'Revising the Theft Acts' [1993] CLJ 191–194; [Mr Glazebrook's article does not in fact 'challenge' these views and the reference to it is omitted in [2001] 2 AC 241 at 244] Simon Gardner 'Property and Theft' [1998] Crim LR 35. The academic criticism of *R v Gomez* provided in substantial measure the springboard for the present appeal. The certified question before the House is as follows: 'Whether the acquisition of an indefeasible title to property is capable of amounting to an appropriation of property belonging to another for the purposes of s 1(1) of the Theft Act 1968'. In other words, the question is whether a person can 'appropriate' property belonging to another where the other person makes him an indefeasible gift of property, retaining no proprietary interest or any right to resume or recover any proprietary interest in the property.

Before the enactment of the 1968 Act English law required a taking and carrying away of the property as the actus reus of the offence. In 1968 Parliament chose to broaden the reach of the law of theft by requiring merely an appropriation. The relevant sections of the Act are as follows:

[Lord Steyn set out the relevant provisions of the Theft Act and the facts of the case, and quoted from the trial judge's summing-up and the judgment of the Court of Appeal; and continued:]

My Lords, counsel for the appellant has not expressly asked the House to depart from the previous decisions of the House. He did, however, submit with the aid of the writings of Sir John Smith that the conviction of a donee for receiving a perfectly valid gift is a completely new departure. Relying on the academic criticism of the earlier decisions of the House counsel submitted that their reach should not be extended. Counsel cited as evidence of the true intention of the draftsman a passage from a note by Sir John Smith on the decision in *R v Hinks* [1998] Crim LR 904. The passage reads as follows (at 904–905):

> 'In a memorandum dated January 15, 1964 the distinguished draftsman of the Theft Act (Mr J.S. Fiennes, as he then was) wrote to members of the Larceny Sub-Committee of the Criminal Law Revision Committee: "I trust the Sub-Committee will not agree with Dr [Glanville] Williams when he says ... that a person appropriates for himself property of which another person is the owner every time he gratefully accepts a gift or buys an apple. If this is what the words mean, then the whole language of the clause ought to be changed, because one really cannot have a definition of stealing which relies on the word 'dishonestly' to prevent it covering every acquisition of property." '

Sir John Smith returned to this point in 'The Sad Fate of the Theft Act 1968', an essay in W Swadling and G Jones *The Search for Principle, Essays in Honour of Lord Goff of Chieveley* (1999) pp 97, 100–101. While this anecdote is an interesting bit of legal history, it is not relevant to the question before the House. Given counsel's use of it, as well as aspects of Sir John Smith's writing on the point in question, which have played such a large role in the present case, it is necessary to state quite firmly how the issue of interpretation should be approached. In *Black-Clawson International Ltd v Papierwerke Waldhof-Aschaffenburg AG* [1975] 1 All ER 810 at 814, [1975] AC 591 at 613 Lord Reid observed:

> 'We often say that we are looking for the intention of Parliament, but that is not quite accurate. We are seeking the meaning of the words which Parliament used. We are seeking not what Parliament meant but the true meaning of what they said.'

This does not rule out or diminish relevant contextual material. But it is the critical point of departure of statutory interpretation. It also sets logical limits to what may be called in aid of statutory interpretation. Thus the published eighth report of the Criminal Law Revision Committee on *Theft and Related Offences* (Cmnd 2977 (1966)), and in particular para 35, may arguably be relevant as part of the background against which Parliament enacted the Bill which became the 1968 Act. How far it in fact takes one is a matter considered in *R v Gomez*. Relevant publicly available contextual materials are readily admitted in aid of the construction of statutes. On the other hand, to delve into the intentions of individual members of the committee, and their communications, would be to rely on material which cannot conceivably be relevant. If statutory interpretation is to be a rational and coherent process a line has to be drawn somewhere. And what Mr Fiennes wrote to the larceny Sub-committee was demonstrably on the wrong side of the line.

V

The starting point must be the words of the statute as interpreted by the House in its previous decisions. The first case in the trilogy is *R v Lawrence* [1971] 2 All ER 1253, [1972] AC 626. The defendant, a taxi driver, had without objection on the part of an Italian student asked for a fare of £6 for a journey for which the correct lawful fare was 10s 6d. The taxi driver was convicted of theft. On appeal the main contention was that the student had consented to pay the fare. But it was clear that the appellant had not told the student what the lawful fare was. With the agreement of all the Law Lords hearing the case Viscount Dilhorne observed:

> 'Prior to the passage of the Theft Act 1968, which made radical changes in and greatly simplified the law relating to theft and some other offences, it was necessary to prove that the property alleged to have been stolen was taken "without the consent of the owner" (Larceny Act 1916, s 1(1)). These words are not included in s 1(1) of the Theft Act 1968, but the appellant contended that the subsection should be construed as if they were, as if they appeared after the word "appropriates". Section 1(1) provides: "A person is guilty of theft if he dishonestly appropriates property belonging to another with the intention of permanently depriving the other of it; and 'thief' and 'steal' shall be construed accordingly." I see no ground for concluding that the omission of the words "without the consent of the owner" was unadvertent and not deliberate, and to read the subsection as if they were included is, in my opinion, wholly unwarranted. Parliament by the omission of these words has relieved the prosecution of the burden of establishing that the taking was without the owner's consent. That is no longer an ingredient of the offence. Megaw LJ, delivering the judgment of the Court of Appeal ([1970] 3 All ER at 935, [1971] 1 QB at 376), said that the offence created by s 1(1) involved four elements: "(i) a dishonest (ii) appropriation (iii) of property belonging to another (iv) with the intention of permanently depriving the owner of it." I agree. That there was appropriation in this case is clear. Section 3(1) states that any assumption by a person of the rights of an owner amounts to an appropriation. Here there was clearly such an assumption. That an appropriation was dishonest may be proved in a number of ways. In this case it was not contended that the appellant had not acted dishonestly.' (See [1971] 2 All ER 1253 at 1254–1255, [1972] AC 626 at 631–632.)

Viscount Dilhorne expressly added that belief that the passenger gave informed consent (ie knowing that he was paying in excess of the fare) 'is relevant to the issue of dishonesty, not to the question whether or not there has been an appropriation' (see [1971] 2 All ER 1253 at 1255, [1972] AC 626 at 632). The appeal was dismissed. The ratio decidendi of *Lawrence*'s case, namely that in a prosecution for theft it is unnecessary to prove that the taking was without the owner's consent, goes to the heart of the certified question in the present case.

The second decision of the House was *R v Morris; Anderton v Burnside* [1983] 3 All ER 288, [1984] AC 320, in 1983, a consolidated appeal involving two cases in each of which the defendant attached a price label to goods in a supermarket which showed a price lower than that which was properly payable for the goods. The defendant intended to pay the lower price at the checkout. In the first case the defendant's deception was detected at the checkout point and in the second he paid the lower prices at the checkout. He was convicted of theft in both cases. The House concluded that the defendant had been rightly convicted of theft on both counts. In each case the certified question was the rolled-up one whether there had been a 'dishonest appropriation' of goods. These questions were answered in the affirmative. However, in the single substantive judgment Lord Roskill made an observation, which was in conflict with the ratio of *Lawrence*'s case and had to be corrected in *R v Gomez*. Lord Roskill said:

> 'If one postulates an honest customer taking goods from a shelf to put in his or her trolley to take to the check-point there to pay the proper price, I am unable to see that any of these actions involves any assumption by the shopper of the rights of the supermarket. In the context of s 3(1), the concept of appropriation in my view involves not an act expressly or impliedly authorised by the owner but an act by way of adverse interference with or usurpation of those rights.' (See [1983] 3 All ER 288 at 293, [1984] AC 320 at 332.)

It will be observed that this observation was not necessary for the decision of the case: absent this observation the House would still have held that there had been an appropriation. Lord Roskill took the view that he was following the decision in *Lawrence*'s case. It is clear, however, that his observation (as opposed to the decision in *R v Morris*) cannot stand with the ratio of *Lawrence*'s case.

And as his observation, cast in terms of 'the honest customer', shows Lord Roskill conflated the ingredients of appropriation and dishonesty contrary to the holding in *Lawrence*'s case.

The third decision of the House was in *R v Gomez* [1993] 1 All ER 1, [1993] AC 442, in 1992. The defendant was employed as an assistant shop manager. He agreed with two accomplices that goods would be supplied by the shop in return for cheques which he knew to be stolen. He told the manager of the shop that the cheques were as good as cash. The Court of Appeal held that there was a voidable contract between the owner of the shop and the dishonest receivers of the goods; that the transfer was with the consent of the owner; and that accordingly there was no appropriation. The Court of Appeal quashed the conviction arising from a plea of guilty. The following question was certified:

> 'When theft is alleged and that which is alleged to be stolen passes to the defendant with the consent of the owner, but that consent has been obtained by a false representation, has, a) an appropriation within the meaning of s. 1(1) of the Theft Act 1968 taken place, or, b) must such a passing of property necessarily involve an element of adverse [interference] with or usurpation of some right of the owner?' (see [1993] 1 All ER 1 at 4, [1993] AC 442 at 444.)

By a majority (Lord Lowry dissenting) the House answered branch (a) of the certified question in the affirmative and branch (b) in the negative. In crystalline terms Lord Keith of Kinkel speaking for all the numbers of the majority ruled the following ([1993] 1 All ER 1 at 12, [1993] AC 442 at 464). (1) The meaning of the relevant provisions must be determined by construing the statutory language without reference to the report which preceded it, namely the eighth report of the Criminal Law Revision Committee on *Theft and Related Offences* (Cmnd 2977 (1966)). (2) The observations of Lord Roskill in *R v Morris* were unnecessary for the decision of that case; that they were in clear conflict with the ratio of *Lawrence*'s case; and that they were wrong. (3) *Lawrence*'s case must be accepted as authoritative and correct, and 'there is no question of it now being right to depart from it'. At the same time Lord Keith ([1993] 1 All ER 1 at 12, [1993] AC 442 at 463), endorsed the judgment of Parker LJ in the civil case of *Dobson v General Accident Fire and Life Assurance Corp plc* [1989] 3 All ER 927, [1990] 1 QB 274 where Parker LJ highlighted the conflict between *Lawrence*'s case and *R v Morris* and chose to follow *Lawrence*'s case. (4) Any act may be an appropriation notwithstanding that it was done with the consent or authorisation of the owner. In *R v Gomez* [1993] 1 All ER 1, [1993] AC 442 at 448 the House was expressly invited to hold that 'there is no appropriation where the entire proprietary interest passes'. That submission was rejected. The leading judgment in *R v Gomez* was therefore in terms which unambiguously rule out the submission that s 3(1) does not apply to a case of a gift duly carried out because in such a case the entire proprietary interest will have passed. In a separate judgment (with which Lord Jauncey of Tullichettle expressed agreement) Lord Browne-Wilkinson observed:

> 'I regard the word "appropriation" in isolation as being an objective description of the act done irrespective of the mental state of either the owner or the accused. It is impossible to reconcile the decision in *Lawrence* (that the question of consent is irrelevant in considering whether this has been an appropriation) with the views expressed in *Morris*, which latter views in my judgment were incorrect.' (See [1993] 1 All ER 1 at 39, [1993] AC 442 at 495–496.)

In other words it is immaterial whether the act was done with the owner's consent or authority. It is true of course that the certified question in *R v Gomez* referred to the situation where consent had been obtained by fraud. But the majority judgments do not differentiate between cases of consent induced by fraud and consent given in any other circumstances. The ratio involves a proposition of general application. *R v Gomez* therefore gives effect to s 3(1) of the 1968 Act by treating 'appropriation' as a neutral word comprehending 'any assumption by a person of the rights of an owner'. If the law is as held in *R v Gomez*, it destroys the argument advanced on the present appeal, namely that an indefeasible gift of property cannot amount to an appropriation.

VI

Counsel for the appellant submitted in the first place that the law as expounded in *R v Gomez* and *Lawrence*'s case must be qualified to say that there can be no appropriation unless the other party (the owner) retains some proprietary interest, or the right to resume or recover some proprietary interest, in the property. Alternatively, counsel argued that 'appropriates' should be interpreted as if the word 'unlawfully' preceded it. Counsel said that the effect of the decisions in *Lawrence*'s case and *R v Gomez* is to reduce the actus reus of theft to 'vanishing point' (see Smith and Hogan *Criminal Law* (9th edn, 1999) p 505). He argued that the result is to bring the criminal law 'into conflict' with the civil law. Moreover, he argued that the decisions in *Lawrence*'s case and *R v Gomez* may produce absurd and grotesque results. He argued that the mental requirements of dishonesty and intention of permanently depriving the owner of property are insufficient to filter out some cases of conduct which should not sensibly be regarded as theft. He did not suggest that the appellant's dishonest and repellent conduct came within such a category. Instead he deployed four examples for this purpose, namely the following. (1) S makes a handsome gift to D because he believes that D has obtained a First. D has not and knows that S is acting under that misapprehension. He makes a gift. There is here a motivational mistake which, it is submitted, does not avoid the transaction. (Glanville Williams *Textbook of Criminal Law* (1978) p 788). (2) P sees D's painting and, thinking he is getting a bargain, offers D £100,000 for it. D realises that P thinks the painting is a Constable, but knows that it was painted by his sister and is worth no more than £100. He accepts P's offer. D has made an enforceable contract and is entitled to recover and retain the purchase price (*Smith and Hogan* pp 507–508). (3) A buys a roadside garage business from B, abutting on a public thoroughfare; unknown to A but known to B, it has already been decided to construct a bypass road which will divert substantially the whole of the traffic from passing A's garage. There is an enforceable contract and A is entitled to recover and retain the purchase price. The same would be true if B *knew* that A was unaware of the intended plan to construct a bypass road. (Compare Lord Atkin in *Bell v Lever Bros Ltd* [1932] AC 161 at 224, [1931] All ER Rep 1 at 30.) (4) An employee agrees to retire before the end of his contract of employment, receiving a sum of money by way of compensation from his employer. Unknown to the employer, the employee has committed serious breaches of contract which would have enabled the employer to dismiss him without compensation. Assuming that the employee's failure to reveal his defaults does not affect the validity of the contract, so that the employee is entitled to sue for the promised compensation, is the employee liable to be arrested for the theft the moment he receives the money? (Glanville Williams 'Theft and Voidable Title' [1981] Crim LR 666 at 672).

My Lords, at first glance these are rather telling examples. They may conceivably have justified a more restricted meaning of s 3(1) than prevailed in *Lawrence*'s case and *R v Gomez*. The House ruled otherwise and I am quite unpersuaded that the House overlooked the consequences of its decision. On the facts set out in the examples a jury could possibly find that the acceptance of the transfer took place in the belief that the transferee had the right in law to deprive the other of it within the meaning of s 2(1)(a) of the 1968 Act. Moreover, in such cases a prosecution is hardly likely and, if mounted, is likely to founder on the basis that the jury will not be persuaded that there was dishonesty in the required sense. And one must retain a sense of perspective. At the extremity of the application of legal rules there are sometimes results which may seem strange. A matter of judgment is then involved. The rule may have to be recast. Sir John Smith has eloquently argued that the rule in question ought to be recast. I am unpersuaded. If the law is restated by adopting a narrower definition of appropriation, the outcome is likely to place beyond the reach of the criminal law dishonest persons who should be found guilty of theft. The suggested revisions would unwarrantably restrict the scope of the law of theft and complicate the fair and effective prosecution of theft. In my view the law as settled in *Lawrence*'s case and *R v Gomez* does not demand the suggested revision.

Those decisions can be applied by judges and juries in a way which, absent human error, does not result in injustice.

Counsel for the appellant further pointed out that the law as stated in *Lawrence*'s case and *R v Gomez* creates a tension between the civil and the criminal law. In other words, conduct which is not wrongful in a civil law sense may constitute the crime of theft. Undoubtedly, this is so. The question whether the civil claim to title by a convicted thief, who committed no civil wrong, may be defeated by the principle that nobody may benefit from his own civil *or* criminal wrong does not arise for decision. Nevertheless there is a more general point, namely that the interaction between criminal law and civil law can cause problems: compare Beatson and Simester 'Stealing One's Own Property' (1999) 115 LQR 372. The purposes of the civil law and the criminal law are somewhat different. In theory the two systems should be in perfect harmony. In a practical world there will sometimes be some disharmony between the two systems. In any event, it would be wrong to assume on a priori grounds that the criminal law rather than the civil law is defective. Given the jury's conclusions, one is entitled to observe that the appellant's conduct *should* constitute theft, the only available charge. The tension between the civil and the criminal law is therefore not in my view a factor which justifies a departure from the law as stated in *Lawrence*'s case and *R v Gomez*. Moreover, these decisions of the House have a marked beneficial consequence. While in some contexts of the law of theft a judge cannot avoid explaining civil law concepts to a jury (eg in respect of s 2(1)(a)), the decisions of the House of Lords eliminate the need for such explanations in respect of appropriation. That is a great advantage in an overly complex corner of the law.

VII

My Lords, if it had been demonstrated that in practice *Lawrence* and *Gomez* were calculated to pro-duce injustice that would have been a compelling reason to revisit the merits of the holdings in those decisions. That is however, not the case. In practice the mental requirements of theft are an adequate protection against injustice. In these circumstances I would not be willing to depart from the clear decisions of the House in *Lawrence* and *Gomez*. This brings me back to counsels' principal submission, namely that a person does not appropriate property unless the other (the owner) retains, beyond the instant of the alleged theft, This submission is directly contrary to the holdings in *Lawrence*'s case and *R v Gomez*. It must be rejected. The alternative submission is that the word 'appropriates' should be interpreted as if the word 'unlawfully' preceded it so that only an act which is unlawful under the general law can be an appropriation. This submission is an invitation to interpolate a word in the carefully crafted language of the 1968 Act. It runs counter to the decisions in *Lawrence*'s case and *R v Gomez* and must also be rejected. It follows that the certified question must be answered in the affirmative. . . .

[**Lord Hutton** made a speech giving reasons why he would allow the appeal and quash the convictions.]

Lord Hobhouse. Rose LJ said ([2000] 1 Cr App Rep 1 at 9):

> 'In our judgment, in relation to theft, one of the ingredients for a jury to consider is not whether there has been a gift, valid or otherwise, but whether there has been appropriation. *A gift may be clear evidence of appropriation*. But a jury should not, in our view, be asked to consider whether a gift has been validly made . . .' (My emphasis.)

The dismissiveness of this reasoning is in itself remarkable but the proposition which needs particularly to be examined is that which I have emphasised bearing in mind that the Court of Appeal draws no distinction between a fully effective gift and one which is vitiated by incapacity, fraud or some other feature which would lead both the man in the street and the law to say that the transfer was not a true gift resulting from an actual intention of the donor to give. Another aspect of the Court of Appeal's reasoning which also has to be examined is the relationship of that proposition to the concept of dishonesty. It is explicit in the Court of Appeal judgment that the relevant definition of the crime of theft is to be found in the element of dishonesty and *R v Ghosh* [1982] 2 All ER 689, [1982] QB 1053 and that this is to receive no greater definition than consciously falling below the standards of an ordinary and decent person and may include anything which such a person would think was morally reprehensible. It may be no more than a moral judgment.

The reasoning of the Court of Appeal therefore depends upon the disturbing acceptance that a criminal conviction and the imposition of custodial sanctions may be based upon conduct which involves no inherent illegality and may only be capable of being criticised on grounds of lack of morality. This approach itself raises fundamental questions. An essential function of the criminal law is to define the boundary between what conduct is criminal and what merely immoral. Both are the subject of the disapprobation of ordinary right-thinking citizens and the distinction is liable to be arbitrary or at least strongly influenced by considerations subjective to the individual members of the tribunal. To treat otherwise lawful conduct as criminal merely because it is open to such disapprobation would be contrary to principle and open to the objection that it fails to achieve the objective and transparent certainty required of the criminal law by the principles basic to human rights.

I stress once more that it is not my view that the resort to such reasoning was necessary for the decision of the present case. I would be reluctant to think that those of your Lordships who favour dismissing this appeal have fallen into the trap of believing that, without adopting the reasoning of the Court of Appeal in this case, otherwise guilty defendants will escape justice. The facts of the present case do not justify such a conclusion nor do the facts of any other case which has been cited on this appeal.

[Lord Hobhouse examined the 1968 Act, ss 1–6 and continued:]

Section 5 and, particularly, s 5(4) demonstrate that the 1968 Act has been drafted so as to take account of and require reference to the civil law of property, contract and restitution. The same applies to many other sections of the 1968 Act. For example, s 6 is drafted by reference to the phrase 'regardless of the other's rights'—that is to say rights under the civil law. Section 28, dealing with the restoration of stolen goods, clearly can only work if the law of theft recognises and respects transfers of property valid under the civil law, otherwise it would be giving the criminal courts the power to deprive citizens of their property otherwise than in accordance with the law.

Section 5 shows that the state of mind of the transferor at the time of transfer may be relevant and critical. Similarly, the degree of the transferee's knowledge will be relevant to the s 5 question quite independently of any question under s 2. For instance, where there has been a mistake on the part of the transferor, the position under s 5(4) can be different depending on whether or not the transferee was aware of the mistake.

Further, it will be appreciated that the situations to which s 5 is relevant can embrace gifts as well as other transactions such as transfers for value. The prosecution must be able to prove that, at the time of the alleged appropriation, the relevant property belonged to another within the meaning given to that phrase by s 5. Where the defendant has been validly given the property he can no longer appropriate property belonging to another. The Court of Appeal does not seem to have had their attention directed to s 5. The question certified on the grant of leave to appeal is self-contradictory. [see [1998] Crim LR at 906. The House of Lords amended the question; above, p **750**] The direction of the trial judge approved by the Court of Appeal is inadequate. There is no law against appropriating your own property as defined by s 5.

[Lord Hobhouse examined s 2(1) of the 1968 Act and continued:]

Although s 2 is headed 'Dishonestly', this quotation shows that it is as much involved with the application of the concepts 'appropriation' and 'property belonging to another'. Paragraph

(a) contemplates that the defendant believes that he has the right to appropriate the property and (b) his belief that he would have the consent of the person to whom the property belongs to appropriate it. If belief in such a right or such consent can prevent the defendant's conduct from amounting to theft (whatever the jury may think of it), how can it be said that his knowledge that he has such a right or the actual consent of the person to whom the property belongs is irrelevant? How can it be said that the right of the defendant to accept a gift is irrelevant—or the fact that the transferor has actually and validly consented to the defendant having the relevant property? Yet it is precisely these things which the judgment of the Court of Appeal would wholly exclude.

Section 2(1) is cutting down the classes of conduct which the jury are at liberty to treat as dishonest. They qualify the *R v Ghosh* approach and show that in any given case the court must consider whether it is adequate to give an unqualified *R v Ghosh* direction as the Court of Appeal held to be sufficient in the present case.

Gifts

The discussion in the present case has been marked by a failure to consider the law of gift. Perhaps most remarkable is the statement of the Court of Appeal that 'a gift may be clear evidence of appropriation'. The making of a gift is the act of the donor. It involves the donor in forming the intention to give and then acting on that intention by doing whatever it is necessary for him to do to transfer the relevant property to the donee. Where the gift is the gift of a chattel, the act required to complete the gift will normally be either delivery to the donee or to a person who is to hold the chattel as the bailee of the donee; money can be transferred by having it credited to the donee's bank account—and so on. Unless the gift was conditional, in which case the condition must be satisfied before the gift can take effect, the making of the gift is complete once the donor has carried out this step. The gift has become the property of the donee. It is not necessary for the donee to know of the gift. The donee, on becoming aware of the gift, has the right to refuse (or reject) the gift in which case it revests in the donor with resolutive effect. (See 20 *Halsbury Laws* (4th edn. reissue) paras 48–49 and the cases cited.)

What consequences does this have for the law of theft? Once the donor has done his part in transferring the property to the defendant, the property, subject to the special situations identified in the subsections of s 5, ceases to be 'property belonging to another'. However wide a meaning one were to give to 'appropriates', there cannot be a theft. For it to be possible for there to be a theft there will have to be something more, like an absence of a capacity to give or a mistake satisfying s 5(4). Similarly, where the donee himself performs the act necessary to transfer the property to himself, as he would if he himself took the chattel out of the possession of the donor or, himself, gave the instructions to the donor's bank, s 5(1) would apply and mean that that constituent of the crime of theft would at that time have been satisfied.

If one treats the 'acceptance' of the gift as an appropriation, and this was the approach of the judge and is implicit in the judgment of the Court of Appeal (despite their choice of words), there are immediate difficulties with s 2(1)(a). The defendant did have the right to deprive the donor of the property. The donor did consent to the appropriation; indeed, he intended it. There are also difficulties with s 6 as she was not acting regardless of the donor's rights; the donor has already surrendered his rights. The only way that these conclusions can be displaced is by showing that the gift was not valid. There are even difficulties with s 3 itself. The donee is not 'assuming the rights of an owner': she has them already.

My Lords, the relevant law is contained in ss 1 to 6 of the 1968 Act. They should be construed as a whole and applied in a manner which presents a consistent scheme both internally and with the remainder of the 1968 Act. The phrase 'dishonestly appropriates' should be construed as a composite phrase. It does not include acts done in relation to the relevant property which are done in accordance with the actual wishes or actual authority of the person to whom the property belongs. This is because such acts do not involve any assumption of the rights of that person within s 3(1) or because, by necessary implication from s 2(1), they are not to be regarded as dishonest appropriations of property belonging to another.

Actual authority, wishes, consent (or similar words) mean, both as a matter of language and on the authority of the three House of Lords cases, authorisation not obtained by fraud or misrepresentation. The definition of theft therefore embraces cases where the property has come to the defendant by the mistake of the person to whom it belongs and there would be an obligation to restore it— s5(4)—or property in which the other still has an equitable proprietary interest—s 5(1). This would also embrace property obtained by undue influence or other cases coming within the classes of invalid transfer recognised in *Re Beaney* (*decd*) [1978] 2 All ER 595, [1978] 1 WLR 770.

In cases of alleged gift, the criteria to be applied are the same. But additional care may need to be taken to see that the transaction is properly explained to the jury. It is unlikely that a charge of theft will be brought where there is not clear evidence of at least some conduct of the defendant which includes an element of fraud or overt dishonesty or some undue influence or knowledge of the deficient capacity of the alleged donor. This was the basis upon which the prosecution of the appellant was originally brought in the present case. On this basis there is no difficulty in explaining to the jury the relevant parts of s 5 and s 2(1) and the effect of the phrase 'assumption of the rights of an owner'....

I would answer the certified question in the negative. But, in any event, I would allow the appeal and quash the conviction because the summing-up failed to direct the jury adequately upon the other essential elements of theft, not just appropriation.

Appeal dismissed

Notes and questions

1. *Aids to interpretation* (above, p **748**). The crucial difference between Lord Keith, speaking for the majority, and the dissenting Lord Lowry, in *Gomez* was that the Lord Keith thought that 'no useful purpose' would be served by looking at the CLRC's 8th Report, whereas Lord Lowry demonstrated convincingly that the CLRC intended that:

   (i) where D, by deception, obtained from V the entire proprietary interest in property, he should be guilty of an offence under s 15 of the Theft Act, but *not* of theft;

  (ii) where D, by deception obtained possession of the property from V, but not ownership, he should be guilty of an offence under s 15 and of theft;

 (iii) where D appropriated property from V without employing any deception he should be guilty of theft.

It was not, in the view of the CLRC, an appropriation of property *belonging to another* (and hence not theft) where D obtained the entire proprietary interest. Was Lord Lowry's investigation 'a useful purpose'? Or was it irrelevant because the House, rightly or wrongly, had, without reference to the relevant passages in the CLRC Report, decided otherwise in *Lawrence*?

2. '*Without the consent of the owner.*' This phrase was included in the Larceny Act because a trespassory taking was an essential element in stealing at common law. It was omitted from the Theft Act so as to avoid unjustified acquittals in cases such as the following. D invites V's employee, E, to assist him to steal V's goods. E pretends to agree but loyally informs V who tells him to go through with the transaction to entrap D. E does so. D was not guilty of larceny because he received *possession* with V's consent—there was no trespass. But D did not receive, nor did he suppose he was receiving, ownership of the property. His intentional assumption of V's entire proprietary interest, without V's consent was clearly an appropriation and is now theft.

3. Notice also that the Larceny Act provided an alternative, statutory, form of stealing, larceny by a bailee, consisting in 'conversion' by the bailee of the goods in his possession. This made no reference to consent. It was unnecessary because conversion with consent would have been a contradiction in terms. 'Conversion' was the model for the definition in the 1968 Act. The CLRC thought that 'appropriation' was a better word for the same thing. The preference for that word did not mean that consent became irrelevant. (See generally, G . Ferris, 'The Origins of Larceny by Trick and Constructive Possession' [1998] Crim LR 17).

4. The first edition of J. C. Smith's *Law of Theft* (published before the 1968 Act came into force) advised prosecutors that the golden rule should be that, whenever property was obtained by any kind of trick or deception, the offender should be charged under s 15 (obtaining property by deception) and not under s 1. If this rule had been observed in *Lawrence* and in *Gomez* would there have been the slightest difficulty in upholding their convictions?

5. *Rights of an owner?* In *Morris*, above, p 752, Lord Roskill rejected an argument that in s 3, above, p 752, 'the rights of an owner' means *all* those rights, saying that the later words 'any assumption of a right' in sub-s (1) and 'no later assumption by him of rights' in sub-s (2) militated strongly against that view: it was sufficient that D assumed one such right, for example, labeling goods. In *Gomez*, Lord Keith said that Lord Roskill was 'undoubtedly right'. Do you agree that this was a correct, or possible, interpretation of s 3? Does not 'a right *to it*' (italicized words omitted by Lord Roskill) mean all the rights?

6. Consider counsel's 'rather telling examples,' above, pp 754–755 Should these cases be theft? Did it follow from the decision in *Gomez* that they must be?

7. D enters a supermarket and picks up a sandwich. He is hungry, so he eats it as he walks towards the cash desk, he intends to offer the packaging displaying its bar code at the cash desk and pay the amount due. When he gets to the cash desk there is no one present. He decides to leave without paying and puts the package in the bin on the way out. Has D committed theft? If so when?

8. Hinks was ordered to pay £19,000 compensation to Dolphin. Compensation for what? For keeping a gift which she was legally entitled to keep? The jury's verdict did not decide that she did not have an *indefeasible* title to the property. Was the judge entitled to decide that her title was defeasible?—for misrepresentation, undue influence, or what? Does Hinks have an argument that the order was contrary to her right to peaceful enjoyment of her possessions under Article 1 protocol 1 of the ECHR?

9. Stolen goods cease to be 'stolen' when the owner ceases to have any right to restitution: Theft Act 1968, s 24(3), p **922**, below. If the gift was indefeasible, Dolphin never had any right to restitution. There were no stolen goods. Is a theft without stolen goods a possibility? Is this a desirable state of affairs for English law to find itself in?

10. Suppose Dolphin had delivered the television to H's house without her knowledge when she was out, with a note saying that it was a gift. Could H have been guilty of theft if, on finding the TV, she had decided 'dishonestly' to retain it? Can it possibly be said that the

TV was 'property belonging to another'? Is the decision limited to the case where there is no interval between a donee's acquisition of an indefeasible title and his 'dishonest appropriation'?

11. For other discussion of *Hinks*, see commentary at [2001] Crim LR 263; A. T. H. Smith, 'Theft as sharp practice: who cares now?' [2001] CLJ 21; and for a defence of the decision, S. Shute, 'Appropriation and the Law of Theft' [2002] Crim LR 445. Shute suggests that dishonest conduct such as that in *Hinks*, although it might not constitute a civil law wrong, 'may nonetheless have a *tendency* to undermine property rights either directly by attacking the interests that they protect, or indirectly by weakening an established system of property rights and so threatening the public good that the system represents.' Do you agree? Is this a sufficiently clear and certain basis on which to construct an offence?

12. In *Gallasso* (1992) 98 Cr App R 284, [1993] Crim LR 459, CA, G was a house leader at a home for the mentally handicapped and was placed in charge of their finances. When cheques were received for patients G would deposit them in trust accounts in the patients' names and was authorized to draw on them to meet the needs of the patients. G received a cheque for £4,250 on behalf of J, a patient, with which she opened a trust account at the Wood Green branch of the Halifax Building Society. With a second cheque for £4,000 received on J's behalf, she opened a further trust account, this time at the St Albans branch of the HBS. With a third cheque for £1,800.32, again received on behalf of J, she opened a second cash card account at the Wood Green branch; this was also a trust account in J's name. G subsequently drew on the St Albans account and the Wood Green cash card account for her own purposes.

   G was convicted on various charges of theft including theft of the cheque for £4,000 and the cheque for £1,800.32. Allowing the appeal and quashing G's convictions, the court said there must still be 'a taking' to give 'appropriation' its ordinary meaning.

   Is this right? For an appropriation what more is required, after *Gomez*, beyond a dealing by the defendant with another's property, whether the dealing is consented to or not, with the dishonest intent to deprive the owner permanently of it?

13. *An act of appropriation?* Consider D who persuades a vulnerable individual, V, to go into her safe and collect her jewels in order to give them to D. At what point has D committed an appropriation? When he tells V to do it? When V touches the jewels? When D first touches them? See *Briggs* [2004] Crim LR 455.

14. *Where does the appropriation occur?* In *Atakpu* [1993] 4 All ER 215, [1994] QB 69, CA, the convictions of the defendants for conspiracy to steal were quashed where they hired cars in Germany and Belgium with the intention of shipping them to England, altering their identity and selling them to unsuspecting purchasers. On the *Gomez* view the cars were stolen in Germany and Belgium and the defendants could not steal again in England property which they had already stolen abroad.

   G. R. Sullivan and C. Warbrick, [1994] Crim LR 650, 659, argue that the Court of Appeal:

reached this undesirable conclusion because it allowed itself to be misled by the familiar language that 'theft abroad is not triable in England' and decided that the cars were stolen in Germany or Belgium. But they were not. The proper explanation is that if the defendants had done in England what they did in Belgium or Germany, the cars would have been stolen here. Because the Theft Act does not reach conduct in Belgium or Germany the cars were not, in this sense, 'stolen' there ... the cars had not been stolen according to English law before they arrived here, and they could be stolen when the defendants kept and dealt with them as owners here, conduct within the reach of the territorial jurisdiction of English criminal law.

Do you agree? The court relied on s 24(1) of the Theft Act 1968 which provides that:

The provisions of this Act relating to goods which have been stolen shall apply whether the stealing occurred in England or Wales or elsewhere, and whether it occurred before or after the commencement of this Act, provided that the stealing (if not an offence under this Act) amounted to an offence where and at the time when the goods were stolen....

Sullivan and Warbrick argue that this points to the opposite conclusion—the subsection provides an extended definition of 'stolen goods' for the purposes of the offence of handling and it acknowledges that stealing goods outside England and Wales is 'not an offence [sc, theft] under this Act'. Might it be argued, to the contrary, that the words in parentheses imply that some stealing outside England and Wales *will be* an offence under the Act? In some jurisdictions, for example, Canada, taking with intent *temporarily* to deprive is theft. Are these words intended to cover cases such as the handling in England of goods stolen in Canada by Canadian law, whether or not there was an intention permanently to deprive? Should such conduct be an offence under English law?

15. As to s 3(2), above, p 749, the CLRC observed (Cmnd 2977, para 37):

A person may buy something in good faith, but may find out afterwards that the seller had no title to it.... If the buyer nevertheless keeps the thing or otherwise deals with it as owner, he could, on the principles stated above, be guilty of theft. It is arguable that this would be right; but on the whole it seems to us that, whatever view is taken on the buyer's moral duty, the law would be too strict if it made him guilty of theft.

In *Adams* (1993) 15 Cr App R (S) 466, [1993] Crim LR 72, CA, D, in good faith, purchased motor cycle parts but did not suspect they were stolen until two or three days later. D's conviction for stealing the parts was quashed. At the time of the acquisition of the parts—the relevant time under s 3(2)—he believed he had become their owner and by thereafter exercising an owner's rights he could not be guilty of theft even though he realized that he had no title to the parts.

Suppose Adams, after discovering the parts are stolen, sells them to V, an innocent purchaser, for £100. May Adams be convicted of (i) stealing the parts; (ii) obtaining £100 from V by deception; (iii) stealing the £100?

(2) THEFT, APPROPRIATION AND CORPORATIONS

Property may belong to a corporation just as much as an individual and may be stolen from the corporation. Such property may be stolen whether the person appropriating it is a stranger to, an employee of, a shareholder in, or the managing director of, the corporation. The dishonest appropriation, with intent permanently to deprive, of a laptop belonging to a university is theft whether the appropriator is a student, a member of staff or the vice-chancellor.

Difficulties arise where the appropriation is done by those who are the sole directors of and shareholders in the company. Supposing that Don and Ed are the sole directors of and shareholders in the company, may they steal the laptop from 'their' company? It may be asked—who cares?—and the answer is that no one is likely to care very much about the appropriation of the laptop but people, most especially creditors, will care if Don and Ed dissipate the company's assets on any considerable scale and thereby deny those assets to their creditors.

If Don is a sole trader he cannot steal *his* assets. Suppose that Don, realizing that the days are numbered for his business, decides that rather than retain what is left for the benefit of creditors, he will spend the remaining £10,000 on a lavish holiday. If Don does so he is not a thief. There is no property belonging to another for him to appropriate.

Suppose that Don is trading in a partnership with Ed. Either may steal from the other by dishonestly appropriating property belonging to the partnership (*Bonner* [1970] 2 All ER 97n, [1970] 1 WLR 838, CA). But if both agree to the appropriation (say both agree to spend the remaining £10,000 on a lavish holiday knowing this will deny that money to their creditors) they are not thieves. It is *their* money and again there is no property belonging to another which they can appropriate.

Now suppose that Don and Ed form a company with themselves as sole directors and shareholders. Although the business is precisely the same as the one they carried on as partners, the company, unlike the partnership, has a distinct and separate legal personality. Acting separately either may steal from the company (note, from the company but not from the fellow director and shareholder). But suppose that acting in concert they withdraw the remaining £10,000 from the company's account for a lavish holiday knowing that this will deny that money to the company's creditors. In this case, unlike the foregoing cases, the money does belong to another, namely, the company and the issue of D and E's liability for theft turns on whether there is an appropriation.

The issue produced different conclusions from the courts in a variety of cases prior to *Gomez* (*McHugh and Tringhamm* (1988) 88 Cr App R 385 (no liability if company authorized payments); cf *Philippou* (1989) 89 Cr App R 290, [1989] Crim LR 559, 585 holding that where D and E, sole directors and shareholders, had used the company's assets for private purposes, they were rightly convicted of theft). In *Gomez* the matter was considered by Lord Browne-Wilkinson who said:

Turning to the company cases, the dictum in *Morris* has led to much confusion and complication where those in de facto control of the company have been charged with theft from it. The argument which has found favour in certain of the authorities runs as follows. There can be no theft within section 1 if the owner consents to what is done: *Morris*. If the accused, by reason of being the controlling shareholder or otherwise, is 'the directing mind and will of the company' he is to be treated as having validly consented on behalf of the company to his own appropriation of the company's property. This is apparently so whether or not there has been compliance with the formal requirements of company law applicable to dealings with the property of a company and even to cases where the consent relied on is ultra vires: see *R v Roffel* [1985] VR 511; *R v McHugh* (1988) 88 Cr App Rep 385.

In my judgment this approach was wrong in law even if the dictum in *Morris* had been correct. Where a company is accused of a crime the acts and intentions of those who are the directing minds and will of the company are to be attributed to the company. That is not the law where the charge is that those who are the directing minds and will have themselves committed a crime against the company: see *A-G's Reference (No 2 of 1982)* [1984] 2 All ER 216, [1984] QB 624 applying *Belmont Finance Corpn Ltd v Williams Furniture Ltd* [1979] 1 All ER 118, [1979] Ch 250.

In any event, your Lordships' decision in this case, re-establishing as it does the decision in *Lawrence*, renders the whole question of consent by the company irrelevant. Whether or not those controlling the company consented or purported to consent to the abstraction of the company's property by the accused, he will have appropriated the property of the company. The question will be whether the other necessary elements are present, viz was such appropriation dishonest and was it done with the intention of permanently depriving the company of such property? In my judgment the decision in *R v Roffel* and the statements of principle in *R v McHugh* at p 393 are not correct in law and should not be followed. As for the case of *A-G's Reference (No 2 of 1982)*, in my judgment both the concession made by counsel (that there had been an appropriation) and the decision in that case were correct, as was the decision in *R v Philippou* (1989) 89 Cr App Rep 290.

I am glad to be able to reach this conclusion. The pillaging of companies by those who control them is now all too common. It would offend both common sense and justice to hold that the very control which enables such people to extract the company's assets constitutes a defence to a charge of theft from the company. The question in each case must be whether the extraction of the property from the company was dishonest, not whether the alleged thief has consented to his own wrongdoing.

The observations of Lord Browne-Wilkinson on the 'company cases' appear to be obiter. Lord Jauncey expressed his agreement with them. Lord Lowry also agreed with Lord Browne-Wilkinson. Lord Lowry observed that:

The company, and the person (or persons) constituting the directing mind are two (or more) separate persons: *Salomon v A Salomon & Co Ltd* [1897] AC 22. That fact should be easily appreciated when the company is the victim of the other person (or persons). The 'directing mind', when taking the company's property, does a unilateral act, to the prejudice of the company, which the company does not authorise or consent to. My Lords, if I may revert to the proposition that a person cannot consent to the theft of property from himself, it is absurd to suppose that a company consents to the theft of its own property, merely because the thief is for most purposes of the company its directing mind. The act of the directing mind is here unilateral and not consensual and bilateral.

Notes and questions

1. Suppose that in January the company, of which Don and Ed are sole directors and shareholders, appears to be doing very well. Profits are high and the order books are full. At a properly constituted board meeting they decide that the company shall donate £10,000 to a charity and the company does so. In February the company's position dramatically alters for the worse. Profits are down and orders have been withdrawn. Realizing that the company faces insolvency, Don and Ed, at another properly constituted meeting, decide that the company shall pay £10,000 for lavish holidays for Don and Ed, aware that, in the event of what seems to be the inevitable insolvency of the company, this will deprive the company's creditors of the £10,000. Are Don and Ed guilty of stealing from the company? When, and how much? In March the economy takes a surprising turn for the better. Profits are again up and orders that were withdrawn in February have been replaced. Don and Ed's company is so successful that in March it is given the Queen's Prize for Industry. But did Don and Ed steal the £10,000 of the company's assets that they used for the holiday in February?

2. Lord Lowry appears emphatically to agree with Lord Browne-Wilkinson's statements that 'Where a company is accused of crime, the acts and intentions of those who are the directing minds and will of the company are to be attributed to the company. That is not the law where the charge is that those who are the directing minds and will themselves have committed a crime against the company . . .' Cf the *Meridian* case, above, p 345.

(3) PROPERTY

Theft Act 1968, s 4

4. 'Property'

(1) 'Property' includes money and all other property, real or personal, including things in action and other intangible property.

(2) A person cannot steal land, or things forming part of land and severed from it by him or by his directions, except in the following cases, that is to say—

(a) when he is a trustee or personal representative, or is authorised by power of attorney, or as liquidator of a company, or otherwise, to sell or dispose of land belonging to another, and he appropriates the land or anything forming part of it by dealing with it in breach of the confidence reposed in him; or

(b) when he is not in possession of the land and appropriates anything forming part of the land by severing it or causing it to be severed, or after it has been severed; or

(c) when, being in possession of the land under a tenancy, he appropriates the whole or part of any fixture or structure let to be used with the land.

For purposes of this subsection 'land' does not include incorporeal hereditaments; 'tenancy' means a tenancy for years or less period and includes an agreement for such a tenancy, but a person who after the end of a tenancy remains in possession as statutory tenant or otherwise is to be treated as having possession under the tenancy, and 'let' shall be construed accordingly.

(3) A person who picks mushrooms growing wild on any land, or who picks flowers, fruit or foliage from a plant growing wild on any land, does not (although not in possession of the land) steal what he picks, unless he does it for reward or for sale or other commercial purpose.

For purposes of this subsection 'mushroom' includes any fungus, and 'plant' includes any shrub or tree.

(4) Wild creatures, tamed or untamed, shall be regarded as property; but a person cannot steal a wild creature not tamed nor ordinarily kept in captivity, or the carcase of any such creature, unless either it has been reduced into possession by or on behalf of another person and possession of it has not since been lost or abandoned, or another person is in course of reducing it into possession.

Notes

Almost anything may be 'property' and, if it is possessed or owned by someone, it 'belongs to' him. While s 4 identifies certain kinds of property which cannot be stolen, it does not otherwise provide a definition of property, whether tangible or intangible, which is capable of being stolen. To determine what is property for this purpose recourse has to be made to the civil law. Merely because something has a value does not mean that it constitutes property.

In summary s 4(1) treats as property: money (that is coins and banknotes); all other property (that is video-recorders, car radios, handbags, etc); things in action (types of property which can only be enforced by bringing a legal action—not things which can be taken physically for example, bank credits) see for example, *Kohn* (1979) 69 Cr App R 395,

Hilton [1997] 2 Cr App R 445, [1997] Crim LR 761; other intangible property (for example, export quotas (*A-G of Hong Kong v Nai Keung* [1987] 1 WLR 1339), patents (Patents Act 1977 s 30), copyright (Copyright, Designs and Patents Act 1988, s 213)).

Intangible property

Intangible property includes such things as debts, copyright, or shares in a company. The most common forms of intangible property that are stolen are 'things in action' that is, types of property that can only be enforced by bringing a legal action for example, a debt.

The main difficulties lie not in determining what constitutes intangible property but in determining how such property is appropriated and the owner permanently deprived of it. Suppose that D without permission publishes V's poems. This is a breach of copyright but is the copyright stolen? Since D does not intend to deprive V *of the copyright* the case would seem to be analogous to a dishonest use by D of V's car which is not theft in the absence of intention permanently to deprive. So how does D set about stealing V's copyright?

One case where it is easy to see how a debt is appropriated is where D causes V's account to be debited and his own credited. See *Chan Man-sin v A-G of Hong Kong* [1988] 1 WLR 196, [1988] 1 All ER 1, PC, below, p **807**. Where a bank account is in credit, the relationship between banker and customer is that of a debtor and creditor. In law, the customer, V, does not have 'money in the bank'; there is no specific pile of money that is designated as his. The property that he has is a 'thing in action', a right to payment by the bank of the sum of money it owes him. If D dishonestly causes a bank to debit V's account, D does not appropriate V's money, he appropriates a thing in action belonging to V (V's right to payment of that sum from the bank) and is guilty of theft of that property. If V has an authorized overdraft with the bank, V has a right to payment from the bank of the sum up to the limit of that agreed overdraft, and that is property—a thing in action—that D may steal by dishonestly causing the to debit V's account. For example, in *Kohn* (1979) 69 Cr App R 395, D, an accountant, drew cheques on the company's account for his own personal items. He was convicted of theft of the company's thing in action (that is, the company's right to sue the back for £x had now been diminished).

What cannot be stolen?

Section 4 provides that some kinds of property cannot be stolen in certain circumstances.

Land—trustees, personal representatives, etc can steal land for which they have responsibility. A person not in possession cannot steal land but can steal anything forming part of the land by severing it or by appropriating it after it has been severed (for example, taking V's tree). A tenant cannot steal the land nor things forming part of the land which he possesses by virtue of the tenancy.

Wild flora—mushrooms, fruit, etc growing wild on V's land constitute property belonging to V which V is entitled to protect by recourse to the civil law but the taker, unless he has a commercial purpose, cannot commit theft if he takes from the plant (but can commit theft of the whole plant).

Wild animals—it is possible to steal wild animals from a zoo or circus, etc. Similarly, D may steal a carcass of a wild animal once it has been shot/hunted, etc.

In addition to those listed in s 4 the following cannot be stolen.

Electricity—while gas is tangible property (which may be stolen by placing a by-pass on the meter) and so is air (it may be theft to let out the air from someone else's compressed air bottle or car tyres), there has always been a doubt as to whether electricity is property capable of being stolen. The CLRC (Cmnd 2977, para 85) thought that 'owing to its nature electricity is excluded from the definition of stealing' and accordingly made separate provision for the dishonest use, wasting or diverting of electricity in s 13. The CLRC view was confirmed in *Low v Blease* [1975] Crim LR 513, DC, where it was held that since electricity was not property capable of appropriation, D could not be convicted of burglary where he entered premises as a trespasser and made an unauthorized telephone call. Oddly enough D may steal a battery but not the electricity it contains though the battery is of no value or use to D without its charge of electricity. Should the offence of theft extend to protect against D who denies V energy for example, by blocks the light to V's solar panels? Is criminalization necessary? Is theft the most appropriate vehicle for criminalization?

Confidential information—confidential information is often of enormous value to the person who possesses it, especially in the context of trade secrets, but it is not treated as 'property'.

Oxford v Moss
[1979] Crim LR 119, Queen's Bench Division

(Lord Widgery CJ, Wien and Smith JJ)

In 1976, M was an engineering student at Liverpool University. He acquired the proof of an examination paper for a civil engineering examination at the University. An information was preferred against him by O, alleging that he had stolen certain intangible property, that is, confidential information, being property of the Senate of the University. It was agreed that he never intended permanently to deprive the owner of the piece of paper on which the questions were printed.

Held, by the stipendiary at Liverpool: on the facts of the case, confidential information is not a form of intangible property as opposed to property in the paper itself, and that confidence consisted in the right to control the publication of the proof paper and was a right over property other than a form of intangible property. The owner had not been permanently deprived of any intangible property. The charge was dismissed.

On appeal by the prosecutor, as to whether confidential information can amount to property within the meaning of section 4 of the Theft Act 1968.

Held: there was no property in the information capable of being the subject of a charge of theft, ie it was not intangible property within the meaning of section 4.

Appeal dismissed

The law here has been affected in many cases by the Computer Misuse Act 1990. The decision gives rise to considerable difficulties in relation to the misappropriation of trade secrets, and reform has been proposed: see Law Commission Consultation Paper No 150, *Legislating the Criminal Code: Misuse of Trade Secrets* (1997) and comment by J. Hull, 'Stealing Secrets: A Review of the Law Commission Consultation Paper' [1998] Crim LR 246. For a recent review of the criminal law's general protection for intellectual property see C. Davies, 'Protection of Intellectual Property—A Myth?' [2004] J Crim Law 398.

Corpses—a rather bizarre anachronism is that there can be no theft of a corpse as the corpse does not, in general belong to anyone.

R v Kelly

[1998] 3 All ER 741, Court of Appeal

(Rose LJ, Ognall and Sullivan JJ)

K, an artist, had access to the Royal College of Surgeons where he was permitted to draw anatomical specimens used by doctors training to be surgeons. He instigated L, a junior technician, to remove 35 to 40 body parts of which K made casts. Most of the parts were buried in a field, a leg was found in K's attic and the remainder in a friend's basement flat. K and L were convicted of theft of the parts from the College. They appealed arguing, inter alia, (i) that the body parts were not property and (ii) that they were not lawfully in possession of the College because they had been retained beyond the period of two years before burial stipulated in the Anatomy Act 1832 and so did not belong to it.

Rose LJ. We return to the first question, that is to say whether or not a corpse or part of a corpse is property. We accept that, however questionable the historical origins of the principle, it has now been the common law for 150 years at least that neither a corpse, nor parts of a corpse, are in themselves and without more capable of being property protected by rights (see eg Erle J, delivering the judgment of a powerful Court of Crown Cases Reserved in *R v Sharpe* (1857) Dears & B 160 at 163, 169 ER 959 at 960, where he said:

> 'Our law recognises no property in a corpse, and the protection of the grave at common law, as contradistinguished from ecclesiastical protection to consecrated ground, depends upon this form of indictment....'

He was there referring to an indictment which charged not theft of a corpse but removal of a corpse from a grave.

If that principle is now to be changed, in our view, it must be by Parliament, because it has been express or implicit in all the subsequent authorities and writings to which we have been referred that a corpse or part of it cannot be stolen.

To address the point as it was addressed before the trial judge and to which his certificate relates, in our judgment, parts of a corpse are capable of being property within s 4 of the Theft Act, if they have acquired different attributes by virtue of the application of skill, such as dissection or preservation techniques, for exhibition or teaching purposes: see *Doodeward v Spence*, in the judgment of Griffith CJ to which we have already referred and *Dobson v North Tyneside Health Authority* [1996] 4 All ER 474 at 479, [1997] 1 WLR 596 at 601, where this proposition is not dissented from and appears, in the judgment of this court, to have been accepted by Peter Gibson LJ; otherwise, his analysis of the facts of *Dobson's* case, which appears at that page in the judgment, would have been, as it seems to us otiose. Accordingly the trial judge was correct to rule as he did.

Furthermore, the common law does not stand still. It may be that if, on some future occasion, the question arises, the courts will hold that human body parts are capable of being property for the purposes of s 4, even without the acquisition of different attributes, if they have a use or significance beyond their mere existence. This may be so if, for example, they are intended for use in an organ transplant operation, for the extraction of DNA or, for that matter, as an exhibit in a trial. It is to be noted that in *Dobson's* case, there was no legal or other requirement for the brain, which was then the subject of lititgation, to be preserved (see the judgment of Peter Gibson LJ [1996] 4 All ER 474 at 479, [1997] 1 WLR 596 at 601).

So far as the question of possession by the Royal College of Surgeons is concerned, in our judgment the learned judge was correct to rule that the college had possession, sufficiently for the purposes of and within s 5(1) of the Theft Act 1968. We are unable to accept that possession, for the purposes of that section, is in any way dependent on the period of possession, ie whether it is for a limited time, or an indefinite time. In our judgment, the evidence, so far as it was material, before the jury, was to the effect that factually, the parts were in the custody of the Royal College of Surgeons. They were, as it seems to us, in their control and possession within the meaning of s 5(1).

That conclusion is, as it seems to us, reinforced by the judgment of the Court of Appeal in *R v Turner (No 2)* [below, p **774**]. We do not accept that the passage in Lord Parker CJ's judgment which we have read is to be regarded as limited to the facts of that particular case. In expressing the view that no other word such as 'lawful' was to be read into s 5(1), by reference to possession, that court was construing s 5 entirely consonantly with the construction which we now place upon it for the purposes of this appeal.

There remains the submission as to the judge's direction that the college was in lawful possession of the parts. It is implicit in what we have already said that the lawfulness of the possession was not a matter for necessary inquiry in the trial. There was, as we have said, evidence before the jury as to the fact of possession of these parts, coming from the inspectors of anatomy. Their views as to the law, as we have already indicated, seem to us to be a matter of no relevance or materiality in relation to any issue which the jury had to determine. It follows that it was not necessary for the judge to direct the jury that the college was in lawful possession rather than merely in possession.

Appeals dismissed

Notes and questions

1. See A. T. H. Smith, 'Stealing the Body and its Parts' [1976] Crim LR 622; P. Skegg, 'Criminal liability for the unauthorised use of corpses for medical education and research' (1992) 32 Med Sci Law 51; M. Pavlowski, 'Dead Bodies as Property' (1996) 146 NLJ 1828; A. Maclean, 'Resurrection of the Body Snatchers' (2000) 150 NLJ 174.

2. Note that parts taken from a living body will belong to someone so that a theft charge might lie (for example, against the taking of a sample of blood or urine given to the police). A magistrates' court once convicted a man of larceny of a girl's hair which he cut from her head without her consent: (1960) The Times, 22 December.

3. D, a surgeon, secretly takes a human kidney from storage in a hospital and transplants it in his patient who was low on the waiting list. Theft?

(4) BELONGING TO ANOTHER

Theft Act 1968, s 5

5. 'Belonging to another'

(1) Property shall be regarded as belonging to any person having possession or control of it, or having in it any proprietary right or interest (not being an equitable interest arising only from an agreement to transfer or grant an interest).

(2) Where property is subject to a trust, the persons to whom it belongs shall be regarded as including any person having a right to enforce the trust, and an intention to defeat the trust shall be regarded accordingly as an intention to deprive of the property any person having that right.

(3) Where a person receives property from or on account of another, and is under an obligation to the other to retain and deal with that property or its proceeds in a particular way, the property or proceeds shall be regarded (as against him) as belonging to the other.

(4) Where a person gets property by another's mistake, and is under an obligation to make restoration (in whole or in part) of the property or its proceeds or of the value thereof, then to the extent of that obligation the property or proceeds shall be regarded (as against him) as belonging to the person entitled to restoration, and an intention not to make restoration shall be regarded accordingly as an intention to deprive that person of the property or proceeds.

(5) Property of a corporation sole shall be regarded as belonging to the corporation notwithstanding a vacancy in the corporation.

Notes

At first sight it is a perfectly obvious proposition that a person may steal only the property of another and, equally, that he cannot steal his own property. Usually the issue of mine-and-thine is clear cut. So D is guilty of theft if, with mens rea, he snatches V's handbag; the handbag being owned and possessed by V and D having no proprietary interest in it whatever. Conversely if D arranges for the 'disappearance' of his own property in order to perpetrate a fraud on insurers (cf *Robinson* [1915] 2 KB 342, p 528, above) it may be that D will commit other offences but it is plain that he cannot be convicted of theft.

But property may 'belong to' more than one person. V may have some interest in the property less than ownership. The handbag snatched from V might have been lent by O (the owner) to P (who thereby acquired possession) and P has in turn asked V to hold it while P unlocks her car door. Here V has mere custody of the handbag but this suffices under s 5(1) and the handbag is stolen from her by D who takes it. It is also stolen from O and P but it is equally stolen from V.

There is no oddity in extending theft to an appropriation of property from someone who is not the exclusive owner of the property. Nor is there any oddity in holding that a person may be guilty of theft though he himself has a proprietary right or interest in the property. If in the illustration concerning the handbag P (the possessor) dishonestly intending to keep it for herself, tells O (the owner) that it was stolen from her by D then both in law and good sense it can be said that P has stolen it from O.

Even a person who is the owner in the strict sense may steal the property if there is another 'owner'. So in *Bonner* [1970] 2 All ER 97n, [1970] 1 WLR 838, CA, it was held that where property is held by a partnership, one partner, even though he is a joint owner of all partnership property, may steal partnership property if he appropriates it to himself intending to defeat the interests of the other partners. The essential idea is that D may be guilty of theft where in respect of particular property he acts so as to usurp the interests that *any* others have in that property.

The onus is on the prosecution to prove that the property in question belonged to another. Frequently this is self-evident and not a live issue, but not always. In *Marshall* [1998] 2 Cr App R 282 D obtained part used Underground tickets and travelcards from members of the public passing through railway barriers and resold them to other potential customers, so depriving London Underground (LUL) of revenue. D was convicted of theft of the tickets from LUL. The court assumed that the tickets, though in the possession of the passengers, continued to belong to LUL because there was a term to that effect on the reverse of each ticket (of the sort 'this ticket remains the property of LUL'). That issue was not contested, but the existence of the term is not conclusive. Whether it was effective was a question which could be answered only by reference to the law of contract. This tells us that the term was not incorporated into the contract unless it was proved that reasonable steps had been taken by LUL to bring that condition to the notice of the passenger. If he had been given sufficient notice, he was not (as he may well have thought) a buyer but a bailee of the ticket: he was in possession of a ticket that is, the piece of paper belonging to LUL. He had not *bought* a ticket, only a right to travel—a thing in action. But if sufficient notice was not given, the ticket belonged only to the passenger, LUL had no proprietary interest in it, and D could not properly be convicted of stealing from LUL. See J. C. Smith, 'Stealing Tickets' [1998] Crim LR 723.

What constitutes possession or control by V?

One difficulty arises when the defendant alleges that the property he has appropriated was abandoned or 'ownerless'.

R v Woodman

[1974] 2 All ER 955, Court of Appeal, Criminal Division

(Lord Widgery CJ, Ashworth and Mocatta JJ)

The judgment of the court was delivered by:

Lord Widgery CJ.. . . . The facts of the case were these. On 20 March 1973 the appellant and his son, and another man called Davey who was acquitted, took a van to some premises at Wick near Bristol and loaded on to the van one ton six cwt of scrap metal, which they proceeded to drive away.

The premises from which they took this scrap metal were a disused factory belonging to English China Clays, and the indictment alleged that the scrap metal in question was the property of English China Clays. Whether that was entirely true or not depends on the view one takes of the events immediately preceding this taking of scrap metal, because what had happened, according to the prosecution evidence, was that the business run by English China Clays at this point had been run down. In August 1970 the business had ceased. There was at that time a great deal of miscellaneous scrap metal on the site, and English China Clays, wishing to dispose of this, sold the scrap metal to the Bird Group of companies, who thereupon had the right and title to enter on the site and remove the scrap metal which they had bought. They or their sub-contractor went on to the site. They took out the bulk of the scrap metal left there by English China Clays, but a certain quantity of scrap was too inaccessible to be removed to be attractive to the Bird Group of companies so that it was left on the site and so it seems to have remained for perhaps a couple of years until the appellant and his son came to take it away, as I have already recounted.

Also in the history of the matter, and important in it, is the fact that when the site had been cleared by the Bird Group of companies a barbed wire fence was erected around it obviously to exclude trespassers. The site was still in the ownership of the English China Clays and their occupation, and the barbed wire fence was no doubt erected by them. Within the barbed wire fence were these remnants of scrap which the Bird Group had not taken away.

English China Clays took further steps to protect their property because a number of notices giving such information as 'Private Property. Keep Out' and 'Trespassers will be prosecuted' were exhibited around the perimeter of the site. A Mr Brooksbank, who was an employee of English China Clays, gave evidence that he had visited the site about half a dozen times over a period of two or three years, and indeed he had visited it once as recently as between January and March 1973. He did not notice that any scrap metal had been left behind, and it is perfectly clear that there is no reason to suppose that English China Clays or their representatives appreciated that there was any scrap remaining on the site after the Bird Group had done their work.

When this matter came on before the Bristol Crown Court, at the close of the prosecution case where evidence had been led to deal with the facts I have referred to, a submission was made to the recorder that there was no case to answer, because it was said that on that evidence there was no ground in law for saying that the theft had been committed.

By now of course it is the Theft Act 1968 which governs the matter, and so one must turn to see what it says. Section 1(1) provides: 'A person is guilty of theft if he dishonestly appropriates property belonging to another...' I need not go further because the whole of the debate turns on the phrase 'belonging to another'.

Section 5(1) of the 1968 Act expands the meaning of the phrase in these terms:

'Property shall be regarded as belonging to any person having possession or control of it, or having in it any proprietary right or interest...'

The recorder took the view that the contract of sale between English China Clays and the Bird Group had divested English China Clays of any proprietary right to any scrap on the site. It is unnecessary to express a firm view on that point, but the court are not disposed to disagree with the conclusion that the proprietary interest in the scrap had passed.

The recorder also took the view on the relevant facts that it was not possible to say that English China Clays were in possession of the residue of the scrap. It is not quite clear why he took that view. It may have been because he took the view that difficulties arose by reason of the fact that English China Clays had no knowledge of the existence of this particular scrap at any particular time. But the recorder did take the view that so far as control was concerned there was a case to go to the jury on whether or not this scrap was in the control of English China Clays, because if it was, then it was to be regarded as their property for the purposes of a larceny charge even if they were not entitled to any proprietary interest.

The contention before us today is that the recorder was wrong in law in allowing this issue to go to the jury. Put another way, it is said that as a matter of law English China Clays could not on these facts have been said to be in control of the scrap.

We have formed the view without difficulty that the recorder was perfectly entitled to do what he did, that there was ample evidence that English China Clays were in control of the site and had taken considerable steps to exclude trespassers as demonstrating the fact that they were in control of the site, and we think that in ordinary and straightforward cases if it is once established that a particular person is in control of a site such as this, then prima facie he is in control of articles which are on the site.

The point was well put in an article written by no less a person than Oliver Wendell Holmes Jnr, in his book *The Common Law* [(1881) pp 222–224], dealing with possession. Considering the very point we have to consider here, he said:

'There can be no *animus domini* unless the thing is known of; but an intent to exclude others from it may be contained in the larger intent to exclude others from the place where it is, without any knowledge of the object's existence ... In a criminal case [*Rowe* (1859) 8 Cox CC 139], the property in iron taken from the bottom of a canal by a stranger was held well laid in the canal company, although it does not appear that the company knew of it, or had any lien upon it. The only intent concerning the thing discoverable in such instances is the general intent which the occupant of land has to exclude the public from the land, and thus, as a consequence, to exclude them from what is upon it.'

So far as this case is concerned, arising as it does under the Theft Act 1968, we are content to say that there was evidence of English China Clays being in control of the site and prima facie in control of articles on the site as well. The fact that it could not be shown that they were conscious of the existence of this or any particular scrap iron does not destroy the general principle that control of a site by excluding others from it is prima facie control of articles on the site as well.

There has been some mention in argument of what would happen if, in a case like the present, a third party had come and placed some article within the barbed wire fence and thus on the site. The article might be an article of some serious criminal consequence such as explosives or drugs. It may well be that in that type of case the fact that the article has been introduced at a late stage in circumstances in which the occupier of the site had no means of knowledge would produce a different result from that which arises under the general presumption to which we have referred, but in the present case there was in our view ample evidence to go to the jury on the question of whether English China Clays were in control of the scrap at the relevant time. Accordingly the recorder's decision to allow the case to go to the jury cannot be faulted and the appeal is dismissed.

Appeal dismissed

Notes and questions

1. Generally possession or control is shown by some measure of control in fact accompanied by an intention to exclude others. Obviously a householder retains possession or control (indeed he retains ownership) of 'unwanted' items which he consigns to his attic or cellar even though he cannot itemize them. Even household rubbish consigned to the dustbin remains in his disposition for he would certainly not want any Tom, Dick or Harry (or *News of the World* journalist) looking for items of value in his dustbin. But what of the men sent by the refuse collection service to empty the dustbins? In *Williams v Phillips* (1957) 41 Cr App R 5, DC, a decision under the former law, it was held that dustmen stole refuse which they placed in the corporation's cart and which they subsequently appropriated. Once placed in the corporation's cart the refuse came into the possession of the corporation and could then be stolen by others, including the corporation's employees. Suppose, though, that the refuse operatives had removed the valuable rubbish before placing it in their employer's vehicle. Would they be guilty of stealing from their employer or from the householder or both?

2. In *Woodman* the appellants were convicted of stealing the metal from English China Clays. The court appeared to lay stress on the facts that the company had erected a barbed wire fence and had erected notices against trespassing. Would it have made any difference if the company had taken neither of these steps?

3. All the scrap on the site had been sold to the Bird Group. What would the position have been if the appellants had been charged with stealing the scrap from the Bird Group?

4. The court in *Woodman* considered, without decisively determining, what the position might have been if some stranger had deposited goods (drugs, explosives) behind the wire fence which the appellants had then appropriated. From the cases (most of them are civil and it can hardly be supposed that different considerations apply in criminal cases) it appears that only exceptionally will a third party acquire a better title to goods than the owner of the land where the goods are found. According to *Parker v British Airways Board* [1982] QB 1004, [1982] 1 All ER 834, CA, the finder of goods on another's property obtains a title better than the owner only where he is lawfully on the owner's premises, the property is not attached to the land and the owner has not manifested an intention to exercise control over the premises and things which may be upon it.

5. D is caught retrieving golf balls from the bottom of the lake at his local club. Is he guilty of theft? From whom? See *Rostron* [2003] EWCA Crim 2206.

6. An unusual case concerned with property on another's land and the theft of 'treasure trove' is *Hancock* [1990] 3 All ER 183, [1990] 2 QB 242, CA. The common law of treasure trove has now been replaced by the Treasure Act 1996 ; J. Marston and L. Ross, 'Treasure and Portable Antiquities in the 1990s still chained to the Ghosts of the Past: The Treasure Act 1996' [1997] Conv 273) but the case is still relevant. Treasure trove was any article of gold or silver hidden by an owner with a view to subsequent recovery. It belonged to the successors in title of the owner but in the likely event these could not be traced the article belonged to, and might be stolen from, the Crown. In *Hancock*, D, surreptitiously using a metal detector on O's land, found some Celtic silver coins on the site of an ancient temple. It was not clear whether the coins constituted treasure trove (they might have been votive offerings left with no intention to recover them) and, at D's trial for theft, the trial judge directed the jury that the Crown had an interest in ascertaining whether the coins were treasure trove and that the key issue was whether there was a real possibility that the coins were treasure trove.

D's conviction was quashed. No doubt the Crown had a very real interest in determining whether the coins constituted treasure trove but that interest did not amount to a proprietary right or interest. D could be convicted of theft only if the jury was satisfied that the coins constituted treasure trove and that D knew that. Clearly the coins could not 'belong to' the Crown until there was a determination that they were treasure trove.

Would the route to conviction in *Hancock* have been easier had D been charged with stealing from the owner of the land?

In *Waverley Borough Council v Fletcher* [1995] 4 All ER 756, [1996] QB 334, CA (Civ Div) F, using a metal detector, found a medieval gold brooch buried nine inches below the surface in a public park owned by the Council. The coroner determined that the brooch was not treasure trove and returned it to F. The Court of Appeal upheld the Council's claim to the brooch. The owner of land in which something is buried has a superior right to the finder. The digging up and removal of the brooch was a trespass. Is the trespassing treasure hunter who knows the law guilty of theft from the landowner if he keeps for himself any buried valuable object he detects and removes, intending to keep it?

7. In *Sullivan and Ballion* [2002] Crim LR 758 the defendants had appropriated the £50,000 they found on their friend who had died (probably from a drugs overdose) in their company the night before. The deceased was a drug dealer and the money represented his takings. Dismissing the charge of theft of the money, the trial judge ruled that the property did not 'belong to another' when it was taken. Surely the property must have belonged to someone other than the thieves (who had no rights to it)? Since there may be a conviction of theft of property of a person unknown, it follows that it should be enough to show that the property must have belonged to someone and that the defendants knew it belonged to someone other than themselves. The money did not belong to those who had purchased drugs from the deceased (in this case a group known as 'The Firm') because, as the judge held, they had parted with their entire proprietary interest in the money; but the proprietary interest can hardly have vanished into thin air—it passed to the deceased or, if he was acting as an agent, his principal. At the time of the alleged theft, the money must have belonged either to D's principal, if any; or to those entitled under his (or their) will or intestacy; or, if they did not exist, to the Crown as *bona vacantia*.

What of D's mens rea in this case? If the defendants supposed, or may have supposed, that the property belonged to no one and could be taken by the first person to come across it, are they guilty? What if they knew it must belong to someone other than themselves, but did not know who?

In what circumstances can D steal property in which he has a proprietary interest?

We have seen that a number of people might simultaneously have an interest in property. Consider D who owns a car and hires it to V for a week, but then sneaks along and takes it back from V after only a day. Is this theft?

R v Turner (No 2)
[1971] 2 All ER 441, Court of Appeal, Criminal Division

(Lord Parker CJ, Widgery LJ and Bridge J)

[**Lord Parker CJ** delivered the judgment of the court:]

… The facts need not be stated at great length, although there is considerable disparity in the accounts given on behalf of the Crown and the defence. The appellant was at the material time living in Seymour Road, East Ham, with a Miss Nelson and their children. Three miles away a man called Arthur Edwin Brown ran a garage in Carlyle Road, Manor Park. There is no doubt that at some time prior to 7 March 1969, the appellant took a Sceptre car of which he was the registered owner to Brown's garage for repairs. It was Mr Brown's case that he did those repairs, that as he was short of space he left the car in Carlyle Road some 10 to 20 yards from the garage. The ignition key had been handed to him by the appellant, and this he retained on the keyboard in his office. According to Mr Brown, on 7 March 1969 the appellant called at the garage and asked if the car was ready. On being told that it was except that it might require to be tuned, the appellant said that he would return on the next day, ie Saturday 8 March 1969, and would pay Mr Brown for the repairs and pick up the car. A few hours later, however, Mr Brown found that the Sceptre car had gone; moreover whoever had taken it had had a key, because the key that Mr Brown had was still on the keyboard. He reported the matter to the police.

Apparently night after night thereafter until 16 March 1969 Mr Brown, according to him, went round the neighbouring streets to see if he could find the car, and sure enough on Sunday 16 March 1969 he found it parked in a street near to the appellant's flat. It was, moreover, his evidence that he did not know the appellant's full name or his address and only knew of him as Frank. What Mr Brown then did was to take the car back to his garage, to take out the engine and then tow it back less the engine to the place from which he had taken it. Meanwhile, the police made enquiries of the appellant and there is no doubt in the light of what happened afterwards, that he, the appellant, told lie after lie to the police. He said that Mr Brown had never had his Sceptre car at all, that the car had never been to the garage, and the only work that Mr Brown had done was to a Zephyr car on an earlier occasion. However, a time came when he abandoned those denials and agreed that he had taken the car to the garage, and that he had taken it away and had never paid for it. In saying that, he however emphasised that he had taken it away with the consent of Mr Brown. It was on those short facts that the jury, as I have said by a majority, found the appellant guilty of the theft of his own car.

The trial lasted, we are told, six days, in the course of which every conceivable point seems to have been taken and argued. In the result, however, when it comes to this court two points, and two only are taken. It is said in the first instance that while Mr Brown may have had possession or control in fact, that is not enough, and that it must be shown before it can be said that the property 'belonged to' Mr Brown, those being the words used in s 1(1) of the Theft Act 1968, that that possession is, as it is said, a right superior to that in Mr Brown. It is argued from that, in default of proof of a lien—and the judge in his summing-up directed the jury that they were not concerned with the question of whether there was a lien—that Mr Brown was merely a bailee at will and accordingly that he had no sufficient possession.

The words 'belonging to another' are specifically defined in s5 of the Act. Section 5(1) provides:

> 'Property shall be regarded as belonging to any person having possession or control of it, or having in it any proprietary right or interest . . .'

As I have said, the judge directed the jury that they were not concerned in any way with lien and the sole question was whether Mr Brown had possession or control. This court is quite satisfied that there is no ground whatever for qualifying the words 'possession or control' in any way. It is sufficient if it is found that the person from whom the property is taken, or to use the words of the Act, appropriated, was at the time in fact in possession or control. At the trial there was a long argument whether that possession or control must be lawful, it being said that by reason of the fact that this car was subject to a hire-purchase agreement, Mr Brown could never even as against the appellant obtain lawful possession or control. As I have said, this court is quite satisfied that the judge was quite correct in telling the jury that they need not bother about lien, and that they need not bother about hire-purchase agreements. The only question was: was Mr Brown in fact in possession or control?

The second point that is taken relates to the necessity for proving dishonesty. Section 2(1) provides:

> 'A person's appropriation of property belonging to another is not to be regarded as dishonest—(a) if he appropriates the property in the belief that he has in law the right to deprive the other of it, on behalf of himself or of a third person . . .'

The judge, in dealing with this matter, said, and I am only taking passages from his summing-up:

> 'Fourth and last, they must prove that [the appellant] did what he did dishonestly and this may be the issue which lies very close to the heart of this case.'

He then went on to give them a classic direction in regard to claim of right, emphasising that it is immaterial that there exists no basis in law for such belief. He reminded the jury that the appellant had said categorically in evidence: 'I believe that I was entitled in law to do what I did.' At the same time he directed the jury to look at the surrounding circumstances. He said this:

> 'The Prosecution say that the whole thing reeks of dishonesty, and if you believe Mr Brown that the [appellant] drove the car away from Carlyle Road, using a duplicate key, and having told Brown that he would come back tomorrow and pay, you may think the Prosecution are right.'

What counsel for the appellant says on this point is this. He says again that if in fact one disregards lien entirely as the jury were told to do, then Mr Brown was a bailee at will, and the car could have been taken back by the appellant perfectly lawfully at any time whether any money was due in regard to repairs or whether it was not. He says, as the court understands it, first that if there was the right, then there cannot be theft at all, and secondly, that if and insofar as the mental element is relevant, namely belief, the jury should have been told that he had this right and be left to judge, in the light of the existence of that right, whether they thought he may have believed, and he said, that he did have a right.

This court, however, is quite satisfied that there is nothing in this point whatever. The whole test of dishonesty is the mental element of belief. No doubt, although the appellant may for certain purposes be presumed to know the law, he would not at the time have the vaguest idea whether he did have in law a right to take the car back again, and accordingly when one looks at his mental state, one looks at it in the light of what he believed. The jury were properly told that if he believed that he had a right, albeit there was none, he would nevertheless fall to be acquitted. This court, having heard all that counsel for the appellant has said, is quite satisfied that there is no manner in which this summing-up can be criticised, and that accordingly the appeal against conviction should be dismissed

...

Appeal and application dismissed

Compare the decision in the following first instance case.

R v Meredith
[1973] Crim LR 253, Manchester Crown Court

(Judge John Da Cunha)

The defendant, who owned a car, left it in a road while he attended a football match. The car was removed to a police station yard under reg 4 of the Removal and Disposal of Vehicles Regulations 1968. After the match the defendant went to the police station adjacent to the yard; it was crowded and he went to the yard not having paid any sum to the police. He found his car with a police Krooklok on the steering wheel and, without consent or authority from the police, he drove the car away. Two days later he was seen by the police, to whom he handed the Krooklok, and he was arrested and charged with its theft contrary to ss 1 and 7 of the Theft Act 1968. While he was at the police station an entry relating to his car in the found property book was signed by him and his having received his car, the column relating to a £4 charge [under reg 17(1)(a)(iii)] being marked 'not paid' by a police officer. Later he was charged also with theft of the car, the property of the police, contrary to ss 1 and 7 of the 1968 Act, and with taking the vehicle without consent of the owner or other lawful authority, contrary to s 12 of the 1968 Act, and he was committed for trial on the three charges. Subsequently he received a demand from the police for £4, the cost of impounding his car. At his trial no evidence was offered on the count under s 12. At the close of the prosecution's evidence he submitted that he had no case to answer.

Held, upholding the submission, that the reality of the situation was that the police were removing the car to another situation for the owner to collect it subsequently. An owner was liable to pay the statutory charge only if the car originally caused an obstruction, and he had three choices on going to the police station: to pay the £4, admitting that his car caused an obstruction; to refuse to pay, whereupon inevitably he would face a prosecution for having caused an obstruction; or to agree to pay, and then, no doubt, receive a bill. In all three eventualities he would be allowed to take the car away, for the police had no right, as against the owner, to retain it. Consequently, a charge of theft against the defendant was improper. As to the count of theft of the Krooklok, not merely was it a (comparatively) minor offence, but so short was the time elapsing between its being taken and the defendant's admission that he had it, that he should no longer be in jeopardy of conviction for dishonesty. Accordingly, the jury would be directed to find the defendant not guilty on all three counts.

Questions

1. Can the decision in *Meredith* be reconciled with the decision in *Turner*?

2. In *Turner* the jury was told to disregard the possibility that the repairer had a lien on the

appellant's car. On that hypothesis how could the car be regarded as 'belonging to another', viz the repairer? Suppose Don lends his copy of *Smith and Hogan* to Vinnie for a day. Several days later Vinnie has still not returned it and Don sees it on Vinnie's desk. Don surreptitiously retakes his book and says nothing to Vinnie. Is Don a thief? Would it make any difference to your answer if Don subsequently charged Vinnie with the loss of the book?

Equitable interests

The section protects 'any proprietary right or interest' and this extends to both legal and equitable proprietary interests. Where property is subject to a trust it belongs to both the trustee (legal interest) and beneficiary (equitable interest) and it may be stolen from either. The question whether V has an equitable interest in property alleged to have been stolen from him may involve difficult issues of civil law.

In *Dyke and Munro* [2002] 1 Cr App R 404, [2002] Crim LR 153, CA, the defendants were trustees of a registered charity. It was alleged that they misappropriated substantial sums of money raised by street collections for the charity. This money never reached the charity's bank account. The prosecutors had doubts about the form the indictment should take. The trustees became the legal owners of the money and the prosecutors were concerned at the prospect of charging D and M with stealing from themselves. They therefore charged them with stealing 'money belonging to a person or persons unknown', that is, the members of the public who put money in the collection boxes. The convictions were quashed. A member of the public parted with his entire proprietary interest when he put his money in the box. It ceased to 'belong to' him. It belonged in law to the trustees who held it on trust for the charitable purpose.

See s 5 (2) of the Theft Act 1968, above. The person who has the right to enforce a charitable trust is the Attorney-General. For this purpose, the money 'belonged to' him. D and M should have been charged with stealing from the Attorney.

What if Fagin were to send out Oliver (aged nine) with a collecting box for Distressed Gentlefolk with the intention of appropriating any money donated for his own use? Would it make any difference whether such a charity existed or not?

Section 5(3)

Despite the breadth of s 5(1), it would not be sufficient to offer protection in all circumstances. Take, for example, the case where V gives D, her flat mate, money on the understanding that D will use it to pay the gas bill. V (probably) has no proprietary right or interest in the money once it has passed and if D spent the money on herself rather than the gas she would not commit theft. Section 5(3) provides a solution to such problems.

R v Hall

[1972] 2 All ER 1009, Court of Appeal, Criminal Division

(Edmund Davies, Stephenson LJJ and Boreham J)

[**Edmund Davies LJ** read the judgment of the court:]

During 1968 the appellant and two others started trading in Manchester as travel agents under the title of 'People to People'. The other partners received no remuneration, played purely insignificant parts, and were called as Crown witnesses. Each of the seven counts related to money received by the appellant as deposits and payments for air trips to America. In some instances a lump sum was paid by school-masters in respect of charter flights for their pupils; in other instances individuals made payments in respect of their own projected flights. In none of the seven cases covered by the indictment did the flights materialise, in none of them was there any refund of the moneys paid, and in each case the appellant admitted that he was unable to make any repayment. In some cases he disputed all liability on the grounds that the other parties had unjustifiably cancelled the proposed trips, in others he denied dishonesty. He claimed to have paid into the firm's general trading account all the sums received by him, asserted that those moneys had become his own property and had been applied by him in the conduct of the firm's business, and submitted that he could not be convicted of theft simply because the firm had not prospered and that in consequence not a penny remained in the bank.

Two points were presented and persuasively developed by the appellant's counsel: (1) that, while the appellant has testified that all moneys received had been used for business purposes, even had he been completely profligate in its expenditure he could not in any of the seven cases be convicted of 'theft' as defined by the Theft Act 1968; there being no allegation in any of the cases of his having *obtained* any payments by deception, counsel for the appellant submitted that, having received from a client, say £500 in respect of a projected flight, as far as the criminal law is concerned he would be quite free to go off immediately and expend the entire sum at the races and forget all about his client; (2) [omitted]...

Point (1) turns on the application of s 5(3) of the Theft Act 1968, which provides:

> 'Where a person receives property from or on account of another, and is under an obligation to the other to retain and deal with that property or its proceeds in a particular way, the property or proceeds shall be regarded (as against him) as belonging to the other.'

Counsel for the appellant submitted that in the circumstances arising in these seven cases there arose no such 'obligation' on the appellant. He referred us to a passage in the Eighth Report of the Criminal Law Revision Committee [*Theft and Related Offences*, Cmnd 2977 (1966), p 127] which reads as follows:

> '*Subsection* (3) [of cl 5 "Belonging to Another"] provides for the special case where property is transferred to a person to retain and deal with for a particular purpose and he misapplies it or its proceeds. An example would be the treasurer of a holiday fund. The person in question is in law the owner of the property; but the sub-section treats the property, as against him, as belonging to the persons to whom he owes the duty to retain and deal with the property as agreed. He will therefore be guilty of stealing from them if he misapplies the property or its proceeds.'

Counsel for the appellant submitted that the example there given is, for all practical purposes, identical with the actual facts in *Pulham*, where, incidentally, s 5(3) was not discussed, the convictions there being quashed, as we have already indicated, owing to the lack of a proper direction as to the accused's state of mind at the time he appropriated. But he submits that the position of a treasurer of a solitary fund is quite different from that of a person like the appellant, who was in general (and genuine) business as a travel agent, and to whom people pay money in order to achieve a certain object—in the present cases, to obtain charter flights to America. It is true, he concedes, that thereby the travel agent undertakes a contractual obligation in relation to arranging flights and at the proper time paying the airline and any other expenses. Indeed, the appellant throughout acknowledged that this was so, although contending that in some of the seven cases it was the other party who was in breach. But what counsel for the appellant resists is that in such circumstances the travel agent 'is under an obligation' to the client 'to retain and deal with ... in a particular way' sums paid to him in such circumstances.

What cannot of itself be decisive of the matter is the fact that the appellant paid the money into the firm's general trading account. As Widgery J said in *Yule* [[1964] 1 QB 5 at 10, [1963] 2 All ER 780 at 784], decided under s20(1)(iv) of the Larceny Act 1916:

'The fact that a particular sum is paid into a particular banking account . . . does not affect the right of persons interested in that sum or any duty of the solicitor either towards his client or towards third parties with regard to disposal of that sum.'

Nevertheless, when a client goes to a firm carrying on the business of travel agents and pays them money, he expects that in return he will, in due course, receive the tickets and other documents necessary for him to accomplish the trip for which he is paying, and the firm are 'under an obligation' to perform their part to fulfil his expectation and are liable to pay him damages if they do not. But, in our judgment, what was not here established was that these clients expected them 'to retain and deal with that property or its proceeds in a particular way', and that an 'obligation' to do so was undertaken by the appellant. We must make clear, however, that each case turns on its own facts. Cases could, we suppose, conceivably arise where by some special arrangement (preferably evidenced by documents), the client could impose on the travel agent an 'obligation' falling within s5(3). But no such special arrangement was made in any of the seven cases here being considered. It is true that in some of them documents were signed by the parties; thus, in respect of counts 1 and 3 incidents there was a clause to the effect that the People to People organisation did not guarantee to refund deposits if withdrawals were made later than a certain date; and in respect of counts 6, 7 and 8 the appellant wrote promising 'a full refund' after the flights paid for failed to materialise. But neither in those nor in the remaining two cases (in relation to which there was no documentary evidence of any kind) was there, in our judgment, such a special arrangement as would give rise to an obligation within s5(3).

It follows from this that, despite what on any view must be condemned as scandalous conduct by the appellant, in our judgment on this ground alone this appeal must be allowed and the convictions quashed. But as, to the best of our knowledge, this is one of the earliest cases involving s 5(3), we venture to add some observations.

(A) Although in *Pulham* [15 June 1971, unreported], s5(3) was not referred to and the case turned on s 2(1)(b) of the Act, it is equally essential for the purposes of the former provision that dishonesty should be present at the time of appropriation. We are alive to the fact that to establish this could present great (and maybe insuperable) difficulties when sums are on different dates drawn from a general account. Nevertheless, they must be overcome if the Crown is to succeed.

(B) Where the case turns, wholly or in part, on s 5(3) a careful exposition of the subsection is called for. Although it was canvassed by counsel in the present case, it was nowhere quoted or even paraphrased by the commissioner in his summing-up. Instead he unfortunately ignored it and proceeded on the assumption that, as the appellant acknowledged the purpose for which clients had paid him money, ipso facto there arose an 'obligation . . . to retain and deal with' it for that purpose. He therefore told the jury:

'The sole issue to be determined in each count is this. Has it been proved that the money was stolen in the sense I have described, dishonestly appropriated by him for purposes other than the purpose for which the moneys were handed over? Bear in mind that this is not a civil claim to recover money that has been lost.'

We have to say respectfully that this will not do, as cases under s 20(1)(iv) of the Larceny Act 1916 illustrate. Thus in *Sheaf* [(1925) 134 LT 127] it was held that whether money had been 'entrusted' to the defendant for and on account of other persons was a question of fact for the jury and must therefore be the subject of an express direction, Avory J saying [(1925) 134 LT 127 at 128]:

> 'It is not sufficient to say that if the question had been left they might have determined it against the appellant. When we once arrive at the conclusion that a vital question of fact has not been left to the jury the only ground on which we can affirm a conviction is that we can say that there has been no miscarriage of justice...'

The same point was made in *Bryce* [(1955) 40 Cr App R 62].

(C) Whether in a particular case the Crown has succeeded in establishing an 'obligation' of the kind coming within s 5(3) of the new Act may be a difficult question. Happily, we are not called on to anticipate or solve for the purposes of the present case the sort of difficulties that can arise. But, to illustrate what we have in mind, mixed questions of law and fact may call for consideration. For example, if the transaction between the parties is wholly in writing, is it for the judge to direct the jury that, as a matter of law, the defendant had thereby undertaken an 'obligation' within s 5(3)? On the other hand, if it is wholly (or partly) oral, it would appear that it is for the judge to direct them that, if they find certain facts proved, it would be open to them to find [but see Note 2, *infra*] that an 'obligation' within s 5(3) had been undertaken—but presumably not that they must so find, for so to direct them would be to invade their territory. In effect, however, the commissioner unhappily did something closely resembling that in the present case by his above-quoted direction that the only issue for their consideration was whether the appellant was proved to have been actuated by dishonesty.

We have only to add that counsel for the Crown submitted that, even if the commissioner's failure to deal with s 5(3) amounted to a misdirection, this was a fitting case to apply the proviso. But point (1), successfully taken by defence counsel, is clearly of such a nature as to render that course impossible. We are only too aware that, in the result, there will be many clients of the appellant who, regarding themselves as cheated out of their money by him, will think little of a law which permits him to go unpunished. But such we believe it to be, and it is for this court to apply it.

Appeal allowed. Conviction quashed

Notes and questions

1. Cf *Re Kumar* [2000] Crim LR 504 where a travel agent business, ARG, was permitted to sell passenger tickets on behalf of IATA members. K, the proprietor and managing director of ARG, agreed to a trustee relationship whereby, after deduction of commission, any moneys received from the sale of tickets would be transferred by direct debit from the bank account of ARG to that of IATA. K knowingly became indebted to his bank but continued to trade with the result that his account was unable to meet the direct debits due for three successive months. In extradition proceedings, it was held that there was evidence that K was guilty of theft. It seems that K had a duty to maintain a credit balance in his trading account, at least to the amount of the direct debits due.

2. Section 5(3) applies only where property is 'received'. Normally this presents no problems. But *Preddy*, below, p **839**, decides that, where funds are 'transferred' by CHAPS order, telegraphic transfer and the like, the property, a thing in action, now in the hands of the 'transferee' is new property, which never belonged to or was in the possession of anyone else. (We have put 'transferred' in quotation marks because it seems to follow from *Preddy* that, just as it is not an 'obtaining' of property from another so it cannot be a 'transfer' or 'receipt' from another.) Funds so 'materialising' were not 'received' from anyone, nor were they the proceeds of property received from anyone. Section 5(3) cannot be invoked against the 'transferee' who dishonestly disposes of the fund.

In *Klineberg* [1999] 1 Cr App R 427, [1999] Crim LR 417 the company of which K was director received payments from intending purchasers of timeshares. The fund was misappropriated and convictions of theft upheld on some counts in reliance on s 5(3). Unlike *Hall*, above, the customers paid on the understanding that the money would be held in independent trusteeship until the apartment in question was ready. Some paid in cash, some by cheque and some by bank transfer. All funds were paid into the company's bank account which was a thing in action belonging to the company. When the cash and cheques were paid into the account, the increased credit was new property (*Preddy*) but it was the proceeds of property received on trust. So it appears that s 5(3) was applicable to the property of those who paid in cash or by cheque but not that of those who paid by bank transfer.

It was however held that the defendants were under a legal obligation to retain the funds which they had received or (in the case of bank transfers) 'come by' and deal with them in a particular way. Was this a mere contractual obligation or did the customers have an equitable interest in the fund? If they did, it belonged to them under s 5(1) and the difficulty is overcome: there is then no need to rely on s 5(3). In *Governor of Brixton Prison, ex p Levin* [1996] 4 All ER 350, [1997] QB 65, DC, D, a dishonest computer operator, caused V's bank account in the United States to be debited and the account of D's accomplice, E, with a different United States bank to be credited. The question was whether E's drawing on this credit would have amounted to theft if done in England. Beldam LJ said that the property appropriated was not a thing in action consisting in V's bank balance but different property as, applying *Preddy*, was undoubtedly so. Yet he held that V had, until his balance was restored, an interest in the funds representing it. The cases are not on all fours. In *Klineberg* the defendants had 'come by' the property without any proven fraud. Whether there is, in these circumstances, a constructive trust is a difficult question of civil law.

In *Klineberg* the court refers critically to the statement in *Smith & Hogan* (8th edn), p 538, concerning s 5(3): 'So where D has received property from or on account of P in the circumstances described in this subsection it will almost always (if not always) be the case that P has a legal or equitable interest in the property or the proceeds'. It is conceded that it would be going too far to assert that, in all cases covered by s 5(3), the victim has a legal or equitable interest. If a railway ticket is sold by V to D on terms that D will return it at the end of the journey, the entire proprietary interest in the ticket may pass to D (he could lawfully destroy it if he decided not to travel) but D's retention of the ticket after the journey, with intent permanently to deprive V of it, could, by virtue of s 5(3), be theft of the ticket (the thing in possession) though not of the thing in action (V's contractual right to have it back). See 'Stealing Tickets' [1998] Crim LR 723, n 5 and p 726 and *Marshall*, below, p **805**.

3. The obligation under s 5(3) must be a legal obligation. Whether, on given facts, a legal obligation arises is a question of law for the judge, but it is for the jury to determine the facts. In *Hall* Edmund Davies LJ said that where the transaction is wholly or partly oral it is for the judge to direct the jury that, if they find certain facts proved, 'it would be open to them to find that an obligation within s 5(3) had been undertaken'. In *Dubar* [1995] 1 Cr App R 280, C-MAC, the court disapproved this observation. Since the law is the exclusive province of the judge, the judge must direct the jury on which finding(s) of fact they must find an obligation and on which finding(s) they must not; there can be no finding(s) of fact on which it would be 'open' to the jury to find that there was or was not an obligation.

4. The question—when is D under an obligation?—can be answered only by reference to the civil law. It may raise complex issues of law, as in *Klineberg* (n2, above) particularly the law of contract and quasi-contract.

In *DPP v Huskinson* [1988] Crim LR 620, DC, for example, whether D was under an obligation turned upon the interpretation of provisions in the Social Security and Housing Benefits Act 1982. It was held that these provisions did not impose an obligation on a recipient of housing benefit to use a cheque made out to him, or its proceeds, to pay his rent even though it was given to him for that purpose, and accordingly D did not steal by spending the money on himself.

In *Lewis v Lethbridge* [1987] Crim LR 59, DC, it was held where D, following a charity event, received money from people who had sponsored him that he was not under an obligation to account to the charity for the *money* or its *proceeds*; he was merely a debtor to the charity for the *amount* received. *Lewis v Lethbridge* was, however, disapproved in *Wain* [1995] 2 Cr App R 660, CA. D was unable to account for some £2,800 which he had received from various contributors during a charity fundraising and which he had initially paid into a separate account before transferring it to his own. Affirming D's conviction for theft the court said that D was plainly under an obligation to retain for the benefit of another (the Trust), if not the actual notes and coins received, at least their proceeds. Putting the matter colloquially, it may be helpful to consider whether the property received by D is earmarked for onward transmission to another.

5. In *A-G's Reference (No 1 of 1985)* [1986] 2 All ER 219, [1986] QB 491, D, the salaried manager of a pub, who was contractually bound to sell only goods supplied by his employer, was found bringing in his own beer, intending to sell it and secretly retain the profit. It was decided that the judge had rightly held that there was no case to answer on a charge of going equipped to steal the profit he would have made. If an employee or agent, D, receives a bribe in contravention of his duty to his employer or principal, P, P may recover the amount of the bribe in a civil action; but whether D can be guilty of stealing the amount of the bribe depends on whether he is a mere debtor or holds the bribe on trust for V. This is a question of civil law. According to the Court of Appeal in *Lister & Co v Stubbs* (1890) 45 Ch D 1, D is a mere debtor; but the Privy Council in *A-G for Hong Kong v Reid* [1994] 1 All ER 1, [1994] 1 AC 324 has held that he is a trustee. See J. C. Smith (1994) 110 LQR 180. If the Hong Kong case is followed by English courts, the scope of the law of theft has been extended by this change in the civil law. The same issues arise where D makes an improper profit through the use of P's property, or his position as P's employee or agent, as in the case of the publican or *Cooke* [1986] 2 All ER 985, [1986] AC 909.

6. Without the existence of a legal obligation it is not enough that D has acted dishonestly, even gravely so. In *Cullen* (1974) unreported, No 968/c/74, D, V's mistress, obviously acted dishonestly where she made off with money given to her by V to pay domestic bills. Roskill LJ said that 'one could hardly imagine a plainer case of theft.' It was of course a plain case of *dishonesty* but was it, bearing in mind *Balfour v Balfour* [1919] 2 KB 571, CA (and the intent to create legal relations for contract), a plain case of theft?

7. It is plain from the terms of s 5(3) that the obligation must be owed by D to the alleged victim of the theft, V. It is not enough to sustain a charge of stealing from V that D was under an obligation to a third party, X, to deal with the property for the benefit of V. In *Floyd v DPP* [2000] Crim LR 411, DC, F collected money in weekly premiums from colleagues at work who had ordered goods from Home Farm Hampers Ltd (HFH). £434 of the money collected by F was not delivered to HFH and cheques later sent by F were not honoured. She was charged with stealing from HFH. It was argued that the money belonged, not to HFH, but to her colleagues. Dismissing her appeal, the court held that F was under a legal obligation to hand over the money to HFH, so that s 5(3) applied. Following *Klineberg*, above, it was unnecessary to establish that HFH had any legal or equitable interest in the money. It was immaterial that there was no 'express contract' between F and HFH. Certainly an implied contract would have sufficed, but it does not appear that there was any finding or, or evidence of, such a contract. Where did the obligation come from? There almost certainly was an implied contract between F and her colleagues that she would 'retain and deal' with the money in particular way—that is, by delivering it to HFH. This would have have justified a charge of theft from the colleagues. But F's obligation would have been only to her colleagues and not to HFH. Under the doctrine of privity of contract, a third party to a contract acquired no rights, even if the contract was made for his benefit.

Note that it may be different since the Contracts (Rights of Third Parties) Act 1999 came into force. When a contract made on or after 11 May 2000, contains a term which 'purports to confer a benefit' on a third party, that party may enforce that term in his own right. Cf *Gee*, below, p **861**.

(5) PROPERTY GOT BY MISTAKE

Of all the provisions in s 5, sub-s (4) certainly appears to be the most complicated and an explanation of its genesis may be helpful. In *Moynes v Coopper* [1956] 1 QB 439, [1956] 1 All ER 450, D, an employee of V, was given an advance of pay by the site agent amounting to £6.19.6d. Unaware that this advance had been made, V's wages clerk paid D his full weekly wage of £7.3.4d and D on discovering the mistake dishonestly decided to keep all of the money. The difficulty with this case is that *in law* ownership of the £7.3.4d passed to D on delivery of the pay packet and hence D had not taken money belonging to another. Section 5(4) was introduced to meet the difficulty by, in effect, deeming the property to belong to V where the property is obtained by mistake and D is under a legal obligation to restore the property, or its proceeds or its value. At law D in *Moynes v Coopper*, although ownership of all the money had passed to him, was at least under an obligation to restore the value of the over-payment; in a civil action V would have been entitled to a judgment for £6.19.6d. But s 5(4) was introduced without consideration of the position in equity.

In *Chase Manhattan Bank NA v Israel-British Bank (London) Ltd* [1979] 3 All ER 1025, [1981] Ch 105, the X bank by mistake paid $2 million to the Y bank for the account of the Z bank. The Z bank subsequently went into liquidation. The X bank was entitled to a dividend in the liquidation but it sought to recover the whole of its loss. It was held by Goulding J that a person who pays money (or, presumably, delivers any property) to another under a mistake of fact retains an equitable interest in the money and the conscience of the recipient is subject to a fiduciary duty to respect his proprietary right. Accordingly the X bank was entitled to the restoration of its money and was not restricted to a creditor's rights in the winding up. If this decision is correct s 5(4) is unnecessary. In *Moynes v Coopper* V, having paid the excess under a mistake of fact, retained an equitable interest in it and the property accordingly belonged to him within s 5(1). In *Shadrokh-Cigari* [1988] Crim LR 465, CA, a bank in the USA in error credited the account of a child at an English bank with £286,000 instead of £286. D, the child's guardian, got the child to sign banker's drafts and when D was arrested only £21,000 remained in the account. Upholding D's conviction for theft from the English bank, the court said that the drafts belonged to the bank and although legal ownership passed to D by delivery, the bank retained an equitable interest by virtue of the principle in *Chase Manhattan*. It was accordingly not necessary to rely on s 5(4) though the subsection provided an alternative route to conviction. But in *Westdeutsche Landesbank Girozentrale v Islington Borough Council* [1996] 2 All ER 961 at 996 Lord Browne-Wilkinson thought *Chase Manhattan* to be wrongly decided and Lord Millett is of the same opinion (114 LQR at p 412). If so, s 5(4) comes into play and the criminal law is unaffected.

Section 5(4) was relied on in *A-G's Reference (No 1 of 1983)* [1984] 3 All ER 369, [1985] QB 182. D, a woman police officer, received her pay from her employer by way of direct debit. On one occasion she was overpaid by £74.74 but when she became aware of this she decided to take no action though she did not subsequently withdraw any of this money. At the close of the prosecution's case the trial judge directed an acquittal. Lord Lane CJ, on behalf of the court, held that he was wrong to do so. Referring to s 5(4) Lord Lane said that D was under no obligation to restore the money or its proceeds (why?) but was under an obligation to restore the value thereof.

But there is another point of interest in this case. D had not spent the overpayment; it remained in her bank account. Lord Lane assumed that D had appropriated the money and pointed out that by virtue of s 5(4) an intention not to make restoration 'shall be regarded accordingly as an intention to deprive that person of the property or proceeds'. But had D appropriated the money? Cf *Stalham* [1993] Crim LR 310, CA.

R v Gilks

[1972] 3 All ER 280, Court of Appeal, Criminal Division

(Cairns, Stephenson LJJ, and Willis J)

Cairns LJ. The judgment I am about to read is the judgment of the court... the appellant was convicted of theft...

The facts were as follows. On 27 March 1971 the appellant went into Ladbrokes' betting shop at North Cheam and placed some bets on certain horses: one of his bets was on a horse called 'Fighting Scot'. 'Fighting Scot' did not get anywhere in the race which was in fact won by a horse called 'Fighting Taffy'. Because of a mistake on the part of the relief manager in the betting shop, the appellant was paid out as if he had backed the successful horse with the result that he was overpaid to the extent of £106.63. He was paid £117.25 when the amount he had won (on other races) was only £10.62. At the very moment when he was being paid the appellant knew that a mistake had been made and that he was not entitled to the money, but he kept it. He refused to consider repaying it, his attitude being that it was Ladbrokes' hard lines.

The questions of law arise under the following sections of the Theft Act 1968. [His Lordship read s 1(1), s 2(1) and s 5(4).]

The deputy chairman gave rulings in law to the following effect. He ruled that at the moment when the money passed it was money 'belonging to another' and that that ingredient in the definition of theft in s 1(1) of the Act was therefore present. Accordingly, s 5(4) had no application to the case. If he was wrong about that then, he said, 'obligation' in s5(4) included an obligation which was not a legal obligation. He told the jury that it was open to them to convict the appellant of theft in respect of the mistaken overpayment. And he directed them that the test of dishonesty was whether the appellant believed that 'when dealing with your bookmaker if he makes a mistake you can take the money and keep it and there is nothing dishonest about it'.

In the grounds of appeal it is contended that all these directions were wrong. The main foundation of one branch of the appellant's case at the trial and in this court was the decision of the Court of Appeal in *Morgan v Ashcroft* [[1937] 3 All ER 92, [1938] 1 KB 49]. In that case a bookmaker, by mistake, overpaid a client £24. It was held that the bookmaker was not entitled to recover the money by action because that would involve taking accounts of gaming transactions which were void under the Gaming Act 1845. The argument proceeded as follows. When Ladbrokes paid the appellant they never supposed that they were discharging a legal liability; even if he had won they need not, in law, have paid him. They simply made him a gift of the money. The deputy chairman was wrong in saying that at the moment of payment the money 'belonged to another'. At that very moment its ownership was transferred and therefore the appellant could not be guilty of theft unless the extension given by s5(4) to the meaning of the words 'belonging to another' could be brought into play. But s 5(4) had no application because under the rule in *Morgan v Ashcroft* the appellant had no obligation to repay.

The deputy chairman did not accept this line of argument. He held that it was unnecessary for the prosecution to rely on s 5(4) because the property in the £106.63 never passed to the appellant. In the view of this court that ruling was right. The sub-s introduced a new principle into the law of theft but long before it was enacted it was held in *Middleton* [(1873) LR 2 CCR 38] that where a person was paid by mistake (in that case by a post office clerk) a sum in excess of that properly payable, the person who accepted the overpayment with knowledge of the excess was guilty of theft. Counsel for the appellant seeks to distinguish the present case from that one on the basis that in *Middleton* the depositor was entitled to withdraw 10s from his Post Office Savings Bank account and the clerk made a mistake in thinking he was entitled to withdraw more than £8, whereas in the present case there was no mistake about the appellant's rights—whether his horse won or lost he had no legal right to payment. In our view this argument is fallacious. A bookmaker who pays out money in the belief that a certain horse has won, and who certainly would not have made the payment but for the belief, is paying by mistake just as much as the Post Office clerk in *Middleton*.

The gap in the law which s 5(4) was designed to fill was, as the deputy chairman rightly held, that which is illustrated by the case of *Moynes v Coopper*. There a workman received a paypacket containing £7 more than was due to him but did not become aware of the overpayment until he opened the envelope some time later. He then kept the £7. This was held not to be theft because there was no *animus furandi* at the moment of taking, and *Middleton* was distinguished on that ground. It was observed that the law as laid down in *Middleton* was reproduced and enacted in s1(2)(i) of the Larceny Act 1916. It would be strange indeed if s 5(4) of the 1968 Act, which was designed to bring within the net of theft a type of dishonest behaviour which escaped before, were to be held to have created a loophole for another type of dishonest behaviour which was always within the net.

An alternative ground on which the deputy chairman held that the money should be regarded as belonging to Ladbrokes was that 'obligation' in s5(4) meant an obligation whether a legal one or not. In the opinion of this court that was an incorrect ruling. In a criminal statute, where a person's criminal liability is made dependent on his having an obligation, it would be quite wrong to construe that word so as to cover a moral or social obligation as distinct from a legal one. As, however, we consider that the deputy chairman was right in ruling that the prosecution did not need to rely on s 5(4), his ruling on this alternative point does not affect the result…

Appeal dismissed

Questions

1. Why did not the ownership in £106.63 pass to Gilks? Did not the manager intend to make Gilks the owner of that sum? *Middleton* was based on the assumption that there was a mistake of identity, either the identity of the payee or the identity of the deposit account from which the money was being withdrawn. Was there any mistake of identity in *Gilks*?

2. What would be the effect, if any, on *Gilks* of *Gomez*, above, p 753 and of *Hinks* above, p 750? If accepting an indefeasible gift is theft, why not receiving the proceeds of a wager which the payer has no right to recover?

(6) DISHONESTY

Theft Act 1968, s 2

2. 'Dishonestly'

> (1) A person's appropriation of property belonging to another is not to be regarded as dishonest—
>
> > (a) if he appropriates the property in the belief that he has in law the right to deprive the other of it, on behalf of himself or of a third person; or
> >
> > (b) if he appropriates the property in the belief that he would have the other's consent if the other knew of the appropriation and the circumstances of it; or
> >
> > (c) (except where the property came to him as trustee or personal representative) if he appropriates the property in the belief that the person to whom the property belongs cannot be discovered by taking reasonable steps.
>
> (2) A person's appropriation of property belonging to another may be dishonest notwithstanding that he is willing to pay for the property.

Section 2 does not define dishonesty. It merely tells us that three specified beliefs negative dishonesty and that the intention specified in sub-s (2) does not necessarily do so. But s 2 makes it clear that where it applies D's *belief* is of paramount importance. If D believes he has a legal right to property he cannot be convicted of theft however unreasonable his belief may be. If he believes that V would have consented to the appropriation he cannot be accounted dishonest though only a fool (which D is) could have believed that V would give consent. If D finds and appropriates property in circumstances in which any man who gave thought to it would realize the owner could be traced by taking reasonable steps, D is not dishonest if this thought does not occur to him. But the definition in s 2 is only partial.

Note that s 2 applies only in relation to theft and not to all offences in which dishonesty is an element. Should it be so limited?

As to belief in legal right note that s 2(1)(a) does not create an exception to the general principle that ignorance of the criminal law is no excuse. Suppose that T, the tenant of furnished premises leased by L, has read s 4 but has misunderstood it. T concludes from his reading that while it is theft for a tenant to appropriate fixtures, it is not theft to appropriate the furniture. If D appropriates a bookcase belonging to L he cannot rely on s 2(1)(a) to negative dishonesty. D has made a mistake of law but his mistake relates to what constitutes the actus reus of theft; it is a mistake as to the *criminal law* and, as such, affords no defence. But if T believes that he has a right in law, the relevant law here being the civil law, then T does not act dishonestly even though the law recognizes no such right. This is not to say that T has necessarily acted dishonestly, only that he cannot rely on s 2(1)(a) to show categorically that he has not. Whether T is dishonest may be considered in the light of the next case.

R v Ghosh

[1982] 2 All ER 689, Court of Appeal, Criminal Division

(Lord Lane CJ, Lloyd and Eastham JJ)

[**Lord Lane CJ** read the following judgment of the court:]

...the appellant was convicted on four counts of an indictment laid under the Theft Act 1968: on count 1, attempting to procure the execution of a cheque by deception; on count 2, attempting to obtain money by deception; on counts 3 and 4, obtaining money by deception. Count 1 was laid under s20(2) and the remainder under s 15(1). He was fined the sum of £250 on each count with a term of imprisonment to be served in default of payment.

At all material times the appellant was a surgeon acting as a locum tenens consultant at a hospital. The charges alleged that he had falsely represented that he had himself carried out a surgical operation to terminate pregnancy or that money was due to himself or an anaesthetist for such an operation, when in fact the operation had been carried out by someone else, and/or under the national health service provisions.

His defence was that there was no deception; that the sums paid to him were due for consultation fees which were legitimately payable under the regulations, or else were the balance of fees properly payable; in other words that there was nothing dishonest about his behaviour on any of the counts.

The effect of the jury's verdict was as follows: as to count 1, that the appellant had falsely represented that he had carried out a surgical operation and had intended dishonestly to obtain money thereby; that as to count 2 he had falsely pretended that an operation had been carried out under the national health service; that as to count 3 he had falsely pretended that money was due to an anaesthetist; and as to count 4 that he had obtained money by falsely pretending that an operation had been carried out on a fee-paying basis when in fact it had been conducted under the terms of the national health service.

The grounds of appeal are simply that the judge misdirected the jury as to the meaning of dishonesty. What the judge had to say on that topic was as follows:

> 'Now, finally dishonesty. There are, sad to say, infinite categories of dishonesty. It is for you. Jurors in the past and, whilst we have criminal law in the future, jurors in the future have to set the standards of honesty. Now it is your turn today, having heard what you have, to consider contemporary standards of honesty and dishonesty in the context of all that you have heard. I cannot really expand on this too much, but probably it is something rather like getting something for nothing, sharp practice, manipulating systems and many other matters which come to your mind.'

The law on this branch of the Theft Act 1968 is in a complicated state and we embark on an examination of the authorities with great diffidence.

When *R v McIvor* [1982] 1 All ER 491, [1982] 1 WLR 409 came before the Court of Appeal, there were two conflicting lines of authority. On the one hand there were cases which decided that the test of dishonesty for the purposes of the Theft Act 1968 is, what we venture to call, subjective, that is to say, the jury should be directed to look into the mind of the defendant and determine whether he knew he was acting dishonestly: see *R v Landy* [1981] 1 All ER 1172 at 1181, [1981] 1 WLR 355 at 365 where Lawton LJ, giving the reserved judgment of the Court of Appeal said:

'An assertion by a defendant that throughout a transaction he acted honestly does not have to be accepted but has to be weighed like any other piece of evidence. If that was the defendant's state of mind, or may have been, he is entitled to be acquitted. But if the jury, applying their own notions of what is honest and what is not, conclude that he could not have believed he was acting honestly, then the element of dishonesty will have been established. What a jury must not do is to say to themselves: "If we had been in his place we would have known we were acting dishonestly, so he must have known he was."'

On the other hand there were cases which decided that the test of dishonesty is objective. Thus in *R v Greenstein; R v Green* [1976] 1 All ER 1 at 6, [1975] 1 WLR 1353 at 1359 the judge in the court below had directed the jury:

'... there is nothing illegal in stagging. The question you have to decide and what this case is all about is whether these defendants, or either of them, carried out their stagging operations in a dishonest way. To that question you apply your own standards of dishonesty. It is no good, you see, applying the standards of anyone accused of dishonesty otherwise everybody accused of dishonesty, if he were to be tested by his own standards, would be acquitted automatically, you may think. The question is essentially one for a jury to decide and it is essentially one which the jury must decide by applying its own standards.'

The Court of Appeal, in a reserved judgment, approved that direction.

In *R v McIvor* [1982] 1 All ER 491 at 497, [1982] 1 WLR 409 at 417 the Court of Appeal sought to reconcile these conflicting lines of authority. They did so on the basis that the subjective test is appropriate where the charge is conspiracy to defraud, but in the case of theft the test should be objective. We quote the relevant passage in full:

'It seems elementary, first, that where the charge is conspiracy to defraud the prosecution must prove actual dishonesty in the minds of the defendants in relation to the agreement concerned, and, second, that where the charge is an offence contrary to s 15 of the Theft Act 1968 the prosecution must prove that the defendant knew or was reckless regarding the representation concerned. The passage in my judgment in *R v Landy* [1981] 1 All ER 1172 at 1181, [1981] 1 WLR 355 at 365 per Lawton LJ to which we have referred should be read in relation to charges of conspiracy to defraud, and not in relation to charges of theft contrary to s 1 of the 1968 Act. Theft is in a different category from conspiracy to defraud, so that dishonesty can be established independently of the knowledge or belief of the defendant, subject to the special cases provided for in s 2 of the Act. Nevertheless, where a defendant has given evidence of his state of mind at the time of the alleged offence, the jury should be told to give that evidence such weight as they consider right, and they may also be directed that they should apply their own standards to the meaning of dishonesty.'

The question we have to decide in the present case is, first, whether the distinction suggested in *R v McIvor* is justifiable in theory and, second, whether it is workable in practice.

In *Scott v Comr of Police for the Metropolis* [1974] 3 All ER 1032, [1975] AC 819 the House of Lords had to consider whether deceit is a necessary element in the common law crime of conspiracy to defraud. They held that it is not. It is sufficient for the Crown to prove dishonesty. In the course of his speech Viscount Dilhorne traced the meaning of the words 'fraud', 'fraudulently' and 'defraud' in relation to simple larceny, as well as the common law offence of conspiracy to defraud. After referring to Stephen's *History of the Criminal Law of England* ((1883) vol 2, pp 121–122) and *East's Pleas of the Crown* ((1803) vol 2, p 553) he continued as follows ([1974] 3 All ER 1032 at 1036, [1975] AC 819 at 836–837):

'The Criminal Law Revision Committee in their eighth report on "Theft and Related Offences" (Cmnd 2977 (1966)) in para 33 expressed the view that the important element of larceny, embezzlement and fraudulent conversion was "undoubtedly the dishonest appropriation of another person's property"; in para 35 that the words "dishonestly appropriates" meant the same as "fraudulently converts to his own use or benefit, or the use or benefit of any other person", and in para 39 that "dishonestly" seemed to them a better word than "fraudulently". Parliament endorsed these views in the Theft Act 1968, which by s 1(1) defined theft as the dishonest appropriation of property belonging to another with the intention of permanently depriving the other of it. Section 17 of that Act replaces ss82 and 83 of the Larceny Act 1861 and the Falsification of Accounts Act 1875. The offences created by those sections and by that Act made it necessary to prove that there had been an "intent to defraud". Section 17 of the Theft Act 1968 substitutes the words "dishonestly with a view to gain for himself or another or with intent to cause loss to another" for the words "intent to defraud". If "fraudulently" in relation to larceny meant "dishonestly" and "intent to defraud" in relation to falsification of accounts is equivalent to the words now contained in s 17 of the Theft Act 1968 which I have quoted, it would indeed be odd if "defraud" in the phrase "conspiracy to defraud" has a different meaning and means only a conspiracy which is to be carried out by deceit.'

Later on in the same speech Viscount Dilhorne continued as follows ([1974] 3 All ER 1032 at 1038, [1975] AC 819 at 839):

'As I have said, words take colour from the context in which they are used, but the words "fraudulently" and "defraud" must ordinarily have a very similar meaning. If, as I think, and as the Criminal Law Revision Committee appears to have thought, "fraudulently" means "dishonestly", then "to defraud" ordinarily means, in my opinion, to deprive a person dishonestly of something which is his or of something to which he is or would or might but for the perpetration of the fraud be entitled.'

In *Scott* the House of Lords were only concerned with the question whether deceit is an essential ingredient in cases of conspiracy to defraud; and they held not. As Lord Diplock said ([1974] 3 All ER 1032 at 1040, [1975] AC 819 at 841), 'dishonesty of any kind is enough'. But there is nothing in *Scott* which supports the view that, so far as the element of dishonesty is concerned, 'theft is in a different category from conspiracy to defraud'. On the contrary the analogy drawn by Viscount Dilhorne between the two offences, and indeed the whole tenor of his speech, suggests the precise opposite.

Nor is there anything in *R v Landy* itself which justifies putting theft and conspiracy to defraud into different categories. Indeed the court went out of its way to stress that the test for dishonesty, whatever it might be, should be the same whether the offence charged be theft or conspiracy to defraud. This is clear from the reference to *R v Feely* [1973] 1 All ER 341, [1973] QB 530, which was a case under s 1 of the Theft Act 1968. Having set out what we have for convenience called the subjective test, the court in *R v Landy* [1981] 1 All ER 1172 to 1181, [1981] 1 WLR 355 at 365 continued:

'In our judgment this is the way *R v Feely* should be applied in cases where the issue of dishonesty arises. It is also the way in which the jury should have been directed in this case ...'

In support of the distinction it is said that in conspiracy to defraud the question arises in relation to an agreement. But we cannot see that this makes any difference. If A and B agree to deprive a person dishonestly of his goods, they are guilty of conspiracy to defraud: see *Scott's* case. If they dishonestly and with the necessary intent deprive him of his goods, they are presumably guilty of theft. Why, one asks respectfully, should the test be objective in the case of simple theft, but subjective where they have agreed to commit a theft?

The difficulties do not stop there. The court in *McIvor* evidently regarded cases under s15 of the Theft Act 1968 as being on the subjective side of the line, at any rate so far as proof of deception is concerned. This was the way they sought to explain *R v Greenstein*. In that case, after directing the jury in the passage which we have already quoted, the judge in the court below continued as follows ([1976] 1 All ER 1 at 7, [1975] 1 WLR 1353 at 1360):

> 'Now in considering whether Mr Green or Mr Greenstein had or may have had an honest belief in the truth of their representations ... the test is a subjective one. That is to say, it is not what you would have believed in similar circumstances. It is what you think they believed and if you think that they, or either of them, had an honest belief to that effect, well then, of course, there would not be any dishonesty. On the other hand, if there is an absence of reasonable grounds for so believing, you might think that that points to the conclusion that they or either of them, as the case may be, had no genuine belief in the truth of their representations. In which case, applying your own standards, you may think that they acted dishonestly and it would be for you to say whether it has been established by the prosecution that they had no such honest belief ...'

The Court of Appeal in *R v Greenstein* appear to have approved that passage. At any rate they expressed no disapproval.

In *R v McIvor* [1982] 1 All ER 491 at 496, [1982] 1 WLR 409 at 415 the court reconciled the two passages quoted from the judge's summing up as follows:

> 'It seems that those two passages are concerned with different points. The first, which follows and adopts the standards laid down in *R v Feely*, is concerned with the element of dishonesty in s 15 offences, whilst the second is specifically concerned with the mental element in relation to the false representation the subject matter of the charge. Clearly, if a defendant honestly believes that the representation made was true the prosecution cannot prove that he knew of, or was reckless as to, its falsity.'

The difficulty with s 15 of the Theft Act 1968 is that dishonesty comes in twice. If a person knows that he is not telling the truth he is guilty of dishonesty. Indeed deliberate deception is one of the two most obvious forms of dishonesty. One wonders therefore whether 'dishonestly' in s 15(1) adds anything, except in the case of reckless deception. But assuming it does, there are two consequences of the distinction drawn in *McIvor*. In the first place it would mean that the legislation has gone further than its framers intended. For it is clear from paras 87–88 of the Criminal Law Revision Committee's eighth report that 'deception' was to replace 'false pretence' in the old s 32(1) of the Larceny Act 1916, and 'dishonestly' was to replace 'with intent to defraud'. If the test of dishonesty in conspiracy to defraud cases is subjective, it is difficult to see how it could have been anything other than subjective in considering 'intent to defraud'. It follows that, if the distinction drawn in *McIvor* is correct, the Criminal Law Revision Committee were recommending an important change in the law by substituting 'dishonestly' for 'with intent to defraud'; for they were implicitly substituting an objective for a subjective test.

The second consequence is that in cases of deliberate deception the jury will have to be given two different tests of dishonesty to apply: the subjective test in relation to deception and the objective test in relation to obtaining. This is indeed what seems to have happened in *R v Greenstein*. We cannot regard this as satisfactory from a practical point of view. If it be sought to obviate the difficulty by making the test subjective in relation to both aspects of s 15, but objective in relation to s1, then that would certainly be contrary to what was intended by the Criminal Law Revision Committee. For in para 88 they say:

> 'The provision in clause 12(1) making a person guilty of criminal deception if he "dishonestly obtains" the property replaces the provision in the 1916 Act, section 32(1) making a person guilty of obtaining by false pretences if he "with intent to defraud, obtains" the things there mentioned. The change will correspond to the change from "fraudulently" to "dishonestly" in the definition of stealing (contained in section 1).'

We feel, with the greatest respect, that in seeking to reconcile the two lines of authority in the way we have mentioned, the Court of Appeal in *McIvor* was seeking to reconcile the irreconcilable. It therefore falls to us now either to choose between the two lines of authority or to propose some other solution.

In the current supplement to *Archbold's, Pleading, Evidence and Practice in Criminal Cases* (40th edn, 1979) para 1460, the editors suggest that the observations on dishonesty by the Court of Appeal in *R v Landy* can be disregarded 'in view of the wealth of authority to the contrary'. The matter, we feel, is not as simple as that.

In *R v Waterfall* [1969] 3 All ER 1048, [1970] 1 QB 148 the defendant was charged under s 16 of the 1968 Act with dishonestly obtaining a pecuniary advantage from a taxi driver. Lord Parker CJ, giving the judgment of the Court of Appeal, said ([1969] 3 All ER 1048 at 1049–1050, [1970] 1 QB 148 at 150–151):

> 'The sole question as it seems to me in this case revolves round the third ingredient, namely, whether that what was done was done dishonestly. In regard to that the deputy recorder directed the jury in this way: "... if on reflection and deliberation you came to the conclusion that [the appellant] never did have any genuine belief that [the appellant's accountant] would pay the taxi fare, then you would be entitled to convict him..." In other words, in that passage the deputy recorder is telling the jury they had to consider what was in this particular appellant's mind; had he a genuine belief that the accountant would provide the money? That, as it seems to this court, is a perfectly proper direction subject to this, that it would be right to tell the jury that they can use as a test, although not a conclusive test, whether there were any reasonable grounds for that belief. Unfortunately, however, just before the jury retired, in two passages of the transcript the deputy recorder, as it seems to this court, was saying that one cannot hold that the appellant had a genuine belief unless he had reasonable grounds for that belief.'

Lord Parker CJ then sets out the passages in question and continues:

> '... the court is quite satisfied that those directions cannot be justified. The test here is a subjective test, whether the appellant had an honest belief, and of course whereas the absence of reasonable ground may point strongly to the fact that that belief is not genuine, it is at the end of the day for the jury to say whether or not in the case of this particular man he did have that genuine belief.'

That decision was criticised by academic writers. But it was followed shortly afterwards in *R v Royle* [1971] 3 All ER 1359, [1971] 1 WLR 1764, another case under s 16 of the 1968 Act. Edmund Davies LJ, giving the judgment of the court, said ([1971] 3 All ER 1359 at 1365, [1971] 1 WLR 1764 at 1769–1770):

> 'The charges being that debts had been dishonestly "evaded" by deception, contrary to s 16(2)(a), it was incumbent on the commissioner to direct the jury on the fundamental ingredient of dishonesty. In accordance with *R v Waterfall* they should have been told that the test is whether the accused had an honest belief and that, whereas the absence of reasonable ground might point strongly to the conclusion that he entertained no genuine belief in the truth of his representation, it was for them to say whether or not it had been established that the appellant had no such genuine belief.'

It is to be noted that the court in that case treated the 'fundamental ingredient of dishonesty' as being the same as whether the defendant had a genuine belief in the truth of the representation.

In *R v Gilks* [1972] 3 All ER 280, [1972] 1 WLR 1341, which was decided by the Court of Appeal the following year, the appellant had been convicted of theft contrary to s 1 of the 1968 Act. The facts were that he had been overpaid by a bookmaker. He knew that the bookmaker had made a mistake, and that he was not entitled to the money. But he kept it. The case for the defence was that 'bookmakers are a race apart'. It would be dishonest if your grocer gave you too much change and you kept it, knowing that he had made a mistake. But it was not dishonest in the case of a bookmaker.

The deputy chairman of the court below directed the jury as follows:

'Well, it is a matter for you to consider, members of the jury, but try and place yourselves in [the appellant's] position at that time and answer the question whether in your view he thought he was acting honestly or dishonestly.'

(See [1972] 3 All ER 280 at 283, [1972] 1 WLR 1341 at 1345.)

Cairns LJ, giving the judgment of the Court of Appeal held that that was, in the circumstances of the case, a proper and sufficient direction on the matter of dishonesty. He continued ([1972] 3 All ER 280 at 283, [1972] 1 WLR 1341 at 1345):

'On the face of it the appellant's conduct was dishonest; the only possible basis on which the jury could find that the prosecution had not established dishonesty would be if they thought it possible that the appellant did have the belief which he claimed to have.'

A little later *R v Feely* came before a court of five judges. The case is often treated as having laid down an objective test of dishonesty for the purpose of s 1 of the 1968 Act. But what it actually decided was (i) that it is for the jury to determine whether the defendant acted dishonestly and not for the judge, (ii) that the word 'dishonestly' can only relate to the defendant's own state of mind, and (iii) that it is unnecessary and undesirable for judges to define what is meant by 'dishonestly'.

It is true that the court said ([1973] 1 All ER 341 at 345, [1973] QB 530 at 537–538):

'Jurors when deciding whether an appropriation was dishonest can be reasonably expected to, and should, apply the current standards of ordinary decent people.'

It is that sentence which is usually taken as laying down the objective test. But the passage goes on:

'In their own lives they have to decide what is and what is not dishonest. We can see no reason why, when in a jury box, they should require the help of a judge to tell them what amounts to dishonesty.'

The sentence requiring the jury to apply current standards leads up to the prohibition of judges from applying *their* standards. That is the context in which the sentence appears. It seems to be reading too much into that sentence to treat it as authority for the view that 'dishonesty can be established independently of the knowledge or belief of the defendant'. If it could, then any reference to the state of mind of the defendant would be beside the point.

This brings us to the heart of the problem. Is 'dishonestly' in s 1 of the 1968 Act intended to characterise a course of conduct? Or is it intended to describe a state of mind? If the former, then we can well understand that it could be established independently of the knowledge or belief of the accused. But if, as we think, it is the latter, then the knowledge and belief of the accused are at the root of the problem.

Take for example a man who comes from a country where public transport is free. On his first day here he travels on a bus. He gets off without paying. He never had any intention of paying. His mind is clearly honest; but his conduct, judged objectively by what he had done, is dishonest. It seems to us that, in using the word 'dishonestly' in the 1968 Act, Parliament cannot have intended to catch dishonest conduct in that sense, that is to say conduct to which no moral obloquy could possibly attach. This is sufficiently established by the partial definition in s 2 of the Theft Act 1968 itself. All the matters covered by s2(1) relate to the belief of the accused. Section 2(2) relates to his willingness to pay. A man's belief and his willingness to pay are things which can only be established subjectively. It is difficult to see how a partially subjective definition can be made to work in harness with the test which in all other respects is wholly objective.

If we are right that dishonesty is something in the mind of the accused (what Professor Glanville Williams calls 'a special mental state'), then if the mind of the accused is honest, it cannot be deemed dishonest merely because members of the jury would have regarded it as dishonest to embark on that course of conduct.

So we would reject the simple uncomplicated approach that the test is purely objective, however attractive from the practical point of view that solution may be.

There remains the objection that to adopt a subjective test is to abandon all standards but that of the accused himself, and to bring about a state of affairs in which 'Robin Hood would be no robber' (see *R v Greenstein*). This objection misunderstands the nature of the subjective test. It is no defence for a man to say, 'I knew that what I was doing is generally regarded as dishonest; but I do not regard it as dishonest myself. Therefore I am not guilty.' What he is, however, entitled to say is, 'I did not know that anybody would regard what I was doing as dishonest.' He may not be believed; just as he may not be believed if he sets up 'a claim of right' under s2(1) of the 1968 Act, or asserts that he believed in the truth of a misrepresentation under s 15 of the 1968 Act. But if he *is* believed, or raises a real doubt about the matter, the jury cannot be sure that he was dishonest.

In determining whether the prosecution has proved that the defendant was acting dishonestly, a jury must first of all decide whether according to the ordinary standards of reasonable and honest people what was done was dishonest. If it was not dishonest by those standards, that is the end of the matter and the prosecution fails. If it was dishonest by those standards, then the jury must consider whether the defendant himself must have realised that what he was doing was by those standards dishonest. In most cases, where the actions are obviously dishonest by ordinary standards, there will be no doubt about it. It will be obvious that the defendant himself knew that he was acting dishonestly. It is dishonest for a defendant to act in a way which he knows ordinary people consider to be dishonest, even if he asserts or genuinely believes that he is morally justified in acting as he did. For example, Robin Hood or those ardent anti-vivisectionists who remove animals from vivisection laboratories are acting dishonestly, even though they may consider themselves to be morally justified in doing what they do, because they know that ordinary people would consider these actions to be dishonest.

Cases which might be described as borderline, such as *Boggeln v Williams* [1978] 2 All ER 1061, [1978] 1 WLR 873, will depend on the view taken by the jury whether the defendant may have believed what he was doing was in accordance with the ordinary man's idea of honesty. A jury might have come to the conclusion that the defendant in that case was disobedient or impudent, but not dishonest in what he did.

So far as the present case is concerned, it seems to us that once the jury had rejected the defendant's account in respect of each count in the indictment (as they plainly did), the finding of dishonesty was inevitable, whichever of the tests of dishonesty was applied. If the judge had asked the jury to determine whether the defendant might have believed that what he did was in accordance with the ordinary man's idea of honesty, there could have only been one answer, and that is No, once the jury had rejected the defendant's explanation of what happened.

In so far as there was a misdirection on the meaning of dishonesty, it is plainly a case for the application of the proviso to s2(1) of the Criminal Appeal Act 1968.

This appeal is accordingly dismissed.

Appeal dismissed

Notes and questions

1. A *Ghosh* direction on dishonesty is not necessary in every case. If D claims that his appropriation of property was not dishonest because he believed that he had in law the right to deprive the other of it, or because he believed the owner would consent, or he believed the owner could not be traced by taking reasonable steps (these are all cases falling

within the partial definition in s 2) then the only issue for the jury or magistrates is whether he did so genuinely believe. Or D may claim that he took the goods (a book from a bookshop say) absent-mindedly and had no intention to steal. In such cases a *Ghosh* direction would be inapt and, indeed, misleading.

2. *Ghosh* clarifies the earlier law in some respects—it confirms that the test is subjective— it still leaves the jury to determine as a matter of fact (i) whether D's conduct would be regarded as dishonest by the ordinary standards of reasonable and honest people; and (ii) whether D knew that.

3. The CLRC said that dishonesty is 'something which laymen can easily recognize when they see it'. Can you easily recognize dishonesty when you see it? Do you think that you would always agree with your friends on what is and what is not dishonest? If not, is it satisfactory to settle the matter by vote after discussion which is presumably what a jury would do where opinions differ?

4. In *Feely* [1973] 1 All ER 341 at 346, CA, Lawton LJ instanced the case of a shop manager, under instructions not to take money from the till, who takes 40p from the till to pay a taxi driver because he has nothing less than a £5 note which the driver cannot change. Assuming that the manager intends to repay the 40p as soon as he has change, Lawton LJ thought that to hold that such a taking was dishonest would bring the law into contempt. Would it? Assume the owner has made it clear that in no circumstances whatever is an employee to take money from the till, does not the manager know that he has not a shred of right to take the 40p? Assuming the manager is not accounted dishonest, at what point do such 'borrowings' become dishonest? Is this to be determined by the amount taken, the time it will take D to restore the amount, or what?

5. While shopping in Megastores Don absent-mindedly placed a bottle of whisky in his overcoat pocket. Arriving home, Don realized that he had taken the bottle of whisky without paying for it. At first Don decided to return to the store, explain what had happened, and pay for the whisky. But, on reflection, he decided that his explanation might not be believed and that he would only get himself into deeper trouble if he did so. Moreover he wondered whether he had been seen and whether the police might call at any moment. In a panic he poured the whisky down the sink and threw the bottle in the dustbin. Five minutes later the police, alerted by Ed, a store detective who had seen Don pocket the bottle of whisky, arrived and arrested Don on suspicion of stealing the whisky. Is Don a thief?

6. Is the definition of dishonesty in English law compatible with Article 7 of the ECHR? Article 7 guarantees not only against retrospective criminalization in strict terms, but also that 'legal provisions which interfere with individual rights must be adequately accessible, and formulated with sufficient precision to enable the citizen to regulate his conduct': *G v Federal Republic of Germany* 60 DR 252, 262 (1989). Can a defendant know before trial whether his conduct qualifies as being dishonest? See *Pattni* [2001] Crim LR 570. The Law Commission in Consultation Paper No 155 *Fraud* (1999) provisionally took the view that a Home Secretary could not safely be advised to make a statement of compatibility in relation to a Bill creating a general dishonesty offence.

7. The present law under *Ghosh* has its critics (see, for example, E. Griew, *Dishonesty and the Jury*, Leicester University Press (1974), and 'Dishonesty, the Objections to *Feely* and *Ghosh*' [1985] Crim LR 341, and D. W. Elliott, 'Dishonesty in Theft: A Dispensable

Concept' [1982] Crim LR 395); but it has its defenders (see A. Samuels '' [1974] Crim LR 493; R. Tur, 'Dishonesty and the Jury Question' in A. Phillips Griffiths (ed) *Philosophy and Practice* (1985).

E. J. Griew, 'Dishonesty, the Objections to *Feely* and *Ghosh*'
[1985] Crim LR 341

There are many objections to the *Feely* question.

A1. More, longer and more difficult trials
If the law is right in principle, so be it; the fact that it tends to multiply and prolong trials cannot be a decisive objection. But as an addition to other objections it is of such practical importance that it should have pride of place. There are several distinct points.

(a) The question tends to increase the number of trials. Whereas a different approach to the dishonesty issue might make clear that given conduct was dishonest as a matter of law and therefore constituted an offence, the *Feely* question leaves the issue open. It may be worth a defendant's while to take his chance with the jury. . . . Defences such as these provide ground for a contest where, before *Feely*, the defendants might have felt constrained to plead guilty.

(b) The question tends to complicate and lengthen contested cases. For it is difficult to say of any - evidence relating to the defendant's state of mind or to the special circumstances in which he acted that it is irrelevant to the *Feely* issue. Moreover, it must be in the interests of some defendants to extend and complicate trials in order to obfuscate the issue. This point is shortly stated but is surely of considerable importance.

(c) At the end of a trial the jury may have to be asked not simply whether the defendant acted with the state of mind he claims to have had, or in other circumstances that, as he suggests, may have rendered his act not dishonest, but also (if he may have done so) whether his act with that state of mind, or in those circumstances, was dishonest according to ordinary standards. If these matters are not kept separate the jury may be seriously misled. But their careful separation shows the complexity of the direction that the *Feely* question will dictate in some cases. Nor can that question be avoided even if a conclusion on it adverse to the defendant is the only one that a jury acting reasonably can reach. The matter must be left to the jury to determine. . . .

(d) The separate matters just referred to, that may need to figure in the judge's direction, must then be handled by the jury in their deliberations. They may find them hard to keep separate. The issues we present to juries should be as simple as possible; jury service, after all, imposes tasks on ordinary people that they are not accustomed to discharge. The *Feely* question involves complications that we are not justified in supposing that all jurors are competent to handle.

A2. Inconsistent decisions
The *Feely* question carries an unacceptable risk of inconsistency of decision. This objection has been voiced by many critics. The problem of inconsistency is likely, of course, to affect only a small proportion of cases. In most cases the issue is one as to the facts: what did D do? what was his state of mind? Once the facts are found there will usually be only one plausible answer to the *Feely* question. It is only in a minority of cases that the matter will truly admit of argument. But within this crucial marginal group different juries, as the presumptive embodiment of ordinary decent standards, may take different views of essentially indistinguishable cases. The law of the relevant offence will then vary as between different defendants. This must be unacceptable.

A3. Fiction of community norms
The *Feely* question implies the existence of a relevant community norm. In doing so it glosses over differences of age, class and cultural background which combine to give the character of fiction to the

idea of a generally shared sense of the boundary between honesty and dishonesty. This is the more obvious in a society with the range of cultural groups that ours now has; and it is the more relevant since jury service was extended to the generality of electors between 18 and 65. It is simply naive to suppose—surely no one does suppose—that there is, in respect of the dishonesty question, any such single thing as 'the standards of ordinary decent people.' Although most people will unite in condemning, or in tolerating, some forms of behaviour, there are others as to which considerable divergence of view will exist. How juries cope with this obvious difficulty we do not know. Presumably some acquittals derive from the triumph of the most relaxed standard represented on the jury. The present objection is not to outcomes, however, but to the illegitimacy of the stated test as resting disreputably on a reference to a fictitious category.

A4. 'Dishonestly' as an 'ordinary word'

The foregoing objection to the *Feely* question is closely related to another. The jury are to consult their sense of ordinary standards because the word 'dishonestly' is 'in common use.' Jurors in their own lives 'have to decide what is and what is not dishonest'; they do not 'require the help of a judge to tell them what amounts to dishonesty.' For 'the meaning of an ordinary word of the English language is not a question of law.' This is the heart of the reasoning in *Feely*. The premise is that the issue is a semantic one; whether the defendant acted 'dishonestly' depends upon what 'dishonestly' means. The conclusion is that the issue requires the application of ordinary 'standards.' Between the premise and the conclusion lies the proposition that the meaning of the word 'dishonestly' will be found by a reference to standards. This silent step in the argument is itself interesting but is not of present concern. What must be expressed here is a doubt about the 'ordinary word.' It simply does not follow from the truth that a word such as 'dishonestly' is an ordinary word that all speakers of the language share the same sense of its application or non-application in particular contexts. Once again, it is to the marginal case, where the issue is live and crucial, that this common sense objection particularly applies. Even judges, a relatively homogeneous group of uniformly high linguistic competence, have been known to differ on the application of the epithet 'dishonest' in a marginal case. It is not acceptable that the meaning of 'dishonestly' should be 'whatever in a particular case it conveys to the mind or minds of the tribunal of fact without any instruction as to the meaning . . .'

A5. Specialised cases

The *Feely* question is in any case unsuitable where the context of the case is a specialised one, involving intricate financial activities or dealings in a specialised market. It is neither reasonable nor rational to expect ordinary people to judge as 'dishonest' or 'not dishonest' conduct of which, for want of relevant experience, they cannot appreciate the contextual flavour. Their answer to the *Feely* question ought sometimes to be that ordinary people have no standards in relation to the conduct in question. Juries do not reply in this rebellious way. Again, we do not know how they cope. Perhaps in some cases they take their cue from the fact of prosecution ('the prosecution are sure it was dishonest; of course the defendant says it was not!') or from the evidence of witnesses who do understand the context; but then they are not applying the *Feely* test. Perhaps in others they acquit because, perforce, they are not satisfied that the arcane activities of which they have heard offend against 'ordinary' standards; and then the test may produce a pernicious result.

A6. Ordinary dishonest jurors

The general understanding is that the jury may be taken to represent the 'ordinary decent people' to whom the *Feely* question refers. That is why, without incurring the disapproval of the Court of Appeal either in his own case or in *Ghosh*, the trial judge in *Greenstein* spoke to the jury of their 'applying [their] own standards.' Yet a vast number of what must surely be theft, handling and minor fraud offences are committed by 'ordinary,' even 'ordinary decent,' people such as serve upon juries: theft at work ('perks'), handling stolen goods being offered in the neighbourhood ('from off the back of a lorry'), inflation of expenses claims, inaccuracy or concealment in the income tax return. These ordinary people, as jurors, will either apply their own standards, as being the prevalent standards of which they know; or they will demand of their defendants higher standards than they themselves attain. To the extent (if at all) that the former occurs, the Court of Appeal in *Feely* and *Ghosh* will have achieved a reduction in the scope of dishonesty offences which it certainly did not intend. We ought not, on the other hand, to view the latter, presumably more common, occurrence with complacency. It is perfectly acceptable for the law to require a jury to apply a standard higher than its own; it is not acceptable that the law should invite a jury to impose such a standard by an act of creative hypocrisy. The law in effect expects many jurors, in relation to very common kinds of offences, to have one conception of ordinary standards outside court and another conception inside. This is disreputable.

A7. 'Anarchic' verdicts
The *Feely* question, offered without qualification to the jury, is 'a question of moral estimation without guidelines' and permits ' "anarchic" verdicts which are not technically perverse'. A jury without stars or compass cannot be accused of bad navigation. The direction it takes may be deplorable but cannot be wrong. A consequence of this, it has been pointed out, is that members of unpopular groups may receive inadequate protection from the law. Nothing, in any case, can prevent a jury from refusing to convict where the victim of the theft or obtaining alleged is someone whom they regard as 'fair game.' Such a disregard of property rights is easier to achieve, however, if it does not involve rebellion against a judicial direction but can pass as the performance of the jurys own evaluative function.

A8. What is 'dishonest' should be a matter of law
Whether an individual defendant was dishonest is, of course, a question for the jury. But it should be so only in the sense that the jury will find the facts upon the strength of which, applying legal principles, they will be able to say whether the defendant acted dishonestly. Whether the facts that they find constitute a case of 'dishonesty' within the meaning of that word in the particular legal context is a matter of legal principle upon which they should be able to turn to the law for clear guidance.

. . . .

A9. Dishonesty and defences
Leaving the dishonesty issue to the untutored application of community standards allows the issue a potentially unlimited function. The jury may be unwilling to condemn a defendant's conduct as 'dishonest' because they sympathise with his motive or are inclined to excuse what he did in the difficult circumstances in which he found himself; they may be still less willing if they are prepared to say that his conduct was justified in the circumstances. Thus the jury may create for their defendant a defence of necessity greater than any known to the law or a defence of pressure of circumstances where the law knows only a plea in mitigation. But the law of defences should develop in a disciplined way under judicial control, save indeed to the extent that it is statutorily defined.

The preceding paragraph assumes that a jury response such as sympathy with the defendant's motive or with his dilemma in an emergency is capable of affecting their judgment of his conduct as 'honest' or 'dishonest.' Similarly, a familiar objection to the *Ghosh* question (B5 below) assumes that it allows a defendant to claim that he did not know that his conduct would be regarded as 'dishonest' because he thought that right-thinking people would approve of it on moral grounds. These assumptions can be challenged. It may be said that sympathy with a motive, or an inclination to condone what is done in an emergency, has nothing to do with a judgment about honesty; that the question 'was it honest according to ordinary standards?' is a narrower question than 'was it justifiable or praiseworthy by ordinary standards?' That would, indeed, be a way of slightly limiting the mischief of *Feely* and *Ghosh*. The difficulty with it is that it would require an explanation to the jury of what is meant by 'dishonest' in the *Feely* question itself. But the jury do not need such an explanation; they know what the word means!

....

B. Objections to the *Ghosh* question

The second question is: Must the defendant have known that what he was doing was dishonest according to the standards of ordinary decent people?

B1. More, longer and more difficult trials

Compare objection A1. The *Ghosh* question (a) creates an additional ground for contested trials; (b) justifies the introduction of additional evidence; (c) further complicates the judge's direction; and (d) adds further to the complexity of the jury's task. There is no need to labour these points.

...

B3. Inept correction of error

Two cases after *Feely* had introduced reference to the question whether the defendant knew or believed that he was acting dishonestly (*Boggeln v Williams* [1978] 2 All ER 1061; *Landy* [1981] 1 All ER 1172)....*Ghosh* was an attempt to reintroduce order into a subject that had become inconsistent and confused. But the job was ineptly performed.

All that needed to be done was to point out that reference to the defendant's belief in the honesty of his own conduct was an inappropriate way of taking into account his 'state of mind.' It is true that, as the Court of Appeal has repeatedly asserted, proof of dishonesty requires reference to the defendant's state of mind. But it does so only in the sense that there must first be a finding as to whether he acted (or may have acted) with a belief (e.g. a claim of right), an intention (e.g. to take the valuable goods he has found to the police station) or an expectation (e.g. of an immediate power to repay) that is relevant under section 2(1) of the Theft Act 1968 or may be regarded by the jury as relevant to the *Feely* question. Once a relevant state of mind has been found, the only question remaining to be answered is whether section 2(1) or the jury's sense of ordinary decent standards makes the defendant's conduct with that state of mind dishonest. This is a question, not as to what state of mind the defendant had, but as to how that state of mind is to be characterised.

The confusion on this point in the *Ghosh* judgment is clear to see in the treatment of the hypothetical of a visitor from a foreign country where public transport is free. He travels on a bus without paying. Does he do so dishonestly? The court says that 'his conduct, judged objectively by what he has done, is dishonest.' The error enters the argument at this point. It cannot be right, as the structure of the court's argument plainly implies, that the visitor's conduct would be regarded as dishonest by ordinary decent standards. If the jury knew that he believed public transport to be free, they would say that, according to ordinary standards, he had not behaved dishonestly. There is no need to go further; his 'state of mind' has already been taken into account. But the court, having declared him dishonest when 'judged objectively,' has to introduce a further 'subjective' element to rescue him. That leads to the question: 'Did he know it was dishonest?'—an entirely unnecessary question.

B4. Mistake of law

The *Ghosh* question 'allows something like a mistake of law to be a defence.' The question is a mere addendum to the *Feely* question; it is the answer to the latter that determines the view to be taken of the defendant's conduct as in principle criminal. The jury's apprehension of current standards makes law for the case; the defendant's misapprehension of those standards is indeed 'something like a mistake of law.' It is not strictly one, of course; his failure to realise that ordinary people would call his conduct dishonest means (taking *Ghosh* literally) that it is not dishonest.

B5. The 'Robin Hood defence'

A person may defend his attack on another's property by reference to a moral or political conviction so passionately held that he believed (so he claims) that 'ordinary decent' members of society would regard his conduct as proper, even laudable. If the asserted belief is treated as a claim to have been ignorant that the conduct was 'dishonest' by ordinary standards (and it has been assumed that it might be so treated, and if the jury think (as exceptionally they might) that the belief may have been held, *Ghosh* produces an acquittal. The result is remarkable. Robin Hood must be a thief even if he thinks the whole of the right-thinking world is on his side.

B6. A further threat to standards

A person reared or moving in an environment in which it is generally regarded as legitimate to take advantage of certain classes of people—perhaps bookmakers or employers—may plausibly claim that he did not realise that his conduct, of which a member of such a class was a victim, was generally regarded as dishonest. It is not acceptable that a claim of that sort should be capable even of being advanced. It has been said that 'the [*Ghosh*] question presents an even greater threat to the standard of honesty than the [*Feely* question].'

Questions

1. Do you find these criticisms convincing? Are there reported instances of juries struggling with the concept? If not, why not?

2. In *Salvo* [1980] VR 401 the Full Court of Victoria declined to follow the approach of English courts to the interpretation of dishonesty. Concluding that it was for the judge to direct the jury on the meaning of dishonesty, Fullagar J said in the context of similar Victorian legislation (at 431):

The alleged proposal of the [CLRC] ... is in my opinion based upon a clear and fundamental fallacy. First, it is simply untrue to say that every citizen 'knows dishonesty when he sees it' or knows the meaning of the word generally, let alone in the context of a ... statute. Secondly, that is simply not the question that arises under the Acts; it is a different question altogether to ask whether a deprivation by deception has been achieved dishonestly. The word 'dishonestly' is in my opinion used in a somewhat special sense in its special context in the Theft Act 1973 and it is simply not true to say that every citizen knows what the word 'dishonestly' means in the context of this statute.... In my opinion the word 'dishonestly' in s 81(1) imports that the accused person must obtain the property (with intent to deprive), without any belief that he has in law the right to deprive the other of the property.

But is it any more satisfactory to leave dishonesty to be defined by the judges? Is Fullagar J's definition a satisfactory one?

3. Would it be possible and desirable to enact an exhaustive definition of dishonesty? Suppose the partial definition in the 1968 Act had been made an exhaustive definition; would this adequately meet the case? Alternatively, consider a provision that a person appropriating property belonging to another *is* to be regarded as dishonest unless one of the three present exceptions applies—

or, (d) he intends to replace the property with an equivalent, having no doubt that no detriment whatever will be caused to the owner by the appropriation.

This would exempt the person who takes money from his employer's till, knowing that he is forbidden to do so, but intending, and having no doubt that he will be able, to replace it before it is missed. *Should* he be exempted from liability for theft?

4. A. Halpin, 'The Test for Dishonesty' [1996] Crim LR 283, at 294 suggests the following redefinition:

1. The treatment by a person of the property of another is to be regarded as dishonest where it is done without a belief that the other would consent to that treatment if he knew of all the circumstances, unless the person believes that the law permits that treatment of the property. 2. The treatment by a person of the property of another is not to be regarded as dishonest if done (otherwise than by a trustee or personal representative) in the belief that the person to whom the property belongs is unlikely to be discovered by taking reasonable steps.

Is this any better?

5. More radically, D. W. Elliott ('Dishonesty in Theft: A Dispensable Concept' [1982] Crim LR 395 at 398) proposes dispensing with the word 'dishonestly' altogether and adding a new sub-s (3) to s 2: 'No appropriation of property belonging to another which is not detrimental to the interests of the other in a significant practical way shall amount to theft of the property.' Is this any improvement?

(7) INTENTION PERMANENTLY TO DEPRIVE

Theft Act 1968, s 6

6. 'With the intention of permanently depriving the other of it'

(1) A person appropriating property belonging to another without meaning the other permanently to lose the thing itself is nevertheless to be regarded as having the intention of permanently depriving the other of it if his intention is to treat the thing as his own to dispose of regardless of the other's rights; and a borrowing or lending of it may amount to so treating it if, but only if, the borrowing or lending is for a period and in circumstances making it equivalent to an outright taking or disposal.

(2) Without prejudice to the generality of subsection (1) above, where a person, having possession or control (lawfully or not) of property belonging to another, parts with the property under a condition as to its return which he may not be able to perform, this (if done for purposes of his own and without the other's authority) amounts to treating the property as his own to dispose of regardless of the other's rights.

The CLRC was firm in its view that, special instances apart (see Chapter 22), dishonest borrowing should not in general be an offence and accordingly retained in the definition of theft the requirement for an intention permanently to deprive as had always been the case with larceny. The CLRC, however, proposed no elaboration of the words 'with the intention of permanently depriving the other of it' and seems to have assumed that the expression would be interpreted as it had been under the earlier law. But someone always knows, or claims to know, better and s 6 was added to the CLRC's Bill. See J. R Spencer, 'The Metamorphosis of Section 6 of the Theft Act' [1977] Crim LR 653.

In the ordinary run of cases the issue presents no problems. If D takes V's car he is a thief if he intends to keep it but guilty only of the offence under s 12 if he intends to return it, or, more likely, abandons it somewhere knowing that it will be recovered by the owner. If D takes V's book he is a thief if he intends to keep it but guilty of no offence if he intends to restore it.

But some cases are not quite ordinary.

R v Lloyd
[1985] 2 All ER 661, Court of Appeal, Criminal Division

(Lord Lane CJ, Farquharson and Tudor Price JJ)

The appellant, a projectionist at a cinema, removed films which were to be shown at the cinema and took them to his accomplices who made a master videotape from which they were able to reproduce large numbers of copies. The films were out of the possession of the owners for only a few hours. The copies would be sold to the great advantage of the accomplices and financial detriment of the owners. The appellant was convicted of conspiracy to steal.

Lord Lane CJ. The trial judge issued his certificate by posing the following question:

> 'Whether the offence of conspiracy to steal is committed when persons dishonestly agree to take a film from a cinema without authority intending it should be returned within a few hours but knowing that many hundreds of copies will be subsequently made and that the value of the film so returned will thereby be substantially reduced?'

The complaint by the appellants is this, that the judge misdirected the jury first of all in leaving the question for them to decide whether the removal of a film in these circumstances could amount to theft, and secondly, in allowing them to consider s6(1) of the Theft Act 1968 as being relevant at all in the circumstances of this case.

The point is a short one. It is not a simple one. It is not without wider importance, because if the judge was wrong in leaving the matter in the way in which he did for the jury to consider, it might mean, as we understand it, that the only offence of which a person in these circumstances could be convicted would be a conspiracy to commit a breach of the Copyright Act 1956. At the time when this particular case was being tried, the maximum penalties available for the substantive offence under the Copyright Act were minimal. Those penalties have now been increased by the provisions of the Copyright (Amendment) Act 1983, and in the light of that Act it can be said that, although Parliament perhaps has not entirely caught up with this type of prevalent pirating offence, it is at least gaining on it.

We turn now to the provisions of the Theft Act 1968, the conspiracy alleged being a breach of that particular Act. Section 1(1) of the 1968 Act provides: [His Lordship read s 1(1)] ... see above, p [748.]

On that wording alone these appellants were not guilty of theft or of conspiracy to steal. The success of their scheme and their ability to act with impunity in a similar fashion in the future, depended, as we have already said, on their ability to return the film to its rightful place in the hands of the Odeon cinema at Barking as rapidly as possible, so that its absence should not be noticed. Therefore the intention of the appellants could more accurately be described as an intention temporarily to deprive the owner of the film and was indeed the opposite of an intention permanently to deprive.

What then was the basis of the prosecution case and the basis of the judge's direction to the jury? It is said that s 6(1) of the Theft Act 1968 brings such actions as the appellants performed here within the provisions of s 1. The judge left the matter to the jury on the basis that they had to decide whether the words of s6(1) were satisfied by the prosecution or not. Section 6(1) reads as follows:

> 'A person appropriating property belonging to another without meaning the other permanently to lose the thing itself is nevertheless to be regarded as having the intention of permanently depriving the other of it if his intention is to treat the thing as his own to dispose of regardless of the other's rights;

and a borrowing or lending of it may amount to so treating it if, but only if, the borrowing or lending is for a period.'

That section has been described by J. R. Spencer in 'The Metamorphosis of Section 6 of the Theft Act' [1977] Crim LR 653 as a section which 'sprouts obscurities at every phrase', and we are inclined to agree with him. It is abstruse. But it must mean, if nothing else, that there are circumstances in which a defendant may be deemed to have the intention permanently to deprive, even though he may intend the owner eventually to get back the object which has been taken . . .

Counsel for the appellants . . . cited to us a series of helpful cases, which are these. First of all, *R v Warner* (1970) 55 Cr App Rep 93, [1971] Crim LR 114. This was a case in which the judgment of the court was delivered by Edmund Davies LJ. Having cited the words in which the chairman directed the jury, Edmund Davies LJ continued (at 96–97):

'But unfortunately his direction later became confused by his references to section 6, the object of which he may himself have misunderstood. There is no statutory definition of the words "intention of permanently depriving", but section 6 seeks to clarify their meaning in certain respects. Its object is in no wise to cut down the definition of "theft" contained in section 1. It is always dangerous to paraphrase a statutory enactment, but its apparent aim is to prevent specious pleas of a kind which have succeeded in the past providing, in effect, that it is no excuse for an accused person to plead absence of the necessary intention if it is clear that he appropriated another's property intending to treat it as his own, regardless of the owner's rights. Section 6 thus gives illustrations, as it were, of what can amount to the dishonest intention demanded by section 1(1). But it is a misconception to interpret it as watering down section 1.'

Those observations we must bear in mind, because that is a decision which of course is binding on this court.

Then counsel for the appellants referred us to *R v Duru* [1973] 3 All ER 715, [1974] 1 WLR 2. That was a case involving cheques. The allegation was that the defendant had obtained certain cheques from the local authority by deception with the intention of permanently depriving the council of them. That was contrary to s 15(1) of the Theft Act 1968, but s 6(1) was equally applicable in that case as it would have been had the allegation been one simply of theft. Megaw LJ, delivering the judgment of the court, said ([1973] 3 All ER 715 at 720, [1974] 1 WLR 2 at 8):

'So far as the cheque itself is concerned, true it is a piece of paper. But it is a piece of paper which changes its character completely once it is paid, because then it receives a rubber stamp on it saying it has been paid and it ceases to be a thing in action, or at any rate it ceases to be, in its substance, the same thing as it was before: that is, an instrument on which payment falls to be made. It was the intention of the appellants, dishonestly and by deception, not only that the cheques should be made out and handed over, but also that they should be presented and paid, thereby permanently depriving the Greater London Council of [the cheques in their substance as things in action]. The fact that the mortgagors were under an obligation to repay the mortgage loans does not affect the appellants' intention permanently to deprive the council of these cheques. If it were necessary to look to s 6(1) of the Theft Act 1968, this court would have no hesitation in saying that that subsection, brought in by the terms of s 15(3), would also be relevant, since it is plain that the appellants each had the intention of causing the cheque to be treated as the property of the person by whom it was to be obtained, to dispose of, regardless of the rights of the true owner.'

Finally counsel for the appellants referred us to *R v Downes* (1983) 77 Cr App Rep 260, [1983] Crim LR 819. That was a case similar in essence to *R v Duru* [1973] 3 All ER 715, [1974] 1 WLR 2. The judgment of the court in *R v Downes* was delivered by Nolan J who said this (at 266–267):

'It is of some interest to note in *Duru* the Court was referred to the earlier case of *Warner* ((1970) 55 Cr App Rep 93, [1971] Crim LR 114), which Mr Lodge cited in support of the narrower reading of section 6(1) for which he contended. *Warner* does not however appear to us, as evidently it did not appear to this Court in *Duru*, to have any significant bearing on the point at issue. It follows that, for substantially the same reasons as those given by the learned judge, we consider that the charge of theft is made out, the vouchers having been dishonestly appropriated with the intention of destroying their essential character and thus depriving the owners, the Inland Revenue, of the substance of their property. In our judgment therefore the appeal must be dismissed.'

In general we take the same view as Professor Griew in his book *The Theft Acts 1968 and 1978* (4th edn, 1982) para 2–73, namely that s 6 should be referred to in exceptional cases only. In the vast majority of cases it need not be referred to or considered at all.

Deriving assistance from another distinguished academic writer, namely Professor Glanville Williams, we would like to cite with approval the following passage from his *Textbook of Criminal Law* (2nd edn, 1983) p 719:

'In view of the grave difficulties of interpretation presented by section 6, a trial judge would be well advised not to introduce it to the jury unless he reaches the conclusion that it will assist them, and even then (it may be suggested) the question he leaves to the jury should not be worded in terms of the generalities of the subsection but should reflect those generalities as applied to the alleged facts. For example, the question might be: "Did the defendant take the article, intending that the owner should have it back only on making a payment? If so, you would be justified as a matter of law in finding that he intended to deprive the owner permanently of his article, because the taking of the article with that intention is equivalent to an outright taking."'

Bearing in mind the observations of Edmund Davies LJ in *R v Warner* (1970) 55 Cr App R 93, [1971] Crim LR 114, we would try to interpret s 6 in such a way as to ensure that nothing is construed as an intention permanently to deprive which would not prior to the 1968 Act have been so construed. Thus the first part of s 6(1) seems to us to be aimed at the sort of case where a defendant takes things and then offers them back to the owner for the owner to buy if he wishes. If the taker intends to return them to the owner only on such payment, then, on the wording of s 6(1), that is deemed to amount to the necessary intention permanently to deprive: see for instance *R v Hall* (1849) 1 Den 381, 169 ER 291, where the defendant took fat from a candlemaker and then offered it for sale to the owner. His conviction for larceny was affirmed. There are other cases of similar intent. For instance. I have taken your valuable painting. You can have it back on payment to me of £X,000. If you are not prepared to make that payment, then you are not going to get your painting back.

It seems to us that in this case we are concerned with the second part of s 6(1), namely the words after the semi-colon: 'and a borrowing or lending of it may amount to so treating it if, but only if, the borrowing or lending is for a period and in circumstances making it equivalent to an outright taking or disposal.'

These films, it could be said, were borrowed by Lloyd from his employers in order to enable him and the others to carry out their 'piracy' exercise.

Borrowing is ex hypothesi not something which is done with an intention permanently to deprive. This half of the subsection, we believe, is intended to make it clear that a mere borrowing is never enough to constitute the necessary guilty mind unless the intention is to return the 'thing' in such a changed state that it can truly be said that all its goodness or virtue has gone. For example *R v Beecham* (1851) 5 Cox CC 181, where the defendant stole railway tickets intending that they should be returned to the railway company in the usual way only after the journeys had been completed. He was convicted of larceny. The judge in the present case gave another example, namely the taking of a torch battery with intention of returning it only when its power is exhausted.

That being the case, we turn to inquire whether the feature films in this case can fall within this category. Our view is that they cannot. The goodness, the virtue, the practical value of the films to the owners has not gone out of the article. The film could still be projected to paying audiences, and, had everything gone according to the conspirators' plans, would have been projected in the ordinary way to audiences at the Odeon cinema, Barking, who would have paid for their seats. Our view is that those particular films which were the subject of this alleged conspiracy had not themselves diminished in value at all. What had happened was that the borrowed film had been used or was going to be used to perpetrate a copyright swindle on the owners whereby their commercial interests were grossly and adversely affected in the way that we have endeavoured to describe at the outset of this judgment. The borrowing, it seems to us, was not for a period, or in such circumstances, as made it equivalent to an outright taking or disposal. There was still virtue in the film.

For those reasons we think that the submissions of counsel for the appellants on this aspect of the case are well founded. Accordingly, the way in which the trial judge directed the jury was mistaken, and accordingly this conviction of conspiracy to steal must be quashed....

Appeals allowed. Convictions quashed

Notes and questions

1. In *Warner* (referred to in *Lloyd*) D removed a toolbox from V's workshop next door and when questioned by the police denied that he had taken it. There had been some ill-feeling between D and V concerning the parking of cars and D later said that it was his intention to return the toolbox and that he told lies to the police because he had panicked. It was held that the trial judge had misdirected the jury in saying that D could be convicted of theft if his intention was that V should lose the use of his tools indefinitely.

2. Consider *Oxford v Moss*, p **766**, above. Was not the borrowing of the paper equivalent to an outright taking in that the examination paper, once its contents were disclosed, was valueless to the university? In *Bagshaw* [1988] Crim LR 321, CA, D was charged with the theft of gas cylinders and claimed that he had borrowed them. His conviction for stealing the cylinders was quashed because the trial judge had not properly explained to the jury that D could be convicted only if he intended to retain the cylinders until all their 'goodness' had gone. But was all their goodness gone by the use of the gas they contained? D was not charged with the theft of the gas (and to such a charge he would appear to have had no defence) but with stealing the cylinders. If the cylinders could be refilled with gas, was all—or any—their goodness gone? The court in *Lloyd* said that the trial judge had given, as an example of permanent deprivation, the case where D takes a torch battery intending to return it only when the charge was exhausted. Do you agree? Would it be different if the battery was rechargeable?

3. A person borrows property when he intends to return that property. This is not the same thing as restoring its equivalent. D, short of money to buy his lunch, 'borrows' money from the petty cash float in his employer's office which he intends to repay with an equivalent amount at a later stage. D may have a defence to a charge of theft in that he is not acting dishonestly but he cannot claim that he has not deprived his employer permanently of the money which he has taken: *Velumyl* [1989] Crim LR 299, CA.

4. When introducing s 6 to an expectant and hushed House of Commons, the Under Secretary of State for the Home Department said:

The case which comes most readily to mind in this connection is that of a person borrowing, say, a season ticket. If he borrows it merely to keep it for any reason whatever as a piece of cardboard having an intrinsic value of a fraction of a penny, no offence can be committed under the [section].

But let us assume that he uses the ticket to gain admittance to a certain performance or series of performances—let us say he uses it for 19 or 20 performances. He has, by that act, used the season ticket in a situation which shows that he is not any longer acting as borrower but as...owner of the ticket.

Do you agree that the taker of the season ticket is (a) not guilty of theft on the first hypothesis—suppose he keeps it in his pocket until the season is over, but (b) guilty of theft on the second?

5. Suppose that D offers to sell to V, an unusually gullible tourist, the Crown jewels for £500. Realizing that this is something of a bargain, V accepts and pays £500. Obviously a case of obtaining by deception, but has D stolen the Crown jewels? Assuming that in such circumstances D has appropriated the property (as to which see *Pitham and Hehl* (1976) 65 Cr App R 45, [1977] Crim LR 285, CA, below, p 930), has D, by virtue of s 6, an intention permanently to deprive the owner? How do you think Lord Lane would answer this question?

6. In *Marshall* [1998] 2 Cr App R 282, [1999] Crim LR 317, above p 769, Mantell LJ said at p 287:

It is submitted [section 6(1)]... is to be construed narrowly and confined to the sort of case of which Lord Lane gave an example and of which the present is not one. However, this Court had to consider a similar situation in the case of *Fernandes* [1996] 1 Cr App Rep 175 where at p 188 Auld LJ giving the judgment of the Court said this:

'In our view section 6(1), which is expressed in general terms, is not limited in its application to the illustrations given by Lord Lane CJ in *Lloyd*. Nor in saying that in most cases it would be unnecessary to refer to the provision, did Lord Lane suggest it should be so limited. The critical notion, stated expressly in the first limb and incorporated by reference in the second is, whether a defendant intended to 'treat the thing as his own to dispose of regardless of the other's rights.' The second limb of subsection (1) and also subsection (2) are merely specific illustrations of the application of that notion. We consider that section 6 may apply to a person in possession or control of another's property who, dishonestly and for his own purpose, deals with that property in such a manner that he knows he is risking its loss.'

In our judgment and following *Fernandes* the subsection is not to be given the restricted interpretation for which the appellants contend.

The principal submission put forward on behalf of the appellants is that the issuing of the ticket is analogous to the drawing of a cheque in that in each instance a *chose in action* is created which in the first case belongs to the customer and in the second to the payee. So by parity of reasoning with that advanced by Lord Goff in *R v Preddy* (below, p **839**), the property acquired belonged to the customer and not London Underground Limited and there can have been no intention on the part of the appellant to deprive London Underground Limited of the ticket which would in due course be returned to the possession of London Underground Limited. Attractive though the submission appears at first blush we do not think that it can possibly be correct.

'A "*chose in action*" is a known legal expression used to describe all personal rights of property which can only be claimed or enforced by action, and not by taking physical possession.' (See *Torkington v Magee* [1902] 2 KB 427, per Channell J at p 430.) On the issuing of an underground ticket a contract is created between London Underground Limited and the purchaser. Under that contract each party has rights and obligations. Theoretically those rights are enforceable by action. Therefore, it is arguable, we suppose, that by the transaction each party has acquired a *chose in action*. On the side of the purchaser it is represented by a right to use the ticket to the extent which it allows travel on the underground system. On the side of London Underground Limited it encompasses the right to insist that the ticket is used by no one other than the purchaser. It is that right which is disregarded when the ticket is acquired by the appellant and sold on. But here the charges were in relation to the tickets and travel cards themselves and a ticket form or travel card and, dare we say, a cheque form is not a *chose in action*. The fact that the ticket form or travel card may find its way back into the possession of London Underground Limited, albeit with its usefulness or 'virtue' exhausted, is nothing to the point. Section 6(1) prevails for the reasons we have given.

7. *Preddy* decided that, because the thing in action represented by the cheque never belonged to anyone but the defendant, *the cheque* could not be stolen or obtained by him. Was the court right to reject the argument that the same principle must apply to the tickets? The cheque and the ticket are both pieces of paper which, when given for consideration, create and represent a thing in action: the right to receive the amount of money for which the cheque is drawn and the right to travel to the named destination, or to enjoy some other service. In both cases the thing in action belongs not to the drawer or supplier, V, but to the recipient, D. In neither case can D be guilty of the offence of obtaining *the thing in action* from V, or stealing it from him for that thing never is, nor could be, property belonging to V. The court did not explain what is the difference between the two pieces of paper. One possible difference is that the ticket continues (because an operative condition on it so provides) to belong to the company, V, throughout, whereas the cheque form belongs to the payee, D, when it is delivered to him. D can lawfully burn it or tear it up if he wants to. But is that a material difference? In the cheque case envisaged in *Preddy*, the cheque form belonged to V at the critical moment—the instant before it was delivered to D. The instant of delivery is the time when offences contrary to ss 1 and 15 of the Theft Act are committed by the dishonest obtainer of property by deception: *Gomez*, above, p 753. The paper on which both the cheque and the ticket is printed is considered to be the property of V at the moment of the alleged theft. What then is the material difference, if any, between the cheque and the ticket? If the cheque is not obtained or stolen, as *Preddy* decides, is the ticket?

Having described the things in action involved, the court says:

But here the charges were in relation to the tickets and travel cards themselves and, dare we say, a cheque form is not a chose in action....No one could doubt that a cheque form is a tangible thing whereas a thing in action is, by definition, intangible.

It would have been really 'daring' if the court had gone on to say:

And it follows that the dicta relating to cheques in *Preddy* are wrong. As in the case of a ticket, there can be no theft or obtaining by deception of the thing in action it evidences, but both offences may be committed in respect of the paper itself because it is, when it is obtained, a valuable thing and the intention of the obtainer is to return it only when it has lost all that value.

The court points out that the company also acquires rights on the issue of the ticket including—

the right to insist that the ticket is used by no one other than the purchaser. It is that right which is disregarded when the ticket is acquired by the appellant and sold on.

The court did not, however, decide that this thing in action belonging to the company is stolen when the ticket is resold. The resale is a breach of the contractual right of the company, but not an assumption of that right. It is like a breach of copyright which is unlawful but not theft of the copyright. The contrary view would appear turn all deliberate breaches of contract into theft. Would that be an acceptable extension of the criminal law?

Intending permanently to deprive without causing loss?

Chan Man-sin v Attorney-General of Hong Kong
[1988] 1 All ER 1, PC

(Lords Brandon of Oakbrook, Ackner, Oliver of Aylmerton, Sir John Stephenson and Sir Edward Eveleigh)

The appellant, employed as an accountant by two Hong Kong companies, forged cheques to a value of nearly $HK5 million which he then deposited in his own account or the account of a company which he owned. He was charged with theft of choses in action, namely the debts owed by the bank to the companies. He appealed against his conviction on the ground that since a bank had no authority to honour a forged cheque the debt owed by the bank to the companies was never diminished so there was no appropriation of it, or any of it.

The following judgment of the Board was delivered.

Lord Oliver of Aylmerton.. . . . The argument for the appellant is a simple one and is founded on the proposition that a bank is not entitled in law, as against its customer, to debit the customer's account with the amount of any cheque which the bank has not, in fact, any authority from the customer to honour. Thus, it is said, if the bank honours a forged cheque and debits the customer's account accordingly, the transaction is, quite simply, a nullity as a matter of law so far as the customer is concerned and the customer, on discovering the unauthorised debit to his account, is entitled to insist on its being reversed. For this proposition reliance is, quite rightly, placed on the decision of their Lordships' Board in *Tai Hing Cotton Mill Ltd v Liu Chong Hing Bank Ltd* [1985] 2 All ER 947, [1986] AC 80. Starting out from this foundation, the appellant argues that the presentation of the ten forged cheques in respect of which he was convicted produced, as a matter of legal reality, no diminution at all of the respective credit balances of the companies. Standard Chartered simply made unauthorised debits to their accounts which they were entitled to have reversed on demand. Thus, it is argued, although the appellant was no doubt guilty of offences of forgery and obtaining a pecuniary advantage by deception with which he was not charged, he could not have been guilty of the offences with which he was charged, namely theft of Merit's or Hunter's choses in action.

The Theft Ordinance of Hong Kong follows, in all respects material to the instant case, the provisions of the English Theft Act 1968. Section 2 provides: '(1) A person commits theft if he dishonestly appropriates property belonging to another with the intention of permanently depriving the other of it . . .' And s 5(1) includes 'things in action and other intangible property' within the statutory definition of 'property'. It is not disputed that the debt due to the customer from his banker is a chose in action capable of being stolen and this equally applies to the sum which a customer is entitled to overdraw under contractual arrangements which he has made with the bank (see *R v Kohn* (1979) 69 Cr App Rep 395, [1979] Crim LR 675), though strictly in the latter case the chose in action is the benefit of the contractual arrangement with the bank. What is argued, however, is that, since as between the customer and the bank an unauthorised debit entry in the customer's account is a mere nullity, the customer is deprived of nothing and therefore there has been no appropriation. Equally, it is said that, since the customer whose property is alleged to have been stolen has not in fact been deprived of anything, there cannot have been an intention permanently to deprive him of the property. Thus, it is argued, there were lacking two essential ingredients of the offences with which the appellant was charged and he was entitled to an acquittal.

Their Lordships can deal very briefly with the second submission. The appellant did not elect to give evidence and if there was, as the prosecution contended, an appropriation of the companies' property there was ample evidence from which the intention permanently to deprive them of it could be inferred. Even if it were possible to infer or assume that the appellant contemplated that the fraud would be discovered and appreciated, also that his employers would or might challenge Standard Chartered's entitlement to payment of the sums debited, he would fall within the provisions of s 7 of the ordinance, which provides:

'(1) A person appropriating property belonging to another without meaning the other permanently to lose the thing itself is nevertheless to be regarded as having the intention of permanently depriving the other of it if his intention is to treat the thing as his own to dispose of regardless of the other's rights...'

Quite clearly here the appellant was purporting to deal with the companies' property without regard to their rights.

Reverting to the appellant's principal ground of appeal, this has an appealing simplicity. The appellant's difficulty, however, is that it entirely ignores the artificial definition of appropriation which is contained in s 4(1) of the ordinance and which reproduces 3(1) of the 1968 Act in the following terms:

'Any assumption by a person of the rights of an owner amounts to an appropriation, and this includes, where he has come by the property (innocently or not) without stealing it, any later assumption of a right to it by keeping or dealing with it as owner.'

The owner of the chose in action consisting of a credit with his bank or a contractual right to draw on an account has, clearly, the right as owner to draw by means of a properly completed negotiable instrument or order to pay and it is, in their Lordships' view, beyond argument that one who draws, presents and negotiates a cheque on a particular bank account is assuming the rights of the owner of the credit in the account or (as the case may be) of the pre-negotiated right to draw on the account up to the agreed figure. Ownership, of course, consists of a bundle of rights and it may well be that there are other rights which an owner could exert over the chose in action in question which are not trespassed on by the particular dealing which the thief chooses to assume. In *R v Morris* [1983] 3 All ER 288, [1984] AC 320, however, the House of Lords decisively rejected a submission that it was necessary, in order to constitute an appropriation as defined by s3(1) of the 1968 Act, to demonstrate an assumption by the accused of all the rights of an owner.

Their Lordships are, accordingly, entirely satisfied that the transactions initiated and carried through by the appellant constituted an assumption of the rights of the owner and, consequently, an appropriation. It is unnecessary, for present purposes, to determine whether that occurred on presentation of the forged cheques or when the transactions were completed by the making of consequential entries in the bank accounts of the companies and the appellant or his business respectively. It is, in their Lordships' view, entirely immaterial that the end result of the transaction may be a legal nullity for it is not possible to read into s 4(1) of the ordinance any requirement that the assumption of rights there envisaged should have a legally efficacious result.

Their Lordships are fortified in the view which they have formed by the recent decision of the English Court of Appeal in *R v Wille* (1987) 86 Cr App Rep 296, of which they have been provided with a transcript and in which the court reached the same conclusion in circumstances not materially dissimilar to those in the instant case. It seems probable that, if that decision had been reported at the time when special leave was applied for, it would not have been granted. Their Lordships will accordingly humbly advise Her Majesty that the appeal should be dismissed.

Appeal dismissed

1. In *Chan Man-sin*, the appellant had caused no loss to the companies so how could it be said that he intended to deprive them permanently of their property when he did not cause them to lose a cent? How does Lord Oliver deal with this point? Does Lord Oliver's view lend support to an argument that the seller of the Crown Jewels in the example given above has stolen them? Cf (1988) 86 Cr App R 303, [1988] Crim LR 319. Is it a relevant difference that, while the companies in *Chan Man-sin* were in some danger of losing their property (the appellant's fraud, as no doubt he hoped, might never have come to light), the Crown is in no danger of losing the jewels?

2. D must *intend* permanent deprivation. Suppose D takes V's car in London which he later abandons in Leeds. D realizes that the car may be restored to V but it is a matter of indifference to him whether it is or not. It would seem that D does not *intend* permanently to deprive V. (Might he be said to be reckless?) But can it be said that he has treated the car as his own 'to dispose of regardless of the other's rights' and this is 'in circumstances making it equivalent to an outright taking or disposal'? Is the abandonment of the car a 'disposal' of it? Cf *Cahill* [1993] Crim LR 141, CA, where it was held insufficient to instruct the jury that D must treat the property as his own; D must treat it as his own 'to dispose of'. The court found it helpful to refer to the following passage from J. C. Smith, *Law of Theft* (6th edn, para 133, now 8th edn, para 2–132):

> The attribution of an ordinary meaning to the language of s6 presents some difficulties. It is submitted, however, that an intention merely to use the property as one's own is not enough and that 'dispose of' is not used in the sense in which a general may 'dispose of' his forces but rather in the meaning given by the Shorter Oxford Dictionary: 'To deal with definitely; to get rid of; to get done with, finish. To make over by way of sale or bargain, sell'.

Intention permanently to deprive by swapping V's property?

In *DPP v Lavender* [1994] Crim LR 297, DC, D had taken two sound doors from council property which was undergoing repair and used them to replace two damaged doors at another council property of which his girlfriend was the tenant. Remitting the case to the justices with a direction to convict of theft, the court said that the issue was whether D had treated the doors as his own to dispose of and took the view that he had. D had dealt with the doors regardless of the owner's rights not to have them removed and in so doing had manifested an intention to treat them as his own. Clearly D had relocated the council's property but had he disposed of it? It does not appear what he did with the two damaged doors which he replaced. What if he had thrown them in a skip for removal to the council's tip. Theft?

Conditional intention

A problem which has much exercised the courts in recent years is whether D may be convicted of theft where his intention permanently to deprive is conditional, as where D has no specific property in mind but has resolved to steal if there is anything worth his while to take. Commonly, for example, rogues enter cars on the look-out for anything that may be of value to them while realizing that there may be nothing in the car that interests them. Obviously the rogue cannot be convicted of theft if in fact he appropriates nothing, but may he be convicted of attempted theft, and, if so, of attempting to steal what? The problem was further complicated by *Haughton v Smith* (p **546**, above) which held that attempt could not be committed where the actus reus was physically impossible to achieve. The difficulty created by *Haughton v Smith* has now been removed by legislation (p **547**, above) and the other difficulties (cf *A-G's References (Nos 1 and 2 of 1979)* [1980] QB 180, [1979] 3 All ER l43, CA) have been shown to be formal rather than substantive. Of course D cannot be convicted of attempting to steal that which he does not intend to steal. If the car contains only articles (tissues, road maps) of no interest to D, D cannot be convicted of attempting to steal these. But if it is D's intention to steal the car radio then he may be convicted of attempting to steal the radio though the car has no radio. And if D is on a fishing expedition having no specific property in mind it appears that he may be convicted of attempting to steal property of V from the car.

2. ROBBERY

Theft Act 1968, s 8

> (1) A person is guilty of robbery if he steals, and immediately before or at the time of doing so, and in order to do so, he uses force on any person or puts or seeks to put any person in fear of being then and there subjected to force.

> (2) A person guilty of robbery, or of an assault with intent to rob, shall on conviction on indictment be liable to imprisonment for life.

Notes and questions

1. Robbery is essentially a form of aggravated stealing so proof of theft is essential to a conviction. In *Robinson* [1977] Crim LR 173, CA, D ran a clothing club to which V's wife owed £7. Meeting V, D and others threatened him and in the fight which followed £5 fell from V's pocket which D took, claiming he was still owed £2. Quashing D's conviction for robbery, it was held that all D had to show was an honest belief in entitlement to the money and not that he honestly believed that he was entitled to take it in the way he did. Should this belief in a right to the property also entitle D to use force to obtain it?

2. Force must be used 'in order to' steal. If D knocks V senseless in a fight and then decides to make off with V's watch which has fallen from his pocket it would not be robbery; it would be assault and theft. Conversely if D steals property without using force but subsequently uses or threatens force to retain it or in effecting an escape it would not be robbery. In *Hale* (1978) 68 Cr App R 415, [1979] Crim LR 596, CA, D and E entered V's house and while D was upstairs stealing a jewellery box, E was downstairs tying up V. The Court of Appeal declined to quash their convictions for robbery though D might have appropriated the jewellery box before the force was used. The court said (at 418):

[T]he act of appropriation does not suddenly cease. It is a continuous act and it is a matter for the jury to decide whether or not the act of appropriation has finished. Moreover, it is quite clear that the intention to deprive the owner permanently, which accompanied the assumption of the owner's rights was a continuing one at all material times. This Court therefore rejects the contention that the theft had ceased by the time [V] was tied up. As a matter of common sense [E] was in the course of committing theft; he was stealing.

What impact has the decision in Gomez (above, p 753) had on this aspect of the offence?

3. The force may be on *any person*. In *Smith v Desmond* [1965] AC 960, [1965] 1 All ER 976, HL, D and E were held to have robbed V and X, respectively nightwatchman and maintenance engineer in a bakery, where force was used on them in order to steal from an office some distance away on the premises. Their employer's property was in their immediate care and protection. The case is obviously within the terms of s 8 which extends to any case in which force is used on any person in order to steal. The threat of force may similarly be made to any person; but the offence is committed only if D seeks to put that person in fear of being subjected to force. It is not sufficient that he seeks to cause that person to fear that someone else will be subjected to force: *Taylor (Richard)* [1996] CLY 1518 (D handing to V, bank cashier, a note saying that D had a gun pointed at a customer).

4. Under the former law it was not sufficient that force was used in the taking of the property: the force had to be used to overpower the person or prevent resistance from him. The CLRC evidently sought to retain this distinction and said it would not regard a mere snatching of property, a handbag for example, from an unresisting owner as a use of force for this purpose. But in *Dawson and James* (1976) 64 Cr App R 170, [1976] Crim LR 692, CA, it was held that a push or nudge causing the victim to lose his balance would suffice and in *Clouden* [1987] Crim LR 56, CA, the court went farther. D wrenched a shopping bag from V's hands and ran off with it. Affirming D's conviction for robbery, the court said that under s 8 the old distinction had gone. The section required only that force be used on a person in order to steal.

5. The robbery is complete when the theft is complete, that is when the appropriation takes place. So in *Corcoran v Anderton* (1980) 71 Cr App R 104, [1980] Crim LR 385, DC, where D and E sought to take V's handbag by force, it was held the theft was complete when D snatched the handbag from V's grasp though it then fell from D's hands and the defendants made off without it. Their contention that this was only an attempt was rejected since the snatching of the handbag from V constituted an appropriation.

6. D is about to go out one day to steal a new suit from a retailer. He tells his wife of his plan and she threatens to telephone the police. D pushes her into the broom cupboard and locks the door and does not free her till he returns later wearing his new suit. Robbery?

7. Ashworth ('Robbery Reassessed' [2002] Crim LR 851) questions whether the offence is necessary:

Robbery is an amalgamated offence. Like burglary, it combines two separate wrongs. Unlike burglary, the two wrongs in robbery are both crimes. The offence combines theft of property with the use or threat of force. It is not specified which wrong should be regarded as more important, but surely the amount of violence should be given the greater significance, on the ground that violence is generally a much greater attack on an individual's well-being. It is possible to conceive of a case where an enormous sum of money is taken by using a small amount of (threatened) force, but even then we should bear in mind that the maximum sentence for theft is seven years. In most cases of street robberies and robberies at building society branches, off-licences and so forth, the robber only sets out to obtain a modest sum and does so, and therefore the theft component of the sentence should be small and well below the maximum for that crime. More significant, surely, is the amount of force.... The law of offences against the person reflects the relative seriousness of violence and threats in a rather unsatisfactory way. If we had a reformed law on violence, it would distinguish the various offences according to the degree of harm and the degree of culpability, and would assign graduated penalties from the least serious up to the most serious. Robbery should mirror this, or have at least two degrees of seriousness.

A more radical proposal would be to abolish the offence of robbery. It would then be left to prosecutors to charge the components of theft and violence separately, which would focus the court's attention on those two elements, separately and then (for sentencing purposes) in combination. The principal difficulty with this is the absence from English law of an offence of threatening injury: between the summary offence of assault by posing a threat of force, and the serious offence of making a threat to kill, there is no intermediate crime. This gap ought to be closed; and, if it were, there would be a strong argument that the crime of robbery would be unnecessary.

Do you agree?

FURTHER READING

Appropriation

J. BEATSON and A. SIMESTER, 'Stealing One's Own Property' (1999) 115 LQR 372

A. L. BOGG and J. STANTON-IFE, 'Protecting the Vulnerable: Legality, Harm and Theft' (2003) 23 LS 402

C. CLARKSON, 'Theft and Fair Labelling' (1993) 56 MLR 554

S. GARDNER, 'Property and Theft' [1998] Crim LR 35

P. R. GLAZEBROOK, 'Revising the Theft Acts' [1993] CLJ 191

R. HEATON, 'Deceiving without thieving' [2001] Crim LR 712

S. SHUTE and J. HORDER, 'Thieving and Deceiving—what is the difference' (1993) 56 MLR 54

S. SHUTE, 'Appropriation and the Law of Theft' [2002] Crim LR 445

J. C. SMITH, 'The Sad Fate of the Theft Act 1968' in W. Swadling and G. Jones (eds) *The Search for Principle, Essays in Honour of Lord Goff of Chieveley* (1999), 97

Property

R. CROSS, 'Protecting Confidential Information under the Criminal Law of Theft and Fraud' (1991) OJLS 264

R. HAMMOND, 'Theft of Information' (1984) 100 LQR 252

J. HULL, 'Stealing Secrets: A Review of the Law Commission Consultation Paper' [1998] Crim LR 246

J. C. SMITH, 'Obtaining Cheques by Deception or Theft' [1997] Crim LR 396

J. C. SMITH, 'Stealing Tickets' [1998] Crim LR 723

Belonging to another

D. W. ELLIOTT, 'Directors' Thefts and Dishonesty' [1991] Crim LR 732

Dishonesty

K. CAMPBELL, 'The Test of Dishonesty in *Ghosh*' [1994] 43 CLJ 349

D. W. ELLIOTT, 'Dishonesty in Theft: A Dispensable Concept' [1982] Crim LR 395

E. J. GRIEW, 'Dishonesty, the Objections to *Feely* and *Ghosh*' [1985] Crim LR 341

E. J. GRIEW, *Dishonesty and the Jury*, Leicester University Press (1974)

A. HALPIN, 'The Test for Dishonesty' [1996] Crim LR 283

A. SAMUELS, 'Dishonesty and the Jury' [1974] Crim LR 493

R. TUR, 'Dishonesty and the Jury Question' in A. Phillips Griffiths (ed) *Philosophy and Practice* (1985)

Intention permanently to deprive

J. R. SPENCER, 'The Metamorphosis of Section 6 of the Theft Act' [1977] Crim LR 653

G. WILLIAMS, 'Temporary Appropriation Should be Theft' [1981] Crim LR 129

Robbery

A. Ashworth, 'Robbery Reassessed' [2002] Crim LR 851

22
Offences involving deception

The various offences involving deception (Theft Act 1968, ss 15, 15A, 16 and 20; Theft Act 1978, ss 1 and 2) differ only in relation to what may be obtained and otherwise they have common features relating to the deception, the obtaining and dishonesty. It is convenient to deal first with these common features.

1. THE DECEPTION

Theft Act 1968, s 15(4)

For purposes of this section 'deception' means any deception (whether deliberate or reckless) by words or conduct as to fact or as to law, including a deception as to the present intentions of the person using the deception or any other person.

This definition is applied to all the foregoing offences.

Director of Public Prosecutions v Ray
[1973] 3 All ER 131, House of Lords

(Lords Reid, MacDermott, Morris of Borth-y-Gest, Hodson and Pearson)

Four men, including the respondent, entered a restaurant and ordered a meal. The respondent did not have enough money to pay but one of the others had agreed to lend him enough to pay for the meal. After eating the meal, and while the waiter was still in the dining room, they all decided not to pay and to run out of the restaurant. Some 10 minutes later, and while the waiter had left the dining room to go into the kitchen, all four ran off without making payment. This was an appeal against the quashing by the Divisional Court of the respondent's conviction for obtaining a pecuniary advantage by deception contrary to s 16(1) of the Act. The court was concerned with determining whether the respondent had obtained a pecuniary advantage within s 16(2)(a). This provision was repealed by the Theft Act 1978 but this does not affect the issues discussed in this case.

Lord Reid..... If a person induces a supplier to accept an order for goods or services by a representation of fact, that representation must be held to be a continuing representation lasting until the goods or services are supplied. Normally it would not last any longer. A restaurant supplies both goods and services: it supplies food and drink and the facilities for consuming them. Customers normally remain for a short time after consuming their meal, and I think that it can properly be held that any representation express or implied made with a view of obtaining a meal lasts until the departure of the customers in the normal course.

In my view, where a new customer orders a meal in a restaurant, he must be held to make an implied representation that he can and will pay for it before he leaves. In the present case the respondent must be held to have made such a representation. But when he made it it was not dishonest: he thought he would be able to borrow money from one of his companions.

After the meal had been consumed the respondent changed his mind. He decided to evade payment. So he and his companions remained seated where they were for a short time until the waiter left the room and then ran out of the restaurant.

Did he thereby commit an offence against s16 of the Theft Act 1968? It is admitted, and rightly admitted, that if the waiter had not been in the room when he changed his mind and he had immediately run out he would not have committed an offence. Why does his sitting still for a short time in the presence of the waiter make all the difference?

The section requires evasion of his obligation to pay. That is clearly established by his running out without paying. Secondly, it requires dishonesty; that is admitted. There would have been both evasion and dishonesty if he had changed his mind and run out while the waiter was absent.

The crucial question in this case is whether there was evasion 'by any deception'. Clearly there could be no deception until the respondent changed his mind. I agree with the following quotation from the judgment of Buckley J in *Re London and Globe Finance Corpn Ltd* [[1903] 1 Ch 728 at 723, [1900–3] All ER Rep 891 at 893]:

> 'To deceive is, I apprehend, to induce a man to believe that a thing is true which is false, and which the person practising the deceit knows or believes to be false.'

So the respondent, after he changed his mind, must have done something intended to induce the waiter to believe that he still intended to pay before he left. Deception, to my mind, implies something positive. It is quite true that a man intending to deceive can build up a situation in which his silence is as eloquent as an express statement. But what did the accused do here to create a situation? He merely sat still... The justices stated that they were of opinion that:

> '...having changed his mind as regards payment, by remaining in the restaurant for a further ten minutes as an ordinary customer who was likely to order a sweet or coffee, the [respondent] practised a deception.'

I cannot read that as a finding that after he changed his mind he intended to deceive the waiter into believing that he still intended to pay. And there is no finding that the waiter was in fact induced to believe that by anything the respondent did after he changed his mind. I would infer from the case that all that he intended to do was to take advantage of the first opportunity to escape and evade his obligation to pay.

Deception is an essential ingredient of the offence. Dishonest evasion of an obligation to pay is not enough. I cannot see that there was, in fact, any more than that in this case. I agree with the Divisional Court that [[1973] 1 All ER 860 at 865, per Talbot J]:

> 'His plan was totally lacking in the subtlety of deception and to argue that his remaining in the room until the coast was clear amounted to a representation to the waiter is to introduce an artificiality which should have no place in the Act.'

I would therefore dismiss this appeal.

Lord MacDermott.... To prove the charge against the respondent the prosecution had to show that he (i) by a deception (ii) had dishonestly (iii) obtained for himself (iv) a pecuniary advantage...

No issue...arises on the ingredients I have numbered (iii) and (iv). Nor is there any controversy about ingredient (ii). If the respondent obtained a pecuniary advantage as described he undoubtedly did so dishonestly. The case is thus narrowed to ingredient (i) and that leaves two questions for consideration. First, do the facts justify a finding that the respondent practised a deception? And secondly, if he did, was his evasion of the debt obtained by that deception?

The first of these questions involves nothing in the way of words spoken or written. If there was deception on the part of the respondent it was by his conduct in the course of an extremely common form of transaction which, because of its nature, leaves much to be implied from conduct. Another circumstance affecting the ambit of this question lies in the fact that, looking only to the period *after* the meal had been eaten and the respondent and his companions had decided to evade payment, there is nothing that I can find in the discernible conduct of the respondent which would suffice in itself to show that he was then practising a deception. No doubt he and the others stayed in their seats until the waiter went into the kitchen and while doing so gave all the appearance of ordinary customers. But in my opinion, nothing in this or in anything else which occurred *after* the change of intention went far enough to afford proof of deception. The picture, as I see it, presented by this last stage of the entire transaction, is simply that of a group which had decided to evade payment and were awaiting the opportunity to do so.

There is, however, no sound reason that I can see for restricting the enquiry to this final phase. One cannot, so to speak, draw a line through the transaction at the point where the intention changed and search for evidence of deception only in what happened before that or only in what happened after that. In my opinion the transaction must for this purpose be regarded in its entirety, beginning with the respondent entering the restaurant and ordering his meal and ending with his running out without paying. The different stages of the transaction are all linked and it would be quite unrealistic to treat them in isolation.

Starting then at the beginning one finds in the conduct of the respondent in entering and ordering his meal evidence that he impliedly represented that he had the means and the intention of paying for it before he left. That the respondent did make such a representation was not in dispute and in the absence of evidence to the contrary it would be difficult to reach a different conclusion. If this representation had then been false and matters had proceeded thereafter as they did (but without any change of intention) a conviction for the offence charged would, in my view, have had ample material to support it. But as the representation when originally made in this case was not false there was therefore no deception at that point. Then the meal is served and eaten and the intention to evade the debt replaces the intention to pay. Did this change of mind produce a deception?

My Lords, in my opinion it did. I do not base this conclusion merely on the change of mind that had occurred for that in itself was not manifest at the time and did not amount to 'conduct' on the part of the respondent. But it did falsify the representation which had already been made because that initial representation must, in my view, be regarded not as something then spent and past but as a continuing representation which remained alive and operative and had already resulted in the respondent and his defaulting companions being taken on trust and treated as ordinary, honest customers. It covered the whole transaction up to and including payment and must therefore, in my opinion, be considered as continuing and still active at the time of the change of mind. When that happened, with the respondent taking (as might be expected) no step to bring the change to notice, he practised to my way of thinking a deception just as real and just as dishonest as would have been the case if his intention all along had been to go out without paying.

Holding for these reasons that the respondent practised a deception, I turn to what I have referred to as the second question. Was the respondent's evasion of the debt obtained by that deception?

I think the material before the justices was enough to show that it was. The obvious effect of the deception was that the respondent and his associates were treated as they had been previously, that is to say as ordinary, honest customers whose conduct did not excite suspicion or call for precautions. In consequence the waiter was off his guard and vanished into the kitchen. That gave the respondent the opportunity of running out without hindrance and he took it. I would therefore answer this second question in the affirmative.

I would, accordingly, allow the appeal and restore the conviction.

Lord Morris of Borth-y-Gest.... In the present case the person deceived was the waiter. Did the respondent deceive the waiter as to what were his intentions? Did the respondent so conduct himself as to induce the waiter to believe that he (the respondent) intended to pay his bill before he left the restaurant whereas at the relevant time he did not so intend? ...

In the present case it is found as a fact that when the respondent ordered his meal he believed that he would be able to pay. One of his companions had agreed to lend him money. He therefore intended to pay. So far as the waiter was concerned the original implied representation made to him by the respondent must have been a continuing representation so long as he (the respondent) remained in the restaurant. There was nothing to alter the representation. Just as the waiter was led at the start to believe that he was dealing with a customer who by all that he did in the restaurant was indicating his intention to pay in the ordinary way, so the waiter was led to believe that that state of affairs continued. But the moment came when the respondent decided and therefore knew that he was not going to pay: but he also knew that the waiter still thought that he was going to pay. By ordering his meal and by his conduct in assuming the role of an ordinary customer the respondent had previously shown that it was his intention to pay. By continuing in the same role and behaving just as before he was representing that his previous intention continued. That was a deception because his intention, unknown to the waiter, had become quite otherwise. The dishonest change of intention was not likely to produce the result that the waiter would be told of it. The essence of the deception was that the waiter should not know of it or be given any sort of clue that it (the change of intention) had come about. Had the waiter suspected that by a change of intention a secret exodus was being planned, it is obvious that he would have taken action to prevent its being achieved. ...

The final question which arises is whether, if there was deception and if there was pecuniary advantage, it was by the deception that the respondent obtained the pecuniary advantage. In my view, this must be a question of fact and the justices have found that it was by his deception that the respondent dishonestly evaded payment. It would seem to be clear that if the waiter had thought that if he left the restaurant to go to the kitchen the respondent would at once run out, he (the waiter) would not have left the restaurant and would have taken suitable action. The waiter proceeded on the basis that the implied representation made to him (ie of an honest intention to pay) was effective. The waiter was caused to refrain from taking certain courses of action which but for the representation he would have taken. In my view, the respondent during the whole time that he was in the restaurant made and by his continuing conduct continued to make a representation of his intention to pay before leaving. When in place of his original intention he substituted the dishonest intention of running away as soon as the waiter's back was turned, he was continuing to lead the waiter to believe that he intended to pay. He practised a deception on the waiter and by so doing he obtained for himself the pecuniary advantage of evading his obligation to pay before leaving. That he did so dishonestly was found by the justices who, in my opinion, rightly convicted him.

I would allow the appeal.

Lord Hodson. ... There is no doubt that the respondent evaded payment of the debt by walking out of the restaurant with his companions, but the prosecution has always accepted that there was no deception in the first instance because the intention was to pay for the meal when ordered. It is argued, however, that a representation having been made at the time the credit was honestly obtained, the respondent later dishonestly decided to evade payment by failing to correct the original representation.

To answer the submitted question it is necessary to follow the definition of deceit which I have cited from s 15(4). The deceit is in essence the same as that long recognised when a person is charged with obtaining property by fraud. There must be some deceit spoken, written or acted to constitute a false pretence: see *Jones* [[1898] 1 QB 119].

There having been no deception in the first instance, since the respondent and his companions intended to pay for the meal, the question is, was a deception practised so as to evade the debt or obligation when having consumed the meal they left without paying for it?

One who enters into a contract is taken to have the intention of carrying it out, but if he changes his mind and decides not to pay he may be guilty of a breach of his contractual obligation but not necessarily of evading the debt by deception. The deception must be proved whereby a pecuniary advantage was obtained.

The vital question is whether by sitting in the restaurant for ten minutes after having consumed the meal the respondent was guilty of deception when he departed without paying.

If he had no intention of paying at the outset *cadit quaestio*. If, on the other hand, his representation made at the outset was honest, I find it difficult to accept that the effect of the original representation continues so as to make subsequent failure to pay his creditor, automatically, so to speak, an evasion of debt obtained by deception.

Whether any evidence was given by a waiter is not disclosed. The case states that the waiter had gone to the kitchen and that during his absence the respondent and his four companions ran out of the restaurant after having been there for nearly an hour and maintaining the demeanour of ordinary customers. Would the reasonable man say that a deception had been practised on him? Evade the debt the respondent did, but no more than any other debtor who, having originally intended to pay for a pecuniary advantage, subsequently changes his mind and evades his contractual obligation by not paying.

In order to succeed the prosecution must rely on the original representation honestly made by the respondent when he entered the restaurant as a continuing representation which operated and lulled the restaurant proprietor into a sense of security so that the respondent was enabled to leave as he did.

I do not recollect that the prosecution put the case in this way but I think it is most formidable if so presented, for if the representation continued it was falsified by the change of mind of the respondent.

It is trite law and common sense that an honest man entering into a contract is deemed to represent that he has the present intention of carrying it out but if, as in this case, having accepted the pecuniary advantage involved in the transaction he does not necessarily evade his debt by deception if he fails to pay his debt.

Nothing he did after his change of mind can be characterised as conduct which would indicate that he was then practising a deception.

To rely on breach of a continuous representation I suggest that in administering a criminal statute this is going too far and seems to involve that the ordinary man who enters into a contract intending to carry it out can be found guilty of a criminal offence if he changes his mind after incurring the obligation to pay unless he has taken a step to bring the change of mind to the notice of his creditor.

The appellant sought to support the argument, that there was a duty on the respondent to correct his original representation, by authority.

With v O'Flanagan [[1936] Ch 575] is good authority for the proposition that if a person who makes a representation, which is not immediately acted on, finds that the facts are changing he must, before the representation is acted on, disclose the change to the person to whom he had made the representation.

That case concerned the sale of a medical practice. The seller, a doctor, represented that his practice was profitable. This was true when the representation was made but by the time the contract was signed the practice had dwindled to practically nothing. This was not disclosed to the purchaser who, on discovery, sought rescission. It was held that the statement made, though true at the time, had become untrue during the negotiations and that there was an obligation to disclose the fact to the purchaser.

The earlier case of *Traill v Baring* [(1864) 4 De GJ & Sm 318] was cited. It contains the following passage from the judgment of Turner LJ [(1864) 4 De GJ & Sm 318 at 329]:

'I take it to be clear, that if a person makes a representation by which he induces another to take a particular course and the circumstances are afterwards altered to the knowledge of the party making the representation, but not to the knowledge of the party to whom the representation is made, and are so altered that the alteration of the circumstances may affect the course of conduct which may be pursued by the party to whom the representation is made it is the imperative duty of the party who has made the representation to communicate to the party to whom the representation has been made the alteration of those circumstances; and that this Court will not hold the party to whom the representation has been made bound unless such a communication has been made.'

This authority does not assist the appellant as to continuity of representation generally. The position there taken was based on a duty to communicate a change of circumstances which had occurred after a representation, true when made, had been falsified by the time the contract was entered into. Here no contract was entered into following a deception of any kind.

The respondent was in breach of his obligation to pay his debt but I agree with the conclusion of the Divisional Court that there was no evidence that he evaded it by deception.

I would dismiss the appeal.

Lord Pearson. . . . In my view, the justices could and did reasonably imply from the course of conduct a representation by the respondent that he had a present intention of paying for his meal before leaving the restaurant. It was a continuing representation in the sense that I have indicated, being made at every moment throughout the course of conduct. Insofar as it was being made before the decision to run out without paying, it was according to the justices' finding a true representation of the respondent's then present intention. Insofar as it was being made after that decision, it was a false representation of the respondent's then present intention, and of course false to his knowledge. That false representation deceived the waiter, inducing him to go to the kitchen, whereby the respondent, with his companions, was enabled to make his escape from the restaurant and so dishonestly evade his obligation to pay for his meal. Thus by deception he obtained for himself the pecuniary advantage of evading the debt.

In my opinion, the respondent was rightly convicted by the justices. I would allow the appeal and restore the conviction and sentence.

Appeal allowed

Notes and questions

1. What was the deception in *Ray*? Did the deception cause the waiter to leave the dining room so that he was in no position to prevent the appellant from decamping without payment?

2. What would the position have been in *Ray* if (a) the respondent had formed the intent not to pay and had decamped while the waiter was in the dining room; or (b) the respondent had formed the intent not to pay while the waiter was in the kitchen and had decamped before the waiter returned to the dining room?

3. The deception must be 'deliberate or reckless'. The now redundant *Caldwell* test for recklessness was once expressly said to be applicable where recklessness appeared in a modern statute but the requirement for dishonesty would appear to rule out its use here. No amount of negligence can make a dishonest man of an honest man (cf *Derry v Peek* (1889) 14 App Cas 337, HL).

4. A deception may be made by conduct other than the use of words. In *Barnard* (1837) 7 C & P 784, D went into an Oxford shop wearing the outfit of the fellow-commoner of the University—a cap and gown—and induced the shopkeeper to give him credit by claiming

to be a fellow-commoner. It was said that there would have been a deception even had he said nothing.

5. Lord Hodson in *Ray* (above, **817**) says that while a party may be under a duty to communicate a relevant change of circumstances before the contract is made, he does not deceive the seller by failing to communicate such change after the contract has been entered into. Is this a relevant distinction? See further the proposed offence of fraudulently failing to disclose information below, **864**.

6. In *Rai* [2000] 1 Cr App Rep 242, [2000] Crim LR 192, D obtained a grant from the city council to provide a bathroom for his disabled mother. Before it was installed, she died. D did not inform the council and allowed the work to proceed. He was convicted of obtaining services by deception. Rai argued that he had no legal or contractual duty to inform the council of his mother's death. But see *With v O'Flanagan* and *Traill v Baring*, above, **818**.

7. In *Silverman* (1987) 86 Cr App R 213, [1987] Crim LR 574, CA, D charged two elderly sisters grossly excessive prices for work done on their flat. The sisters trusted D and assumed that the price was a fair one. D's conviction for deception was quashed for other reasons but the court said, 'In such circumstances of mutual trust, one party depending on the other for fair and reasonable conduct, the criminal law may apply if one party takes dishonest advantage of the other by representing as a fair charge that which he but not the other knows is dishonestly excessive.' Suppose a car dealer, aware that the buyer doesn't know the first thing about cars, sells the buyer a car for £10,000 which he knows to be worth not more than £2,500. Deception? Would it make any difference that the seller was the buyer's father-in-law? To what extent to the deception offences conflict with capitalist ideals of sharp business practice?

8. In *Charles* [1976] 3 All ER 112 at 116, Viscount Dilhorne said, 'Until the enactment of the Theft Act 1968 it was necessary in order to obtain a conviction for false pretences to establish that there had been a false pretence of an existing fact'. Has the Theft Act dispensed with this requirement? By s 15(4) 'deception' includes 'a deception as to the present intentions of the person using the deception'. Where this qualification applies, is it unnecessary for the prosecution to prove a deception as to an existing fact? What statement as to existing fact did the defendants make in *Greenstein* below, **821**?

9. A statement of opinion is not a statement of fact but there is usually implicit in a statement of opinion a statement of fact. If D says that in his opinion X is honest or that certain spoons are made of silver these assertions contain the implicit statement of fact that he knows of nothing that makes his assertion untrue.

(1) CHEQUES AND DECEPTION

What is represented?

A common form of obtaining by deception is where D, in return for goods or services provided by V, gives a cheque which D knows will not be met, or has reason to believe may not be met, when presented by V. In giving a cheque D does not represent that he has funds in his account to meet the cheque there and then, for he may have a facility to overdraw his account (who hasn't?!), or intend himself to pay in sufficient funds before the cheque is presented or expect a third party to do so.

In *Hazelton* (1874) LR 2 CCR 134, it was thought to be settled law that a person tendering a cheque impliedly makes three representations: (i) that he had an account at the bank on which the cheque is drawn; (ii) that he has had authority to draw on the bank for the amount specified; and (iii) that the cheque as drawn is a valid order for that amount but in *Metropolitan Police Comr v Charles* [1976] 3 All ER 112, [1977] AC 177, HL, it was held that in substance there is only one representation, namely, that 'the existing state of facts is such that in the ordinary course the cheque will be met'—per Lord Edmund-Davies quoting with approval the words of Pollock B in *Hazelton*. The 'existing facts' may thus include D's present intention to pay money into the account, or his belief that someone else will do so. It makes no difference that the cheque is post-dated: *Gilmartin* [1983] 1 All ER 829, [1983] QB 953, CA.

A case which is not at first sight easy to reconcile with these principles is *Greenstein* [1976] 1 All ER 1, [1975] 1 WLR 1353, CA. D and others applied to V for large numbers of shares and with each application they enclosed a cheque to cover the purchase price. They knew that they did not have funds in the bank to meet the cheque *at the time of the application,* but they also knew from experience that they would be allocated only a proportion of the shares applied for and that when the shares were allocated V would return a cheque for the difference between their cheque for the full purchase price and the actual purchase price. V's cheque would then be promptly paid into the defendants' account so that their own cheque, which was presented by V after the allocation of shares, would be met either on first or, at worst, second presentation. To put this simply: suppose D had £5,000 in his bank account. He applies to V for £10,000's worth of shares knowing that the issue will be oversubscribed and that at best he will be allocated 40% of his application. V allocates D 40%, confirms this allocation to D and encloses a cheque for £6,000. D promptly banks this so that he has £11,000 standing to his credit when D's cheque for £10,000 is presented by V for payment.

The defendants had been told by their bankers that this practice (known as 'stagging') was irregular, and the defendants knew that V would not have issued the shares had they realized that by this scheme the defendants were getting for themselves a larger number of shares than bona fide applicants. Indeed to combat the practice of stagging V had in some cases asked applicants to give an assurance that their cheques would be met on first presentation and, when asked, the defendants had given this assurance.

The defendants claimed that they did not dishonestly obtain the shares by deception since their experience in these stagging operations showed that the cheques would be met (it was only in 14 out of 136 transactions that the defendants' cheques were not met on first presentation because V's return cheque had not been cleared in time). But it was held that, in so far as the defendants represented that each cheque was a valid order, it was not because, as they knew, they had no authority whatever to draw cheques for such large amounts—cheques which could only be met if the defendants succeeded in deceiving V into thinking their applications were genuine. But does a cheque cease to be a valid order because D does not have the funds in the bank to meet it at the time it is drawn if he expects that there will be sufficient funds at the time of presentation? Does it follow from *Greenstein* that if D buys goods from V with a cheque for £10,000 he is guilty of obtaining by deception if he has only £5,000 to his account but believes that a rich uncle will pay into his account a further £5,000 before V presents his cheque?

In those cases where the defendants had given an undertaking that their cheques would be met on first presentation the case against them seems clearer. They might have hoped that their cheques would be met on first presentation but they were aware of the risk (since in 14 cases their cheques had not been so met) that they might not, hence it could be said that there was a reckless deception.

Obtaining a cheque from a corporation

Where it is alleged that D obtained a cheque from a limited company, it must be proved that a person whose state of mind was that of the company (apparently a person with authority to sign cheques, not, for example, the typist who made out the cheque) was deceived: *Rozeik* [1996] 3 All ER 281, [1996] 1 WLR 159. The case proceeds on the assumptions (1) that managers who signed the cheques were the proper persons to authorize, and that they did authorize all the relevant transactions; but, (2) that the managers were not deceived because they knew that the representations were false, and (3) that they were, nevertheless, not parties to the fraud. It followed that it did not avail the Crown to prove that anyone else was deceived. The managers *were* the company for this purpose, so the company was not deceived.

The result might have been different if it had been proved that the managers were parties to the fraud of the company: 'The company will not be fixed with knowledge where the employee or officer has been defrauding it'. So it would then have been sufficient to prove that other employees concerned in providing the cheque were deceived.

If you deceive the waiter at the Savoy into supplying you with a meal you have obtained it by deception from the company that owns that hotel because the waiter is the person with the authority of the company to take your order and deliver your meal. But if the waiter is a party to the fraud, no one is deceived and the only charge is theft.

The court in *Rozeik* said that theft or conspiracy to defraud would probably have been better charges. The facts implied in the verdict of the jury seem to amount to theft of the cheque and, if the cheques were presented, of the thing in action constituted by the company's bank balance which would have been depleted by the honouring of the cheques.

2. THE OBTAINING

The obtaining (or the 'securing' or 'procuring' in the language in some of the offences) must be by a deception. Thus there is a requirement of causation. Something done by D must cause V to do something.

R v Lambie
[1981] 2 All ER 776, House of Lords

(Lords Diplock, Fraser of Tullybelton, Russell of Killowen, Keith of Kinkel, Roskill)

Their Lordships concurred in the speech of Lord Roskill.

Lord Roskill. My Lords, on 20th April 1977 the respondent was issued by Barclays Bank Ltd ('the bank') with a Barclaycard ('the card'). That card was what today is commonly known as a credit card. It was issued subject to the Barclaycard current conditions of use, and it was an express condition of its issue that it should be used only within the respondent's credit limit. That credit limit was £200 as the respondent well knew, since that figure had been notified to her in writing when the card was issued. The then current conditions of use included an undertaking by the respondent, as its holder, to return the card to the bank on request. No complaint was, or indeed could be, made of the respondent's use of the card until 18th November 1977. Between that date and 5th December 1977 she used the card for at least 24 separate transactions, thereby incurring a debt of some £533. The bank became aware of this debt and thereupon sought to recover the card. On 6th December 1977 the respondent agreed to return the card on 7th December 1977. She did not, however, do so. By 15th December 1977 she had used the card for at least 43 further transactions, incurring a total debt to the bank of £1,005.26.

My Lords, on 15th December 1977 the respondent entered into the transaction out of which this appeal arises. She visited a Mothercare shop in Luton. She produced the card to a departmental manager at Mothercare named Miss Rounding. She selected goods worth £10.35. Miss Rounding completed the voucher, checked that the card was current in date, that it was not on the current stop list and that the respondent's signature on the voucher corresponded with her signature on the card. Thereupon, the respondent took away the goods which she had selected. In due course, Mothercare sent the voucher to the bank and were paid £10.35 less the appropriate commission charged by the bank. On 19th December 1977 the respondent returned the card to the bank.

My Lords, at her trial at the Crown Court at Bedford on 1st and 2nd August 1979 before his Honour Judge Counsell and a jury, the respondent faced two charges of obtaining a pecuniary advantage by deception contrary to s 16(1) of the Theft Act 1968. These were specimen charges. The first related to an alleged offence on 5th December 1977 and the second to the events which took place at the Mothercare shop at Luton which I have just related. The particulars of each charge were that she dishonestly obtained for herself a pecuniary advantage 'namely, the evasion of a debt for which she then made herself liable by deception, namely, by false representations that she was authorised to use a Barclaycard...to obtain goods to the value of £10.35'.

The jury acquitted the respondent on the first charge. She was, however, convicted on the second. The evidence of dishonesty in relation to the Mothercare transaction which was the subject of the second charge was overwhelming, and before your Lordships' House counsel for the respondent did not seek to suggest otherwise. Presumably the acquittal on the first count was because the jury were not certain that at the earlier date, 5th December 1977, the respondent was acting dishonestly.

My Lords, during the hearing in this House your Lordships inquired of counsel for the appellant prosecutor why no count of obtaining property by deception on 15th December 1977 contrary to s15 of the Theft Act 1968 had been included in the indictment. Your Lordships were told that such a charge had indeed been preferred at the magistrates' court during the committal proceedings but had been rejected by the magistrates on a submission made on behalf of the respondent during those proceedings. My Lords, if this be so, I find it difficult to see on what basis such a submission could properly have succeeded, or what defence there could have been had such a charge been the subject of a further count in the indictment once the jury were convinced, as they were, of the respondent's dishonesty on 15th December 1977. Had that course been taken, the complications which in due course led to the Court of Appeal, Criminal Division, quashing the conviction on the second count, and consequently, to the prosecutor's appeal to this House, with your Lordships' leave, following the grant of a certificate by the Court of Appeal, Criminal Division, would all have been avoided. But the course of adding a count charging an offence against s15 of the Theft Act 1968 was not followed, and accordingly your Lordships have now to determine whether the Court of Appeal, Criminal Division, was correct in quashing the conviction on the second count. If it was, then, as that court recognised in the concluding paragraph of its judgment, a gateway to successful fraud has been opened for the benefit of the dishonest who in circumstances such as the present cannot be proceeded against and punished at least for offences against s16 of the Theft Act 1968.

My Lords, the committal proceedings were what is sometimes called 'old fashioned', that is to say, that advantage was not taken of s1 of the Criminal Justice Act 1967. Witnesses were called in the magistrates' court and cross-examined. These witnesses included Miss Rounding, the departmental manager. Your Lordships were shown a copy of her deposition. Miss Rounding was not called at the trial at the Crown Court. Her deposition was read to the jury. It emerged from her evidence, and other evidence given or read, that, as one would expect, there was an agreement between Mothercare and the bank. That agreement does not appear to have been properly proved at the trial, but, by consent, your Lordships were given a pro forma copy of what is known as a 'merchant member agreement' between the bank and its customer, setting out the conditions on which the customer will accept and the bank will honour credit cards such as Barclaycards.

My Lords, at the close of the case for the prosecution, counsel for the respondent invited the judge to withdraw both counts from the jury on, it seems from reading the judge's clear ruling on this submission, two grounds: first, that as a matter of law there was no evidence from which a jury might properly draw the inference that the presentation of the card in the circumstances I have described was a representation by the respondent that she was authorised by the bank to use the card to create a contract to which the bank would be a party, and, second, that as a matter of law there was no evidence from which a jury might properly infer that Miss Rounding was induced by any representation which the respondent might have made to allow the transaction to be completed and the respondent to obtain the goods. The foundation for this latter submission was that it was the existence of the agreement between Mothercare and the bank that was the reason for Miss Rounding allowing the transaction to be completed and the goods to be taken by the respondent, since Miss Rounding knew of the arrangement with the bank, so that Mothercare was in any event certain of payment. It was not, it was suggested, any representation by the respondent which induced Miss Rounding to complete the transaction and to allow the respondent to take the goods.

My Lords, the judge rejected these submissions. He was clearly right to do so, as indeed was conceded in argument before your Lordships' House, if the decision of this House in *Metropolitan Police Comr v Charles* [1976] 3 All ER 112, [1977] AC 177 is of direct application. In that appeal this House was concerned with the dishonest use, not as in the present appeal of a credit card, but of a cheque card. The appellant defendant was charged and convicted on two counts of obtaining a pecuniary advantage by deception, contrary to s 16 of the Theft Act 1968. The Court of Appeal, Criminal Division, and your Lordships' House both upheld those convictions. Your Lordships unanimously held that where a drawer of a cheque which is accepted in return for goods, services or cash, uses a cheque card he represents to the payee that he has the actual authority of the bank to enter on its behalf into the contract expressed on the card that it would honour the cheque on presentation for payment.

My Lords, I venture to quote in their entirety three paragraphs from the speech of my noble and learned friend Lord Diplock ([1976] 3 All ER 112 at 114, [1977] AC 177 at 182–183) which, as I venture to think, encapsulate the reasoning of all those members of your Lordships' House who delivered speeches:

> 'When a cheque card is brought into the transaction, it still remains the fact that all the payee is concerned with is that the cheque should be honoured by the bank. I do not think that the fact that a cheque card is used necessarily displaces the representation to be implied from the act of drawing the cheque which has just been mentioned. It is, however, likely to displace that representation at any rate as the main inducement to the payee to take the cheque, since the use of the cheque card in connection with the transaction gives to the payee a direct contractual right against the bank itself to payment on presentment, provided that the use of the card by the drawer to bind the bank to pay the cheque was within the actual or ostensible authority conferred on him by the bank.
> By exhibiting to the payee a cheque card containing the undertaking by the bank to honour cheques drawn in compliance with the conditions endorsed on the back and drawing the cheque accordingly,

the drawer represents to the payee that he has actual authority from the bank to make a contract with the payee on the bank's behalf that it will honour the cheque on presentment for payment.

It was submitted on behalf of the accused that there is no need to imply a representation that the drawer's authority to bind the bank was actual and not merely ostensible, since ostensible authority alone would suffice to create a contract with the payee that was binding on the bank; and the drawer's possession of the cheque card and the cheque book with the bank's consent would be enough to constitute his ostensible authority. So, the submission goes, the only representation needed to give business efficacy to the transaction would be true. This argument stands the doctrine of ostensible authority on its head. What creates ostensible authority in a person who purports to enter into a contract as agent for a principal is a representation made to the other party that he has the actual authority of the principal for whom he claims to be acting to enter into the contract on that person's behalf. If (1) the other party has believed the representation and on the faith of that belief has acted on it and (2) the person represented to be his principal has so conducted himself towards that other party as to be estopped from denying the truth of the representation, then, and only then, is he bound by the contract purportedly made on his behalf. The whole foundation of liability under the doctrine of ostensible authority is a representation, believed by the person to whom it is made, that the person claiming to contract as agent for a principal has the actual authority of the principal to enter into the contract on his behalf.'

If one substitutes in the passage the words 'to honour the voucher' for the words 'to pay the cheque', it is not easy to see why mutatis mutandis the entire passages are not equally applicable to the dishonest misuse of credit cards as to the dishonest misuse of cheque cards.

But the Court of Appeal in a long and careful judgment delivered by Cumming-Bruce LJ felt reluctantly impelled to reach a different conclusion. The crucial passage in the judgment which the learned Lord Justice delivered reads thus ([1981] 1 All ER 332 at 339–340, [1981] 1 WLR 78 at 86–87):

'We would pay tribute to the lucidity with which the learned judge presented to the jury the law which the House of Lords had declared in relation to deception in a cheque card transaction. If that analysis can be applied to this credit card deception, the summing up is faultless. But, in our view, there is a relevant distinction between the situation described in *Metropolitan Police Comr v Charles* and the situation devised by Barclays Bank for transactions involving use of their credit cards. By their contract with the bank, Mothercare had bought from the bank the right to sell goods to Barclaycard holders without regard to the question whether the customer was complying with the terms of the contract between the customer and the bank. By her evidence Miss Rounding made it perfectly plain that she made no assumption about the appellant's credit standing at the bank. As she said: "The company rules exist because of the company's agreement with Barclaycard." The flaw in the logic is, in our view, demonstrated by the way in which the judge put the question of the inducement of Miss Rounding to the jury: "Is that a reliance by her, Miss Rounding of Mothercare, on the presentation of the card as being due authority within the limits as at that time as with count 1?" In our view, the evidence of Miss Rounding could not found a verdict that necessarily involved a finding of fact that Miss Rounding was induced by false representation that the appellant's credit standing at the bank gave her authority to use the card.'

I should perhaps mention, for the sake of clarity, that the person referred to as the appellant in that passage is the present respondent.

It was for that reason that the Court of Appeal, Criminal Division, allowed the appeal, albeit with hesitation and reluctance. That court accordingly certified the following point of law as of general public importance; namely:

'In view of the proved differences between a cheque card transaction and a credit card transaction, were we right in distinguishing this case from that of *Metropolitan Police Comr v Charles* [1976] 3 All ER 112, [1977] AC 177 on the issue of inducement?'

My Lords, as the appellant says in his printed case, the Court of Appeal, Criminal Division, laid too much emphasis on the undoubted, but to my mind irrelevant, fact that Miss Rounding said she made no assumption about the respondent's credit standing with the bank. They reasoned from the absence of assumption that there was no evidence from which the jury could conclude that she was 'induced by a false representation that the [respondent's] credit standing at the bank gave her authority to use the card'. But, my Lords, with profound respect to Cumming-Bruce LJ, that is not the relevant question. Following the decision of this house in *Charles*, it is in my view clear that the representation arising from the presentation of a credit card has nothing to do with the respondent's credit standing at the bank but is a representation of actual authority to make the contract with, in this case, Mothercare on the bank's behalf that the bank will honour the voucher on presentation. On that view, the existence and terms of the agreement between the bank and Mothercare are irrelevant, as is the fact that Mothercare, because of that agreement, would look to the bank for payment.

That being the representation to be implied from the respondent's actions and use of the credit card, the only remaining question is whether Miss Rounding was induced by that representation to complete the transaction and allow the respondent to take away the goods. My Lords, if she had been asked whether, had she known the respondent was acting dishonestly and, in truth, had no authority whatever from the bank to use the credit card in this way, she (Miss Rounding) would have completed the transaction, only one answer is possible: 'No'. Had an affirmative answer been given to this question, Miss Rounding would, of course, have become a participant in furtherance of the respondent's fraud and a conspirator with her to defraud both Mothercare and the bank. Leading counsel for the respondent was ultimately constrained, rightly as I think, to admit that had that question been asked of Miss Rounding and answered, as it must have been, in the negative, this appeal must succeed. But both he and his learned junior strenuously argued that as Lord Edmund-Davies pointed out in his speech in *Charles* [1976] 3 All ER 112 at 122, [1977] AC 177 at 192–193, the question whether a person is or is not induced to act in a particular way by a dishonest representation is a question of fact, and, since what they claimed to be the crucial question had not been asked of Miss Rounding, there was no adequate proof of the requisite inducement. In her deposition, Miss Rounding stated, no doubt with complete truth, that she only remembered this particular transaction with the respondent because someone subsequently came and asked her about it after it had taken place. My Lords, credit card frauds are all too frequently perpetrated, and if conviction of offenders for offences against s15 or s16 of the Theft Act 1968 can only be obtained if the prosecution are able in each case to call the person on whom the fraud was immediately perpetrated to say that he or she positively remembered the particular transaction and, had the truth been known, could never have entered into that supposedly well-remembered transaction, the guilty would often escape conviction. In some cases, of course, it may be possible to adduce such evidence if the particular transaction is well remembered. But where as in the present case no one could reasonably be expected to remember a particular transaction in detail, and the inference of inducement may well be in all the circumstances quite irresistible, I see no reason in principle why it should not be left to the jury to decide, on the evidence in the case as a whole, whether that inference is in truth irresistible as to my mind it is in the present case. In this connection it is to be noted that the respondent did not go into the witness box to give evidence from which that inference might conceivably have been rebutted.

My Lords, in this respect I find myself in agreement with what was said by Humphreys J giving the judgment of the Court of Criminal Appeal in *R v Sullivan* (1945) 30 Cr App Rep 132 at 136:

> 'It is, we think, undoubtedly good law that the question of the inducement acting upon the mind of the person who may be described as the prosecutor is not a matter which can only be proved by the direct evidence of the witness. It can be, and very often is, proved by the witness being asked some question which brings the answer: "I believed that statement and that is why I parted with my money"; but it is not necessary that there should be that question and answer if the facts are such that it is patent that there was only one reason which anybody could suggest for the person alleged to have been defrauded parting with his money, and that is the false pretence, if it was a false pretence.'

It is true that in *R v Laverty* [1970] 3 All ER 432 Lord Parker CJ said that the Court of Appeal, Criminal Division, was anxious not to extend the principle in *Sullivan* further than was necessary. Of course, the Crown must always prove its case and one element which will always be required to be proved in these cases is the effect of the dishonest representation on the mind of the person to whom it is made. But I see no reason why in cases such as the present, where what Humphreys J called the direct evidence of the witness is not and cannot reasonably be expected to be available, reliance on a dishonest representation cannot be sufficiently established by proof of facts from which an irresistible inference of such reliance can be drawn.

My Lords, I would answer the certified question in the negative and would allow the appeal and restore the conviction of the respondent on the second count in the indictment which she faced at the Crown Court.

Certified question answered in the negative; order appealed from reversed; conviction on count 2 of the indictment restored

Notes and questions

1. Lord Roskill refers to *Metropolitan Police Comr v Charles*, *Sullivan* and *Laverty*. In *Charles*, D was provided by his bank with a cheque book and cheque card and authorized to overdraw his account up to £100. The cheque card provided the usual conditions such as an undertaking by the bank that any cheque not exceeding £30 would be honoured by the bank if the specified conditions were met. In the course of one evening at a gambling club D drew 25 cheques for £30 each made out to Mr Cersell, the manager of the club, for which he received gaming chips. In *Sullivan*, D represented that he was the 'actual maker' of dartboards which he offered for sale and for which he received a number of orders. No purchaser ever received a dartboard nor was any money returned and D had neither premises nor plant for making dartboards. D's conviction for obtaining by false pretences was upheld though no purchaser said he had parted with his money because of D's claim that he was the 'actual maker' and those that were asked why they had said that it was because they wanted a dartboard. The Court of Appeal, Criminal Division held that there was no conceivable reason for their parting with the money other than the language of the advertisement which began with the words 'actual maker'. In *Laverty*, D changed the number plates on a car which he then sold to V. It was held that this constituted a representation that the car was the original car to which these numbers had been assigned. D's conviction for obtaining by deception was quashed because it was not proved that this deception had operated on V's mind. In each of these cases is it true to say that there is an operative deception? Have the courts extended the concept to include 'constructive' deceptions?

2. In *Charles*, Mr Cersell said that it was 'totally irrelevant' to him whether D had authority to draw the cheque and in *Lambie* Miss Rounding was, if anything, even more adamant on this. 'We will honour the card,' she said, 'if the conditions are satisfied whether the bearer has authority to use it or not'. So how could it be said that the deception in either case was an operative cause of the obtaining? In both cases reliance is placed on the fact that had Mr Cersell or Miss Rounding known that the defendants were acting without authority they would not have entered into the transaction. Is this a relevant consideration? Suppose Miss Rounding had said to D, 'I would not enter into this transaction if I thought you had no authority to use the credit card but you look honest enough to me and I'll assume that you are authorized'. Would she then have been deceived by D's representation of authority?

Does it follow from *Charles* and *Lambie* that the deception in *Laverty* equally caused V to buy the car? He had no reason to question the number plates but if he had known that they were not the number plates belonging to that car he would presumably have declined to buy the car.

3. Is it desirable that the law should invoke a strained, or even fictitious, notion of deception in cases like *Charles* and *Lambie*? Would it be better if the law provided specifically for this kind of dishonest conduct? The wrongdoing of these individuals was to cause a legal obligation to pay money to be imposed on a person (the bank) without his consent, knowing that they had no right to do so. Consider the proposed offences below, p 861.

R v Fitzeal Nabina

[2000] Crim LR 481, Court of Appeal

(Lord Bingham CJ, Alliott and Steele JJ)

The appellant by false pretences induced banks and credit card companies to issue credit cards to him. He used the cards to finance purchases from a number of outlets. [Though the matter is not mentioned in the transcript, presumably he failed to settle accounts submitted by the companies.] He was charged with obtaining property from the various outlets, contrary to s 15 of the 1968 Act by deception, namely by falsely representing that he was [for example] the legitimate holder of a Mastercard number 543 6806 5767 0083. The appellant conceded that the cards had been fraudulently obtained, but he was not charged with obtaining the cards. He contended that he held the cards under a voidable contract. The judge directed the jury that they must be sure that he had obtained the cards by deception from the companies but omitted to direct them that they must be satisfied that the representation charged had been made to any sales outlet.

Bingham CJ [having pointed out that there was no direct evidence of the making of any such representation]. So the case must in our judgment rest on either necessary or irresistible inference or implication of law. It is not enough that an inference was possibly open to the jury because the representation is the crux of the offence and the jury could not convict unless the offence were proved to the criminal standard.

In our judgment the Crown, in seeking to uphold this conviction, face an insuperable problem. The drawing of an inference from the facts proved was a matter for the jury, and the jury were never directed to consider whether this ingredient of the offence was met and whether the inference should be drawn or not....

We have the gravest possible doubt whether the jury could properly, even if fully directed, have regarded the making of the representation charged as a necessary inference from the facts before them. The use of a card to obtain goods and services is of course an everyday act. Broadly speaking, suppliers are concerned to ensure that they will receive payment from the issuers of the card. For that reason it is normal to require a signature from the customer, to compare the signature on the card with the signature on the voucher, and to make sure that the card is not on a stop list. There is, however, in our judgment room for doubt whether a supplier is interested in how a holder comes to be the holder of the card, provided (and this we emphasise) the transaction is one which will be honoured by the issuer of the card. In this connection the observations of Lord Diplock in *R v Charles* [1977] AC 177, 182 are very relevant. [See above, pp **824–825**.]

On all these counts there was evidence that the issuer, had it known at the time of issue what it knew later, would not have issued the card. But there was no evidence from any of the issuing institutions that any of the transactions had not been, or would not be, honoured, nor that in the circumstances they regarded the appellant as acting outside the authority which they had respectively conferred on him. It is indeed in our judgment doubtful whether the appellant by his conduct could be said to have represented anything more than that he had authority to bind the bank and that the transaction would be honoured. There is room for argument (to say no more) as to whether such a representation, if made, would have been false.

We refer, as the judge did, to *R v Lambie* [above, p **822**], and draw attention to the facts on which that case was based.

[**Bingham LCJ** discussed *Lambie*, quoting from the speech of Lord Roskill, above.]

In that case therefore the customer did not have the actual authority of the bank to warrant that the bank would honour the voucher upon presentation because she was in excess of her limit, and her authority to use the card had been revoked by the bank's request for its return and her agreement to return it. Here, so far as the evidence went, the appellant did have the actual authority of the issuing institutions to warrant that they would honour the vouchers upon presentation because the cards had been issued to the appellant and even if the banks would have been entitled to revoke his authority to use the cards, they had not done so.

The appellant relies on the general principle that a contract (here the granting by the issuing company to the appellant of a right to use the card) is voidable until rescinded. In *Lambie* that contract had been rescinded. Here Mr McCullough for the appellant argues that it had not. Thus, he says, the appellant was entitled to exercise the right conferred on him by the issuers even if those rights had been obtained by dishonestly misleading statements until the issuers terminated the appellant's rights as, on the hypothesis of dishonest misleading, they were undoubtedly entitled to do. But Mr McCullough says that the issuers had not done so, and accordingly the appellant remained a person authorised to bind the bank or (if the language of the indictment is adopted) he remained for purposes of the sales outlet a legitimate holder of the card. There was no evidence that the issuers did not regard the appellant as having authority to bind them. Nor was there evidence that these transactions would not be honoured by the issuers.

On behalf of the Crown Mr O'Byrne did not take fundamental issue with the principles of law on which Mr McCullough relied. He cited no authority which threw doubt on those contentions. He accepted that, in the sense contended for, the appellant was a lawful holder of the cards. But he submitted that there was a rule of the civil law, not of the criminal law, and that this was a case concerned with allegations of dishonesty where different considerations applied. It is of course true that this was a prosecution concerned with dishonesty, but the dishonest misrepresentation alleged against the appellant concerned his civil law rights, and the issue whether the representation was correct or incorrect could not in our judgment be avoided.

We are on this question reluctant to express a concluded view since we have no knowledge of the contract between the issuers and appellant, which could be relevant, and other questions could arise which might have a bearing on the question. We are mindful that the correct resolution of this issue could have potentially far-reaching implications and we are reluctant to express concluded views in an appeal which must in our judgment, because of what we regard as a fatal omission in the summing-up, be allowed. Reluctantly, since it seems clear on all the facts that the appellant certainly was acting in a dishonest manner, we feel compelled to allow this appeal.

Notes and questions

1. If the question is material at all, is it (i) whether V believed D had *authority*, or (ii) whether he believed D had *power*, to bind the company? Which of these was Mr Cersell (*Charles*) or Ms Rounding (*Lambie*) interested in?

2. Should the conduct in *Nabina* be criminal? Is this a case of obtaining the cards by deception, contrary to s 15. Why did not the prosecution charge that? Was it perhaps because it was thought not to represent the full criminality of what had been done? Is it impossible because the cards remain the property of the credit card company? On conviction of obtaining a card from the company, could the court have taken into account in sentencing the financial damage which had resulted to the company?

3. Note that the court has no truck with the argument that the rules of civil law should be ignored when we are faced with dishonesty in a criminal case. See *Hinks*, above, p 750.

4. Was not Nabina clearly guilty of theft of the property he received (as the jury found) dishonestly, under *Hinks*, above, p 750?

5. Compare the approach in *Sofroniou* below, p 853. Is the wrongdoing of these individuals better reflected in charges relating to their being allowed to borrow by way of overdraft, etc? Or by their obtaining the banking services by the deception? Or by their deception of the retailers?

R v Doukas
[1978] 1 All ER 1061, Court of Appeal, Criminal Division

(Geoffrey Lane LJ, Milmo and Watkins JJ)

The applicant, a waiter employed at an hotel, was found in the hotel with six bottles of wine. The wine was not of a type stocked or sold by the hotel. A search of his car revealed bottles of spirits. On a charge under s 25(1), below, p 915, the prosecution's case was that the applicant intended, on receipt of orders by customers for the hotel's wine, to substitute his own and pocket the money. The applicant was convicted.

[**Geoffrey Lane LJ** delivered the judgment of the court:]

... The only criticism which is levelled against the conviction is that the judge was wrong in law in rejecting the submission, made by the defence at the close of the prosecution case, that the evidence could not prove the offence alleged; the facts of this case, in all material respects, were the same as in *Rashid* [[1977] 2 All ER 237, [1977] 1 WLR 298]. Then it goes on to a second ground which must be dealt with hereafter. This court has to decide whether the judge was wrong in law in rejecting the applicant's submission.

[His Lordship referred to s 25(1) and s 15.]

Combining those two sections of the 1968 Act, ss 25 and 15, which are apposite, one reaches this result: 'A person shall be guilty of an offence if, when not in his place of abode, he has with him any article for use in the course of or in connection with, any deception, whether deliberate or reckless, by words or conduct, as to fact or as to law, for purposes of dishonestly obtaining property belonging to another with the intention of permanently depriving the other of it'.

If one analyses that combined provision, one reaches the situation that the following items have to be proved. First of all that there was an article for use in connection with the deception; here the bottles. Secondly, that there was a proposed deception: here the deception of the guests into believing that the proffered wine was hotel wine and not the waiter's wine. Thirdly, an intention to obtain property by means of the deception, and the property here is the money of the guests which he proposes to obtain and keep. Fourthly, dishonesty. There is twofold dishonesty in the way the Crown put the case. First of all the dishonesty in respect of his employers, namely putting into his pocket the money which really should go to the hotel and, more important, the second dishonesty, vis-à-vis the guests, the lying to or misleading of the guests into believing that the wine which had been proffered was the hotel wine and not the waiter's wine. Fifthly, there must be proof that the obtaining would have been, wholly or partially, by virtue of the deception.

The prosecution must prove that nexus between the deception and obtaining. It is this last and final ingredient which, as we see it in the present case, is the only point which raises any difficulty. Assuming, as we must, and indeed obviously was the case, that the jury accepted the version of the police interviews and accepted that this man had made the confession to which I have referred, then the only question was, would this obtaining have in fact been caused by the deception practised by the waiter?

We have, as in the notice of appeal, been referred to the decision in *Rashid* which was a decision by another division of this court. That case concerned not a waiter in a hotel, but a British Railways waiter who substituted not bottles of wine for the railway wine but his own tomato sandwiches for the railway tomato sandwiches; and it is to be observed in that case the basis of the decision was that the summing-up of the judge to the jury was inadequate. On that basis the appeal was allowed. But the court went on [[1977] 2 All ER 237 at 240, [1977] 1 WLR 298 at 302, per Bridge LJ] to express its views obiter on the question whether in these circumstances it could be said that the obtaining was by virtue of deception and it came to the conclusion, as I say obiter, that the answer was probably No.

Of course each case of this type may produce different results according to the circumstances of the case and according, in particular, to the commodity which is being proffered. But, as we see it, the question has to be asked of the hypothetical customer: why did you buy this wine? or, if you had been told the truth, would you or would you not have bought the commodity? It is, at least in theory, for the jury in the end to decide that question.

Here, as the ground of appeal, is simply the judge's action in allowing the case to go to the jury, we are answering that question, so to speak, on behalf of the judge rather than the jury. Was there evidence of the necessary nexus fit to go to the jury? Certainly so far as the wine is concerned, we have no doubt at all that the hypothetical customer, faced with the waiter saying to him: 'This of course is not hotel wine, this is stuff which I imported into the hotel myself and I am going to put the proceeds of the wine, if you pay, into my own pocket', would certainly answer, so far as we can see, 'I do not want your wine, kindly bring me the hotel carafe wine'. Indeed it would be a strange jury that came to any other conclusion, and a stranger guest who gave any other answer, for several reasons. First of all the guest would not know what was in the bottle which the waiter was proffering. True he may not know what was in the carafe which the hotel was proffering, but he would at least be able to have recourse to the hotel if something was wrong with the carafe wine, but he would have no such recourse with the waiter; if he did, it would be worthless.

It seems to us that the matter can be answered on a much simpler basis. The hypothetical customer must be reasonably honest as well as being reasonably intelligent and it seems to us incredible that any customer, to whom the true situation was made clear, would willingly make himself a party to what was obviously a fraud by the waiter on his employers. If that conclusion is contrary to the obiter dicta in *Rashid*, then we must respectfully disagree with those dicta. It is not necessary to examine the question any further whether we are differing from *Rashid* or not. But it seems to us beyond argument that the judge was right in the conclusion he reached and was right to allow the matter to go to the jury on the basis which he did.

There are two other matters which are raised on behalf of the applicant. The first is the question of the gin, whisky, brandy and Cointreau which was found in the applicant's car, which was also included in the indictment as being part of the articles which were being used for cheating. The jury were invited, if they wished, to come to a separate conclusion on the spirits from that which they reached on the wine. They did not make any distinction and counsel for the applicant suggests that they must have been wrong so far as the spirits were concerned on the basis that any customer who was proffered a sealed bottle of a proprietary brand of spirits, either brandy, whisky or gin, would be certain, or might reasonably be expected to say 'Yes' to the waiter's offer, although he may have said 'No' so far as the wine was concerned. We think that the same reasoning can be applied to that. No reasonable customer would lend himself to such a swindle, whether the basis of the swindle was wine or spirits.

Finally, the last part of the notice of appeal reads:

> '…the terms of the [applicant's] alleged confession, which was the basis of the prosecution case, did not preclude the possibility that the customers would be willing parties to the defendant's scheme.'

With respect to counsel for the applicant it is not altogether clear what that means but I think the way he explained it to us was this. The way in which the applicant answered the questions of the police in the passage which I have read, did not preclude his giving the customers a choice, namely 'There is carafe wine of the hotel if you wish it. There is also the wine which I have here, which is my wine, if you wish that. Kindly select which you would prefer.' It seems to us that that is an unreal hypothetical situation which would never, in the circumstances of this case, have arisen.

For the reasons which we have endeavoured to explain in this judgment, we are of the view that there is no basis on which this application can properly be founded. Consequently the application is refused.

Application refused

R v King

[1987] 1 All ER 547, Court of Appeal, Criminal Division

(Neill LJ, Waterhouse and Saville JJ)

The appellants were convicted of attempting to obtain property by deception. Falsely representing themselves as belonging to a reputable firm of tree surgeons they persuaded a 68-year-old widow to agree to pay £500, or £470 in cash, for the removal of two trees by further falsely representing that the removal of the trees was necessary to prevent damage to the gas supply and the house foundations. When the widow was withdrawing the money from her building society account she told the cashier what had happened and the police were informed.

[The judgment of the court was delivered by **Neill LJ**:]

In support of the appeal against conviction counsel for the appellants argued that the judge erred in rejecting the motion to quash the indictment, or alternatively the submission that there was no case to answer. The argument was developed on the following lines: (1) that, as the appellants were charged with an attempt, it was incumbent on the prosecution to prove that if the relevant conduct had been completed it would have constituted a criminal offence; (2) that if the appellants had received £470 for cutting down the trees they would have been paid by reason of the work they had done, and not by reason of any representation they had made to secure the work; (3) that since the decision in *R v Lewis* (January 1922, unreported) it had been generally recognised that conduct of the kind complained of in the present case did not constitute the criminal offence of obtaining property by false pretences or by deception because, as a matter of causation, the relevant property was obtained by reason of the work carried out rather than by reason of any representation or deception. Our attention was directed to statements on the subject in some leading textbooks; (4) that the offence of obtaining a pecuniary advantage by deception contrary to s 16 of the Theft Act 1968 had no relevance in the present case (a) because the appellants were not given the opportunity to earn the remuneration 'in an office or employment'; on the facts of this case the appellants were independent contractors and (b) because during the course of the argument at the trial the prosecution stated in terms that they were not relying on the provisions of s 16.

In order to examine these arguments it is necessary to start by setting out the particulars of offence as stated in the indictment, as amended. The particulars read as follows:

'David King and Jimmy Stockwell on the 5th day of March 1985 in Hampshire, dishonestly attempted to obtain from Nora Anne Mitchell, £470 in money with the intention of permanently depriving the said Nora Anne Mitchell thereof by deception, namely by false oral representations that they were from J F Street, Tree Specialists, Pennington, that essential work necessary to remove trees in order to prevent damage to the gas supply and house foundations would then have to be carried out.'

It will be remembered that the word 'then' towards the end of the particulars was added by way of amendment on 18 February.

The argument advanced on behalf of the appellants on causation or remoteness was founded on the decision in *R v Lewis*, and on commentaries on that decision by academic writers. The report of the decision in *R v Lewis* is scanty and, as far as we are aware, is contained only in a footnote in *Russell on Crime* (12th edn, 1964) vol 2, p1186, n66.

In that case (which was a decision at Somerset Assizes in January 1922) a school-mistress obtained her appointment by falsely stating that she possessed a teacher's certificate. She was held to be not guilty of obtaining her salary by false pretences, on the ground that she was paid because of the services she rendered, and not because of the false representation.

It was submitted on behalf of the appellants that the principle underlying the decision in *R v Lewis* could be applied in the present case. It was further submitted that the authority of *R v Lewis* was implicitly recognised by the enactment of para (c) of s16(2) of the Theft Act 1968. Section 16 is concerned with the obtaining of a pecuniary advantage by deception; s 16(2) provides:

'The cases in which a pecuniary advantage within the meaning of this section is to be regarded as obtained for a person are cases where … (c) he is given the opportunity to earn remuneration or greater remuneration in an office or employment…'

It is to be observed, however, that Professor Glanville Williams in his *Textbook of Criminal Law* (2nd edn, 1983) p 792 has this to say of the decision in *R v Lewis*:

'Yet *Lewis* would not have got the job and consequently her salary, if it had not been for the pretence. Her object in making the pretence was to get the salary. Assuming, as is likely, that the employer would not have made her any payment of salary if a lie had not been operating on his mind, there was certainly a factual causal connection between the lie and the obtaining of salary. Why should it not be a causal connection in law? We have seen that when the defendant produces a consequence intentionally, it is generally regarded as imputable to him. Why should it not be so here?'

Furthermore, the learned author of *Russell on Crime* p 1187 (immediately after the footnote already referred to) continued:

'But it is submitted that cases of this kind could be placed beyond doubt if the indictment were worded carefully. The essential point in this crime is that in making the transfer of goods the prosecutor must have been influenced by the false pretence as set out in the indictment.'

We have given careful consideration to the argument based on causation or remoteness, and have taken account of the fact that some support for the argument may be provided by the writings of a number of distinguished academic lawyers. Nevertheless, we have come to the conclusion that on the facts of the present case the argument is fallacious.

In our view, the question in each case is: was the deception an operative cause of the obtaining of the property? This question falls to be answered as a question of fact by the jury applying their common sense.

Moreover, this approach is in accordance with the decision of the Court for Crown Cases Reserved in *R v Martin* (1867) LR 1 CCR 56, where it was held that a conviction for obtaining a chattel by false pretences was good, although the chattel was not in existence at the time that the pretence was made, provided the subsequent delivery of the chattel was directly connected with the false pretence. Bovill CJ said:

'What is the test? Surely this, that there must be a direct connection between the pretence and the delivery—that there must be a continuing pretence. Whether there is such a connection or not is a question for the jury.'

The decision in *R v Martin* was referred to with approval in *R v Moreton* (1913) 8 Cr App Rep 214, cf [1911–13] All ER Rep 699 at 700, where Lord Coleridge J said:

'*Martin* leaves the law in no doubt; it was held there that the fact that the goods were obtained under a contract does not make the goods so obtained goods not obtained by a false pretence, if the false pretence is a continuing one and operates on the mind of the person supplying the goods.'

In the present case there was, in our judgment, ample evidence on which the jury could come to the conclusion that had the attempt succeeded the money would have been paid over by the victim as a result of the lies told to her by the appellants. We consider that the judge was correct to reject both the motion to quash the indictment and the submission that there was no case to answer.

For the reasons which we have set out, we consider that the appellants were rightly convicted in this case, and the appeals must therefore be dismissed.

Appeals dismissed

A. T. H. Smith, 'The Idea of Criminal Deception',
[1982] Crim LR 721 (footnote references omitted)

.... in a number of recent decisions, the courts have extended the concept of deception beyond what it meant when the Theft Act was framed in 1968, to mean something much more like fraud. This might be seen as an objectionable exercise in judicial creativity in the criminal law. But even if we can shrug off such theoretical objections to the interstitial development of the law as being somehow inevitable (particularly in the light of increased fraudulent misuse of cheque cards and credit cards) it is as well that we should be aware of the metamorphosis which criminal deception is undergoing. To give their new creature a protective screen the courts have employed crude 'but for' principles of causation. Whereas elsewhere in the criminal law the conduct objected to must be an 'operating and substantial cause' the courts are now saying that a man has been deceived when he has been told an untruth (verbally, or by conduct) and where it may be assumed that he would have done otherwise had he known the truth. This applies even though the victim may have been unconcerned to ascertain the truth or falsity of what is said, or even unaware that a statement has been made at all. They are also being urged to hold that a person commits deception where he takes advantage of another's mistaken belief, having in no way contributed to the formation of that mistake in the first place. It will be argued that these developments are objectionable because they pay insufficient regard to the notion of deception, and that the courts must evolve more acceptable limits to the breadth of the causal nexus in criminal deception.

Deception defined
Deception could have been explained by the legislators in the Theft Act, but it was not. The Act confines itself to the somewhat unhelpful observation that ' "deception" means any deception, the remainder of the section being devoted to reversing certain of the old common law rules surrounding the former "false pretences" '. To some extent this left the courts free to apply their own gloss to the word as the need to do so arose. But 'deception' already had, by the time the Theft Act became law in 1968, acquired a reasonably settled meaning, classically that stated by Buckley J. in *Re London and*

Globe Finance Corporation. 'To deceive is, I apprehend, to induce a man to believe that a thing is true which is false...to deceive is by falsehood to induce a state of mind.' The Criminal Law Revision Committee explained its use of 'deception' by saying:

> 'The substitution of "deception" for "false pretence" is chiefly a matter of language. The word "deception" seems to us (as to the framers of the American Law Institute's Model Penal Code) to have the advantage of directing attention to the effect that the offender deliberately produced on the mind of the person deceived, whereas "false pretence" makes one think of what exactly the offender did in order to deceive. "Deception" seems also more apt in relation to deception by conduct.'

This reinforces the suggestion in Buckley J.'s definition that it is essential that the representation must operate on the conscious mind of the victim and cause him to believe that the facts are otherwise than they really are.

Apart from being inherent in the very notion of deception, there is an additional reason why the motivation of the victim must be examined in deception cases. It must be shown by the prosecution that the obtaining was caused by the deception, since in all the deception offences it must be established that the obtaining was effected 'by' the deception.... This analysis shows that, as classically understood, there are at least two links in the causal chain. It must be shown that the victim was induced into a certain affirmative belief, and that as a result of his belief, he behaved in a certain way, as a further result of which property (or a service or other protected interest) was obtained.

Where the deception takes the form of an express representation, it will be relatively easy to show that the victim heard it and was influenced by it. But the deception may be 'by words or conduct', and it is deception by conduct that occasions all the difficulties. Three recurrent situations will be discussed. In the first, the victim never consciously adverts to the matter about which he is alleged to have been duped. He makes an assumption of which the cheat takes advantage. In the second case, the victim is aware that he might be being told an untruth, but he does not consider it material, and his behaviour is not influenced by it. In the third situation, the victim makes a definite mistake of which the fraudster is aware, but he does not contribute to its formation.

...

It is suggested that if a duty of disclosure is to be imposed in the criminal law, this should be done expressly. Although the civil law forms the back-drop against which the criminal law must operate, it is too uncertain to be a reliable source for obligations of disclosure. Even where the civil law says that there is an obligation to disclose a material fact (as in the law of insurance, the obtaining of which by deception constitutes an offence), it does not follow that the criminal law must arrive at the same conclusion. Certainly, if the civil law indicates that a party to an agreement is entitled to remain silent on a particular matter, the criminal law should not hold otherwise.

The criminal law might approach the obligation to disclose in two different ways, both of which methods are employed in the American Model Penal Code. It may state general principles, as in section 231 (c) which provides that a person commits deception if he: '(c) fails to correct a false impression which the deceiver previously created or reinforced, or which the deceiver knows to be influencing another to whom he stands in a fiduciary or confidential relationship.'; In terms of eradicating vagueness from the law, this does not help much. The question whether or not a person 'stands in a fiduciary or confidential relationship' to another is notoriously vague. Even if it is obviously intended to exclude the purely contractual relationship, it does not identify with sufficient precision the added ingredient that transforms the transaction from the civil to the criminal.

The second approach is to identify particular facts about which candour is necessary. Section 231 '(d) adds that deception occurs where a person: "(d) fails to disclose a known lien, adverse claim or other impediment to the enjoyment of property which he transfers or encumbers in consideration for the property obtained, whether such impediment is or is not valid, or is or is not a matter of official record." The provision seems simple, clear and concise, leaving little room for doubt about what must be disclosed, and when. It is suggested that until the legislature in this country enacts a similar provision, the courts should continue to decline to hold that silence can by itself constitute deception, even though the silence may be misleading. And it is suggested that if the law is to impose obligations of candour in connection with sexual relations, it would do better to say so expressly.'

Notes and questions

1. Suppose the customers had said after the arrest of Doukas, 'We never gave any thought to whose wine it was but had we thought about it we would have assumed it was the proprietor's'. Would they have been deceived?

2. D buys a knife to murder his wife but he does not tell the seller this since he assumes (correctly) that the seller would not sell him the knife if he knew this. Has the knife been obtained by deception? Is there an implicit representation by D that he requires the knife for a lawful purpose? Has D stolen the knife? Cf *Hinks*, above, p 750.

3. In *Miller* (1992) 95 Cr App R 421, [1992] Crim LR 744, CA, D, by representing that he was operating a licensed taxi and that by inference his fares would be reasonable, inveigled foreign visitors arriving at Heathrow or Gatwick to travel in his car. He then charged excessive fares, in one case 10 times what a licensed taxi driver would have been entitled to charge. In each case the visitor had realized to some extent that D had lied but had nevertheless paid the extravagant sum demanded out of a feeling of compulsion or obligation or fearing the consequences if he did not. On appeal against convictions for deception, D's counsel argued that in order to prove the money had been obtained by deception it had to be proved that when the money changed hands the victims still believed the lie to be true: that is, that the deception had to be a continuing and operative cause. Dismissing the appeal the court said it was not legitimate to isolate the moment when the money was handed over from the rest of the story. If it could legitimately be said that D's various deceptions had caused the money to be handed over it was irrelevant that the victim at the final moment suspected or even believed that he had been swindled. But how can it be said that property is obtained by deception if at the time of delivery of the property the victim no longer believes the lies he was told by the rogue? But was D in *Miller* in any case guilty of an attempt to obtain by deception? Or theft? Cf *Hinks*.

4. For a deception to take place it would seem implicit that some human mind must be deceived. 'For a deception to take place', said Lord Morris in *DPP v Ray* [1973] 3 All ER 131 at 137, 'there must be some person or persons who will have been deceived'. It follows that a machine cannot be deceived. If, however, D uses a washer to get goods from a machine he may be convicted of stealing the goods just as much as if he had used a jemmy to force the machine open: *Hands* (1887) 16 Cox CC 188. Cf *Goodwin* [1996] Crim LR 262 (going equipped with Kenyan shillings for stealing from gaming machines).

5. In *Holmes* [2004] EWHC 2020 Admin, D faced extradition for his conduct when working as an official in a German bank. He used a co-worker's password to credit an account under his control in a Dutch bank. In the course of construing the offence under s 15A of the 1968 Act, the Administrative Court did not find it necessary to resolve whether s 15A could be committed where the transaction is entirely automated. Counsel for the applicant relied on the decision of the Divisional Court in *Davies v Flackett* [1973] RTR 8 as an

authority for the proposition that there can be no operative deception of a machine. The court observed at para. 12.

Davies v Flackett is not binding authority for the proposition that deception of a machine or computer is not deception for the purposes of the Theft Act. Ackner J so stated in terms in his judgment in that case. We nonetheless accept that 'The prevailing opinion is that it is not possible in law to deceive a machine': see Professor J.C. Smith's The Law of Theft, 8th Edition, at paragraph 4–12; and see Professor Griew's *The Theft Acts* 7th Edition, at paragraph 8–12 and 8–13. In the modern world, where internet banking involves the transfer of funds by the use of passwords and PIN numbers, and within banks and other organisations funds can be transferred by the misuse of passwords (as in the present case), it is regrettable that obtaining by means of PIN numbers, passwords and the like operating on computers by a person who knows that he has no right to do so is not a substantive offence of theft or a cognate offence; and we note that Professor Griew thought that it should be. So far as the alleged deception of the bank's computer in the present case is concerned, we say no more about it, other than to draw attention to the provisions of section 2 of the Computer Misuse Act 1990, which might have been used to frame a charge in the present case: c.f. *Attorney General's Reference (No. 1 of 1991)* [1993] QB 94.

6. Where D uses some trick to obtain services or property from a machine or via a computer can it be argued that he deceives the programmer? Cf *R (O) v Coventry* [2004] Crim LR 948 (a case on incitement of a company to distribute child pornography).

3. DISHONESTY

All offences of deception require dishonesty. Although no definition of dishonesty is provided for the deception offences under ss 15 and 16 of the 1968 Act or for ss 1 and 2 of the 1978 Act, nor is there any adaptation of the partial definition of dishonesty relating to theft in s 2, the CLRC seems to have thought that dishonesty for the purposes of ss 15 and 16 should bear, so far as the case admits, the same meaning for these offences as it has for theft. 'Owing to the words "dishonestly obtains", ' said the Committee (Cmnd 2977, para. 88):

a person who uses deception in order to obtain property to which he believes himself entitled will not be guilty; for though the deception may be dishonest the obtaining is not. In this respect…the offence will be in line with theft, because a belief in legal right to deprive an owner of property is for the purpose of theft inconsistent with dishonesty and is specifically made a defence by the partial definition of 'dishonestly' in [s]2(1)(a). (The partial definition of 'dishonestly' in [s]2(1) is not repeated in [s] 15(1). It would be only partly applicable to the offence of criminal deception, and it seems unnecessary and undesirable to complicate the [Act] by including a separate definition in [s] 15.)

It can hardly be supposed that the CLRC had some different meaning of dishonesty in mind for the (remaining) offences under s 16 of the 1968 Act or for the offences under ss 1 and 2 of the 1978 Act.

In cases not involving a claim of right *Ghosh* (p 787, above) where the charge was laid under s 15, governs the issue of dishonesty. *Greenstein* (p 821, above) may illustrate the practical difficulties of the test. How is a jury to determine whether the conduct in question would be regarded as dishonest by the standards of ordinary men? How many ordinary men know the first thing about stagging and by what yardstick is it to be regarded as dishonest? Is it to be settled by reference to what bankers and issuing houses think? See the criticisms of *Ghosh* levelled by Professor Griew as extracted above, p 795.

In *Greenstein*, the Court of Appeal said that it would be no bar to the conviction of the defendants that no one lost a penny by the scheme. In *Potger* (1970) 55 Cr App R 42, CA, where D induced V to subscribe for magazines by the false representation that he was a student taking part in a points competition, it was no answer that the magazines to be delivered were worth what was asked for them. Cf s 2(2) of the 1968 Act—'A person's appropriation of property may be dishonest notwithstanding that he is willing to pay for the property'.

Deception without dishonesty?

Deception and dishonesty are separate elements of the obtaining offences. If D practises a deliberate deception in order to recover from V property which, as D knows, V is wrong-fully withholding from him, he commits no offence because he is not dishonest. Similarly where D mistakenly, but honestly, believes the property is being wrongfully withheld. The deception may be dishonest but the obtaining is not. In *Talbott* [1995] Crim LR 396 D, in order to conceal from her landlord that she was obtaining housing benefit, obtained a lease in her stage name and applied for benefit in her real name to the local authority (the LA), giving to the LA her stage name as that of her landlady. The LA's officers testified that they would not have paid had they known the truth. D seems to have believed, and perhaps she was right, that she was entitled to benefit, whatever the identity of her land-lord. It was held that she was guilty of obtaining. She was certainly behaving dishonestly towards her landlord but was she dishonest vis-à-vis the LA? Following *Gomez*, would theft have been a better charge? The prosecution would not have had to prove an opera-tive deception. Would not attention have been concentrated on what should have been the real issue?

4. WHAT MAY BE OBTAINED

Most commonly it is tangible property (money or goods) that is obtained by deception but there would be serious gaps in the law if only tangible property could be the subject of a charge. D may by deception obtain gains to himself or inflict losses on another other than in terms of tangible property. He may, for example, by deception persuade V to forgo a debt which D owes to V, or he may obtain a service by deception. Separate provision is made in the Theft Acts 1968 and 1978 according to the nature of what is obtained. It should not be thought, however, that these provisions are mutually exclusive and on given facts D may fall foul of more than one provision. Take what might be one of the most common frauds of all where D obtains goods on credit having no intention to pay. Here D commits an offence under s 15 of the Theft Act 1968 in obtaining goods by deception but he also commits an offence under s 1 of the 1978 Act because he has caused V to do an act (deliver the goods) which confers a benefit on D and this amounts to a service.

A word of explanation about the Theft Act 1978. Before this Act, cases where D obtained by deception something other than tangible property were provided for mainly, though not exclusively, in s 16(2)(a) of the 1968 Act. This provision which was not the work of the CLRC was drafted in some haste as the Bill was going through Parliament. Its interpreta-tion was attended by so much difficulty (Edmund Davies LJ once referred to it as a 'judicial nightmare') that it was repealed and replaced by ss 1 and 2 of the 1978 Act. It is a complex statute and the reform proposals discussed below would repeal s 1 and replace it with a very simple offence of obtaining a service dishonestly (with no requirement of deception).

(1) PROPERTY BELONGING TO ANOTHER

Theft Act 1968, s 15

(1) A person who by any deception dishonestly obtains property belonging to another, with the intention of permanently depriving the other of it, shall on conviction on indictment be liable to imprisonment for a term not exceeding ten years.

(2) For purposes of this section a person is to be treated as obtaining property if he obtains ownership, possession or control of it, and 'obtain' includes obtaining for another or enabling another to obtain or to retain.

(3) Section 6 above shall apply for purposes of this section, with the necessary adaptation of the reference to appropriating, as it applies for purposes of section 1.

By s 34(1) of the 1968 Act, the definitions of 'property' and 'belonging to another' in s 4(1), above, p 764, and s 5(1), above, p 768, respectively are applied for the purpose of s 15.

So far as the definition of property is concerned the qualifications to the general definition in s 4(1) do not apply to the s 15 offence so that land, things growing wild on land, and wild creatures not reduced into possession, though they may not be stolen may be obtained by deception. Why?

It is sufficient that by deception D obtains 'ownership, possession or control' but D commits the offence only if he intends permanently to deprive V. D does not commit this offence where by deception he obtains a car on hire intending to return it. Why? (See the CLRC's observations, Cmnd 2977, para 89.)

R v Preddy, Slade and Dhillon
[1996] 3 All ER 481, House of Lords

(Lord Mackay, LC, Lords Goff, Jauncey, Slynn and Hoffmann)

The facts appear sufficiently in the speech of Lord Goff.

Lord Goff:

The first question
Against the above background, I now turn to the first question which your Lordships have to consider, which is whether the debiting of a bank account and the corresponding crediting of another's bank account brought about by dishonest misrepresentation, amount to the obtaining of property within s 15 of the 1968 Act.

Under each count, one of the appellants was charged with dishonestly obtaining, or attempting to obtain, from the relevant lending institution an advance by way of mortgage in a certain sum. In point of fact it appears that, when the sum was paid, it was sometimes paid by cheque, sometimes by telegraphic transfer, and sometimes by the CHAPS (Clearing House Automatic Payment System) system. However, in the cases where the sum was paid by cheque the appellants were not charged with dishonestly obtaining the cheque. A useful description of the CHAPS system is to be found in the Law Commission's Report *Criminal Law: Conspiracy to Defraud* (Law Com No 228) (1994) p 39, n 83. It involves electronic transfer as between banks, and no distinction need be drawn for present purposes between the CHAPS system and telegraphic transfer, each involving a debit entry in the payer's bank account and a corresponding credit entry in the payee's bank account.

The Court of Appeal in the present case concentrated on payments by the CHAPS system. They considered that the prosecution had to prove that the relevant CHAPS electronic transfer was 'property' within s 15(1) of the 1968 Act. They then referred to the definition of property in s 4(1) of the Act as including 'money and all other property, real or personal, including things in action and other intangible property'; and they concluded, following the judgment of the Court of Appeal in *R v Crick* (1993) Times, 18 August, that such a transfer was 'intangible property' and therefore property for the purposes of s 15(1).

The opinion expressed by the Court of Appeal in *R v Williams* on this point was, in fact, obiter. The case related to a mortgage advance, the amount having been paid by electronic transfer. The court however concluded that a sum of money represented by a figure in an account fell within the expression 'other intangible property' in s 4(1), and that the reduction of the sum standing in the lending institution's account, and the corresponding increase in the sum standing to the credit of the mortgagor's solicitor's account, constituted the obtaining of intangible property within s 15(1).

In holding that a sum of money represented by a figure in an account constituted 'other intangible property', the court relied upon the decision of the Privy Council in *A-G of Hong Kong v Nai-Keung* [1987] 1 WLR 1339, in which an export quota surplus to a particular exporter's requirements, which under the laws of Hong Kong could be bought and sold, was held to constitute 'other intangible property' within s 5(1) of the Hong Kong Theft Ordinance (Laws of Hong Kong, 1980 rev, c 210) (identical to the English 1968 Act). I feel bound to say that that case, which was concerned with an asset capable of being traded on a market, can on that basis be differentiated from cases such as the present. But in any event, as I understand the position, the Court of Appeal were identifying the sums which were the subject of the relevant charges, as being sums standing to the credit of the lending institution in its bank account. Those credit entries would, in my opinion, represent debts owing by the bank to the lending institution which constituted choses in action belonging to the lending institution and as such fell within the definition of property in s 4(1) of the 1968 Act.

My own belief is, however, that identifying the sum in question as property does not advance the argument very far. The crucial question, as I see it, is whether the defendant obtained (or attempted to obtain) property *belonging to another*. Let it be assumed that the lending institution's bank account is in credit, and that there is therefore no difficulty in identifying a credit balance standing in the account as representing property, ie a chose in action, belonging to the lending institution. The question remains, however, whether the debiting of the lending institution's bank account, and the corresponding crediting of the bank account of the defendant or his solicitor, constitutes obtaining of that property. The difficulty in the way of that conclusion is simply that, when the bank account of the defendant (or his solicitor) is credited, he does not obtain the lending institution's chose in action. On the contrary, that chose in action is extinguished or reduced pro tanto, and a chose in action is brought into existence representing a debt in an equivalent sum owed by a different bank to the defendant or his solicitor. In these circumstances, it is difficult to see how the defendant thereby obtained *property belonging to another*, ie to the lending institution.

Professor Sir John Smith, in his commentary on the decision of the Court of Appeal in the present case, has suggested that:

> 'Effectively, the victim's property has been changed into another form and now belongs to the defendant. There is the gain and equivalent loss which is characteristic of, and perhaps the substance of, obtaining.' (See [1995] Crim LR 564 at 565–566.)

But even if this were right, I do not for myself see how this can properly be described as obtaining property belonging to another. In truth, the property which the defendant has obtained is the new chose in action constituted by the debt now owed to him by his bank, and represented by the credit entry in his own bank account. This did not come into existence until the debt so created was owed to him by his bank, and so never belonged to anyone else. True, it corresponded to the debit entered in the lending institution's bank account; but it does not follow that the property which the defendant acquired can be identified with the property which the lending institution lost when its account was debited. In truth, s 15(1) is here being invoked for a purpose for which it was never designed, and for which it does not legislate.

I should add that, throughout the above discussion, I have proceeded on the assumption that the bank accounts of the lending institution and the defendant (or his solicitor) are both sufficiently in credit to allow for choses in action of equivalent value to be extinguished in the one case, and created in the other. But this may well not be the case; and in that event further problems would be created, since it is difficult to see how an increase in borrowing can constitute an extinction of a chose in action owned by the lending institution, or a reduction in borrowing can constitute the creation of a chose in action owned by the defendant. It may be that it could be argued that in such circumstances it was the lending institution's bank whose property was 'obtained' by the defendant but, quite apart from other problems, that argument would in any event fail for the reasons which I have already given. For these reasons, I would answer the first question in the negative.

Payment by cheque

Before I leave this topic, I wish to turn briefly to cases in which a mortgage advance has been made, not by telegraphic or electronic transfer, but by cheque. It appears that, in the case of some of the mortgage advances made in the present cases, the money was in fact advanced by cheque. Strictly speaking, cases concerned with payment by cheque do not fall within the scope of the three questions posed for your Lordships' consideration, and they were not considered by the Court of Appeal. Even so, they provide a common alternative to cases of payment under the CHAPS system and raise very similar problems. It would, therefore, be unrealistic to ignore them and, since they were the subject of argument before the Appellate Committee, I propose to consider them.

None of the appellants was charged with obtaining the cheques themselves by deception. They were, even in the cases in which payment was made by cheque, charged with the obtaining by deception of the relevant advance. But whether they had been charged with obtaining the cheques by deception, or (as they were) with obtaining the advances by deception, the prosecution was, in my opinion, faced with the same insuperable difficulty as that which I have already discussed, viz that the defendant must have obtained property belonging to another to be convicted of obtaining property by deception under s 15(1) of the 1968 Act.

The point in question has been much discussed in the literature on the subject, and there now appears to be a broad consensus on the point, with which I find myself to be in agreement. I can therefore consider the point relatively shortly.

I start with the time when the cheque form is simply a piece of paper in the possession of the drawer. He makes out a cheque in favour of the payee, and delivers it to him. The cheque then constitutes a chose in action of the payee, which he can enforce against the drawer. At that time, therefore, the cheque constitutes 'property' of the payee within s 4(1) of the 1968 Act. Accordingly, if the cheque is then obtained by deception by a third party from the payee, the third party may be guilty of obtaining property by deception contrary to s 15(1).

But if the payee himself obtained the cheque from the drawer by deception, different considerations apply. That is because, when the payee so obtained the cheque, there was no chose in action belonging to the drawer which could be the subject of a charge of obtaining property by deception. This was decided long ago in *R v Danger* (1857) Dears & B 307, 169 ER 1018. There, the defendant was charged with obtaining a valuable security by false pretences, on the basis that he had presented a bill to the prosecutor who accepted it and returned it to the defendant, his acceptance having been induced by false pretences, on the part of the defendant. The court held that in these circumstances the defendant was not guilty of the offence with which he was charged because, before the document came into his possession, the prosecutor had no property in the document as a security, nor even in the paper on which the acceptance was written. Lord Campbell CJ, delivering the brief judgment of the court, said ((1857) Dears & B 307 at 324, 169 ER 1018 at 1025):

> '...we apprehend that, to support the indictment, the document must have been a valuable security while in the hands of the prosecutor. While it was in the hands of the prosecutor it was of no value to him, nor to any one else unless to the prisoner. In obtaining it the prisoner was guilty of a gross fraud; but we think not of a fraud contemplated by this Act of Parliament [7 & 8 Geo 4 c 29, s 53].'

Unfortunately, this authority does not appear to have been cited in *R v Duru* [1973] 3 All ER 715, [1974] 1 WLR 2. There, the defendants were involved in mortgage frauds perpetrated on a local authority. The advances were made by cheque, and the defendants were charged with obtaining the cheques by deception. The principal question for consideration was whether there was an intention on the part of the defendants to deprive the council of the property. The Court of Appeal held that there was such an intention. Megaw LJ, who delivered the judgment of the court, had this to say ([1973] 3 All ER 715 at 720, [1974] 1 WLR 2 at 8):

> 'So far as the cheque itself is concerned, true it is a piece of paper. But it is a piece of paper which changes its character completely once it is paid, because then it receives a rubber stamp on it saying it has been paid and it ceases to be a thing in action, or at any rate it ceases to be, in its substance, the same thing as it was before: that is, an instrument on which payment falls to be made. It was the intention of the appellants, dishonestly and by deception, not only that the cheques should be made out and handed over, but also that they should be presented and paid, thereby permanently depriving the Greater London Council of the cheque in substance as their things in action.'

That decision was followed and applied by the Court of Appeal in *R v Mitchell* [1993] Crim LR 788.

Both these decisions have been the subject of academic criticism, notably by Professor Smith in his commentary on *Mitchell* in the Criminal Law Review (in which he withdrew the support which he had previously given to the decision in *Duru*). The point is simply that, when the cheque was obtained by the payee from the drawer, the chose in action represented by the cheque then came into existence and so had never belonged to the drawer. When it came into existence it belonged to the payee, and so there could be no question of his having obtained by deception 'property belonging to another'. This is the point which was decided in *Danger*. The case of a cheque differs from *Danger* only in the fact that the cheque form, unlike the paper on which the bill was written in *Danger*, did belong to the drawer. But there can have been no intention on the part of the payee permanently to deprive the drawer of the cheque form, which would on presentation of the cheque for payment be returned to the drawer via his bank.

For these reasons I am satisfied that *Duru* and *Mitchell* are to this extent wrongly decided, and that the prosecution of the appellants in cases where the advance was made by cheque would have been equally flawed if they had been charged with obtaining the cheque in question by deception, as they were when charged with obtaining the advance itself by deception, contrary to s 15(1). Whether they could have been charged with dishonestly procuring the execution of a valuable security by deception contrary to s 20(2) of the 1968 Act does not arise for consideration in the present appeals.

The second question

I turn next to the second question which your Lordships have to consider, which is (in effect) whether the answer to the first question would be different where the transfer is to a firm of solicitors acting in a mortgage transaction. . . . the same difficulties arise here as they do where the money has been paid direct to the mortgagor by electronic transfer, or by cheque. This is because any chose in action which comes into existence by the crediting of the solicitor's bank account (simultaneously with the debiting of the lending institution's bank account), or by the receipt by the solicitors of a cheque from the lending institution, can never have belonged to the lending institution or its bank and so can never have belonged to another as required by s 15(1).

I turn next to the release of the money by the solicitor, with the lending institution's authority, to the vendor's solicitor in the form of a banker's draft. Presumably the solicitor's bank will debit the solicitor's general account with the amount of the draft, and in due course the solicitor will effect an adjustment in his own accounts as between his client account and his general account. The banker's draft will be made payable to the vendor's solicitor who will, on receipt of the draft, obtain property in the form of a chose in action represented by the draft; but once again that chose in action never belonged to another—either to the solicitor acting in the mortgage transaction or his bank, or to the lending institution itself. It is true that the consequence will have been that the lending institution's equitable interest, such as it was, was extinguished. But the identification of that equitable interest is not altogether easy. True the solicitor acting in the mortgage transaction received the money as trustee, but the money itself was paid directly into the solicitor's client account where it was 'mixed' with other money and its identity lost. I suppose that, if the solicitor became bankrupt, the lending institution could assert an equitable proprietary claim in the form of an equitable lien upon the chose in action represented by the credit balance (if any) in the account; but that contingency did not occur and, in any event, despite the broad words of s 15(1) of the 1968 Act, applicable in the case of obtaining property by deception by virtue of s 34(1), I find great difficulty in conceiving the possibility of the mortgagor 'obtaining' any such interest, which is not transferred to the mortgagor or to the vendor, but is simply extinguished, being replaced in due course by the lending institution's rights as mortgagee. In truth, the more one examines this problem, the more inapt does s 15 of the 1968 Act appear to be in cases of this kind.

[**Lord Goff** declined to answer the third question regarding the intention permanently to deprive as it did not arise for decision.]

Lord Mackay LC, and **Lords Jauncey, Slynn** and **Hoffmann** agreed with the speech of Lord Goff.

Notes and questions

1. The decision of the House had enormous repercussions, including the quashing of numerous convictions under s 15 of persons undoubtedly guilty of mortgage fraud. It led to the speedy enactment of the Theft (Amendment) Act 1996, creating the offence of obtaining a money transfer by deception, infra. Was it a necessary decision? Could the House have fairly held that there was, *in substance*, an obtaining of property belonging to another, as suggested in [1995] Crim LR at 565–566 (above, p **840**)? Was it relevant that prosecutors and courts had, for years, proceeded on the assumption that this was the law?

2. The dicta regarding the obtaining of cheques are obiter. Three issues need to be considered:

 (i) Where D deceives V into drawing and delivering a cheque made payable to D, he does not obtain 'property belonging to another' in the form of the thing in action represented by the cheque. That thing belonged to D from the moment of its creation and never belonged, or could belong, to V. *Duru*, deciding that D obtained the thing in action, was rightly overruled.

 (ii) Where D deceives V into drawing and delivering a cheque made payable to D, he does not obtain 'property belonging to another' in the form of the piece of paper on which the cheque is written. It will, in the normal course, be returned to V's bank after presentation so D, if he understands banking practice, does not intend permanently to deprive V of the paper.

(iii) Where D deceives V into drawing and delivering a cheque made payable to D, he *does* obtain 'property belonging to another' in the form of the tangible thing (not the thing in action) of real value—'a valuable security'. It is in effect a key to V's bank balance. But when the paper is returned to V, it has been cancelled, it is not longer a valuable security. V has therefore been permanently deprived of it. In this respect the court in *Duru* was right. So why should not D be convicted of obtaining the valuable security by deception—just as, under the Larceny Act 1916, he could be convicted of obtaining it by false pretences? See arguments by J. C. Smith in 'Obtaining Cheques by Deception or Theft' [1997] Crim LR 396, which was, in effect, applied by the Supreme Court of Victoria in *Parsons* [1998] 2 VR 478; affd (1999) 73 ALJR 27, HC of A. But the dictum in *Preddy* continues to be applied in England. In *Horsmann* [1997] 3 All ER 385, [1998] Crim LR 128 it was 'common ground' that, because there could be no obtaining of the thing in action, there could be no obtaining of the cheque.

In *Clark* [2001] Crim LR 572 the court, like the court in *Parsons* found the above article 'highly persuasive', but held they were precluded by *Preddy* from following it. In commenting on that case J. C. Smith stated:

Until the Theft Act 1968 came into force there was no doubt that a cheque could be stolen or obtained from the drawer by the false pretences of the payee.... Before 1969 there was no possibility of stealing a thing in action—larceny could be committed only of tangible property, something capable of being taken and carried away. The same rule applied to obtaining by false pretences: Russell on Crime (12th ed., 1964, by J.W.C. Turner) 1167. The Theft Act changed that, providing that: '"Property" includes money and all other property, real or personal, including things in action and other intangible property.' It would be hard to find a more comprehensive definition and, plainly, the object of the Act was to extend the range of property capable of being stolen and not to diminish it in any way. The courts however, soon went off the rails. In *Duru*, the court, in a judgment delivered by Megaw L.J. held that a cheque was obtained by deception because the defendants had obtained the thing in action represented by the cheque. The reason given was obviously wrong because that thing in action was not 'property belonging to another'—it belonged to the defendant from the start. The commentators pounced on this error with enthusiasm (see, e.g. commentary at [1973] Crim.L.R. 701 (where *Duru* was reported under the name of *Asghar*)). Over the next 20 years much ink was spilt trying to persuade the courts that Duru was wrongly decided but this was not achieved until the decision of the House of Lords in *Preddy*, when this ageing penny at last dropped. In the meantime, almost everyone seems to have become so bemused by things in action that sight was lost of the fact that cheques could be stolen or obtained from the drawer long before it was possible to steal things in action. The thing that was stolen was the physical thing that could be taken and carried away, the valuable security.

Throwing out the baby with bathwater. We have now reached the ludicrous result that since 1968, cheques cannot be stolen or obtained by deception from the drawer although they had been so capable at least since 1827 and probably before that. The House in *Preddy* was right to throw out *Duru*'s dirty bathwater but, if the baby has gone with it, their Lordships were surely in error. The law of theft seems to have gone completely mad when a person can be guilty of stealing property which is entirely his (*Hinks*) but cannot be guilty of stealing someone else's cheque. It may be arguable that, following *Hinks*, the dishonest acquisition of the thing in action now is theft of it; but in *Hinks* the victim was at least the owner of the property until he delivered it, whereas the drawer of the cheque was never the owner of the thing in action.

3. In *Danger*, above, p **841**, the paper on which the bill of exchange was written was never owned or possessed by V. It belonged to D and was merely put in front of V to be signed. D obtained V's signature by deception, but that was all. Was Lord Goff right to conclude that this made no difference?

(2) A MONEY TRANSFER

Theft Act 1968, s 15A

Obtaining a money transfer by deception

(1) A person is guilty of an offence if by any deception he dishonestly obtains a money transfer for himself or another.

(2) A money transfer occurs when—
(a) a debit is made to one account,
(b) a credit is made to another, and
(c) the credit results from the debit or the debit results from the credit.

(3) References to a credit and to a debit are to a credit of an amount of money and to a debit of an amount of money.

(4) It is immaterial (in particular)—
(a) whether the amount credited is the same as the amount debited;
(b) whether the money transfer is effected on presentment of a cheque or by another method;
(c) whether any delay occurs in the process by which the money transfer is effected;
(d) whether any intermediate credits or debits are made in the course of the money transfer;
(e) whether either of the accounts is overdrawn before or after the money transfer is effected.

(5) A person guilty of an offence under this section shall be liable on conviction on indictment to imprisonment for a term not exceeding ten years.

Section 15A: Supplementary

(1) The following provisions have effect for the interpretation of section 15A of this Act.

(2) 'Deception' has the same meaning as in section 15 of this Act.

(3) 'Account' means an account kept with—
(a) a bank; or
(b) a person carrying on a business which falls within subsection (4) below.

(4) A business falls within this subsection if—
(a) in the course of the business money received by way of deposit is lent to others; or
(b) any other activity of the business is financed, wholly or to any material extent, out of the capital of or the interest on money received by way of deposit;
and 'deposit' here has the same meaning as in section 35 of the Banking Act 1987 (fraudulent inducement to make a deposit)....

(5) For the purposes of subsection (4) above—
(a) all the activities which a person carries on by way of business shall be regarded as a single business carried on by him; and
(b) 'money' includes money expressed in a currency other than sterling or in the European currency unit (as defined in Council Regulation No 3320/94/EC or any Community instrument replacing it).

This section describes Preddy's conduct and enacts it is an offence. The Act is not retrospective, so only money transfers obtained after 18 December 1996 may be prosecuted under s 15A1(2). See Section 1(2) of the Theft (Amendment) Act 1996. Subsection (3) limits the offence to 'money', meaning an obligation to pay money, notably the obligation of a banker to his customer. It would not therefore apply to transfers of other things in action, such as bonds and securities, a limitation which was criticized in Parliament by Lord Donaldson (Hansard, HL, vol 576, col 796).

In *Holmes* [2004] EWHC 2020 Admin, D faced extradition for his conduct when working as an official in a German bank. He used a co-worker's password to credit an account under his control in a Dutch bank. The banking practice, of which the court took judicial notice, was such that the transfer was not complete until the Dutch bank received confirmation from the German bank. The Administrative Court held that 'credit' in s 15A is to be construed as an 'unconditional credit' so that for the purposes of the offence the credit only occurred once the Dutch bank received confirmation. In other respects the court took a broad approach to interpretation, holding that it was not necessary to identify which account had been debited or whether it was in credit at the time.

Sub-section (4) excludes possible unmeritorious defences which might have been raised. It is not an exclusive list, as the words, 'in particular', are intended to make clear. A court may properly hold other matters, not listed in the subsection, to be immaterial. As we have already noticed, *Preddy* decided that where D induces V to draw and deliver a cheque in favour of D, D is not guilty under s 15 of the 1968 Act of obtaining by deception the thing in action represented by the cheque. The new offence covers that case. When D presents the cheque and it is honoured a debit is made to V's account and a corresponding credit to D's, so a money transfer as defined in s 15A(1) occurs. It might be argued that the *transfer* has not been obtained by deception but by D's presentation of the cheque (as where a key is obtained by deception and used to open a safe and steal: the money taken from the safe has been stolen, not obtained by deception). But sub-s (4)(b) appears to assume that the transfer has been obtained by deception and, for practical purposes, probably puts the matter beyond all doubt. The offence is not committed until the cheque is honoured but D will be guilty of an attempt to commit it when he presents, or attempts to present the cheque. Until then, he has probably done no act which is 'more than merely preparatory' (above, Ch 15) to the commission of the s 15A offence. Nor will D be guilty of obtaining a transfer of funds if he negotiates the cheque to E for cash. V's account has not yet been debited and no account has been credited. The offence will be committed only when E, or some subsequent holder of the cheque presents it, and it is honoured. It is therefore still important to know whether D has obtained the cheque, as a valuable security, contrary to s 15 (above, p 839).

The Law Commission, when proposing the clause which became s 15A, rejected the apparently obvious course of amending s 15 because this would have involved a great deal of undesirable 'deeming'. But, in Law Com Consultation Paper 155 (1999), they provisionally recommend (para 7.7) that 'for the purposes of the offence of obtaining property by deception, it should be sufficient that the person to whom the property belongs is deprived of it by deception, whether or not anyone else obtains it'. The offence would of course cease to be one of 'obtaining' and become one of procuring or causing, more closely akin to theft than the present s 15. Is that a good solution? Note that the property which was created in favour of D, being neither obtained by deception nor stolen, would not be 'stolen goods'. See now the more radical proposals for reform discussed below.

Preddy and theft

It will be recalled that *Preddy* decided that where funds are transferred from V's bank account to D's by telegraphic transfer, CHAPS order or similar means, D does not obtain any property belonging to V and so cannot be guilty of obtaining property by deception contrary to s 15 of the Theft Act 1968. A thing in action belonging to V (property X) has been diminished (or destroyed) and a thing in action belonging to D (property Y) has been increased (or created). If property Y did not belong to V, obviously it could not be stolen from him—but the possibility that V has an equitable interest in property Y which could be stolen from him was not considered in *Preddy* or subsequent cases and that remains a possibility. Cf *Governor of Brixton Prison, ex p Levin* [1996] 4 All ER 350, [1977] QB 65, above, p 781.

In *Holmes* (above, p 846), the court made interesting obiter observations on the availability of a theft charge. The court found that there was insufficient evidence to conclude that there was a theft of a thing in action from the German bank. However it suggested that a theft conviction might be upheld on the following basis:

21. If the recipient bank account had been situated in England [and thereby subject to the rules of equity], [the Dutch bank] and the account holder would have held the monies credited to it on a constructive trust for the defrauded party [the German bank]. In *West Deutsche Landesbank Grozentrale v Islington London Borough Council* [1996] AC 669, Lord Browne-Wilkinson said: 'Although it is difficult to find clear authority for the proposition, when property has been obtained by fraud equity imposes a constructive trust on the fraudulent recipient: the property is recoverable and traceable in equity.'

22. The beneficial interest on property held on constructive trust is 'property' within the meaning of the Theft Act 1968, and is regarded as belonging to the person entitled to that beneficial interest: see section 4 read with section 5. The Applicant was under a legal duty to return the funds transferred into the account [in the Dutch bank] to [the German bank], to whom they belonged in equity. Accordingly, section 5(3). The monies in the account [in Holland] were, on the basis of the facts set out in the arrest warrant, dishonestly appropriated by the Applicant when he caused them to be remitted out of that account to various company accounts.

23. This analysis avoids what would otherwise be an irrational distinction between the obtaining of property by another's mistake (section 5(4)) and the obtaining of property by fraud. It remains to consider the decision of the Court of Appeal in *Attorney-General's Reference (No. 1 of 1985)* [1986] 1 QB 491. That case concerned an employee who had made a secret profit by selling his own goods on his employer's premises, thereby breaking the terms of his contract of employment. The Court held that the moneys the employee received from his private customers were not received on account of his employer within the meaning of section 5(4), that the profits made by the employee were not the subject of a constructive trust, and that if they were, that constructive trust did not give the employer a proprietary right or interest in the secret profit within the ambit of section 5(1). The present case is not concerned with a secret profit, but with the fraudulent taking of property (the chose in action constituted by the credit in the bank account at [Dutch bank]) obtained as a result of fraud on

the employer and belonging to it. In *Attorney-General's Reference (No. 1 of 1985)*, the Court stated, at 503:

> '...if the contentions of the Crown are well founded and if in each case of secret profit a trust arises which falls within section 5, then a host of activities which no layman would think were stealing will be brought within the Theft Act 1968. As this court pointed out in *Kaur v Chief Constable for Hampshire* [1981] 1 W.L.R. 578, 583:
>
> > "the court should not be astute to find that a theft has taken place where it would be straining the language so to hold, or where the ordinary person would not regard the defendant's acts, though possibly morally reprehensible, as theft."
>
> The second matter is this. There is a clear and important difference between on the one hand a person misappropriating specific property with which he has been entrusted, and on, the other hand a person in a fiduciary position who uses that position to make a secret profit for which he will be held accountable. Whether the former is within section 5, we do not have to decide. As to the latter we are firmly of the view that he is not, because he is not a trustee.'

24. This case is of conduct that any ordinary person would regard as theft, and is far closer to the misappropriation of specific property entrusted to an accused than to the making of a secret profit in breach of a contract of employment. We do not think that the Court of Appeal's decision in that case was intended to apply, or does apply, to facts such as those of the present.

Nor did *Preddy* decide that property X (the thing in action which is diminished), which certainly did belong to V, was not stolen from him. The obstacle to so holding is that the diminution in V's thing in action—his right to sue his bank for a sum of money—is effected by V or by V's agents and it is not easy to discern the necessary act of appropriation by D: J. C. Smith, *Archbold News* (Issue 9, 14/11/96) and commentary on *Caresana* [1996] Crim LR 667. The court in *Cummings-John* [1997] Crim LR 660 said:

We are not satisfied that a misrepresentation which persuades the account holder to direct payment out of his account is an assumption of the rights of the account holder as owner such as to amount to an appropriation of his rights within s 3(1) of the 1968 Act.

The case where D induces V to make a telegraphic transfer is materially different from that where D dishonestly presents a cheque drawn on V's account, causing it to be debited. The latter is an appropriation by D of the thing in action belonging to V and is theft. If the transaction is fully automated, that seems obvious. If it is carried out by bank clerks, they are innocent agents. It is the same in principle as where a person commits the offence of false accounting by giving false information to a clerk who innocently enters it into his employer's accounts: *Butt* (1884) 15 Cox CC 564, CCR. It is true that in the telegraphic transfer case D procures the whole course of events resulting in V's account being debited; but the telegraphic transfer is initiated, not by D, but by V. It can be argued that V's voluntary intervening acts break the chain of causation and that it is the same as if V is induced by deception to take money out of his safe to pay to D. D does not at that moment 'appropriate' it—V is not acting as his agent. D commits theft only if and when the money is put into his hands.

In contrast, in *Hilton* [1997] 2 Cr App R 445, [1997] Crim LR 761, D had direct control of a bank account belonging to a charity. He caused payments to be made from that account to settle his personal debts. This was a completely straightforward case of theft of the thing in action belonging to another. It made no difference whether the payments were by a cheque drawn by D or by telegraphic or other transfers which he directed. The Court of

Appeal recently affirmed this view in *Briggs* [2004] Crim LR 495 where D had, by deception, induced solicitors to transfer to her account proceeds of the sale of her parents' house. The Court of Appeal quashed a conviction for theft of the credit balance representing the proceeds of the sale. The court held that the word 'appropriation' connoted a physical act rather than a more remote action triggering the payment that gave rise to the charge.

It is submitted that while *Gomez* and *Hinks* do not expressly preclude this approach they do make it very much harder to draw any clear distinction between (i) D's direct acts towards V's property, with V's fraudulently obtained consent (*Hilton*), and (ii) D's acts causing V to transfer his property (or extinguish his chose in action) with V's fraudulently obtained consent. Arguably they are distinguishable on the basis that V's act of transfer in (ii) breaks the chain of causation since V will not be acting in a free informed manner (having been deceived). However, if D used an innocent agent, E, to effect the transfer of V's property, or to extinguish it, there would be no difficulty in establishing a theft charge at the moment that E assumes any right in relation to V's property. Why are things different when D causes V to act towards his own property in a way that will lead to its being destroyed or transferred to D? Both the agent and V appear to have been deceived. The fact that V has the authority to act in this way by transferring the property and is consenting is, according to *Gomez* and *Hinks*, irrelevant. D's setting in motion the transaction could be regarded as the commencement of the continuing act of appropriation. It is therefore arguable that where D, by deceit of V, causes a transfer of property that act is itself an appropriation.

(3) PECUNIARY ADVANTAGE

Theft Act 1968, s 16

(1) A person who by any deception dishonestly obtains for himself or another any pecuniary advantage shall on conviction on indictment be liable to imprisonment for a term not exceeding five years.

(2) The cases in which a pecuniary advantage within the meaning of this section is to be regarded as obtained for a person are cases where:

    (a) [*Repealed.*]

    (b) he is allowed to borrow by way of overdraft, or to take out any policy of insurance or annuity contract, or obtains an improvement of the terms on which he is allowed to do so;

    (c) he is given the opportunity to earn remuneration or greater remuneration in an office or employment, or to win money by betting.

(3) For purposes of this section 'deception' has the same meaning as in section 15 of this Act.

All that remains of s 16 are the two particular cases instanced in paras (b) and (c).

Paragraph (c) was presumably introduced to meet what were thought to be the difficulties caused by the decisions in *Lewis* (referred to in the decision in *King*, above, p 832) and *Clucas* [1949] 2 All ER 40, CCA. So far as *Lewis* is concerned, *King* shows that the draftsman's precaution was largely unnecessary. Under para (c) of course a person acting as Lewis did commits the offence once the office or employment is secured by deception and before any remuneration is paid but it would seem that by securing the office or employment he is guilty of an attempt to obtain by deception: *King*.

In *Clucas* D induced a bookmaker to accept a large bet by falsely representing that he was making a number of bets on behalf of others. The horse backed in this way by D won and

D was paid the winnings. It was held that D did not obtain the winnings by false pretences; he got them by backing the winning horse. It was accepted by the court in that case that the bookmaker would not have accepted the bet, nor paid the winnings, had he not been deceived. Clucas is now guilty of the offence under para (c) when he places the bet. Does it follow from *King* that when he placed the bet he was guilty of attempting to obtain by deception?

Paragraph (b) of s 16 deals with the sort of case where D, say, obtains an overdraft by representing that he needs it for urgent repairs to his house when his intent is to use it to buy a new car, or where he gets better terms on an insurance policy by falsely representing that he is a non-smoker. In the former case D is guilty of obtaining by deception when he obtains the facility to overdraw and it is not necessary that he should have drawn on the account: *Watkins* [1976] 1 All ER 578 (Crown Court).

(4) VALUABLE SECURITIES

Theft Act 1968, s 20(2), (3)

(2) A person who dishonestly, with a view to gain for himself or another or with intent to cause loss to another, by any deception procures the execution of a valuable security shall on conviction on indictment be liable to imprisonment for a term not exceeding seven years; and this subsection shall apply in relation to the making, acceptance, indorsement, alteration, cancellation or destruction in whole or in part of a valuable security, and in relation to the signing or sealing of any paper or other material in order that it may be made or converted into, or used or dealt with as, a valuable security, as if that were the execution of a valuable security.

(3) For purposes of this section 'deception' has the same meaning as in section 15 of this Act, and 'valuable security' means any document creating, transferring, surrendering or releasing any right to, in or over property, or authorising the payment of money or delivery of any property, or evidencing the creation, transfer, surrender or release of any such right, or the payment of money or delivery of any property, or the satisfaction of any obligation.

In *Danger* (1857) 7 Cox CC 303 it was held that D was not guilty of obtaining a valuable security by false pretences where he drew up a bill of exchange payable to himself and by false pretences induced V to accept it by signing it. The court held that for a valuable security to be the subject of the charge it must be the property of someone other than D. Neither the thing in action nor even the paper on which the bill was written belonged to V. The paper was probably never even in V's possession. All that D obtained was V's signature. Parliament quickly amended the law to plug the gap disclosed by *Danger*; the provision made, subsequently amended and enlarged in later Acts, now appears in s 20. The section is not well drafted.

The reach of this provision was considered in *Kassim* [1991] 3 All ER 713, [1992] 1 AC 9, HL. D opened an account at the V bank in a false name and address. He was given cheque books, a cheque guarantee card and an Access card. Not surprisingly he went on a spending spree and when apprehended he had overdrawn his account by £8,338 and had a debit of £943 on his Access account. The V bank was of course obliged to foot the bill. D was charged with, and convicted of, offences under s 20(2). The Court of Appeal upheld these convictions on the ground that D had by deception procured the execution of the cheques by obliging the bank to honour them. Quashing D's convictions, Lord Ackner, with whom all their Lordships agreed, said that while s 20(2) was concerned with a wide range of documents, it was concerned only with acts done to or in connection with such documents and was not concerned with giving effect to such documents by carrying out the instructions (such as delivering goods or paying money) which the documents may contain.

The offence is a valuable one since it can be prosecuted when the conduct involved would at most amount to an attempt to commit an obtaining or theft.

(5) SERVICES

Theft Act 1978, s 1

(1) A person who by any deception dishonestly obtains services from another shall be guilty of an offence.

(2) It is an obtaining of services where the other is induced to confer a benefit by doing some act, or causing or permitting some act to be done, on the understanding that the benefit has been or will be paid for.

(3) Without prejudice to the generality of subsection (2) above, it is an obtaining of services where the other is induced to make a loan, or to cause or permit a loan to be made, on the understanding that any payment (whether by way of interest or otherwise) will be or has been made in respect of the loan.

On conviction on indictment the offence is punishable with five years' imprisonment.

J. R. Spencer, 'The Theft Act 1978'
[1979] Crim LR 24 at 28 (footnote references omitted)

The definition of obtaining services requires the victim of the offence not merely to 'do some act, or cause or permit some act to be done', but to *confer a benefit* thereby. It seems, therefore, that P must be induced to do something which is of some use to somebody. Possibly, this means that P must be induced to do something which is of *economic value* to D or someone else—meaning that he must, at the end of the day, be financially better off than he would otherwise have been, To some extent as yet uncertain, therefore, the use of the word 'benefit' cuts down the extreme wideness of the phrases which follow it.

The benefit which P is induced to confer must involve 'doing some act, or causing or permitting some act to be done'. In many or most of the cases at which section 1 is aimed, P will be induced to confer a benefit by doing some act: repairing D's car, painting D's house, carrying D in his taxi, or doing some other sort of work for him. Were the benefit limited to the doing of some act, however, certain recurrent cases would fall outside the section. Where D lies his way into P's hotel, cinema or car park, for example, P's acts in providing the benefit are done for a large number of people, and would be done whether or not D told P lies in order to share it; P is not induced to show his film or to make up the hotel beds solely because D deceives him. The only thing which D actually induces P to do which he would not have done anyway—and hence the only conduct of P's causally linked to D's deception—is to *allow* D to use the facility, and this D would no doubt have argued was an omission, not an act. Presumably it was with this problem in mind that the section includes conferring a benefit by 'permitting some act to be done'. Presumably the benefit may also be conferred by 'causing some act to be done' in order to make it obtaining services from P where P, an employer or manager, is deceived into commanding one of his servants or underlings to do some act of benefit to D—as where a garage proprietor is deceived into telling his mechanic to service D's car. 'Doing some act' might have been sufficient to produce this result without the addition of 'causing some act to be done', but the addition of 'causing' relieves the courts of the need to construe 'doing' in an extensive sense.

A person 'is induced to confer a benefit by doing some act' inter alia where he is persuaded to hand over property to another. Thus there appears to be a considerable overlap between this offence and obtaining property by deception contrary to section 15 of the Theft Act 1968. *Some* overlap is desirable. Two mutually exclusive offences would be excessively inconvenient, because many transactions involve both materials and services: the trickster who obtains bed and breakfast by deception would have to be charged under section 15 of the Theft Act 1968 for the breakfast and under section 1 of the Theft Act 1978 for the bed, and the man who by deception gets a silicone damp-course injected into the walls of his house would be guaranteed an appeal to the House of Lords, whichever offence he were charged with! If *any* transfer of property counts as 'conferring a benefit by doing some act' and hence performing services, so that any contravention of section 15 of the Theft Act 1968 is automatically a breach of section 1 of the Theft Act 1978 as well, no great injustice would result, since section 1 carries only half the punishment available under section 15. However, an offence of obtaining services by deception that also included all cases of obtaining property by deception would be unsightly. This result can be avoided if subsection (2) is interpreted as *limiting*, but not extending, the word 'services' in subsection (1) On this view, conduct would only amount to 'services' if it could fairly be described as 'services' in normal speech. The new offence would then cover obtaining property by deception where work was provided as well, but not obtaining property pure and simple.

'…*on the understanding that the benefit has been or will be paid for*'

This phrase imposes an important limitation on what conduct conferring a benefit amounts to 'services' within the section. If P's intention were to do something for D free of charge, then, notwithstanding the fact that D might in everyday language be said to have dishonestly obtained services by deception, he has not in law committed the criminal offence. Thus if D gets P, his neighbour, to drive him to the station free of charge by telling him a lie about a dying relative that he has to visit, D would not contravene section 1 of the Theft Act 1978. It would be no different even if P were a taxi-driver who normally charges his passengers, but was induced to make an exception in this case—though here there would appear to be an offence under section 2(1)(c) of this Act.

The range of dishonesty which this limitation leaves unpunished depends on when a benefit is 'paid for'. At its narrowest, a benefit would only be 'paid for' when a specific fee was paid in respect of a specific benefit. Thus where a motorist paid an annual fee to the Automobile Association for example, and was then entitled to the 'free' use of their breakdown service if he needed it, the benefit would not on this view be 'paid for'. On a broader view of 'paid for', however, this sort of indirect payment would be sufficient. It is to be hoped that the broader view will be adopted.

It is sufficient if P believes either that he will be paid, or that he *has been paid*. Thus provision is made for the man who gets into a rugby international by lying that he has lost his ticket.

A benefit counts as services if it is conferred 'on the understanding' that it has been or will be paid for, not 'on the *mis*understanding'. The phrase occurs, be it noted, in the definition of what amounts to 'obtaining services' not in a limitation of what sort of deception is necessary to commit the offence. Thus, unless the courts are willing to read in words in favour of the accused, the offence does not require D's deception to be as to payment. So D commits an offence if, on payment of the appropriate fee, he obtains a service available only to a member of a restricted group to which he falsely pretends to belong: if he gets the use of a bed in a YHA hostel on payment, for example, having pretended to be a YHA member; or if he impersonates a member of a trade association in order to obtain, on payment, confidential information about debtors available only to members.

It appears to be enough that P should understand that the benefit has been or will be paid for. It does not seem to be necessary for P to believe that D can be, or could have been, legally made to pay. Thus an offence appears to be committed even where D tricks P into performing an unlawful act for him, as long as P understands that he has been or will be paid. So the man who induces a prostitute to have intercourse with him on a false promise of payment seems to be guilty of obtaining services by deception.

Notes and questions

1. In *Widdowson* (1986) 82 Cr App R 314, CA, it was said, obiter, that the obtaining of goods on hire purchase could amount to an obtaining of services since a benefit (the delivery of possession of the goods to the hirer) is conferred on the hirer on the understanding that the hirer had or would pay the deposit and instalments. Suppose D by deception (say the presentation of a cheque that D knows will be dishonoured) induces V to hire a car to D. All V does is to hand the car keys to D so that D can take the car from the premises. Is handing over the car keys a 'service'? If it is a service, is it a service given on the understanding that it has been or will be 'paid for'? When the hirer uses the car this is undoubtedly a benefit to him given on the understanding that it has or will be paid for. Is V's provision of the use of the car a 'service'?

2. Does a rogue who commits the offence of obtaining property by deception contrary to s 15 of the 1968 Act inevitably commit the offence of obtaining services by deception? Does not the victim invariably deliver property (a service?) to the rogue or allow the rogue to take possession (a service?) of it?

3. Section 1(3) was inserted by the Theft (Amendment) Act 1996 to reverse the effect of *Halai* [1983] Crim LR 624 which decided that a mortgage advance is not 'services', apparently because it is a lending of money for property, which would be an offence under s 15 of the 1968 Act. *Halai* was heavily criticized and was distinguished in *Widdowson* [1986] RTR 124 where the court said that an agreement to let on hire purchase would be a service. The new subsection does not apply to anything done before 18 December 1996, but in *Cooke* [1997] Crim LR 436 the Court of Appeal held that *Halai* was wrongly decided and had never been the law. Later, however, in *Naviede* [1997] Crim LR 662 *Halai* was merely distinguished, implying that it remains law for events before 18 December 1996. Probably the better view is that it was wrongly decided. The result is that the offence heavily overlaps other Theft Acts offences, but that is the effect of the section properly construed.

Sofroniou
[2004] Crim LR 381, [2003] EWCA Crim 3681, Court of Appeal, Criminal Division

(May LJ, Mckinnon J and HH Judge Jeremy Roberts QC)

May LJ. S used a false identity to deceive or attempt to deceive banks into providing him with banking services and credit cards. There was no charge for opening the bank accounts or issuing the cards. S overdrew on one account and exceeded the limit on one credit card. He was convicted under s 1, and appealed on the basis that there was no evidence that the 'benefit' would be paid for. The Court of Appeal dismissed the appeal acknowledging that the ambit of the necessary understanding as to payment for services was problematic.

This appeal raises difficult issues relating to the extent to which banking and credit card services are 'services' within s 1 of the 1978 Act; what amounts to obtaining those services; and what is the ambit of the words 'on the understanding that the benefit has been or will be paid for' in s 1(2). In form, the definition of 'an obtaining of services' in section 1(2) is composite. But there are two parts to the definition comprised in the words (1) 'where the other is induced to confer a benefit by doing some act, or causing or permitting some act to be done', and (2) 'on the understanding that the benefit has been or will be paid for'. The concept of services is in the first of these. An understanding as to payment is also necessary, but only indirectly affects the question whether what is obtained constitutes services. It is to be supposed that obtaining services is to be contrasted with obtaining property. In ordinary use, 'services' has a wide range of meaning. Inducing someone to confer a benefit is also capable of wide application.

... The decision in *Halai* that a mortgage advance was not a service was widely regarded as wrong (see *Preddy* at 839G and *R v Graham* [1997] 1 Cr App R 302 at 315E to 317C.) It had become a 'sunken wreck, impeding navigation but difficult, laborious and expensive to remove'—see *Graham* at 317A. Section 1(3) of the 1978 Act now provides that inducing a bank or building society to make a loan, or to cause or permit a loan to be made, constitutes the obtaining of services within the section. It also provides that an understanding that any payment, by way of interest or otherwise, will be or has been made in respect of the loan is sufficient for the purposes of sub-section (2).

The appellant no longer pursues his appeal against his conviction on count 3. This charged him with dishonestly obtaining services from American Express. He used a false identity to obtain a credit card with a £2000 limit. He completed and sent application documents to the bank. He subsequently used the card that was issued to him. There was evidence that the agreement with American Express provided for an annual charge of £12. Mr Cousens accepted that these facts constituted obtaining services by deception within section 1 of the 1978 Act. He accepted that the obtaining of a credit card by deception constituted obtaining services within the section. We consider that he was correct to do so. Obtaining a credit card comprises obtaining access to the familiar structure of services which a credit card supports. The card itself is not a service or services. The services are those which underlie the card holder's use of the card. Mr Cousens also accepted that the stipulation as to payment established by the evidence satisfied the statutory requirement that the person providing the services should be induced to confer a benefit on the understanding that the benefit had been or would be paid for.

Mr Cousens accepted by extension that the opening of a bank account, where this is obtained by deception, could constitute obtaining services by deception. In so far as this is an acceptance that the second limb of *Halai* has not survived the amendment to section 1 of the 1978 Act, we think this is correct. The second limb included that inducing the opening of a savings account did not constitute the offence within the unamended section. Opening a bank account comprises obtaining access to the familiar structure of services which the retail banking system supports. But Mr Cousens submits that it would be necessary for the prosecution also to establish positively that the account was opened upon an understanding or agreement that the account holder would make some payment to the bank for the services obtained. If the prosecution did not positively establish this, the statutory offence was not made out.

Mr Cousens submitted that, once a bank account or credit card has been initially obtained, different considerations apply for each of them. He accepted that the dishonest use of a credit card would be capable of being the obtaining of services within the section, provided that the necessary understanding as to payment was also established. He did not, however, accept that the continuing dishonest use of a bank account, once it had been opened, constituted obtaining services by deception. The obtaining of the services comprising the ability to use the bank account occurred when the account was opened. The subsequent operation of the account did not constitute obtaining services within the section. The obtaining of a loan to be credited to the bank account could, however, come within the section, if the requisite understanding as to payment were also established. These are fine and troublesome distinctions. If they are correct, they would require intellectual gymnastics by judges and juries which a workable criminal justice structure could well do without. We do not see any substantial difference, in the context of obtaining services by deception, between the dishonest use of a credit card and the dishonest operation of a bank account. To be fair, we did not understand Mr Cousens to have been consistent in his oral submissions in maintaining this distinction.

When the appeal in *Preddy* came before the House of Lords, the appellate committee was invited to hear argument, in the light of the by then discredited (but not overruled) decision of this court in *Halai*, as to the proper ambit of section 1 of the 1978 Act in its then unamended form. The House declined to make any ruling, but Lord Goff of Chieveley rehearsed the strong academic and judicial criticisms of *Halai*. He epitomised these criticisms as founded essentially upon sub-section (2) of section 1 of the 1978 Act. It was said that, in the context of obtaining mortgage advances from building societies, the 'act' is the making of the advance, and that that act is plainly to be paid for because interest is to be charged for the advance. Lord Goff then said at page 840B:

> 'There is considerable force in this criticism; and certainly, if accepted, it would close a manifest gap in our criminal law. I feel bound to comment however, that, although a wide definition of "services" appears to have been intended (see Professor Smith's *The Law of Theft*, 7th ed., p 112), nevertheless if sub-section (2) were to be construed in the literal manner which is understandably urged upon us in the literature on the subject, it would follow that the ambit of section 1 of the Act of 1978 would be remarkably wide. It would stretch far beyond what is ordinarily included in the notion of services as generally understood. In particular, although we have become used to the expression "financial services" as describing a range of services available for those involved in that service industry, it is not altogether natural to think of the simple making of a loan upon interest as itself constituting a service. Moreover on this approach it is, I suppose, arguable that, for example, the supply of goods (at an underpayment) or procuring the execution of a valuable security might also fall within this section, which could lead to an overlap between the section and sections 15(1) and 20(2) of the Act of 1968. The effect is that section 1 of the Act of 1978 is exposed to some of the criticisms which led to the rejection of clause 12(3) of the Criminal Law Revision Committee's original Bill (Eighth Report: Theft and Related Offences (Cmnd. 2977)), though its scope is restricted by the requirement that the relevant benefit should be conferred on the understanding that it has been or will be paid for.'

The subsequent addition of sub-section (3) to section 1 of the 1978 Act, in our judgment, justifies a modification to Lord Goff's caution as to the ambit of 'services'. Parliament was persuaded that dishonestly inducing a bank or building society to make a loan, on the understanding that interest or other payment would be made in respect of it, should constitute obtaining services within the section. In our judgment, there should no longer be any doubt but that dishonestly inducing a bank or building society to provide banking or credit card services is also within the section, provided the requirement as to payment is also satisfied. We consider that Mr Cousens is right to accept that inducing a bank or building society to open an account constitutes obtaining services; and that inducing a bank or other organisation to issue a credit card constitutes obtaining services. We also consider that the dishonest operation of a bank or building society account over a period and a dishonest use of a credit card over a period constitutes obtaining services within the section. We reach this conclusion, having due regard to Lord Goff's caution as to the width of the section and its possible overlap with other provisions of the 1968 Act, but seeing no proper distinction between the opening of a bank account and its subsequent operation. What the bank provides in each instance is the benefit of their participation in the banking system which can in our judgment properly be described as a service or services. We do not need to decide for the purposes of the present appeal whether dishonestly inducing a bank to negotiate a single cheque or the dishonest use of a credit card on a single occasion would constitute obtaining services within the section. Mr Cousens was inclined to concede that it would and we can see that logically it might, given our earlier decisions. But we do not so decide and do not encourage prosecutors to bring proceedings on this basis. For facts such as these, it should usually be possible, depending on the facts, to formulate a more appropriate charge under one of the related sections of the 1968 Act.

Since we consider that the dishonest operation of a bank or building society account over a period is capable, subject to the necessary understanding as to payment, of constituting dishonestly obtaining services by deception within the section, we also consider that the judge was correct to rule that this was capable of being a continuous offence encompassing the whole operation of the accounts...

The ambit of the necessary understanding as to payment is problematic. Mr Causer, for the prosecution, submits that the words 'on the understanding that the benefit has been or will be paid for' are only intended to limit the ambit of the section to commercial transactions. The section is not intended to encompass obtaining gratuitous services by deception. Banks and building societies are commercial organisations. They are not in business to provide gratuitous services and it may be assumed that, if a customer opens and operates an account, he will pay for the services so provided by some means. Banks habitually make charges for running their customers' accounts. They charge interest on overdrawn accounts. They often pay no interest on accounts which are in credit; or, if they do, the rate of interest is less than they themselves obtain on the same money in the market. Credit card providers sometimes make charges for operating the account, whether there is prompt repayment in full or not. American Express did this for count 3 of the present indictment. Credit card operators also charge interest, if the account is not paid in full after a stipulated short period. Even if a particular customer pays his credit card balance in full within the stipulated period, the card provider may still be taken to make a charge to the supplier of goods purchased by means of the card, so that the amount which the customer pays for the goods is greater than it would be if the credit card service were not provided.

Mr Causer further submits that the 'understanding' is that of the person providing the services, that is the bank or the credit card company, and that the understanding does not have to be mutual. Banks, building societies and credit card companies do operate on the understanding that their services are paid for by some means or other and that should be sufficient. Somewhere within the system there is a charge sufficient to comprise an understanding that the benefit has been or will be paid for.

Section 1(2) refers to an understanding, not an agreement. This is, we think, intended to cover situations where nothing explicitly is said about payment, but where there is a common understanding that the services will not be provided gratuitously. I can induce someone to mow my lawn on the understanding that he will do so for nothing: or the understanding may be that he will be paid. If, in the latter instance, I induce him to mow my lawn dishonestly by deception, as for instance by representing that I am able to pay him when I am not, I commit an offence within the section. This would be so even if there is no explicit articulation of the understanding as to payment.

We accept that in a subjective sense the understanding may not in truth be mutual. The section is concerned with dishonest deception and the deception may well relate to the deceiver's intention and ability to pay. A dishonest person may well not have a subjective intention or understanding that he will pay. But we do consider that the section envisages a putative objective mutual understanding as to payment on the assumption that the inducement was not dishonest. We consider that an understanding which is mutual in this sense is the natural meaning of the use of the word 'understanding' in its context. We also consider that payment has to be an identifiable payment or payments made or to be made by or on behalf of the person obtaining the services. We recognise that there are some indications in favour of a looser construction. The words in sub-section (2) 'has been or will be paid for' do not by themselves positively require that the payment has to be by or on behalf of the person obtaining the services. The words '*any* payment' and 'by way of interest *or otherwise*' in sub-section (3) are wide. But we consider that the general sense of the section is that the payment is to be made by or on behalf of the person obtaining the services. And we consider that the words in sub-section (3) 'on the understanding that any payment...will be or has been made in respect of the loan' positively connote payment by the borrower in respect of the loan. Just as we consider that the introduction of sub-section (3) clarified the ambit of 'services' beyond the specific instance of a loan; so we consider that the introduction of the sub-section clarified the meaning 'has been or will be paid for'.

This construction means that, in our judgment, an understanding as to payment under the section will not be satisfied unless there is an agreement or sufficient understanding that an identifiable payment or payments have been or will be made by or on behalf of the person receiving the services to the person providing them. Although it is a common understanding that banks often make charges on accounts which are in credit and charge interest on accounts which are overdrawn, this is not invariably so. Likewise, although it is common for credit card providers to make charges and to charge interest on debit balances which are not promptly paid, it is not to be assumed that every credit card provider makes a charge irrespective of when the balance is repaid; and many people are careful to pay off their balances promptly and thus avoid interest charges. It may therefore be possible to have the benefit of a credit card without ever making any identifiable direct payment to the credit card provider.

In *Shortland* [[1995] Crim LR 893], the appellant opened two bank accounts under an assumed name. There was no direct evidence of any understanding that the provision of banking services had been or would be paid for. The trial judge rejected a submission of no case to answer saying that it would be an affront to commonsense to think that banking services would be provided free of charge. He ruled that the jury could infer from the opening of the bank accounts that the benefit conferred would be paid for, and he directed them accordingly. This court allowed the appellant's appeal, holding that the matter should have been withdrawn from the jury. The inference which the jury were invited to draw was not something that they could conclude with any safety or satisfaction. Mr Causer points out that the Crown did not resist the appeal and that the decision was before the amendment introducing sub-section (3) to section 1 of the 1978 Act. As to the latter, we have explained our view that sub-section (3) clarifies the requirement as to payment in the way we have indicated. Professor Smith's commentary on *Shortland* states that what was missing in that case was any evidence as to the terms of the contract made when the appellant opened the account. These terms would probably have shown that the service was to be paid for but it was not possible to infer with the necessary degree of certainty that this was so from the mere fact of the opening of the account.

It might be possible to submit, from the brevity of the report and the fact that the Crown did not resist the appeal, that we are not strictly bound by the decision in *Shortland*. We consider on balance that we are bound by that decision, but in any event it accords with our view as to the construction of the section as amended. We do not consider that inferred indirect commercial advantages to a bank, building society or credit card provider are capable of providing the necessary ingredient as to payment. These will include the difference between interest paid by a bank to an account holder and interest earned by the bank on the same money; or a charge by the credit card provider to the seller of goods bought by means of a credit card. Nor can it be safely inferred from the mere opening of a bank account or the mere obtaining of a credit card that there will be charges. But the facts of the present appeal well illustrate circumstances in which a jury could surely infer the necessary understanding as to payment. The appellant was comprehensively dishonest. He intentionally used the bank accounts in counts 1 and 2 so that they became overdrawn. For count 1 he obtained a substantial loan. The services he obtained were not just the use of bank accounts, but of bank accounts which he dishonestly intended to overdraw. It was open to the jury to infer that the banks would charge interest on accounts overdrawn in this way. Although in different circumstances an inference that interest would be charged might not safely be drawn, it did not require direct evidence that banks invariably charge interest on substantial unauthorised overdrafts to draw such an inference in the present case. Such an inference would be a sufficient putative objective mutual understanding as to payment for the purposes of the offence charged in each of these counts. For counts 4 and 5, where the appellant was charged with attempting to open a bank account and with obtaining the shop card, it was open to the jury to infer from the evidence as a whole that the appellant's intention in each instance was to overdraw the accounts so that interest would be charged. Here again the inference was capable of supporting the necessary understanding as to payment.

Appeal dismissed

Notes and questions

1. In a case such as this has D obtained the cards from the bank by deception? Has D committed an offence under s16 of the 1968 Act?

2. Is having a bank account a 'benefit' to the account holder? Is that sufficient to trigger s 1?

3. Some years ago the press reported the case of an enterprising sixth form student who, lacking confidence in the education he was receiving at school A, acquired the uniform of students at school B and attended classes there. (i) Were the teachers at school B providing a 'service'? (ii) What if the teaching at school B had been even worse than the teaching at school A so that the enterprising student learned nothing from it; would the teaching at school B have conferred any benefit on the enterprising student? (iii) Would it make any difference that school B was a fee charging public school or a non-fee charging state school? (iv) Were the teachers at school B deceived if they were unaware that the enterprising student sitting quietly in the back row was not entitled to be there? (v) Was there any 'understanding' between the enterprising schoolboy and school B as to payment?

4. John Spencer in the extract given above says that 'the man who induces a prostitute to have intercourse with him on a false promise of payment seems to be guilty of obtaining services by deception'. Do you agree? Could this be held in law to be a 'benefit' to the user of the prostitute's services? Suppose that H hires V, giving in payment a cheque that H knows will not be honoured, to kill H's wife, W, and V does so. Has H obtained V's services by deception? Have V's services conferred a 'benefit' on H?

(6) EVASION OF LIABILITY

Theft Act 1978, s 2

(1) Subject to subsection (2) below, where a person by any deception:
   (a) dishonestly secures the remission of the whole or part of any existing liability to make a payment, whether his own liability or another's; or
   (b) with intent to make permanent default in whole or in part on any existing liability to make a payment, or with intent to let another do so, dishonestly induces the creditor or any person claiming payment on behalf of the creditor to wait for payment (whether or not the due date for payment is deferred) or to forgo payment; or
   (c) dishonestly obtains any exemption from or abatement of liability to make a payment; he shall be guilty of an offence.

(2) For purposes of this section 'liability' means legally enforceable liability; and subsection (1) shall not apply in relation to a liability that has not been accepted or established to pay compensation for a wrongful act or omission.

(3) For purposes of subsection (1)(b) a person induced to take in payment a cheque or other security for money by way of conditional satisfaction of a pre-existing liability is to be treated not as being paid but as being induced to wait for payment.

(4) For purposes of subsection (1)(c) 'obtains' includes obtaining for another or enabling another to obtain.

On conviction on indictment the offence is punishable with five years' imprisonment. The section is not as well drafted as it might be. In short:

Section 2(1)(a) is focused on remission of liability—that is, where V accepts that the liability ceases to exist. An example might be where D, having taken a taxi home, falsely tells the driver on arrival that he must have had his wallet stolen and that he has no money to pay. If the driver believes him and agrees to let him off the fare, D commits the para (1)(a) offence.

Section 2(1)(b) deals with forgoing or waiting for payment—that is, where V stops his present demands for payment of the liability, but the liability continues to exist. In the above example, if D had deceived the taxi driver by explaining that his wallet was stolen but that he would pay at the cab office the next day, secretly intending never to pay, he would commit the offence.

Section 2(1)(c)—this is significantly different since it deals with prospective liability.

CLRC, Thirteenth Report, paras 13–16

13. Clause 1 of the draft Bill at Annex 1 deals with the common frauds to which section 16(2)(a) applies where there is a deception at the outset of a transaction. In our Working Paper we suggested that part of the balance of section 16(2)(a) could be brought within the scope of an offence of obtaining relief from debt by deception and we suggested that this offence should be limited to cases where by deception a debtor obtains remission of the whole or part of any liability to make payment, including a liability that would be incurred but for the remission, and cases where there is an existing liability to make payment and the debtor by deception induces the creditor to wait for payment intending never to pay. When we subsequently worked on the detail of this proposal we found it convenient to divide this offence into three parts and to use 'liability' throughout rather than 'debt'. The resulting provision appears as clause 2 of our draft Bill. Subsection (1)(a) covers the deception which dishonestly secures the remission of the whole or part of an existing liability to make a payment. An example would be where a man borrows £100 from a neighbour and, when repayment is due, tells a false story of some family tragedy which makes it impossible for him to find the money; this deception persuades the neighbour to tell him that he need never repay the loan.

14. Clause 2(1)(b) is concerned with the stalling debtor. It provides that a creditor who by deception dishonestly induces his creditor to wait for payment or to forego payment is guilty of an offence if, and only if, he intends to make permanent default in whole or in part of his liability to pay. This final limitation makes the offence narrower than the corresponding offence in section 16(2)(a) for the reasons which have been given in paragraph 6 above. We recognise that the practical difficulties of proving an intention never to pay will have the consequence that there will be few prosecutions under this head, but this is consistent with our view that the criminal law should not apply to the debtor who is merely trying to delay making a payment. Sir Rupert Cross and Professor Williams are opposed to the inclusion of clause 2(1)(b) in the draft Bill. Professor Williams' views are set out in the Note at the end of this Report.

15. Clause 2(1)(c) is concerned with a type of fraud which can conveniently be brought within the scope of the offence of obtaining relief from liability by deception although it differs from the other cases covered by the offence in that it can include frauds where the offender has been acting dishonestly from the outset of the transaction. In paragraph 7 of Appendix 2 we note that certain enactments creating offences of fraudulently evading charges or obtaining allowances or relief were repealed by the Theft Act 1968 on the basis that the conduct at which they were aimed would involve offences under section 16. Clause 2(1)(c) will ensure that such conduct remains an offence. For there to be an offence under this provision there must be dishonesty and a deception which obtains any exemption from or abatement of liability to make a payment. To take an example, section 49(8) of the General Rate Act 1967 (one of the enactments repealed in 1968) provided a penalty for false statements made to obtain rate rebates. The ratepayer who makes a false statement in order to obtain a rebate to which he is not entitled is acting dishonestly and is practising a deception in order to obtain an abatement of his liability to pay rates and, accordingly, would be guilty of an offence under clause 2(1)(c). The wording of this provision, 'where a person by any deception...dishonestly obtains any exemption from or abatement of liability to make a payment' is intended to cover cases where the deception has induced the victim to believe that there is nothing due to him or that the amount due to him is less than would be the case if he knew the true facts. [It is the 'liability to make a payment' from which exemption (or of which abatement) is obtained and it is not necessary for there to be 'any existing liability' which is reduced or extinguished.] Another example of the application of this part of clause 2 is the case where a person by deception obtains services at a reduced rate (for example, air travel at a special rate for students when the traveller is not a student)....

16. Subsection (2) of clause 2 makes it clear that the clause does not apply in relation to a liability that has not been accepted or established to pay compensation for a wrongful act or omission. Without this provision there would be room for argument that subsection (1)(a) of the clause applies where, for example, a person lies about the circumstances of an accident in order to avoid the bringing of civil proceedings for negligence against him. We think that the dividing line is reached where liability is not disputed even though the amount of that liability is. On this basis it would be an offence under clause 2(1)(a) for an antique dealer to lie about the age and value of jewellery sent to him for valuation which had been lost as a result of his admitted negligence, but not for him to lie about the circumstances of the loss in disputing an allegation of negligence. We see no justification for extending the criminal law to cases where the existence of any liability is disputed: the claimant can launch civil proceedings if he thinks he had been deceived when he absolved the other from liability.

Notes and questions

1. At the end of para 13 the CLRC gives an example of the operation of s 2(1)(a). In such a case D does not secure the 'remission' of an existing liability to make a payment if remission means the extinction in law of the debt. In civil law D continues to owe his neighbour £100 and the neighbour would no doubt enforce that liability once he becomes aware of the fraud so how can it be said that D has secured the remission of an existing liability? E. Griew, however, argues (*The Theft Acts*, paras 10–11) that, 'It must be immaterial that the creditor's agreement is not binding on him, because it was obtained by fraud and that the debtor whose fraud is uncovered may in the result...gain temporary relief only'. The same issue arises in connection with s 2(1)(c) in that there would in law be no exemption from the prospective liability. The Court of Appeal had the opportunity to consider these problems in *Dawson* [2001] EWCA Crim 1554 where D had secured the agreement of his creditors by entering into an individual voluntary agreement (IVA). It was argued that the creditors' agreement to the IVA when it was proposed by D had removed any existing liability so that by the time Vs were finally induced to agree to it in its final form (by D's deception), there was no enforceable liability. The court sidestepped the issue by concluding that by reference to the obligations imposed under the Insolvency Act, s 264 and s 276, an existing liability remained at the time of the final IVA and that a charge under s 2(1)(b) was appropriate.

2. The operation of s 2(1)(b) may be illustrated by reference to the facts of *DPP v Turner* [1974] AC 357, [1973] 3 All ER 124, HL. D, who owed V some £38 for work done and was being pressed for payment, told V that he had no ready cash and persuaded V to accept a cheque knowing that it would be dishonoured. Such conduct falls within s 2(1)(b) if, and only if, D intends to make permanent default. If, as seemed likely in *Turner*, D simply wanted to give himself a breathing space, and was bent on settling the debt at a later stage, he would not commit the offence.

3. Is the offence objectionable in terms of its criminalization of debtors?

4. Does D commit an offence, and if so under which provision relating to deception, in the following circumstances? T bought a tractor. He financed the purchase by a conditional sale agreement with the H Finance Co. Later, with the concurrence of H, T agreed to sell the tractor to Gee for £9,500. Gee gave T a banker's draft for £2,825 and agreed to pay H the remaining charge of £8,090. T gave Gee a receipt for the full amount. Gee did not pay H. When H approached him, he said that he had paid the full amount to T and produced the receipt. He was charged under s 2(1)(b) with inducing H to wait for payment by falsely representing that his liability had been discharged. His conviction was quashed. H was 'not the creditor or any person claiming payment on behalf of the creditor,' the prescribed victim of this offence. H, not being a party to the contract between T and Gee had no legal right against Gee that the money should be paid to him: *Gee* [1999] Crim LR 397. Since the Contracts (Rights of Third Parties) Act 1999 came into force, it might be different. Cf *Floyd v DPP*, above, p 783.

5. The offences created by s 2 of the 1978 Act have been heavily criticised as ambiguous, confusing and overlapping. Consider whether subsection (1) could be adequately replaced by a much simpler provision:

'A person is guilty of an offence where, by any deception, he dishonestly induces another to agree—
  (i) to remit the whole or part of any existing or future liability to make a payment (whether his own liability or another's), or
  (ii) to defer payment of any such liability, intending never to pay.'
    See J. C. Smith, 'Reforming the Law of Theft', (1996) 28 Bracton LJ 27.

4. FRAUD REFORM PROPOSALS

The Government proposals for change are based mainly on the Law Commission Report, *Fraud*, published in 2002 (Cm 5560).

Part III The need for simplification and rationalization (footnote references omitted)

3.10 At present, there is a multitude of overlapping but distinct statutory offences which can be employed in fraud trials. As Griew noted: No one wanting to construct a rational, efficient law of criminal fraud would choose to start from the present position. The law … is in a very untidy and unsatisfactory condition. The various offences are not so framed and related to each other as to cover, in a clearly organised way and without doubt or strained interpretation, the range of conduct with which the law should be able to deal.

3.11 Arguably, the law of fraud is suffering from an 'undue particularisation of closely allied crimes'. Over-particularisation or 'untidiness' is undesirable in itself, but it also has undesirable consequences.

3.12 First, it allows technical arguments to prosper. When the original Theft Act deception offences were first proposed by the CLRC in their Eighth Report, this problem was foreseen by a minority of the committee members: To list and define the different objects which persons who practise deception aim at achieving is unsatisfactory and dangerous, because it is impossible to be certain that any list would be complete. Technical distinctions would also inevitably be drawn—as they have been drawn under [the Larceny Act] 1916 s 32—between conduct which did and which did not fall within the list. …

3.20 The second difficulty that arises from over-particularisation is that a defendant may face the wrong charge, or too many charges.…

3.23 We do not argue that all the Theft Act offences could or should be combined into one. The fewer there are, however, the easier it is for prosecutors to choose the right one, thus decreasing the likelihood of mistakes. At present, in order to avoid mistakes, prosecutors may take the 'belt and braces' approach.…

3.24 The over-particularisation of fraud offences can result in indictments made complex by the charging of alternative offences. A clearer, simpler law of fraud would make it easier for prosecutors to pursue one correct charge, which in turn would give fraud trials greater focus and structure.

The Home Office consultation paper (below) sets out the Law Commission's proposals and further policy questions. The main proposal is for a general offence toward fraud which can be committed in three different ways by: false representation; wrongfully failing to disclose information; abuse of office. In each case the behaviour must be dishonest, and must aim at securing a gain for the defendant or a loss for another. The gain does not actually have to take place, which changes existing statutory offences.

Home Office Consultation Paper on Fraud (2004)

2. The statutory offences are specific and overlapping, yet are not related to each other to cover the variety of fraudulent behaviour in an organised way. This state of untidiness in the law allows technical arguments to prosper. It is not always clear which offence should be charged, and defendants have successfully argued that the consequences of their particular deceptive behaviour did not fit the definition of the offence with which they had been charged. A general offence of fraud will benefit juries by making fraud law easier to understand. This could prove particularly beneficial in complex and serious fraud cases.…

5 .…the current statutory offences are highly specific and fail to define what 'fraud' actually means, whereas 'conspiracy to defraud' is so wide that it provides little guidance on the difference between lawful and fraudulent conduct. This makes fraud cases extremely difficult for juries. Repealing the current statutory and common law offences, and replacing them with a general offence of fraud will benefit juries by making fraud law easier to understand. This could prove particularly beneficial in complex and serious fraud cases.

6. It is not a realistic solution to continue plugging loopholes in fraud law by the addition of more specific offences. Not only does this piecemeal law reform lead to further complexities and potential

for charging defendants wrongly, but it means that the law will always be lagging behind any developments in technology or new methods of committing fraud.

Background to the reform

7. In 1999 the Law Commission issued a consultation paper (No 155), which distinguished between two forms of a general offence of fraud: one based on dishonesty, and the other based on deception. It concluded that while the concerns expressed about existing law were valid they could be met by extending the existing (deception based) offences in preference to creating a single offence of fraud.

8. The Commission reconsidered their conclusions in the light of reactions to the 1999 paper and their criminal law team issued an informal discussion paper in 2000. This paper accepted the view of respondents that the requirement of dishonesty should be retained and proposed the introduction of a general offence which would cover the infliction, by a false pretence, of any kind of financial loss and the making, by deception, of any financial gain. The paper suggested that it was desirable to shift the focus to the behaviour of the defendant (who makes a false pretence) rather than the mind of the victim (who may, or may not, be 'deceived' by the pretence).

9. Responses to this paper suggested that the element of pretence (or misrepresentation) was not essential to constitute a fraud. For example if an employee misuses company information to steal money from his employers, without making a misrepresentation (for example by altering or falsifying accounts) his behaviour can still be described as fraud. The Commission accepted this argument and misrepresentation will be one, but only one, of the 3 ways in which the proposed new fraud offence can be committed. Dishonesty, however, is a requirement for all 3.

10. The test of dishonesty was established in the case of Ghosh ([1982] QB 1053). Fact finders have first to decide whether the behaviour of the defendant was dishonest according to the ordinary standards of reasonable, honest people. If the answer is yes, then they have then to decide whether the defendant realised that it was dishonest according to those standards (as opposed to his or her own standards). It is a useful test, but if the offence of fraud were to be constituted solely by this test, then legitimate activity could become fraudulent if the jury is prepared to define it as dishonest. Different juries could also potentially draw different conclusions on similar types of behaviour, leading to a lack of consistency in convictions. We agree with the Law Commission that dishonesty is a necessary, though not sufficient, ingredient of any fraud.

The Law Commission's proposals

11. The Law Commission's final report was published in 2002. It contained a draft Bill (at pages 95—106 of Cm 5560) and references in this paper to clauses are to that Bill. This report will form the basis of the Government's Bill. The full report, and the draft Bill, are available on the Law Commission website at http://www.lawcom.gov.uk

12. As mentioned above, dishonesty is not sufficient in itself to define the crime. Fraud cannot be defined as dishonest conduct which causes loss, as that would cover, for example, shoplifting and burglary. We thus propose to create a general offence of fraud, with 3 different ways of committing it. A person will be guilty of the general offence if he is dishonest and either: (1) makes a false representation; or (2) wrongfully fails to disclose information; or (3) secretly abuses a position of trust. In each case the act must be done with the intention of making a gain or causing loss or risk of loss to another. In contrast to the existing statutory offences, the gain or loss does not actually have to take place. (Though investigators will need to establish the level of the gain or loss, whether actual or potential, in each case, as that is relevant to mode of trial and to sentencing.) The maximum sentence for the new offence would be 10 years, as for the main existing offences in the Theft Act 1968 and for conspiracy to defraud. This new general offence of fraud does not focus upon very specific acts as

previous fraud statutes have done, rather it defines three broad ways in which fraud can be committed. The aim is to encompass the full variety of fraudulent behaviour, and that the offence should continue to be relevant as methods of committing crime and technology change and develop.

Fraud by false representation

13. False representation (or fraudulent misrepresentation) is a well-established concept in law. It consists of the assertion of a proposition which is wrong or misleading. The person making this assertion must know that it is wrong or misleading, or be aware that it might be. This proposition can be clearly stated, implied in written or spoken word, or in non-verbal conduct. The proposition may be one of fact or law. It may be as to the current intentions or other state of mind of the defendant or any other person.

14. There are distinct similarities between fraud by false representation and deception. Both involve behaviour that is carried out dishonestly and causes a financial loss, and obviously constitute one of the ways that fraud can be committed. However, in certain examples of this offence, false representation is a more appropriate description than deception.

15. The current concept of deception implies that the victim believes the truth of the assertion made by the defendant. However in cases where a false representation is made to a shop assistant (for example by using a credit card or debit cards without authorisation), it is not always the case that the person accepting the payment needs to believe the truth of the representation. By using the card, the defendant is falsely representing that he has the authority to use the card for that transaction. But the shop assistant who accepts the card for payment is not necessarily interested in whether the defendant has authority to use it—he may only be concerned that the payment is cleared. Therefore we cannot say that he has actually been deceived if the defendant has no authority. False representation would be a more accurate way to describe this form of conduct: the customer who offers the card is implying that he has the authority to use it.

16. For a representation to be false, the Law Commission propose that the defendant should know that the representation is untrue or misleading or be 'aware that it might be'. While this phrase may be unusual in criminal law, we believe that it fits the policy need: it can be difficult to prove that a fraudster knows in advance that his claims for any particular scheme (eg a 'High Yield Investment') are untrue, whilst it should be possible to show that he was 'aware that' his prospectus 'might' be untrue, by—for example—providing evidence of previous failures.

17. An alternative approach is provided by section 15(4) of the Theft Act 1968, which provides that a deception must be 'deliberate or reckless'. Recklessness is a concept wellrecognised and accepted in criminal law. (Clearly this would be so-called *Cunningham* recklessness, where the defendant must foresee a risk and unreasonably go on to take that risk). However, the addition of a 'recklessness' criterion might prove troublesome. The Law Commission argued in their report that it was preferable to avoid the use of 'reckless' as it is 'somewhat problematic,' in view of the different meanings it can have.

Fraud by wrongfully failing to disclose information

18. Fraudulent conduct can arise as a result of positive steps being taken to create a false impression. However, a false impression can also be created by the failure to challenge or dispute such an impression arising naturally, or through failure to reveal information. Non-disclosure can constitute deception, particularly where there is a legal duty to disclose.

19. In their 1999 Consultation Paper, the Law Commission suggested that omission should not be enough to constitute deception. It was argued against this that, from the victim's point of view, a failure to reveal facts could have the same essential effect as deception by conduct. The Law

Commission accordingly redefined their position to state that the concept of fraud should be wide enough to include cases of dishonest nondisclosure and we agree with this view.

20. The legislation will make clear that there are two cases where dishonest non-disclosure of information would qualify as fraud. The first is when there is a legal duty to disclose. This may be a legal duty in statute, from a contract, from express or implied terms of a contract, from custom of a particular trade or market, or from the existence of a fiduciary relationship between the parties. In the second case, there is no legal duty to disclose but there are 3 conditions which must be satisfied:
  • the information is of a kind which the person trusts the defendant to disclose to him;
  • the defendant knows the other person is trusting him to disclose information or is 'aware that he might be'; and
  • any reasonable person would expect the defendant to disclose the information to the other person.

21. While the first case, where there is a legal duty, is relatively uncomplicated, we recognise that there could be concern about the scope of the second case. No offence is committed, in either case, unless the requirement of dishonesty is also fulfilled. However, where there is no legal duty, much will depend on the facts of each situation and so much will be left to the discretion of the jury. Take for example the situation where a householder papers over a crack in a lintel and later sells the house without mentioning this. If it was a minor crack, and the house was sold 2 years later we do not think this particular case would fall within the new offence as there is no duty to disclose and no reasonable person would expect disclosure. But it does very much depend on the detail: a major crack, papered over just prior to sale, might be a different issue. A lot of weight is placed on the jury's interpretation of 'trust' and 'what any reasonable person would expect'.

22. Another example of this second case is where an antique dealer calls on vulnerable elderly people and buys their valuable furniture at exceptionally low prices. He makes no misrepresentation regarding the true value of the items, and has no legal duty to disclose what that might be. However it is clear that he has a moral duty to do so. The Law Commission believes that if his failure to disclose is regarded by fact-finders as dishonest, than he should be guilty of fraud. Again, much depends on the circumstances of each case.

Fraud by abuse of position

23. Some types of behaviour amount to fraud as they are essentially an abuse of an existing position of trust. The necessary situation for an offence of this type to take place is where the victim has put the perpetrator into a privileged position where he would be expected to safeguard the victim's interests (for example he has been given access to the victim's premises, equipment, records or customers). The defendant does not need to induce the victim to any further action (either by misrepresentation or non-disclosure) because his co-operation has already been secured.

24. The type of relationships that may give rise to this situation are those between employer and employee, trustee and beneficiary, director and company, professional person and client, agent and principal, and between 2 partners. This type of offence is also possible within family relationships or the context of voluntary work. In almost all cases the relationship will involve fiduciary duties, however these duties are not essential to the commission of the offence. The judge will be able to rule, or give directions to the jury, as to whether an appropriate relationship existed between victim and defendant.

25. An example of this type of fraudulent conduct is where a bar manager uses the premises of the establishment where he works to sell barrels of his own beer, rather than the beer belonging to the landlord. Abuse of position can also be committed by omission. An example given by the Law Commission is that of an employee who fails to take up the opportunity of a crucial contract, in order that an associate of his can take it up instead (to the detriment of the employer).

26. As with other types of fraud, this offence always requires proof of dishonesty. However, dishonest abuse of position alone is not enough to constitute fraudulent behaviour. The Law Commission proposes that there should also be an element of secrecy—the victim must be unaware of what is happening. If the victim is aware of the abuse, then the action cannot rightly be described as fraud, though it may be theft.

27. It is possible that the defendant may intend to disclose his action in the future. If this is the case then the activity cannot necessarily be construed as fraudulent. However there are difficulties in defining the limits of this. If the defendant intends to disclose the information as soon as possible, then the conduct should not be described as fraudulent. However if he intends to disclose after a considerable time period, for example once the action is completed and the victim can no longer influence the outcome, then the activity could be considered fraud.

28. It is very difficult to formulate a set of criteria flexible enough to fit this variety of situations. The Law Commission recommend that, with one exception, the abuse of position must occur without the victim's knowledge. The exception is where the perpetrator believes that the victim is unaware of the abuse. The fact he may be wrong in his belief should not excuse his conduct.

29. The requirement of secrecy can give rise to difficulties of interpretation, and hence legal argument, and we would be glad to have views on this. There is one respect in which we think the Law Commission Bill requires modification. 'Secretly' is defined, in Clause 4 (2), as where the offender believes that the person (P) whose interests he is meant to be safeguarding, *and any person acting on P's behalf*, is ignorant of the abuse. But an abuse of position may be carried out with the knowledge of subordinates who fear the consequences of complaining—and these subordinates might arguably be 'acting on P's behalf'. We think that amendment of this particular provision is therefore necessary. A solution might be to state that the abuse is secret if the defendant believes that P is ignorant of it *and/or if he believes that the only people who act for P who know about it are not in a position to withhold authorisation or countermand his abuse*. That should ensure that an offence is committed if a subordinate knows about the abuse but fears the consequences of complaining to the boss.

30. The Law Commission propose to define 'gain' and 'loss' in the same way as in the Theft Act 1968 (sections 4 and 34). We agree that it is right to align the definitions used for theft and fraud in this way. ...

31. Gain and loss, as for the law of theft, refer only to money and other property (real or personal). An example of a case that cannot be prosecuted at present, or under the Bill, is the fraudulent obtaining of answers to exam papers. There may be a case for devising a new definition of property to cover all obtaining and manipulation of data for gain. However there are different views on this: most confidential information is stored on computers, so that unauthorised access would give rise to offences under the Computer Misuse Act 1990, whilst lawful access for an improper use is a matter rightly left to civil law. In our view changing the definition of property for fraud would also require re-examination of the definition for theft. If we do so we doubt that this exercise will remain manageable.

Obtaining services dishonestly

32. We also propose to create a specific offence of obtaining services dishonestly. Deception is not a condition for committing this offence. This provision would replace section 1 of the Theft Act 1978 (obtaining services by deception). The 1978 Act provision proved necessary because the 1968 Act definition of property does not include services, so that no fraud or theft offence might be committed when services are obtained. However the 1978 provision has not proved sufficient and the Law Commission set out in their report 4 cases in which services can be obtained without deceiving a person.

33. One of these cases is where services are obtained from a machine—and no deception has taken place, as a machine cannot be deceived. This behaviour might also be caught by the new

offence of false representation, but we believe that nevertheless we need a new offence of obtaining services, because services could be obtained by other means than by deceiving machines. An example of this, which is certainly not caught by the new general fraud offence, is where someone helps himself to a service—e.g. a spectator who leaps over a wall and sees a football match for free.

34. The proposed new offence of obtaining services dishonestly is a 'theft-like' offence: the benefit has to be obtained, and that is, and should be, the substantive point of the offence. So perhaps it is easiest to see this as a 'theft of services' offence, which is not necessary for other types of property, as they are all dealt with adequately by the law of theft already.

35. The defendant must either know that the services are made available on the basis that they are chargeable, or be 'aware that they might be'. It can be argued that when certain services are obtained (e.g. over the Internet) the position regarding payment may be very unclear. So, it might be preferable to require that the defendant knows that payment should be made, rather than just being 'aware that it might be'. On the other hand the element of dishonesty will always need to be proved. The maximum sentence will be 5 years.

Notes and questions

1. Consider how much easier it would be to prosecute cases such as *Charles* and *Lambie* under the proposed new offence of false representation.

2. Is it possible to define with certainty when a sufficient relationship of trust exists for the proposed new offence of failing to disclose information? Should the householder papering over the crack in the wall be guilty of an offence—in all cases or only where the crack is a large one and the sale is imminent? Is the offence being made to turn on questions of fact alone?

3. Do the offences depend too heavily on the element of dishonesty? (see Ch **21** above).

FURTHER READING

D. C. ORMEROD, 'A Bit of A Con: The Law Commission's Proposals on Fraud' [1999] Crim LR 789

A. T. H. SMITH, 'The Idea of Criminal Deception' [1982] Crim LR 721

J. C. SMITH, 'Obtaining Cheques by Deception or Theft' [1997] Crim LR 396

23

Making off without payment

Theft Act 1978, s 3

(1) Subject to sub-section (3) below, a person who, knowing that payment on the spot for any goods supplied or service done is required or expected from him, dishonestly makes off without having paid as required or expected and with intent to avoid payment of the amount due shall be guilty of an offence.

(2) For purposes of this section 'payment on the spot' includes payment at the time of collecting goods on which work has been done or in respect of which service has been provided.

(3) Sub-section (1) above shall not apply where the supply of the goods or the doing of the service is contrary to law, or where the service done is such that payment is not legally enforceable.

(4) Any person may arrest without warrant anyone who is, or whom he, with reasonable cause, suspects to be, committing or attempting to commit an offence under this section.

On conviction on indictment the offence is punishable with two years' imprisonment.

CLRC, Thirteenth Report, paras. 19–21

18. In our Working Paper we discussed *DPP v Ray* [[1973] 3 All ER 131, [1974] AC 370]. The facts were that the defendant ordered a meal in a restaurant and after he had eaten it waited until the waiter went out into the kitchen before running out of the restaurant without paying his bill. The magistrates' court found that when the defendant ordered the meal he intended to pay for it and that his conduct in remaining seated at the table after he had finished eating amounted to a deception which obtained for him the opportunity of evading his liability by running out of the restaurant. If the defendant had entered the restaurant with the intention of not paying for his meal he would have been guilty of an offence under section 15, and in our Working Paper we asked whether that section is, in practice, an adequate weapon to use against restaurant bilking and similar frauds or whether there are sufficient cases where the accused claims an original innocent intention to make it necessary to consider creating a new offence. We explained that any new offence should not be an offence of deception, because the mischief would have been as great in *DPP v Ray* if the diner had run out of the restaurant immediately he decided not to pay the bill; and we commented that it must be very rare to be able to allege any deception of the waiter. The comments which we received from those with practical experience of the conduct of prosecutions showed that there were many cases in which the accused claimed an original innocent intention; and there was general support for our suggestion that where the customer knows that he is expected to pay on the spot for goods supplied to him or services done for him it should be an offence for him dishonestly to go away without having paid and intending never to pay. We have developed this proposal into clause 3 of our draft Bill and have given the offence the label 'making off without payment'.

19. The proposed new offence is confined to circumstances where goods are supplied or a service is done on the basis that payment will be made there and then. The obvious example is the restaurant

where everyone knows that the meal is supplied on the understanding that the bill will be paid before the diner leaves the restaurant. The clause also covers hotel bills which the traveller is expected to pay before he leaves. The clause will equally apply to bills for board and lodging alone, in boarding houses or elsewhere, where the arrangements are such that payment on the spot is required. It will not apply where there is a lease of premises because the lease will not require the tenant to pay the rent on the premises when it is due and before he goes away from them. In the discussion of this proposal in our Working Paper we commented that it could be represented as producing a risk that the threat of prosecution would be used by the creditors to enforce their claims, in particular where lodgers leave their lodgings without paying the outstanding rent. Comments on our proposal made it clear that there is a need for an offence to deal with the dishonest guest who leaves an hotel without paying his bill but who cannot be proved to have practised any deception on the hotel management. We have found it impossible to devise a satisfactory limitation on the scope of the offence which would apply it to hotels but exclude payment for accommodation in other premises. We have concluded that the advantages of extending the criminal law as we propose in clause 3 outweigh the possible risks to which we referred in our Working Paper. The clause applies also to the collection of goods on which work has been done or in respect of which service has been provided: examples are the collection from a shop of shoes which have been repaired or clothes which have been cleaned, and for the purposes of the clause it does not matter whether the work was done on the premises. As the new offence is essentially a protection for the legitimate business we have not thought it right that it should extend to transactions where the supply of the goods or the doing of the service is contrary to law, or where the service done is such that payment is not legally enforceable, and clause 3(3) imposes this limitation.

20. Further examples of the application of the clause are the passenger who at the end of his journey in a taxi runs off without paying his fare; and the motorist who has had his car's petrol tank filled at a garage and when the attendant is called to the telephone drives off without paying for the petrol.

21. Among the comments on our Working Paper was the suggestion that this proposed offence should be extended to cover obtaining entry to premises without paying the admission charge. We were told that young people frequently enter cinemas through fire exits or cloakroom windows and that they cannot be prosecuted when they are caught. We can see that there is a case for creating a summary offence to deal with that and similar misconduct (eg climbing over the wall into a football ground to avoid paying at the turnstiles). The essence of that offence would be *entering* premises knowing that a charge was made for admission and without paying that charge. This cannot be combined in one provision with the offence in clause 3 of *making off* without paying when payment on the spot for goods or services is required or expected. Clause 3 is a natural extension of our proposals for replacing section 16(2)(a) but we do not think it right to go any further away from the offences of deception which our terms of reference required us to review and so we must leave it to others to decide whether it would be desirable to create a summary offence of entering premises without paying the admission charge.

Notes and questions

1. According to the OED 'makes off' means to depart suddenly 'often with a disparaging implication'. But while making off is usually thought of as having the disparaging implication of cowardice or secrecy or stealth, it is not confined to such cases. It simply means to decamp and in *Brooks and Brooks* (1982) 76 Cr App R 66 at 69, CA, the court said that it 'may be an exercise accompanied by the sound of trumpets or a silent stealing away after a folding of tents'.

2. How easy is it to identify the 'spot' at which payment is expected or required: in the case of a taxi ride; a large department store?

3. Does D make off when he leaves proof of identity by which V can enforce the debt? J. R. Spencer writes ([1983] Crim LR 573):

Obviously, s 3 is partly concerned to prevent the legitimate expectations of restaurateurs, hoteliers, etc being disappointed by people failing to pay their bills. But equally obviously, the section is aimed at some specific mischief narrower than this. If non-payment had been all that Parliament was concerned with, presumably it would have phrased the offence as 'dishonestly failing to pay'. If mere failure to pay was the true mischief of the offence, there was no need for 'making off' as an ingredient in it at all, whether it means 'leaves' as Professor Smith and others say, or whether it means 'leaves with guilty haste' as Francis Bennion suggests. So we must assume, surely, that 'makes off' points to some additional element of mischief which renders the case significantly worse than simply failing to pay, and to see what 'making off' really is, we ought to consider what conduct is, in practical terms, significantly worse than merely failing to pay. It can hardly be *leaving* without paying, because this, as such, does not worsen the creditor's position. It must surely be *disappearing: leaving in a way that makes it difficult for the debtor to be traced.*

On this view, 'making off' would cover, obviously, the man who runs away. It would also cover the man who tells a lie to get outside, and then runs away. It would also cover a man who leaves a cheque signed in a false name. But it would not cover the person who leaves his correct name and an address at which he may readily be found. Nor would it usually cover the person who leaves behind him a cheque, drawn on his own account, in circumstances where it is likely to be dishonoured. In this case, although D has left, he has not as a rule made it difficult for P to trace him.

I also think this interpretation of 'makes off' is the right one because it solves a problem which otherwise arises in connection with s 3(4): 'Any person may arrest without warrant any one who is, or whom he, with reasonable cause, suspects to be, committing or attempting to commit an offence under this section.' Years ago the common law set its face against giving hoteliers, restaurateurs and suchlike the power to arrest those who merely fail to pay their bills. Yet if we interpret 'makes off' as synonymous with 'leaves' we give them precisely this. On this view, any customer who sought to leave having failed to pay his bill would—subject to what the jury make of 'dishonestly'—commit the offence of making off without payment, and the hotelier or restaurateur would be able lawfully to detain him. To me, at least, it seems highly undesirable that hoteliers, etc should be given this power, at any rate when they know who the non-paying customer is and where he may later be found. On the other hand, if 'makes off' is limited as I suggest, there is no question of the hotelier having the power to arrest a customer who leaves his name backed with some plausible identification.

4. In *Vincent* [2001] 2 Cr App R 150, [2001] Crim LR 488 D stayed at two hotels in Windsor and left without paying his bills. His defence was that he had arranged with the proprietors of the hotels to pay when he could and payment was not expected on the spot when he left; that he had not acted dishonestly and that he had no intention of avoiding payment. The judge directed that a dishonestly obtained agreement to postpone payment could not be relied on to negate the expectation of payment on the spot and D was convicted. His conviction was quashed: the section did not permit or require an analysis whether the agreement was obtained by deception. The fact that the agreement was dishonestly obtained did not reinstate the expectation of payment on the spot.

Would this decision apply to all cases where consent is obtained by fraud? If D 'pays' with counterfeit money or a forged cheque, including a handsome tip, and departs with the warm good wishes of the hotelier, has he paid 'as required or expected'? Has he 'made off'? Does it make any difference that he has left his true name and address in the hotel register?

5. The court in *Vincent* said that the remedy for fraudulently obtaining agreement to postpone payment must be sought elsewhere in the Theft Acts. Where? Section 2(1)(b) of the 1978 Act?

6. D, being well known to V, a restaurateur, decides not to pay his bill and departs via the cloakroom window. Would he be guilty according to Professor Spencer? Is there anything in the section to justify acquittal? (See also *Bennion* [1980] Crim LR 670.)

7. Goods may be supplied, or services done, though many or all of the physical acts are done by D. All commentators are agreed that petrol is supplied by V at self-service filling stations though the customer serves himself. Similarly a service is done by V at a self-service car wash though V is not on the premises and the machinery is operated by D.

A more difficult case is the self-service store. Suppose that D takes goods from the shelves which he places in his pocket and leaves the store with them. Obviously theft but does he also commit the offence under s 3? A. T. H. Smith ([1981] Crim LR 590) thinks that this case is to be distinguished from the self-service petrol station in that in the latter 'the customer does not just take possession of the petrol, but makes himself owner of it by pouring it into his tank'.

8. Payment ordinarily presents no problems. One problem concerns payment by cheque. If the cheque is supported by a cheque card which the bank must then honour it would seem clear that V has been paid though D has exceeded his authority as between himself and the bank, and the same would follow where a credit card is used. But what if V accepts a cheque from D which D knows will not be honoured? There is a suggestion in *Hammond* [1982] Crim LR 611 that V has been paid because a cheque taken without a banker's card is always taken at risk by the recipient. The judge in *Hammond* added that he did not see how in such a case it could be said that D made off.

9. D and E visit a 'club' in a disreputable part of town. D uses the services of a prostitute on the premises, and E orders and eats a meal. Subsequently, D and E leave refusing to pay, both claiming that they found the services substandard. Are they liable under s 3?

10. It was settled by *Allen* [1985] 2 All ER 641, [1985] AC 1029, HL, that s 3 requires an intention to make permanent default. Lord Hailsham said, at 643:

The judgment of the Court of Appeal, with which I agree, was delivered by Boreham J. He said ([1985] 1 All ER 148 at 154, [1985] 1 WLR 50 at 57):

'To secure a conviction under s 3 of the 1978 Act the following must be proved: (1) that the defendant in fact made off without making payment on the spot: (2) the following mental elements: (a) knowledge that payment on the spot was required or expected of him: and (b) dishonesty: and (c) intent to avoid payment [sc 'of the amount due']'.

I agree with this analysis. To this the judge adds the following comment:

'If (c) means, or is taken to include, no more than an intention to delay or defer payment of the amount due, it is difficult to see what it adds to the other elements. Anyone who knows that payment on the spot is expected or required of him and who then dishonestly makes off without paying as required or expected must have at least the intention to delay or defer payment. It follows, therefore, that the conjoined phrase "and with intent to avoid payment of the amount due" adds a further ingredient: an intention to do more than delay or defer, an intention to evade payment altogether'.

My own view, for what it is worth, is that the section thus analysed is capable only of this meaning. But counsel for the Crown very properly conceded that, even if it were equivocal and capable of either meaning, in a penal section of this kind any ambiguity must be resolved in favour of the subject and against the Crown. Accordingly, the appeal falls to be dismissed either if on its true construction it means unambiguously that the intention must be permanently to avoid payment, or if the clause is ambiguous and capable of either meaning. Even on the assumption that, in the context, the word 'avoid' without the addition of the word 'permanently' is capable of either meaning, which Boreham J was inclined to concede, I find myself convinced by his final paragraph, which reads:

> 'Finally, we can see no reason why, if the intention of Parliament was to provide, in effect, that an intention to delay or defer payment might suffice, Parliament should not have said so in explicit terms. This *might* have been achieved by the insertion of the word "such" before payment in the phrase in question. It *would* have been achieved by a grammatical reconstruction of the material part of s 3(1) thus," dishonestly makes off without having paid and with intent to avoid payment of the amount due as required or expected". To accede to the Crown's submission would be to read the section as if it were constructed in that way. That we cannot do. Had it been intended to relate the intention to avoid "payment" to "payment as required or expected" it would have been easy to say so. The section does not say so. At the very least it contains an equivocation which should be resolved in favour of [the respondent]'.

There is really no escape from this argument. . . .

Do you agree?

FURTHER READING

F. Bennion, Letter, 'The Drafting of Section 3 of the Theft Act 1978' [1980] Crim LR 670

P. Rowlands, 'Minors: Can they make off without payment' (1981) JP 410

A. T. H. Smith, 'Shoplifting and the Theft Acts' [1981] Crim LR 586

J. R. Spencer, 'The Theft Act 1978' [1979] Crim LR 24

J. R. Spencer, Letter, 'Making off without Payment' [1983] Crim LR 573

G. Syrota, 'Statutes: Theft Act 1978' (1979) 42 MLR 301

G. Syrota, 'Are Cheque Frauds covered by Section 3 of the Theft Act 1978?' [1980] Crim LR 413

24

Temporary deprivation offences

A temporary deprivation of property invariably causes inconvenience to the owner that in some cases may be hardly less serious than permanent deprivation. Most students will have experienced the problem when a book or article that they are recommended to read disappears from the library shelves and is not returned until it is too late to make use of it. More serious still, it has been known for one student to borrow another student's well-prepared notes and return them (or rather leave them where they will be returned) to the owner after the examinations. Is it arguable in the latter case that the notes are stolen because, when returned, they have no value to the owner (cp *Lloyd*, above, p **801** and *Oxford v Moss*, above, p **766**)?

More generally, why should it not be theft to appropriate (that is, to act as owner of) property for a week, a month, or a year, as well as permanently to do so? For an argument to delete the words 'with the intention of permanently depriving the other of it' from the definition of theft and to accordingly make dishonest use theft. (See G. Williams, 'Temporary Appropriation should be Theft' [1981] Crim LR 129.) What are the arguments for and against? Arguably it has become increasingly common for property to be of value precisely because of its availability for immediate use, and the law may need to respond by creating a temporary deprivation offence.

The common law always required an intention permanently to deprive as a constituent of theft though many legal systems do not have this requirement. The CLRC, however, decided against either extending theft to include temporary deprivation or of creating a general offence of temporary deprivation. The former seemed wrong because 'an intention to return property, even after a long time, makes the conduct essentially different from stealing' (Cmnd 2977, para 56). How?

'Apart from this,' the Committee said (loc cit):

... either course would be a considerable extension of the criminal law, which does not seem to be called for by any existing serious evil. It might moreover have undesirable social consequences. Quarrelling neighbours and families would be able to threaten one another with prosecution. Students and young people sharing accommodation who might be tempted to borrow one another's property in disregard of a prohibition by the owner would be in danger of acquiring a criminal record. Further, it would be difficult for the police to avoid being involved in wasteful and undesirable investigations into alleged offences which had no social importance. It is difficult to see how the provision could be framed in a way which would satisfactorily exclude trivial cases and meet these objections. If cases of temporary deprivation should become common, or if it should become too easy a defence to a charge of theft that the intention was to return the property in the end, it might be necessary, notwithstanding these formidable difficulties, to create an offence of temporary deprivation with a high enough maximum penalty for serious cases.

One case where temporary deprivation had already been recognized as an 'existing serious evil' was of motor vehicles and the temporary deprivation of motor vehicles was first made an offence by the Road Traffic Act 1930. This was followed by a similar offence in relation to the taking of vessels in 1967. The Theft Act 1968, s 12, continues to penalize such temporary deprivations and extends it to a greater range of conveyances. In addition the CLRC recommended the creation of an entirely new offence of removing articles from public places.

Why should the law only offer protection against temporary deprivation of these types of property? Are these offences, which are defined in terms of the type of property affected rather than the manner of commission of the harm, consistent with the law's approach to dishonesty offences generally?

The Law Commission's provisional view now is that 'temporary deprivation is wrong in principle, and, unless there is a significant countervailing argument, should be criminal': Law Com Consultation Paper No 155 (1999).

1. REMOVAL OF ARTICLES FROM PLACES OPEN TO THE PUBLIC

Theft Act 1968, s 11

(1) Subject to sub-sections (2) and (3) below, where the public have access to a building in order to view the building or part of it, or a collection or part of a collection housed in it, any person who without lawful authority removes from the building or its grounds the whole or part of any article displayed or kept for display to the public in the building or that part of it or in its grounds shall be guilty of an offence.

For this purpose 'collection' includes a collection got together for a temporary purpose, but references in this section to a collection do not apply to a collection made or exhibited for the purpose of effecting sales or other commercial dealings.

(2) It is immaterial for purposes of sub-section (1) above, that the public's access to a building is limited to a particular period or particular occasion; but where anything removed from a building or its grounds is there otherwise than as forming part of, or being on loan for exhibition with, a collection intended for permanent exhibition to the public, the person removing it does not thereby commit an offence under this section unless he removes it on a day when the public have access to the building as mentioned in sub-section (1) above.

(3) A person does not commit an offence under this section if he believes that he has lawful authority for the removal of the thing in question or that he would have it if the person entitled to give it knew of the removal and the circumstances of it.

(4) A person guilty of an offence under this section shall, on conviction on indictment, be liable to imprisonment for a term not exceeding five years.

While the CLRC recommended the creation of this offence, the Committee did not include a provision dealing with it in its draft Bill. The section was drafted at a subsequent stage and, as a glance will show, it is not one which a student of the criminal law is likely to find transparently clear! As Griew (*The Theft Acts 1968 and 1978*, 7th edn, 5–02) observes, 'The section is drafted with a complexity disproportionate to the importance of the offence'.

The creation of the offence was inspired by a number (there seems to have been barely a handful of them) of 'removals' such as the removal of Goya's portrait of the Duke of Wellington from the National Portrait Gallery and the removal of the Coronation Stone from Westminster Abbey. The thinking behind the CLRC's recommendation (Cmnd 2977, para 57(ii)) appears to be that articles displayed to the public are often irreplaceable and are not as easily protected as articles on private premises. But are they any more vulnerable than books kept on the shelves of a university library, many of which are equally irreplaceable?

Questions

1. D enters the grounds of a stately home that is open to the public (on payment of a fee). As a prank, he removes a statute from the garden and hides it in a groundsman's shed. Has he committed an offence under s 11? Does it matter whether the stately home is open for business?

2. Bloggs owns a shop specializing in selling books on art. He hosts an exhibition in his back room allowing Tracy, an artist, to exhibit her latest pieces. Tracy hopes they will generate interest and will sell. Bloggs is hosting the exhibition in the hope that it will generate more trade for him. Damien, an art lover, removes one of Tracy's pieces from the display and takes it home, believing it to be unworthy of being labelled as 'art'. Edna, the cleaner, removes another of Tracy's pieces entitled 'Rubbish' and places it in the skip outside. Discuss any criminal liability arising under the Theft Act 1968.

2. TAKING CONVEYANCES

Theft Act 1968, s 12. Taking motor vehicle or other conveyance without authority

(1) Subject to sub-sections (5) and (6) below, a person shall be guilty of an offence if, without having the consent of the owner or other lawful authority, he takes any conveyance for his own or another's use or, knowing that any conveyance has been taken without such authority, drives it or allows himself to be carried in or on it.

(2) A person guilty of an offence under sub-section (1) above shall be liable on summary conviction to a fine not exceeding level 5 on the standard scale, to imprisonment for a term not exceeding six months, or to both.

(3) [Repealed.]

(4) If on the trial of an indictment for theft the jury are not satisfied that the accused committed theft, but it is proved that the accused committed an offence under sub-section (1) above, the jury may find him guilty of the offence under sub-section (1) and if he is found guilty of it, he shall be liable as he would have been liable under sub-section (2) above on summary conviction.

(5) Sub-section (1) above shall not apply in relation to pedal cycles; but, subject to sub-section (6) below, a person who, without having the consent of the owner or other lawful authority, takes a pedal cycle for his own or another's use, or rides a pedal cycle knowing it to have been taken without such authority, shall on summary conviction be liable to a fine not exceeding level 3 on the standard scale.

(6) A person does not commit an offence under this section by anything done in the belief that he has lawful authority to do it or that he would have the owner's consent if the owner knew of his doing it and the circumstances of it.

(7) For purposes of this section—

    (a) 'conveyance' means any conveyance constructed or adapted for the carriage of a person or persons whether by land, water or air, except that it does not include a conveyance constructed or adapted for use only under the control of a person not carried in or on it, and 'drive' shall be construed accordingly; and

    (b) 'owner', in relation to a conveyance which is the subject of a hiring agreement or hire-purchase agreement, means the person in possession of the conveyance under that agreement.

For s 12A, 'Aggravated vehicle-taking', see below, p 885.

R v Bow

(1976) 64 Cr App R 54, Court of Appeal, Criminal Division

(Bridge LJ, Wien and Kenneth Jones JJ)

The appellant, together with his brother and father, drove in the brother's motor car to a country estate; all had air rifles. At the estate they were approached by gamekeepers who asked for their names and addresses. When these were refused, the head gamekeeper sent for the police and parked his Land Rover so as to obstruct the only escape route for the brother's car. Since the head gamekeeper refused to remove the Land Rover, the appellant got into it, released the handbrake and allowed it to coast some 200 yards so that his brother could drive his car away. The appellant was convicted of an offence under s 12(1).

[**Bridge LJ** delivered the judgment of the court:]

...Mr Toulson, for whose interesting and careful argument we are extremely grateful, makes two submissions in summary. First, he submits that the case should have been withdrawn from the jury on the footing that there was indeed no evidence that the taking of the Land Rover was for the appellant's own use. Secondly, and alternatively, if he is wrong on the first submission he says that in any event the issue raised a question of fact which should have been left by the judge to be determined by the jury.

It is convenient to say at the outset that no point turns in this appeal on the fact that the Land Rover's engine was not used by the appellant. Mr Toulson does not suggest that the case falls to be decided any differently because the appellant was able to coast downhill for 200 yards than if he had driven 200 yards using the engine.

It is appropriate to recall that the present statutory offence created by section 12 of the Act of 1968 is defined in two respects in significantly different language from the language which was used in earlier statutes, the latest embodiment prior to 1968 having been in section 217 of the Road Traffic Act 1960. Under that Act the offence was defined as committed by 'a person who takes and drives away a motor vehicle without having either the consent of the owner or other lawful authority.'

Some arguments have been addressed to us with respect to the supposed intention of the legislature in effecting those changes in the definition of the offence, but in the event, having regard to the conclusion the Court has reached on a narrow point which we think is decisive of this appeal, it is unnecessary for us to express any opinion on those wider arguments.

Mr Toulson's basic submission is in these terms. He contends that if a person moves a vehicle for the sole reason that it is in his way and moves it no further than is necessary to enable him to get past the obstruction, he is not taking that vehicle for his own use. The starting point of the argument is the decision of this court in *Bogacki* (1973) 57 Cr App R 593, [1973] QB 832. In that case the three defendants were charged with attempting to take without authority a motor bus. The evidence showed that they had gone to a bus garage late at night and attempted to start the engine of a bus without success. The trial judge directed the jury as follows, adverting specifically to the change of language between section 12 of the Act of 1968 and section 217 of the Act of 1960. He said:

> 'The offence is not, I repeat, the offence is not taking and driving away, it is merely taking and "taking", members of the jury, means assuming possession of an object for your own unauthorised use, however temporary that assumption of possession might be. May I give you an example. Suppose that you left your motorcar parked in the car park behind a cinema, and you forgot to lock the door but you shut the door, and suppose that a man and a woman, some time later, when the motorcar was unattended, came along, opened the door, got into the car, and had sexual intercourse in the car. This particular offence would then have been committed by them'.

Later he said with respect to the defendants before him: 'The question is: Did they, without the permission of the owners, acquire possession, for however short a time, for their own unauthorised purpose? That is the question.'

In giving the judgment of this Court in that case Roskill LJ said at pp 598 and 837 of the respective reports:

> 'The word "take" is an ordinary simple English word and it is undesirable that where Parliament has used an ordinary simple English word elaborate glosses should be put upon it. What is sought to be said is that "take" is the equivalent of "use" and that mere unauthorised use of itself constitutes an offence against section 12. It is to be observed that if one treats "takes" as a synonym for "uses", the sub-section has to be read in this way: "if...he uses any conveyance for his own or another's use...." That involves the second employment of the word "use" being tautologous, and this court can see no justification where Parliament has used the phrase "if...he takes any conveyance for his own or another's use" for construing this language as meaning if he "uses any conveyance for his own or another's use", thus giving no proper effect to the words "for his own or another's use". For those reasons the court accepts Mr Lowry's submission that there is still built in, if I may use the phrase, to the word "takes" in the sub-section the concept of movement and that before a man can be convicted of the completed offence under section 12(1) it must be shown that he took the vehicle, that is to say, that there was an unauthorised taking possession or control of the vehicle by him adverse to the rights of the true owner or person otherwise entitled to such possession or control, coupled with some movement, however small...of that vehicle following such unauthorised taking'.

Basing himself on that decision, Mr Toulson submits, cogently as we think, that since the concept of taking in the definition of the offence already involves moving the vehicle taken, the words 'for his own or another's use' must involve something over and above mere movement of the vehicle. What then is the concept embodied in this phrase 'for his own or another's use'?

On this point the argument ranged widely, but we hope that at the end of the day it is an adequate summary of the final submission made on it by Mr Toulson to say that he contends that what is involved is that the conveyance should have been used as a conveyance, ie should have been used as a means of transport. That submission seems to us to be well founded. Mr Toulson points out that the mischief at which this section is aimed has been appropriately defined as 'stealing a ride'. The interpretation of the phrase 'for his own or another's use' as meaning 'for his own or another's use as a conveyance' would fall into line, we think, with the discriminations suggested in Smith and Hogan's *Criminal Law*, 3rd edn (1973) at p 462, where the following passage occurs:

> 'But subject to the requirement of taking, the offence does seem, in essence, to consist in stealing a ride. This seems implicit in the requirement that the taking be for "his own or another's *use*". Thus if D releases the handbrake of a car so that it runs down an incline, or releases a boat from its moorings so that it is carried off by the tide this would not as such be an offence within the section'.

Pausing at that point in the quotation from the textbook, the reason why neither of those examples would constitute an offence within the section would be that in neither case, although the conveyance had been moved, would it have been used as a conveyance.

The quotation from the textbook goes on: 'The taking must be for D's use or the use of another and if he intends to make no use of the car or boat there would be no offence under section 12. But it would be enough if D were to release the boat from its moorings so that he would be carried down-stream in the boat.' In that case, since he would be carried downstream in the boat there would be a use of the boat as a conveyance, as a means of transporting him downstream.

So far the court is in agreement with Mr Toulson's submissions. But then the next step has to be taken. The next step is, as Mr Toulson submits, that merely to move a vehicle which constitutes an obstruction so that it shall be an obstruction no more cannot involve use of the vehicle as a conveyance. It is at this point that the submission requires to be carefully analysed.

Clearly one can envisage instances in which an obstructing vehicle was merely pushed out of the way a yard or two which would not involve any use of it as a conveyance. But the facts involved in the removal of the obstructing vehicle must be examined in each case.

Mr Matheson, for the Crown, meets this submission squarely by pointing to the circumstance that here the Land Rover was in the ordinary sense of the English language driven for 200 yards. Attention has already been drawn to the fact that no distinction was relied upon by Mr Toulson between a vehicle driven under its own power and a vehicle driven by being allowed to coast down hill. Mr Matheson says that again, as a matter of ordinary use of English, in the course of driving the vehi-cle a distance of 200 yards the appellant was inevitably using it as a conveyance and that his motive for so doing is immaterial. This submission for the Crown, it is pointed out to us, is in line with another suggestion by Professor Smith in his textbook on the *Law of Theft*, 2nd edn (1972), paragraph 317, where he says: 'Probably driving, whatever the motive, would be held to be "use".'

In reply, Mr Toulson submits that even if it be right that the appellant had in the ordinary sense of the word to drive the Land Rover for 200 yards, and even if that did involve its use as a conveyance, nevertheless the offence was still not made out because the purpose of the taking was not to use the conveyance as a conveyance but merely to remove it as an obstruction. He emphasises that the words of the section are: 'takes for his own use', not 'takes and uses'. This is in our judgment a very subtle and refined distinction and if it were admitted it would open a very wide door to persons who take conveyances without authority and use them as such to dispute their guilt on the ground that the motive of the taking was something other than the use of the conveyance as such.

The short answer, we think, is that where as here, a conveyance is taken and moved in a way which nec-essarily involves its use as a conveyance, the taker cannot be heard to say that the taking was not for that use. If he has in fact taken the conveyance and used it as such, his motive in so doing is, as Mr Matheson submits, quite immaterial. It follows, in our judgment, that the trial judge was right, not only to reject the submission of no case, but also to direct the jury, as he did, that on the undisputed facts the appellant had taken the Land Rover for his own use. Accordingly the appeal will be dismissed.

Appeal dismissed

McKnight v Davies
[1974] RTR 4, Queen's Bench Division

(Lord Widgery CJ, Bridge and May JJ)

Lord Widgery CJ. . . . The justices convicted the defendant and found the following facts. The defend-ant was employed as a lorry driver. His duty was to deliver goods from his employer's depot to shops, and on completion of deliveries to return the lorry to the depot. On the evening of 30 November 1972 the defendant, having completed his deliveries, was driving the lorry back to the depot when the roof of the lorry struck a low bridge. When he saw the damage to the lorry he was scared, and he drove it to a public house and had a drink. After that he drove three men to their homes on the outskirts of

Cardiff, drove back to the centre of the city and had a drink at another public house, and then drove to the area where he lived and parked the lorry near his home. He drove the lorry to his employer's depot at 6.20 am on 1 December, the following day.

The question for this court is whether on those relatively simple facts the defendant was guilty of the offence charged.

Section 12 of the Theft Act 1968, so far as relevant, reads:

'(1) Subject to sub-sections (5) and (6) below, a person shall be guilty of an offence if, without having the consent of the owner or other lawful authority, he takes any conveyance for his own or another's use…'

There can, I think, be little doubt that the lorry was being used, following the accident with the bridge, for the defendant's own use, and the argument centres on whether on the facts found he can be said to have 'taken' the conveyance at all.

A similar question arose under s 28 of the Road Traffic Act 1930 in *Mowe v Perraton* [1952] 1 All ER 423. In that case a lorry driver had made an unauthorised deviation from his route in the course of his working day in order to pick up a radiogram and take it to the address of a friend. He had no authority from his employers to use the vehicle for a private purpose of that character, and he was charged with a breach of the corresponding provision in the Road Traffic Act 1930. In this court it was held that he had not committed the offence charged, Lord Goddard CJ pointing out that s 28 of the Act of 1930—and, I quote, (1952) 35 Cr App Rep 194 at 196:

'…was intended to deal with a case where a person takes a motor car which does not belong to him, drives it away and then abandons it…This is a case of a man who took and drove a motor vehicle during his work. What he did was an unauthorised thing, but that does not make the taking or the driving away a criminal offence under section 28'.

That authority on its face suggests that the offence could not be committed by a man who was lawfully entrusted with a vehicle for a limited purpose, but subsequently used it in excess of the purpose for which it had been given to him.

The point was next raised in this court in *Wibberley* [1966] 2 QB 214, [1965] 3 All ER 718, where a driver employed to drive a vehicle had taken it home at the end of the day and parked it outside his house. It was within the authority of his employers to leave the vehicle outside overnight instead of taking it back to the depot. Having so parked it, and after an interval, the defendant took the vehicle out on a private mission of his own, and it was held that he was properly convicted of taking the vehicle for the purpose of the present legislation. The earlier decision in *Mowe v Perraton* [1952] 1 All ER 423 was distinguished on the footing that, since the driver had finished his working day and parked the vehicle in the place where it should be parked for the night, it was possible to say that when he returned to the vehicle and began to drive it he had taken it for present purposes.

The third authority to which I would refer is *Phipps, McGill* [1970] RTR 209, a decision of the Court of Appeal. That case fell to be decided under s 12 of the Theft Act 1968, and I will read the headnote, in (1970) 54 Cr App Rep 301:

'Where a defendant has been given permission by the owner of a motor vehicle to take and use it for a limited purpose, but on the completion of that purpose fails to return it and thereafter uses it without any reasonable belief that the owner would consent, the defendant is guilty of taking the vehicle without the consent of the owner, contrary to s 12 of the Theft Act 1968.'

That decision, as I understand it, is inconsistent with the judgment of Lord Goddard CJ, in *Mowe v Perraton* [1952] 1 All ER 423. In *Phipps, McGill* [1970] RTR 209 the Court of Appeal clearly rejected the argument that a lawful acquisition of possession or control of the vehicle meant that an unauthorised use by the driver could never amount to a taking for the purpose of s 12.

In my judgment we must choose between those two decisions, and I have no hesitation in saying that we should follow the decision of the Court of Appeal in *Phipps, McGill* [1970] RTR 209. It is, therefore, not in itself an answer in the present case for the defendant to say that he was lawfully put in control of the vehicle by his employers. The difficulty which I feel is in defining the kind of unauthorised activity on the part of the driver, whose original control of the vehicle is lawful, which will amount to an unlawful taking for the purpose of s 12. Not every brief, unauthorised diversion from his proper route by an employed driver in the course of his working day will necessarily involve a 'taking' of the vehicle for his own use. If, however, as in *Wibberley* [1966] 2 QB 214, [1965] 3 All ER 718, he returns to the vehicle after he has parked it for the night and drives it off on an unauthorised errand, he is clearly guilty of the offence. Similarly, if in the course of his working day, or otherwise while his authority to use the vehicle is unexpired, he appropriates it to his own use in a manner which repudiates the rights of the true owner, and shows that he has assumed control of the vehicle for his own purposes, he can properly be regarded as having taken the vehicle within s 12.

As Professor Smith puts it (in Smith's *Law of Theft*, 2nd edn (1972), p 113) he has

> '…altered the character of his control over the vehicle, so that he no longer held as servant but assumed possession of it in the legal sense'.

In the present case I think that the defendant took the vehicle when he left the first public house. At that point he assumed control for his own purposes in a manner which was inconsistent with his duty to his employer to finish his round and drive the vehicle to the depot. I think that the justices reached the correct conclusion and I would dismiss the appeal.

I am authorised by Bridge J to say that he agrees with the judgment that I have just delivered.

May J. I also agree.

Appeal dismissed

Questions

1. *Bow* suggests that to fall within the provision the conveyance must be taken for use as a conveyance. In *Pearce* [1973] Crim LR 321, CA, a conviction was upheld where D took an inflatable rubber dinghy from outside a lifeboat depot, putting it on a trailer and driving it away. The court rejected D's contention that the conveyance must be moved in its own element, water in this case. Perhaps D had it in mind to use the dinghy as a conveyance at some future stage, but what if he was minded to use it as a paddling pool for his children? Cf *Stokes* [1983] RTR 59, CA, where it was held that D did not commit the offence when, as a practical joke, he pushed V's car round the corner so that V would think it had been stolen.

2. In *Bow*, Bridge LJ said that clearly there would be cases in which an obstructing vehicle was moved a yard or two which would not involve the use of the vehicle as conveyance. Suppose D lives in a cul-de-sac and finds that V's car obstructs his access to the highway. Is it to make a difference if in order to gain access to the highway D has to move V's car two yards, 20 yards or 200 yards?

Whittaker v Campbell
[1983] 3 All ER 582, Queen's Bench Division

(Robert Goff LJ and Glidewell J)

Two brothers, Wilson Coglan Whittaker and Stewart Whittaker, purchased coal cheaply but were required to provide their own means of transporting it. Wilson had no driving licence while Stewart had only a provisional licence and neither had a vehicle of his own. Somehow they came into the possession of a full driving licence belonging to Derek Dunn. They then hired a van by Wilson's representing himself as Derek Dunn and by producing to the van hirer the driving licence in that name. The hirer said that he believed Wilson Whittaker to be Derek Dunn and the holder of a full licence; had he known that this was not the case the brothers would not have been allowed to hire any of their vehicles.

The judgment of the court was delivered by:

Robert Goff LJ.... The case raises for decision a point of construction of s 12(1) of the Theft Act 1968, relating to the meaning of the words 'without having the consent of the owner' in the offence which is committed under that sub-section if a person, without having the consent of the owner or other lawful authority, takes any conveyance for his own or another's use... The justice's convicted the two appellants of such an offence....

Before the Crown Court it was contended by the appellants that they had the consent of the owner to take the conveyance, that consent having been given by Mr Robson to the persons with whom he was dealing, namely the appellants, and that consent not having been vitiated by the misrepresentation of Wilson Coglan Whittaker that he was in fact Derek Dunn and the holder of a full driving licence. The misrepresentations as to identity and the holding of a full driving licence were not fundamental so as to vitiate the consent given, but were merely misrepresentations as to the representor's attributes, such as to render a contract voidable and not void ab initio. The mere fact that Mr Robson would not have consented to parting with possession of the vehicle if he had known of the true position was not conclusive against the appellants; nor was the fact that the appellants would not be insured to drive the vehicle.

The respondent, on the other hand, contended that the appellants were guilty of the offence because in law and in fact they did not have the consent of the vehicle owner or other lawful authority to take the vehicle in question. Although the vehicle owner gave his de facto consent to the appellants taking the vehicle, that consent was not a true consent or a consent at all in law or in fact because it was vitiated by the fraudulent misrepresentations as to identity and the holding of a full driving licence made by the appellants which induced the owner to part with possession of his vehicle. These misrepresentations were fundamental to the transaction in that the owner would not have parted with possession had he known of the true position because the hirer would not have been insured to drive the vehicle.

These arguments were repeated and developed in the submissions made by counsel before this court. We, like the Crown Court, were referred to certain authorities, some of which we shall consider later in this judgment. The conclusion of the Crown Court was that the appellants' misrepresentations were fundamental in that the vehicle owner would not have contemplated handing over the vehicle had he known the true position, and that his consent was therefore vitiated by the fraudulent misrepresentation of the appellants. We quote from the case:

> 'The question in the present appeals was whether the vehicle owner gave his consent to the Appellants taking the vehicle. In my opinion he did not. He consented to someone called Derek Dunn with a full driving licence taking the vehicle. I accordingly held that in law the Appellants were guilty of the offence under section 12(1) of the Theft Act 1968'.

The following questions were stated for the opinion of the court:

> '(1) Whether in law the de facto consent to take a conveyance namely a motor vehicle given by the vehicle owner to a person hiring that vehicle is vitiated by reason of its being induced by the false representations of the person hiring the vehicle as to his identity and the holding of a full driving licence, so that the person taking the vehicle under the contract of hire is guilty of taking a conveyance

without the owner's consent or other lawful authority contrary to section 12(1) of the Theft Act 1968. (2) Whether, on the facts found by me and having regard to the cases cited, the Crown Court was wrong in law in rejecting the appeals of the Appellants'.

We are concerned in the present case with the construction of certain words, viz 'without having the consent of the owner', in their context in a particular sub-section of a criminal statute. However, the concept of consent is relevant in many branches of the law, including not only certain crimes but also the law of contract and the law of property. There is, we believe, danger in assuming that the law adopts a uniform definition of the word 'consent' in all its branches....

What is the effect of fraud? Fraud is, in relation to a contract, a fraudulent misrepresentation by one party which induces the other to enter into a contract or apparent contract with the representor. Apart from the innocent party's right to recover damages for the tort of deceit, the effect of the fraud is simply to give the innocent party the right, subject to certain limits, to rescind the contract. These rights are similar to (though not identical with) the rights of a party who has been induced to enter into a contract by an innocent, as opposed to a fraudulent, misrepresentation, though there the right to recover damages derives from statute, and the limits to rescission are somewhat more severe. It is plain, however, that in this context fraud does not 'vitiate consent', any more than an innocent misrepresentation 'vitiates consent'. Looked at realistically, a misrepresentation, whether fraudulent or innocent, induces a party to enter into a contract in circumstances where it may be unjust that the representor should be permitted to retain the benefit (the chose in action) so acquired by him. The remedy of rescission, by which the unjust enrichment of the representor is prevented, though for historical and practical reasons treated in books on the law of contract, is a straightforward remedy in restitution subject to limits which are characteristic of that branch of the law...

Similar criteria to those applied in order to ascertain whether property in goods had passed in circumstances such as these were at one time of particular relevance in criminal law. This was because, under the old law of larceny, the crime of larceny as the result of a mistake was only committed if the mistake was sufficient to prevent the property from passing to the accused; and the crime of larceny by a trick was only committed if the accused, having the relevant mens rea, induced the owner to transfer possession of the goods to him, though the owner did not intend to convey the property to the accused. If the owner was induced to convey the property to the accused, the latter could not be guilty of larceny but could be guilty of obtaining by false pretences. The nature of the mistake in cases of larceny as the result of a mistake and the distinction between larceny by a trick and obtaining by false pretences were, not surprisingly, fruitful sources of dispute and of nice distinctions. But one purpose of the Theft Act 1968 was to avoid, as far as possible, problems of this kind. And even under the old law of larceny it could not be said that fraud 'vitiated consent', for the existence of the crime of larceny as the result of a mistake demonstrates that the 'vitiating' of the consent of the owner to part with the property in the goods was not dependent on fraud on the part of the accused.

It is against this background that we turn to the problem in the instant case. There being no general principle that fraud vitiates consent, we see the problem simply as this: can a person be said to have taken a conveyance for his own or another's use 'without having the consent of the owner or other lawful authority' within those words as used in s 12(1) of the Theft Act 1968 if he induces the owner to part with possession of the conveyance by a fraudulent misrepresentation of the kind employed by the appellants in the present case?

Now there is no doubt about the mischief towards which this provision (like its predecessors, ss 28(1) and 217(1) of the Road Traffic Acts 1930 and 1960, respectively) is directed. It is directed against persons simply taking other persons' vehicles for their own purposes, for example, for use in the commission of a crime, or for a joyride, or just to get home, without troubling to obtain the consent of the owner but without having the animus furandi necessary for theft. In the vast majority of circumstances, no approach is made to the owner at all: the vehicle is just taken. But is the crime committed when the owner is approached, and when he is compelled to part with his possession by force, or when he is induced to part with his possession by fraud?

Now it may be that, if the owner is induced by force to part with possession of his vehicle, the offence is committed, because a sensible distinction may be drawn between consent on the one hand and submission to force on the other. This is a point which, however, we do not have to decide, though we comment that, in the generality of such cases the accused is likely to have committed one or more other offences with which he could perhaps be more appropriately charged.

But where the owner is induced by fraud to part with the possession of his vehicle, no such sensible distinction can be drawn. In commonsense terms, he has consented to part with the possession of his vehicle, but his consent has been obtained by the fraud. In such a case no offence under this sub-section will have been committed unless, on a true construction, a different meaning is to be placed on the word 'consent' in the sub-section. We do not however consider that any such construction is required.

It is to be observed, in the first instance, that the presence or absence of consent would be as much affected by innocent as by fraudulent misrepresentation. We do not however regard this point as persuasive, for the answer may lie in the fact that, where the misrepresentation is innocent, the accused would lack the mens rea which, on the principle in *R v Tolson* (1889) 23 QBD 168, [1886–90] All ER Rep 26, may well be required as a matter of implication (a point which, once again, we do not have to decide). It is also to be observed that the owner's consent may, to the knowledge of the accused, have been self-induced, without any misrepresentation, fraudulent or innocent, on the part of the accused. More compelling, however, is the fact that it does not appear sensible to us that, in cases of fraud, the commission of the offence should depend not on the simple question whether possession of the vehicle had been obtained by fraud but on the intricate question whether the effect of the fraud had been such that it precluded the existence of objective agreement to part with possession of the car, as might for example be the case where the owner was only willing to part with possession to a third party and the accused fraudulently induced him to do so by impersonating that third party.

We find it very difficult to accept that the commission of an offence under this sub-section should depend on the drawing of such a line, which, having regard to the mischief to which this sub-section is directed, appears to us to be irrelevant. The judge in the Crown Court felt it necessary to inquire, on the appeal before him, whether this line had been crossed before he could hold that the appellants had committed the offence. An inquiry of this kind is by no means an easy one, as is demonstrated by, for example, the disagreement on a similar point among the members of the Court of Appeal in *Ingram v Little* [1960] 3 All ER 332, [1961] 1 QB 31, and by the subsequent preference by the Court of Appeal in *Lewis v Averay* [1971] 3 All ER 907, [1972] 1 QB 198, for the dissenting judgment of Devlin LJ in the earlier case. Indeed, we would (had we thought it necessary to do so) have reached a different conclusion on the point from that reached by the judge in the Crown Court in the present case, considering that the effect of the appellants' fraud was not that the owner parted with possession of his vehicle to a different person from the one to whom he intended to give possession but that the owner believed that the person to whom he gave possession had the attribute, albeit a very important attribute, of holding a driving licence. However, on our view of the sub-section, the point does not arise.

In circumstances such as those of the present case, the criminality (if any) of the act would appear to rest rather in the fact of the deception, inducing the person to part with the possession of his vehicle, rather than in the fact (if it be the case) that the fraud has the effect of inducing a mistake as to, for example, 'identity' rather than 'attributes' of the deceiver. It would be very strange if fraudulent conduct of this kind has only to be punished if it happened to induce a fundamental mistake; and it would be even more strange if such fraudulent conduct has only to be punished where the chattel in question happened to be a vehicle. If such fraudulent conduct is to be the subject of prosecution, the crime should surely be classified as one of obtaining by deception, rather than an offence under s 12(1) of the 1968 Act, which appears to us to be directed to the prohibition and punishment of a different form of activity. It was suggested to us in argument that, in the present case, the appellants could have been accused of dishonestly obtaining services by deception contrary to s 1(1) of the Theft Act 1978; the submission was that, having regard to the broad definition of 'services' inherent in s 1(2) of the 1978 Act, the hiring of a vehicle could, untypically, be regarded as a form of services. Since we did not hear full argument on the point, we express no opinion on it, commenting only that, in a comprehensive law of theft and related offences, a decision of policy has to be made whether a fraudulent obtaining of temporary possession of a vehicle or other goods should be punishable, irrespective of any of the nice distinctions which the Crown Court felt required to consider in the present case.

We are fortified in our conclusion by the opinion expressed by Sachs LJ in *R v Peart* [1970] 2 All ER 823, [1970] 2 QB 672. In that case, on comparable facts, the Court of Appeal held that no offence had been committed under s 12(1) of the 1968 Act, because the fraudulent misrepresentation did not relate to a fact which was sufficiently fundamental. But Sachs LJ, in delivering the judgment of the court, expressly reserved the question whether, in any case where consent had been induced by fraud, an offence would be committed under the sub-section; and it is plain from his comments that he had serious misgivings whether any such offence would be committed in those circumstances ([1970] 2 All ER 823 at 825, [1970] 2 QB 672 at 676). These misgivings we share in full measure, and it is our conclusion that the sub-section on its true construction contemplates no such offence.

We wish to add that our judgment is confined to the construction of s 12(1) of the Theft Act 1968. We are not to be understood to be expressing any opinion on the meaning to be attached to the word 'consent' in other parts of the criminal law, where the word must be construed in its own particular context.

It follows that we answer the first question posed for our decision in the negative and the second question in the affirmative, and that the convictions of the appellants under s 12(1) of the Theft Act 1968 will be quashed.

Appeal allowed. Convictions quashed. Leave to appeal to the House of Lords refused

Notes and questions

1. In *Peart* [1970] 2 QB 672, [1970] 2 All ER 823, CA, D had persuaded V to lend him a van by saying that he needed it for an urgent appointment in Alnwick and that he would be able to return it by 7.30 pm. In fact D wanted the van for a journey to Burnley where he was found with the van by the police at 9.30 pm. D knew all along that V would not have consented to lending the van for a trip to Burnley but it was held that V's consent was not vitiated by the deception. It should be noted that the court had to consider the situation at 2.30 pm when the van was borrowed in the afternoon since no issue was left to the jury as to whether there might not have been a fresh taking at some time after 2.30 pm. But if D admits, as he did in *Peart*, that it was his intention all along to go to a destination not agreed to by V, why should this not be a taking for his own use from the outset?

2. Assume that in *Whittaker v Campbell* the brothers had told the hirer that they required the van to transport coal and the hirer agreed to this. Supposing the brothers intended all along to transport stolen goods, would they commit the offence? What sorts of fraud as to the conduct ought to vitiate consent in this context? See J. Birds, 'Consent of the Owner under a Motor Policy' [1998] J Bus Law 421.

3. 'Conveyance' has been held to connote a mechanical contrivance of some kind; it does not include a horse since this ancient form of transport is not 'constructed or adapted' for

the carriage of persons: *Neal v Gribble* (1978) 68 Cr App R 9, [1978] Crim LR 500. What of the student who uses a lift reserved for the Vice-Chancellor? What of someone who borrows a parachute? What of someone who borrows another's roller-blades? Note that while pedal cycles are excluded from the definition of conveyance, provision is made in s 12(5) for the taking of them.

4. An offence under s 12 may be committed not merely by one who takes the conveyance (primary taker) but also by one who, knowing the conveyance has been taken without authority, drives it or allows himself to be carried in or on it. If the taking by D is aided by E then E is a secondary party in the ordinary way. Section 12 also allows for E's conviction where, after D's taking, E becomes aware that the conveyance has been taken without consent or other lawful authority and allows himself to be carried in or on it.

Aggravated vehicle-taking

The taking of motor vehicles (sometimes called 'joyriding' or 'twocking') increased dramatically in the 1990s to an extent where it was described as 'epidemic'. There are significant risks attendant upon takers demonstrating their driving 'skills' and high speed chases when takers are pursued by police. The government felt it had to respond to the growing mischief and the Aggravated Vehicle-Taking Act 1992 adds a further section, s 12A, to the Theft Act 1968 which creates the offence of aggravated vehicle-taking (the offence is confined to the taking of mechanically propelled vehicles). This requires proof:

(i) that D has committed the offence under s 12(1) of the 1968 Act (the 'basic offence') and

(ii) that after the vehicle was taken and before it was recovered, the vehicle was driven or injury or damage was caused in one or more of the aggravating circumstances:
   (a) that the vehicle was driven dangerously;
   (b) that, owing to the driving of a vehicle, an accident occurred by which injury was caused to any person. (In *Marsh* [1997] 1 Cr App R 67 held that the words 'owing to the driving of the vehicle' were plain and simple and no gloss ought to be provided by referring the jury to the manner of the driving. See [1997] Crim LR 205 and comment. If D has used the car as a weapon, he will still be caught by the section: accident includes deliberate causing of injury: *B* [2005] Crim LR 388.) If injury is caused it matters not if it was caused deliberately or without fault);
   (c) that, owing to the driving of the vehicle, an accident occurred by which damage was caused to any property, other than the vehicle;
   (d) that damage was caused to the vehicle.

There are two offences (one punishable on indictment by imprisonment for two years, and one by imprisonment for 14 years where death is caused). Both offences are draconian. While aggravating circumstance (a) requires a degree of fault (see above, p **168**), liability is totally strict in relation to the others and the offence is committed though the vehicle taken was driven with due care. Is this fair? Is it necessary? Moreover liability for the offence extends not only to the driver but to all of the participants in the basic offence. Is this fair? It seems that if D slashes the seats of the taken vehicle, E is guilty of the offence though he seeks to dissuade D from damaging the seats or even if he seeks to prevent him. See *Dawes v DPP* [1995] 1 Cr App R 65 at 72. Is this fair? Is it necessary?

FURTHER READING

J. SPENCER, 'The Aggravated Vehicle Taking Act 1992' [1992] Crim LR 69

S. WHITE, 'Taking the Joy out of Joy-Riding' [1980] Crim LR 60

25
Blackmail

Theft Act 1968, s 21

(1) A person is guilty of blackmail if, with a view to gain for himself or another or with intent to cause loss to another, he makes any unwarranted demand with menaces; and for this purpose a demand with menaces is unwarranted unless the person making it does so in the belief:
   (a) that he has reasonable grounds for making the demand; and
   (b) that the use of the menaces is a proper means of reinforcing the demand.

(2) The nature of the act or omission demanded is immaterial, and it is also immaterial whether the menaces relate to action to be taken by the person making the demand.

(3) A person guilty of blackmail shall on conviction on indictment be liable to imprisonment for a term not exceeding fourteen years.

Originally the word blackmail was used to describe the tribute paid to Scottish chieftains by landowners in the border countries to secure immunity from raids on their lands. In the early years of its development it seems to have been pretty well coextensive with robbery and attempted robbery (the simplistic money-or-your-life approach) but over the years it has been extended to more subtle forms of extortion. It includes cases where D:

 (i) demands that V pay money to D or another E, or that V destroy his own property, under threat that otherwise D will commit some crime against him or another X;

 (ii) demands that V pay money to D or E or else D will make true or untrue revelations about V's immoral activity;

 (iii) demands that V pay D a debt owed or else D will truthfully expose V's immoral behaviour.

Ordinarily the blackmailer's demand is for money or other property but s 21(2) provides that 'the nature of the act or omission demanded is immaterial'. The demand can be for paid employment or for the destruction of V's property. The absence of a limitation on what may be demanded is not as far-reaching as may appear because the offence may be committed only where D has a view to gain or an intent to cause loss, and this refers to gain and loss in money or other property. The Theft Act 1968 is concerned with the invasion of economic interests so if D by menaces demands, say, sexual favours, other provisions of the criminal law must be looked to.

1. DEMAND

The demand may take any form and may be implicit as well as explicit. The essence of the matter is that D's communication to V, however phrased, conveys to V the message that a menace will materialize unless V complies with the demand. The demand could be in writing, orally, by gestures or by D's demeanour provided, objectively viewed it is a demand.

The offence is committed when and where D 'makes any . . . demand'. The offence is thus complete when the demand is made irrespective of whether V hears it or understands it as a demand or is not intimidated by it. In *Treacy v DPP* [1971] AC 537, [1971] 1 All ER 110, HL, it was held that a demand is made when it is posted so that D could be convicted of blackmail where his demand, addressed to V in Germany, was posted in England. (The case is now covered by the Criminal Justice Act 1993, ss 1 and 2.)

The offence is a form of inchoate offence, since there need not be any compliance by V, and the demand need not even have succeeded in being communicated. In what circumstances might D be appropriately charged with attempted blackmail?

Since there need not be a demand for property (although the demand must be made with a view to gain or loss) to what extent is blackmail a property offence? Is it accurately placed in the theft acts? Or is it more appropriately viewed as an offence against the person?

2. MENACES

R v Harry
[1974] Crim LR 32, Chelmsford Crown Court

(Judge Francis Petre)

H was indicted on two counts of blackmail. As treasurer of a college rag committee he sent letters to 115 shopkeepers asking them to buy indemnity posters for amounts between £1 and £5, the money to go to charity. The purchase of a poster was to 'protect you from any Rag Activity which could in any way cause you inconvenience'. The letter continued: 'The Committee sincerely hope that you will contribute, as we are sure you will agree that these charities are worthy causes which demand the support of all the community.' The poster read 'These premises are immune from all Rag 73 activities whatever they may be.' Fewer than six traders complained about the letter. None who complained had paid. One witness said in evidence that his objection was to the veiled threat contained in the words 'protect you from . . . inconvenience'. The President of the local Chamber of Trade said that he thought the letter was ill-conceived but that he took no serious view about it; because it was so loosely worded it was apt to be misconstrued.

The prosecution submitted that the letter contained 'the clearest threat or menace however nicely it was couched, and that there was no need for direct evidence that anyone thought it was a threat.'

Defence counsel submitted that there was no, or no *sufficient* evidence to leave to the jury. Not every threat, veiled or otherwise, was within the section but only if it satisfied the test in *Clear* [1968] 2 WLR 122 at 130 of being 'of such a nature and extent that the mind of an ordinary person of normal stability and courage might be influenced or made apprehensive so as to accede unwillingly to the demand.' There was no evidence from any victim or possible victim that the letter had that effect at all.

The judge ruled that he was not satisfied there were any menaces within the definition in *Clear*. That case had stiffened the law as previously laid down in *Thorne v Motor Trade Association* [1937] AC 797 at 817. Normally a demand with menaces was made to one person;

in this case it was made to over 100 people. To some extent one could be guided by their reaction. Exercising a broad general judgment commonsense indicated that no menaces had been proved such as fell within the Act. In directing the jury to return verdicts of not guilty on both counts, Judge Petre said: 'Menaces is a strong word. You may think that menaces must be of a fairly stern nature to fall within the definition.'

Notes and questions

1. In *Thorne v Motor Trade Association* [1937] AC 797, [1937] 3 All ER 157, HL, Lord Wright said, at 167: 'I think the word menace is to be liberally construed, and not as limited to threats of violence, but as including threats of any action detrimental to or unpleasant to the person addressed. It may also include a warning that, in certain events, such action is intended.' The CLRC, however, said (*Eighth Report*, para 113).

We have chosen the word 'menaces' instead of 'threats' because, notwithstanding the wide meaning given to 'menaces' in *Thorne's* case . . . we regard that word as stronger than 'threats' and the consequent slight restriction on the scope of the offence seems to us right.

But is there any discernible distinction between 'threat' and 'menace'?

2. 'Words or conduct which would not intimidate or influence anyone to respond to the demand would not be menaces . . . but threats and conduct of such a nature and extent that the mind of an ordinary person of normal stability and courage might be influenced or made apprehensive so as to accede unwillingly to the demand would be sufficient for a jury's consideration. The demand must be accompanied . . . by menaces . . . There may be special circumstances unknown to an accused which would make the threats innocuous and unavailing for the accused's demand, but such circumstances would have no bearing on the accused's state of mind and his intention. If an accused knew that what he threatened would have no effect on the victim it might be different.' —*Clear* [1968] 1 All ER 74 at 80, CA, considering the offence of demanding with menaces contrary to s 30 of the Larceny Act 1916. See also *Lawrence and Pomroy* (1971) 57 Cr App R 64, p **900**, below. If D can be held to have blackmailed someone as soon as the demand is made, even if the victim is unaware of the communication, why should the court be interested in the susceptibilities of the particular victim?

3. In *Harry* the trial judge pointed out that D's letters had been sent to over 100 people and only a handful had complained. The judge obviously thought that regard must be had to the general reaction. Was the judge directing himself to the right question? The shopkeepers might well have thought themselves capable of dealing with any trouble caused by students but were they not threatened by D with 'action detrimental or unpleasant' to themselves? The majority of shopkeepers did not view the threat seriously but then nor did Wellington when he replied, 'Publish and be damned.' In *Garwood* [1987] 1 WLR 319, [1987] Crim LR 476, CA, the court said:

[I]t is only rarely that a judge will need to enter upon a definition of the word menaces. It is an ordinary word of which the meaning will be clear to any jury.... It seems to us that there are two possible occasions upon which a further direction on the meaning of the word menaces may be required. The first is where the threats might affect the mind of an ordinary person of normal stability but did not affect the person addressed. In such circumstances that would amount to a sufficient menace: see *R v Clear*.... The second situation is where the threats in fact affected the mind of the victim, although they would not have affected the mind of a person of normal stability. In that case … the existence of menaces is proved providing that the accused man was aware of the likely effect of his actions upon the victim.

Is the question whether something is a menace an objective or a subjective question? Is it an element of actus reus or mens rea?

3. UNWARRANTED DEMAND

If D believes that he is owed money by V and that the threat to reveal a true fact about V is a legitimate means of leverage to persuade V to pay, should D be exposed to prosecution for an offence of blackmail?

CLRC, Eighth Report, Theft, paras 121–122

…

The essential feature of the offence will be that the accused demands something with menaces when he knows either that he has no right to make the demand or that the use of the menaces is improper. This, we believe, will limit the offence to what would ordinarily be thought should be included in blackmail. The true blackmailer will know that he has no reasonable grounds for demanding money as the price of keeping his victim's secret: the person with a genuine claim will be guilty unless he believes that it is proper to use the menaces to enforce his claim. It is likely that, as at present, only those kinds of cases which resemble blackmail in the generally accepted sense will be prosecuted. In doubtful cases the test proposed will, we believe, be one which a jury will find easy to apply. Obviously much would depend on the circumstances. The size of the demand may show whether the accused was seeking genuine compensation or merely trying to make money; and a repetition of a demand once met is likely to be strong evidence of the latter. On this test we should expect that Dymond probably (assuming that the facts were as the defence wished to prove), and Bernhard certainly, would easily establish that they believed that they had reasonable grounds for making the demand. Whether they would establish that they believed that the use of the menaces was a proper means of reinforcing the demand would depend on the facts. A deliberate and unjustified refusal to pay a debt might cause a creditor to believe that he could properly threaten to tell the debtor's wife or employer about the debt. A threat to do some harm disproportionate to the amount of a disputed claim would be strong evidence of the absence of any belief in the propriety of the threat.

At first we proposed to include a requirement that a person's belief that he has reasonable grounds for making the demand or that the use of the menaces is proper should be a reasonable belief. There would be a case for this in policy; for it may be thought that a person who puts pressure on another by menaces of a kind which any reasonable person would think ought to be blackmail should not escape liability merely because his moral standard is too low, or his intelligence too limited, to enable him to appreciate the wrongness of his conduct. The requirement might also make the decision easier for a jury; for if they found that the demand was unwarranted or that the menaces were improper, they would not have to consider whether the accused believed otherwise. But we decided finally not to include the requirement. To require that an honest belief, in order to be a defence, should be reasonable would have the result that the offence of blackmail could be committed by mere negligence (for example, in not consulting a lawyer or, as did Bernhard, in consulting the wrong kind of lawyer). The requirement would also be out of keeping with the rest of the Bill, because all the major offences under it depend expressly or by implication on dishonesty. In particular, the provision in clause 2(1) making it a defence to a charge of theft that the defendant believed that he had the right to deprive the owner does not require that the belief should be reasonable.

…

Notes and questions

1. In the above passage the CLRC refers to the cases of *Dymond* [1920] 2 KB 260, CCA, and *Bernhard* [1938] 2 All ER 140, [1938] 2 KB 264, CCA, both decided under the former law of blackmail. In the former case D wrote to V accusing him of having indecently assaulted her and added, 'I leave this to you to think what you are going to do, paid or gett summons . . . if you don't send to and apologize I shall let everybody knowed in the town it.' In the latter case V, some time after D had ceased to be his mistress, promised her money but later failed to honour his promise. D was informed, incorrectly, that she was legally entitled to the money but having been refused payment she threatened to expose him to his wife and to the press.

2. Should D have a defence to blackmail in all cases in which his demand was reasonable? Should he have a defence if he mistakenly believed his demand was reasonable? However outrageous his beliefs?

3. Should D have a defence to blackmail in all cases in which his use of threats is a legitimate means of enforcing the demand? Only if the demand is reasonable? Even if he mistakenly believes the demand is reasonable? What if it is clear to most people that the use of threats is not a legitimate means of enforcing the demand, but D believes it is? Does it matter if D's belief is reasonable?

Sir Brian MacKenna, 'Blackmail'
[1966] Crim LR 467 at 468

4. The two issues, the reasonableness of the grounds and the propriety of using menaces, are each to be decided by a subjective test. In other words the question for the jury will be whether the defendant believed that he had reasonable grounds and that it was proper to use the menaces. Had the test been objective the question would have been whether the jury, as reasonable men, believed that the defendant's grounds were reasonable and that his menaces were properly used.

5. A man's belief that he has reasonable grounds for making a demand depends on two matters:

    (a) his belief that the facts of the case are such-and-such; and
    (b) his opinion upon these facts that it would be reasonable to make the demand.

In a particular case one man's belief that there are reasonable grounds for making a demand may differ from another's because of a difference in their beliefs about the facts (one believing the facts to be X, the other to be Y), or because of a difference in their opinions upon the same facts (one opining that those facts give a reasonable ground for making the demand, the other that they do not).

6. 'Reasonable grounds' ... cannot be limited to such as are believed to give a legally enforceable claim. To many it would seem reasonable to demand satisfaction of a claim recognised by the law as valid though unenforceable by legal action for some technical reason, such as the want of a writing or the expiration of the period of limitation. To some it would seem equally reasonable to demand payment of a claim incapable in any circumstances of being enforced by action, such as the claim to be paid a winning bet. There may be many other cases in which a moral, as distinct from a legal right, would seem to some at least a reasonable ground for making a demand. On these questions there could be differences of opinion, particularly as to whether on the facts of the case the person

demanding had a moral right to the thing demanded. There could be similar 'moral' differences about the propriety of using threats.

7. The Committee intend that the test shall be subjective in both the respects indicated in 5 above: (i) the facts shall be taken to be those which the defendant believed to exist, and (ii) his opinion as to whether those facts gave him a reasonable ground for making a demand (or made it proper for him to use threats) will be the only relevant one. His own moral standards are to determine the rightness or wrongness of his conduct. This appears from a sentence in paragraph 122 where the Committee discuss (and dismiss) the possible objection ... that 'it may be thought that a person who puts pressure on another by menaces of a kind which any reasonable person would think ought to be blackmail should not escape liability merely because his moral standard is too low, or his intelligence too limited, to enable him to appreciate the wrongness of his conduct.'

8. That a sane man's guilt or innocence should depend in this way on his own opinion as to whether he is acting rightly or wrongly is, I think, an innovation in our criminal law.

9. The claim of right which excuses a taking that might otherwise be theft under s 1 of the Larceny Act 1916, may of course be a mistaken claim, and the mistake may be one of law or of fact. A man's mistaken belief that the rules of the civil law make him the owner of a certain thing is as good an excuse as his mistaken belief that the thing is X when it is in fact Y. But clause 17(1) goes further than this, and gives efficacy to the defendant's moral judgments whatever they may be. That is surely something different. It is one thing to hold that the defendant is excused if he believes the civil law to be X when it is Y. It is another to excuse him in any case where he thinks that what he is doing is morally right, though according to ordinary moral notions he may be doing something very wrong.

10. Dr Glanville Williams observes [*Criminal Law, General Part*, 2nd edn, p 100] that negligence has an objective meaning in the law of tort, and that the same rule prevails in criminal law. I am sure that this is so. If it is, then the analogy is much against the proposed new rule for blackmail. If on a charge of manslaughter by negligence it is no defence for the defendant to prove that he thought it reasonable to act as he did in a case where the ordinary man would think his conduct unreasonable, why should a different rule prevail in blackmail?

11. The Committee give their reasons in paragraph 118 which I shall now examine (I have numbered the sentences for convenient reference):

'118. [1]As to the illegality of making the demand we are decidedly of the opinion that the test should be subjective, namely whether the person in question honestly believes that he has the right to make the demand. [2] This means in effect adopting the test whether there is a claim of right, as in 1916 s30 and not the test whether there is in fact a reasonable cause for making the demand, as in 1916 s29(1)(i). [3] Since blackmail is in its nature an offence of dishonesty, it seems wrong that a person should be guilty of the offence by making a demand which he honestly believes to be justified. [4] Moreover to adopt the objective test seems to involve almost insuperable difficulty. [5] It would be necessary either to set out the various kinds of demands which it was considered should be justified or to find an expression which would describe exactly these kinds but not others. [6] The former course might in theory be possible; but the provision would have to be very elaborate, and it would involve the risk which attends any attempt to list different kinds of conduct for the purpose of a criminal offence—that of including too much or too little. [7] Moreover, there is much room for disagreement as to what kinds of demand should or should not be treated as justified. [8] The latter course seems impossible having regard to the results which have followed from making liability depend on the absence of a 'reasonable or probable cause'. [9] Any general provision would probably have to use some such uninformative expression, and it would be almost bound to cause similar difficulty and uncertainty.' [Similar reasons are said to justify clause 17(1)(b), op cit, para 120.]

12. Sentences [1] to [3] must be read with the following passage from paragraph 122 in which the Committee justify their rejection of the requirement that the defendant's belief as to the reasonableness of his grounds should be a reasonable one:

'The requirement would also be out of keeping with the rest of the Bill, because all the major offences under it depend expressly or by implication on dishonesty. In particular, the provision in clause 2(1) making it a defence to a charge of theft that the defendant believed that he had the right to deprive the owner does not require that the belief should be reasonable....'

13. In paragraph 118 the Committee apparently treat as one and the same thing the defendant's belief that he has a legal right to that which is demanded and his belief that he has reasonable grounds for demanding it. But the two things are different, as I have tried to show in 7 and 9 above. The difference is between mistaking the law and making a wrong moral judgment. Clause 2(1) would be analogous to clause 17(1) only if it provided that the appropriation of anything should not be theft if the person making the appropriation thought it reasonable to do so. That is not what clause 2(1) provides.

14. Sentence [5] states the draftsman's alternatives, either to express his thought in general or in particular terms. Sentences [6] and [7] point out the objection to the use of particular terms: (a) too much or too little may be included, and (b) those listing the cases which are to be included may have difficulty in agreeing about them. Sentences [8] and [9] point out the objection to the use of general terms: there may be difficulty in interpreting them, the kind of difficulty which caused the disagreement between the Court of Criminal Appeal in *Denyer* [1926] 2 KB 258 and the Court of Appeal in *Hardie and Lane Ltd v Chilton* [1928] 2 KB 306. Sentence [4] suggests that all these difficulties may be eliminated by the use of a subjective test. But is this so? Whether the justification for the demand is to be (a) the existence of a state of things (the objective test), or (b) the defendant's belief that that state of things exists (the subjective test), the draftsman must still describe the state of things, using either general or particular terms to do so. Whether the form of the enactment is 'if X exists' or 'if X is believed to exist', X must still be given a value, and there is no means of doing this except by words, which must be either general or particular.

15. The objections to the use of general terms are not fully stated in sentences [8] and [9]. As in the case of particular term, there is a danger of too much or too little being included. If when general words are used there are fewer disagreements among the drafting committee about particular cases, it can only be that the members understand the same general words in different senses or that in choosing those words they do not advert to the particular cases which the words may (or may not) include. These are not necessarily good things.

16. The Committee's solution is to choose the most general expressions ('reasonable grounds' in (a) and 'proper means' in (b)) and to make the defendant himself the judge of what are 'reasonable grounds' under (a) and of what is a 'proper means' under (b). This solution perhaps reduces the possibility of disagreement at the drafting stage and certainly eliminates it at any subsequent stage. When Denyer decides for himself what is reasonable or proper, there is no possibility of any conflict on the point between the two Courts of Appeal. Though this may be convenient, there are disadvantages. These are twofold. If a defendant has acted disgracefully by making a certain demand reinforced by threats of a particular kind, I see no injustice in holding him responsible in a criminal court, even though he may have acted according to his own standard in these matters. On the other hand I see some danger to our general standards of right and wrong if each man can claim to act according to his own, however low that standard may be. That is one objection. Another is the difficulty of the jury's ascertaining the defendant's standard, so that it may be decided whether in the case

before them he acted in accordance with it. A man whose standard is below the general may fail in a particular case to observe even his own standard in which event he would, I suppose, be punishable under clause 17. (What is the position to be if his standard is above the general and he does not act in accordance with it?) But are questions of this kind triable?

Question

Daffid's former girlfriend Vicky left owing him a considerable sum of money. Is Daffid guilty of blackmail if he demands payment of the amount due from Vicky and threatens:

    (i) to send to her parents pornographic photos of Vicky taken with her consent when they cohabited?

    (ii) to send to her parents a photo of Vicky smoking a cigarette, knowing that Vicky is particularly scared that her parents will discover her vice?

    (iii) to damage the few items of property Vicky left in the attic at Daffid's flat for safe storage?

R v Harvey, Uylett and Plummer
(1981) 72 Cr App R 139, Court of Appeal, Criminal Division

(Shaw LJ, Wien and Bingham JJ)

The appellants had entered into a supposed transaction with a rogue named Scott, the basis of which was that Scott would procure a large quantity of cannabis for a sum in excess of £20,000. Scott had no intention of supplying the cannabis but he produced a purported sample, which was in fact cannabis, and followed that up by delivering what turned out to be a load of rubbish. The appellants were accountable to others who had made their contribution to the £20,000 and were much enraged. They then kidnapped Scott's wife and small child. They also kidnapped Scott and subjected him to threats of what would happen to him, and his wife and child, if he did not give them their money back. The appellants were convicted of various offences against the person and of blackmail. The judgment of the court was delivered by:

Bingham J. Section 21(1) of the Theft Act 1968 is in these terms: [his Lordship read s 21(1)]. The learned judge in his direction to the jury quoted the terms of the subsection and then continued as follows:

> 'Now where the defence raise this issue, in other words, where they say that the demand is warranted and where they say they believe they had reasonable cause for making the demand and that the use of the menaces was a proper way of reinforcing the demand, it is for the prosecution to negative that allegation. It is not for the defendants to prove it once they have raised it. It is for the prosecution to prove that they had no such belief. Now is that clear? It is not easy and I do not want to lose you on the way. It has been raised in this case so you have got to ask yourself this. Has the prosecution disproved that these defendants or those who have raised the matter believed that they had *reasonable* grounds for making the demand? Certainly you may say to yourselves that they had been ripped off to the tune of £20,000. They had been swindled ... As I say, on this question of reasonable ground for making a demand, you may say to yourselves: "Well, they did have reasonable ground for making the demand in this sense, that they had put money into this deal, they had been swindled by Scott, and it was reasonable to demand the return of their money." So you may say: "Well, the prosecution have not negatived that but what about the second leg of the proviso, the belief that the use of menaces is a proper method of reinforcing the demand?" Now it is for you to decide what, if any, menaces were made, because that is a question of evidence. If you decide that the threats or menaces made by these

accused, or any of them, were to kill or to maim or to rape, or any of the other matters that have been mentioned in evidence—I mention about three that come into my mind—then those menaces or threats are threats to commit a criminal act, a threat to murder, a threat to rape, or a threat to blow your legs or kneecaps off, those are threats to commit a criminal offence and surely everybody in this country, including the defendants, knows those are criminal offences. The point is that this is a matter of law. It cannot be a proper means of reinforcing the demand to make threats to commit serious criminal offences. So I say to you that if you look at these two counts of blackmail and you decide that these defendants, or any of them, used menaces, dependent upon the menaces you decide were used, the threats that were used, but if you decide that these threats were made by these men to commit criminal offences against Scott, they cannot be heard to say on this blackmail charge that they had reasonable belief that the use of those threats was a proper method of reinforcing their demand.'

Later, when prosecuting counsel drew attention to the learned judge's erroneous reference to 'reasonable' belief, he added the following:

'I do not think it affects the point I was seeking to make, that where the demand or the threat is to commit a criminal offence, and a serious criminal offence like murder and maiming and rape, or whatever it may be, it seems hard for anybody to say that the defendants had a belief that was a proper way of reinforcing their demand. That is the point.'

For the appellants it was submitted that the learned judge's direction, and in particular the earlier of the passages quoted, was incorrect in law because it took away from the jury a question properly falling within their province of decision, namely, what the accused in fact believed. He was wrong to rule as a matter of law that a threat to perform a serious criminal act could never be thought by the person making it to be a proper means. While free to comment on the unlikelihood of a defendant believing threats such as were made in this case to be a proper means, the judge should nonetheless (it was submitted) have left the question to the jury. For the Crown it was submitted that a threat to perform a criminal act can never as a matter of law be a proper means within the subsection, and that the learned judge's direction was accordingly correct. Support for both these approaches is to be found in academic works helpfully brought to the attention of the Court.

The answer to this problem must be found in the language of the subsection, from which in our judgment two points emerge with clarity: (1) The subsection is concerned with the belief of the individual defendant in the particular case: '. . . a demand with menaces is unwarranted unless *the person making it* does so in the belief . . .' (added emphasis). It matters not what the reasonable man, or any man other than the defendant, would believe save in so far as that may throw light on what the defendant in fact believed. Thus the factual question of defendant's belief should be left to the jury. To that extent the subsection is subjective in approach, as is generally desirable in a criminal statute. (2) In order to exonerate a defendant from liability his belief must be that the use of the menaces is a 'proper' means of reinforcing the demand. 'Proper' is an unusual expression to find in a criminal statute. It is not defined in the Act, and no definition need be attempted here. It is, however, plainly a word of wide meaning, certainly wider than (for example) 'lawful'. But the greater includes the less and no act which was not believed to be lawful could be believed to be proper within the meaning of the subsection. Thus no assistance is given to any defendant, even a fanatic or a deranged idealist, who knows or suspects that his threat, or the act threatened, is criminal, but believes it to be justified by his end or his peculiar circumstances. The test is not what he regards as justified, but what he believes to be proper. And where, as here, the threats were to do acts which any sane man knows to be against the laws of every civilised country no jury would hesitate long before dismissing the contention that the defendant genuinely believed the threats to be a proper means of reinforcing even a legitimate demand.

It is accordingly our conclusion that the direction of the learned judge was not strictly correct. If it was necessary to give a direction on this aspect of the case at all (and in the absence of any evidence by the defendants as to their belief we cannot think that there was in reality any live issue concerning it) the jury should have been directed that the demand with menaces was not to be regarded as unwarranted unless the Crown satisfied them in respect of each defendant that the defendant did not make the demand with menaces in the genuine belief both: (a) that he had had reasonable grounds for making the demand; and (b) that the use of the menaces was in the circumstances a proper (meaning for present purposes a lawful, and not a criminal) means of reinforcing the demand.

The learned judge could, of course, make appropriate comment on the unlikelihood of the defendants believing murder and rape or threats to commit those acts to be lawful or other than criminal.

On the facts of this case we are quite satisfied that the misdirection to which we have drawn attention could have caused no possible prejudice to any of the appellants. Accordingly, in our judgment, it is appropriate to apply the proviso to section 2(1) of the Criminal Appeal Act 1968, and the appeals are dismissed.

Appeals against conviction dismissed

Notes and questions

1. In *Lambert* [1972] Crim LR 422, D suspected his wife, W, to be having an affair with V, W's sales manager. D contacted V and informed him that for £250 V could buy D's rights to W (!) and that if V did not accept this offer D would inform V's employer and V's wife of his suspicions. D was charged with blackmail and in directing the jury the trial judge (Deputy Circuit Judge John Arnold) said that a demand was unwarranted unless D made it in the belief that he had reasonable grounds. This did not mean that D's belief be reasonable, only that he honestly thought that it was reasonable. 'The defendant's belief,' the judge continued,

> need not be reasonable. The question whether the defendant held this belief is to ask the question—what did the defendant himself believe? His guilt or innocence depends upon his own opinion whether he was acting rightly or wrongly in the circumstances.... The main question in the case was this. Was the demand with menaces unwarranted? Did the defendant honestly believe he had the right on reasonable grounds for making the demand, and did he honestly believe it was proper to reinforce that demand?... The prosecution must establish that the defendant did not have that belief. The defendant's guilt or innocence depends on his own opinion as to whether he was acting rightly or wrongly at the time.

The defendant was acquitted.

2. Is the effect of s 21, as Sir Brian MacKenna suggests, that the defendant's 'own moral standards are to determine the rightness or wrongness of his conduct'? How does the test compare with that for dishonesty under *Ghosh* (above p **786**).

3. No doubt a lawyer (and even the ordinary man in the street?) would have appreciated in *Harvey* that the defendants were not in law entitled to recover the £20,000 paid for the cannabis. But the court said that it was for the jury to determine as a matter of fact whether they believed their demand to be reasonable. How is the jury to set about this task? How can a jury answer the question: in what circumstances may a person involved in illegal drug trafficking believe that it is reasonable to recover a payment for drugs not delivered? Is not the only possible answer: Never?

4. The court in *Harvey* appears to assume that if D knows that his menace constitutes a threat of action that is criminal then the menace is necessarily improper. Why? If the reasonableness of his demand, however divorced from legal niceties, is to be judged as a matter of fact, why not the menace? If the standards of the Mafia are to be accepted in relation to what they consider to be a reasonable demand, why should not their standards be equally applicable to what they consider to be a proper menace?

4. THE PARADOX OF BLACKMAIL

If it is lawful to demand from B money that he owes you, and it is lawful to expose B to be a homosexual (if he is such), how can it be a crime of such seriousness to do both together? This paradox was first examined by Williams in [1954] Crim LR 79–92, 162–172, 240–246:

The two things that taken separately are moral and legal whites together make a moral and legal black. Although D has a liberty to demand money and a liberty to speak the truth concerning others, and even to threaten to speak the truth, he is not at liberty to demand money under threat of speaking the truth.

Since then it has been the subject of a wealth of literature. See especially, J. Feinberg, *Harmless Wrongdoing (The Moral Limits of the Criminal Law, vol 4)*, 238–276; J. Lindgren, 'Unraveling the Paradox of Blackmail' (1984) 84 Col L Rev 670. An interesting review of many of the theories can be found in Joseph Isenbergh, 'Blackmail from A to C' (1993) 141 U Pa L Rev 1905. The issue was considered by the CLRC who stated that:

A may be owed £100 by B and be unable to get payment. Perhaps A needs the money badly and B is in a position to pay; or perhaps A can easily afford to wait and B is in difficulty. Should it be blackmail for A to threaten B that, if he does not pay, A will assault him; or slash the tyres of his car; or to tell people that B is a homosexual, which he is (or which he is not); or tell people about the debt and anything discreditable about the way in which it was incurred? On one view none of these threats should be enough to make the demand amount to blackmail. For it is no offence merely to utter the threats without making the demand (unless for some particular reason such as breach of the peace or defamation); nor would the threat become criminal merely because it was uttered to reinforce a demand of a kind quite different from those associated with blackmail. Why then should it be blackmail merely because it is uttered to reinforce a demand for money which is owed? On this view no demand with menaces would amount to blackmail, however harsh the action threatened, unless there was dishonesty. This is a tenable view, though an extreme one. In our opinion it goes too far and there are some threats which should make the demand amount to blackmail even if there is a valid claim to the thing demanded. For example, we believe that most people would say that it should be blackmail to threaten to denounce a person, however truly, as a homosexual unless he paid a debt. It does not seem to follow from the existence of a debt that the creditor should be entitled to resort to any method, otherwise non-criminal, to obtain payment. There are limits to the methods permissible for the purpose of enforcing payment of a debt without recourse to the courts. For example, a creditor cannot seize the debtor's goods; and in *Parker* it was held that a creditor who forged a letter from the Admiralty to a sailor warning him to pay a debt was guilty of forgery notwithstanding the existence of the debt.

Some of the theories seeking to explain the extension of the offence to these circumstances include:

(i) Criminalization to protect privacy. See further P. Alldridge, 'Attempted Murder of the Soul: Blackmail, Privacy and Secrets' (1993) 13 OJLS 368. Alldridge argues that 'the essence of the offence of blackmail is intimately connected to secrets, and especially to secrets of a sexual nature'. Alldridge views it as 'a crime of empowerment by the powerless which disrupts and transgresses normal power relationships in a way which is far more serious (since it lingers) than a short act of violence'. He concludes: 'Blackmail concerns the relationship between truth and power: law regards the making of threats as being a province of which it is the sole legitimate occupant. Blackmail threatens to reveal a weakness in that supposed monopoly by threatening to speak truth against it. So, appropriately, a crime based in the threat to reveal (sexual) truth reveals truth about the institution of law'.

(ii) Economic theories defending the criminalization of the paradoxical cases as efficient. See further: D. H. Ginsburg and P. Shechtman, *Blackmail: An economic analysis of the law* (1993) U Pa L Rev 1849. 'The paradox, then, is that of a legal system that gives B the right to reveal information, but prevents him from seeking remuneration in exchange for his forbearance'. They argue:

that the apparent paradox of blackmail, that one may not threaten to do what one has a lawful right to do, is an economically rational rule. If such threats are lawful, there would be an incentive for people to expend resources to develop embarrassing information about others in the hope of then selling their silence. In that case, some people would be deterred from engaging in embarrassing (but lawful) conduct, while some others who were undeterred would find that their business or social acquaintances or family were informed of their activity. Neither such deterrence nor such information can be counted as a good in many situations, however. These particularly include social and family relations in which the concern of one individual for another is altruistic rather than self-interested; i.e., where one might be distressed to learn another's secret, but was not harmed by ignorance of it.

(iii) Criminalizing the blackmailer for gaining advantage to which he is not entitled. Lindgren sees the blackmailer as seeking to bargain with something that does not belong to him or her: 'In effect, the blackmailer attempts to gain an advantage in return for suppressing someone else's actual or potential interest. The blackmailer is negotiating for his own gain with someone else's leverage or bargaining chips'. See further on this J. Lindgren *Unravelling the Paradox of Blackmail* (1984) 84 Col L Rev 670.

(iv) Securing appropriate 'punishment' of the victim as well as the offender. 'Under this theory, the prohibition of blackmail promotes disclosure of information. Bargaining between B [blackmailer] and A [victim], to the extent it is successful, denies to C [the public] information in which C has an interest. If the information has greater value to C than A, the bargaining leads to a net loss. In this theory of blackmail, A and B are to some degree in complicity as wrongdoers and C is their victim'. See J. Isenbergh (1993) 141 U Pa L Rev 1905.

(iv) Preventing private law enforcement. 'If A has done a bad thing that B knows about, B's threat to disclose it is a form of punishment of A. B is collecting a fine of sorts, as well as inflicting a measure of pain'. See further J. G. Brown, *Blackmail as Private Justice* (1993) U Pa L Rev. Brown poses the question 'if people could legally blackmail criminals by threatening to reveal their criminal activity unless paid a fee, would we have less crime?'

(v) Preventing coercion and exploitation. See further, S. Altmann, *A Patchwork Theory of Blackmail* (1993) 141 U Pa L Rev 1639 who argues that blackmail 'is coercive when the blackmailer would have kept silent had the opportunity to demand payment been unavailable. Blackmail is exploitative when the blackmailer obtains a premium over other uses for her information because of the victim's hardship'.

Two leading American academics have offered theories of blackmail as a paradigmatic crime: See G. Fletcher, *Blackmail: The Paradigmatic Crime* (1993) U Pa L Rev 1617 and L. Katz, *Blackmail and Other Forms of Arm-Twisting* (1993) U Pa L Rev 1567. Professor Fletcher argues that 'blackmail is not an anomalous crime but rather a paradigm for understanding both criminal wrongdoing and punishment'. He looks to the earlier works on the paradox, finds that all the earlier theories have flaws and that 'The proper test . . . is whether the transaction with the suspected blackmailer generates a relationship of dominance and subordination'. He concludes that 'Blackmail occurs when, by virtue of the demand and the action satisfying the demands, the blackmailer knows that she can repeat the demand in the future. Living with that knowledge puts the victim of blackmail in a permanently subordinate position'. Taking his theory of blackmail, Fletcher attempts to analyse all criminal conduct in a similar vein: 'Becoming a victim of violence beyond the law means that what we all fear becomes a personal reality; exposure and vulnerability take hold and they continue until the offender is apprehended. It would be difficult to maintain that all crimes are characterised by this feature of dominance. We can say, however, that this relationship of power lies at the core of the criminal law. It is characteristic of the system as a whole'.

L. Katz, in *Blackmail and Other Forms of Arm-Twisting* (1993) U Pa L Rev 1567, argues that blackmail is linked to our more general ideas of punishment. The essence of his argument is that:

When a wrongdoer puts his victim to the choice between two wrongs, the degree of blameworthiness is not much affected by the preferences of the victim. Hence, even though the threatened wrong is non-criminal, the level of blameworthiness is no less than it would be if the threatened wrong were a criminal one—the level of blameworthiness is determined by the wrong committed, not the wrong threatened.

He calls this the 'punishment puzzle'.

Question

Does the answer lie in redrafting the offence of blackmail to exclude the paradox cases, but replacing it with an offence of making illegal threats? J. Feinberg, *The Paradox of Blackmail* (1988) 1 Ratio Juris 83, 89 suggests that:

To preserve the coherence of a criminal code, *either* the threatened disclosure should be made independently illegal, that is, illegal in its own right quite antecedent to any blackmail threat, in which case the threat, to make that disclosure unless one is paid hush money could be unparadoxically prohibited, *or* the disclosure as such should continue to be independently permissible (a valid exercise of free speech), in which case blackmail could be unparadoxically permitted. In other words, if we make disclosure independently illegal then we can ban blackmail because it uses the threat to do something illegal to extract a gain, and if we legalise the disclosure as such, then we must legalise blackmail too since it only uses a threat to do what is legally permitted, in order to extract a gain.

Do you agree?

5. VIEW TO GAIN OR INTENT TO CAUSE LOSS

Theft Act 1968, s 34(2)

For purposes of this Act:

    (a) 'gain' and 'loss' are to be construed as extending only to gain or loss in money or other property but as extending to any such gain or loss whether temporary or permanent: and:

        (i) 'gain' includes a gain by keeping what one has, as well as a gain by getting what one has not: and

        (ii) 'loss' includes a loss by not getting what one might get as well as a loss by parting with what one has . . .

Notes and questions

Normally the blackmailer intends a gain to himself and a loss to the victim but either will suffice. D may commit blackmail where he secures paid employment by V (view to gain) through menaces though his intention is to restore the failing fortunes of V's firm (not to cause loss to V). Conversely D might by menaces cause V to do something, revoke a will for example, which confers no benefit on D but causes loss to others (or might cause them not to get something to which they might get).

In *Bevans* (1987) 87 Cr App R 64, [1988] Crim LR 236, CA, D, crippled by osteo-arthritis, called a doctor, V, and at gunpoint demanded a pain-killing injection which V administered. D was convicted of blackmail and his appeal was dismissed. The drug was property which D had demanded with a view to gain for himself; it was irrelevant that D's ulterior motive was the relief of pain rather than economic gain.

One question which arises here is whether D has an intention to gain or cause loss where he has, or believes he has, a claim of right to the property demanded. In *Lawrence and Pomroy* (1971) 57 Cr App R 64, D and E were convicted of blackmail where they threatened to use force in order to collect a debt owed for roofing repairs effected by D. That D may have had a claim of right to the money demanded was not discussed but in *Parkes* [1973] Crim LR 358, the trial judge (Judge Dean QC) rejected a submission that D could not be guilty of blackmail where by menaces he demanded what was lawfully owing to him. Cf B. Hogan, 'Blackmail' [1966] Crim LR 474.

A person cannot be convicted of theft nor of robbery where he appropriated property under a claim of legal right (p 786, above). The CLRC characterised blackmail as an offence of dishonesty but, if so, does s 21 of Theft Act 1968 carry out their intentions? Is there an invasion of V's economic interests where D demands that V pay a debt that is due or believed to be due? In *Robinson* [1977] Crim LR 173, CA, p 811, above, D could not be convicted of robbery. But can he be convicted of blackmail?

Note also in this connection the offence under s 40 of the Administration of Justice Act 1970 of unlawful harassment of debtors. This deals (see Payne Committee Report, 1969, Cmnd 3909) with the coercing of debtors by reprehensible means calculated to subject the debtor to 'alarm, distress or humiliation'. Instances given to the Payne Committee include calling at the debtor's house with an alsatian dog, threatening to paint over a motor car with the statement that it is the creditor's property, and informing neighbours of the debtor's indebtedness under the guise of seeking information. The offence overlaps with but is wider than blackmail. The offence under s 40 is summary only and is punishable by a level 5 fine.

FURTHER READING

Blackmail—A Symposium (1993) 141(5) U Pa L Rev

R. EPSTEIN, 'Blackmail, Inc' (1983) 50 U Chicago LR 553

L. KATZ, Ill-Gotten Gains: Evasion, Blackmail, Fraud And Kindred Puzzles Of The Law (1996)

26

Burglary and related offences

1. BURGLARY

Theft Act 1968, s 9

(1) A person is guilty of burglary if:
   (a) he enters any building or part of a building as a trespasser and with intent to commit any such offence as is mentioned in subsection (2) below; or
   (b) having entered any building or part of a building as a trespasser he steals or attempts to steal anything in the building or that part of it or inflicts or attempts to inflict on any person therein any grievous bodily harm.

(2) The offences referred to in subsection (1)(a) above are offences of stealing anything in the building or part of a building in question, of inflicting on any person therein any grievous bodily harm [. . .], and of doing unlawful damage to the building or anything therein.

(3) A person guilty of burglary shall on conviction on indictment be liable to imprisonment for a term not exceeding—
   (a) where the offence was committed in respect of a building or part of a building which is a dwelling, fourteen years;
   (b) in any other case, ten years.

(4) References in subsections (1) and (2) above to a building, and the reference in subsection (3) above to a building which is a dwelling, shall apply also to an inhabited vehicle or vessel, and shall apply to any such vehicle or vessel at times when the person having a habitation in it is not there as well as at times when he is.

Note that burglary included entering a building as a trespasser with intent to rape a person therein, until this element of the offence was replaced by s 63 of the Sexual Offences Act 2003—trespassing with intent to commit a sexual offence (see below p **915**).

R v Collins
[1972] 2 All ER 1105, Court of Appeal, Criminal Division

(Edmund Davies, Stephenson LJJ and Boreham J)

[**Edmund Davies LJ** delivered the judgment of the court:]

This is about as extraordinary a case as my brethren and I have ever heard either on the Bench or while at the Bar. Stephen William George Collins was convicted on 29 October 1971 at Essex Assizes of burglary with intent to commit rape and he was sentenced to 21 months' imprisonment. He is a 19 year old youth, and he appeals against that conviction by the certificate of the trial judge. The terms in which that certificate is expressed reveals that the judge was clearly troubled about the case and the conviction.

Let me relate the facts. Were they put into a novel or portrayed on the stage, they would be regarded as being so improbable as to be unworthy of serious consideration and as verging at times on farce. At about two o'clock in the early morning of Saturday, 24 July 1971, a young lady of 18 went to bed at her mother's home in Colchester. She had spent the evening with her boyfriend. She had taken a certain amount of drink, and it may be that this fact affords some explanation of her inability to answer satisfactorily certain crucial questions put to her. She has the habit of sleeping without wearing night apparel in a bed which is very near the lattice-type window of her room. At one stage in her evidence she seemed to be saying that the bed was close up against the window which, in accordance with her practice, was wide open. In the photographs which we have before us, however, there appears to be a gap of some sort between the two, but the bed was clearly quite near the window. At about 3.30 to 4.00 am she awoke and she then saw in the moonlight a vague form crouched in the open window. She was unable to remember, and this is important, whether the form was on the outside of the window sill or on that part of the sill which was inside the room, and for reasons which will later become clear, that seemingly narrow point is of crucial importance. The young lady then realised several things: first of all that the form in the window was that of a male; secondly that he was a naked male; and thirdly that he was a naked male with an erect penis. She also saw in the moonlight that his hair was blond. She thereupon leapt to the conclusion that her boyfriend, with whom for some time she had been on terms of regular and frequent sexual intimacy, was paying her an ardent nocturnal visit. She promptly sat up in bed, and the man descended from the sill and joined her in bed and they had full sexual intercourse. But there was something about him which made her think that things were not as they usually were between her and her boyfriend. The length of his hair, his voice as they had exchanged what was described as 'love talk', and other features led her to the conclusion that somehow there was something different. So she turned on the bedside light, saw that her companion was not her boyfriend and slapped the face of the intruder, who was none other than the appellant. He said to her, 'Give me a good time tonight', and got hold of her arm, but she bit him and told him to go. She then went into the bathroom and he promptly vanished.

The complainant said that she would not have agreed to intercourse if she had known that the person entering her room was not her boyfriend. But there was no suggestion of any force having been used on her, and the intercourse which took place was undoubtedly effected with no resistance on her part.

The appellant was seen by the police at about 10.30am later that same morning. According to the police, the conversation which took place then elicited these points: He was very lustful the previous night. He had taken a lot of drink, and we may here note that drink (which to him is a very real problem) had brought this young man into trouble several times before, but never for an offence of this kind. He went on to say that he knew the complainant because he had worked around her house. On this occasion, desiring sexual intercourse—and according to the police evidence he had added that he was determined to have a girl, by force if necessary, although that part of the police evidence he challenged—he went on to say that he walked around the house, saw a light in an upstairs bedroom, and he knew that this was the girl's bedroom. He found a step ladder, leaned it against the wall and climbed up and looked into the bedroom. What he could see inside through the wide open window was a girl who was naked and asleep. So he descended the ladder and stripped off all his clothes, with the exception of his socks, because apparently he took the view that if the girl's mother entered the bedroom it would be easier to effect a rapid escape if he had his socks on than if he was in his bare feet. That is a matter about which we are not called on to express any view, and would in any event find ourselves unable to express one. Having undressed, he then climbed the ladder and pulled himself up on to the window sill. His version of the matter is that he was pulling himself in when she awoke. She then got up and knelt on the bed, she put her arms around his neck and body, and she seemed to pull him into the bed. He went on:

'. . . I was rather dazed, because I didn't think she would want to know me. We kissed and cuddled for about ten or fifteen minutes and then I had it away with her but found it hard because I had so much to drink.'

The police officer said to the appellant:

'It appears that it was your intention to have intercourse with this girl by force if necessary and it was only pure coincidence that this girl was under the impression that you were her boyfriend and apparently that is why she consented to allowing you to have sexual intercourse with her.'

It was alleged that he then said:

'Yes, I feel awful about this. It is the worst day of my life, but I know it could have been worse.'

Thereupon the officer said to him—and the appellant challenged this—'What do you mean, you know it could have been worse?' to which he is alleged to have replied:

'Well, my trouble is drink and I got very frustrated. As I've told you I only wanted to have it away with a girl and I'm only glad I haven't really hurt her.'

Then he made a statement under caution, in the course of which he said:

'When I stripped off and got up the ladder I made my mind up that I was going to try and have it away with this girl. I feel terrible about this now, but I had too much to drink. I am sorry for what I have done.'

In the course of his testimony, the appellant said that he would not have gone into the room if the girl had not knelt on the bed and beckoned him into the room. He said that if she had objected immediately to his being there or to his having intercourse he would not have persisted. While he was keen on having sexual intercourse that night, it was only if he could find someone who was willing. He strongly denied having told the police that he would, if necessary, have pushed over some girl for the purpose of having intercourse.

There was a submission of no case to answer on the ground that the evidence did not support the charge, particularly that ingredient of it which had reference to entry into the house 'as a trespasser'. But the submission was overruled, and, as we have already related, he gave evidence.

Now, one feature of the case which remained at the conclusion of the evidence in great obscurity is where exactly the appellant was at the moment when, according to him, the girl manifested that she was welcoming him. Was he kneeling on the sill outside the window or the inner sill? It was a crucial matter, for there were certainly three ingredients that it was incumbent on the Crown to establish. Under s 9 of the Theft Act 1968, which renders a person guilty of burglary if he enters any building or part of a building as a trespasser and with the intention of committing rape [note that this version of the offence has been repealed by the Sexual Offences Act 2003], the entry of the appellant into the building must first be proved. Well, there is no doubt about that, for it is common ground that he did enter this girl's bedroom. Secondly, it must be proved that he entered as a trespasser. We will develop that point a little later. Thirdly it must be proved that he entered as a trespasser with intent at the time of entry to commit rape therein.

The second ingredient of the offence—the entry must be as a trespasser—is one which has not, to the best of our knowledge, been previously canvassed in the courts. Views as to its ambit have naturally been canvassed by the textbook writers, and it is perhaps not wholly irrelevant to recall that those who were advising the Home Secretary before the Theft Bill was presented to Parliament had it in mind to get rid of some of the frequently absurd technical rules which had been built up in relation to the old requirement in burglary of a 'breaking and entering'. The cases are legion as to what this did or did not amount to, and happily it is not now necessary for us to consider them. But it was in order to get rid of those technical rules that a new test was introduced, namely that the entry must be 'as a trespasser'.

What does that involve? According to the learned editors of Archbold [*Criminal Pleading, Evidence and Practice* (37th edn, 1969), p 572, para 1505]:

'Any intentional, reckless or negligent entry into a building will, it would appear, constitute a trespass if the building is in the possession of another person who does not consent to the entry. Nor will it make any difference that the entry was the result of a reasonable mistake on the part of the defendant, so far as trespass is concerned.'

If that be right, then it would be no defence for this man to say (and even were he believed in saying), 'Well, I honestly thought that this girl was welcoming me into the room and I therefore entered, fully believing that I had her consent to go in'. If Archbold is right, he would nevertheless be a trespasser, since the apparent consent of the girl was unreal, she being mistaken as to who was at her window. We disagree. We hold that, for the purpose s 9 of the Theft Act 1968, a person entering a building is not guilty of trespass if he enters without knowledge that he is trespassing or at least without acting recklessly as to whether or not he is unlawfully entering.

A view contrary to that of the learned editors of Archbold was expressed in Professor J C Smith's book on *The Law of Theft* [then in its first edition (1968), pp 123, 124, para 462], where, having given an illustration of an entry into premises, the learned author comments:

'It is submitted that . . . D should be acquitted on the ground of lack of mens rea. Though, under the civil law, he entered as a trespasser, it is submitted that he cannot be convicted of the criminal offence unless he knew of the facts which caused him to be a trespasser or, at least, was reckless.'

The matter has also been dealt with by Professor Griew [then in its first edition *The Theft Act 1968*, pp 52, 53, para 4–05] who in his work on the Theft Act 1968 had this passage:

'What if D wrongly believes that he is not trespassing? His belief may rest on facts which, if true, would mean that he was not trespassing: for instance, he may enter a building by mistake, thinking that it is the one he has been invited to enter. Or his belief may be based on a false view of the legal effect of the known facts: for instance, he may misunderstand the effect of a contract granting him a right of passage through a building. Neither kind of mistake will protect him from tort liability for trespass. In either case, then, D satisfies the literal terms of section 9(1): he "enters . . . as a trespasser". But for the purposes of criminal liability a man should be judged on the basis of the facts as he believed them to be, and this should include making allowances for a mistake as to rights under the civil law. This is another way of saying that a serious offence like burglary should be held to require mens rea in the fullest sense of the phrase: D should be liable for burglary only if he knowingly trespasses or is reckless as to whether he trespasses or not. Unhappily it is common for Parliament to omit to make clear whether mens rea is intended to be an element in a statutory offence. It is also, though not equally, common for the courts to supply the mental element by construction of the statute.'

We prefer the view expressed by Professor Smith and Professor Griew to that of the learned editors of Archbold. In the judgment of this court, there cannot be a conviction for entering premises 'as a trespasser' within the meaning of s 9 of the Theft Act 1968 unless the person entering does so knowing that he is a trespasser and nevertheless deliberately enters, or, at the very least, is reckless whether or not he is entering the premises of another without the other party's consent.

Having so held, the pivotal point of this appeal is whether the Crown established that the appellant at the moment that he entered the bedroom knew perfectly well that he was not welcome there or, being reckless whether he was welcome or not, was nevertheless determined to enter. That in turn involves consideration as to where he was at the time that the complainant indicated that she was welcoming him into her bedroom. If, to take an example that was put in the course of argument, her bed had not been near the window but was on the other side of the bedroom, and he (being determined to have her sexually even against her will) climbed through the window and crossed the bedroom to reach her bed, then the offence charged would have been established. But in this case, as we have related, the layout of the room was different, and it became a point of nicety which had to be conclusively established by the Crown as to where he was when the girl made welcoming signs, as she unquestionably at some stage did.

How did the learned judge deal with this matter? We have to say regretfully that there was a flaw in his treatment of it. Referring to s 9, he said:

> '...there are three ingredients. First is the question of entry. Did he enter into that house? Did he enter as a trespasser? That is to say, did he—was the entry, if you are satisfied there was an entry, intentional or reckless? And, finally, and you may think this is the crux of the case as opened to you by [counsel for the Crown], if you are satisfied that he entered as a trespasser, did he have the intention to rape this girl?'

The judge then went on to deal in turn with each of these three ingredients. He first explained what was involved in 'entry' into a building. He then dealt with the second ingredient. But he here unfortunately repeated his earlier observation that the question of entry as a trespasser depended on 'was the entry intentional or reckless?' We have to say that this was putting the matter inaccurately. This mistake may have been derived from a passage in the speech of counsel for the Crown when replying to the submission of 'No case'. Counsel for the Crown at one stage said:

> 'Therefore, the first thing that the Crown have got to prove, my Lord, is that there has been a trespass which may be an intentional trespass, or it may be a reckless trespass.'

Unfortunately the trial judge regarded the matter as though the second ingredient in the burglary charged was whether there had been an intentional or reckless entry, and when he came to develop this topic in his summing-up that error was unfortunately perpetuated. The trial judge told the jury:

> 'He had no right to be in that house, as you know, certainly from the point of view of [the girl's mother], but if you are satisfied about entry, did he enter intentionally or recklessly? What the Prosecution say about this is, you do not really have to consider recklessness because when you consider his own evidence he intended to enter that house, and if you accept the evidence I have just pointed out to you, he, in fact, did so. So, at least, you may think, it was intentional. At the least, you may think it was reckless because as he told you he did not know whether the girl would accept him.'

We are compelled to say that we do not think the trial judge by these observations made it sufficiently clear to the jury the nature of the second test about which they had to be satisfied before the appellant could be convicted of the offence charged. There was no doubt that his entry into the bedroom was 'intentional'. But what the appellant had said was, 'She knelt on the bed, she put her arms around me and then I went in'. If the jury thought he might be truthful in that assertion, they would need to consider whether or not, although entirely surprised by such a reception being accorded to him, this young man might not have been entitled reasonably to regard her action as amounting to an invitation to him to enter. If she in fact appeared to be welcoming him, the Crown do not suggest that he should have realised or even suspected that she was so behaving because, despite the moonlight, she thought he was someone else. Unless the jury were entirely satisfied that the appellant made an effective and substantial entry into the bedroom without the complainant doing or saying anything to cause him to believe that she was consenting to his entering it, he ought not to be convicted of the offence charged. The point is a narrow one, as narrow maybe as the window sill which is crucial to this case. But this is a criminal charge of gravity and, even though one may suspect that his *intention* was to commit the offence charged, unless the facts show with clarity that he in fact committed it he ought not to remain convicted.

Some question arose whether or not the appellant can be regarded as a trespasser ab initio. But we are entirely in agreement with the view expressed in Archbold [*Criminal Pleading, Evidence and Practice* (37th edn, 1969) p 572, para 1505] that the common law doctrine of trespass ab initio has no application to burglary under the Theft Act 1968. One further matter that was canvassed ought perhaps to be mentioned. The point was raised that, the complainant not being the tenant or occupier of the dwelling-house and her mother being apparently in occupation, this girl herself could not in any event have extended an effective invitation to enter, so that even if she had expressly and with full knowledge of all material facts invited the appellant in, he would nevertheless be a trespasser. Whatever be the position in the law of tort, to regard such a proposition as acceptable in the criminal law would be unthinkable.

We have to say that this appeal must be allowed on the basis that the jury were never invited to consider the vital question whether this young man did enter the premises as a trespasser, that is to say knowing perfectly well that he had no invitation to enter or reckless of whether or not his entry was with permission. The certificate of the trial judge, as we have already said, demonstrated that he felt there were points involved calling for further consideration. That consideration we have given to the best of our ability. For the reasons we have stated, the outcome of the appeal is that this young man must be acquitted of the charge preferred against him. The appeal is accordingly allowed and his conviction quashed.

Appeal allowed. Conviction quashed

R v Jones; R v Smith
[1976] 3 All ER 54, Court of Appeal, Criminal Division

(James, Geoffrey Lane LJJ and Cobb J)

Two television sets were removed in the early hours of the morning from the home in Farnborough of Mr Alfred Smith without his knowledge or consent. The sets were subsequently found in the possession of the appellants, Christopher Smith (who lived in Arborfield and was the son of Alfred Smith) and his friend John Jones. At their trial for burglary Alfred Smith said that Christopher would not be a trespasser in his house at any time. The appellants were convicted of burglary.

[**James LJ** delivered the judgment of the court:]

... The next ground of appeal relied on by counsel for the appellants in his argument is that which is put forward as the first ground in each of the appellant's grounds. It is the point on which counsel had laid the greatest stress in the course of his argument. The argument is based on the wording of the Theft Act 1968, s9(1) [his Lordship read s9(1)]. ...

The important words from the point of view of the argument in this appeal are 'having entered any building ... as a trespasser'.

It is a section of an Act of Parliament which introduces a novel concept. Entry as a trespasser was new in 1968 in relation to criminal offences of burglary. It was introduced in substitution for, as an improvement on, the old law, which required considerations of breaking and entering and involved distinctions of nicety which had bedevilled the law for some time.

Counsel for the appellants argues that a person who had a general permission to enter premises of another person cannot be a trespasser. His submission is as short and as simple as that. Related to this case he says that a son to whom a father has given permission generally to enter the father's house cannot be a trespasser if he enters it even though he had decided in his mind before making the entry to commit a criminal offence of theft against the father once he had got into the house and had entered that house solely for the purpose of committing that theft. It is a bold submission. Counsel frankly accepts that there has been no decision of the court since this Act was passed which governs particularly this point. He had reminded us of the decision in *Byrne v Kinematograph Renters Society*

Ltd [[1958] 2 All ER 579, [1958] 1 WLR 762], which he prays in aid of his argument. In that case persons had entered a cinema by producing tickets not for the purpose of seeing the show, but for an ulterior purpose. It was held in the action, which sought to show that they entered as trespassers pursuant to a conspiracy to trespass, that in fact they were not trespassers. The important words in the judgment are [[1958] 2 All ER 579 at 593 per Harman J]: 'They did nothing that they were not invited to do . . .' That provides a distinction between that case and what we consider the position to be in this case.

Counsel has also referred us to one of the trickery cases, *Boyle* [[1954] 2 All ER 721, [1954] 2 QB 292], and in particular to a passage in the judgment of that case [at 722]. He accepts that the trickery cases can be distinguished from such a case as the present because in the trickery cases it can be said that that which would otherwise have been consent to enter was negatived by the fact that consent was obtained by a trick. We do not gain any help in the particular case from that decision.

We were also referred to *Collins* [[1972] 2 All ER 1105, [1973] QB 100] and in particular to the long passage of Edmund Davies LJ [at 1109] where he commenced the consideration of what is involved by the words 'the entry must be "as a trespasser"'. Again it is unnecessary to cite that long passage in full; suffice it to say that this court on that occasion expressly approved the view expressed in Professor Smith's book on the *Law of Theft* [(1968) 123, 124], and also the view of Professor Griew [(1968) 52, 53] in his publication on the Theft Act 1968 on this aspect of what is involved in being a trespasser.

In our view the passage there referred to is consonant with the passage in the well-known case of *Hillen and Pettigrew v ICI (Alkali) Ltd* [[1936] AC 65 at 69] where, in the speech of Lord Atkin, these words appear:

> 'My Lords, in my opinion this duty to an invitee only extends so long as and so far as the invitee is making what can reasonably be contemplated as an ordinary and reasonable use of the premises by the invitee for the purposes for which he has been invited. He is not invited to use any part of the premises for purposes which he knows are wrongfully dangerous and constitute an improper use. As Scrutton LJ has pointedly said [*The Calgarth* [1927] P 93 at 110]: "When you invite person into your house to use the staircase you do not invite him to slide down the banisters." '

That case of course was a civil case in which it was sought to make the defendant liable for a tort.

The decision in *Collins* in this court, a decision on the criminal law, added to the concept of trespass as a civil wrong only the mental element of mens rea, which is essential to the criminal offence. Taking the law as expressed in *Hillen and Pettigrew v ICI (Alkali) Ltd* and in *Collins*, it is our view that a person is a trespasser for the purpose of s 9(1)(b) of the Theft Act 1968 if he enters premises of another knowing that he is entering in excess of the permission that has been given to him, or being reckless whether he is entering in excess of the permission that has been given to him to enter, providing the facts are known to the accused which enable him to realise that he is acting in excess of the permission given or that he is acting recklessly as to whether he exceeds that permission, then that is sufficient for the jury to decide that he is in fact a trespasser.

In this particular case it was a matter for the jury to consider whether, on all the facts, it was shown by the prosecution that the appellants entered with the knowledge that entry was being effected against the consent or in excess of the consent that had been given by Mr Alfred Smith to his son Christopher. The jury were, by their verdict, satisfied of that. It was a novel argument that we heard, interesting but one without, in our view, any foundation.

Finally, before parting with the matter, we would refer to a passage of the summing-up to the jury which I think one must read in full. In the course of that the recorder said:

> 'I have read out the conversations they had with Detective Sergeant Tarrant and in essence Smith said, "My father gave me leave to take these sets and Jones was invited along to help." If that account may

be true, that is an end of the case, but if you are convinced that that night they went to the house and entered as trespassers and had no leave or licence to go there for that purpose and they intended to steal these sets and keep them permanently themselves, acting dishonestly, then you will convict them. Learned counsel for the prosecution did mention the possibility that you might come to the conclusion that they had gone into the house with leave or licence of the father and it would be possible for you to bring in a verdict simply of theft but, members of the jury, of course it is open to you to do that if you felt that the entry to the house was as a consequence of the father's leave or licence, but what counts of course for the crime of burglary to be made out is the frame of mind of each person when they go into the property. If you go in intending to steal, then your entry is burglarious, it is to trespass because no one gave you permission to go in and steal in the house.'

Then the recorder gave an illustration of the example of a person who is invited to go into a house to make a cup of tea and that person goes in and steals the silver and he went on:

'I hope that illustrates the matter sensibly. Therefore you may find it difficult not to say, if they went in there they must have gone in order to steal because they took elaborate precautions, going there at dead of night, you really cannot say that under any circumstances their entry to the house could have been other than trespass.'

In that passage that I have just read the recorder put the matter properly to the jury in relation to the aspect of trespass and on this ground of appeal as on the others we find that the case is not made out, that there was not misdirection, as I have already indicated early in the judgment, and in those circumstances the appeal will be dismissed in the case of each of the appellants.

Appeals dismissed

(1) ENTRY

At common law the insertion of any part of D's body, however small—a finger through an opening—was a sufficient entry. In *Collins* Edmund Davies LJ appears to suggest that this has changed by requiring a 'substantial and effective' entry. In *Brown* [1985] Crim LR 212, however, there was a sufficient entry where D's feet were on the ground outside a shop and the top half of his body was inside the broken shop window, as if he was rummaging for goods displayed there. The court said that the word 'substantial' did not materially assist but the entry must be 'effective' and here it was. Perhaps D was already in a position to steal. But in *Ryan* [1996] Crim LR 320 D became trapped by the neck with only his head and right arm inside the window. His argument that his act was not capable of constituting an entry because he could not have stolen anything was rejected. In what sense could this be said to be 'effective'?

It cannot have been intended that D must have got so far into the building as to be able to accomplish his unlawful purpose. D who enters intending to cause grievous bodily harm to V is surely guilty of burglary when he enters through the ground floor window though V is on the fourth floor. Thus it is hard to see that there is any requirement that the act be either an 'effective' or a 'substantial' entry. *Ryan* decided only that there was evidence on which a jury could find that D had entered, suggesting that it is open to a jury to find he had not. It is in principle unsatisfactory that it should be open to a jury to find that there is no entry when such facts are established. Is the best course to accept the continued existence of the common law rule?

Has D 'entered' when he: (a) uses his 9-year-old child to climb through the window to steal? (b) uses a trained animal to do so? (c) pokes a telescopic grab handle through the letter box to seize property inside the building? (d) sends a letter bomb to V's house through the post?

(2) AS A TRESPASSER

1. What must D do to render him a trespasser for the purpose of burglary?

2. What must D know to render him a trespasser for the purpose of burglary?

3. For the purposes of staging a sit-in, students enter the main administrative offices of the university. They believe (wrongly) that, as students of the university, they are entitled to go anywhere on university premises. One of them steals a file from the registry office. Is he a burglar?

4. Dan, who is courting Stella, knows that Peter, Stella's father, has formed a strong dislike for him and has forbidden him ever to enter Peter's house. But, at Stella's invitation, he enters the house one evening without Peter's knowledge. Just before he leaves, Dan steals Peter's riding boots. Is Dan a burglar? Would it make any difference to your answer if Dan had accepted Stella's invitation only because he wished to steal Peter's riding boots?

5. It appears from the report of *Collins* that D 'knew the complainant because he had worked around her [sic] house.' Presumably he knew that the complainant lived there with her mother. If he did and was aware that the mother was the owner of the house, did he enter as a trespasser?

6. Suppose that in *Jones and Smith* Smith had lived at the Farnborough house with his parents. Would he have been guilty of burglary? Would Jones?

7. 'The decision [in *Jones and Smith*] runs counter to *Collins*, where it must have been held . . . that the defendant was not a trespasser although, since he intended to commit rape if necessary, he knew that his intention was "in excess of the permission". The court in *Jones and Smith* evidently did not realise this aspect of *Collins*. If *Jones and Smith* is right, Collins should have been convicted of burglary—Glanville Williams, *Textbook of Criminal Law* (2nd edn) at p 849. Do you agree? Cf *Barker* (1983) 57 ALJR 426, High Court of Australia, where D, asked to look after V's house during V's absence, entered and stole certain goods. His conviction for burglary was upheld. Murphy J, dissenting, said that to regard such a case as one of burglary would depart very far from the traditional concept of burglary; it would mean that one who accepted an invitation to dinner would be guilty of burglary if he intended to steal a teaspoon. Is the guest a burglar? See further P. J. Pace, 'Burglarious Trespass' [1985] Crim LR 716.

8. Where it is open to the prosecution to do so (for example, where the burglar steals or attempts to steal in the building) the prosecution will normally rely on s 9(1)(b) rather than s 9(1)(a) because, under the former, it is not necessary to prove that D *entered* with the relevant intent. But, whichever limb is relied on, the prosecution must prove that D entered as a trespasser. It is not enough that D becomes a trespasser as by hiding in a store until after closing time: *Laing* [1995] Crim LR 395, CA. D may, of course, thereafter commit burglary by entering another 'part' of the store as a trespasser.

(3) BUILDING OR PART OF A BUILDING

1. In *Stevens v Gourley* (1859) 7 CBNS 99, a question arose whether a wooden structure measuring 16 by 13 feet and intended to be used as a shop was a building for the purposes of the Metropolitan Building Act 1855 though it was not let into the ground and merely rested on timbers laid on the surface. In his judgment Byles J said, at 112:

The only question is, whether the subject-matter of this contract was a 'building' within the fair meaning and contemplation of the Act. And that brings us to the very difficult inquiry, What is a 'building'? Now, the verb 'to build' is often used in a wider sense than the substantive 'building'. Thus, a ship or a barge-builder is said to build a ship or a barge, a coach-builder to build a carriage; so, birds are said to build nests: but neither of these when constructed can be a 'building'. It is a well-established rule, that the words of an Act of Parliament, like those of any other instrument, must if possible be construed according to their ordinary grammatical sense. The imperfection of human language renders it not only difficult, but absolutely impossible, to define the word 'building' with any approach to accuracy. One may say of this or that structure, this or that is not a building; but no general definition can be given; and our lexicographers do not attempt it. Without, therefore, presuming to do what others have failed to do, I may venture to suggest, that, by 'a building' is usually understood a structure of considerable size, and intended to be permanent, or at least to endure for a considerable time. A church, whether constructed of iron or wood, undoubtedly is a building. So, a 'cowhouse' or 'stable' has been held to be a building the occupation of which as tenant entitles the party to be registered as a voter under the . . . Reform Act . . . On the other hand, it is equally clear that a bird-cage is not a building, neither is a wig-box, or a dog-kennel, or a hen-coop—the very value of these things being their portability. It seems to me that the structure in question, which was erected for a shop, and is of considerable dimensions, and intended for the use of human creatures, is clearly a 'building', in the common and ordinary understanding of the word. If we look at the object and intention of the Act, we find that this construction is the only one which will bear it out. The intention—the main intention—was, to prevent the metropolis from being covered with combustible structures. Looking, therefore, at the ordinary meaning of the word, and at the intention of the legislature, I think we are well warranted in coming to the conclusion that this was a 'building' within the prohibition of the statute. . . .

Byles J says of a building that it must be 'intended to be permanent, or at least to endure for a considerable time'. So what of the portable cabins placed at building sites to provide eating and toilet facilities for those working on the site? Can it make any difference that the works are planned to take months or only a matter of days? In *B and S v Leathley* [1979] Crim LR 314, Carlisle Crown Court, a freezer container had been placed in a farmyard for goods storage. For some two or three years it had been resting on sleepers, was connected to the mains electricity and the doors were equipped with locks. It was held to be a building. Cf *Norfolk Constabulary v Seekings and Gould* [1986] Crim LR 167, Norwich Crown Court. Needing extra storage space, a supermarket had two lorry trailers towed to the site. There they were unhitched, left standing on their wheeled chassis and connected to the mains electricity. Steps were provided for access and entry was made by unlocking the trailer shutters. They had been in use for a year when D and E tried to effect an entry. It was held that the trailers remained vehicles and had not become buildings. What if their tyres had been removed to prevent anyone taking them from the site? Would a wedding marquee set up on the lawn of the bride's parents be capable of being burgled? Why should it matter that the trespass is to a building? Should there be an offence of trespassing on property with intent to commit specified offences thereon? Why?

2. The issue of a part of a building was addressed in *Walkington* [1979] 2 All ER 716, [1979] 1 WLR 1169, CA. D entered the 'counter area' (a rectangle made up from movable counters which housed a till and which was reserved to staff) of a department store and was there observed to open and shut the till drawer. It was held, upholding D's conviction for burglary, that whether the counter area was sufficient to amount to an area from which the public were excluded was a matter for the jury; there was ample evidence from which the jury could conclude that it was such an area and that D knew it.

3. Does Dan, a law student, commit burglary in any of the following cases?
   (i) He enters a telephone kiosk with intent to break open the coin box and steal its contents.
   (ii) He enters the law library and, seeing that no one is around, he goes behind the library counter and steals a bottle of juice that the library assistant had brought for her lunch.
   (iii) He enters the departmental secretary's room intending to pass through into the office of the Head of Department in order to steal an examination paper, but is stopped by the secretary before he reaches the office.
   (iv) He enters a hall of residence, intending to enter any study that might have been left unlocked, in order to steal therein.
   (v) He falls asleep in a cinema and wakes to find the building closed. On his way out through the foyer he helps himself to some cigarettes from the kiosk which stands near the entrance.
   (vi) He enters the Department's computing facility intending to use a computer to order goods over the internet using an unauthorized credit card as payment for them.

(4) MENS REA

1. The mens rea involves two elements: (i) as to the trespassory entry and (ii) as to the ulterior offence.

As to (i) *Collins* shows that D must be proved to know (or be reckless as to) the facts which constitute him a trespasser.

As to (ii) it must be shown that D either:

- in respect of s 9(1)(a) entered with intent to steal, or to inflict grievous bodily harm, or to do unlawful damage to the building or anything therein, or

- in respect of s 9(1)(b) entered and committed, or attempted to commit, the offence of stealing or of inflicting grievous bodily harm.

It is not immediately apparent why D if he enters a building as a trespasser without intent to commit any offence is not a burglar if he thereafter decides to set it alight but is a burglar if he steals some trinket. Under the draft Bill proposed by the CLRC, the commission of rape or unlawful damage after a trespassory entry would also have been burglary. The Bill was amended in Parliament. Was that a wise amendment? See commentary on *Jenkins* [1983] Crim LR 386, (1983) 76 Cr App R 313.

2. Stealing clearly means theft contrary to s 1 of the 1968 Act. So was D in *Morris* (p 752, above) a burglar? Are all shoplifters? Was D in *Gomez*, above, p 753 a burglar? What of D, a

plumber, who on arriving at V's house realizes she is vulnerable and confused. He decides to deceive her as to the extent of the repair necessary. When, if at all, does he become a burglar?

3. Grievous bodily harm must extend to those offences where the infliction of grievous bodily harm is an offence (viz ss 20 and 23 of the Offences Against the Person Act 1861). Following the decision in *Mandair* [1995] 1 AC 208 (removing the distinction between causes and inflicts) it surely extends to the s 18 offence which uses 'causes' rather than inflicts. Whether it extends to murder, is undecided but it would certainly be surprising if it did not do so: the greater may be taken to conclude the less. There are differences depending on whether reliance is placed on s 9(1)(a) or s 9(1)(b). Under the former *intent* must be proved, and thus the offence must be that under s 18 (grievous bodily harm with intent to do gbh). Under s 9(1)(b), offences of ss 18, 20 or 23 OAPA would suffice. Another distinction seems to be suggested by *Jenkins* [1983] 1 All ER 1000, CA. It will be noticed that while s 9(1)(a) refers to 'offences of . . . inflicting on any person therein any grievous bodily harm' s 9(1)(b) merely refers to the infliction (or attempt to inflict) any grievous bodily harm without specifying that it must be an offence. This led the Court of Appeal in *Jenkins*, at 1004, to give the following example:

An intruder gains access to the house without breaking in (where there is an open window for instance). He is on the premises as a trespasser and his intrusion is observed by someone in the house of whom he may not even be aware, and as a result that person suffers a severe shock with a resulting stroke. . . . Should such an event fall outside the provisions of s 9 when causing some damage to property falls fairly within it?

What arguments are there for saying that this event should fall within or without s 9? The House of Lords allowed the appeal in *Jenkins* [1984] AC 242, [1983] 3 All ER 448, without expressing any opinion on this matter. Clause 147 of the Draft Criminal Code would make it clear that the causing of the harm must amount to an offence.

4. Must there be some nexus between the invasion of the building and the commission of the ulterior crime? If D and E, two tramps, squat for the night in V's empty building, does D become a burglar because he attacks E and inflicts on him grievous bodily harm? Should he be?

(5) BURGLARY IN RESPECT OF A DWELLING

1. Since the Criminal Justice Act 1991, burglary of a dwelling—a domestic burglary—is a separate offence. 'Dwelling' is not defined but it presumably means substantially the same as 'dwelling house' in the former offence of burglary at common law and under the Larceny Acts. Is D guilty of domestic burglary by entering as a trespasser with the necessary ulterior intent: a block of flats? a hotel room? a prison cell?

2. As 'dwelling' is an aggravating element in the offence warranting a higher maximum sentence of imprisonment, it should, in principle, import a requirement of mens rea. D enters a dilapidated house believing it to be uninhabited, does he commit a domestic burglary? Is it sufficient that D realizes that the house might be used as a dwelling?

3. What are the advantages of singling out the offence of domestic burglary? Does this re-categorization provide any insight into the principal harm against which burglary is designed to protect?

2. AGGRAVATED BURGLARY

Theft Act 1968, s 10

(1) A person is guilty of aggravated burglary if he commits any burglary and at the time has with him any firearm or imitation firearm, any weapon of offence, or any explosive; and for this purpose:

    (a) 'firearm' includes an airgun or air pistol, and 'imitation firearm' means anything which has the appearance of being a firearm, whether capable of being discharged or not; and

    (b) 'weapon of offence' means any article made or adapted for use for causing injury to or incapacitating a person, or intended by the person having it with him for such use; and

    (c) 'explosive' means any article manufactured for the purpose of producing a practical effect by explosion, or intended by the person having it with him for that purpose.

(2) A person guilty of aggravated burglary shall on conviction on indictment be liable to imprisonment for life.

Notes and questions

1. It must be proved that D had the article of aggravation with him *at the time* of the commission of the burglary. Where the charge is one of entry with intent (s 9(1)(a)) this is the time of the entry; where it is one of committing a specified offence, having entered, etc, (s 9(1)(b)) it is the time of commission of the specified offence. In *Francis* [1982] Crim LR 363, CA, the Ds who were armed with sticks were allowed by V to enter after they noisily demanded entry. They then discarded their sticks and subsequently stole articles in the house. Their convictions for aggravated burglary were quashed; they may have entered with weapons of offence but there was no evidence that at the point of entry they intended to steal. But in *O'Leary* (1986) 82 Cr App R 341, CA, D's conviction for aggravated burglary was upheld where, having entered as a trespasser, he took a knife from the kitchen, went upstairs and forced the occupants to part with property at knifepoint. At the time of committing the offence under s 9(1)(b) he had with him the weapon of offence.

2. 'Has with him' has been interpreted to require knowledge by D that he has the article with him since what aggravates the burglary, and attracts the higher penalty, must be D's decision to have the article of aggravation with him: *Stones* (1989) 89 Cr App R 26, CA.

3. What appears to aggravate the burglary under s 10 is not the *use* of the firearm, weapon of offence or explosive but the possession of any of these articles at the time of the commission of the burglary. If at the time of commission D 'has with him' a firearm or a kilo of semtex it can be no defence that D did not use them in the course of the burglary and never intended to do so. With 'weapon of offence' the position is slightly more complicated. Two categories must be distinguished.

    (i) If the article is one made or adapted for use for causing injury or for incapacitating D may be convicted of aggravated burglary though he neither uses nor intends to use the weapon in the course of the burglary.

    (ii) If the article is intended by D for use for causing injury or for incapacitating, D may be convicted of aggravated burglary only if he had it with him for such use. But if D does have the article with him for such use he may be convicted of aggravated burglary though he does not and does not intend to use the article for such use during the course of the burglary. So D's conviction for aggravated burglary was upheld in

Stones (1989) 89 Cr App R 26, CA even though, as he claimed, he carried a knife in case he was attacked by a rival gang and had no intention of using it during the burglary. The mischief aimed at by s 10, the court said, included the case where the weapon was carried to injure a person unconnected with the burglary because D, if challenged, might use it during the burglary.

4. But the section requires that D 'has with him' the firearm, etc at the time of the commission of the offence. In *O'Leary* D, it may fairly be said, 'has with him' a weapon, the kitchen knife, at the time he threatened the householders since he had possession of it for some moments. But suppose D has been in the kitchen in the course of stealing the food processor when he is surprised by the householder. D seizes a rolling pin and threatens the householder with this. Aggravated burglary? Cp *Kelly* (1992) 97 Cr App R 295, [1993] Crim LR 763, CA, and commentary.

3. TRESPASS WITH INTENT TO COMMIT A SEXUAL OFFENCE

Sexual Offences Act 2003, s 63

63 Trespass with intent to commit a sexual offence

    (1) A person commits an offence if—
        (a) he is a trespasser on any premises,
        (b) he intends to commit a relevant sexual offence on the premises, and
        (c) he knows that, or is reckless as to whether, he is a trespasser.

    (2) In this section—

    'premises' includes a structure or part of a structure;
    'relevant sexual offence' [is all those in that Part of the Act];
    'structure' includes a tent, vehicle or vessel or other temporary or movable structure.

Note the significant differences from burglary: (i) the offence is wider, since any trespass is sufficient and there is no need to prove a trespassory entry; (ii) the trespass relates to 'premises', which is wider than the concept of a building or part of a building; (iii) the concept of 'structure' is widely defined; (iv) as with s 9(1)(a) there is no need for the ulterior offence to occur; (v) the ulterior offences are all those in part 1 of the Act. Would Collins have committed this offence?

4. POSSESSION OF HOUSEBREAKING IMPLEMENTS, ETC

Theft Act 1968, s 25

    (1) A person shall be guilty of an offence if, when not at his place of abode, he has with him any article for use in the course of or in connection with any burglary, theft or cheat.

    (2) A person guilty of an offence under this section shall on conviction on indictment be liable to imprisonment for a term not exceeding three years.

(3) Where a person is charged with an offence under this section, proof that he had with him any article made or adapted for use in committing a burglary, theft or cheat shall be evidence that he had it with him for such use.

(4) Any person may arrest without warrant anyone who is, or whom he, with reasonable cause, suspects to be, committing an offence under this section.

(5) For purposes of this section an offence under section 12(1) of this Act of taking a conveyance shall be treated as theft, and 'cheat' means an offence under section 15 of this Act.

Notes and questions

1. In *Bundy* [1977] 2 All ER 382, [1977] 1 WLR 914, CA, the appellant had been convicted under s 25(1) where the articles had been found in his car. He argued that his car was his 'place of abode' because he lived in it travelling from place to place. Affirming his conviction, the court said (at 384):

In that context [*sc* s25(1)] it is manifest that no offence is committed if a burglar keeps the implements of his criminal trade in his 'place of abode'. The phrase 'place of abode'... connotes, first of all, a site. That is the ordinary meaning of the word 'place'. It is a site at which the occupier intends to abide. So, there are two elements in the phrase 'place of abode', the element of site and the element of intention. When the appellant took the motor car to a site with the intention of abiding there, then his motor car on that site could be said to be his 'place of abode', but when he took it from that site to another site where he intended to abide, the motor car could not be said to be his 'place of abode' during transit. When he was arrested by the police he was not intending to abide on the site where he was arrested. It follows that he was not then at his 'place of abode'.

2. The requirement 'for use in the course of or in connection with' refers to a future use. In *Ellames* [1974] 3 All ER 130, [1974] 1 WLR 1391, CA, where it had been proved that the appellant was in possession of certain articles after but not before a robbery, his conviction was quashed:

An intention to use must necessarily relate to use in the future.... the words 'for use' govern the whole of the words which follow. The object and effect of the words 'in connection with' is to add something to 'in the course of'. It is easy to think of cases where an article could be intended for use 'in connection with' though not 'in the course of' a burglary, etc, eg articles intended to be used while doing preparatory acts or while escaping after the crime.... In our view, to establish an offence under s 25(1) the prosecution must prove that the defendant was in possession of the article, and intended the article to be used in the course of or in connection with some future burglary, theft or cheat; it is enough to prove a general intention to use it for *some* burglary, theft or cheat; we think that this view is supported by the use of the word 'any' in s 25(1). Nor, in our view, is it necessary to prove that the defendant intended to use it himself; it will be enough to prove that he had it with him with the intention that it should be used by someone else. For example, if in the present case it had been proved that the defendant was hiding away these articles, which had already been used for one robbery, with the intention that they should later be used by someone for some other robbery, he would be guilty of an offence under s25(1).

But cf *Minor v DPP* (1987) 86 Cr App R 378, [1988] Crim LR 55, CA. D was disturbed as he and another were about to syphon petrol from a car using a syphoning tube and a petrol can. D was convicted of attempted theft and of going equipped. The justices found, perhaps somewhat strangely, that there was no evidence that D had taken the articles, the tube and can, to the car. D appealed, the question being whether a person carrying out an act of preparation for the offence (in this case theft) could be convicted of going equipped when his possession of the article took place only at the time of the theft or the attempt. The conviction was upheld. Mann J, distinguishing *Ellames*, said, at 381, 'In *Ellames* the crime had been committed before possession was acquired. That is not this case. In this case the theft (which was not in the event committed) was to be posterior to the acquisition of possession of the articles. In that circumstance it seems to me that the offence is made out. It is in my judgment immaterial as to whether or not theft is in fact achieved.' Does it follow that D commits the offence of going equipped if to gain entry to V's house he picks up a brick lying in V's garden and uses this to break a window? Can it properly be said that D 'has with him' the brick, or that D in *Minor* 'has with him' the tube and can?

3. While s 25 does not in terms require an *intent* to use in the course of any burglary, etc, it seems clear that only an intended use is contemplated. No doubt it would suffice that D intended to use the article should the occasion for its use present itself, but it is not enough to prove that D had the article and that he might have used it: *Hargreaves* [1985] Crim LR 243, CA.

4. CLRC, *Theft*, para 148:

[T]he offence under the [section] applies to possessing articles of any kind. There is no reason for listing particular kinds of articles...anything intended for use in committing any of the offences referred to should be included. The offence will apply, for example, to firearms and other offensive weapons, imitation firearms, housebreaking implements, any articles for the purpose of concealing identity (for example masks, rubber gloves and false car number-plates) and...[a variety of] car keys and confidence tricksters' outfits. The reference to the offender having the article for use 'in the course of or in connection with' any of the offences mentioned will secure that the offence under the clause will apply to having an article (for example a motor car) for getting to the place of the crime or getting away afterwards.

See *R v Doukas* [1978] 1 All ER 1061, Court of Appeal, Criminal Division (Geoffrey Lane LJ, Milmo and Watkins JJ). The case is set out at p **830**, above.

5. In *Cooke and Sutcliffe* [1985] Crim LR 215, CA, which also involved the provision by a British Rail steward of his own sandwiches, the court said that the ownership of the sandwiches would matter vitally to the customers if they were poisonous since the Board could pay damages when the steward could not. In the House of Lords ([1986] 2 All ER 985) Lord Bridge said: 'Upright citizens as the ordinary run of British Rail passengers may be presumed to be, I am not prepared to assume that they would necessarily refuse to take and pay for refreshments even if they knew perfectly well that the buffet staff were practising the kind of "fiddle" here involved.' But the opinion of the majority of the House seems to be that in circumstances like those of *Rashid*, *Doukas* and *Cooke* itself there is a case to leave to the jury. If the defendant goes into the witness box and says: 'I believe that no passenger cares a jot whether the sandwiches are mine or British Rail's,' how should the judge direct the jury? Whose belief as to the reaction of the passengers is material—that of the judge, the jury, or the defendant?

6. The CLRC considered that a car may fall within the offence if it is used 'for getting to the place of the crime or getting away afterwards.' What if D drives to a shop with a view to ordering goods for which he does not intend to pay?

7. The offence is described in the side-note (which is not part of the section but may be used as an aid to interpretation) as 'Going equipped for stealing etc.' It was aimed at the person who goes abroad from the place of abode equipped to steal, etc. In *Re McAngus* [1994] Crim LR 602, DC, an extradition case, it was however held that the justices were right to conclude that D had with him counterfeit shirts which were kept in a bonded ware-house to which D had taken two customers (they were in fact undercover agents) and where he agreed to sell them the shirts. The case seems to fall literally within s 25 but if account is taken of the side-note and the intentions of the framers of the section, where had D *gone* with the shirts?

8. Cp s 3 of the Criminal Damage Act 1971 (below, p **962**) which makes it an offence for a person to have 'anything in his custody or control intending without lawful excuse to use it or permit another to use it' for the purpose of committing an offence under s 1 of the Criminal Damage Act. This offence is not limited, as is the offence under s 25 of the Theft Act, by the words 'when not at his place of abode'. Is there any justification for this distinction between the offences? There is no general offence of possessing 'anything' with intent to kill or cause other bodily harm. Should there be such an offence? Should it be an offence to possess 'anything' with intent to commit any offence, or, at least, with intent to commit any arrestable offence?

9. The Home Office propose the introduction of a new subsection within s 25, rendering it an offence to possess equipment to commit frauds whether at home or elsewhere. The proposal is that the new offence will criminalize the possession of articles (defined so as to include computer software) 'for use in the course of or in connection with' the commission or facilitation of a fraud, with a defence to show that there was lawful authority or reasonable excuse. It is also proposed to create an offence of manufacturing, selling or supplying equipment designed for the commission of frauds. D possesses at home a computer, a printer and a hifi system capable of making multiple recordings from CDs. What more, if anything, should be necessary to render him liable for an offence of possessing equipment to facilitate fraud?

FURTHER READING

P. J. Pace, 'Burglarious Trespass' [1985] Crim LR 716

27

Handling stolen goods

Theft Act 1968

22 Handling stolen goods

(1) A person handles stolen goods if (otherwise than in the course of the stealing) knowing or believing them to be stolen goods he dishonestly receives the goods, or dishonestly undertakes or assists in their retention, removal, disposal or realisation by or for the benefit of another person, or if he arranges to do so.

(2) A person guilty of handling stolen goods shall on conviction on indictment be liable to imprisonment for a term not exceeding fourteen years.

24 Scope of offences relating to stolen goods

(1) The provisions of this Act relating to goods which have been stolen shall apply whether the stealing occurred in England or Wales or elsewhere, and whether it occurred before or after the commencement of this Act, provided that the stealing (if not an offence under this Act) amounted to an offence where and at the time when the goods were stolen; and references to stolen goods shall be construed accordingly.

(2) For purposes of those provisions references to stolen goods shall include, in addition to the goods originally stolen and parts of them (whether in their original state or not),—

 (a) any other goods which directly or indirectly represent or have at any time represented the stolen goods in the hands of the thief as being the proceeds of any disposal or realisation of the whole or part of the goods stolen or of goods so representing the stolen goods; and

 (b) any other goods which directly or indirectly represent or have at any time represented the stolen goods in the hands of a handler of the stolen goods or any part of them as being the proceeds of any disposal or realisation of the whole or part of the stolen goods handled by him or of goods so representing them.

(3) But no goods shall be regarded as having continued to be stolen goods after they have been restored to the person from whom they were stolen or to other lawful possession or custody, or after that person and any other person claiming through him have otherwise ceased as regards those goods to have any right to restitution in respect of the theft.

(4) For purposes of the provisions of this Act relating to goods which have been stolen (including sub-sections (1) to (3) above) goods obtained in England or Wales or elsewhere either by blackmail or in the circumstances described in section 15(1) of this Act shall be regarded as stolen; and 'steal', 'theft' and 'thief' shall be construed accordingly.

1. STOLEN GOODS

What constitutes 'stolen goods'?

'Goods' are defined in s 34(2)(b) of the 1968 Act to include 'money and every other description of property except land, and includes things severed from the land by stealing'. The effect seems to be that with minor exceptions the property which can be the subject of handling is co-extensive with that which can be the subject of theft. While things in action are not expressly mentioned in s 34(2) they must be included in the words 'every other description of property except land'. Perhaps a thing in action cannot be 'received' (a word more apt to describe taking control of tangible property) but there would seem to be no reason why a thing in action cannot be 'realised' or 'disposed of'. In *A-G's Reference (No 4 of 1979)* [1981] 1 All ER 1193 at 1198, CA, the court said:

[I]t is clear that a balance in a bank account, being a debt, is itself a thing in action which falls within the definition of goods and may therefore be goods which directly or indirectly represent stolen goods for the purposes of s 24(2)(a).

This makes sense. If D steals £500 and gives £250 in cash to E while opening a bank account in F's favour for the remainder it would be absurd that E might be a handler while F could not. Cf *Forsyth* below.

Proceeds as stolen goods

A stolen article—for example, an Audi car—may pass through many hands by way of sale or exchange but it continues to be stolen goods until it is restored to its owner or other lawful custody or until the owner ceases to have a right to restitution in respect of it: s 24(3). Any person acquiring the stolen car may be convicted of handling it if he acquires it knowing or believing it to be stolen. But the law goes further. See s 24(2) above. If D exchanges the Audi with E for a BMW, the BMW is now notionally stolen because it directly represents the proceeds of the stolen Audi *in the hands of the thief*, D. If E is aware that the Audi was stolen and he exchanges it with F for a Citroën, the Citroën is now also notionally stolen because it represents the proceeds of the stolen Audi *in the hands of the handler*, E.

If D has a voidable title to the BMW (because he obtained it by deception from E) and he sells it to H who buys in good faith for £5,000, the BMW now ceases to be stolen goods; and, once stolen goods cease to be stolen goods, they cannot revert to being stolen because they are subsequently acquired by someone aware of their provenance.

The £5,000 in D's hands, however, is 'stolen' because it indirectly represents the stolen goods in the hands of the thief, provided that the true owner has a right to restitution of the money which now represents his car. If so, anyone to whom he gave it would, if aware of its provenance, be guilty of handling.

The position is more complex where D banks the £5,000. If the £5,000 represents all that D has in the account, money which D draws from the account is stolen goods and a person receiving it from D, having the requisite knowledge, would be guilty of handling. Where, however, D has other innocently acquired money in his account, say a further £5,000 it may be difficult to prove that a cheque drawn for £2,000 represented proceeds of the stolen £5,000—that it represented his share of the ill-gotten £5,000. This will establish the recipient's mens rea, which would be enough to convict him of an attempt. It may be that the full offence is established if it can be proved that D intended the £2,000 to represent the proceeds of the stolen money: *A-G's Reference (No 4 of 1979)* [1981] 1 All ER 1193 at 1199.

The problems which can arise when a stolen thing in action is assigned or converted into cash and vice versa are well illustrated by the next case.

R v Forsyth
[1997] 2 Cr App R 299, Court of Appeal

(Beldam LJ, Bracewell and Mance JJ)

Because of the complexity of the facts, the following note is provided in place of the judgment of the court.

Forsyth (F) was convicted of handling stolen goods. The 'goods' alleged to be stolen were a thing in action, £400,000 of a balance in Polly Peck International (PPI)'s account at the M bank in London. It was alleged that Asil Nadir (N), chairman and chief executive of PPI, stole it on 17/10/89 by ordering the transfer of that sum, via other banks, to the X bank in Geneva. F, in Geneva collected that sum, less commission, in cash from the X bank and deposited it with the Y bank also in Geneva. On her instructions, the Y bank transferred £307,000 to a bank in England and F brought back the balance (after commission) of £88,050 in cash to England. It was alleged she dishonestly handled the proceeds of the theft by N, comprising (i) the thing in action of £307,000 and (ii) £88,050 in cash, by undertaking or assisting in the retention, removal, etc, of this property. F's handling of the thing in action was taken to continue until credit was made to the Bank in England, so the offence was committed within the jurisdiction.

When the M bank opened for business on 17/10/89 PPI's account was in debit to the extent of £7m. There was no thing in action to steal. But the M bank was aware that very large sums of overnight interest were regularly credited to PPI's account and, indeed some £11m was credited that day. If, when the M bank transferred the £400,000, PPI's account was overdrawn, the overdraft was increased (apparently without prior authority), there was no theft and no stolen goods to handle. The evidence as to whether the account was in debit or in credit at the time of the transfer was, in the court's word, 'inconclusive'. Nevertheless, the court held that there was evidence on which the jury could be sure that the account was in credit at that time. There was another problem of timing. It was argued that F may have been allowed to withdraw the cash before the electronic transfer of that sum to the X bank was complete so the cash could not be the proceeds of any disposal or realisation of the stolen thing in action. Again, it appears that the judge ruled that there was evidence on which the jury could find that the transfer was completed before the withdrawal and the Court of Appeal agreed; but they thought it at least arguable that, where a sum is 'credited out of order in well-founded anticipation of an imminent receipt which then follows', the credit directly or indirectly represents the thing in action.

Between the trial and the appeal came the decision of the House of Lords in *Preddy* [above, p **839**], which was invoked by the appellant. When funds are transferred from A to B by CHAPS order or telegraphic transfer, etc, *Preddy* establishes that B does not obtain property 'belonging to' A. B has acquired a new thing in action which never belonged to anyone but him. The property in B's bank account cannot, as Lord Goff said ([1996] 3 All ER 481 at 490), be 'identified' with that which was in A's account; but it does not necessarily follow that it does not 'represent' it. The difficulty for the prosecution in this case was that the bank (or succession of banks) to which the £400,000 was transferred was not dishonest—it was neither thief nor handler. That difficulty was overcome by the court's decision that the words of s 24(2), 'in the hands of', mean 'in the possession or under the control of' and that the new credit balance, including that in the X bank, remained under the control of the thief, N. Although it was a new, different, property, it indirectly represented the stolen goods in the hands of N and was 'stolen'.

But F was not charged with handling the stolen thing in action consisting in the credit in the X bank. That *credit* may have been under the control of N and so 'stolen'; but the X bank's banknotes certainly were not. When they were set aside for the purpose, they perhaps represented the stolen thing in action but they were quite separate property, not in the hands or under the control of any thief or handler. When the bank's cashier counted out £400,000 in notes to pay to F, he was counting money which was the property of, and under the exclusive control of, the bank, which was certainly neither a handler nor a thief. The £400,000 which was passed across the counter to F represented the stolen thing in action but it was not stolen goods while in the hands of the bank clerk. F, however, was acting as N's agent in cashing the cheque. If N, the thief, had done it himself, the cash he received would have represented the stolen goods in the hands of the thief—himself—and so it would have been stolen goods. As F was N's agent, it was the same as if N had done it himself. F was not a *receiver* of stolen goods; the cash was not stolen before she received it. She was in possession of stolen goods but that is not an offence. F was however guilty of handling if, knowing or believing it to be stolen she assisted in the retention, removal, etc, of the stolen cash for the benefit of another person, N. F's conviction was, however, quashed because of an inadequate direction on the meaning of the word 'belief' [below, p 934.]

Note the significance of the fact that F was cashing the cheque as agent for the alleged thief. If A steals money, pays it into a new bank account and, in payment of a debt, gives B a cheque, B, if he cashes the cheque does not receive *or have* stolen money in his hands. The cash in the hands of the bank is not stolen and it is not possible to argue that B is a handler and therefore the goods are stolen because they are in his hands. That would be circular argument. If B believes the money to be stolen, it is arguable that he is guilty of an attempt to handle but it may be that this is not so because his 'mens rea' arises from a mistake of criminal law, not merely one of fact or civil law: above, p 180.

2. WHEN GOODS CEASE TO BE STOLEN

Re Attorney-General's Reference (No 1 of 1974)
[1974] 2 All ER 899, Court of Appeal, Criminal Division

(Lord Widgery CJ, Ashworth and Mocatta JJ)

Lord Widgery CJ. . . . The facts of the present case . . . are these:

> 'A Police Constable found an unlocked unattended car containing packages of new clothing which he suspected, and which in fact subsequently proved to be, stolen. The Officer removed the rotor arm from the vehicle to immobilise it, and kept observation. After about ten minutes, the accused appeared, got into the van and attempted to start the engine. When questioned by the Officer, he gave an implausible explanation, and was arrested.'

On those facts two charges were brought against the respondent: one of stealing the woollen goods, the new clothing, which was in the back of the car in question, and secondly and alternatively of receiving those goods knowing them to be stolen. The trial judge quite properly ruled that there was no evidence to support the first charge, and that he would not leave that to the jury, but an argument developed whether the second count should be left to the jury or not. Counsel for the respondent in the court below had submitted at the close of the prosecution case that there was no case to answer, relying on s 24(3) of the Theft Act 1968. . . .

After hearing argument, the judge accepted the submission of the respondent and directed the jury that they should acquit on the receiving count. That has resulted in the Attorney-General referring the following point of law to us for an opinion under s 36 of the 1977 Act. He expresses the point in this way:

'Whether stolen goods are restored to lawful custody within the meaning of s 24(3) of the Theft Act 1968 when a Police Officer, suspecting them to be stolen, examines and keeps observation on them with a view to tracing the thief or a handler.'

One could put the question perhaps in a somewhat different way by asking whether on the facts set out in the reference the conclusion as a matter of law was clear to the effect that the goods had ceased to be stolen goods. In other words, the question which is really in issue in this reference is whether the trial judge acted correctly in law in saying that those facts disclosed a defence within s 24(3) of the 1968 Act.

Section 24(3) is not perhaps entirely happily worded. It has been pointed out in the course of argument that in the sentence which I have read there is only one relevant verb, and that is 'restore'. The section contemplates that the stolen goods should be restored to the person from whom they were stolen or to other lawful possession or custody. It is pointed out that the word 'restore', although it is entirely appropriate when applied to restoration of the goods to the true owner, is not really an appropriate verb to employ if one is talking about a police officer stumbling on stolen goods and taking them into his own lawful custody or possession.

We are satisfied that despite the absence of another and perhaps more appropriate verb, the effect of s 24(3) is to enable a defendant to plead that the goods had ceased to be stolen goods if the facts are that they were taken by a police officer in the course of his duty and reduced into possession by him.

Whether or not s 24(3) is intended to be a codification of the common law or not, it certainly deals with a topic on which the common law provides a large number of authorities. I shall refer to some of them in a moment, although perhaps not all, and it will be observed that from the earliest times it has been recognised that if the owner of stolen goods resumed possession of them, reduced them into his possession again, that they thereupon ceased to be stolen goods for present purposes and could certainly not be the subject of a later charge of receiving based on events after they had been reduced into possession. It is to be observed that in common law nothing short of a reduction into possession, either by the true owner or by a police officer acting in the execution of his duty, was regarded as sufficient to change the character of the goods from stolen goods into goods which were no longer to be so regarded. . . .

[Lord Widgery discussed *Dolan* (1855) 6 Cox CC 449 and *Schmidt* [1866] LR 1 CCR 15.]

Then there is a helpful case, *Villensky* [[1892] 2 QB 597]. Again it is a case of a parcel in the hands of carriers. This parcel was handed to the carriers in question for conveyance to the consignees, and whilst in the carriers' depot it was stolen by a servant of the carriers who removed the parcel to a different part of the premises and placed on it a label addressed to the prisoners by a name by which they were known and at a house where they resided. The superintendent of the carriers, on receipt of information as to this and after inspection of the parcel, directed it to be replaced in the place from which the thief had removed it and to be sent with a special delivery receipt in a van accompanied by two detectives to the address shown on the label. At that address it was received by the prisoners under circumstances which clearly showed knowledge on their part that it had been stolen. The property in the parcel was laid in the indictment in the carriers and an offer to amend the indictment by substituting the names of the consignees was declined. The carriers' servant pleaded guilty to a count for larceny in the same indictment. It was there held by the Court of Crown Cases Reserved:

'that as the person in which the property was laid [ie the carriers] had resumed possession of the stolen property before its receipt by the prisoners, it had then ceased to be stolen property, and the prisoners could not be convicted of receiving it knowing it to have been stolen.'

In the same report there is a brief and valuable judgment by Pollock B, in these terms [[1892] 2 QB 597 at 599]:

'The decisions in *Dolan* and *Schmidt* are, in my judgment, founded on law and on solid good sense, and they should not be frittered away. It is, of course, frequently the case that when it is found that a person has stolen property he is watched; but the owner of the property, if he wishes to catch the receiver, does not resume possession of the stolen goods; here the owners have done so, and the result is that the conviction must be quashed.'

We refer to that brief judgment because it illustrates in a few clear words what is really the issue in the present case. When the police officer discovered these goods and acted as he did, was the situation that he had taken possession of the goods, in which event, of course, they ceased to be stolen goods, or was it merely that he was watching the goods with a view to the possibility of catching the receiver at a later stage? I will turn later to a consideration of those two alternatives.

Two other cases should, I think, be mentioned at this stage. The next one is *King* [[1938] 2 All ER 662]. We are now getting to far more recent times because the report is published in 1938. The appellant here was convicted with another man of receiving stolen goods knowing them to have been stolen. A fur coat had been stolen and shortly afterwards the police went to a flat where they found the man Burns and told him they were enquiring about some stolen property. He at first denied that there was anything there, but finally admitted the theft and produced a parcel from a wardrobe. While the policeman was in the act of examining the contents of the parcel, the telephone bell rang. Burns answered it and the police heard him say: 'Come along as arranged'. The police then suspended operations and about 20 minutes later the appellant arrived and being admitted by Burns, said: 'I have come for the coat. Harry sent me.' This was heard by the police, who were in hiding at the time. The coat was handed to the appellant by Burns, so that he was actually in possession of it. It was contended that the possession by the police amounted to possession by the owner of the coat, and that, therefore, the coat was not stolen property at the time the appellant received it. It was held by the Court of Criminal Appeal that 'the coat had not been in the possession of the police, and it was therefore still stolen property when the appellant received it.'

Counsel for the Attorney-General, appearing in support of this reference, showed some hesitation in relying on this case, because he clearly took the view that it was perhaps a rather unlikely decision, the policemen having started to examine the coat and then stopped for 20 minutes until the prisoner arrived and then claiming that the coat was not in their possession. It might be thought to be a rather bold decision to say that the police action in that case had not reduced the coat into their possession. But nevertheless that was the view of this court in the judgment of Humphreys J. All the authorities, as I say, point in the same direction.

The most recent case on the present topic, but of little value in the present problems is *Haughton v Smith* [[1975] AC 476, [1973] 3 All ER 1109; p **545**, above]. The case being of little value to us in our present problems, I will deal with it quite briefly. It is a case where a lorry-load of stolen meat was intercepted by police, somewhere in the north of England, who discovered that the lorry was in fact full of stolen goods. After a brief conference they decided to take the lorry on to its destination with a view to catching the receivers at the London end of the affair. So the lorry set off for London with detectives both in the passenger seat and in the back of the vehicle, and in due course was met by the defendant at its destination in London. In that case before this court it was conceded, as it had been conceded below, that the goods had been reduced into the possession of the police when they took possession of the lorry in the north of England, so no dispute in this court or later in the House of Lords was raised on that issue. It is, however, to be noted that three of their Lordships, when the matter got to the House of Lords, expressed some hesitation as to the propriety of the prosecution conceding in that case that the goods had been reduced to the possession of the police when the lorry was first intercepted. Since we cannot discover on what ground those doubts were expressed either from the report of the speeches or from the report of the argument, we cannot take advantage of that case in the present problem.

Now to return to the present problem again with those authorities in the background did the conduct of the police officer, as already briefly recounted, amount to a taking of possession of the woollen goods in the back seat of the motor car? What he did, to repeat the essential facts, was: seeing these goods in the car and being suspicious of them because they were brand new goods and in an unlikely position, he removed the rotor arm and stood by in cover to interrogate any driver of the car who might subsequently appear. Did that amount to a taking possession of the goods in the back of the car? In our judgment it depended primarily on the intentions of the police officer. If the police officer seeing these goods in the back of the car had made up his mind that he would take them into custody, that he would reduce them into his possession or control, take charge of them so that they could not be removed and so that he would have the disposal of them, then it would be a perfectly proper conclusion to say that he had taken possession of the goods. On the other hand, if the truth of the matter is that he was of an entirely open mind at that stage as to whether the goods were to be seized or not and was of an entirely open mind as to whether he should take possession of them or not, but merely stood by so that when the driver of the car appeared he could ask certain questions of that driver as to the nature of the goods and why they were there, then there is no reason whatever to suggest that he had taken the goods into his possession or control. It may be, of course, that he had both objects in mind. It is possible in a case like this that the police officer may have intended by removing the rotor arm both to prevent the car from being driven away and to enable him to assert control over the woollen goods as such. But if the jury came to the conclusion that the proper explanation of what had happened was that the police officer had not intended at that stage to reduce the goods into his possession or to assume the control of them, and at that stage was merely concerned to ensure that the driver, if he appeared, could not get away without answering questions, then in that case the proper conclusion of the jury would have been to the effect that the goods had not been reduced into the possession of the police and therefore a defence under s 24(3) of the 1968 Act would not be of use to this particular defendant.

In the light of those considerations it has become quite obvious that the trial judge was wrong in withdrawing the issue from the jury. As a matter of law he was not entitled to conclude from the facts which I have set out more than once that these goods were reduced into the possession of the police officer. What he should have done in our opinion would have been to have left that issue to the jury for decision, directing the jury that they should find that the prosecution case was without substance if they thought that the police officer had assumed control of the goods as such and reduced them into his possession. Whereas, on the other hand, they should have found the case proved, assuming that they were satisfied about its other elements, if they were of the opinion that the police officer in removing the rotor arm and standing by and watching was doing no more than ensure that the driver should not get away without interrogation and was not at that stage seeking to assume possession of the goods as such at all. That is our opinion.

Determination accordingly

Notes and questions

1. In determining whether goods have ceased to be stolen which issues are for the judge and which for the jury? Considering *Haughton v Smith*, do you think that, had the prosecution not conceded the point, it would have been successfully argued that the goods on the lorry remained stolen goods, that is, they had not been restored to the possession or control of the police?

2. In *A-G's Reference (No 1 of 1974)* was not the only possible interpretation of the police officer's conduct, and especially his immobilization of the car, that he had taken 'custody' of the car and its contents? If so, was not the trial judge right to withdraw the case from the jury? The police officer's intention may have been conditional (I will let D drive away with the goods in the back of the car only if he satisfies me that they are not stolen) but even if it was so conditioned, should this make any difference?

3. FORMS OF HANDLING

Under the old law before the Theft Act 1968 it was an offence to 'receive' stolen property. This was interpreted as requiring that D should have exclusive control over the property or should be acting in concert with the thief so as to have joint control of the property. This meant that if, say, D helped E to load stolen goods onto a lorry, or allowed E to leave them in D's garage overnight, or put E into contact with a prospective buyer, D did not thereby become guilty of receiving. The CLRC was in favour of enlarging the offence and s 22 extends not only to receiving but to what the CLRC referred to (Cmnd 2977, para 127) as 'other kinds of meddling with stolen property'. The offence may be committed in the following ways: (i) by *receiving* the goods; (ii) by *undertaking* the retention, removal, disposal or realisation of the goods for the benefit of another person; (iii) by *assisting* in the retention, removal, disposal or realisation of the goods by another person, and (iv) by *arranging* to do (i), (ii) or (iii). The words of the section, it was said in *Deakin* [1972] 3 All ER 803 at 808, 'are obviously intended to throw the net very wide'.

R v Kanwar

[1982] 2 All ER 528, Court of Appeal, Criminal Division

(Dunn LJ, Cantley and Sheldon JJ)

[**Cantley J** read the following judgment of the court:]

In counts 7 and 9 of an indictment on which she was tried with others, the appellant was charged with dishonestly assisting in the retention of stolen goods for the benefit of Maninder Singh Kanwar, who was her husband. She was convicted and by way of sentence was given a conditional discharge. She now appeals against her conviction.

Her husband had brought the stolen goods to their house where the goods were used in the home. It was conceded that the appellant was not present when the goods were brought to the house. She was in hospital at the time.

On 2 November 1978 police officers, armed with a search warrant, came to the house to look for and take away any goods which they found there which corresponded with a list of stolen goods in their possession. The appellant arrived during the search and was told of the object of the search. She replied: 'There's no stolen property here.'

She was subsequently asked a number of questions with regard to specific articles which were in the house and in reply to those questions, she gave answers which were lies. It is sufficient for present purposes to take two examples. She was asked about a painting which was in the living room and she replied: 'I bought it from a shop. I have a receipt.' The officer said: 'That's not true.' She said: 'Yes. I have.' He said: 'If you can find a receipt, please have a look.' She made some pretence of looking for the receipt but none was produced and ultimately she at least tacitly admitted there was none. The painting is one of the articles in the particulars to count 9.

She was also asked about a mirror which was in the kitchen. This is one of the articles in the particulars to count 7. The officer said: 'What about the mirror?' She said: 'I bought it from the market.' The officer asked: 'When?' She said: 'Sometime last year.' There is no dispute that that answer was a lie as was the answer about the painting. Later on, she was warned that she was telling lies and that the property was stolen. She said: 'No, it isn't. We're trying to build up a nice home.' Ultimately, although the officer had had no intention of arresting her when he came to the house, he did arrest her and she was subsequently charged.

The appellant did not give evidence and the evidence of the police officer stood uncontradicted.

In *R v Thornhill*, decided in this court on 15 May 1981, and in *R v Sanders*, decided in this court on 25 February 1982, both unreported, it was held that merely using stolen goods in the possession of another does not constitute the offence of assisting in their retention. To constitute the offence, something must be done by the offender, and done intentionally and dishonestly, for the purpose of enabling the goods to be retained. Examples of such conduct are concealing or helping to conceal the goods, or doing something to make them more difficult to find or to identify. Such conduct must be done knowing or believing the goods to be stolen and done dishonestly and for the benefit of another.

We see no reason why the requisite assistance should be restricted to physical acts. Verbal representations, whether oral or in writing, for the purpose of concealing the identity of stolen goods may, if made dishonestly and for the benefit of another, amount to handling stolen goods by assisting in their retention within the meaning of s 22 of the Theft Act 1968.

The requisite assistance need not be successful in its object. It would be absurd if a person dishonestly concealing stolen goods for the benefit of a receiver could establish a defence by showing that he was caught in the act. In the present case, if, while the police were in one part of the house, the appellant, in order to conceal the painting had put it under a mattress in the bedroom, it would not alter the nature of her conduct that the police subsequently looked under the mattress and found the picture because they expected to find it there or that they caught her in the act of putting it there.

The appellant told these lies to the police to persuade them that the picture and the mirror were not the stolen property which they had come to take away but were her lawful property which she had bought. If that was true, the articles should be left in the house. She was, of course, telling these lies to protect her husband, who had dishonestly brought the articles there but, in our view, she was nonetheless, at the time, dishonestly assisting in the retention of the stolen articles.

In his summing up, the judge directed the jury as follows:

> 'It would be quite wrong for you to convict this lady if all she did was to watch her husband bring goods into the house, even if she knew or believed that they were stolen goods because, no doubt, you would say to yourselves, "What would she be expected to do about it?" Well, what the Crown say is that she knew or believed them to be stolen and that she was a knowing and willing party to their being kept in that house in those circumstances. The reason the Crown say that, and we shall be coming to the evidence, is that when questioned about a certain number of items, [the appellant] gave answers which the Crown say were not true and that she could not possibly have believed to be true and that she knew perfectly well were untruthful. So, say the prosecution, she was not just an acquiescent wife who could not do much about it, she was, by her conduct in trying to put the police officers as best she could off the scent, demonstrating that she was a willing and knowing part of those things being there and that she was trying to account for them. Well, it will be for you to say, but you must be satisfied before you can convict her on either of these counts, not only that she knew or believed the goods to be stolen, but that she actively assisted her husband in keeping them there; not by just passive acquiescence in the sense of saying, "What can I do about it?" but in the sense of saying, "How nice to have these things in our home, although they are stolen goods".'

In so far as this direction suggests that the appellant would be guilty of the offence if she was merely willing for the goods to be kept and used in the house and was thinking that it was nice to have them there, although they were stolen goods, it is a misdirection. We have considered whether on that account the conviction ought to be quashed. However, the offence was established by the uncontradicted evidence of the police officer which, looked at in full, clearly shows that in order to mislead the officer who had come to take away stolen goods, she misrepresented the identity of the goods which she knew or believed to be stolen. We are satisfied that no miscarriage of justice has occurred and the appeal is accordingly dismissed.

Appeal dismissed

R v Pitchley

(1972) 57 Cr App R 30, Court of Appeal, Criminal Division

(Cairns LJ, Nield and Croom-Johnson JJ)

On 5 November the appellant was handed £150 by his son, Brian, and was asked to look after it. On 6 November the appellant paid the money into his post office savings account. The money was in fact stolen but the appellant claimed that his son told him that he had won the money on the horses and, while he thought this explanation strange, he did not become aware that it was stolen until 7 November. Having become aware of this he had no wish to take his son to the police so he allowed the money to remain in his account and it was still there when he was seen by the police on 11 November. The appellant was convicted of handling the money.

Cairns LJ. . . . The main point that has been taken by Mr Kalisher, who is appearing for the appellant in this Court, is that, assuming that the jury were not satisfied that the appellant received the money knowing it to have been stolen, and that is an assumption which clearly it is right to make, then there was no evidence after that, that from the time when the money was put into the savings bank, that the appellant had done any act in relation to it. His evidence was, and there is no reason to suppose that the jury did not believe it, that at the time when he put the money into the savings bank he still did not know or believe that the money had been stolen—it was only at a later stage that he did. That was on the Saturday according to his evidence, and the position was that the money had simply remained in the savings bank from the Saturday, to the Wednesday when the police approached the appellant. It is fair to say that from the moment when he was approached he displayed the utmost frankness to the extent of correcting them when they said it was £100 to £150 and telling them where the post office savings book was so that the money could be got out again and restored to its rightful owner.

But the question is: Did the conduct of the appellant between the Saturday and the Wednesday amount to an assisting in the retention of this money for the benefit of his son Brian? The Court has been referred to the case of *Brown* (1969) 53 Cr App Rep 527 which was a case where stolen property had been put into a wardrobe at the appellant's house and when police came to inquire about it the appellant said to them: 'Get lost'. The direction to the jury had been on the basis that it was for them to consider whether in saying: 'Get lost', instead of helping the police constable, he was dishonestly assisting in the retention of stolen goods. This Court held that that was a misdirection but there are passages in the judgment in the case of *Brown* (supra) which, in the view of this Court, are of great assistance in determining what is meant by 'retention' in this section. I read first of all from p 528 setting out the main facts a little more fully: 'A witness named Holden was called by the prosecution. He gave evidence that he and others had broken into the cafe and had stolen the goods, and that he had brought them to the appellant's flat, where, incidentally, other people were sleeping, and had hidden them there; and he described how he had taken the cigarettes out of the packets, put them in the plastic bag and hidden them in the wardrobe. Holden went on to say that later and before the police arrived he told the appellant where the cigarettes were; in other words, he said that the appellant well knew that the cigarettes were there and that they had been stolen.' There was no evidence that the appellant had done anything active in relation to the cigarettes up to the time when the police arrived. The Lord Chief Justice, Lord Parker, in the course of his judgment at p 530 said this: 'It is urged here that the mere failure to reveal the presence of the cigarettes, with or without the addition of the spoken words "Get lost", was incapable itself of amounting to an assisting in the retention of the goods within the meaning of the sub-section. The Court has come to the conclusion that that is right. It does not seem to this Court that the mere failure to tell the police, coupled if you like with the words: "Get lost", amounts in itself to an assisting in their retention. On the other hand, those matters did afford strong evidence of what was the real basis of the charge here, namely, that knowing that they have been stolen, he permitted them to remain there or, as it has been put, provided accommodation for these stolen goods in order to assist Holden to retain them.' Having said that the direction was incomplete, the Lord Chief Justice went on to say: 'The Chairman should have gone on to say: "But the fact that he did not tell the constable that they were there and said 'Get lost' is evidence from which you can infer, if you think right, that this man was permitting the goods to remain in his flat, and to that extent assisting in their retention by Holden."'

In this present case there was no question on the evidence of the appellant himself, that he was permitting the money to remain under his control in his savings bank book, and it is clear that this Court in the case of *Brown* (supra) regarded such permitting as sufficient to constitute retention within the meaning of retention. That is clear from the passage I have already read, emphasised in the next paragraph, the final paragraph of the judgment, where the Lord Chief Justice said (at p 531): 'It is a plain case in which the proviso should be applied. It seems to this Court that the only possible inference in these circumstances, once Holden was believed is that this man was assisting in their retention by housing the goods and providing accommodation for them, by permitting them to remain there.' It is important to realise that that language was in relation to a situation where there was no evidence that anything active had been done by the appellant in relation to the goods.

In the course of the argument, Nield J cited the dictionary meaning of the word 'retain'—keep possession of, not lose, continue to have. In the view of this Court, that is the meaning of the word 'retain' in this section. It was submitted by Mr Kalisher that, at any rate, it was ultimately for the jury to decide whether there was retention or not and that even assuming that what the appellant did was of such a character that it could constitute retention, the jury ought to have been directed that it was for them to determine as a matter of fact, whether that was so or not. The Court cannot agree with that submission. The meaning of the word 'retention' in the section is a matter of law in so far as the construction of the word is necessary. It is hardly a difficult question of construction because it is an ordinary English word and in the view of this Court, it was no more necessary for the Deputy Chairman to leave to the jury the question of whether or not what was done amounted to retention, than it would be necessary for a judge in a case where goods had been handed to a person who knew that they had been stolen for him to direct the jury it was for them to decide whether or not that constituted receiving...

Appeal dismissed

Notes and questions

1. In *Coleman* [1986] Crim LR 56, CA, it was proved that D's wife was stealing from her employers and was using the money as part of the living expenses of herself and D. D was convicted of handling on a count which alleged that his wife had paid £650 in solicitors' fees in relation to the purchase of a flat in their joint names. D admitted that he knew the £650 was stolen. Quashing D's conviction, the court said that the actus reus of the offence lay in *assisting* in the disposal of the money. This meant helping or arranging. It was not enough that D derived a benefit from what his wife did unless he had told his wife so to use the money or agreed that she should do so. Suppose that D's wife had asked him what she should do with the money and he told her to invest it in shares. Would D have assisted in its disposal?

2. Are *Pitchley* and *Brown* authority for the proposition that handling may be constituted by omission?

3. Dan's wife, Ena, makes her living by stealing fur coats which she keeps in the garage to Dan's house. Dan is well aware of this but considers it no business of his to interfere so long as he can get his car in and out of the garage. Is Dan a handler?

4. OTHERWISE THAN IN THE COURSE OF THE STEALING: THE RELATIONSHIP BETWEEN HANDLING AND THEFT

'It should be noted,' said the CLRC (Eighth Report, *Theft*, para 132) '. . . that a person guilty of handling stolen goods will often be guilty of stealing them at the same time. This is because what he does in relation to them will be likely to amount to an appropriation within the meaning of [section] 3 as it would if they had not been stolen.'

So why have an offence of handling if the handler is ordinarily guilty of theft? The CLRC gave two reasons. One was that the penalty is higher for handling than for theft (14 years as against then 10, now seven). Why should the penalty be higher for handling than for theft? *Archbold* (2005); paras 21–279, observes that 'Many defendants, who are, in truth, thieves, see themselves as doing well if either the prosecution accepts a plea of guilty of handling, or the jury convicts of handling rather than stealing. This, no doubt, is merely a reflection of what has been the everyday experience in the criminal courts that usually the handler is more leniently dealt with than the thief'. The second was that certain evidence (relating to other stolen goods found in his possession and to previous convictions for handling or theft) may be given against D under s 27 on a charge of handling which is inadmissible on a charge of theft. Again, why should this be so? See also the Sentencing Advisory Panel, *Handling Stolen Goods* (2001).

Given the decision to retain handling as a specific offence, it became necessary to find a formula to mark off handling from theft. Suppose, for example, that D and E enter an unlocked car; D removes the radio and hands this to E. D and E are clearly guilty of theft but unless some special provision is made both would become handlers; E by receiving goods which he knows to be stolen and D by assisting in the disposal of the stolen goods. The special provision is to be found in the words 'otherwise than in the course of the stealing'. Since D and E in this illustration are both clearly in the course of the stealing they cannot be convicted of handling though they may of course be convicted of theft.

In *Pitham and Hehl* (1976) 65 Cr App R 45, [1977] Crim LR 285, CA, one Millman, knowing that his friend McGregor was in prison and in no position to interfere, planned to steal the furniture from McGregor's house. He told the appellants that he had some furniture to sell, took them with him to McGregor's house, and there sold them such furniture as they wished to buy at a considerable undervalue. Millman was convicted of stealing the furniture and the appellants of handling it. They argued that as their handling was 'in the course of the stealing' they could not be convicted of handling. Affirming the conviction, the court said, at 48:

Section 22(1) of the Theft Act provides: 'A person handles stolen goods if (otherwise than in the course of the stealing)'—I emphasise the words 'otherwise than in the course of the stealing'— 'knowing or believing them to be stolen goods he dishonestly receives the goods, or dishonestly undertakes or assists in their retention, removal, disposal or realisation by or for the benefit of another person, or if he arranges to do so.' Now, the two conflicting academic views can be summarised in this way. Professor Smith's view in his book [*The Law of Theft* (3rd edn, 1977)], para 400, seems to be that 'in the course of the stealing' can be a very short time or it can be a very long period of time. Professor Griew in his book [*The Theft Act 1968* (2nd edn, 1974)] paras 8–18, 8–19, seems to be of the opinion that, 'in the course of the stealing', embraces not only the act of stealing as defined by section 1 of the Theft Act 1968, but in addition making away with the goods. In the course of expounding their differing views in their books on the Theft Act the two professors have both referred to ancient authorities. Both are of the opinion that the object of the words, 'otherwise than in the course of the stealing' was to deal with the situation where two men are engaged in different capacities in a joint enterprise. In those circumstances, unless some such limiting words as those to which I have referred were included in the definition of handling, a thief could be guilty of both stealing and receiving. An illustration of the sort of problem which arises is provided by Professor Smith's reference to the old case of *Coggins* (1873) 12 Cox CC 517. In his book on the Theft Act at paragraph 400, he summarises the facts of *Coggins* (supra) in these terms: 'If a servant stole money from his master's till and handed it to an accomplice in his master's shop, the accomplice was guilty of larceny and not guilty of receiving.' He added another example. It was the case of *Perkins* (1852) 5 Cox CC 554. He summarises that case as follows: 'Similarly, if a man committed larceny in the room in which he lodged and threw a bundle of stolen goods to an accomplice in the street, the accomplice was guilty of larceny and not guilty of receiving.'

In our judgment the words to which I have referred in section 22(1), were designed to make it clear that in those sorts of situations a man could not be guilty under the Theft Act of both theft and handling. As was pointed out to Mr Murray by my brother, Bristow J, in the course of argument, the Theft Act in section 1 defines theft. It has been said in this Court more than once that the object of that definition was to make a fresh start so as to get rid of all the subtle distinctions which had arisen in the past under the old law of larceny. Sub-section (1) of section 1 has a side heading, 'Basic definition of theft'. That definition is in these terms: 'A person is guilty of theft if he dishonestly appropriates property belonging to another with the intention of permanently depriving the other of it; and "thief" and "steal" shall be construed accordingly.' What Parliament meant by 'appropriate' was defined in section 3(1): 'Any assumption by a person of the rights of an owner amounts to an appropriation, and this includes, where he has come by the property (innocently or not) without stealing it, any later assumption of a right to it by keeping or dealing with it as owner.'

Mr Murray's submission—a very bold one—was that the general words with which section 3(1) opens, namely, 'Any assumption by a person of the rights of an owner amounts to an appropriation,' are limited by the words beginning 'and this includes'. He submitted that those additional words bring back into the law of theft something akin to the concept of appropriation, which was one of the aspects of the law of larceny which the Theft Act 1968 was intended to get rid of. According to Mr Murray, unless there is something which amounts to 'coming by' the property there cannot be an appropriation. We disagree. The final words of section 3(1) are words of inclusion. The general words at the beginning of section 3(1) are wide enough to cover any assumption by a person of the right of an owner.

What was the appropriation in this case? The jury found that the two appellants had handled the property *after* Millman had stolen it. That is clear from their acquittal of these two appellants on count 3 of the indictment which had charged them jointly with Millman. What had Millman done? He had assumed the right of the owner. He had done that when he took the two appellants to 20 Parry Road, showed them the property and invited them to buy what they wanted. He was then acting as the owner. He was then, in the words of the statute, 'assuming the rights of the owner'. The moment he did that he appropriated McGregor's goods to himself. The appropriation was complete. After this appropriation had been completed there was no question of these two appellants taking part, in the words of section 22, in dealing with the goods 'in the course of the stealing'.

It follows that no problem arises in this case. It may well be that some of the situations which the two learned professors envisage and discuss in their books may have to be dealt with at some future date, but not in this case. The facts are too clear.

Mr Murray suggested the learned judge should have directed the jury in some detail about the possibility that the appropriation had not been an instantaneous appropriation, but had been one which had gone on for some time. He submitted that it might have gone on until such time as the furniture was loaded into the appellant's van. For reasons we have already given that was not a real possibility in this case. It is no part of a judge's duty to give the jury the kind of lecture on the law which may be appropriate for a professor to give to a class of undergraduates. We commend the judge for not having involved himself in a detailed academic analysis of the law relating to this case when on the facts it was as clear as anything could be that either these appellants had helped Millman to steal the goods, or Millman had stolen them and got rid of them by sale to these two appellants. We can see nothing wrong in the learned judge's approach to this case and on that particular ground we affirm what he did and said.

Questions

1. In the light of *Pitham and Hehl*, do you think the accomplices in *Coggins* and *Perkins* could be convicted of handling?

2. D and E, employed by V, agree to steal goods belonging to V. D is to steal the goods and place them in E's locker for removal by E. D steals the goods in the morning and places them in E's locker. E removes them just before leaving at 5.00 pm. Is E a handler? Cf *Atakpu*, p **760**, above.

5. BY OR FOR THE BENEFIT OF ANOTHER

A thief steals property most often to dispose of it for his own benefit by selling it to another. The CLRC was concerned that the thief should not become a handler by disposing, etc for his own benefit the goods he had stolen and sought to do this by introducing the requirement that the disposal, etc be 'by or for the benefit of another'. In *Bloxham* [1983] 1 AC 109, [1982] 1 All ER 582, HL, D, having purchased a car which he subsequently discovered had been stolen, sold it at an undervalue to E. The trial judge rejected a submission that he had no case to answer on a charge of handling and he pleaded guilty. His conviction was upheld by the Court of Appeal on the ground that another person, the buyer E, had been benefited by D's disposal of the car at an undervalue. The House of Lords quashed D's conviction, holding that the sale of the car by D was not 'for the benefit of another' and thus gave the section its intended effect. Cf J. R. Spencer [1981] Crim LR 682, 684, '[Bloxham] did not "undertake . . . for the benefit of another" in that he did not act on another's behalf. And although he assisted another in the *acquisition* of the stolen goods that is not the same thing as assisting in their removal, retention, disposal or realisation by another'.

The drafting of s 22 (above, p **919**) is clumsy in some respects and in the Draft Criminal Code handling is, by cl 172, defined as follows:

A person is guilty of handling stolen goods if (otherwise than in the course of the stealing) knowing or believing them to be stolen goods, he dishonestly:

   (a) receives or arranges to receive the goods; or
   (b) undertakes or arranges to undertake their retention, removal, disposal or realisation for the benefit of another; or
   (c) assists or arranges to assist in their retention, removal, disposal or realisation by another.

6. MENS REA

The mens rea contains two elements: (i) dishonesty; and (ii) knowledge or belief that the goods are stolen.

Dishonesty

Dishonesty bears the same meaning as it does for other offences under the Act, see above, p 786, (but note that s 2 of the Act does not apply). If D intends to restore the goods to the owner he is obviously not acting dishonestly. In *Roberts* (1986) 84 Cr App R 117, [1986] Crim LR 122, CA, insurers advertised a reward for the return of stolen paintings. D contacted them offering to return the paintings provided no attempt was made to arrest him. He was arrested as he collected the £10,000 reward and subsequently convicted of handling, the prosecution's case being that he was involved with the thieves. D appealed, inter alia, on the ground that dishonesty in s 22 must involve dishonesty vis-à-vis the owner of the property and not dishonesty in a more general way. Dismissing D's appeal, the court said that whether D acted dishonestly in relation to the owner would in some circumstances be important, the question whether D was dishonest was a subjective one and it was not necessary that the jury must consider whether D was dishonest vis-à-vis the owner. But in the context of s 22 in respect of whom other than the owner can the act be said to be dishonest? The go-between presents problems. The owner is often anxious to recover his property and is willing to pay for it. Suppose he employs D to contact the thieves to arrange for restoration of the property and D does so (see [1972] Crim LR 213). Literally D assists in its disposal for the benefit of the thieves but his conduct cannot be accounted dishonest at least if he gets no more from the owner than fair remuneration for his services. Is D dishonest if, knowing of the great sentimental value of the property to the owner, he makes an extravagant charge for his services? What if in *Roberts* the thieves had approached D saying that the paintings would be delivered to him for restoration to the insurers, D to pay them £9,000 and keep £1,000 for himself?

Knowing or believing

The interpretation of 'knowing or believing' has occasioned not a little difficulty. It has been held a misdirection to tell the jury that it suffices that D suspected the goods were stolen, or that he believed it more likely than not that the goods were stolen, or that he closed his eyes to the obvious. In *Harris* (1986) 84 Cr App R 75 at 78, CA, it was said, 'In our judgment the words "knowledge or belief" are words of ordinary usage in English. In most cases, but not all, all that need be said to a jury is to ask them whether that which is alleged by the prosecution, namely receipt, knowing or believing that the goods were stolen, has been established.' In *Hall* (1985) 81 Cr App R 260, 264, CA, the court had this to say:

We think that a jury should be directed along these lines. A man may be said to know that goods are stolen when he is told by someone with first hand knowledge (someone such as the thief or the burglar) that such is the case. Belief, of course, is something short of knowledge. It may be said to be the state of mind of a person who says to himself: 'I cannot say I know for certain that these goods are stolen, but there can be no other reasonable conclusion in the light of all the circumstances, in the light of all that I have heard and seen.' Either of those two states of mind is enough to satisfy the words of the statute. The second is enough (that is, belief) even if the defendant says to himself: 'Despite all that

I have seen and all that I have heard, I refuse to believe what my brain tells me is obvious.' What is not enough, of course, is mere suspicion. 'I suspect that these goods may be stolen, but it may be on the other hand that they are not.' That state of mind, of course, does not fall within the words 'knowing or believing'.

In *Forsyth*, above, p **921**, the judge based his direction on *Hall* and the conviction was quashed because it was potentially confusing. Judges have to be careful not to tell juries that 'mere suspicion is not enough' because that might lead them to think that great suspicion is enough. The very greatest suspicion is, apparently, not enough, even when coupled with the fact that D deliberately shut his eyes to the circumstances. In fact this seems to be exactly the situation which the Criminal Law Revision Committee thought would be covered by 'believing'—their example is of a man who buys goods at a ridiculously low price from an unknown seller whom he meets in a pub: Eighth Report, Cmnd 2977 at 64). Is the best practical advice to the judge now that he should avoid any explanation of what 'believing', as distinct from 'knowing', means? Any explanation he gives it almost bound to be wrong. The Court of Appeal constantly tells us what 'believing' is not, but never tells us (except unsuccessfully, as in *Hall*) what it is.

Hall suggests that if D had direct evidence, he knows; if he has mere circumstantial evidence, he believes, but, it would surely be more accurate to describe knowledge in terms of the accuracy of the belief, not the directness of the evidence leading to the belief? Shute has recently suggested that the distinctions between the two concepts are twofold: knowledge constitutes a true belief, and belief includes acceptance of the proposition in question whereas knowledge does not (S. Shute, 'Knowledge and Belief in the Criminal Law' in S. Shute and A. Simester (eds) *Criminal Law Theory: Doctrines of the General Part* (2002) 171 at 194).

What the judge may do is to tell the jury that turning a blind eye to the obvious inference that the goods were stolen is *evidence* that he believed they were stolen; but then he would be advised to stress that they must be sure that he really did believe that. If the jury ask him what *is* this state of mind of which they must be sure, probably all he can properly do is to tell him that 'believing' is an ordinary word of the English language and that, provided they remember it is not suspicion, however great, its meaning is a matter for them, not him.

What is the right solution? Should the law require nothing less than that D knows that the goods are stolen? Or should it be sufficient that D has deliberately turned a blind eye to the possibility; or merely that he is aware that it is (a) highly probable, (b) probable or (c) possible that they are stolen? Would there be a stronger argument for criminalizing reckless handling if the offence was specifically subdivided into offences treating separately professional handling and single incidents of low value 'dodgy trading'?

7. DISHONESTLY RETAINING A WRONGFUL CREDIT

The increased credit balance procured by *Preddy*, above, p **839**, would, before the decision of the House, have been 'stolen goods', and could be the subject of an offence of handling, contrary to s 22 of the 1968 Act. That is no longer so. The 1996 Act filled this lacuna by a new s 24A of the 1968 Act, creating an offence of 'Dishonestly retaining a wrongful credit'.

(1) A person is guilty of an offence if—
  (a) a wrongful credit has been made to an account kept by him or in respect of which he has any right or interest;
  (b) he knows or believes that the credit is wrongful; and
  (c) he dishonestly fails to take such steps as are reasonable in the circumstance to secure that the credit is cancelled.

(2) References to a credit are to a credit of an amount of money.

(3) A credit to an account is wrongful if it is the credit side of a money transfer obtained contrary to section 15A of this Act.

(4) A credit to an account is also wrongful to the extent that it derives from
  (a) theft;
  (b) an offence under section 15A of this Act;
  (c) blackmail; or
  (d) stolen goods.

The effect is that D, a person who has committed an offence under s 15A, commits a second offence under s 24A, if he does not take steps within a reasonable time to divest himself of his ill-gotten gains. The provision is not aimed at him but at E, where D has, without E's connivance, procured the crediting, not of his own, but of E's account; or F, where D has obtained 'a wrongful credit' and transferred it, or part of it, to F's account. The latter case would be covered by s 24(4)(b). But the effect of s 24A(4)(a), (c) and (d) is that the section has a wider application, embracing cases not covered even before *Preddy*.

If D pays into his bank account money which he has stolen, or obtained by blackmail, or by selling stolen goods, and transfers the credit thereby created to F's account, the credit in F's account is a new item of property—a thing in action belonging to F—which has never been 'in the hands' of a thief or handler and so is not 'stolen goods' within s 24(2). F, however, now commits an offence under s 24A(1) if he dishonestly fails to surrender 'the wrongful credit' within a reasonable time. Any money which is withdrawn from a wrongful credit will be stolen goods and subject to the general law of handling: s 24A(8).

There is no provision in s 24A corresponding to s 24(3). Nor is there any exemption for the bona fide purchaser such as is to be found in s 3, above p 761. D sells goods to A who pays him with stolen banknotes. D receives the money in good faith, not knowing or believing it to be stolen. D then learns that the money is stolen. He spends it. He is not guilty of theft—s 3(2)—or any other offence. But if A had paid D by a cheque, drawing on the stolen money, or if D has paid the cash into his own bank account, he then has a wrongful credit and it appears that he will (subject to proof of dishonesty) commit an offence under s 24A when he spends the money because he has failed to take reasonable steps to disgorge. Arguably, that would create not only an unsatisfactory anomaly but also a conflict with the civil law. A transferee of stolen currency for value and without notice gets a good title: *Miller v Race* (1758) 1 Burr 452. The money, whether in cash or in the bank, is surely D's to dispose of as he chooses. It may be that a court will think it necessary to read into s 24A(1) some such qualification as 'except where no person has any right to restitution of the credit', on the ground that Parliament could not have intended to change, or create a conflict with, such a fundamental rule of the civil law. This would introduce a limitation to the same effect as that relating to stolen goods generally in s 24(4).

8. REWARDS FOR RETURN OF STOLEN GOODS

By s 23 of the Theft Act 1968 it is an offence publicly to advertise for the return of stolen goods indicating that no questions will be asked about how the person returning the goods came by them. Should it be? Who does this offence seek to punish and why?

FURTHER READING

L. Blake, 'The Innocent Purchaser and Section 22 of the Theft Act' [1972] Crim LR 494

D. W. Elliott, 'Theft and Related Problems—England, Australia and the USA Compared' (1977) 26 ICLQ 110, 135–144

E. Griew, 'Consistency, Communication and Codification—Reflections on Two Mens Rea Words' in P. R. Glazebrook (ed) *Reshaping the Criminal Law* (1978)

A. T. H. Smith, 'Theft and/or Handling' [1977] Crim LR 517

J. R. Spencer, 'Handling, Theft and the Mala Fide Purchaser' [1985] Crim LR 92

J. R. Spencer, 'The Mishandling of Handling' [1981] Crim LR 682

28

Offences of damage to property

The principal offences of damage to property are governed by the Criminal Damage Act 1971 which is in the main the work of the Law Commission: see The Law Commission (Law Com No 29) *Criminal Law: Report on Offences of Damage to Property* (1970), hereinafter referred to as Law Com No 29.

1. DESTROYING OR DAMAGING PROPERTY OF ANOTHER

Criminal Damage Act 1971, s 1(1)

A person who without lawful excuse destroys or damages any property belonging to another intending to destroy or damage any such property or being reckless as to whether any such property would be destroyed or damaged shall be guilty of an offence.

Where the damage is caused other than by fire (see below, p **962**) the offence is punishable by imprisonment for 10 years.

(1) DESTROY OR DAMAGE

The Act does not define 'destroy or damage'. The *OED* defines 'damage' as 'Injury, harm, *esp* physical injury to a thing such as impairs its value or usefulness'.

In *Samuels v Stubbs* [1972] 4 SASR 200 at 203, Walters J said:

It seems to me that it is difficult to lay down any very general and, at the same time, precise and absolute rule as to what constitutes 'damage'. One must be guided in a great degree by the circumstances of each case, the nature of the article and the mode in which it is affected or treated. ... It is my view, however, that the word ... is sufficiently wide in its meaning to embrace injury, mischief or harm done to property, and that in order to constitute 'damage' it is unnecessary to establish such definite or actual damage as renders the property useless, or prevents it from serving its normal function. ...

And the learned judge then held that a 'temporary functional derangement' of a policeman's cap resulting from it being trampled upon constituted damage though there was no evidence that the cap might not have been restored to its original shape at no cost and without any real trouble to the owner.

Under the former law it was held that a machine may be damaged by removing an integral part (*Tacey* (1821) Russ & Ry 452); or by tampering with it so that it will not work (*Fisher* (1865) LR 1 CCR 7, DC); or by running it in a manner to cause impairment (*Norris* (1840) 9 C & P 241); or by dismantling it (*Getty v Antrim County Council* [1950] NI 114).

In *Hardman v Chief Constable of Avon and Somerset Constabulary* [1986] Crim LR 330 (Judge Llewellyn Jones and justices) it was held that pavement drawings in water soluble paint constituted damage when the local authority was involved in expense in removing them with high-pressure water jets; and in *Roe v Kingerlee* [1986] Crim LR 735, DC it was held that where D had smeared mud and graffiti on the wall of a police cell the justices were wrong to conclude that this was incapable of amounting to damage.

In *A (a juvenile) v R* [1978] Crim LR 689 (Kent CC) D's conviction for damaging a police officer's raincoat by spitting on it was quashed. 'Spitting at a garment,' Judge Streeter said:

could be an act capable of causing damage. However, one must consider the specific garment which has been allegedly damaged. If someone spat upon a satin wedding dress, for example, any attempt to remove the spittle might in itself leave a mark or stain. The court would find no difficulty in saying that an article had been rendered 'imperfect' if, after a reasonable attempt at cleaning it, a stain remained. An article might also have been rendered 'inoperative' if, as a result of what happened, it had been taken to dry cleaners. However, in the present case, no attempt had been made, even with soap and water, to clean the raincoat, which was a service raincoat designed to resist the elements. Consequently, there was no likelihood that if wiped with a damp cloth, the first obvious remedy, there would be any trace or mark remaining on the raincoat requiring further cleaning.

The tenor of the cases under the Act indicates that, as under the former law, 'damage' embraces not only physical damage to the property but also any impairment, temporary or permanent, with the value of usefulness of the property (*Morphitis v Salmon* [1990] Crim LR 48, DC). So to remove the rotor arm or electronic ignition component from a car constitutes damage to the car (though not to the rotor arm if this is removed without damaging it) since without the rotor arm the car will not go. But a mere denial of use of property does not constitute damage. If a landowner finding a car parked on his premises choose to lock up his premises for the night there is no damage to the car though its owner will have to wait until the following morning before he can drive it away.

As to damage to computers, see below, p 962.

Notes and questions

1. Was Judge Streeter right in *A (a juvenile)* to rule that the raincoat was not damaged because it could be wiped clean with a damp cloth? What if the police officer had insisted (perhaps not unreasonably) that the coat be dry-cleaned before he wore it again? Can it sensibly be said that the cap in *Samuels v Stubbs* was damaged if it could be pressed back into shape in a matter of moments? Is there (should there be) a principle of de minimis in relation to criminal damage?

2. In *Hardman* the council clearly incurred expense in washing down the pavement. Would the pavement have been damaged had the council left it to the next downpour to wash away the paint?

3. What if D, as a practical joke, hides the ignition key to V's car and the key to V's house? Is the car damaged because V cannot drive it away? Is V's house damaged because V cannot gain access? Is the door to the house damaged because V cannot open it?

4. What of clamping a car? In *Lloyd v DPP* [1992] 1 All ER 982, DC, the court rejected a submission that, in the absence of any evidence that the clamping caused damage to the car,

this constituted criminal damage. *Lloyd* was followed in *Drake v DPP* [1994] RTR 411, [1994] Crim LR 855 and commentary, the court holding that clamping involved no intrusion into the physical integrity of the car. Deflating the tyres of a car would presumably amount to damage since the car, albeit temporarily, is deprived of its usefulness. So why not clamping? Additionally in *Lloyd*, D's car had 'a large yellow sticker affixed to its windscreen' alerting D to the clamping. Might this have constituted damage to the car?

5. Is a car damaged by (a) disconnecting the battery terminals; (b) removing the ignition key?

6. Is what constitutes 'damage' a question of fact or of law? In *Henderson and Battley* (unreported but noted in *Cox v Riley* (1986) 83 Cr App R 54, [1986] Crim LR 460) the Court of Appeal said that ultimately whether damage was done was a question of fact for the jury; and in *Roe v Kingerlee* the Divisional Court said that what constitutes damage is 'a matter of fact and degree and it is for the justices to decide whether what occurred was damage or not'. In *Samuels v Stubbs* counsel for D submitted that the finding 'of fact' by the trial court that the hat had not been damaged ought not to be disturbed. Walters J said that not only was it the practice of Australian courts to distinguish between the determination of the evidence (a matter of fact) and the determination of the inferences to be drawn from those facts (a matter of law) but that this view was based on respected English authorities. Which view is to be preferred?

7. Does D damage property by improving it (a) in his eyes? (b) in the reasonable man's eyes (eg by whiting out offensive slogans: *Fancy* [1980] Crim LR 171)? See also M. Watson, 'Graffiti—Popular Art, Anti Social Behaviour or Criminal Damage' (2004) 168 JP 668.

(2) PROPERTY

Criminal Damage Act 1971, s 10(1)

In this Act 'property' means property of a tangible nature, whether real or personal, including money and:

    (a) including wild creatures which have been tamed or are ordinarily kept in captivity, and any other wild creatures or their carcasses if, but only if, they have been reduced into possession which has not been lost or abandoned or are in the course of being reduced into possession; but

    (b) not including mushrooms growing wild on any land or flowers, fruit or foliage of a plant growing wild on any land.

For the purposes of this sub-section 'mushroom' includes any fungus and 'plant' includes any shrub or tree.

Law Com No 29, paras 34, 35

Offences of criminal damage to property in the context of the present law connote physical damage in their commission, and for that reason we have not included intangible things in the class of property, damage to which should constitute an offence. On the other hand, in the context of damage to property there is no reason to distinguish, as does the Theft Act between land and other property... We recommend, therefore, that the property which can be the subject of an offence of criminal damage should be all property of a tangible nature, whether real or personal.

Question

Why should D be liable for rotivating his neighbour's lawn, but not for stealing it?

(3) BELONGING TO ANOTHER

Criminal Damage Act 1971, s 10(2)

Property shall be treated for the purposes of this Act as belonging to any person:

   (a) having the custody or control of it;

   (b) having in it any proprietary right or interest (not being an equitable interest arising only from an agreement to transfer or grant an interest); or

   (c) having a charge on it.

   (3) Where property is subject to a trust, the persons to whom it belongs shall be so treated as including any person having a right to enforce the trust.

   (4) Property of a corporation sole shall be so treated as belonging to the corporation notwithstanding a vacancy in the corporation.

The offence under s 1(1) may be committed only where D destroys or damages property 'belonging to another'. Since there are similar policy considerations s 10(2) of the Criminal Damage Act is similar to, though not identical with, s 5 of the Theft Act 1968. It is accordingly enough that V has some proprietary interest in the property which D damages and it does not have to be shown that V is the owner of the property; D may, for example, damage property of which V is the lessee or bailee. Further, D may commit an offence where he is the owner of the property provided that V also has a proprietary interest in the property and that D acts with mens rea.

But if no third party has any interest in the property D cannot by destroying that property, nor by authorizing its destruction, commit an offence under s 1(1) even if this is done in order to perpetrate a fraud by making a claim against insurers.

Question

D falls out with his wife and out of spite defaces the original Picasso which she bought him as a present. Is D liable for criminal damage? Should he be?

(4) INTENTION AND RECKLESSNESS

Intention, unlike recklessness, appears to have no objective connotations. It is not enough to prove that D intentionally did the act (threw the stone, fired the gun) which caused damage, nor that D intended to damage property; it must be proved that D intended to damage property of *another*.

R v Smith (David Raymond)

[1974] 1 All ER 632, Court of Appeal, Criminal Division

(Roskill, James LJJ and Talbot J)

[**James LJ** read the following judgment of the court:]

. . . The question of law in this appeal arises in this way. In 1970 the appellant became the tenant of a ground floor flat at 209 Freemasons Road, London, E16. The letting included a conservatory. In the conservatory the appellant and his brother, who lived with him, installed some electric wiring for use with stereo equipment. Also, with the landlord's permission, they put up roofing material, and asbestos wall panels and laid floor boards. There is no dispute that the roofing, wall panels and floor boards became part of the house and, in law, the property of the landlord. Then in 1972 the appellant gave notice to quit and asked the landlord to allow the appellant's brother to remain as tenant of the flat. On 18 September 1972 the landlord informed the appellant that his brother could not remain. On the next day the appellant damaged the roofing, wall panels and floorboards he had installed in order—according to the appellant and his brother—to gain access to and remove the wiring. The extent of the damage was £130. When interviewed by the police, the appellant said, 'Look, how can I be done for smashing my own property. I put the flooring and that in, so if I want to pull it down it's a matter for me.' The offence for which he was indicted is in these terms:

> 'Damaging property contrary to section 1(1) of the Criminal Damage Act 1971. *Particulars of Offence*: [The appellant] and Steven John Smith on the 19th day of September 1972 in Greater London, without lawful excuse, damaged a conservatory at 209, Freemasons Road, E16, the property of Peter Frank Frand, intending to damage such property or being reckless as to whether such property would be damaged.'

... The appellant's defence was that he honestly believed that the damage he did was to his own property, that he believed that he was entitled to damage his own property, and therefore he had a lawful excuse for his action causing the damage.

In the course of his summing-up the deputy judge directed the jury in these terms:

> 'Now, in order to make the offence complete, the person who is charged with it must destroy or damage that property belonging to another, "without lawful excuse", and that is something that one has got to look at a little more, members of the jury, because you have heard here that, so far as each defendant was concerned, it never occurred to them, and, you may think, quite naturally never occurred to either of them, that these various additions to the house were anything but their own property...But, members of the jury, the Act is quite specific, and so far as the [appellant] is concerned...lawful excuse is the only defence which has been raised. It is said he had a lawful excuse by reason of his belief, his honest and genuinely held belief that he was destroying property which he had a right to destroy if he wanted to. But, members of the jury, I must direct you as a matter of law, and you must, therefore, accept it from me, that belief by the [appellant] that he had the right to do what he did is not lawful excuse within the meaning of the Act. Members of the jury, it is an excuse, it may even be a reasonable excuse, but it is not, members of the jury, a lawful excuse, because, in law, he had no right to do what he did. Members of the jury, as a matter of law, the evidence, in fact, discloses, so far as [the appellant] is concerned, no lawful excuse at all, because, as I say, the only defence which he has raised is the defence that he thought he had the right to do what he did. I have directed you that that is not a lawful excuse, and members of the jury, it follows from that that so far as [the appellant] is concerned, I am bound to direct you as a matter of law that you must find him guilty of this offence with which he is charged.'

It is contended for the appellant that that is a misdirection in law, and that, as a result of the misdirection, the entire defence of the appellant was wrongly withdrawn from the jury...

The offence created [by s 1(1) of the Criminal Damage Act] includes the elements of intention or recklessness and the absence of lawful excuse. There is in s5 of the Act a partial 'definition' of lawful excuse.... [His Lordship referred to s5(2), s5(3) and s5(5).]

It is argued for the appellant that an honest, albeit erroneous, belief that the act causing damage or destruction was done to his own property provides a defence to a charge brought under s 1(1). The argument is put in three ways. First, that the offence charged includes the act causing the damage or destruction and the element of mens rea. The element of mens rea relates to all the circumstances of the criminal act. The criminal act in the offence is causing damage to or destruction of 'property belonging to another' and the element of mens rea, therefore, must relate to 'property belonging to another'. Honest belief, whether justifiable or not, that the property is the defendant's own negatives the element of mens rea....

It is conceded by counsel for the Crown that there is force in the argument that the element of mens rea extends to 'property belonging to another'. But, it is argued, the section creates a new statutory offence and that it is open to the construction that the mental element in the offence relates only to causing damage to or destroying property. That if in fact the property damaged or destroyed is shown to be another's property the offence is committed although the defendant did not intend or foresee damage to, another person's property.

We are informed that so far as research has revealed this is the first occasion on which this court has had to consider the question which arises in this appeal.

It is not without interest to observe that under the law in force before the passing of the Criminal Damage Act 1971, it was clear that no offence was committed by a person who destroyed or damaged property belonging to another in the honest but mistaken belief that the property was his own or that he had a legal right to do the damage. In *Twose* [(1879) 14 Cox CC 327] the prisoner was indicted for setting fire to furze on a common. Persons living near the common had occasionally burned the furze in order to improve the growth of grass but without the right to do so. The prisoner denied setting fire to the furze and it was submitted that even if it were proved that she did she could not be found guilty if she bona fide believed she had a right to do so whether the right were a good one or not. Lopes J ruled that if she set fire to the furze thinking she had a right to do so that would not be a criminal offence.

On the facts of the present appeal the charge, if brought before the 1971 Act came into force, would have been laid under s 13 of the Malicious Damage Act 1861, alleging damage by a tenant to a building. It was a defence to a charge under that section that the tenant acted under a claim of right to do the damage.

If the direction given by the deputy judge in the present case is correct, then the offence created by s 1(1) of the 1971 Act involves a considerable extension of the law in a surprising direction. Whether or not this is so depends on the construction of the section. Construing the language of s 1(1) we have no doubt that the actus reus is 'destroying or damaging any property belonging to another'. It is not possible to exclude the words 'belonging to another' which describe the 'property'. Applying the ordinary principles of mens rea, the intention and recklessness and the absence of lawful excuse required to constitute the offence have reference to property belonging to another. It follows that in our judgment no offence is committed under this section if a person destroys or causes damage to property belonging to another if he does so in the honest though mistaken belief that the property is his own, and provided that the belief is honestly held it is irrelevant to consider whether or not it is a justifiable belief.

In our judgment, the direction given to the jury was a fundamental misdirection in law. The consequence was that the jury were precluded from considering facts capable of being a defence to the charge and were directed to convict . . .

Appeal allowed. Conviction quashed

R v Appleyard

(1985) 81 Cr App R 319, Court of Appeal, Criminal Division

(Lord Lane CJ, Skinner and Macpherson JJ)

The Lord Chief Justice. . . . There is no need to detail the facts relating to the offences other than those alleged in count 4. Count 4 was based upon an allegation made by the Crown that on 15 June 1982, allegedly with a man called Lawford, who was acquitted, this man set fire to a store belonging to a limited company called Pontefract Tape Ltd.

The appellant and Lawford were seen at the premises shortly after 5.30 pm in a Volvo motor car. The fire brigade was called some 20 minutes later by a neighbour who had seen smoke issuing from the premises. The engine arrived at 5.57 pm and there was no doubt upon the scientific examination of the premises that the fire had been deliberately started, because traces of paraffin were found upon the floor. According further to the scientific evidence, the fire had not been burning for very much longer than 20 minutes before the fire engine arrived. Consequently it was at least possible, if not strongly probable, that the appellant had something to do with the starting of the fire.

He was seen by police officers on two occasions. On the second occasion he agreed that he was at the store at 5.30 pm or just after. He said he had left in a hurry because he had to go and see his solicitor some distance away and he denied having anything to do with the starting of the fire.

At the close of the prosecution case Mr Steer, appearing for the defendant then as he does for him as the appellant now, submitted that there was no case to answer, amongst other counts, on count 4. It was argued by him that since the appellant was in effect the owner of the premises, he must be entitled to set fire to them if he wanted to. It could not therefore be said that he was acting without lawful excuse as the statute requires. After a very lengthy submission indeed, the learned Judge rejected that submission, the trial continued and, as already indicated, the jury convicted.

The first and main issue at the trial was the question whether it was proved to the satisfaction of the jury so that they felt sure that this man had started the fire. The jury came to the conclusion, not surprisingly, that they were so satisfied.

The next problem was that raised by the words of the statute itself. Let me therefore read the terms of section 1 of the Criminal Damage Act 1971: '(1) A person who without lawful excuse destroys or damages any property belonging to another intending to destroy or damage any such property or being reckless as to whether any such property would be destroyed or damaged shall be guilty of an offence.... (3) An offence committed under this section by destroying or damaging property by fire shall be charged as arson.'

The submission made by Mr Steer and rejected by the learned judge, has been repeated here today. The only point of this appeal is whether the judge was right in rejecting that submission or not. Mr Steer confines his argument today to section 1 and does not rely on the provisions of section 5(2), to which it is, therefore, not necessary for us to refer.

The basis of Mr Steer's submission, as he was eventually driven to concede, was a statement by this Court in *Denton* (1981) 74 Cr App Rep 81. Let me just read the headnote relating the facts of that case in order to show the way it is distinguished from the present circumstances. It reads as follows: 'The appellant, who was employed by one T, set fire to T's business premises and was charged with arson contrary to section 1(1) and (3) of the Criminal Damage Act 1971. At his trial he gave evidence that T had asked him to start the fire because T's company was in difficulties and a fire might improve the financial circumstances of the company. The appellant relied on section 5(2) of the Act of 1971 providing him with a defence to the charge in that T had consented to the damage caused by the fire and intended to make a fraudulent insurance claim in respect of it. The trial judge ruled that 'entitled' in section 5(2)(a) carried a connotation of general lawfulness and that T could not be said to have been entitled to consent to damage for a fraudulent purpose, so that the defence under section 5(2) was not open to the appellant, whereupon the latter changed his plea to one of guilty. On appeal against the judge's ruling,

'*Held*, that no offence was committed under section 1(1) and (3) of the Criminal Damage Act 1971 by a person who burnt down his own premises; nor could that act become unlawful because of an inchoate intent to defraud the insurers; accordingly, the judge's ruling was wrong; and as the appellant's plea of guilty had been based upon that ruling, the appeal would be allowed and the conviction quashed.'

It will therefore be seen that the point at issue in that case was nothing to do with the point in issue in the present case. Moreover in that case it was the servant of the company who had set light to the machinery and not T. In the present case it is the managing director or, as Mr Steer chooses inaccurately to call him, the proprietor of the business who had, according to the jury's finding, set fire to the property.

Therefore in order to support his argument and, as he concedes, as the basis of his argument, Mr Steer relies upon a passage in the judgment of *Denton* (1981) 74 Cr App Rep 81, 84, which runs as follows: 'It was agreed on all hands for the purpose of this case that T was the person who, any evil motives apart, was entitled to consent to the damage. It was likewise conceded that the appellant Denton honestly believed that T occupied that position and was entitled to consent.'

Basing himself upon that and basing himself upon the similarity of the position of T to the position of the appellant in the present case, Mr Steer argues that therefore this appellant must be taken to have been entitled to consent to the damage.

The fundamental fallacy of that argument scarcely needs pointing out. It was a concession in *Denton* (supra) that was assumed for the purposes of argument, for the simple reason that it was the servant and not the so called proprietor who was being charged. To seek to base a proposition of law upon a concession which was made simply for the purpose of argument in another case, is a fruitless exercise.

There is nothing in this appeal and it is dismissed.

Appeal dismissed

Question

Smith made an error in thinking that the wiring he had installed belonged to him and not to the landlord but so long as he did believe this he could not be convicted of damaging property 'belonging to another'. How does *Appleyard*'s case differ? If he believed that he was 'in effect' the owner of the company and its premises, and however unreasonable his belief was, was he not entitled to an acquittal since he did not intend to destroy property belonging to another?

R v G
[2003] UKHL 50, [2004] AC 1034

The case is set out at and discussed in full above, p 140.

The two defendants aged 11 and 12, when on a camping expedition without their parents' consent, entered the yard of a shop set fire to bundles of newspapers, leaving some lit newspaper under a large plastic wheelie-bin. The newspapers set fire to the wheelie-bin and the fire spread causing £1m worth of damage. The boys had expected the fires to extinguish themselves on the concrete floor; neither had appreciated that there was any risk of the fire spreading in the way that it did. They were convicted applying the *Caldwell* formula of recklessness [above p 144], although the jury acknowledged some difficulty in applying fairly an objective standard to children whose capacity to see risk was limited by their immaturity.

The House of Lords, quashed their convictions, overruling *Caldwell*.

Lord Bingham observed that:

section 1 as enacted followed, subject to an immaterial addition, the draft proposed by the Law Commission. It cannot be supposed that by 'reckless' Parliament meant anything different from the Law Commission. The Law Commission's meaning was made plain both in its Report (Law Com No 29) and in Working Paper No 23 which preceded it. These materials (not, it would seem, placed before the House in *R v Caldwell*) reveal a very plain intention to replace the old-fashioned and misleading expression 'maliciously' by the more familiar expression 'reckless' but to give the latter expression the meaning which *R v Cunningham* ... and Professor Kenny had given to the former. In treating this authority as irrelevant to the construction of 'reckless' the majority fell into understandable but clearly demonstrable error. No relevant change in the mens rea necessary for proof of the offence was intended, and in holding otherwise the majority misconstrued section 1 of the Act.

Lord Bingham confirmed that the definition of recklessness to be applied in criminal damage is now that found in cl 18(c) of the Draft Criminal Code:

A person acts recklessly within the meaning of section 1 of the Criminal Damage Act 1971 with respect to—

  (i) a circumstance when he is aware of a risk that it exists or will exist;

  (ii) a result when he is aware of a risk that it will occur;

  and it is, in the circumstances known to him, unreasonable to take the risk.

Question

Consider *Smith* (above), which elements of the crime are circumstances and which results? On an allegation of reckless criminal damage what must be proved in relation to each?

(5) TRANSFERRED FAULT

The common law doctrine of 'transferred malice' or, to use a more modern term, 'transferred fault,' is considered above, p 34, with particular reference to the law of murder and other offences against the person. The Law Commission assumed that the doctrine would apply to their proposed Criminal Damage Act.

For the simple offence we think that the necessary mental element should be expressed as an intention to destroy or damage the property of another or as recklessness in that regard. The intention or the recklessness need not be related to the particular property damaged, provided that it is related to another's property. If, for example, a person throws a stone at a passing motor car intending to damage it, but misses and breaks a shop window, he will have the necessary intention in respect of the damage to the window as he intended to damage the property of another. But if in a fit of anger he throws a stone at his own car and breaks a shop window behind the car he will not have the requisite intention. In the latter case the question of whether he has committed an offence will depend upon whether he was reckless as to whether any property belonging to another would be destroyed or damaged.

Glanville Williams agrees that the doctrine 'almost certainly' applies to the Act: *Textbook of Criminal Law* (2nd edn) 907. But, while accepting that it may be right for offences against the person, he has argued that, in principle, it should not apply to criminal damage: [1983] CLJ 85. He argued that it results in 'unfair labelling' where the property damaged is more valuable than that which D intended to damage or foresaw that he might damage; whereas injury to one person—for example, a broken leg—is presumably as bad as the same injury to any other person. (Cf Andrew Ashworth, 'Transferred Malice and Punishment for Unforeseen Consequences' in P. Glazebrook (ed) *Reshaping the Criminal Law* (1978) 77, at 92.)

Notes and questions

1. D throws a stone intending to smash V's cheap vase. Unforeseeably, the stone bounces off that cheap, but very solid, vase which is undamaged, and smashes V's priceless Ming vase. *Should* D be guilty of criminally destroying the Ming vase? Is the case materially different from that where D smashes the vase he aims at, believing it to have been bought by V at Woolworths, when in fact it is priceless Ming? Assuming D is convicted, should the sentence, in either case, be related to the value of the Ming vase, or the cheap vase—or something in between?

2. Suppose that D, bent on stealing from a gas meter, knowingly fractures the gas pipe and this leads to a fire in which the premises are destroyed. D is clearly guilty of criminal damage to the pipe but is he guilty of arson? Though fire is only another means of causing criminal damage, Glanville Williams thinks not ([1983] CLJ 85 at 86) because arson carries a higher maximum punishment. 'The reasonable view,' he says, 'is that arson is a separate offence, so that the intention cannot be transferred.' (Cf *Courtie*, above, p **44**). But what if the gas leak caused an explosion, without any attendant fire, which destroyed the premises? Jeremy Horder ('A Critique of the Correspondence Principle in Criminal Law' [1995] Crim LR 759, 769–770) argues that what really matters is 'the representative label: is it right to label D as an arsonist if he did not intend to start a fire . . .'? Do you agree? Is this a sufficiently precise concept for the law to operate effectively?

Obviously mens rea cannot be supplied by an afterthought. If D inadvertently breaks V's window he cannot be liable when, having learned that V is a tax inspector, he rejoices in the harm caused. On the other hand, as *Miller* [1983] 2 AC 161, [1983] 1 All ER 978, HL, p **93**, above shows, if D inadvertently sets fire to V's property and subsequently becomes aware that he has done so, he may be criminally liable if, intending or being reckless that *further* damage may ensue to V's property, he lets the fire take its course when it lies within his power to prevent or minimise that further damage.

(6) LAWFUL EXCUSE

Criminal Damage Act 1971, s 5

(1) This section applies to any offence under section 1(1) above and any offence under section 2 or 3 above other than one involving a threat by the person charged to destroy or damage property in a way which he knows is likely to endanger the life of another or involving an intent by the person charged to use or cause or permit the use of something in his custody or under his control so to destroy or damage property.

(2) A person charged with an offence to which this section applies shall, whether or not he would be treated for the purposes of this Act as having a lawful excuse apart from this sub-section, be treated for those purposes as having a lawful excuse:

(a) if at the time of the act or acts alleged to constitute the offence he believed that the person or persons whom he believed to be entitled to consent to the destruction of or damage to the property in question had so consented, or would have so consented to it if he or they had known of the destruction or damage and its circumstances; or

(b) if he destroyed or damaged or threatened to destroy or damage the property in question or, in the case of a charge of an offence under section 3 above, intended to use or cause or permit the use of something to destroy or damage it, in order to protect property belonging to himself or another or a right or interest in property which was or which he believed to be vested in himself or another, and at the time of the act or acts alleged to constitute the offence he believed:

   (i) that the property, right or interest was in immediate need of protection; and
   (ii) that the means of protection adopted or proposed to be adopted were or would be reasonable having regard to all the circumstances.

(3) For the purposes of this section it is immaterial whether a belief is justified or not if it is honestly held.

(4) For the purposes of sub-section (2) above a right or interest in property includes any right or privilege in or over land, whether created by grant, licence or otherwise.

(5) This section shall not be construed as casting doubt on any defence recognised by law as a defence to criminal charges.

Law Com No 29, para 49:

In most cases there is a clear distinction between the mental element and the element of unlawfulness, and in the absence of one or the other element no offence will be committed, notwithstanding that damage may have been done to another's property. For example, a police officer who, in order to execute a warrant of arrest, has to force open the door of a house is acting with a lawful excuse although he intends to damage the door or the lock. On the other hand a person playing tennis on a properly fenced court who inadvertently hits a ball on to a greenhouse roof, breaking a pane of glass, acts without lawful excuse, but will escape liability because he has not the requisite intention.

Notes and questions

1. The Law Commission says that in most cases there is a clear distinction between 'the mental element' and 'the element of unlawfulness' and the Act deals separately with these elements. Is there any such clear distinction? Was the conviction in *Smith (DR)* quashed because D lacked the mental element or because he had a lawful excuse? Does it matter to determine which? Cf *Jaggard v Dickinson*, p 209, above.

2. In *Denton* [1982] 1 All ER 65, [1981] 1 WLR 1446, CA, p **943**, above, D obviously contemplated a fraudulent claim against insurers and the trial judge ruled that he could not rely on s 5(2) because the section carried a general connotation of lawfulness and it could not be said that the owner was 'entitled' to consent to damage for a fraudulent purpose. Quashing D's conviction the Court of Appeal pointed out that had T been charged he would (on the admission made in that case) have to be acquitted since it is no crime for a man to set fire to his own property. But if the Crown's contention was right someone whom the owner directed to set fire to the property could be convicted. The court concluded (at 68):

Quite apart from any other consideration, that is such an anomalous result that it cannot possibly be right. The answer is this: that one has to decide whether or not an offence is committed at the moment that the acts are alleged to be committed. The fact that somebody may have had a dishonest intent which in the end he was going to carry out, namely to claim from the insurance company, cannot turn what was not originally a crime into a crime. There is no unlawfulness under the 1971 Act in burning a house. It does not become unlawful because there may be an inchoate attempt to commit fraud contained in it; that is to say it does not become a crime under the 1971 Act, whatever may be the situation outside of the Act.

Consequently it is apparent to us that the judge, in his ruling in this respect, was wrong. Indeed it seems to us, if it is necessary to go as far as this, that it was probably unnecessary for the defendant to invoke s 5 of the 1971 Act at all, because he probably had a lawful excuse without it, in that T was lawfully entitled to burn the premises down. The defendant believed it. He believed that he was acting under the directions of T and that on its own, it seems to us, may well have provided him with a lawful excuse without having resort to s 5.

On the face of it the conduct of Denton falls four-square with s 5(2)(a) but the court thought he probably had a lawful excuse without it. On this view is s 5(2)(a) superfluous?

3. *Smith (DR)* is overtly based on the premise (and *Denton* implicitly so) that the mens rea of criminal damage lies not merely in intentionally or recklessly damaging property but in intentionally or recklessly damaging property of *another*. 'It is not possible', the court said in *Smith (DR)*, 'to exclude the words "belonging to another" which describe the "property". Applying the ordinary principles of *mens rea*, the intention and recklessness and the absence of lawful excuse required to constitute the offence have reference to property belonging to another.' No doubt D would commit an offence where, not sure whether property which was really V's belonged to himself or V, he nevertheless went ahead and destroyed the property.

4. Clearly a belief that the owner has consented to the destruction or damage constitutes a lawful excuse within s 5(2)(a). In *Blake v DPP* [1993] Crim LR 586, DC, D, a vicar, protesting against allied action against Iraq in the Gulf War, wrote a biblical quotation on a concrete pillar at the perimeter of the Houses of Parliament. Charged with criminal damage D claimed that he was carrying out the instructions of God and that he had a lawful excuse because he believed God was 'the person . . . whom he believed to be entitled to consent to the . . . damage to the property in question . . .' Perhaps not surprisingly the court held that a belief, however genuinely held, that D had God's consent was not a defence under 'the domestic law of England'. Rumpole would commit no offence if he sets fire to the Old Bailey on the instructions of his wife—'she who must be obeyed'—if he believes, however unreasonably, that his wife is the owner or has been authorized by the owner. Suppose Rumpole gets what he believes a message from God to set fire to the Old Bailey. Rumpole, being Rumpole, is hesitant but God assures him that He has consulted with the Lord Chancellor and the Lord Chief Justice and both have agreed. Rumpole sets fire to the Old Bailey. Advise Rumpole.

R v Hunt

(1977) 66 Cr App R 105, Court of Appeal, Criminal Division

(Roskill LJ, Wein and Slynn JJ)

Roskill LJ. . . . The appellant was convicted . . . of arson contrary to section 1(1) and (3) of the Criminal Damage Act 1971. . . .

[His Lordship read sections 1(1) and 1(3) of the Act above, p **937** and below, p **962**.]

Therefore quite correctly, by virtue of sub-section (3), this man was charged with arson.

Now, two defences were raised: the first was that he had a lawful excuse for what he did; secondly it was said that he was not reckless whether any such property would be destroyed. The learned judge withdrew the first defence from the jury after hearing an interesting argument, as we have heard, from Mr Marshall-Andrews, by whom this man was represented at the trial as in this Court. He left the issue of recklessness to the jury, and the jury, by a majority verdict, convicted him. Obviously, on the judge's direction, there was no lawful excuse.

Lawson J gave leave to appeal, in order that this Court might consider whether the judge was right in withdrawing the defence of lawful excuse from the jury.

That defence arises under section 5 of the same Act and it is necessary, in order to make the point plain, to read the whole section.

[His Lordship read s 5 of the Act above, p **946**.]

Let me now go back and try to select from those rather long and complicated sub-sections of section 5 the relevant parts: '(1) This section applies to any offence under section 1(1) above…(2) A person charged with an offence to which this section applies shall…be treated for those purposes as having a lawful excuse—…(b) if he…damaged…the property in question…in order to protect property belonging…to another…and at the time of the act or acts alleged to constitute the offence he believed—(i) that the property, right or interest was in immediate need of protection; and (ii) that the means of protection adopted or proposed to be adopted were or would be reasonable having regard to all the circumstances.'

I have already read sub-section (3) which makes it immaterial whether a belief is justified or not provided it is honestly held.

The facts can be very shortly stated. The appellant married his wife in 1970; in August 1976 his wife took up a job as a deputy warden in a block of old people's flats. The appellant was unemployed, but he helped his wife and his wife's employers by doing jobs at the flats. He discovered that, regrettably one is bound to say, the fire alarm and the emergency alarm did not work. He thought that the warden had written to the Council but the Council did nothing about it.

On 22 October 1976, when the warden was away, the appellant set fire to a bed in the guest room in a comparatively isolated part of the block of flats. He then went to his wife and told her he could smell smoke: he then led her past the guest room in their search for the fire. The appellant then 'discovered' the fire in the guest room and told his wife to get the people out. He then telephoned for the fire brigade. He then broke the fire alarm in order to show that it was not working.

His main ground of appeal was that the trial judge was wrong in ruling that the defence provided by section 5 of the Criminal Damage Act 1971 was not open to him on the facts of the case.

Let it be assumed in the appellant's favour that he honestly believed that the council were failing in their duty in not having repaired the fire alarm. The question is whether, on those bare facts which I have related and assuming an honest belief in this case, he is entitled to say that he had a lawful excuse for that which he did? I should add that he originally denied having set fire to anything.

This must depend upon the true construction of section 5(2)(b). As I said earlier, there was an interesting argument before the learned judge and the learned judge said that those facts were incapable, as a matter of law, of entitling this man to the benefit of that defence. Therefore, he withdrew that defence from the jury. Mr Marshall-Andrews has strenuously argued in this Court that the learned judge was wrong and that the appellant was entitled to the benefit of the statutory defence.

It is known that some of the sections in the Criminal Damage Act 1971 can give rise to difficulties. Some of the problems are helpfully discussed at pp532 to 536 of Smith and Hogan's *Criminal Law* (3rd edn, 1973).

Mr Marshall-Andrews' submission can be put thus: If this man honestly believed that that which he did was necessary in order to protect this property from the risk of fire and damage to the old people's home by reason of the absence of a working fire alarm, he was entitled to set fire to that bed and so to claim the statutory defence accorded by section 5(2).

I have said we will assume in his favour that he possessed the requisite honest belief. But in our view the question whether he was entitled to the benefit of the defence turns upon the meaning of the words 'in order to protect property belonging to another.' It was argued that those words were subjective in concept, just like the words in the latter part of section 5(2)(b) which are subjective.

We do not think that is right. The question whether or not a particular act of destruction or damage or threat of destruction or damage was done or made in order to protect property belonging to another must be, on the true construction of the statute, an objective test. Therefore we have to ask ourselves whether, whatever the state of this man's mind and assuming an honest belief, that which he admittedly did was done in order to protect this particular property, namely the old people's home in Hertfordshire?

If one formulates the question in that way, in the view of each member of this Court, for the reason Slynn J gave during the argument, it admits of only one answer: this was not done in order to protect property; it was done in order to draw attention to the defective state of the fire alarm. It was not an act which in itself did protect or was capable of protecting property. The learned trial judge, during the argument, mentioned quite correctly, that one, though not necessarily the only, purpose of this sub-section was to make provision whereby a person, in order to protect his own property, might destroy or damage the property of another without being guilty of criminal damage. There are cases of which it is easy to think of examples, in which a person, in order to protect his property in actual or imminent danger of damage, will take steps, maybe drastic steps, legitimately protecting either his property or the property of another. It is that kind of protective action to which this particular sub-section is directed though we do not suggest that that is exhaustive. But the sub-section, on its proper construction, cannot possibly extend to the situation which arose in this present case.

During the argument after the adjournment Slynn J gave an example of the position which might arise were the argument for the appellant to succeed. Let it be supposed that the roof of some famous cathedral or building, like Westminster Abbey, was in danger due to a defective beam suffering from dry rot; let it be supposed that the authorities are doing nothing to repair it; let it be supposed that some person, acting in good faith, is horrified at this lack of attention. In order to draw attention to what he regards as a dangerous position, he goes and sets fire to a hassock. Is that seriously to be said not to be an offence of criminal damage because it is done to draw attention to the defective beam on the roof of the Abbey? Mr Marshall-Andrews says that the section would, on those facts, provide a defence. We think that the question has only to be asked to be answered in the negative.

In those circumstances the learned judge was absolutely right in his decision and for the reasons which he gave. As Slynn J pointed out, even if, contrary to our view, the test were subjective, the appellant did not set fire to the bed in order to protect property: he merely did that act in order to draw attention to what was in his view an immediate need for protection by repairing the alarm.

I would only add that we had some discussion about the scope of the words 'in immediate need of protection' in paragraph (b)(i) of sub-section (2). That question is touched upon on p 534 of Smith and Hogan, *Criminal Law* (3rd edn, 1973). No question arises for decision under that part of section 5(2)(b) and we express no view about it.

In those circumstances the appeal against conviction is dismissed.

Appeal dismissed

Notes and questions

1. In *Ashford and Smith* [1988] Crim LR 682, CA, D and E were convicted under s 3 of the Act of possessing articles with intent to damage property. They were found in possession of equipment with which they had tried to cut a wire fence surrounding an RAF base as part of a demonstration against nuclear weapons. They claimed they had done this to protect the property of persons abroad and in this country by lessening the risk of nuclear war. The Court of Appeal held the trial judge was right to rule that their conduct did not fall within the definition of lawful excuse since whether an act was done to protect property was to be objectively determined and there was no evidence that any property was in immediate need of protection. *R v Hill; R v Hall* (1988) 89 Cr App R 74, [1989] Crim LR 136, CA, were factually similar cases. D and E, also convicted under s 3, were carrying equipment to cut the fence surrounding a US base. At her trial D claimed that the base was used to monitor the movements of Soviet submarines and thus was a prime target for a retaliatory or even pre-emptive Soviet nuclear strike which would devastate the property of herself and her neighbours. By cutting the wire the security of the base might be compromised and force its removal. The trial judge directed the jury that what D had done was really part of a political campaign and, objectively, could not be said to be done to protect property. Moreover, on D's own testimony, there was no evidence that she believed the property to be in *immediate* need of protection. Upholding the convictions, the CA reaffirmed the correctness of *Hunt*.

The trial judge, [said the court] had to decide (i) what was in [D's] mind (subjective test); (ii) whether it could be said, as a matter of law that, on the facts as believed by her, cutting the strand of wire could amount to something done to protect her own home or the homes of adjacent friends (objective test). The judge had rightly concluded that the proposed act was too remote from the eventual aim at which she had targeted her actions to satisfy the test. He had also to determine whether on the facts, as stated by [D], there was any evidence on which it could be said that there was a need of protection from immediate danger.

Similarly in *Blake*, p **948**, above, the defence was rejected because, said the court, adopting 'an objective view', the action taken by D was not capable of protecting property in the Gulf States.

2. However misguided or ineffective the conduct of Hunt, Ashford, Smith, Hill and Hall and Blake might be thought to be, to the question—what was your object in doing what you did?—each could have honestly answered: to protect property belonging to myself or another. Does not this meet the requirements in the first part of s 5(2)(b)? What warrant is there for saying that the action taken by them must be in some way causally effective in protecting the property?

3. Consider the example given by Roskill LJ in *Hunt* of the hassock burner. Roskill LJ said, 'Mr Marshall-Andrews says that the section would, on those facts, provide a defence. We think the question has only to be asked to be answered in the negative'. Do you agree with Roskill LJ that the question has only to be asked to be answered in the negative?

4. In *Kelleher* [2003] EWCA Crim 2486, D decapitated a statue of Baroness Thatcher, and explained his motive as being that he held her responsible for developments in world politics with which he disagreed and that he genuinely feared for the future of his son being brought up in such a world. Should the defence under s 5(2)(b) be available to him? What property is he protecting?

5. D must also believe, however, that the property is in 'immediate' need of protection within s 5(2)(b)(i). This suggests that the property must be immediately and not remotely threatened. So in *Hill and Hall* the trial judge ruled that there was no evidence that D believed that the former Soviet Union was about to declare war or launch a pre-emptive strike. Nor could Hunt believe that a fire would break out next day, next month, or even that a fire would ever occur. What Hunt no doubt believed was that *if* a fire ever did occur it might bring with it, in view of the fact that the alarms were not working, disastrous consequences. He had done, in writing to the warden and the council, all that he could do but this had been to no avail. Why could he not claim, within the section, that he believed the property was in *immediate* need of protection albeit the risk was a future one? Had the relevant fire authority been consulted they would surely have insisted on the alarms being repaired immediately and not at any remoter time. So was not the property in immediate need of protection? In *Johnson v DPP* [1994] Crim LR 673, DC, D, a squatter, chiselled off the lock of the door of the house he was occupying and replaced it with his own lock. Charged with criminal damage D claimed that the action he had taken was done to protect his property, viz the furniture he had moved into the squat. Upholding his conviction, the court said that D's property was not in 'immediate' need of protection as opposed to a 'speculative future need'. But the risk of theft, like the risk of fire, is always a future risk and neither may ever materialize. But does any reasonable person wait until the burglar calls before securing the door?

6. How far is subjectivity to be taken? Would D have a lawful excuse for burning down a factory because he believed that effluent from the factory was ruining his tomatoes so long as D believed this to be reasonable?

7. Section 5(5) makes it clear that the definition of lawful excuse in the section is not exhaustive so that general defences such as self-defence, duress and necessity are available on a charge of criminal damage.

8. Could a defendant plead that his conduct which caused criminal damage was an act of expression for the purposes of Article 10 of the ECHR?

In *Steele v UK* (1999) 28 EHRR 603 S, with 60 others, attempted to obstruct a grouse shoot. She was arrested for breach of the peace for impeding the progress of a member of the shoot by walking in front of him as he lifted his shotgun. At trial S was convicted of the Public Order Act 1986, s 5 offence and for breach of the peace. Other defendants were convicted for various other unrelated peaceful protest activities. S argued that this infringed her right to freedom of expression under Article 10.

Article 10 reads, so far as relevant, as follows:

1. Everyone has the right to freedom of expression. This right shall include freedom to hold opinions and to receive and impart information and ideas without interference by public authority and regardless of frontiers. . . .

2. The exercise of these freedoms, since it carries with it duties and responsibilities, may be subject to such formalities, conditions, restrictions or penalties as are prescribed by law and are necessary in a democratic society, . . . for the prevention of disorder or crime, . . . [or] for the protection of the reputation or rights of others. . . .

The European Court held:

Para 90. The Government submitted that the protest activity . . . was not peaceful, and that Article 10 was not, therefore, applicable.

91. The Commission found that the measures taken against each of the .. applicants amounted to interferences with their rights under Article 10.

92. The Court recalls that the applicants were arrested while protesting against a grouse shoot and the extension of a motorway respectively. It is true that these protests took the form of physically impeding the activities of which the applicants disapproved, but the Court considers nonetheless that

they constituted expressions of opinion within the meaning of Article 10. The measures taken against the applicants were, therefore, interferences with their right to freedom of expression.

The Court found that in relation to S, the infringement of her freedom of expression was necessary and proportionate to a legitimate aim under Article 10(2). See [1998] Crim LR 893.

9. Protestors charged with criminal damage have also sought to rely on a defence that they were acting to prevent illegality in international law. In *Pritchard and others* [2005] QB 259 [2004] 4 All ER 955. DD had been charged with conspiracy to cause criminal damage and with offences under s 3(b) of the Act. DD had been involved in causing and attempting to cause damage at the military base at RAF Fairford. The defence asserted that the UK's attack on Iraq was an unlawful act and that their acts at the airforce base were to prevent that illegality. DD sought to rely on the defences of duress of circumstance, necessity, lawful excuse under s 5(2)(b) and the prevention of crime under s 3 of the 1967 Act. The court, on a preliminary ruling held that the international crime of aggression could not constitute a crime for the purposes of s 3 of the 1967 Act (see above, p **450**), and that under s 5(2)(b) the jury was only concerned with the question of DD's honestly held beliefs. Therefore, no issue could arise in relation to the defence under s 5(2)(b) of whether the war in Iraq was illegal.

As noted in the commentary in the *Criminal Law Review*:

...the court's conclusion that the legality of the war is irrelevant to the *availability* of the section 5(2) defence seems correct. But, is the illegality relevant to its *application*? Surely the circumstances—the immediacy, potency, lawfulness etc—of the action will be important to the jury in its evaluation of D's belief that his conduct is 'reasonable' as the statute requires? The success of the defence on facts such as these nevertheless remains debatable. Is there sufficient immediacy of threat to property, particularly where the charges of conspiracy to damage? Which item of property (the defence does not apply to protect people: *Baker* [1997] Crim LR 497) is D seeking to protect? [2005] Crim LR 122.

In *Hutchinson v Newbury Magistrates Court* [2000] 9 October, DC, H appealed against her conviction for criminal damage after cutting a perimeter fence at an atomic weapons establishment. H contended that (1) the production of weapons at the establishment was unlawful in customary international law pursuant to an opinion of the International Court of Justice in 1996 on the legality of the threat of use of nuclear weapons; (2) the establishment's activities were therefore also unlawful in English domestic law and since H's actions had been intended to impede that unlawful activity they were therefore not a criminal act; (3) by English domestic law the forbidden conduct of the establishment was not only unlawful but also criminal. Buxton LJ observed that:

It originally seemed to be contended, ...that the fact that Mrs Hutchinson was acting to impede, alternatively to protest about, activities that were unlawful under international law in itself provided her with a lawful excuse in English criminal law. No authority was cited for a claim as broad as that. That is because no authority supports it. It is clear that the claim, when scrutinised, is hopelessly wide. If D commits a crime only to stop X doing an unlawful but not criminal act, he cannot claim the latter unlawfulness alone as an excuse for his own criminal conduct. Quite apart from the lack of authority, the practical implications of such an argument, were it correct, are obvious. What D must do in such a situation is bring his conduct, if he can, under one of the recognised heads of public or private defence, such as the heads that were set out by the judge in the second of her two questions for the opinion of this Court.

See also *Ayliffe v DPP* [2005] EWHC 684 (Admin), [2005] Crim LR (Dec).

10. In *Lloyd v DPP* [1992] 1 All ER 982, [1991] Crim LR 904, DC, D, a trespasser, had parked his car on private land aware of notices that said the cars of trespassers would be clamped and that a charge of £25 would be made for their removal. He returned that evening to find his car clamped but refused to pay the £25 for its removal. The following day D returned to remove the clamp using a disc cutter. D was charged with criminal damage to the clamp.

On D's behalf it was argued that he could rely on s 5(5) because at common law the clamping of his car constituted a trespass and he was accordingly entitled to take reasonable steps to recover his property. If this argument was correct, said Nolan LJ:

... the only remedy open to a landowner who finds a car parked without authority on his land is to remove the car using as little force as may be required and to place it either on the highway or, if he knows who the owner of the car is, back at the owner's property. The practical difficulties and dangers which that remedy would involve can readily be imagined: breaking into the car if locked in the first place; propelling it by some means onto the road with or without insurance cover; leaving it where it might cause obstruction at least, if not danger to other road users.

I mention that only to illustrate the problems inherent in this branch of the law and the need to my mind for them to be fully explored in civil proceedings. This court, exercising its criminal jurisdiction, is not concerned with the question whether Mr Lloyd could sue the landowners for trespass to his car and for the inconvenience caused to him or with the precise remedies open in civil law to the landowner. We are solely concerned with the question whether Mr Lloyd had a lawful excuse for damaging the property of South Coast Securities. We are concerned with the civil law only to the extent necessary for determining whether such an excuse existed for the purpose of the criminal law.

For that purpose it is sufficient to decide, as I do, that [the prosecutor's] alternative submission is well founded. It substantially reflects the conclusion of the justices in para 6(d) of the case [In para 6(d) the justices had said: 'The clamping of the appellant's motor vehicle, whether lawful or unlawful, and we considered it to be a trespass, was not such an act that the appellant could not in law consent to it. He consented to the risk of his vehicle being clamped. In this regard the signs erected around the car park were sufficiently clear and unambiguous.'] although that conclusion might more accurately have been expressed by saying that since the applicant had consented to the risk of his car being clamped the clamping was not a trespass. Mr Sharp submits that this conclusion cannot carry the day for the respondent because the appellant's consent to the clamping ceased on his return to the car park at 10.00 pm. Mr Sharp submits that the immobilisation of the car was plainly unlawful thereafter and the appellant was at liberty to exercise his right of recaption using such reasonable force as was necessary to do so.

To my mind, it would be a truly absurd state of affairs if the appellant, having consented to the risk of clamping, was at liberty to withdraw his consent with immediate effect once clamping had occurred and to proceed at once to recover his car by force. I am satisfied that this is not the law. Even assuming in the appellant's favour that the refusal of South Coast Securities to let him remove his car save on payment of £25 was an unlawful restraint, it would by no means follow that there was a lawful excuse for his subsequent action. He had a choice. He could have paid the £25 under protest, removed his car and taken action against South Coast Securities in the county court. Instead he chose to re-enter the car park, once again quite plainly as a trespasser, and to retrieve his car by causing some £50-worth of damage to the property of South Coast Securities.

In my judgment, the suggestion that there was a lawful excuse for his action is wholly untenable. At the worst what he had suffered was a civil wrong. The remedy for such wrongs is available in the civil courts. That is what they are there for. Self-help involving the use of force can only be contemplated where there is no reasonable alternative. ...

Situations like those which have arisen in the present case are becoming increasingly common. They can cause intense irritation both to the motorist deprived of the use of his car, as he thinks, unreasonably, and to the landowner or other victim of the motorist's unauthorised parking. That makes it all the more necessary for it to be clearly stated that, at any rate as a general rule, if a motorist parks his car without permission on another person's property knowing that by doing so he runs the risk of it being clamped, he has no right to damage or destroy the clamp. If he does so he will be guilty of a criminal offence....

Question

Consent to being clamped negatives trespass; but does 'consenting' to the risk?

2. RACIALLY OR RELIGIOUSLY AGGRAVATED CRIMINAL DAMAGE

The Crime and Disorder Act 1998 created a new category of racially aggravated crimes. A person commits an offence under s 30 of the 1998 Act if he commits an offence within s 1(1) of the Criminal Damage Act which is 'racially aggravated' for the purposes of s 29. As with racially aggravated offences against the person (above, p 703), this offence is racially aggravated if, at the time of committing it, or immediately before or after doing so (*Parry v DPP* [2004] EWHC 3112 (Admin) (20-minute delay between throwing nail varnish on V's door and calling him an Irish so-and-so)), D demonstrated hostility to V (the person to whom the property belongs or is treated as belonging), based on V's membership or presumed membership of, or his association with, a racial group; or the offence is motivated wholly or partly by hostility towards members of a racial group based on their membership of, or association with, that group. The offence is punishable summarily by imprisonment for six months or a fine not exceeding the statutory maximum and, on indictment, by imprisonment for 14 years, or a fine, or both.

The Anti Terrorism, Crime and Security Act 2001 s 39 extended s 28 to 'religiously aggravated' offences. By s 39(5) 'religious group' means a group of persons defined by reference to religious belief or lack of religious belief.

The offence has of course been used in diverse circumstances as where D spat and urinated on the Stephen Lawrence Memorial in London, *Guardian*, 20 July 1999.

The case law dealing with these aggravating factors is examined in the context of offences against the person above.

3. DESTROYING, ETC PROPERTY WITH INTENT TO ENDANGER LIFE

Criminal Damage Act 1971, s 1

(2) A person who without lawful excuse destroys or damages any property, whether belonging to himself or another:

(a) intending to destroy or damage any property or being reckless as to whether any property would be destroyed or damaged; and

(b) intending by the destruction or damage to endanger the life of another or being reckless as to whether the life of another would be thereby endangered;

shall be guilty of an offence.

Law Com No 29, paras 21–27:

This proposed offence gives effect to our view that the policy of the criminal law is, and should continue to be, to select certain offences as attracting exceptionally high maximum penalties, because these offences are accompanied by aggravating factors. There are examples of this approach in ss 8–10 of the Theft Act 1968 dealing with robbery, burglary and aggravated burglary, which may be regarded as theft accompanied by aggravating circumstances…None of our commentators suggested that the test should be objective in the sense that one should look only to the consequences or potential consequences of the offender's conduct. All were agreed that the criterion for the aggravated offence was to be found in the offender's state of mind, namely, his intention to endanger the personal safety of another or his recklessness in that regard…[I]f no such offence is created, a considerable gap in the law is left, especially where the offender is reckless as to endangering personal safety and yet no injury is caused. In such a case the offender cannot be convicted of an attempt to commit an offence under the Offences against the Person Act 1861, in an attempt to commit an offence, intention and not merely recklessness is necessary…We think that the proper criterion should be related to the endangering of life, a concept which appears in s2 of the Explosive Substances Act 1883 and in s16 of the Firearms Act 1968. It is not, therefore, a novel one likely to give rise to difficulties of interpretation, and we think that it correctly expresses the necessary seriousness. It is true that in adopting the criterion of endangering life there may still be some overlapping with offences against the person….

See further D. W. Elliott, 'Endangering life by destroying or damaging property' [1997] Crim LR 382.

R v Steer

[1987] 2 All ER 833, House of Lords

(Lords Bridge of Harwich, Griffiths, Ackner, Oliver of Aylmerton and Goff of Chieveley)

All their Lordships concurred in the speech delivered by:

Lord Bridge of Harwich. My Lords, in the early hours of 8 June 1985 the respondent went to the bungalow of his former business partner, David Gregory, against whom he bore some grudge. He was armed with an automatic .22 rifle. He rang the bell and woke Mr and Mrs Gregory, who looked out of their bedroom window. The respondent fired a shot aimed at the bedroom window. He then fired two further shots, one at another window and one at the front door. Fortunately no one was hurt. It was never suggested that the first shot had been aimed at Mr or Mrs Gregory.

Arising from this incident the respondent was arraigned on an indictment containing three counts. He pleaded not guilty to possession of a firearm with intent to endanger life, contrary to s16 of the Firearms Act 1968 (count 1) and to an offence of damaging property with intent, contrary to s1(2) of the Criminal Damage Act 1971, which was alleged in the particulars as originally framed as having been committed 'intending by the said damage to endanger the lives of David Gregory and Tina Gregory or being reckless as to whether the lives of David Gregory and Tina Gregory would be thereby endangered' (count 2). He pleaded guilty to a separate offence of damaging property, contrary to s1(1) of the 1971 Act (count 3).

[His Lordship read section 1 of the Act.]

It is to be observed that the offence created by sub-s(2), save that it may be committed by destroying or damaging one's own property, is simply an aggravated form of the offence created by sub-s(1), in which the prosecution must prove, in addition to the ingredients of the offence under sub-s(1), the further mental element specified by sub-s(2)(b). In this case presumably count 2 was intended to relate to the damage done by the shot fired at the bedroom window and count 3 to the damage done by one or other or both the other two shots. It is also significant to note the maximum penalties attaching to the three offences charged. For an offence under s16 of the 1968 Act it is 14 years' imprisonment, for an offence under s1(2) of the 1971 Act life imprisonment, and for an offence under s1(1) of the 1971 Act 10 years' imprisonment.

At some stage in the trial the particulars of count 2 were amended by deleting the words alleging an intent to endanger life and leaving only recklessness in that regard as the mental element relied on to establish the offence under s1(2). The prosecution, it appears, presented the case on the footing that counts 1 and 2 were alternatives and, if the case had been left to the jury, the judge would presumably have directed them that if they found that the respondent intended to endanger the lives of Mr and Mrs Gregory they should convict on count 1, but if they found that he was merely reckless with regard to such danger they should acquit on count 1 and convict on count 2.

At the conclusion of the case for the prosecution, however, counsel for the respondent submitted that there was no case to answer on count 2 on the ground that, in so far as the lives of Mr and Mrs Gregory had been endangered, the danger had not been caused by the damage done to the bungalow, but by the shot fired from the respondent's rifle. Of course, it is obvious that any danger to life in this case was caused by the shot from the rifle itself, not by any trifling damage done to the bedroom window or to any property in the bedroom. But the judge rejected counsel's submission and accepted the submission made for the Crown that the phrase in s 1(2)(b) of the 1971 Act 'by the destruction or damage' refers on its true construction not only to the destruction or damage to property as the cause of the danger to life on which the mental element in the aggravated offence under the sub-section depends, but also to the act of the defendant which causes that destruction or damage. On the basis of the judge's ruling the respondent changed his plea to guilty on count 2. He appealed against conviction on the ground that the judge's ruling was erroneous. The Court of Appeal, Criminal Division (Neill LJ, Peter Pain and Gatehouse JJ) ([1986] 3 All ER 611, [1986] 1 WLR 1286) allowed the appeal, but certified that the decision involved a question of law of general public importance in the following terms:

> 'Whether, upon a true construction of s1(2)(b) of the Criminal Damage Act 1971, the prosecution are required to prove that the danger to life resulted from the destruction of or damage to the property, or whether it is sufficient for the prosecution to prove that it resulted from the act of the defendant which caused the destruction or damage.'

The Crown now appeals by leave of your Lordships' House.

We must, of course, approach the matter on the footing, implicit in the outcome of the trial, that the respondent, in firing at the bedroom window, had no intent to endanger life, but accepts that he was reckless whether life would be endangered.

Under both limbs of s1 of the 1971 Act it is the essence of the offence which the section creates that the defendant has destroyed or damaged property. For the purpose of analysis it may be convenient to omit reference to destruction and to concentrate on the references to damage, which was all that was here involved. To be guilty under sub-s(1) the defendant must have intended or been reckless as to the damage to property which he caused. To be guilty under sub-s(2) he must additionally have intended to endanger life or been reckless whether life would be endangered 'by the damage' to property which he caused. This is the context in which the words must be construed and it seems to me impossible to read the words 'by the damage' as meaning 'by the damage or by the act which caused the damage'. Moreover, if the language of the statute has the meaning for which the Crown contends, the words 'by the destruction or damage' and 'thereby' in sub-s(2)(b) are mere surplusage. If the Crown's submission is right, the only additional element necessary to convert a sub-s(1) offence into a sub-s(2) offence is an intent to endanger life or recklessness whether life would be endangered simpliciter.

It would suffice as a ground for dismissing this appeal if the statute were ambiguous, since any such ambiguity in a criminal statute should be resolved in favour of the defence. But I can find no ambiguity. It seems to me that the meaning for which the respondent contends is the only meaning which the language can bear.

The contrary construction leads to anomalies which Parliament cannot have intended. If A and B both discharge firearms in a public place, being reckless whether life would be endangered, it would be absurd that A, who incidentally causes some trifling damage to property, should be guilty of an offence punishable with life imprisonment, but that B, who causes no damage, should be guilty of no offence. In the same circumstances, if A is merely reckless but B actually intends to endanger life, it is scarcely less absurd that A should be guilty of the graver offence under s1(2) of the 1971 Act, B of the lesser offence under s16 of the Firearms Act 1968.

Counsel for the Crown did not shrink from arguing that s1(2) of the 1971 Act had created, in effect, a general offence of endangering life with intent or recklessly, however the danger was caused, but had incidentally included as a necessary, albeit insignificant, ingredient of the offence that some damage to property should also be caused. In certain fields of legislation it is sometimes difficult to appreciate the rationale of particular provisions, but in a criminal statute it would need the clearest language to persuade me that the legislature had acted so irrationally, indeed perversely, as acceptance of this argument would imply.

It was further argued that to affirm the construction of s 1(2)(b) adopted by the Court of Appeal would give rise to problems in other cases in which it might be difficult or even impossible to distinguish between the act causing damage to property and the ensuing damage caused as the source of danger to life. In particular, it was suggested that in arson cases the jury would have to be directed that they could only convict if the danger to life arose from falling beams or similar damage caused by the fire, not if the danger arose from the heat, flames or smoke generated by the fire itself. Arson is, of course, the prime example of a form of criminal damage to property which, in the case of an occupied building, necessarily involves serious danger to life and where the gravity of the consequence which may result as well from recklessness as from a specific intent fully justifies the severity of the penalty which the 1971 Act provides for the offence. But the argument in this case is misconceived. It is not the match and the inflammable materials, the flaming firebrand or any other inflammatory agent which the arsonist uses to start the fire which causes danger to life, it is the ensuing conflagration which occurs as the property which has been set on fire is damaged or destroyed. When the victim in the bedroom is overcome by the smoke or incinerated by the flames as the building burns, it would be absurd to say that this does not result from the damage to the building.

Counsel for the Crown put forward other examples of cases which he suggested ought to be liable to prosecution under s 1(2) of the 1971 Act, including that of the angry mob of striking miners who throw a hail of bricks through the window of the cottage occupied by the working miner and that of people who drop missiles from motorway bridges on passing vehicles. I believe that the criminal law provides adequate sanctions for these cases without the need to resort to s 1(2) of the 1971 Act. But, if my belief is mistaken, this would still be no reason to distort the plain meaning of that sub-section.

Some reference was also made to damage caused by explosives. This is the subject of specific provision under the Explosive Substances Act 1883 as amended. The offence created by s 3(1)(a) of that Act, as substituted by s7(1) of the Criminal Jurisdiction Act 1975, of doing 'any act with intent to cause ... by an explosive substance an explosion of a nature likely to endanger life, or cause serious injury to property ...' obviates the need to resort to the 1971 Act when explosives are used. ...

I can well understand that the prosecution in this case thought it necessary and appropriate that, even if they could not establish the intent to endanger life necessary to support a conviction under s16 of the 1968 Act, they should include a count in the indictment to mark in some way the additional gravity of an offence of criminal damage to property in which a firearm is used. But they had no need to resort to s1(2) of the 1971 Act. A person who, at the time of committing an offence under s1 of the 1971 Act, has in his possession a firearm commits a distinct offence under s17(2) of the 1968 Act: see Sch 1 to the 1968 Act, as amended by s11(7) of the 1971 Act. If the respondent had been charged with that offence in addition to the offence under s1(1) of the 1971 Act, he must have pleaded guilty to both and, if the prosecution were content to accept that there was no intent to endanger life, this would have been amply sufficient to mark the gravity of the respondent's criminal conduct in the incident at the Gregory's bungalow.

I would accordingly dismiss the appeal. The certified question should be answered as follows: on the true construction of s1(2)(b) of the Criminal Damage Act 1971 the prosecution are required to prove that the danger to life resulted from the destruction of or damage to property; it is not sufficient for the prosecution to prove that it resulted from the act of the defendant which caused the destruction or damage.

Appeal dismissed

Notes and questions

1. Do you agree with the Law Commission, above, p **956**, that but for the creation of this offence 'a considerable gap is left in the law'? How does the offence differ from attempted murder?

2. Ought there to be an offence of recklessly endangering life whether by damaging property or otherwise? In *Meah v Roberts* [1978] 1 All ER 97, [1977] 1 WLR 1187, DC, D, after cleaning pipes in a bar, put some caustic soda 'stronger than that needed to remove paint from woodwork' in a lemonade bottle and left the bottle standing with other lemonade bottles. At this stage, and assuming that D does not intend to kill but is aware of the risk to life, it seems that D commits no offence if the bottle is empty but commits the offence under s 1(2) if the bottle had contained some lemonade. On endangerment offences generally, see the discussion in K. J. M. Smith, 'Liability for Endangerment: English Ad Hoc Pragmatism and American Innovation' [1983] Crim LR 127; D. Lanham, 'Danger Down Under' [1999] Crim LR 960.

3. Consider *Webster, Warwick* [1995] 2 All ER 168, CA. In the first case the defendants and others pushed a coping stone from the parapet of a bridge onto a passenger train passing beneath. The stone penetrated the roof but did not strike anyone; passengers were, however, showered with, though not physically injured by, debris dislodged from the roof by the falling stone. The court said the judge was wrong to direct the jury that the defendants could be convicted of the s 1(2) offence if they intended that life would be endangered *by the falling stone*. The conviction was upheld, however, on the ground that the jury's verdict implied that the defendants must have been reckless to the lives of the passengers being endangered by falling debris. Would that still be the case now that *G* has overruled *Caldwell*?

In the second case D, in a stolen car, repeatedly rammed pursuing police vehicles while E, D's passenger, threw bricks at passing police cars, one of which shattered a windscreen and showered the officers therein with broken glass. It was held that D was properly convicted of the s 1(2) offence. D intended that property be damaged and was at least reckless as to the endangering of life since either action—the ramming of the police cars or the breaking of the window—caused damage which in turn might have put the lives of the police officers at risk.

4. The offence under s 1(2) requires that some property be intentionally or recklessly damaged. Given that, however, it is not necessary to show that life was in fact endangered if D in fact intended, or was reckless as to, such endangerment. D may be accordingly convicted, if he has the relevant mens rea, though a house in which he starts a fire is unoccupied (*Sangha* [1988] 2 All ER 385, [1988] 1 WLR 519, CA) or the fire which he starts is doused before any endangerment in fact arises (*Dudley* [1989] Crim LR 57, CA). The brick thrown at the police car in *Warwick* might have missed the windscreen and caused only trivial damage to the police car. D would still be liable if it was thrown with the requisite *mens rea*; otherwise, said the court in *Warwick*, liability would depend on whether D was a good shot.

5. The offence under s 1(2) may be committed though the property damaged is D's own property or is damaged with D's permission: *Merrick* [1996] 1 Cr App R 130, [1995] Crim LR 802, CA.

Attorney-General's Reference (No 3 of 1992)
(1993) 98 Cr App R 383

(Lord Taylor CJ, Schiemann J and Wright J)

The complainants, V, maintained a night watch over their premises from a motor car. Early one morning the respondents arrived in a vehicle containing petrol bombs and threw towards V's car a lighted petrol bomb which passed over the car and smashed against a wall. They were charged with attempted aggravated arson, the particulars alleging recklessness whether life would be endangered. The trial judge ruled that, on a charge of attempt, intent to endanger life was required; recklessness was not sufficient. That was the point of law referred by the Attorney-General. See above, p 525. Before considering the attempts problem, however, the court considered what has to be proved for the completed offences of criminal damage and aggravated criminal damage.

Schiemann J. So far as the completed simple offence is concerned, the prosecution needs to prove:

(1) Property belonging to another was damaged by the defendant.

(2) The state of mind of the defendant was one of the following:
    (a) he intended to damage such property, or
    (b) he was reckless as to whether any such property would be damaged.

In the case of the completed aggravated offence the prosecution needs to prove:

(1) the defendant in fact damaged property, whether belonging to himself or another;

(2) that the state of mind of the defendant was one of the following:
    (a) he intended to damage property, and intended by the damage to endanger the life of another, or
    (b) he intended to damage property and was reckless as to whether the life of another would be thereby endangered, or
    (c) he was reckless as to whether any property would be damaged and was reckless as to whether the life of another would be thereby endangered.

It is to be noted that the property referred to under 1 (to which we shall hereafter refer as the first-named property) is not necessarily the same property as that referred to in 2 (to which we shall refer as the second-named property), although it normally will be. Thus a man who—

(1) owns a crane from which is suspended a heavy object and

(2) cuts the rope (the first-named property) which holds the object with the result that

(3) the object falls and hits the roof of a passing car (the second-named property) which roof

(4) collapses killing the driver—

would be guilty if it could be shown that he damaged the rope, was reckless as to whether this would damage the car, and was reckless as to whether the life of the driver of the car would be endangered by the damage to the car.

All the foregoing is common ground. The problem which has given rise to this reference relates to an attempt to commit the aggravated offence in circumstances where the first-named property is the same as the second-named property—in the instant case a car. It amounts to this: whether, if the state of mind of the defendant was that postulated in 2(b) above, namely that he intended to damage property and was reckless as to whether the life of another would thereby be endangered, and whilst in that state of mind he did an act which was more than merely preparatory to the offence, he is guilty of attempting to commit that offence.

We turn to the law of attempt....

The difference between the full offence and the attempt seems to be minimal. If the attempt is committed at all, it is committed as soon as D does an act more than merely preparatory to damaging the crane by cutting the rope—for example, taking out his knife and moving to make the cut. If the full offence is committed, it is done as soon as he cuts the rope. The only remaining questions for both attempt and full offence concern D's state of mind.

The court seems to assume that D would be guilty of neither offence unless he was reckless (which applying G means that he foresaw that there was a risk) that, someone's life might be endangered by a crushed car roof or some other property damaged by the falling object, distinct from the danger from the falling object itself. The object is treated like the ricocheting bullet in Steer (p 956, above). But is this right? The ricochet was not the product of any criminal damage. The object falls as the direct result of criminal damage to the crane. Would not the full offence have been committed if D foresaw that the object was likely to fall on a pedestrian? If D damages the braking system of a car is it not sufficient to prove that he was reckless whether the damaged car might endanger the lives of pedestrians by running into them? Is it really necessary to prove that he foresaw that the car might damage some other property which would endanger life, as by knocking down a lamp post which might hit a pedestrian?

(1) RECKLESSNESS

R v Martin Alan Cooper
[2004] EWCA Crim 1382, Court of Appeal, Criminal Division

(Rose LJ, Hughes and Gloster JJ)

D was a resident in a hostel which provides support for people with mental health problems. One evening, after warning the staff that there would be 'trouble later', badly burnt bedding was found outside D's room. There was smoke in D's room and a mattress was found to be scorched on the underside. D had used lighter fuel as an accelerant. When interviewed he was asked, 'Had it crossed your mind that you might have hurt anyone else while you were doing it?' He replied, 'I don't think, it did cross my mind a bit but nobody would have got hurt anyway.' [The officer:] 'I know that no-one did get hurt, but obviously you could have been hurt.' The defendant replied: 'That is what my intention was.' The trial judge directed the jury in accordance with *Caldwell* and D was convicted. On appeal, the conviction was quashed.

Rose LJ stated:

In the light of the House of Lords speeches in *G*, the *Caldwell* direction was a misdirection. It is now, in the light of *G*, incumbent on a trial judge to direct a jury, in a case of this kind, that the risk of danger to life was obvious and significant to the defendant. In other words, a subjective element is essential before the jury can convict of this offence. Mr Tizzano [counsel for D] also put the matter in this way, in the light of those answers in interview to which we have rehearsed: 'If he realised there was a risk, but dismissed it as negligible, it cannot be said he realised he was taking an obvious and significant risk.' With that submission we agree.

4. ARSON

The Law Commission recommended that there should be no separate offence of damaging property by fire (see Law Com No 29, paras 28–33) but this recommendation proved unacceptable to Parliament and s 1(3) of the Act provides 'An offence committed under this section by destroying or damaging property by fire shall be charged as arson'. Since arson is punishable with life imprisonment, arson contrary to s 1(1) must be a separate offence under *Courtie*, above, p 44.

A person may therefore be charged with an offence under s 1(1) and (3), to which the definition of lawful excuse in s 5 applies; or with an offence under s 1(2) and (3), to which the definition in s 5 does not apply. In order to constitute arson there must be some damage, however slight, done by fire.

5. OTHER OFFENCES

By s 2 of the Criminal Damage Act it is an offence to threaten to destroy, etc property, and by s 3 it is an offence to possess anything intending to destroy, etc property.

6. A NOTE ON THE COMPUTER MISUSE ACT 1990

Computers, like any other machines, may be damaged as by taking a hammer to them and such damage falls within the Criminal Damage Act. But they are much more likely to be 'damaged' or interfered with by the alteration of programs or the deletion of data by electronic means which, unlike the use of a hammer, leave no visible signs of damage to the computer or its software.

In *Cox v Riley* (1986) 83 Cr App R 54, [1986] Crim LR 460, DC, D blanked (that is, erased by electronic means) the programs from a plastic circuit card which was used to operate a saw to cut wood to programmed designs. The card bore no visible signs of damage and could have been re-programmed, after the expenditure of time and money, to perform its original function. D's counsel argued ('gallantly' it was said) that because the programs could not be seen or touched in the ordinary physical sense they were not 'property of a tangible nature' within the Criminal Damage Act.

The court thought that this argument failed to take account of the fact that D was charged not with damaging the programs but with damaging the plastic circuit card. The value and usefulness of the card had been impaired because it would no longer perform the function for which it had been designed. In principle the decision seems defensible. The card, like a key which has been physically deformed, would not perform its function and the card, like the key, is no less damaged because it can be re-formed, by whatever means, to perform its original function. *Cox v Riley* was followed by the Court of Appeal in *Whitely* (1991) 93 Cr App R 25, [1991] Crim LR 436.

The Law Commission (see Law Com Working Paper No 10, *Computer Misuse* and Law Com Report No 186, *Computer Misuse*, Cmnd 819, 1989) took the view that the problem of computer misuse should be tackled directly and the outcome was the Computer Misuse Act 1990. This Act is not concerned merely with harm caused *to* computers but with harms caused *by* their use and accordingly creates offences of unauthorized access (hacking) and unauthorized access with intent to commit, or facilitate the commission by another, of arrestable offences. So far as interference with computers is concerned s 3 provides:

(1) A person is guilty of an offence if:
   (a) he does any act which causes an unauthorised modification of the contents of any computer; and
   (b) at the time when he does the act he has the requisite intent and the requisite knowledge.

(2) For the purposes of sub-section (1)(b) above the requisite intent is an intent to cause a modification of the contents of any computer and by so doing—
   (a) to impair the operation of any computer;
   (b) to prevent or hinder access to any program or data held in any computer; or
   (c) to impair the operation of any such program or the reliability of any such data.

(3) The intent need not be directed at—
   (a) any particular computer;
   (b) any particular program or data or a program or data of any particular kind; or
   (c) any particular modification or a modification of any particular kind.

(4) For the purposes of sub-section (1)(b) above the requisite knowledge is knowledge that any modification he intends to cause is unauthorised.

Had the matter been left there, and assuming that *Cox v Riley* and *Whitely* were correctly decided, there would have been an overlap between the offence of criminal damage carrying 10 years' imprisonment and the offence under s 3 carrying five years' imprisonment. The Law Commission wished to eliminate this overlap partly because of the 'theoretical difficulties posed by applying the concept of damage to intangible property such as data programs' and partly because while criminal damage could be committed recklessly the Law Commission did not think that the new offence should apply to a person who recklessly modified computer material. Section 3(6) accordingly provides—

For the purposes of the Criminal Damage Act 1971 a modification of the contents of a computer shall not be regarded as damaging any computer or computer storage medium unless its effect on that computer or computer storage medium impairs its physical condition.

The Law Commission was, with respect, entirely right to tackle the problem of computer misuse directly but the relationship of the Criminal Damage Act and the Computer Misuse Act raises a number of questions.

Why is it an offence carrying 10 years' imprisonment to take a hammer to a computer but an offence carrying only five years' imprisonment to cause harm by interference with programs and data? The Law Commission instanced the case of a hacker (Law Com No 186, para 3) whose electronic vandalism required 10,000 hours of skilled work to repair.

Why should D be liable to 10 years' imprisonment if by recklessly wielding a hammer he damages a computer while E who recklessly damages a computer by electronic means cannot be convicted of criminal damage, nor of an offence under s 3 of the Computer Misuse Act?

The Home Office is currently reviewing the need for further legislation, particularly an offence to deal with denial of service attacks. A Denial-of-Service (DoS) attack occurs 'when a deliberate attempt is made to stop a machine from performing its usual activities by having another computer create large amounts of specious traffic. The traffic may be valid requests made in an overwhelming volume or specially crafted protocol fragments that cause the serving machine to tie up significant resources to no useful purpose. In a Distributed Denial-of-Service (DDoS) attack a large number of remote computers are orchestrated into attacking a target at the same time.' [All Party Internet Group www.apig.org.uk/computer_misuse_act_inquiry.htm, para 56] These are extremely common at over 4,000 reported instances a week.

FURTHER READING

Criminal Damage

D. W. Elliott, 'Criminal Damage' [1988] Crim LR 403

Law Com No 29, *Offences of Damage to Property* (1970)

See also Law Commission Working Paper No 23, *Malicious Damage*

Computer Misuse Act 1990

Y. Akdeniz, 'Cybercrime' in *E-Commerce Law & Regulation Encyclopaedia* (2003)

Y. Akdeniz, 'Section 3 of the Computer Misuse Act 1990—An Antidote for Computer Viruses' [1996] Web Jnl CLI

A. Charlesworth, 'Addiction and Hacking' (1993) 143 NLJ 540

R. Essen, 'Cybercrime: a Growing Problem' (2002) J Crim L 269

G. Fearon, 'All Party Internet (APIG) Report on the Computer Misuse Act' (2004) 15 Comps and Law 36

C. Holder, 'Staying one step ahead of the criminals' (2002) 10(3) IT Law 17

M. Klang, 'A Critical Look at the Regulation of Computer Viruses' (2003) Int J of Law and IT 162

D. Thomas, and B. D. Loader, *Cybercrime* (2000)

O. Ward, 'Cyber Policing' (2000) 150 NLJ 1812

M. Wasik, 'The Computer Misuse Act 1990' [1990] Crim LR 767

M. Wasik, *Crime and the Computer* (1991)

M. Wasik, 'Law Reform Proposals on Computer Misuse' [1989] Crim LR 257

See further Internet Crime Forum. www.internetcrimeforum.org.uk

Index